AMERICAN GUNSMITHS

2nd EDITION

by Frank M. Sellers

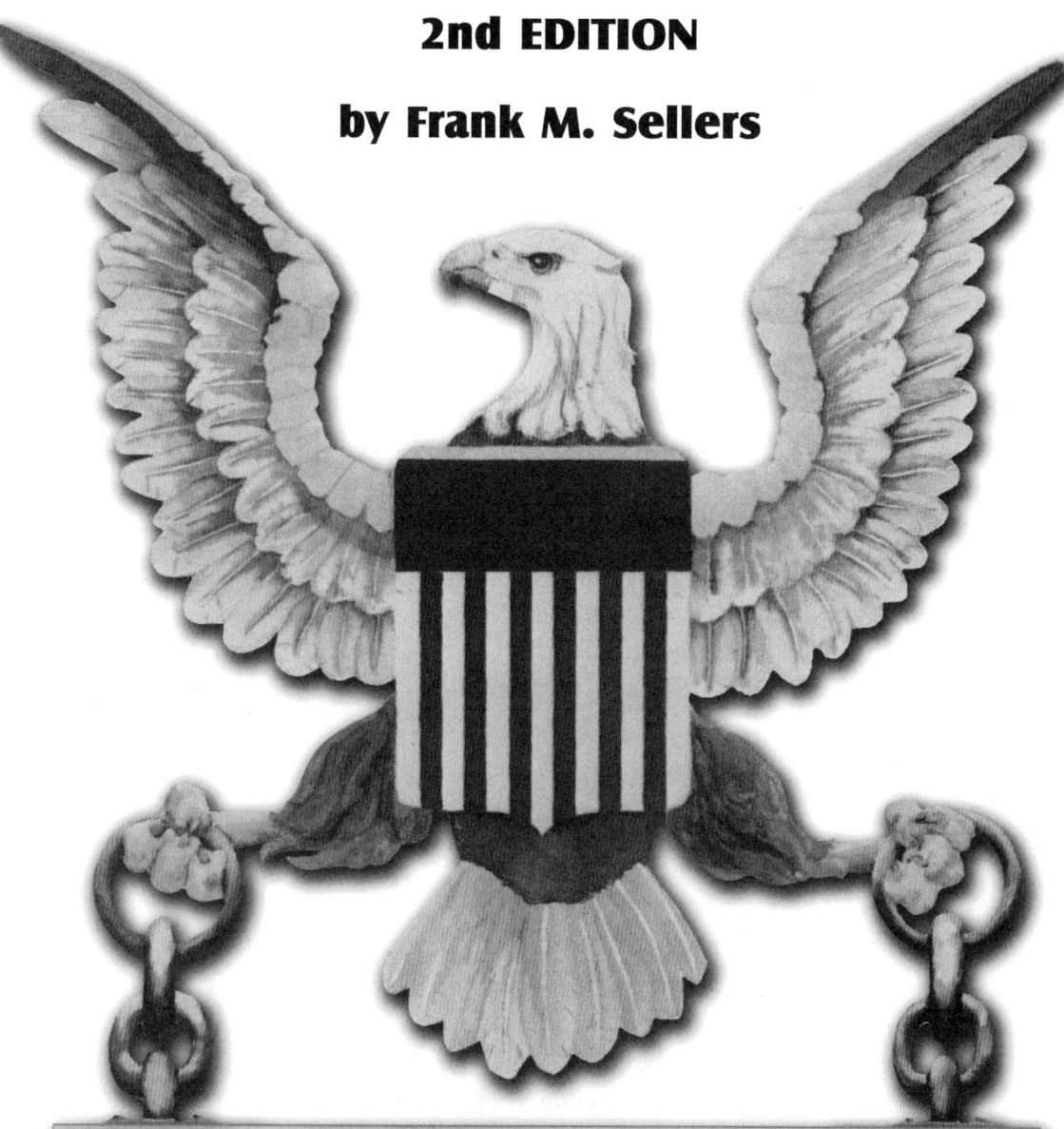

A comprehensive listing of American manufacturers, trademarks, gunsmiths, brands, and other trade names from the mid-16th century to present day.

Blue Book Publications, Inc.
8009 34th Ave. S., Ste. 175
Minneapolis, MN 55425 USA

American Gunsmiths
Second Edition

This book is the result of nonstop and continuous firearms research obtained by attending and/or participating in trade shows, gun shows, auctions, and also communicating with contributing editors, gun dealers, collectors, company historians, and other knowledgeable industry professionals worldwide each year.

All Rights Reserved
Copyright 2008 by Karen Sellers

Published and Printed by:
Blue Book Publications, Inc.
8009 34th Avenue South, Suite 175
Minneapolis, MN 55425 U.S.A.

Orders Only: 800-877-4867, ext. 3 (domestic only)
Phone No.: 952-854-5229
Fax No.: 952-853-1486
General Email: bluebook@bluebookinc.com
Web site: www.bluebookinc.com

Published and printed in the United States of America
ISBN 10: 1-886768-80-2
ISBN 13: 978-1-886768-80-3

Distributed in part to the book trade by Ingram Book Company and Baker & Taylor.

Distributed throughout Europe by Deutsches Waffen Journal
Rudolf-Diesel-Strasse 46
Blaufelden, D-74572 Germany
Fax No.: 011-497-919566919
Website: www.dwj-verlag.de

No part of this publication may be reproduced in any form whatsoever, by photograph, mimeograph, fax transmission or any other mechanical or electronic means. Nor can it be broadcast or transmitted, by translation into any language, nor by electronic recording or otherwise, without the express written permission from the publisher - except by a reviewer, who may quote brief passages for critical articles and/or reviews.

TABLE OF CONTENTS

Title Page 1
Copyright/Publisher's Note 2
Table of Contents 3
Foreword 4-8
How To Use This Book 9-10
Introduction to the 2nd Edition 11
A-Z Sections .... 12 - 375
    A Section 12-22
    B Section 23-62
    C Section 63-86
    D Section 87-102
    E Section 103-111
    F Section 112-126
    G Section 127-144
    H Section 145-173
    I Section 174-175
    J Section 176-182
    K Section 183-195
    L Section 196-212
    M Section 213-240
    N Section 241-246
    O Section 247-250
    P Section 251-267
    Q Section 268
    R Section 269-286
    S Section 287-328
    T Section 329-339
    U Section 340-341
    V Section 342-345
    W Section 346-370
    X-Y Section 371-373
    Z Section 374-375
Bibliography 376-384

FOREWORD
by Frank Sellers

Among the ever expanding crop of books relating to the gun collecting field, there have been many lists of gunsmiths. From the pioneering efforts of Charles W. Sawyer in 1910 to the recent studies on the makers of the individual states, more than fifty lists have been published.

Unfortunately, most of these are long out of print and not available to the average collector. Those that are available are either incomplete or limited in scope. This work is an attempt to give the collector basic information on the names, initials, and other markings that appear on American guns.

The decision to limit this work to the American gunsmiths was made for two reasons: first, the vast numbers of gunsmiths in this country's first three centuries. Second, the lack of research facilities available on European, Asian, and African gunsmiths.

The late Frank Sellers, surrounded by a small portion of his extensive collection. Image courtesy R.I.A.

There are many sources of information about America's gunsmiths. Perhaps the most important is the guns themselves. Most guns, especially those of the 19th Century, which comprise the largest surviving group of American antique guns, carry the name of the maker and in many instances, the location in which it was made. This is usually enough information for further study if one has the time and inclination to do so.

The next step in researching a gun is to check out the published material that may relate to it. Several thousand books have been written on guns. There are also periodicals devoted to the subject. Some of these, both books and magazines, are more scholarly than others, and thus have more reliable information.

For the past fifty years, most collector interest has focused on the guns of the 18th and 19th centuries. Consequently, more books have been written on the makers of these centuries. Naturally, there is more information published on the more popular subjects (over 60 books on Colt alone), but with enough searching, some information is available on most American gunsmiths. Perhaps the most useful books for the basic researcher are the lists of gunsmiths. These give the researcher an idea of the area in which to search for more information.

Of the many lists that have been published, only a few are available to the average collector. Some of these are more useful than others, but all have some information not found in others. A brief look at these is necessary to understand their relative usefulness.

Sawyer, Charles W., *FIREARMS IN AMERICAN HISTORY*, Sawyer, Boston, Massachusetts, 1910. A basic coverage of guns made and used in America up to 1800, now completely superceded by later books.

Sawyer, Charles W., *OUR RIFLES*, The Cornhill Co., Boston, Massachusetts, 1920. Basic coverage of rifles, with emphasis on Kentucky rifles, now obsolete.

Dillin, John, *THE KENTUCKY RIFLE*, National Rifle Association, Washington, D.C., 1924. A standard reference on the subject, still in print in its seventh edition.

Satterlee, L.D., *A CATALOG OF FIREARMS FOR THE COLLECTOR*, Satterlee, Detroit, Michigan, 1927. First published information on machine made or "manufactured" guns, now largely out of date.

Gardner, Robert E., *AMERICAN ARMS AND ARMS MAKERS*. The F.J. Heer Printing Co., Columbus, Ohio, 1938. Biographical information on many gunsmiths, mostly 19th century. Superceded by his own 1963 book.

Roberts, Ned H., *THE MUZZLE-LOADING CAP LOCK RIFLE*, The Granite State Press, Manchester, New Hampshire, 1940. Biographical information on later muzzle loading makers.

Gluckman, Arcadi and Satterlee, L.D., *AMERICAN GUN MAKERS*, Otto Ulbrich Co., Buffalo, New York, 1940. A comprehensive list of gunsmiths known at the time.

Van Rensselaer, Stephen, *AMERICAN FIREARMS*, Century House, Watkins Glen, New York, 1940. Another list of makers, many of whom are undocumented.

Gluckman, Arcadi, *UNITED STATES MUSKETS, RIFLES, AND CARBINES*, Otto Ulbrich Co., Buffalo, New York, 1948. Information on the makers of these guns, from revolutionary times to the 20th century.

Swinney, Holman J., *NEW YORK STATE GUNMAKERS*, The Freeman's Journal Press, Cooperstown, New York, 1951. A checklist of New York makers, with brief biographical information.

Gardner, Robert E., *SMALL ARMS MAKERS*, Crown Publishers, New York, New York, 1963. A large general listing of gunsmiths and cutlers, about 7,000 of whom are American. The best general listing available to date.

These represent the early works. More recent efforts in this area have followed the lead of Holman Swinney and concentrated on the makers of one state or area. Most representative of these are:

Kauffman, Henry, *THE PENNSYLVANIA KENTUCKY RIFLE*, The Stackpole Co., Harrisburg, Pennsylvania, 1960.
Lindert, Albert, *GUNMAKERS OF INDIANA*, Albert Lindert, Indianapolis, Indiana, 1968.
Bivins, John, *LONGRIFLES OF NORTH CAROLINA*, George Shumway, York, Pennsylvania, 1968.
Demeritt, Dwight, *MAINE MADE GUNS AND THEIR MAKERS*, Paul Plummer, Hallowell, Maine, 1973.
Hutslar, Donald, *GUNSMITHS OF OHIO*, George Shumway, York, Pennsylvania, 1973.
Horn, Warren, *GUNSMITHS AND GUNMAKERS OF VERMONT*, The Horn Co., Burlington, Vermont, 1975.
Shelton, Lawrence, *CALIFORNIA GUNSMITHS*, Far West Publishers, Fair Oaks, California, 1977.

These can all be considered the prime source for the areas they cover. Work covering other areas is in progress, and some are approaching publication, but much remains to be done.

A large amount of data is available in more obscure, published sources: newspapers, magazines, city directories, dealer catalogs, collector's club bulletins, museum, and government publications.

Like that from books, information from these sources can range from miniscule to extremely good. Of course, the information from collector's publications, whether they be periodicals, club, dealer, or museum publications, will be better for the researcher than the more general publications such as newspapers and city directories which cover all areas of interest to the populace.

Even in the periodicals devoted to guns, one seldom finds a constant diet of articles of interest to the student of antique arms. Some, directed to the "popular" taste, almost never have an article of value to the student. Of the more than 100 periodicals past and present devoted to some phase of collecting, only those listed here were found to have a sufficient number of scholarly articles to be considered "useful" to the researcher.

American Arms Collectors, The Collectors Press, Towson, Maryland, 1957-1958.
Arms Gazette, Beinfeld Publications, North Hollywood, California, 1973-1981.
The Gun Collector, G.C. Harrison, Madison, Wisconsin, 1946-1957.
Gun Report, World Wide Gun Report, Inc., Aledo, Illinois, 1955-present.

Another category of periodicals is the "bulletins," "magazines," "annuals," etc. of the various collecting and shooting organizations. These are available only to members and in most cases have a very limited circulation. The articles are usually researched in more depth than those in other periodicals.

AMERICAN RIFLEMAN, National Rifle Association, Washington D.C., 1886-present.
ASAC BULLETINS, American Society of Arms Collectors, Cincinnati, Ohio, 1955-present.

FOREWORD, cont.

C.G.C.A. Annual, Colorado Gun Collectors Association, Denver, Colorado, 1972-present.
KRA Bulletins, Kentucky Rifle Association, Lancaster, Pennsylvania, 1964-present.
MUZZLE BLASTS, National Muzzle Loading Rifle Association, Friendship, Indiana, 1939-present
THE TEXAS GUN COLLECTOR, Texas Gun Collectors Association, Dallas, Texas, 1950-present.
W.G.C.A. Annual, Wisconsin Gun Collectors Association, Madison, Wisconsin, 1960-present.

The government publication most useful to the researcher is probably the *PATENT OFFICE REPORT*, printed by the Patent Office since 1849. Besides the name and address of each patentee, it gives a brief description and one or more drawings of the patented item. This enables the identification of some patented guns, even though they are not marked with the patent information.

There are two major "unpublished" sources, the government archives and the data gathered by many researchers over the years that has never found its way into print.

Both state and federal governments maintain archives. Many kinds of documents relating to guns are held in these repositories. The sections with the most information for the collector are: patent, legal, ordnance, taxes, and census. Of these, the ordnance and census sections are probably the most useful.

Tax records are only available in a few areas. Those of Pennsylvania are the only ones that have been examined to any extent. Samuel E. Dyke and Henry Kauffman did much work in these records to establish the identity and location of many of the makers of "Kentucky" rifles.

The records of both the Army and Navy Ordnance Departments in the National Archives contain a vast amount of gun related material. There are more than 16,000 cubic feet of documents in this section. To give an idea of the immensity of this, the average city library contains about one third of this amount.

One source that has been neglected in the past is the census reports. Starting in 1790 and conducted every 10 years, these reported the name, location, age, origin, net worth, and occupation of each person in the country. From 1850-1880 a separate "industrial census" was also conducted, dividing all of the workers into various categories. One of these categories was gunsmith and in 1850 over 3800 were listed in this occupation.

There are two major problems in using the raw data from the census reports. The first, and by far the more important is that all of the people reported as "gunsmiths" may not have worked as gunsmiths themselves, but as employees of others. (In 1860, the 200 employees of Colt were all listed as "pistol makers"). The second problem is that not all gunsmiths were so listed. To use the 1860 census for example again, Carlos Gove, the most prolific of the Colorado gunsmiths, was listed as a merchant. Christian Sharps, a name familiar to most gun collectors, was listed as an "industrialist". These same problems exist when using newspapers and city directories.

The following list of nearly 2,000 state and local business directories are only a small part of those personally examined while doing research for this book. It is felt that no useful purpose would be served in giving the full bibliographical citation for each directory. They can be found in those libraries that have them under "Business directory" or "Gazeteer."

Alabama	1885; Mobile 1839, 1844, 1855, 1859, 1870, 1874, 1879, 1887, 1892.
Arkansas	1884, 1885.
California	1866, 1867, 1877, 1878, 1881, 1893; S.F. 1850-1900; L.A. 1875-1900.
Colorado	1859, 1866, 1871, 1873-1900; Denver 1876-1900.
Connecticut	1849, 1856, 1860, 1865, 1866, 1867, 1868, 1871, 1873-1889; Bridgeport 1865, 1871-1891; Derby 1883-1887; Hartford 1849, 1850, 1851, 1855-1879, 1881, 1884-1899.
Dakota Territory	1880, 1882, 1884, 1886, 1888, 1892.
Delaware	1859, 1872, 1874, 1882, 1884, 1891; Wilmington 1894.
D.C.	1822, 1830, 1832, 1834, 1840, 1853, 1855, 1858-60, 1862-1880.
Florida	1883, 1884, 1885, 1886, 1895.
Georgia	1854, 1879, 1881, 1883, 1885; Atlanta 1888-1895; Augusta 1888, 1895-1899; Columbus 1886-1898.
Idaho	1866, 1881, 1886, 1889, 1891.

FOREWORD, cont.

Illinois	1854, 1860, 1864-65, 1866, 1867, 1878, 1880, 1882, 1884, 1886, 1888, 1890, 1893; Aurora 1868, 1872,1895-1899; Bloomington 1870, 1872, 1873, 1885-1899; Chicago 1854, 1855, 1857, 1859, 1867, 1870-1900; Joliet 1870, 1885-1894; Springfield 1866, 1892.
Indiana	1858, 1860, 1862, 1890; Evansville 1866-1873.
Iowa	1865, 1875, 1880, 1882, 1884, 1887, 1889, 1892, 1895, 1897; Burlington 1890; Des Moines 1871, 1879, 1889-1899; Davenport 1858, 1880, 1882; Dubuque 1867, 1868, 1870, 1877, 1880, 1884, 1888; Council Bluffs 1868, 1869, 1871, 1873, 1876, 1884.
Kansas	1866, 1870, 1871, 1872, 1878, 1882, 1884, 1888, 1894; Fort Scott 1879, 1888, 1897; Topeka 1878; Atchison 1865, 1880, 1891-1899; Kansas City 1859, 1867, 1868, 1869, 1871, 1886, 1891, 1899; Leavenworth 1860, 1866, 1869, 1870, 1872, 1873, 1874.
Kentucky	1859, 1879, 1883, 1896; Louisville 1844, 1851, 1859, 1862, 1864, 1868-1890; Covington 1876, 1882, 1884, 1886, 1888, 1890, 1892, 1895, 1899; Newport 1882, 1884, 1886, 1888, 1890, 1895, 1899.
Louisiana	New Orleans 1805, 1822, 1823, 1834, 1838, 1841, 1842, 1844-1861, 1867-1900; Shreveport 1882.
Maine	1849, 1855, 1856, 1860 1862, 1865, 1867-1900; Bangor 1851, 1869, 1871, 1874-80; Portland 1823, 1830, 1844, 1850, 1852, 1866, 1869, 1871, 1877.
Maryland	1878, 1880, 1882, 1887; Baltimore 1800, 1810, 1812-1824, 1831-1860, 1866-1900.
Massachusetts	1849, 1853, 1860, 1868, 1869, 1874, 1878, 1885, 1888, 1890, 1892; Boston 1849-1860, 1872-1899; Bristol Co. 1867, 1870, 1872, 1876, 1878, 1881, 1883, 1885, 1888; Charleston 1854, 1856, 1858, 1860, 1868, 1870, 1872, 1874; Clinton 1890-1899; Fall River 1882-1888; Essex Co. 1866, 1870-1891; Fitchburg 1877-1899; Hampden Co. 1872, 1874, 1876, 1885, 1889, 1897; Haverhill 1859, 1860, 1867, 1869; Holyoke 1882; Hampshire Co. 1887.
Michigan	1860, 1863, 1865, 1867, 1870, 1872, 1873, 1875, 1877, 1879, 1883, 1884, 1887, 1891, 1895, 1899; Adrian 1865, 1867, 1890; Alpena 1883, 1889, 1891, 1893; Bay City 1883-1900; Calhoun Co. 1860, 1869; Detroit 1852-1860; 1863, 1882-1900; Flint 1888-1898; Jackson 1869-1897; Lansing 1883, 1887, 1891, 1892.
Minnesota	1865, 1867, 1872, 1875, 1878, 1882, 1884, 1886, 1888, 1898; Duluth 1883-1890.
Mississippi	1885.
Missouri	1854, 1860, 1879, 1889, 1891, 1893, 1898.
Montana	1871, 1880, 1884, 1886, 1888, 1892.
Nebraska	1872, 1879, 1882, 1884, 1886, 1893; Omaha 1866, 1869, 1870, 1873, 1875, 1877, 1878, 1879.
Nevada	1867, 1871, 1878, 1880.
New Hampshire	1849, 1856, 1860, 1865, 1868, 1872, 1874, 1875, 1877, 1878, 1887, 1889; Concord 1844, 1850, 1853, 1856, 1867, 1870, 1872; Dover 1884-1898.
New Jersey	1860, 1866, 1878, 1882, 1885; Atlantic City 1886; Burlington Co. 1883, 1887, 1889, 1893, 1895; Camden 1879, 1884, 1885, 1886, 1889-1899; Elizabeth 1866, 1868-1897; Essex Co. 1859, 1866, 1870-1899.
New York	1850, 1859, 1861, 1864, 1865, 1867, 1869, 1870, 1874, 1876, 1880, 1882; New York City 1800,1810,1814-1818, 1822-1830, 1836, 1838, 1841, 1846, 1849-1860, 1867-1900; Albany 1858, 1859, 1860, 1880-1891; Auburn 1869-1874, 1879-1900; Binghamton 1857, 1859, 1869-1899; Brooklyn 1872, 1877-1896; Buffalo 1855-1860, 1880-1889; Elmira 1857, 1863, 1866, 1871, 1872, 1874, 1878, 1880, 1882, 1884, 1889, 1891; Hudson 1862, 1870, 1876, 1880-1895; Jefferson Co. 1890; Oswego 1866; Rochester 1827, 1834, 1838, 1841, 1844, 1845, 1847, 1849, 1851-1899; Westchester Co. 1866.
North Carolina	1866, 1877, 1884, 1885, 1890; Durham 1887-1890.
Ohio	1853, 1857, 1859, 1860, 1864, 1866, 1867, 1868, 1870, 1872, 1875, 1878, 1881, 1883, 1885, 1887, 1888, 1889, 1890, 1892, 1896, 1899; Cincinnati 1816, 1819, 1820, 1829, 1836, 1837, 1846-1900.
Oregon	1866, 1867, 1871, 1873, 1878, 1880, 1881, 1886, 1889, 1891.
Pennsylvania	1860, 1861, 1868, 1874, 1882, 1887, 1890; Bedford, 1877, 1886; Lancaster 1857, 1859, 1869,

	1884, 1894; Philadelphia 1805, 1818, 1822, 1823, 1824, 1830-1849, 1853, 1856-1899; West Chester 1884, 1888, 1889, 1896-1900.
Rhode Island	1849, 1856, 1860, 1865; Providence 1860-1889.
South Carolina	1885-1886.
Tennessee	1834, 1860, 1871, 1873, 1876, 1881, 1885, 1887, 1889, 1891, 1897; Chattanooga 1884; Memphis 1860, 1870-1888.
Texas	1878, 1884, 1885, 1890, 1892, 1896; Austin 1872, 1881; Ft. Worth 1877-1885; Galveston 1868, 1870, 1872, 1874, 1875, 1878; Houston 1866, 1872, 1878, 1882, 1884, 1886, 1887, 1889; San Antonio 1879, 1880, 1887-1897; Waco 1878.
Utah	1871, 1878, 1880.
Virginia	1871, 1873, 1877, 1880, 1882, 1884, 1888, 1890, 1893, 1897; Charlottesville 1888; Richmond 1860, 1872.
Vermont	1849, 1856, 1860, 1865, 1868; Franklin Co. 1882; Orleans Co. 1883; Rutland Co. 1881; Washington Co. 1889; Windham Co. 1884; Windsor Co. 1883.
Washington	1866, 1871, 1878, 1880, 1886, 1889, 1891.
West Virginia	1884.
Wisconsin	1857, 1865, 1868, 1872, 1873, 1875, 1878, 1879, 1884, 1888, 1891, 1895: Eau Claire 1885, 1888-1896; Fond du Lac 1890; La Crosse 1866.

As has been stated many times in the past, a book such as this can never be complete. New guns turn up, new sources of information are found, more detailed studies are made in a given area, and so on. Most collectors and researchers are interested in the disemination of information in their chosen field and have been very helpful in furnishing information for this work. I would like to take this opportunity to thank: Samuel E. Dyke for the detailed studies on the early Pennsylvania and New York makers, both published and unpublished; Edward L. Eich, for his study of the Rochester, New York gunsmiths; Charles H. Elias, for the work on Arkansas makers; Ronald Gabel, for his work on the makers of Northhampton and Lehigh Counties; Curtis L. Johnson, for information on Illinois gunsmiths; Merrill Lindsay, for access to his unpublished manuscript material gathered over the years and the loan of his secretaries, Jean Starke and Jane Ellen Pfeifer, for the comparison of the manuscripts; Robert McAfee for census data from various states; John J. Malloy, for the use of the patent files of the Winchester Repeating Arms Co; George Moller, for his study of U.S. martial arms makers; William Myers, for access to the manuscript compiled by Herman Dean and C.W. Sawyer; R.E. Neville, Jr., for his study of Alabama makers; DeWitt Pourie and Gordon Lewis for notes on the gunsmiths of St. Louis; Holman Swinney, for information from the files gathered in the 55 years since his book was published; and the many others who furnished lists or information on individual guns.

INTERESTED IN CONTRIBUTING?

This new Second Edition of *American Gunsmiths* by Frank Sellers is the result of 24 years worth of revisions and additions to the First Edition, which was published in 1983. If you have a trademark, brand name, manufacturer, or gunsmith which is not listed in this publication, we may be interested in including it in our database, if you provide sufficient documentation.

Please supply us with as much information as you can about a missing trademark/manufacturer at:

Blue Book Publications, Inc.
Attn: AG revisions
8009 34th Ave. S., Ste. 175
Minneapolis, MN 55425 USA
Fax No.: 952-853-1486
Email: guns@bluebookinc.com

HOW TO USE THIS BOOK

by David Kosowski, Copy Editor

When originally published during 1983, *American Gunsmiths* quickly gained acceptance as the only single publication with not hundreds, but thousands of listings consisting of firearms manufacturers, trademarks, gunsmiths, and trade names from the mid-17th century to the 20th century. Many of these listings were previously unresearched, and as a result, many of America's smaller and previously unknown gunsmiths finally had some information provided on them.

In the following A-Z sections, the first and last listing will appear at the top of the page within the header indicating the alphabetical range of listing on each page. Within the individual listings, abbreviations will appear first, if possible, and may refer you to the complete name. In general, all listings have a standardized format, which is as follows:

B. & S. - BADGER & ABBOTT   AMERICAN GUNSMITHS   21

B SECTION

1c — **B. & S.** see Blunt & Syms.

B. see Marmaduke Blackwood for flintlock locks only.

B.A. Co. see Brooklyn Arms Co.

B.A. Co. unidentified. Percussion 1/2 stock.

B.B. unidentified. Flintlock Kentucky.

B.B. unidentified. Percussion fullstock dated 1863.

B.B. unidentified. Percussion pistol with folding trigger.

B.E. see Barney Engle.

B.F.S. unidentified. Flintlock Kentucky.

B.I. unidentified. Flintlock Kentucky.

B.L. unidentified. Percussion fullstock.

B.M. unidentified. Percussion fullstock.

B.T. unidentified. Flintlock Kentucky.

B.T. unidentified. Percussion fullstock.

1d — **B.W.** see Benjamin Wright.

BABBITT, A.S., & CO. Plattesburg, New York. Made first model Robinson rifles.

2 — **BABBITT, BENJAMIN T.** New York, New York. Patents #31,291 February 25, 1861, cannon, #34,472 February 25, 1862, cannon, and #209,014 October 15, 1878, air gun.

BABBITT, L.W. Cleveland, Ohio, 1832-1838, Burlington, Iowa, 1839-1844. Percussion rifles.

BABCOCK & CO. Evansville, Indiana, 1860d.

BABCOCK PATENT, marking on muzzle loading rifles and shotguns with center mounted safety hammers similar to John Byer's patent.

BABCOCK, ALBERT H. Boston, and Charlestown, Massachusetts, 1855d-1861. Percussion 1/2 stock.

Hoboken, New Jersey, 1878d.

1a — **BACH, JOHN,** (1824-1905), San Francisco, California, 1852-1874. Derringer. (Shelton)

BACHE, JOSEPH, (1815-?), Stockton, California, 1850-1853, Sonora, California, 1853-1885. (Shelton)

BACHMAN, F.M. Fredricksburg, Pennsylvania, 1880d. (C&W)

BACHMAN, HEINRICH, Lancaster, Pennsylvania. Patent #none August 21, 1833, safety for gun locks.

2 — **BACHNER BROTHERS,** Minneapolis, Minnesota, 1868-1884d.

BACKER, JACOB JR. Dauphin Co., Pennsylvania, 1800. (C&W)

BACKER, JACOB, Macungie, Pennsylvania, 1779t-1805t. (KRA II-3)

BACKERS, J. Grand de Tour, Illinois, 1860d.

BACKHOUSE, RICHARD, Easton, Pennsylvania, 1727-1781. Owner of Durham Iron Works which produced musket barrels during Revolutionary War. (Boehrett)

BACKMAN, Galena, Illinois, 1848-1849. (Johnson)

BACKMAN, G. Indiana. Percussion 1/2 stock. (Lindert)

BACKMAN, J.H. Rushford, Minnesota, 1886d-1892d.

BACON & CO. Norwich, Connecticut, 1852-1858. Thomas K. Bacon. Predecessor to Bacon Mfg. Co. (Nutter)

2 — **BACON ARMS CO.** Norwich, Connecticut, 1868-1888. Percussion and cartridge revolvers, and shotguns under their own or other names. Shotguns only in 1888. Bankrupt, 1888. Crescent Fire Arms Co. purchased the fac-

BABCOX, J.T. Syracuse, New York. Percussion 1/2 stock.

BABJOE, BERNARD, Jerseyville, Illinois, 1860d.

1b — **BABY HAMMERLESS,** trade name of Henry Kolb and R.F. Sedgely on revolvers.

BABY RUSSIAN, trade name of American Arms Co. on revolvers.

---

1. **NAME** (in bold print and upper case) - may be any one of the following:
   a. A specific person who was a gunsmith, an owner/partner/officer of a business, or a notable contributor in firearms development, technology, manufacturing, or distribution.
   b. A "trade name" used by a person or business, or found on a firearm.
   c. One or more initials, which were found on a firearm or commonly used by the person, business, or other entity.
   d. A marking or stamping on a firearm, such as a model name, maker's name or location, etc., or used in some identifying manner.

Note: "unidentified" may follow a NAME, and it indicates a dual status; not known and not located.

2. **BUSINESS/TRADE NAME** - a proprietorship, partnership, company, corporation, or other form of organization.

3. **YEAR OF BIRTH-DEATH** - for specific persons only. If either year is unknown, a question mark is displayed, and always in parentheses. In some cases, a lower case suffix may appear after the date(s) which indicates that the person/company was listed in the census (c), tax records (t), or directory (d), and will not appear in parentheses.

4. **LOCATION, YEAR(S)** - place and time span of NAME's firearm-relevant activity. If location(s) are unknown, nothing is displayed,

How to Use this Book, cont.

---

52   AMERICAN GUNSMITHS   *BROWNING & BREMER - BRUCE, T.*

BROWNING & BREMER, San Francisco, California, 1881-1900. (Kelver)

BROWNING & HEBER, San Francisco, California, 1873-1876. Percussion 1/2 stock. (Shelton)

BROWNING ARMS CO. St. Louis, Missouri, 1890-date. Sales organization for Browning patent guns made in Belgium.

BROWNING, ABEL S. (1854-?), Garett Co., Maryland, 1875-1940s. Also worked in West Virginia. (Hartzler)

BROWNING, AUGUST, (1837-?), San Francisco, California, 1867-1900. With Schneider & Browning, 1867-1870, Browning & Heber, 1873-1877, and Browning & Bremer, 1881-1900. (Shelton)

BROWNING, DAVID, (1829-?), Kanesville, Iowa, 1850c. Son of Jonathan Browning.

BROWNING, GEORGE, Philadelphia, Pennsylvania, 1780-1782. Continental Armory. (Moller)

BROWNING, JOHN MOSES, (1855-1926), Ogden, Utah. Patents #220,271 October 7, 1879, breechloading firearm, #261,667 July 25, 1882, magazine gun, #282,839 August 7, 1883, magazine gun, #306,577 October 14, 1884, magazine gun, #312,183 February 10, 1885, magazine gun, #324,296 August 11, 1885, magazine gun, #324,297 August 11, 1885, magazine gun, #336,287 February 16, 1886, magazine gun, #345,881 July 20, 1886, magazine gun, #345,882 July 20, 1886, magazine gun, #346,021 July 20, 1886, magazine gun, #356,271 January 18, 1887, magazine gun, #359,917 March 22, 1887, breechloading firearm, #367,336 July 26, 1887, magazine gun, #376,576 January 17, 1888, magazine gun, #385,238 June 26, 1888, magazine gun, #409,599 August 20, 1889, magazine gun, #409,600 August 20, 1889, magazine gun, #421,663 February 18, 1890, magazine gun, #428,887 May 27, 1890, magazine gun, #436,965 September 23, 1890, breechloading firearm, #441,390 November 25, 1890, magazine gun, #465,339 December 15, 1891, magazine gun, #465,340 December 15, 1891, magazine gun, #471,782 March 29, 1892, automatic gun, #471,783 March 29, 1892, machine gun, #471,782 March 29, ...272 November 15, 1892,

zine gun, #730,870 June 16, 1903, automatic gun, #747,585 December 22, 1903, automatic gun, #781,765 February 7, 1905, magazine gun, #808,003 December 19, 1905, magazine gun, #812,326 February 13, 1906, recoil brake, #818,739 April 24, 1906, automatic gun, #853,438 May 14, 1907, automatic gun, #864,608 August 27, 1907, automatic gun, and #864,609 August 27, 1907, automatic gun. Son of Jonathan Browning. Most of his patents were used by the large gun companies - Winchester, Colt, and Remington in this country and Fabrique Nationale d'Armes de Guerre in Belgium. He and his brother Matthew made about 600 single shot rifles on his 1879 patent before selling its rights to Winchester.

BROWNING, JONATHAN, M. (1805-1879), Sumner Co., Tennessee, 1826-1834, Adams Co., Illinois, 1834-1842, Nauvoo, Illinois, 1842-1846, Kanesville, Iowa, 1846-1851, Ogden, Utah, 1851-1879. Made percussion rifles, both muzzle loading and repeating. The repeating guns were of the harmonica and revolver types. Four of his sons, David, John M., Matthew S., and Wesley, were gunsmiths. (GR 5-61)

BROWNING, MATTHEW S. Ogden, Utah. Operated Browning Bros. shop in Ogden with his brother John M. Browning with whom he held three patents.

BROWNING, WESLEY, (1832-?), Kanesville, Iowa, 1850c, Ogden, Utah, 1851-?. Son of Jonathan Browning. (MB 8-64)

BROWNSON, HOPKINS & SLOCUMB, New Orleans, Louisiana. Percussion guns.

BROWNUP, JAMES, Philadelphia, Pennsylvania, 1779-1780. (Dean)

BROYHIER, F. McGregor, Iowa, 1865d.

BROYLES, G.E. Ringgold, Georgia, 1879d-1883d.

BROYLES, JAMES C. Tupelo, Mississippi. Patents #338,247 March 23, 1886, breechloading firearm, and #653,613 July 10, 1900, choke device. Columbus, Mississippi. Patent #685,669 October 29, 1901, choke device. Birmingham, Alabama. Patent #778,629 December 27, 1904, single trigger.

---

or "unlocated" appears. If either year in a span is unknown, a question mark is displayed. Year(s) will not be in parentheses.

5. **RELEVANT INFORMATION** - a listing may have none, some, or many of the following:
   a. Firearm type produced/designed/sold/associated with the listing NAME. As a general rule, especially in conjunction with the terms flintlock, percussion, 1/2 stock, fullstock, and Kentucky, the author was describing a rifle. "Rifle" appears in listings as an exception rather than the rule.
   b. Patents (typically with numbers).
   c. Limited personal or business information.
   d. Business ownership - name(s) of co-owner(s) and business name. Denoted by the presence of "with person(s) as XYZ entity" for a specific person. A business listing may have no names, or several.
   e. Employment by a person or business, usually indicated by "for NAME".
   f. Predecessor/successor businesses.
   g. Familial relationships.
   h. Other.

6. **BIBLIOGRAPHY CODE** - always at the end of a listing, always in parentheses. Short alpha-numeric or author last name for sources of listing content. For some "new" post-1983 listings or updates, the bibliography references may be incomplete but have been transcribed as they appeared in Frank Sellers' master copy. The Bibliography can be found in the back of this text.

It is also important that you understand what will not be found within these pages. The A-Z sections do not have listings for absolutely every American gunsmith, past or present - that is impossible. A specific person's listing may provide very limited information, and no listing has comprehensive or fully detailed information. This Second Edition is not merely a reprint of the original. There are many new listings, and thousands of corrections, amendments, updates, and edits. The primary source for "new" content was the author's pre-publication master copy of the First Edition, with his handwritten notations entered since 1983. A caution to those fortunate owners of the First Edition - the scanner/optical character recognition technology used to convert a pre-computer era book into an e-publishing version has not deleted any listings. However, its alphabetization logic has noticeably repositioned listings within alphabetic sections, or transferred listings to another section.

EDITOR'S COMMENTARY:

I wish to formally express my appreciation and gratitude to S.P. Fjestad for his confidence in my editorial and proofing qualifications, and for the opportunity to participate in publishing this edition. Thanks also to Sara Lange, Kelsey Fjestad, Clint H. Schmidt, John Andraschko, and John Allen, for their invaluable assistance.

INTRODUCTION TO THE 2ND EDITION
by S.P. Fjestad

Over the years, learning to trust my initial instincts on a new project has been more helpful than anything else to evaluate its potential. Some new ventures take forever and seem to move slower than even a climate change glacier. Other first time endeavors leap out of the gate, only to quickly slow down or stop all together.

The inception date on this Second Edition was approximately 8:45 am on July 27, 2007. Larry Riling from Ray Riling Arms Books Co., Inc. walked up to our corner table at the annual Missouri Valley Collectors Association show in Kansas City, MO, and gave me a mint, signed copy of *American Gunsmiths* by Frank Sellers, who was only 75 feet away down the aisle from our tables. It was graciously accepted, as the previous copy Frank had signed to me years earlier was virtually worn-out from daily use and a little abuse.

Fully knowing that a rare copy like the one Frank had just signed was currently selling in the $250-$300 range, I immediately sensed a unique opportunity to get a new Second Edition published. However, an agreement would have to be reached between Blue Book Publications, Inc. and Frank and Karen Sellers. Walking down the aisle, Frank was in his regular spot, doing his usual things in his own inimitable style, which was always laced with wit and humor.

Striking up a conversation with both of them, we reached a preliminary agreement shortly, even though I knew that publishing a Second Edition was going to be difficult, since there were no word processing files or even film to work with. The key was to edit and update it using Frank's original handwritten notes accumulated since 1983, and to competitively price it, assuring everyone who needed a copy could easily afford it.

Returning to Minneapolis after the show, a contractual agreement was drawn up, but there was one big problem - Frank had been diagnosed with cancer, and his health was failing fast. In October, Frank sent his original First Edition proof copy with handwritten notes, which thankfully contained hundreds of listings that had come up since the First Edition was published. In order to get a needed word processing manuscript for publishing, my original First Edition was scanned by a process called OCR (optical character recognition). After scanning, this is when the real work began.

David Kosowski, a long-time member of our proofing staff and meticulous copy editor, who hates even an extra space after a comma, was given the job to proof/edit the entire A-Z sections. This meant changing and editing a lot of entries, re-alphabetizing when necessary, and in general, cleaning up a lot of inconsistencies from the First Edition. As he put it, "It was like trench warfare during WWI, and I didn't leave the trenches for a long time."

After hundreds of hours, David completed his task, and an extensively revised word processing manuscript was now available for us to publish. Another huge benefit is that the A-Z sections were also adaptable to an advanced database environment, which is why this publication is also available online.

Throughout the entire process, while Frank's health deteriorated rapidly, Karen Sellers helped us out tremendously with her constant flow of communication and attention to the overall project, even the details. Frank Sellers passed away peacefully on the last day of January, 2008. At that point, we were well into the proofing/editing process, but it saddened me knowing that Frank could not sign a new Second Edition for me.

Maybe the greatest memory I have of Frank Sellers occurred during an Antique Arms show decades ago at the Sahara Hotel in Las Vegas. Frank had his usual spread of hundreds of handguns and rifles, many of them from some of America's more obscure gunmakers and gunsmiths. An attorney walked up to his table and told Frank that he needed to decorate his law office in town, and would prefer to use antique guns over wallpaper. Frank quickly replied, "How long is the hallway, and how many feet high do you want them?" The attorney had to think about this for awhile, and then told Frank, "It's probably 40 feet long and I think four feet high would be fine." Again, Frank quickly replied, "OK, so you need 160 square feet of guns. Do you have any preferences?" The attorney's answer was "Not really", so Frank wrote him out a receipt for 160 square feet of antique handguns, and then proceeded to pick them out.

In closing, I feel fortunate to have known Frank Sellers, and even more fortunate to have published this new and revised Second Edition. I think Frank would be proud of our work, and Blue Book Publications, Inc. is very proud to have been involved in his final publication. Additionally, the entire staff would like to thank Karen Sellers for making our job go as easily as it could during this difficult time. In my original First Edition, Frank signed it "Steve, glad I can help you sound smarter everyday." It's still true today.

Sincerely,

S.P. Fjestad
Publisher
Blue Book Publications, Inc.

A SECTION

A & B see Amos & Border.

A*T*W unidentified. Percussion fullstock.

A. & B. Co. see Amos & Border.

A.A. Co. grip marking on suicide special.

A.A. see Adam Angstadt.

A.B. see Abija Fairchild.

A.C. unidentified. Flintlock pistols.

A.C.T. unidentified. Percussion Tennessee rifle.

A.D. see Adam Daniels.

A.D.R. see A.D. Reger.

A.E. see Adam Ernst.

A.E. unidentified. Percussion fullstock.

A.F. see Alfred Field.

A.F. see Andrew Figthorn.

A.G. unidentified. Percussion fullstock.

A.H. unidentified. Flintlock Kentucky.

A.J. unidentified. Flintlock Kentucky.

A.J.S. unidentified. Percussion fullstock.

A.K. see A. Kiser.

A.K. see Andrew Klay.

A.K. see Andrew Klineinst.

A.K. see Andrew Kopp.

A.L. see Andrew Long.

A.M. unidentified. Percussion fullstock.

A.P. unidentified. Percussion 1/2 stock.

A.P.F. unidentified. Percussion 1/2 stock.

A.P.W. unidentified. Percussion fullstock.

A.R.F. unidentified. Flintlock Kentucky.

A.S. see Asa Stilgenbauer.

A.S.-O.H. unidentified. Percussion 1/2 stock (possibly Stilgenbauer and Hartington).

A.S.T. Co. see American Standard Tool Co.

A.T. unidentified. Percussion 1/2 stock.

A.W. see Abraham Welshantz.

A.W. unidentified. Flintlock Kentucky.

AARON, ABRAHAM Virginia, 1774-1778. Militia repairs. (Gill)

AARON, GEORGE W. Washington, D.C., 1858d. (Hartzler)

ABBEY, FREDERICK J., & CO. Chicago, Illinois, 1858-1878d. Patent #114,081 April 25, 1871, breechloading firearm. Muzzle and breechloading rifles, shotguns, pistols. Company included J.H. Foster, 1870-1872, and C. Olson and W. Foss, 1876-1878.

ABBEY, GEORGE T. (1823-?), Utica, New York, 1845-1852, Chicago, Illinois, 1852d-1874d. Patent #87,814, March 16, 1869, breechloading firearm. Successor to Peacock & Thatcher. Percussion and breechloading firearms.

ABBEY, OREN Middlebury, Vermont, 1865d-1911. (Horn)

ABBEY, ROBERT Augusta, Georgia, 1842-1860. Percussion 1/2 stock. As Rogers & Abbey, 1842.

ABBOTT see Badger & Abbott.

ABBOTT, A.M. Oquawka, Illinois, 1845, Summit Hill, Illinois, 1860d.

ABBOTT, JAMES M. Welchville, Maine. Percussion 1/2 stock.

ABBOTT, JOSEPH S. Columbus, Ohio, 1845-1855. As Gere & Abbott. (Hutslar)

ABBOTT, L.N. Clarksville, Texas, 1896d.

ABBOTT, SAMUEL C. Zanesville, Ohio. Patent #25,795 October 11, 1859, shotgun wads.

ABBOTT, WILLIAM W. Philadelphia, Pennsylvania, 1890d. (C&W)

ABBOTT, WILLIAM Grand Rapids, Michigan 1875d.

ABBOTT, WILLIAM Henniker, New Hampshire, 1874d.

ABBY, R. Albion, New York, 1848-1850d.

ABE, AUGUSTUS St. Louis, Missouri, 1869-1895d.

ABEL, HENRY Williamsport, Pennsylvania, 1882d.

ABEL, J.B. Alfordsville, Indiana, 1860d.

ABELL, JUDSON Clove Valley, New York, 1874d. Percussion fullstock.

ABENDROTH, ANDREW Defiance, Ohio, 1872d. Percussion 1/2 stock. (Hutslar)

ABENDSHEN, JOSEPH Pittsburgh, Pennsylvania, 1850-1860d. Percussion 1/2 stock.

ABENDSHEN, MRS. JOSEPH Wheeling, West Virginia, 1867d.

ABERCROMBIE & FITCH New York, New York, 1892-1978. Dealers only.

ABERCROMBIE Seneca, South Carolina. Percussion fullstock.

ABILL, ROSS Putnam Co., Missouri. Percussion era.

ABLY, HENRY Sheffield, Iowa, 1887d-1897d.

ABRAHAM, GUSTAVE C. Flint, Michigan, 1887d-1899d.

ABRAHAM, THOMAS (1808-?), Delaware County, Indiana. (Lindert)

ABRAMSON, G. Scandinavia, Wisconsin, 1857d.

ACCELERATING FIRE ARMS CO. New York, New York, 1857-1860. Lyman patent rifles. (GR 10-69)

ACCLES, JAMES G. Hartford, Connecticut, 1880-1888. Patents #290,622 December 18, 1883, machine gun feeder, #348,180 August 31, 1886, machine gun carriage, #396,523 January 22, 1889, magazine (London), #426,356 April 22, 1890, machine gun (London), and #487,238 December 6, 1892, machine gun feeder (London). Patents used by Gatling Gun Co.

ACFIELD, JACOB unlocated. Pennsylvania Committee of Safety. (Kauffman)

ACHOR, ALEXANDER (1821-?), York, Pennsylvania, 1847, Harrison County, Ohio, 1850c. (Hutslar)

ACHOR, ELIAS Indianola, Iowa, 1889d.

ACKERMAN, HERMAN Peru, Illinois, 1867-1890d, Marysville, Kansas, 1894d.

ACKERMAN, JASPER, L. Monon, Indiana. Patents #633,939 September 26, 1899, safety lock, and #667,051 January 29, 1901, lever lock.

ACKERMAN, LOUIS New Orleans, Louisiana, 1871d.

ACKLEY, LUTHER (?-1948), Caldwell, Ohio, 1890-1948. Percussion 1/2 stock.

ACME ARMS CO. trade name of Cornwall Hardware Co., New York, on shotguns and revolvers.

ACME trade name of Davenport Arms Co. on shotguns.

ACME trade name of Hopkins & Allen on hammerless safety revolvers.

ACME trade name of Hopkins & Allen on spur trigger revolvers.

ACME trade name of Maltby, Henley & Co. on revolvers.

ACME trade name of Merwin, Hulbert & Co. on owlhead revolvers.

ADAIR, JAMES A. (1829-?), Syracuse, New York, 1850c-1856, Manlius, New York, 1856-1859, Sacramento, California, 1860-1861, 1865-1870, Red Bluff, California, 1871-1875. Percussion rifles. For Andrew Flohr and George Kingsley in California. (Shelton)

ADAM, ANTHONY New Orleans, Louisiana, 1899d.

ADAM, P. unlocated. Percussion over/under rifle.

ADAMS & EAYRS Bridgeport, Connecticut, 1876-1878d. Percussion rifles.

ADAMS & MCCOY Utica, New York, 1840-1850. Percussion rifles. Lyman Adams and Daniel McCoy. (Swinney)

ADAMS & SON Mexia, Texas, 1890d.

ADAMS REVOLVING ARMS CO. New York, New York, 1857-1861. Promotional company for Adams revolvers which were made by Massachusetts Arms Co.

ADAMS, C.M. Bridgeport, Connecticut, 1880d-1881d.

ADAMS, CHARLES W. Haverhill, Massachusetts, 1879d.

ADAMS, CHARLES Leadville, Colorado, 1886-1890. (Sellers-3)

ADAMS, CHRISTOPHER (1848-?), San Francisco, California, 1870-1895. (Shelton)

ADAMS, D.E. Lapeer, Michigan, 1860d.

ADAMS, DANIEL (1806-?), Somerset, Pennsylvania, 1837 (Kauffman), Crawford, Pennsylvania, 1860c. (Whisker-II)

ADAMS, DAVID Junction, Oregon, 1878d.

ADAMS, DUMMER J. Kittery, Maine, 1873-1900. (Demeritt)

ADAMS, H.E. Los Angeles, California, 1893d.

ADAMS, HENRY W. New York, New York. Patent #11,685, September 19, 1854, breechloading firearms.

ADAMS, J.H. Cincinnati, Ohio, 1880c. Percussion 1/2 stock rifle.

ADAMS, JAMES Bloomfield, Pennsylvania, 1871d-1874d, Riceville, Pennsylvania, 1879d-1890. Riceville was a village in Bloomfield Township.

ADAMS, JOHN S. St. Charles, Missouri, 1820.

ADAMS, JOHN S. Taunton, Massachusetts, 1861-1865. Patents #39,455 August 11, 1863, breechloading firearm, #44,377 September 27, 1864, breechloading firearm, #45,806 January 10, 1865, hand grenade, and #48,010 May 30, 1865, cartridge.

ADAMS, JOSEPH Cleveland, Ohio. Patents #15,797 September 30, 1856, firearm, and #25,929 October 25, 1859, cannon.

ADAMS, LYMAN Utica, New York, 1832-1850. Percussion 1/2 stock. As Adams & McCoy, 1840-1850. (Swinney)

ADAMS, N.R. trade name of N.R. Davis on shotguns. (Hinman)

ADAMS, P. Antioch, California. Patent #257,085 April 3, 1883, magazine gun with S. Adams and John Simmons.

ADAMS, R.C. Milan, Tennessee, 1885d.

ADAMS, RALPH (1829-?), Chicago, Illinois, 1848, Galena, Illinois, 1858-1859. (Johnson)

ADAMS, RICHARDSON & CO. Salem, Massachusetts, 1867d. Importers and dealers.

ADAMS, SALMON Richmond, Virginia, 1860-1865. Master armorer at Virginia Manufactory, 1862-1865.

ADAMS, SAMUEL Antioch, California. Patent #275,085 April 3, 1883, magazine gun with John P. Simmons.

ADAMS, SAMUEL Battle Creek, Michigan, 1860d-1899d. Percussion fullstock.

ADAMS, SAMUEL Springfield, Massachusetts. Patent #960 October 3, 1838, barrels. Percussion 1/2 stock with removable barrel liner for converting shotguns produced by C.B. Allen.

ADAMS, SAMUEL Troy, New York, 1838-1840. Flintlock Kentucky. Probably same as Samuel Adams of Massachusetts.

ADAMS, TOWER Washington County, Pennsylvania, 1826-1859. Negro gunsmith. (Kauffman)

ADAMS, W. Dunstable, Massachusetts. Flintlock Kentucky. (ASAC 44)

ADAMS, W.A. Quincy, Illinois, 1858, Denver, Colorado, 1859. As Hightower & Adams. (Sellers-3)

ADAMSON, WILLIAM C. Atlanta, Georgia, 1887d.

ADCOCK, ALLEN Columbia, Tennessee, 1881d-1887d.

ADDAMS, THOMAS, JR. Richmond, Virginia, 1862. Altered guns for the Confederacy. (Albaugh-1)

ADDICKS, D.C. Augusta, Georgia. Mostly 20th century. (AR 12-32)

ADGER, J.E., & CO. Charleston, South Carolina. Percussion double shotgun.

ADIRONDACK ARMS CO. Plattsburg, New York, 1870-1874. Produced Robinson's patent repeating rifles until purchased by Winchester in 1874. (ST 11-62)

ADKINS, JOSIAH Connecticut, 1777. Committee of Safety lockmaker.

ADLON, J.C. Albia, Iowa, 1880d.

ADVANCE trade name on spur trigger revolver.

AETNA ARMS CO. New York, New York, 1869-1883. Copies of Smith & Wesson revolver Models 1, 2, and 3.

AETNA suicide special by Harrington & Richardson.

AFFLEBAUGH, HENRY Philadelphia, Pennsylvania, 1816d-1819d. (C&W)

AFFLERBACH, J. Philadelphia, Pennsylvania, 1860c-1861d. Derringers.

AFFLERBACH, JOHN C. Philadelphia, Pennsylvania, 1876d-1892d. Son of William Afflerbach.

AFFLERBACH, WILLIAM H. Philadelphia, Pennsylvania, 1880d-1890d. Son of William Afflerbach.

AFFLERBACH, WILLIAM Philadelphia, Pennsylvania, 1846d-1891d. Percussion guns.

AGER, ALEXANDER (1821-1898), New Rumly, Ohio, 1848-1886. Percussion rifles and shotguns.

AGER, WILLIAM (1794-?), King George County, Virginia, 1850c. (MB 10-63)

AGER, WILSON New York, New York. Reputed inventor of the "Union Coffee Mill" and holder of British patents on it. (Chinn)

AGNEW, ANDREW Orange, New Jersey, 1865d, New Brunswick, New Jersey, 1866d-1878d. Percussion 1/2 stock.

AGOSTINO, JOSEPH New York, New York, 1867d-1871d.

AGY Pennsylvania, 1780. Flintlock Kentucky rifles. Could be Haga?

AHART, A. Davidson County, Tennessee. Percussion Tennessee rifle.

AHLEPUDT, THOMAS Red Wing, Minnesota, 1867d.

AHLES, W. unlocated. Flintlock swivel breech rifle.

AHNER, CHRISTIAN Lancaster, Pennsylvania, 1857d.

AHRENS, JAMES H. Oswego, New York, 1866d-1870d. Percussion guns.

AICHELE, CHARLES G. Kendallsville, Indiana, 1867d. Percussion fullstock.

AIKEN, B.F. Freetown, Massachusetts, 1867, Patent #66,913, July 16, 1867, breechloading firearm with D.C. Thrasher.

AILER, LEWIS Philadelphia, Pennsylvania, 1813d-1819d.

AINSWORTH, W.H. Benicia, California, 1871-1872. (Shelton)

AIRS, SAMUEL Beaver Creek, Illinois, 1860d.

AKE, SIMON McConnellsburgh, Pennsylvania, 1845. (C&W)

AKINS, THOMAS (1826-1887), Sebastopol, California, 1860, Santa Rosa, California, 1867, Salinas, California, 1869, Cloverdale, California, 1873-1887. (Shelton)

ALABAMA ARMS CO. Montgomery, Alabama, 1862. Produced parts only. (Albaugh & Simmons)

ALASKA suicide special by Hood Fire Arms Co.

ALB, J. see Jacob Albright.

ALBEE, GEORGE E. New Haven, Connecticut. Patents #354,371 December 14, 1886, magazine gun, and #852,152 April 30, 1907, sight.

ALBERTSON, DOUGLAS & CO. New London, Connecticut, 1840-1860. Whaling guns.

ALBERTSON, NATHAN Guilford Co., North Carolina, 1844. (Bivins)

ALBIG, GEORGE New York, New York, 1879d-1896d.

ALBRECHT, ANDREW see Andrew Albright.

ALBRECHT, ANTON (?-1816), Lancaster, Pennsylvania. Flintlock Kentucky. (Dean)

ALBRECHT, CHARLES Pittsburgh, Pennsylvania, 1870d.

ALBRECHT, JOHN Northhampton Co., Pennsylvania, 1745. (Kauffman 2)

ALBRICH, FRANK M. Chicago, Illinois, 1890d.

ALBRIGHT & RUDOLPH St. Louis, Missouri, 1872-1873. William Albright and Victor Rudolph.

ALBRIGHT & SON Alamance Co., North Carolina. Elias and John Albright. (Bivins)

ALBRIGHT, A. Lancaster, Pennsylvania, 1820c. Flintlock Kentucky.

ALBRIGHT, ANDREW (1718-1802), Nazareth, Pennsylvania, 1750, Lancaster, Pennsylvania, 1767-1802. Flintlock Kentucky. Born Andreas Albrecht. (ASAC7)

ALBRIGHT, DAVID (1823-?), Wooster, Ohio, 1850c. (Hutslar)

ALBRIGHT, ELIAS (1793-?), Alamance Co., North Carolina, 1820-1850. Flintlock and percussion rifles. (Bivins)

ALBRIGHT, H. unlocated. Percussion fullstock (but not John Henry Albright's "Henry Albright" signature).

ALBRIGHT, HENRY (1772-1845), Lancaster, Pennsylvania, 1792-1794, Chambersburg, Pennsylvania, 1796, Shippensburg, Pennsylvania, 1800, Gnadenhutten, Ohio, 1805-1808, Nazareth, Pennsylvania, 1810-1845. Son of Andrew Albright, born John Henry, but signed all guns just "Henry Albright". (Kindig)

ALBRIGHT, JACOB (1759-?), Northcumberland Co., Pennsylvania, 1800, Center Co., Pennsylvania, 1802t. Son of Andrew Albright. (Kauffman-Dyke)

ALBRIGHT, JACOB, JR. (1803-?), Mifflin Co., Pennsylvania, 1825-1830, Wooster, Ohio, 1830-1850. (Hutslar)

ALBRIGHT, JOHN ANDREW (1770-1822), Nazareth, Pennsylvania, 1790-1822. Son of Andrew Albright. (Dyke)

ALBRIGHT, JOHN HENRY see Henry Albright.

ALBRIGHT, JOHN P. Burlington, North Carolina, 1877d-1890d.

ALBRIGHT, JOHN (1826-?), Alamance Co., North Carolina, 1850c. Son of Elias Albright. (Bivins)

ALBRIGHT, JOSHUA Otsego, Missouri, 1850c-1855d.

ALBRIGHT, LOUIS Ottawa, Ohio, 1859-1863. Patent #38,366 May 5, 1863, breechloading firearm.

ALBRIGHT, MATHIAS Lancaster Co., Pennsylvania, 1771.

ALBRIGHT, PETER Lancaster Co., Pennsylvania, 1771.

ALBRIGHT, THOMAS JOHN (1808-1890), Stroudsburg, Pennsylvania, 1835t-1840, St. Louis, Missouri, 1842d-1877d. Joined by his sons William A. and Thomas, Jr. in 1849. (Dyke-Pourie)

ALBRIGHT, THOMAS JOHN, JR. St. Louis, Missouri, 1849d-1866d.

ALBRIGHT, WILLIAM St. Louis, Missouri, 1849d-1883d.

ALBRIGHT, ZACHARIA JR. (1821-?), Bedford County, Pennsylvania, 1845-1848, Buckeye, Illinois, 1850c. (C&W)

ALBRIGHT, ZACHARIA Bedford Co., Pennsylvania, 1846, Centre Co., Pennsylvania, 1850c, Williamstown, Iowa 1865d. Percussion fullstock signed "Z.A.". (KRA 1)

ALBRO, ALFRED Chicago, Illinois, 1845, Columbus, Kansas, 1882d.

ALBRO, HENRY, & CO. Cincinnati, Ohio, 1840-1856. Locks and parts.

ALBRO, MARK (1800-?), Nauvoo, Illinois, 1850c. (Johnson)

ALDEN, E.B. Claremont, New Hampshire, 1863-1868d.

ALDEN, L.M. Middleboro, Massachusetts, 1892d.

ALDENDERFER, HENRY Lancaster, Pennsylvania, 1810t-1818t. Listed only as a gunsmith in tax records but Kentucky rifles carry his signature.

ALDENDERFER, JOEL Lancaster, Pennsylvania, 1815-1855. Flintlock Kentucky.

ALDENDERFER, METSCHL Lancaster, Pennsylvania, 1763-1814, Colbrookdale, Pennsylvania, 1817t-1820t. Flintlock Kentucky. (Kindig-Dyke)

ALDERMAN, RILEY (1808-?), Brookfield, Ohio, 1850-1861d. Muzzleloading rifles. (Hutslar)

ALDERMAN, WILLIAM Rock Cave, West Virginia, 1900d. (Whisker IV)

ALDINGER, D. Galveston, Texas, 1878d.

ALDRICH, JAMES T. Norwich, Connecticut, 1881-1884. Patents #283,185 August 14, 1883, revolver, and #308,231 November 18, 1884, revolver.

ALDRICH, ROBERT Blackstone, Massachusetts. Patent #459,732 September 22, 1891, airgun.

ALDRICH, WALES Cleveland, Ohio. Patent #38,455 May 12, 1863, breechloading firearm.

ALEK, J. unlocated. Flintlock Kentucky rifle.

ALERT suicide special by Hood Firearms Co.

ALEXANDER GUN CO. trade name on imported shotgun.

ALEXANDER, CHARLES WILLIAM Moorefield, Virginia. Patents #20,315 May 25, 1858, breechloading firearm, and Confederate #163 April 18, 1863, breechloading firearm. (Albaugh-1)

ALEXANDER, DONALD Allegheny Co., Pennsylvania, 1790-1838. (Whisker II)

ALEXANDER, F.M. Martinsburg, Iowa, 1897d.

ALEXANDER, FREDERICK W. Baltimore, Maryland. Patents #45,009 November 15, 1864, bayonet, and #74,478 February 18, 1868, cannon.

ALEXANDER, WILLIAM (?-1797), Augusta Co., Virginia, 1775-1776, Lexington, Virginia, 1797. Eight rifles for Virginia, 1776. (Gill)

ALEXANDER, ZENAS (?-1826), Charlotte, North Carolina, 1805-1826. Flintlock Kentucky rifles. (Bivins)

ALEXIA suicide special by Hood Fire Arms Company.

ALEXIS suicide special by Hood Fire Arms Company.

ALFORD & BERKELE New York, New York, 1883-1888d.

ALFORD, A.G., & CO. Baltimore, Maryland, 1880d-1889d. (Hartzler)

ALFORD, ALBRO Crete, Illinois, 1864d.

ALFORD, ALONZO New York, New York, 1869d-1888d. As Alford, Farr & Clapp, 1869 and Alford & Berkele, 1883-1888, dealers and importers.

ALFORD, FARR & CLAPP New York, New York, 1869d. Successors to Morgan & Clapp.

ALFORD, NELSON E. Baltimore, Maryland, 1880-1887d. (Hartzler)

ALFSON, ANDREW Chicago, Illinois. Patents #638,677 December 5, 1899, magazine gun, and #716,976 December 30, 1902, revolving rifle.

ALISON, J.H. unlocated. Percussion 1/2 stock.

ALISS, JOHN J. Washington D.C. Patent #44,586 October 11, 1864, barrel cleaner.

ALKIN, CHARLES St. Louis, Missouri, 1848d. Probably Charles Altinger.

ALLBRIGHT, ISRAEL unlocated. Early flintlock Kentucky.

ALLEBAUGH, WILLIAM (1822-?), Fayette County, Pennsylvania, 1850c. (Whisker)

ALLEGHENY GUN WORKS Allegheny (Pittsburgh), Pennsylvania, 1831-1898. Percussion rifles and shotguns. John and William Fleeger.

ALLEGRA BROTHERS Brooklyn, New York, 1892d-1899d. Breechloading shotguns.

ALLEGRA, FRANCISCO Brooklyn, New York, 1891d-1899d. As Allegra Bros., 1892-1899.

ALLEMAN, A.B. unlocated. Percussion swivel breech.

ALLEMAN, WILLIAM Bushkill, Pennsylvania, 1835t. (KRA II-3)

ALLEN & BALL Springfield, Massachusetts, 1835-1836. C.B. Allen and Charles Ball.

ALLEN & DIAL Columbia, S.C. Importers and dealers.

ALLEN & HILLE New Orleans, Louisiana, 1842d-1859d. Percussion guns. Joseph Allen and Charles Hille.

ALLEN & THURBER Grafton, Massachusetts, 1837-1842, Norwich, Connecticut, 1842-1847, Worcester, Massachusetts, 1847-1856. Allen patent pepperboxes, pistols, rifles, and shotguns. (Mouillesseaux)

ALLEN & TUCKER Wichita, Kansas, 1884d.

ALLEN & WHEELOCK Worcester, Massachusetts, 1856-1865. Allen patent pepperboxes, percussion, and cartridge guns. (Mouillesseaux)

ALLEN PATENT FIRE-ARMS MFG. CO. North Scituate, Massachusetts, 1867-1879. Assigned patents of Charles E. Bailey, but no production known.

ALLEN'S SONS, S. Greenfield, Massachusetts, 1878-1893, moved from Shrewsbury in 1878.

ALLEN, A. Kalamazoo, Michigan, 1865d-1867d. As Sweet & Allen in 1867.

ALLEN, A.E. Taylor, New York. Percussion 1/2 stock.

ALLEN, ALEXANDER Massilon, Ohio, 1859-1868. (Hutslar)

ALLEN, ALEXANDER Urbana, Ohio, 1811. (Hutslar)

ALLEN, AMASA Walpole, New Hampshire, 1790-1810. Kentucky rifles, and Model 1798 contract muskets with Joseph Barnard and Samuel Grant. (Gluckman)

ALLEN, BENJAMIN F. Fairfield County, Ohio, 1877. (Hutslar)

ALLEN, BENJAMIN F. Lancaster, Ohio, 1894. (Hutslar)

ALLEN, BRADFORD Providence, Rhode Island, 1872d.

ALLEN, BROWN & LUTHER Worcester, Massachusetts, 1848-1858. Rifle and musket barrels. Fredrick Allen, Andrew J. Brown, and John Luther.

ALLEN, CHARLES H. Norwich, Connecticut, 1857-1880. As Hopkins & Allen, 1867-1880. (ASAC 20)

ALLEN, CYRUS BULLARD (?-1840), Springfield, Massachusetts, 1830-1840. Many patent guns, including Elgin Cutlass pistols and Cochran turret pistols. As Allen & Barber, 1830-1835, and Allen & Ball, 1835-1836. (GC 30)

ALLEN, DANIEL C. (1814-?), Bellevue, Iowa, 1850c. Brother of Henry Allen.

ALLEN, DANIEL L. Morristown, New Jersey, 1882d.

ALLEN, EDWARD T. (1839-?), San Francisco, California, 1875-1900. Dealer. (Shelton)

ALLEN, EDWARD Kansas City, Missouri, 1891d-1893d. Dealer.

ALLEN, ELIAS (1775-?), Shrewsbury, Massachusetts, ?-1840. Flintlock fowlers and muskets.

ALLEN, ENOS G. Boston, Massachusetts. Patents #39,024 June 30, 1863, gain twist rifling, #41,590 February 16, 1864, cartridge, and #45,306, December 6, 1864, bullet.

ALLEN, ETHAN (1806-1871), Grafton, Massachusetts, 1835-1842, Norwich, Connecticut, 1842-1847, Worcester, Massachusetts, 1847-1871. Patents #461 November 11, 1837, pistol, #2,919 January 16, 1843, engraving machine, #3,998 April 16, 1845, pepperbox, #13,154 July 3, 1855, firearm, #15,454 July 29, 1856, bullet mold, #16,367 January 13, 1857, revolver, #18,836 December 15, 1857, revolver, #21,400 September 7, 1858, revolver, #22,005 November 9, 1858, revolver, #27,094 February 14, 1860, cartridge machinery, #27,415 March 13, 1860, firearm, #28,951 July 3, 1860, revolver, #30,033 September 18, 1860, breechloading firearm, #30,109 September 25, 1860, cartridge, #31,695 March 19, 1861, cartridge machinery, #33,328 September 24, 1861, revolver, #33,509 October 22, 1861, revolver, #35,067 April 29, 1862, revolver, #36,760 October 28, 1862, sight, #46,617 March 7, 1865, extractor, #47,688 May 16, 1865, cartridge, #48,249 June 20, 1865, firearms, #49,491 August 22, 1865, breechloading, #55,596 June 19, 1866, barrels, and #84,929 December 15, 1968, breechloading firearm. Allen was a founder and partner in several gun companies; all of which carried his name. (Mouilleseaux).

ALLEN, ETHAN, & CO. Worcester, Massachusetts, 1863-1871. Allen patent guns.

ALLEN, FRANK H. Norwich, Connecticut. Patents #168,549 October 11, 1875, revolvers, #239,634 April 5, 1881, palm pistol, #273,335 March 6, 1883, palm pistol, and #294,950 March 11, 1884, revolvers. Pistols made under these last two patents for Minneapolis Fire Arms Co. Son of Charles Allen.

ALLEN, FRANK Carrollton, Illinois, 1890d-1893d.

ALLEN, FREDERICK Worcester, Massachusetts, 1845-1858. Percussion muskets. As Allen, Brown & Luther.

ALLEN, G.F. Utica, New York, 1846-1851, New York, New York, 1851-1855. Telescopes exhibited at Crystal Palace in 1851. (Swinney)

ALLEN, GEORGE Brooklyn, New York, 1885d-1887d.

ALLEN, HARVEY S. (1816-1897), Burlington, Iowa, 1844-1849, Placerville, California, 1869-1897. (Shelton)

ALLEN, HENRY S. (1816-?), Burlington, Iowa, 1849, Bellevue, Iowa, 1850c. Brother of Daniel Allen. (MB 8-64)

ALLEN, HENRY New York, New York, 1812-1851. Percussion guns. (Swinney)

ALLEN, HIRAM J. Arkadelphia, Arkansas. Patent #113,963 April 25, 1871, breechloading firearm.

ALLEN, J. Tecumseh, Michigan, 1865d.

ALLEN, J.M. Trenton, New Jersey, 1882d-1885d. As J.M. Allen & Son, 1885.

ALLEN, J.P. Dawson, Georgia, 1881d-1883d.

ALLEN, JACAMIAH Richmond County, New York, 1768.

ALLEN, JACOB New York, New York, 1773. (Swinney)

ALLEN, JAMES Kalamazoo, Michigan, 1863d-1883d, Detroit, Michigan, 1888d-1895d. Percussion rifles.

ALLEN, JEROME Goshen, Indiana, 1870-1892. (MB 4-54)

ALLEN, JOHN New York, New York, 1876-1878.

ALLEN, JOSEPH New Orleans, Louisiana, 1838d-1861d. Percussion rifles. As Allen & Hille, 1842-1859.

ALLEN, L.A. Bristol, Rhode Island, 1876d.

ALLEN, MARTIN V.B. New York, New York, 1899d-1907. Patents #741,754 October 20, 1903, safety, #793,382 June 13, 1905, safety, and #849,825 April 9, 1907, safety.

ALLEN, OLIVER Norwich, Connecticut, 1841-1848. Patent #1,202 September 19, 1846, bomb lance. Percussion 1/2 stock.

ALLEN, ROBERT (1809-?), Dixon, Ohio, 1850c. (Hutslar)

ALLEN, ROBERT Norwich, Connecticut, circa 1840. Whaling guns.

ALLEN, SAMUEL Dansville, New York, 1874d-1880d.

ALLEN, SCOTT Baptistown, New Jersey, 1860d.

ALLEN, SILAS M. Shrewsbury, Massachusetts, 1856d-1859d. Son of Silas Allen Jr.?

ALLEN, SILAS (1750-1834), Shrewsbury, Massachusetts. Flintlock Kentucky. (GR 3-76)

ALLEN, SILAS, JR. (1785-1868), Shrewsbury, Massachusetts, 1806-1845. Flintlock and percussion guns. (GR 3-76)

ALLEN, SYD E. Raleigh, North Carolina. Patent #60,897 January 1, 1867, alarm gun with Al Johnson.

ALLEN, THOMAS New York, 1768-1775. Flintlock guns.

ALLEN, THURBER & CO. Worcester, Massachusetts, 1856-1865. Allen patent pepperboxes and other guns. (Mouillesseaux)

ALLEN, W. Sutton, Massachusetts, circa 1800. Kentucky rifle. (Lindsay)

ALLEN, W.C., & CO. San Francisco, California, 1853d-1870d. Agent for Deringer.

ALLEN, WILLIAM C. Lewistown, Illinois, 1878d-1880d.

ALLEN, WILLIAM (?-1822), New York, New York, 1782-1822. Flintlock guns. (Swinney)

ALLEN, Y.S. Nashville, Arkansas, 1888d.

ALLEN-22 suicide special by Hopkins and Allen.

ALLENBREN, JOHN unlocated. Flintlock Kentucky.

ALLENDER, HENRY Detroit, Michigan. Patents #303,411 August 12, 1884, breechloading firearms, #323,997 August 11, 1885, machine gun, and #372,191 October 25, 1887, machine gun.

ALLERS, CHARLES H. Pittsburgh, Pennsylvania, 1884d.

ALLEY, CASSIUS Metamora, Indiana. Patent #372,191 October 25, 1887, machine gun. (Lindert)

ALLFEATHER, JOHN Berlin, Pennsylvania, 1850. (Whisker II)

ALLIN, ERSKINE S. (1809-1879), Springfield, Massachusetts. Patent #49,959 September 19, 1865, breechloading firearms. Master armorer at Springfield Armory 1847-1878. Patent used on "Trapdoor" Springfields.

ALLING Henrietta, New York, 1870d.

ALLING see McKinney & Alling.

ALLING, EDWARD D. Rochester, New York, 1861-1875. As Green & Alling, 1873-1875. (Eich)

ALLISON, J.H. unlocated. Percussion fullstock.

ALLISON, PETER & CO. Buffalo, New York, 1825.

ALLISON, RICHARD (1796-?), Allegheny County, Pennsylvania, 1860c. (Whisker II)

ALLISON, THOMAS (1786-1836), Pittsburgh, Pennsylvania, 1810-1816, New Sweickly, Pennsylvania, 1816-1836. Flintlock and percussion rifles. (MB 12-70)

ALLISON, WILLIAM (1788-1855), Fayette County, Pennsylvania, 1811t-1834t. (Kauffman)

ALLOWAY, ELMER Philadelphia, Pennsylvania, 1829d.

ALLOWAYS, AXARIAH York County, Pennsylvania, 1807c. Flintlock Kentucky. (Kauffman)

ALLSWORTH, SAMUEL Anne Arundel County, Maryland, 1769. Convict, gunstocker. (Hartzler)

ALSOP, CHARLES H. Middleton, Connecticut. Patents #33,770 November 26, 1861, revolver, and #76,374 April 7, 1868, breechloading firearm. (Sellers-1)

ALSOP, CHARLES R. Middleton, Connecticut. Patents #28,433 May 22, 1860, detachable stock, #29,213 July 17, 1860, revolver, #29,538 August 1, 1860, revolver, #32,333 May 14, 1861, revolver, #34,226 January 21, 1862, revolver, #34,803 March 25, 1862, revolver, #37,193 December 16, 1862, rifled muzzle, and #37,481 January 27, 1863, cartridge. Made revolvers in small quantities, 1862-1865. (Sellers-1)

ALSOP, JOSEPH W. Middleton, Connecticut. Father of the Alsops and owner of the factory which produced Alsop revolvers. Moved to New York City at the end of the Civil War. (Sellers-1)

ALSTON, WILLIAM F. Walker County, Texas. Patent #358,915 March 8, 1887, firearms.

ALT Salt Lake City, Utah, 1871d. As Whittemore & Alt.

ALTER, I. B. Elk Falls, Kansas, 1884d.

ALTHOFF, HERMAN C. Aurora, Illinois, 1888d-1899d.

ALTINGER, CHARLES Lebanon, Illinois, 1864d.

ALTINGER, CHARLES St. Louis, Missouri, 1842-1870d, Springfield, Missouri, 1879d. Percussion 1/2 stock. As Charles Altinger & Sons, 1870.

ALTINGER, CHARLES Stockton, California, 1867d. (Shelton)

ALTINGER, GEORGE St. Louis, Missouri, 1847d. Percussion double shotgun.

ALTINGER, IGNATIUS St. Louis, Missouri, 1842. (Kauffman)

ALTINGER, JOSEPH St. Louis, Missouri, 1838-1845d.

ALTLAND, ANDREW (1810-1878), York County, Pennsylvania. Son of Jacob Altland. (Kindig)

ALTLAND, JACOB (1785-1830), Orts Mill, Pennsylvania, 1802-1830. Kentucky rifles. (Kindig)

ALTLAND, JOHN (?-1853), Adams County, Pennsylvania. Flintlock Kentucky. (Bowers)

ALTMAIER, PETER A. Harrisburg, Pennsylvania, 1868-1887. Patents #261,648 July 25, 1882, breechloading firearm, #261,802, July 25, 1882, safety, #320,038 June 16, 1885, safety, #334,731 January 26, 1886, magazine gun, #343,883 June 15, 1886, magazine gun, and #370,032 September 20, 1887, magazine gun. Breechloading rifles and cane guns. (ST 10-62)

ALTMAIER, PETER Lewiston, Pennsylvania, 1855-1861d. Patent #24,774 July 12, 1859, breechloading firearm. Listed as Peter Altman in 1860 census.

ALTMAN, JOHN unlocated. Flintlock Kentucky.

ALTMAN, JONATHAN Armstrong County, Pennsylvania, 1857, Kittaning, Pennsylvania, 1867-1880. Patent #16,634 February 17, 1857, set trigger. (Kauffman)

ALTMAN, PETER see Peter Altmaier.

ALTON, JESSE Frankfort, Indiana, 1866-1870. (Lindert)

ALTON, RYLEY Howard County, Indiana, 1846-1850. (Lindert)

ALVORD, J.J. unlocated. Percussion 1/2 stock.

ALWORTH, SAMUEL Philadelphia, Pennsylvania, 1793d-1808d. See Samuel Allsworth.

AMADON, L.M. Bellows Falls, Vermont, 1861-1900. Percussion target rifles and telescopes. (Horn)

AMBACHER, JACOB (1843-?), Sandusky, Ohio, 1878-1890. (Hutslar)

AMBLER, J.J. Mount Pleasant, Iowa, 1867d.

AMBLER, JOHN, JR. South New Berlin, New York. Patent # none October 16, 1827, gun lock.

AMBLER, NATHAN H. Cleveland, Ohio. Patent #106,246 August 9, 1870, magazine gun.

AMBOLD, H.E. Waco, Texas, 1884d-1896d.

AMEN, JOHN unlocated. Percussion fullstock.

AMERICA suicide special by Crescent Arms Co.

AMERICAN ARMS CO. Boston, Massachusetts, 1870-1901, Milwaukee, Wisconsin, 1893-1904 (?), Bluffton, Alabama, 1890-1901. Owned by George H. Fox, this company made Wheeler patent derringers, Fox and Whittemore patent shotguns and revolvers under patents of Fox, F.W. Hood, A.S. Hood, and H.F. Wheeler. A second factory was opened in Alabama in 1890, but references to a move to Milwaukee are unverified. Successor to American Nut & Arms Co. (AR 4-70)

AMERICAN AUTOMATIC ARMS CO. Saco, Maine, 1899-1910. Patents of Franklin Young.

AMERICAN BOY suicide special. (Webster)

AMERICAN BULLDOG trade name of Iver Johnson on double action revolver.

AMERICAN CARTRIDGE AND ARMS CO. Chicago, Illinois, 1892d, sales only.

AMERICAN EAGLE suicide special and double action revolver, both by Hopkins & Allen.

AMERICAN ELECTRIC ARMS & AMMUNITION CO. New York, New York, 1884-1888. Produced a few guns under Samuel Russell's patents. Samuel Russell was the company's president.

AMERICAN GUN CO. New York, New York. Trade name of H.& D. Folsom Arms Co. on shotguns. (GR 7-74)

AMERICAN MACHINE WORKS Chicopee Falls, Massachusetts, 1843-1865. Name appears on Smith carbines made by Ames.

AMERICAN NUT & ARMS CO. Boston, Massachusetts, 1867-1870. Wheeler's patent derringers. Became American Arms Co., in 1870. (AR 4-70)

AMERICAN PRIMING & ARMS CO. New York, New York. Sales organization for Gedney's patent priming hammers.

AMERICAN REPEATING RIFLE CO. Boston, Massachusetts, 1869. Fogarty Repeating Rifle Co. was reorganized under this name, shortly before being purchased by Winchester.

AMERICAN STANDARD ORDNANCE CO. New York, New York, 1888d-1889d. Breechloading shotguns.

AMERICAN STANDARD TOOL CO. Newark, New Jersey, 1868-1873. Successors to Manhattan Fire Arms Co., producing identical revolvers and single shot pistols. (Nutter)

AMERICAN STEAM WORKS New York, New York. Pecare & Smith pepperboxes. (Gluckman & Satterlee)

AMERICAN TOOL & MACHINE CO. Boston, Massachusetts, 1865d-1867. Wheeler derringers. Became American Nut & Arms Co.

AMERICAN suicide special by Ely & Wray.

AMERICAN trade name of Hyde & Shattuck on shotguns, and Harrington & Richardson on revolvers.

AMERICUS trade name of Hopkins & Allen on revolvers.

AMES MFG. CO. Cabotsville, Massachusetts, 1834-1840, Chicopee Falls, Massachusetts, 1841-1883. Cannons, swords, model 1843 pistols, Jenks carbines, Lowell Machine Guns, and Chicago Palm Pistols. Succeeded by Ames Sword Co., 1883. Nathan P. Ames, Jr. (GR 12-64)

AMES SWORD CO. Chicago Palm pistols. Successor to Ames Mfg. Co. in 1883.

AMES, DAVID (1761-1847), Bridgewater, Massachusetts, 1780-1795 and 1810-1830, Springfield, Massachusetts, 1795-1802. Flintlock muskets marked only "Bridgewater" with his father John Ames and brother Oliver Ames. First superintendent of Springfield Armory, 1795-1802.

AMES, GEORGE Portland, Maine, 1832-1834. (Demeritt)

AMES, JAMES T. (1810-1883), Chicopee Falls, Massachusetts. Son of Nathan P. Ames, Sr. (GR 12-64)

AMES, JOHN B. Providence, Rhode Island, 1849d-1865d. Percussion shotguns.

AMES, JOHN (1738-1803), Bridgewater, Massachusetts, 1776-1803. Flintlock muskets. Father of David and Oliver.

AMES, NATHAN P. (?-1832), Chelmsford, Massachusetts, 1808-1829. Retired in 1829 and turned business over to his two sons Nathan, Jr., and James T.

AMES, NATHAN P., JR. (1803-1847), Chicopee Falls, Massachusetts, 1829-1847. Successor to his father's business, moved to Chicopee Falls in 1829, and founded the Ames Mfg. Co. in 1834.

AMES, OLIVER West Bridgewater, Massachusetts, 1803-1806, North Easton, Massachusetts, 1806-circa 1820. Flintlock muskets. Son of and successor to John Ames.

AMES, S.G. Spencer, Massachusetts, 1874d. Listed as "Proprietor of Spencer Gun".

AMES, WASHINGTON Omro, Wisconsin, 1884d-1888d.

AMESBOON Canton, Illinois, 1850. Percussion 1/2 stock. (Johnson)

AMICK, WILLIAM Howard County, Missouri, 1850c. (MB 11-66)

AMIET, AUGUST Koch's, Ohio, 1883-1886. Percussion shotgun. (Hutslar)

AMODEO-SALVATORE, EMANUEL U.S. Navy. Patents #350,096 October 5, 1886, cartridge, and #350,098 October 5, 1886, magazine gun.

AMORY & WILKINSON Goshen, New York. Percussion shotgun. (Swinney)

AMORY, JOHN Fond du Lac, Wisconsin, 1850-1857, and 1866-? Brother of Samuel Amory, worked for him and Thomas Weeks. (WGCA 6)

AMORY, SAMUEL B. (1822-1896), Goshen, New York, 1843-1850, Fond du Lac, Wisconsin, 1850-1860. Percussion 1/2 stock. (WGCA 6)

AMOS & BORDER Bedford, Pennsylvania. John Amos and his brother-in-law, Daniel Border.

AMOS, JOHN (1800-1867), Bedford, Pennsylvania, 1849-1867. Percussion "Bedford" rifles. Partner of Daniel Border. (Hetrick)

AMOSKEAG MFG. CO. Manchester, New Hampshire, 1862-1869. 1861 contract musket, Lindner and Straw carbines.

AMSDEN, BENJAMIN W. (?-1882), Saratoga Springs, New York, 1850c-1882. Percussion guns. (Swinney)

ANDERS, D. Nelsonville, Ohio, 1888d. (Hutslar)

ANDERSON & COYLE St. Louis, Missouri, 1840d.

ANDERSON, ANDREW J. Fort Worth, Texas, 1866d-1884d, Henrietta, Texas, 1884d, Colorado, Texas, 1884d-1892d. Percussion and cartridge guns.

ANDERSON, GEORGE Barnesville, Ohio, 1880. Percussion 1/2 stock.

ANDERSON, GEORGE Dalles, Oregon, 1880d-1889d.

ANDERSON, J. Saxeville. Wisconsin, 1857d.

ANDERSON, JAMES (1740-1798), Williamsburg, Virginia, 1762-1798. Armorer in public magazine, 1776-1783. (Gill)

ANDERSON, JAMES New York, New York, 1798. Flintlock guns and pistols, swords.

ANDERSON, JAMES Virginia, 1820. Flintlock Kentucky.

ANDERSON, JOHN (1807-?), Lawrence County, Illinois, 1832-1850. (Johnson)

ANDERSON, N.M. Omaha, Nebraska, 1886d.

ANDERSON, R.S. (1818-?), Carondelet, St. Louis, Missouri, 1850c. (Lewis)

ANDERSON, SILAS Mayfield, Tennessee, 1881d.

ANDREW, LYMAN (1829-?), Napa, California, 1860c. (Shelton)

ANDREW, R.G. unlocated. Percussion fullstock.

ANDREWS & HILLS El Paso, Texas, 1890d. Nelson S. Andrews, 1884. (El Paso Lone Star)

ANDREWS Denver, Colorado. See Henderson & Andrews. (Sellers-3)

ANDREWS, D.C. Winstead, Connecticut, 1883d-1892d.

ANDREWS, E. Santa Fe, New Mexico, 1873d.

ANDREWS, EBEN Boston, Massachusetts, 1840. (Kauffman 2)

ANDREWS, EDWARD W. (1809-1899), Cleveland, Ohio, 1825-1853, Oberlin, Ohio, 1854-1860c. Percussion double rifle. (Hutslar)

ANDREWS, F. Medina, Ohio, 1896-1897. (Hutslar)

ANDREWS, FERRY & CO. Stafford, Connecticut. Underhammer pistol. Robert W. Andrews. (Logan)

ANDREWS, J.D. Eufala, Alabama, 1855d.

ANDREWS, JACKSON (1835-?), Alexander County, Illinois, 1850. (Johnson)

ANDREWS, JACOB Dauphin County, Pennsylvania, 1807. Barrelmaker. (Kauffman)

ANDREWS, JOEL W. Norristown, Pennsylvania. Patent #33,731 November 19, 1861, gun and bayonet.

ANDREWS, N.D. Stevens Point, Wisconsin, 1884d-1891d.

ANDREWS, PHILLIP B. (1796-?), Cleveland, Ohio, 1820-1832, Detroit, Michigan, 1832-?. Flintlock rifles. Brother of Edward.

ANDREWS, ROBERT W. Stafford, Connecticut. Patent #328 July 31, 1837, attaching knives to pistols. (Frost)

ANDREWS, T.H. Minneapolis, Minnesota, 1867d, Mankato, Minnesota, 1878d-1886d.

ANDREWS, THOMAS (1795-?), Alexander County, Illinois, 1850. (Johnson)

ANDREWS, WILLIAM Buckhannon, West Virginia, 1890-1910. (Whisker)

ANDRUS & NAEDELE Hartford, Connecticut, 1884d.

ANDRUS & OSBORN Canton, Connecticut, 1863-1867, Southbridge, Massachusetts, 1850-1860. Underhammer pistols. (Logan)

ANGEL, CARL H. (1821-?), New Orleans, Louisiana, 1850c. (MB 9-65)

ANGEL, JOHN Philadelphia, Pennsylvania, 1816d-1836d.

ANGEL, JOSEPH & JOHN New Haven, Connecticut, 1840-1848. (Kauffman 2)

ANGELE, GEORGE (1827-1869), Buffalo, New York, 1850c-1859d, San Francisco, California, 1860-1861, Sacramento, California, 1864-1869. (Shelton)

ANGELL, A. Oxford, Pennsylvania, 1830-1840. Flintlock and percussion rifles.

ANGELL, GILBERT Erieville, New York. Percussion bench gun.

ANGELL, NORMAN Erieville, New York. Percussion 1/2 stock.

ANGER, SINACIUS Madison, Indiana, 1858d-1880. (Lindert)

ANGLIN, J. Mount Vernon, Kentucky, 1856-1860. Percussion fullstock.

ANGLIN, PHILIP Springfield, Tennessee, 1860d. Flintlock and percussion Tennessee rifles.

ANGSTADT, ABRAHAM (1784-?), Germantown, Indiana, 1850-1860. (Lindert)

ANGSTADT, ADAM (1826-?), Germantown, Indiana, 1850. Son of Abraham. (Lindert)

ANGSTADT, ADAM Kutztown, Pennsylvania, 1800-1817. Flintlock pistols and rifles, both military and civilian, most signed "A.A.". (Kindig)

ANGSTADT, DAVID Lewisburg, Pennsylvania. Flintlock Kentucky rifles. (Gabel)

ANGSTADT, GIDEON (1800-1854), Lewisburg, Pennsylvania. Late flint and percussion period. (Gabel, C&W)

ANGSTADT, JOSEPH Kutztown, Pennsylvania, 1800-1817. Flintlock Kentucky signed "Jos. An." - son of Adam? Flintlock contract pistols with Adam Angstadt. (Kindig)

ANGSTADT, PETER (1809-?), Montgomery County, Ohio, 1850c. (Hutslar)

ANGSTADT, PETER Berks County, Pennsylvania, 1800. Flintlock Kentucky signed "Peter Anstat". (Kauffman)

ANGUSH, JAMES Lancaster, Pennsylvania, 1771. Flintlock Kentucky rifles. (Gluckman & Satterlee)

ANN, ERICK Bishop Hill, Illinois, 1880d-1884d.

ANNAN, C.F. Starke, Florida, 1895d.

ANNELY, EDWARD New York, New York, 1748, Trenton, New Jersey, 1770-1777. Queen Anne style pistol marked "Ed & Thos ANNELY" (converted to percussion). Armorer for the Colony of New Jersey. (Kauffman 2)

ANNELY, JOHN New York, New York. Percussion shotgun.

ANNELY, THOMAS Trenton, New Jersey, 1770-1777, Philadelphia, Pennsylvania, 1796d-1798. Contract pistols, 1797-1798. Armorer to Colony of New Jersey. (Gluckman)

ANSCHETS, LEO Lancaster, Wisconsin, 1857d.

ANSCHUTZ, A. Watertown, Wisconsin, 1857d.

ANSCHUTZ, A.W. Stevens Point, Wisconsin, 1879d.

ANSCHUTZ, AUGUST Chillicothe, Missouri, 1879d-1881d.

ANSCHUTZ, E. Madison, Wisconsin, 1856-1860d. As Herfurth & Anschutz, 1860.

ANSCHUTZ, EDWARD Philadelphia, Pennsylvania, 1860d-1882d. High quality percussion guns.

ANSCHUTZ, F. Cleveland, Ohio, 1868-1872.

ANSCHUTZ, F. Sauk Center, Wisconsin, 1857d.

ANSETH, AUDEN Black River Falls, Wisconsin, 1888d-1895d.

ANSON, COMSTOCK Danbury, Connecticut, 1869-1875. Percussion 1/2 stock.

ANSON, GEORGE (1813-?), Medina, Ohio, 1850c-1857d. Quasqueton, Iowa, 1865d. (Hutslar)

ANTENEN, CHRISTIAN Toledo, Ohio, 1898d.

ANTES, WILLIAM (1735-1810), Philadelphia, Pennsylvania, 1775-1780, Northumberland County, Pennsylvania, 1781-1785, Sunbury, Pennsylvania, 1785-1806, Canandaigua, New York, 1806-1810. Flintlock pistols and rifles. (AAC 10-57)

ANTHIS, WILLIAM Auburn, New York, 1829-1836. Colburn revolving rifles and percussion fullstock rifles. Son of William Antes. (AAC 10-57)

ANTHONY, JAMES Escanaba, Michigan, 1872d-1878.

ANTHONY, JOHN W. (1827-1885), Stilesville, Iowa, 1856-1885. Percussion guns. (MB 10-64)

ANTHONY, JOHN W. Dayton, Ohio, 1850. (Hutslar)

ANTIS, ROBERT Canandaigua, New York, 1842d-1855c. Percussion 1/2 stock. (Swinney)

APPLE, J. Alden, New York, 1872-1874d.

APPLEBAY, ALEXANDER (1832-1906), Wellsburg, West Virginia, 1848?, Steubenville, Ohio, 1850, Lowell, Ohio, 1884-1906. Percussion 1/2 stock. As Keesey & Applebay, 1873-1875. (Gluckman & Satterlee)

APPLEBAY, HARDEN D. (1865-1932), Sisterville, West Virginia, Lakulpa, Illinois, Lowell, Ohio, 1886-1932. Percussion and cartridge guns. Son of Alexander. (Hutslar)

APPLEBAY, WILEY P. (1863-1927), Sisterville, West Virginia, Lakulpa, Illinois, Lowell, Ohio, 1905-1913. (Hutslar)

APPLEBEE, ALLEN Friendship, New York, 1863-1882d. Percussion guns.

APPLEBY, JOHN F. Mazomanie, Wisconsin. Patent #45,466 December 20, 1864, magazine gun.

APPLEYARD, AUSTIN New York, New York, 1886d-1896d.

ARAB, THE trade name on shotguns by Harrington & Richardson.

ARBOGAST, SOLOMON (1827-?), Valley Head, West Virginia, 1870-1884d. (Whisker IV)

ARCHBOLD, ISRAEL N. Ridge Farm, Illinois. Patents #476,590 June 7, 1892, machine gun, and #476,591 June 7, 1892, revolver.

ARCHER, J.A. Eureka, California, 1880-1881d. (Shelton)

ARCHER, JAMES A. (1821-?), Monroe County, Indiana, 1850c. (Lindert)

ARCHER, JAMES (1822-?), Guilford, North Carolina, 1850c. (Bivins)

ARCHER, JOHN Wellsburg, Virginia. Percussion fullstock.

ARDEN & SMITH Philadelphia, Pennsylvania. Percussion(?) 1/2 stock.

ARDNESER, A. Butte, Montana, 1884d.

ARDUESSER, ABRAHAM Dubuque, Iowa, 1884d.

AREIS, FRANCIS Philadelphia, Pennsylvania, 1823d-1831d. (Kauffman 2)

AREND BROTHERS Sandusky, Ohio, 1883. Sales only. (Hutslar)

ARENDT, FRANCIS Kingston, New York, 1856-1859. Percussion guns.

ARGALL, M.W. Grass Valley, California, 1893d.

ARGOTE, EDMOND New Orleans, Louisiana, 1822d-1823d.

ARICK, JOHN Philadelphia, Pennsylvania, 1846d.

ARISTOCRAT suicide special by Hopkins & Allen.

ARKADELPHIA ORDNANCE WORKS Arkadelphia, Arkansas, 1861-1863. Rifles for the Confederacy. (Albaugh)

ARKINS, J.P. unlocated. Percussion fullstock.

ARKMAN, HENRY Annville, Pennsylvania, 1860d.

ARMBRUSTER, WILLIAM Brooklyn, New York, 1871-1883d.

ARMENDT, GEORGE Baltimore, Maryland, 1851-1856d. (Hartzler)

ARMENDT, JOHN E. Baltimore, Maryland, 1866-1886d. (Hartzler)

ARMFIELD, ITHAMAR (1819-?), Jamestown, North Carolina, 1850c. Son of Joseph Armfield. (Bivins)

ARMFIELD, JOHN (1830-?), Jamestown, North Carolina, 1850c. (Bivins)

ARMFIELD, JOSEPH S. Jamestown, North Carolina, 1850c-1884d. As J.S. Armfield & Son, 1877-1884.

ARMINGTON, WILLIAM W. Norwich, Connecticut. Patent #429,110 June 3, 1890, firearm with Horace Briggs.

ARMITSTEAD, THOMAS E. Mazomanie, Wisconsin. Patent #504,696 September 5, 1893, sight.

ARMSBY & HARRINGTON Worcester, Massachusetts, 1862-1865. Rifles under C.B. Holden's patents.

ARMSTRONG & TAYLOR Augusta, Kentucky. James W. Armstrong and John Taylor patented a carbine produced by Norwich Arms Co.

ARMSTRONG, A.H. unlocated. Percussion 1/2 stock.

ARMSTRONG, AARON Mercer, Pennsylvania, 1843-1887d. Same as A.H. Armstrong?

ARMSTRONG, ALLEN Philadelphia, Pennsylvania, 1840d. Flintlock Kentucky rifles and locks.

ARMSTRONG, CRAWFORD Pittsburgh, Pennsylvania, 1852. Barrel maker. (Kauffman)

ARMSTRONG, G.A. Youngstown, Ohio, 1880-1890. Repairs only. (Hutslar)

ARMSTRONG, J. & E.L. Morristown, New Jersey, 1868-1869. Percussion pistols.

ARMSTRONG, JAMES W. Augusta, Kentucky. Patent #37,025 November 25, 1862, breechloading firearm with John Taylor.

ARMSTRONG, JAMES (1800-?), Harrison County, Indiana, 1850. (Lindert)

ARMSTRONG, JAMES Emmitsburg, Maryland. Son of John Armstrong. (Hartzler)

ARMSTRONG, JOEL (1820-?), Marysville, Ohio, 1859-1864. (Hutslar)

ARMSTRONG, JOHN (?-1827), Gettysburg, Pennsylvania, 1813-1827. (Kauffman)

ARMSTRONG, JOHN (1772-?), Emmitsburg, Maryland, 1793-1841. Flintlock Kentucky rifles. (Hartzler)

ARMSTRONG, JOHN Gettysburg, Pennsylvania, 1855. Son of John Armstrong.

ARMSTRONG, JOHN Terre Haute, Indiana, 1882-1885. (Lindert)

ARMSTRONG, L. Dwight, Illinois, 1860d.

ARMSTRONG, RANSOM H. Hudson, Michigan, 1863d-1895d. Percussion target rifle.

ARMSTRONG, ROBERT Emmitsburg, Maryland. Son of John Armstrong. (Hartzler)

ARMSTRONG, SAMUEL F. Adamsville, Michigan, 1865-1891d. Percussion 1/2 stock.

ARMSTRONG, SAMUEL Emmitsburg, Maryland. Flintlock Kentucky. Son of John Armstrong. (Hartzler)

ARMSTRONG, STEWART Clear Creek, West Virginia, 1900d. (Whisker IV)

ARMSTRONG, WILLIAM (1797-?), Washington, D.C., 1822d, Harpers Ferry, Virginia, circa 1830. Inspector at Harpers Ferry. (Hartzler)

ARN, EDWARD Marietta, Ohio, 1862-1865, Booneville, Missouri, 1870-1889d.

ARN, F.E. Booneville, Missouri, 1891d-1898d. Son of Edward Arn.

ARN, FREDERICK (1845-?), Pleasant County, West Virginia, 1880c. (Whisker IV)

ARNAUD, VINCENT New Orleans, Louisiana, 1834d.

ARNO, OLIVER H. Boston, Massachusetts. Patent #473,808 April 26, 1892, spring gun.

ARNOLD & COOLEY Wadesboro, North Carolina, 1861-1862. Confederate contractors, Earle Cooley. (Bivins)

ARNOLD, ALBAN Providence, Rhode Island, 1859-1876d, Colville, Washington, 1886d.

ARNOLD, JAMES Lake City, Minnesota, 1867d.

ARNOLD, L. Cannelton, Indiana, 1871-1872. (Lindert)

ARNOLD, O.B. Liverpool, Ohio, 1881-1897. (Hutslar)

ARNOLD, T.H. Owensboro, Kentucky, 1879d-1884d.

ARNOLD, W.G. Brooklyn, New York, 1892d-1895d.

ARNOLD, WILLIAM H. Washington, D.C. Patents #23,538 April 12, 1859, projectile, and #26,076 November 15, 1859, breechloading firearms. Two rifles made for experiment at Harper's Ferry.

ARNOLD, WILLIAM Cadez, Ohio, 1812-1815. Flintlock Kentucky rifle.

ARNTZ, ADOLPH Muskegon, Michigan, 1883d-1895d.

ARONSON, JOSEPH N. New York, New York. Patent #59,540 November 13, 1866, breechloading firearms.

ARPERMANN, CHRISTIAN (1783-?), Philadelphia, Pennsylvania, 1807-1814.

ARRIS, JAMES (1883-?), Petersburg, Virginia, 1850c. (MB 10-63)

ARRONSON, C.A. Stillwater, Minnesota, 1884d.

ARROWSMITH, GEORGE A. New York, New York. Was one of the original promoters of the Jennings repeater.

ARROWSMITH, W.K. Bement, Illinois, 1880d-1886d.

ARTHUR, A.C. Parkersburg, West Virginia, 1888d-1896d. (Whisker IV)

ARTHUR, BENJAMIN Virginia, 1781. Committee of Safety repairs. (Gill)

ARTZ, CHARLES Pittsburgh, Pennsylvania, 1826. (Kauffman)

ARTZ, NICHOLAS Winona, Minnesota, 1884d-1892d.

ARVIDSSON, CHARLES JOHN (1818-1905), Placerville, California, 1857-1905. With A.C. Arvidsson in 1862. (Shelton)

ASBILL, A. Middle Fabius, Missouri, 1860d.

ASBILL, J. Winston, Kentucky, 1874d-1880d.

ASBILL, W.H. Winston, Kentucky, 1883d-1896d. Son of J. Asbill.

ASH, JOHN Logan, Utah, 1871d-1886d. As Ash & Sons, 1879-1886.

ASH, JOSEPH (1808-?), Indiana County, Pennsylvania, 1850c-1860c. (Whisker II)

ASHBA, ELI Canton, Ohio, 1865. Percussion rifles. (Hutslar)

ASHCROFT, EDWARD H. Boston, Massachusetts. Patent #38,645 May 26, 1863, breechloading firearm. (GR 5-80)

ASHEVILLE ARMORY Asheville, North Carolina, 1862-1865. Enfield pattern muskets and Mississippi rifles. (Hill-Anthony)

ASHFIELD, JOHN Buffalo, New York, 1834-1850. Percussion 1/2 stock. Worked for himself only 1842-1843, with Joseph Haberstro, 1834-1841, with Patrick Smith, 1844-1850.

ASHFIELD, WILLIAM (1828-1859), Rochester, New York, 1849-1851, Maryville, California, 1854-1859. (Shelton-Eich).

ASHLEY, GEORGE Washingtonville, New York, 1880-1882d.

ASHLEY, JACOB Rochester, New York, 1841d. For Joseph Medbury. (Eich)

ASHLEY, JOHN Rochester, New York, 1841d, Dansville, New York, 1850c. With John Brunker. (Eich)

ASHMAN, HENRY (1820-?), Richmond, Virginia, 1850c, Annville, Pennsylvania, 1861d. (MB 10-63)

ASHTON, PETER H. Middleton, Connecticut, 1850. Underhammer pistol.

ASHTON, WILLIAM Kenton, Ohio. Lock marking. (Hutslar)

ASHTON, WILLIAM Middleton, Connecticut. Patent #12,774 May 1, 1855, bullet mold. Underhammer pistols.

ASHTON, WILLIAM Springfield, Massachusetts, 1861d-1868d. At Springfield Armory, 1861-1865.

ASHWORTH, ALBERT W. St. Cloud, Minnesota. Patent #542,983 July 23, 1895, magazine gun.

ASKEW & PAXSON Philadelphia, Pennsylvania. Locks, flintlock.

ASNAHL, JOHN Charles City, Virginia, 1677. (Gill)

ASSANTI, JEAN New Orleans, Louisiana, 1841d.

ASSMANN, G.P. Austin, Texas, 1884d-1896d. Son of and successor to Paul Assmann.

ASSMANN, PAUL Austin, Texas, 1878d-1883d.

ASSMUS, A. Chicago, Illinois. Patent #145,478 December 16, 1873, magazine gun.

ASSONET GUN FACTORY Assonet, Massachusetts, 1893-1894. Shotguns.

ASTER, J. New York, New York. Patent #641,620 January 16, 1900, foot operated revolver.

ASTOL, J. & W. New Orleans, Louisiana, 1805-1812.

ASTON, HENRY (1803-?), Middleton, Connecticut, 1843-1852. U.S. Model 1842 pistols marked, "H. ASTON & CO.".

ATCHLEY, T.V. Oakland, Missouri, 1860d.

ATHERTON, CORNELIUS (1736-1809), Boston, Massachusetts, 1769-1775, Amenia, New York, 1775-1777, Plymouth, Pennsylvania, 1777-1786, Taylorville, Pennsylvania, 1786-1806, South Bainbridge, New York, 1806-1809. Committee of Safety muskets with John Chamberlain, flintlock Kentucky rifles and pistols alone. (AAC 4-58)

ATHERTON, WILLIAM Northville, New York, 1874d. Percussion guns.

ATHEY, GEORGE (1829-?), Washington County, Ohio, 1850c. Son of Thomas Athey. (Hutslar)

ATHEY, THOMAS (1805-?), Washington County, Ohio, 1850c. (Hutslar)

ATKIN, RALPH Painsville, Ohio, 1883-1896, Thompson, Ohio, 1878. (Hutslar).

ATKINSON, JAMES W. Milpitas, California. Patent #477,982 June 28, 1892, trap gun.

ATKINSON, JAMES Washington County, Pennsylvania, 1833-1836. (Whisker II)

ATKINSON, JOEL Parkesburg, Kentucky, 1877-1883. Percussion guns. (Gluckman-Satterlee)

ATKINSON, PETER Monticello, Kentucky, circa 1880. (MB 6-60)

ATKINSON, S.W. Lawrence, Massachusetts, 1878d-1891d.

ATKINSON, WYATT (1877-1964), Parkesburg, Kentucky. Son of Joel Atkinson. (MB 12-64)

ATLAS GUN CO. Ilion, New York, 1890-1906. .22 rifles.

ATLEMAN, B., & CO. Clearfield, Pennsylvania, 1873-1875. Percussion shotgun.

ATLEY, CONRAD Bedford, Pennsylvania, 1797t-1850t. Bedford Kentucky rifles.

ATMAR, RALPH, JR. Charleston, South Carolina, 1800. (Kauffman 2)

ATWATER, JOHN B. Ripon, Wisconsin, 1850-1865. Patents #27,342 March 6, 1860, priming plate, and #36,592 September 30, 1862, rifling, cannon. Percussion target rifle.

AUBER, DANIEL Fayette County, Pennsylvania, 1804. (Kauffman)

AUBREY, ALBERT J. Meriden, Connecticut, 1904-1906, Hopkinton, Massachusetts, 1906-1908. Patents 835,091 November 6, 1906, sight, #839,535 December 25, 1906, sight, #859,477 July 9, 1907, firearm, #908,552 January 5, 1908, firearm, #908,553 January 5, 1908, firearm, and #911,362 February 2, 1908, firearm. Made cheap revolvers and rifles for Sears, Roebuck & Co. (AR 2-74)

AUER, BALTHAZAR I. Louisville, Kentucky, 1859d-1869d, Owensboro, Kentucky, 1883d-1896d. Percussion guns.

AUER, CHARLES Philadelphia, Pennsylvania, 1880d.

AUER, FRANCIS XAVIER Portland, Oregon, 1867d-1881d.

AUER, XAVIER New Orleans, Louisiana, 1860d-1861d.

AUGHE, F.M. Frankfort, Indiana, 1886d.

AUGHENBAUGH, ROBERT M. Glenfield, Pennsylvania. Patents #381,821 April 24, 1888, magazine gun, and #399,464 March 12, 1899, magazine gun, both with George Ruffley.

AUGHINBAUGH & SON Dayton, Ohio. Lockmakers only.

AUGUSTA GUN WORKS Augusta, Georgia, 1885d.

AUGUSTA MACHINE WORKS Augusta, Georgia, 1862. Confederate copy of Colt model 1851. (Albaugh 3)

AUGUSTIN see Gall & Augustin.

AUGUSTINE, A. unlocated. Percussion 1/2 stock.

AUGUSTINE, SAMUEL (1815-?), Chauncy, Ohio, 1830-1860c. Flintlock Kentucky. (Hutslar)

AULENBACH, JOHN C. (1837-?), Lebanon County, Pennsylvania, 1863d-1887d. Percussion fullstock.

AULEY, O.G. Lisbon, Dakota Territory, 1884d-1886d.

AULT, FREDERICK J. Washington County, Pennsylvania, 1791-1818. (Whisker II)

AULTLAND, H.G. unlocated. Percussion fullstock.

AUMOCK, JOHN Matawan, New Jersey, 1878d.

AUSTERSNELL, LOUIS Hermann, Missouri, 1854d.

AUSTIN, CORNELIUS unlocated. Armorer to New Jersey, 1776-1778.

AUSTIN, DEAN C. Chicago, Illinois, 1858. (Johnson)

AUSTIN, F.J. Weld, Maine, 1871d. Dealer.

AUSTIN, THOMAS K. New York, New York. Patent #21,730 October 12, 1858, revolver. Basic patent for Pettengill revolvers. (Sellers-1)

AUSTIN, THOMAS Charleston, Massachusetts, 1774-1778. Armorer to Colony of Massachusetts Bay, 1775.

AUTOMATIC trade name of Forehand & Wadsworth, Iver Johnson, and Harrington & Richardson on revolvers.

AUTRY, C.W. Yoakum, Texas, 1896d.

AUXILIARY RIFLE BARREL CO. New Haven, Connecticut, 1880d-1886d. Rifle barrels for shotguns under C.R. Shelton's patents.

AVENGER suicide special.

AVERETT, G.W.G. Washington, Utah, 1871d.

AVERILL, J.R. Pomfret, New York, 1856-1860.

AVERY & WOOLFOLK Pensacola, Florida, 1884d-1886d.

AVERY, A.M. Pensacola, Florida, 1884d-1895d. As Avery & Woolfolk, 1884-1886.

AVERY, G. Hamburg, Pennsylvania. Percussion 1/2 stock and fullstock.

AVERY, GEORGE Pound Ridge, New York, 1870d.

AVERY, JAMES L. Madison Court House, Florida. Patent #153,924 August 11, 1874, mounting guns.

AVERY, O.J. Adrian, Michigan, 1883d.

AVERY, STEPHEN North Anson, Maine, 1849-1879. (Demeritt)

AVERY, WILLIS Salisbury, New York, 1850c. Percussion fullstock.

AVET, F. New Orleans, Louisiana, 1853d.

AVIS, S. St. Louis, Missouri. Percussion 1/2 stock.

AX, JOHN JOSEPH Waterloo, Indiana, 1870-1890. (Lindert)

AX, JOSEPH (1817-?), Millersburg, Ohio, 1850c. Flintlock Kentucky. (Hutslar)

AX, WILLIAM (1810-?), Deardorff's Mills, Ohio, 1846-1853. (Hutslar)

AXER, JOHN Lancaster, Pennsylvania, 1843t-1844t (Dyke), Baltimore, Maryland, 1845d. (Hartzler)

AXTELL, JOSHUA Alden, New York, 1857-1860, Medina, New York, 1860-1867d.

AYERS, E. unlocated. Percussion 1/2 stock.

AYERS, GEORGE Alexandria, Virginia, 1890d-1897d.

AYERS, ROBERT, JR. Venango County, Pennsylvania, 1828. (Kauffman)

AYERS, T.G. Rapp's Mill, Virginia, 1890d-1893d.

AYERS, WILLIAM (1805-1845), Venango County, Pennsylvania, 1828-1845. (Kauffman)

AYLSWORTH & HOLMES unlocated. Percussion lock marketing.

AYRES, HENRY Virginia, 1776. Committee of Safety repairs. (Gill)

AYRES, J.W. Plum Creek, Nebraska, 1884d-1886d.

AYRES, R.A. (1820-?), Franklin County, Indiana, 1850. (Lindert)

AYRES, WILLIAM G. Brooklyn, New York. Patent #187,244 February 13, 1877, revolver with G. Wittacker.

AYRES, WILLIAM Leon, Wisconsin, 1857d.

B SECTION

B. & S. see Blunt & Syms.

B. see Marmaduke Blackwood for flintlock locks only.

B.A. Co. see Brooklyn Arms Co.

B.A. Co. unidentified. Percussion 1/2 stock.

B.B. unidentified. Flintlock Kentucky.

B.B. unidentified. Percussion fullstock dated 1863.

B.B. unidentified. Percussion pistol with folding trigger.

B.E. see Barney Engle.

B.F.S. unidentified. Flintlock Kentucky.

B.I. unidentified. Flintlock Kentucky.

B.L. unidentified. Percussion fullstock.

B.M. unidentified. Percussion fullstock.

B.T. unidentified. Flintlock Kentucky.

B.T. unidentified. Percussion fullstock.

B.W. see Benjamin Wright.

BABBITT, A.S., & CO. Plattesburg, New York. Made first model Robinson rifles.

BABBITT, BENJAMIN T. New York, New York. Patents #31,291 February 25, 1861, cannon, #34,472 February 25, 1862, cannon, and #209,014 October 15, 1878, air gun.

BABBITT, L.W. Cleveland, Ohio, 1832-1838, Burlington, Iowa, 1839-1844. Percussion rifles.

BABCOCK & CO. Evansville, Indiana, 1860d.

BABCOCK PATENT marking on muzzle loading rifles and shotguns with center mounted safety hammers similar to John Byer's patent.

BABCOCK, ALBERT H. Boston, and Charlestown, Massachusetts, 1855d-1861. Percussion 1/2 stock.

BABCOCK, C.B. Hoboken, New Jersey, 1878d.

BABCOCK, E. Decatur, New York, 1850c. (Swinney)

BABCOCK, J. unlocated. Underhammer pistol.

BABCOCK, MOSES (?-1789), Charlestown, Massachusetts, 1777-1786. Committee of Safety muskets. (Lindsay)

BABCOCK, MOSES (?-1886), Charlestown, Massachusetts, 1849d-1873. Underhammer pistols. (Logan)

BABCOCK, MOSES Forrestville, Iowa, 1865d.

BABCOCK, N.L. New Haven, Connecticut. Patent #27,509 March 20, 1860, breechloading firearm. Pistols under this patent made by T.J. Stafford.

BABCOCK, O.W. Fowlerville, Michigan, 1875d.

BABCOCK, W.L. Toledo, Ohio. Patent #323,810 August 4, 1885, alarm gun with H. Herrick. (Bugle 72)

BABCOX, J.T. Syracuse, New York. Percussion 1/2 stock.

BABJOE, BERNARD Jerseyville, Illinois, 1860d.

BABY HAMMERLESS trade name of Henry Kolb and R.F. Sedgely on revolvers.

BABY RUSSIAN trade name of American Arms Co. on revolvers.

BACH, JOHN (1824-1905), San Francisco, California, 1852-1874. Derringer. (Shelton)

BACHE, JOSEPH (1815-?), Stockton, California, 1850-1853, Sonora, California, 1853-1885. (Shelton)

BACHMAN, F.M. Fredricksburg, Pennsylvania, 1880d. (C&W)

BACHMAN, HEINRICH Lancaster, Pennsylvania. Patent #none August 21, 1833, safety for gun locks.

BACHNER BROTHERS Minneapolis, Minnesota, 1868-1884d.

BACKER, JACOB JR. Dauphin Co., Pennsylvania, 1800. (C&W)

BACKER, JACOB Macungie, Pennsylvania, 1779t-1805t. (KRA II-3)

BACKERS, J. Grand de Tour, Illinois, 1860d.

BACKHOUSE, RICHARD Easton, Pennsylvania, 1727-1781. Owner of Durham Iron Works which produced musket barrels during Revolutionary War. (Boehrett)

BACKMAN Galena, Illinois, 1848-1849. (Johnson)

BACKMAN, G. Indiana. Percussion 1/2 stock. (Lindert)

BACKMAN, J.H. Rushford, Minnesota, 1886d-1892d.

BACON & CO. Norwich, Connecticut, 1852-1858. Thomas K. Bacon. Predecessor to Bacon Mfg. Co. (Nutter)

BACON ARMS CO. Norwich, Connecticut, 1868-1888. Percussion and cartridge revolvers, and shotguns under their own or other names. Shotguns only in 1888. Bankrupt, 1888. Crescent Fire Arms Co. purchased the factory in 1892 and used Bacon Arms Co. as a brand name. (Sellers-1)

BACON MFG. CO. Norwich, Connecticut, 1858-1868. Percussion revolvers. Predecessor to Bacon Arms Co.

BACON, AUGUSTUS M. Washington, D.C., 1858d-1868. Patent #56,846 July 31, 1868, magazine gun. (Hartzler)

BACON, GEORGE R. Providence, Rhode Island. Patent #39,270 July 21, 1863, breechloading firearm.

BACON, PHILLIP Samsbury, Connecticut. Patent #12,810 May 8, 1855, fuse.

BACON, THOMAS K. Norwich, Connecticut, 1846-1888. As Bacon & Co., 1852-1858, Bacon Mfg. Co., 1858-1868, and Bacon Arms Co., 1868-1888. Made a large variety of both percussion and cartridge guns before going bankrupt in 1888. (Nutter, Sellers-1)

BACON, WILLIAM New York, New York, 1840d-1843d.

BADE, AUGUST 1827-1912, Sandusky, Ohio, 1878-1896. Percussion 1/2 stock. (Hutslar)

BADENHAUSEN, HENRY New York, New York, 1873d.

BADENHAUSEN, JOHN New York, 1870d.

BADENHAUSEN, PHILIP New York, New York, 1875d-1876d.

BADER, C.B. Massillon, Ohio, 1888. (Hutslar)

BADER, HENRY Saint Martinsville, Louisiana. Patent #216,012 June 3, 1879, breechloading firearm.

BADGER & ABBOTT Concord, New Hampshire, 1868d. George A. Badger.

BADGER, C.L. unlocated. Percussion target rifle.

BADGER, GEORGE A. Quincy, Massachusetts. Patent #209,600 November 5, 1878, registering attachment.

BADGER, GEORGE A., & CO. Concord, New Hampshire, 1865-1868d. Underhammer pistol.

BADGER, J.R. Ballston Spa, New York, 1848-1874d.

BADGER, O. unlocated. Flintlock duelling pistol.

BAE, I.T. Syracuse, New York. Percussion 1/2 stock.

BAEDER, FREDERICK Quincy, Illinois, 1867d-1868d.

BAER, JACOB Lancaster, Pennsylvania, 1871d.

BAER, JOHN York, Pennsylvania, 1807-1840. Flintlock Kentucky rifles. (Kauffman)

BAGGETT, ELIJAH Attleboro, Massachusetts, 1798-1805. Model 1798 contract muskets, no delivery. (Gluckman)

BAGLEY, ALBERT G. unlocated. Breech loading percussion rifles, dated 1852.

BAHN, B. & BRO. Cape Girardeau, Missouri, 1879d-1889d. Percussion 1/2 stock.

BAHN, G.W. Cape Girardeau, Missouri, 1867d.

BAHNEY, I.S. Osage Mission, Kansas, 1884d.

BAHRMANN, G. Louisville, Kentucky. Percussion 1/2 stock.

BAIERS, H. unlocated. Flintlock barrel maker.

BAILEY & DOW Ann Arbor, Michigan, 1891d-1895d.

BAILEY & EDMUNDS Ann Arbor, Michigan, 1899d.

BAILEY & WARREN Stockbridge, Michigan, 1895d.

BAILEY BROTHERS Stockbridge, Michigan, 1899d.

BAILEY, B.A. unlocated. Underhammer pistol. (Logan)

BAILEY, CHARLES E. North Scituate, Massachusetts, 1866-1879, 1885d-1890d, Springfield, Massachusetts, 1879-1885. Patents #72,777 December 31, 1867, relining barrels, and #320,613 June 23, 1885, straightening barrels.

BAILEY, CYRIL G. Metamora, Illinois, 1878d.

BAILEY, D. New Orleans, Louisiana, 1853d. Importer and dealer.

BAILEY, ELMER E. Sennamakoning, Pennsylvania. Patents #487,169 November, 29, 1892, air gun, #507,470 October 24, 1893, air gun, and #603,549 May 3, 1898, air gun with T.A. Mark.

BAILEY, F. Perham, Minnesota, 1878-1882, Bluffton, Minnesota, 1882d-1884d.

BAILEY, F.T. North Scituate, Massachusetts, 1892d. Son of Charles E. Bailey.

BAILEY, FORTUNE L. Indianapolis, Indiana. Patents #173,751 and 173,752 February 22, 1876, machine gun, and #206,852 August 13, 1878. (Lindert)

BAILEY, GASTON Butte, Montana, 1898d.

BAILEY, GEORGE Philadelphia, Pennsylvania, 1829d.

BAILEY, GILBERT L. Portland, Maine, 1850d-1904. Percussion 1/2 stock, held several patents on reloading tools. (Demeritt)

BAILEY, GOFF Kincheloe, West Virginia, 1890-1942. Percussion rifles. (Dean)

BAILEY, H.C. Newton Falls, Ohio, 1857-1861. (Gardner)

BAILEY, ISAAC Chester Co., Pennsylvania, 1786-1790. (Gardner)

BAILEY, JOHN E. New Orleans, Louisiana, 1867d-1887d, Gretna, Louisiana, 1888d-1894d. Son of Thomas Bailey.

BAILEY, JOHN Bristol, Pennsylvania, 1880d.

BAILEY, JOHN Chicago, Illinois, 1896d-1900d.

BAILEY, JOHN Jonesville, Michigan. 1863d.

BAILEY, JOHN Philadelphia, Pennsylvania, 1870d-1876d. With his son Samuel as J. & S. Bailey, 1874.

BAILEY, L.O. Metamora, Illinois, 1864d.

BAILEY, LEBBEUS Portland, Maine. Patent #1084 February 20, 1839, magazine rifle with John Ripley and William Smith. (Demeritt)

BAILEY, LYMAN M. North Landgrove, Vermont, 1872-1879. (Horn)

BAILEY, NATE Forked Run, Ohio. (Hutslar)

BAILEY, NATHAN New London, Connecticut, 1775. Armorer to State of Connecticut. (Kauffman 2)

BAILEY, ROBERT Yorktown, Pennsylvania, 1777-1783. (Kauffman)

BAILEY, S.O. Metamora, Illinois, 1875d, Minonk, Illinois, 1890d-1893d. See L.O. Bailey.

BAILEY, SAMUEL Philadelphia, Pennsylvania, 1874d-1889d. With his father John as J. & S. Bailey, 1874.

BAILEY, SYLVESTER C. Middletown, Connecticut, 1845. (Dean)

BAILEY, THOMAS New Orleans, Louisiana, 1850-1863 and 1879d-1884d, London, England(?), 1863-?. Percussion 1/2 stock rifles and revolvers. Patents #24,274 June 7, 1859, revolver, and #24,437 June 14, 1859, breechloading firearm.

BAILEY, W.A. Metamora, Illinois, 1880d. Underhammer percussion target pistol.

BAILEY, W.J. Greenville, Alabama, 1885d.

BAINBRIDGE, JOHN Lower Lake, California, 1893d.

BAIR, JOHN Jefferson, Pennsylvania, 1807-1815. Flintlock Kentucky. See John Baer. (Kindig)

BAIR, W.R. Camas Valley, Oregon, 1881d.

BAIRD, A.W. unlocated. Percussion 1/2 stock rifle.

BAIRD, ABRAHAM (1821-?), Columbiana County, Ohio, 1850c. (Hutslar)

BAIRD, CHARLES Chittenden, Vermont, 1850-1865. Percussion 1/2 stock. Older brother of Stephen. For J. Hapgood, 1828-1832. (Horn)

BAIRD, JAMES Auburn, Missouri, 1860d.

BAIRD, JOHN T. Olney, Illinois. Patent #652,583 June 26, 1900, folding gun.

BAIRD, STEPHEN S. Chittenden, Vermont, 1832-1881. Underhammer rifle, percussion 1/2 stock.

BAIRD, WALLACE Marshall, Illinois, 1893d.

BAISCH, C.G. Grand Rapids, Michigan, 1883d-1899d.

BAISCH, JOHN F. Detroit, Michigan, 1868-1899d.

BAKER & MOSS Philadelphia, Pennsylvania. Imported percussion pistol.

BAKER & SKINNER Rockford, Illinois, 1883-1884. (Johnson)

BAKER GUN & FORGING CO. Batavia, New York, 1889-1933. Automatic .22 cal. rifles under patent of F.M. Farwell and shotguns under patent of Frank Hollenbeck, George Shafer, and Edward Watson.

BAKER GUN CO. Batavia, New York, 1903-1933. Sales organization for Baker Gun & Forging Co. until purchased by H. & D. Folsom Arms Co. in 1933.

BAKER GUN CO. Marathon, New York, 1881-1885, Syracuse, New York, 1885-1889. Breechloading shotguns. W.H. Baker and L.H. Smith (also used W.H. Baker & Co. marking).

BAKER GUN CO. trade name of H. & D. Folsom Arms Co. on imported guns. (AR 2-69)

BAKER, ALBERT Bark River, Wisconsin, 1857d.

BAKER, ALPHEUS, JR. Marietta, Ohio, 1871d. (Hutslar)

BAKER, ANDREW (1808-1887), Bedford Co., Pennsylvania, 1832, Huntington Co., Pennsylvania, 1833t-1845t, Blair Co. (Newry, 1845-1861 and East Freedom, 1861-1887), Pennsylvania, 1845-1887. Percussion fullstock. (Whisker II)

BAKER, ANDREW East Freedom, Pennsylvania, 1861d.

BAKER, ANDREW Newry, Pennsylvania, 1836t-1861d. Percussion fullstock.

BAKER, B.B. Winchester, Virginia, 1888d-1897d.

BAKER, C. Albany, New York. Percussion fowler dated 1839, percussion lock marking.

BAKER, C.E. Chagrin Falls, Ohio, 1881-1886.

BAKER, CALEB Lancaster, Pennsylvania, 1728-1741. Son of Robert Baker. (Dyke)

BAKER, CHARLES Bedford Co., Pennsylvania, 1849-?. (Dean)

BAKER, D. Wells, Minnesota, 1878d, Sherman, Dakota Territory, 1884d.

BAKER, EDWARD D. Claremont, New Hampshire. Patent #24,287 February 4, 1862, cannon.

BAKER, EDWARD Albany, New York, 1816, Chester, Pennsylvania, 1819. Patent #none Oct. 10, 1816, gun lock.

BAKER, ELIAS Danby, Vermont, 1870-1875d.

BAKER, G. Batavia, New York. Percussion pistol. (Swinney)

BAKER, GEORGE W. Burlington, Vermont. Patent #18,117 September 1, 1857, capper. (Horn)

BAKER, GEORGE (?-1821), Lancaster Co., Pennsylvania, 1786, Fayette Co., Pennsylvania, 1802-1821. (Kauffman)

BAKER, GEORGE Morgantown, Virginia, 1811. Contract rifles for Virginia. (Cromwell)

BAKER, H.A. Bowen's Mills, Michigan, 1875d. Corunna, Michigan, 1883d.

BAKER, I.C. Princeton, Kentucky, 1854-1860. Percussion fullstock rifle.

BAKER, I.F. New Haven, Connecticut, 1881d.

BAKER, ISAAC (1730-?), Frederick, Maryland, 1758-1779, Washington Co., Maryland, 1779-1786, Washington Co., Virginia, 1786-1792. Son of Joshua Baker. (Hartzler)

BAKER, J.E. unlocated. Percussion 1/2 stock.

BAKER, J.H. Ripley, Ohio. Percussion 1/2 stock.

BAKER, JACOB S. Philadelphia, Pennsylvania, 1819d-1836d. Flintlock Kentucky.

BAKER, JAMES S. Fayetteville, North Carolina, 1854. See Galt & Baker. (Bivins)

BAKER, JAMES Mill Creek, Pennsylvania, 1820-1825.

BAKER, JOHN G. Philadelphia, Pennsylvania. Patent #343,560 June 15, 1886, spring gun.

BAKER, JOHN Lancaster, Pennsylvania, 1728-1750. (Dyke)

BAKER, JOHN Norristown, Pennsylvania, 1768-1776. Committee of Safety muskets.

BAKER, JOHN, JR. New Berlin, Pennsylvania. Flintlock Kentucky rifles. (Gabel)

BAKER, JOSEPH Blair Co., Pennsylvania, 1859-1861. (Kauffman)

BAKER, JOSEPH Philadelphia, Pennsylvania. Flintlock and percussion guns.

BAKER, JOSHUA (1680-1754), Lancaster, Pennsylvania, 1754. Flintlock guns. Son of John Baker. (Dean)

BAKER, JOSHUA, II (?-1765), Lancaster, Pennsylvania, 1753-?, Winchester, Virginia, 1755-1765. Son of Joshua Baker. (Hartzler-Gill)

BAKER, M.A. Fayetteville, North Carolina, 1857-1863. Rifles & muskets for the Confederacy, percussion 1/2 stock rifles. (Hill- Anthony)

BAKER, MELCHOIR Fayette Co., Pennsylvania, 1781-1809. Muskets and swords, Model 1798 contract muskets for Pennsylvania with Albert Gallatin.

BAKER, NICHOLAS Fayette Co., Pennsylvania, 1799-1804. (Kauffman)

BAKER, R.F. unlocated. Percussion 1/2 stock.

BAKER, ROBERT (?-1728), Lancaster Co., Pennsylvania, 1719-1728. (Dyke)

BAKER, S. Philadelphia, Pennsylvania. Percussion 1/2 stock.

BAKER, SAMUEL Lancaster, Pennsylvania. (Dyke)

BAKER, T.J. Gradyville, Kentucky, 1879d-1880d.

BAKER, THOMAS Ft. Collins, Colorado, 1874. Armorer at Ft. Collins Army Post, stayed in Ft. Collins as a gunsmith. (Sellers-3)

BAKER, W. Port Gibson, Mississippi, 1885d.

BAKER, W.S. Carthage, Illinois, 1880d.

BAKER, WALTER Ilion, New York. Patents #41,669 February 23, 1864, gun barrels, and #206,762 August 6, 1878, gun bands. Employed by Remington.

BAKER, WILLIAM G. Stueben, Maine, circa 1870. (Demeritt)

BAKER, WILLIAM H. (1835-1889), Greene, New York, 1858-1859, Marathon, New York, 1863-1870, Lisle, New York, 1870d-1876d, Syracuse, New York, 1877-1889. Patents #40,809 December 8, 1863, lock, #167,293 August 31, 1875, breechloading firearm, #198,333 December 18, 1877, gun barrel, #199,773 January 29, 1878, gun lock, #202,397 April 16, 1878, breechloading firearm, #228,020 May 25, 1880, gun lock, #228,165 June 1, 1880, breechloading firearm, and #248,249 October 11, 1881, breechloading firearm. Operated W.H. Baker & Co., in Marathon and Syracuse. Became Baker Gun Co. in Syracuse and Baker Gun & Forging Co. in Batavia in 1889. Percussion and cartridge guns. (AR 6-68)

BAKER, WILLIAM Chicot Co., Arkansas, 1850. (Elias)

BAKER, WILLIAM Visalia, California, 1865. (Shelton)

BAKEWELL, WILLIAM Pittsburgh, Pennsylvania. Patent #39,109 July 7, 1863, cartridge.

BAKEWOOD, GEORGE Philadelphia, Pennsylvania, 1780-1785. Repaired U.S. arms. (Moller)

BALCH, FREDERICK E. East Charlestown, Vermont, 1863-1875d. (Horn)

BALD, FREDERICK W. Baltimore, Maryland, 1847-1888d. (Hartzler)

BALDWIN, A. & CO. New Orleans, Louisiana. Imported percussion and cartridge shotguns.

BALDWIN, AARON Newark, New Jersey, 1841-1842. (Kauffman 2)

BALDWIN, CHARLES St. Joseph, Missouri, 1860d. As Baldwin & Bro.

BALDWIN, CYRUS W. Boston, Massachusetts. Patent #85,897 January 19, 1869, breechloading firearm.

BALDWIN, DAVID Jay County, Indiana, 1835-1850, Kansas, circa 1855. (MB 7-67)

BALDWIN, E.A. Tidioute, Pennsylvania, 1873d-1887d.

BALDWIN, EDEN A., JR. Shelburne Falls, Massachusetts. Patent #11,283 July 11, 1854, magazine gun. Percussion over/under rifle/shotgun. Established E. A. Baldwin & Co. at Worcester in 1855 to make these guns, but no known production.

BALDWIN, ELIHU Branford, Connecticut, 1776. Committee of Safety muskets.

BALDWIN, GEORGE E. West Meriden, Massachusetts. Patent #23,223 March 15, 1859, adjustable worm.

BALDWIN, GEORGE New Westfield, Ohio, 1860c.

BALDWIN, J.H. Sparta, Wisconsin, 1867d-1895d.

BALDWIN, JACOB West Chester, Pennsylvania, 1775-1776. Committee of Safety muskets. (Hobbies 4-38).

BALDWIN, JOHN Dalton, Indiana, 1863-1865. (Lindert)

BALDWIN, N.J. Ione, California, 1893d.

BALES Ipswich, Massachusetts, 1826. (Dean)

BALES, JOHN Penn Yann, New York. Percussion fullstock. As Gilbert & Bales.

BALL & BALLARD Worcester, Massachusetts, 1855-1859. Tool makers, R. Ball and Charles H. Ballard. (AR 8-27)

BALL & WILLIAMS Worcester, Massachusetts, 1859-1865. Ballard carbines and rifles. Charles H. Ballard was superintendent. Successor to Ball & Ballard. (AR 8-27)

BALL, A.L. Prosper, Kansas, 1882d.

BALL, ALBERT (1835-1927), Worchester, Massachusetts. Patents #38,935 June 23, 1863, magazine gun, #43,827 August 16, 1864, magazine gun, #45,307 December 6, 1864, magazine gun, #47,484 May 23, 1865, bullet machine, and #60,664 January 1, 1867, extractor. Guns made by E.G. Lamson & Co. (GR 7-66)

BALL, CHARLES Springfield, Massachusetts, 1835-1840. As Allen & Ball, 1835-1836 (GC 30)

BALL, ELISHA North Carolina, 1821. Flintlock Kentucky rifles. (Dillin)

BALL, H.D. Morganfield, Kentucky, 1896d.

BALL, JOSEPH T. Malta, Ohio, 1848-1853. (Gardner)

BALL, WILSON Rochester, New York, 1872d. (Eich)

BALLAGH & GOODMAN Lynchburg, Virginia, 1871d-1875d. See M.L. Goodman.

BALLANTINE, JOHN Charleston, South Carolina, 1720-1725. Son of Patrick Ballantine. (Kauffman 2)

BALLANTINE, PATRICK (?-1720), Charleston, South Carolina, 1720. (Kauffman 2)

BALLARD & CO. Worcester, Massachusetts, 1861-1872.

BALLARD & FAIRBANKS Worcester, Massachusetts, 1870-1872. Made Fairbanks patent derringer now known as "Ballard".

BALLARD, A.W. Oshkosh, Wisconsin, 1883-1895d. Percussion 1/2 stock.

BALLARD, ALVIN S. Waterville, New York. Patent #209,444 October 29, 1878, firearm.

BALLARD, CHARLES HENRY (1822-1901), Worcester, Massachusetts. Patents #33,631 November 5, 1861, breechloading firearm, and #63,605 April 9, 1867, extractor. Guns produced under these patients by Ball & Williams, Marlin, and others. (AR 8-27)

BALLARD, J.M. unlocated. Percussion 1/2 stock.

BALLARD, JOHN K. Grayling, Michigan. Patent #337,916 March 16, 1886, gun barrels.

BALLARD, JORDAN Red Rock, Iowa, 1865d.

BALLARD, T.M. Montezuma, Iowa, 1889d-1897d.

BALLARD, WILLIAM Pleasantville, Iowa, 1865d.

BALLINGER, J.H. Clayton, West Virginia, 1884d.

BALLS, C. Sharpsburg, Kentucky, 1854-1860. Percussion 1/2 stock rifle.

BALLS, R.R. (1836-1863), Sonora, California, 1856-1863. (Shelton)

BALLWEG, AMBROSE (1830-?), Indianapolis, Indiana, 1857-1885. Percussion fullstock. (Lindert)

BALSER, A.L., & CO. Cincinnati, Ohio, 1857-1859.

BALSLEY, CHRISTIAN Cumberland Co., Pennsylvania, 1781-1793. (Bowers)

BALSLEY, T. Connellsville, Pennsylvania. Percussion 1/2 stock.

BALTIMORE ARMS CO. Baltimore, Maryland, 1895-1902. Hammerless shotguns. (Hartzler)

BALTZOR & ESLINGER Virgil City, Missouri, 1893d.

BALZER Hayneville, Alabama. Percussion 1/2 stock, two pin, alligator inlay.

BAMES, S. unlocated. Percussion fullstock.

BAMSON, R.B. Wynne, Arkansas, 1892d-1898d.

BANCROFT, CHARLES F. Baltimore, Maryland, 1882-1886d. (Hartzler)

BANDLE GUN CO. Cincinnati, Ohio, 1865-1902. Made parlor guns under J.C. Bandle's patent. P.C. Bandle, J.C. Bandle (son of P.C.) and, after 1885, Al Bandle (son of J.C.). (Hutslar)

BANDLE, AL Cincinnati, Ohio, 1887-1888. Son of J.C. (Hutslar)

BANDLE, JACOB CHARLES (?-1899), Cincinnati, Ohio. Patent #117,367 July 25, 1871, parlor gun with E.P. Christner. Percussion, cartridge, and air guns produced by Bandle Arms Co. (Hutslar)

BANDLE, P.C. Cincinnati, Ohio, 1865d-1866d. (Hutslar)

BANG suicide special.

BANGASSER & LOBERT Buffalo, New York, 1850c.

BANGUP suicide special by Harrington & Richardson.

BANKS Harper's Ferry, Virginia. Invented priming magazine for Hall's rifle, 1828.

BANKS, JOHN Bushkill, Pennsylvania, 1835t. (KRA II-3)

BANKS, JOHN Chester Co., Pennsylvania, 1779, Westmoreland Co., Pennsylvania, 1794. (C&W)

BANKS, URI Hebron, Connecticut, 1775. Committee of Safety locks.

BANNACKER, GEORGE Philadelphia, Pennsylvania, 1800d. (Kauffman)

BANNEN, MICHAEL (1789-?), Darke County, Ohio, 1850c. (Hutslar)

BANNERMAN, F. New York, New York, 1866-1970. Dealers, also made Spencer pump shotguns.

BANNISTER, GEORGE W. Boston, Massachusetts, 1880d-1884d.

BANNON, WILLIAM Fredricksburg, Virginia, 1873-1875.

BANTA, JACOB J. Jersey City, New Jersey. Patent #16,860 March 17, 1857, loading rod with John Foster.

BARBA, G. Houston, Texas, 1890d-1899d. With son, Angelo, 1892-1899.

BARBER & LEFEVER Syracuse, New York, 1875d-1876d. 45/70 tip-up rifle. Successor to L. Barber & Co. (Swinney)

BARBER, D.L. Wallingford, Connecticut, 1887d-1888d.

BARBER, H.B. Scott, New York, 1870d. Patent #101,586 April 5, 1870, sight.

BARBER, JOHN M. Canaan, New Hampshire, 1872-1879. Percussion 1/2 stock.

BARBER, JOSEPH Bridesburg, Pennsylvania. Patent #23,224 March 15, 1859, breechloading firearm with P.C. Reinfried.

BARBER, L. & CO. Syracuse, New York, 1873-1875.

BARBER, ROYAL F. Palmyra, Michigan, 1863d.

BARBER, SAMUEL Lancaster County, Pennsylvania, 1800c-1813t. (Dyke)

BARBER, WALLACE Waterloo, Iowa, 1880d-1895d.

BARBERET, J.I. (1792-?), Edenton, North Carolina, 1820, New Orleans, Louisiana, 1821d.

BARBERET, THEON New Orleans, Louisiana, 1822d-1823d.

BARBEY, JULIUS Greenville, Illinois, 1893d.

BARBOUR, J.M. Rushville, Indiana, 1860d.

BARCLAY, J. New York, New York. Percussion 1/2 stock.

BARD, GEORGE Lancaster, Pennsylvania, 1777t. (Dyke)

BARD, JOHN (?-1894), Barzil, Indiana, 1860-1894. Percussion 1/2 stock. (Lindert)

BARDER, WILLIAM Spring Hope, Pennsylvania, 1882d.

BARE, ALEXANDER Bellmont, Illinois, 1888d-1895d.

BARE, L. Lancaster, Pennsylvania, 1794. Delivered four Model 1792 contract rifles. (Moller)

BARENT, COVERT New Amsterdam, New York, 1646. (Satterlee & Gluckman)

BARGDOLL, JOEL Chillicothe, Missouri, 1850c-1860d.

BARGDOLL, LOUIS Chillicothe, Missouri, 1889d-1898d. Son of Joel Bargdoll.

BARGER, FREDERICK N. (1813-?), Champaign Co., Ohio, 1836, Urbana, Ohio, 1881. Percussion fullstock dated 1870. (Hutslar)

BARIE, WILLIAM Red Cliffe, Pennsylvania. 1887d-1890d.

BARKER, C.M. Albion, Michigan. Patent #404,779 June 4, 1889, breechloading firearm, with William Dicer.

BARKER, CYRUS (1787-1870), Providence, Rhode Island. Converted fullstock.

BARKER, JOHN G. Walnut Valley, Tennessee, 1860d.

BARKER, JOSEPH New Orleans, Louisiana, 1859d-1870d, Salt Lake City, Utah, 1878d-1886d.

BARKER, MILAN S. Eugene, Oregon, 1889d-1906d. Patent #509,716 November 28, 1893, trap gun.

BARKER, T. trade name of H. & D. Folsom Arms Co. on imported and Crescent shotguns. (AR 2-65).

BARKER, THOMAS alternate trade name, see T. Barker.

BARKHIMER see Birkhimer.

BARKHOLDER, JACOB Albany, Oregon, 1867d.

BARKLEY, J.J. Port Andrew, Wisconsin, 1857d.

BARKLEY, W.C. Lichfield, Illinois, 1893d.

BARKMAN, JOE (?-1907), Browstown, Indiana, 1875-1907. Percussion 1/2 stock rifle signed "JB" in script. (Lindert)

BARKMAN, JOEL CHARLES (1829-?), St. Louis, Missouri, 1850c. (Lewis)

BARLOW, JESSE M. (1805-1892), Moscow, Indiana, 1831-1882. Kentucky and 1/2 stock rifles. (Lindert)

BARLOW, JOHN H. New Haven, Connecticut. Patent #659,953 October 16, 1900, extractor.

BARLOW, JOHN W. Moscow, Indiana. Son of Jesse. MB 10-50 says James M. Barlow was at Moscow. (Lindert)

BARLOW, JOHN Point of Fork, Viringia, 1786-1790. Public armory. (Gill)

BARLOW, SAMUEL Greenbush, Illinois, 1864d.

BARLOW, THOMAS H. Lexington, Kentucky. Patent #12,230 May 29, 1855, firearm.

BARN, B., & BRO. Cape Girardeau, Missouri, 1879d-1889d. Percussion 1/2 stock.

BARNABY, JOHN Elktown, Maryland, 1776. (Dean)

BARNARD, HENRY H. Rochester, New York. Patent #189,417 April 10, 1877, shot cartridge.

BARNARD, JOSEPH Walpole, New Hampshire. Model 1798 contract muskets with Amasa Allen and Samuel Grant. (Gluckman)

BARNEKOV, KIEL V. Cornwall, New York. Patent #104,100 June 14, 1870, breechloading firearm. Guns made by G.W. Greene, who submitted them to the 1872 trials.

BARNES & GREEN Vassar, Michigan, 1890d. T.W. Barnes and Saul Green.

BARNES & ONION New York, New York, 1851d. Importers and dealers.

BARNES, A.D. Hyde Park, Illinois, 1888d.

BARNES, A.T. Wilson, North Carolina, 1884d.

BARNES, ABNER Delaware, Ohio, 1870-1888. (Hutslar)

BARNES, CHARLES EMERSON Lowell, Massachusetts. Patent #15,315 July 8, 1856, automatic cannon.

BARNES, DAVIS Chillicothe, Ohio, 1822. (Dean)

BARNES, ERI Marengo, Illinois, 1860d.

BARNES, GEORGE W. Vassar, Michigan. (Roberts)

BARNES, HENRY Wilson, North Carolina, 1858-1860c. Patent #19,121 January 19, 1858, lock. (Bivins)

BARNES, JOHN N. Orange, Massachusetts, 1869-1874d, Salem, Massachusetts, 1885d. Percussion 1/2 stock.

BARNES, JOSEPH (1796-?), Richmond, Virginia, 1850c. (MB 10-63)

BARNES, SAMUEL (1833-?), Waterford, Michigan.

BARNES, T. Greensburg, Indiana, 1857-1860d. Percussion 1/2 stock.

BARNES, THOMAS C. Cedarton, Georgia, 1881d.

BARNES, THOMAS N. (1764-?), North Brookfield, Massachusetts, 1790-1800.

BARNES, THOMAS WASHINGTON (1840-1909), Vassar, Michigan, 1863d-1909. Mule-ear over/under. As Barnes & Green, 1890.

BARNES, TURNER Boston, Massachusetts, 1866-1869, Terre Haute and Franklin, Indiana, 1880-1885. Percussion 1/2 stock. (Lindert)

BARNES, W.H. Boston, Massachusetts. Percussion 1/2 stock.

BARNES, W.H. Penfield, Ohio, 1880-1890. (Hutslar)

BARNET, HENRY Youngstown, Ohio, 1850c. (Hutslar)

BARNET, PETER Watsons, Virginia, 1781. Committee of Safety repairs. (Gill)

BARNETT, JOHN New Lexington, Ohio, 1872-1877. Patent #176,276 April 18, 1876, breechloading firearm.

BARNETT, M.L. unlocated. Percussion fullstock.

BARNEWALT, ADOLPH Peoria, Illinois, 1878d-1882d.

BARNEY & FERRIS Sandusky, Ohio, 1882-1888. Sales only.

BARNEY, G.L. Eureka, Illinois, 1888d-1890d.

BARNEY, H.W. Waterville, Maine, 1856d-1860d.

BARNEY, WILLIAM C. Yuma, Arizona Territory, 1881.

BARNHART, A.W. unlocated. Percussion fullstock.

BARNHART, D.A. Reedsburg, Wisconsin, 1857d-1886d.

BARNHART, GEORGE A. New Rumley, Ohio, 1844-1881. (Hutslar)

BARNHART, GEORGE (1791-1844), Jackson, Ohio, ?-1844. (Hutslar)

BARNHART, MATTHIAS Jackson, Ohio, 1810-?. (Hutslar)

BARNHART, NEHEMIAH (1831-1888), Jackson, Ohio and Columbus, Nebraska, 1852-1875, Hallsville and Chillicothe, Ohio, 1875-1888. Percussion 1/2 stock. Son of William. (MB 8-40)

BARNHART, SIMON Kingstown, Ohio, 1845. Son of George Barnhart. (MB 8-40)

BARNHART, WASHINGTON Chambersburg, Ohio, 1872-1882. (Hutslar)

BARNHART, WILLIAM J. (1802-1867), Ross Co., Ohio, 1850c. Percussion 1/2 stock. Brother of George, father of Nehemiah. (MB 9-40)

BARNHART, WILLIAM (1825-1891), Ross Co., Ohio. Pill lock fullstock. Son of George. (MB 9-40)

BARNHILL, ROBERT Philadelphia, Pennsylvania, 1795-1800d. (Kauffman)

BARNHIZLE, CHRISTOPHER Frederick Town, Maryland. Delivered 235 muskets under contract of 1798 in association with Nicholas White, Thomas Crabbe, and Jacob Metzger. (Gluckman)

BARNS, LUTHER Philadelphia, Pennsylvania, 1800d-1810d. (Kauffman)

BARNUM, WILLIS S. Syracuse, New York, 1874d-1882d.

BARNWELL, R.M. Little Prairie, Missouri, 1860d.

BARR BROTHERS Umpqua Ferry, Oregon, 1881d, Dexter, Oregon, 1886d-1891d.

BARR, FREDERICK New York, New York, 1801-1804.

BARR, H. G. Skowhegan, Maine, circa 1870. (Demeritt)

BARR, JACOB Lancaster Co., Pennsylvania, 1829. Barrelmaker. (Dyke)

BARR, JAMES New York, New York, 1850c.

BARR, JOHN H. Camden, New Jersey, 1850d. (Dean)

BARR, JOHN Lancaster, Pennsylvania, 1857d.

BARR, RICHARD New York, New York, 1847d-1854d. Percussion guns.

BARR, WILLIAM New York, New York, 1841d-1858d. As W. & R. Barr, 1851-1853.

BARRETT, A.R. & CO. Wytheville, Virginia, 1861-1864. Rifles for the Confederacy. (Hill-Anthony)

BARRETT, CONRAD Marron, Pennsylvania, 1887d-1890d.

BARRETT, F.J. Lenox, Massachusetts, 1888d.

BARRETT, JOHN B. Wytheville, Virginia, 1862-1880. Patent #110,233 December 20, 1870, repeating cannon. Confederate muskets and carbines made from Hall parts. (Hill-Anthony)

BARRETT, LOCKHART Brattleboro, Vermont, 1853-1878. As Pike & Barrett, 1856. (Horn)

BARRETT, M.L. Assumption, Illinois, 1867d-1893d.

BARRETT, SAMUEL (1749-1804), Concord, Massachusetts, ?-1800. Committee of Safety muskets, son of Thomas Barrett. (GR 4-75)

BARRETT, THOMAS (1702-1779), Concord, New Hampshire, 1734-1779. Flintlock muskets. (GR 4-75)

BARRIETT, SAMUEL L. Houston, Texas, 1886d.

BARRINGER New York, New York. Very fancy percussion rifles, marked with old English lettering, so the name may be "Warringer".

BARRINGER, DANIEL M. Philadelphia, Pennsylvania. Patent #484,240 March 28, 1893, sight.

BARRINGTON, A.C. Lebanon, New Hampshire. Underhammer.

BARRON, E. Metz, Indiana, 1860d-1885d.

BARRON, THOMAS J. Newnan, Georgia, 1879d-1885d.

BARROW, BENJAMIN D. Donville, Virginia. Patent #496,589 May 2, 1893, safety.

BARROWS, A. Castleton, Vermont, 1849d-1894d.

BARROWS, E. unlocated. Flintlock Kentucky.

BARROWS, F.A. Castleton, Vermont, 1890d. (Horn)

BARRY, DANIEL Providence, Rhode Island, 1872d.

BARRY, ELIJAH Philadelphia, Pennsylvania, 1860c-1875d. Stocks only.

BARRY, THOMAS C. Philadelphia, Pennsylvania, 1886d-1894d.

BARSTOW, CHARLES CHAUNCEY Exeter, New Hampshire, 1808-1820. Patent #none November 21, 1820, ramrods. Model 1808 muskets with brother Joshua, marked "J. & C.B./EXETER.".

BARSTOW, FREDERICK S. Baltimore, Maryland, 1883-1886. As Marriott & Barstow. (Hartzler)

BART, FREDERICK (1816-?), Quincy, Illinois, 1850. (Johnson)

BARTH, W. Milton, Kentucky, 1896d.

BARTHEL, ALBRECHT EDWARD Detroit, Michigan. Patents #168,823 October 19, 1875, firearm implement, #220,785 October 21, 1879, lock, #221,145 November 4, 1879, lock, and #221,146 November 4, 1879, revolver.

BARTHOLOMEW, H.M. Troy, Kansas, 1884d.

BARTLETT BROS. Binghamton, New York, 1829-1851. Joseph and Robert Bartlett.

BARTLETT FIELD trade name of Hibbard, Spencer & Bartlett on imported shotguns.

BARTLETT Lancaster, Pennsylvania. Flintlock Kentucky.

BARTLETT, A. & P. Springfield, Massachusetts, 1760-1814. Model 1808 contract muskets. Asher and Pliny Bartlett. (Gluckman)

BARTLETT, A. Baltimore, Maryland, 1817d. (Hartzler)

BARTLETT, A.H. New York, New York, 1857d.

BARTLETT, GEORGE M. Hallowell, Maine, 1850c. (Demeritt)

BARTLETT, GEORGE S. Anaconda, Montana. Patent #464,060 December 1, 1891, shotgun.

BARTLETT, I.W. Otterville, Illinois, 1878d-1895d.

BARTLETT, ITHAMAR Boston, Massachusetts, 1816. (Lindsay)

BARTLETT, JOSEPH Chenago Point (Binghamton), New York, 1829-1851. Kentucky and 1/2 stock rifles. With his brother Robert. (Swinney)

BARTLETT, ROBERT see Joseph Bartlett.

BARTLETT, S.B. Little Rock, Illinois, 1864d.

BARTLETT, WILLIAM (1816-?), Plainfield, Illinois, 1850c. (Johnson)

BARTLEY, ROBERT Norwalk, Ohio, 1853-1866. (Hutslar)

BARTLEY, T.D. Norwalk, Ohio, 1852-1856, Sandusky, Ohio, 1860-1864. Percussion 1/2 stock. (Hutslar)

BARTLEY, THEODORE D. Dresden, New York, 1871d-1880d. Patent #232,919 October 5, 1880, breechloading firearms.

BARTON & CAMPBELL Pinckney, Michigan, 1887d-1891d. S.A. Barton and Eugene Campbell.

BARTON & RUTTER San Francisco, California, 1870-1872. Percussion 1/2 stock. (Shelton)

BARTON New Lisbon, New York. (Swinney)

BARTON, GEORGE W. Springfield, Ohio, 1870-1884. (Hutslar)

BARTON, HENRY Pinckney, Michigan, 1879d-1891d. As Barton & Campbell, 1887-1891.

BARTON, S.A. Pinckney, Michigan, 1863d-1891d. As Barton & Campbell, 1887-1891.

BARTON, S.D. Milford, Kansas, 1888d.

BARTON, SAMUEL Thornton, Indiana, 1884-1885. (Lindert)

BARTON, SILAS H. Enon, Ohio, 1890d. Patents #543,336 July 23, 1895, ejector, and #676,809 June 18, 1902, magazine gun, both with Charles A. Young. Patent #713,276 November 11, 1902, magazine gun.

BARTON, SILAS Unadilla, Michigan, 1863d-1867d.

BARTON, THOMAS J. Enon, Ohio, 1869-1875, Springfield, Ohio, 1875-1891. Percussion fullstock. (Hutslar)

BARTON, W.M. De Leon, Texas, 1892d.

BARTON, WILLIAM H. 1817-?, Bloomington, Indiana, 1850-1886. (Lindert)

BARZ, CARL La Crosse, Wisconsin, 1865d-1895d. With brother, George, 1875.

BASCOM, HENRY C. LaCrosse, Wisconsin, 1866d-1868, Bay City, Michigan, 1870-1879d, Lansing, Michigan, 1887d-1899d. Patent #75,839 March 24, 1868, powder flask. Operated as Bascom & Powell, 1891d and Bascom & Schilling, 1892-1899.

BASEL, JOHN C. Galveston, Texas, 1868d-1896d.

BASEMANN, HENRY Fort Scott, Kansas, 1879d-1884d.

BASEMANN, WILLIAM Fort Scott, Kansas, 1878d-1888d.

BASILIO, LAOGIER Stockton, California, 1852c-1858d. (Shelton)

BASINAIT, LOUIS Albion, New York, 1858-1882d. Percussion 1/2 stock.

BASLER & DENK St. Louis, Missouri, 1859d. Air guns. John Basler and Emanuel Denk. (Wolff)

BASLER, A.L., & CO. Cincinnati, Ohio, 1857-1959. (Hutslar)

BASLER, JOHN New York, New York, 1855d, St. Louis, Missouri, 1859-1860d, Sacramento, California, 1863-1868, Hamilton, Nevada, 1871d, Ely, Nevada, 1872d, Ward, Nevada, 1878d-1880d. Air guns and percussion rifles. As Basler & Denk in St. Louis. (Shelton)

BASS, J. Arkadelphia, Arkansas, 1850. (Elias)

BASSELL, JOHN C. Calvert, Texas, 1878d.

BASSELL, W. New Orleans, Louisiana, 1869d.

BASSETT, EARNEST A. Boston, Massachusetts. Patent #325,901 September 8, 1885, breechloading firearms.

BASSETT, F.E. unlocated. Single shot target pistol, brass frame.

BASSETT, JOHN E. New Haven, Connecticut, 1905d.

BASSETT, JOHN FRANKLIN Bolwar, New York, 1870. Lever action magazine rifle. (AG 12-79)

BASSETT, S. unlocated. Underhammer. (Logan)

BASTMAN, TOM (1821-?), St. Louis, Missouri, 1850c. (Lewis)

BASTROM, HENRY Chicago, Illinois, 1853-1854. (Johnson)

BATAVIA LEADER trade name of Baker Gun Co. on shotguns.

BATAVIA trade name of Baker Gun Co. on shotguns.

BATCHELLER, J.W. St. Joseph, Missouri, 1891d-1898d.

BATCHELLER, JAMES D. Madison, Wisconsin, 1855-1859. (Kauffman 2)

BATCHELOR, WILLIAM R. Philadelphia, Pennsylvania, 1807-1814, Northern Liberties, Pennsylvania, 1819.

BATCHES, C. (1825-?), Sacramento, California, 1860c. (Shelton)

BATEMAN, THOMAS Lawrenceville, Pennsylvania, 1847. (Kauffman)

BATEMAN, THOMAS St. Louis, Missouri, 1842-1866d. For T.J. Albright, 1854-1857.

BATES VICTORIA trade name on suicide special by Hopkins & Allen.

BATES, C.A. Ellington, New York, son of Cord Bates.

BATES, CORD Ellington, New York, Thornton, New York, 1867d-1882d. Percussion 1/2 stock.

BATES, E. Mount Ephraim, Ohio, 1858-1860, Kellogsville, Ohio, 1860-1866. Percussion 1/2 stock. (Hutslar)

BATES, F.G. Springfield, Massachusetts. Patent #138,439 April 29, 1873, magazine gun, with Louis Rodier.

BATES, FRANCIS Pittsburgh, Pennsylvania, 1850c-1858d. (Kauffman, C&W)

BATES, HENRY New London, Connecticut. Patents #18,568 November 10, 1857, projectile, and #29,573 August 14, 1860, projectile, with Richard Cranston.

BATES, JACOB unlocated. Percussion mule ear fullstock, superposed loads.

BATES, JOHN C. Sparta, Illinois, 1860d.

BATES, M.S. Taylorville, Illinois, 1880d-1893d.

BATES, R. North Carolina, 1820. Flintlock Kentucky. (Satterlee & Gluckman)

BATES, RICHARD Fair Grove, Michigan, 1867d.

BATES, W.C. unlocated. Model 1841 pistol. (GR 6-69)

BATIE, GEORGE (1812-?), Shelby Co., Ohio, 1852c. (Hutslar)

BATISTIE, M.B. Montgomery, Texas, 1896d.

BATTESON, WILLIAM Springfield, Illinois, 1850, Illiopolis, Illinois, 1860. (Johnson)

BATTLEFIELD, R. unlocated. Flintlock Kentucky rifles.

BATTLES, C.G. Wellington, Ohio. (Hutslar)

BATTLS, JOHN Whittier, North Carolina. Percussion rifles. (Bivins)

BATTON, W.A. New Paris, Ohio, 1858-1866. (Hutslar)

BAUER, CHARLES G. (1815-1862), Sacramento, California, 1852-1862. As Klepzig & Co., 1856-1859. (Shelton)

BAUER, E.F. Chillicothe, Ohio, 1878. (Hutslar)

BAUER, GEORGE Lancaster, Pennsylvania, 1770-1781. (Satterlee & Gluckman, not in Dyke)

BAUER, J. unlocated. Flintlock Kentucky rifle.

BAUER, J.C. Battle Creek, Michigan, 1895d-1899d.

BAUER, JACOB Leavenworth, Kansas, 1874d-1878d.

BAUER, W.J. Jackson, Michigan, 1887d-1899d.

BAUGH, JOHN Philadelphia, Pennsylvania, 1780-1783. (Whisker III)

BAUGHMAN, SAMUEL (1827-?), Valparaiso, Indiana, 1850-1860. (Lindert)

BAUM & CO. Hummell's Wharf, Pennsylvania, 1887d-1890d.

BAUM Xenia, Ohio. (Hutslar)

BAUM, ADAM Dauphin Co., Pennsylvania, 1750-1761. (Shumway)

BAUM, CHARLES New Berlin, Pennsylvania. Flintlock and percussion Kentucky rifles. (Gabel)

BAUM, CHARLES Pottsville, Pennsylvania, 1850c. Percussion swivel breech.

BAUM, DANIEL (1759-?), Dauphin Co., Pennsylvania. Son of Adam Baum. (Shumway)

BAUM, J. Northumberland Co., Pennsylvania, 1800-1821. Flintlock Kentucky.

BAUM, JOHN (1761-?), Dauphin Co., Pennsylvania. Son of Adam Baum. (Shumway)

BAUM, SAMUEL New Berlin, Pennsylvania, 1789-1840. Flintlock Kentucky rifles. (Gabel)

BAUM, SAMUEL Northumberland Co., Pennsylvania, 1800c, Columbia Co., Pennsylvania, 1811-1820c. Flintlock Kentucky. (Kauffman)

BAUM, SAMUEL, JR. New Berlin, Pennsylvania. Flintlock Kentucky rifles. (Gabel)

BAUMAN, JOSEPH San Francisco, California, 1870-1874. (Shelton)

BAUMANN, JACOB St. Louis, Missouri, 1842d.

BAUMBACH, HENRY EMIL St. Louis, Missouri, 1879d-1908d.

BAUMGARTNER, JOSEPH Barron, Wisconsin, 1888d.

BAUMLEY, W.D. Senecaville, Ohio, 1883. (Hutslar)

BAUNELL, WILLIAM Somerset Co., Pennsylvania, 1853. (Kauffman)

BAUR, GEORGE Philadelphia, Pennsylvania, 1847d.

BAURMAN, GUSTAV Louisville, Kentucky, 1864d-1871d. Percussion 1/2 stock.

BAXTER, A.P. Waterville, Maine. Underhammer pistol. (Demeritt)

BAXTER, ARCHIBALD Campbellsburg, Indiana, 1858-1870c. (Lindert)

BAXTER, ARTHUR T. Baltimore, Maryland, 1827d-1840d. Flintlock Kentucky rifles and percussion double shotgun. (Hartzler)

BAXTER, H., & SON Philadelphia, Pennsylvania, 1858d. Lockmakers. Listed in the 1859 directory for Philadelphia New York.

BAXTER, HENRY Colon, Michigan, 1867-1879d.

BAXTER, NATHAN L. Mason City, Illinois, 1878d.

BAXTER, R.C. East Liverpool, Ohio, 1888. (Hutslar)

BAY STATE ARMS CO. Uxbridge, Massachusetts, 1870-1874, Worcester, Massachusetts, 1875-1887. Complete line of cheap guns, purchased by Hopkins & Allen who continued to use the name. (Lindsay)

BAYARD ARMS CO. trade name on imported shotguns.

BAYER, HENRY (1780-1850), Pittsburgh, Pennsylvania, 1820-1850. Barrelmaker. (Kauffman, Whisker II)

BAYER, JOHN New York, New York, 1869d-1873d. Air guns. (Wolff)

BAYES, STEPHEN G. Wauseon, Ohio. Patents #86,723 February 9, 1869, magazine gun, and #242,809 June 14, 1881, sight.

BAYLES, JOHN Georgia, 1820c. (Gluckman & Satterlee)

BAYLESS Ft. Smith, Arkansas, 1870. (Elias)

BAYLEY, OLIVER W. Somerville, Massachusetts. Patent #35,008 April 22, 1862, breechloading firearms.

BAYLISS, S. unlocated. Percussion pepperbox dated 1853.

BAZZURO, JOHN Washington, D.C., 1885d.

BEACH & PITTINGER Marshall, Michigan. Percussion three-barrel rifle.

BEACH, ALBERT Hartford, Connecticut, 1854-1880. Sights.

BEACH, CLAUDIUS H. (?-1888), Marshall, Michigan, 1860-1888. Percussion guns.

BEACH, J. Perry Co., Pennsylvania, 1815. (Gluckman & Satterlee)

BEACH, J.J. Celina, Ohio, 1835-1860. (Gluckman & Satterlee)

BEACH, SAMUEL O. Mt. Vernon, Ohio, 1855-1883d. (Hutslar)

BEACH, T. Perry Co., Indiana, 1815.

BEACHLER & BRO. Ironton, Ohio. Percussion 1/2 stock. Also used "G. & P. Beachler" marking.

BEACHLER, G.W. Miamisburg, Ohio, 1883-1896. (Hutslar)

BEACHLER, JACOB Anderson, Indiana, 1860d-1862d.

BEADLE Maumee Valley, Ohio, 1840-1890. (Gluckman & Satterlee)

BEAKLEY, DANIEL Pittsburgh, Pennsylvania, 1860d. (C&W)

BEAL, BARNEY Muscatine, Iowa, 1850c. (MB 8-64)

BEAL, O.H. Bismarck, Dakota Territory, 1877-1881.

BEAL, S.L. Seymour, Indiana, 1860d.

BEALE & BRO. Rockford, Illinois, 1883-1888. Joseph and Thomas Beale. (Johnson).

BEALE, JEREMIAH Hingham, Massachusetts, 1675. (Dean)

BEALE, ROBERT Washington, D.C. Patents #none January 13, 1835, lock for cannon, and #none February 20, 1835, lock for cannon.

BEALL, HOWARD C. St. Louis, Missouri, 1900d. (Pourie)

BEALL, O.W. Colon, Michigan, 1895d.

BEALS, A.C. unlocated. Submitted a lever action rifle to the 1872 trials.

BEALS, FORDYCE New Haven, Connecticut. Patents #11,715 September 26, 1854, revolver, #15,617 June 24, 1856, revolver, #17,359 May 26, 1857, revolver, #21,478 September 14, 1858, revolver, #37,329 June 23, 1863, revolver, #43,284 June 28, 1864, breechloading firearm, #45,202 November 22, 1864, breechloading firearm, #46,207 February 7, 1865, breechloading firearm, and #52,258 January 30, 1866, breechloading firearm. The first patent was used by Eli Whitney, the rest by Remington.

BEALS, WILLIAM A. Trump, Tennessee, 1887d-1891d.

BEAMAN, W.A. Athol, Massachusetts, 1892d.

BEAN & DAY Biddeford, Maine, 1866-1880. Samuel Bean and Benjamin F. Day. (Demeritt)

BEAN, BAXTER Jonesboro, Tennessee, 1812-1834, Washington Co., Tennessee, Nashville, Tennessee (killed there). Flintlock rifles. Son of Russell. (MB 10-46)

BEAN, C.R. Indian Creek, Tennessee, 1881d-1891d.

BEAN, CHARLES Jonesboro, Tennessee, 1830-?. Son of Russell. His son Charles Bean, Jr., succeeded to the shop, 1840-1920, and guns were marked *** on rear sight and muzzle. (MB 10-46)

BEAN, CHARLES, JR. (1840-1920), Jonesboro and Erwin, Tennessee, 1861-1920. Percussion fullstock (MB 10-46)

BEAN, DANIEL V. Plover, Wisconsin. Patent #382,130 May 1, 1888, sight.

BEAN, EDMUND Bean's Station, Tennessee. Son of William Bean. (MB 10-46)

BEAN, EDWARD D. Boston, Massachusetts, 1885, Arlington, Massachusetts, 1888. Patents #329,430 November 3, 1885, cane gun, and #380,975 April 10, 1888, cane gun.

BEAN, GEORGE Bean's Station, Tennessee, 1792-?. Son of William Bean. (MB 10- 46)

BEAN, J. Lawrence, Massachusetts. Percussion target rifles. (MB 4-63)

BEAN, J. Old Town, Maine. Percussion 1/2 stock. (Demeritt)

BEAN, J.H. Cincinnati, Ohio. Patent #141,624 August 12, 1873, magazine gun.

BEAN, JAMES Jonesboro, Tennessee, 1814-1834. With Baxter Bean. (MB 10-46)

BEAN, JESSE Bean's Station, Tennessee. Son of William Bean. (MB 10-46)

BEAN, JOAB Memphis, Tennessee. (MB 10-46)

BEAN, JOHN Bean's Station, Tennessee. Son of William Bean. (MB 10-46)

BEAN, JOSEPH R. (1808-?), Davies Co., Illinois, 1835-1850. (Johnson)

BEAN, JOSEPH Rock Creek, Tennessee. Son of Russell Bean. (MB 10-46)

BEAN, ROBERT Jonesboro, Tennessee. Son of Russell Bean. Sold tools in 1835. (MB 10-46)

BEAN, RUSSELL (1769-?), Jonesboro, Tennessee, 1790, Memphis, Tennessee. Son of William Bean, made flintlock rifles. (MB 10-46)

BEAN, SAMUEL Biddeford, Maine, 1867-1902. As McKenney & Bean, 1867-1871 and Bean & Day, 1873-1884. (Demeritt)

BEAN, WILLIAM (1745-1799), Granger Co., Tennessee, 1768-1799. Flintlock rifles. (MB 10-46)

BEAN, WILLIAM Granger Co., Tennessee, 1790. Son of William Bean. (MB 10-46)

BEANERLEE, JOHN Jonesville, Michigan, 1865d.

BEAR, GEORGE see George Beer.

BEAR, ISAAC Margaretta Furnace, Pennsylvania, 1860d-1861d. Percussion fullstock.

BEAR, JACOB Lancaster, Pennsylvania, 1825t-1871d. (Dyke)

BEAR, JOHN Lancaster Co., Pennsylvania, 1825t-1840t. Flintlock and percussion rifles. See John Baer. (KRA IV-4)

BEAR, JOSEPH Lancaster, Pennsylvania, 1825-1834. Barrelmaker. (Dyke)

BEAR, PETER Lancaster, Pennsylvania, 1840-1850. (Dyke)

BEAR, SAMUEL Lancaster, Pennsylvania, 1809-1850. Barrelmaker. (Dyke)

BEARCOCK, THOMAS W. Pittston, Pennsylvania. Patents #190,543 May 8, 1877, revolver with John Brooks, and #195,562 September 25, 1877, revolver.

BEARD BROTHERS Boise, Idaho, 1889d-1891d.

BEARD, A.W. Salem, Ohio, 1861-1865. Percussion 1/2 stock. (Hutslar)

BEARD, BENJAMIN, E. Florence, New York, 1870-1874d.

BEARD, CHARLES Manlius Station, New York, 1880d.

BEARD, G.L. Arkansas City, Kansas, 1894d.

BEARD, JAMES Woodburn, Illinois, 1860d.

BEARD, WILLIAM T. Parsons, Kansas, 1878d, Seattle, Washington, 1880d, Salt Lake City, Utah, 1886d.

BEARDEN, ALFRED Robinson's Store, Tennessee, 1860d.

BEARDEN, L.J.E. Galveston, Texas. Agent on Slotter & Co. derringer.

BEARDEN, N.M. Robinson's Store, Tennessee, 1860d.

BEARDON, ELIAS M. Green Co., Missouri, 1850c. (MB 11-66)

BEARDSLEY MFG. CO. Brooklyn, New York, 1865-1867. Percussion muskets. (Gluckman & Satterlee)

BEATTY, CORNELIUS E. Baltimore, Maryland, 1835-1842d. Importer. As Norris & Beatty. (Hartzler)

BEATTY, WILLIAM T. Calhoun, Missouri, 1860d.

BEAUCHEE, FRANCIS Charleston, South Carolina, 1807d. (Kauffman)

BEAUDROT, JOSEPH Charleston, South Carolina, 1852-1859. (Kauffman)

BEAUMONT, ISRAEL G. Green Bay, Wisconsin. Patent #152,452 June 30, 1874, breechloading firearm.

BEAUPRE, PETER R. Metropolis, Illinois. Patent #76,58 April 14, 1868, cannon.

BEAUTY suicide special and imported shotgun.

BEAUVAIS, RENAULT (aka Reno), St. Louis, Missouri, 1840-1874. Percussion 1/2 stock. As R & A Beauvais in 1847. Reno and brother Augustus were silversmiths as well as gunsmiths.

BEBOUT, WILLIAM Belmont Co., Ohio, 1858-1876. (Hutslar)

BECHMAN, ROBERT Hamilton, Ohio, 1861. (Hutslar)

BECHTLER, AUGUSTUS Rutherford, North Carolina, 1831-1846. Worked with his father, Christopher, in his mint and gun shop. (Bivins)

BECHTLER, CHRISTOPHER (?-1852), Rutherford, North Carolina, 1831-1852. Made "double ender" percussion pistols with his son, Augustus. (Bivins)

BECK, A.S. unlocated. Flintlock Kentucky rifles.

BECK, ASBUNY (spelling of first name in doubt), Washington Co., Pennsylvania, 1827-1829. (Whisker II)

BECK, AUGUST (1845-?), San Francisco, California, 1874-1882. (Shelton)

BECK, C. Lancaster Co., Pennsylvania, 1780-1820. Flintlock Kentucky rifles. (Gluckman & Satterlee)

BECK, CHRISTIAN (1787-1845), Dauphin Co., Pennsylvania, 1807t-1811t, Franklin Co., Pennsylvania, 1813-1821, Martinsburg, Virginia, 1827, Cinncinati, Ohio, 1841-1845. Flintlock Kentucky. (Bowers)

BECK, CHRISTIAN Lebanon Co., Pennsylvania, 1787-1810. Flintlock Kentucky. Brother of J.P. Beck. (Kauffman-Kindig)

BECK, CHRISTIAN, JR. (1813-1886), Indianapolis, Indiana, 1835-1886. Brother of Samuel. (Lindert, Gluckman & Satterlee)

BECK, CHRISTIAN, JR. Cincinnati, Ohio, 1841-1845. (Hutslar)

BECK, D. unlocated. Flintlock Kentucky.

BECK, DANIEL Bath, New York, 1868d-1882d. Percussion over/under rifle/shotgun.

BECK, GIDEON Lancaster, Pennsylvania, 1780-1788.

BECK, H. New Orleans, Louisiana, 1853d.

BECK, HENRY Ripon, Wisconsin, 1870-1876. (WGCA6)

BECK, HERMAN Cincinnati, Ohio, 1888-1900. (Hutslar)

BECK, I.L. Lehigh Co., Pennsylvania. Flintlock and percussion rifles. (Gabel)

BECK, I.P. see John P. Beck.

BECK, ISAAC Mifflinburg, Pennsylvania, 1835. Flintlock and percussion rifles. (Dillin)

BECK, J.P. Union County, Pennsylvania, flintlock period. (Gluckman & Satterlee)

BECK, J.W. unlocated. Flintlock Kentucky rifles.

BECK, JACOB (1820-?), Indianapolis, Indiana, 1850-1860, Hillsboro, Illinois, 1864d-1893d. Percussion 1/2 stock. (Lindert)

BECK, JOHN PHILIP (1751-1811), Lebanon, Pennsylvania, 1772-1811. Flintlock Kentucky rifles and pistols, Committee of Safety muskets. Two different J.P. Becks, one northern style (Bucks Co.) and one southern (Lancaster Co.). Kindig says John Philip is the "southern" style. (Kindig)

BECK, JOHN VALENTINE (1731-1791), Bethabara, North Carolina, 1764-1791. (Bivins)

BECK, JOHN Lancaster County, Pennsylvania, 1772-1777.

BECK, M. Columbus, Texas, 1878d.

BECK, MICHAEL Minneapolis, Minnesota. Patent #645,932 March 27, 1900, machine gun, with Emil Ferrant.

BECK, S., & SONS Indianapolis, Indiana. Rifles and shotguns. (Lindert)

BECK, SAMUEL (1810-?), Indianapolis, Indiana, 1833-1885. Percussion and cartridge guns. Brother of Christian Beck. (Lindert)

BECK, SIMON Boscobel, Wisconsin, 1884d-1888d.

BECK, W.E. Winston, North Carolina, 1885d-1890d.

BECK, W.M. Lawrenceville, Pennsylvania, 1856-1857d.

BECK, WILLIAM (1819-?), Indianapolis, Indiana, 1850c. (Lindert)

BECK, WILLIAM LaCrosse, Wisconsin, 1895d.

BECK, WILLIAM Portland, Oregon, 1866d-1889d. Percussion 1/2 stock. As William Beck and Son, 1878-1889. (MB 11-48)

BECK, WILLIAM Westmoreland Co., Pennsylvania, 1802-1812. (Whisker II)

BECKER, A. Cincinnati, Ohio, 1880c. Percussion revolver.

BECKER, CHARLES, JR. Lexington, Illinois, 1884d-1886d.

BECKER, FREDERICK JOHN (1823-1879), Oroville, California, 1856-1879. (Shelton)

BECKER, FREDERICK Ironton, Ohio, 1884-1891. (MB 3-55)

BECKER, GEORGE Lancaster, Pennsylvania, 1785t. (KRA IV-4)

BECKER, J. Lebanon, Pennsylvania, 1800. Kentucky rifles. (Gluckman and Satterlee)

BECKER, J.E. Rocky Comfort, Arkansas, 1888d-1898d.

BECKER, J.S. Lebanon, Pennsylvania, 1887d.

BECKER, JOSEPH Wilkes-Barre, Pennsylvania, 1886d-1890d.

BECKER, N. Montgomery, Alabama, 1854d.

BECKER, O.C. East Saginaw, Michigan, 1879d.

BECKER, PETER Hanover Center, Indiana, 1882-1885. (Gardner)

BECKER, WILLIAM (1800-?), Illinois, 1836-1844. (Johnson)

BECKETT, WILLIAM St. Louis, Missouri, 1858d.

BECKHAM, JAMES Gordonsville, Virginia, 1885d.

BECKLEY, ELIAS (1735-1816), Berlin, Connecticut, 1800-1816. (Gluckman & Satterlee)

BECKLEY, ELIAS, JR. (?-1828), Berlin, Connecticut, 1816-1828. Son of Elias.

BECKMAN, JOHN F. Charleston, South Carolina, 1886d.

BECKMAN, R.E. Franklin, New Hampshire, 1874d-1879d.

BECKWITH Mansfield, Ohio. Percussion 1/2 stock. (Hutslar)

BECKWITH, MARION F. (1829-?), Mansfield, Ohio, Stockton, California, 1860c. (Shelton)

BECKWITH, ROBERT New York, New York. Patent #19,674 March 23, 1858, cane gun.

BECKWITH, SAMUEL Whitneyville, Connecticut, 1871d-1874d.

BEDDIE, GEORGE Tuscarawas Co., Ohio, 1815-1871. Flintlock rifles. (Gluckman & Satterlee)

BEDDOW, JOSIAH Philadelphia, Pennsylvania, 1890d.

BEDFORD, AUGUSTUS New York, New York. Patent #172,376 January 18, 1876, air gun.

BEDFORD, WILLIAM H. Rosendale, New York, 1870d.

BEDGER, CHARLES Sacramento, California, 1856-1862. (Shelton)

BEE, BENJAMIN Horton's, Pennsylvania, 1861d.

BEE, ELIAS Cherokee, Kansas, 1882d.

BEEBE BROS. Denison, Texas, 1879. A.L. and H.R. Beebe.

BEEBE, A. HENRY Pine Run, Michigan, 1863d-1892d.

BEEBE, A.L. (1853-?), Denison, Texas, 1878-1880c. As Sheeder & Beebe, 1878 and Beebe Bros., 1879.

BEEBE, A.L. see Fergus & Beebe.

BEEBE, FRANK N. Columbus, Ohio. Patent #230,224 July 20, 1880, extractor.

BEEBE, GEORGE Albany, New York, 1846-1850d. Underhammer pistol.

BEEBE, H. Fort Scott, Kansas, 1878d. Son of Richard Beebe.

BEEBE, H.R. Denison, Texas, 1879. As Beebe Brothers.

BEEBE, RICHARD Springfield, Ohio, 1853-1870, Fort Scott, Kansas, 1871d-1875d. Percussion 1/2 stock.

BEEBE, WILLIAM S. Philadelphia, Pennsylvania. Patent #63,834 April 19, 1867, fuse.

BEECH, G.H. Litchfield, Minnesota, 1898d.

BEECHER, SANFORD (1819-?), Lawrence Co., Illinois, 1849-1850c. (Johnson)

BEECK, C. Walker, Illinois, 1860d.

BEEMAN, ANDREW M. Rochester, New York, 1853d. (Eich)

BEEMAN, JOHN Lancaster, Ohio, 1815-1826. Flintlock Kentucky pistol. As Beeman & Sights, 1826. (Hutslar)

BEEMAN, MARTIN Lancaster, Ohio, 1831. Converted fullstock. (Gluckman & Satterlee)

BEEMAN, O.H. Kirksville, Missouri, 1893d-1898d.

BEEMAN, WILLIAM Boston, Massachusetts, 1775-1776. Flintlock pistol. Committee of Safety muskets. (Gluckman & Satterlee)

BEER see Bear. (Sellers)

BEER, GEORGE Westmoreland Co., Pennsylvania, 1808-1819. Flintlock Kentucky. (Kauffman, Whisker II)

BEERGER, WILLIAM Aurora, Indiana, 1858d-1862d. Percussion fullstock.

BEERS, J. Hudson Valley, New York, 1830-1840. Percussion fullstock. (Swinney)

BEERSTECHER, FREDERICK (1812-1890), Philadelphia, Pennsylvania, 1848-1856d, Lewisburg, Pennsylvania, 1857-1868, Centreville, Michigan, 1868-1879, San Francisco, California, 1879-1890. Patent #13,592 September 28, 1855, superposed loads. Derringers and rifles both with and without patent mechanism. Percussion four-shot rifle. (Winant, Shelton)

BEESON BROTHERS Metropolis, Illinois, 1884d-1886d.

BEESON, JESSE B. Metropolis, Illinois, 1860d-1893d. Son of Matthew Beeson. As Beeson Bros., 1884-1886.

BEESON, MARTIN Metropolis, Illinois, 1860d-1886d. Son of Matthew Beeson. As Beeson Bros., 1884-1886.

BEESON, MATTHEW Metropolis, Illinois, 1854d.

BEETON, JOHN Lexington, Virginia, 1871d-1873d. Percussion fullstock.

BEETON, R. & J. Lexington, Virginia. Percussion duelling pistol.

BEETON, R.E., & SON Lexington, Virginia, 1897d.

BEETON, ROBERT Lexington, Virginia, 1871d.

BEFORD, ARTER Jefferson City, Missouri. (Dean)

BEHMER, DANIEL (1855-1944), Lima, Ohio, 1875d, San Francisco, California, 1875-1877, Santa Rosa, California, 1877-1919. (Shelton)

BEHMER, DANIEL Niles Michigan, 1872d-1877d.

BEHR, J.J. Baltimore, Maryland. Brown Bess musket. (Hartzler)

BEHR, PETER N. St. Louis, Missouri, 1894d. (Pourie)

BEHRENS, CHRISTIAN F. Baltimore, Maryland, 1833-1841d. (Hartzler)

BEIDEL, JACOB Bushkill, Pennsylvania, 1828-1835t. (KRA II-3)

BEIDENHARDT, CHRISTOPHER Lancaster Co., Pennsylvania, 1770t-1773t. (Dyke)

BEIG, S. unlocated. Flintlock Kentucky rifle.

BEIGH, S. unlocated. Percussion 1/2 stock.

BEIGHTLE, J.L. Valley Falls, Kansas, 1888d-1906d.

BEIL, BORNHART Muscatine, Iowa, 1865d. With H. Molis & Co.

BEINCIKER, JOHN Sacramento, California, 1856d. (Shelton)

BEINERT & SON Racine, Wisconsin, 1879d.

BEISEL, JOHN Bushkill, Pennsylvania, 1820t, Philadelphia, Pennsylvania, 1829d. (KRA II-3)

BEISEL, SIMON Philadelphia, Pennsylvania, 1829d. See Samuel Birsel.

BEISHEIM, HENRY Rochester, New York, 1873-1886. Patent #151,953 June 16, 1874, air gun. Made air guns with brother, Jacob. (Eich)

BEIST, JACOB (1811-?), Stark County, Ohio, 1850c. (Hutslar)

BEITZEL, P.M. Canton, Ohio, 1859d. (Hutslar)

BEKEART, FRANK (1822-1890), New York, New York, 1842-1845, Natchez, Mississippi, 1846, Coloma, California, 1849-1859, Placerville, California, 1860-1864, San Francisco, California, 1865-1890. Born Jules Francois Bekeart. Percussion and cartridge target pistols. (Shelton)

BEKEART, PHILIP B. (1850-1936), San Francisco, California, 1890-1920. Sales mostly, son of and successor to Frank Bekeart. (Shelton)

BELAMY, EMERY and GAY Mobile, Alabama, 1844d. (Neville)

BELBI, H. Springfield, Ohio, 1845. (Dean*)

BELDEN, SALMON Visalia, California. Patents #76,587 April 14, 1868, lock, and #85,268 December 29, 1868, breechloading firearm. Both with John F. Crabtree.

BELISLE, ROBERT S. Philadelphia, Pennsylvania. Patent #342,563 May 25, 1886, spring gun.

BELKNAP HARDWARE CO. Louisville, Kentucky. Dealers only.

BELKNAP trade name of Belknap Hardware Co. on shotguns made by Crescent.

BELKNAP, AMASA (1786-1874), Cherry Valley, New York, 1830-1874. Percussion rifles. (MB 8-52)

BELKNAP, JOHN S. St. Johnsbury, Vermont, 1879-1887. Percussion 1/2 stock. (Horn)

BELKNAP, LEVERETT Hartford, Connecticut, 1850d. (Kauffman 2)

BELKNAP, N. Columbia, South Carolina. Agent on Allen pepperbox and single shots.

BELL see Burgess & Bell.

BELL, BOAZ (1827-?), Lawrenceburgh, Indiana, 1860. (Lindert)

BELL, C.J. Bainbridge, Georgia, 1883d.

BELL, CONDER unlocated. Kentucky rifles.

BELL, DANIEL Stark Co., Ohio, 1858-1861. Percussion guns. (Hutslar)

BELL, ELIAS unlocated. Flintlock Kentucky rifle dated 1818.

BELL, F.F. Marysville, California, 1853d. (Shelton)

BELL, FRANCIS H. (1810-?), Washington, D.C., 1858-1860d. Patent #23,545 April 12, 1859, self priming lock. (Hartzler)

BELL, GEORGE W. Elizabeth City, North Carolina, 1877d-1890d.

BELL, HILLIARD Raleigh, North Carolina, 1866-1885d. (Bivins)

BELL, J.P. Pleasant Grove, Georgia, 1879d.

BELL, JAMES Pennsylvania, 1778. Committee of Safety gunsmith. (C&W)

BELL, JOHN Boston, Massachusetts, 1745-1754. Flintlock musket.

BELL, JOHN Carlisle, Pennsylvania, 1800-1850. (Bowers)

BELL, LLOYD C. Washington, D.C., 1858-1860d. New Orleans, Louisiana, 1883d-1892d.

BELL, ROBERT Yancy, North Carolina. (Bivins)

BELL, THOMAS H. (1842-?), Washington, D.C., 1860c. Son of Francis Bell. (Hartzler)

BELL, WALTER Baltimore, Maryland, 1847-1867d. (Hartzler)

BELL, WILLIAM C. Cincinnati, Ohio, 1825-1826. For John Keating. (Hutslar)

BELL, WILLIAM C. Leadville, Colorado, 1881-1882. As Miller & Bell. (Sellers-3)

BELL, WILLIAM H. Fortress Monroe, Virginia, 1829-1835, Washington D.C., 1835-1860d, Baltimore, Maryland, 1880. Patents #none December 8, 1829, cannon, #none December 8, 1829, primer for cannon, #none October 1, 1830, percussion lock, #none May 14, 1836, cannon, #22,618 January 18, 1858, primer, #27,518 March 20, 1860, revolver, and #228,859 June 15, 1880, revolver. Bell was a member of the Ordnance Corps. (Sellers-1)

BELL, WILLIAM H., JR. (1834-?), Washington, D.C., 1860c, Baltimore, Maryland. Patents #223,100 December 30, 1879, cartridge holder, and #223,101 December 30, 1879, revolver. (Hartzler)

BELL, WILLIAM (1815- ?), New Massilon, Illinois, 1858-1860d.

BELL, WILLIAM Raleigh, North Carolina, 1870c. (Bivins)

BELLAMY, JOHN A. Mobile, Alabama, 1839d. (Neville)

BELLESON, WILLIAM Baltimore, Maryland. (Hartzler)

BELLEW, ROBERT Yancey Co., North Carolina. (Bivins)

BELLINGER, ARTHUR F. Mohawk, New York. Patent #251,344 December 27, 1881, magazine gun.

BELLIS see Hathaway & Bellis.

BELLIS, PETER Dauphin Co., Pennsylvania, 1831-1834. Flintlock Kentucky. (MB 1-66)

BELLMORE GUN CO. trade name of Crescent Arms Co. on shotguns. (Hinman)

BELLMORE, C.S. Skowhegan, Maine, 1896. As Phillips & Bellmore. (Demeritt)

BELLOWS, JOSIAH Walpole, New Hampshire. Contracts for 1,000 Model 1798 muskets with Gordon Huntington, John Livingston, and David Stone. (Gluckman)

BELSCHNER, JOHN L. Manchester, Maryland, 1878d. (Hartzler)

BELTON, JOSEPH Philadelphia, Pennsylvania. Multiple loading invention. 100 authorized by Congress May 3, 1777. (see Bugle 42 for Joseph Belton, Lumberton, Massachusetts, 1799, same invention) (AR 9-58)

BEMIS, AMASA Worcester, Massachusetts, 1861d. Armorer.

BEMIS, EDMUND (1720-1810), Boston, Massachusetts, 1745-1785. Flintlock pistol. (Gluckman & Satterlee)

BEMIS, JAMES E. Jaffrey, New Hampshire, 1878d-1879d.

BENCH, WILLIAM Oshkosh, Wisconsin, 1876.

BENDER, AMOS unlocated. Flintlock Kentucky.

BENDER, CHRISTIAN Lancaster, Pennsylvania, 1785-1814t. Flintlock Kentucky. For Michael Bender. (Kauffman) (Dyke)

BENDER, IGNATIUS Mobile, Alabama, 1870d-1873d.

BENDER, JACOB Cambria Co., Pennsylvania, 1808-1816. Flintlock Kentucky rifles. (Kauffman)

BENDER, JOHN (1782-1815), Lancaster, Pennsylvania, 1808-1815. Flintlock Kentucky rifles. (Dean)

BENDER, JOHN Mobile, Alabama, 1874d-1904d. Son of and successor to Ignatius Bender.

BENDER, MICHAEL Lancaster, Pennsylvania, 1785. (Kauffman)

BENDER, PHILIP Lancaster Co., Pennsylvania, 1786t-1793t. (Dyke)

BENDERITTER, JOSEPH (1803-?), Bellevue, Ohio, 1846-1853. (Hutslar)

BENEDICT see Unger & Benedict.

BENEDICT, ALBERT Lincoln Co., Missouri, 1850c. (MB 11-66)

BENEDICT, E.B. Spearfish, Dakota Territory, 1884d, Wadena, Minnesota, 1892d.

BENEDICT, INHOFF Berks Co., Pennsylvania, 1781-1784. (Dean)

BENESH, JOSEPH Chicago, Illinois, 1874-1888d.

BENFER, AMOS (1841-1916), Beavertown, Pennsylvania, Troxelville, Pennsylvania, 1861-1893. Flintlock and percussion rifles. Brother of Arnig Benfer. (MB 1-50)

BENFER, ARNIG Beavertown, Pennsylvania. Late flintlock rifles. Brother of Amos. (Gluckman & Satterlee)

BENFER, MOSES Beavertown, Pennsylvania, 1840-1880. (Chandler 2)

BENGAL suicide special by Iver Johnson.

BENGTSON, ANDREW Chicago, Illinois, 1875d-1888d.

BENHAM trade name of Keith, Benham & Dezendorf on imported shotguns.

BENHAM, W.B. Bozeman, Montana, 1888d.

BENJAMIN, AMADEE J. Valley Falls, Rhode Island. Patent #325,042 August 25, 1885, magazine gun.

BENJAMIN, REUBEN Chicago, Illinois. Patent #664,074 December 18, 1900, light.

BENNET & BIGALO Chenango, New York, 1824. (MB 6-45)

BENNET, SILAS C. Chenango, New York, 1824. As Bennet & Bigalo. (MB 6-45)

BENNETT & CALDWELL Windsor Locks, Connecticut, 1860d. Percussion pistols.

BENNETT & HANFORD St. Cloud, Minnesota, 1867d.

BENNETT & PACKSON Kent Island, Maryland Colony, 1629-1631. (Hartzler)

BENNETT Kent Island, Maryland Colony, 1621-?. As Bennett & Packson, 1629-1631. (Carey, Hartzler)

BENNETT, AUGUSTUS A. Cincinnati, Ohio, 1861-1900. With Benjamin Kittredge 1861-1865. (Hutslar)

BENNETT, DANIEL K. Montpelier, Vermont, 1855-1875. (Horn)

BENNETT, EDWARD E. Groveland, New York. Patent #551,251 December 10, 1895, breechloading firearm.

BENNETT, EPENSTUS A. Waterville, Maine. Patent #603 February 15, 1838, repeating gun, with Frederick Haviland.

BENNETT, G.A. Erie, Pennsylvania, 1850c. (GR 11-60)

BENNETT, H.P. St. Cloud, Minnesota, 1867d-1886d. As Bennett & Hanford, 1867d.

BENNETT, J.M. Harper's Ferry, Iowa, 1865d.

BENNETT, JOAB W. Pulaski Co., Missouri, 1850c. (MB 11-66)

BENNETT, JOB Pawtucket, Rhode Island, 1855-1875d.

BENNETT, JOHN R. Palmyra, New York, 1858-1861d, Nunda, New York, 1870d-1882d. Percussion shotguns and rifles.

BENNETT, JOSEPH A. Hartford, Connecticut, 1865d. Patent #643,935 February 20, 1900, magazine gun. Basic Ross rifle patent.

BENNETT, L. Providence, Rhode Island, 1859-1868. (Dean)

BENNETT, OLIVER H. Jamestown, North Dakota. Patent #478,214 July 5, 1892, magazine gun.

BENNETT, ORRA (1800-?), Lyon, New York, 1848-1865d. Percussion 1/2 stock.

BENNETT, R. Mt. Vernon, Missouri, 1860d.

BENNETT, S.F. Youngstown, Ohio, 1841-1855. Percussion 1/2 stock. (Hutslar)

BENNETT, T. unlocated. Flintlock Kentucky.

BENNETT, T. unlocated. Underhammer.

BENNETT, THOMAS GRAY (1845-1930), New Haven, Connecticut, 1870-1924. Patents #188,844 March 27, 1877, magazine gun, #190,264 May 1, 1877 magazine gun with W.W. Wetmore, #209,748 November 12, 1878, magazine gun, #211,691 January 28, 1879, charger for magazine guns, #223,797 January 27, 1880, lock, #224,366 February 10, 1880, magazine gun with W.W. Wetmore, #343,423 June 8, 1886, magazine gun, #352,292 November 9, 1886, breechloading firearm, #355,121 December 28, 1886, sight, #386,290 July 17, 1888, magazine gun, #487,465 and #487,466 December 6, 1892, takedown barrels, #537,598 April 16, 1895, bolt action gun, #545,766 September 3, 1895, magazine gun, #549,343 November 5, 1895, machine gun, #551,572 December 17, 1895, magazine gun, #557,947 April 7, 1896, fore stock, #564,420 July 21, 1896, magazine gun, #564,421 July 21, 1896, magazine gun, #588,315 August 17, 1897, locking mechanism, #589,201 August 31, 1897, locking mechanism, #589,687 September 7, 1897, locking mechanism, #599,587 February 22, 1898, magazine gun with William Mason, #632,090 August 29, 1899, bolt action gun, #695,784 March 18, 1902, automatic gun with William Mason, #710,660 October 7, 1902, automatic gun with Thomas C. Johnson, #747,645 December 22, 1903, extractor, #781,179 January 31, 1905, breechloading firearm, #782,716 February 14, 1905, bolt action gun, #798,866 September 5, 1905, bolt action gun with Frank F. Burton, #814,511 March 6, 1906, shot spreader, and #836,554 November 20, 1906, magazine gun. Bennett was the son-in-law of Oliver Winchester and succeeded him as president and later chairman of the board of the Winchester Repeating Arms Co. All of his patents were assigned to Winchester. (Williamson)

BENNETT, THOMAS Pulaski Co., Missouri, 1850c.

BENNETT, WILLIAM N. (1827-1888), Elgin, Iowa, 1856-1888. California, 1849-1856. (MB 10-46)

BENNING, A. Abbott, Iowa, 1887d.

BENSON & COLLINS Fairmont, West Virginia. Sliding barrel rifle. M.M. Benson.

BENSON, AARON Madison, Florida, 1885d.

BENSON, EZRA D. (1836-1909), Terra Alta, West Virginia, 1870c. Percussion 1/2 stock. (MB 11-66) (Whisker IV)

BENSON, H.J. Dalles, Oregon, 1873d.

BENSON, ISAAC Hume, New York, 1847-1851. Percussion fullstock rifle.

BENSON, M.M. (?-1911), Bruceton Mills, West Virginia, 1884d. Morgantown, West Virginia. Brother of Ezra, also as Benson & Collins, date unknown. (MB 4-63)

BENSON, MADISON (1854-?), Grant, West Virginia, 1880c.

BENSON, P.P. Green Hill, Tennessee, 1860d.

BENSON, WILLIAM M. Rice's Landing, Pennsylvania, Fairmont, West Virginia. (Dean)

BENTHAL, W.H. Canton, Mississippi, 1885d.

BENTLEY & HURST Bloomington, Illinois, 1895d-1899d. P.W. Bentley and Richard E. Hurst.

BENTLEY & RAMEY Bloomington, Illinois, 1867d-1870d.

BENTLEY, PRESTON W. Bloomington, Illinois, 1864d-1899d. As Bentley & Ramey, 1867-1870 and Bentley & Hurst, 1895-1899.

BERDAN FIRE ARMS MFG. CO. Hartford, Connecticut, 1866-1868, New York, New York, 1868-1874. Promotional company for Hiram Berdan's inventions.

BERDAN, HIRAM Hartford, Connecticut. Patents #45,898 January 10, 1865, rifling, #45,899 January 10, 1865, breechloading firearm, #45,901 January 10, 1865, bayonet attachment, #46,292 February 7, 1865, cartridge, #51,991 January 8, 1866, breechloading firearm, #52,818 February 27, 1866, cartridge, #52,925 February 27, 1866, breechloading firearms, #53,388 March 20, 1866, cartridge, #82,587 September 29, 1868, cartridge, #85,162 December 22, 1868, breechloading firearm, #88,436 March 30, 1869, breechloading firearm, #101,418 April 5, 1870, breechloading firearm, #108,869 November 1, 1870, breechloading firearm, #157,783 December 15, 1874, breechloading firearm, and #478,215, July 5, 1892, submarine gun. Commander of "Berdan's Sharpshooters" during Civil War. Guns made by Colt and others.

BERG, ADOLPH (1836-?), Davenport, Iowa, 1857-1861, Santa Cruz, California, 1864-1865, Gilroy, California, 1868-1872. Percussion 1/2 stock. (Shelton)

BERG, ANTON H. Akron, Ohio, 1857-1886. Percussion 1/2 stock. (Hutslar)

BERG, CHARLES J. St. Louis, Missouri, 1889d-1898d.

BERG, EMIL (1859-1931), Davenport, Iowa, 1868-1931. Son of Henry Berg, rebarreled guns. (Kelver)

BERG, HART O. Brick Church, New Jersey. 1880d-1887, New York, New York, 1887d-1888d. Patent #363,577 May 24, 1887, hammerless gun with Adolph De Cortis of Liege, Belgium.

BERG, HENRY Davenport, Iowa, 1858d-1887d. Patent #34,729 March 25, 1862, breechloading firearm. Took sons Frank and Emil into firm of H. Berg & Sons in 1868. Most work was done on schuetzen rifles. (Kelver)

BERGEN, ALEXANDER J. Brooklyn, New York. Patents #45,202 November 22 1864, breechloading firearm with D. Williamson, #62,465 February 26, 1868, breechloading firearm, #62,466 February 26, 1867, cartridge, and #62,467 February 26, 1867, cartridge. (Gardner)

BERGEN, CORNELIUS J. Brooklyn, New York. Patent #42,815 May 17, 1864, cartridge, assigned to Moore's Patent Fire Arms Co.

BERGER, ANTON Menominee, Wisconsin, 1857d.

BERGER, BARNHART (1823-?), Reading, Pennsylvania, 1850c. (Kauffman)

BERGER, CASPAR Detroit, Michigan, 1858-1864. Percussion 1/2 stock.

BERGER, CHARLES B. Bay City, Michigan, 1868d-1879d. As Berger & Co., 1868.

BERGER, F. AUGUSTUS East Saginaw, Michigan, 1872d-1895d.

BERGER, RICHARD ALFRED Baltimore, Maryland. Patent #340,192 April 20, 1886, breechloading firearm.

BERGER, W. (1829-?), Aurora, Indiana, 1860c. Percussion 1/2 stock. (Lindert)

BERGERSEN, PEDER (1848-1930), Chicago, Illinois, 1870c, Cheyenne, Wyoming, 1876-1915d. Patent #215,557 May 20, 1879, magazine gun. Custom work on breechloaders.

BERGESOIDES, RUDOLPH St. Genevieve, Missouri, 1854d.

BERGHOUSEN, CHARLES Kansas City, Missouri, 1891d-1893d.

BERGLEY, WILLIAM Lancaster, Pennsylvania, 1875d.

BERGMAN, HENRY Appleton, Wisconsin, 1888d-1895d.

BERGNER, GEORGE Washington, Missouri, 1879d. Son of Henry Bergner.

BERGNER, HENRY Washington, Missouri, 1860d.

BERGSTON, ANDREW Chicago, Illinois, 1882d-1888d.

BERINGER, JOHN Philadelphia, Pennsylvania, 1861d. See John Biringer.

BERKELE, JOHN Atlanta, Georgia, 1877d-1890d. As Heinz & Berkele.

BERKLEY, JOHN R. Globe, Missouri, 1860d.

BERKSHIRE trade name of Shapleigh Hardware Co. on shotguns. (Hinman)

BERLIN, ABRAHAM Easton, Pennsylvania, 1763t-1786t. Flintlock Kentucky rifles, barrelmaker. (Dyke)

BERLIN, ISAAC (1755-1831), Easton, Pennsylvania, 1775-1793 and 1811-1831, Abbottstown, Pennsylvania, 1793-1803. Flintlock rifles and swords. Probably two men of same name as tax lists of Crawford Co., 1826 and Lehigh Co., 1835, also list him. (Kindig, KRA 11-3)

BERLIN, LOUIS Buffalo, New York, 1854. (Gluckman-Satterlee)

BERNAL, LEON Laredo, Texas, 1890d-1896d.

BERNARD, F.N. (1805-?), Crescent City, California, 1850-1856, Orleans Bar, California, 1857. (Shelton)

BERNARD, JOSEPH Walpole, New Hampshire, 1799-1801. Contract muskets with Amasa Allen and Samuel Grant. (Gluckman)

BERNDS, PHILIP Trumbaursville, Pennsylvania, 1860d-1861d.

BERNE, W. (1806-?), Paddocks Grove, Illinois, 1860c. (Johnson)

BERQUR, E. Detroit, Michigan. (Roberts)

BERRIER, JACOB (1865-1907), Big Spring, Pennsylvania. Percussion fullstock. (Chandler 2)

BERRIER, T. Thibodeaux, Louisiana, 1885d.

BERRY & BINHEIMER Olympia, Washington, 1891d.

BERRY, A.P. Lancaster Co., Pennsylvania, 1770t-1795t. Flintlock Kentucky. (KRA IV-4).

BERRY, B. Painted Post, New York, 1820-1825. Probably Barry Wood. Flintlock Kentucky rifles. (Dillin)

BERRY, GEORGE G. Rochester, New York, 1849. For William Billinghurst. (Eich)

BERRY, GILBERT Kingston, New York, 1849-1874d.

BERRY, PETER (?-1796), Dauphin Co., Pennsylvania, 1786-1796. Flintlock Kentucky. (Kindig)

BERRY, PETER Annville, Pennsylvania, 1800-1807. Son of Peter Berry. (Kindig)

BERRY, R.B. unlocated. Flintlock Kentucky.

BERRY, S. unlocated. Flintlock Kentucky.

BERRY, WILLIAM J. (1818-?), Crescent City, California, 1856, Petaluma, California, 1860c, Prescott, Arizona, 1864-1866, Las Cruces, New Mexico, 1884d, El Paso, Texas, 1884d-1885d. Was also a lawyer. (Shelton)

BERRY, WILLIAM Kewana, Indiana, 1860d.

BERRY, WILLIAM Poughkeepsie, New York, 1834-1851, Albany, New York, 1853-1855. Cochran turret pistols and other percussion guns. (Gluckman & Satterlee)

BERSTRO, H.T. Buffalo, New York, 1830-1840. Flintlock Kentucky. Worked alone and with his brother, J.H. Berstro. (Dean)

BERSTRO, I.W. Buffalo, New York. Percussion 1/2 stock, probably J.H. Berstro. (Gluckman & Satterlee)

BERSTRO, J.H. Buffalo, New York, 1832-1838. Flintlock Kentucky. Employed his brother, H.T. Berstro, who also operated alone. (Swinney)

BERTHOLF, JAMES New York, New York, 1840d-1854d.

BERTHOUD, EDWARD L. Golden, Colorado. Patent #298,659 May 13, 1884, sight. (Sellers-3)

BERTRAM, THEODORE F. Philadelphia, Pennsylvania, 1875d.

BERTSCHE Sandusky, Ohio, 1859d. As Leidke & Bertsche. (Hutslar)

BERY, P. unlocated. Flintlock Kentucky rifle.

BEST, CHARLES E. Jordan, New York. Patent #216,370 June 10, 1879, lock.

BEST, JOHN ISRAEL (1832-?), Edinboro, Pennsylvania 1856d. Percussion fullstock.

BEST, LEONARD Lancaster, Pennsylvania. Flintlock Kentucky rifle. (Gluckman & Satterlee)

BEST, M. unlocated. Late flintlock Kentucky.

BEST, M. unlocated. Superposed load mule ear percussion rifle.

BEST, ROBERT Cincinnati, Ohio, 1812-1826. (Hutslar)

BEST, SAMUEL Cincinnati, Ohio, 1812. Brother of Robert Best. (Hutslar)

BEST, THE suicide special.

BEST, WILLIAM T. Minneapolis, Minnesota, 1884d-1886d.

BESTGEN, CHRISTIAN Ashland, Pennsylvania, 1871d-1880d.

BESUCHET, FRANCOIS New Orleans, Louisiana, 1841d.

BESWICK, ANDREW J. West Bergen, New Jersey, 1852-1859d.

BESWICK, H. West Bergen, New Jersey, 1871-1874d.

BETCHER, N. Mountain Grove, Pennsylvania, 1890d.

BETTEN, WILLIAM San Francisco, California, 1881-1884. (Shelton)

BETTIS, PHILIP P. Vickery's Creek, Georgia, 1879d-1881d.

BETTLEY Buffalo, New York, 1860. (Gluckman & Satterlee)

BETTS, JESSE F.P. Bowling Green, Missouri, 1860d, Louisiana, Missouri 1879d.

BETZ, ANDREAS (1727-1795), Wachovia, North Carolina, 1754-1767, Salisbury, North Carolina, 1767-1795. (Bivins)

BETZ, GEORGE Salisbury, North Carolina, 1795-1804. Brother of Andreas. (Bivins)

BETZ, J. Franklin Square, Ohio, 1870-1880. Percussion 1/2 stock. (Hutslar)

BETZER, CALVIN St. Mary's, Ohio, 1884-1886. (Hutslar)

BEUTLER & TRAVER Ann Arbor, Michigan, 1865d-1867d. Percussion rifles. Charles Beutler and Richard C. Traver. (MB 9-66)

BEUTTENMULLER, FREDERICK (1832-?), Joliet, Illinois, 1853-1886d. As Keen & Beuttenmuller, 1853-1859, Beuttenmuller & Bro., 1884-1886. Retired in 1886, but business continued as Beuttenmuller & Spelter until 1916.

BEUTTENMULLER, GEORGE B. (1821-?), Chicago, Illinois, 1854-1893d. Percussion double shotgun.

BEUTTENMULLER, JOHN Joliet, Ill., 1884d-1886d. As F. Beuttenmuller & Bro.

BEUTTER BROTHERS New Haven, Connecticut, 1850d, Meriden, Connecticut, 1856d. Percussion target rifles.

BEUTTER, H. Hartford, Connecticut. Percussion 1/2 stock.

BEVANS, A.L. Flushing, New York. Percussion 1/2 stock. (Gluckman & Satterlee)

BEVER, L.G. Portage, Wisconsin, 1857d-1879d. Percussion 1/2 stock.

BEVIER, JAMES Plymouth, Ohio, 1867-1869. (Hutslar)

BEVILL, THOMAS Guilford, North Carolina, 1820. (Bivins)

BEYER, DAVIT Lebanon, Pennsylvania, 1800t. (Dyke)

BEYER, JESSE Benton, Pennsylvania, 1882d-1890d.

BEYER, NICHOLAS (1780-1850), Lebanon Co., Pennsylvania, 1805-1815. Flintlock Kentucky rifles. (Kindig) (Whisker III)

BEYOR, I. unlocated. Flintlock Kentucky rifle.

BEYRY, A. Akron, Ohio, 1859d-1860c. (Hutslar)

BEZ, MICHAEL Lancaster Co., Pennsylvania, 1758-1759. (Dyke)

BIBER, ALBERT Newton, Iowa, 1880d-1884d.

BICAISE, BENJAMIN Charleston, South Carolina, 1831-1859. (Kauffman 2)

BICAISE, L.W. Charleston, South Carolina, 1885d-1902d. Percussion and cartridge guns.

BICKEL & HERROLD Akron, Ohio, 1881d. (Hutslar)

BICKEL, LOUIS Akron, Ohio, 1883-1892. (Hutslar)

BICKFORD, F.A. Batavia, New York, ?-1874d. Percussion 1/2 stock.

BICKFORD, H.W. Flint, Michigan, 1895d.

BICKFORD, J.C. Dunlap, Iowa, 1887d-1897d.

BICKFORD, N.G., & SON Mount Holly, New York, 1889d.

BICKNELL, THOMAS Philadelphia, Pennsylvania, 1799d-1803d.

BICKNELL, THOMAS Vergennes, Vermont, 1799-1801. Model 1798 contract muskets. Was located in Providence, Rhode Island according to some sources.

BICYCLE trade name of Harrington & Richardson on revolvers.

BIDDLE, C. Holmes Co., Ohio, 1832. Percussion fullstock. (Hutslar)

BIDDLE, D. Muskegum Co., Ohio. Percussion fullstock. (Hutslar)

BIDDLE, FREDERICK (?-1868), Chambersburg, Pennsylvania, 1805-1816. Tuscarawas Co., Ohio, 1815-1868. (Hutslar) (AOLR IV-2)

BIDDLE, GEORGE (1791-1871), Chambersburg, Pennsylvania, 1815-1823, Tuscarawas Co., Ohio, 1823-1860. Brother of and successor to Frederick in Chambersburg. (Hutslar)

BIDDLE, LEVI, JR. (1831-1894), Shanesville, Ohio, 1850-1893. Percussion 1/2 stock. (AOLR IV-2)

BIDDLE, R. & W.C. Philadelphia, Pennsylvania, 1847d-1861d. Locks and barrels only. (Kauffman)

BIDDLE, S. Scioto Co., Ohio. (Hutslar)

BIDDLE, T. & W.C. Philadelphia, Pennsylvania. Lockmaker.

BIDDLE, W.C., & CO. Philadelphia, Pennsylvania. Locks only.

BIDEMAN, DANIEL Philadelphia, Pennsylvania, 1837d. (Kauffman 2)

BIDWELL, OLIVER (1732-?), Hartford, Connecticut, 1770-1808, Middletown, Connecticut, 1812. Model 1808 contract muskets. (Gluckman)

BIEDELL, MARK (?-1877). Kit Carson, Colorado, 1870-1874, Saugauche, Colorado, 1874-1877. (Sellers-3)

BIEDENBACH, GEORGE London, Ohio, 1880-1899. Percussion 1/2 stock. (Hutslar)

BIEDERMANN, CARL F. Milwaukee, Wisconsin, 1879d, Ottawa, Kansas, 1882d-1894d.

BIELEY Colchester, Connecticut, 1800. (Lindsay)

BIELRY & CO. unlocated. Locks only.

BIENAIME, ANTOINE P. New Orleans, Louisiana, 1822d. See Dorion & Bienaime.

BIERMANN, FREDERICK J. Ann Arbor, Michigan, 1895d-1909d. As Wagner & Biermann, 1895-1896.

BIETZE, CHARLES Worcester, Massachusetts, 1874-1875d.

BIG ALL RIGHT trade name of Wright Arms Co. on shotguns. (Hinman)

BIG BONANZA suicide special. (Webster)

BIGALO, MYRON Chenango, New York, 1824. As Bennett & Bigalo. (MB 6-45)

BIGELOW & HEYWOOD Concord, Massachusetts, 1878-1880.

BIGELOW, BENJAMIN B. (1824-1888), Rochester, New York, 1845-1849 and 1852-1857, San Francisco, California, 1850-1851, Marysville, California, 1858-1888. Miller patent revolving rifles. (Shelton-Eich)

BIGELOW, GEORGE W. New Haven, Connecticut. Patents #27,772 April 10, 1860, alarm gun, and #38,000 March 24, 1863, rifling machine.

BIGELOW, GIDEON L. Rochester, New York, 1853d. Brother of Benjamin Bigelow, who moved to California. (Eich)

BIGGS, T. Albion, Wisconsin, 1857d. Percussion 1/2 stock.

BIGOT, LEON San Francisco, California, 1859d. (Shelton)

BIJUR, DANIEL Alma, Michigan, 1863d.

BILAN, LOUIS Iowa City, Iowa, 1882d.

BILBEE, W.H. Trenton, New Jersey, 1882d-1885d.

BILHARTZ, HALL & CO. Pittsylvania Court House, Virginia, 1862-1863. Confederate carbines. (Gluckman & Satterlee)

BILL, CHARLES H. Waltham, Massachusetts, 1857-1860.

BILLIG, H. Lehigh Co., Pennsylvania, 1850t. (Gabel)

BILLINGHURST, WILLIAM B. (1807-1880), Rochester, New York, 1827-1880. Patents #24,987 August 9, 1859, fishing reel, and #36,448 September 16, 1862, battery gun. Worked for Joseph Medbery, 1827, J. & J. Miller, 1834-1838. Made high quality target and revolving rifles as well as fishing reels. (Eich)

BILLINGHURST, WILLIAM B., JR. (1842-1873), Rochester, New York, 1863-1873. Percussion target pistol. (Eich)

BILLINGS & SPENCER CO. Hartford, Connecticut, 1869-1876. C.E. Billings and C.M. Spencer, mostly made parts for other makers.

BILLINGS Moretown, Vermont. Underhammer pistols. (Horn)

BILLINGS, CHARLES ETHAN (1835-?), Hartford, Connecticut, 1865-1876. Patents #54,100 April 24, 1866, breechloading firearm, #56,885 August 7, 1866, dies for pistol frames, #82,279 September 22, 1868, combined pistol & sword, and #169,335 November 2, 1875, breechloading firearm. President of Roper Repeating Rifle Co., 1865-1869, formed Billings & Spencer in 1869.

BILLINGS, CLARK E. Warren, Vermont, 1872-1879. (Horn)

BILLINGS, F.C. Kansas City, Missouri, 1898d.

BILLS, ALFRED (1815-?), West Co., West Virginia, 1840-1860c. (Whisker IV)

BILLUPS & HASSELL Mound Prairie (Plenitude Post Office), Texas, 1862-1865. Rifles for the State of Texas. John D. Billups and D.D. Hassell. Name changed to Billups & Son on Hassell's death late in 1862. (Holloway)

BILZ, OTTO Denver, Colorado, 1888d-1893d. As Steuck & Bilz, 1889. (Sellers-3)

BIMERT, JOHN Richland City, Wisconsin, 1857d.

BINCKELY, JOHN Hope, North Carolina, 1790-1801. (Bivins)

BINDER, G.D. Philadelphia, Pennsylvania, 1860c.

BINGAL, L. Terre Haute, Indiana, 1858d.

BINGHAM, BENJAMIN (1817-?), Richmond, Virginia, 1850c. (MB 10-63)

BINGHAM, HENRY unlocated (Pennsylvania?), 1775. Committee of Safety flintlock.

BINGHAM, PLINY Dedham, Massachusetts, 1855. (Dean*)

BINGHAM, W. Cleveland, Ohio, 1880-1900. Dealer only.

BINNIO, L. (1817-?), Tuolumme Co., California, 1852c. (Shelton)

BINNSTON, WILLIAM Bedford Co., Pennsylvania, 1846-1847. (C & W - questionable)

BINZ, FREDERICK Floris, Iowa, 1889d-1892d.

BIRCHER, CASPER St. Louis, Missouri, 1875d. Percussion rifle.

BIRCHMILLER, ROBERT Lancaster, Pennsylvania, 1850-1869. (Whisker III)

BIRD & ASHMORE Philadelphia, Pennsylvania, 1800c. Flintlock lockmakers.

BIRD BROS. Philadelphia, Pennsylvania, 1812-1818. Flintlock locks only. Charles and Amos?

BIRD, A. NOBLE (1820-1872), Kenton, Ohio, 1853-1865. Percussion fullstock. (Hutslar)

BIRD, C.L. Shelby, Michigan, 1891d.

BIRD, CHARLES, & CO. Philadelphia, Pennsylvania, 1790-1814d. Locks only.

BIRD, ELIAS (1817-?), Muskingum Co., Ohio, 1850c. Oscaloosa, Iowa, 1865d-1889d. Percussion fullstock. As E. Bird & Son, 1887-1889.

BIRD, JOHN W. (1832-1917), Oscaloosa, Iowa, 1858-1898. Son of Elias Bird.

BIRD, JOSEPH Alexander, Indiana, 1859-1863. Percussion 1/2 stock. (Lindert)

BIRD, MARK Birdsboro, Pennsylvania, 1775-1788. Committee of Safety muskets and cannon. (Gluckman)

BIRD, N. Kenton, Ohio, 1847-1853d. Percussion fullstock rifle.

BIRD, NIGHTINGALE & NEFF Baltimore, Maryland, 1819-1823. Importers of guns and locks. (Hartzler)

BIRD, W.E. Geneva, New York, 1877-1882, Luddington, Michigan, 1891d-1895d. Over/under mule ear rifle.

BIRD, WILLIAM Overton, Pennsylvania, 1858d, Campbellville, Pennsylvania, 1887d-1890d. Percussion over/under rifle.

BIRINGER, JOHN (1830-?), Philadelphia, Pennsylvania, 1850-1861d, Leavenworth, Kansas, 1860d-1878d. Percussion guns.

BIRKENBEUEL, W.E. La Salle, Illinois, 1884d.

BIRKENFIELD, ADOLPH Helena, Montana, 1876-1886d.

BIRKENHEAD, JOHN Ilion, New York. Patent #41,472 February 9, 1864, safety. Trigger cover applied to Remington revolvers. (Sellers-1)

BIRKHIMER, JAMES (1829-?), Tyler Co., Virginia, 1850c. Son of Thomas. (MB 10-63)

BIRKHIMER, JOHN (1828-?), Tyler Co., Virginia, 1850c. Son of Thomas. (MB 10-63)

BIRKHIMER, THOMAS (1805-?), Norwich, Ohio, 1828-1839, Tyler Co., Virginia, 1850c. Percussion fullstock. (Hutslar)

BIRRCHER, H. New Orleans, Louisiana, 1871d.

BIRSEL, SAMUEL Philadelphia, Pennsylvania, 1837d. (Kauffman 2)

BISBEE, DEPLURA H. (1818-1893), Norway, Maine, 1840-1860, Buckfield, Maine, 1860d-1865d. Percussion 1/2 stock. (Demeritt)

BISBEE, J. Kalamazoo, Michigan. Percussion swivel breech rifles.

BISBEE, WILLIAM North Buckfield, Maine, 1865d.

BISBING, AMOS S. Tannersville, Pennsylvania, 1861d, White Haven, Pennsylvania, 1870d-1890d. High quality percussion swivel rifles.

BISCH, C. New Braunfels, Texas, 1885d.

BISCHENS, BENJAMIN St. Louis, Missouri, 1847d. (Kauffman)

BISCOE, WILLIAM S.N. Tyler, Texas, 1862-1865. As Short, Biscoe & Co., 1862-1864. (Albaugh 2)

BISH, MIZE & STILLMAN HARDWARE CO. Atchison, Kansas, 1880-1900. Dealers only.

BISHIP, M. Linesville, Pennsylvania, 1879-1880. (Kauffman)

BISHLEY, ANDREW Lancaster Co., Pennsylvania, 1771. (Dyke)

BISHOP Sand Spring, Iowa, 1865d.

BISHOP, A. Centerville, Pennsylvania. Flintlock Kentucky. (Dillin)

BISHOP, A.J. Manchester, Michigan, 1879d.

BISHOP, A.J. New Market, Missouri, 1860d.

BISHOP, ADDISON G. Hillsdale, Michigan, 1872d-1899d. Percussion rifle.

BISHOP, ALBERT L. Sylvanus, Michigan, 1863d-1867d.

BISHOP, ALEXANDER Union Co., Pennsylvania, 1850c. Flintlock Kentucky rifles. (Kauffman)

BISHOP, ALEXANDER. Penns Creek, Pennsylvania. Percussion fullstock. (Gabel)

BISHOP, ALMON D. (1814-1882), Decatur, New York, 1850-1874d, Worcester, New York, 1875-1882d. Percussion guns. (Swinney)

BISHOP, B. Poland, Ohio, 1860-1865. (Hutslar)

BISHOP, BENJAMIN Boardman, Ohio, 1861-1865. (Gardner)

BISHOP, C.L. Kaufman, Texas, 1892d-1896d.

BISHOP, D.D. unlocated. Percussion over/under rifle/shotgun.

BISHOP, DAVID (1816-?), Morgan Valley, West Virginia, 1860c. (Whisker IV)

BISHOP, E.C. Worcester, New York. Percussion 1/2 stock.

BISHOP, EDWARD Penns Creek, Pennsylvania. Percussion fullstock. (Gabel)

BISHOP, GEORGE (1825-1907), Westbrook, Maine, 1870-1907. Percussion target rifle. (Demeritt)

BISHOP, HENDERSON (1806-1873), Charleston, West Virginia, 1850c. (Bowers)

BISHOP, HENRY H. Boston, Massachusetts, 1818-1857d. Worked on Artemus Wheeler's guns. (Mass Arms)

BISHOP, HENRY W. Boston, Massachusetts, 1820-1860. Son of Henry H. Bishop. (Mass Arms)

BISHOP, J. Philadelphia, Pennsylvania, 1790c. Flintlock lockmaker only. (Gluckman & Satterlee)

BISHOP, J.C. Petersburg, Illinois, 1886d-1898d. Son of, and successor to, Robert Bishop.

BISHOP, JOHN Charleston, West Virginia. Son of Henderson Bishop. Percussion 1/2 stock. (Bowers)

BISHOP, L.W. Lisbon, Dakota Territory, 1884d.

BISHOP, LOUIS C. Brooklyn, New York, 1888d.

BISHOP, M., JR. unlocated. Percussion 1/2 stock.

BISHOP, MOSES Pine, Pennsylvania, 1874d, Lineville, Pennsylvania, 1882d.

BISHOP, R. Poland, Ohio, 1862-1865. Percussion fullstock rifle.

BISHOP, ROBERT (1815-?), St. Louis, Missouri, 1840-1841d, Petersburg, Illinois, 1841-1884d.

BISHOP, THOMAS New York, New York, 1857d.

BISHOP, WILLIAM (1818-?), Springfield, Illinois, 1857d-1868d. As William Bishop & Son, 1867-1868 (were listed separately in 1859).

BISHOP, WILLIAM Boston, Massachusetts, 1818-1860. Father of William Bishop Jr. and Henry Bishop. (Dean)

BISHOP, WILLIAM, JR. Boston, Massachusetts, 1845-1848. (Kauffman)

BISKER, WILLIAM (1866-1939), Canal Fulton, Ohio. (Hutslar)

BISLE, SAMUEL Westmoreland Co., Pennsylvania, 1817-1818. (Whisker II)

BISMARCK unidentified copy of Smith & Wesson revolver Models 1, 2, and 3.

BISMARK suicide special. (Webster)

BISSANIET, B. Houston, Texas, 1868d-1872d.

BISSE, JOHN Philadelphia, Pennsylvania, 1857d.

BISSELL, ANDREW J. (1827-?), Holly and Pontiac, Michigan, 1867d.

BISSELL, CHARLES H. Chicago, Illinois, 1876d-1898d. Dealer.

BISSIG, VINCENT New York, New York, 1881d-1884d.

BISSONET, LOUIS Houston, Texas, 1878d.

BITNER, WILLIAM G. (1800-?), Washington, D.C., 1837-1867d. (Hartzler)

BITTERLICH & LEGLER Nashville, Tennessee, 1867-1879. Percussion derringers and rifles. Franz J. Bitterlich and Joseph P. Legler.

BITTERLICH, FRANZ J. (1829-1880), Lockport, Illinois, 1850-1860c, Nashville, Tennessee, 1861-1879d. Percussion derringers and rifles. With Joseph P. Legler as Bitterlich & Legler, 1867-1879. (ASAC 21)

BITTINGER, PETER Ashland Co., Ohio, 1825. (Knittle)

BIVENS, J. Woodbury, Missouri, 1860d.

BIXLER & IDDINGS Lafayette, Indiana, 1850-1880, LaPorte, Indiana. Percussion 1/2 stock. John Bixler and Samuel Iddings. (Lindert)

BIXLER, JACOB Lancaster, Ohio, 1820c. (Hutslar)

BIXLER, JOHN E. Lafayette, Indiana, 1889-1900. Son of John Bixler. (Lindert)

BIXLER, JOHN (1823-1891), Lafayette, Indiana, 1850-1891. With Samuel Iddings as Bixler & Iddings, 1850-1881. With his son John E. Bixler as Bixler & Son, 1889-1891. (Lindert)

BJERKNESS, CARL J. Arkdale, Wisconsin. Patent #357,170 February 8, 1887, magazine gun.

BLACE, HORACE Lenton, Indiana, 1876-1880.

BLACHETTER, HENRY (1830-?), Cincinnati, Ohio, 1850c. (Hutslar)

BLACK & OWEN Detroit, Michigan. Dealers for suicide special made by Hopkins & Allen.

BLACK BEAUTY trade name of Sears, Roebuck & Co. on imported shotguns. (Hinman)

BLACK DIAMOND trade name on shotguns.

BLACK DIANA trade name of Baker Gun Co. on shotguns.

BLACK PRINCE trade name on shotguns and suicide specials made by Hopkins & Allen.

BLACK Springfield, Ohio. Percussion rifle. (Gluckman & Satterlee)

BLACK, A. unlocated. Flintlock Kentucky, dated 1787.

BLACK, A.M. Linn, Illinois, 1890d.

BLACK, CENAS St. Louis, Missouri, 1848d.

BLACK, HENRY Fayette Co., Pennsylvania, 1807-1816. (Kauffman)

BLACK, HENRY St. Louis, Missouri, 1847d.

BLACK, JAMES (1813-?), Doncannon, Pennsylvania, 1850c-1861d. (McAfee)

BLACK, JOHN (1764-?), Charlotte, North Carolina. Apprenticed 1778. (Bivins)

BLACK, MICHAEL Huntingdon Co., Pennsylvania, 1799-1800. (Whisker II)

BLACK, SAMUEL Lewistown, Maine, 1878d-1888d. (Demerritt)

BLACK, THOMAS Virginia, 1777. Committee of Safety repairs. (Gill)

BLACKBURN, ELI B. (1839-?), Mt. Yonah, Georgia, 1861, Rome, Georgia, 1870-1880. Percussion 1/2 stock.

BLACKBURN, JOHN (1786-?), Emmittsburg, Maryland. Apprenticed to John Armstrong. (Hartzler)

BLACKETT, JOHN New York, New York, 1853d-1857d.

BLACKFIELD trade name of Hibbard, Spencer & Bartlett on shotguns.

BLACKHAWK suicide special.

BLACKMAN, ANSON Elkland, Pennsylvania, 1850.

BLACKMAN, ANSON Woodhill, New York, 1870d-1874d.

BLACKMAN, ELIJAH Middletown, Connecticut, 1776. Committee of Safety locks.

BLACKMAN, G.R. Ellicottville, New York, 1870d-1882d. Son of George Blackman.

BLACKMAN, GEORGE Ellicottville, New York, 1848-1850d.

BLACKMAN, J. unlocated. Flintlock Kentucky pistols.

BLACKMAN, SAIN Ellicottville, New York, ?-1874d. See G.R. Blackman.

BLACKWELL, O. Skowhegan, Maine, 1873. (Demeritt)

BLACKWELL, WILLIAM (1836-?), Guilford, North Carolina. Apprenticed 1849. (Bivins)

BLACKWOOD, MARMADUKE Philadelphia, Pennsylvania, 1775. Committee of Safety locks. (Hobbies 4-38)

BLAETTERLEIN, JOHN Brooklyn, New York, 1868-1877d. Air guns and percussion pistols.

BLAFORD, R. unlocated. Percussion 1/2 stock.

BLAINE, WILLIAM Westmoreland Co., Pennsylvania, 1838. Percussion fullstock.

BLAIR, ANDREW Washington Co., Pennsylvania, 1799t, St. Clairsville, Ohio, 1802-1812, with Jonathan Hunt, 1812. (Hutslar) (Whisker II)

BLAIR, CHARLES Amherst, Massachusetts, 1836-1839. With Henry A. Morrill and Silas Mosman Jr. as Morrill, Mosman & Blair.

BLAIR, D. Akron, Indiana, 1860d-1862d.

BLAIR, DAVID F. Owosso, Michigan, 1870d-1895d. Percussion over/under rifle/shotgun.

BLAIR, DAVID Bladenburgh, Ohio, 1852-1860. Percussion 1/2 stock.

BLAIR, DAVID Washington Co., Pennsylvania, 1785-1800. (Whisker II)

BLAIR, JOSEPH Rupellville, Kentucky, 1820c.

BLAIR, M.F. Marquette, Michigan, 1895d.

BLAIR, WILLIAM Somerset Co., Pennsylvania, 1823. (Kauffman)

BLAIR, WILLIAM Wabash, Indiana, 1870c. (Lindert)

BLAISDEL, DAVID (?-1756), Amesbury, Massachusetts. (Dean*)

BLAISDEL, DAVID Cambridge, Massachusetts, 1775. Committee of Safety repairs. (Dean*)

BLAISDEL, JOHNATHAN Amesbury, Massachusetts, 1775. Committee of Safety muskets.

BLAKE, AMAZIAH Clarkson, New York, 1850c-1870d.

BLAKE, AMOS S. Waterbury, Connecticut. Patent #55,233 June 5, 1866, cartridge.

BLAKE, BURDINE (1823-?), London, Ohio, 1864-1896. (Hutslar)

BLAKE, JOHN E. Norwich, Connecticut. Patent #66,072 June 25, 1867, breechloading firearm.

BLAKE, JOHN HENRY New York, New York, 1893-1904. Patent #608,023 July 26, 1898, magazine gun. Small quantities of both military and sporting rifles made; submitted two guns to 1892 trials.

BLAKE, JOHN Watertown, New York, 1856-1869. Percussion 1/2 stock.

BLAKE, P. & E.W. New Haven, Connecticut, 1825-1842. Patent #none February 5, 1836, lock mortice. Philo and Eli Whitney Blake were nephews and partners of Eli Whitney. After Eli Whitney's death, contract muskets were made and marked with Philo and Eli W. Blake's names until Eli Whitney, Jr. reached 21. (Fuller)

BLAKE, R. Center Montville, Maine, 1877. (Demeritt)

BLAKE, THOMAS Boone Co., Indiana, 1850. (Lindert)

BLAKE, THOMAS Cumberland Co., Tennessee, 1817-1827.

BLAKELEE, B.E. Cambridge, Delaware, 1882d. See B.E. Blakslee.

BLAKELY, JOHN New York, New York, 1844-1853d.

BLAKEMORE, CHARLES C. (1849-?), Washington Court House, Ohio, 1878-1883. (Hutslar)

BLAKER, JOHN D. Newton, Pennsylvania. Patent #93,403 August 10, 1869, breechloading firearm.

BLAKESLEE, ERASTUS Plymouth, Connecticut. Patent #45,469 December 20, 1864, cartridge box for Spencer rifles and carbines.

BLAKESLY, STEPHEN (1811-?), Peoria Co., Illinois, 1842-1850. (Johnson)

BLAKLEY, MATTHEW New York, New York, 1844-1845d. (Kauffman 2)

BLAKSLEE, B.E. Cambridge, Maryland, 1878-1887d. (Hartzler)

BLALOCK, J.A. New Whatcom, Washington, 1891d.

BLALOCK, ROBERT (1800-?), Albemarle, North Carolina, 1830-1850. (Bivins)

BLANCH, W.H. unlocated. Percussion 1/2 stock.

BLANCHARD, ALBERT D. Wichita, Kansas, 1887-1894d. Patents #369,313 September 6, 1887, breechloading gun, and #572,520 December 8, 1896, breechloading gun.

BLANCHARD, D.D. Hutchinson, Kansas, 1878d-1882d.

BLANCHARD, DWIGHT Harperfield, Ohio, 1875-1888. Percussion 1/2 stock. (Hutslar)

BLANCHARD, FRED Baton Rouge, Louisiana, 1867d.

BLANCHARD, ROBERT North Yarmouth, Maine, 1811-1819. Made Hall sporting rifles.

BLANCHARD, THOMAS (1788-1864), Middlebury, Massachusetts. Patents #none, September 6, 1819, gun stock, and #none January 20, 1820, gun stock. (GR 6-90)

BLANCHARD, WELLMAN Allegan, Michigan, 1868-1879d, Kalamazoo, Michigan, 1883d.

BLANCHEMIN, PIERRE New Orleans, Louisiana, 1841d-1844d.

BLANKENSHIP, W.S. (1865-1940), Hot Springs, North Carolina, 1884-1917. Percussion rifles signed "WSB". (Cline)

BLANKMAN, JOHNS Washington, D.C. Patents #395,944 January 8, 1889, sight, #403,242 May 14, 1889, sight, #416,554 December 3, 1889, sight, and #420,261 January 28, 1890, sight.

BLASIRUS, PETER unlocated. Flintlock Kentucky rifle.

BLATTER, JOHN Cincinnati, Ohio, 1855-1866, Ripley, Ohio, 1868-1896. (Hutslar)

BLAUTZ, JOHN Brickerville, Pennsylvania, 1861d.

BLAZE, JOHN K. Springfield, Massachusetts. Patent #72,949 December 31, 1867, double-barrel shotgun with D.B. Wesson.

BLEGARD, ROBERT Linden, Missouri, 1898d.

BLEHA, WILLIAM V. St. Louis, Missouri. Patents #633,949 September 26, 1899, breechloading firearm, and #657,052 August 28, 1900, breechloading firearm.

BLEOU, JOSEPH (1826-?), Vienna, Illinois, 1853-1860. (Johnson)

BLESSING, JOHN (1830-?), Denver, Colorado, 1860c. (Sellers-3)

BLEVINS, JOHN M. Washington Co., Arkansas, 1850. (Elias)

BLEWITT & JOHNSON San Francisco, California, 1864-1866. Isaac Blewitt and Edwin H. Johnson. (Shelton).

BLEWS, SAMUEL (?-1779), Norfolk, Virginia, 1776-1779. State repairs. (Gill).

BLEZARD, R.H. Atchison, Kansas, 1888d.

BLICKENSDOERFER & SCHILLING St. Louis, Missouri, 1869-1874. Percussion target rifle.

BLICKENSDOERFER, A. St. Louis, Missouri, 1864d.

BLICKENSDOERFER, JOHN St. Louis, Missouri, 1863d-1874d. Percussion rifles and airguns. As Blickensdoerfer & Schilling, 1869-1874.

BLISS & GOODYEAR New Haven, Connecticut, 1859-1860. Small percussion revolvers. (Sellers-1)

BLISS & HUTCHINSON 61 Chambers St., New York, New York. Agent for Allen pepperboxes.

BLISS suicide specials attributed to Bliss were made under William Bliss' patent, but the maker (certainly not Bliss & Goodyear) is not known, but may have been Norwich Arms Co.

BLISS, CHARLES Warren, Massachusetts, 1878d.

BLISS, FRANK D. New Haven, Connecticut, 1856-1863. Small percussion revolvers as Bliss & Goodyear and nearly identical cartridge revolvers by himself.

BLISS, GEORGE Providence, Rhode Island, 1650. (Achtermier)

BLISS, WILLIAM H. Norwich, Connecticut. Patents #202,627 April 23, 1878, revolver, #283,854 August 28, 1883, revolver, #294,188 February 26, 1884, revolver, and #313,048 March 3, 1885, revolver. All patents used on suicide specials.

BLITTKOWSKIE, GUSTAVE ADOLPH New York, New York. Patents #14,488 March 25, 1856, breechloading firearm gun, #14,710 April 22, 1856, revolver with Frederick W. Hoffman, and #17,136 April 28, 1857, breechloading firearm.

BLODGET, DAMON Sherwood, Michigan, 1863d-1865d.

BLODGETT, L. Harrisburg, New York, 1882d.

BLOM, JOHN H. Houston, Texas, 1897d-1899d. Rebarreled Winchester Highwall.

BLOOD HOUND suicide special. (Webster)

BLOODWORTH, TIMOTHY North Carolina, 1776. Committee of Safety muskets. (Bivins)

BLOOM, DAVID Ganges, Ohio, 1870c. Percussion rifles (Hutslar)

BLOOM, GEORGE unlocated. Flintlock Kentucky.

BLOOM, H. Dot, Washington, 1889d.

BLOOM, JACOB unlocated. Flintlock and percussion Kentucky rifles.

BLOQUELL, GUSTAV Manitowoc, Wisconsin, 1857d-1895d.

BLORE, SAMUEL Rahway, New Jersey, 1882d.

BLOSSER, PETER New Springfield, Ohio, 1870-1880. Percussion rifles. (Hutslar)

BLOW, GEORGE P. Norfolk, Virginia. Patent #544,696 February 13, 1894, revolver.

BLOXAM, A.S. Faribault, Minnesota, 1880d-1898d.

BLUE JACKET suicide special by Hopkins & Allen.

BLUE LEADER suicide special.

BLUE WHISTLER suicide special by Hopkins & Allen.

BLUEFIELD trade name of Davenport on shotguns.

BLUEGRASS trade name on percussion locks and .22 rifles sold by Belknap Hardware Co., Louisville, Kentucky.

BLUEHER, FRANZ Mascoutah, Illinois, 1878d-1890d.

BLUEMEL, JULIUS (?-1892), San Francisco, California, 1872-1892. Patent #210,905 December 11, 1878, breechloading firearm. (Shelton)

BLUM, CHRISTIAN (1784-?), Salem, North Carolina. Apprenticed to C. Vogeler, 1798. (Bivins)

BLUM, EPHRAIM Easton, Northhampton Co., Pennsylvania, 1763t-1783t. (KRA II-3) (Dyke)

BLUNT & SYMS New York, New York, 1837d-1867d. (Mass. Arms)

BLUNT, ORISON (1817-?), New York, New York, 1837-1867. Patent #6,966 December 25, 1849, gunlock. As Blunt & Syms made pistols and muskets. (Mass. Arms)

BLUNT, WILLIAM G. San Francisco, California, 1868-1869. (Shelton)

BLUNT, WILLIAM S. Bay Ridge, New York, Patent #219,845 September 23, 1879, hammer guard for revolvers.

BLURTON, JOHN, JR. Queen City, Missouri, 1889d.

BLYMIRE, GEORGE York Co., Pennsylvania, 1776. Committee of Safety rifles and pistols. (Gluckman & Satterlee)

BOALER, JOSEPH Newark, New Jersey. Percussion pistols. (Gluckman & Satterlee)

BOARD, R. Cloverport, Kentucky, 1856-1860. Percussion 1/2 stock.

BOARDLEAR, SAMUEL Boston, Massachusetts, 1796. See Samuel Broadlear.

BOARDMAN, ABEL (?-1752), Ipswich, Massachusetts.

BOARDMAN, EDWARD P. Lawrence, Massachusetts. Patent #172,243 January 18, 1876, revolver, with A.J. Peavey. "Little Allright" revolvers made by Wright Firearm Co.

BOAS, A.W. unlocated. Percussion fullstock.

BOATWRIGHT & GLAZE see Palmetto Armory.

BOBB, ANTHONY Reading, Pennsylvania, 1776-1781. Flintlock Kentucky rifle. (Gluckman & Satterlee)

BOCH, PHILIPP H. New York, New York. Patents #272,636 February 20, 1883, magazine gun, #276,522 April 24, 1883, magazine gun, and #287,090 October 23, 1883, magazine gun. Slide action single shot rifle. (Grant)

BODDINGTON unlocated. Percussion double rifle.

BODENHEIMER, WILLIAM (1779-1876), Lancaster, Ohio, 1815-1859. Percussion 1/2 stock. As Bodenheimer & Matlock, 1815-1817. (Hutslar)

BODENHEIMER, WILLIAM, JR. (1824-?), Lancaster, Ohio, 1850c. (Hutslar)

BODINE, S. Camden, New Jersey, 1850d.

BODWELL, DUNWICKE G. Philadelphia, Pennsylvania, 1780-1785. Repaired U.S. arms. (Moller)

BOECKLEY, ANDREW Cincinnati, Ohio, 1858-1864. Also Bokley, Buckely. (Hutslar)

BOECKLEY, HENRY Cincinnati, Ohio, 1861d. (Hutslar)

BOEHME, LOUIS Chicago, Illinois, 1874-1886d.

BOENTGEN, GUS Astoria, Oregon, 1889d.

BOENZLI, ANDREAS Lancaster, Pennsylvania. Flintlock Kentucky rifles. (Dillin)

BOERSTLER, DANIEL Funkstown, Maryland, 1814-1832. (Hartzler)

BOESCH, GUSTAV S. Freetown, Massachusetts. Patent #408,453 August 6, 1889, breechloading firearm.

BOESCHLER, C. Canton, Ohio. (Hutslar)

BOESSEL Ogden, Utah, 1871d. As Parpe & Boessel.

BOETCHER, CHRISTOPHER (1813-?), Cambridge, Ohio, 1850c-1853d. (Hutslar)

BOETCHER, FREDERICK Shelbyville, Missouri, 1850c. (MB 11-66)

BOETIGER, FRANZ F. (1828-?), Quincy, Illinois, 1860c. (Johnson)

BOGAN, ANDREW (1802-1862), Kirklin, Indiana, 1830-1862. Percussion fullstock. (Lindert)

BOGARDUS CLUB GUN trade name on imported shotgun. (Hinman)

BOGART, A.S. Union Pier, Michigan, 1883d.

BOGART, ORLANDO H. San Francisco, California, 1853-1859. Percussion 1/2 stock. (Shelton)

BOGER, B. unlocated. Percussion 1/2 stock.

BOGERT & OAKLEY New York, New York, 1867d-1868d. Dealers.

BOGERT, HENRY K. Mesa, Colorado, 1898-1900. (Sellers-3)

BOGGESS, JOHN S. Wiggonsville, Ohio, 1820-1860. Percussion fullstock. (Hutslar)

BOGGS, ANDREW Braxton Co., West Virginia, circa 1880. (Whisker II)

BOGGS, WESLEY Rock Cave, West Virginia, 1884d.

BOGGS, WILLIAM H. (1852-?), Webster Co., West Virginia, 1880c-1886d. (Whisker IV)

BOGGUS, J. Aspen Grove, Kentucky, 1860d.

BOHM, C.F. Wonewoc, Wisconsin, 1879d.

BOHR, WILLIAM M. Union Forge, Pennsylvania. Percussion fullstock.

BOICLAIRE, ETIENNE New Orleans, Louisiana, 1834d.

BOICOURT, THOMAS (1818-?), Madison, Indiana, 1849-1862. Also Bicourt, Boycourt. (Lindert)

BOIN, DANIEL Delaware, Ohio, 1863-1866. Percussion 1/2 stock. (Gardner)

BOISDORE, L. New Orleans, Louisiana, 1841d-1842d.

BOISSECQ, JULES New Orleans, Louisiana, 1841d-1842d.

BOIXEL, PETER New Orleans, Louisiana, 1822d-1823d.

BOKLEY, ANDREW Cincinnati, Ohio, 1858d.

BOLAND, JAMES Norwich, Connecticut. Patents #317,965 May 19, 1885, revolver, #333,725 January 5, 1886, revolver, #353,914 December 7, 1886, revolver, and #505,569 September 26, 1893, revolver with C.M. Hopkins. All produced by Hopkins & Allen.

BOLCH, F.E. Charlestown, Vermont, 1868-1873. (Horn)

BOLEN, JOHN G. New York, New York, 1837-1857. Patent #8,439 October 21, 1851, alarm gun. Made single shot percussion pistols and retailed Allen pepperboxes.

BOLICH, LOGAN (1821-?), Catawba, North Carolina, circa 1850. (Bivins)

BOLIN, WILLIAM G. California, Missouri, 1879d-1891d.

BOLKENIUS, ALBERT (1829-1890), Milwaukee, Wisconsin, 1848-1890. Percussion and cartridge rifles. (WGCA 4)

BOLLES, NATHAN H. Philadelphia, Pennsylvania, 1854-1856. Partner of C. Sharps.

BOLLES, WILLIAM E. Mattapoisett, Massachusetts, 1888d.

BOLLINGER, GEORGE Barrien Springs, Michigan. Percussion fullstock.

BOLLINGER, PETER Lancaster Co., Pennsylvania, 1776. (Dyke)

BOLSER, JOSEPH Philadelphia, Pennsylvania, 1799. Flintlock Kentucky. (Dillin)

BOLTON, ENOCH Charlestown, Massachusetts, 1665. (Gluckman & Satterlee)

BOLTON, ROBERT Savannah, Georgia, 1770-1773. State Armorer. (Dean)

BOLYARD, STEVE Preston Co., West Virginia, circa 1900. (Whisker IV - questionable)

BOMAR, R.F. Sherman, Texas, 1890d-1896d. As Bomar & Loving, 1890d.

BOMEN, WILLIAM see William Bowman.

BON, WILLIAM unlocated. Percussion fullstock.

BONA, G.L. Cincinnati, Ohio, 1888-1890. (Hutslar)

BONANZA suicide special by Bacon.

BONAWITZ, JOHN Womelsdorf, Pennsylvania, 1772-1810. "I.B." (like an inspector's mark) sometimes used as signature. (Kindig)

BOND & VAN KEUREN Allegan, Michigan, 1899d. J. Van Keuren.

BOND & WINSLOW Pontiac, Michigan, 1869d-1871d. Percussion side by side double rifle. William F. Bond.

BOND, F. unlocated. Contract musket dated 1811.

BOND, H. Rusted, Ohio, 1860-1890. Percussion fullstock. (Hutslar)

BOND, N. Maryland, 1776. (Dean*)

BOND, RICHARD Cecil Co., Maryland, 1776-1782. Committee of Safety barrels. (Hartzler)

BOND, WILLIAM F. Pontiac, Michigan, 1869d-1875d. As Bond & Winslow, 1869-1871.

BONE, SAMUEL (1833-?), Waterford, Michigan.

BONEBRAKE, TOBIAS MILLER (1820-?), Kingman, Indiana, 1860-1885. Percussion 1/2 stock. (Lindert)

BONER, ALBERT Eaton, Ohio, 1875-1886. (Hutslar)

BONER, T.D. West Alexandria, Ohio, 1860-1875. Percussion 1/2 stock. (Hutslar)

BONHAJO, LOUIS Newport, Kentucky, 1879d-1882d.

BONHAM, JOHN L. (1821-1903), Hellam, Pennsylvania, 1862, Kersey, Pennsylvania, 1865-1896, Olean, New York, 1896-1903. Patent #36,555 September 30, 1862, revolving cannon. (Bowers) (Whisker II)

BONKER, GEORGE Sedalia, Missouri, 1898d.

BONNET, ANTHONY Clarion, Pennsylvania, 1868-1875, Brookville, Pennsylvania, 1887d-1890d. Percussion fullstock.

BONNETT, HENRY A. (1835-1907), Brookville, Pennsylvania, 1861-1875. Same as Anthony Bonnet? (Whisker II)

BONNETTI, G. San Jose, California, 1870-1875. (Shelton)

BONSE, THOMAS Mojave City, Arizona, 1884d.

BONSHOFF, GEORGE W. Lancaster, Pennsylvania, 1875d.

BONTEMPS, CHARLES Camden, New Jersey, 1850d. Percussion rifles.

BOOKER, W.H. Gardiner, Maine, 1892. (Demeritt)

BOOKMAN, WILLIAM (1815-?), Wilmington, North Carolina, 1850c. (Bivins)

BOOM trade name of C.S. Shattuck on revolvers.

BOOM, BIRCH S. Mt. Vernon, Ohio. (Hutslar)

BOOMHOWER, ELI E. Morrisville, Vermont, 1876-1884. (Horn)

BOONE, DANIEL trade name of Belknap Hardware Co. on shotguns. (Hinman)

BOONE, E. Oley Valley, Pennsylvania, 1815-1818. Flintlock Kentucky rifle. (Dillin)

BOONE, RATLIFF (?-1844), Booneville, Indiana, 1807-1816. (Lindert)

BOONE, SAMUEL Berks Co., Pennsylvania, 1768-1776, Frederick, Maryland, 1777-1778. Manager of Maryland State Gun Lock Factory and purchaser of part of the equipment when it was sold in 1778. (Hartzler)

BOONE, SQUIRE Frederick, Maryland, 1776, Harrodsburg, Kentucky, 1800. Brother of Daniel Boone. (Dean)

BOONE, THOMAS Berks Co., Pennsylvania, 1790-1801. Flintlock Kentucky rifles, barrels and bayonets for U. S. contract muskets. (Gluckman & Satterlee) (Moller)

BOORN, BURCH S. Mt. Vernon, Ohio. (MB 11-44)

BOOSEY, JAMES Weathersfield, Connecticut, 1639. (Dean*)

BOOTH & CO. Philadelphia, Pennsylvania, 1799d-1814d. Locks only. Richard and William Booth. (Kauffman)

BOOTH, C.W. Cincinnati, Ohio, lockmaker only. See R.W. Booth & Co.

BOOTH, POMEROY Hartford, Connecticut, 1848-1850. (Kauffman 2)

BOOTH, RALPH W., & CO. Cincinnati, Ohio, 1856-1875. Percussion lockmaker. (Hutslar)

BOOTH, RICHARD Philadelphia, Pennsylvania, 1813d-1816d.

BOOTH, S.W. Madison, Georgia, 1879d-1885d.

BOOTH, WILLIAM Philadelphia, Pennsylvania, 1798-1816. Flintlock pistols. (Gluckman & Satterlee)

BOOTHBY, DAVID Livermore, Maine, 1870-1884, E. Wilton, Maine, circa 1890. (Demeritt)

BOOTHBY, EDWARD K. (1819-?), Portland, Maine, 1858-1899. Airguns. (Demeritt)

BOOTS, ELI Panora, Iowa, 1865d.

BOOTS, SAMUEL Pike Co., Illinois, 1844-1850. (Johnson)

BORCHARDT, HUGO Bridgeport, Connecticut, 1876-1881, Peekskill, New York, 1881-1886. Patents #185,721 December 26, 1876, breechloading firearm, #197,319 November 20, 1877, sight, #206,217 July 23, 1878, breechloading firearm, #254,453 March 7, 1882, magazine for Lee rifle, and #273,44, March 6, 1883, magazine. The first three patents were produced by the Sharps Rifle Co., the last by Remington. Borchardt went to England and Germany where he patented the pistol which became the Luger. Another 25 patents were issued to him after he left this country.

BORCHERDING, H. Cincinnati, Ohio, 1880c.

BORDEN, DANIEL (1783-?), Taneytown, Maryland. Apprenticed to P. Creamer, 1799. (Hartzler)

BORDEN, JEFFERSON, JR. Fall River, Massachusetts. Patent #243,842 July 5, 1881, breechloading firearm.

BORDEN, WILLIAM Baltimore, Maryland, 1833-1851d. (Hartzler)

BORDER, DANIEL B. (1826-1891), Bedford, Pennsylvania, 1848-1884. Percussion fullstock rifles signed "D.B." or "D.B.B.". Son of William Border. (Whisker)

BORDER, ENOS (1820-?), Bedford, Pennsylvania, 1843t. (Hetrick)

BORDER, GEBALD Bedford, Pennsylvania, 1769. (Gluckman & Satterlee)

BORDER, JOHN (1825-?), Bedford, Pennsylvania, 1850-1861. Son of William Border. Percussion fullstock rifles signed "J.B.". (Whisker) (see C&W)

BORDER, SAMUEL G. (1815-1865), Bedford, Pennsylvania, 1841t, Somerset Co., Pennsylvania, 1843-1853. Son of John Border. (Whisker)

BORDER, WILLIAM (1800-1881), Bedford, Pennsylvania, 1820-1881. Percussion fullstock signed "W.B.". (Whisker)

BORDER, WILLIAM (1848-1929), Bedford Co., Pennsylvania, 1877d-1929. (Whisker)

BORGER, PETER (1829-?), Chillicothe, Illinois, 1856-1860. (Johnson)

BORING, GEORGE (1802-?), Tamaroa, Illinois, 1834-1860. (Johnson)

BORMER, BARNABY Augusta, Virginia, 1774-1775. (Gill)

BORNS, H. unlocated. Percussion 1/2 stock.

BORSSER, WILLIAM Shrewsbury, Pennsylvania, 1880d. (Whisker II)

BORTNER, PHILIP Bedford Co., Pennsylvania, 1814. (C&W)

BORTREE, WILLIAM Philadelphia, Pennsylvania, 1819-1833d.

BOSA, WILLIAM Higginsville, Illinois, 1860d.

BOSHAM, J. Woodbury, Tennessee, 1860d.

BOSLER, A.L. Cincinnati, Ohio, 1857d-1858d.

BOSLER, JOSEPH Philadelphia, Pennsylvania, 1800. Flintlock Kentucky rifles.

BOSLEY & HOWE Baltimore, Maryland, 1887-1889. (Hartzler)

BOSLEY, J.L. Gainesville, Texas, 1896d.

BOSS 4th of July pistol marked patent 1876.

BOSSELL, V.E. Annapolis, Maryland. Percussion target rifle. (Hartzler)

BOSSERT, JACOB Philadelphia, Pennsylvania, 1860c.

BOSTLEMAN, W. Nashville, Tennessee, 1853d.

BOSTON & SPRINGFIELD MFG. CO. Chicopee, Massachusetts, 1822-1828. Became Chicopee Falls Mfg. Co., owned by Ames Bros. (GR 4-64)

BOSTON, GEORGE Portersville, Pennsylvania, 1882d-1887d.

BOSTON, J.A. David City, Nebraska, 1893d.

BOSTWICK, HENRY Denver, Colorado, 1884d-1917d. (Sellers-3)

BOSTWICK, SEYMOUR Graniteville, Massachusetts. Patent #36,891 November 11, 1862, breechloading firearm, with Charles G. Sargent.

BOSWELL, AARON Rochester, New York, 1827d. (Eich)

BOSWORTH Lancaster, Pennsylvania, 1800-1805. (Gluckman & Satterlee)

BOSWORTH, B.M. Norwich, Connecticut, 1845, Warren, Rhode Island, 1849. All metal underhammer pistol.

BOSWORTH, H.C., & SON Norwich, New York, 1859d-1882d. Percussion target pistol. Hendrick C. Bosworth.

BOSWORTH, HENDRICK C. Norwich, New York, 1859d-1882d. As H.C. Bosworth & Son in 1880-1882. Percussion target pistol signed "H Bosworth & Son".

BOSWORTH, NATHANIEL C. Shrewsbury, Massachusetts, 1828-1832. Worked for Hapgood. (GR 7-76)

BOTCHFORD, BENJAMIN Waterford, Iowa, 1865d.

BOTELER, JOHN D. Washington, D.C., 1822d-1830d. (Hartzler)

BOTTS, WILLIAM Jackson Co., Missouri, 1850c. (MB 11-66)

BOTTUM, ALBERT Bridgeport, Connecticut, 1853d-1870d, Easton, Connecticut, 1871d-1874d. Percussion pistols.

BOUCHARD, JACOB Rochester, New York, 1857d. For William Billinghurst. (Eich)

BOUCHETTE, JOHN Philadelphia, Pennsylvania, 1819d.

BOUDORE, CHEVASIER (1810-?), New Orleans, Louisiana, 1850c. (MB 9-65)

BOUGHMER, GEORGE Jacksonville, Pennsylvania, 1880d.

BOUIS, J.V. St. Louis, Missouri, 1819. (Hanson)

BOULON, W.S. Kentucky, 1800-1840. (Gluckman & Satterlee)

BOULT, J.W. Spokane, Washington, 1891d.

BOURBON, PHILIP (1835-?), New Orleans, Louisiana, 1850c-1875.

BOURBON, WILLIAM New Orleans, Louisiana, 1866-1875.

BOURDEREAUX & SON Peoria, Illinois, 1878d-1884d.

BOURDEREAUX, G.C. Peoria, Illinois, 1878d-1888d. Son of J. Bourdereaux.

BOURDEREAUX, J. Peoria, Illinois, 1860-1884d. Percussion 1/2 stock.

BOURDEREAUX, PIERRE New York, New York, 1866-1873d, Peoria, Illinois, 1876d-1884d. Percussion schuetzen rifle and cartridge shotguns. Patents #59,706 November 13, 1866, breechloading firearm, and #141,198 July 29, 1863, breechloading firearm. As Bourdereaux & Son, 1878-1884.

BOUREAU, ANTHONY Charleston, South Carolina, 1686-1696. (Kauffman 2)

BOURG, MATTHEW Chicago, Illinois, 1859d.

BOURGIN, PETER (1824-?), Oakland, California, 1874-1882. (Shelton)

BOURNE, WILLIAM Savannah, Georgia, 1860. Percussion revolvers of doubtful authenticity-marked "W.B.". (Sellers-1)

BOURON, LOUIS L. New Orleans, Louisiana, 1861-1943. Son of Philipe Bouron. As P. Bouron Sons. (Gluckman & Satterlee)

BOURON, PHILIPE (1835-1905), New Orleans, Louisiana, 1851-1899d. Air, percussion, and cartridge guns. (MB 9-65)

BOURON, PHILIPE GEORGE New Orleans, Louisiana, 1859-1929. Son of Philipe Bouron. (Gluckman & Satterlee)

BOUSHINGER, HENRY Somerset Co., Pennsylvania, 1805-1813. (Kauffman)

BOUTEL, S.M. Orleans, Missouri, 1860d.

BOUTON, RICHARD M. West Troy, New York. Patent #6,196 March 20, 1849, machine for making percussion caps.

BOVEE, GEORGE Madison, Wisconsin, 1859-1885. (Kauffman 2)

BOVEE, N. Madison, Wisconsin, 1865d. With Theodore Bovee.

BOVEE, THEODORE Madison, Wisconsin, 1855-1885.

BOVY, NATHANIEL Carlisle, Pennsylvania, 1817. (Whisker III)

BOVY, VICTOR New York, New York. Patents #191,563, June 5, 1877, breechloading firearm, #196,781, November 6, 1877, breechloading firearm, #363,043 May 17, 1887, breechloading firearm, and #473,903 May 3, 1892, revolvers.

BOWEN, ANDRUS Providence, Rhode Island, 1832.

BOWEN, BENJAMIN B. Bethel, Vermont, 1849d-1881d, Tunbridge, Vermont, 1875d.

BOWEN, J.R. Edina, Missouri, 1889d-1898d.

BOWEN, JAMES L. Fremont, Ohio, 1897- ?. (Hutslar)

BOWEN, WILLIAM D. Augusta, Georgia, 1840-1899d. As Rogers & Bowen before the Civil War.

BOWEN, WILLIAM Trent, Michigan, 1872d-1879d.

BOWER & KAISER Fremont, Ohio, 1890d. (Hutslar)

BOWER, E. FRED Chillicothe, Ohio, 1872-1888. (Hutslar)

BOWER, GEORGE Philadelphia, Pennsylvania, 1846d. (Whisker III)

BOWER, HENRY (1812-?), San Francisco, California, 1852. (Shelton)

BOWER, ISAAC G. Fremont, Ohio, 1888-1897. With John Kaiser as Bower & Kaiser, 1890. (Hutslar)

BOWERMAN, J.J. Seymour, Wisconsin, 1879d-1886d.

BOWERMAN, JACOB Steelville, Illinois, 1868.

BOWERS, EDWARD Charleston, South Carolina, 1855d. (Kauffman)

BOWERS, J.C.F. DeWitt, Arkansas, 1892d.

BOWERS, J.W. Barryville, New York, 1847-1850d.

BOWERS, JOHN E. Charleston, South Carolina, 1837-1838d. (Kauffman 2)

BOWERS, JOHN Jonestown, Pennsylvania, 1860d-1861d.

BOWERS, RALPH St. Johns, Iowa, 1865d.

BOWERS, SOL Pickerington, Ohio, 1878-1883. (Hutslar)

BOWERS, W.H. Philadelphia, Pennsylvania. Lockmaker only.

BOWERS, WILLIAM Middlebury, Vermont, 1840-1843. (Horn)

BOWIE, C. San Francisco, California, 1856-1857d. Worked for Klepzig & Co. (Shelton)

BOWKER, JAMES Exeter, New Hampshire, 1887d.

BOWLBY, GEORGE W. (1826-?), Pontiac, Michigan, 1863d-1867d. Breechloading rifle. Patent #64,941 May 21, 1867, ejector. (GR 5-80)

BOWLES, JOHN Washington, D.C. Patent #213,616 March 25, 1879, breechloading.

BOWLES, WILLIAM H. unlocated. Percussion 1/2 stock dated 1886.

BOWLIN, THOMAS (1812-?), El Dorado Co., California, 1852c. (Shelton)

BOWLING, C. Berrien Springs, Michigan, 1873d.

BOWLING, J.W. Pilot Point, Texas, 1890d-1892d.

BOWMAN see Peck & Bowman.

BOWMAN, FRANK Oshkosh, Wisconsin, 1869-1870.

BOWMAN, JEREMIAH (1848-?), Shellsburg, Pennsylvania, 1866-1888.

BOWMAN, JOHN Warren, Ohio, 1841d, Kalida, Ohio, 1859-1865. (Hutslar)

BOWMAN, L.M. Mineola, Texas, 1892d-1896d.

BOWMAN, MARK H. Pinkstaff, Illinois. Patent #662,761 November 27, 1900, machine gun, with William Hughes.

BOWMAN, PETER Worcester, Pennsylvania, 1860d-1861d.

BOWMAN, W.F. Antigo, Wisconsin, 1884d-1888d.

BOWMAN, WILLIAM (1838-1903), Loundonville, Ohio, 1855-1902. With Peter Reinhard, 1855-1878. Guns stamped "WM BOMEN". (MB 9-44)

BOWN & TETLEY Pittsburgh, Pennsylvania, 1848-1862. Large manufacturer of muzzle loading guns using the trade name "Enterprise Gun Works". (MB 1-46)

BOWN, ALBERT Salem, Ohio, 1868, Newcastle, Pennsylvania, 1869, Titusville, Pennsylvania, 1876d-1882d. Percussion 1/2 stock. (Hutslar)

BOWN, JAMES (1823-?), Pittsburg, Pennsylvania, 1848-1887d. As Bown & Tetley, 1848-1862, James Bown, 1862-1871, and James Bown & Son (William H. Bown, 1847-?) 1871-1887, when they sold out to Brown & Hirth. Used "Enterprise Gun Works" as a trade name. (MB 1-46)

BOWN, WILLIAM H. Pittsburgh, Pennsylvania, 1874-1875, Salem, Ohio, 1880-1890. Son of James Bown. (Hutslar)

BOWNESS, JAMES Boston, Massachusetts. Patent #43,733 August 2, 1864, breechloading firearm.

BOWSHINGER, HENRY Somerset Co., Pennsylvania, 1820-1823. (Kauffman)

BOX Bedford, Indiana. (Lindert)

BOYCE, MATTHEW (1816-?), Anaheim, California, 1879-1882. (Shelton)

BOYCE, T. unlocated. Percussion underhammer pistol.

BOYCOURT, THOMAS see Boicourt.

BOYD BREECH-LOADING ARMS CO. Boston, Massachusetts, 1870-1872. Francis Boyd and S.D. Stevens. (GR 11-74)

BOYD unlocated. Percussion 1/2 stock.

BOYD, D. Gonzales, Texas, 1878d. Eagle Lake, Texas, 1890d.

BOYD, FRANCIS E. Hyde Park, Massachusetts, 1866-1874d. Patents #73,494 January 21, 1868, breechloading firearm, and #88,540 April 6, 1869, breechloading firearm. Both with P.S. Tyler. Made Boyd & Tyler shotguns. As Boyd & Stevens, 1874. (GR 11-74)

BOYD, J.S. Greenville, Texas, 1884d-1896d.

BOYD, JAMES St. Mary's Co., Maryland, 1776. Committee of Safety muskets. (Hartzler)

BOYD, JOSEPH Columbia, Lane Co., Pennsylvania, 1780. (Whisker III - questionable)

BOYD, ROBERT New Windsor, New York, 1772-1776. Committee of Safety muskets with Henry Watkeys. (Dean)

BOYD, T.P. (1835-?), Golden, Colorado, 1860c. (Sellers-3)

BOYD, WILLIAM Harrisburg, Pennsylvania, 1811. (Kauffman)

BOYD, WILLIAM Mansfield, Ohio. Patent #175,590 April 4, 1876, alarm gun. (Bugle 72)

BOYDEN, ALEXANDER Newark, New Jersey. Patent #none January 10, 1824, method of constructing gun.

BOYDSTUN, B.F. Jefferson, Texas, 1884d.

BOYER, BENJAMIN Hamburg, Pennsylvania, 1850c. (Kauffman)

BOYER, DANIEL (1818-?), Harrisville, Ohio, 1850c. (Hutslar)

BOYER, DANIEL Alma, Michigan, 1858-1871. Percussion slug gun.

BOYER, DAVID (OR DANIEL) Orwigsburg, Pennsylvania, circa 1820. Flintlock Kentucky. Son of M. Boyer. (Kindig)

BOYER, DAVID Orwigsburg, Pennsylvania, 1880d.

BOYER, DAVID Schuykill Co., Pennsylvania. Flintlock Kentucky rifle. (Gluckman & Satterlee)

BOYER, GEORGE (1840-?), Orwigsburg, Pennsylvania, 1862. Son of David Boyer. (Kauffman)

BOYER, HENRY Lebanon, Pennsylvania, 1807-1842. (Kauffman)

BOYER, J. unlocated. Flintlock Kentucky rifle.

BOYER, M. Lehigh Co., Pennsylvania. Flintlock Kentucky rifles. (Dillin)

BOYER, NICHOLAS Lebanon, Pennsylvania, 1807-1842. (Kauffman)

BOYINGTON, JOHN South Coventry, Connecticut, 1850. Percussion breechloading rifles. (Gluckman & Satterlee)

BOYLAN, KINNEY (1836-?), Guilford Co., North Carolina. Apprenticed to N. Albertson, 1844. (Bivins).

BOYLES, D. Moore's Prairie, Illinois, 1860d.

BOYNTON, JOHN S. East Hartford, Connecticut. Patent #30,714 November 27, 1860, breechloading firearm. Brass frame needle fire carbine.

BOYNTON, PAUL Canton, New York. Patents #23,226 March 15, 1859, magazine gun, and #26,646 January 3, 1860, magazine gun. Percussion magazine pistols. (GR 2-60)

BOYS CHOICE suicide special by Hood Fire Arms Co.

BOYSELL, BENJAMIN Dinwiddie Court House, Virginia, 1781. Committee of Safety repairs. (Gill)

BOYSON, G.G. Willmar, Minnesota, 1882d.

BOZEMAN, DAVID W. Central, Alabama, 1862-1864. As Davis & Bozeman. (Gluckman & Satterlee)

BRACE, D.R. Hannibal, Missouri. Patent #426,916 April 29, 1890, automatic gun with Robert W. Cash.

BRACEY, W.H. Gainesville, Florida, 1895d.

BRACH, H.D. Huron, Dakota Territory, 1884d-1886d.

BRACK, WILLIAM Providence, Rhode Island, 1826d.

BRACKEN Cleburne, Texas, 1890d. With John H. Derrough as Derrough & Bracken, 1890-1892.

BRACKETT, F. Albany, Texas, 1890d.

BRACKLOW, THEODORE (1814-?), St. Louis, Missouri, 1850-1855d, Pekin, Illinois, 1860d-1880d. Percussion 1/2 stock with St. Louis address.

BRAD, H. Greencastle, Indiana, 1860d.

BRADA, CONRAD Baltimore, Maryland, 1859-1864. (Hartzler)

BRADBERRY, J.E. Longview, Texas, 1878d.

BRADFORD, L.H. Boston, Massachusetts. Patent #42,741 May 17, 1864, nipple primer.

BRADFORD, SAMUEL New Orleans, Louisiana, 1841d-1842d.

BRADLEY, AMBROSE Polk Co., Missouri, 1850c. (MB 11-66)

BRADLEY, C. Navasota, Texas, 1878d.

BRADLEY, C.B. Hempstead, Texas, 1890d-1892d.

BRADLEY, C.H. West Chester, Pennsylvania. Patent #34,235 January 28, 1862, muzzle.

BRADLEY, H. Liverpool, New York. (Van Rensselaer)

BRADLEY, H.P. Dundee, Illinois, 1890d-1895d.

BRADLEY, HAZEN W. Ilion, New York. Patent #572,102 December 1, 1896, breechloading firearm.

BRADLEY, ISAAC Hartford, Connecticut. Patent #56,890 August 7, 1866, breechloading firearm.

BRADLEY, J.M. Pittsburgh, Texas, 1890d-1896d.

BRADLEY, JOHN (1797-?), Lovington, Illinois, 1860-1870. (Johnson)

BRADLEY, R. unlocated. Flintlock Kentucky.

BRADLEY, SIMON (1848-?), Liverpool, Pennsylvania, 1870c. Converted Kentucky rifle. (Chandler 2)

BRADLEY, T. Lexington, Kentucky. Underhammer pistol.

BRADSHAW, BURTON Hermitage, Missouri, 1879d.

BRADT, WILLIAM H. Leadville, Colorado, 1877-1883. Percussion fullstock. (Sellers-3)

BRADY, A.V. unlocated. Percussion 1/2 stock.

BRADY, FREEMAN W., JR. Washington, Pennsylvania. Patent #34,126 January 14, 1862, magazine gun, with J.C. Noble.

BRADY, ISAAC D. Katonah, New York, 1866d.

BRAGDON, M. unlocated. Percussion 1/2 stock.

BRAIN, JAMES Elko, Nevada, 1878d.

BRAINARD, CHESTELTON PRIEST Munson, Ohio, 1830-1910. Percussion full stock, signed "CPB". (Hutslar)

BRAINARD, ROBERT L. Meriden, Connecticut. Patent #175,875 April 11, 1876, soldering barrels.

BRAKE, WILLIAM (1808-?), St. Louis, Missouri, 1850c. (Lewis)

BRAKEMAN, P. Edgerton, Ohio, 1860-1865. (Hutslar)

BRAMAN, GARDNER Newport, Rhode Island, 1852-1856.

BRAMES, HENRY (1863-1948), Jasper, Indiana, 1880-1948. Unmarked percussion rifles. (Lindert)

BRAMLEY, E.D. Logans Creek, Missouri, 1860d.

BRAMMER, GEORGE LAFAYETTE (1861-1947), Huntington, West Virginia, 1883-1937, Chesapeake, Ohio, 1937-1941. Percussion and flintlock fullstock. (MB 7-44)

BRANCH, J.Y. Petersburg, Virginia, 1893d-1897d. As Butler & Branch, 1893.

BRANCH, JOSEPH Massachusetts, 1775. Committee of Safety repairs. (Dean*)

BRAND ARMS CO. Norwich, Connecticut, 1850-1875. Whaling guns and other firearms patented by Christopher C. Brand.

BRAND, CHRISTOPHER C. Norwich, Connecticut, 1855d-1874d. Patents #17,312 May 19, 1857, whaling projectile, #35,989 July 29, 1862, breechloading firearm, #36,505 September 23, 1862, revolving firearm, #38,279 April 28, 1863, pistol, #38,280 April 28, 1863, breechloading firearm, and #38,943 June 23, 1863, breechloading firearm. Carbines made by E. Chamberlin and E. Robinson, whaling guns by Brand. Guns sold by Brand until 1875 when his son took over the business. (GRI-78)

BRAND, JUNIUS A. Norwich, Connecticut, 1876d-1889d. Son of, and successor to, C.C. Brand.

BRAND, PETER Lancaster, Pennsylvania, 1801. Contract muskets for Pennsylvania. (Whisker III)

BRAND, WALTER H. (1830-?), Chico, California, 1871-1873, 1878-1879, Santa Rosa, California, 1874-1875. (Shelton)

BRANDAGEEZ Grahamsville, New York. Early flintlock period. (Dillin)

BRANDEL, JAMES Salem, North Carolina, 1854. (Bivins)

BRANDIS, G.A. Chicago, Illinois, 1880d.

BRANDON, CHARLES F. Pittsfield, Massachusetts, 1878d.

BRANDON, J.W. Pittsfield, Massachusetts, 1869d-1874d. As Sedgewick & Brandon, 1869.

BRANDON, WALTER H.F. Visalia, California, 1866. (Shelton)

BRANDSTELER, J. Smithland, Kentucky, 1857-1860. (Gardner)

BRANDT, JACOB F. see Jacob F. Brant.

BRANDT, JOHN Lancaster, Pennsylvania, 1834. (Kauffman)

BRANHAM, JOHN Monroe Co., Missouri, 1850c. (MB 11-61)

BRANN, PERRY Clarksville, Arkansas, 1884d.

BRANNAN, LUKE Norwich, Connecticut, 1875. Pistol maker. (Gluckman & Satterlee)

BRANNAN, WILLIAM Fredericksburg, Virginia, 1871d-1893d.

BRANSFORD HARDWARE CO. Nashville, Tennessee, 1865-1900. Sold percussion and cartridge guns marked with their name.

BRANSHAW, GEORGE (1833-?), Omaha, Nebraska Territory, 1860c.

BRANSON, BENJAMIN (1832-?), Visalia, California, 1860-1864. (Shelton)

BRANT, G. unlocated. Flintlock Kentucky.

BRANT, JACOB F. (1811-1872), Uniontown, Pennsylvania, 1835-1852, Pittsburgh, Pennsylvania, 1852-1865. As "Pittsburgh Gun Works" with Samuel McCosh, 1852-1855. Guns marked "J.F.B.". (Kauffman)

BRANT, JOHN G. (1809-?), Romney, Virginia, 1850c. (Bowers)

BRANT, JOHN Stevensburg, Virginia, 1800. With George Wheeler. (Gluckman)

BRANTLEY, S.H. Fairburn, Georgia, 1883d.

BRANTLINGER, DANIEL (1825-?), Pittsfield, Illinois, 1850c. (Johnson)

BRASHERS, ROBERT A. Venango Co., Pennsylvania, 1834-1856. (Kauffman)

BRASHIER, S.D. unlocated. Percussion 1/2 stock.

BRASIRUS, JOSEPH Buffalo, New York, 1820. Flintlock Kentucky. (Dean*)

BRASIRUS, PETER Buffalo, New York. Flintlock pistol. Brother of Joseph Brasirus.

BRASK, F.H. Baltimore, Maryland, 1835-1836. Worked for Pearson on Colt revolvers. (Sellers-1)

BRASS, ANDREW (1832-?), Harrodsburg, Kentucky, 1850c. For Benjamin Mills.

BRASS, G.W. Tiffin, Ohio, 1872d. (Hutslar)

BRAUN, AUGUSTUS San Francisco, California. Patents #54,021 April 17, 1866, lock, and #55,716 June 19, 1866, lock. Both with William Rudolph. (Shelton)

BRAUN, LEO Arkadelphia, Arkansas, 1878d. Percussion double shotgun with J. Overton.

BRAWLEY, JOHN Reynolds Co., Missouri, 1850c. (MB 11-66)

BRAY, ASA Benoni, Michigan, 1883d.

BRAY, C.T. Olathe, Kansas, 1882d.

BRAY, EDWARD P. see Merwin & Bray.

BRAY, SOLON A. Carrol, Idaho. Patent #661,031 November 6, 1900, sight.

BRAYMAN, GARDNER Newport, Rhode Island, 1828-1856. (Achtermier)

BREATH, WILLIAM L. Brooklyn, New York. Patent #599,549 February 22, 1898, pneumatic gun, assigned to Dynamite Ordnance & Armaments Co.

BREATHED, JOHN Bedford Co., Pennsylvania, 1823-1825. (C&W)

BRECHT, GUSTAVUS V. St. Charles, Missouri, 1850c-1875d. Air gun. (Wolff)

BRECK, WILLIAM (1800-?), St. Louis, Missouri, 1845d-1850, Santa Barbara, California, 1850-1870. (Shelton)

BRECKENRIDGE, J.H. Mendan, Connecticut. Patent #19,342 February 16, 1858, powderflask.

BREECH, E. unlocated. Percussion 1/2 stock.

BREEDLOVE, A.C. Horseshoe Falls, Tennessee, 1881d, Holder's Store, Tennessee, 1887d.

BREEDLOVE, MADISON Fredrickburg, Virginia, 1778. At state armory. (Gill)

BREEDON, J.C. Adrian, Michigan, 1883d-1895d.

BREESE, ALFRED Greenup, Illinois, 1864d.

BREETS, H.V. unlocated. Converted Kentucky rifle.

BREFFEIHL, J.M. Charleston, South Carolina, 1831d. New Orleans, Louisiana 1834d-1838d.

BREFFEILEL, T. M. Wilmington, North Carolina, 1829. (Bivins)

BREHINE, A. Chicago, Illinois, 1880d.

BREHM, EDUARD Jersey City, New Jersey. Patent #110,194 December 20, 1870, revolver.

BREICK, HENRY W. (?-1848), San Francisco, California. (Gluckman & Satterlee)

BREIDENHART, CHRISTOPHER Pennsylvania, 1775 1776. Committee of Safety muskets and Kentucky rifles. (Gluckman & Satterlee)

BREIGLE, JACOB G. (1831-1895), Bedford Co., Pennsylvania, 1852-1868, Dubuque, Iowa, 1868d, Maple Grove, Missouri, 1870-1895. Percussion fullstock. (Whisker) (see C&W for new information)

BREIHAN, CHRISTOPHER Lancaster, Pennsylvania, 1759-1770. (Dyke)

BREITENBAUGH, MARTIN St. Louis, Missouri, 1842d.

BREITENSTEIN, JACOB Farmington, Iowa, 1865d, St. Louis, Missouri, 1871-1873, Warsaw, Illinois, 1874-1903. Air gun.

BREITENSTEIN, WILLIAM Quincy, Illinois, 1884d, Little Rock, Arkansas, 1897d.

BRELSFORD, JONATHAN (1800-?), Zanesville, Ohio, 1814-1890. (Hutslar)

BREMER, OTTO A. San Francisco, California, 1872-1916. Stockmaker. As Browning & Bremer (schuetzen stocks), 1882-1899, and Bremer-Lewis Co., 1907. (Kelver)

BREMERMAN, GEORGE St. Louis, Missouri, 1854d-1864d. As Bremerman, Raschoe & Co. in 1854.

BREMERMAN, RASCHOE & CO. St. Louis, Missouri, 1854d. Dealers.

BREN, GEORGE H. Leavenworth, Kansas, 1867d, Junction City, Kansas, 1870d.

BRENBERGER, FREDERICK Lancaster Co., Pennsylvania, 1813-1815t. Barrelmaker. (Kauffman)

BRENISE, GEORGE York, Pennsylvania, 1800t-1819t. "Breneissen" in 1800 tax list. Flintlock Kentucky. (Kauffman)

BRENNAN, HUGH St. Louis, Missouri, 1857d-1859d. Percussion 1/2 stock.

BRENNEMAN, JACOB Lancaster Co., Pennsylvania, 1828t. (Dyke)

BRENNER, MARTIN Lancaster, Ohio, 1820-1830. (Hutslar)

BRENTZEL, WILLIAM Bloomfield, Missouri, 1898d.

BRETON, RUDOLPH B. Keokuk, Iowa, 1887d-1897d.

BRETT, JAMES Matteawan, New York. Patent #42,552 May 3, 1864, many-barreled gun.

BRETTELL, FRANCIS S. Allegheny City, Pennsylvania. Patent #16,575 February 10, 1857, revolver with Joseph Frisbie. (Sellers-1)

BREWER, J.T. Marlin, Texas, 1890d-1896d.

BREWER, M. Gonzales, Texas, 1884d.

BREWER, NELSON W. Williamsport, Pennsylvania, 1860-1882d. Patent #28,646 June 12, 1860, self capping firearm.

BREWER, R. unlocated. Converted Kentucky pistol.

BREWER, ROLAND L. Pittston, Pennsylvania. Patents #239,914 April 5, 1881, revolver, #279,324 June 12, 1883, breechloading firearm, #307,263 October 28, 1884, magazine gun, and #307,626 November 4, 1884, magazine gun.

BREY, ELIAS (1817-1891), Pennsburg, Pennsylvania, 1840, Kraussdale, Pennsylvania, 1860. Patent #20,757 June 29, 1858, double action lock. Percussion rifles and cane guns. (KRA II-4)

BRIANT, C.W. Franklin, Kentucky, 1879d-1884d.

BRICE, JAMES Philadelphia, Pennsylvania, 1760-1775. (Kauffman)

BRICH, MATHIAS (1799-?), Chicago, Illinois, 1860c. (Johnson)

BRICKER, ADAM Lancaster Co., Pennsylvania, 1863d.

BRICKLEY, D.J. Nola, Pennsylvania, 1887d-1890d.

BRICKLEY, ELMER E. Anita, Iowa. Patent #370,601 September 27, 1887, spring gun.

BRICKLEY, VIRGIL (1828-?), Harrodsburg, Kentucky, 1860c. For Benjamin Mills.

BRICKNER & VAN NETTE Tiffin, Ohio, 1888d. (Hutslar)

BRICKNER, JULIUS Delphos, Ohio, 1875, Tiffin, Ohio, 1888-1897. As Brickner & Van Nette in 1888. (Hutslar)

BRICKSEY, WILLIAM Waldo, Missouri, 1854d.

BRIDEMAN, DAVID Philadelphia, Pennsylvania, 1835d.

BRIDESBURG MACHINE WORKS Bridesburg, Pennsylvania, 1840-1869. Model 1863 contract muskets. Alfred and Barton Jenks.

BRIDGE GUN CO. trade name of Shapleigh Hardware Co. on shotguns. (Hinman)

BRIDGEMAN, QUARTERS E., Flushing, Michigan, 1863d-1865d. St. Johns, Michigan, 1867d-1883d.

BRIDGEPORT ARMS CO. trade name of Fred Beffar & Co. on imported shot guns. (Hinman)

BRIDGER, B. B. & W. B. Blandville, Kentucky, 1860d.

BRIDGES, ISAAC (1814-?), Newton Falls, Ohio, 1850-1860. Percussion 1/2 stock. (Hutslar)

BRIDGES, JOHN R. Castine, Maine, 1855-1880. Percussion 1/2 stock. (Demeritt)

BRIDGEWATER see Adam Kinsley and James Perkins for Model 1798 contract muskets.

BRIDGEWATER see John Ames for Model 1798 contract muskets.

BRIDGEWATER see Rufus Perkins for Model 1808 contract muskets.

BRIDGFORD & SON Salem, Illinois, 1890d.

BRIDGFORD, AARON Salem, Illinois, 1884d-1890d. As Bridgford & Son, 1890.

BRIEGMANN see Brugman.

BRIGGLE, JACOB G. Bedford, Pennsylvania. See Jacob Breigle.

BRIGGS, E. G. Baltimore, Maryland, 1840d. (Hartlzer)

BRIGGS, ETHAN Philadelphia, Pennsylvania, 1837-1847d.

BRIGGS, GEORGE W. New Haven, Connecticut. Patent #58,937 October 16, 1866, magazine gun. Produced by Winchester.

BRIGGS, HENRY Philadelphia, Pennsylvania. Patent #327,860 October 6, 1885, breechloading firearm.

BRIGGS, HORACE A. Norwich, Connecticut, 1850-1899. Patents #41,117 January 5, 1864, revolver with Samuel Hopkins, #429,110 June 3, 1890, revolver with William Armington, and #498,366 January 3, 1893, firearm with Charles W. Hopkins. Single shot "Flobert" pistols. President of Hopkins & Allen, 1868-1897.

BRIGGS, ISAAC Ithaca, New York, 1850-1860. Percussion 1/2 stock.

BRIGGS, JOHN Portsmouth, Rhode Island, 1643. (Achtermier)

BRIGGS, STERRY & CO. Norwich, Connecticut, 1854-1856. Breechloading pistols.

BRIGGS, T.L. Chester, Pennsylvania, 1890d. Son of William Briggs.

BRIGGS, W.M. Pottsdam, New York. Percussion six-barreled rifle.

BRIGGS, WILLIAM H. Chicopee Falls, Massachusetts. Patents #245,799 August 16, 1881, breechloading firearm.

BRIGGS, WILLIAM (?-1889), Norristown, Pennsylvania, 1848-1889d. Patents #25,244 August 30, 1859, gunlock, and #88,605 April 6, 1869, breechloading firearm. Made all metal underhammer rifles and shotguns under his 1859 patent marked "W. B." or fully marked. (GR 9-70)

BRIGH, SAMUEL unlocated. Flintlock Kentucky rifles.

BRIGHAM, JOHN Jerome, Ohio, 1853d, Lewis Center, Ohio, 1859-1861. (Hutslar)

BRIGHT, JACOB Washington, D. C., 1822d. (Hartzler)

BRIGHT, JOHN HENRY Logan, Ohio, 1883-1914. Son of and successor to Simon Bright. (Hutslar)

BRIGHT, SIMON H. Logan, Ohio. (Hutslar)

BRILES, J.C. Dun, Kansas, 1894d.

BRILHART, JACOB (1802-1867), Georgeville, Pennsylvania, 1832-1867. (Whisker II)

BRILLAN, W. unlocated. Flintlock fullstock.

BRIMFUL, JAMES Jerome, Indiana, 1858d.

BRINDLE, JOHN F. Philadelphia, Pennsylvania, 1847-1855d. Percussion fullstock. (Dean)

BRINKER, GEORGE (1747-1785), Frederick Co., Virginia, 1769-1785. Apprenticed to Adam Haymaker, 1764. (Gill)

BRINKLEY GEORGE M. (1865-1937), Sigel, Pennsylvania, 1886-1937. (Whisker II)

BRINKMAN, FREDERICK New Haven, Connecticut, 1881d.

BRINSON, A.A. Madison, Florida, 1885d.

BRISBAN, VICTOR (1833-?), Madison, Indiana, 1850c. (Lindert)

BRISCOE, JOHN Brunswick, Missouri, 1850c. (MB 11-66)

BRISON, BENJAMIN St. Louis, Missouri, 1842d-1859d.

BRISON, H.M. St. Louis, Missouri, 1842d.

BRISSON, JOSHUA (1828-?), Wabash Co., Indiana, 1850c. (Lindert)

BRISTOL FIRE ARMS CO. Bristol, Rhode Island, 1856d-1860d. Made first model Burnside carbines.

BRISTOL, RICHARD C. Chicago, Illinois. Patent #34,730 March 25, 1862, breechloading cannon.

BRISTOW, JAMES Dover, Tennessee, 1860d.

BRITISH BULLDOG trade name of many companies on revolvers.

BRITTELL, HARRY Rock Elm, Wisconsin, 1884d-1895d.

BRITTIN, J.S. Muskegon, Michigan, 1895d.

BRITTON, JOHN Little Rock, Arkansas, 1873d. With A. E. Linzell.

BRITTON, WILLIAM (1794-?), Romney, Virginia, 1850c. (Bowers)

BRITTON, WILLIAM Terre Haute, Indiana. "W. Brittan" percussion fullstock. (Lindert)

BRITZ, ADAM York Co., Pennsylvania, 1807-1810. (Kauffman)

BROAD, I. unlocated. Model 1808 contract musket.

BROADLEAR, SAMUEL Boston, Massachusetts, 1795. Flintlock powder.

BROADWELL, LEWIS WELLS New Orleans, Louisiana. Patents #49,583 August 22, 1865 breechloading firearms, #55,761 June 19, 1866, projectile, #55,762 June 19, 1866, breechloading ordnance, #22,872 December 10, 1861, breechloading ordnance, #110,338 December 20, 1870, repeating firearm, #167,981, September 21, 1875, gas check, #172,382 January 18, 1876, projectile, #174,770 March 14, 1876, gun carriage, and #174,771 March 14, 1876, projectile.

BROBST, JACOB Corning, Arkansas, 1884d.

BROCK, ANTHONY J. Galveston, Texas, 1867-1890d.

BROCK, JACOB Lancaster, Pennsylvania, 1857d.

BROCK, STEPHEN Greene Co., Pennsylvania, 1795-1799. (Whisker II)

BROCK, W.J. Old Jamestown, Arkansas, 1873. (Elias)

BROCKUS, W.K. Indian Creek, Tennessee, 1860d-1883. Percussion 1/2 stock dated 1883.

BROCKWAY, CHAUNCEY JR. (1821-1910), Brockway, Pennsylvania. Percussion and cartridge rifles.

BROCKWAY, NORMAN S. (1841-1936), Bellows Falls, Vermont, 1866-1900. Percussion match rifles. (Cline)

BROCKWELL, THOMAS F. Raleigh, North Carolina, 1884d-1890d.

BRODEN, WILLIAM H. Oakland, California. Patent #217,770 July 22, 1879, sight.

BRODERICK, CLEMENT M. Hartford, Connecticut. Patents #504,516 September 5, 1893, machine gun, and #504,517 September 5, 1893, machine gun, with J. Vankiersbilk. Used by Gatling Gun Co.

BRODERICK, JOHN Lancaster, Pennsylvania, 1857d.

BROEFFLE, G.H. Alpena, Michigan, 1887d-1889d.

BROMM, FRED (1859-1934), Ferdinand, Indiana, 1880-1934. (Lindert)

BRONG, JOSEPH Lancaster, Pennsylvania, 1760-1805. Flintlock Kentucky rifles. (Gluckman & Satterlee)

BRONG, PETER (?-1817), Lancaster, Pennsylvania, 1790-1817. Kentucky rifles, muskets and pistols. Had contracts with U.S., Pennsylvania, and Virginia for muskets and pistols. (Gluckman)

BRONOUP, JAMES Philadelphia, Pennsylvania, 1779. See Brownup.

BROOK Norwich, New York, 1845-1865. (Dean*)

BROOKE, EDWARD St. Louis, Missouri, 1870d. (Pourie)

BROOKE, I. I. & N. Chester Co., Pennsylvania. Model 1808 contract muskets. James, John, and Nathan Brooke. (Gluckman)

BROOKE, JOHN B. St. Louis, Missouri, 1845-1870d. (Pourie)

BROOKES, RICHARD Boston, Massachusetts, 1675. (Dean)

BROOKFIELD see Daniel Gilbert.

BROOKINS, EUGENE Boscohel, Wisconsin, 1891d.

BROOKLYN ARMS CO. Brooklyn, New York, 1863-1867. Made Slocum "sliding sleeve" revolvers marked "B.A.Co.".

BROOKS, C.C. Augusta, Maine, 1854-1860. With Larkin M. Leland as Leland & Brooks (see Larkin M. Leland, business timeframe shown as 1830-1860).

BROOKS, CHAPIN C. East Wilton, Maine, 1888-1903. Patents #441,389 November 25, 1890, drilling, #688,383 October 15, 1901, magazine gun, and #726,251 April 28, 1903, magazine gun. Guns made by Brooks under the name C. C. Brooks Arms & Tool Co., Portland, Maine. (Demeritt)

BROOKS, ENOCH Philadelphia, Pennsylvania. Patent #20,776 July 6 1858, breechloading firearm with G. Walker.

BROOKS, F.C. Janesville, Wisconsin, 1884d-1886d. Son of Oscar Brooks.

BROOKS, FRANCIS Philadelphia, Pennsylvania, 1787-1791. (Kauffman)

BROOKS, GEORGE F. Worcester, Massachusetts. Patent #466,952 January 12, 1892, revolver.

BROOKS, GEORGE Colusa, California, 1874-1881. (Shelton)

BROOKS, HENRY Saugatuck, Michigan, 1863d.

BROOKS, J.A., SR. Jones Valley, Tennessee, 1881d.

BROOKS, JOHN Canton, Massachusetts. Patent #12,411 February 20, 1855, bullet mold with J.S. Keith.

BROOKS, JOHN Lancaster, Pennsylvania, 1800-1803, Harrisburg, Pennsylvania, 1807-1817. Flintlock Kentucky. (Kindig)

BROOKS, JOHN Pittston, Pennsylvania. Patent #190,543 May 8, 1877, revolver, with Thomas Bearcock.

BROOKS, OSCAR M. Janesville, Wisconsin, 1866d-1879d.

BROOKS, WILLIAM F. New York, New York, 1861-1865. Made Gibbs patent carbines during the Civil War.

BROOM, FRED see Fred Bromm.

BROOMSCOTCH, ISAIAH Chambersburg, Ohio, 1882. With Washington Barnhart. (Hutslar)

BROSCHERT, GEORGE F. Williamsport, Pennsylvania, 1880d.

BROSSIUS, LEVI Steeleville, Pennsylvania, 1887d-1890d.

BROSWELL, JOSEPH West Brownsville, Pennsylvania, 1861d.

BROTHERHOUSE, WILLIAM Baltimore, Maryland, 1819d. (Hartzler)

BROTHIER, FRANK McGregor, Iowa, 1867d.

BROUGHTON, JOHN New York, New York. Patents #76,595 March 14, 1864, breechloading firearm, and #158,899 January 19, 1875, breechloading firearm. Hartford, Connecticut. Patent #76,595 April 14, 1868, breechloading firearm. Submitted this and two other actions to the 1872 breechloading trials.

BROWER, JOSEPH Lexington, Kentucky, 1879d-1896d. Dealer after 1885.

BROWN & GMEHLIN Chicago, Illinois, 1856d.

BROWN & HIRTH Pittsburgh, Pennsylvania, 1887-1894d. Purchased Enterprise Gun Works from James Brown in 1887.

BROWN & MANZANARIS see Chick, Brown, & Co.

BROWN & RAY unlocated. Flintlock Kentucky rifle.

BROWN & STEELE unlocated. Percussion target rifle.

BROWN MFG. CO. incorporated February 18, 1869, New York, New York. Factory located in Newburyport, Massachusetts, 1869-1885 (per AR 8-27 was sold at auction July 23, 1873). Ballard rifles, Merrill bolt action rifles, "Brown Standard" rifles, and Southerner derringers. John Hamilton Brown. Also see Brown Standard Firearms Co. (dealer for "Brown Standard" rifles?).

BROWN STANDARD FIREARMS CO. New York, New York. See John Hamilton Brown, and Brown Mfg. Co..

BROWN, A. & E. New York, New York. Made Lindner patent revolving rifles. (Sellers-1)

BROWN, A.F. Rushville, Illinois, 1882d-1888d.

BROWN, AARON Scio, New York, 1870d-1876d.

BROWN, ALBERT Newcastle, Pennsylvania, 1865d-1873d.

BROWN, ALDEN B. Rochester, New York, 1847d, for Billinghurst. (Eich)

BROWN, ALEXANDER T. (1854-1929), Syracuse, New York. Patents #234,749 November 23, 1880, lock, #261,663 July 25, 1882, breechloading firearm, #274,435 March 20, 1883, breechloading firearm, #282,838 August 7, 1883, breechloading firearms, #289,062 November 27, 1883, lock, #291,288 January 1, 1884, electric firearm, #345,362 July 13, 1886, lock, #350,109 October 5, 1886, lock, #367,089 July 26, 1887, breechloading firearm, and #381,109 April 17, 1888, airgun. Worked for L.C. Smith.

BROWN, ALEXANDER (1832-?), Monroe, Indiana, 1850c. Worked for James Archer. (Lindert)

BROWN, ANDREW J. Worcester, Massachusetts, 1852. As Allen, Brown & Luther.

BROWN, ANDREW Fremont, New Hampshire, 1860d-1879, Poplin, New Hampshire, 1880. Son of John F. Brown. (MB 3-62)

BROWN, ANTHONY Z. Philadelphia, Pennsylvania, 1841d-1847d. (Dean)

BROWN, BERKLEY T. (1810-?), Lebanon, Ohio, 1849-1891. (Hutslar)

BROWN, C.E. Grand Ledge, Michigan, 1872d-1879d.

BROWN, C.W. unlocated, percussion rifles.

BROWN, CHARLES F. Warren, Rhode Island. Patents #12,942 May 29, 1855, cartridge, #13,249 July 17, 1855, mounting cannon, #29,055 July 10, 1860, cannon wheels, #30,045 September 18, 1860, cannon, #33,378 October 1, 1861, projectile, #36,273 August 26, 1862, mounting cannon, and #82,284 September 22, 1868, projectile.

BROWN, CHARLES H. (1830-?), Warren, Ohio, 1850c. Worked for John Day. (Hutslar)

BROWN, CHARLES HENRY Bristol, Vermont, 1871-1885. (Horn)

BROWN, CHARLES LISTON New York, New York. Patent #26,919 January 24, 1860, "Conical Repeater" rifle with William Hopkins Morris. Rifles made by Morris & Brown (William Hopkins Morris and Charles Liston Brown).

BROWN, CHARLES S. Newburyport, Massachusetts, 1869d.

BROWN, D. B. Cambridge, Massachusetts, 1860, Southbridge, Massachusetts. Underhammer pistol.

BROWN, DANIEL J. (1836-?), Norwich, Connecticut, 1884d-1896d, Cranston, Rhode Island, 1898-1904. Patents #698,440 April 29, 1902, lock, #699,487 May 6, 1902, shot spreader, and #771,806 October 11, 1904, set trigger lock.

BROWN, DANIEL Umatilla, Oregon, 1866d.

BROWN, DAVID P. Lancaster, Pennsylvania, 1838d-1857d. Percussion rifles.

BROWN, DEHN Stark Co., Ohio, 1850c.

BROWN, ELISHA Providence, Rhode Island, 1799-1804. Model 1798 contract muskets. (Gluckman)

BROWN, EVAN B. Savannah, Missouri, 1850c. (MB 11-61)

BROWN, F. EBAN Dartmouth, Massachusetts, 1850. Whaling guns. (Dean)

BROWN, F.B. Lancaster, Pennsylvania, 1840. Flintlock Kentucky. (Dillin)

BROWN, FRANK E. Three Rivers, Michigan, 1872d-1899d.

BROWN, GEORGE A. Rochester, New York, 1847-1850, Dansville, New York, 1850-1853. For Billinghurst and Miller in Rochester. Miller patent revolving rifle. (Eich)

BROWN, GEORGE Winchester, Illinois. (Johnson)

BROWN, H.B. Galesburg, Michigan, 1867d.

BROWN, H.D. Scio, New York, 1874d.

BROWN, H.S. unlocated. Percussion shotgun.

BROWN, HARRY Grinnel, Iowa. Patent #624,620 May 9, 1899, firearm.

BROWN, HENRY CHARLES Bristol, Vermont, 1871-1885. Possibly same as Charles Brown. (Horn)

BROWN, HENRY M. (1814-?), St. Louis, Missouri, 1838-1850c. (Pourie)

BROWN, HIRAM (1819-?), Montgomery Co., Illinois, 1850c. (Johnson)

BROWN, IRA Cincinnati, Ohio, 1855-1868. With Palemon Powell as Powell & Brown, 1855-1858. (Hutslar)

BROWN, ISAAC West Springfield, Massachusetts. Patent #11,470 August 8, 1854, revolver. (Sellers-1)

BROWN, J.C. Savannah, Illinois, 1867d-1868d.

BROWN, J.F. Raymond, New Hampshire, 1874-1880. Son of John F. Brown.

BROWN, J.H. Dayton, Ohio. (Hutslar)

BROWN, J.L. Boston, Massachusetts, 1840-1848.

BROWN, J.N. Dayton, Ohio. Percussion fullstock. (Dean)

BROWN, JAMES (1817-?), Metropolis, Illinois, 1850c. (Johnson)

BROWN, JAMES Philadelphia, Pennsylvania, 1829d.

BROWN, JARED (1830-?), Columbiana Co., Ohio, 1850c. (Hutslar)

BROWN, JEHU Argo, Illinois, 1860d.

BROWN, JEREMIAH (1820-?), Carmi, Illinois, 1855-1860d.

BROWN, JESSE H. Syracuse, New York. Patent #423,521 March 18, 1890, breechloading firearm with Daniel Lefever.

BROWN, JOHN B. Pittsburgh, Pennsylvania, 1824d.

BROWN, JOHN C. Avon, Illinois, 1867d-1888d.

BROWN, JOHN F. (1824-1904), Poplin, New Hampshire, 1840-1856, Fremont, New Hampshire, 1856-1859, Haverhill, Massachusetts, 1859d-1904. Operated as John Brown & Sons, 1865-1874, with Andrew and John F., Jr. The shop is now at Greenfield Village. (MB 3-62)

BROWN, JOHN F. Philadelphia, Pennsylvania, 1855. (Kauffman)

BROWN, JOHN H. New York, New York. Patent #430,061 June 10, 1890, magazine gun. Probably John Hamilton Brown.

BROWN, JOHN H. Reading, Pennsylvania. Patent #653,208 July 10, 1900, explosive charge.

BROWN, JOHN HAMILTON (1837-?), Liberty, Maine, 1855-1860, Newburyport, Massachusetts, 1860-1903. Patent #290,737 December 25, 1883, breechloading firearm. As Brown Mfg. Co., 1860-1885 made Ballard, Merrill, and "Brown Standard" rifles. (Demeritt)

BROWN, JOHN JR. (1833-?), Stark Co., Ohio, 1850c. (Hutslar)

BROWN, JOHN N. Norwich, Vermont, 1869-1875d, Hanover, New Hampshire, 1877d-1880d.

BROWN, JOHN (1791-?), Stark Co., Ohio, 1821-1850. (Hutslar)

BROWN, JOHN (1800-?), Guernsey County, Ohio, 1850c. (Hutslar)

BROWN, JOHN Athens, Ohio, 1865-?. Negro gunsmith. (Hutslar)

BROWN, JOHN Fortville, Indiana, 1881-1886. (Gardner)

BROWN, JOHN Washington Co., Pennsylvania, 1831. (Kauffman)

BROWN, JONAS Buffalo, New York, 1836. Worked for Haberstro. (Kauffman 2)

BROWN, JOSEPH M., & CO. San Francisco, California. Importers & Dealers.

BROWN, JOSEPH Sabetha, Kansas, 1894d.

BROWN, L.G. Wilmington, Ohio, 1878d. (Hutslar)

BROWN, LARS Orcas, Washington, 1860-1880. (MB 12-65)

BROWN, LEVI S. Portland, Maine, circa 1860. (Demeritt)

BROWN, LOWELL N. Danville, New Hampshire, 1872d-1874d.

BROWN, MARMADUKE Fauquier Co., Virginia, 1762-1785. (Gill)

BROWN, MURRAY Luzerne, Michigan, 1887d.

BROWN, OTIS Portland, Maine, 1852-1889. (Demeritt)

BROWN, PIERCE Argo, Illinois, 1860d.

BROWN, R.H. Hopkinton, New York, 1874d.

BROWN, R.H., & CO. Westville, Connecticut, 1883, New Haven, Connecticut, 1884-1904. Shotguns and yacht guns.

BROWN, REUBEN Nicholville, New York. Percussion rifles. (Swinney)

BROWN, ROBERT New London, Connecticut. Patent #24,371 June 14, 1859, whaling projectile. Percussion whaling guns.

BROWN, S.C. Hartford, Connecticut, 1847-1850. (Kauffman 2)

BROWN, T. YARDLEY Reading, Pennsylvania, 1880d.

BROWN, T.H. Corry, Pennsylvania, 1882d-1890d. Sidehammer percussion target rifles.

BROWN, TAYLOR (1831-?), Montgomery Co., Indiana, 1850c. (Lindert)

BROWN, THEODORE Cascade, Iowa, 1865d.

BROWN, W.S. Pittsburgh, Pennsylvania, 1890d.

BROWN, W.T. Springfield, West Virginia, Romney, West Virginia, 1900d. (Whisker IV)

BROWN, WILLIAM H. (1803-?), Dayton, Ohio, 1827-1837, Perryville, Indiana, 1846-1850. Percussion fullstock rifle. (Lindert, Hutslar)

BROWN, WILLIAM H. (1811-?), San Francisco, California, 1849-1859. Percussion 1/2 stock. (Shelton)

BROWN, WILLIAM H. Perryville, Indiana, 1850c.

BROWN, WILLIAM H. Pittsburgh, Pennsylvania, 1838-1841. (Kauffman)

BROWN, WILLIAM H. Worcester, Massachusetts. Patent #34,561 March 4, 1862, breechloading firearm.

BROWN, WILLIAM Norton, Ohio, 1860-1891. (Hutslar)

BROWN, WILLIAM Santa Clara, California. Patent #52,966 March 6, 1866, bullet machine with Lewis Hebard.

BROWN, WILLIAM Youngstown, Ohio, 1881-1884. (Gardner)

BROWNE, JOHN New Jersey, 1664-1691. (Gluckman & Satterlee)

BROWNELL, C.W. Quincy, Michigan, 1899d.

BROWNELL, M.J. unlocated. Percussion 1/2 stock.

BROWNIE trade name on Mossberg four-shot pistol.

BROWNING & BREMER San Francisco, California, 1881-1900. (Kelver)

BROWNING & HEBER San Francisco, California, 1873-1876. Percussion 1/2 stock. (Shelton)

BROWNING ARMS CO. St. Louis, Missouri, 1890-date. Sales organization for Browning patent guns made in Belgium.

BROWNING, ABEL S. (1854-?), Garett Co., Maryland, 1875-1940s. Also worked in West Virginia. (Hartzler)

BROWNING, AUGUST (1837-?), San Francisco, California, 1867-1900. With Schneider & Browning, 1867-1870, Browning & Heber, 1873-1877, and Browning & Bremer, 1881-1900. (Shelton)

BROWNING, DAVID (1829-?), Kanesville, Iowa, 1850c. Son of Jonathan Browning.

BROWNING, GEORGE Philadelphia, Pennsylvania, 1780-1782. Continental Armory. (Moller)

BROWNING, JOHN MOSES (1855-1926), Ogden, Utah. Patents #220,271 October 7, 1879, breechloading firearm, #261,667 July 25, 1882, magazine gun, #282,839 August 7, 1883, magazine gun, #306,577 October 14, 1884, magazine gun, #312,183 February 10, 1885, magazine gun, #324,296 August 11, 1885, magazine gun, #324,297 August 11, 1885, magazine gun, #336,287 February 16, 1886, magazine gun, #345,881 July 20, 1886, magazine gun, #345,882 July 20, 1886, magazine gun, #346,021 July 20, 1886, magazine gun, #356,271 January 18, 1887, magazine gun, #359,917 March 22, 1887, breechloading firearm, #367,336 July 26, 1887, magazine gun, #376,576 January 17, 1888, magazine gun, #385,238 June 26, 1888, magazine gun, #409,599 August 20, 1889, magazine gun, #409,600 August 20, 1889, magazine gun, #421,663 February 18, 1890, magazine gun, #428,887 May 27, 1890, magazine gun, #436,965 September 23, 1890, breechloading firearm, #441,390 November 25, 1890, magazine gun, #465,339 December 15, 1891, magazine gun, #465,340 December 15, 1891, magazine gun, #471,782 March 29, 1892, automatic gun, #471,783 March 29, 1892, machine gun, #471,782 March 29, 1892, machine gun, #486,272 November 15, 1892, breechloading firearm, #486,273 November 15, 1892, breechloading firearm, #486,274 November 15, 1892, magazine gun, #487,659 December 6, 1892, magazine gun, #492,459 February 28, 1893, magazine gun, #499,005 June 6, 1893, magazine gun, #499,006 June 6, 1893, magazine gun, #499,007 June 6, 1893, magazine gun, #502,549 August 1, 1893, gas operated gun, #511,677 December 26, 1893, breechloading firearm, #544,659 August 20, 1895, machine gun, #544,660 August 20, 1895, automatic gun, #544,661 August 20, 1895, automatic gun, #545,671 September 3, 1895, magazine gun, #545,672 September 3, 1895, magazine gun, #547,986 October 15, 1895, cartridge box, #549,345 November 5, 1895, magazine gun, #550,778 December 3, 1895, magazine gun, #552,864 January 7, 1896, magazine gun, #577,281 February 16, 1897, magazine gun, #580,923 April 20, 1897, magazine gun, #580,924 April 20, 1897, magazine gun, #580,925 April 20, 1897, magazine gun, #599,595 February 22, 1898, magazine gun, #619,132 February 7, 1899, magazine gun, #621,747 March 21, 1891, automatic gun, #632,094 August 29, 1899, bolt action gun, #659,507 October 9, 1900, automatic gun, #659,786 October 16, 1900, automatic gun, #678,937 July 23, 1901, automatic gun, #689,283 December 17, 1901, automatic gun, #701,288 June 3, 1902, automatic gun, #701,289 June 3, 1902, sight, #708,794 September 9, 1902, automatic gun, #710,094 September 30, 1902, magazine gun, #730,870 June 16, 1903, automatic gun, #747,585 December 22, 1903, automatic gun, #781,765 February 7, 1905, magazine gun, #808,003 December 19, 1905, magazine gun, #812,326 February 13, 1906, recoil brake, #818,739 April 24, 1906, automatic gun, #853,438 May 14, 1907, automatic gun, #864,608 August 27, 1907, automatic gun, and #864,609 August 27, 1907, automatic gun. Son of Jonathan Browning. Most of his patents were used by the large gun companies - Winchester, Colt, and Remington in this country and Fabrique Nationale d'Armes de Guerre in Belgium. He and his brother Matthew made about 600 single shot rifles on his 1879 patent before selling its rights to Winchester.

BROWNING, JONATHAN, M. (1805-1879), Sumner Co., Tennessee, 1826-1834, Adams Co., Illinois, 1834-1842, Nauvoo, Illinois, 1842-1846, Kanesville, Iowa, 1846-1851, Ogden, Utah, 1851-1879. Made percussion rifles, both muzzle loading and repeating. The repeating guns were of the harmonica and revolver types. Four of his sons, David, John M., Matthew S., and Wesley, were gunsmiths. (GR 5-61)

BROWNING, MATTHEW S. Ogden, Utah. Operated Browning Bros. shop in Ogden with his brother John M. Browning with whom he held three patents.

BROWNING, WESLEY (1832-?), Kanesville, Iowa, 1850c, Ogden, Utah, 1851-?. Son of Jonathan Browning. (MB 8-64)

BROWNSON, HOPKINS & SLOCUMB New Orleans, Louisiana. Percussion guns.

BROWNUP, JAMES Philadelphia, Pennsylvania, 1779-1780. (Dean)

BROYHIER, F. McGregor, Iowa, 1865d.

BROYLES, G.E. Ringgold, Georgia, 1879d-1883d.

BROYLES, JAMES C. Tupelo, Mississippi. Patents #338,247 March 23, 1886, breechloading firearm, and #653,613 July 10, 1900, choke device. Columbus, Mississippi. Patent #685,669 October 29, 1901, choke device. Birmingham, Alabama. Patent #778,629 December 27, 1904, single trigger.

BRUBAKER, JOHN Lancaster Co., Pennsylvania, 1802t-1820t. (Dyke)

BRUCE & DAVIS Webster, Massachusetts, 1840c. Agents for Allen pistols.

BRUCE, GEORGE Ossining, New York, 1861-1870d. Patent #32,349 May 21, 1861, alarm gun. As George Bruce & Sons, 1870.

BRUCE, GEORGE, & SONS Ossining, New York, 1870d.

BRUCE, JOHN H. (1853-?), Eureka, California, 1879. (Shelton)

BRUCE, JOHN Springfield, Massachusetts. Patent #none October 15, 1824, gun barrels.

BRUCE, LUCIEN F. Springfield Massachusetts. Patents #247,158 June 14, 1881, cartridge feeder for machine gun, #273,249 March 6, 1883, cartridge feeder for machine gun, #341,371 May 4, 1886, cartridge feeder for machine gun, #343,532 June 8, 1886, cartridge feeder for machine gun, #351,960 November 2, 1886, cartridge feeder for machine gun, #432,507 July 22, 1890, magazine gun, #452,447 May 19, 1891, cartridge box, #462,298 November 3, 1891, magazine, and #708,311 September 2, 1902, magazine. Early patents used by Gatling Gun Co.

BRUCE, T. Sparta, Georgia, 1883d.

BRUCE, W.A. Santa Rosa, California, 1872-1873, St. Helena, California, 1874-1878. (Shelton)

BRUCE, WILLIAM A. Louisiana, Missouri, 1867d. Same as W. A. Bruce?

BRUCKLACHER, F.W. Elizabeth, New Jersey, 1879d-1897d. As Brucklacher Bros., 1889-1897. He worked for his brother before 1889.

BRUCKLACHER, JACOB Elizabeth, New Jersey, 1866d-1897d. As Brucklacher Bros., 1889-1897.

BRUDER, JOHN Lancaster, Pennsylvania, 1871d.

BRUEGMAN BROTHERS Manistee, Michigan, 1899d.

BRUEGMAN, OTTO Manistee, Michigan, 1895d-1899. As Bruegman Bros., 1899.

BRUEHLER, FRANK East St. Louis, Illinois, 1888d-1893d.

BRUEN, LEWIS B. Brooklyn, New York. Patent #37,491 January 27, 1863, shot cartridge.

BRUENINGSEN, FREDERICK Hastings, Nebraska, 1882d-1893d.

BRUFF BRO. & SEAVER New York, New York, 1858d-1861d. Derringer.

BRUFF, RICHARD P. New York, New York, 1858d-1875d. Derringer. As Bruff Bro. & Seaver, 1858d-1861d.

BRUFF, THOMAS Charlestown, Maryland, 1793. (Dean)

BRUFF, THOMAS Washington, D.C. Patents #none October 5, 1808, shot manufacture, and #none June 4, 1813, shot manufacture.

BRUGMANN, HEINRICH Waterloo, Michigan, 1872d, Fowler, Michigan, 1879d, Reed City, Michigan, 1883d-1887d. Patent #129,312 July 16, 1872, breechloading firearm.

BRUMBACK, C. Little Rock, Arkansas, 1832.

BRUMFIELD, J. & W. Connersville, Indiana, 1860c. James and William Brumfield also worked in other locations. (Lindert)

BRUMFIELD, JAMES R. (1837-?), Connersville, Indiana, 1860c, Terre Haute, Indiana, 1882-1885. Converted Kentucky. (Lindert)

BRUMFIELD, W.E. Brownsburg, Indiana, 1860d-1862d.

BRUMFIELD, W.H. (1803-1890), Perrysville, Indiana, 1846-1875. (Lindert)

BRUMLEY, SAMUEL Marion, Indiana, 1858d, Jonesboro, Indiana, 1860d-1862d.

BRUMLEY, SAMUEL Senecaville, Ohio, 1852-1865.

BRUMLEY, WILLIAM D. Senecaville, Ohio, 1853-1886. (Hutslar)

BRUNDAGE, H. Virginia City, Montana, 1871d.

BRUNDEL, JOHN H. Philadelphia, Pennsylvania, 1847d.

BRUNER, CHARLES Galesburgh, Illinois, 1890d-1893d.

BRUNER, GEORGE (1720-1793), Lebanon, Pennsylvania, 1739-1748, Salisbury, North Carolina, 1750-1793. Also Brunner. (Bivins)

BRUNER, HENRY (1719-1769), Salisbury, North Carolina, ?-1769. Flintlock Kentucky rifle. Brother of George Bruner. (Bivins)

BRUNER, HENRY, III (1789-1819), Salisbury, North Carolina, 1816-1819. (Bivins)

BRUNER, HENRY, JR. (?-1803), Salisbury, North Carolina, 1785-1803. Flintlock Kentucky rifle. (Bivins)

BRUNER, J. Woodville, Missouri, 1860d.

BRUNER, J.S. Corydon, Indiana. (Lindert)

BRUNER, JACOB Camden, New Jersey, 1866d-1882d.

BRUNKER & BUSCHICK Ottawa, Illinois, 1850-1852. (Johnson)

BRUNKER & EBERSOL Ottawa, Illinois, 1865. (Johnson)

BRUNKER & MITCHELL Ottawa, Illinois, 1856-1858. (Johnson)

BRUNKER & ROSE Ottawa, Illinois, 1866-1871. (Johnson)

BRUNKER, H. Leavenworth, Kansas, 1860d.

BRUNKER, HENRY P. Ottawa, Illinois, 1871d.

BRUNKER, JOHN (?-1843), Rochester, New York, 1841, Lockport, New York, 1842-1843. (Eich)

BRUNKER, PETER Ottawa, Illinois, 1840-1872. Percussion 1/2 stock. (MB 4-43)

BRUNNER see Bruner.

BRUNNER, EMIL Calvert, Texas, 1884d-1896d.

BRUNNER, JOSEPH (1801-?), St. Louis, Missouri, 1840-1852d. (Lewis)

BRUNNER, JOSEPH, JR. (1834-?), St. Louis, Missouri, 1850c. (Lewis)

BRUNSON, PETER, E. Trumbull, Ohio, 1870c. (Hutslar)

BRUNTY, JESSE Carrol Co., Missouri, 1850c. (MB 11-66)

BRUNTY, WILLIAM Carrol Co., Missouri, 1850c. (MB 11-66)

BRUSH, E.A. Hydesville, California, 1893d.

BRUSH, JOHN (?-1726), Williamsburg, Virginia, 1717-1726. (Gill)

BRUTON, JACKSON W. Guthrie, Missouri. Patent #440,538 November 11, 1890, target gun.

BRUTUS suicide special by Hood Fire Arms Co.

BRYAN, C.M. La Harpe, Illinois, 1860d.

BRYAN, DANIEL North Carolina. Although this nephew of Daniel Boone is listed as a gunmaker in several sources, there is no documentary evidence to support it.

BRYAN, FRANCIS Baltimore, Maryland, 1814d. (Hartzler)

BRYAN, JAMES Lancaster, Pennsylvania, 1801. (Kauffman)

BRYAN, JOHN Philadelphia, Pennsylvania, 1847d. Worked for Henry Deringer. (Dean)

BRYAN, L. & W. unlocated. Flintlock Kentucky rifle.

BRYAN, P.O. Harrodsburg, Kentucky, 1856-1860.

BRYAN, S. Independence, Kentucky, 1858-1860.

BRYAN, T. unlocated. Barrel maker.

BRYANT, I.W. Altamont, Tennessee, 1860d.

BRYANT, J.E. Richmond, Virginia, 1870-1873.

BRYANT, J.H. Chicago, Illinois, 1893d.

BRYANT, SILAS Cincinnati, Ohio, 1818d-1837d.

BRYCE & BUDD Chatham, New Jersey, 1881-1885. Cartridge shotguns under patents of William Budd.

BRYCE, JAMES New York, New York. Percussion full-stock.

BRYCE, JOHN Philadelphia, Pennsylvania, 1775. (Kauffman)

BRYCE, WILLIAM, & CO. New York, New York, 1842d-1886d. Wholesale hardware dealers, agent for Sharps percussion revolver. (Sellers-4)

BRYCHE, B. (1823-?), Jerseyville, Illinois, 1853-1860. (Johnson)

BUBSER, F. unlocated. Percussion 1/2 stock.

BUBSER, MICHAEL Jersey City, New Jersey, 1878d.

BUCHALEW, S. Rowlesburg, West Virginia. Percussion Kentucky rifle. (Gluckman & Satterlee)

BUCHAN, A. Delphi, New York, 1874d. See Andrew Buckingham.

BUCHANAN, GEORGE (1782-1860), Blair Co., Pennsylvania, 1850c-1860. (Whisker II)

BUCHANAN, JACOB Charleston, South Carolina, 1794. (Kauffman 2)

BUCHANAN, JAMES Malden, Missouri 1879d.

BUCHANAN, JOHN (1775-1864), Laurel Hill, North Carolina, ?-1864. Flintlock and percussion fullstock rifles. Son of William Buchanan. Operated gun factory with son-in-law Murdoch Morrison during the Civil War. Rifles signed "J.B.". (Hill-Anthony)

BUCHANAN, JOHN Pocahontas, Missouri, 1860d.

BUCHANAN, L. unlocated. Flintlock Kentucky rifle.

BUCHANAN, SAMUEL Dauphin Co., Pennsylvania, 1814. (Kauffman)

BUCHANAN, THOMAS Rich, West Virginia, 1900d. (Whisker IV)

BUCHANAN, WILLIAM Laurel Hill, North Carolina, flintlock Kentucky rifles. (Hill-Anthony)

BUCHEL, CHRISTIAN W. New York, New York. Patent #6136 February 20, 1849, repeating firearm.

BUCHLEY, JOSEPH Bayou Meto, Arkansas, 1884d.

BUCHMILLER, D.F. Lancaster, Pennsylvania, 1875d-1890d. Son of Robert Buchmiller.

BUCHMILLER, ROBERT Lancaster, Pennsylvania, 1861d-1870. Lockmaker who made a few guns. (Kauffman)

BUCHMILLER, W.C. Lancaster, Pennsylvania, 1860-1870. (Dean)

BUCHNER, HEINRICH New York, New York. Patent #114,259 May 20, 1870, breechloading firearm.

BUCK, CHARLES New York, New York, 1858d.

BUCK, DANIEL unlocated. Flintlock Kentucky rifle.

BUCK, E. De Pere, Wisconsin, 1867d.

BUCK, H.A., & CO. see Henry Buck.

BUCK, HENRY A. West Stafford, Connecticut, 1879-1883. Patent #214,098 April 8, 1879, breechloading firearms. Rolling block rifles made by H.A. Buck & Co., West Stafford.

BUCK, PETER Pennsylvania, ?-1776. Committee of Safety repairs. (C&W)

BUCKEL, GEORGE Monroe, Michigan. Patents #14,597 April 8, 1856, shotgun, and #15,369 July 22, 1856, cartridge with Edward Dorsch.

BUCKEYE GUN STORE Cincinnati, Ohio, 1856-1858. H.L. Seibert. (Hutslar)

BUCKEYE suicide special by Hopkins & Allen.

BUCKHALTER, JOHN Philadelphia, Pennsylvania, 1875d. (Whisker III)

BUCKHAM, A. see Andrew Buckingham.

BUCKINGHAM, ANDREW Delhi, New York, 1850-1882d. Percussion guns-also listed as Buckan and Buckham. (Swinney)

BUCKLAND, ALMANGOR A. Springfield, Massachusetts, 1867d-1876d. Pistols. As E.H. Buckland & Co., 1867-1870 and Buckland Bros., 1870-1874.

BUCKLEY, ANTON Cincinnati, Ohio, 1854-1862.

BUCKLEY, H.P. New Orleans, Louisiana, 1867d. For Thomas Bailey.

BUCKLEY, SAMUEL & CO. trade name of J. Palmer O'Neal on imported shotguns. (Hinman)

BUCKLIN, F.R. New Hampshire, Breechloading shotgun similar to Lawrence.

BUCKMAN, ALEXANDER see Edward Buckman.

BUCKMAN, C.F. Gibson City, Illinois, 1884d.

BUCKMAN, EDWARD Brooklyn, New York, 1869-1872d. Patents, with Alexander Buckman (brother?), #85,638 January 5, 1869, magazine pistol, and #107,442 September 20, 1870, magazine pistol.

BUCKMAN, IRA New York, New York. Patent #17,915 August 4, 1857, cane gun.

BUCKMINSTER, LEONARD M. Craig, Missouri, 1881d.

BUCKNER Maquoketa, Iowa. (MB 1-46)

BUCKNUM, J.R. Atchison, Kansas, 1878d.

BUCKWALTER, ABRAHAM Lancaster, Pennsylvania, 1771-1779. Brother of Henry and John Buckwalter.

BUCKWALTER, DAVID B. (1850-1928), Antes Fort, Pennsylvania, 1870-1885, Houtsdale, Pennsylvania, 1885-1895. (Gluckman & Satterlee)

BUCKWALTER, HENRY Lancaster, Pennsylvania, 1771-1779. Brother of Abraham & John Buckwalter. (Gluckman & Satterlee)

BUCKWALTER, JOHN Lancaster, Pennsylvania, 1771. Brother of Abraham and Henry Buckwalter. (Gluckman & Satterlee)

BUDD, BERN L. New York, New York. Patents #34,724 March 18, 1862, cartridge, #34,725 March 18, 1862, cartridge, #34,744 March 25, 1862, cartridge, and #34,806 March 25, 1862, cartridge. First three with R. Ogden Doremus.

BUDD, LEWIS ROSS Oskaloosa, Iowa. Patent #38,557 May 19, 1863, capper.

BUDD, SAMUEL O. (1830-?), Fayette Co., Indiana, 1850c, Muncie, Indiana, 1858d-1860c. (Lindert)

BUDD, WILLIAM E. Chatham, New Jersey. Patents #240,653 April 26, 1881, breechloading firearm, #259,361 June 13, 1882, breechloading firearm, and #291,980 January 15, 1884, breechloading firearm. Shotguns made by Bryce & Budd.

BUDDENHAGEN, JOHN Sandusky, Ohio, 1866-1889. (Hutslar)

BUDDLE, JOHN (1801-?), Canajoharie, New York, 1850c-1864d.

BUDENBAUGH, MARTIN (1780-?), Hagerstown, Maryland. Apprenticed to George Kreps, 1797. (Hartzler)

BUE, PETER Titusville, Pennsylvania, 1887d.

BUELL, ELISHA Hebron, Connecticut, 1776-1797, Marlborough, Connecticut, 1797-1830. Flintlock muskets of Revolutionary War and Model 1808 pattern, flintlock Kentucky. (Gluckman)

BUELL, ENOS Marlborough, Connecticut, 1819-1850. Successor to his father, Elisha.

BUFFALO ARMS CO. Buffalo, New York, 1886d-1889d. Dealers.

BUFFALO BILL all brass suicide special by Iver Johnson and Hood.

BUFFALO trade name of Western Arms Co. for .22 cal. rifle.

BUFFINGTON, ABRAHAM (1785-?), Jefferson Co., Illinois, 1823-1850. (Johnson)

BUFFINGTON, HERBERT Putnam, Connecticut, 1869-1873d.

BUFFLER, H. Darrtown, Ohio, 1860-1866. (Gardner)

BUFFLER, ROMAN Darrtown, Ohio, 1857-1866. (Gardner)

BUGLES, GEORGE H. San Francisco, California, 1854. Worked for P.B. Comino. (Shelton)

BUHL, JOSEPH (1820-?), Freeport, Illinois, 1850c. (Johnson)

BUIE, MALCOM Cumberland, North Carolina, 1806. (Bivins)

BUJAC & HENSLER New Orleans, Louisiana, 1858-1861d. M.J. Bujac and John Hensler.

BUKLEY, D. see Daniel Beakley.

BULFIELD, JOHN Cedarburg, Wisconsin, 1857d.

BULL DOG suicide special by Forehand & Wadsworth.

BULL DOZER suicide special by Norwich Pistol Co. and Forehand & Wadsworth.

BULL DOZER trade name occasionally found on Hammond Bulldog.

BULL FROG trade name on Hopkins & Allen rifle.

BULL, DANIEL (1816-?), Hancock Co., Illinois, 1844. (Johnson)

BULL, ELISHA Morristown, Tennessee. Flintlock and percussion Tennessee rifles and pistols.

BULL, HENRY C. New York, New York. Patents #169,413 November 2, 1875, breechloading firearm, #195,882 October 9, 1877, boring barrels, and #209,010 October 15, 1878, breechloading firearm.

BULL, JOHN Bulls Gap, Tennessee, 1784-1829. Flintlock Kentucky.

BULL, MILAN W. Springfield, Massachusetts, 1888d-1889d. Successor to L.H. Mayott.

BULLARD BROTHERS Vernon, New York, 1872-1882.

BULLARD REPEATING ARMS CO. Springfield, Massachusetts, 1882-1890. Lever action rifles under patents of J.H. Bullard, Solomon Hindley, and Edwin Field. (NRA GCN #8)

BULLARD, FRED Rowe, Massachusetts, 1888d.

BULLARD, IRA Clinton, Massachusetts, 1899d.

BULLARD, JAMES HERBERT (1842-1914), Springfield, Massachusetts. Patents #187,269 February 20, 1877, revolver, #187,689 February 20, 1877, revolver, and #198,228 December 18, 1877, revolver, all with D.B. Wesson. Patents #227,481 May 11, 1880, revolver, #245,700 August 16, 1881, magazine gun, and #287,229 October 23, 1883, magazine gun. Revolvers made by Smith & Wesson, single shot and magazine rifles produced by Bullard Repeating Arms Co.

BULLARD, L. O. Bourne, Massachusetts, 1892d.

BULLARD, R. Litchfield, Michigan, 1860d.

BULLOCK, W.C.A. Boston, Massachusetts. Patent #320,910 June 30, 1885, revolver.

BULLS EYE suicide special by O.A. Smith.

BULOW, CHARLES Lancaster, Pennsylvania, 1779-1800. (Dillin)

BUNCH, JEFF P. (1807-?), El Monte, California, 1868-1876. (Shelton)

BUNCH, JOSEPH (1818-?), Green Co., Indiana, 1850c. (Lindert)

BUNCHMAN, FRANKLIN Oroville, California, 1860c. (Shelton)

BUNDLE, JOHN F. see John F. Brindle.

BUNDLE, WILLIAM (1822-?), Muskingham Co., Ohio, 1850c. (Hutslar)

BUNGE, CHARLES Geneva, New York, 1860d-1900d. Patents #94,179 August 13, 1869, air gun, and #433,323 July 29, 1890, sight. Made percussion revolving rifles and revolving airguns along with other guns.

BUNKER, WILLIAM J. Thomaston, Maine, 1880. (Demeritt)

BUNNELL, MERRITT Ridgeville, Ohio, 1853d, Waynesville, Ohio, 1878-1886. Son of Stephen Bunnell (Hutslar)

BUNNELL, STEPHEN Cincinnati, Ohio, 1788-1812. (Hutslar)

BUNSEN & RANDEGGER Belleville, Illinois, 1869. Percussion revolving rifles.

BUNSEN, GEORGE C. Belleville, Illinois, 1864-1869. Patent #51,690 December 26, 1865, revolving rifle. As Bunsen & Randegger, 1869. Clockwork revolving rifles. School superintendent, 1860. (Sellers-1)

BURBANK, A.L. Worcester, Massachusetts, 1873-1876.

BURBANK, J.H. Springfield, Massachusetts, 1882d-1888d.

BURCH, W.H. Bowling Green, Kentucky, 1883d.

BURCHDAUGH, H. Vernon, Oregon, 1871d.

BURCHETT, THEODORICK (1803-?), Polk Co., Iowa, 1850c. (MB 8-64)

BURD, C. Philadelphia, Pennsylvania. Flintlock Kentucky rifle. See Bird or Burden.

BURDEN, B.H. unlocated. Percussion fullstock.

BURDEN, CALVIN Philadelphia, Pennsylvania, 1819d.

BURDEN, EDMUND C. (1826-1913), Carlisle, Kentucky, 1854-1860, Elizabethtown, Kentucky, 1860-1878, Raymond, Kansas, 1878-1900. (MB 5-55)

BURDEN, JAMES M. Mount Olivet, Kentucky, 1854-1860. Brother of Edmund Burden.

BURDICK trade name of H & D Folsom on shotgun imported for Sears Roebuck & Co.

BURDICK, I.L. Janesville, Wisconsin, 1857d-1867d.

BURDICK, J.B. Danville, Vermont, 1875d.

BURDICK, JESSE A. East Saginaw, Michigan, 1875d.

BURDICK, S. unlocated. Percussion 1/2 stock.

BURDIS, PETER Maumee City, Ohio, 1851-1860. (Hutslar)

BURDO, PETER (1807-?), Waynesville, Ohio, 1850c, Maumee City, 1853d. (Hutslar)

BURG, WILLIAM Freeport, Pennsylvania, 1876-1878. (Kauffman)

BURGAN, EMANUEL St. Louis, Missouri, 1860d.

BURGAN, L.C. (1826-?), Terre Haute, Indiana, 1850c-1867d. (Lindert)

BURGANS, CHARLES E. (1839-?), San Francisco, California, 1868-1885, Oakland, California, 1885-?. Patent #344,896 July 6, 1886, trigger. (Shelton)

BURGE, D.H. Trimble, Kentucky, 1896d.

BURGE, WILLIAM Freeport, Pennsylvania, 1880d.

BURGEN, E. (1838-?), Central City, Colorado, 1860c, Golden Gate, Colorado, 1861d. (Sellers-3)

BURGEN, FRED A. Denver, Colorado, 1887-1896. Partner of George Schoyen. (Sellers-3)

BURGER & SMITH Charleston, South Carolina, 1774. (Kauffman 2)

BURGER, DAVID (?-1804), Charleston, South Carolina, 1775-1804. (Kauffman 2)

BURGES, DAVID Philadelphia, Pennsylvania, 1780-1785. Repaired U.S. Arms. (Moller)

BURGESS GUN CO. Buffalo, New York, 1892-1899. Made Andrew Burgess shotguns. (Maxwell)

BURGESS, A.J. Manchester, Virginia, 1893d.

BURGESS, ANDREW (1837-1908), Buffalo, New York. Patents #119,115 September 19, 1871, magazine gun, #119,218 September 26, 1871, breechloading firearm, #127,737 June 11, 1872, breechloading firearm, #128,208 June 25, 1872, magazine gun, #129,523 July 16, 1872, magazine gun, #134,589 January 7, 1873, magazine gun, #168,966 October 19, 1875, magazine gun, #169,083 October 26, 1875, magazine gun, #210,091 November 19, 1878, magazine gun, #210,181 November 26, 1878, magazine gun, #210,182 November 26, 1878, magazine gun, #210,294 November 26, 1878, magazine gun, #210,295 November 26, 1878, magazine gun, #213,865 April 1, 1879, magazine gun, #213,866 April 1, 1879, magazine gun, #213,867 April 1, 1879, magazine gun, #213,868 April 1, 1879, magazine gun, #213,869 April 1, 1879, magazine gun, #216,080 June 3, 1879, magazine gun, #217,987 July 29, 1879, magazine gun, #222,008 November, 25, 1879, magazine gun, #224,994 March 2, 1880, magazine gun, #235,204 December 7, 1880, magazine gun, #250,825 December 13, 1881, magazine gun with J.M. Marlin, #250,880 December 13, 1881, magazine gun, #251,694 January 3, 1882, magazine gun, #289,972 December 11, 1883, magazine gun, #290,393 December 18, 1883, magazine gun, #290,394 December 18, 1883, magazine gun, #290,529 December 18, 1883, magazine gun, #290,848, December 25, 1883, magazine gun, #290,968, December 25, 1883, #303,262 August 12, 1884, magazine gun, #337,239 March 2, 1886, magazine gun, #340,479 April 20, 1886, magazine gun, #357,458 February 8, 1887, magazine gun, #357,459 February 8, 1887, magazine gun, #357,460 February 8, 1887, magazine gun, #357,461 February 8, 1887, magazine gun, #357,462 February 8, 1887, magazine gun, #357,517 February 8, 1887, magazine gun, #357,518 February 8, 1887, magazine gun, #357,519 February 8, 1887, magazine gun, #366, 558 July 12, 1887, magazine gun, #366,559 July 12, 1887, magazine gun, #366,560 July 12, 1887, magazine gun, #366,561 July 12, 1887, magazine gun, #366,562 July 12, 1887, #366,563 July 12, 1887, #366,564 July 12, 1887, magazine gun, #366,565 July 12, 1887, magazine gun, #373,438 November 22, 1887, magazine gun, #458,333 August 25, 1891, magazine gun, #463,225 November 17, 1891, magazine gun, #476,246 June 7, 1892, magazine gun, #478,220 July 5, 1892, magazine gun, #478,221 July 5, 1892, magazine gun, 478,222 July 5, 1892, magazine gun, #520,752 May 29, 1894, magazine gun, #520,753 May 29, 1894, magazine gun, #557,358 March 31, 1896, magazine gun, #557,359 March 31, 1896, magazine gun, #557,360 March 31, 1896, magazine gun, #589,117 August 31, 1897, automatic gun, #589,118 August 31, 1897, automatic gun, #589,119 August 31, 1897, automatic gun, #589,120 August 31, 1897, automatic gun, #591,525 October 12, 1897, automatic gun, #636,196 October 31, 1899, automatic gun, #663,954 December 18, 1900, automatic gun, #663,955 December 18, 1900, automatic gun, #663,956 December 18, 1900, automatic gun, #666,084 January 15, 1901, automatic gun, #687,448 November 26, 1901, automatic gun, #693,105 February 11, 1902 automatic gun, #693,106 February 11, 1902, automatic gun, #715,971 December 16, 1902, automatic gun, #726,399 April 28, 1903, automatic gun, #821,921 May 29, 1906, automatic gun, #821,922 May 29, 1906, automatic gun, and #821,851 June 5, 1906, automatic gun. Burgess designed guns for Whitney, Marlin, and Colt before forming the Burgess Gun Co. in 1892. He only operated it seven years before selling out to Winchester. (Maxwell)

BURGESS, G.P. Post Huron, Michigan, 1887d-1895d.

BURGESS, HIRAM Mt. Gilead, Tennessee, 1887d-1891d.

BURGESS, HIRAM Whitehall, New York, 1856-1859d.

BURGESS, JONATHAN Champaign, Illinois, 1880d-1890d.

BURGESS, JONATHAN, JR. (1821-?), Staunton, Ohio, 1850c, Leesburg, Ohio, 1859d. (Hutslar)

BURGESS, SAMUEL (1819-?), Staunton, Ohio, 1850-1854. Percussion fullstock. (Hutslar)

BURGESS, SAMUEL Sandyville, Iowa, 1865d.

BURGESS, WILLIAM STARLING Brookline, Massachusetts. Patent #591,155 October 5, 1897, breechloading gun.

BURGET, G. Homerville, Ohio, 1868d. (Hutslar)

BURGET, WASHINGTON (1824-?), Circleville, Ohio, 1850c. Percussion 1/2 stock. (Hutslar)

BURGHART, WILLIAM Lawrence, Massachusetts, 1858-1880d. Patent #19,063 January 12, 1858, breechloading needle gun.

BURGMAN, H. Woodland, Michigan, 1872d-1878.

BURGMAN, HENRY Appleton, Wisconsin, 1889d.

BURGON, L.C. Casey, Illinois, 1875d. See L.C. Burgan.

BURGOYNE, JAMES Helena, Arkansas, 1884d-1885d.

BURGOYNE, JOSEPH R. Memphis, Tennessee, 1876d-1881d.

BURGOYNE, W.J. Memphis, Tennessee, 1891d.

BURGWIN, JOSEPH Belleville, Illinois, 1882d.

BURK, J. Plover, Wisconsin, 1857d.

BURK, W.H. Cincinnati, Ohio, 1894d. (Hutslar)

BURKE, JOHN Courtland, Illinois, 1865-1868. Patents #54,680 May 15, 1866, breechloading firearm, and #55,613 June 19, 1866, breechloading firearm.

BURKE, JOHN Hearne, Texas, 1892d.

BURKE, MICHAEL L. Ilion, New York. Patent #307,175 October 28, 1884, magazine gun.

BURKEBILE, HENRY Palestine, Ohio, 1875. (Hutslar)

BURKETT, ABRAHAM (1862-1943), Punxatawney, Pennsylvania, 1883-1943. Percussion and cartridge guns. (Whisker II)

BURKHARD, J.J. Galena, Illinois, 1868d-1882d. Son of and successor to William R. Burkhard.

BURKHARD, JOHN St. Paul, Minnesota. Patents #288,618 November 20, 1883, breechloading firearm, with P. Novotny and Frank Novotny, and #288,619 November 20, 1883, safety.

BURKHARD, WILLIAM R. Galena, Illinois, 1864d-1867d.

BURKHARD, WILLIAM R. St. Paul, Minnesota, 1856-1898d. Percussion schuetzen rifle.

BURKHARDT, PHILIP, & CO. Baltimore, Maryland, 1870c-1887d. (Hartzler)

BURLINGAME, IRA Woodstock, Vermont, 1840-1872. (Horn)

BURLINGAME, WARREN Alabama, New York, 1859-1882d. Double percussion rifle/ shotgun.

BURLINGTON, JAMES Nashville, Tennessee, 1853d.

BURLINGTON, JOHN Nashville, Tennessee, 1855d-1860d. Percussion fullstock.

BURLY, WILLIAM Washington Co., Pennsylvania, 1854-1855. (Kauffman)

BURMAN, ADAM Lancaster, Ohio, 1820-1903. (Hutslar)

BURMAN, P.H. Van Buren, Ohio, 1868d. (Hutslar)

BURMEN, S. Carol, Ohio, 1831-?, Flaggs Corners, Ohio. Percussion fullstock. (Hutslar)

BURN, J. Eustace, Missouri. Derringer.

BURNET, HENRY (1834-?), Youngstown, Ohio, 1850c. Son of Stephen Burnet. (Hutslar)

BURNET, STEPHEN F. (1805-?), Youngstown, Ohio, 1850c. Percussion 1/2 stock. (Hutslar)

BURNET, WILLIAM (1830-?), Youngstown, Ohio, 1850-1900. Son of Stephen Burnet. (Hutslar)

BURNETT, EDWARD H. (1860-?), Eureka, California, 1882-1895. Brother of Thomas Burnett. (Shelton)

BURNETT, F.L. unlocated. Flintlock Kentucky.

BURNETT, GARLAND Baltimore, Maryland, 1819-1833d. (Hartzler)

BURNETT, GEORGE H. Waukegan, Illinois, 1875d-1893d.

BURNETT, HENRY M. (1854-?), Eureka, California, 1876-1880.

BURNETT, HENRY Greene Co., Pennsylvania, 1817-1830. (Whisker II)

BURNETT, S.F. unlocated. Percussion fullstock rifles, probably Stephen Burnet.

BURNETT, THOMAS (1832-?), Eureka, California, 1866-1895. Patent #250,495 December 6, 1881, breechloading firearm. Brother of Edward Burnett. (Shelton)

BURNETT, WILLIAM Boston, Massachusetts. Patent #34,103 January 7, 1862, rifle stock.

BURNHAM & FORD Duquoin, Illinois, 1867d.

BURNHAM, ELISHA Hartford, Connecticut, 1777-1781. Committee of Safety repairs. (Gluckman & Satterlee)

BURNHAM, FREDERICK I. Saginaw City, Michigan, 1868-1881d, Harrisville, Michigan, 1891d.

BURNHAM, GEORGE Hartford, Connecticut, 1777-1779. Committee of Safety repairs. (Gluckman & Satterlee)

BURNS, HENRY C. (1825-1890), Dayton and Lewisburg, Ohio, 1850-1890. Percussion rifles. (Hutslar)

BURNS, HENRY S. New Haven, Connecticut. Patent #232,238 September 14, 1880, cartridge loader.

BURNS, J.W. Atchison, Kansas, 1894d-1899d.

BURNS, J.W. Cherry Creek, New York. Percussion 1/2 stock. Same as J.W. Burns of Atchison, Kansas?

BURNS, JAMES Philadelphia, Pennsylvania, 1814d-1816d. (Kauffman)

BURNS, JOHN B. Camden, New Jersey. Patent #568,560 September 29, 1896, spring gun.

BURNS, JOHN M. (1832-?), Columbiana Co., Ohio, 1850c. Percussion 1/2 stock. (Hutslar)

BURNS, JOHN (1825-?), Detroit, Michigan, 1850c.

BURNS, JOHN Grafton, Illinois, 1893d.

BURNS, JOSEPH (1820-?), Knox Co., Ohio, 1850c. (Hutslar)

BURNS, O.J. Sidell, Illinois, 1890d-1893d.

BURNS, R.H. Jamestown, New York, 1883d.

BURNS, WILLIAM (1832-?), Jacksonville, Illinois, 1860c. (Johnson)

BURNS, WILLIAM St. Louis, Missouri, 1864d-1866d.

BURNS, WILLIAM Uhrichsville, Ohio, 1870c. (Hutslar)

BURNSIDE RIFLE CO. Providence, Rhode Island, 1860-1866. Successor to Bristol Fire Arms Co., made Burnside and Spencer carbines.

BURNSIDE, AMBROSE E. (1824-1881), Bristol, Rhode Island. Patents #14,491 March 25, 1856, breechloading firearm, and #17,261 May 12, 1857, gas seal. Large quantities of Burnside carbines made during the Civil War.

BURNSTEN, RICHARD Uniontown, Indiana, 1840-1860. (Lindert)

BURNSTON, WILLIAM Bedford Co., Pennsylvania, 1846t. (Dean)

BURR, DAVID J. Atlanta and Macon, Georgia, 1862-1865. Revolvers for the Confederacy. With Edward N. Spiller as Spiller & Burr.

BURRETTE, LOUIS H. (1863-?), Santa Barbara, California, 1890-1896. (Shelton)

BURRIER, THOMAS A. Knoxville, Tennessee, 1876d-1891d.

BURROWS, EDMUND F. Mystic River, Connecticut. Patent #131,845 October 1, 1872, safety.

BURSLEM, FRED Hutchinson, Kansas, 1888d.

BURSON, H.J. Ashland, Oregon, 1886d-1891d.

BURSON, I.L. Dallas, Oregon, 1889d.

BURSON, J.S. Mt. Vernon, and Wabash, Indiana, 1858d-1862d. Percussion 1/2 stock. (Lindert)

BURSON, SETH Stayton, Oregon, 1881d.

BURT, A.M. New York, New York. Model 1861 contract muskets marked "Trenton". (Fuller)

BURT, EDWIN Washington, D.C., 1865d-1875. Patent #160,748 March 16, 1875, breechloading firearm. (Hartzler)

BURT, HENRY Orwell, Vermont, 1876-1879. (Horn)

BURT, I.J. Camden, Arkansas, 1884d.

BURT, JAMES Boston, Massachusetts, 1774. (Dean*)

BURT, JOHN Howard Co., Indiana. (Lindert)

BURT, MILTON Oakland, Illinois, 1860d.

BURTIS, J.H. El Paso, Illinois, 1884d-1888d.

BURTLEY, ROBERT (1806-?), Norwalk, Ohio, 1850c. (Hutslar)

BURTLEY, THEODORE (1831-?), Norwalk, Ohio, 1850c, Sandusky, Ohio, 1859d. Son of Robert. (Hutslar)

BURTON BROTHERS Dallas, Texas, 1878d.

BURTON, BETHEL (?-1904), Brooklyn, New York. Patents #26,475 December 20, 1859, breechloading firearm, #81,056 August 11, 1868, cartridge, #81,057 August 11, 1868, waterproof percussion caps, #81,058 August 11, 1868, cartridge, #81,059 August 11, 1868, breechloading firearm, #92,013 June 29, 1869, breechloading firearm, #136,130 February 25, 1873, cartridge, #143,495 October 7, 1873, bayonet, #143,614 October 14, 1873, breechloading firearm with W.G. Burton, #232,880 October 5, 1880, magazine gun, #390,114 September 25, 1888, magazine gun, #594,853 December 7, 1897, magazine gun, #613,240 November 1, 1898, sight, #613,241 November 1, 1898, bayonet/gun rest, #622,443 April 4, 1899, magazine gun, #640,627 January 2, 1900, magazine gun, #656,807 August 28, 1900, and #785,085 March 21, 1905, automatic gun. Ward-Burton rifles and carbines made at Springfield Armory. See William G. Ward.

BURTON, CHARLES E. (1808-?), Cincinnati, Ohio, 1850c. (Hutslar)

BURTON, CHARLES H. Norwich, Connecticut, 1877d.

BURTON, CLINTON Marneville, Ohio, 1867-1891. (Hutslar)

BURTON, F.A. Elkhorn, Wisconsin, 1895d.

BURTON, ISAAC C. Hokinsville, Ohio, 1857-1865. (Hutslar)

BURTON, J.G. Brownwood, Texas, 1892d.

BURTON, JAMES HENRY (1823-1894), Harpers Ferry, Virginia, 1844-1854. Patent #27,539 March 20, 1860, gun barrels. Burton was in charge of the Richmond Armory and involved in the Spiller & Burr contracts. Went to England after the Civil War. (Albaugh 3)

BURTON, JARRETT (?-1833), Stafford Co., Virginia, 1777-1781, Mason Co., Kentucky, ?-1833. (Gill)

BURTON, JOHN (1840-?), Denver, Colorado, 1870c-1871d. Worked for M.L. Rood. (Sellers-3)

BURTON, JOSEPH Waukon, Iowa, 1889d-1895d.

BURTON, L. Norwalk, Ohio, 1871-1886. (Hutslar)

BURTON, LEMUEL Pigeon, Illinois, 1888d.

BURTON, WINGFIELD G. Brooklyn, New York. Patent #143,614 October 14, 1873, breechloading firearm with Bethel Burton. Operated sales organization for Ward-Burton rifles in New York City.

BUSCH Fred, New Orleans, Louisiana, 1875d.

BUSCH, F.L. Lancaster, Pennsylvania, 1775. Flintlock Kentucky rifle. (Dillin)

BUSCH, LOUIS Lancaster, Pennsylvania, 1776. With brother Michael, Committee of Safety rifles. Sons of F.L. Busch. (Dean)

BUSCH, MICHAEL Lancaster, Pennsylvania, 1776. With brother Louis, Committee of Safety rifles. Sons of F.L. Busch. (Dean)

BUSCH, OSCAR Union, Missouri, 1869d-1898d. Percussion 1/2 stock.

BUSCHICK, E. (1828-?), Ottawa, Illinois, 1850-1852. As Brunker & Buschick. (Johnson)

BUSCHOR, GILBERT Effingham, Illinois, 1882d-1888d.

BUSELMEIER, ANSLOW (1843-?), Quincy, Illinois, 1859, 1867d. Denver, Colorado, 1859d-1864, San Francisco, California, 1865-1866, Healdsburg, California, 1867-1877, Ukiah, California, 1877-1878, Roseburg, Oregon, 1878-?. Percussion 1/2 stock. (Sellers-3, Shelton)

BUSELMEIER, H. Healdsburg, California, 1868. (AAC 10-58)

BUSEY, CHARLES E. Applegate, Oregon, 1889d-1891d.

BUSH, ABIEL P. Youngsville, New York, 1880-1882d.

BUSH, H.E. McPherson, Kansas, 1888d.

BUSHMAN, CHARLES West Chester, Pennsylvania, 1857d.

BUSHMAN, M. West Chester, Pennsylvania, 1868d.

BUSHNELL, DAVID Saybrook, Connecticut. Patent #none February 2, 1776, torpedo.

BUSHONG, JACOB (1754-1818), Point of Forks, Virginia, 1786-1793. Public armory. (Gill)

BUSLER BROS. Jersey Shore, Pennsylvania, 1850-1860. (Whisker III)

BUSLER, JAMES Lycoming Co., Pennsylvania. Flintlock Kentucky rifles. (Dillin)

BUSS, CHARLES Marlborough, New Hampshire. Patent #10,821 April 25, 1854, revolver. Made only about 20 of these revolvers. (Sellers-1)

BUSSE, F. Corpus Cristi, Texas, 1878d.

BUSSE, W. Madera, California, 1893d.

BUSSEY, J.F. Boston, Massachusetts, 1844d-1852d.

BUSWELL unlocated. New England flintlock Kentucky. (Sellers-2)

BUSWELL, JAMES Glens Falls, New York, 1849-1859. Percussion over/under rifle/ shotgun.

BUSWELL, MARTIN L. (1823-1908), Glens Falls, New York, 1849-1874d. Son of James Buswell. Percussion guns. (Swinney)

BUTCHER, F.T. Shelbyville, Missouri, 1860d, Kansas City, Missouri, 1891d.

BUTLAND, S.B. Philadelphia, Pennsylvania, 1882d.

BUTLER & BRANCH Petersburg, Virginia, 1893d.

BUTLER & CO. Chicago, Illinois, 1870-1874.

BUTLER & FIRCKELTON Cherryvale, Kansas, 1884d.

BUTLER & WEBER Chicago, Illinois, 1859d-1862d. Joseph Butler and Matthias Weber.

BUTLER, A.B. Chico, California, 1866-1867d. (Shelton)

BUTLER, EDWARD S. New York. Patent #382,455 May 8, 1888, cartridge feed indicator.

BUTLER, ENOCH Haverhill, Massachusetts, 1857-1861.

BUTLER, H.A. (1820-?), Sacramento, California, 1852. (Shelton)

BUTLER, J.C. unlocated. Flintlock Tennessee rifle.

BUTLER, J.G. Atlanta, Texas, 1878d.

BUTLER, JOHN (1764-1834), King William Co., Virginia, 1780-1784.

BUTLER, JOHN Lancaster, Pennsylvania, 1775-1778. Committee of Safety muskets. (Dillin)

BUTLER, JOSEPH (1830-?), Chicago, Illinois, 1857-1886d. As Butler & Weber Co., 1859-1862.

BUTLER, M.A. Eldorado, Kansas, 1882d-1884d.

BUTLER, MARTIN J. unlocated. Percussion revolving rifle. (Sellers-1)

BUTLER, RICHARD Pittsburgh, Pennsylvania, 1765-1767. Son of Thomas Butler. (Bowers)

BUTLER, SUGDEN & CO. Rocky Hill, Connecticut, 1857-1860. Made William S. Butler's patent pistols.

BUTLER, T.M. Villa Rica, Georgia, 1861.

BUTLER, THOMAS (1720-1791), Lancaster, Pennsylvania, 1754t, Carlisle, Pennsylvania, 1759-1791. (Bowers)

BUTLER, THOMAS Philadelphia, Pennsylvania, 1777-1778. Continental Armorer from December 1777 to April 1778. Son of Thomas Butler of Carlisle. (Bowers)

BUTLER, W.E. Union, Iowa, 1887d.

BUTLER, WALTER E. Haverhill, Massachusetts, 1849-1855. (Lindsay)

BUTLER, WALTER T.B. Houston, Texas, 1889d-1899d.

BUTLER, WILLIAM R. Richmond, Virginia, 1877d.

BUTLER, WILLIAM S. Rocky Hill, Connecticut. Patent #16,571 February 3, 1857, pistol barrel and frame in one piece. Made by Butler, Sugden & Co., and Wm. S. Butler.

BUTLER, WILLIAM Pittsburgh, Pennsylvania, 1766. (Kauffman)

BUTLER, WILLIAM Waukegan, Illinois, 1867d-1874.

BUTNER, EDWARD Bethania, North Carolina, 1815. (Bivins)

BUTNER, FRANCIS A. (1831-?), Bethania, North Carolina, 1850c. Son of Herman Butner. (Bivins)

BUTNER, HERMAN H. (1793-?), Bethania, North Carolina, 1815-1850c. (Bivins)

BUTNER, SAMUEL (1818-?), Bethania, North Carolina, 1850c. (Bivins)

BUTSCHER, JOSEPH Parkesburgh, West Virginia, 1882d-1896d. With his brother Louis as L. Butscher & Bro., 1886.

BUTSCHER, LOUIS Parkersburg, West Virginia, 1888d. With his brother Joseph as L. Butscher & Bro., 1888d. (Whisker IV)

BUTT, DANIEL W. Denver, Colorado, 1884d-1887d. Partner of George Schoyen. (Sellers-3)

BUTT, ISRAEL Corydon, Indiana, 1810-1830. (Lindert)

BUTTERFIELD, BENJAMIN (?-1861), Philadelphia, Pennsylvania, 1831-1861d. Hall sporting rifle with H. Keith (GC-31)

BUTTERFIELD, D. Townsend, Massachusetts, 1870-1879.

BUTTERFIELD, ELON B. Brattleboro, Vermont. Patent #1,106 March 16, 1839, revolving rifle. (Sellers-1)

BUTTERFIELD, JESSE S. Philadelphia, Pennsylvania, 1852d-1865d. Patents #12,124 January 2, 1855, lock and primer, #14,850 May 13, 1856, cartridge opener with Simeon Marshall, #24,372 (mo/day/yr?) revolver, and #? April 30, 1861, breechloading cannon. Son of Benjamin Butterfield. Derringers and revolvers were made with the Butterfield primer.

BUTTERFIELD, JOSEPH B. Philadelphia, Pennsylvania, 1861d-1865d. Son of Jesse Butterfield.

BUTTERFIELD, LEVI Lynn, Massachusetts, 1855-1871d, Townsend, Massachusetts, 1874d-1878d.

BUTTON, NATHAN P. Barclay, Iowa, 1865d.

BUTTS, F.W. Milledgeville, Georgia, 1885d.

BUTZ & SCHIFFER Chicago, Illinois, 1852-1856d.

BUXTON, ALFRED C. (1843-1924), Nashville, Michigan, 1865d-1924. Breechloading over/under rifle/shotgun.

BUYERS, ROBERT Lancaster Co., Pennsylvania 1801t. (Dyke)

BUYSLEY, JOHN Allentown, Pennsylvania, 1850t. (Gabel)

BUZZARD, GEORGE Northampton Co., Pennsylvania, 1820t-1822t. (Gabel)

BUZZARD, J. Scott's Depot, West Virginia, circa 1900. (Whisker IV)

BUZZINI, SALVATORE J. New York, New York. Patents #284,815 September 11, 1883, firearm, and #340,482 April 20, 1886, firearm.

BYC see Bartlett Couch.

BYE, MARTIN Worcester, Massachusetts. Patents #176,003 April 11, 1876, air gun, with Iver Johnson, #176,004 April 11, 1876, air gun with Iver Johnson, #204,438 June 4, 1878, revolver with Iver Johnson, #212,606 February 25, 1879, revolver with Iver Johnson, #253,292 February 7, 1882, revolver with Iver Johnson, #375,799 January 3,1888, revolver, #378,355 February 21, 1888 breechloading firearm, #441,395 November 25, 1890, breechloading firearm, #490,065 January 17, 1893, breechloading firearm with Edward Perry, #495,298 April 11, 1893, safety with Edward Perry, #535,528 March 12, 1895, ejector,

#562,455 June 23, 1896, magazine pistol, #582,776 May 18, 1897, frame, #644,040 February 20, 1900, ejector, #644,402 February 27, 1900, mainspring, #658,314 September 18, 1900, safety, #674,957 May 28, 1901, ejector, #795,816 August 1, 1905, safety, #812,015 February 6, 1906, automatic, #812,016 February 6, 1906, grip, and #818,075 March 17, 1906, revolver. Formed Johnson, Bye & Co. in 1871, sold out to Iver Johnson in 1883, worked for himself until 1900 when he went to work for Harrington & Richardson.

BYERS, FREDERICK (1733-1801), Cumberland Co., Pennsylvania, 1771-1801. (Bowers)

BYERS, GEORGE W. (1866-?), South Bend, Indiana, 1886-1900. (Lindert)

BYERS, JOHN J. Delta, New York, Patents #131,961 September 24, 1872, safety lock, and #128,015 June 8, 1872, lock. Percussion 1/2 stock with internal hammer.

BYERS, N. unlocated. Flintlock Kentucky rifle. (possibly Nicholas Boyer)

BYERS, NOAH T. Washington-on-Brazos, Texas, 1836. Probably confused with Noah Smithwick. (GR 8-59)

BYINGTON, GEORGE S. Salisbury Center, New York, 1870d-1874d.

BYLES, L. unlocated. Flintlock Kentucky.

BYMAN & ELLIS Nashville, Tennessee. Derringer. See Kirkman & Ellis.

BYOR, BERNHARDT Girard, Illinois, 1878d-1886d.

BYRKETT, ABIJAH R. Troy, Ohio. Patent #336,289 February 16, 1886, magazine gun.

BYRKIT & RANDLE Centerville, Iowa, 1880d-1883d.

BYRKIT, ARCHIBALD R. Fairfield, Iowa, 1866d-1880d and 1884d-1897d, Centerville, Iowa 1880d-1883d. Patent #146,651 January 20, 1874, stock swivel. Small quantities of swivel stock over/under rifles were made by Byrkit as well as more normal percussion guns. (GR 6-68)

BYRNE, PATRICK Pittsburgh, Pennsylvania, 1861d-1864d.

BYROM, HENRY (?-1718), Essex Co., Virginia, 1696-1718. (Gill)

BYROM, PETER (?-1719), Essex Co., Virginia, 1696-1719. Brother of Henry Byrom. (Gill)

BYROME, JOHN Culpepper, Virginia. (MB 3-72)

C SECTION

C.B. see Charles Baum.

C.B. unidentified. Converted Tennessee rifle.

C.D. see Christian Derr.

C.D. unidentfied. Percussion fullstock.

C.E.I. see Cornelius Inman.

C.F. see Charles Flowers.

C.G. unidentified. Flintlock Kentucky.

C.H. unidentified. Flintlock Kentucky.

C.K. unIdentified. Percussion 1/2 stock.

C.M. see Charles Meissner.

C.M. unidentified. Flintlock rifle.

C.M.H. unidentified. Percussion 1/2 stock.

C.M.K. see Charles M. Knupp.

C.M.S. see Charles M. Siebert.

C.N. unidentified. Flintlock Kentucky.

C.N.M. unidentified. Percussion fullstock.

C.P. mark of the Commonwealth of Pennsylvania.

C.P.B. see C.P. Brainard.

C.R. Colony of Rhode Island inspector's mark.

C.S. Confederate States of America, also C.S.A.

C.S.A. Confederate States of America, also C.S.

CABLE, WILLIAM Lawrenceville, Pennsylvania, 1847. (Kauffman)

CADE, EPHRAIM D. (1814-?), Sullivan Co., Illinois, 1854-1860. (Johnson)

CADET trade name of Crescent Fire Arms Co. on rifles and revolvers.

CADMAN, ANTHONY Columbus, Georgia, 1861-1881d. Derringer and percussion revolver. (Sellers-1)

CADMAN, GEORGE Dixon, California, 1877-1881d. (Shelton)

CADY, F.R. South Haven, Michigan, 1891d-1899d.

CADY, JOHN New Haven, Connecticut, 1837-1840. (Kauffman)

CADY, N.O. Hudson, Michigan, 1887d-1891d.

CAHOON, C.E. Taunton, Massachusetts, 1885d.

CAIN, PETER see Peter Kane. (Hutslar)

CAINE, JAMES Buena Vista, Ohio, 1850c. Probably James Kane. (Hutslar)

CAIRNS, JAMES Madelia, Minnesota, 1892d.

CAIRNS, THOMAS Clear Lake, Wisconsin, 1888d.

CALBETZER, GEORGE New Berlin, Pennsylvania. Flintlock Kentucky rifles. (Gabel)

CALDERWOOD, HUGH Lawrence Co., Pennsylvania, 1840-1883. (Whisker II)

CALDERWOOD, THOMAS A. Baltimore, Maryland, 1853-1874d. (Hartzler)

CALDERWOOD, WILLIAM (1780-1860), Philadelphia, 1807-1819. Contract flintlock pistols and duelling pistols. (ASAC, see C&W)

CALDERWOOD, WILLIAM Pittsburgh, Pennsylvania, 1819-1846. Percussion fullstock. (Kauffman)

CALDWELL, HOMER M. Springfield, Massachusetts, 1872d, Worcester, Massachusetts, 1881-1910. Patents #246,940 September 13, 1881, revolver, #370,926 October 4, 1887, revolver, #383,701 May 29, 1888, revolver, #395,119 December 25, 1888, revolver, #408,457 August 6, 1889, revolver, #415,444 November 19, 1889, revolver, #419,412 January 14, 1890, revolver, #425,979 April 22, 1890, revolver, #427,833 May 13, 1890, revolver, #453,421 June 2, 1891, revolver, #511,406 December 26, 1893, revolver, #561,963 August 25, 1896, revolver, #644,660 March 6, 1900, safety, #649,809 May 15, 1900, safety. Employed by Harrington & Richardson.

CALDWELL, T.R. Burke Co., North Carolina, 1857. (Bivins)

CALHOUN, W.H. Atchison, Kansas, 1867d.

CALHOUN, W.H. Nashville, Tennessee, 1839-1860, Atchison, Kansas, 1867d. Agent on Philadelphia Deringer.

CALIFORNIA ARMS CO. Eureka, California, 1877-1886, San Francisco, California, 1877-1879. Finch repeating rifle. (Shelton)

CALKINS BROS. Grand Rapids, Michigan, 1872d-1883d. Percussion 1/2 stock.

CALKINS, WILLIAM H. Grand Rapids, Michigan. Patent #614,532 November 22, 1898, air gun with C.A. Lindberg.

CALL, G. unlocated. Flintlock Kentucky.

CALLAGHAN, CORNELIUS Brooklyn, New York. Patent #74,888 February 25, 1868, breechloading firearm.

CALLART unlocated. Harmonica pistol, .22 cal.

CALLENDER, W.L. Clinton, Iowa, 1882d-1897d.

CALLEY, ANDREW Tully, New York, 1870d. (Syracuse directory)

CALLIAN, CHRIS (1851-?), San Bernadino, California, 1878-1888. (Shelton)

CALLOWAY, ZACHARIAH Virginia, 1777. Public repairs. (Gill)

CALVER, GEORGE W.H. Burlington, New Jersey. Patent #103,013 May 17, 1870, revolver.

CALVERT & PARKHURST Washington, D.C., 1867d. (Hartzler)

CALVERT, GEORGE W. Perrysville, Kentucky, 1879d-1884d.

CALVERT, J.O. (1816-1897), Mayhill, Ohio. Percussion fullstock rifle. (Hutslar)

CALVERT, JAMES (?-1890), McKean, Pennsylvania. (Gluckman & Satterlee)

CALVERT, W.H. (?-1909), Beloit, Wisconsin, 1857d-1909. Percussion 1/2 stock. (GC-1)

CALVIN, MARVIN S. see M.S. Colvin.

CAMANT, JOHN M. Wellsburg, Virginia. Percussion 1/2 stock dated 1850.

CAMBELL Cincinnati, Ohio, 1788. (Hutslar)

CAMBRON, S. Boston, Kentucky, 1857-1861.

CAMEL & CO. Troy, New York, 1840. Kentucky rifles. (Gluckman & Satterlee)

CAMERON, A.J. Cobbville, Georgia, 1883d.

CAMERON, E.P. Albany, Missouri, 1889d.

CAMERON, J. Princeton, Kentucky, 1883d.

CAMERON, JOHN Cadiz, Kentucky, 1854d.

CAMERON, S. Scott, Ohio, 1860-1864. (Hutslar)

CAMP, BEN Mt. Pleasant, Pennsylvania. Percussion hunting rifles. (Gluckman & Satterlee)

CAMP, CHAUNCEY W. Hartford, Connecticut. Patent #9,687 July 12, 1853, shot chargers.

CAMP, T.P. Portage, Wisconsin, 1888d-1895d.

CAMP, W.J. Covington, Georgia, 1855-1861.

CAMPBELL & HUGHES unlocated. Percussion fullstock.

CAMPBELL, ABNER C. (1824-1868), Hamilton, Ohio, 1859-1862. Patent #36,709 October 21, 1862, breechloading firearm with Edward Gwyn. Carbines made by Cosmopolitan Arms Co. (Hutslar)

CAMPBELL, B. unlocated. Flintlock Kentucky.

CAMPBELL, CHARLES C. Hallowell, Maine, 1860-1880. (Demeritt)

CAMPBELL, DAVID (1819-?), Ashland City, Ohio, 1850c. (Hutslar)

CAMPBELL, EUGENE Pinckney, Michigan, 1887d-1899d. As Barton & Campbell, 1887-1891.

CAMPBELL, GEORGE W. Belleville, New Jersey. Patent #2,809 November 20, 1847, bullet making.

CAMPBELL, ISAAC Martinsburgh, Pennsylvania, 1887d.

CAMPBELL, JAMES C. New York, New York. Patent #39,032 June 30, 1863, revolver pike. (Frost)

CAMPBELL, JAMES (1805-1856), Middletown, Pennsylvania, 1826-1856. (Dean)

CAMPBELL, JAMES Uniontown, Pennsylvania, 1809-1814, Wheeling, West Virginia, 1817-1833. (C&W)

CAMPBELL, JOSEPHUS (1830-?), Hardin, Illinois, 1860c. (Johnson)

CAMPBELL, R. & A. Baltimore, Maryland. Imported converted pistol.

CAMPBELL, ROBERT Disco, Michigan, 1891d-1899d.

CAMPBELL, ROBERT St. Louis, Missouri, 1864d.

CAMPBELL, SAMUEL Bedford Co., Virginia, 1774-1776. (Gill)

CAMPBELL, STRIKER & CO. New Orleans, Louisiana. Cased percussion duellers, dated 1834.

CAMPBELL, THOMAS Frederick Co., Virginia, 1765. (Gill)

CAMPBELL, THOMAS Lincoln, Illinois. Patent #35,504 January 7, 1862, revolving cannon.

CAMPBELL, TRISTRAM St. Louis, Missouri, 1842-1860d, Denver, Colorado, 1860c. Patent #16,327 January 6, 1857, bullet mold, with Henry B. Poorman. Worked both for himself and Sam Hawken. As Hawken & Campbell, 1854d. (Hanson 2)

CAMPBELL, WILLIAM H. Cincinnati, Ohio, 1856d. (Hutslar)

CAMPBELL, WILLIAM Annapolis, Maryland, 1780. Committee of Safety muskets and flintlock pistols. (Hartzler)

CAMPBELL, WILLIAM Frederick Co., Virginia, 1766-1775. Committee of Safety rifles. (Gill)

CAMPBELL, WILLIAM Mt. Pulaski, Illinois, 1860d.

CAMPER & MONSON South Bend, Indiana, 1870-1871d. (MB 4-54)

CAMPER & STEDMAN South Bend, Indiana. James Camper and his nephew, F.J. Stedman.

CAMPER, JAMES W. (1836-1918), South Bend, Indiana, 1868-1918. (Lindert)

CAMRON, W. Smithville, Tennessee, 1860d.

CANADAY, J.W. Oakland, Oregon, 1881d.

CANADY & ROMINES Marshall, Illinois, 1853. (Johnson)

CANADY, CHARLES Philadelphia, 1820d-1833d.

CANADY, M.N. Marshall, Illinois, 1853. (Johnson)

CANDRAIN, CHRISTIAN Springfield, Massachusetts. Patent #660,361, October 23, 1900, sight guard.

CANFIELD & BRO. Baltimore, Maryland, 1835-1881. Derringers and Allen pepperboxes. As Canfield, Bro. & Co., 1860-1888. (Hartzler)

CANFIELD, W. Pine Run, Michigan, 1863d.

CANNAN, JAMES C. East Saginaw, Michigan, 1872d-1877d, Escanaba, Michigan, 1877-1878.

CANNEY, W. Tuftonboro, New Hampshire, 1871-1879d.

CANNON BREECH trade name of Hopkins & Allen on shotguns.

CANNON, H.T. Florence, Kansas, 1894d.

CANNON, JAMES Mt. Morris, Pennsylvania, 1876d-1890d.

CANNON, P.G. Orangeburg, South Carolina, 1885d-1886d.

CANNON, RICHARD Washington, D.C. Patent #274,269 March 20, 1883, sight.

CANTZMAN, CHARLES (1822-?), Chicago, Illinois, 1860c. (Johnson)

CAPLINGER, LYONS Sinking Springs, Ohio, 1820. (Hutslar)

CAPPER & CO. unlocated. Flintlock lock.

CAPPS, EDWIN M. San Diego, California. Patents #632,098 August 29, 1899, machine gun, and #709,301 September 16, 1902, machine gun.

CAPRON, LYMAN Williamstown, Vermont, 1875. (Horn)

CAPT. JACK suicide special by Hopkins & Allen.

CAPWELL, GEORGE A. Woodbury, Connecticut, 1875-1880.

CAPWELL, JOSEPH T. Woodbury, Connecticut. Patent #14,151 January 27, 1856, shot chargers.

CAPY, A.W. Dallas, Texas. Patent #658,934 October 2, 1900, barrel attachment with Reade Washington.

CARBOTT, J.A. unlocated. Percussion fullstock.

CARD, MILTON E. Cazenovia, New York. Patent #340,273 April 20, 1886, breechloading firearm with W. H. Cruttenden.

CARD, S.W. unlocated. Underhammer pistol.

CARDEN, ARCHIBALD Munfordville, Kentucky, 1820c.

CARDIFF, J. Savannah, Georgia, 1881d.

CARDIFF, JOHN Toledo, Ohio, 1863-1872. (Hutslar)

CARDIS, THOMAS unlocated. Flintlock Kentucky.

CARDONA & COOK New Orleans, Louisiana, 1884d. Louis Cook.

CAREY, A.C. Malden, Massachusetts. Patents #178,233 June 6, 1878, spring air gun, #178,509 June 13, 1876, spring air gun.

CAREY, G.R. Boston, Massachusetts. Patent #184,698 November 28, 1876, spring air gun.

CAREY, H. & W.T. Xenia, Ohio. Percussion fullstock. Hardware dealers. (Hutslar)

CAREY, JOHN (1826-?), Martinsville, Ohio, 1850-1882. (Dean)

CAREY, M. Lexington, Ohio, 1859-1869. (Hutslar)

CAREY, W.T. Xenia, Ohio, 1878d. (Hutslar)

CAREY, WILLIAM, & CO. New York, New York. Percussion shotguns. See William Cary. (Gluckman & Satterlee)

CARGILL, BENJAMIN Goshen, Connecticut, 1770-1800. Committee of Safety muskets, with Elisha Child and Nathan Frink. (Gluckman & Satterlee)

CARLETON, MICHAEL Haverhill, New Hampshire, Grafton, New Hampshire. Patent #none December 22, 1830, underhammer. Guns made by M. Carleton & Co.

CARLINE, WILLIAM Hancock, Michigan, 1879d-1895d. As Kruger & Carline, 1879-1883.

CARLISLE, HENRY (?-1847), Shippensburg, Pennsylvania, 1818-1847. Flintlock and percussion Kentucky rifles. (Bowers)

CARLISLE, JOHN W. Columbia, Missouri, 1879d-1898d.

CARLSON, ANDERS G. Rico, Colorado. Patent #539,470 May 21, 1895, sight. (Sellers-3)

CARLTON & HAGGARD Oxford Mills, Iowa, 1889d.

CARLTON Marlborough, Connecticut, 1750. (Lindsay)

CARLTON, CHARLES C. Portland, Maine, 1823-1834. (Demeritt)

CARLTON, W.E. Salem, Massachusetts, 1884d.

CARLTON, WALES D. Woodstock, Vermont, 1857-1861. (Horn)

CARMAN, D. Quapaw, Missouri, 1879d.

CARMICHAEL, ABRAHAM St. Croix, Indiana, 1881. (Lindert)

CARNAHAN, A. Little Rock, Arkansas, 1826. Percussion fullstock. (Elias)

CARNAHAN, J.C. Creekside, Pennsylvania, 1882d.

CARNES, PHILOM P. Cleveland, Ohio. Patent #206,164 July 23, 1878, sight.

CARNET, GEORGE J. Lowell, Massachusetts. Patents #236,304 January 4, 1881, gun wad, #240,088 April 12, 1881, gun wad.

CARNEY, JAMES N. McAllisterville, Pennsylvania, 1861d.

CARNMAN, D. Aaronsburg, Pennsylvania, 1861d.

CARNS, A. Ayersville, Missouri, 1860d.

CARNS, LEWIS (1816-?), Licking Co., Ohio, 1850c. (Hutslar)

CAROLINA ARMS CO. trade name of Crescent on shotguns for Smith-Wadsworth Hardware Co., Charlotte, North Carolina. Also see Virginia Arms Co. (AR 2-69)

CARPENTER, A.B. Dalston, Illinois, 1878d-1886d. Percussion 1/2 stock.

CARPENTER, F.J. (1822-?), Jamestown, North Carolina, 1850c, West Las Animas, Colorado, 1884d.

CARPENTER, JOHN Lancaster, Pennsylvania, 1771-1790. (Gluckman & Satterlee)

CARPENTER, JOHN Oakford, Michigan, 1863d.

CARPENTER, JOHN Pine Bank, Pennsylvania, 1890d.

CARPENTER, JULIUS Louisville, Kentucky, 1879d.

CARPENTER, L.A. Baldwin, Michigan, 1883d-1891d.

CARPENTER, M.A. Addison, Vermont, 1884-1885. (Horn)

CARPENTER, NICHOLAS J. Louisville, Kentucky, 1868d-1874d.

CARPENTER, NICHOLAS (?-1791). Virginia, 1775-1776, Marietta, Ohio, 1788-1791. Virginia militia repairs. (Gill)

CARPER see Whisker IV for others who may not have been gunsmiths.

CARPER, JOHN Nashville, Tennessee, 1874d.

CARPER, JOSEPH (1802-1880), Cashmere Co., West Virginia, 1825, Raleigh Co., West Virginia, 1849-1880. Percussion 1/2 stock. (Whisker IV)

CARPER, SAMUEL HOUSTON (1853-1923), Grandview, West Virginia, 1874-1923. Percussion guns. (Whisker IV)

CARPER, SAMUEL West Virginia. Percussion 1/2 stock.

CARPS & MILHAIN Philadelphia, Pennsylvania. Lockmakers.

CARR, CHARLES A. (1851-?), San Francisco, California, 1888-1903. With George Washington Shreve, 1889d-1891. (Shelton)

CARR, CHARLES Philadelphia, Pennsylvania, 1855d-1859d.

CARR, D.C. Fowlerville, Michigan, 1887d.

CARR, H. unlocated. Flintlock Kentucky.

CARR, HENRY (1820-?), Phillipstown, Illinois, 1845-1864d. (Johnson)

CARR, HOWARD W. San Francisco, California, 1880-1910. Patents #281,341 July 17, 1883, magazine gun, #368,130 August 9, 1887, magazine gun, #547,189 December 29, 1896, automatic gun, #584,153 June 8, 1897, automatic gun, and #681,439 August 27, 1901, magazine gun. With George Washington Shreve, 1889d-1891, and various other partnerships prior to 1895. As San Francisco Arms Co., 1895-?. (Shelton)

CARR, JAMES J. Auburn, New York, 1887d-1907d.

CARR, JOHN J. Portsmouth, Virginia, 1870-1875. Percussion double 1/2 stock.

CARR, JOHN S. Frankfort, Illinois, 1860d-1864d.

CARR, JOHN Parrish, Illinois, 1860d.

CARR, SAMUEL Newport, Rhode Island, 1733-1739. (Achtermier)

CARR, SAMUEL Philadelphia, Pennsylvania, 1819d.

CARRELL, GEORGE Northampton Co., Pennsylvania, 1828-1835t. (KRA II-3)

CARRELL, LAWRENCE Philadelphia, Pennsylvania, 1786-1790c. (Dean)

CARRIER, ASHBEL J. (1830-?), Hartford, Connecticut, 1870, Trinidad, Colorado, 1875-1882. As Ramage & Carrier, 1875-1879. With Edwin A. Curtis as Carrier & Curtis, 1881-1882. (Sellers-3)

CARRIGAN, W.T. Corsicana, Texas, 1896d.

CARROLL, J.P. New Haven, Kentucky, 1883d, Campbellsville, Kentucky, 1896d.

CARROLL, LAWRENCE Philadelphia, Pennsylvania, 1771-1790. See Lawrence Carrell.

CARROLL, THERON S. Winsted, Connecticut, 1881d.

CARROLL, W. Philadelphia, Pennsylvania. Derringer.

CARRUTH, ADAM Greenville, South Carolina, 1809-1823. Model 1812 contract muskets under Elias Earle's contract. (Hobbies 9-34)

CARRUTHERS, JOHN Savannah, Georgia, 1847

CARSON & BALDWIN Cherryvale, Kansas, 1884d.

CARSON, SILAS Pinckneyville, Illinois, 1860d.

CARSON, WILLIAM Virginia, 1815. Contract rifles for Virginia. (Cromwell)

CARTER, A. Mullett Lake, Michigan, 1879d-1883d.

CARTER, CHARLES Fitchburg, Massachusetts, 1844-1851. Percussion 1/2 stock.

CARTER, EPHRAIM Erroll, New Hampshire, 1876-1880. Percussion 1/2 stock.

CARTER, FRANK C. (?-1830), Concord, New Hampshire. (Gluckman & Satterlee)

CARTER, GARNETT, CO. Chattanooga, Tennessee. Dealers only.

CARTER, GEORGE B. Petersburg, Virginia, 1897d.

CARTER, HENRY (1803-?), Benton Co., Missouri, 1850c. (MB 11-66)

CARTER, HENRY West Jefferson, Ohio, 1862-1865. (Gardner)

CARTER, JAMES F. Benton Co., Missouri, 1850c. (MB 11-66)

CARTER, JOHN R. Greensboro, North Carolina, 1835. (Bivins)

CARTER, THOMAS Salt Lake City, Utah, 1884d.

CARTRELL, A.J. Como, Tennessee, 1860d.

CARTWRIGHT, GEORGE K. Wheeling, West Virginia, 1867d.

CARTWRIGHT, J. Wheeling, West Virginia, 1867d.

CARTWRIGHT, JOHN Attica, Ohio, 1859d, Ottawa, Ohio, 1860-1865. (Hutslar)

CARTWRIGHT, THOMAS Wheeling, West Virginia, 1882d. Dealer.

CARUSO trade name of Hibbard, Spencer, Bartlett & Co. on shotguns by Crescent.

CARUTHERS, GREENUP see Greenup Correthers.

CARUTHERS, JOSEPH Netherland, Texas, 1860d.

CARVER, GEORGE N. Colchester, Connecticut, 1872-1880d.

CARVER, J.L. unlocated. Percussion 1/2 stock.

CARVER, JAMES W. Pawlet, Vermont, 1860-1900. Patents #387,282 August 7, 1888, sight, #388,166 August 21, 1888, sight with George W. Wood, #404,598 June 4, 1889, sight, #404,599, June 4, 1889, sight, #424,640 April 1, 1890, sight, #453,828 June 9, 1891, sight, #460,120 September 22, 1891, rifle barrel, #466,599 January 5, 1892, sight, #649,194 May 8, 1900, sight.

CARY, PATRICK New York, New York, 1852d-1853d.

CARY, TRAVERSE & CO. Thief River Falls, Minnesota, 1898d.

CARY, WILLIAM W. Alton, Illinois, 1851-1858d.

CARY, WILLIAM, & CO. New York, New York. Percussion double shotgun.

CARZER, HENRY Douglas Co., Missouri, 1860c.

CASE, C.G. Thornton, Indiana, 1858d, Greencastle, Indiana, 1860d. Percussion 1/2 stock.

CASE, EDWARD N. Chicago, Illinois. Patents #589,930 September 14, 1897, padlock gun, #607,831 July 26, 1898, padlock gun, #609,212 September 20, 1898, padlock gun, and #611,992 October 4, 1898, padlock gun.

CASE, GEORGE Conesville, New York, 1870d-1882d.

CASE, H. Angola, Indiana, 1860d-1862d.

CASE, I.J. Norwich, New York. Percussion target rifle. (Swinney)

CASE, WILLARD, & CO. New Hartford, Connecticut. Underhammer pistols.

CASEY, D.F. Harrisonville, Ohio, 1890-1896. (Hutlsar)

CASEY, J.J. Locust Grove, Illinois, 1880d-1882d.

CASH, ROBERT W. Hannibal, Missouri, 1879d-1893d. Patent #426,916 April 29, 1890, self cocking gun with D.R. Brace.

CASHMORE, SAMUEL (?-1757), Gloucester, Massachusetts.

CASHWELL, R. Frederick, Maryland, 1814. (Hartzler)

CASKELL, E. Natchez, Mississippi, 1850. (Gluckman & Satterlee)

CASPAR, FREDERICK Plainfield, New Jersey. Patent #255,141 March 21, 1883, spring gun.

CASPARI, CHARLES St. Louis, Missouri, 1866d. (Pourie)

CASPARI, FREDERICK (1804-?), St. Louis, Missouri, 1850c-1866d.

CASPARI, WILLIAM St. Louis, Missouri, 1866d-1909d. Son of Frederick Caspari.

CASPER, JOHN Nashville, Tennessee, 1870-1875.

CASS, MILO M. Utica, New York. Patent #5,814 September 26, 1848, repeating frearm.

CASS, O.D. Denver, Colorado, 1859-1865. Cass was not a gunsmith, but sold 12 revolvers "of his own make" to the U.S. Ordnance Dept. in 1861. (Sellers-3)

CASSELL, GEORGE Van Wert, Ohio, 1888-1890. (Gardner)

CASSELL, JOHN FRANKLIN Clayton, Illinois, 1848-1886. (Johnson)

CASSELL, JOSEPH (1830-?), Richland Co., Ohio, 1850c, Van Wert, Ohio, 1868-1896. As Joseph Cassell & Son, 1879-1883. (Hutslar)

CASSELL, LEE Celina, Ohio, 1883-1891. (Gluckman & Satterlee)

CASSITY & DODD Auburn, Illinois, 1884d.

CASTEEL, C.W. Clarksville, Texas, 1880c. Re-barreled Sharps.

CASTER, MATTHEW Northampton Co., Pennsylvania, 1800t. (KRA II-3)

CASTERLINE, HORACE Elmira, New York, 1871-1880d.

CASTERLINE, ISAAC Elmira, New York, 1866-1884d.

CASTERLINE, MORRIS A. Elmira, New York, 1885d-1891d. Isaac was listed as manager in 1891.

CASTLE Berlin Crossroad, Ohio, 1890c. Negro gunsmith. (Hutslar)

CASTLE, HORACE A. Ilion, New York. Patents #144,190 November 4, 1873, breechloading firearm, #182,557 September 26, 1876, breechloading firearm.

CASTLE, J.S. Quincy, Illinois, 1880d.

CASTLE, W.D. Ashtabula, Ohio, 1878-1891. (Hutslar)

CASTOR, HENRY (1790-?), Pulaski Co., Illinois, 1850c. (Johnson)

CASTRO, P. Coulterville, California, 1878-1881. (Shelton)

CASWELL & DODGE Lansingburgh, New York, 1806-1807. Model 1798 pattern muskets (no contract found). (Gluckman)

CASWELL & GAYLORD Milwaukee, Wisconsin, 1858. (WGCA 4)

CASWELL & WAGGONER Lansingburgh, New York. Percussion fullstock. H.A. Caswell.

CASWELL, ASA L. Lansingburgh, New York. Patent #25,806 October 18, 1859, gun carriage. Son of John Caswell.

CASWELL, ELI E. (1795-?), Albany, New York, 1837d-1843d, Lansingburgh, New York, 1859d. Percussion fullstock rifle with O.H. Herbert in Albany and H.A. Caswell in Lansingburgh.

CASWELL, H.A. & E.E. Lansingburgh, New York, 1857-1859. Percussion 1/2 stock.

CASWELL, HIRAM A. Lansingburgh, New York, 1843d-1859d. With E.E. Caswell, 1857-1859.

CASWELL, J.M. Lansingburgh, New York. There is some disagreement over which of the Caswells used the "J.M." signature, James or John. Both were gunsmiths. Most authorities use John as the most likely as he produced large numbers of guns according to the 1850 census.

CASWELL, J.M., & SON Lansingburgh, New York.

CASWELL, JAMES Lansingburgh, New York. Late flintlock period. (MB 6-68)

CASWELL, JEDEDIAH Manlius, New York, 1822-1828. Patent #none May 8, 1828, percussion lock. Over/under rifle and underhammer pistols.

CASWELL, JOHN M. Lansingburgh, New York, 1812-1850. Model 1808 contract muskets marked "JMC". Son of Thomas Caswell. (Dean)

CASWELL, JOHN M., JR. Lansingburgh, New York, 1850-1851. Percussion 1/2 stock target. (Clow)

CASWELL, JOHN Albany, New York, 1815. (Kauffman 2)

CASWELL, NELSON Manlius, New York, 1850c-1881d. Son of Jedediah Caswell. (Swinney)

CASWELL, THOMAS (?-1836), Lansingburgh, New York, 1812-1836. Model 1808 muskets and Model 1814 rifles on state contracts. (Gluckman)

CATELY, ANDREW Tully, New York, 1855-1868d.

CATHEY, RICHARD Rowan Co., North Carolina, 1791. (Bivins)

CATLAND, THOMAS R. Lewiston, Maine, 1880. (Demeritt)

CATLIN, ROBERT MAYO Tuscarora, Nevada. Patents #454,993 June 30, 1891, magazine gun, and #574,350 December 29, 1896, magazine gun. Both used by San Francisco Arms Co.

CATLIN, WILLIS Bay City, Michigan, 1883d-1887d. As Russell & Catlin.

CATON, C. Ohio. Percussion targer rifle. (Hutslar)

CATON, JAMES Boston, Massachusetts, 1850-1860. Importer, percussion shotguns and rifles.

CATTANA, ALBERT New Orleans, Louisiana, 1889d-1899d.

CATTEY, EDWARD Baltimore, Maryland, 1847d. (Hartzler)

CAULKING, A.F. Cleveland, Ohio, 1857d. (Hutslar)

CAUP, LEVI West Buffalo, Pennsylvania. Flintlock Kentucky rifles. (Dillin)

CAVE, CHRISTOPHER Philadelphia, Pennsylvania, 1776-1799. (Kauffman)

CAVENY, J. Newton, Kansas, 1878d.

CAWTHON, J. unlocated. Percussion fullstock.

CAYWOOD, SAMUEL Farmington, Illinois, 1886d-1893d.

CEBRIAN, ENCARNACION (1833-?), Santa Clara Co., California, 1852c. (Shelton)

CEDERBRAND, JOHN (1816-?), Pontiac, Illinois, 1860d-1874d, Streator, Illinois 1880d-1886d.

CELLAR, THOMAS C. Franklin Co., Pennsylvania. Flintlock rifles and muskets. (Dean) (Sellers)

CENTENNIAL 1876, suicide special by Hood Fire Arms Co.

CENTENNIAL 1876 trade name of Deringer Pistol Co. on revolvers.

CENTER, JOSEPH H. Boston, Massachusetts, 1826. Rufus Porter's revolving rifle. (Sellers-1)

CENTRAL ARMS CO. St. Louis, Missouri. Trade name of Davenport Fire Arms Co. on shotguns for Shapleigh Hardware Co. (AG 4-75)

CENTURY ARMS CO. St. Louis, Missouri. Trade name of Shapleigh Hardware on shotguns.

CERWENKA, M. Milwaukee, Wisconsin. Percussion pepperbox. (Logan)

CH.D. see Christian Duerr.

CHABOT, CYPRIEN Philadelphia, Pennsylvania. Patents #47,163 April 4, 1865, breechloading gun, #49,718 September 5, 1865, breechloading gun.

CHACE & BROWN Warren, Rhode Island, 1854-1856d.

CHACON, PAUL Baltimore, Maryland, 1817d.

CHADD, GEORGE W.M. (1822-1888), Stockton, California, 1870-1888. (Shelton)

CHADDOCK, J. Brownsville, Nebraska, 1879d.

CHADWICK & CRIGLER Monroe City, Missouri, 1889d.

CHADWICK, WILLIAM (1797-?), Terre Haute, Indiana, 1850c.

CHAFFEE, NOAH Athen, Pennsylvania. Patent #542,407 July 9, 1895, alarm gun.

CHAFFEE, REUBEN SHIPLEY Springfield, Massachusetts. Patents #161,480 March 30, 1875, magazine gun, #211,887 February 4, 1879, magazine gun, #216,657 February 25, 1879, magazine gun, #314,363 March 24, 1885, magazine gun, #314,515 March 24, 1885, magazine gun, #342,338 May 25, 1886, magazine gun, and #368,933 August 30, 1887, magazine gun. 1,000 Chaffee-Reece rifles made at Springfield Armory in 1884.

CHAFFIN, R. unlocated. Percussion target rifle dated 1842.

CHAIN, BILL Scottsdale, Pennsylvania, percussion period. (Gluckman & Satterlee)

CHALLENGE suicide special.

CHALLENGE trade name on shotguns by Meriden.

CHAMBER BROS. Pniladelphia, Pennsylvania, 1862-1863. Converted flintlock muskets to percussion.

CHAMBERLAIN & TAPP Louisville, Kentucky, 1857-1860d.

CHAMBERLAIN, DEXTER H. Boston, Massachusetts, 1832-1858. Patents #none August 17, 1835, harpoon, #168 April 17, 1837, breechloading firearms with Elijah Fisher, #7,300 April 23, 1850, pepperbox, and #7,360 May 14, 1850, pepperbox. Rifles under 1837 patent made by C.B. Allen.

CHAMBERLAIN, E. Southbridge, Massachusetts, 1850. Underhammer pistol. (Logan)

CHAMBERLAIN, HIRAM M. Springfield, Massachusetts. Patent #60,998 January 8, 1867, breechloading firearm with Martin Chamberlain.

CHAMBERLAIN, JOHN (1815-?), Monterey, California, 1867-1879. (Shelton)

CHAMBERLAIN, JOSEPH Albany, New York, 1815. (Kauffman)

CHAMBERLAIN, LYMAN B. Ellisburgh, New York, 1866d-1890d.

CHAMBERLAIN, MARTIN J. Springfield, Massachusetts. Patents #60,998 January 8, 1867, breechloading firearm with H.M. Chamberlain, #111,814 February 14, 1871, breechloading firearm with Dexter Smith, #112,505 March 7, 1871, breechloading firearm with Dexter Smith, #129,393 July 16, 1872, breechloading firearm, and #135,405 February 4, 1873, breechloading firearm.

CHAMBERLAIN, WILLIAM T. Norwich, Connecticut. Patents #229,868 July 13, 1880, air gun, #279,538 June 19, 1883, air gun, and #279,540 June 19, 1883, air gun.

CHAMBERLIN & FARNAN Cleveland, Ohio, 1860c. While listed as gunsmith this firm actually made gunpowder. (Hutslar)

CHAMBERLIN, E. New York, New York, 1862. Brand patent carbines. (GR 1-78)

CHAMBERS, BENJAMIN Washington, D.C. Patents #6,423 April 21, 1849, lock, and #6,612 July 31, 1849, breechloading firearm.

CHAMBERS, E.L. Milan, Tennessee, 1885d.

CHAMBERS, JAMES (1738-1763), Lancaster, Pennsylvania, ?-1763. (Dyke)

CHAMBERS, JOSEPH C. West Middleton, Pennsylvania, 1810-1815. Patent #none March 23, 1813, repeating gun. The Chambers guns worked on the "Roman Candle" principle. Also see Belton. (AR 9-58)

CHAMBERS, JOSIAH Philadelphia, Pennsylvania, 1780-1785. Repaired US arms. (Moller)

CHAMBERS, WILLIAM Washington, D.C., 1862d. (Hartzler)

CHAMNESS, ANTHONY (1838-1935), Elwood, Indiana, 1858-1935. (Lindert)

CHAMNESS, CLINTON Elwood, Indiana. Father of Anthony Chamness. (MB 3-44)

CHAMP, EDWIN Red Oak, Iowa, 1889d-1897d.

CHAMPE, R.E. Nashville, Tennessee, 1891d.

CHAMPION suicide special by Norwich Arms Co.

CHAMPION trade name of H.C. Squires on shotguns, 1877. (Hinman)

CHAMPION trade name of Iver Johnson on suicide specials, air guns, and shotguns. (Hinman)

CHAMPION trade name of J.P. Lovell on shotguns, 1883. (Hinman)

CHAMPION, J.H. Pittsburg, Kansas, 1894d.

CHAMPIROUX, AUGUST New Orleans, Louisiana, 1841d-1842d.

CHAMUSS, M. Alexandria, Indiana, 1860d.

CHANDLER, ELISHA Samantha, Ohio, 1849, Howard Co., Indiana, 1850c. (Lindert, Hutslar)

CHANDLER, F.L. Hamburg, Iowa, 1887d.

CHANDLER, GEORGE W. Ayer, Massachusetts, 1888d-1890d.

CHANDLER, GEORGE W. Manhatton, Kansas. Patents #631,951 August 29, 1899, revolver, and #632,235 September 5, 1899, magazine gun.

CHANDLER, J. unlocated. Fullstock Kentucky rifle.

CHANDLER, JAMES New Ipswich, New Hampshire, 1869-1875d. Percussion fullstock.

CHANDLER, STEPHEN Hartford, Connecticut, 1770-1776. Committee of Safety muskets. (Gluckman & Satterlee)

CHANEY Levine, Kentucky, U.S. Army (?),1840-1860. (Hist. KY, V3, P259)

CHANNEL, AARON (1821-?), Utica, Ohio, 1851-1860. (Hutslar)

CHAPIN, A.H. Earlville, New York, 1845-1874d. Percussion 1/2 stock. (Swinney)

CHAPIN, C.J. St. Louis, Missouri. Double-barrel hammer shotgun.

CHAPIN, DWIGHT & CO. see Dwight, Chapin & Co.

CHAPIN, ETHAN S. Stafford Springs, Connecticut. Patent #816 July 17, 1837, lock.

CHAPIN, HENRY A. Bridgeport, Connecticut, 1860-1867d. Ballard rifles as Dwight, Chapin & Co. Later became superintendent of New Haven Arms Co.

CHAPIN, JOHN Windsorville, Connecticut, 1740. (Dean*)

CHAPIN, LINUS N. New Lisbon, New York. Patent #42,748 May 17, 1864, breechloading firearm.

CHAPIN, LUTHER Philadelphia, Pennsylvania, 1847d. (Kauffman)

CHAPIN, LYMAN Rochester, New York, 1834d. (Eich)

CHAPMAN & HERDER Green Bay, Wisconsin, 1872d.

CHAPMAN, ALFRED J. Schenectady, New York, 1857-1867d. Percussion fowler.

CHAPMAN, C. unlocated. Derringer, percussion revolver, and Confederate rifles.

CHAPMAN, C.M. unlocated. Percussion over/under rifle/shotgun.

CHAPMAN, DANIEL P. Ionia, Michigan, 1863d-1867d.

CHAPMAN, E.F. Eugene, Oregon, 1878d.

CHAPMAN, G. & J. Philadelphia, Pennsylvania. Early cartridge revolver.

CHAPMAN, GEORGE (1825-?), Galena, Illinois, 1850c. (Johnson)

CHAPMAN, HERBERT W. Newark, New Jersey. Patent #190,820 May 15, 1877, breechloading firearm. Harpoon guns under this patent.

CHAPMAN, J. Schnectady, New York, 1862-1865. See Alfred J. Chapman.

CHAPMAN, JAMES Bucks Co., Pennsylvania, 1770-1776. Committee of Safety muskets.

CHAPMAN, JOHN Amelia, Virginia, 1781-?.

CHAPMAN, JOSIAH Frederickstown, Maryland. Committee of Safety muskets.

CHAPMAN, THOMAS (1834-?), Peru, Indiana, 1860c. (Lindert)

CHAPMAN, W.D., & SON Rochester, New York, 1888d-1893d. Percussion duelling pistol. (Swinney)

CHAPMAN, W.J. Rutland, Vermont, 1898. (Horn)

CHAPMAN, WARD Grand Forks, Dakota Territory, 1882d.

CHAPMAN, WILLARD Saranac, Michigan, 1860d-1867d.

CHAPPLE, THOMAS New York, New York. Percussion fullstock. (Swinney)

CHARLES, A. Canisteo, New York, 1872-1874d.

CHARLES, H.J. Canisteo, New York, 1880-1882d.

CHARLOTTESVILLE RIFLE WORKS Charlottesville, North Carolina, 1740-1777. Committee of Safety muskets.

CHARLUT, F. Dallas, Texas, 1878d.

CHARNLEY, W.J. Helena, Arkansas, 1884d.

CHARPE, P.F. unlocated. Percussion fullstock marked "TENN".

CHARPIE, A.B. Helena, Montana Territory, 1888d., Kingman, Kansas 1894d. Converted Sharps Rifle.

CHARPIE, FREDERICK P. (1815-?), Mt. Vernon, Ohio, 1850c-1858. Patents #9,934, August 16, 1853, lock, #18,387, October 13, 1857, trigger. Percussion 1/2 stock and underhammer pistol. (Hutslar)

CHARRIER, JACQUES Baltimore, Maryland, 1812-1824d. (Hartzler)

CHARRIER, JAMES Baltimore, Maryland, 1816-1818. (Hartzler)

CHARRIER, JOHN Baltimore, Maryland, 1822-1836d. As J. & P. Charrier, 1831-1836. (Hartzler)

CHARRIER, P. & I. Baltimore, Maryland, 1831-1835. Percussion 1/2 stock, (MB 4-63)

CHARRIER, PETER Baltimore, Maryland, 1831d-1845d. As J. & P. Charrier, 1831-1836 and Cleaveland & Charrier, 1845. (Hartzler)

CHASE, A.C. Baltimore, Maryland, 1889d. (Hartzler)

CHASE, A.S. Seabrook, New Hampshire, 1868d.

CHASE, ABRAM Wolcott, New York, 1867d-1882d. (Swinney)

CHASE, ANSON Enfield, Massachusetts, 1820-1830, Hartford, Connecticut, 1830-1834, New London, Connecticut, 1834-1877d. Worked on prototype Colt revolvers. (Sutherland)

CHASE, CALEB J. Newcomb, New York, 1860c-1870d. Percussion guns. (Swinney)

CHASE, CARLISLE (1815-?), Pleasant Vale, Illinois, 1850-1860d.

CHASE, CHARLES Cherry Creek, New York, 1870d.

CHASE, HENRY G. Burlington, Vermont, 1870-1900. Percussion 1/2 stock. (Horn)

CHASE, HORACE Worcester, Massachusetts. Converted Southerner pistols.

CHASE, J. unlocated. Fullstock underhammer pistol.

CHASE, JACOB J. Newburyport, Massachusetts, 1869-1876d. Percussion pistols. As Dyer & Chase, 1873.

CHASE, TIMOTHY (?-1875), Belfast, Maine, 1854-1875. (Dillin)

CHASE, WILLIAM S. Pandora, Ohio, 1854-1891. Percussion guns. (Hutslar)

CHASTAIN, ROBERT Freetown, Indiana, 1868-1896. (MB 4-55)

CHATELET, HENRY Newton, Kansas, 1882d-1894d.

CHATENS, CHARLES Baltimore, Maryland, 1810. (Gluckman & Satterlee)

CHATHAM ARMS CO. trade name on shotgun.

CHATTAWAY, JAMES Springfield, Massachusetts. Patents #15,063 June 10, 1856 and #15,370 July 22, 1856, tape priming.

CHATTERTON, C. Milwaukie, Oregon, 1871d.

CHAUDFOSSE, GUSTAVUS Omaha, Nebraska, 1875d.

CHEDESTER, JOSEPH New Madrid, Missouri, 1879d.

CHEEK, J.B. Mineola, Texas, 1890d.

CHEELEY, SAMUEL Thief River Falls, Minnesota, 1898d.

CHEENEY, WILLIAM Pike, New York, 1874d.

CHEEVER & BURGHARD CUTLERY CO. St. Louis, Missouri, 1880-1881d. Single barrel shotgun and suicide special by T.J. Ryan.

CHENERLY, O.S.C. Jamestown, Dakota Territory, 1886d.

CHENEY, ELISHA see Simeon North.

CHENEY, FRANK Winamac, Indiana, 1882-1885. (Gardner)

CHENEY, H.H. Holly, Michigan, 1863d, Saginaw, Michigan, 1867d-1873d.

CHERINGTON, A. unlocated, 1847. Percussion rifle.

CHERIX, DAVID New York, New York, 1860d. Percussion schuetzen.

CHEROKEE ARMS CO. trade name of Crescent on shotguns made for C.M. McClung & Co., Knoxville, Tennessee. (AR 2-69)

CHERRINGTON, THOMAS P. Jr., Catawissa, Pennsylvania, 1815-1858, Rochester, New York, 1859d, Ashland, Pennsylvania, 1861d. Successor to his father, worked for Billinghurst and later made revolving rifles. (Gluckman & Satterlee)

CHERRINGTON, THOMAS P. Sr., Cattawissa, Pennsylvania, 1790-1815. Flintlock Kentucky rifles and pistols.

CHERRINGTON, WILLIAM Missemer's Mills, Pennsylvania, 1861d. Barrelmaker.

CHERRY, JOHN Westmoreland Co., Pennsylvania, 1802-1813. See also John Sherry. (Kauffman)

CHERRY, MOSES Frederick Co., Virginia. Apprenticed to Thomas Campbell.

CHESAPEAKE GUN CO. trade name of Crescent on shotguns. (AR 2-69)

CHESEBROUGH & CO. Ithaca, New York, 1857-1861. Door jamb guns made under patent of David Coon.

CHEVALIER, AUGUSTA (1806-?), LaGrange, California, 1856, Mokelumme Hill, California, 1860c. (Shelton)

CHEYNEY, CHARLES Birmingham, Pennsylvania, 1839.

CHEYNEY, FRANK Winnimac, Indiana, 1885. (Lindert)

CHICAGO ARMS CO. Chicago, Illinois, 1883d-1893d.

CHICAGO FIRE ARMS CO. Chicago, Illinois, 1880-1884, "Creedmore" suicide special.

CHICAGO FIRE ARMS CO. Chicago, Illinois, 1892-1897. Distributors of Chicago palm or "Protector" pistols made by Ames Sword Co. Trademark registered on May 29, 1894. (GR 10-66, 1-67)

CHICAGO GUN & CUTLERY CO. Chicago, Illinois, 1884d-1895d. Sales only.

CHICAGO LEDGER suicide special by Chicago Firearms Co.

CHICAGO LONG RANGE WONDER trade name of Sears, Roebuck & Co. on shotguns by Crescent.

CHICAGO REPEATING FIREARMS CO. Chicago, Illinois, 1883-1885. Chaffee Reese rifles and A.E. Whittemore shotguns. Not to be confused with Chicago Fire Arms Co. of the same period.

CHICAGO trade name of Hibbard, Spencer, Bartlett, & Co. on air rifles and shotguns.

CHICHESTER RIFLE CO. see Lewis S. Chichester.

CHICHESTER trade name on taxidermy gun made by various companies for Chichester Rifle Co.

CHICHESTER, GEORGE New York, New York, 1887d-1888d.

CHICHESTER, LEWIS S. Jersey City, New Jersey, 1878-1890. Patent #310,283 January 6, 1885, air gun. Made by Chichester Rifle Co. which also distributed taxidermy guns.

CHICK, BROWN & CO. La Junta, Colorado, 1872-1875, Granada, Colorado, 1875, El Moro, Colorado, 1876-1885. As Brown & Manzenaris, 1879-1885. (Sellers-3)

CHICOPEE ARMS CO. trade name used by H. & D. Folsom Arms Co.

CHICOPEE FALLS MFG. CO. Chicopee Falls, Massachusetts, 1828-1841. Flintlock muskets and Jenks carbines. Became Ames Mfg. Co. (GR 7-64)

CHIDESTER, M. Judsonia, Arkansas, 1888d-1898d.

CHIEFTAIN suicide special.

CHILCOTE, J.A. Dry Run, Pennsylvania. Percussion rifle.

CHILCOTT, WILLIAM S. Houstontown, Pennsylvania, 1887d. Percussion rifles.

CHILD, ALONZO Lowell, Massachusetts, St. Louis, Missouri, 1838-1863, Pittsburgh, Pennsylvania, 1863-1865. Percussion 1/2 stock marked "CHILD' only. As A. Child & Co. 1838-1847, Child, Farr & Co., 1847-1850, Child & Pratt 1850-1863, and Child Pratt & Co., 1863-1865. (MB 9-67)

CHILD, ELISHA Goshen, Connecticut, 1770-1780. Committee of Safety muskets with Benjamin Cargell and Nathan Frink. (Gluckman)

CHILD, FARR & CO. St. Louis, Missouri, 1847-1850d. Hardware dealers.

CHILD, J.C. Rochester, New York, 1847d-1850d.

CHILD, PRATT & CO. Pittsburgh, Pennsylvania. Lockmakers only.

CHILD, PRATT & CO. St. Louis, Missouri, 1850-1863d. Percussion 1/2 stock, sales only.

CHILDERS, M. unlocated. Percussion 1/2 stock.

CHILDRESS, H. unlocated. Percussion 1/2 stock.

CHILDS, EDWARD Conway, Massachusetts. Patent #707 April 24, 1838, revolver with Rufus Nichols. Pistols and rifles under this patent made by Nichols & Childs. (Sellers-1)

CHILLINGWORTH, FELIX Providence, Rhode Island. Patents #125,720 April 16, 1872, bayonet with Ira Merrill, #151,238 May 26, 1874, bayonet with Henry Metcalfe, and #170,988 December 14, 1875, safety. Chillingworth bayonets made at Springfield Armory. (AG 9-74)

CHINN, FRANK Ravenden Springs, Arkansas, 1898d.

CHIPMAN, DARIUS (1758-1820). Rutland, Vermont, 1798-1816, New York, New York, 1816-1820. Model 1798 contract muskets with Royal Crafts, Thomas Hooker, and John Smith. (Gluckman)

CHIPMAN, SAMUEL Vergennes, Vermont, 1789-1804. Model 1798 muskets with Thomas Towsey. (Gluckman)

CHISHOLM, ARCHIBALD Annapolis, Maryland, 1776-1781. Committee of Safety muskets with John Shaw, 1776-1777. (Hartzler)

CHISHOLM, JAMES C. Savannah, Georgia, 1879d-1885d.

CHISLER, NICHOLAS Morgantown, Virginia, 1811. Contract rifles for Virginia under contract of James Laidley. (Cromwell)

CHISM, ELISHA Albion, Illinois, 1886d.

CHISMORE, ALBERT Oswagatchie, New York, 1850c, Ogdensburgh, New York, 1850c-1882d. (Swinney)

CHISMORE, HENRY Rockford, Illinois, 1859d.

CHITTENDEN, EBENEZER (?-1783), Hartford, Connecticut, 1776-1783. Committee of Safety muskets and repairs. (Gluckman & Satterlee)

CHITTLE, FREDERICK Buffalo, New York, 1832. (Gluckman & Satterlee)

CHITTUM, W.H. Paris, Texas, 1896d.

CHOATE, NATHANIEL W. Auburn, New York, 1856d-1880d. High quality percussion guns.

CHORD, DANIEL (1830-?), St. Joseph Co., Indiana, 1850c, St. Helena, California, 1866-1875, Ukiah, California, 1880. (Lindert, Shelton)

CHOTARD, HENRY (1787-?), Natchez, Mississippi, 1860d.

CHRIST, ALBERT California, Ohio. Patent #57,864 September 11, 1866, double-barrel eighteen-shot revolver.

CHRIST, D. Lancaster, Pennsylvania. Flintlock Kentucky rifles. (Gluckman & Satterlee)

CHRIST, D. Reading, Pennsylvania. Barrels only. (Kindig)

CHRIST, I. see Jacob Christ.

CHRIST, JACOB Graceham, Maryland, 1803-185. Flintlock Kentucky rifles marked I. Christ. (Bowers)

CHRISTENSON, CHRISTIAN Wilimar, Minnesota, 1882d-1898d.

CHRISTIAN, J.B. Mt. Carroll, Illinois, 1875d-1878d.

CHRISTIAN, W.J. Bryan, Texas, 1896d.

CHRISTIAN, W.T. Lynn, Massachusetts, 1886d-1889d.

CHRISTIE, ANDREW (1798-?), Wyandot Co., Ohio, 1850c. (Hutslar)

CHRISTMAN, JACOB Clark, Pennsylvania, 1880d-1890d. Percussion target rifle.

CHRISTMAN, T.F. Raleigh, North Carolina, 1860. (Bivins)

CHRISTOPHER, J. (1817-?), Washington, D.C., 1845-1850c. (Hartzler)

CHRISTY, WILLIAM J. Philadelphia, Pennsylvania. Patent #58,064 September 18, 1866, pepperbox.

CHURCH, FRANK Denver, Colorado, 1875-1889, New York, New York, 1894. With C. Gove & Co., 1875-1884, and Church & Bostwick, 1884-1889. (Sellers-3)

CHURCH, J. unlocated. Flintlock Kentucky.

CHURCH, LOUIS J. Tecumseh, Michigan, 1863d-1878, St. Joseph, Michigan, 1879d-1891d. Percussion double rifle.

CHURCH, RANDALL Bath, Maine, 1867-1872. (Demeritt)

CHURCH, WILLIAM H. Norwich, New York, 1847-1851. Percussion 1/2 stock. (Clow)

CHURCHILL, BELA Buckfield, Maine, 1820s-1860. (Demeritt).

CHURCHILL, JOSIAH Belle Plaine, Minnesota, 1864-1866. Percussion 1/2 stock. (Gluckman & Satterlee)

CHURCHILL, OTIS Albany, New York, 1839-1860d. Percussion rifles, underhammer pistol.

CILLEY, GEORGE W. Norwich, Connecticut. Patents #215,721 May 27, 1879, revolver, #254,798 March 14, 1882, revolver, #263,684 September 5, 1882, lock, #270,204 January 9, 1883, revolver, #336,894 March 2, 1886, revolver, #339,149 April 6, 1886, revolver, #350,346 October 5, 1886, revolver, and #450,448 April 14, 1891, barrel.

CISKUY, CHARLES Chicago, Illinois, 1873d.

CISSNA, JOSEPH Rockport, Indiana. (Lindert)

CLABROUGH & GOLCHER San Francisco, California, 1883-1905. (Shelton)

CLABROUGH, JOHN P. St. Louis, Missouri, 1860d, San Francisco, California, 1863-1896. As Clabrough & Bros., 1870-1883, including John P., Joseph, and George Claybrough. William Golcher bought a 50% interest in 1883 and it became Clabrough & Golcher. (Shelton)

CLAFLIN, CHARLES C. Verndale, Minnesota, 1886d-1892d.

CLAFLIN, GEORGE W. New York, New York, 1889d-1890d.

CLAGGETT, ALEXANDER (1744-1821), Hagerstown, Maryland, 1778-1817. Model 1798 contract muskets. (Hartzler)

CLALLCH, H.M. Pennsylvania. Flintlock and percussion rifles. (Dillin)

CLAMBALL, EUGENE (1842-?), Freeport, Illinois, 1860c. (Johnson)

CLANTON, A.J. & T.O. Panola, Mississippi. Confederate patent #111 October 3, 1862, breechloading firearm. (Albaugh 1)

CLAPHAM & Co. Point of Rocks, Virginia, 1739-1777. Committee of Safety rifles and muskets. Josiah Clapham. (Gluckman & Satterlee)

CLAPP, GATES & CO. Whitsett, North Carolina, 1862-1865. Rifles and muskets for Confederacy. (Hill-Anthony)

CLARE, R.S. Ithaca, New York. Percussion 1/2 stock. See R. Clark.

CLARK & BLYMYER unlocated. Locks.

CLARK & EDGERLY Biddeford, Maine, 1880. Charles B. Clark, and Samuel Edgerly. (Demeritt)

CLARK & HORNE Waldens Ridge, Tennessee. Flintlock Tennessee rifle. (ASAC 21)

CLARK & LAMB Deep River, North Carolina, 1861-1865. Arms for the Confederacy. Firm continued by Anderson Lamb until 1877. (Bivins)

CLARK & RANKIN unlocated. Barrelmakers.

CLARK & SNEIDER Baltimore, Maryland, 1873-1884. Duncan C. Clark and Charles E. Sneider. Breechloading guns.

CLARK, A. Utica, New York. Percussion over/under rifle/shotgun with Robert Roberts.

CLARK, A.B. Whiterock Prairie, Missouri, 1860d.

CLARK, A.B. Wilmington, Vermont, 1875d.

CLARK, A.S. Dallas, Texas, 1866d-1867d. Advertised as "Formerly with Clark, Sherrard & Co.".

CLARK, ALBERT Fitchburg, Michigan, 1863d-1865d, Blissfield, Michigan, 1875d, Hastings, Michigan, 1879d-1883d, Bay City, Michigan, 1899d.

CLARK, ALVAN Montpelier, Vermont, 1832-1838, Cambridge, Massachusetts, 1839-1841, Boston, Massachusetts, 1841-1848. Patent #1,565 April 24, 1840, false muzzle. Made rifles using his muzzle and licensed others to use it. (Horn)

CLARK, ANDREW Detroit, Michigan, 1817. Flintlock Kentucky rifles. (Dillin)

CLARK, BARNES (1812-1892), Clarksdale, Missouri, 1836-1882. Percussion 1/2 stock, percussion double rifle/shotgun. (MB 10-62)

CLARK, BENJAMIN Waukesha, Wisconsin, 1875d-1879d.

CLARK, C.C. San Angelo, Texas, 1892d-1896d.

CLARK, C.L. unlocated. Percussion 1/2 stock.

CLARK, CARLOS C. (1809-?), Windsor, Vermont, 1832-1865, Nashua, New Hampshire, 1865d-1868, Manchester, New Hampshire, 1868d-1889d. Flintlock, percussion, and cartridge guns.

CLARK, CHARLES B. Biddeford, Maine, 1868-circa 1880. (Demeritt)

CLARK, CHARLES D. unlocated. Flintlock Kentucky rifles.

CLARK, D. Vernon, Michigan, 1860d. Converted fullstock rifles.

CLARK, D.E. Omro, Wisconsin, 1888d-1895d.

CLARK, DANIEL Philadelphia, Pennsylvania, 1823d-1856d. Derringer.

CLARK, DANIEL Rochester, New York, 1867-1868. (Eich)

CLARK, DUNCAN C. see Clark & Sneider.

CLARK, E. New York, New York. Percussion 1/2 stock rifle and shotgun. (Clow)

CLARK, EDWARD Flint, Michigan, 1860d-1883d. Percussion guns.

CLARK, EZRA Hartford, Connecticut, 1850c. Employed nineteen men making rifles.

CLARK, F.H., & CO. Memphis, Tennessee. Agent on Deringer.

CLARK, FRANCES Pennsylvania Committee of Safety muskets. (Hobbies 4-38)

CLARK, FRANCIS North Oxford, Massachusetts, 1860-1864, Auburn, Massachusetts, 1865-1867. Patents #43,571 July 19, 1864, breechloading firearm, #45,701 January 3, 1865, breechloading firearm, and #53,522 March 27, 1866, breechloading firearm.

CLARK, FRANCIS Philadelphia, Pennsylvania, 1862d-1863d. As Quinn and Clark.

CLARK, FRANK Augusta, Maine, 1894-1900. (Demeritt)

CLARK, H.L. Delavan, Wisconsin, 1884d-1888d.

CLARK, HENRY F. Poughkeepsie, New York. Patents #286,387 October 9, 1883, bullet, #319,068 June 2, 1885, sight, and #328,005 October 13, 1885, breechloading firearms.

CLARK, HIRAM (1793-?), Allegany Co., Maryland, 1850c. Percussion fullstock. (Bowers)

CLARK, HIRAM (1820-?), Florida, Ohio, 1850c-1866. Percussion fullstock. (Hutslar)

CLARK, HYDE & CO. Charleston, South Carolina, 1854d. Importer and dealer.

CLARK, I. JONES Philadelphia, Pennsylvania, 1879d-1881d. Son-in-law of Henry Deringer, operated Deringer Rifle & Pistol Works.

CLARK, I. Lebanon, Ohio. Very fancy silver inlaid fullstock rifle sold at Sotheby's, Sussex, England for $32,000.00, October 1986.

CLARK, J.J. Elgin, Illinois. Percussion underhammer rifle.

CLARK, J.W. Engleman, Texas 1896d.

CLARK, J.W. Iola, Kansas, 1878d-1882d.

CLARK, J.W. Tunkhannock, Pennsylvania. Three-barrel percussion rifle.

CLARK, JAMES H. Tecumseh, Michigan, 1879d-1895d.

CLARK, JAMES Bedford Co., Pennsylvania, 1804-1821. Flintlock Kentucky. (Hetrick)

CLARK, JAMES Bedford Co., Pennsylvania, 1877d.

CLARK, JAMES Cincinnati, Ohio, 1807-1831. (Knittle)

CLARK, JAY Licking Co., Ohio, 1850-1930. Percussion 1/2 stock. (Hutslar)

CLARK, JOHN G. Augusta, Georgia. Patents #24,177 May 24, 1859, alarm gun, and #24,349 June 7, 1859, alarm pistol.

CLARK, JOHN (1789-?), Canton, Ohio, 1821-1850c, West Brookfield, Ohio, 1853d. Patents #none May 17, 1832, button rifling, and #none May 17, 1832, magazine gun with Joseph Plummer. (Hutslar)

CLARK, JOHN Marshall, Michigan, 1853-1860, for M.L. Rood, 1853-1857.

CLARK, JOHN Newport, Rhode Island, 1764. (Achtermier)

CLARK, JOHN Reading, Pennsylvania, 1804, Shippensburg, Pennsylvania, 1811-1817. (Kindig)

CLARK, JOHN Sidney, Ohio, 1872d. (Hutslar)

CLARK, JONATHAN (1856-?), Gunnison, Colorado, 1880c.

CLARK, JOSEPH ANDRE Detroit, Michigan, 1814.

CLARK, JOSEPH Danbury, Connecticut, 1798-1801. Model 1798 contract muskets. (Gluckman)

CLARK, L. Lodi, Ohio. Percussion 1/2 stock. (MB 6-58)

CLARK, L. unlocated. Flintlock Kentucky.

CLARK, LORENZO (1809-?), Alabama, New York, 1848-1867d. Percussion 1/2 stock. (Swinney)

CLARK, LYMAN Council Bluffs, Iowa, 1889d.

CLARK, M.O. St. Louis, Missouri. Percussion pistol.

CLARK, M.S. (1832-?), Napoleon, Indiana, 1860c. Brother of Walter Clark. (Lindert)

CLARK, MARTIN (1801-?), Elyria, Ohio, 1850-1860. (Hutslar)

CLARK, MILTON Delaware, Indiana, 1860d.

CLARK, N. unlocated. Southern fullstock rifle.

CLARK, NELSON (1801-1859), Miamisburg, Ohio, 1825-1859. Percussion 1/2 stock. (Hutslar)

CLARK, PETER Pennsylvania, 1777. Committee of Safety rifles. (C&W)

CLARK, PHILO, & SON Hartford, Connecticut, 1876d.

CLARK, R. Albany, New York. Percussion 1/2 stock. (Clow)

CLARK, RICHARD Salinas, California, 1877-1878. (Shelton)

CLARK, S. unlocated. Percussion fullstock.

CLARK, S.D., & SONS Ottawa, Kansas, 1882d.

CLARK, SAMUEL E. Philadelphia, Pennsylvania. Patent #288,548 November 13, 1883, spring gun.

CLARK, SHERRARD & CO. Lancaster, Texas, 1865. Colt Dragoon copies after the Civil War. Successors to Tucker, Sherrard & Co. (GR 11-62)

CLARK, T. Philadelphia, Pennsylvania. Patent #176,367 April 18, 1876, safety with Adolph Skerl.

CLARK, W.N. Cleburne, Texas, 1884d.

CLARK, W.W. Raleigh, North Carolina, 1855. (Bivins)

CLARK, WALTER A. New Milford, Connecticut, 1876-1880.

CLARK, WALTER (1825-?), Napoleon, Indiana, 1860. Brother of M.S. Clark. (Lindert)

CLARK, WARREN M. Waverly, New York. Patent #198,080 December 11, 1877, breechloading firearms.

CLARK, WIDDIFIELD & CO. Cincinnati, Ohio, 1883-1888. (Hutslar)

CLARK, WILLIAM A. Bethafly, Connecticut. Patent #34,944 April 15, 1862, bullet mold.

CLARK, WILLIAM B. Haverhill, New Hampshire, 1878-1886.

CLARK, WILLIAM H. Denver, Colorado, 1880c-1904d. (Sellers-3)

CLARK, WILLIAM Philadelphia, Pennsylvania, 1783-1790. (Kauffman 2)

CLARKE, GEORGE Jamestown, Virginia, 1623. (Gill)

CLARKE, JOHN Columbia, Pennsylvania. Flintlock Kentucky rifle.

CLARKE, JOSEPH DANIEL Rochester, New York, 1869d. (Eich)

CLARKE, N. Columbia, Pennsylvania, 1830-1869.

CLARKE, THOMAS H. Lafayette, Indiana, 1850-1860. Percussion 1/2 stock. (Lindert)

CLARY, A. Dimple, Missouri, 1898d.

CLASPILL, GEORGE W. (1802-?), Lancaster, Ohio, 1831-1853. (Hutslar)

CLASS, DANIEL Berks Co., Pennsylvania, 1850c. Barrelmaker. Probably Daniel Glass.

CLASS, JAMES Monticello, Illinois, 1868. (Johnson)

CLAUDE, E. New York, New York. Patent #22,348 December 21, 1858, revolver.

CLAUS, DANIEL Lancaster, Pennsylvania, 1875d.

CLAUSE, DANIEL Berks Co., Pennsylvania, 1850c-1855d(?). (C&W)

CLAUSE, GEORGE Bedford Co., Pennsylvania, 1850-1855. Also spelled Clouse. (Kauffman)

CLAUSE, HENRY Bedford Co., Pennsylvania, 1850c. (Kauffman)

CLAUSE, HENRY Lehigh Co., Pennsylvania, 1821t. (KRA II-3)

CLAUSE, NATHAN unlocated. Flintlock Kentucky rifle.

CLAUSSEN, J.H. Wilson, Kansas, 1888d.

CLAW, R.H. Thomas Fork, Idaho, 1891d.

CLAY, EDWARD C. Newton, Massachusetts. Patent #105,057 July 5, 1870, breechloading firearms with Alfred B. Ely.

CLAY, LEE Gunnison, Colorado, 1899d-1914. (Sellers-3)

CLAYTON, EVANS unlocated. Percussion over/under rifle/shotgun.

CLAYTON, JOHN Lancaster, Pennsylvania, 1779. Furnished 100 rifle locks to the Continental Armory. (Moller)

CLEAVELAND & CHARRIER Baltimore, Maryland, 1845d. George W. Cleaveland and Peter Charrier. (Hartzler)

CLEAVELAND, WILLIAM M. Spring, Georgia, 1861. Confederate gunsmith convention.

CLEAVES, CHARLES J. Biddeford, Maine, 1880-1889. (Demeritt)

CLEELAND, W.M. Great Falls, Montana, 1892d.

CLEFF, HENRY R. Lexington, Missouri, 1850c. (MB 11-66)

CLEGG, A.W. & E.P. Galveston, Texas, 1870d. Percussion fullstock. Hardware dealers in 1870 directory. (T3)

CLEGG, W.B. Cisco, Texas, 1890d.

CLEMENT ARMS CO. see John B. Clement.

CLEMENT, BURTON H. Chester, Wisconsin. Patent #572,290 December 1, 1896, breechloading firearm.

CLEMENT, CHARLES H. Northville, Michigan. Patent #434,862 August 19, 1890, air gun.

CLEMENT, JOHN B. Cincinnati, Ohio, 1887-1900. Imported shotguns marked "J. B. Clement" and "Clement Arms Co.". With Palemon Powell as Powell & Clement, 1887-1900. (Hutslar)

CLEMENT, SURGY New Orleans, Louisiana, 1841d.

CLEMENT, W.H. Monclava, Ohio, 1860-1864. Percussion fullstock. (Hutslar)

CLEMENT, WILLIAM T. Greenfield, Massachusetts, 1836-1865d, Northhampton, Massachusetts, 1866-1878. Percussion rifles and pistols. Model 1863 contract muskets for Massachusetts Militia marked "S.N. & W.T.C. MASS." with Samuel Norris as Norris & Clement, Springfield, Massachusetts, 1862-1865. As Clement & Hawkes Mfg. Co. in Northhampton. (ASAC 44, Carey)

CLEMENTS & PATEY Virginia, 1776. Committee of Safety repairs. (Gill)

CLEMENTS, JOHN W. Soddy, Tennessee. Son of John Clements, used signature "J.W.C." on percussion guns.

CLEMENTS, JOHN Soddy, Tennessee. Percussion era.

CLEMENTS, NATHAN S. Worcester, Massachusetts, 1848-1865. Patents #14,949 May 27, 1856, breechloading firearm, #44,127 September 6, 1864, breechloading firearm with Frederick Townsend, and #50,334 October 10, 1865, breechloading firearm.

CLEMONS, WILLIAM H. Hiram, Maine, 1868-1873.

CLENNEY, JOHN (1830-?), Baltimore, Maryland, 1850c. Apprenticed to A. McComas. (Hartzler)

CLERK, WILLIAM Philadelphia, Pennsylvania, 1780-1782. Continental Armory. (Moller)

CLEVELAND, S.R. Milwaukee, Wisconsin, 1867d.

CLEVELAND, W.H. Norwalk, Ohio, 1875-1897. As W.H. Cleveland & Son, 1888-1897. (Hutslar)

CLEVELAND, WILLIAM Trenton, Michigan, 1863d-1867d.

CLEVER, P.J. Brunswick, Missouri, 1879d-1898d.

CLEVERLY, ASA Randolph, Vermont, 1880-1888. (Horn)

CLEWELL, JACOB Hanover, Northampton Co., Pennsylvania, 1799-1802t. (KRA II-3)

CLEWELL, JESSE Bustleton, Pennsylvania, 1861d.

CLEWELL, PHILIP Bushkill, Pennsylvania, 1820-1835t. (KRA II-3)

CLEWELL, WILLIAM Bushkill, Pennsylvania, 1814t-1835t. Flintlock locks. (KRA II-3)

CLEWFLIN, W. unlocated. Flintlock Kentucky rifle.

CLEWS, WILLIAMS Ilion, New York. Patent #136,134 February 25, 1873, revolver.

CLICK, SAMUEL Kendrick's Creek, Pennsylvania, 1887d.

CLIFFORD, WILLIAM Ligonier, Pennsylvania. Percussion fullstock. (AR 11-28)

CLINE, C. Lancaster, Pennsylvania. Flintlock Kentucky rifles and flintlock military pistol.

CLINE, JACOB Saltsburg, Pennsylvania, 1861d. Percussion fullstock.

CLINES, JOHN St. Louis, Missouri, 1860d.

CLING Spring Run, Pennsylvania. (Gluckman & Satterlee)

CLINGER, REUBEN (1833-?), Napa Co., California, 1871-1875. (Shelton)

CLIPPER suicide special. (Webster)

CLIPPINGER, JOSEPH LEONARD (1852-1929), New Franklin, Ohio. (Hutslar)

CLIPPINGER, JOSEPH (1800-?), Franklin Co., Pennsylvania, 1821t-1830t, New Carlisle, Ohio, 1846-1880. (Hutslar-Bowers)

CLIVE, ALBERT A. (1870-1919), Ilion, New York, 1898-1901. Patents #472,251 April 5, 1892, magazine gun, and #592,196 October 19, 1897, breechloading gun. Guns made by Remington, but carry only Clive's name. (Perkins)

CLONCH, WILLIAM unlocated. 1/2 stock.

CLOSON, CHARLES Baton Rouge, Louisiana, 1850c. (MB 9-65)

CLOSSMAN, ISAAC N. Zanesville, Ohio, 1885-1900. (Hutslar)

CLOSSON, CHARLES Philadelphia, Pennsylvania, 1829d.

CLOUGH, CYRUS Concord, New Hampshire, 1889d.

CLOUGH, JEFFERSON M. Belchertown, Massachusetts. Patents #294,481 March 4, 1884, magazine gun, #337,247 March 2, 1886, gun barrel machine, and #833,872 October 23, 1906, magazine gun.

CLOUS, CHRISTIAN Northampton Co., Pennsylvania, 1795-1807t. (KRA II-3)

CLOUSE, GEORGE (?-1897), Bedford, Pennsylvania, 1840-1875. Brother of Henry Clouse. (Whisker)

CLOUSE, HENRY VALENTINE Bedford, Pennsylvania, 1850c. Percussion fullstock marked "H.V.C.". (Whisker)

CLOUSE, VALENTINE FELTUS (1850-1936), Bedford Co., Pennsylvania, 1875-1936. Son of George Clouse. Signed "V.F.C.", on percussion fullstock. (Whisker)

CLOYD, W.S. McKinney, Texas, 1878d-1884d.

CLOYES, B.F. Jacksonville, Tennessee, 1860d.

CLUTZ, C. Millwood, Ohio, Massilon, Ohio, 1858-1866. Percussion 1/2 stock.

CLUTZ, JOSIAH (1831-?), Millwood, Ohio, 1850c, Massilon, Ohio, 1858-1886. Percussion 2 stock. (Hutslar)

COALMAN, B. unlocated. Percussion 2 stock.

COATS, J.A. Richland Center, Wisconsin, 1895d.

COATS, JAMES Philadelphia, Pennsylvania, 1810-1814d.

COBB, AMOS E. Norwich, Connecticut, 1880d. Pistols.

COBB, EBENEZER Providence, Rhode Island, 1850. (Achtermier)

COBB, HENRY Norwich, Connecticut, 1796-1801. Model 1798 contract muskets with his brother Nathan. (Gluckman)

COBB, J. Johnstown, Wisconsin, 1857d.

COBB, JOHN Taunton, Massachusetts, 1775. (Kauffman 2)

COBB, LYMAN South Portland, Maine, Fitchburg, Massachusetts. Patents #629,770 August 1, 1899, breechloading firearm, #782,827 February 21, 1905, breechloading firearm, #999,209 August 1, 1911, revolvers, and #1,046,268 December 3, 1912, revolvers. Shotguns under the first patent made by Lovell Arms Co., Portland, Maine, balance by H & R. (Demeritt).

COBB, NATHAN Norwich, Connecticut, 1799-1801. Model 1798 contract muskets with his brother Henry. (Gluckman)

COBBS, SAMUEL Williamsburg, Virginia, 1726. (Gill)

COBLE, JACOB South West, Indiana, 1881-1885. (Gardner)

COBURN, BENJAMIN Lancaster Co., Pennsylvania, 1816t. (Dyke)

COBURN, E.W. Waterloo, Iowa, 1887d-1895d.

COCHENNOUR, JOHN S. Olney, Illinois, 1874. (Johnson)

COCHENS, H. Easton, Pennsylvania, 1880d.

COCHRAN BROS. Chico, California, 1881d. R.L. & C.J. Cochran. (Shelton)

COCHRAN, C.J. Chico, California, 1881d. As Cochran Bros. (Shelton)

COCHRAN, CHARLES Worthington, West Virginia, 1830-1870. (Whisker II)

COCHRAN, FREDERICK G. St. Louis, Missouri. Patent #116,559 July 4, 1871, revolver.

COCHRAN, GEORGE P. Fulton, Tennessee, 1876d.

COCHRAN, GEORGE T. (1821-?), Troy, Illinois, 1850c, Galena, Illinois, 1850c, Sullivan, Indiana, 1854-?, Evansville, Indiana, 1863d. (Lindert, Johnson)

COCHRAN, I. unlocated. Percussion double rifle.

COCHRAN, JAMES (1822-?), Galena, Illinois, 1850c. (Johnson)

COCHRAN, JOHN WEBSTER (1814-1874), New York. Patents #none October 22, 1834, revolving cannon, #180 April 28, 1837, turret gun, #183 April 28, 1837, turret gun, #1,649 April 30, 1840, rocket staffs, #22,412 December 12, 1858, revolver, #25,951 November 1, 1859, projectile, #26,016 November 8, 1859, projectile, #26,017 November 8, 1859, projectile, #26,256 November 29, 1859, breechloading firearm, #26,337 December 6, 1859, projectile, #27,428 March 13, 1860, cartridge, #30,123 September 25, 1860, projectile, #37,275 January 6, 1863, explosive shell, #37,675 February 7, 1863, explosive shell, #39,120

July 7, 1863, breechloading firearm, #40,553 November 10, 1863, revolver, #40,992 December 22, 1863, breechloading firearm, #47,088 April 4, 1865, breechloading firearm, #47,396 April 25, 1865, breechloading firearm, #52,679 February 20, 1866, breechloading firearm, #63,217 March 26, 1867, breechloading firearm, #75,627 March 17, 1868, breechloading firearm, #85,645 January 5, 1869, breechloading firearm, #126,446 May 7, 1872, breechloading firearm, #127,308 May 18, 1872, cartridge, #153,748 August 4, 1874, breechloading firearm, #157,793 December 15, 1874, cartridge, and #184,145 November 7, 1876, revolver. Cochran's turret guns made by C.B. Allen were the only ones produced in quantity. Cartridge carbines made by Whitney.

COCHRAN, JOHN (1834-?), Terre Haute, Indiana, 1860c, Sacramento, California, 1870-1889. Percussion 1/2 stock. (Lindert, Shelton)

COCHRAN, LANDON (1795-?), Brownsville, Pennsylvania, 1825, Vigo Co., Indiana, 1850c. Flintlock Kentucky pistol. (Lindert)

COCHRAN, R.L. Chico, California, 1881d. As Cochran Bros. (Shelton)

COCHRAN, ROBERT Philadelphia, Pennsylvania, 1814-1833. (Kauffman)

COCHRAN, SAMUEL Connellsville, Pennsylvania, 1834-1835. (Whisker II)

COCHRAN, WILLIAM (1790-1884), Worthington, West Virginia, 1830-1870. (Whisker II)

COCK ROBIN suicide special by Hood.

COCK, JAMES Piqua, Ohio, 1841-1846, Burlington, Iowa, 1850c. Percussion 1/2 stock. (Hutslar)

COCKBURN, J. New Orleans, Louisiana, 1841d-1843d.

COCKBURN, L.E. New Orleans, Louisiana, 1841d-1845d.

COCKCROFT, A.B. Lake de Funiak, Florida 1883d-1886d.

COCKE, SANFORD B. (1822-?), Richmond, Virginia, 1850c. Percussion shotguns. (MB 10-63)

COCKERAL, G.W. unlocated. Percussion 1/2 stock.

COCKLER, P. Lewisburg, Pennsylvania. Percussion over/under rifle/shotgun.

COCKLIN, NICHOLAS New York, New York, 1834-1843. See Nicholas Concklin. (Swinney)

COCKS, C.C. Ft. Worth, Texas, 1892d-1896d.

COCKS, WILLIAM Virginia, 1778. Committee of Safety repairs. (Gill).

COCLARE, SAMUEL McMinnville, Oregon, 1891d.

COE, J. unlocated. Pill lock fullstock rifle.

COFER, THOMAS W. Portsmouth, Virginia, 1861-1862, Norfolk, Virginia, 1862-1880d. Confederate patent #9 August 12, 1861, revolver. Brass frame percussion revolvers under his Confederate patent and other percussion guns. (Albaugh 3)

COFFERS, AUGUSTUS Lancaster, Pennsylvania, 1848d-1857d.

COFFIN, JOSEPH W. Providence, Rhode Island. Patent #302,893 August 5, 1884, lock with J. Maloney. Treasurer of Davenport Arms Co., which used this patent.

COGGIN, C. unlocated. Percussion 1/2 stock.

COGSHALL, CALEB Little Black, Missouri, 1879d.

COGSWELL, SMITH Troy, New York, 1800, Albany, New York, 1813-1820. Model 1808 contract muskets for New York, Model 1814 contract rifles for New York. (Gluckman)

COHN, J. see Marston & Cohn.

COIT, J.A. Marshall, Texas, 1878d-1885d.

COLBEE, A. Windsor, Vermont. Percussion underhammer rifle.

COLBURN, A.E. Pueblo, Colorado, 1890d. (Sellers-3)

COLBURN, BENJAMIN Lancaster, Pennsylvania, 1816t. (Dyke)

COLBURN, DAVID G. Port Byron, New York, 1832, Canton, New York, 1833. Patents #none October 25, 1832, revolver, and #7620X June 29, 1833, revolving rifle. (Sellers-1)

COLBY, CYRUS D. St. Peter, Minnesota, 1864-1869, Denver, Colorado, 1879-1901. As Frazier & Colby, 1864-1865.

COLBY, JOHN N. New London, Connecticut. Patent #341,884 May 18, 1886, air gun.

COLDREIN, JONATHAN Fayette Co., Pennsylvania, 1822-1837.

COLDREN, SAMUEL Lancaster, Pennsylvania, 1838-1857d. Gun barrels. (Dyke)

COLDWELL, J.W. Reading, Michigan, 1863d.

COLE, B. Indiana. Flintlock Kentucky. (Lindert)

COLE, C.O. Charles City, Iowa, 1875d, Grandview, Iowa, 1882d. Cartridge rifles and shotguns. (Kelver)

COLE, C.W. unlocated. Percussion 1/2 stock.

COLE, DAVID S. (1836-?), Columbus Junction, Iowa, 1882d-1884d, Wapello, Iowa, 1884d. Patents #289,070 November 27, 1883, breechloading firearm, and #291,153 January 1, 1884, breechloading firearm. Single shot dropping block rifles. (Kelver)

COLE, HENRY North Brownsville, Michigan, 1863d-1867d.

COLE, J.J. Rockford, Illinois, 1884d-1893d.

COLE, JOHN S. (1851-?), South Fork, California, 1879-1880. (Shelton)

COLE, OTIS F. Norwich, Connecticut. Patent #171,506 December 28, 1875, revolver extractor.

COLE, WILLIAM Caledonia, Missouri, 1854d-1860d.

COLE, WILLIAM. Detroit, Michigan, 1870d-1875d. As Hagadorn & Cole.

COLEMAN, BARTLEY B. (1825-?), McConnelsville, Ohio, 1850-1860. (Hutslar)

COLEMAN, CHARLES C. (?-1865), Worcester, Massachusetts, 1860-1865. Patents #35,217 May 20, 1862, breechloading firearm, and #59,500 November 6, 1866, breechloading firearm.

COLEMAN, HENRY Boston, Massachusetts, 1847d. Converted 1816 North pistol.

COLEMAN, J.P. Carrollton, Georgia, 1861. Confederate gunsmith convention.

COLEMAN, WILLIAM Deer Lodge, Montana, 1876-1878, Butte, Montana, 1878-1886.

COLES, B. unlocated. Percussion fullstock dated 1845.

COLES, JOHN K. (1803-?), Brooklyn, New York, 1837d-1872d. (Swinney)

COLKMAN & DUKE Cahaba, Alabama. Agents for Deringer.

COLLEY, J. unlocated. Flintlock Kentucky.

COLLIER, ELISHA HAYDON Boston, Massachusetts, 1810-1819. Collier patented Artemus Wheeler's revolver in England and had small quantities made there.

COLLINS & PETTY Omaha, Nebraska, 1876-1883d.

COLLINS, J.G. Garden City, Kansas, 1894d.

COLLINS, JAMES Henderson, Illinois, 1864d.

COLLINS, JOHN H. Creston, Ohio, 1888d. (Hutslar)

COLLINS, LINDSEY unlocated. Percussion fullstock.

COLLINS, ROBERT Netherland, Tennessee, 1860d.

COLLINS, W.R. Colorado Springs, Colorado, 1883d. (Sellers-3)

COLLINS, WILLIAM (1821), Portland, Oregon, 1852d, Olympia, Washington, 1853d, Crescent City, California, 1860-1867. (Shelton)

COLLINS, WILLIAM Beech Creek, West Virginia, 1882d. (Whisker II)

COLLMAN, JOHN Freeport, Illinois, 1857-1860d, Cedar Falls, Iowa, 1866-1889d. Percussion 1/2 stock.

COLLUM, DAVID Youngstown, Pennsylvania (?), 1832-1840. (Whisker II)

COLLYER, BENJAMIN Easton, Kansas, 1866-1867d.

COLMAN, H. Boston, Massachusetts, 1849d.

COLMAN, JOHN M. Philadelphia, Pennsylvania, 1847. Agent for Bacon. (Logan)

COLONEY, MYRON New Haven, Connecticut. Patents #213,976 April 8, 1879, spring gun, #225,462 March 16, 1880, machine gun, #225,466 March 16, 1880, machine gun, #231,65, August 31, 1880, magazine gun, #231,653 August 31, 1880, machine gun, #282,499 August 7, 1883, magazine gun, #282,548 August 7, 1883, machine gun, and #282,549 August 7, 1883, machine gun. The last two patents were with James H. McLean and all assigned to McLean. (McLean)

COLONGIN Charleston, South Carolina, 1819-1822. (Kauffman)

COLORADO ARMORY see George Freund.

COLQUITH, JOSEPH JR. Richmond, Virginia, 1870-1876. (Gardner)

COLSON, DWIGHT H. Eaton, New York, 1875d-1878d. Underhammer pistol. (Swinney)

COLT PATENT FIRE ARMS MFG. CO. Hartford, Connecticut, 1848-date. Colt patent revolvers and other guns.

COLT, SAMUEL (1814-1862), Hartford, Connecticut, 1848-1862. Patents #9530X February 25, 1836, revolver, #1,304 August 29, 1839, revolver, #7,613 September 3, 1850, revolver, #7,629 September 10, 1850, revolver, #14,905 May 20, 1856, revolver, #16,683 February 24, 1857, revolver, #16,716 March 3, 1857, lubricator, #18,678 November 24, 1857, revolver, #20,144 May 4, 1858, revolver, #22,626 January 18, 1859, stock, #22,627 January 18, 1859, stock, and #23,230 March 15, 1859, packing cartridges. (Sutherland)

COLTON & SNOW Hartford, Connecticut, 1832-1835. (Mass. Arms)

COLTON ARMS CO. trade name used by Shapleigh Hardware Co., St. Louis, Missouri on imported guns.

COLTON FIREARMS CO. Toledo, Ohio, 1894-1897. double-barrel shotgun. (Hutslar)

COLTON, DANIEL (1830-?), Russell, New York, 1862d-1882d.

COLTON, E.B. Poynette, Wisconsin, 1895d.

COLTON, FRANCIS Hartford, Connecticut, 1832-1833, Glastonbury, Connecticut, 1840-1856, Meriden, Connecticut, 1833, Marlboro, Connecticut, 1834-1836, Middletown, Connecticut, 1836-1840. As Colton & Snow in Hartford, Connecticut. (Sellers-1).

COLTON, WILLIAM M. Leonminster, Massachusetts, 1850. (Lindsay)

COLTRIN, WILLIAM H. Neosho, Missouri, 1889d.

COLUMBIA ARMORY Columbia, South Carolina. Made a few guns for the Confederacy. (Gluckman & Satterlee)

COLUMBIA suicide special.

COLUMBIA trade name of Henry Squires on imported shotguns. (Hinman)

COLUMBIAN FIRE ARMS MFG. CO. Philadelphia, Pennsylvania 1896d. Owlhead revolvers. Successors to, and used trade name of, Foehl & Weeks.

COLUMBIAN FIREARMS CO. trade name of Crescent on double shotgun.

COLUMBIAN FIREARMS CO. trade name of Maltby, Henley & Co. on owlhead revolvers.

COLUMBIAN suicide special. (Webster)

COLUMBUS FIRE ARMS MFG. CO. Columbus, Georgia, 1862-1865. Copies of Colt Navy revolver for the Confederacy. Louis and Elias Haiman. (Albaugh 3)

COLVILLE, ALEXANDER A. Little River, Maine. Patent #none April 28, 1820, lock.

COLVIN, DAVIS Green Grove, Pennsylvania, 1861d.

COLVIN, GEORGE H. Sioux City, Iowa, 1880d-1895d.

COLVIN, HENRY W. Falmouth, Kentucky. Patent #25,389 September 13, 1859, sight.

COLVIN, JOHN R. Oliphant, Pennsylvania, 1880d. (same as John Colvin of Peckville, Pennsylvania?)

COLVIN, JOHN Peckville, Pennsylvania, 1880d-1890d.

COLVIN, MARVIN S. Syracuse, New York, 1872-1873, East Randolph, New York, 1870-1874, Salamanca, New York, 1875d-1882d, Elmira, New York, 1884d-1889d. Percussion 1/2 stocks at all four locations. Cartridge tip-up pistol. (Clow)

COLVIN, ROBERT J., JR. Lancaster, Pennsylvania. Patent #34,740 March 25, 1862, pistol sword. (Sellers-1)

COLVIN, ROBERT K. Lancaster, Pennsylvania. Patent #44,784 October 24, 1864, pistol bayonet. (Sellers-1)

COLWELL, J.W. Reading, Michigan, 1867d.

COLWELL, WADE Reading, Michigan, 1860d.

COLWILL, THOMAS (1825-?), Gambier, Ohio, 1852-1863.

COMBS, C.E. Carson City, Michigan, 1899d.

COMBS, GEORGE Pipestone, Minnesota, 1898d.

COMER, HARVEY Peru, Indiana, 1881-1885. (Lindert)

COMET suicide special by Prescott Pistol Co.

COMINS, LORING (1832-?), San Francisco, California, 1855-1857, Napa, California, 1867-1875. Son of, and successor to, Pascal Comins. (Shelton)

COMINS, PASCAL B. (1810-1876), Sacramento, California, 1850-1852, San Francisco, California, 1852-1876. (Shelton)

COMLEY, A.A. Albany, Oregon, 1891d.

COMMANDER suicide special by Norwich Arms Co.

COMMERCIAL suicide special made by O.A. Smith.

COMMINGE & GEISLER Houston, Texas, 1882d-1894d. Frank Comminge and Anton H. Geisler.

COMPEER trade name of Crescent on guns for Van Camp Hardware, Indianapolis. (AR 2-69)

COMPETITON trade name of John Meunier on shotguns. (Hinman)

COMPTON, ALEXANDER Hagerstown, Maryland. Apprenticed to John Gonter, 1794. (Hartzler)

COMPTON, B.H. Cass, Tennessee, 1860d.

COMPTON, JOHN Wabash, Indiana. (Lindert)

COMPTON, ORSEMUS (1815-1897), Brownstown, Indiana, 1840-1884. Percussion 1/2 stock. (MB 4-55)

COMPTON, PHINEAS M. (1804-1858), Berlin, Pennsylvania, 1830-1858.

COMPTON, SAMUEL (?-1902), Berlin, Pennsylvania, 1858-1902. Son of, and successor to, Phineas Compton.

COMSTOCK, ANSON Danbury, Connecticut, 1869-1879.

COMSTOCK, HARRY Fulton, New York. Patents #409,017 August 13, 1889, breechloading guns, #414,796 November 12, 1889, lock, #414,797 November 12, 1889, lock, and #422,731 March 4, 1890, firearm. L.C. Smith employee.

CONANT, HEZEKIAH Hartford, Connecticut. Patents #12,258 January 16, 1855, bullet, and #14,554 April 1, 1856, gas seal. The gas seal was used on Sharps rifles throughout the percussion period. (Sellers-4)

CONCKLIN, NICHOLAS New York, New York, 1841d-1845.

CONCORD GUN MANUFACTORY Concord, New Hampshire, 1841-1845. Owned by Cutchins & Crosby.

CONDIT, J.H. Stockton, California, 1880-1881d. (Shelton)

CONDO Milesburg, Pennsylvania. (Dean)

CONDOR, A. Philadelphia, Missouri, 1860d.

CONDRAY, W.P. Portsmouth, Virginia. Percussion 1/2 stock.

CONE & COLLINS Warren, Pennsylvania, 1882d.

CONE, ALFRED MARION (183 1-1903). Corry, Pennsylvania, 1873-1881d, Warren, Pennsylvania, 1882d-1903. Percussion rifles. As Cone & Collins, 1882. (MB 6-45)

CONE, CYRUS L. Shellburne, Massachusetts, 1884.

CONE, D.D. Washington, D.C. Patent attorney who had his name stamped on revolvers made by William Uhlinger.

CONE, SAMUEL A. West Chesterfield, Massachusetts, 1868-1874d.

CONESTOGA RIFLE WORKS Lancaster, Pennsylvania. Trade name used by Henry Eicholtz Leman on contract rifles and muskets.

CONKLE, JOHN, JR. Westmoreland Co., Pennsylvania, 1831-1846. (Whisker II)

CONKLIN & HAUSER Chicago, Illinois. Burglar alarm gun. (Winans)

CONKLIN, H.M. unlocated. Percussion fullstock.

CONKLIN, ISAIAH B. Baltimore, Maryland. Patent #86,971 February 16, 1869, breechloading firearm.

CONKLIN, LEVI New Orleans, Louisiana, 1871d-1875d.

CONKLIN, PERCIVAL Kenton, Michigan, 1891d.

CONLEY, DAVID Lowery Stand, Tennessee, 1815-1825. Flintlock pistols. (Gardner)

CONLEY, J.C. Linville, North Carolina. Late percussion rifles. (Bivins)

CONN, L. unlocated. Percussion 1/2 stock.

CONNECTICUT ARMS & MFG. CO. Naubuc, Connecticut, 1863-1873d. B. L. Hammond patent pistols.

CONNECTICUT ARMS CO. Norfolk, Connecticut, 1864d-1866d. Stephen Wood's patent front loading cartridge revolvers.

CONNELL, M. Brooklyn, New York, 1871-1876. See M. O'Connell.

CONNELLY & MATTHIS San Antonio, Texas, 1850-1855.

CONNELLY, E.J. San Antonio, Texas, 1850-1860. Percussion 1/2 stock. As Connelly & Matthis, 1850-1855.

CONNELLY, WILLIAM Philadelphia, Pennsylvania, 1824d.

CONER, ARMSTRONG Jackson Co., Missouri, 1850c. (MB 11-66)

CONER, DAVID Groton, Connecticut. Patent #493,352 March 14, 1893, firearm.

CONNER, H. Mobile, Alabama. See Hugh Connor.

CONNER, J.M. Tuskeegee, Alabama, 1885d.

CONNER, JOHN (1802-?), Guilford, North Carolina. (Bivins)

CONNER, WILLIAM Charleston, South Carolina, 1852d. (Dean)

CONNER, WILLISTON Rensselaerville, New York. Patent #63,022 March 19, 1867, sight.

CONNING, JAMES Mobile, Alabama, 1841d-1875d. Duellers (imported), swords. Agent for Deringer. (ASAC 39)

CONNOR, DAVID New Haven, Connecticut. Patent #160,880 March 16, 1875, breechloading firearm.

CONNOR, HUGH Mobile, Alabama, 1855d-1870d. For James Ferrie, 1855-1859.

CONNOR, JOSEPH New York, New York. Patent #464,215 December 1, 1891, lock.

CONOVER, C.E. Cincinnati, Ohio 1896d-1897d.

CONOVER, JACOB A. New York, New York. Patent #56,669 July 24, 1866, breechloading firearm.

CONOW, WILLIAM Grand Island, Nebraska, 1879d-1893d. As W. Conow & Son, 1879-1884.

CONQUEROR suicide special by Bacon.

CONRAD, R. Elida, Ohio, 1860-1868. (Hutslar)

CONRAD, R. Trenton, Michigan, 1863d.

CONRAD, SAMUEL Brothers Valley, Pennsylvania, 1832-1834, Berlin, Pennsylvania, 1837-1853. (Kauffman)

CONRATH, C.H. Hannibal, Missouri, 1854d.

CONROY, LAUGHLIN New York, New York. Patents #72,803 December 31, 1867, breechloading firearm, #91,421 June 15, 1869, breechloading firearm, #145,154 December 2, 1873, and #437,574 September 30, 1890, breechloading firearm. (ASAC-40)

CONSTABLE, JAMES unlocated. Percussion rifles and shotguns.

CONSTABLE, RICHARD Philadelphia, Pennsylvania, 1817d-1851d. Flintlock double shotgun, flintlock duellers, percussion duellers, derringer. Successor to Booth & Co.

CONSTANS, FRED Paris, Illinois, 1876d-1880d.

CONSTANT suicide special. (Webster)

CONSTANTINE & SMART Dover, New Hampshire, 1868d. S.W. Constantine and Eugene Smart.

CONSTANTINE, S.W. Dover, New Hampshire, 1868d, Thorton, New Hampshire, 1876-1880. As Constantine & Smart, 1868.

CONTINENTAL ARMS CO. Norwich, Connecticut, 1866-1867. Cartridge pepperboxes under Converse & Hopkins patent.

CONTINENTAL trade name of Great Western Gun Works on suicide specials and shotguns.

CONVERSE, A.T. Norwich, Connecticut, 1873d. Pistols.

CONVERSE, CHARLES A. Norwich, Connecticut. Patent #57,622 August 28, 1866, revolver with Samuel S. Hopkins. Used by Bacon and Continental Arms Co.

CONVERSE, E. A. Norwich, Connecticut. Single barrel shotgun.

CONVERSE, EUGENE Oswego, New York. 1866d-1870d.

CONVERSE, JESSE Laramie City, Wyoming, 1884d.

CONVERSE, WILLIAM F. (1812-?), Cincinnati, Ohio, 1836-1839, Harrison, Ohio, 1839-1845. (Hutslar)

CONVERSE, WILLIAM H. Colorado Springs, Colorado, 1875-1882, Newton, Kansas, 1884d. (Sellers-3)

CONWAY, B.H. Sharon Grove, Kentucky, 1896d.

CONWAY, JOSEPH Hannibal, Missouri, 1850c. (MB 11-66)

CONWAY, THOMAS G. New York, New York, 1879d-1881d. Importer.

COOK & BROTHER New Orleans, Louisiana, 1861-1863, Athens, Georgia, 1863-1865. Percussion carbines for the Confederacy. Ferdinand and Francis Cook. (Hill-Anthony)

COOK & BROWN unlocated. Percussion fullstock.

COOK & RICHARDS Lansing, Michigan, 1872d-1878.

COOK, ABRAM (1803-?), Catawba, North Carolina, 1850c. Flintlock Kentucky. (Bivins)

COOK, ALEXANDER Philadelphia, Pennsylvania, 1790c. (Gluckman & Satterlee)

COOK, ASHBEL Clayton, New York, 1866-1890d. Percussion guns.

COOK, B.E. Warrenton, North Carolina, 1867-1875. (Bivins)

COOK, C.E. Boone, Iowa, 1880d-1897d.

COOK, CHARLES Baltimore, Maryland, 1847-1854d. (Hartzler)

COOK, D. Shalersville, Ohio, 1883d. (Hutslar)

COOK, EDGAR Grass Valley, California, 1874d. (Shelton)

COOK, ELLIOTT W. (?-1877), Lockport, New York, 1848-1877. Percussion 1/2 stock. (Swinney)

COOK, HEZEKIAH (1835-1904), Allen Co., Kentucky. (Hist. KY, V4, P606)

COOK, ISAAC Paola, Kansas, 1884d.

COOK, J. Thornton, Texas, 1884d-1896d.

COOK, JACOB Lancaster, Pennsylvania, 1807-1813, Foulton Co., Pennsylvania, 1825. Flintlock Kentucky and contract pistols. (ASAC 3) (C&W - Bedford Co., Pennsylvania, 1819-1834?)

COOK, JOHN W. Hennepin, Illinois, 1881d, Quitman, Missouri, 1898d.

COOK, JOHN Cooperstown, New York, 1874d, Oneida, New York, 1876d-1881d.

COOK, JOHN McConnellsburg, Pennsylvania, 1825-1829t. Percussion fullstock. (Bowers)

COOK, JOSEPH Porter, Maine, 1868-1874.

COOK, JOSHUA (1821-?), Piqua, Ohio, 1848-1850. Percussion 1/2 stock. (Hutslar)

COOK, JOSHUA (1834-?), Nebraska City, Nebraska, 1860c. For William Rotton.

COOK, L.C. Belvidere, Illinois, 1867d.

COOK, LOUIS New Orleans, Louisiana, 1881d-1885d. As Hall & Cook, 1881-1882 and Cardona & Cook, 1884.

COOK, LOUIS Shalersville, Ohio, 1890d. Son of D. Cook? (Hutslar)

COOK, M.L. Marshalltown, Iowa, 1882d-1897d.

COOK, MICHAEL (1755-1839). Franklin Co., Pennsylvania, 1824-1839. Barrelmaker only. Successor to Leonard Snider. (Bowers)

COOK, NATHAN B. Chicago, Illinois, 1842-1852. Patent #7,596 August 27, 1850, lock. Percussion rifles.

COOK, R. Stockton, California, 1852d. (Shelton)

COOK, ROBERT Shreveport, Louisiana, 1882d.

COOK, ROSWELL F. West Pottsdam, New York, 1850-1862, Watertown, New York, 1863-1868, Ilion, New York, 1868-1900. Patents #29,340 July 24, 1860, breechloading firearm, #37,854 March 10, 1863, breechloading firearm, #215,507 May 20, 1879, revolver with Joseph Rider, #224,651 February 17, 1880, sight, #305,050 September 16, 1884, magazine, #313,851 March 17, 1885, magazine gun, #378,661 February 28, 1888, magazine gun, #539,037 May 14, 1895, magazine gun, and #539,035 May 14, 1895, magazine gun. Percussion 1/2 stock and revolving rifles. For Remington after 1868.

COOK, THOMAS R. Noblesville, Indiana, 1891, Marion, Indiana, 1896. Patents #458,268 August 25, 1891, machine gun, and #560,842 May 26, 1896, machine gun.

COOK, THOMAS New York, New York, 1852d-1854. Patent #10,520 February 14, 1854, firearm.

COOK, THOMAS Philadelphia, Pennsylvania, 1814d.

COOK, V. I. Belfast, New York, 1874d-1882d. Percussion 1/2 stock.

COOK, W.M., & BRO. Nashville, Tennessee 1873d-1876d.

COOK, WILLIAM Rochester, New York, 1827d-1838d. For Ephraim Gilbert, 1827. (Eich)

COOKE, J., & CO. Terre Haute, Indiana. Lockmaker only. (Lindert)

COOKE, JACOB New London, Virginia, 1796-1800. Contract for pistols, 1807-1808, and Model 1798 contract muskets. (Gill)

COOKE, JAMES C. Middletown, Connecticut. Patent #35,488 June 23, 1862, breechloading firearms.

COOKMAN, WILLIAM Hagerstown, Maryland, 1841, Philadelphia, Pennsylvania, 1846d. (Hartzler)

COOKSON, JOHN (?-1762), Boston, Massachusetts, 1701-1762. Repeating flintlock rifles. Left his shop to his grandsons, John and Samuel Cookson. (USCC)

COOKSON, SAMUEL Boston, Massachusetts, 1762-1775, Halifax, Nova Scotia, 1776-1784. Grandson and successor to John Cookson. (Gluckman & Satterlee)

COOLEY, ALOMSON L. (1820-?), Marshfield, Ohio, 1850-1878. (Hutslar)

COOLEY, DAVID (1790-1856), Adams Co., Pennsylvania, 1814t-1856. Flintlock Kentucky rifles. (Bowers)

COOLEY, HENRY B. Hartford, Connecticut. Patent #541,654 June 25, 1895, automatic feeding device with John M. Noble and J.E. Trevor.

COOLEY, THOMAS (1790-?), St. Charles, Illinois, 1860c. (Johnson)

COOLIDGE BROTHERS Bonaparte, Iowa, 1882d.

COOLLEY, T.C. Capella, California, 1867d. (Shelton)

COON, DAVID Ithaca, New York, 1845-1858. Patent #17,406 May 26, 1857, burglar alarm, made by Cheseborough & Co. Percussion 1/2 stocks and revolving rifles. Son of Levi Coon. (Clow)

COON, JESSE Hope, Ohio, 1860-1865. (Hutslar)

COON, JOHN DENNIS Centerville, Ohio. Patent #208,889 October 15, 1878, breechloading firearm. Nathrop, Colorado. Patent #603,218, April 26, 1898, breechloading firearm. (Sellers-3)

COON, L. & SONS Ithaca, New York, 1850-1851. Levi, Levi Jr., and David Coon.

COON, L. Owego, New York. Percussion 1/2 stock. (Swinney)

COON, LEVI (1792-?), Ithaca, New York, 1821-1850. Flintlock and percussion rifles. (Swinney)

COON, LEVI, JR. Ithaca, New York, 1842-1850. Percussion 1/2 stock. (Clow)

COON, SIMEON Ithaca, New York. Patent #18,236 September 22, 1857, burglar alarm.

COONEY, JAMES Brooklyn, New York, 1889d.

COONEY, T.F. Sterling, Kansas, 1882d.

COONS, E. Philadelphia, Pennsylvania. Flintlock Kentucky rifles. Last name possibly Kuntz. (Dillin)

COONS, HARRIS Union Co., Ohio, Columbus, Ohio. (Hutslar)

COONS, JOHN unlocated. Flintlock Kentucky rifle.

COONS, JOSEPH Philadelphia, Pennsylvania, 1810-1817.

COONTS, ANDREW J. (1850-?), Barbour Co., West Virginia, 1880c.

COOPER & LAVELY Pittsburgh, Pennsylvania, 1861-1862. Josiah Ells' and Cooper revolvers. J. Maslin Cooper and James Lavely. (Kauffman)

COOPER & POND New York, New York, 1858d-1867d. Importers and dealers. Joseph Cooper and C.H. Pond.

COOPER FIREARMS MFG. CO. Pittsburgh, Pennsylvania, 1859-1864, Philadelphia, Pennsylvania, 1864-1869. Double action revolvers under Cooper's patents. (Sellers-1)

COOPER, A.J. Colt, Arkansas, 1892d.

COOPER, ANDERSON Columbus, Ohio. (Hutslar)

COOPER, B. & J. New York City, New York, 1800-1840d. Flintlock and percussion guns. Dealers and importers.

COOPER, F.J. Emporia, Kansas, 1894d.

COOPER, GEORGE Lancaster Co., Pennsylvania, 1834t. (Dyke)

COOPER, HARRIS & HODGKINS New York, New York, 1868d-1874d. Importers and dealers. Joseph Cooper, Edwin Harris, and Walter Hodgkins.

COOPER, HENRY T. New York, New York, 1841d-1852d. Percussion guns. Successor to B. & J. Cooper. As H.T. & A. Cooper 1852. Agent for Bacon in 1847.

COOPER, ISAIAH Chetopa, Kansas, 1888d.

COOPER, J.J. unlocated. Flintlock Kentucky rifle.

COOPER, J.M. Pittsburgh, Pennsylvania, 1839-1859. Locks only. Father of James Maslin Cooper. (GR 6-59)

COOPER, JAMES MASLIN Pittsburgh, Pennsylvania. Patents #27,526 March 20, 1860, revolver, #29,864 September 4, 1860, revolver, #40,021 September 22, 1863, revolver, and #45,319 December 6, 1864, cartridge. (Sellers-1)

COOPER, JEREMIAH New York, New York, 1815d-1820d. Flintlock Kentucky.

COOPER, JOHN A. Adair, Iowa. Patent #607,344 July 12, 1898, sight.

COOPER, JOSEPH New York, New York, 1831d-1874d. As Cooper & Pond, 1858-1867 and Cooper, Harris & Hodgkins, 1868-1874d.

COOPER, L. unlocated. Percussion 1/2 stock.

COOPER, N.A. Winchester, Virginia, 1897d.

COOPER, SAMUEL D. New York, New York, 1867d-1880d.

COOPER, SAMUEL (1833-?), Waterford, Michigan.

COOPER, W. Sharpsburg, Pennsylvania. Percussion fullstock.

COOPER, W.C. Trenton, New Jersey, 1866d-1869d.

COOPER, WALTER (1843-1924), Bozeman, Montana, 1870-1886. Patent #267,497 November 14, 1882, sight. As "Montana Armory" until succeeded by Gottschalck Bros., 1886.

COOPER. THOMAS New York, New York, 1803. Lockmaker.

COPE, JACOB unlocated. Flintlock Kentucky rifle.

COPE, JAMES West Plains, Missouri, 1898d.

COPELAND, FRANK H. (1856-?), Elbert Co., Colorado, 1880d.

COPELAND, FRANK (1833-1927). Worcester, Massachusetts, 1863-1867, Sterling, Massachusetts, 1867-1888d. Cartridge pistols and revolvers. (GR 11-72)

COPELAND, JOHN (?-1773), Edentown, North Carolina, 1769-1773. (Bivins)

COPP, G. unlocated. Percussion fullstock.

COPPE, CHARLES (1820-?), Canton, Ohio, 1850c. (Hutslar)

COPPUCK, W.M. Petersburg, Indiana, 1860d.

CORBETT, ROBERT New York, New York, 1798. (Gardner)

CORBETT, THOMAS St. Louis, Missouri, 1860-1863d.

CORBETT, WALTER S. Quincy, Illinois, 1864d, Little Rock, Arkansas, 1876d-1880d. (Elias)

CORBIN, H. Ozark, Missouri, 1860d.

CORBLEY, D. York Co., Pennsylvania. (Kauffman)

CORBY, JOHN Bethel, New York, 1870d.

CORD, ARTHUR Accomack, Virginia, 1891d.

CORDES, DIETRICH Defiance, Ohio, 1885d. (Hutslar)

CORDES, JOHN D. Defiance, Ohio, 1878d. (Hutslar)

CORDES, R.G. unlocated. Percussion fullstock.

CORDIS, THOMAS unlocated. Flintlock lockmaker.

CORDUAN, BENJAMIN F. Jersey City, New Jersey, 1878d.

COREY, A.W. Lapeer, Michigan, 1872d-1895d.

COREY, CHESTER Reynolds Co., Missouri, 1850c. (MB 11-66)

CORLEY, CHRISTOPHER New York, New York, 1818-1820. (Gardner)

CORLISS, JOHN Philadelphia, Pennsylvania, 1837d-1841d.

CORMAN, HENRY De Soto, Illinois, 1860d. Percussion 1/2 stock.

CORNAY, FRANCIS Philadelphia, Pennsylvania, 1814d-1816d. Possibly Cornet? (Kauffman)

CORNELL, D.O. New York, New York, 1860c. Derringer. See Daniel O'Connell.

CORNELL, J.W. Princeton, Illinois, 1877. (Johnson)

CORNER, PAUL Lancaster, Pennsylvania, 1759. Lockmaker. (Dyke)

CORNET, CHARLES Philadelphia, Pennsylvania, 1814d.

CORNMAN, HENRY (1831-?), Logan Co., Ohio, 1850c. Percussion 1/2 stock. With William Gardner. (Hutslar)

CORNS, ABRAHAM Lancaster, Pennsylvania, 1857d.

CORNWELL, WILLIAM A. Trenton, Tennessee, 1887d.

COROLUS Lancaster Co., Pennsylvania, 1801t. (Dyke)

CORR, A.L. unlocated. Percussion 1/2 stock.

CORRELL, GEORGE Kunkletown, Pennsylvania, 1861d.

CORRETHERS, GREEN see Greenup Correthers.

CORRETHERS, GREENUP (1820-1892), Springfield, Illinois, 1847d-1892d.

CORRETHERS, Z.J. Springfield, Illinois, 1892d.

CORWIN, W.H. Titusville, Pennsylvania, 1874d.

CORY, JOHN C. (?-1845), Beaver Co., Pennsylvania, 1803-1845. (Whisker II)

CORY, RANDOLPH P. Union City, Indiana, 1881, St. Louis, Missouri, 1890-1907. Patents #245,792 August 1881, revolver, #555,432 February 28, 1896, choke attachment, #633,428 September 19, 1899, choke attachment, and #847,911 March 19, 1907, choke attachment. Cartridge shotguns.

COSAT see Davis & Cosat.

COSEY, B. unlocated. Barrelmaker.

COSGROVE, GEORGE Whitneyville, Connecticut, 1871d.

COSMOPOLITAN ARMS CO. Hamilton, Ohio, 1860-1865. Made Henry Gross Jr. patent rifles and carbines. Owned by Gwyn & Campbell, who put their own name on later guns.

COSS, WARREN Bark River, Wisconsin, 1857d.

COSTER, ABRAHAM Philadelphia, Pennsylvania, 1810-18 14.

COSWELL, JOHN (1830-?), Terre Haute, Indiana, 1860c. (Lindert)

COTHRELL, W.H. Davisburgh, Michigan, 1860d.

COTHREN, J. Illiopolis, Illinois, 1860d.

COTHRON, W.F. Eureka, Kentucky, 1879d-1884d.

COTTEN, CHRISTOPHER Albion, Michigan. Patent #457,812 August 18, 1891, spring gun.

COTTEN, I.F. Topeka, Kansas, 1894d-1910d.

COTTEN, WILLIAM Topeka, Kansas, 1888d-1894d.

COTTON, WILLIAM M. Leominster, Massachusetts, 1820-1850. Percussion 1/2 stock. (Lindsay)

COTTON, Z.L. Rocky Comfort, Arkansas, 1884d.

COTTRELL, ABRAHAM Lansing, Michigan. Patent #345,120 July 6, 1886, gunstock.

COUCH, BARTLETT Y. (1826-?), Jamestown, North Carolina, 1850c. Signature "BYC" on flintlock rifle. (Bivins)

COUCH, ELBERT M. Northhampton, Massachusetts. Patents #516,476 March 13, 1894, Chicago palm pistol, #530,823 December 11, 1894, machinery for making palm pistol, and #530,824 December 11, 1894, palm pistol. (GR 1-67)

COUCH, JOHN D. Middletown, Connecticut. 1859d-1860d. Patent #24,573 June 28, 1859, trap gun with Henry North.

COUCH, MILTON Jamestown, North Carolina, 1853. (Bivins)

COUCH, QUINCY Jamestown, North Carolina. (Bivins)

COUCH, WILLIAM H.C. (1841-?), Jamestown, North Carolina. (Bivins)

COULANOY, J. Philadelphia, Pennsylvania, 1781. Committee of Safety repairs.

COULAUX, JULIEN Philadelphia, Pennsylvania, 1796d-1798d. Same as above? (Kauffman)

COULTAS, CHARLES Winchester, Illinois, 1868-1910. (Johnson)

COULTHARD, J. Natchez, Mississippi. Percussion 1/2 stock. See Chotard.

COULTRUP, DAVID Belvidere, Illinois, 1878d-1893d.

COUNTS, JACK A. Coshocton, Ohio, 1893-1945. (Hutslar)

COURTER, DAVID A. Beloit, Wisconsin. Patent #34,625 March 11, 1862, pistol sword.

COURTLEYOW, JACOB Chariton, Iowa, 1882d-1895d.

COURTNEY, R. Memphis, Missouri, 1860d.

COURTNEY, R.A. Canton, Missouri, 1867d. Same as R. Courtney, Memphis, Missouri?

COURTNEY, TENNANT & CO. Charlestown, South Carolina, 1854d. Importers and dealers. Beware of fake markings.

COURTNEY, WILLIAM T. Oswego, New York, 1850d-1859d.

COUSINS, H.D. Surrey, Maine, 1871-1874d.

COUTTY, SAMUEL (?-1795), Philadelphia, Pennsylvania, 1779-1794. Flintlock pistols. Repaired US arms, 1780-1785. (Kauffman)

COVE, CHRISTOPHER Philadelphia, Pennsylvania, 1780-1782. Continental Armory. (Moller)

COVELL, JOSEPH Buchanan, Michigan, 1883d-1891d.

COVER, JOHN Connellsville, Pennsylvania, 1859-1861d.

COVERT, W.M. Bluffton, Indiana, 1871-1875. (Lindert)

COVEY, WARREN Richburgh, New York, 1880-1882d.

COVODE, JACOB Hiawatha, Kansas, 1882d-1884d, Hot Springs, Arkansas, 1885d.

COWAN, JOHN (1723-1789), Salisbury, North Carolina, 1750-1789. (Bivins)

COWAN, W.H.C. Atlanta, Georgia, 1861. Confederate gunsmith convention.

COWAN, WILLIAM III (1776-1844), Rowan Co., North Carolina, ?-1844. (Bivins)

COWBOY trade name of Hibbard, Spencer & Bartlett on imported revolvers.

COWDAN, JAMES F. Chandlerville, Pennsylvania, 1860d-1861d.

COWELL, EBENEZER Allentown, Pennsylvania, 1774-1779, Philadelphia, Pennsylvania, 1779-1782. Committee of Safety muskets at the State Arms Factory at Allentown and on his own in Philadelphia. (Dillin)

COWELL, JOSEPH Boston, Massachusetts, 1745-1775. (Gluckman & Satterlee)

COWELL, P. unlocated. Flintlock Kentucky rifle dated 1783.

COWEN, JOSEPH (1826-?), Carlisle, Ohio, 1850c. (Hutslar)

COWGIL, ADDISON J.H. Little Rock, Arkansas, 1845-1850. (Elias)

COWLES & SMITH Chicopee, Massachusetts, 1863-1870. Percussion and cartridge pistols. W.W. Cowles. Succeeded by Cowles & Son in 1871.

COWLES & SON Chicopee, Massachusetts, 1871-1876. Cartridge derringers.

COWLES, THOMAS Virginia, 1775. Committee of Safety repairs. (Gill)

COX & SON Atlanta, Georgia, 1847. Percussion underhammer and derringer pistols. (Logan)

COX, A.D. Charlottesville, Virginia, 1877d-1880d.

COX, ABIEL Cincinnati, Ohio, 1820-1862. As A. Cox & Co. 1855-62. Percussion 1/2 stock. (Hutslar)

COX, ABNER Belmond, Iowa, 1865d.

COX, CALVIN Coxville, North Carolina. Patents #20,041 April 27, 1858, breechloading firearm, and #27,778 April 10, 1860, breechloading firearm.

COX, GEORGE Mifflinville, Pennsylvania, 1870-1898. Percussion 1/2 stock. (C&W)

COX, J.G. Yates Center, Kansas, 1888d-1894d.

COX, JESSE R. Knox Co., Missouri, 1850c. (MB 11-66)

COX, L.W. Charlottesville, Virginia, 1867-1875d.

COX, MARTIN Philadelphia, Pennsylvania, 1819d.

COX, R.C., GUN CO. Milwaukee, Wisconsin, 1894-1895. (MB 5-49)

COX, T.B. Reagan, Texas, 1892d.

COX, WILLIAM H. Elyria, Ohio, 1878d. (Hutslar)

COX, WILLIAM Bloomington, Indiana, 1870c. (Lindert)

COXFORD, WILLIAM F. New York, New York, 1875d-1881d. Successor to B.S. Moulton.

COY, S.S. East Lewiston, Ohio, 1885-1900. (Hutslar)

COYFE, CHARLES Jamestown, Virginia, 1619. (Gill)

COZAD, WILLIAM (1824-?), Perrysville, Indiana, 1850c. (Lindert)

COZART, J.Y. St. Cloud, Minnesota, 1892d.

COZENS, JOHN Mattoon, Illinois, 1888d-1890d.

COZINE, SAMUEL McMinnville, Oregon, 1881d-1886d.

CRABB, THOMAS Fredericktown, Maryland, 1790-1808. Model 1798 contract muskets with Jacob Metzger, Nicholas White, and Christopher Barnhizle. (Hartzler)

CRABBS, J.C. Morenci, Michigan, 1879d.

CRABEN, WILLIAM Warren Co., Missouri, 1850c. (MB 11-66)

CRABILL, CHARLES E. Strasburg, Virginia, 1884d-1897d.

CRABTREE, ABSALOM Buffalo Creek, Tennessee. Flintlock Kentucky rifles. (Dillin)

CRABTREE, JOHN F. (1839-?), Visalia, California, 1868-1874. Patents #75,248 March 10, 1868, lock with William Crabtree, #76,587 April 14, 1868, lock with Salmon Belden, and #85,268 December 29, 1868, breechloading firearm with Salmon Belden. (Shelton)

CRABTREE, WILLIAM M. Visalia, California, Porterville, California. Patents #75,248 March 10, 1868 lock, with John Crabtree, and #229,383 June 29, 1880, lock. Brother of John Crabtree. (Shelton)

CRACK SHOT trade name of J. Stevens Arms Co., on .22 cal. rifles.

CRACKER JACK trade name of J. Stevens Arms Co., on .22 cal. rifles. (Perkins)

CRADDOCK, JOHN (1814-?), Springfield, Illinois, 1839-1854d. (Johnson)

CRADDOCK, JOHN Brownsville, Nebraska, 1882d-1893d.

CRADDOCK, WILLIAM F. Brownsville, Nebraska, 1872d.

CRADDOCK, WILLIAM (1836-?), Springfield, Illinois, 1860c. (Johnson)

CRADDOCKE, D. unlocated. Flintlock Kentucky.

CRAE, PETER Paterson, New Jersey, 1860d.

CRAFT, D.S. Brush Valley, Pennsylvania, 1861d.

CRAFT, GEORGE W. Prosperity, Pennsylvania, 1861d-1875. Percussion 1/2 stock signed "GWC". (Kauffman)

CRAFT, JACOB Philadelphia, Pennsylvania, 1813d. (C&W)

CRAFT, P.W. Columbia, South Carolina. Percussion duelling pistol.

CRAFT, PARKER Scotland, Illinois, 1890d-1893d.

CRAFT, WILLIAM H. Sevastopol, Indiana, 1862-1865.

CRAFTS, ROYAL Rutland, Vermont. Model 1798 contract muskets with Darius Chipman, Thomas Hooker, and John Smith. (Gluckman)

CRAIG & MUSGRAVE Pittsburgh, Pennsylvania, 1861d. William Craig.

CRAIG & PERDUE Wilmington, North Carolina, 1869-1875. (Bivins)

CRAIG see Malcolm & Craig.

CRAIG, ANDREW Mansfield, Ohio, 1812, Delaware Co., Ohio, 1820c. Brother of David. (Hutslar)

CRAIG, DAVID Mansfield, Ohio, 1812. Brother of Andrew Craig. (Hutslar)

CRAIG, GEORGE Pittsburgh, Pennsylvania, 1846-1875, Foxburg, Pennsylvania, 1875-1877. For his father William. As Craig & Son in Foxburg.

CRAIG, J.B. Calais, Ohio, 1872-1881. (Hutslar)

CRAIG, JOHN W. Knoxville, Illinois, 1867d-1868d, Kirkwood, Illinois, 1870-1910. Percussion 1/2 stock. (Johnson)

CRAIG, JOSEPH ALLEN (1822-1899), Pittsburgh, Pennsylvania, 1842-1857, Shasta, California, 1857-1859, Weaverville, California, 1859-1873, San Bernadino, California, 1873-1899. Percussion rifles. Brother of William. (Shelton)

CRAIG, ROBERT Philadelphia, Pennsylvania, 1775-1776. Committee of Safety locks. (Gluckman & Satterlee)

CRAIG, W. & J. Pittsburgh, Pennsylvania, 1847. Percussion fullstock. Probably William & Joseph Craig.

CRAIG, WILLIAM (1820-1877), Pittsburgh, Pennsylvania, 1844-1850c, Sonora, California, 1857-1860, Allegheny, Pennsylvania, 1867-1868, Rochester, Pennsylvania, 1868d, Foxburg, Pennsylvania, 1877. Over/under rifle/shotgun, percussion 1/2 stock target. Brother of Joseph Craig. (Shelton)

CRAIGHEAD, JAMES A. Nashville, Tennessee, 1853d-1854d. (James B. in 1853)

CRAIN, GEORGE M. Mansfield, Connecticut, 1872-1881d.

CRAM, WILLIAM H. Penawawa, Washington. Patent #501,765 July 18, 1893, spring gun.

CRAMER, HOWARD Williamsport, Pennsylvania. Patent #610,123 August 30, 1898, magazine.

CRAMER, I. Askum, Illinois, 1890d-1893d.

CRAMER, J.B. Walnut Grove, Illinois, 1860d.

CRAMER, PHILLIP unlocated. Flintlock Kentucky rifles. (probably Phillip Creamer)

CRAMER, W.H. Madison, Florida, 1885d-1886d.

CRAMERI, DOMINGO (1830-?), San Jose, California, 1866-1870. (Shelton)

CRAMPTON, H.L. (?-1890), Amboy, Illinois, 1878d-1890d.

CRANDALL, CARL Springville, New York, 1882d.

CRANDALL, GEORGE E. Springville, New York, 1848-1850d.

CRANDALL, JOSEPH C. unlocated. Percussion locks.

CRANDALL, MARVIN F. (1830-?), Gowanda, New York, 1850c-1882d, Persia, New York, 1864d. Percussion guns. (Swinney)

CRANE Blair, Nebraska, 1879d. As Hammond & Crane.

CRANE, ASHLEY B. Shalerville, Ohio, 1852-1883d. (Hutslar)

CRANE, F.A. Shalerville, Ohio, 1890d. (Hutslar)

CRANE, S.E. Monroe Center, Michigan, 1875d.

CRANER, W.M. unlocated. Percussion fullstock.

CRANMER, T.J. Vallicita, California. Patent #74,994 March 3, 1868, self loading cannon.

CRANSTON, JAMES F. Springfield, Massachusetts. Patents #73,877 January 28, 1868, cartridge, and #81,478 August 25, 1886, cartridge.

CRANSTON, RICHARD New London, Connecticut. Patent #29,573 August 14, 1860, projectile.

CRASKE, CHARLES (1823-1857), Rochester, New York, 1849-1857. For Christopher (?) Passage in 1849 and Billinghurst in 1851. (Eich)

CRASS, H. & F.L. Ithaca, New York. Patent #593,615 November 16, 1897, ejector with Leroy H. Smith.

CRAVALTY & DUGAN Frederickstown, Maryland, 1776. Committee of Safety locks. (Dean)

CRAVEN, JESSE (1815-?), Forsythe Co., North Carolina, 1850c. (Bivins)

CRAW, J. South Norwalk, Connecticut, 1869-1874d.

CRAWFORD, HUGH Charleston, South Carolina, 1776. (Dean)

CREAGER, GEORGE L. Dayton, Ohio, 1843. (Hutslar)

CREAMER, B. Philadelphia, Pennsylvania. Flintlock rifles and pistols.

CREAMER, C.W. Cranesville, West Virginia, 1900d. (Whisker IV)

CREAMER, J.N. St. Louis, Missouri. Percussion pistol.

CREAMER, PHILLIP Taneytown, Maryland, 1792-1805, St. Louis, Missouri, 1820, St. Clair Co., Illinois, 1820. Flintlock Kentucky rifle and pistols. (Johnson, Hartzler)

CREAMER, WILLIAM Morgan Co., Missouri, 1850c. (MB 11-66)

CREASEY, MASON Mexico, Missouri, 1893d.

CREASON, N.B. Sullivan Co., Missouri, 1850c. (MB 11-66)

CREECIER New Orleans, Louisiana, 1838d.

CREEDMOOR trade name of Hopkins & Allen on revolvers.

CREEDMOOR trade name on William Wurfflein parlor guns.

CREEDMORE ARMORY trade name of A.D. McAusland.

CREEDMORE ARMS CO. trade name on imported shotgun.

CREEDMORE suicide special by Chicago Fire Arms Co. and others.

CREESY, GEORGE Garden, Ohio, 1883-1886. Percussion 1/2 stock. (Hutslar)

CREGG, J.W. Kirkwood, Illinois, 1880d.

CREIDER, S.S. Sterling, Illinois, 1880d-1893d.

CREPIN, EMILE A. Hollister, California. Patent #274,279 March 20, 1883, trap gun with F. Rochat.

CRESCENT FIRE ARMS CO. Norwich, Connecticut, 1888-1931. Revolvers, rifles, and shotguns under many names. Controlled by H. & D. Folsom Arms Co., from 1893-1931. (GR 7-74)

CRESCENT GUN CO. Saginaw, Michigan, 1899d. Air guns.

CRESCENT PISTOL CO. Hatfield, Massachusetts, 1874-1877. Trade name of Prescott Pistol Co., sold out to Hyde & Shattuck. (AG 6-78)

CRESCENT suicide special by Crescent Fire Arms Co.

CRESON, V.B. Jackson Corners, Missouri, 1860d.

CRESS, GEORGE Hamilton, Pennsylvania, 1818t-1823t. (Gabel)

CRESS, NICHOLAS (?-1799), Wythe Co., Virginia, ?-1799. (Gill)

CRESSON, JAN, JR., & CO. Philadelphia, Pennsylvania. Percussion 1/2 stock.

CRESSY, E.H. Saline, Michigan, 1891d.

CREVE COEUR trade name of Isaac Walker Hardware Co. on imported shotguns. (Hinman)

CREWS, RODMAN Monroe Co., Kentucky, 1816-1821. (Gardner)

CREWS, WILLIAM Monroe Co., Kentucky, 1816-1821. (Gardner)

CRIDER, C. North Carolina. Flintlock Kentucky.

CRIDER, C.W. Beaver Creek, Pennsylvania. (According to C&W)

CRIDER, FELIX (1838-1924), West Virginia. (MB 10-58)

CRIGLER see Chadwick & Crigler.

CRINER, A. see Abraham Croner.

CRINER, WILLIAM see William Greiner.

CRIPPEN, HOSEN (1820-?), Morgan Co., Ohio, 1850c. (Hutslar)

CRISP, J.A. Jefferson, Ohio, 1883-1886. (Hutslar)

CRISPIN, SILAS New York, New York. Patents #40,978 December 15, 1863, cartridge, #42,329 April 12, 1864, cartridge, #49,237 August 8, 1865, cartridge, #50,224 October 3, 1865, revolver, #60,698 January 1, 1867, breechloading firearm, #61,722 February 5, 1867, breechloading firearms, #64,701 May 14, 1867, breech-loading firearm with Thomas Poultney, and #84,616, December 1, 1868, cartridge box.

CRISSEY, ELIAS (1835-1915), Hooversville, Pennsylvania, 1855-1895. Percussion fullstock. (Hetrick)

CRIST, JOHN Lancaster, Pennsylvania, 1805. Barrelmaker. (Dyke)

CRISWELL, JOSEPH (?-1891), Keedysville, Maryland, 1834-1891. (Hartzler)

CRISWELL, SAMUEL (?-1810), Carlisle, Pennsylvania, 1780t-1810. (Bowers)

CRITCHETT, JAMES C. Clint, Texas. Patent #595,046 December 7, 1897, lock.

CROCKER, DAVID Grove City, Pennsylvania, 1890d.

CROCKER, JAMES A. Providence, Rhode Island. Patent #194,653 August 28, 1877, revolver.

CROCKETT, JAMES M. Newburn, Virginia. Patent #68,609 September 10, 1867, cartridge.

CROCKETT, SAMUEL Tennessee. (ASAC-21)

CROCKETT, THOMAS Bath Co., Kentucky, 1800. Flintlock Kentucky rifles. (Dillin)

CROFT, J.H. Fairfield, Nebraska, 1879d-1882d.

CROISSANT, MARTIN Albany, New York, 1857-1885d.

CROLL, DANIEL Montgomery Co., Pennsylvania, 1790c-1800c. (C&W)

CROLL, HENRY (1817-?), Bridgeville, Ohio, 1850c. (Hutslar)

CROLL, JEFFERSON Monterey, Illinois, 1860d.

CROMWELL, L., SON & CO. Baltimore, Maryland, 1872-1878d. Levi Cromwell, T. Elvin Cromwell, and John Bishop. (Hartzler)

CROMWELL, LEVI Baltimore, Maryland, 1822d-1880d. Percussion shotgun. (Hartzler)

CROMWELL, OLIVER Baltimore, Maryland, 1850-1856. Son of Levi. (Hartzler)

CROMWELL, SIMON Edgecomb, Maine. Patent #none February 3, 1827, lock.

CROMWELL, T. ELVIN Baltimore, Maryland, 1872-1880. Son of Levi Cromwell, operated business after Levi retired. (Hartzler)

CRONENBERGER, A. Bucyrus, Ohio, 1848-1854. (Hutslar)

CRONER, ABRAHAM Cross Creek, Pennsylvania, 1847-1861d.

CROOKER, GEORGE R. New York, New York. Patent #18,486 October 20, 1857, revolver.

CROOM, I. unlocated. Percussion 1/2 stock.

CROSBEE, EDWARD Philadelphia, Pennsylvania, 1880d.

CROSBEE, WALTER E. Philadelphia, Pennsylvania, 1880d.

CROSBY & KELLOGG New Haven, Connecticut, 1860-1863. Percussion target rifle. C.O. Crosby and Henry Kellogg.

CROSBY, G.C. Great Barrington, Massachusetts, 1851. Percussion 1/2 stock target.

CROSBY, J. Springfield Armory. Model 1818 flintlock pistol locks. (MB 6-49)

CROSBY, JOSEPH R. Washington, Arkansas, 1850. (Elias)

CROSBY, L. unlocated. Flintlock Kentucky.

CROSBY, THOMAS Philadelphia, Pennsylvania, 1874d.

CROSS, AMBROSE (1804-?), West Virginia, 1880c (retired).

CROSS, DANIEL, & CO. unlocated. Flintlock lockmakers.

CROSS, M.F. Neodesha, Kansas, 1884d.

CROSS, S. Bloomville, Ohio, 1860-1864d. (Hutslar)

CROSS, W.C. Boston, Massachusetts. Patent #182,899 October 3, 1876, spring air gun.

CROSS, WILLIAM Memphis, Tennessee, 1881d-1887d.

CROSSLAND, JOHN M. (1819-?), Uniontown, Pennsylvania, 1841-1898. (Whisker II)

CROTHERS, ROBERT Philadelphia, Pennsylvania, 1780-1785. Repaired US arms. (Moller)

CROUCH, RICHARD (1832-?), Richmond, Virginia, 1855-1872.

CROUSE, PETER (1762-?), Salisbury, North Carolina. Apprenticed to Andreas Betz. (Bivins)

CROW, ALLISON T. Lima, Ohio, 1888-1893. (Hutslar)

CROW, ANDREW Middlefield, Massachusetts. Patent #28,160 May 8, 1860, cane gun.

CROW, C.A. Lima, Ohio, 1860-1920. (Hutslar)

CROW, JOHN Van Buren, Iowa, 1850c. (MB 8-64)

CROWELL, CHAUNCEY L. Jonesboro, Illinois, 1860d, Peoria, Illinois, 1864d.

CROWELL, E.M. Jay, Indiana, 1860d. Percussion fullstock.

CROWELL, EBENEZER Easton, Pennsylvania, 1775t. (Dyke)

CROWELL, GEORGE G. Lime Rock, Connecticut. Patent #53,955 April 17, 1866, revolver.

CROWELL, S.A. Hastings, Michigan, 1899d.

CROWN JEWEL suicide special by Bliss.

CROWN suicide special by Harrington & Richardson.

CROYSDALE, THOMAS Baltimore, Maryland, 1810. (Gluckman & Satterlee)

CROZIER, L.W. Knoxville, Iowa, 1884d-1889d.

CRUCHLEY, FRED Boston, Massachusetts, 1882d-1883d.

CRUM, DANIEL (1841-1926), Newport, Pennsylvania, 1887d-1890d, Harrisburg, Pennsylvania, 1892. Percussion swivel breech and percussion pistol. (Chandler 2)

CRUM, SAMUEL (1840-1924), Sugar Run, Pennsylvania, 1860-1924. (Chandler 2)

CRUM, SAMUEL Perry Co., Pennsylvania, 1860. Percussion fullstock.

CRUM, T. unlocated. Flintlock Kentucky rifle.

CRUM, WILLIAM Hare's Valley, Pennsylvania, 1890d.

CRUMM Huntingdon Co., Pennsylvania, 1860. (Dean)

CRUSO trade name of Crescent Fire Arms Company on guns made for Hibbard, Spencer, Bartlett & Co. (AR 2-69)

CRUSON, ANDREW Angola, Indiana, 1882-1884, Lantana, Tennessee, 1884-1887. (Gardner)

CRUSSELL, FRANK R. (1815-?), San Francisco, California, 1852-1875. (Shelton)

CRUTTENDEN, W.H. Cazenovia, New York, 1883d-1886. Patent #340,283 April 20, 1886, breechloading firearm with M.E. Card.

CRUVER, JAMES W. (1820-1881), Ulsterville, New York, 1860-1881. Percussion three-barrel, percussion 1/2 stock. (GR 4-67)

CRUZEN, JACOB Washington, D. C., 1822d-1830d. (Hartzler)

CRYSCHER, DANIEL Lancaster Co., Pennsylvania, 1830. Barrelmaker. (Dyke)

CRYTH, JOHN Lancaster, Pennsylvania, 1778-1800. Committee of Safety locks. Flintlock Kentucky rifles. (Dillin)

CUBBERLY, CHARLES M. Keosauqua, Iowa, 1865d-1897d.

CULBERTSON, ALEXANDER Venango, Pennsylvania, 1802-1805. (Whisker II)

CULBERTSON, JAMES Kenton Co., Kentucky. Patent #7,178 March 12, 1850, rifling machine.

CULLEN, THOMAS (1825-1885), New Orleans, Louisiana, 1851-1854, San Francisco, California, 1859-1885. Patents #72,982 January 7, 1868, cartridge, #88,853 April 13, 1868, magazine gun, and #333,307 December 29, 1885, magazine gun. (Shelton)

CULLMAN, CARL CHARLES (1829-1903), Columbus, Ohio, 1847-1900. (MB 1-53)

CULLMAN, G. Cleveland, Ohio, 1840. (Knittle)

CULP, ANDREW B. Victor, Michigan, 1863d.

CULPEPPER, DAVID W. Columbus, Georgia, 1886d-1889d.

CULVER, EDWARD Bushkill, Pennsylvania, 1835t-1850c. (KRA II-3)

CULVER, JOSEPH Westfield, New York, 1866-1874d. Percussion 1/2 stock.

CULVER, N. Warren, Indiana, 1860d.

CULVERHOUSE, WILLIAM Ligonier, Indiana, 1882-1885. (Lindert)

CUMBERLAND ARMS CO. trade name of Crescent Fire Arms Company on guns made for Gray & Dudley Hardware Co., Nashville, Tennessee. (AR 2-69)

CUMINGS, TATE Matlock, Georgia, 1879d.

CUMMINGS & LANE Worcester, Massachusetts, 1869-1872. Charles A. Cummings.

CUMMINGS, ALEXANDER (1819-?), Mendocino Co., California, 1866-1871. (Shelton)

CUMMINGS, CHARLES A. Worcester, Massachusetts, 1860-1872d. As Cummings & Lane, 1869-1872.

CUMMINGS, JOHN Hartford, Connecticut, 1841-1843. (Gardner)

CUMMINGS, O.S. Lowell, Massachusetts, 1877-1880. Copies of the S & W Model 1 Third Issue revolver.

CUMMINGS, WILLIAM Philadelphia, Pennsylvania, 1829d-1855d.

CUMMINS, ALEXANDER Bellevue, Iowa, 1850c. (MB 8-64)

CUNARDEN, HENRY A. (1826-?), Richmond, Virginia, 1850c. (MB 10-63)

CUNDIFF, R.J. Lynchburg, Virginia, 1871d-1888d.

CUNES, JACOB Virginia, 1775-1776. Committee of Safety repairs. (Gill)

CUNHAIN, TIMOTHY (1835-?), Petersburg, Virginia, 1850c. Apprentice. (MB 10-63)

CUNIE, ROBERT Augusta Co., Virginia, 1777. Committee of Safety repairs. (Whisker IV)

CUNKLE, GEORGE Harrisburg, Pennsylvania, 1840-1861d. Percussion fullstock.

CUNKLE, L.G. unlocated. Flintlock Kentucky pistol.

CUNNINGHAM & COGAN New Bedford, Massachusetts. Whaling gun on Patrick Cunningham's patent.

CUNNINGHAM, ALEXANDER (1754-?), Falling Creek Church, Virginia, 1781. Army gunsmith. (Gill)

CUNNINGHAM, ALEXANDER Fayette Co., Pennsylvania, 1802-1805. (Kauffman)

CUNNINGHAM, GEORGE W. Detroit, Michigan, 1872d-1888d.

CUNNINGHAM, JAMES Virginia, 1776. Committee of Safety muskets and repairs. (Gill)

CUNNINGHAM, JOHN Harford Co., Maryland, 1776. Committee of Safety muskets with Isaac Thomas. (Gluckman & Satterlee)

CUNNINGHAM, PATRICK New Bedford, Massachusetts. Patents #256,548 April 18, 1882, whaling gun, and #294,017 February 26, 1884, whaling gun.

CUNNINGHAM, SAMUEL (1820-?), Canton, Ohio, 1850c. (Hutslar)

CUNNINGHAM, W.A. Mt. Vernon, Ohio, 1852-1865. Percussion 1/2 stock. (Hutslar)

CUPP, CHRISTIAN (1800-?), Ashland Co., Ohio, 1850c. (Hutslar)

CUQUA, CHARLES (1811-?), Mt. Carmell, Illinois, 1840-1860. (Johnson)

CURD & HARVEY Louisville, Kentucky, 1858-1860.

CURRAN see Farrelly & Curran.

CURRENS & OWENS Maysville, Kentucky, 1857-1860.

CURRY, CHARLES (?-1863). Philadelphia, Pennsylvania, 1837-1852, San Francisco, California, 1852-1863. Derringers and percussion rifles. (Shelton)

CURRY, CHARLES Tulare, California, 1893d. Son of Charles Curry.

CURRY, GEORGE M. (1827-?), Simpson Creek, West Virginia, 1880c-1884d.

CURRY, JOHN San Francisco, California, 1863-1886. Brother of Charles and Nathaniel Curry. (Shelton)

CURRY, NATHANIEL (1825-?), San Francisco, California, 1854-1886. Inherited the business from brother, Charles, in 1863. As N. Curry & Bro. entire time. Percussion and cartridge guns, usually made by others. (Shelton)

CURRY, PETER D. Dubois, Illinois, 1860d-1864d.

CURRY, WILLIAM (1739-1820). Carlisle, Pennsylvania, 1778-1883t, Washington Co., Pennsylvania, 1783t-1820. (Bowers-Kauffman)

CURTAIN, JOSEPH St. Louis, Missouri, 1842d-1848d.

CURTIN, TIMOTHY Roxton, Texas, 1884d.

CURTIS, A.B. Dayton, Ohio, 1856d. Percussion bench gun with W.W. Hackney. (Hutslar)

CURTIS, D. Mauston, Wisconsin, 1857d.

CURTIS, EDWIN A. Trinidad, Colorado, 1880-1890. With Ashbel J. Carrier as Carrier & Curtis, 1880-1882. With Alphonso T. Sturtevant as Curtis & Sturtevant, 1882-1885. (Sellers-3)

CURTIS, FREDERICK Saugus Center, Massachusetts. Patent #22,940 February 15, 1859, breechloading firearm, Newton, Massachusetts. Patents #33,317 September 17, 1861, breechloading firearm, #41,281 January 19, 1864, breechloading firearm, and #41,489, February 9, 1864, breechloading firearm. (GR 5-80)

CURTIS, HORACE H. Jackson, Tennessee, 1881d.

CURTIS, ISAAC New Haven, Connecticut. Patent #316,880 April 28, 1885, magazine gun.

CURTIS, J.P. Bristol, Virginia, 1880d.

CURTIS, JESSE Waterbury, Connecticut, 1778-1779. Committee of Safety muskets with Thomas Fancher in 1779. (Gluckman & Satterlee)

CURTISS, EDWARD Jackson, Tennessee, 1887d-1891d.

CURTISS, G. Litchfield, Connecticut. Percussion 1/2 stock.

CURTISS, J.W. Chicago, Illinois, 1844d.

CURTISS, N.P. Paso Robles, California, 1893d.

CUSHING & PRATT unlocated. Flintlock New England fowler.

CUSHING, ALVIN D. Troy, New York, 1829-1850d. Patent #none July 20, 1831, cane gun. Percussion fullstock.

CUSHING, HARRY C. New London, Connecticut. Patent #294,770 March 11, 1884, sight.

CUSHING, ROYAL J. Boothbay, Maine, 1884. (Demeritt)

CUSHING, RUEL J. Bangor, Maine. Patent #439,271 October 28, 1890, sight.

CUSHMAN, MATHEW SMITH (1777-1811), Providence, Rhode Island. (Achtermier)

CUSHMAN, N.B. (1817-?), Warsaw, Illinois, 1853-1860. (Johnson)

CUSTER, A.H. Eastwood, Michigan, 1883d.

CUSTER, NICHOLAS Montgomery Co., Pennsylvania, 1800. (Kauffman)

CUSTER, RICHARD, JR. (1790-1858), Rockingham Co., Virginia, 1810-1858. Flintlock Kentucky. (Dean)

CUSTOPHE, FRANCOIS (1817-?), Santa Clara Co., California, 1852c. (Shelton)

CUTCHALL, I.W. unlocated. Percussion fullstock.

CUTCHINS & CROSBY see Concord Gun Manufactory.

CUTLER, BENJAMIN P. Boston, Massachusetts. Patent #76,058 January 7, 1868, safety.

CUTLER, EBEN J. Cleveland, Ohio, 1884-1890. Patents #392,108 October 30, 1888, sight, and #398,315 February 19, 1889, sight. (Hutslar)

CUTLER, J.R. Canandaigua, New York, 1850c-1859d.

CUTLER, JOHN Boston, Massachusetts, 1757. (Lindsay)

CUTLIP, DAVID H. (1848-?), Mingo, West Virginia, 1872-1882d.

CUTTER, ABIJAH Lowell, Massachusetts, 1849d-1878d. Match rifles. With O.A. Richardson as Richardson & Cutter, 1849-1873.

CUTTER, BENJAMIN P. Boston, Massachusetts, 1866-1868.

CUTTER, CHARLES N. Worcester, Massachusetts, 1877-1886d. Patent #193,060 July 10, 1877, breechloading firearm with Frank Wesson, for whom he worked before going on his own in 1880. Single shot rifles on various patterns.

CUTTER, ERASTUS W. Providence, Rhode Island, 1847-1855. With William R. Pope as Pope & Cutter. (Achtermier)

CUTTINO, BENJAMIN T. Georgetown, South Carolina, 1825. (Kauffman 2)

CYPHERS, M.B. Showhegan, Maine, 1859-1868, Greenville, Michigan, 1870-1906. Percussion and cartridge guns. (Demeritt-Grant 2)

CZAR suicide special by Hopkins & Allen, and Hood Fire Arms Co., retailed by Turner and Ross. (Webster)

CZERNY, G. Lyons, New York, 1874d-1880d.

CZISCHKI, CHARLES Crown Point, Indiana, 1882-1885. (MB 5-54)

D SECTION

D. & B. see Davis & Bozeman.

D.B. see Daniel Border.

D.B. see Daniel Boyer.

D.B.B. see Daniel Border.

D.B.W. see David Wagner.

D.C. & CO. see Denny, Campbell & Co.

D.C. & CO. see Dickson, Clark & Co.

D.D. see David Defibaugh.

D.G. see Daniel Gilbert for Model 1798 contract musket.

D.G. unidentified. Flintlock Kentucky.

D.K. unidentified. Flintlock Kentucky

D.K.M. unidentified. Percussion swivel.

D.N. unidentified. Percussion fullstock.

D.S. see David Shepherd.

D.V.S. unidentified. Percussion fullstock.

D.W. unidentified. Percussion 1/2 stock.

D.W. unidentified. Percussion fullstock.

D.Y. see D. Yokum.

DABBS, WILLIAM Little Rock, Arkansas, 1869-1900. As Trumpler & Dabbs, 1873-1874. (Elias)

DADE & RAYNOLDS Mobile, Alabama. Flintlock and percussion guns.

DAFFRY, PETER Buffalo, New York, 1852d. (Dean)

DAFT, ALEXANDER (1826-?), St. Louis, Missouri, 1850c-1852d. As Daft & Hague, 1852. (Lewis)

DAFT, ROBERT (1824-?), St. Louis, Missouri, 1850c. (Lewis)

DAGG, THOMAS (?-1780), Prince William Co., Virginia. (Gill)

DAGGETT, C. Sherman, Maine, 1875. (Demeritt)

DAGGETT, ROBERT P. Indianapolis, Indiana. Patent #230,693 August 3, 1880, safety.

DAHL, ALBERT Marshalltown, Iowa, 1880d, Aurora, Nebraska, 1884d.

DAHL, S.A. Aurora, Nebraska, 1886d-1893d.

DAIGLE, MARCELLUS Houma, Louisiana. Patent #189,305 April 10, 1877, cane gun.

DAISY suicide special by Bacon.

DAKIN, THOMAS Harpers Ferry, Virginia. Patent #none July 28, 1820, gun barrel machine.

DALBEY, H.C. Berlin, Ohio, 1857-1881. Percussion 1/2 stock. (Hutslar)

DALBY, ALEXANDER Millsboro, Pennsylvania, 1858-1865. (Kauffman)

DALBY, ENOCH Millsboro, Pennsylvania, 1841-1865. Percussion 1/2 stock. (Kauffman)

DALBY, HENRY Millsboro, Pennsylvania, 1838.

DALBY, JAMES M. (1837-1906), Millsboro, Pennsylvania, 1865-1882d. Son of Enoch Dalby.

DALBY, WILLIAM (?-1828), Fredrickstown, Pennsylvania, 1815-1828. (Whisker II)

DALEY, A.J. Scio, Oregon, 1867d-1871d.

DALEY, PETER Greene Co., Pennsylvania, 1782-1796, Wheeling, West Virginia, 1797-1804. (Whisker II)

DALEY, S.P. Hartsville, Indiana, 1882-1885. (Lindert)

DALHOUSE, RICHARD Maryland, 1776. Committee of Safety muskets.

DALL, JOSHUA unlocated. Percussion fullstock dated 1839.

DALLAM, RICHARD Harford Co., Maryland, 1776. Committee of Safety muskets. (Hartzler)

DALLIS, J.R. Gale's Creek, Oregon, 1891d.

DALLY, W.H., (H.H., or H.C.) Newton Falls, Ohio, 1852-1888. (Hutslar)

DALTON, PETER Jersey City, New Jersey, 1866-1869. Percussion 1/2 stock.

DALY ARMS CO. trade name of Schoverling, Daly & Gales on imported guns.

DALY, CHARLES New York, New York, 1873d-1939. Importer and dealer.

DAMER, HENRY Lancaster, Pennsylvania, 1857d.

DAMMAN, C.A. Cheyenne, Wyoming, 1880. Temporarily purchased the Freund Bros. store.

DAMSEAUX, JEAN H. (1820-?), San Andreas, California, 1870-1882. (Shelton)

DANA, DANIEL Canton, Massachusetts. Patent #none August 24, 1818, barrel lathe with A. Holmead. Model 1798 muskets, Model 1814 rifles.

DANA, I. Canton, Massachusetts, 1798-1825. Flintlock and percussion Kentucky rifles.

DANA, J. unlocated. Flintlock Kentucky.

DANA, JACOB Canton, Massachusetts, 1777-1815. Flintlock muskets and rifles, Hall patent sporting rifles. (Huntington)

DANBURY see Joseph Clark.

DANBURY, JACOB Maineville, Ohio, 1867. Shotgun. With Clinton Burton. (Hutslar)

DANCE BROTHERS Columbus, Texas, 1863-1865, Anderson, Texas. Confederate revolvers. David, George, and James Dance. (GC 22)

DANCER, GEORGE Croton, Michigan, 1863d.

DANCER, GEORGE Richland Co., Ohio, 1850c.

DANCER, JOSIAH (1829-?), Richland Co., Ohio, 1850c. (Hutslar)

DANE, JOSEPH C. La Crosse, Wisconsin, 1870-1885. Patents #146,658 January 20, 1874, breechloading firearm, and #150,538 May 5, 1874, breechloading firearm. Breechloading shotgun.

DANGERFIELD & LEFEVER Syracuse, New York. Large caliber single shot rifles and double-barrel shotguns. Francis Dangerfield and Daniel Lefever.

DANGERFIELD, FRANCIS S. Auburn, New York, 1870-1874. Patent #130,984 September 3, 1872, breechloading firearm. The "Destroyer", produced by Dangerfield & Lefever, was a tip-up .58 caliber rifle based on this patent.

DANGERFIELD, LEONARD H. (1804-?), Tazewell, Virginia, 1830-1850c. Flintlock match rifle. (Dillin)

DANHAM, L.M., & SONS Mapleton, Pennsylvania, 1887d-1890d.

DANIEL BOONE GUN CO. trade name of Belknap Hardware Co. on rifles.

DANIEL, ADAM Cochranton, Pennsylvania, 1874d. (C&W)

DANIEL, ADDINGTON Northhampton, Massachusetts, 1856-1861. Percussion fullstock.

DANIEL, C. Galveston, Texas. Percussion 1/2 stock.

DANIEL, JOHN Saidora, Illinois, 1860. (Johnson)

DANIEL, PHINEAS Philadelphia, Pennsylvania. Patent #none March 31, 1804, shot tower. The Daniel shot tower was later purchased by Thomas Sparks.

DANIEL, SAMUEL Middlesex Co., Virginia, 1776. Committee of Safety repairs. (Gill)

DANIELS, ADAM Lancaster, Pennsylvania, 1820-1840. Flintlock Kentucky rifles marked "A.D.".

DANIELS, ADAM Wayne, Pennsylvania, 1874d.

DANIELS, CHARLES Chester, Connecticut. Patents #610 February 15, 1838, breechloading firearm, and #677 April 5, 1839, revolver, both with his brother Henry. Guns made by Henry.

DANIELS, GEORGE M. (1831-?), Barbour Co., Virginia, 1850c. Son of Joseph Daniels.

DANIELS, HENRY C. Chester, Connecticut. Patents #610 February 15, 1838, breechloading firearm, and #677 April 5, 1839, revolver, both with his brother Charles. Guns made by Henry.

DANIELS, JOSEPH (1804-?), Barbour Co., Virginia, 1850c. Percussion double rifle.

DANIELS, VERIEN (1800-?), Jacksonville, Illinois, 1831-1850. (Johnson)

DANNAN, W.S. & G. Richmond, Virginia. Derringer. (Eberhart)

DANNE & ZEPERNICK Mobile, Alabama, 1870d. Single shot pistol.

DANNE, JOHN F. Ray Co., Missouri, 1850c. (MB 11-66)

DANNE, JOHN W. Mobile, Alabama, 1859d-1887d. For Gelbke & Bro., 1859. As Danne & Zepernick, 1870. (Neville)

DANNEFELSER, JOHN P. New York, New York, 1884d-1896d. Shotguns.

DANNER, JACOB (1795-1844), Canton, Ohio, 1818-1844. (Hutslar)

DANSETH, ANDREW Pittsburgh, Pennsylvania, 1799, Cincinnati, Ohio, 1800-1820. (Hutslar)

DANTZ, H.A. New Haven, Connecticut, 1873-1876.

DANY, W. Red Cloud, Nebraska, 1884d-1886d.

DAPLYN, THOMAS Dover, Ohio, 1832-1836. Patent #none February 20, 1835, lock. Percussion rifles. (Hutslar)

DARBY, ISAAC Lancaster, New Hampshire, 1783-1840. Flintlock.

DARBY, JOHN V. Newburg, Indiana, 1860d.

DARLING see Harris & Darling.

DARLING, BARTON & BENJAMIN M. (1808-1890), Bellingham, Massachusetts, Woonsocket, Rhode Island. Patent #9,591X April 13, 1836, pepperbox. Made only iron frame pepperboxes; those with brass frames were made in Sweden. (Achtermier)

DARLING, DEXTER H. Guilford, New York. Patent #638,007 November 28, 1899, sight.

DARLING, E.C. New Orleans, Louisiana, 1846. Submitted a repeating rifle to Ordnance Department.

DARLING, EDMUND R. Woonsocket, Rhode Island, 1877-1921.

DARLING, W.K. Otsego, Michigan, 1863d-1867d. Percussion rifles. As Harris & Darling, 1867.

DARLINGTON, BENJAMIN Pittsburgh, Pennsylvania, 1816d. Importer and dealer.

DARNELL, MORGAN (?-1726), King George Co., Virginia. (Gill)

DARNS, HERMAN A. Napa, California. Patents #590,411 September 21, 1897, rifle tube, and #611,062 September 20, 1898, rifle tube.

DARR, H.L. Portland, Oregon, 1871d.

DARR, JOHANN C. (1825-?), San Francisco, California, 1870-1881. (Shelton)

DARRAGH, JOHN Aurora, Illinois, 1867d.

DARROW, H. Mayville, New York, 1880-1882d.

DARROW, L.F. Mayville, New York, 1865-1882. Percussion 1/2 stock. (Clow)

DART & WATKINSON New Orleans, Louisiana, 1867d. Importers and dealers. Successors to Kittredge & Folsom.

DART, D. Carbondale, Kansas, 1878d.

DART, JOHN P. Enfield, Illinois, 1864d.

DASH suicide special.

DASHER, C.M. Point Pleasant, West Virginia, 1900d. See C.M. Daschner.

DASHIELL, GEORGE V. Norfolk, Virginia, 1888d-1897d.

DASHNER, C.M. Renault, Illinois, 1890d.

DASHNOW, PETER Rossie, New York, 1871-1874.

DAUB, J. Berks Co., Pennsylvania. Flintlock Kentucky rifle. (Dillin)

DAUGHERTY, ABSALOM Annville, Pennsylvania, 1842. (Kauffman)

DAUGHERTY, J.S. Atkins, Arkansas, 1898d.

DAUGHERTY, THOMAS North Manchester, Indiana, 1860d, Bourbon, Indiana, 1862d.

DAUSETT, ANDREW unlocated. Flintlock Kentucky rifle.

DAVENPORT ARMS CO. Providence, Rhode Island, 1880-1884. Single shot rifles and shotguns. Sold to Bay State Arms Co. (GR 9-72)

DAVENPORT FIRE ARMS CO. Norwich, Connecticut, 1890-1909. Single and double-barrel shotguns, single shot rifles. Used many trade names. (GR 9-72)

DAVENPORT, ARCHIBALD B. (?-1909), Ft. Scott, Kansas, 1890-1909. Rented guns which he stamped with his name. (GR 2-65)

DAVENPORT, JOSEPH Williamsburg, Virginia, 1747-1760. (Gill)

DAVENPORT, W.H., & CO. Providence, Rhode Island, 1878-1880. Barrels for Sharps Rifle Co.

DAVENPORT, WALTON C. Norwich, Connecticut. Patent #5 12,434, January 9, 1894, firearm. Son of William H. Davenport.

DAVENPORT, WILLIAM H. (1828-1905), Milbury, Massachusetts. Patents #237,432 February 8, 1881, breechloading firearm, #243,222 June 21, 1881, breechloading firearm, #243,223 June 21, 1881, breechloading firearm, #251,099 December 20, 1881, breechloading firearm, #290,751 December 25, 1883, breechloading firearm, #300,851 June 24, 1884, breechloading firearm, #300,852 June 24, 1884, breechloading firearm, #320,637 June 23, 1885, breechloading firearm, #326,276 September 15, 1885, breechloading firearm, #334,570 January 19, 1886, breechloading firearm, #390,286 October 2, 1888, set trigger, #406,031 July 2, 1889, breechloading firearm, #406,032 July 2, 1889, removable barrels, #442,106 December 9, 1890, extractor, #465,354 December 15, 1891, breechloading firearm, #549,706 November 12, 1895, cocking device, #565,605 August 11, 1896, extractor, #565,606 August 11, 1896, extractor, #580,679 April 13, 1897, magazine gun, #592,239 October 26, 1897, ejector, #615,958 December 13, 1898, ejector, #624,187 May 2, 1899, breechloading firearm, #638,322 December 5, 1899, extractor, #701,158 May 27, 1902, breechloading firearm, and #701,159 May 27, 1902, breechloading firearm. Employed by Allen, Brown & Luther, 1850-1853, Burnside Rifle Co., 1862-1865, Providence Tool Co., 1865-1878, W.H. Davenport & Co., 1878-1880, Davenport Arms Co., 1880-1883, Bay State Arms Co., 1883-1887, Hopkins & Allen, 1887-1890, and W.H. Davenport Fire Arms Co., 1890-1905. (OR 9-72)

DAVID, SAMUEL (1813-?), Jeffersonville, Indiana, 1860c. (Lindert)

DAVIDSON, C.H. Union, California, 1854. (Shelton)

DAVIDSON, ESTELL W., & CO. Cincinnati, Ohio. Percussion fullstock.

DAVIDSON, HEZEKIAH Hart Co., Kentucky, 1820c.

DAVIDSON, JOHN (1757-1832), Rockbridge Co., Virginia, 1790-1832. Flintlock Kentucky rifles and Virginia contract rifles. (Gill)

DAVIDSON, JOHN Manchester, Ohio, 1798-1859. (Hutslar)

DAVIDSON, OTIS E. Nashville, Tennessee, 1866-1877d.

DAVIDSON, PETER Chicago, Illinois, 1839. (Johnson)

DAVIDSON, SAMUEL Travisville, Tennessee, 1860d.

DAVIDSON, T., & CO. Cincinnati, Ohio, 1834-1866. Lockmakers only. Tyler Davidson.

DAVIDSON, THOMAS H. (1823-?), Monmouth, Illinois, 1850c-1880d.

DAVIES, EVAN G. (1810-?), Bouckville, New York, 1850c-1882d. Percussion rifles. See Evan Davis. (Swinney)

DAVIES, WILLIAM Boston, Massachusetts, 1650-1683.

DAVIS & BOZEMAN Central, Alabama, 1862-1864. Mississippi rifles, marked "D & B", and repaired arms (also marked "D & B"), for the Confederacy. Henry J. Davis and David Bozeman. (Hill-Anthony)

DAVIS & COSAT Perrysville, Indiana. J.S. Davis. (Lindert)

DAVIS & HURST Paris, Illinois, 1874-1877. James S. Davis and J.M. Hurst.

DAVIS & THRASHER Freetown, Massachusetts, 1856-1860. N.R. Davis and David Thrasher.

DAVIS BROTHERS Glencoe, Minnesota, 1886d.

DAVIS Canfield, Ohio. Percussion over/under rifle. (Hutslar)

DAVIS, A., JR. Stafford, Connecticut. Underhammer pistol. (Logan)

DAVIS, ABBOT R. East Cambridge, Massachusetts. Patent #12,545 March 20, 1855, shot cartridge.

DAVIS, AMOS R. (1818-1894), Deposit, New York, 1846-1882d. Flintlock and percussion rifles. (Swinney)

DAVIS, ARI Washington, D.C. Patent #10,788 April 18, 1854, box. Gun cases made by William Kidder under this patent.

DAVIS, ARMENIUS Shelbyville, Indiana, 1860d-1862d. Patent #29,676 August 21, 1860, cane gun. (Lindert)

DAVIS, B.F., Beech Grove, Indiana, 1860d.

DAVIS, C.A. Halcottville, New York. Percussion 1/2 stock. (Swinney)

DAVIS, CASPER EARLY (1848-1928), New Paris, Pennsylvania, 1870-1928. (Whisker II)

DAVIS, CHARLES W. Taylorville, Illinois, 1864d.

DAVIS, CHARLES (1836-?), Logansport, Indiana, 1860c. Son of W.R. Davis. (Lindert)

DAVIS, CHARLES Vandalia, Illinois, 1864d.

DAVIS, DANIEL Albemarle Co., Virginia, 1801, Orange Co., Virginia, 1810-1815. Contract rifles for Virginia. (Cromwell)

DAVIS, E.J. Winona, Minnesota, 1898d.

DAVIS, E.L. Hinkley, Illinois, 1860.

DAVIS, EALY C. Bedford, Pennsylvania, 1884d. See Casper E. Davis.

DAVIS, ELI (1827-?), Porter Co., Indiana, 1850c. (Lindert)

DAVIS, ESBON B. Buffalo, New York, 1857d. Son of James Davis.

DAVIS, EVAN G. Madison, New York, 1863-1874, Bouchsville, New York, 1874-1882. See Evan Davies.

DAVIS, FLORIAN Brooklyn, New York. Patent #43,709 August 2, 1864, revolver with Charles Robitaille; produced as the Pettengill. (Sellers-1)

DAVIS, G.W. Unionville, Missouri, 1898d.

DAVIS, GEORGE (1795-?), Louisburg, North Carolina, 1850c. (Bivins)

DAVIS, H.R. Hartford, Michigan, 1863d.

DAVIS, HENRY J. see Davis & Bozeman.

DAVIS, ISAAC (1740-1775), Acton, Massachusetts, 1763-1775. Was the first officer killed at the battle of Concord.

DAVIS, J.D. unlocated. Percussion 1/2 stock.

DAVIS, J.F. Fall River, Massachusetts, 1871-1885d.

DAVIS, J.G. De Kalb, Illinois, 1882.

DAVIS, J.M. Butlerville, Indiana, 1858d, Bryantsville, Indiana, 1860d.

DAVIS, J.N. New Paris, Pennsylvania, 1860. (Gluckman & Satterlee)

DAVIS, J.S. Perrysville, Indiana. Percussion fullstock. As Davis & Cosat.

DAVIS, JACOB Buffalo, New York, 1844. For Patrick Smith. (Dean)

DAVIS, JAMES B. Washington, D.C. Patents #315,253 April 7, 1885, breechloading firearm, and #318,093 May 19, 1885, gas check.

DAVIS, JAMES H. Buffalo, New York, 1844-1859d.

DAVIS, JAMES S. (1830-?), Danville, Illinois, 1859-1862. (Johnson)

DAVIS, JAMES T. Big Oak Flat, California, 1860c. (Shelton)

DAVIS, JAMES Philadelphia, Pennsylvania, 1780-1785. Repaired US arms. (Moller)

DAVIS, JAMES St. Louis, Missouri, 1847d.

DAVIS, JARVIS Buffalo, New York, 1848-1870. Patents #37,544 January 27, 1863, breechloading firearm, #39,198 July 7, 1863, breechloading firearm, #42,529 April 26, 1864, breechloading firearm, #51,258 November 28, 1865, breechloading firearm, and #103,154 May 17, 1870, breechloading firearm. All used by Patrick Smith.

DAVIS, JOHN G. (1821-?), Belvidere, Illinois, 1854d-1860d.

DAVIS, JOHN N. (1814-1882), Bedford Co., Pennsylvania, 1835-1882. Percussion fullstock. (Whisker)

DAVIS, JOHN S. Paris, Illinois, 1874d-1896d.

DAVIS, JOSHUA Limestoneville, Pennsylvania. Patents #112,127 February 28, 1871, magazine gun, #132,357 October 22, 1872, revolver, and #182,646 September 26, 1876, revolver.

DAVIS, JOSHUA Muskegon, Michigan, 1863d.

DAVIS, M.O. unlocated. Percussion 1/2 stock.

DAVIS, MARVEL C. Mayville, New York. Patent #none February 20, 1827, lock.

DAVIS, N.R., & CO. Assonet, Freetown, Massachusetts, 1853-1917. Percussion and cartridge guns. Nathan R. Davis. Assonet was a section of Freetown.

DAVIS, NATHAN RUSSELL Freetown, Massachusetts. Patents #81,348 August 25, 1868, attaching gun barrels, #217,001 July 1, 1879, firearms, #293,719, February 19, 1884, breechloading firearms, #294,772 March 11, 1884, breechloading firearm, and #346,536 August 3, 1886, breechloading firearm. Formed N.R. Davis & Co. in 1853.

DAVIS, OBEDIAH Battle Creek, Michigan, 1873d-1875d.

DAVIS, POWHATAN (1821-?), Southwark, Virginia, 1850c. (MB 10-63)

DAVIS, R.L. Eldorado, Kansas, 1894d.

DAVIS, SAMUEL L. St. George, Maine, 1840-1880. (Demeritt)

DAVIS, SAMUEL (1763-1849), Delaware Co., Ohio, 1808, Franklin Co., Ohio, 1809-1849. (Hutslar)

DAVIS, SYLVANUS Lincoln, Maine, 1867-1873. (Demeritt)

DAVIS, THEODORE B. Portland, Maine, 1874-1939. Primarily imported guns. As T.B. Davis Arms Co., 1894-1939. (Demeritt)

DAVIS, THOMAS New York, New York, 1847-1851. (Gardner)

DAVIS, W.H. Blue Earth City, Minnesota, 1898d.

DAVIS, W.P., & SON Kansas City, Missouri, 1878d.

DAVIS, WILLIAM H. Linneus, Maine, 1868-1873.

DAVIS, WILLIAM R. (1808-?), Logansport, Indiana, 1836-1880. (Lindert)

DAVIS, WILLIAM T. Battle Creek, Michigan, 1879d-1891d. Patent #278,688 June 15, 1883, firearm.

DAVIS, WILLIAM Albany, New York, 1834-1836.

DAVIS, WILLIAM Little Rock, Arkansas, 1873d.

DAVIS, WILLIAM Savannah, Illinois, 1878d.

DAVIS, ZENO P. (1818-1902), Nevada City, California, 1849-1900. (Shelton)

DAVISON & JONES Allegheny, Pennsylvania, 1887d.

DAW, REUBEN (1806-?), Washington, D.C., 1834d-1872d. (Hartzler)

DAWIN BROTHERS Peekskill, New York, 1868-1874.

DAWLEY & WHEELOCK Montpelier, Vermont, 1891d.

DAWLEY, FRANK K. Montpelier, Vermont, 1889d-1891d. As Dawley & Wheelock, 1891.

DAWSON, I. unlocated. Flintlock Kentucky rifle.

DAWSON, J.G. Lecoma, Missouri, 1898d.

DAWSON, T.K. Williamsport, Indiana. Fancy percussion fullstock rifle.

DAWSON, THOMAS Point of Fork, Virginia, 1786-1790. (Gill)

DAY & HALSEY New York, New York, 1867d-1880d. Breechloading shotgun, dealers.

DAY, BARNEY Catlin, Illinois, 1872, Ellis and Sheridan, Kansas, 1873, Georgetown, Colorado, 1876d, Hot Sulphur Springs, Colorado, 1877d, Boulder, Colorado, 1878-1884d. Brother of John Day.

DAY, BENJAMIN F. Cherryfield, Maine, 1848-1856, Bangor, Maine, 1859, Biddeford, Maine, 1874-1880. See also Bean & Day. (Demeritt)

DAY, E.N. Mesopotamia, Ohio, 1860-1864. (Hutslar)

DAY, JAMES Louisville, Kentucky, 1843-1890. Percussion and cartridge guns. For Joseph Griffith, 1843-1849. (MB 12-46)

DAY, JESSE (1818-?), Trumbull Co., Ohio, 1850c. (Hutslar)

DAY, JOHN (1816-?), Central City, Colorado, 1870d-1874d, Boulder, Colorado, 1874d-1884d. (Sellers-3)

DAY, JOHN (1817-?), Warren, Ohio, 1850-1865. Percussion rifles. (Hutslar)

DAY, JOHN Point of Fork, Virginia, 1781. (Gill)

DAY, JOSEPH C. Hackettstown, New Jersey, 1849-1865. Patents #11,477 August 8, 1854, breechloading firearm, #13,941 December 18, 1855, breechloading firearm, #14,095 January 15, 1856, breechloading firearm. Made rifles and pistols under his patents.

DAY, RICHARD Philadelphia, Pennsylvania, 1835d-1846d.

DAY, SILAS New York, New York, 1831-1840. Patents #364 August 31, 1837, breechloading firearm, #1,461 December 31, 1839, self capping firearms with Samuel Hall, and #1,810 October 8, 1840, breechloading firearm.

DAY, THOMAS St. Louis, Missouri, 1848d-1867d, New York, New York, 1867d-1880d. As Shapleigh, Day & Co. in St. Louis and Day & Halsey in New York.

DAY, WILLIAM E. Georgetown, Massachusetts, 1876d-1892d.

DAY, WILLIAM Gillespieville, Ohio, 1831-1860. Percussion 1/2 stock. (Hutslar)

DAYTON, FREDERICK New Buffalo, Michigan, 1860d.

DAYTON, W.H. Stamford, Connecticut, 1885d.

DE BENDER, GEORGE Philadelphia, Pennsylvania, 1855d-1867d.

DE HODIAMONT, GEORGE St. Louis, Missouri, 1857d.

DE LA RUE Madisonville, Ohio, 1878d. (Hutslar)

DE LAVEN, H.W., & CO. unlocated. Lockmakers only.

DE LONG, EBENEZER (?-1879), Parish, New York, 1850c-1879. (Swinney)

DE LONG, LUCIUS Chattanooga, Tennessee, 1860d-1891d. Percussion and cartridge guns. As De Long & Son, 1869-91.

DE LONG, W.E. Dardanelle, Arkansas, 1884d.

DE LORME, FRANK New York, New York. Patent #269,023 December 12, 1882, sight.

DE REINER, MICHAEL Lancaster, Pennsylvania, 1773-1777. Committee of Safety muskets. Worked for William Henry, 1777. (Hobbies 4-38)

DE SINGER, VALENTINE Philadelphia, Pennsylvania, 1837d.

DEACON, EDWARD unlocated. Percussion pistol similar to Allen design.

DEADSHOT trade name of Meriden Fire Arms Co. on single shot .22 cal. rifle.

DEADSHOT trade name on spur trigger revolvers made from Bacon pepperboxes.

DEAN, CHARLES Ft. Walla Walla, Washington. Lever action rifle in 1882 trials.

DEAN, E. Phillipsburgh, Kansas, 1888d.

DEAN, JOHN (1774-1857), Rochester, New York, 1842-1857. (Eich)

DEAN, JOHN Huntingdon Co., Pennsylvania, 1795-1805. (Whisker II)

DEAN, S.O. Brown Hill, Pennsylvania, 1882d-1890d.

DEARBORN, OTIS R. Limerick, Maine, 1871. (Demeritt)

DEARTH, LACY (1812-?), Brownsville, Pennsylvania, 1840-1860. (Whisker II)

DEASHNER see Deschner.

DEBARBIERIS, HENRY New Orleans, Louisiana, 1867d-1897d.

DEBARRIER, HENRY see Henry Deberier.

DEBEAUGRINE, J.W. Warrenton, Georgia, 1879d-1883d.

DEBERIER, HENRY Philadelphia, Pennsylvania, 1769-1780. (Kauffman)

DEBERRY, HENRY Montgomery Co., North Carolina, 1770-1805. (Bivins)

DEBOLT, HENRY Mapleton, Pennsylvania, 1869-1876. (Kauffman)

DEBOND, NOWELL (1830-?), Harrison, Indiana, 1850c. (Lindert)

DEBRAME, J.A. New York, New York. Patents #32,685 July 2, 1861, revolver, #34,024 December 24, 1861, breechloading cannon, and #34,025 December 24, 1861, revolving cannon. (Sellers-1)

DEBRULER, JOSEPH Ashboro, Indiana, 1862d.

DECHART, JACOB Lancaster, Pennsylvania, 1753. See also Dickert. (Dillin)

DECKARD, H.H. Gamaliel, Kentucky, 1883d.

DECKARD, J. Fairfax, Indiana, 1879-1885. (Gardner)

DECKER, ALONZO T. New York, New York. Patent #198,279 December 18, 1877, sight.

DECKER, WILLIAM Millstadt, Illinois, 1864d.

DECORTINS, JOSEPH Badus, Dakota Territory, 1886d.

DECOURSEY, JOHN G. Philadelphia, Pennsylvania. Patent #53,582 April 3, 1866, bullet.

DECUMBUS, OLIVER H. Newark, New Jersey. Patent #358,734 March 1, 1887, sight protector.

DECURTIN, A. Stillwater, Minnesota, 1878d.

DEDER, G. unlocated. Percussion fullstock.

DEEDS, HENRY W. (1811-1888), Reading, Pennsylvania, 1850c, Lancaster Co., Pennsylvania, 1860c-1888. Barrelmaker.

DEEDS, W. unlocated. Flintlock Kentucky rifle.

DEEMER, JACOB Northampton Co., Pennsylvania, 1850c. Percussion fullstock of Bedford Co. style.

DEER SLAYER trade name on percussion 1/2 stock, by J. Henry & Son.

DEFENDER knife pistol by U.S. Small Arms Co.

DEFENDER suicide special by Iver Johnson.

DEFIANCE suicide special by Norwick Arms Co.

DEFIBAUGH, DANIEL (1830-?), Bedford Co., Pennsylvania, 1852-1864. Brother of William Defibaugh. (Whisker)

DEFIBAUGH, DAVID (1841-1914), Everett, Pennsylvania, 1864-1880. Percussion rifles signed "D.D.". Son of William Defibaugh.

DEFIBAUGH, JAMES LAWRENCE Everett, Pennsylvania, 1860-1880. Son of William Defibaugh. (Whisker)

DEFIBAUGH, L. Bedford Co., Pennsylvania, 1871. See James Defibaugh.

DEFIBAUGH, L. Nebraska City, Nebraska, 1879d-1886d.

DEFIBAUGH, MILTON (1848-1931), Everett, Pennsylvania, 1870-1931. Son of William Defibaugh.

DEFIBAUGH, WILLIAM (1814-1891), Bedford, Pennsylvania, 1840-1860. Percussion fullstock. (Hetrick)

DEFORD, ISAAC Forest City, Missouri, 1898d.

DEFRAITAS, JOHN J. Springfield, Illinois, 1857d-1875d.

DEFREES, J.H. Piqua, Ohio, 1813-1906. Percussion fullstock.

DEGRESS, FRANCIS Bloomfield, New Jersey. Patent #150,229 April 28, 1874, metal pistol grips. (GR 1-72)

DEHAVEN & WELLS Philadelphia, Pennsylvania, 1780. Peter DeHaven & Richard Wells.

DEHAVEN, HUGH Philadelphia, Pennsylvania, 1775-1779. Committee of Safety muskets. (Gluckman & Satterlee)

DEHAVEN, PETER Philadelphia, Pennsylvania, 1775-1790. Operated State Gun Lock Factory, 1776-1778, and on his own thereafter.

DEHUFF, ABRAHAM Lancaster, Pennsylvania, 1779. (Gluckman & Satterlee)

DEHUFF, HENRY (1770-?), Lancaster, Pennsylvania, 1800-1808. Model 1798 contract muskets for Pennsylvania, Model 1807 contract rifles for U.S. with Jacob Dickert and Peter Gonter. Flintlock Kentucky. (Gluckman)

DEHUFF, JOHN Pittsburgh, Pennsylvania, 1787-1793, Washington, Pennsylvania, 1793-1803, Lancaster Co., Pennsylvania, 1813-1816. Father and son? (Kauffman)

DEISINGER, J. Kokomo, Indiana. Percussion 1/2 stock.

DEISINGER, WENDELL Philadelphia, Pennsylvania, 1861d. See Wendel Diesinger.

DEITERICH, LOUIS Wittenburg, Missouri, 1879d.

DEITZ, ADAM Warren, Pennsylvania, 1822-1833. (Whisker II)

DEIVIT, ELIJAH Clay City, Illinois, 1860d.

DEIZMAN, O. Hennepin, Illinois, 1860d.

DELAGNEAU, GEORGE Hastings, Nebraska, 1893d.

DELAND, F.A. Memphis, Michigan, 1895d-1899d.

DELANEY, I.F. Reading, Pennsylvania, 1890d.

DELANEY, NELSON Bethlehem, Pennsylvania, 1847-1848, Reading, Pennsylvania, 1848-1885. Percussion rifles and pistols. (Kauffman)

DELANEY, PIERRE Lynnville, Illinois, 1866-1875. (Johnson)

DELANO, N. Duxbury, Massachusetts, 1876-1880.

DELAROCHE, THEODORE Denver, Colorado, 1874-1875d. (Sellers-3)

DELARUE, M.E. Richmond, Virginia, 1870c-1873d. Percussion 1/2 stock.

DELASSIZE, L.T. New Orleans, Louisiana. Patent #92,799 July 20, 1869, breechloading firearm.

DELATORRE, ANTONIO New Orleans, Louisiana, 1877d-1879d.

DELAVILLITTE, ALFRED Butte, Montana, 1886d.

DELCKER, FREDERICK Dubuque, Iowa, 1865d-1888d.

DELENISTEZ, JAMES Los Angeles, California. (Shelton)

DELLETT, PETER Lancaster, Pennsylvania, 1854-1857d.

DELONG, L. Parish, New York, 1870d.

DELOP, A. (1814-?), Marysville, California, 1852c. (Shelton)

DELPH, W.H. Metamora, Illinois, 1860d-1864d.

DELPHIAN ARMS CO. trade name of Supplee-Biddle Hardware Co. on imported shotguns. (Hinman)

DELPHIAN MANUFACTURING CO. trade name of Crescent on shotguns.

DELVEY, JOHN Gill, Massachusetts. Percussion target rifle.

DEMAREST, NICHOLAS P. (1809-1879), Rochester, New York, 1841d, Bergen Point, New Jersey, 1879. (Eich)

DEMAY, EUGENE Richmond, Texas, 1884d.

DEMERITT, JOHN (1809-1896), Dover, New Hampshire, 1860-1863, Montpelier, Vermont, 1866-1889d. Underhammer pistols. (Horn)

DEMETZ, J.M. see J.M. Diemetz.

DEMILLY, L.C. Tallahassee, Florida, 1884d-1886d.

DEMILLY, W.A. Tallahassee, Florida, 1883d.

DEMING, BYRON (1826-?), San Francisco, California, 1850, Union Town, California, 1856. (Shelton)

DEMING, H. unlocated. Flintlock Kentucky.

DEMING, JAMES unlocated. Flintlock Kentucky.

DEMOUSTIER, JOSEPH New Orleans, Louisiana, 1841d-1842d.

DEMPSEY, A.B. Sedalia, Missouri, 1879d-1893d.

DEMPSEY, GEORGE Rochester, New York, 1849d. (Eich)

DEMPSEY, H.H. Denison, Texas, 1896d.

DEMPSEY, J.W. New Orleans, Louisiana, 1855-1872d. As Gerteis & Dempsey, 1860.

DEMPSEY, JAMES W. Detroit, Michigan, 1875d-1882d.

DEMPSEY, JOHN see John Demsey.

DEMPSTER, BADWIN Dale (rural), Ohio, 1857-1863, Zanesville, Ohio, 1863-1878. Percussion 1/2 stock. (Hutslar)

DEMSCHELL, JOSEPH (1823-?), Cincinnati, Ohio, 1850c. (Hutslar)

DEMSEY, JOHN Cambria Co., Pennsylvania, 1852t-1854t. (Kauffman)

DEMSEY, MATTHEW Cambria Co., Pennsylvania, 1834-1835. (Kauffman)

DEMUTH, CHRISTOPHER Lancaster Co., Pennsylvania, 1790t-1804t. (Dyke)

DEMUTH, H. unlocated. Flintlock swivel breech.

DEMUTH, JOHN (1771-?), Lancaster, Pennsylvania, 1794-?, Frederick Co., Maryland, 1796. Flintlock Kentucky. (Hartzler)

DEMUTH, JONATHAN Bushkill, Pennsylvania, 1828t. Percussion lock. (Dyke)

DEMUTH, JOSEPH Lancaster Co., Pennsylvania, 1800t-1813t. (Dyke)

DEMUTH, WILLIAM Bushkill, Pennsylvania, 1820t. (KRA II-3)

DENCH, J.W. Placerville, California, 1880-1881. (Shelton)

DENING, H. unlocated. Flintlock Kentucky.

DENISON, JOHN Findlay, Ohio, 1875d. (Hutslar)

DENISTON, A. Montrose, Colorado, 1895d. (Sellers-3)

DENIZOT, R. Stuebenville, Ohio, 1861-1865. (Hutslar)

DENK, EMANUEL St. Louis, Missouri, 1859d. As Basler & Denk.

DENMAN, WILLIAM unlocated. Percussion 1/2 stock underhammer.

DENNELL, PETER Athens, New York, 1869-1874d.

DENNER, A. Santa Cruz, California, 1859-1862. (Shelton)

DENNIS, E.B. South Bradford, New York, 1880d.

DENNIS, E.M. David City, Nebraska, 1880d.

DENNIS, E.M. Saline, Michigan, 1887d.

DENNIS, JOHN (?-1778), Williamsburg, Virginia, 1741-?, Halifax Co., Virginia, ?-1778. (Gill)

DENNIS, JOHN Bedford, New York, 1871-1882. Percussion 1/2 stock.

DENNIS, WALTER L. Bridgeport, Connecticut, 1865d-1877.

DENNIS, WILLIAM La Grange, Missouri, 1860d.

DENNIS, WILLIAM Wilkes-Barre, Pennsylvania, 1818, Montrose, Pennsylvania, 1818-1832. (Kauffman)

DENNISON, G.W. unlocated. Percussion 1/2 stock target.

DENNISON, JAMES St. Francois Co., Missouri, 1850c. (MB 11-66)

DENNISON, JOSEPH W. Freeport, Maine, 1871. (Demeritt)

DENNISON, WILLIAM C. Haverhill, Massachusetts, 1865d-1871d. As Sawyer & Dennison.

DENNY, CAMPBELL & CO. Cincinnati, Ohio, 1857d. Wholesale hardware, locks. (Hutslar)

DENNY, WALTER West Augusta, Virginia, 1775. State repairs. (Gill)

DENNY, WILLIAM Glencoe, Minnesota, 1875d-1884d, Anoka, Minnesota, 1886d-1898d.

DENSLANS, R. unlocated. Percussion 1/2 stock.

DENSLOW, CHARLES A. (1848-?), San Diego, California, 1869-1877. (Shelton)

DENSMORE, CHARLES A. Chelsea, Vermont, 1868-1888. (Horn)

DENT, I.C. unlocated. Percussion fullstock.

DENT, WILLIAM North Carolina, 1793. Committee of Safety muskets and flintlock Kentucky rifle. (MB 10-65)

DENZLER, FREDERICK New York, New York. Patent #35,086 April 29, 1862, parlor gun.

DEOBLER, HENRY New Berlin, Pennsylvania. Flintlock and percussion Kentucky rifles. (Gabel)

DEPAUGH & HEFFLY Nebraska City, Nebraska, 1872-1875.

DERBY, DAVID B. Erie Co., Pennsylvania, 1850c. (GR 11-60)

DERINGE, DEERRINGER, (AND OTHER VARIANTS OF DERINGER) trade names on copies of Henry Deringer's pistols.

DERINGER RIFLE & PISTOL WORKS Philadelphia, Pennsylvania, circa 1870. Cartridge revolvers and single shot rifles. (GR 6-75)

DERINGER, BRONAUGH W., & CO. Philadelphia, Pennsylvania. Son of and successor to Henry Deringer. (Bugle 49)

DERINGER, HENRY Richmond, Virginia, ?-1769, Philadelphia, Pennsylvania, 1769-1814, Easton, Pennsylvania, 1786-1798t. Flintlock Kentucky rifles.

DERINGER, HENRY, JR. (1786-1868), Richmond, Virginia, 1807-1808, Philadelphia, Pennsylvania, 1808-1868. Many U.S. government contracts for rifles (in 1814[two], 1821, 1823, 1832, and 1840), Indian guns (in 1809, 1815, 1831, 1832, 1833, and 1839), muskets (in 1828), and pistols (in 1841). Also made "Deringers", which ensured his name and handgun type a permanent status in firearms history. Son of and successor to Henry Deringer. (Parsons)

DERINGER, JACOB Philadelphia, Pennsylvania, 1860c. Derringers.

DERN, H. Philadelphia, Pennsylvania. Spurious marking on derringer.

DERR, CHRISTIAN Berks Co., Pennsylvania, 1805. (Kauffman)

DERR, CHRISTIAN, JR. Union Co., Pennsylvania. Flintlock and percussion Kentucky rifles signed "C.D.". (Gabel)

DERR, DANIEL Bellefonte, Pennsylvania, 1861d-1868d. Percussion fullstock.

DERR, JOHANNES Weisenberg, Pennsylvania, 1800-1807, Oley Valley, Pennsylvania, 1818-1831. Flintlock Kentucky rifle. (Kauffman)

DERR, JOHN Lancaster, Pennsylvania, 1810-1844. Flintlock Kentucky.

DERR, PETER Tulpehocken, Pennsylvania, 1860d-1861d.

DERRINGER, PHILIP Reading, Pennsylvania, 1860d-1861d.

DERRINGER, T.T. Philadelphia, Pennsylvania, 1841d-1847d. (Dean)

DERROUGH, JOHN H. (1825-?), Rusk, Texas, 1862-1864, Sweetwater, Texas, 1880d, Cleburne, Texas, 1884d-1892d, Dublin, Texas, 1892d. As Derrough & Bracken, 1890-1892.

DERTH, G. unlocated. Flintlock Kentucky pistol. (Dean)

DERUNK, JOSEPH (1810-?), Chicago, Illinois, 1859, Anaheim, California, 1871-1876. (Shelton)

DESANY, NELSON Lehigh Co., Pennsylvania, 1846t-1849t. Probably Nelson Delany. (Dyke)

DESCHNER, THEODORE (?-1876), Rochester, New York, 1855-1859d, Ithaca, New York, 1863-1876. Percussion 1/2 stock. For Billinghurst, 1855-1859, and as T. Deschner & Sons, 1863-1867. (Eich)

DESCHNER, THEODORE Bellefonte, Pennsylvania, 1871-1887d. Son of Theodore Deschner?

DESCHNER, THEODORE Seattle, Washington, 1891d. Same as above?

DESENGLES, FRANCOIS New Orleans, Louisiana, 1879d.

DESHERA, WILLIAM Jersey Shore, Pennsylvania, 1882d.

DESPATCH suicide special by Iver Johnson.

DESTROYER trade name of Dangerfield & Lefever.

DESVERNEYS, ANTHONY, JR. Charleston, South Carolina, 1785. (Kauffman)

DESVERNEYS, PIERRE FRANCOIS Charleston, South Carolina, 1777-1798. Used Francis Deverney as his professional name. (Kauffman 2)

DETERER, ADAM Lancaster, Pennsylvania, 1775-1778. Committee of Safety muskets. For William Henry. (Hobbies 4-38)

DETREISON, REUBEN Lancaster Co., Pennsylvania, 1850t. (KRA IV-4)

DETROIT ARMS CO. Detroit, Michigan, circa 1880. Cartridge shotguns. (Hinman)

DETTMAR, WILLIAM (1832-?), Salem, North Carolina, 1850c-1896d. (Bivins)

DETWILER, ANDREW Springfield Furnace, Pennsylvania, 1861d.

DETWILER, ANTHONY Bedford, Pennsylvania, 1870d, Bloomfield, Pennsylvania, 1886d.

DETWILER, CHRISTIAN Bellville, Pennsylvania, 1844-1870. (Dillin, Whisker II)

DETZ, GEORGE (1831-1904), San Francisco, California, 1852, Stockton, California, 1852-1858 and 1879-1887. (Shelton)

DEUKERT & BROCKHAUS Milwaukee, Wisconsin, 1858.

DEUNCKEL, GEORGE F.S. St. Louis, Missouri, 1864-1899d. Percussion double shotgun.

DEUTTENMULLER see Beuttenmuller.

DEVANE, JAMES (1757-1832), New Hanover, North Carolina, 1776-1832. Committee of Safety muskets and rifles with Richard Herring. (Bivins)

DEVANE, JOHN Wilmington, North Carolina, 1776-1778. Public gun factory.

DEVAUX, FERDINAND Robertsville, Ohio, 1865-1898. Percussion 1/2 stock. As Frank N. DeVaux in 1898 directory. (Hutslar)

DEVECE, JOHN Fayette Co., Pennsylvania, 1816-1820. (Whisker II)

DEVENDORF, LEWIS (1809-1887), Cedarville, New York, 1847-1874d. Percussion rifles and pistols.

DEVERSON, RICHARD Boston, Massachusetts, 1810-1814.

DEVOL, ED Sullivan Co., Indiana, circa 1880. Son of J.B. Devol. (Lindert)

DEVOL, J.B. Middletown, Indiana, 1858d, Sullivan, Indiana, 1880. (Lindert)

DEVOL, NOEL B. (1831-?), Marshall, Illinois, 1860c. (Johnson)

DEVORE, BENJAMIN Somerset Co., Pennsylvania, 1840. (Kauffman)

DEVORE, SAMUEL A. New Rumley, Ohio, 1855-1861. With Alexander Ager. (AOLRC 1)

DEWALT, PETER Wequoit, Wisconsin, 1857d.

DEWERSON, RICHARD C. Boston, Massachusetts, 1846d-1855d. See Richard Deverson.

DEWEY, C. Saranac, Michigan, 1863d.

DEWEY, EBENEZER Amber, New York, 1850c-1882d. Percussion over/under rifle/shotgun. (Clow)

DEWEY, H. Otisco, New York, 1870d-1882. Percussion 1/2 stock. (Clow)

DEWEY, MAURICE Clarendon, New York, 1856-1873d. Percussion 1/2 stock.

DEWEY, SAMUEL Hebron, Connecticut, 1774-1777. Committee of Safety muskets. (Kauffman 2)

DEWING, A.W. Lompoc, California, 1893d.

DEWIT, GEORGE C. (1801-?), Wapakoneta, Ohio, 1850c. (Hutslar)

DEWITT & SCRIBER Elmira, New York, 1866d.

DEWITT, ALFRED (1821-?), Crawford Co., Ohio, 1850c. (Hutslar)

DEWITT, D.G. Elmira, New York. Percussion rifles.

DEWITT, ELIJAH (1798-?), Louisville, Illinois, 1860c-1864d.

DEWITT, HIRAM (1816-?), Crawford Co., Ohio, 1850c. (Hutslar)

DEWITT, JAMES Wapakoneta, Ohio, 1848-1860. (Hutslar)

DEWITT, WILLIAM P. Elmira, New York, 1848-1891d. As DeWitt & Scriber, 1866. Percussion guns.

DEWITZLEBEN, ARTHUR Washington, D.C. Patent #16,220 February 7, 1865, ball puller.

DEWSNAP, E.L. Shelbourne Falls, Massachusetts, 1874d-1890d.

DEXTER suicide special.

DEY & DEWELL Norfolk, Virginia, 1893d-1897d. Dealers.

DEY, JOHN Norfolk, Virginia, 1870d-1897d. As Sorey & Dey, 1870-1875 and Dey & Dewell, 1893-1897.

DEYO, JEREMIAH Denton, Michigan. Patent #290,867 December 25, 1883, safety.

DEYOE & FROMAN BROS. Albany, Oregon, 1891d.

DEZENG, HENRY L. Geneva, New York. Patent #16,910 March 31, 1857, bullet molds.

DHOUDT, EUGENE H. Portland, Oregon, 1867d.

DIAMOND ARMS CO. trade name of Shapleigh Hardware Co. on shotguns. (Hinman)

DIAMOND suicide special.

DIAZ, FAUSTINO VALDEZ New York, New York. Patent #94,577 September 7, 1869, breechloading firearm.

DIBBLE, ALMON (1825-?), Denver, Colorado, 1860c-1879d. Repaired U.S. arms with G.W. Hightower in 1861. (Sellers-3)

DIBBLE, HORACE P. New York, New York, 1884d.

DIBBLE, WILLIAM H. Middletown, Connecticut. Patent #40,092 September 29, 1863, cartridge.

DICER, WILLIAM Albion, Michigan. Patent #404,779 June 4, 1889, breechloading firearm.

DICK, DAVID New York, New York, 1777. (Gardner)

DICK, FREDERICK R. Buffalo, New York, 1853-1874d. Percussion 1/2 stock and air guns. (Gluckman & Satterlee)

DICK, WALTER Charleston, South Carolina, 1774. (Kauffman)

DICKENS, FOWLER Philadelphia, Pennsylvania, 1829d-1841d.

DICKENS, JOHN Philadelphia, Pennsylvania, 1829d.

DICKENS, RICHARD Philadelphia, Pennsylvania, 1835d-1841d.

DICKENSON, EDWARD Richmond, Indiana, 1860d-1865. Percussion fullstock. (Lindert)

DICKENSON, JOHN Russell Co., Virginia, 1847-1851. Flintlock rifles. (Dillin)

DICKENSON, L.R. Elkhart, Indiana, 1884-1885d. (MB 4-54)

DICKERMAN BROTHERS Plainview, Minnesota, 1898d.

DICKERMAN, AMOS New Haven, Connecticut, 1881-1888. Patents #323,501 August 4, 1885, breechloading firearm, #354,890 December 28, 1886, breechloading firearm, and #369,437 September 6, 1887, breechloading firearm. Single barrel shotguns and rifles made by Strong Firearm Co., and later by himself. (Grant 2)

DICKERSON & HART Appleton, Wisconsin, 1865d. A.H. Hart, Jr.

DICKERSON, A. unlocated. Derringer.

DICKERSON, JOHN S. Trenton, Tennessee, 1871d-1876d.

DICKERSON, WILLIAM R. (1828-?), Jamestown, North Carolina, 1850c. (Bivins)

DICKERT & GILL Lancaster, Pennsylvania, 1787-1800. Flintlock Kentucky rifles. Jacob Dickert and James Gill, his son-in-law. (Kauffman)

DICKERT, JACOB (1740-1822), Lancaster, Pennsylvania, 1755-1822. Flintlock Kentucky rifles, Model 1792 contract rifles with Peter Gonter and John Groff, Model 1807 contract rifles with Peter Gonter and Henry DeMuff, Model 1801 contract musket for Pennsylvania with Matthew Llewellin. As Dickert & Gill.

DICKEY, DAVID Middletown, Pennsylvania, 1778-1791. (Bowers)

DICKEY, JOHN (1724-1808), Iredale Co., North Carolina, 1759-1808. Committee of Safety member. (Bivins)

DICKEY, MOSES Westmoreland Co., Pennsylvania, 1801-1812. (Whisker II)

DICKINS, A.J. Smyrna, Michigan, 1863d.

DICKINSON ARMS CO. Little Rock, Arkansas, 1893d-1895d. Dealers only.

DICKINSON, A. Philadelphia, Pennsylvania, 1841d. Derringer.

DICKINSON, CHARLES S. Cleveland, Ohio. Patent #24,997 August 9, 1859, centrifugal gun. (Hartzler)

DICKINSON, E.L. & J. Springfield, Massachusetts, 1863d-1868d. Single shot pistol.

DICKINSON, EDMUND Richmond, Indiana, 1860d. See Edward Dickenson.

DICKINSON, EDWIN L. Springfield, Massachusetts, 1863d-1885d. Single shot pistols and suicide specials. As E.L. & J. Dickinson, 1863-1868.

DICKINSON, GEORGE W. Providence, Rhode Island, 1870d.

DICKINSON, J., & SONS Bangor, New York, 1843-1850d.

DICKINSON, L.R., & CO. Elkhart, Indiana, 1882-1885. Percussion 1/2 stock.

DICKSON & GILMORE Louisville, Kentucky, 1848-1860. Percussion rifles and derringers. Moses Dickson and J.B. Gilmore. (MB 12-49)

DICKSON, CLARK & CO. Cincinnati, Ohio, 1865. Percussion locks marked "D.C. & Co.".

DICKSON, H. Bear, Wisconsin, 1879d.

DICKSON, J.S. Viroqua, Wisconsin, 1895d.

DICKSON, JOSEPH Montpelier, Ohio, 1850c-1880. (Hutslar)

DICKSON, MOSES Louisville, Kentucky, 1848-1860, Liberty, Missouri, 1860d-1867d. As Dickson & Gilmore, 1848-1860.

DICKSON, NELSON & CO. Dickson, Alabama, 1861, Rome, Georgia, 1862, Adairsville, Georgia, 1863, Dawson, Georgia, 1864-1865. Also known as Shakanoosa Arms Manufacturing Co. Mississippi rifles and carbines for the Confederacy. William Dickson, Owen O. Nelson, and Dr. L.H. Sadler. (Hill-Anthony)

DICKSON, W. Adams, New York. Percussion 1/2 stock.

DICKSON, W.H. (1894-?), Corry, Pennsylvania, 1864-1869, Erie, Pennsylvania, 1869-1890d. (C&W)

DICTATOR suicide special by Hopkins & Allen.

DICTATOR trade name on percussion and conversion revolvers by Hopkins & Allen.

DIEBERGER, HENRY Philadelphia, Pennsylvania, 1770. (Kauffman)

DIECKMAN, C. Galveston, Texas, 1848.

DIECKOW, CHARLES Utica, New York, 1860c-1880d. Percussion bench gun. (Swinney)

DIECO, C.P. Owensboro, Kentucky, 1896d.

DIEFENDERFER, PHILIP Lehigh Co., Pennsylvania, 1847t-1880d. (Gabel)

DIEHL, PHILIP New Britain, Connecticut, 1885d.

DIEMAR, FRANCIS San Francisco, California, 1850d. (Shelton)

DIEMAR, RICHARD Taunton, Massachusetts, 1856d-1878d, Boston, Massachusetts, 1878d-1879d. Percussion 1/2 stock.

DIEMER, JACOB Northampton Co., Pennsylvania, 1828-1835t. (KRA II-3)

DIEMER, PETER Cleveland, Ohio, 1856. Needlefire carbine.

DIEMER, PETER Northampton Co., Pennsylvania, 1807-1835t. (KRA II-3)

DIEMETZ, J.M. Kankakee, Illinois, 1878d-1886d.

DIESBOCK, JOHN unlocated. Flintlock Kentucky. (Dillin)

DIESINGER, WENDEL Philadelphia, Pennsylvania, 1847d-1863. Percussion fullstock, converted flintlock muskets for U.S. government.

DIETERICHS, FREDERICK New Paltz, New York, 1870d.

DIETTRICH, JOHN F. (1827-?), St. Louis, Missouri, 1850c. See Dittrich.

DIETZ, ERNST Hagerstown, Maryland, 1786-1798. Lockmaker. (Bowers)

DIETZ, JOHN Somerset Co., Pennsylvania, 1800. (Kauffman)

DIEZMAN, OSCAR Providence, Illinois, 1864d.

DIFFENDERFER, JOHN Lancaster, Pennsylvania, 1779. (Dillin)

DIFFENDERFER, LUDWIG Lancaster, Pennsylvania, 1796-1801. Barrels for U.S. contract muskets. (Moller)

DIFFENDERFER, MICHAEL Lancaster, Pennsylvania, 1779. (Dillin)

DIKE, ANTHONY Bridgewater, Massachusetts, 1775-1776. Committee of Safety musket. (Gluckman & Satterlee)

DILG Belleville, Illinois. As Walter & Dilg. (Johnson)

DILL, JAMES Gainsville, Texas, 1860d.

DILL, Z.T. Milton, Texas, 1873d.

DILLENBURG, M. Lemont, Illinois, 1884d.

DILLEY, W.T. Scio, Oregon, 1896d.

DILLINGHAM, H.P. Norwalk, Ohio, 1883d. (Hutslar)

DILLON, C. Grant, Indiana, 1860d.

DILLON, GEORGE B. McArthur, Ohio, 1876-1880. Percussion 1/2 stock.

DILLON, H.A. (1816-?), Natchez, Mississippi, 1860c.

DILLON, JAMES Bedford Co., Pennsylvania, 1844t. (Kauffman)

DILLON, JOAB (1825-?), Guernsey Co., Ohio, 1850c. (Hutslar)

DILLON, MOSES (1734-1828), Muskingum Co., Ohio, 1806-1828. (Hutslar)

DILLY, LEVANT (1830-?), Chestnut, Illinois, 1860c. (Johnson)

DIMICK & FOLSOM see Horace Dimick.

DIMICK, HORACE E. (1809-1873), Lexington, Kentucky, 1838d, St. Louis, Missouri, 1849-1873. Patents #16,377 January 13, 1857, rifling cannon, and #39,216 July 14, 1863, cannon projectile. Plains rifles and derringers; retailed many guns made by others, but marked with his name. As H.E. Dimick & Co., 1849-1864, Eaton & Dimick, 1849-1851, and Dimick & Folsom, 1854-1861. (AR 4-58)

DIMITT, FRANK C. Rocheport, Missouri. Patent #306,593 October 14, 1884, shotgun.

DIMMRICK, H.C. (1821-?), St. Louis, Missouri, 1850c. (Lewis)

DIMOCK, LUCIUS Leeds, Massachusetts. Patent #172,716 January 25, 1876, firing pin.

DIMON, C.A.R. New Haven, Connecticut. Patents #213,887 April 1, 1879, loading tool, and #351,747 November 2, 1886, loading tool. Tools made by Sharps and U.S. Cartridge Co.

DIMOND, DANIEL Pershing, Pennsylvania, 1861d.

DIMOND, LEVI South Fork, Pennsylvania, 1850-1870. Percussion fullstock.

DINGEE, ROBERT New York, New York, 1832-1870. Patent #none August 15, 1835, cartridge box. Military leather goods during the Civil War.

DINGLER, JOHN Easton, Pennsylvania, 1807t-1814t. Flintlock Kentucky. (KRA II-3)

DINGLER, SAMUEL Easton, Pennsylvania, 1823t. (Gabel)

DINGLER, WILLIAM Philadelphia, Pennsylvania, 1847d-1855d. (Kauffman)

DINKLE, CHRIS Howard Co., Missouri, 1850c. (MB 11-66)

DINNAN, JOHN J. New Haven, Connecticut, 1882d-1906.

DINNEN, JOHN Brooklyn, New York, 1850c.

DINSMAN, JOHN Philadelphia, Pennsylvania, 1813d-1819d.

DINSMORE, ROBERT Weston, West Virginia. Patents #444,666 January 13, 1891, magazine gun, #455,034 June 30, 1891, magazine gun, #492,864 March 7, 1893, magazine gun, #560,348 May 19, 1896, magazine gun, and #601,708 April 5, 1898, magazine gun.

DIPPEBERGER, HENRY Philadelphia, Pennsylvania, 1773. (Kauffman 2)

DIRK, D.C. Terrell, Texas, 1884d.

DIRKER, WILLIAM Brownstown, Indiana, 1875-1907. (MB 4-55)

DISBROW, LACY T. Eaton Rapids, Michigan, 1872d-1899d.

DISS, LOUIS P. Ilion, New York. Patents #295,563 March 25, 1884, magazine gun with J.P. Lee, #303,992 August 26, 1884, magazine gun, #304,712 September 9, 1884, magazine gun, #313,856 March 17, 1885, magazine gun, #356,274 January 18, 1887, magazine gun, #356,275 January 18, 1887, magazine gun, #356,276 January 18, 1887, cartridge packet, #356,277 January 18, 1887, magazine gun, #367,199 July 26, 1887, magazine gun, and #383,108 May 22, 1888, magazine gun. Diss was employed by Remington and all of his patents were assigned to them.

DISSTON, HENRY Philadelphia, Pennsylvania, 1862-1863. Converted fullstock muskets. (ASAC)

DISTELBART, GEORGE Baltimore, Maryland, 1868-1879d. (Hartzler)

DITMAR, VALENTINE Fosterdale, New York, 1868-1874d.

DITMER, GEORGE Pittsburgh, Ohio. (Hutslar)

DITTMAN, JOHN F. (1834-?), Polo, Illinois, 1860c, Freeport, Illinois, 1863-1885. As Pelck & Dittman, 1863-1883. (MB 4-46)

DITTRICH, HENRIETTA New Orleans, Louisiana, 1876d-1878d. Widow and successor to John F. Dittrich.

DITTRICH, JOHN F. (1827-1875), St. Louis, Missouri, 1850c-1859, Mobile, Alabama, 1861d-1868d, New Orleans, Louisiana, 1868-1875d. Made and imported percussion guns.

DITZ BROS. Stockton, California, 1893d.

DITZEL, JOHN Newark, New Jersey, 1866-1869.

DIXON & BRO. Rockford, Illinois, 1866-1869. B. and George L. Dixon. (Johnson)

DIXON, B. Mt. Aerial, Kentucky, 1854-1860.

DIXON, BENJAMIN Natchez, Mississippi, 1860-1880. Percussion 1/2 stock. (Dean)

DIXON, C.P. New York, New York, 1852d-1853d. Agent for Jennings rifles.

DIXON, GEORGE L. Rockford, Illinois, 1866-1878d. As Dixon & Bro., 1866-1869.

DIXON, GEORGE Greenbrier Co., Virginia, 1810. Contract rifles for Virginia with Nathaniel Kelly. (Cromwell)

DIXON, HENRY ST. JOHN Washington Co., Virginia, 1809-1819. Contract rifles for Virginia. (Cromwell)

DIXON, O.M. Jamestown, North Carolina. Percussion 1/2 stock. (Bivins)

DIXON, R.E.L. Waynesboro, Georgia, 1881d-1885d.

DIXON, THERON S.E. Chicago, Illinois. Patent #249,240 November 8, 1881, trigger, with Lysander Hill.

DIXON, WILLIAM Adams, New York, 1864d-1890d. Percussion 1/2 stock.

DOBBELL, FREDERICK W. Purissima, California. Patents #462,475 November 3, 1891, sight, and #548,801 October 29, 1895, sight.

DOBBIN, GEORGE W. Baltimore, Maryland. Patent #none March 23, 1833, shot charge.

DOBBINS, A.N. Jacksonville, Florida, 1883d-1895d. As A.N. Dobbins & Bro., 1883.

DOBBINS, ALBERT N. Atlanta, Georgia, 1880d.

DOBBS, JOSEPH Lancaster Co., Virginia, 1780. Committee of Safety repairs. (Gill)

DOBLER, RICHARD (1819-1895), Wheeling, West Virginia, 1859d-1895d. (MB 9-60)

DOBLER, ROMAN Wheeling, West Virginia, 1867. Son of Richard Dobler. (MB 9-60)

DOBROWSKY, ERNEST (1838-?), Douglas City, California, 1861-1864, Shasta City, California, 1865. (Shelton)

DOBSON, JOHN New York, New York, 1795-1804.

DOCKWEILER, J.B. Jonesboro, Arkansas, 1898d.

DODD, JOHN (?-1770), Pon Pon, South Carolina, 1754, Charleston, South Carolina, 1755-1770. (Dean)

DODDRIDGE, JOHN (1745-1791), Bedford Co., Pennsylvania, 1771-1773. (Whisker IV)

DODDS, JAMES Xenia, Ohio, 1864-1868, Dayton, Ohio, 1869-1908. Rebarreled Sharps rifles, percussion and cartridge guns. (Hutslar)

DODGE, GROVER Woodstock, Vermont, 1840-1843. (Horn)

DODGE, JOSEPH Duluth, Minnesota, 1888d-1892d.

DODGE, JOSIAH Dummerston, Vermont. Patents #15,357 July 15, 1856, cannon, and #17,920 August 4, 1857, discharging cannon.

DODGE, PHILIP TELL Washington, D.C. Patents #112,694 March 14, 1871, breechloading firearm, #118,350 August 22, 1871, breechloading firearm, and #127,683 June 11, 1872, breechloading firearm. All patents with his brother William C. Dodge.

DODGE, WILLIAM C. Washington, D.C. Patents #42,755 May 17, 1864, revolver extractor, #44,290 September 20, 1864, breechloading firearm, #45,912 January 17, 1865, revolving extractor, #45,983 January 24, 1865, revolver, #52,547 February 13, 1866, breechloading firearm, #54,436 July 4, 1865, cartridge, #58,790 October 16, 1866, magazine gun, #112,694 March 14, 1871, breechloading firearm, #112,763 March 14, 1871, breechloading firearm, #113,408 April 4, 1871, breechloading firearm, #114,653 May 9, 1871, breechloading firearm, #118,350 August 22, 1871, breechloading firearm, and #127,683 June 11, 1872, breechloading firearm. Many patents with his brother Philip T. Dodge.

DODGE, WILLIAM W. Washington, D.C. Patent #210,506 December 3, 1878, revolver. Son of William C. Dodge.

DODSWORTH, ROBERT St. Louis, Missouri, 1857d-1870d.

DODT, FRANK (1822-?), Mendota, Illinois, 1860d-1888d.

DOELL, FREDERICK G. (1842-1909), Boston, Massachusetts, 1872d-1909d.

DOELL, FREDERICK H. Boston, Massachusetts, 1895. Son and successor to Frederick G. Doell.

DOELLBOT, F. Philadelphia, Pennsylvania, 1863. Converted flintlock muskets.

DOERMER, CHARLES (1819-1894), Washington, D.C., 1846-1852, San Jose, California, 1860-1894. (Hartzler-Shelton)

DOGARTHY, GEORGE Charleston, South Carolina, 1802-1806d. (Kauffman 2)

DOHERTY & EVANS Petersburg, Virginia. James Doherty and Daniel Evans. Derringer.

DOHERTY, JAMES (1810-?), Petersburg, Virginia, 1850-1875. Percussion guns. As Doherty & Evans, circa 1860. (MB 10-63)

DOHN, N.A. Dittmer's Store, Missouri, 1893d.

DOHRMAN, FREDERICK St. Louis, Missouri, 1840-1842d.

DOLAN, THOMAS J. New York, New York. Patent #584,629 June 15, 1897, sight.

DOLBY Morgantown, West Virginia. Percussion rifles.

DOLL, CASPER (1724-1793), Northampton Co., Pennsylvania, 1750-1793. (Whisker III)

DOLL, DANIEL Yorktown, Pennsylvania, 1799-1800. (Kauffman)

DOLL, JACOB (?-1847), York, Pennsylvania, 1792-1847. Model 1798 contract muskets for Pennsylvania with Henry Pickel and Conrad Welshanze, and flintlock Kentucky rifles. (Kauffman)

DOLLAR, LAWRENCE (1823-?), Baltimore, Maryland, 1849-1854d. (Hartzler)

DOLLMAN, JOHN Thebes, Illinois, 1860d-1864d.

DOMINICK, W.F. Chicago, Illinois, 1852-1853d.

DOMINION PISTOL CO. suicide special.

DONACK, GEORGE New York, New York, 1858d. Percussion 1/2 stock.

DONAHO, JAMES (1807-?), Iredale Co., North Carolina. Apprenticed to Jacob Kibler, 1814. (Bivins)

DONALD, ALEXANDER Allegheny Co., Pennsylvania, 1800-1813. (Whisker II)

DONALDSON, JOSIAH Caro, Michigan, 1887d-1891d.

DONHAM, LEWIS N. (1833-1902), Greensboro, Pennsylvania, 1876-1890, Bowlby, West Virginia, 1890-1900. Percussion fullstock; guns marked "LND".

DONN, JAMES (1839-1911), Canton, Illinois, 1859-1886d, Peoria, Illinois, 1886d-1893d. As James Donn & Bro., 1878d-1886d and Peoria Model Works, 1890-1893.

DONNAN, W.S. & G. Richmond, Virginia. Hardware dealer-locks.

DONP, G. Hope, Arkansas, 1885d.

DOOLEY Scranton, Pennsylvania. Flintlock Kentucky. (Dean)

DOOLITTLE, F.H. Anawauk, Minnesota, 1882d.

DOOLITTLE, ISAAC Milford, Connecticut, 1776-1777. Committee of Safety locks.

DOOLITTLE, JAMES B. Seymour, Connecticut. Patents #35,996 July 29, 1862, magazine gun, and #54,065 April 17, 1866, revolver.

DOOLITTLE, MILTON R. (1837-1904), Homerville, Ohio, 1858-1897. Percussion and cartridge rifles. (Hutslar)

DOOLITTLE, MILTON Cowlesville, New York, 1870d.

DOOLITTLE, T.B. New Haven, Connecticut. Patent #54,065 April 17, 1866, revolver. See James B. Doolittle.

DOOR & CO. York, Nebraska, 1886d.

DOPLIER, ROBERT Wheeling, West Virginia. Flintlock and percussion guns. See Robert Dobler.

DORAN, JAMES E. Ashtabula, Ohio, 1881-1910. (Hutslar)

DORCHESTER & ROSE Geneva, New York, 1877d.

DORCHESTER, EDWARD G. Sioux City, Iowa, 1876, Geneva, New York, 1877-1884. Patents #183,255 October 17, 1876, breechloading firearm, and #305,160 September 16, 1884, breechloading firearm. As Dorchester & Rose, 1877.

DOREMUS, R. OGDEN New York, New York. Patents, with Bern L. Budd, #34,724 March 18, 1862, cartridge, #34,725 March 18, 1862, cartridge, and #34,744 March 25, 1862, cartridge.

DORIAN, CHARLES Shreveport, Louisiana, 1882d.

DORION & BIENAIME New Orleans, Louisiana, 1822d. Pierre Dorion and Antoine Bienaimé.

DORION, PIERRE New Orleans, Louisiana, 1822d-1834d. As Dorion & Bienaimé, 1822.

DORIOT, VICTOR (1800-?), Wyoming Co., West Virginia, 1860c.

DORMAN, HARMON (1797-?), Clearfield Co., Pennsylvania, 1850c. (Whisker II)

DORMAN, ROBERT Belltown, Pennsylvania. Flintlock Kentucky rifles. (Dillin)

DORN Huntington, Pennsylvania, 1830. Flintlock Kentucky. (Dillin)

DORN, CHRISTOPHER ANDREW (1832-1890), Drytown, California, 1856-1890. (Shelton)

DORNBACH, ANTHONY Lancaster Co., Pennsylvania, 1803t. (Dyke)

DORNER, JOHN (1796-?), Sabbath Rest, Pennsylvania, 1859-1870. (Kauffman, C&W)

DOROTHY, THOMAS Lineville, Iowa, 1882d-1884d.

DORR, J.W. Alpena, Michigan, 1899d.

DORR, STEPHEN unlocated. Flintlock Kentucky.

DORRIS, JAMES Ft. Smith, Arkansas, 1855. Percussion 1/2 stock. (Elias)

DORRIS, THOMAS Cumberland, Maryland, 1887d. (Hartzler)

DORSCH, EDWARD Monroe, Michigan. Patents #14,597 April 8, 1856, shotgun, and #15,369 July 22, 1856, cartridges, both with George Bucknell.

DORSETT, B.D. Harris, Georgia, 1883d.

DORSETT, BRANSON Alton, Illinois, 1884d-1888d.

DORSEY, JOHN E. Baltimore, Maryland, 1813-1822. Cannon. (Hartzler)

DORWART, BENJAMIN K. Rockland, Rhode Island. Patent #142,376 September 2, 1873, revolver.

DOTSON, R.F. Paw Paw, Kentucky, 1883d.

DOTZERT, CONRAD Newburgh, New York, 1850d.

DOTZERT, JAMES H. Newburgh, New York, 1880c-1882d.

DOTZERT, JOHN Newburgh, New York, 1863-1874d.

DOUBLE HEADER trade name of Perry & Goddard on derringer made by E.S. Renwick. Also known as the "Perpetual Revolver". (GR 3- 59)

DOUD, JOHN Goshen, Connecticut, 1777-1800.

DOUDAL, J. Morris, Illinois, 1860d-1867d.

DOUGAN & CO. Leadville, Colorado, 1882-1889. David H. and George B. Dougan. (Sellers-3)

DOUGHERTY, ABSOLOM Annville, Pennsylvania, 1844. See Absalom Daugherty. (Kauffman 2)

DOUGHERTY, ALBERT G. Chambersburg, Indiana. Patents #529,521 November 20, 1894, breechloading gun, and #547,717 October 8, 1895, machine gun.

DOUGHERTY, H.F. Galesburg, Illinois, 1855-1859. (Johnson)

DOUGHTY, C.M. St. Cloud, Minnesota, 1867d-1878d.

DOUGHTY, F. (1826-?), Indianapolis, Indiana, 1850c. (Lindert)

DOUGHTY, SAMUEL Bloomington, Illinois, 1850-1851. (Johnson)

DOUGLAS ARMS CO. trade name of Hopkins & Allen on shotguns.

DOUGLAS, BOONE Phillipsburgh, Kansas, 1894d.

DOUGLAS, DANIEL Clarksville, Missouri, 1879d. Percussion fullstock.

DOUGLAS, JACOB East Springfield, Ohio, 1834-1840. (Knittle)

DOUGLAS, JOHN A. Fordtown, Tennessee, 1873d.

DOUGLAS, JOHN Danbury, Connecticut. Committee of Safety repairs. (Gluckman & Satterlee)

DOUGLAS, JOSEPH Tyrone, Pennsylvania, 1850c, Huntingdon Co., Pennsylvania, 1856-1880. (Dillin, Whisker II))

DOUGLAS, L., & LAUDENSLAGER unlocated. Percussion swivel breech.

DOUGLAS, ROBERT Buffalo, New York, 1852d. For Rector & Robson. (Dean)

DOUGLAS, ROBERT East Springfield, Ohio, 1832d-1850c. Possibly father and son (same name); but the individual in the 1850 census was 15 years old in 1832. (Hutslar)

DOUGLAS, THOMAS McConnellstown, Pennsylvania, 1833-1840. Percussion fullstock. (Whisker II)

DOUGLAS, WILLIAM Cocke Co., Tennessee. Percussion guns. (ASAC 21)

DOUGLASS, JAMES Tyrone, Pennsylvania, 1840. (Whisker II)

DOUGLASS, A.B. Beech, Missouri, 1860d.

DOUGLASS, ARTHUR R. Chariton, Iowa. Patent #644,901 March 6, 1900, sight.

DOUGLASS, DAVID Warner, Pennsylvania, 1850-1867. Percussion fullstock. (Kauffman)

DOUGLASS, J.D. unlocated. Percussion fullstock.

DOUGLASS, JOHN (?-1775), Montgomery Co., Virginia, 1775. (Gill)

DOUGLASS, JOHN Huntington, Pennsylvania, circa 1830. Flintlock and percussion rifles.

DOUGLASS, JOHN Jonesboro, Tennessee. Percussion fullstock. (Roberts)

DOUGLASS, THOMPSON (1815-?), Richmond, Ohio, 1850-1864. Percussion 1/2 stock. (Hutslar)

DOUGLASS. WILLIAM Corry, Pennsylvania. Patent #43,903 August 23, 1864, cannon.

DOULAR, JOHN Philadelphia, Pennsylvania, 1823d.

DOUP, G. Hope, Arkansas, 1888d. See G. Donp.

DOUTHERT, JOHN Indiana Co., Pennsylvania, 1823-1828. (Kauffman)

DOVER, SAMUEL B. (1803-?), Dayton, Ohio, 1850c. (Hutslar)

DOW, ELI S. Dayton, Ohio, 1856-1900. (Hutslar)

DOW, H.K. Franklin, Vermont, 1865d, Newbury, Vermont, 1870-1873.

DOW, S. unlocated, 1837-1840. Percussion fullstock rifles.

DOWART, B.K. Rockland, New York. Patent #142,376 September 2, 1873, revolver.

DOWDLE, FREDERICK Seneca, Illinois, 1882d-1886d, Marseilles, Illinois, 1888d-1890d.

DOWDY, RANDOM Richmond, Virginia, 1850c. (MB 10-63)

DOWELLE, FREDERICK (1824-?), Morris, Illinois, 1860c-1867d. See Doudel and Dowdle.

DOWLER, FRANCIS Wayne Co., Ohio. Patent #none, April 9, 1832, lock.

DOWLER, JOHN Philadelphia, Pennsylvania, 1819d-1833d. See John Doular.

DOWLER, THOMAS Edenton, North Carolina, 1829. (Bivins)

DOWLING, JESSE Jefferson Co., Missouri, 1850c. (MB 11-66)

DOWN, J. Canton, Illinois, 1860d.

DOWNEY, J. Joliet, Illinois, 1882d.

DOWNEY, JOHN Jackson, Ohio, 1851-1876. (Gluckman)

DOWNEY, NATHANIEL (?-1913), Jackson, Ohio, 1869-1902. Percussion fullstock. (MB 6-41)

DOWNEY, WILL Jackson, Ohio, 1880-1913. (MB 6-41)

DOWNIE, D.P. Denver, Colorado 1882d. (Sellers-3)

DOWNING, LEVINUS Troy, New York, 1842-1843. (Kauffman 2)

DOWNING, THOMAS Paulina, Iowa, 1895d-1897d.

DOWNS, SIMON T. Lynn, Massachusetts, 1883d-1884d.

DOWNWARD, JOHN Fayette Co., Pennsylvania, 1820-1834. (C&W)

DOWNWARD, THOMAS (?-1825), Fayette Co., Pennsylvania, 1799-1804. (Kauffman, C&W)

DOYLE, JOHN (1750-?), Lancaster, Pennsylvania, 1784, Cincinnati, Ohio, 1800-1801. (Hutslar)

DRABLING, HENRY Kellersville, Indiana, 1882-1885. (Gardner)

DRAEGER, CHARLES Indianapolis, Indiana. Patent #34,922 April 8, 1862, revolver. (Sellers-1)

DRAKE, ADOLPHUS M. (1851-1855), Everett, Pennsylvania, 1880-1950. Son of Isaac Drake. Percussion & cartridge rifles. (Whisker)

DRAKE, AUGUSTINE J. Boston, Massachusetts, 1862-1867d. Altered Model 1841 rifles for Massachusetts. (Moller)

DRAKE, ISAAC Allegheny Co., Maryland, 1853-1874. (Hetrick)

DRAKE, MATTHEW Baltimore, Maryland, 1817-1836. Flintlock fowling piece. (Hartzler)

DRAKE, R.R. Shabonier, Illinois, 1860d.

DRAPER, J.J. Rock Island, Illinois, 1847, Arkansas Co., Arkansas, 1850. (Johnson-Elias)

DRAPER, JOEL Northville, Michigan, 1863d.

DRAPER, JOHN Williamsburg, Virginia, 1769-1789. Repairs. (Gill)

DRAYTON & EDMANSON Charleston, South Carolina, 1770-1772. John Drayton and Jacob Edmanson. (Kauffman 2)

DRAYTON, JOHN Charleston, South Carolina, 1770-1800. As Drayton & Edmanson, 1770-1772. (Kauffman)

DREADNOUGHT suicide special by Hopkins & Allen.

DREADNOUGHT trade name of Stevens on shotguns, 1911-1936.

DREHER, EMIL New York, New York. Patent #465,248 December 15, 1891.

DREHER, GOTTLIEB Louisville, Kentucky, 1868d-1869d.

DREIKOSEN, JOHN L. Ashford, Wisconsin, 1857d.

DREISBACH, JOHN (1793-?), Mifflinburg, Pennsylvania, 1814-1861d. Son of John Dreisbach. Flintlock Kentucky rifles, sometimes signed "J.D.". (Gabel)

DREISBACH, JOHN Union Co., Pennsylvania, 1801-1820. (Hutslar)

DREISBACH, SAMUEL (1790-?), Mifflinburg, Pennsylvania, 1814-1838, Circleville, Ohio, 1850-1865, London, Ohio, (dates?). Percussion fullstock. (Hutslar)

DREON, GEORGE Detroit, Michigan, 1860d.

DREPPARD, ANDREW Lancaster, Pennsylvania, 1848-1857d. (Dyke)

DREPPARD, HENRY Lancaster, Pennsylvania, 1760.

DREPPARD, JOHN Lancaster, Pennsylvania, 1834-1869d. Percussion guns.

DREPPARD, WILLIAM (1827-?), Delphi, Indiana, 1850c. (Lindert)

DREPPERD, GEORGE (1787-?), Lancaster, Pennsylvania, 1849. (Dyke)

DREPPERD, HENRY (1803-?), Lancaster, Pennsylvania, 1840. (Dean)

DREPPERD, JACOB (1766-?), Lancaster, Pennsylvania, 1787t.

DREPPERD, JACOB (1782-?), Lancaster, Pennsylvania, 1810t.

DREPPERD, JOHN (1784-1840), Lancaster, Pennsylvania. (Whisker II)

DREPPERD, JOHN (1803-?), Lancaster, Pennsylvania, 1834d-1873d.

DREPPERD, MICHAEL (1818-?), Lancaster, Pennsylvania.

DREPPERD, WILLIAM (1816-?), Lancaster, Pennsylvania, 1843t. (Dyke)

DRESBACH see Dreisbach.

DRESCHER, EMIL Houston, Texas, 1892d, Caldwell, Texas, 1896d.

DRESSER, SAMUEL R. Mt. Pleasant, Missouri, 1866-1868. Percussion 1/2 stock.

DREW, ALVA (1835-?), Dixon, Illinois, 1860c. (Johnson)

DREW, DAN (1791-?), St. Louis, Missouri, 1832-1850c. (Lewis)

DREW, DANIEL (1793-?), Sagetown, Illinois, 1870c. (Johnson)

DREW, F.H. Cedar Rapids, Iowa, 1887d-1889d.

DREW, FRANK H. Leadville, Colorado, 1883d.

DREW, HENRY J. (1824-?), Dixon, Illinois, 1857-1886d. Patents #112,563 March 14, 1871, magazine gun, and #114,564 March 14, 1871, magazine gun.

DREW, J.H. unlocated. Underhammer pistol.

DREW, REUBEN W. Lowell, Massachusetts. Patent #63,450 April 2, 1867, ejector, used by Rollin White Arms Co.

DREYAC, A. Baltimore, Maryland, 1817d.

DREYER, C.W. (1791-?), Belvidere, Illinois, 1850c. (Johnson)

DREYSE, A. Baltimore, Maryland, 1845-1865. (Dean)

DRIGGS, LOUIS LABADIE New York, New York, 1893-1929. Patents #613,195 October 25, 1898, breech loading firearm, #698,472 April 29, 1902, automatic gun, and #781,503 January 31, 1905, automatic gun. Operated as Driggs-Seaburg Gun and Ammunition Co. and Driggs Ordnance Co. (after 1905).

DRINKEL, JOHN Reading, Pennsylvania, 1790t. (KRA 76)

DRINKER, A.C. Scranton, Pennsylvania, 1880d.

DRINKER, C.M. Bloomsburgh, Pennsylvania, 1887d-1890d.

DRIPPARD, F. Lancaster, Pennsylvania, 1767-1773. (Gluckman & Satterlee)

DRISCOLL unlocated. Flintlock Kentucky rifle.

DRISCOLL, J.B. Springfield, Massachusetts. Single shot cartridge derringer.

DRIVER, SAMUEL Philadelphia, Pennsylvania. Patent #18,424 Oct. 13, 1857, shell.

DRUCK, CONRAD (1818-?), Washington, D.C., 1846-1850c. (Hutslar)

DRUM, GEORGE Detroit, Illinois, 1860. (Johnson)

DRUMMOND, JOHN New York, New York. Patent #5,563 May 9, 1848, bullet machine.

DRUMMOND, S. Chicago, Illinois, 1895d.

DRUMMOND, SIEGELE Butler, Missouri, 1879d-1883d.

DRURY, ALVIN Barre, Vermont, 1867-1873. (Horn)

DRURY, MOSES A. Dayton, Ohio, 1827. (Hutslar)

DUARDS, WILLIAM (1832-?), Ft. Wayne, Indiana, 1860c. Percussion 1/2 stock. (Lindert)

DUBBS, A. Pine Grove, Pennsylvania, 1880d.

DUBBS, DANIEL (1748-1828), Northampton Co., Pennsylvania, 1812t. Son of Jacob Dubbs. (KRA II-3)

DUBBS, JACOB (1710-1775), Northampton Co., Pennsylvania, 1732-1775. (Dyke)

DUBEL, MICHAEL Moorestown, New Jersey, 1889d.

DUCHESS suicide special by Hopkins & Allen.

DUCKWORTH, JAMES Springfield, Massachusetts. Minneapolis Fire Arms Co. "Protector" palm pistols. (GR 1-67)

DUDDEN, E. H. Philadelphia, Pennsylvania, 1827-1834. Repairs only. (Dean)

DUDEN, DANIEL Gettysburg, Pennsylvania, 1801-1807, McConnellstown, Pennsylvania, 1808-1837, Martinsburg, Pennsylvania, 1841. (Whisker II)

DUDLEY, ALBERT Menominee, Michigan, 1891d.

DUDLEY, DANA Lynn, Massachusetts. Patents #407,475 July 23, 1889, pneumatic gun, and #407,476 July 23, 1889, pneumatic gun. Produced as the Dudley-Simms dynamite gun.

DUDLEY, GEORGE (1835-?), San Francisco, California, 1870-1887. (Shelton)

DUDLEY, M. Carrollton, Illinois, 1860d.

DUDLEY, OLIVER Topeka, Kansas, 1866d.

DUDMAN, WILLIAM Xenia, Illinois, 1860d.

DUENKEL, AUGUSTUS Boonville, Missouri, 1860d.

DUENKEL, FREDERICK (1822-?), Cincinnati, Ohio, 1850c. (Hutslar)

DUENKEL, FREDERICK Sheboygan, Wisconsin, 1872d-1895d.

DUERR, CHRISTIAN Philadelphia, Pennsylvania, 1755-1780. Flintlock Kentucky rifles signed "CH.D.". (Kauffman)

DUERR, WILLIAM F. Orange, New Jersey, 1878d.

DUFF, GEORGE J. Pittsburgh, Pennsylvania. As Whittemore, Wolfe, Duff & Co., dealers.

DUFFEY, BARTHOLOMEW (1820-?), St. Louis, Missouri, 1847-1850c. (Lewis)

DUFFORD, JOSEPH (1804-?), Butler Co., Pennsylvania, 1850c.

DUFFY, FRANK Everett, Pennsylvania, 1886d.

DUFORT, AUGUSTUS Charlestown, South Carolina, 1855-1860. (Kauffman)

DUGAN, GEORGE B. Leadville, Colorado, 1884d. See George Dougen.

DUGGINS, WILLIAM Hanover, Virginia, 1781. (Gill)

DUHART, A. New Orleans, Louisiana, 1834d-1853d.

DUHEM, CONSTANT LOUIS (1840-1933), San Francisco, California, 1859, Oroville, California, 1889-1933. (Shelton)

DUKE suicide special.

DULANEY, ALEXANDER Maud, West Virginia, 1900d.

DULANEY, D.E. Georgetown, Colorado, 1880d. (Sellers-3)

DULANEY, MARSHALL (1821-?), Carrollton, Illinois, 1844-1886d.

DULIBAR, CHRISTIAN Lancaster Co., Pennsylvania, 1847t-1850c. (Dyke)

DULLY, HENRY H. (1832-?), Warren, Ohio, 1850c. For John Day. (Hutslar)

DUMONT, WORTHINGTON Biddeford, Maine, 1852-1856. (Demeritt)

DUNBAR & PRENTISS Union Village, New York. Percussion 1/2 stock, locks, hardware. H. Prentiss. (Union Village became West Greenwich in 1878.)

DUNBAR, ALEXANDER Montgomery Co., Pennsylvania, 1800c. (Kauffman)

DUNBAR, CHARLES Detroit, Michigan, 1887d.

DUNCAN & BRO. Crawfordsville, Iowa, 1867d, Council Bluffs, Iowa, 1868d-1871d.

DUNCAN & GARNIER Kansas City, Kansas, 1889d.

DUNCAN BROS. Philadelphia, Pennsylvania, 1820. Dealers and importers.

DUNCAN Jenkins Ridge, Missouri, 1860d.

DUNCAN, ALFRED Sullivan Co., Tennessee, circa 1825. Flintlock Kentucky. (KRA 76)

DUNCAN, DAVID B. New Richmond, Ohio. Patent #249,598 November 15, 1881, breechloading firearm.

DUNCAN, JOSEPH (?-1793), Fauquier Co., Virginia, 1781-1793. (Gill)

DUNCAN, T.J.C. Pardee, Kansas, 1866d.

DUNCAN, W. Osceola, Missouri, 1860d.

DUNCAN, WILLIAM, E. Dorrett's Run, Kentucky, 1883d.

DUNCAN, WILSON (1833-1913), St. Louis, Missouri, 1850c, St. Joseph, Missouri, 1852-1854, Council Bluffs, Iowa, 1854 and 1857-1913, Quincy, Illinois, 1854d-1857. For T.J. Albright in St. Louis, Carlos Gove in St. Joseph and Council Bluffs until 1862. As Duncan & Bro., 1868-1871. (Sellers-3)

DUNCKLEY, GEORGE W. Covington, Kentucky, 1876d.

DUNHAM, A.C. unlocated. Underhammer pistol.

DUNHAM, A.W. Willimantic, Connecticut, 1886d-1890d. As Martin & Dunham, 1886.

DUNHAM, C.L. Oroville, California, 1893d.

DUNHAM, E.L. Greeley, Colorado, 1880d-1886d. (Sellers-3)

DUNHAM, GEORGE F. Plymouth, Massachusetts, 1860d-1869d.

DUNHAM, H.E. unlocated. Underhammer pistol.

DUNHAM, HENRY, & CO. Norwich, Connecticut, 1853-1856d.

DUNHAM, JOB New Geneva, Pennsylvania, 1861d.

DUNHAM, LEWIS N. (1833-1902), Green Co., Pennsylvania, 1869-1876. See Lewis Donham. (Kauffman, Whisker II)

DUNHAM, THOMAS Strawberry Point, Iowa, 1884d-1887d.

DUNKLE, GEORGE (1805-?), Shippensburg, Pennsylvania, 1825-1828t, Upper Strasburg, Pennsylvania, 1829t-1853t. Flintlock and percussion rifles. (Bowers)

DUNKLE, GEORGE Oxford, Illinois, 1860d. Same as George Dunkle of Pennsylvania?

DUNKLE, H. unlocated. Percussion swivelbreech.

DUNKLE, JACOB Frederick, Maryland, 1778. For Jacob Reaser.

DUNKLE, WILLIAM Bow, New Hampshire. Percussion 1/2 stock.

DUNKLE, WILLIAM Hooksett, New Hampshire, 1872d-1879d.

DUNKLE, WILLIAM Oxford, Illinois, 1864d.

DUNKLIS, JOHN (1826-?), Nash Co., North Carolina, 1850c. (Bivins)

DUNLAP SPECIAL trade name of Dunlap Hardware Co., Macon, Georgia, on shotguns by Crescent. (Hinman)

DUNLAP Salisbury, New Hampshire. (Gluckman & Satterlee)

DUNLAP, ADOLPHUS (1816-1889), Rock Island, Illinois, 1835-1856. (Johnson)

DUNLAP, ALFRED Harrisonville, Ohio, 1859d. Percussion 1/2 stock. (Hutslar)

DUNLAP, G. Philadelphia, Pennsylvania. Owner of Pennsylvania Rifle Works, sometimes marked guns with his name. (MB 3-66)

DUNLAP, H.C. Kossuth, Ohio, 1848-1854. Percussion 1/2 stock.

DUNLAP, JEPTHAH G. Cedarville, Ohio. Patent #236,791 January 18, 1881, breechloading firearm.

DUNLAP, ROBERT, JR. Pittsburgh, Pennsylvania, 1841. Percussion fullstock. (Kauffman)

DUNLAY & GEISLER Houston, Texas, 1894d. J.S. Dunlay and A.H. Geisler.

DUNLAY, J.S. Houston, Texas, 1894d-1914d. As Dunlay & Geisler, 1894 and Dunlay Hardware Co. after 1897.

DUNMEYER, DAVID Somerset Co., Pennsylvania, 1856-1872. (Kauffman)

DUNMEYER, JONATHAN (1828-1885), Somerset, Pennsylvania, circa 1840-1885. Son of Peter. (Kauffman)

DUNMEYER, PETER (1795-1859), Cambria Co., Pennsylvania, 1826-1832, Somerset Co., Pennsylvania, 1844-1859. (Kauffman)

DUNN, J.E. (1849-?), Pitkin, New York, 1880c.

DUNN, JAMES Big Rock, Tennessee, 1860d.

DUNN, JAMES Buffalo, New York, 1832-1835. (Gluckman & Satterlee)

DUNN, V.G. Fort Smith, Arkansas, 1898d.

DUNNING, ELIJAH Bridgeport, Connecticut. Patent #34,713 March 18, 1862, cartridge.

DUNSETH, ANDREW see Andrew Danseth.

DUNSETH, JOHN Cincinnati, Ohio, 1817-1820. (Hutslar)

DUNSTONE, THOMAS Santa Cruz, California. Patent #158,577 January 12, 1877, sight.

DUNTZE, HENRY A. New Haven, Connecticut, 1845d-1880d.

DUNWALD, JOHN P. Corning, New York, 1855-1859d.

DUNWICK, WILLIAM Philadelphia, Pennsylvania, 1775-1785. Committee of Safety muskets and repaired U.S. arms. (Hobbies 4-38)

DUNWICKE, WILLIAM see William Dunwick.

DUPARCK, LUCIUS H. Albion, Michigan, 1863d.

DUPAS New Orleans, Louisiana, 1842d.

DUPAS, A. Virginia City, Nevada, 1878d.

DUPAS, OCTAR Virginia City, Nevada, 1878d-1880d.

DUPLER, SAMUEL (1825-?), Athen Co., Ohio, 1850c. (Hutslar)

DUPLEX trade name of Osgood Gun Works on double-barrel revolvers.

DUPONT, JOSEPH (1821-?). New Orleans, Louisiana, 1850c. (MB 9-65)

DUPRE, JAMES Wilmington, North Carolina, 1776. Committee of Safety muskets. (Bivins)

DUPREZ, S. Del Norte, Colorado, 1873-1879. (Sellers-3)

DUPUY, BERNARD New Orleans, Louisiana, 1822d-1837d. Dealer.

DURAND MFG. CO. Durand, Michigan, 1890-1892. Bolt action .22 cal. rifle. (Perkins)

DURAND, F.O. Goldsboro, North Carolina, 1884d-1885d, Durham, North Carolina, 1887d-1890d.

DURBIN, LUKE (1830-?), Knox Co., Ohio, 1850c. (Hutslar)

DURFEE, S.S. Red Bud, Illinois, 1880d-1886d.

DURHAM IRON WORKS Bucks Co., Pennsylvania. Produced musket barrels during the Revolutionary War.

DURIN, S.F.C. (1819-1898), San Juan, California, 1851-1898. (Shelton)

DURKEE, J.H. Lebanon, New Hampshire. Underhammer pistol. (Logan)

DURRINGER see Wolf & Durringer.

DURST, MURRAY H. Wheatland, California. Patent #502,812 August 8, 1893, magazine gun. Bolt action rifle, 1891 trials. (Shelton)

DURWOOD, D. Boston, Massachusetts. double-barrel/hammer shotgun.

DURY, JOHN San Antonio, Texas, 1896d.

DURYEA & HEYER unlocated. Percussion 1/2 stock.

DUSTIN, D.H. Manchester, New Hampshire. Percussion 1/2 stock.

DUTTON, JOHN S. (?-1881), Jaffrey, New Hampshire, 1856-1881. Percussion rifles and pistols. (Hobbies 8-34)

DUTTON, REED (1825-?), Richland Co., Ohio, 1850c, Tomales, California, 1878. (Hutslar)

DUTTON, SAMUEL (1833-?), Waterford, Michigan.

DUTY, HIRAM LaFayette Co., Missouri, 1850c. (11-66)

DUVALL, ALFRED Baltimore, Maryland. Patent #678 May 8, 1838, shot manufacture.

DUVICE, JOHN Springhill, Pennsylvania, 1818-1819. (Kauffman)

DWARA unlocated. Flintlock Kentucky.

DWIGGENS, WILLIAM W. Arkadelphia, Arkansas, 1885-1910. (Elias)

DWIGHT, CHAPIN & CO. Bridgeport, Connecticut, 1862-1864. Ballard rifles under contract for Merwin & Bray. Henry Chapin.

DWIGHT, H.D. Belchertown, Massachusetts, 1845-1850. Percussion 1/2 stock.

DYER & CHASE Newburyport, Massachusetts, 1873d.

DYGERT, A.S. Buffalo, New York, 1828-1832, Detroit, Michigan. Percussion fullstock. (MB 4-65)

DYNAMITE ORDNANCE & ARMAMENTS CO. see William Breath and Sims-Dudley.

DYSON, ABRAHAM Garrettsville, Ohio, 1803-1820. (Hutslar)

E SECTION

E * L unidentified. Flintlock Kentucky.

E.B. see Enos Border.

E.D. & CO. unidentified. Flintlock muskets dated 1800.

E.D. unidentified. Percussion fullstock.

E.E. see E. Eley.

E.P.W. unidentified. Flintlock Kentucky.

E.R. see Elijah Ross.

E.S. unidentified. Percussion fullstock.

E.S. unidentified. Percussion swivel.

E.T.B. unidentified. Percussion fullstock.

E.W.B. unidentified. Percussion derringer.

EACHUS, F.H. West Chester, Pennsylvania, 1884d-1899d. As Mayer & Eachus.

EADELMAN, CHARLES Lehigh Co., Pennsylvania, 1847t. (KRA II-3)

EADELMAN, WILLIAM Lehigh Co., Pennsylvania, 1847t. (KRA II-3)

EAGLE ARMS CO. Hartford, Connecticut. Trade name on suicide specials by Harrington & Richardson.

EAGLE ARMS CO. New York, New York, 1865-1869. Made Plant revolvers after New Haven factory destroyed in 1866.

EAGLE ARMS CO. Sterling, Massachusetts. Trade name on Copeland revolver.

EAGLE CO. trade name used on Whitney revolvers.

EAGLE FOUNDRY Cincinnati, Ohio, 1829-1890. Gatling guns, cannon, muskets, and carbines during the Civil War. Operated by Miles Greenwood, and also known as Eagle Iron Works, and as Greenwood Iron Works.

EAGLE IRON WORKS see Miles Greenwood, Eagle Foundry, and Greenwood Iron Works.

EAGLE MFG. CO. Norwich, Connecticut, 1890. Double action revolvers.

EAGLE MFG. CO. Norwich, Connecticut. Model 1861 contract muskets. (Fuller)

EAGLE REVOLVER MFG. CO. Norwich, Connecticut, 1892-1893. (Dean*)

EAGLE RIFLE WORKS Philadelphia, Pennsylvania, 1830-1870. Owned and operated by James Golcher. (MB 4-65)

EAGLE suicide special by Iver Johnson.

EAGLE, CONRAD Lancaster, Pennsylvania, 1871d.

EAGLE, GEORGE (1783-?). Carbarrus Co., North Carolina, 1850c. (Bivins)

EAGLE, ISAAC Carbarrus Co., North Carolina. (Bivins)

EAGLE, JOHN Rowan Co., North Carolina, 1819. Flintlock Kentucky. (Bivins)

EAGLE, JOHN, II (1813-?), Carbarrus Co., North Carolina, 1850c. Son of John Eagle. (Bivins)

EAGLE, MALACHI McCandless, Pennsylvania, 1890d.

EALER, F.A. (1832-?), Lancaster, Pennsylvania, 1857d. Son of Lewis Ealer.

EALER, LEWIS W. (1791-?), Lancaster, Pennsylvania, 1822-1857d, Baltimore, Maryland, 1822d-1833d, Philadelphia, Pennsylvania, 1837d-1856d. (Hartzler)

EARFERT, RODNEY Ridge Post, Tennessee, 1876d.

EARL, ALBERT St. Louis, Michigan, 1872d-1887d.

EARL, WILL (1821-?), St. Louis, Missouri, 1850c. (Lewis)

EARLE, ELIAS Centerville, South Carolina. Model 1812 contracts, but made no guns. (Hobbies 9-34)

EARLE, ETHAN Middlebury, Massachusetts, 1847d.

EARLE, IRA M. Guilford Center, Vermont. Patents #178,363 June 6, 1876, breechloading firearms, and #189,026, April 3, 1877, breechloading firearms.

EARLE, REUBEN Leicester, Massachusetts, 1780-1800. Flintlock musket.

EARLE, THOMAS (1737-1819), Leicester, Massachusets, 1767-1810. Flintlock musket. (Lindsay)

EARLEY, AMOS (1840-1905), West Hanover, Pennsylvania, 1860d-1861d. Son of Jacob Earley.

EARLEY, AMOS, JR. West Hanover, Pennsylvania, 1882d-1890d. Percussion fullstock.

EARLEY, JACOB Dauphin Co., Pennsylvania. Flintlock Kentucky rifle. (Gluckman & Satterlee)

EARLHOOD suicide special by E.L. Dickinson.

EARLY, J.F. Wilbur, Nebraska, 1879d.

EARLY, JACOB H. (1816-1886), Bent's Fort, Colorado, 1839, West Point, Missouri, 1850c, Ft. St. Vram, Colorado, 1855, Marias des Cygnes, Kansas, 1860, Atchison, Kansas, 1864-1886d. Used his initials on percussion fullstock guns. (Sellers-3)

EARNEST, GEORGE H. Springfield, Ohio. Patent #129,115 July 16, 1872, breechloading firearm.

EARNEST, GEORGE Philadelphia, Pennsylvania, 1810d.

EARNEST, JACOB (1805-1884), Westmoreland Co., Pennsylvania, 1836-1884. Flintlock Kentucky rifle. (Bowers)

EARNEST, JOHN (1827-1904), Delmont, Pennsylvania.

EARNEST, SIMON PETER Delmont, Pennsylvania.

EARNEY, C. unlocated. Flintlock pistol.

EARNHARD, JOHN Northampton Co., Pennsylvania, 1814t. (KRA II-3)

EARNHART, CHARLES Philadelphia, Pennsylvania, 1847d. See Charles Ernhart.

EARNHART, JOHN Cromwell, Indiana, 1860d.

EARNHEART, WILLIAM unlocated. Flintlock Kentucky.

EARPS & BRO. unlocated. Flintlock and percussion locks.

EARPS & MCMAIN Philadelphia, Pennsylvania. Lockmakers.

EARTHQUAKE suicide special by Dickinson.

EAST, E.D. Weatherford, Texas, 1884d-1896d.

EASTER, ALLEN Pettis Co., Missouri, 1850c. (MB 11-66)

EASTERLEY, CHRISTOPHER Baltimore, Maryland, 1840d. (Hartzler)

EASTERN ARMS CO. suicide special.

EASTERN ARMS CO. trade name of Sears, Roebuck & Co. on shotguns by Meriden Mfg. Co. and, after 1915, by J. Stevens Arms & Tool Co.

EASTMAN, A.F. Blue Earth City, Minnesota, 1880d.

EASTMAN, A.G. Rochester, New York. Percussion rifles. (Roberts)

EASTMAN, ALBERT Ashtabula, Ohio. Patent #307,449 November 4, 1884, breechloading firearm.

EASTMAN, AMOS Penacock, New Hampshire, 1770, Hollis, New Hampshire, 1775. (Dean*)

EASTMAN, F.S. Hardwick, Vermont, 1884-1885. (Horn)

EASTMAN, GEORGE Concord, New Hampshire. (Roberts)

EASTMAN, IVAN F. Lewiston, Maine, 1893-1898. As Nason & Eastman, 1896-1898. (Demeritt)

EASTMAN, JOHN I. Jaffrey, New Hampshire, 1863-1860, Concord, New Hampshire, 1860d-1874d. Percussion bench rifles. As Utley & Eastman, 1858-1860.

EASTMAN, ROBERT Brunswick, Maine. Patent #none December 7, 1829, lock and priming pills.

EASTON, JOHN Winfield, Kansas, 1882d-1888d.

EATON & DIMICK see Horace Dimick.

EATON & FOLSOM New York, New York, 1856d-1857d. James Eaton and Charles Folsom, dealers.

EATON & KITTREDGE Cincinnati, Ohio, 1850c. Benjamin Kittredge and Daniel Eaton.

EATON, CALVIN Rochester, New York, 1827d. (Eich)

EATON, CHARLES A. Chicago, Illinois, 1860d-1862d.

EATON, D. Chicago, Illinois, 1853-1859d.

EATON, D.S. Moravia, New York. Percussion era. (Swinney)

EATON, DANIEL E. Cincinnati, Ohio, 1849d-1853d, Chicago, Illinois, 1853d-1859d, St. Louis, Missouri, 1860-1866. Partner of Dimick in St. Louis and Kittredge in Cincinnati. (Hanson-Hutslar)

EATON, E.D. unlocated. Virginia contract rifle.

EATON, E.E. Chicago, Illinois, 1872-1884d. Dealer.

EATON, GILBERT C. Cleveland, Ohio. Patent #37,159 December 16, 1862, centrifugal gun with Samuel Turner. (Hutslar)

EATON, J. Boston, Massachusetts, 1847-1860, Concord, New Hampshire, 1860-1916. Agent for Allen in Boston, made underhammer guns in Concord.

EATON, R.H. unlocated. Flintlock Kentucky.

EATON, WILLIAM unlocated. "EATON, WILLIAM, Norwich, New York. Pat'd Aug. 9, 1870." marking on revolving shotgun.

EBBERT, D. unlocated. Percussion fullstock.

EBERHARD Baltimore, Maryland, 1853d. (Hartzler)

EBERHARDT, WILLIAM (1838-1906), Sacramento, California, 1868-1906. Breechloading shotguns. (Shelton)

EBERLE, ANDREW (?-1867), Cincinnati, Ohio, 1855-1867. (Hutslar)

EBERLE, JACOB Lancaster, Pennsylvania, 1810c. (Dyke)

EBERLING, FRED Linn, Kansas. Patent #531,168 July 18, 1894, machine gun.

EBERLING, L. Chicago, Illinois, 1848. (Johnson)

EBERLY, HENRY Lancaster, Pennsylvania. Son-in-law of Andrew Kauffman. (Dean)

EBERLY, JACOB see Jacob Eberle.

EBERLY, JOHN Lancaster, Pennsylvania, 1775-1777, for William Henry. (Hobbies 4-38)

EBERLY, JOSEPH Jefferson Co., Ohio, 1820c. (Hutslar)

EBERMAN, HENRY Lancaster, Pennsylvania, 1820-1840. Flintlock Kentucky. (Kindig)

EBERMAN, JOHN Lancaster, Pennsylvania, 1859. (Dyke)

EBERSOL & KROUSE Ottawa, Illinois, 1872-1880. Daniel S. Ebersol and David Krouse. (Johnson)

EBERSOL, DANIEL S. (1820-1880), Ottawa, Illinois, 1855-1880. Underhammer pistol. With David Krouse, 1878-1880. (T 58)

EBERSOL, J.W. Ottawa, Illinois, 1866. (Johnson)

EBERSOLE, DAVID S. Burlington, Iowa, 1850c. (MB 8-64)

EBERSOLE, W.H. (1846-1920), Duncannon, Pennsylvania, 1870-1920.

EBERT, A. Knoxville, Tennessee, 1871d-1873d.

EBERT, BENJAMIN, & SONS Frederick, Maryland, 1886-1895. (Hartzler)

EBERTS, ADAM Lehigh Co., Pennsylvania, 1822. Flintlock Kentucky. (KRA 76)

EBERTS, GEORGE JOHN Northampton Co., Pennsylvania, 1800-1807t. (KRA II-3)

EBNER, FERDINAND (1831-?), Burlington, Iowa, 1856-1890. Successor to D.S. Ebersol, and as F. Ebner & Sons, 1883-1890.

EBSWORTH, WILLIAM Davenport, Iowa, 1858d.

EBY, ABRAM Lancaster Co., Pennsylvania, 1781t. (Dyke)

EBY, CHRISTIAN Lancaster Co., Pennsylvania, 1768. (Dyke)

EBY, JOHN Lancaster Co., Pennsylvania, 1801t. (Dyke)

ECCLESTON & BROTHER Kankakee, Illinois, 1867d.

ECKEL, CHARLES Cincinnati, Ohio, 1855d-1896d.

ECKEL, FREDERICK Cincinnati, Ohio, 1866. For Kittredge. (Hutslar)

ECKEL, ROBERT Cincinnati, Ohio, 1897d-1900d.

ECKENRODE, DAVID E. Upper Amberson, Pennsylvania, 1890d.

ECKER, SEVEREN F. San Diego, California, 1878-1890. (Shelton)

ECKHARDT & HOPKINS St. Joseph, Missouri, 1869d. Henry Eckhardt and Frank Hopkins.

ECKHARDT & REIN St. Joseph, Missouri, 1866-1867. Percussion 1/2 stock. William Eckhardt.

ECKHARDT BROS. St. Joseph, Missouri, 1860d-1866d. Henry and William Eckhardt.

ECKHARDT, HENRY (1833-1909), St. Joseph, Missouri, 1860d-1869d, Sacramento, California, 1870-1896. As Eckhardt Bros., 1860-1866 and Eckhardt & Hopkins, 1869. Percussion and breechloading shotguns. (Shelton)

ECKHARDT, WILLIAM St. Joseph, Missouri, 1860d-1879d. As Eckhardt Bros., 1860-1866 and Eckhardt & Rein, 1866-1867.

ECKLER, HENRY (?-1862), Pine Grove, Pennsylvania, 1861d. Flintlock Kentucky rifles. (Kindig)

ECLIPSE trade name of E.C. Meacham on imported shotguns.

ECLIPSE trade name on .22 cal. derringer.

EDDINGS & CRUM Nacogdoches, Texas, 1896d.

EDDINGS, A.W. Garrison, Texas, 1890d, Marlin, Texas, 1892d-1896, Nacogdoches, Texas, 1896d. As Schimming & Eddings, 1892-1896 and Eddings & Crum, 1896d.

EDDY, HENRY L. West Chesterfield, Massachusetts, 1885d.

EDDY, IRA B. Philadelphia, Pennsylvania, 1854-1857. In partnership with Christian Sharps in 1855. Also made percussion fullstock pistols. (Sellers-4)

EDDY, JAMES Philadelphia, Pennsylvania, 1812-1814.

EDDY, SAMUEL Bristol, Wisconsin, 1857d.

EDDY, SAMUEL West Chesterfield, Massachusetts, 1888d.

EDDY, W.G. New Britain, Connecticut. Patent #245,888 August 16, 1881, breechloading firearm with Charles Street.

EDELMANN, JOSEPH San Francisco, California, 1878-1879d. (Shelton)

EDEN, T.M. Americus, Georgia, 1879d-1885d.

EDENS, FRANK Waterbury, Connecticut, 1888d-1896d.

EDEY, ALFRED S. Des Moines, Iowa, 1887d-1892d. As Edey Bros., 1892.

EDEY, CHARLES E.C. Des Moines, Iowa, 1889d-1895d. As Edey Bros., 1892.

EDGAR, MOSES Condit, Oregon, 1867d.

EDGECOMB, EDWARD F. Mechanics Falls, Maine. Patent #205,066 June 18, 1878, magazine gun. (Demeritt)

EDGELL, J.G. Brooklyn, New York, 1870d.

EDGERLY, BINGHAM Greenfield, Maine, 1869-1874.

EDGERLY, MOODY O. Bristol, New Hampshire, 1877d-1886d.

EDGERLY, SAMUEL see Clark & Edgerly. (Demeritt)

EDGERTON, H.S. East Germany, New York, 1874d-1882d, Chenango, New York. Percussion rifles.

EDGERTON, PHILIP Rutland, Vermont, 1873-1874. (Horn)

EDGINGTON, DANIEL Brownsville, Pennsylvania, 1829. Flintlock Kentucky. (Whisker II)

EDLER, FREDERICK ADOLPH (1836-1892), Folsom, California, 1862-1872, Auburn, California, 1872-1886. (Shelton)

EDMANSON, JACOB Charleston, South Carolina, 1770-1780. As Drayton & Edmanson, 1770-1772. (Kauffman 2)

EDMONDS, JACOB Aaronsburg, Pennsylvania, 1861d. Flintlock Kentucky rifle.

EDMONDS, JOHN Bushkill, Pennsylvania, 1850c. (Gabel)

EDMONDS, WILLIAM Monroe Co., Pennsylvania, 1850c. (Gabel)

EDWARD, E. unlocated. Raised carved Kentucky.

EDWARDS & GOODRICH New Haven, Connecticut. Model 1840 contract muskets, none delivered. (Gluckman)

EDWARDS & SHEPPARD Milan, Tennessee, 1885d.

EDWARDS, ANTROBUS GEORGE Rochester, New York, 1849-1853d, Corunna, Michigan, 1855-1879d. Purchased John Miller's shop in 1852 after working for him several years. Made Miller patent revolving rifles and normal percussion rifles. (Sellers-1)

EDWARDS, DANIEL New York, New York. Patent #242,517 June 7, 1881, sight.

EDWARDS, DAVID Zanesville, Ohio, 1835-1840. Patent #1,134 April 25, 1839, revolver. (Sellers-1)

EDWARDS, FRANK Granville Co., North Carolina, 1870c. (Bivins)

EDWARDS, H. unlocated. Flintlock Kentucky.

EDWARDS, JOHN Morris, New York, 1870d.

EDWARDS, MICHAEL (1767-1826), York, Pennsylvania, 1788-1801, Washington, Pennsylvania, 1801-1826. For Conrad Welshans in York, Pennsylvania. (Bowers)

EDWARDS, MICHAEL, JR. Washington, Pennsylvania, 1807-1836, Moundsville, West Virginia, 1838-1860. Son of Michael Edwards. (Bowers)

EDWARDS, SAMUEL Connecticut, 1800c.

EDWARDS, WILLIAM E. (1825-?), Nash Co., North Carolina, 1850c. (Bivins)

EDWARDS, WILLIAM Washington, Pennsylvania, 1834t-1836t, Moundsville, West Virginia, 1838-1860. (Bowers)

EFFINGER, AUGUST Canton, Ohio, 1883-1898. Percussion 1/2 stock. (Hutslar)

EFFINGER, BERNARD New Orleans, Louisiana, 1875d-1883d.

EFFINGER, GEORGE Henderson, Kentucky, 1855-1860, Hickman, Kentucky, 1879d-1896d. Percussion 1/2 stock.

EGAR, WILLIAM (1835-?), Los Angeles, California, 1870c. (Shelton)

EGE, CHARLES Detroit, Michigan, 1891d-1895d.

EGE, FREDERICK Detroit, Michigan, 1860d-1895d. Percussion 1/2 stock.

EGELSTON, ANDREW Egelston, Michigan, 1863d-1865d.

EGENER, HENRY New York, New York. Patent #178,749 June 16, 1876, breechloading firearm.

EGER, WILLIAM (1834-?), San Francisco, California, 1867-1871, Santa Rosa, California, 1872-1875, Eureka, California, 1876-1878. (Shelton)

EGGERS, SELMAR New Bedford, Massachusetts, 1836-1888d. Patents #17,370 May 26, 1857, bomb lance with Julius Grudchos, and #200,338 February 12, 1878, breechloading gun with Ebenezer Pierce. Whaling guns and explosive harpoons with Grudchos & Eggers, 1850-1860, percussion 1/2 stock and air guns alone.

EGLE, GEORGE Watertown, Wisconsin, 1879c-1895d.

EGLER, JACOB D. Pittsburg, Pennsylvania. Patent #403,096 May 14, 1889, spring gun.

EHBETTS, CARL J. Hartford, Connecticut. Patents #303,135 August 5, 1884, revolver, #303,827 August 19, 1884, revolver, #306,596 October 14, 1884, lock, #311,732 February 3, 1885, safety lock, #316,761 April 28, 1885, magazine gun, #318,711 May 26, 1885, magazine gun, #335,517 February 2, 1886, magazine gun with William B. Franklin, #341,227 May 4, 1886, breechloading firearm, #343,800 June 15, 1886, magazine gun, #373,277 November 15, 1887, magazine gun, #392,503 November 6, 1888, revolver, #402,423, April 30, 1889, lock, #415,451 November 19, 1889, breechloading firearm, #469,465 February 23, 1892, revolver, #550,261 November 26, 1895, safety, #550,262 November 26, 1895, machine gun, #570,388 October 27, 1896, machine gun, #580,935 April 20, 1897, firearm, #599,835 March 1, 1898, magazine gun, #650,931 June 5, 1900, revolver with James G. Peard, #734,524 July 28, 1903, automatic, and #917,723 April 6, 1908, safety. Worked for Colt.

EHLE, J.B. Janesville, Wisconsin, 1879d.

EHLERS unlocated. Flintlock Kentucky.

EHLERS, JOHN New York, New York, 1846d. Acquired the assets of Patent Arms Mfg. Co., Paterson, New Jersey, after its failure. See also Samuel Colt, Colt Patent Fire Arms Mfg. Co., and Patent Arms Mfg. Co. (Phillips)

EHRET, JOHN Philadelphia, Pennsylvania, 1862-1863. Converted flintlock muskets.

EHRMANN, PHILIP Ottumwa, Iowa, 1897d. Son of Wendell Ehrmann.

EHRMANN, WENDELL Ottumwa, Iowa, 1880d-1882d. Percussion 1/2 stock.

EHRMON, H. unlocated. Flintlock Kentucky rifle.

EICHOLTZ & BRO. Lancaster, Pennsylvania, 1840-1888d. Henry C. & Robert L. Eicholtz.

EICHOLTZ, HENRY C. Lancaster, Pennsylvania, 1840-1888d. As Eicholtz & Bro.

EICHOLTZ, JOHN Lancaster, Pennsylvania, 1840. (Kauffman)

EICHOLTZ, ROBERT L. Lancaster, Pennsylvania, 1840-1888. As Eicholtz & Bro.

EICHSTAEDT, ROMAN Michigan City, Michigan, 1881-1887d. (MB 4-54)

EICKHORN, CHRISTOPHER Cleveland, Ohio, 1848d. (Hutslar)

EIDERKIN, C.W. Anaconda, Montana, 1898d.

EIFLER, PHILLIP Columbus, Georgia, 1881d-1889d. (Derringer)

EINOR, M., JR. unlocated. Flintlock Kentucky. (Dean)

EISAMAN BROS. St. Mary's, Ohio, 1888d. (Hutslar)

EISAMANK, JERRY LaRue, Indiana, 1882-1885. (Lindert)

EISENHARD, HENRY Lehigh Co., Pennsylvania, 1850c. (Gabel)

EISENHOWER, ISRAEL Union Deposit, Pennsylvania, 1880d.

EISHOFF & VOGT Cincinnati, Ohio, 1878d. Possibly Christian Vogt? (Hutslar)

EISTER, GEORGE (1762-1831), York Co., Pennsylvania, 1787-1802. Flintlock Kentucky. (Kindig)

EIZENHEIMER, EMIL Toledo, Ohio, 1869d. (Hutslar)

ELBE, HENRY Niagara Falls, New York. Patent #477,187 June 14, 1892, repeating gun.

ELBERTSON, NATHAN Plainfield, Indiana, 1862d.

ELDER, EDWARD H. Chicopee Falls, Massachusetts. Patents #663,604 December 11, 1900, ejector, #690,568 January 7, 1902, ejector, #822,886 June 5, 1906, forend, #824,535 June 26, 1906, ejector, and #847,659 March 19, 1907, breechloading firearm. All patents used by Stevens.

ELDER, JOHN Indiana Co., Pennsylvania, 1826-1828. (Kauffman)

ELDER, W.J. Watkinsville, Georgia, 1861. Confederate gunsmith convention.

ELDIN, M. Cardington, Ohio, 1853d. Percussion fullstock rifle. (Hutslar)

ELDRED, EDWARD Carrollton, Illinois, 1884d.

ELDREDGE, J.W. unlocated. Percussion lock.

ELDRIDGE & SCHENCK Angelica, New York, 1850c. Henry W. Eldridge and William Schenck.

ELDRIDGE, HENRY W. Angelica, New York, 1850c-1859d. As Eldridge & Schenck, 1850.

ELDRIDGE, W.H. Rushford, New York. Percussion.

ELDRIDGE, WILLIAM Hightstown, New Jersey, 1878d-1882d.

ELECTOR suicide special.

ELECTRIC CITY trade name of Wyeth Hardware Co., St. Joseph, Missouri.

ELECTRIC HAMMERLESS trade name of Eagle Mfg. Co.

ELECTRIC suicide special.

ELERMAN, CARL Cincinnati, Ohio, 1886d and 1898d.

ELEY, E. Mt. Gilead, Ohio, 1859d. Percussion fullstock, marked "E.E.". (Hutslar)

ELGALL, JOSEPH (1842-?), Wheeling, West Virginia, 1870c. (Whisker IV)

ELGAR & SMITH Mineral Point, Wisconsin. Percussion revolvers and 1/2 stock rifle. William Elgar and R.M. Smith. (Sellers-1)

ELGIN ARMS CO. trade name of Crescent on guns made for Fred Biffar & Co., and Strauss & Schran, both of Chicago. (AG 4-75)

ELGIN, GEORGE New York, New York. Patent #254 July 5, 1837, cutlass pistol. Made by C.B. Allen and Morrill, Mosman & Blair. (GC-30)

ELITA trade name of Davenport Arms Co. on shotguns. (Hinman)

ELLENWOOD, D.J., & SON Stevens Point, Wisconsin, 1895d.

ELLER, H.O. Cairo, Illinois, 1870. Percussion target rifle. (Johnson)

ELLINGER, HENRY St. Louis, Missouri, 1894-1907. (Pourie)

ELLINGWOOD, E.M. Rowe, New York, 1880d.

ELLIOTT & HOWELL Socorro, New Mexico, 1884d.

ELLIOTT ARMS CO. New York, New York, 1863. Promotional name for guns made by Remington.

ELLIOTT, D.R. Murphysborough, Illinois, 1893d.

ELLIOTT, H. New Lebanon, Indiana, 1860d.

ELLIOTT, JOSEPH (1838-?), San Diego, California, 1886-1887d. (Shelton)

ELLIOTT, MATTHEW & NATHAN Kent, Connecticut, 1798-1801. Model 1798 contract muskets marked only with the city name. (Gluckman)

ELLIOTT, MICHAEL Washington Co., Pennsylvania, 1854-1856.

ELLIOTT, WILLIAM H. Plattsburg, New York, 1858-1869, New York, New York, 1870-1888. Patents #21,188 August 17, 1858, revolver, #28,460 May 29, 1860, breechloading firearm, #28,461 May 29, 1860, revolver, #28,951 July 3, 1860, revolver, #32,378 November 6, 1860, revolver, #33,382 October, 1, 1861, revolver, #33,932 December 17, 1861, revolver, #35,284 May 13, 1862, breechloading firearm, #35,872 July 15, 1862, patched cartridges, #37,329 January 6, 1863, revolver, #39,136 July 7, 1863, breechloading firearm, #41,510 February 9, 1864, breechloading firearm with R.J. Howland, #42,648 May 10, 1864, many-barreled firearm, #42,649 May 10, 1864, many-barreled firearm, #43,840 August 16, 1864, double-barreled firearm, #46,225 February 7, 1865, revolver, #47,372 April 18, 1865, breechloading firearm, #47,707 May 16, 1865, revolver, #47,809 May 23, 1865, breechloading firearm, #50,232 October 3, 1865, many-barreled firearm, #51,440 December 12, 1865, many-barreled firearm, #68,292 August 27, 1867, hammer, #110,024 December 13, 1870, breechloading firearm, #111,827 February 14, 1871, magazine, #114,540 May 9, 1871, breechloading firearm, #118,916 September 12, 1871, magazine, #121,499 December 5, 1871, breechloading firearm, #125,127 April 2, 1872, breechloading firearm, #163,646 May 25, 1875, breechloading firearm, #168,562 October 11, 1875, breechloading firearm, #218,37, August 12, 1879, magazine gun, #224,522 February 17, 1880, magazine gun, #225,750 March 23, 1880, magazine gun, #229,812 July 13, 1880, magazine gun, #232,178 September 14, 1880, magazine gun, #239,748 April 5, 1881, magazine gun, #240,649 April 26, 1881, magazine gun, #250,650 December 13, 1881, magazine gun, #255,153 March 21, 1882, magazine gun, #258,731 May 30, 1882, magazine gun, #262,023 August 1, 1882, magazine gun, #274,578 March 27, 1883, magazine gun, #278,003 May 22, 1883, magazine gun, #278,324 May 29, 1883, magazine gun, #285,020 September 18, 1883, magazine gun, #293,315 February 12, 1884, #307,531 November 14, 1884, magazine gun, #309,213 December 16, 1884, magazine gun, #309,834 December 30, 1884, magazine gun, #314,570 March 31, 1885, magazine gun, #323,922 August 11, 1885, magazine gun, #325,513 September 1, 1885, magazine gun, and #377,549 February 7, 1888, magazine gun. All of Elliott's patents were used by Remington, for whom he worked.

ELLIS, BENSON Corinna, Maine, 1871. (Demeritt)

ELLIS, DARWIN New Haven, Connecticut. Patents #48,056 June 6, 1865, cartridge machine, Whitestone, New York, and #101,845 April 12, 1870, magazine gun.

ELLIS, GEORGE New Brunswick, New Jersey, 1866-1870. Percussion 1/2 stock target rifle.

ELLIS, H. unlocated. Percussion over/under rifle/shotgun.

ELLIS, J.B. Woodbury, Connecticut, 1896d.

ELLIS, JAMES A. Honoeye and Canandaigua, New York, 1868-1880d, Waterloo, New York, 1880-1882d. Percussion mule ear rifles. (Clow)

ELLIS, JAMES Buck, Illinois, 1860d.

ELLIS, R.T., & CO. New York, New York, 1838-1851. Lockmakers and importers. Reuben T. Ellis.

ELLIS, REUBEN T. Albany, New York, 1815-1837, New York, New York, 1838-1851. Repeating flintlock rifles with sliding lock (Jennings patent) made for Ellis by R. & D. Johnson on U.S. contract. As R.T. Ellis & Co., importer, in New York. (Fuller)

ELLIS, SALAS (1823-?), Muskingum Co., Ohio, 1850c. Percussion 1/2 stock. (Hutslar)

ELLIS, WILLARD C. Springfield, Massachusetts. Patents #23,762 April 26, 1859, breechloading firearm, #24,726 July 12, 1859, revolver with John N. White, and #39,318 July 21, 1863, revolver with John N. White. Patents used on Plant revolvers.

ELLIS, WILLIAM Scott Co., Missouri, 1850c. Flintlock fowlers. (MB 11-66)

ELLISON, W.W. unlocated. Percussion fullstock.

ELLS, JOSIAH Allegheny, Pennsylvania, 1855-1858. Patents #10,812 April 25, 1854, revolver, #11,419 August 1, 1854, revolver, #17,032 April 14, 1857, revolver, and #17,143 April 28, 1857. Made several models of percussion revolvers before selling out to J.M. Cooper in 1858. (Sellers-1)

ELLSWORTH, EUGENE Sumner, Iowa, 1889d.

ELLSWORTH, JOSEPH Richland Co., Ohio, 1800-1810. (Knittle)

ELLSWORTH, WILLIAM New York, New York, 1771.

ELLY, C. DAVIS Bedford Co., Pennsylvania, 1884. (Kauffman)

ELMIRA ARMS CO. Elmira, New York, 1890-1920. Shotguns.

ELMORE, ELIJAH Magnolia, Arkansas, 1888d.

ELMORE, NORMAN Granby, Connecticut, 1871-1879. (Gardner)

ELSHOFF & VOGT Cincinnati, Ohio, 1877d-1878d.

ELSON, JULIUS Boston, Massachusetts. Patents #64,650 May 14, 1867, breechloading firearm, #67,033 July 23, 1867, breechloading firearm, #71,149 November 19, 1867, breechloading firearm, and #86,378 February 2, 1869, breechloading firearm with William R. Schaefer.

ELSTER, O. Meriden, Connecticut, 1887d.

ELSTON, ALLAN Lincoln Co., Georgia, 1820c.

ELSTON, P.L. Cambridge, Illinois, 1888d.

ELSWORTH, ALEX Geneva, Michigan, 1863d-1865d.

ELSWORTH, L. Fairfield, Michigan, 1860d.

ELTERICH, OTTO P. New York, New York. Patent #594,863 December 7, 1897, lock.

ELTON & JOHNS Philadelphia, Pennsylvania, 1780. Thomas Elton and Isaac Johns. (Gluckman & Satterlee)

ELTON, A. Philadelphia, Pennsylvania, 1814d. (Kauffman)

ELTON, THOMAS Philadelphia, Pennsylvania, 1780. As Elton & Johns. (Kauffman)

ELUERE, PROSPER (1812-1891), Vincennes, Indiana, 1842-1891. As P. Eluere & Sons in 1888. (Lindert)

ELVINS, RALPH Farmington, Missouri, 1893d-1898d.

ELWELL, HENRY Seneca Co., Ohio, 1810-1812. Lockmaker. (Hutslar)

ELY & WRAY Springfield, Massachusetts, 1883d. Suicide specials.

ELY, A.F. Mt. Vernon, Ohio, 1830-1859. With F. Lemon as Ely & Lemon, 1858-1859. (Hutslar)

ELY, ALFRED B. Newton, Massachusetts. Patents #34,626 March 11, 1862, chain shot, and #105,058 July 5, 1870, breechloading firearm with E.C. Clay.

ELY, G.B. Baird, Texas, 1892d.

ELY, L.M. Nevada, Missouri, 1879d.

ELY, LEWIS A. (1819-1911), Chesterville, Ohio, 1847-1856, St. Joseph, Missouri, 1856-1870, Leadville, Colorado, 1870d-1872d, Cardington, Ohio, 1896d. Made guns only in Ohio and Missouri. (Hutslar)

ELY, MARTIN Springfield, Massachusetts, 1770-1776. Committee of Safety muskets. (Gluckman & Satterlee)

ELY, O.S. Buchanan, Michigan, 1873d.

EMBERTON, H. Tompkinville, Kentucky 1896d.

EMBRICK, C. Lancaster, Pennsylvania, 1875d.

EMCH, FREDERICK (1831-1903), Tiffin, Ohio, 1850-1858, Woodville, Ohio, 1858-1865. (Hutslar)

EMERSON, FRANK L. Brentwood, California. Patent #355,602 January 4, 1887, gopher gun.

EMERY, CHARLES A. U.S. Army. Patent #54,743 May 15, 1866, breechloading firearm with T.T.S. Laidley.

EMERY, N. Chatfield, Minnesota, 1859-1865. (Gluckman & Satterlee)

EMLAW, ANDREW J. Grand Rapids, Michigan. Patents #429,106 May 27, 1890, spring gun, and #430,572 June 17, 1890, spring gun.

EMMES, NATHANIEL Boston, Massachusetts, 1789-1825. (Gluckman & Satterlee)

EMMES, NATHANIEL, JR. Boston, Massachusetts, 1816-1825. (Gluckman & Satterlee)

EMPIRE ARMS CO. trade name of Crescent on guns for Sears, Roebuck & Co. (AR 2-69)

EMPIRE BREECH LOADING FIRE ARMS CO. New York, New York, 1866. Promotional organization for Conover patent rifles.

EMPIRE STATE ARMS CO. trade name of Crescent on guns made for Sears, Roebuck & Co. (AR 2-69)

EMPIRE suicide special by Rupertus.

EMPIRE trade name of Crescent on shotguns. (AR 2-69)

EMPRESS suicide special.

EMRICK, DAVID Tama City, Iowa, 1884d.

EMRY, STEPHEN Frederick Co., Virginia, 1753. (Gill)

ENCORE suicide special by Iver Johnson.

ENDECOTT, GABRIEL Chetopa, Kansas, 1888d-1894d.

ENDERS trade name of Crescent on guns for Shapleigh Hardware Co. (Perkins)

ENDSLY, M. Cohutta Springs, Georgia, 1883d.

ENGELN, MATTHIAS McHenry, Illinois, 1878d-1890d.

ENGELS, DAN (1814-?), St. Louis, Missouri, 1850c. (Lewis)

ENGLAND, WELTDEN PARRY (1838-?), Santa Cruz, California, 1874-1886. (Shelton)

ENGLAND, WILLIAM (1834-?), Omaha, Nebraska, 1860c. Born in Kent, Great Britain.

ENGLE, BARNEY (?-1887), Greensboro, Pennsylvania, 1833-1878. Son of Peter Engle, percussion guns marked "B.E.". (Hartzler)

ENGLE, CHARLES (1838-?), Tyler Co., West Virginia, 1860c, Elizabeth, West Virginia, 1880c, Reedy Ripple, West Virginia, 1882d. Son of Ezra Engle. (Whisker IV)

ENGLE, CHRISTIAN A. (1817-?), Ready Ripple, West Virginia, 1850c-1884d. Son of Ezra Engle. (MB 10-63)

ENGLE, CHRISTIAN Greene Co., Pennsylvania. Son of Peter Engle.

ENGLE, EZRA (1791-?), Greene Co., Pennsylvania, 1817-1838, Tyler Co., West Virginia, 1850c. From 1835-1838 two men named Ezra Engle in Greene County; one was a son of Peter Engle. (MB 10-63)

ENGLE, EZRA Greene Co., Pennsylvania, 1817-1838. From 1835-1838 two men named Ezra Engle in this location; one was a son of Peter Engle. (Kauffman)

ENGLE, JAMES E. (1832-?), Tyler Co., West Virginia, 1860c, Sisterville, West Virginia, 1880c. Guns marked "J.E.E.".

ENGLE, JOHN Monocacy, Maryland, 1760-1800. (Hartzler)

ENGLE, PETER (1755-1833), Monocacy, Maryland, 1767-1790, Allegheny Co., Maryland, 1796-1800, Greene Co., Pennsylvania, 1803-1823. Son of John Engle. (Kauffman, Hartzler)

ENGLE, PETER, JR. Greene Co., Pennsylvania. Son of Peter. (Hartzler)

ENGLE, STEPHEN D. Hazelton, Pennsylvania. Patents #320,643 June 23, 1885, spring gun, #334,575 January 19, 1886, spring gun, and #442,025 December 2, 1890, air gun. Guns made by Engle Spring Gun Co., Hazelton, Pennsylvania, 1886-1890. (GR 9-66)

ENGLEHART, F.A. Raleigh, North Carolina, 1884d.

ENGLEHART, J. Nazareth, Pennsylvania, 1832-1837.

ENGLES, CHRISTIAN Greene Co., Pennsylvania, 1824-1829.

ENGLES, JOHN see John Engle.

ENGLISH, B.C. Hartford, Connecticut. Patent #33,528 October 8, 1861, cartridge.

ENGLISH, CASTLEMAN & CO. Alexandria, Virginia, 1855d.

ENHOLM, J.H. St. Louis, Missouri. Patent #28,977 July 3, 1860, alarm gun.

ENKE, E. Norma, Missouri, 1879d.

ENNES, ROBERT B. Calhoun, Iowa, 1865d.

ENNS, F.F. St. James, Minnesota, 1882d-1896d.

ENSLEY, MESSER Claronaton, Tennessee, 1887d. Percussion 1/2 stock.

ENSMINGER, L. Laurel, Indiana, 1860d.

ENTEBROUK, CHARLES H. see Charles Eutabrouk.

ENTERPRISE GUN WORKS trade name of James Bown, 1848-1890. (Kauffman)

ENTERPRISE suicide special by Enterprise Gun Works. (Webster)

ENTERS, LEWIS Philadelphia, Pennsylvania, 1818-1829d. Stocks.

ENTLER, JACOB (?-1822), Shepherdstown, Virginia, 1808-1822. Flintlock fowler. (Bowers)

EOFF, HORACE Elmira, Michigan, 1884d.

EPIVLET, DENSION San Andreas, California, 1860c. (Shelton)

ERB, WILLIAM Denver, Colorado, 1885d. (Sellers-3)

ERELL, O.A. Forrest City, Arkansas, 1884d.

ERHARDT, LOUIS Atchison, Kansas, 1882d-1894d.

ERHARDT, PAUL Salem, New Jersey, 1860d-1885d.

ERICHSON, ALEXANDER Houston, Texas, 1866d-1878d. For his father, Gustave Erichson, 1866-1872. With his brother, Otto, as O. & A. Erichson, 1878.

ERICHSON, GUSTAVE Houston, Texas, 1838-1872d. Percussion guns. (T36)

ERICHSON, OTTO Houston, Texas, 1866d-1890d. Son of and successor to Gustave Erichson. With his brother, Alexander, as O. & A. Erichson, 1878. As O. Erichson & Co., 1882-1883. For L.T. Noyes, 1884-1886, and for Michael Floeck, 1887-1888.

ERICK, JOHN (1804-?), Wood Co., Virginia, 1850c. (MB 10-63)

ERICK, WILLIAM (1803-?), Franklin Co., West Virginia, 1870c-1880c.

ERICKSON, L. unlocated. Percussion fullstock.

ERICSON, ERIC Florence, Wisconsin. Patent #610,675 September 13, 1898, cane gun.

ERN, ABRAHAM Virginia, 1777. Committee of Safety repairs. (Gill)

ERNEST, J. unlocated. Flintlock Kentucky. Possibly Jacob or John Earnest. (Sellers)

ERNHART, CHARLES Philadelphia, Pennsylvania, 1841d. See C. Earnhart.

ERNST, ADAM (1781-1857), Berwick, Pennsylvania, 1803t-1811, York Co., Pennsylvania, 1813-1857. Flintlock Kentucky marked "A.E.". (Kindig)

ERNST, JACOB Frederick, Maryland, 1772-1790c. (Hartzler)

ERNST, JACOB New Salem, Pennsylvania, 1854-1862. See Jacob Earnest

ERNST, JACOB York Co., Pennsylvania, 1820. (Kindig)

ERRIES, FRANCOIS New Orleans, Louisiana, 1850c-1853d.

ERSKINE, HENRY M. Ilion, New York. Patent #207,168 August 20, 1878, revolver.

ESCH, H. Manitowoc, Wisconsin, 1857d-1867d.

ESCHELMAN, JOHN (1819-?), Lancaster, Pennsylvania, 1843d-1850c, Pittsburgh, Pennsylvania, 1856-1857d. (Dean)

ESCHERICH, ANTON Baltimore, Maryland, 1856-1866d. High quality percussion guns. (Hartzler)

ESCHERICH, AUGUST W. (1822-?), Chicago, Illinois, 1860d-1862d.

ESCHERICH, CHARLES Washington, D.C., 1866d, Baltimore, Maryland, 1869d-1873d. (Hartzler)

ESCHERICH, FERDINAND Baltimore, Maryland, 1864-1870d. Brother of Francis. (Hartzler)

ESCHERICH, FRANCIS H. Baltimore, Maryland, 1864-1870d. Patent #78,519 June 2, 1868, breechloading firearm. Percussion and cartridge guns. As Escherich & Co. Son of Anton. (Hartzler)

ESCHERICH, FRANCIS X. Buffalo, New York, 1879-1885d.

ESCOBEDO, JUSTO Lampasas, Texas, 1890d-1896d.

ESGENBACH, HENRY Washington, D.C., 1858d. (Hartzler)

ESPER, JOHN Griffin, Georgia, 1861. Confederate gunsmith convention.

ESPICH, CHARLES Ragersville, Ohio, 1828, New Philadelphia, Ohio, 1828. (Hutslar)

ESSEX REPEATING ARMS CO. trade name of (and successor to?) Turner & Ross.

ESSEX trade name of Crescent on guns made for Belknap Hardware Co., Louisville, Kentucky.

ESSEX, JESSE, JR. (1812-?). Perryville, Indiana, 1850c. (Lindert)

ESTABROOK, J. MASON Milford, Massachusetts, 1854d-1860d. Percussion slug gun.

ESTABROOK, WILLIAM W. Armada, Michigan. Percussion over/under rifle/shotgun.

ESTEP, CORNELIUS Washington Co., Pennsylvania, 1849-1850. (Kauffman)

ESTERLOO, CHRIS Virden, Illinois, 1893.

ESTES, EDWARD Clarksville, Tenneseee, 1871d-1876d.

ESTES, H.E. Columbia, Tennessee. Percussion pistol.

ESTILL, D.R. Poplar Plains, Kentucky, 1856-1860. Percussion fullstock.

ETERLE, JOSEPH St. Louis, Missouri, 1869-1870d. (Pourie)

ETHERTON, J.P. Brushy, Kentucky, 1883d.

ETHERTON, WILLIAM F. Brushy, Kentucky, 1883d.

ETON, THOMAS Philadelphia, Pennsylvania, 1780-1785. Repaired U.S. arms with Isaac Johns. (Moller)

ETTINGER, MARTIN Wilmington, North Carolina, 1799. (Bivins)

EUBANK & STONE Charleston, South Carolina. Percussion 1/2 stock.

EUBANKS, JAMES Circleville, Texas, 1884d.

EUREKA GUN WORKS see John F. Longanecker.

EUREKA air gun by Quackenbush.

EUREKA suicide special by Iver Johnson.

EUREKA trade name on Bretell & Frisbie percussion revolver.

EUSTACE, B.J., & CO. Missouri. Derringer.

EUSTACE, THOMAS F. St. Louis, Missouri. Patent #488,627, December 27, 1892, cartridge.

EUSTIS, WILLIAM Arizona, and New Mexico, 1870-1880. (Sellers)

EUTABROUK, CHARLES H. Boston, Massachusetts, 1876d-1879d, Cambridge, Massachusetts, 1880-1892d. Patents #187,462 February 20, 1877, breechloading firearm, #193,150 July 17, 1877, reloading tools, #230,409 July 27, 1880, breechloading firearm, and #289,521, December 4, 1883, breechloading firearm.

EVANS & SPENCER Salt Lake City, Utah 1884d.

EVANS RIFLE MANUFACTURING CO. Mechanic Falls, Maine, 1873-1881. (Demeritt)

EVANS, BROOKE Valley Forge, Pennsylvania, 1821-1825. Model 1816 contract muskets with John Rogers. (Gluckman)

EVANS, CALEB Union City, Indiana. Patents #507,757 September 26, 1893, magazine gun, #650,829 June 5, 1900, magazine gun, and #676,181 June 11, 1901, shotgun.

EVANS, DANIEL Petersburg, Virginia. Percussion 1/2 stock. As Doherty & Evans.

EVANS, DANIEL Philadelphia, Pennsylvania, 1775. (Kauffman)

EVANS, DANIEL Washington Co., Pennsylvania, 1817-1824. (Whisker II)

EVANS, E.J. Hastings, Michigan, 1899d.

EVANS, EDWARD Evansburg, Pennsylvania, 1800-1815. Model 1801 contract muskets for Pennsylvania with James Evans, and Model 1808 contract muskets with Owen Evans. With Owen Evans as O. & E. Evans, 1800-1812. (Gluckman)

EVANS, FRANKLIN JAMES Iowa Falls, Iowa. Patents #283,089 August 14, 1883, magazine gun, and #300,856 June 24, 1884, magazine gun. Made rifles similar to the Winchester-Lee.

EVANS, FREEMAN Portland, Maine, 1846-1850. Also as Bailey & Evans. (Demeritt)

EVANS, GEORGE FRANKLIN (1842-1904), Mechanics Falls, Maine. Patents #189,848 April 24, 1877, magazine gun, #192,749 July 3, 1877, magazine gun, #207,350 August 27, 1878, magazine gun, and #213,555 March 25, 1879, magazine gun. (Demeritt)

EVANS, H.B. (1824-?), Shasta Co., California, 1852c. (Shelton)

EVANS, ISAAC G. Galena, Illinois, 1854d. Marshall, Michigan, 1869d-1877d, Monroe, Michigan, 1879d-1891d. Percussion 1/2 stock.

EVANS, J.L. Tacoma, Washington, 1891d.

EVANS, JAMES E. (1825-1870), Philadelphia, Pennsylvania, 1850d-1870. Derringers, rifles, and shotguns. (AG 6-78)

EVANS, JAMES Evansburg, Pennsylvania, 1800-1805. Model 1801 contract muskets for Pennsylvania with Edward Evans. (Gluckman)

EVANS, JERRY (1810-?), Nash Co., North Carolina, 1850c. (Bivins)

EVANS, JOHN R. (1828-?), Sacramento, California, 1854-1874. As Wilson & Evans. (Shelton)

EVANS, JOSEPH (1804-?), Caledonia, Illinois, 1850c-1860d.

EVANS, JOSEPH Bell Center, Wisconsin, 1857d.

EVANS, JOSEPH Philadelphia, Pennsylvania, 1847d.

EVANS, LEWIS Morgantown, West Virginia. Patents #30,054 September 10, 1860, bullet mould, and #30,307 October 9, 1860, breechloading cannon.

EVANS, O. & E. Evansburg, Pennsylvania, 1800-1812. Model 1795 contract muskets and Model 1808 contract muskets. Owen and Edward Evans. (Gluckman)

EVANS, OWEN (1758-1812), Evansburg, Pennsylvania, 1790-1812. Model 1797 contract muskets for Pennsylvania, Model 1798 contract muskets, and Model 1808 contract muskets with Edward Evans. (Hobbies 10-38)

EVANS, SILAS W. West Davenport, New York, 1874d-1882d.

EVANS, STEPHEN Valley Forge, Pennsylvania, 1742-1800. (Gardner)

EVANS, THOMAS Lancaster, Pennsylvania, 1779. (Gluckman & Satterlee)

EVANS, W.S. Philadelphia, Pennsylvania. Derringer. (Eberhart)

EVANS, WARREN R. (1835-1912), Thomaston, Maine. Patents #84,685 December 8, 1868, magazine gun, and #119,020 September 19, 1871, magazine gun. Guns made by Evans Rifle Mfg. Co. (Demeritt)

EVANS, WILLIAM L. (1797-1851), Valley Forge, Pennsylvania, 1825. Model 1822 contract muskets and Model 1826 contract pistols. Son of Owen Evans. (Gluckman)

EVANS, WILLIAM S. Leechburg, Pennsylvania. Patent #660,496 October 23, 1900, barrel.

EVATT, COLUMBUS (1813-?), Baltimore, Maryland, 1831-1853. Son of Edward Evatt. (Hartzler)

EVATT, EDWARD Baltimore, Maryland, 1804-1831. (Hartzler)

EVATT, EDWARD, II Baltimore, Maryland, 1827d-1871d. As Evatt Bros., 1827, and with E. & C. Scott, 1831-1835. Son of Edward Evatt (Hartzler)

EVATT, JOHN Baltimore, Maryland, 1827-1835. Son of Edward Evatt. (Hartzler)

EVENS, P. Cincinnati, Ohio. Agent on Allen pepperbox.

EVERETT, EDWARD Baltimore, Maryland, 1804. (Gluckman & Satterlee)

EVERETT, THOMAS Lehigh Co., Pennsylvania, 1848t-1850t. (KRA II-3)

EVERETT, WILLIAM Camden, New Jersey, 1847d-1850d.

EVERHART, P. Breckenridge, Missouri, 1881d.

EVERSON, LEWIS Cincinnati, Ohio, 1848-1853. Percussion fullstock. (Hartzler)

EVERSON, OLE Chetek, Wisconsin, 1891d-1895d.

EVERSON, WASHINGTON Belle Vernon, Pennsylvania, 1834t-1836t, Logan, Indiana, 1860d.

EVERSON, WILLIAM Dayton, Ohio. Percussion 1/2 stock. (Hutslar)

EVICK, WILLIAM unlocated. Percussion fullstock.

EVITT, WOODWARD Frederick, Maryland, 1776. For Jacob Reaser.

EWELL, H.F. unlocated. Multi-barrel percussion rifles.

EWING, WILLIAM D. (1831-?), Staunton, Virginia, 1860c.

EXCEL trade name of Montgomery Ward on shotguns made by Crescent and Iver Johnson. (Hinman)

EXCELSIOR air gun by Quackenbush.

EXCELSIOR shotgun by Iver Johnson.

EXCELSIOR suicide special.

EXETER marking on Model 1808 contract muskets made by I. & C.C. Barstow.

EXPERT .22 cal. single shot derringer.

EXPERT single barrel shotgun made by Davenport for Witte Hardware Co. in St. Louis.

EXPRESS suicide special by Bacon.

EYLAND & HAYDEN Charleston, South Carolina, 1832-1835. Importers.

EYSTER, GEORGE see George Eister.

EYSTER, JOHN Sandy Mount, Maryland. (Hartzler)

EZELL, GUSTAVUS Forrest City, Arkansas, 1878d.

EZELL, OTTO A. Forrest City, Arkansas, 1884d-1898d.

F SECTION

F. & P. unidentified. 1818 flintlock musket.

F.A.M. unidentified. Flintlock Kentucky rifle.

F.B. see Frederick Biddle.

F.J.H. see Filson Hampton.

F.Y. see Frederick Yerian.

FAAS, RUDOLPH Chicago, Illinois, 1868d-1875d, Decatur Illinois, 1884d-1886d. See Foss Bros. & Co., also Rudolph Foss.

FABER, E. & F. Pittsburgh, Pennsylvania, 1835. Barrel makers. (Kauffman)

FABER, ROBERT F. New York, New York, 1867d-1890d.

FACH, JACOB New York, New York, 1848-1851.

FAH, JOHN Chippewa Falls, Wisconsin, 1857d.

FAHNESTOCK, SAMUEL Chambersburg, Pennsylvania, 1814-1829. Percussion 1/2 stock. Hardware dealer, locks, and barrels.

FAHRINGER, HERMAN Macungie, Pennsylvania, 1799t. (KRA I-3)

FAIGLE, JOSEPH Jerseyville, Illinois, 1888d.

FAINOT, FREDERICK Lancaster, Pennsylvania, 1780. (Kauffman)

FAINOT, GEORGE FREDERICK (1728-1818), Lancaster, Pennsylvania, 1779-1794. Flintlock Kentucky and Model 1794 contract rifles.

FAINOT, JACOB Lancaster, Pennsylvania, 1779-1783. Flintlock Kentucky rifles. (Dillin)

FAIR, JAMES Dayton, Ohio, 1872-1876. (Hutslar)

FAIRBANKS & HODGES Newburyport, Massachusetts, 1853.

FAIRBANKS & LOVELL Boston, Massachusetts, 1835-1841. All metal rifles and pistols. A.B. Fairbanks and John P. Lovell.

FAIRBANKS, AARON B. (?-1841), Boston, Massachusetts, 1827-1841. All metal pistols. As Fairbanks & Lovell after 1835. (Gluckman & Satterlee)

FAIRBANKS, GEORGE E. Haverhill, Massachusetts, 1867d-1878d.

FAIRBANKS, HENRY (1814-?), Harrison, Indiana, 1847-1859. (Lindert)

FAIRBANKS, JAMES A. Augusta, Maine, 1875-1887. (Demeritt)

FAIRBANKS, LOUIS T. Worcester, Massachusetts. Patent #91,616 June 22, 1869, breechloading firearm. Made as the Ballard derringer.

FAIRBANKS, MANDAL W. Booneville, California. Patent #511,940 January 2, 1894, pistol attachment.

FAIRCHILD, ABIJAH Sneedville, Tennessee, 1860d. Percussion fullstock marked "A.B.". (MB 9-54)

FAIRCHILD, ENOCH Johnson Co., Kentucky, 1870. (Hist. Ky., V1, P128)

FAIRFIELD, EDWARD Portland, Maine, 1858. (Demeritt)

FAIVRE, ALEXANDER C. Meadville, Pennsylvania. Patents #19,553 March 9, 1858, magazine gun, and #172,008 January 11, 1876, breechloading firearm.

FALES, JAMES M., JR. New Bedford, Massachusetts, 1859-1885d.

FALK, FRANK Laredo, Texas, 1885d-1892d.

FALKENRATH, RUDOLPH St. Louis, Missouri, 1887d-1913d.

FALL & CUNNINGHAM Nashville, Tennessee, 1853-1865. Hardware dealers, locks, and guns. Alexander Fall. (GR 6-77)

FALL, ALEXANDER (1815-?), Nashville, Tennessee, 1846-?. Hardware dealer. As Fall & Cunningham, 1846-1865, and Fall & Gray, 1866-1870. (GR 6-77)

FALL, J.H., & CO. Nashville, Tennessee, 1880-1916. Hardware dealer. Son of Alexander Fall. (GR 6-77)

FALLEY, RICHARD (1740-1808), Montgomery, Massachusetts, 1760, Westfield, Massachusetts, 1761-1808. Model 1798 contract muskets. (Gluckman)

FALLS ARMS CO. trade name on Stevens shotguns.

FANCHER, THOMAS Waterbury, Connecticut, 1776-1779. Committee of Safety muskets with Jesse Curtis. (Gluckman & Satterlee)

FANCHER, W.H. Waterloo, New York. Patent #35,600 June 17, 1862, gun plow with C.M. French.

FANE, JOHN C. Chester, Pennsylvania, 1879d.

FANN, J.W. Independence, Missouri, 1889d-1898d.

FANNER, THOMAS Philadelphia, Pennsylvania, 1824d.

FARIES, SAMUEL L. Middletown, Ohio, 1826-1837. Patents #none May 29, 1828, selfpriming lock, and #none October 10, 1829, turret gun. Flintlock fullstock.

FARISH, NED Jackson, Mississippi, 1885d.

FARKKER Ravenna, Ohio. Percussion 1/2 stock and center hammer rifles. (Hutslar)

FARLEMAN, HENRY Juniata Co., Pennsylvania, 1852. (Whisker III)

FARLOW & AMES Forrest City, Iowa 1882d.

FARLOW, L. & SON Forrest City, Iowa, 1884d.

FARMER, C.H. New York, New York. Patent #609,211 August 16, 1898, magazine gun with George L. Putnam.

FARMER, E. Alma, Arkansas, 1878d.

FARMER, EDWIN Greenville, Ohio, 1875d, Carthage, Missouri, 1879d-1898d.

FARMER, NATHAN Cornucopia, Indiana, 1860d.

FARNAM, JAMES M. (1825-?), Monroe Co., Illinois, 1850c. (Johnson)

FARNAM, R.E. Flint, Michigan, 1883d-1891d.

FARNHAM, W. Jamesville, Wisconsin. Patent #60,160 December 4, 1866, alarm gun.

FARNOT see Fainot.

FARNSWORTH, L.T. Steamboat Springs, Colorado, 1880d. (Sellers-3)

FARO percussion pistol by Manhattan.

FARR, ASA New York, New York, 1869d-1873d. As Alford, Farr & Clapp, 1869.

FARRAR, MARTIN La Porte, Colorado, 1898-1900d. (Sellers-3)

FARRAR, WILLIAM J. Cleveland, Ohio, 1875d, Toledo, Ohio, 1878. (Hutslar)

FARRAR, WILLIAM Galena, Illinois, 1860d. See William J. Farrar.

FARRELL & STRIPLING Doctortown, Georgia, 1881d.

FARRELL, M. West Hoboken, New Jersey, 1878d.

FARRELL, MICHAEL Pittsburgh, Pennsylvania, 1864d.

FARRELLY & CURRAN Little Rock, Arkansas, 1819.

FARRER, WILLIAM (1828-?), Galena, Illinois, 1860c. (Johnson)

FARRINGTON, DE WITT C. Lowell, Massachusetts. Patents #165,318 July 6, 1872, machine gun, #179,450 July 4, 1876, machine gun, #185,510 December 19, 1876, machine gun, #198,366 December 18, 1877, machine gun, #198,367 December 18, 1877, machine gun, #198,368 December 18, 1877, machine gun, #205,179 June 25, 1878, machine gun carriage, #205,180 June 25, 1878, cartridge clip, and #241,130 August 16, 1881, machine gun. All patents relevant to the Lowell machine gun.

FARRINGTON, JAMES M. Concord, New Hampshire. Patent #285,474, September 25, 1883, sight.

FARRINGTON, W.S. Sanford, Florida, 1884d, Kissimee, Florida, 1886d. As Loud & Farrington, 1884.

FARRINGTON, WILLIAM B. Lebanon, Concord, and Andover, New Hampshire, 1855-1879. Percussion guns, mostly underhammer. (Roberts)

FARRO, FRANK Worcester, Massachusetts, 1867d.

FARROW ARMS CO. see William Milton Farrow.

FARROW, WILLIAM MILTON (1848-1934), Holyoke, Massachusetts, 1878-1887d, Brattleboro, Vermont, 1887, Mason, Tennessee, 1889-1904, Washington, D. C., 1904-1917, West Palm Beach, Florida, 1917-1928. Patents #306,391 October 14, 1884, breechloading firearm, #372,213, October 25, 1887, breechloading firearm, and #387,868 August 14, 1888, capping tool. Made single shot target rifles under his patent as Farrow Arms Co. (Grant 2)

FARVER, JOHN (1788-1870), Millerstown, Pennsylvania, 1818-1850. (Chandler 2)

FARVER, WILLIAM (1818-1863), Millerstown, Pennsylvania, 1839-1848, Hollidaysburg, Pennsylvania, 1848-1849, Elkhart, Indiana, 1850c, Ripley, Ohio, 1853d, Millerstown, Pennsylvania, 1860c, Newport, Pennsylvania, 1861d. Percussion fullstock. (Chandler 2)

FARWELL ARMS CO. trade name of Farwell, Ozmun, Kirk & Co., St. Paul, Minnesota on shotguns. (Hinman)

FARWELL GUN CO. New York, New York. Promotional name for William B. Farwell.

FARWELL, F.O. Cresco, Iowa, 1882d.

FARWELL, I.M. Sibley, Iowa, 1895d-1897d.

FARWELL, WILLARD B. New York, New York. Patents #137,428 April 1, 1873, machine gun (New York), #154,596 September 1, 1874, machine gun, #169,686, November 9, 1875, machine gun (San Francisco, California), and #715,773 December 16, 1902, magazine gun.

FASER, J. Macon, Mississippi, 1885d.

FASHION suicide special.

FASOLDT, BERNARD Albany, New York, 1873-1886. Patents #164,642 June 22, 1875, breechloading firearm, #181,566 August 29, 1876, breechloading firearm, and #195,496 September 25, 1877, breechloading firearm. Single shot rifles under his patents.

FASOLDT, E.C. Albany, New York. Patent #504,820 September 12, 1893, air gun with John Thatcher.

FAUCHERAUD, GIDEON Charleston, South Carolina, 1708. (Hobbies 7-42)

FAULCON, NICHOLAS Virginia, 1776. Committee of Safety repairs. (Gill)

FAULK, ADAM see Adam Foulke.

FAULKNER BROS. New Brunswick, New Jersey, 1885d.

FAULTLESS suicide special.

FAULTLESS trade name of Crescent on guns made for Smythe Hardware Co., Chicago. (Webster-Hinman)

FAUNCE, Z.W. Monrovia, California, 1893d.

FAUNCE, ZINAS Duxbury, Massachusetts, 1869d-1879d.

FAUNTLEROY, ROBERT H. New Harmony, Indiana, 1829-1840. Patent #none August 15, 1833, underhammer lock. (Lindert)

FAUST & McCRAN unlocated. Percussion 1/2 stock.

FAUST & WIN... unlocated. Lock marking.

FAUST, ANTHONY Berks Co., Pennsylvania, 1767. (Whisker III)

FAUST, HENRY Deming, New Mexico, 1884d.

FAUST, JOSEPH H. (1818-?), Alsace, Pennsylvania, 1844-1880. Percussion rifles and shotguns. (Hobbies 5-37)

FAUST, W.E. La Fontaine, Indiana, 1870-1910. (Lindert)

FAVIELL, S.A. Jefferson, Texas, 1890d-1892d.

FAVIER, PETER A. Baltimore, Maryland, 1837-1853d. (Hartzler)

FAVORITE NAVY suicide special by Iver Johnson.

FAVORITE suicide special by Iver Johnson.

FAVORITE trade name of Stevens on single shot rifles.

FAXON, A.M. St. Francis, Missouri, 1854d, Athens, Missouri, 1867d-1881d.

FAY, A. Altoona, Pennsylvania, 1868d.

FAY, EDWARD Albany, New York, 1831-1842. Percussion fullstock rifle. (Gluckman & Satterlee)

FAY, EDWIN T. Hartford, Connecticut, 1848-1860, Marshfield, Massachusetts, 1871-1873. Fine percussion rifles and pistols. Later president of Stevens Arms & Tool Co. (Roberts)

FAY, GEORGE H. Morrison, Illinois. Patent #226,505 April 13, 1880, breechloading firearm.

FAY, GEORGE Blair Co., Pennsylvania, 1850c, Gaysport, Pennsylvania, 1859, Hollidaysburg, Pennsylvania, 1860c-1861d, Duncansville, Pennsylvania, 1861d, Altoona, Pennsylvania, 1862-1890. Percussion fullstock and 1/2 stock. (Kauffman)

FAY, HENRY C. Lancaster, Massachusetts. Patent #203, May 22, 1837, firearm.

FAY, RICHARD Philadelphia, Pennsylvania. Patent #209,613, November 5, 1878, breechloading firearm.

FAY, RIMMON C. Ilion, New York. Patents #547,602 October 8, 1895, magazine gun, and #547,603 October 8, 1895, magazine gun.

FAY, W.M. Cresco, Iowa, 1889d.

FAY, WILLIAM (?-1864), Altoona, Pennsylvania, 1864. (Kauffman)

FAYE, G. see George Fay.

FAYETTEVILLE ARSENAL Fayetteville, North Carolina, 1861-1865. Rifles, pistols, and muskets for the Confederacy. (Hill-Anthony)

FEA & HAMILTON St. Louis, Missouri, 1854d. Thomas Fea and John Hamilton.

FEA, THOMAS St. Louis, Missouri, 1854d-1859d. As Fea & Hamilton, 1854.

FEATHER, GEORGE Lancaster Co., Pennsylvania, 1820t-1822t. (Dyke)

FEATHERLIGHT trade name of Sears Roebuck on shotguns. (Hinman)

FEAY, GEORGE see George Fay.

FEBIGER ARMS CO. New Orleans, Louisiana, 1886d-1914d. Importers until 1900 when they made and sold rifles under Henry Febiger's patents.

FEDER, G. unlocated. Flintlock Kentucky. Possibly George Feather? (Sellers)

FEDERAL ARMS CO. trade name of Meriden on owlhead revolvers.

FEDERAL trade name of Hopkins & Allen on .22 rifles.

FEEL, JAMES E. Havana, Missouri, 1879d.

FEHR, J. Nazareth, Pennsylvania, 1830-1835. Flintlock Kentucky.

FEHR, JOHN Northampton Co., Pennsylvania, 1850c. Same as J. Fehr, Nazareth, Pennsylvania?

FEHR, R.H. Bethlehem, Pennsylvania, 1882d-1890d.

FEHR, W. unlocated. Percussion swivel.

FEHRMAN, C.H. Chicago, Illinois, 1872-1873.

FEINBECKER, DANIEL Lancaster Co., Pennsylvania, 1796t. (Dyke)

FEINOUR, ALFRED Baltimore, Maryland, 1847. (Hartzler)

FEIS, CELESTINE Stillwater, Minnesota, 1867d.

FELL, THOMAS Hartford, Connecticut, 1852-1853d.

FELLOW, MATTHEW New Orleans, Louisiana, 1868d-1869d. Fellen in 1868.

FELLOWS, J. OTIS Hornellsville, New York, 1877-1883.

FELSHAW, F. see Frank Telshaw.

FELSHAW, HIRAM T. Constableville, New York, 1878-1882.

FELSHAW, JEROME Constableville, New York, 1858-1874d. Percussion 1/2 stock and pistol.

FELSTED & ARTZ Winona, Minnesota, 1878d-1880d. Double shotgun.

FELSTED BROS. Winona, Minnesota, 1884d.

FELSTED, THEODORE I. Winona, Minnesota, 1875d-1884d. As Felsted & Artz, 1878-1880 and Felsted Bros., 1884.

FELTMAN, WILLIAM H. (1799-?), Cincinnati, Ohio, 1850c. (Hutslar)

FELTON, FRANK B. Hartford, Connecticut. Patent #535,097 March 5, 1895, revolver safety.

FELTON, S. Phelps Co., Missouri, 1860d.

FENDERSON & COLE Biddeford, Maine, 1896d. Dealers. (Demeritt)

FENNER, ALBERT Baltimore, Maryland, 1851d. (Hartzler)

FENNER, R.M. Jamesville, Wisconsin, 1879d.

FENNER, THOMAS Philadelphia, Pennsylvania, 1824d-1839d.

FENNO Lancaster, Pennsylvania, 1779. Committee of Safety muskets (Hobbies 4-38).

FENNO, WILLIAM D. Worcester, Massachusetts, 1853d.

FENSEL, PETER (1842-1930), Marysville, Ohio, 1887-1930. (Gluckman & Satterlee)

FENSTERMAKER, W.E. Lincoln, Kansas, 1888d.

FENWICK, ROBERT Charlestown, South Carolina, 1699. (Lindsay 3)

FERGUS & BEEBE Pine Bluff, Arkansas, 1888d.

FERGUSON, ALFRED B. (1805-?), Washington, D.C., 1841-1853d. (Hartzler)

FERGUSON, CHARLES Troy, New York, 1830-1845. Flintlock Kentucky rifles. (Dillin)

FERGUSON, D. Aurora, Illinois, 1899d.

FERGUSON, ELIAS H. (1809-?), Buffalo, West Virginia, 1870c-1880c.

FERGUSON, P. Bowling Green, Kentucky, 1855-1860. Percussion 1/2 stock.

FERGUSON, R. Island Grove, Florida, 1886d.

FERGUSON, S.F. Franklin, Texas, 1884d-1896d.

FERGUSON, WILLIAM (1798-?), McDonough Co., Illinois, 1840-1850. (Johnson)

FERRANT, EMIL Minneapolis, Minnesota. Patent #645,932 March 27, 1900, automatic (type ?) with Michael Beck.

FERREE, GEORGE SPENCER (1818-1896), Clinton, Pennsylvania, 1838-1852, Danville, Indiana, 1852-1868, Corydon, Indiana, 1869-1871, Laconia, Indiana, 1871-1896. Son of Isaac Ferree. (Lindert)

FERREE, ISAAC (1786-1822), Peter's Creek, Pennsylvania, 1807-1812, Corydon, Indiana, 1815, Baton Rouge, Louisiana, 1818-1822. Son of Jacob Ferree, operated his shop after his father's death and then followed the Ohio and Mississippi rivers. (Kauffman)

FERREE, JACOB (1750-1807), Strasburg, Pennsylvania, 1774-1784, Peter's Creek, Pennsylvania, 1784-1807. Flintlock Kentucky rifle. (Dean)

FERREE, JOEL THORNTON (1815-1882), Clinton, Pennsylvania, 1838-1840, Corydon, Indiana, 1882. Son of Isaac Ferree, percussion fullstock. (Lindert)

FERREE, JOEL (1731-1784), Lancaster, Pennsylvania, 1752-1784. Committee of Safety muskets and flintlock Kentucky rifles. (Gluckman)

FERREE, JOEL (1771-1813), Peter's Creek, Pennsylvania, 1785-1813. Son of Jacob Ferree, worked with him until Jacob's death in 1807, alone thereafter. (Kauffman)

FERREE, JOEL (1806-1883), Bridgeville, Pennsylvania, Cumberland, Ohio, 1850-1883. Son of Joel (1771) Ferree, listed as Joel Free in 1853 directory. (Kaufmann, Hutslar)

FERREE, MANUEL Lancaster, Pennsylvania, 1779. (Gluckman & Satterlee)

FERRELL, CLEMENT Harrisburg, Illinois, 1860d.

FERRELL, WYATT C. (1829-1918), Marion, Illinois, 1870-1900. (Johnson)

FERRIE, JAMES Mobile, Alabama, 1855d-1859d. (Neville)

FERRILL, WILLIAM C. (1815-?), Hardin Co., Illinois, 1838-1850c. (Johnson)

FERRINGTON, SOLOMON Rowan Co., North Carolina, 1820c-1829. (Bivins)

FERRIS Sandusky, Ohio, 1882-1888. As Barney & Ferris. (Hutslar)

FERRIS, BENJAMIN Peekskill, New York, 1865-1874d. Percussion 1/2 stock.

FERRIS, CHARLES H. Sing Sing, New York, 1870-1882. Percussion target pistol.

FERRIS, FRED G. Utica, New York, 1859-1863. (Roberts).

FERRIS, GEORGE H. Utica, New York, 1848-1882. Patents #41,984 March 22, 1864, breechloading cannon, #42,571 May 3, 1864, cannon, #118,849 September 12, 1871, cartridge loader, #119,834 October 10, 1871, breechloading firearm, and #149,456 April 7, 1874, breechloading firearm. Percussion target rifles. (Roberts)

FERRIS, HUDSON Chicago, Illinois. Patent #286,598 October 16, 1883, alarm gun.

FERRIS, JAMES Litchfield, Illinois, 1864d.

FERRIS, R.B. Columbus Junction, Iowa, 1882d.

FESIG, CONRAD Reading, Pennsylvania, 1778-1785. (Gluckman & Satterlee)

FESLER, WILLIAM S. Carrollton, Illinois, 1868. (Johnson)

FETE, ALFRED Horton, Kansas, 1894d.

FETTER, ANDREW Ridgeville, Indiana, 1881-1885. (Lindert)

FETTER, GEORGE Lancaster Co., Pennsylvania, 1831t-1848t. (Dyke)

FETTER, GEORGE, JR. Lancaster Co., Pennsylvania, 1844t-1850t. (Dyke)

FETTER, HENRY Lancaster Co., Pennsylvania, 1847t-1848t. Son of George Fetter. (Dyke)

FETTER, JOHN Pittsburgh, Pennsylvania, 1819.

FETTER, PERRY Kratzerville, Pennsylvania, 1860-1908. Percussion match rifles. (Chandler 2)

FETTER, PETER Lancaster Co., Pennsylvania, 1837t-1850t. (Dyke)

FETTER, SAMUEL (1806-?), Ohio, 1840, Goshen, Indiana, 1850c. (Lindert)

FETTER, WILLIAM Philadelphia, Pennsylvania, 1776. For Lewis Prahl. (Gluckman & Satterlee)

FEUTZ, EDWARD Highland, Illinois, 1882d.

FEW, RICHARD Bethel, Pennsylvania, 1770s.

FIBRICK, CHARLES R. Chicago, Illinois, 1867. Submitted breechloading rifle to ordnance trials.

FICK, GEORGE A. New Orleans, Louisiana, 1869d.

FIDDLER, F. see Squire Fidler.

FIDIAN unlocated. Flintlock Kentucky rifle.

FIDLER, SQUIRE (1809-1886), Mt. Washington, Kentucky, 1830-1859, Orleans, Indiana, 1859-1886. Percussion fullstock. Listed in both Pimento and Quincy, Indiana directories for 1860. (Lindert)

FIEDLER, JOSEF Pittsburgh, Pennsylvania. Patent #181,830 September 5, 1876, breechloading firearm.

FIEDLER, JOSEPH Stanton, Texas, 1896d.

FIEHL, F. New Orleans, Louisiana, 1896d.

FIELD & LANGSTROTH Philadelphia, Pennsylvania, 1846d-1870d. Lockmakers to 1850, locks and derringers thereafter. Became Field, Langstroth & Co. in 1855.

FIELD, ALFRED Statesville, North Carolina. Worked for Daniel Speck. Signed flintlock barrels "A.F.". (Bivins)

FIELD, ARROWSMITH Pulaski, Tennessee. Confederate Model 1841 rifles (GR8-72.)

FIELD, EDWIN S. Springfield, Massachusetts. Patents #345,058 July 6, 1886, breechloading firearm, and #391,953 October 30, 1888, breechloading firearm, both with Solomon Hindley.

FIELD, EVAN DES (1832-?), Ottawa, Illinois, 1850c. (Johnson)

FIELDS, I. Philadelphia, Pennsylvania. Flintlock Kentucky.

FIELDS, WILLIAM Wilmington, Delaware. Patent #113,996 April 25, 1871, battery gun.

FIERSCH, JOSEPH Bushkill, Pennsylvania, 1828-1829t. (KRA II-3)

FIFE, HARMON (?-1845), North Pembroke, New Hampshire, 1835-1845. Percussion revolvers. (AR 9-55)

FIFIELD & RICHARDSON Boston, Massachusetts, 1850-1863d. Percussion double shotgun.

FIFIELD, B. Boston, Massachusetts. Underhammer rifle.

FIGG, A. unlocated. Percussion fullstock.

FIGTHORN, ANDREW (?-1827), Reading, Pennsylvania, 1779-1827. Flintlock Kentucky rifles, signed "A. F.". (Kindig)

FIGTHORN, ANDREW, JR. Reading, Pennsylvania, 1803-1805. (Kindig)

FIGURES, BARTHOLOMEW (?-1699), Surry Co., Virginia. (Gill)

FIKENTSCHER, ADAM Newport, Kentucky, 1892d.

FILMAN, WILLIAM A. Milton, Pennsylvania, 1820-1861d. Flintlock and percussion rifles. (Kauffman)

FILMORE, W. unlocated. Percussion fullstock.

FINCH, JOSEPH N. Mercer Co., New York, 1850c. (GR 11-60)

FINCH, JOSEPH (?-1825), New York, New York, 1818-1825. Patent #none April 12, 1823, percussion guns.

FINCH, JOSEPH Venango Co., Pennsylvania, 1850. (Kauffman)

FINCH, WILLIAM ROSE (1832-1906), Eureka, California, 1869-1906. Patents #200,042 February 5, 1878, breechloading firearm, #215,445 May 20, 1879, breechloading firearm, #229,035 June 22, 1880, breechloading firearm, #306,144 October 7, 1884, magazine gun, and #452,699 May 19, 1891, breechloading firearm. Guns made under his patents by California Arms Co. and himself. (Shelton)

FINDLAY, ROBERT & CO. Baltimore, Maryland, 1887d. (Hartzler)

FINDLEY, TUNIS (1823-?), Cincinnati, Ohio, 1850c. (Hutslar)

FINDLEY, WASHINGTON Jackson Co., Indiana 1850c.

FINE, WILLIAM R. Wilsonville, Tennessee, 1860.

FINK, A. L. unlocated. Percussion 1/2 stock.

FINLEY, ABE Cortland, Indiana, 1850-1893. (MB 4-55).

FINNEGAN, PETER H. Springfield, Massachusetts. Patent #504,154 August 29, 1893, palm pistol, used by Chicago Fire Arms Co.

FINNEY, F.R. Sulphur Springs, Texas, 1884d-1890d.

FIRCKELTON see Butler & Firckelton.

FISCHER, CHRISTIAN A. Grand Forks, North Dakota, 1898d. Patent #636,650 November 7, 1899, ejector.

FISCHER, GEORGE unlocated. Percussion over/under rifle/shotgun.

FISCHER, GUSTAVE New York, New York. Breechloading rifles.

FISCHER, MICHAEL Hastings, Minnesota, 1877-1880.

FISCHER, SOPHIAN E. Hayward, California. Patents #606,452 June 28, 1898, sight, #658,708 September 25, 1900, sight, #658,709 September 25, 1900, sight, and #689,476 December 24, 1901, sight.

FISH & FURBER Gardiner, Maine, 1898d. (Demeritt)

FISH & SIMPSON New York, New York, 1875d-1876d.

FISH, DANIEL (?-1875), New York, New York, 1844d-1875d. Percussion pistols and rifles.

FISH, ISAAC L. (1821-?), Ohio, 1849, Aurora, Indiana, 1850c. (Lindert)

FISH, J.E. Bath, Maine, 1896d.

FISH, MARSHALL unlocated. Flintlock Kentucky.

FISH, P.A. New York, New York, 1875d-1876d.

FISH, T.B., & CO. New York, New York, 1874d-1875d. Same address as Daniel Fish.

FISHBURN, HENCE Lancaster, Pennsylvania, 1785. (Dean)

FISHBURN, PHILIP (1722-1795), Dauphin Co., Pennsylvania. Flintlock muskets. (Gardner)

FISHEL, A. County Line, Iowa, 1884d.

FISHEL, JACOB (?-1863), Bedford Co., Pennsylvania, 1846-1863. Fullstock Bedford rifle. (Whisker)

FISHER & LONG Detroit, Michigan, 1867d-1875d. Percussion double shotgun. Elam J. Fisher and John E. Long. Both worked for William Wingert, and acquired his shop when he retired. (MB 6-61)

FISHER & SHAEFFER Washington, D.C., 1867d. G. Frederick Fisher. (Hartzler)

FISHER trade name of Cyrus Fisher on shotguns and revolvers.

FISHER, A.R. Cumberland, Maryland, 1887d. (Hartzler)

FISHER, C.B. Aurora, Illinois, 1880d.

FISHER, C.R. Greenville, Texas, 1884d, Front Royal, Virginia, 1893d.

FISHER, CYRUS (1820-?). Lynchburg, Virginia, 1850c-1877d, with William B. Fisher, 1859-1863.

FISHER, DANIEL (1813-?), Pike Co., Illinois, 1844-1850. Percussion fullstock. (Johnson)

FISHER, DAVID Macungie, Pennsylvania, 1887d.

FISHER, E.C. unlocated. Flintlock New England rifle.

FISHER, E.E. Concord, New Hampshire, 1874d-1878d.

FISHER, E.M. Fostoria, Ohio, 1855-1881. Percussion 1/2 stock. (Hutslar)

FISHER, ELAM J. see Fisher & Long.

FISHER, ELIJAH Springfield, Massachusetts. Patent #168 April 17, 1837, firearms with Dexter Chamberlain.

FISHER, ELKANS (1834-?), Lynchburg, Virginia, 1850c-1888d. Apprenticed to his father, Cyrus, whom he succeeded in 1877. (MB 10-63)

FISHER, F.G. Bellvue, Evans, La Porte, and Greeley, Colorado, 1876-1884d. Percussion schuetzen rifles. (Sellers-3)

FISHER, FRANCIS Allegheny, Pennsylvania, 1859-1860. (Kauffman)

FISHER, FRANK G. Bellvue, Iowa, 1865d, McGregor, Iowa, 1875d-1897d. (Same as F.G. Fisher?)

FISHER, G. FREDERICK Washington, D.C., 1864-1867d. As Fisher & Shaeffer, 1867. (Hartzler)

FISHER, G. New York, New York. Air gun.

FISHER, GEORGE A. Modesto, California, 1883-1893. As Pereira & Fisher, 1883-1884. (Shelton)

FISHER, GEORGE W. (1835-?), Clark Co., West Virginia, 1856-1880c.

FISHER, GEORGE (?-1821), Cadiz, Ohio, 1808-1821. (Hutslar)

FISHER, GEORGE Washington, Pennsylvania, 1803-1805. (Kauffman)

FISHER, H. Sandy, Oregon, 1889d-1891d.

FISHER, HARRISON Berks Co., Pennsylvania, 1850c, Lancaster, Pennsylvania, 1871d. Barrel maker. (Kauffman)

FISHER, HENRY Frederick, Maryland, 1776. For Jacob Reaser.

FISHER, HOMER New York, New York, 1855-1888d. Mostly retail sales, but made a few percussion guns.

FISHER, JACOB (?-1849), Bedford Co., Pennsylvania, 1846-1848. (Whisker)

FISHER, JACOB Canton, Ohio. Percussion 1/2 stock.

FISHER, JAMES Baltimore, Maryland, 1817-1818d. (Hartzler)

FISHER, JOHN H. New York, New York, 1841d-1858d. Percussion double shotgun.

FISHER, JOHN (1811-?), Seneca Co., Ohio, 1850c. Percussion fullstock. (Hutslar)

FISHER, JOHN (1821-?), Cincinnati, Ohio, 1850c. (Hutslar)

FISHER, JOHN (1834-?), Lynchburg, Virginia, 1850c. (MB 10-63)

FISHER, JOSEPH FRANCIS (1830-1906). San Luis Obispo, California, 1869-1905. (Shelton)

FISHER, JOSEPH (1827-?), Placerville, California, 1861-1880. (Shelton)

FISHER, JOSHUA Meigsville, Ohio, 1860-1864. (Hutslar)

FISHER, M.M. David City, Nebraska, 1886d.

FISHER, MARVIN W. Washington, D.C. Patent #5,928 November 21, 1848, percussion caps.

FISHER, MICHAEL Hastings, Minnesota, 1875d-1886d.

FISHER, P.C. Arcadia, Ohio, 1883d. (Hutslar)

FISHER, PAUL White Deer, Pennsylvania, 1861d.

FISHER, SAMUEL O. Lynchburg, Virginia, 1877d-1893d. Son of Cyrus Fisher.

FISHER, SEBASTIAN New York, New York, 1858d-1880d. Percussion and air guns.

FISHER, T.L. Warren Co., Missouri, 1850c. (MB 11-66)

FISHER, URIAH Shenandoah Co., Virginia. Percussion fullstock. (KRA 76)

FISHER, W.B. & C. Lynchburg, Virginia, 1861-1862. William B. Fisher and his brother Cyrus. Altered flintlocks for the Confederacy and made percussion guns.

FISHER, WILLIAM B. (1814-?), Lynchburg, Virginia, 1850c-1863. Percussion fullstock.

FISK, C.A. Camden, Arkansas, 1884d-1888d, Brinkley, Arkansas, 1892d.

FISK, JAMES H. Chicago, Illinois, 1885-1889d.

FISKE & TUTTLE New Haven, Connecticut, 1874d. H.W. Fiske and C.W. Tuttle.

FISKE, H.W. New Haven, Connecticut, 1873d-1874d. As Fiske & Tuttle, 1874. Percussion 1/2 stock.

FISTER, H. unlocated. Flintlock Kentucky rifle.

FITCH & WALDO New York, New York, 1860-1867d. Retailers for Bacon percussion revolvers. James Fitch.

FITCH, ARDEN S. New York, New York. Patent #624,317 May 2, 1899, grip.

FITCH, G.A. Media, Kansas, 1888d.

FITCH, GEORGE A. Kalamazoo, Michigan. Patent #58,800 October 16, 1866, priming cartridges.

FITCH, JAMES L. Orangeville, Indiana, 1870c. (Gardner)

FITCH, JAMES P. New York, New York, 1858-1865. Dealer for James Reid and others. With Fitch & Waldo in 1860, and Fitch, Van Vechten & Co. after 1863.

FITCH, JOHN (1743-1798), Trenton, New Jersey, 1769-1776, Bucks Co., Pennsylvania, 1777-1798. Committee of Safety muskets, also invented steam boat. (Boerhet)

FITCH, JOHN New York, New York, 1844-1851.

FITTING, JACOB Denver, Colorado, 1883-1914. With Gustave Winter, 1883-1890. (Sellers-3)

FITTON & BRIERLY Worcester, Massachusetts, 1871-1874.

FITTRELL, PATRICK Philadelphia, Pennsylvania, 1780-1785. Repaired U.S. arms. (Moller)

FITZGERALD, R. Cambridge, Massachusetts, 1861d. All iron pistol.

FITZGERALD, WALTER Boston, Massachusetts. Patent #45,919 January 17, 1865, magazine gun.

FITZPATRICK, DANIEL Chicago, Illinois, 1890d.

FITZPATRICK, L. Natchez, Mississippi, 1885d. Son of Rees Fitzpatrick.

FITZPATRICK, REES (1808-1868), Baton Rouge, Louisiana, 1829-1840, Natchez, Mississippi, 1840-1868. Partner of Stephen O'Dell, 1840-1843. Made percussion guns and Bowie knives.

FITZPATRICK, SAMUEL Helena, Arkansas, 1884d-1898d.

FITZWATER, L. Philadelphia, Pennsylvania, 1847d. For G. W. Palmer.

FLAGG, BENJAMIN (1807-1882), Milbury, Massachusetts, 1849-1852. Model 1842 contract muskets as B. Flagg & Co. Sold out to William Glaze of Palmetto Armory. (Reilly)

FLAGG, EDWARD (1818-?), Peoria, Illinois, 1850c. (Johnson)

FLAGG, JOHN S. Berkeley Springs, West Virginia, 1870-1890. (Whisker IV)

FLAGLER, JOHN Pittsburgh, Pennsylvania, 1837d. (Kauffman)

FLAHARTY, JAMES West Liberty, West Virginia, 1794-1822. (Dean)

FLAIG, EDWARD Danville, Kentucky, 1883d.

FLANDERS, CHARLES E. Leon, Iowa, 1880d-1887d, Chariton, Iowa, 1895d.

FLANIGAN, WILLIAM (1831-?), Holmes Co., Ohio, 1850c. (Hutslar)

FLATHER, HENRY Bridesburg, Pennsylvania. Patent #49,463 August 15, 1865, breechloading firearm with W.T. Wilson.

FLAUGHER, JOHN North Jackson, Ohio, 1859-1864. (Hutslar)

FLAUTT, JERRY A. Somerset, Ohio, 1881d. (Hutslar)

FLECK, GEORGE K. (1796-1880), Barrville, Pennsylvania, 1840-1877, Mt. Union, Pennsylvania, 1880. Percussion swivel. (Whisker II)

FLECK, VALENTINE (1805-1880), Memmo, Pennsylvania, 1850c-1880. (Whisker II)

FLEEGER, CHRISTIAN McCandless, Pennsylvania, 1861d.

FLEEGER, I or **J.**, Dauphin Co., Pennsylvania, 1790.

FLEEGER, JOHN Allegheny, Pennsylvania, 1831-1886. Operated Allegheny Gun Works, with son, William A. Fleeger after 1870. Percussion fullstock. (Gluckman & Satterlee)

FLEEGER, PETER Allegheny, Pennsylvania, 1856-1857d. (Kauffman)

FLEEGER, WILLIAM A. Allegheny, Pennsylvania, 1861-1886. With his father, John, at Allegheny Gun Works.

FLEEK, S.B. Cedar Rapids, Iowa, 1880d-1882d, Grand Island, Nebraska, 1886d-1893d.

FLEENOR, JAMES (1832-1899), Fleenortown, Indiana, 1853-1893. Percussion fullstock and 1/2 stock. (MB 3-51)

FLEGEL, GEORGE Philadelphia, Pennsylvania, 1814-1835, at U.S. Arsenal 1814-1819. (Hartzler)

FLEGEL, J.G. Philadelphia, Pennsylvania, 1829d-1835d.

FLEHART, JAMES Fayette Co., Pennsylvania, 1801-1804. (Kauffman)

FLEISCHEL, LOUIS Jersey City, New Jersey, 1878d.

FLEMING, BENJAMIN F. (1803-?), Kenton, Ohio, 1850c. (Hutslar)

FLEMING, JOHN W. Union, Ohio, 1859d, Luray, Indiana. Percussion fullstock. (Hutslar)

FLEMING, L.M. unlocated. Percussion 1/2 stock, percussion fullstock.

FLEMING, SILAS M. Richmond, Indiana, 1850-1852, New Paris, Ohio, 1853d. (Hutsiar, Lindert)

FLEMING, THOMAS Luray, Indiana, 1840-1860. Percussion fullstock rifle marked TF. (Lindert)

FLEMING, THORNTON (1871-1953), Great Bend, Ohio, 1892-1947. (Hutslar)

FLEMMING Union City, Indiana, 1860d.

FLEMMING, THOMAS M. Washington, D.C. Patent #185,224 December 12, 1876, hammer.

FLERON, L.J. Paterson, New Jersey, 1878d-1882d.

FLESH, MARTIN (1829-?), St. Louis, Missouri, 1850c. (Lewis)

FLESHER, PETER Edmiston, West Virginia, 1900d. (Whisker IV)

FLETCHER HARDWARE CO. Wilmington, North Carolina. Dealers only.

FLETCHER see Hendricks & Fletcher.

FLETCHER, HENRY (1806-?), Cincinnati, Ohio, 1850-1855. (Hutslar)

FLETCHER, HENRY, JR. (1831-?), Cincinnati, Ohio, 1850c, Mound City, Illinois, 1859-1860d. (Hutslar)

FLETCHER, WILLIAM F. Baltimore, Maryland, 1876-1879. Worked with William G. Fletcher. (Hartzler)

FLETCHER, WILLIAM G. (1821-?), Baltimore, Maryland, 1847d-1889d. (Hartzler)

FLICK, JOHN (1859-1958), Ellsworth, Ohio, 1880-1930. Worked with David Leonard. (MB 4-60)

FLIEGE, WILLIAM Nashville, Tennessee, 1887d.

FLING, G.F. (1806-?), Napa, California, 1852c. (Shelton)

FLINT, GEORGE V. (1871-1921), Lee, Illinois, 1894-1921.

FLIPPIN, THOMAS Bedford Co., Virginia, 1777. Committee of Safety repairs. (Gill)

FLODIN, L.T. Burlington, Iowa, 1887d-1889d.

FLOECK, MICHAEL Houston, Texas, 1882d-1888d. Successor to Otto Erichson.

FLOERL, BALTHAZAR St. Genevieve, Missouri, 1879d-1891d.

FLOHR & WENDELL San Francisco, California, 1858. Needlefire shotgun.

FLOHR, ALEXANDER (1852-?), Sacramento, California, 1870-1880. Son of Andrew Flohr. (Shelton)

FLOHR, ANDREW (1824-1896), Missouri, 1850, Sacramento, California, 1851-1893. As Flohr & Wendell, 1858-1860, percussion and breechloading rifles and shotguns. (Shelton)

FLOHR, CHARLES (1852-1903), Sacramento, California, 1873-1900. Nephew of Andrew Flohr, but operated his own shop. (Shelton)

FLOHR, RHEINHART (1862-?), Sacramento, California, 1880-1895. Son of Andrew Flohr, worked for his father. (Shelton)

FLOHR, T.T. Wooster, Ohio, 1878d. (Hutslar)

FLOHR, WILLIAM MORRIS (1852-?), Madison, Wisconsin, 1879d, Sacramento, California, 1889-1892. Not related to other Flohrs. (Shelton)

FLORA, JOSEPH Dycusburg, Kentucky, 1883d-1885d.

FLORENCE, L. Big Plain, Ohio, 1859d. (Hutslar)

FLORUS, PETER Lehigh Co., Pennsylvania, 1845t. (KRA II-3)

FLORUS, WILLIAM Lehigh Co., Pennsylvania, 1856t. (Gabel)

FLOWERS, AARON Cromwell, Indiana, 1860d.

FLOWERS, CHARLES (1821-1897), Harmony, Pennsylvania, 1866-1890d. Percussion rifles. Sometimes used "C.F." instead of full signature. (Kauffman)

FLOYD, J.O. Des Moines, Iowa, 1871d.

FLOYD, T. Circleville, Ohio, 1853d. (Hutslar)

FLOYD, THOMAS Charleston, South Carolina, 1767. (Dean)

FLOYD, THOMAS Warsaw, Indiana, 1860d.

FLOYD, W. South Perry, Ohio. Patent #33,842 December 3, 1861, alarm gun with P. Kane.

FLOYD, WILLIAM Rock House, Ohio. Patent #16,761 March 3, 1857, cane gun with John Tilton.

FLUCK, ADAM Alexandria, Louisiana, 1885d.

FLUERY, JOHN Omaha, Nebraska, 1878d.

FLUES, E.F. Buffalo, New York. Percussion over/under shotgun.

FLUES, EMIL F. Bay City, Michigan, 1887d-1900d. Patent #546,516 September 17, 1895, safety. As Wrege & Flues, 1887.

FLUKER, W.T. Washington, Georgia, 1879d-1883d. As Fluker & Bro., 1881d-1883d.

FLYNN, JOHN Philadelphia, Pennsylvania, 1780-1782. Continental Armory. (Moller)

FOBES, GEORGE Nashua, Iowa, 1884d-1897d.

FOEHL & WEEKS FIRE ARMS MFG. CO. Philadelphia, Pennsylvania, and Camden, New Jersey, 1889-1900. Successors to Deringer Pistol Co. Single shot rifles and cheap double action revolvers.

FOEHL, CHARLES Philadelphia, Pennsylvania, 1863d-1912. Patents #139,461 June 3, 1873, revolver, #180,216 July 25, 1876, breechloading firearm, #222,991 December 30, 1879, breechloading firearm, #417,672 December 17, 1889, revolver, #444,823 January 20, 1891, revolver with Charles A. Weeks, #447,219 February 24, 1891, revolver with Charles A. Weeks, #468,243 February 2, 1892, revolver with Charles A. Weeks, #471,112 March 22, 1892, revolver with Charles A. Weeks, #530,759 December 11, 1894, revolver, #554,058 February 4, 1896, revolver, #818,177 April 17, 1906, revolver with Henry Kolb, #826,788 July 24, 1906, revolver with Henry Kolb, #847,011 March 12, 1907, revolver with Henry Kolb, and #1,019,446 March 5, 1912. After working for the Deringer Pistol Co., made percussion rifles and pistols on his own, revolvers and single shot rifles were made by Foehl & Weeks.

FOGERTY REPEATING RIFLE CO. Boston, Massachusetts, 1867-1869. Valentine Fogerty repeating rifles.

FOGERTY, GEORGE F. Cambridge, Massachusetts, 1889-1895. Patents #482,305 September 6, 1892, magazine gun, and #533,949 February 12, 1895. magazine gun. double-barrel shotgun.

FOGERTY, VALENTINE Cambridge, Massachusetts. Patents #46,459 February 21, 1865, magazine gun, #59,126 October 23, 1866, magazine gun, #82,819 October 6, 1868, magazine gun, #86,520 February 2, 1889, breechloading firearm, and #117,398 July 25, 1871, breechloading firearm.

FOGG, G.E. Manchester, New Hampshire. Percussion rifles and pistols.

FOGG, GILMAN B. Manchester, New Hampshire, 1845-1879. Percussion rifles and pistols. (Roberts)

FOGLE, HEINRICH Lancaster, Pennsylvania, 1857d.

FOGLESON, SCHILLER Marion, Ohio, 1895-1900. (Hutslar)

FOGLESONG, JOHN Richland Co., Ohio, 1810-1820. (Hutslar)

FOHRER, LEWIS see Ludwig Fohrer.

FOHRER, LUDWIG Philadelphia, Pennsylvania, 1775-1785. Commitee of Safety muskets, and as Lewis Fohrer, 1780-1785, repaired U.S. arms. (Moller)

FOLAND, J. Dandridge, Tennessee, 1860d.

FOLEY, T. Catskill, New York. Percussion fullstock.

FOLGER, H. unlocated. Percussion fullstock.

FOLGER, LAMB & CO. unlocated. Percussion locks.

FOLGER, WILLIAM H. (1813-?), Barnesville, Ohio, 1838-1886. Percussion 1/2 stock, percussion fullstock. (MB 6-64)

FOLIART, WILLIAM unlocated. Percussion 1/2 stock.

FOLK, WILLIAM and SAMUEL E. Bryan Ohio, 1876-1896. Patent #308,482 November 25, 1884, breechloading firearm. As Folk's Gun Works, 1886-1896, brass frame rifles. (Hartzler)

FOLKART, WILLIAM Helena, Montana, 1871d.

FOLKER, I. Ravenna, Ohio. Percussion 1/2 stock.

FOLLANSBEE & PRESTON Manchester, New Hampshire, 1867d.

FOLLECHT Lancaster, Pennsylvania, 1770c. Flintlock Kentucky rifle. (Dillin)

FOLLECK, JOHN Johnstown, New York, 1769-1775.

FOLLETT, JOSEPH L. New York, New York. Patent #192,751 July 3, 1877, spring gun.

FOLSOM BROS. Chicago, Illinois, 1868-1869d, New Orleans, Louisiana, 1870-1875d.

FOLSOM, CHARLES New York, New York, 1852d-1888d. As H. Tomes & Co., 1852-1856, Eaton & Folsom, 1856-1857, Folsom & Stevens, 1858-1860. Also had a branch office in St. Louis. Importer and dealer.

FOLSOM, DAVID St. Louis, Missouri, 1865-1869d. Son of Henry Folsom.

FOLSOM, E.A. New Haven, Connecticut, 1880d-1885d. As E.A. Folsom & Co., 1885.

FOLSOM, H. & D. ARMS CO. New York, New York, 1877-1934(?). Other offices in St. Louis and New Orleans. Percussion rifles and breechloading shotguns under many names. Sons of Henry Folsom. Owned Crescent Fire Arms Co. and were wholesalers and importers of rifles and shotguns. (Hinman)

FOLSOM, HENRY (?-1887), St. Louis, Missouri, 1849-1879d, Memphis, Tennessee, 1862-1866, New Orleans, Louisiana, 1864-1899. As Dimick & Folsom, 1849-1853, and Henry Folsom & Co. to 1887. Firm taken over by his sons who operated as H. & D. Folsom Arms Co.

FOLSOM, JOHN G. Winchendon, Massachusetts. Patent #370,329 September 20, 1887, air gun.

FOLSOM, N.D. New Haven, Connecticut, 1886d-1888d. Successor to E.A. Folsom & Co.

FOLTZ, GEORGE (1798-?), Salem, North Carolina, 1826-1850. (Bivins)

FONCANNON, M.B. Columbus, Ohio, 1848-1849, New Lexington, Ohio, 1849-1854. As Hood & Foncannon in 1848-1849. (Hutslar)

FONDERGRIFT unlocated. Flintlock Kentucky.

FONDERSMITH, GEORGE (1814-?), Licking Co., Ohio, 1850c. (Hutslar)

FONDERSMITH, GEORGE Champaign, Illinois, 1884d-1890d.

FONDERSMITH, GEORGE Strasburg, Pennsylvania, 1803-1825. Son of John Fondersmith. (Kauffman)

FONDERSMITH, ISAAC (1835-?), Burgettstown, Pennsylvania, 1860-1870. (Whisker II)

FONDERSMITH, J. (1809-?), Mason, Ohio, 1839-1853. (Hutslar)

FONDERSMITH, JACOB Adams Co., Pennsylvania, 1819-1821t, East Liberty, Pennsylvania, 1833-1843, Lawrenceville, Pennsylvania, 1847. (Bowers) (Whisker II)

FONDERSMITH, JOHN (1749-1805), Strasburg, Pennsylvania, 1776-1805. Model 1798 contract muskets for Pennsylvania, Kentucky rifles and pistols. (Kindig-Gluckman)

FONDERSMITH, LOUIS Strasburg, Pennsylvania, 1803-1825. Son of John Fondersmith, percussion fullstock.

FONDERSMITH, SAMUEL G. (1819-?), Licking Co., Ohio, 1850c, Gratiot, Ohio, 1853d. (Hutslar)

FONDERSMITH, VALENTINE (1746-?), Lancaster Co., Pennsylvania, 1777t-1804t. Flintlock Kentucky. (Dyke)

FONDERSMITH, WILLIAM Washington Co., Pennsylvania, 1856-1859. (Kauffman)

FONG, AUGUST F. South Chicago, Illinois, 1884d-1888d.

FONSHILL, JOHN Baltimore, Maryland, 1815-1819. See John Fornshell.

FOOTE, JOSEPH Milwaukee, Wisconsin, 1895d.

FOOTE, JOSEPH Philadelphia, Pennsylvania, 1780-1785. Repaired U.S. arms. (Moller)

FOPAY, FREDERICK St. Louis, Missouri, 1860d.

FORBES, F.F. trade name of Crescent on shotguns. (AR 2- 69)

FORBES, GILBERT New York, New York, 1767-1776. Flintlock muskets, rifles, pistols. (Gluckman & Satterlee)

FORBES, HERBERT Danville, Kentucky. Patent #112,795 March 21, 1871, magazine gun.

FORBES, HORACE B. Ogden, Utah. Patent #467,089 January 12, 1892, revolving magazine gun.

FORBES, JOHN W. Worcester, Massachusetts, 1847-1851.

FORBES, JOHN Ripon, Wisconsin, 1857d.

FORBES, NATHAN Plymouth, New Hampshire, 1795-1805. Patent #none December 22, 1804, barrel boring.

FORBES, WILLIAM B. Morristown, New Jersey. Patents #466,778 January 12, 1892, machine gun, and #466,779 January 12, 1892, breechloading firearm.

FORBIS, HARBERT K. New York, New York. Patent #112,795 March 21, 1871, magazine gun.

FORD BROS. unlocated. Lock makers.

FORD see Burnham & Ford.

FORD, AMAN Washington Co., Ohio, 1833-1860. No fixed location, shop was on a boat. (Hutslar)

FORD, DAVID Abbeyville, Ohio, 1860d. (Hutslar)

FORD, GEORGE (1805-?), Peoria, Illinois, 1860c. (Johnson)

FORD, J. unlocated. Flintlock Kentucky.

FORD, JOHN (1780-1862), Harrisburg, Pennsylvania, 1810-1862. Percussion fullstock. Son of Peter Ford, see Burnham & Ford. (Bowers)

FORD, P.J. Torrington, Connecticut. Percussion target rifle.

FORD, PETER York Co., Pennsylvania, 1780. Primarily a silversmith. (Bowers)

FORD, R.E.L. unlocated. Percussion fullstock.

FORD, W.B. Atlanta, Georgia, 1883d.

FORDER, MATTHIAS San Antonio, Texas 1891d-1892d. As Forder & Nagel, 1891.

FORDING, JOHN J. Pittsburgh, Pennsylvania, 1860d.

FORDNEY, CASPAR (1807-?), Lancaster, Pennsylvania, 1828-1835, Mt. Vernon, Ohio, 1835-1850c. Percussion fullstock. (Hutslar)

FORDNEY, CHARLES Lancaster, Pennsylvania, 1871d-1875d.

FORDNEY, HENRY Lancaster, Pennsylvania, 1833t-1838t. (KRA IV-4)

FORDNEY, ISAAC Lancaster, Pennsylvania, 1840t.

FORDNEY, JACOB H. (1835-?), Mt. Vernon, Ohio, 1850. Son of Caspar Fordney. (Hutslar)

FORDNEY, JACOB (?-1819), Lancaster, Pennsylvania, ?-1819. Flintlock Kentucky. (Kindig)

FORDNEY, JACOB (1808-1878), Lancaster, Pennsylvania, 1830-1878. Indian contract rifles and Kentucky rifles. (Kauffman)

FORDNEY, JOHN J. Lancaster, Pennsylvania, 1875d-1894d.

FORDNEY, JOHN Lancaster, Pennsylvania, 1843d-1853d. Percussion fullstock.

FORDNEY, MELCHIOR (1789-1846), Lancaster, Pennsylvania, 1809-1846. Flintlock Kentucky rifles. (Kauffman)

FORDNEY, PHILIP Lancaster, Pennsylvania, 1836t. (Dyke)

FOREHAND & WADSWORTH Worcester, Massachusetts, 1871-1890. Successors to Ethan Allen. Sullivan Forehand and Henry C. Wadsworth were sons-in-law of Allen.

FOREHAND ARMS CO. Worcester, Massachusetts, 1890-1903. Successor to Forehand & Wadsworth.

FOREHAND, SULLIVAN (1831-1898), Worcester, Massachusetts. Son-in-law and successor (with his brother-in-law Henry Wadsworth) to Ethan Allen. Patents #116,422 June 27, 1871, #143,566 October 14,1873, #162,162 April 20, 1875, and #193,367 July 24, 1877, all revolvers with Henry Wadsworth. Patents #121,606 December 5, 1871, cartridge, #178,133 May 30, 1876, revolver, #245,620 August 16, 1881, lock, and #355,761 January 11, 1887, revolver. (Mouilleseaux)

FOREMAN, S. & WILLIAM C. Bidwell's Bar, California. Patent #414,306 November 5, 1889, animal gun.

FORESTER, CHESTER East Dubuque, Iowa, 1884d-1888d.

FORESTER, JOHN Greene Co., Pennsylvania, 1824-1838. (Kauffman)

FORKEL, AUGUST Waterloo, Illinois, 1882d, Murphysboro, Illinois, 1888d.

FORKER, ISRAEL Ravenna, Ohio, 1852-1866.

FORKER, JOHN Mercer, Pennsylvania, 1816-1861d. Brother of Samuel Forker, percussion fullstock. (GR 9-57)

FORKER, JOHN Philadelphia, Pennsylvania, 1875. (Kauffman)

FORKER, JOSEPH (1829-?), Mercer, Pennsylvania, 1848-1857. Son of John Forker. (Kauffman)

FORKER, SAMUEL (1798-1860), Meadville, Pennsylvania, 1823-1890d. Patent #none February 13, 1830, percussion lock. Brother of John Forker. Repeating rifle. (GR 9-57)

FORKER, WILLIAM H. (1828-1899), Meadville, Pennsylvania, 1859-1880. Percussion 1/2 stock and salon guns. Son of Samuel Forker. (GR 9-57)

FORMAN, JOHN Philadelphia, Pennsylvania, 1860d-1861d.

FORNSHELL, JOHN Baltimore, Maryland, 1814d-1853d. (Hartzler)

FORNSHIL, JOHN Alexandria, Virginia, 187 ld-1873d.

FORREST, CASPAR Lancaster, Pennsylvania, 1857d-1875d.

FORREST, WILLIAM Marlborough, Tennessee, 1860d.

FORRESTER, HARRISON (1840-?), Tyler Co., West Virginia, 1860c. Son of John Forrester. (Whisker IV)

FORRESTER, JACOB (1835-?), Tyler Co., West Virginia, 1860c. Son of John Forrester. (Whisker IV)

FORRESTER, JAMES (1839-?), Tyler Co., West Virginia, 1860c, Booker's Mills, West Virginia, 1882d. Son of John Forrester. (Whisker IV)

FORRESTER, JOHN (1802-?), Tyler Co., West Virginia, 1850c. (MB 10-63)

FORRESTER, JOHN (1828-?), Tyler Co., West Virginia, 1850c. (MB 10-63)

FORRESTER, WILLIAM (1845-?), Tyler Co., West Virginia, 1860c. Son of John Forrester. (Whisker IV)

FORSTNER, ADOLPHUS H. Salem, Oregon. Patent #649,829 May 15, 1900. Breechloading firearm.

FORSTNER, BENJAMIN Albany, Oregon, 1867d, Salem, Oregon, 1878d-1886d.

FORSYTH, JOSEPH Somerset Co., Pennsylvania, 1802-1803.

FORT, FREDERICK Ashford, Wisconsin, 1857d.

FORT, GEORGE Virginia, 1636. (Gill)

FORT, LUKE Hooks, Texas, 1896d.

FORTE, M. North Adams, Michigan, 1879d.

FORTENBURY, BENJAMIN (1802-?), Bartholomew Co., Indiana, 1850c. (Lindert)

FORTIER, FRANCIS New Orleans, Louisiana, 1720.

FORTIER, PETER Quincy, Illinois, 1888d-1905d.

FORTNEY, PETER Chilicothe, Ohio, 1804. (Hutslar)

FORTSON, M.F. Stansell, Georgia, 1883d.

FORTUNE, THOMAS L. Mt. Pleasant, Kansas, 1890-1910. (Gluckman & Satterlee)

FOSDICK, CHARLES LaPorte, Indiana, 1882-1885. (Lindert)

FOSDICK, JAMES Vinton, Iowa, 1865d.

FOSDICK, JOHN Elkhorn Grove, Illinois, 1854d-1860d.

FOSDICK, SAMUEL J. LaPorte, Indiana, 1850-1890d. Percussion 1/2 stock. (Lindert)

FOSS BROS. & CO. Chicago, Illinois, 1878-1882d. Successors to Frederick J. Abbey & Co. (Chicago, Illinois, 1858-1878d). Rudolph and William H. Foss.

FOSS, RUDOLPH Chicago, Illinois, 1868d-1880d. As Foss Bros. & Co., 1878-1880. Sometimes listed as Faas.

FOSS, WILLIAM H. Chicago, Illinois. Miller type revolving rifle.

FOSTER & MARTIN Bowling Green, Kentucky, 1879d.

FOSTER & SCHAFFLER South Bend, Indiana, 1900. (Lindert)

FOSTER CORNELIUS C. (1807-?), West Franklin, Indiana, 1850c-1858d.

FOSTER, A.W. unlocated. Percussion target rifle.

FOSTER, ALEXANDER Mansfield, Massachusetts, 1824. Son of and worked for George Foster. (MB 4-48)

FOSTER, ANDREW Machias, Maine, 1856d-1879. Percussion 1/2 stock.

FOSTER, CHARLES E. Washington, D.C. Patent #565,678 August 11, 1896, revolver.

FOSTER, DANIEL Rowan Co., North Carolina, 1816. (Bivins)

FOSTER, F. unlocated. Percussion 1/2 stock.

FOSTER, FRANK A. Norwich, Connecticut. Patents #361,819 April 26, 1887, revolver, #545,355 August 27, 1895, safety, and #645,705 March 20, 1900, ejector.

FOSTER, GEORGE F. Mohawk, New York. Patents #49,994 September 19, 1865, ejector, and #56,399 July 17, 1866, breechloading firearm, both with George P. Foster, his father.

FOSTER, GEORGE J. Alameda, California. Patent #343,706 April 6, 1886, cartridge loading machine.

FOSTER, GEORGE PRATT (1810-1874), Taunton, Massachusetts, 1849-1855, Providence, Rhode Island, 1855-1861, Bristol, Rhode Island, 1861-1867. Patents #27,791 April 10, 1860, cartridge, #27,874 April 10, 1860, breechloading firearm, #49,994 September 19, 1865, breechloading firearm, and #56,399 July 17, 1866, breechloading firearm. Patent #49,994 and #56,399 with G. F. Foster. Made percussion rifles and many patent rifles, including Burnside, Klein, and Howard. Son of George Foster, brother of Alexander Foster; worked for his father 1824-1830. (MB 4-48)

FOSTER, GEORGE Attleboro, Massachusetts, 1815-1824, Mansfield, Massachusetts, 1824-1840. Flintlock guns. (MB 4-48)

FOSTER, HENRY Lubec, Maine, 1871-1875. (Demerrit)

FOSTER, HOPESTILL Dorchester, Massachusetts, 1694. (Dean*)

FOSTER, J.H., & CO. Chicago, Illinois, 1855-1879. Percussion target rifle. James H. Foster and J.D Hargill.

FOSTER, J.T. Buena Vista, Oregon, 1873d, Scio, Oregon, 1881d.

FOSTER, JACOB East Machias, Maine, 1871-1874d.

FOSTER, JAMES H. Chicago, Illinois, 1855-1879. Patent #114,081 April 25, 1871, breechloading firearm with Frederick J. Abbey. Shotguns under this patent made by Frederick J. Abbey & Co. Percussion target rifles with J.D. Hargill. As partner in F.J. Abbey & Co. with Frederick J. Abbey. As J.H. Foster & Co. with J.D. Hargill, 1855-1879.

FOSTER, JAMES (1806-?), Newbern, Indiana, 1850c-1860d.

FOSTER, JAMES (1837-?), McElroy, West Virginia, 1880c.

FOSTER, JOHN T. Jersey City, New Jersey. Patent #16,860 March 17, 1857, loading rod with Jacob J. Banta.

FOSTER, JOHN York Co., Pennsylvania. Flintlock Kentucky and Committee of Safety muskets. (Dean)

FOSTER, JOSEPH Philadelphia, Pennsylvania, 1780-1785. Repairs U.S. arms. (Boehret)

FOSTER, R.B. Clay Center, Kansas, 1888d.

FOSTER, T.M. Philadelphia, Pennsylvania, 1856d. Percussion 1/2 stock.

FOSTER, THOMAS Fayette Co., Pennsylvania, 1812-1825. (Kauffman)

FOSTER, THOMAS Philadelphia, Pennsylvania, 1841d-1865d.

FOSTER, W.E. Norfolk, Virginia, 1855. (Albaugh 1)

FOSTER, WHITE Columbia, Ohio, 1868d. (Hutslar)

FOSTER, WILLIAM (1809-?), North Liberty, Pennsylvania, 1850c-1861d. Percussion fullstock.

FOTE, J. unlocated. Flintlock Kentucky rifle.

FOTTRELL, PATRICK French Creek, Pennsylvania, 1776-1778. Worked for Peter DeHaven at State gun factory. (Gluckman & Satterlee)

FOUGHT, GEORGE M. Parkersburg, West Virginia, 1882d-1896d. Dealer. (Whisker IV)

FOULK, WILLIAM (1737-1812), Lancaster, Pennsylvania, 1758-1769, Harrisburg, Pennsylvania, 1769-1812. Flintlock Kentucky rifle. Same as William Foulks? (Dyke)

FOULKE Philadelphia, Pennsylvania. Flintlock locks only.

FOULKE, ADAM Easton, Allentown, and Philadelphia, Pennsylvania, 1770-1794. Committee of Safety muskets with John Young.

FOULKROD, JOSEPH Philadelphia, Pennsylvania. Patent #555,602 March 3, 1896, adjustable stock.

FOULKS, WILLIAM Lancaster, Pennsylvania, 1775. Flintlock Kentucky rifles. (Dillin)

FOUQUET, E. New Orleans, Louisiana, 1860d-1861d.

FOURCHER, VICTOR Augusta, Georgia, 1879d-1883d.

FOUSNIQUER, CHARLES Providence, Rhode Island, 1880d-1886d. (Achtermier)

FOWLER, B., JR. Hartford, Connecticut, 1835-1838. Underhammer guns, made in Connecticut State prison.

FOWLER, C.E. Butte, Montana, 1886d.

FOWLER, D. Shrewsbury, Massachusetts, 1835. (Lindsay)

FOWLER, HENRY (1802-?), Raleigh, North Carolina. Apprenticed 1816. (Bivins)

FOWLER, JOHN S. (1808-?), Belmont Co., Ohio, 1850c. Percussion 1/2 stock. (Hutslar)

FOWLER, JOHN (1822-?), New Frankfort, Indiana, 1850. (Lindert)

FOWLER, JOHN Lancaster, Pennsylvania, 1807-1810. Patent #none January 4, 1810, gun plating.

FOWLER, M.L. Ludington, Michigan, 1883d-1887d.

FOWLER, ROBERT (1746-1794), Hampshire Co., Virginia, 1781-?, Point of Fork, Virginia, 1786-1790, Fluvanna Co., Virginia, 1791-1794. (Gill)

FOWLER, S.J. Wheeling, West Virginia, 1839d. (Whisker IV)

FOWLER, STACY Philadelphia, Pennsylvania, 1829d-1833d.

FOWLER, WILLIAM M. New York, New York, 1874d-1884d.

FOX, ALLEN H. (1801-?), San Francisco, California, 1852-1861. (Shelton)

FOX, ANSLEY H. Baltimore, Maryland. Patents #563,153 June 30, 1896, breechloading gun, Philadelphia, Pennsylvania, #714,688 December 2, 1902, breechloading gun, #796,119 August 1. 1905, breechloading gun, #801,862 October 17, 1905, breechloading gun, #810,046 January 16, 1906, breechloading gun, and #921,220 May 11, 1908, breechloading gun with G.A. Home. Fox formed the Philadelphia Gun Company in 1900 and changed its name to A.H. Fox Gun Co. in 1904. In 1933, the company was bought by Savage Repeating Arms Co., which was, in turn, absorbed by Stevens.

FOX, B. & CO. Lancaster, Pennsylvania. Percussion fullstock, also locks.

FOX, BENJAMIN Lancaster, Pennsylvania, 1843t. (KRA IV-4)

FOX, CHARLES J. Council Bluffs, Iowa, 1861d.

FOX, D. Carrothers, Ohio, 1881d. (Hutslar)

FOX, G. New Lisbon, Ohio. (MB 3-53)

FOX, GEORGE HENRY (1819-1901), Boston, Massachusetts, 1853-1901. Patents #98,579 January 4, 1870, breechloading firearm, #196,748 November 5, 1877, breechloading firearm, #196,749 November 5, 1877, breechloading firearm with Henry F. Wheeler, #198,973 January 8, 1878, breechloading firearm, #255,274, March 21, 1882, lock, #278,423 May 29, 1883, forend, #278,424 May 29, 1883, extractor, #342,507 May 25, 1886, revolver, #422,930 March 11, 1890, revolver, with Henry F. Wheeler. As G.H. Fox & Co., 1853-1865, American Tool & Machine Co., 1865-1867, American Nut & Arms Co., 1867-1870, and American Arms Co., 1870-1901. All patents produced by American Arms Co. of Boston, which he founded. (AR 4-70)

FOX, GEORGE W. Barre, Vermont, 1890-1891. (Horn)

FOX, GEORGE Lawrenceville, Pennsylvania, 1847d. (Kauffman)

FOX, GEORGE Trinity Springs, Indiana, 1880-1886. Converted muskets. (Lindert)

FOX, H.A. New York, New York, 1842-1845.

FOX, HARVEY Raleigh Co., West Virginia, 1880-1900. (Whisker IV)

FOX, HORACE (1815-1882), Tionesta, Pennsylvania, 1850c, Corry, Pennsylvania, Hydetown, Pennsylvania, Jamestown, New York, Carroll, New York, 1860c, Frewsburg, New York, 1870-1882d. Percussion rifles and pistols, specializing in multi-barrels. (GR 11-60)

FOX, IRVING W. Rochester, Minnesota, 1877-1881.

FOX, JOHN NICHOLAS New Orleans, Louisiana, 1834d.

FOX, JOHN (1835-?), Logan, Ohio, 1850c. Apprentice with William Stalter. (Hutslar)

FOX, JOHN Reading, Pennsylvania, 1775-1790. Repairs for Committee of Safety.

FOX, JOHN Zeeland, Michigan, 1891d-1895d.

FOX, PHILIP Lancaster, Pennsylvania, 1843t. (Dyke)

FOX, REUBEN (1794-?). Corry, Pennsylvania, 1818-1835, Canton, Ohio, 1840c-1860c. Flintlock and percussion rifles. (Hutslar)

FOX, REUBEN Bolivar, Ohio, 1830c-1859d. Percussion 1/2 stock. (Hutslar)

FOX, WESLEY B. Willimantic, Connecticut, 1871d.

FOY, JAMES (1813-?), Baltimore, Maryland, 1849-1875. As James Foy & Son, 1870-1875. (Hartzler)

FRAHNER & SCHAF Paris, Texas, 1890d.

FRAILEY, ANDREW J. Lancaster, Pennsylvania, 1850c-1857d.

FRAILEY, HENRY Pennsylvania, 1775-1777. Committee of Safety muskets. (Gluckman)

FRAIZER, A. unlocated. Flintlock, Kentucky.

FRALEY, H.J. Lovelton, Pennsylvania, 1882d-1890d.

FRALEY, HENRY Philadelphia, Pennsylvania, 1816d. See Henry Frailey.

FRALEY, SAMUEL Salisbury, North Carolina, 1823. (Bivins)

FRALICK A. Plymouth, Michigan, 1863d.

FRANCE, DAVID (1827-?) Clinton, Ohio, 1850c. (Hutslar)

FRANCE, JOSEPH A. Cobbleskill, New York, 1857-1862. Patent #33,244 September 10, 1861, breechloading cannon. Percussion pistol.

FRANCE, JOSEPH Shreve, Ohio, 1853d. (Hutslar)

FRANCES, S.E. (1795-?), Powhatten Point, Ohio, 1850-1860. (Hutslar)

FRANCIS & TILLINGHAM Philadelphia, Pennsylvania, 1775. Committee of Safety. (Dean)

FRANCIS, ANDREW J. (1829-1863), Zanesville, Ohio, 1850c. (Hutslar)

FRANCIS, SEBASTIAN E. (1802-?), Zanesville, Ohio, 1850c. (Hutslar)

FRANCISCO, JOHN New Providence, Tennessee, 1860d.

FRANCK Lancaster, Pennsylvania, 1775. Flintlock Kentucky rifle. (Dillin)

FRANCK, A. unlocated. Percussion over/under rifle.

FRANCKE, FREDERICK Long Prairie, Minnesota, 1888d.

FRANK, ABRAM Newberry, Pennsylvania, 1861d.

FRANK, JOHN Chicago, Illinois, 1877d.

FRANK, MARTIN Dubuque, Iowa, 1870d-1888d.

FRANK, WILLIAM (1819-?), Buckhorn, Illinois, 1853-1860, Walker's Neck, Illinois, 1860d, Mount Sterling, Illinois, 1861. Patent #33,245 September 10, 1861, lock.

FRANKE, BERNARD New York, New York. Patent #35,998 July 29, 1862, revolver.

FRANKE, CHARLES H. Chicago, Illinois, 1873d.

FRANKLIN, C.W. trade name of H & D Folsom on imported shotguns. (AR 2-69)

FRANKLIN, EDWIN Wilson Co., North Carolina, 1870. (Bivins)

FRANKLIN, WILLIAM B. Hartford, Connecticut. Patents #307,285 October 28, 1884, magazine gun, #314,823 March 31, 1885, magazine gun, #326,491 September 15, 1885, magazine gun, #335,517 February 2, 1886, magazine gun, and #372,531 November 1, 1887, magazine gun. Patents #335,517 and #372,531 with Carl J. Ehbetts. Franklin was president of Colt's Patent Fire Arms Mfg. Co. and guns under his patents were produced by Colt.

FRANKS & WATT New Prospect, Ohio, 1853d. (Hutslar)

FRANKS, BENJAMIN R. Scottsborough, Alabama. Patent #239,238 March 22, 1881, extractor.

FRANSE, J.A. Lancaster, Pennsylvania, 1850t. (Dyke)

FRANTORNO, CHRISTOPHER (1827-?), Holmes Co., Ohio, 1850c. (Hutslar)

FRANZ, G.C. Grafton, Nebraska, 1886d.

FRASER, THOMAS (1790-?), Montgomery Co., North Carolina, 1850c. (Bivins)

FRAVEL, JOHN (1824-?), Corydon, Indiana. Flintlock fullstock rifle. (Lindert)

FRAZER, G. Jackson, Mississippi, 1885d.

FRAZER, R.J. Lawrence, Kansas, 1870d.

FRAZER, THOMAS Dresden, Ohio, 1859-1864. Percussion 1/2 stock. (Hutslar)

FRAZER, TROY Trenton, Tennessee, 1860d.

FRAZIER & COLBY St. Peter, Minnesota, 1864-1867d. Aaron Frazier and C.D. Colby.

FRAZIER, AARON St. Peter, Minnesota, 1864-1880. As Frazier & Colby, 1864-1865.

FRAZIER, AARON Troupsburgh, New York, 1891d.

FRAZIER, ALBERT (1830-?), Randolph Co., North Carolina, 1850c. Son of Alexander Frazier. (Bivins)

FRAZIER, ALEXANDER (1797-?), Randolph Co., North Carolina, 1850c. Flintlock Kentucky rifle. (Bivins)

FRAZIER, FRANCIS Dunnings, Pennsylvania, 1861d.

FRAZIER, HENRY Knox Co., Ohio, 1838-1846. (MB 4-49)

FRAZIER, JOHN (?-1773), Lancaster, Pennsylvania, 1746, Venango Co., Pennsylvania, 1750, Turtle Creek, Pennsylvania, 1753-1756, Bedford, Pennsylvania, 1773. Flintlock Kentucky rifles. (Hetrick)

FRAZIER, JOSEPH W. New York, New York, 1860-1895. Patent #290,636 December 18, 1883, magazine gun. Frazier was a retailer who specialized in the development and sales of new inventions.

FRAZIER, PERRY (1832-?), Randolph, North Carolina, 1850c, Dubois, Nebraska. Patent #753,384 March 1, 1904, breechloading firearm. Son of Alexander Frazier. (Bivins)

FRED BIFFAR & CO. Chicago, Illinois. Dealers only.

FREDERICK, A. Dalles City, Oregon, 1866d-1867d.

FREDERICK, HENRY Washington D.C., 1872d.

FREDERICK, JOHN Goughlersville, Pennsylvania, 1859d-1879d.

FREDERICK, SAMUEL Lewisburg, Pennsylvania. Flintlock Kentucky rifles. (Gabel)

FREDERICK, WILLIAM Locke, Michigan, 1863d, Pontiac, Michigan, 1867d.

FREDERICKS, FRED Kansas City, Missouri, 1869d-1884d.

FREDERICKSBURG GUN FACTORY Fredericksburg, Virginia, 1775-1781. Muskets. (Gluckman & Satterlee)

FREED, DAVID Philadelphia, Pennsylvania, 1846d.

FREELAND, JESSE E. (1834-1915), Barrackville, West Virginia, 1900d. (Whisker IV)

FREEMAN, A.A. San Luis Rey, California, 1880-1881d. (Shelton)

FREEMAN, AUSTIN TYLER (1838-?), Binghamton, New York. Patents #37,091 December 9, 1862, revolver, #122,717 January 16, 1872, breechloading firearm, #133,770 December 10, 1872, breechloading firearm, and #148,555 February 17, 1874, magazine gun. Freeman revolvers made by Hoard's Armory. (AG 12-79)

FREEMAN, B.A. Charlotte, North Carolina, 1884d.

FREEMAN, J. Coulter's Store, Missouri, 1860d.

FREEMAN, JAMES S. Salem, Illinois, 1864d, Saco, Maine, 1870d-1877d.

FREEMAN, ROBERTSON (1776-1831), Rutherford Co., North Carolina, 1831. (Bivins)

FREEMAN, SAMUEL Ashland, Ohio, 1872-1886. (Hutslar)

FREEMAN, THOMAS Harwich, Massachusetts, 1868-1892d. Percussion 1/2 stock.

FREEMAN, W.C. Worcester, Massachusetts, 1861-1865. Made Joslyn revolvers. (Sellers-1)

FREEMONT ARMS CO. trade name on shotgun.

FREESTONE, ROBERT Smyrna, Delaware 1859d.

FREETH, T.B. Little Falls, Minnesota, 1898d.

FREITAG, A.J. Camden, South Carolina, 1886d.

FREITAS, JOHN Springfield, Illinois, 1860d.

FREIVERLY, JOSEPH Bushkill, Pennsylvania, 1835t. (KRA II-3)

FRENCH, C.M. Waterloo, New York. Patent #35,600 June 17, 1862, gun plow with W.H. Fancher.

FRENCH, FRANK Littleton, New Hampshire, 1874d-1875d.

FRENCH, M.H. Marshall, Michigan, 1860d.

FRENCH, N. Canton, Massachusetts. NewEngland flintlock musket dated 1835.

FRENCH, SIDNEY Cambridge, Vermont, 1900. (Horn)

FRENCH, THOMAS (1778-1862), Canton, Massachusetts, 1808-1820. Model 1808 contract muskets with Adam Kinsley and P.E. Blake. (Gluckman)

FRENCH, WILLIAM Dumerstown, Vermont. Early flintlock New England rifle.

FRENZEL, E.R. Ledbetter, Texas, 1884d-1896d.

FRESH, JOSEPH Wilmore, Pennsylvania, 1861-1867, Summerhill, Pennsylvania, 1845-1861d. Flintlock and percussion fullstock. (Kauffman)

FRESHETTE, L. Lincoln, Nebraska, 1893d.

FRESHOUR, HENRY Washington Co., Arkansas, 1835-1855. (Elias)

FREUND, FRANK W. (1837-1910), Nebraska City, Nebraska, 1865-1867, Julesburg, Colorado, 1867, Cheyenne, Wyoming, 1867-1870 and 1875-1885, Denver, Colorado, 1870-1875, Jersey City, New Jersey, 1886-1910. Patents #153,432 July 28, 1874, breechloading firearm, #160,762 March 16, 1875, breechloading firearm, #160,763 March 16, 1875, cartridge, #160,819 March 16, 1875, sight, #162,224 April 20, 1875, breechloading firearm, #162,373 April 20, 1875, attached pistol grip, #162,374 April 20, 1875, lever guard, #180,567 August 1, 1876, breechloading firearm, #183,389 October 17, 1876, revolver, #184,202 November 7, 1876, breechloading firearm, #184,203 November 7, 1876, breechloading firearm, #184,854 November 28, 1876, cartridge, #185,911 January 2, 1877, breechloading firearm, #189,721 April 17, 1877, front sight, #211,728 January 28, 1879, breechloading firearm, #216,084 June 3, 1879, breechloading firearm, #229,245 June 29, 1880, sight with George Freund, #268,090 November 28, 1882, sight, and #409,051 April 25, 1893, sight. Operated as Freund & Bro., 1865-1880. Made percussion and cartridge rifles of his own patterns, but is best known for his alterations of Sharps and Remington rifles. (Ballentine)

FREUND, GEORGE (1842-1911), Nebraska City, Nebraska, 1867, Julesburg, Colorado 1867, Denver, Colorado, 1871-1875, Cheyenne, Wyoming, 1875-1880, Durango, Colorado, 1881-1911. Patents #229,245 June 29, 1880, sight with Frank Freund, #297,375 April 22, 1884, knife, and #313,414 March 3, 1885, knife. As Freund & Bro., 1867-1880. (Ballentine)

FREY see Fry.

FREY, MARTIN (1769-?), York, Pennsylvania, 1799-1804. (Kauffman)

FRIAL, JOHN unlocated. Flintlock Kentucky.

FRIBELY, CHRISTIAN Northampton Co., Pennsylvania, 1850c. (Gabel)

FRICHLE, WILLIAM (1832-?), Paxton, Illinois, 1852-1860. (Johnson)

FRICK, HENRY (?-1890), St. Louis, Missouri, 1879d-1890d. His wife and minor son carried on the business for two years after his death.

FRICK, JOHN Laramie, Wyoming. Patents #426,004 April 22, 1890, lock, #426,373 April 22, 1890, cane gun, and #428,597 May 27, 1890, breechloading firearm.

FRICKER, JOHN Berks Co., Pennsylvania. Flintlock Kentucky rifles. (Dean)

FRICKEY, SAMUEL New York, New York, 1801.

FRIDDLEY, CHARLES (1817-?), Allegheny Co., Virginia, 1850c. (MB 10-63)

FRIE, FREDERICK Warsaw, Illinois, 1878d, Bellevue, Iowa, 1880d-1823d. Son of W.H. Frie, operated as Frie & Sons, 1892d-1923.

FRIE, WILLIAM H. Bellvue, Iowa, 1870-1878d.

FRIEBELE, CHRISTIAN Northampton Co., Pennsylvania, 1835t. See Fribley. (KRA II-3)

FRIEDE, MEYER St. Louis, Missouri, 1851d-1860d.

FRIEDERICK, HENRY Washington, D.C., 1872d. (Hartzler)

FRIEDRICH, JOSEPH Galveston, Texas. Agent for Arden & Smith 1/2 stock.

FRIEND, GABRIEL Frederick, Maryland, 1759. (Hartzler)

FRIEND, ISRALE A. Braxton Co., West Virginia, 1890-1910. Signed cowbells "I.A.F.". (Whisker IV)

FRIEND, JOSIAH Roanoke, Virginia, 1888d.

FRIEND, THOMAS W. Rochester, New York, 1868d. (Eich)

FRIER, I.C. Abilene, Texas, 1892d, Cisco, Texas, 1896d.

FRIES, WILLIAM Lancaster Co., Pennsylvania, 1850t. (Dyke)

FRIESENER, PAUL Texarkana, Texas, 1884d-1890d.

FRINK, NATHAN Goshen, Connecticut. Committee of Safety muskets with Elisha Child and Benjamin Cargill.

FRISBEE, J. Cork, Ohio, 1848-1854. (Dean)

FRISBIE & MILES Newton, Iowa, 1889d.

FRISBIE, ALONZO Manistee, Michigan, 1883d.

FRISBIE, JOSEPH B. Allegheny, Pennsylvania. Patent #16,575 February 10, 1857, revolver with Francis S. Brettell. (Sellers-1)

FRISBIE, L. Fowler, Michigan, 1873d-1875d. Same as L. Frisbie from Harpersfield, Ohio?

FRISBIE, L. Harpersfield, Ohio, 1860-1865. (Hutslar)

FRISBIE, THEODORE Cork, Ohio, 1853d. (Hutslar)

FRISBY, WILLIAM (?-1708), Philadelphia, Pennsylvania.

FRISH, A.D. unlocated. Percussion fullstock.

FRISON, C.W. (1823-?), Summum, Illinois, 1860c. (Johnson)

FRITTS, JOHN Soddy, Tennessee. (ASAC 21)

FRITZ, GEORGE Rowan Co., North Carolina, 1820c. (Bivins)

FROCK, J. unlocated. Flintlock Kentucky rifle.

FROEHLICH, LOUIS St. Louis, Missouri, 1880d-1900d. Dealer.

FROGDIN, EMSIAH T. (1837-?), Jamestown, North Carolina. Apprenticed to William Lamb. (Bivins)

FROGGATT, WILLIAM Philadelphia, Pennsylvania, 1847d.

FROHER, LUDWIG see Ludwig Fohrer.

FRONTFIELD, JOHN (1770-1853), Montgomery Co., Pennsylvania, 1800c, Chester Co., Pennsylvania, 1853. (Kauffman)

FRONTIER suicide special by Norwich Falls Pistol Co.

FROST, EDWARD J. New York, New York. Patent #65,742 June 11, 1867, revolver.

FROST, ELMER F. Waterloo, Iowa, 1880d, Alcester, South Dakota, 1888d-1898d.

FROST, GIDEON Boston, Massachusetts, 1775-1777. Committee of Safety musket. (Gluckman & Satterlee)

FROST, J.W. Lawrence, Massachusetts, 1869d-1891d. As J.W. Frost & Co., 1875-1891.

FROST, JOSEPH W. New York, New York. Patent #319,898 June 9, 1885, electric gun.

FROTHINGHAM, JOPSEPH (?-1801), Newbury Port, Massachussetts.

FRUCHEY, ISAAC Columbus Grove, Ohio, 1872d. (Hutslar)

FRY & EDGAR Sidney, Ohio, 1878d. Robert L. Fry. (Hutslar)

FRY, DANIEL (1823-?), Porter Co., Indiana, 1850c. (Lindert)

FRY, EDWARD (1869-1955), Ligonier, Pennsylvania, 1890-1930d. Son of Joseph Fry.

FRY, FRANCIS Doniphan Co., Kansas, 1855. (Gluckman & Satterlee)

FRY, GEORGE W. Mt. Pisgah, Iowa, 1887d-1889d.

FRY, GEORGE Bedford Co., Pennsylvania, 1840. (Kauffman)

FRY, GUY Mercerville, Ohio, 1888d. (Hutslar)

FRY, H.L. Ringgold, Georgia, 1879d.

FRY, ISAAC (1791-?), Greene Co., Indiana, 1850. (Lindert)

FRY, JOHN (1820-1889), Ligonier, Pennsylvania, 1843-1852.

FRY, JOHN Latrobe, Pennsylvania. Patent #84,912, December 15, 1868, choke.

FRY, JOHN Ligonier, Indiana, 1850. Percussion fullstock.

FRY, JOSEPH (1825-1891), Ligonier, Pennsylvania, 1861d-1891d. Brother of John Fry.

FRY, MARTIN Carlisle, Pennsylvania, 1821t. (Bowers)

FRY, MARTIN, III (1769-?), York, Pennsylvania, 1799-1809. Model 1808 contract pistols. See Martin Frey. (ASAC 3)

FRY, MARTIN, JR. (1739-1780), York, Pennsylvania, 1760-1780. Flintlock Kentucky. See Martin Frey. (Kindig)

FRY, ROBERT L. Sidney, Ohio, 1862-1878. As Fry & Edgar in 1878, percussion 1/2 stock. (Hutslar)

FRYBERGER, JOHN Goshen, Ohio, 1868. (Hutslar)

FRYMAN, WILLIAM C. Venus, Kentucky, 1865d-1884d.

FRYMER, JOHN Lancaster Co., Pennsylvania, 1850t. (Dyke)

FRYMIER, S. unlocated. Flintlock Kentucky rifle.

FUCH, GEORGE Huntington Co., Pennsylvania, 1850. (Kauffman)

FUCHS, A.M. Evansville, Indiana, 1882-1885. (Gardner)

FUGITT, THOMAS M. (1813-?), Washington, D.C., 1837-1850c. (Hartzler)

FUGNA, JOHN W. Willow, Iowa, 1865d.

FUHR, GEORGE N. Alliance, Ohio, 1875-1878d. (Hutslar)

FULLER, BENJAMIN F. St. Clair, Michigan, 1863d-1878d.

FULLER, E.F. St. Clair, Michigan, 1858-1867d. Probably same as Benjamin Fuller.

FULLER, GUSTAVE New York, New York, 1858d.

FULLER, J.S. Montville, Massachusetts, 1869d.

FULLER, W.S. Milbury, Massachusetts. Percussion 1/2 stock.

FULLER, WEBSTER Bowie, Texas, 1896d.

FULLER, WILLIAM Ipswich, Massachusetts, 1635. (Dean)

FULLER, WILLIAM Ontario, Wisconsin, 1879d.

FULLERTON, F.W. St. Paul, Minnesota, circa 1900. Single shot .22 pistol.

FULMER, JONATHAN Easton, Pennsylvania. (Whisker III)

FULTON ARMS CO. trade name of Davenport Fire Arms Co. on shotguns.

FULTON barrel marking used by Charles and Clayton Myers on their percussion 1/2 stock guns.

FULTON trade name of Hunter Arms Co. on shotguns. (AG 4-75)

FULTON, ROBERT (1765-?), Lancaster, Pennsylvania. The Inventor of the steamboat also invented an air gun and worked on Committee of Safety muskets in 1779.

FULTON, SIEBERT Perry Co., Pennsylvania. Percussion fullstock with John Watts. (Chandler 2)

FUNCK, C. Trenton, New Jersey, 1866-1869.

FUNDERSMITH see Fondersmith.

FUNDERSMITH, JACOB Allegheny, Pennsylvania, 1847d. (Kauffman)

FUNK, AMOS B. (1807-?), Harrison Co., Indiana, 1850c. (Lindert)

FUNK, D. unlocated. Flintlock Kentucky pistol. (KRA 76)

FUNK, JACOB Muskingum Co., Ohio, 1810. (Knittle)

FUNK, L.B. Warsaw, Indiana, 1882-1885. (Gardner)

FUNK, M. Cove, Pennsylvania. Percussion over/under rifle.

FUNKE, CHARLES Union, Missouri, 1879d.

FUNKE, LEOPOLD East St. Louis, Illinois, 1882d-1886d.

FUNKHAUSER, ABRAHAM (1816-1854), Beaver Co., Pennsylvania, 1834-1854. (Whisker II)

FUNKHAUSER, JONATHAN (1808-1875), Beaver Co., Pennsylvania, 1831-1875. (Whisker II)

FUQUA, T.G. Coffeyville, Kansas, 1878d, Independence, Oregon, 1891d.

FURBER, CHARLES B. Gardiner, Maine, 1894-1898. As Fish & Furber, 1898. (Demeritt)

FURBY, GEORGE W. Waterford, Vermont, 1855-1887d. (Horn)

FURLER, W.F.D. Loysville, Pennsylvania, 1886-1940. (Dean)

FURLONG, HENRY (1829-?), St. Louis, Missouri, 1850c. (Lewis)

FURLONG, MARTIN Carthage, Missouri, 1879d.

FURNES. CHARLES (1799-?), Sycamore, Illinois, 1860c. (Johnson)

FURNEY, DANIEL (1815-?), Tuscarawas Co., Ohio, 1850c-1860c. (Hutslar)

FURNEY, JOHN (?-1885), Bedford Co., Pennsylvania, 1829t-1885. Flintlock and percussion fullstock rifles signed "J.F.". (Whisker)

FURNEY, WILLIAM Mahoning Co., Ohio, 1815. (Gluckman & Satterlee)

FURNISH, A.D. Alexandria, Kentucky, 1856-1860.

FURNISH, J.T. Alexandria, Kentucky, 1870d-1884d. Son of A.D. Furnish.

FURST BROS. Gutenberg, Iowa, 1865d. Frederick and William Furst.

FUSS, FRANCIS J. Baltimore, Maryland. Patent #146,445 January 13, 1874, breechloading firearm with John Week.

FYRBERG, ANDREW Worcester, Massachusetts, 1886-1902, Hopkinton, Massachusetts, 1902-1910. Patents #339,301 April 6, 1886, revolver with Iver Johnson and R.T. Torkalson, #345,974 July 20, 1886, revolver with Iver Johnson and R.T. Torkalson, #350,681 October 12, 1886, breechloading firearm with Iver Johnson, #357,085 February 1, 1887, revolver with Iver Johnson, #362,631 May 10, 1887, revolver with Iver Johnson, #362,632 May 10, 1887, revolver with Iver Johnson, #379,225 March 13, 1888, revolver with Iver Johnson, #379,226 March 13, 1888, revolver with Iver Johnson, #379,227 March 13, 1888, revolver with Iver Johnson, #391,153 October 16, 1888, revolver with Iver Johnson, #391,154 October 16, 1888, revolver with Iver Johnson, #391,155 October 16, 1888, revolver with Iver Johnson, #391,156, October 16, 1888, revolver with Iver Johnson, #465,179 December 15, 1891, revolver with Iver Johnson, #469,387 February 23, 1892, revolver, #498,427 May 30, 1893, breechloading firearm, #505,918 October 3, 1893, revolver with Iver Johnson, #536,618 April 2, 1895, revolver with Iver Johnson, #566,393 August 25, 1896, revolver, #566,399 August 25, 1896, revolver, #574,409 January 5, 1897, breechloading firearm, #624,321 May 2, 1899, lock, #624,322 May 2, 1899, ejector, #642,688 February 6, 1900, lock, #669,520 March 12, 1901, breechloading firearm, #728,890 May 26, 1903, revolver, #735,490 August 4, 1903, revolver, #754,210 March 8, 1904, breechloading firearm, #841,240 January 15, 1907, ejector, #869,967 November 5, 1907, breechloading firearm, #887,784 May 19, 1908, revolver, #935,102 September 28, 1908, breechloading firearm, #945,320 January 4, 1910, revolver, and #975,685 November 15, 1910, revolver. After working for Iver Johnson, Fyrberg formed his own company in 1896 and made cheap revolvers and break open shotguns. Sears Roebuck & Co. bought a part interest in the company in 1902 and moved it to Hopkinton. Sears bought the entire company in 1905, and Fyrberg continued to design guns.

G SECTION

G. & W. see Goetz & Westphall.

G.A. unidentified. Flintlock Kentucky.

G.B. unidentified. Flintlock Kentucky.

G.C. see George Clouse.

G.C.B. unidentified. Flintlock Kentucky.

G.D. & CO. see Gaston, Dickson, & Co.

G.D. & CO. unidentified. Percussion 1/2 stock.

G.D. & W. see Gaston, Dickson & Wallingford.

G.E.H. see George E. Hilliard.

G.F. unidentified. Percussion fullstock.

G.G. unidentified. Flintlock Kentucky.

G.H. see G. Harrison, signed on stock.

G.H. unidentified. Percussion swivel, signed on barrel.

G.J. unidentified. Flintlock Kentucky.

G.L. unidentified. Percussion fullstock.

G.M. unidentified. Percussion fullstock.

G.M.H. unidentified. Flintlock Kentucky dated 1840.

G.P.W. unidentified. Percussion fullstock.

G.S. see George Schroyer.

G.S. see George Slaysman.

G.S. see George Smith.

G.S. see George Spangle.

G.T. unidentified. Percussion fullstock.

G.W.C. see G.W. Craft.

G.W.S. unlocated. Flintlock Kentucky.

G.W.T. & R. see Turner & Ross.

GABBOTT, JACOB Frederick Co., Virginia, 1758, Augusta Co., Virginia, 1777. With Humphrys, Perry and Simpson, 1777. (Gill)

GABEL, LUCIAN Richmond, Indiana. Patent #35,093 April 29, 1862, sword pistol. (Frost)

GABKNECHT unlocated. Flintlock Kentucky.

GABLE & ALLEN Williamsport, Pennsylvania, 1882d.

GABLE, HENRY Williamsport Pennsylvania, 1850-1890, Son of Henry Gable. As Gable & Allen, 1882.

GABLE, HENRY Williamsport, Pennsylvania, 1817-1880d. Flintlock Kentucky rifles and percussion fullstock rifles. Became Henry Gable & Son, around 1850. (Gluckman & Satterlee)

GABLE, THOMAS Lancaster, Pennsylvania, 1871d.

GABREL, LOUIS (1805-?), New Orleans, Louisiana, 1850c.

GABRIEL, DAVID (1819-?), Wayne Co., Ohio, 1850c. (Hutslar)

GAFFORD, JOHN Baltimore, Maryland, 1816d-1829d. Flintlock shotguns. (Hartzler)

GAGE, JAMES EDWIN (1850-1924), Rochester, New York, 1872-1873, Ontario, New York, 1875-1895, Concord, New Hampshire, 1895-1924. Patents #296,325 April 8, 1884, breechloading firearm, and #409,188 August 20, 1889, breechloading firearm. Percussion and cartridge rifles, and pistols for Billinghurst, 1872-1873. (Eich)

GAGE, WILLIAM M. Coldwater, Michigan, 1863d-1887d. Percussion rifles.

GAGER, GEORGE W. Sharon, Connecticut, 1876-1882d.

GAHM, GUSTAVUS Titusville, Pennsylvania, 1882d.

GAHN, V. (1810-?), Portsmouth, Ohio, 1840-1850c. V. Ghan per industrial census. (Hutslar)

GAISCHER, H.R. Gardi, Georgia, 1879d.

GALASPY, WILLIAM J. (1810-?), San Diego Co., California, 1871-1879. (Shelton)

GALBRAITH, JAMES Philadelphia, Pennsylvania, 1792. Sold 24 pistols to the Purveyor of Public Supplies.

GALBREATH, J.H. Grafton, Ohio, 1850-1870. (Hutslar)

GALBREATH, J.H. Lancaster, Pennsylvania, 1851-1858. Percussion rifle.

GALBREATH, JOHN Chester Co., Pennsylvania, before 1757. Apprenticed to Henry Willis.

GALBREATH, SAMUEL Newton, Pennsylvania, 1800c, Strasburg, Pennsylvania, 1804-1809, Pittsburgh, Pennsylvania, 1810-1813. (Kauffman)

GALE, WILLIAM Northumberland Co., Pennsylvania, 1826. (Kauffman)

GALENBECK, J. Lebanon, Pennsylvania. Flintlock Kentucky. (Dillin)

GALL, C. Madison, Indiana, 1860d-1863. As Gall & Augustin 1860.

GALL, G. unlocated. Early flintlock Kentucky rifles.

GALL, JOHN Lancaster, Pennsylvania, 1857d, Washington, Pennsylvania, 1859-1861d.

GALLAGER, MAHLON J. Savannah, Georgia. Patents #17,733 July 7, 1857, self priming lock, #24,730 July 12, 1859, breechloading firearm with W.H. Gladding, and #29,157 July 17, 1860, breechloading firearm. Gallager carbines made by Richardson & Overman in Philadelphia.

GALLAGHER, R.H. Washington, D.C., 1859-1862d.

GALLATIN, ALBERT Fayette Co., Pennsylvania, 1799-1803, Clarksburg, West Virginia, 1804-1808. Model 1798 contract muskets for Pennsylvania with Melchior Baker. (Gluckman)

GALLESPY, WILLIAM (1813-?), San Diego, California, 1869-1879. (Shelton)

GALLET, EMILE (1829-?), Yuba City, California, 1867-1876. (Shelton)

GALLISON, WILLIAM Lawrence, Massachusetts, 1886d-1888d.

GALLOUP, L.C. Lodi, New York, 1877-1882d.

GALLOWAY, BENJAMIN C. Richmond, Virginia, 1868-1885d.

GALLOWAY, HENRY Greene Co., Pennsylvania, 1807-1819. (Kauffman)

GALLOWAY, ROBERT M. New York, New York. Patent #462,859 November 10, 1891, safety.

GALLOWAY, T.L. Richmond, Virginia, 1885d-1890d. Son of, and successor to, B.C. Galloway.

GALT & BAKER Fayetteville, North Carolina. Miller patent revolving rifle and percussion 1/2 stock. (Sellers-1)

GALT, M.W. & BRO. Washington, D.C., 1853d. Importers and dealers. Agent on Derringer.

GALYON SEVIER CO. Tennessee, 1861. Confederate rifles.

GAME GETTER trade name of Marble Arms & Mfg. Co. on combination rifle/shotgun.

GAMLOS, JOHN M. Summerfield, Ohio, 1881d. Percussion 1/2 stock. (Hutslar)

GAMMA, FRANZ Elizabeth, New Jersey, 1882, Newark, New Jersey, 1885d. Patent #269,660 December 26, 1882, magazine gun.

GAMMELL, WILLIAM Houston, Texas. 1853-1866, Chapmanville, Texas, 1866d. Percussion fullstock rifles.

GANDER, PETER Lancaster, Pennsylvania, 1779-1782. Flintlock Kentucky rifle. See Peter Gonter. (Gluckman & Satterlee)

GANNAUN, CHRISTIAN Buffalo, New York, 1844d. (Dean)

GANO, HOWELL, & CO. Cincinnati, Ohio, 1844-1900. Hardware dealers, locks only marked "H.G. & Co.". (Hutslar)

GANOE, T.W. unlocated. Percussion fullstock rifle.

GANON, THOMAS Huntington Co., Pennsylvania, 1850c. (Kauffman)

GANT, SHEROD Lincoln Co., North Carolina, 1838. (Bivins)

GANTER see Gonter.

GANTT, W.M. Cleveland Co., North Carolina, 1850. (Bivins)

GAPEN, MICHAEL Wiley, Pennsylvania, 1887d.

GAPPEN, MICHAEL Greene Co., Pennsylvania, 1841-1869. Same as Michael Gapen? (Whisker II)

GARAND, JOHN C. (1888-1974), Springfield, Massachusetts. Ordnance engineer at Springfield Armory; designed the .30-06 cal. M1 semi-automatic rifle, adopted in 1936 by the U.S. military. (Carey)

GARBER, MICHAEL Lancaster, Pennsylvania, 1776. Committee of Safety musket. (Dean)

GARCELON, CHARLES E., JR. Lewiston, Maine, 1893. (Demeritt)

GARCH, R. Washington, D.C., 1867-1872.

GARCIA, A.D.E. New Orleans, Louisiana, 1853d.

GARDINER, C.L. Geneva, New York, 1848-1850d.

GARDINER, JAMES A. Staunton, Virginia, 1850c.

GARDNER & SCHUTTE Chillicothe, Ohio. Percussion fullstock.

GARDNER GUN CO. Cleveland, Ohio, 1887-1895. Sales organization for Gardner machine guns, which were made by Pratt & Whitney. (Hutslar)

GARDNER, ALFRED (1829-?), Jamestown, North Carolina, 1850c. (Bivins)

GARDNER, AMOS H. Milwaukee, Wisconsin, 1857d-1892d.

GARDNER, C. Lima, Ohio, 1855-1861. (Knittle)

GARDNER, C.A. Milan, Michigan, 1891d.

GARDNER, C.L. Flint, Michigan, 1860d.

GARDNER, CHARLES L. Rochester, New York, 1844d-1855d. Percussion 1/2 stock. Successor to A.G.Edwards. (Eich)

GARDNER, D. Homeworth, Ohio, Georgetown, Ohio, circa 1870. (Hutslar)

GARDNER, FREDERICK J. Cincinnati, Ohio. Patent #259,844, June 20, 1882, sight.

GARDNER, G. Geneva, New York. Flintlock Kentucky rifle, pill lock mule ear fullstock marked "Gardner's Patent" on lock. (Dillin)

GARDNER, G.W. Troy, New York. Patent #34,262 December 3, 1861, shell.

GARDNER, GEORGE H. New York, New York. Patent #47,712 May 16, 1865, revolver with 2 cylinders. (Sellers-1)

GARDNER, GEORGE Lima, Ohio, 1859-1885. Percussion 1/2 stock. (Hutslar)

GARDNER, GRAFTON see Mendenhall, Jones and Gardner.

GARDNER, H. Geneva, New York. Pill lock fullstock.

GARDNER, H. Soddy, Tennessee. (ASAC 23)

GARDNER, HENRY L. Springfield, Massachusetts. Patent #186,470 January 23, 1877, automatic ejector for revolver.

GARDNER, J.F. Charleston, South Carolina, 1885d.

GARDNER, J.W. Hyde Park, Pennsylvania, 1882d.

GARDNER, JAMES A. (1824-?), Augusta Co., Virginia, 1850c.

GARDNER, JOHN N. Scranton, Pennsylvania, 1865-1894. Percussion target rifle.

GARDNER, JOHN Columbus, Ohio, 1856-1892. Two men, father and son. Air gun. (Hutslar)

GARDNER, M.H. unlocated. Percussion 1/2 stock.

GARDNER, THADEUS (1774-1851), Jamestown, North Carolina, 1814-1851. (Bivins)

GARDNER, WILLIAM C. Guilford Co., North Carolina, 1850c. (Bivins)

GARDNER, WILLIAM MCKINLEY Ada, Ohio, 1878-1886. (Hutslar)

GARDNER, WILLIAM (1821-?), Lima, Ohio, 1850-1868. Percussion 1/2 stock. (Hutslar)

GARDNER, WILLIAM Geneva, New York, 1848-1850d. Percussion fullstock rifle, percussion 1/2 stock. As Gardiner in 1850 directory. (Clow)

GARDNER, WILLIAM Philadelphia, Pennsylvania, 1780-1782. Continental Armory. (Moller)

GARDNER, WILLIAM Toledo and Cleveland, Ohio. Patents #87,038 February 16, 1869, magazine gun, #174,130 February 29, 1876, machine gun, #174,798 March 14, 1876, machine gun, #216,266 June 10, 1879, machine gun, #235,627 December 31, 1880, machine gun with Edward G. Parkhurst, #245,710 August 16, 1881, machine gun, and #271,836 (date?), breechloading firearm. Gardner machine guns made by Pratt & Whitney. (Chinn)

GARFIELD, JOHN M. Lake City, Minnesota. Patent #152,839 July 7, 1874, lock.

GARITT, ROBERT A. Adair Co., Missouri, 1850c. (MB 11-66)

GARLAND, FRANK M. New Haven, Connecticut. Patents #430,206 June 17, 1890, machine gun. #457,276 August 2, 1892, machine gun, #479,799 May 17, 1892, machine gun. #513,995 February 6, 1894, machine gun, #623,003 April 11, 1899, machine gun, #636,974 November 14, 1899, machine gun, #636,976 November 14, 1899, machine gun, #636,977 November 14, 1899 machine gun, #643,118 February 13, 1900, machine gun, #643,119, February 13, 1900, machine gun, #669,236 March 5, 1901, machine gun, and #693,386 February 18, 1902, machine gun.

GARMON, JOHN (1803-?), Rushville, Illinois, 1860c. (Johnson)

GARNER, GUSTAVE New Orleans, Louisiana, 1850c. (MB 9-65)

GARNER, JAMES M. (1820-?), Bellefontaine, Ohio, 1860d-1864d. Percussion 1/2 stock. (Hutslar)

GARNER, JOSEPH (1816-?), Eldora, Illinois, 1850-1860. (Johnson)

GARNER, L. Pomeroy, Ohio, 1867d.

GARNER, LEWIS (1791-?), Fayette Co., Pennsylvania, 1830c, Butler Co., Pennsylvania, 1850c. (Whisker II)

GARNER, LEWIS (1795-?), Moore Co., North Carolina, 1850c. (Bivins)

GARNER, SILAS (1820-?), Pomeroy, Ohio, 1850c. (Hutslar)

GARNIER, F.A. Kansas City, Kansas, 1894d.

GARNIER, GUSTAVE (1823-?), New Orleans, Louisiana, 1850c.

GARRATT, WILLIAM Lowville, New York, 1870d-1874d.

GARRET, HERMAN Boston, Massachusetts, 1650-1677. (Kauffman 2)

GARRETSON, A.T. Mount Pleasant, Iowa. Patent #40,256 October 13, 1863, sight.

GARRETT, AMOS Hartford City, Maryland, 1776. Committee of Safety. (Dean)

GARRETT, J.F. & CO. Greensboro, North Carolina, 1861-1865. Made Tarpley carbines and brass frame pistols. (Albaugh 1)

GARRETT, JACOB F. Orbisonia, Pennsylvania, 1861d. See Jacob F. Gehrett.

GARRISON suicide special. (Webster)

GARRISON, ELIAS Clifford, Indiana, 1830-1886.

GARRISON, G.H., & CO. Chicago, Illinois, 1895d-1897d.

GARRISON, GEORGE H. Chicago, Illinois, 1895d-1897d, Rockford, Illinois, 1903-1905. Patents #732,540 June 30, 1903, subcaliber gun, #804,804 November 14, 1905, sight. As G.H. Harrison & Co. in Chicago.

GARRISON, GEORGE H. Sumas City, Washington, 1893, Olympia, Washington, 1907. Patents #509,727 November 28, 1893, firearm, and #873,535 December 10, 1907, sight.

GARRISON, SAMUEL (1817-?), Perkinsville, Indiana, 1850-1886. (Lindert)

GARROUTTE, S.J. Adel, Iowa, 1865d.

GARTMAN, T.B. Youngsport, Tennessee, 1884d-1896d.

GARVER, BROWN & CO. Hamilton, Ohio, 1863d. Jacob L. Garver. (Hutslar)

GARVER, HENRY Sugar Creek, Indiana, 1882-1886. (Gardner)

GARVER, JACOB L. Rossville, Ohio, 1843-1853. (Hutslar)

GARVER, JOHN Norristown, Pennsylvania, 1860d-1861d.

GARWOOD, L.C. Champaign, Illinois, 1880d-1886d.

GARY, SOLOMON (1830-?), Bloomfield, California, 1870c. (Shelton)

GARY, W.H. Plum Creek, Nebraska, 1886d.

GASH, R. Washington, D.C., 1885d.

GASKILL, B. (1770-?), Fayette Co., Pennsylvania, 1793-1829, Washington Co., Pennsylvania, 1840-1843, Crawford Co., Pennsylvania, 1850c-1890c. (Whisker II)

GASKILL, HENRY (1810-?), Belle Vernon, Pennsylvania, 1831-1832, Washington Co., Pennsylvania, 1834-1851, Crawford Co., Pennsylvania, 1860c. (Whisker II)

GASKINS & IVES Edenton, North Carolina, 1841. (Bivins)

GASKINS, RADFORD Tarboro, North Carolina, 1833. (Bivins)

GASPARD Lancaster, Pennsylvania, 1770. Flintlock Kentucky. (Dillin)

GASS, VALENTINE Dry Run, Pennsylvania, 1861d.

GASTEN, DICKSON & CO. Cincinnati, Ohio, 1859-1861. Imported locks and guns, marked "G.D. & Co.". (Hutslar)

GASTEN, DICKSON & WALLINGFORD Cincinnati, Ohio, 1856-1859. Imported locks marked "G.D. & W.".

GASTER, ROBERT Ohio, 1834, Maheska Co., Iowa, 1850c. (MB 9-64)

GASTON & JAEDICKE Lawrence, Kansas, 1867d.

GATES, A. unlocated. Percussion fullstock.

GATES, FREDERICK (1839-?), Derby, England, 1875, San Francisco, California, 1876-1878, Salinas, California, 1878-1898. (Shelton)

GATES, M.D. Andover, Ohio, 1875-1878d. (Hutslar)

GATES, THOMAS J. Griswold, Connecticut, 1871d-1874d.

GATES, WILLIAM H. Worcester, Massachusetts. Patent #566,513 August 25, 1896, automatic pistol.

GATLING GUN CO. Hartford, Connecticut, 1866-1909. Sales organization for Gatling guns made by Colt.

GATLING, RICHARD JORDAN (1818-1903), Hartford, Connecticut. Patents #36,402 September 9, 1862, steam ram, #36,836 November 4, 1862, Gatling gun, #47,631 May 9, 1865, Gatling gun, #78,953 June 16, 1868, cartridge, #112,138 February 28, 1871, Gating gun, #125,563 April 9, 1872, Gatling gun #145,563 December 16, 1873, traversing mechanism, #311,974 February 10, 1885, breechloading gun, #311,973 February 10, 1885, breechloading cannon, #427,847 May 13, 1890, pnematic gun, #427,848 May 13, 1890, pneumatic gun, #434,662 August 19, 1890, pneumatic gun, #497,781 May 23, 1893, machine gun, #499,534 June 13, 1893, machine gun, #502,185 July 25, 1893, machine gun, #502,882 August 8, 1893, machine gun, and #504,831 September 12, 1893, machine gun. (Wahl)

GATSCHET, J. unlocated. Percussion 1/2 stock (a "Mr. Gauchez" entered a shotgun in the 1858 St. Louis fair). (Pourie).

GATZWILLER, GUSTAVE Niagara Falls, New York, 1865-1867d.

GAUGLER, GEORGE Selinsgrove, Pennsylvania. Flintlock Kentucky rifles. (Gabel)

GAUGLER, NICHOLAS Selinsgrove, Pennsylvania. Flintlock Kentucky rifles. (Gabel)

GAULENBECK, J. Lebanon, Pennsylvania. (Dean)

GAUMER, JACOB Salem, Ohio, 1811-1823. (Hutslar)

GAUNT & MONET Philadelphia, Pennsylvania, 1813. Contract for Chamber guns. (AR 12-49)

GAUNT, NICHOLAS Philadelphia, Pennsylvania, 1813-1819d. As Gaunt & Monet, 1813.

GAUTEC, PETER Lancaster, Pennsylvania, 1780. See Peter Gonter.

GAUYTER, GEORGE unlocated. Flintlock Kentucky. See George Gaugler.

GAVITT, JAMES K.G. Philadelphia, Pennsylvania. Patent #332,071 December 8, 1885, electric gun.

GAWLEY, ROBERT Deming, New Mexico, 1882d.

GAY & PARSONS Augusta, Maine, 1880-1884. George E. Gay and John H. Parsons. (Demeritt)

GAY, ELDRIDGE Binghamton, New York, 1869d-1905d. As Stuart & Gay, 1869. Percussion and cartridge guns.

GAY, FREDERICK Mobile, Alabama, 1844d-1859d. (Neville)

GAY, GEORGE E. Augusta, Maine, 1877d-1885d.

GAY, JOHN Cameron, Illinois, 1860d.

GAY, LODOWICK W. Wardner, Idaho. Patent #402,918 May 17, 1889, trigger.

GAYLORD, B. Battle River, Michigan, 1860d.

GEARSON, JOSEPH Philadelphia, Pennsylvania, 1829d. Locks only.

GEARY, WILLIAM Philadelphia, Pennsylvania, 1833. (Kauffman)

GEBHART, DANIEL (1809-?), Fremont, Ohio, 1850c. (Hutslar)

GEBHART, JACOB (1827-?). Ashland Co., Ohio, 1850c. (Hutslar)

GEBHART, JOHN R. (1833-?), Fremont, Ohio, 1850c-1886c. Son of Daniel Gebhart. (Hutslar)

GEDDY, DAVID Spottsylvania Co., Virginia, 1744-1751, Williamsburg Co., Virginia, 1751. Son of James Geddy. (Gill)

GEDDY, JAMES (?-1744), Williamsburg, Virginia, 1736-1744. (Gill)

GEDDY, WILLIAM (?-1784), Williamsburg, Virginia, 1744-1784. Committee of Safety repairs. Son of James Geddy. (Gill)

GEDNEY, GEORGE W.B. New York, New York. Patents #23,241 March 15, 1859, priming lock, #33,344 September 24, 1861, air gun, and #35,999, July 29, 1862, revolver. Gedney locks purchased by U.S. government in small quantities. (Sellers-1)

GEEHR, BALSER (1740-?), Berks Co., Pennsylvania, 1767-1779. (Boehret)

GEHBE, ERNEST Bethlehem, Pennsylvania, 1799-1800t. (KRA II-3)

GEHRETT, JACOB F. Orbisonia, Pennsylvania, 1850d-1903d. Percussion fullstock. Son of John Gehrett. (Whisker II)

GEHRETT, JAMES W. (1832-?), Huntingdon, Pennsylvania, 1850c-1887d. (Whisker II)

GEHRETT, JAMES W. Huntingdon Co., Pennsylvania, 1810. Flintlock Kentucky. (Dillin)

GEHRETT, JOHN (1806-?), Orbisonia, Pennsylvania, 1840c-1850c. Flintlock Kentucky. (Dillin)

GEHRETT, SAMUEL (1789-1854), Huntingdon Co., Pennsylvania, 1820-1828, and Armstrong Co., Pennsylvania, 1850c-1854. (Kauffman)

GEHRIG, F.D. Peru, Illinois, 1860d, Centralia, Illinois, 1878d.

GEIGER, J.V. Towanda, Pennsylvania, 1861d-1890d. Flintlock and percussion fullstock rifle.

GEIGER, JOSEPH unlocated. Percussion 1/2 stock.

GEIGER, LEONARD Hudson, New York. Patent #37,501 January 27, 1863, breechloading firearm. E. Remington & Sons purchased this patent for rolling block guns.

GEIGER, PETER Pandora, Ohio, circa 1850. (Hutslar)

GEIRSACH, CHRISTIAN Bushkill, Pennsylvania, 1804t-1814t. (KRA II-3)

GEIRSCH, CHARLES Bushkill, Pennsylvania, 1835t. (Dyke)

GEIRSH, WILLIAM Bushkill Centre, Pennsylvania, 1861d.

GEISE, GEORGE Northampton Co., Pennsylvania, 1800t. (KRA II-3)

GEISER, J.G. San Antonio, Texas, 1862d-1878d.

GEISINGER, HENRY Philadelphia, Pennsylvania, 1856-1860.

GEISLER, ANTON H. Houston, Texas, 1882d-1894d. As Comminge & Geisler, 1882-1893 and Dunlay & Geisler, 1894.

GELBKE, FREDERICK L. Mobile, Alabama, 1859d-1887d. As Gelbke & Bro., 1859.

GELLER, WARD & HASNER St. Louis, Missouri. Dealers only.

GEM derringer by Stevens.

GEM suicide special by Bacon.

GEMMER, JOHN PHILLIP (1838-1919), Boonville, Missouri, 1855-1859, St. Louis, Missouri, 1859-1915. Purchased the Hawken businesss, 1864, and operated it until 1915. (Hanson)

GEMMILL, GEORGE W. (?-1914), Troy, New York, 1860-1914. Flintlock and percussion fullstock. (Swinney)

GENERAL suicide special by Rupertus.

GENERETH, DANIEL Bedford Co., Pennsylvania, 1820t. (Hetrick)

GENESTE, WILLIAM New Orleans, Louisiana, 1877d-1899d.

GENEZ, AUGUST G. New York, New York, 1850-1890d. Percussion pistols and rifles. (GR 7-57)

GENITZ, F. Bridgeport, Connecticut, 1888d-1891d.

GENNER, ELIJAH Rochester, New York, 1838d. See Elijah Jenner.

GENTER, MICHAEL (?-1779), New York, New York, 1776-1779. Flintlock fullstock rifle.

GENTZ, PETER Cleveland, Ohio, 1844-1857. (Hutslar)

GEORGE & NICHOL Hagerstown, Maryland, 1802-1804. Flintlock Kentucky and locks. (Bowers)

GEORGE, ASA Charlotte, North Carolina. Confederate patent #178 June 10, 1863, revolver. (Sellers-1)

GEORGE, CHARLES Maxatawney, Pennsylvania, 1850c-1880d. Percussion fullstock.

GEORGE, HENRY Molltown, Berks Co., Pennsylvania, 1850c-1861d, There was another Henry George, at Nora, Berks Co., 1861d.

GEORGE, ISAAC Ohio, 1837, Kenosha, Wisconsin, 1850c-1857d.

GEORGE, ISAAC Rochester, New York, 1809-1834d. Flintlock Kentucky rifle. (Eich)

GEORGE, J.S. Monterey, Pennsylvania, 1832. Percussion fullstock rifle. (Gardner)

GEORGE, JACOB Berks Co., Pennsylvania, 1793-1850. Flintlock Kentucky. (Kauffman)

GEORGE, JAMES (?-1819), Mifflin Co., Pennsylvania, 1812-1819. Barrel maker. (Whisker III)

GEORGE, JOHN Hagerstown, Maryland, 1802-1804. As George & Nichol. (Bowers)

GEORGE, PATRICK Marysville, California, 1893d.

GEORGE, PETER (1827-1895), Marysville, California, 1855-1895. Percussion 1/2 stock and percussion shotgun. (Shelton)

GEORGIA ARMORY Milledgeville, Georgia, 1861-1864. Mississippi rifles for the Confederacy marked, "GA. ARMORY". (Hill-Anthony)

GERAGHTY, MICHAEL F. Jersey City, New Jersey. Patent #39,642 August 25, 1863, revolver.

GERBER, JOHN T. Taylorsville, Utah, 1878d-1880d.

GERDON, GREGORY Sandy Hook, New Jersey. Patents #539,733 May 21, 1895, breechloading cannon, and #809,107 January 2, 1906, breechloading cannon.

GERE & ABBOTT Columbus, Ohio, 1845-1855. Gunsmith supplies. (Hutslar)

GERHART, DANIEL (1844-?), Reading, Pennsylvania, 1868-1872 and 1882d-1898d, Tamaqua, Pennsylvania, 1872-1881d. For Nelson Delaney, 1868-1872. As Gerhart Bros., 1880-1882.

GERMAN, CHRISTIAN Buffalo, New York, 1836-1851. (Kauffman)

GERMAN, HENRY Hermann, Missouri, 1891d.

GERNER, CHARLES New Haven, Connecticut. Patents #93,149 July 27, 1869, breechloading firearm with Eli Whitney and Frank W. Tiesing, #113,470 April 4, 1871, breechloading firearm with Frank Tiesing, and #114,230 April 25, 1871, breechloading firearm with Frank Tiesing.

GERNGROSS, STEPHEN St. Louis, Missouri. Patent #110,353 December 20, 1870, breechloading firearm.

GERNUNDER, ALBERT Springfield, Massachusetts. Patent #19,086 January 12, 1858, spring gun.

GERRINS & PETERS Buffalo, New York, 1885d. Nicholas Gerrins and Casper Peters.

GERRINS, NICHOLAS Buffalo, New York, 1885d-1889d. As Gerrins & Peters, 1885.

GERRISH, JOHN Boston, Massachusetts, 1709-1725. (Gluckman & Satterlee)

GERTEIS, LOUIS New Orleans, Louisiana, 1855d-1879d. As Gerteis & Dempsey in 1860.

GERTEIS, LOUIS, JR. New Orleans, Louisiana, 1880d-1899d. Succeeded his father.

GERTNER, XAVIER St. Louis, Missouri, 1893d.

GERY & BROS. Philadelphia, Pennsylvania, 1813d. Importers.

GESAMAN, JACOB (1856-1941), Canal Fulton, Ohio. Percussion 1/2 stock. (Hutslar)

GETCHELL, JAMES M. Bath, Maine, 1867-1872. (Demeritt)

GETTIG, H. Williamsport, Pennsylvania. Flintlock Kentucky.

GETZ, FREDERICK (?-1810), Lancaster, Pennsylvania, 1795-1810. See Goetz. (Whisker III)

GETZ, FREDERICK (?-1813), Philadelphia, Pennsylvania, 1813d. See Goetz. (Whisker III)

GETZ, JACOB F. Philadelphia, Pennsylvania, 1860d-1889d.

GETZ, JOHN Lancaster, Pennsylvania, 1833t. (Dyke)

GETZ, PETER Lancaster, Pennsylvania, 1799-1810. Pennsylvania inspector. (Gluckman & Satterlee)

GHERSKIN, G. Nauvoo, Illinois, 1875d.

GHIO, J.A. Hot Springs, Arkansas, 1892d-1898d.

GHORKY, JOHN (1809-?), Portsmouth, Ohio, 1850c. (Hutslar)

GHRISKEY, LEWIS Philadelphia, Pennsylvania, 1812-1819. Contract and flintlock Kentucky rifles. (Gluckman)

GIBBON, H.E. Brooklyn, New York. Patent #46,100 January 31, 1865, safety.

GIBBONS, CHARLES L. Mansfield, Ohio, 1891-1894. (Hutslar)

GIBBONS, HENRY Fayette Co., Pennsylvania, 1857-1870. (Kauffman)

GIBBONS, JOSEPH S. Brownsville, Pennsylvania, 1856-1882d. Flintlock and percussion rifles. (Kauffman)

GIBBONS, ROBERT Yorktown, Virginia, 1776-1783. (Gill)

GIBBONS, THOMAS Covington, Kentucky, 1850c, St. Louis, Missouri, 1859-1879d. Percussion 1/2 stock and locks at both locations.

GIBBS & FOSTER Sturbridge, Massachusetts, 1840-1845. Underhammer pistols. (Logan)

GIBBS ARMS CO. New York, New York. Promotional outfit for Lucius Gibbs' guns.

GIBBS, ABRAHAM Lancaster, Pennsylvania, 1847-1857. (Kauffman 2)

GIBBS, D.H. Portsmouth, Ohio, 1850c.

GIBBS, E.K. Painesville, Ohio, 1865-1883d. (Hutslar)

GIBBS, EDWIN Macon City, Missouri, 1860d,

GIBBS, G. Bristol, Connecticut. Percussion 1/2 stock.

GIBBS, HENRY (?-1843), Lancaster, Pennsylvania, 1812-1843. Flintlock and percussion Kentucky. (Kauffman)

GIBBS, HENRY (1820-1880), Lancaster, Pennsylvania, 1843-1880. Son of Henry Gibbs. Percussion rifles and derringers. (Kauffman)

GIBBS, JOHN (1797-?), Lancaster, Pennsylvania, 1819, Honesdale, Pennsylvania, 1824, Lancaster, Ohio, 1826-1853. (Kauffman)

GIBBS, L. unlocated. Percussion 1/2 stock.

GIBBS, LUCIUS H. Oberlin, Ohio. Patents #5,316 October 2, 1847, breechloading firearm, #14,057 January 8, 1856, breechloading firearm, and #21,924 October 26, 1858, patching balls. Gibbs carbines made by William Brooks during the Civil War.

GIBBS, THOMAS Fort Cumberland, Virginia, 1754, Yorktown, Virginia, 1781. (Gill)

GIBBS, TIFFANY & CO. Sturbridge, Massachusetts, 1820-1838. Underhammer guns. Enoch Gibbs and Lucian Tiffany. (Logan)

GIBBS, WILLIAM Lancaster, Pennsylvania, 1834-1840. (Kauffman)

GIBRALTER trade name of Sears, Roebuck & CO. on shotguns made by Meriden.

GIBSON, A.J. Worcester, Massachusetts. Patents #28,437 May 22, 1860, revolver, #29,126 July 10, 1860, revolver, and #30,309 October 9, 1860, revolver. Lucius Willson Pond made revolvers under these patents.

GIBSON, B.M. Osceola, Iowa, 1884d, Corning, Iowa, 1889d, Bedford, Iowa, 1892d.

GIBSON, CHARLES R. Madison, Indiana, 1881-1885d.

GIBSON, D. Columbus, Indiana, 1876-1880.

GIBSON, FRANCIS Carlisle, Pennsylvania, 1805-1830. (Bowers)

GIBSON, HENRY Washingtonville, Pennsylvania, 1850c-1870c.

GIBSON, I. unlocated. Flintlock Tennessee rifle.

GIBSON, JAMES Philadelphia, Pennsylvania, 1816d.

GIBSON, L.L. Rock Prairie, Missouri, 1879d, French Village, Missouri, 1889d.

GIBSON, PETER Yorktown, Virginia, 1699-1706. (Gill)

GIBSON, SAMUEL Albany, New York, 1832-1834. Worked on Colt prototypes. (Phillips)

GIBSON, STEPHEN Knoxville, Tennessee, 1812-1860. Percussion fullstock marked "S.G.". (Dillin)

GIBSON, THOMAS O. Wilmington, Delaware. Patent #90,164, May 18, 1869, projectile.

GIBSON, THOMAS Philadelphia, Pennsylvania, 1845-1847d. (Kauffman)

GIBSON, THOMAS Taneytown, Maryland, 1796-1827. Flintlock muskets. (Hartzler)

GIBSON, THOMAS Yonkers, New York. Patent #42,435 April 19, 1864, revolver. Single action Starr patent.

GIBSON, WILEY (1866-1940), Sevierville, Tennessee, 1890-1940. Son of William Gibson. (AR 12-40)

GIBSON, WILLIAM Sevierville, Tennessee, 1860-1880. Son of Stephen Gibson (AR 12-40)

GIBSON, WILLIAM Wheeling, West Virginia, 1884d. Percussion 1/2 stock.

GIDDINS, FRANCIS Louisa Co., Virginia, 1776-1784. Committee of Safety repairs, (also spelled Gideon). (Gill)

GIERSCHKE, EDWARD Detroit, Michigan, 1895d.

GIFFORD, JOHN H. Springfield, Massachusetts, 1867-1896d.

GIFFORD, JOSEPH Baltimore, Maryland, 1819. (Gluckman & Satterlee)

GILASPY, ALEXANDER Virginia, 1761. (Gill)

GILBERT & BALES Penn Yann, New York, 1848-1890d. Percussion rifles.

GILBERT, C.N. Edinburg, Ohio, 1861-1865. (Hutslar)

GILBERT, D.H. Chester, Connecticut, 1876-1880.

GILBERT, DANIEL (1729-1820), Brookfield, Massachusetts, 1770-1820. Model 1798 and 1808 contract muskets marked "Brookfield". (Gluckman)

GILBERT, DANIEL Boston, Massachusetts, 1685-1700. Flintlock fowler. (Lindsay)

GILBERT, EPHRAIM (1791-1847), Rochester, New York, 1822-1837. Flintlock and percussion rifles. Patent #none April 3, 1829, mule-ear lock. With Samuel Marckley until 1822. (Eich)

GILBERT, JOHN B. Penn Yann, New York, 1880-1890d. As Gilbert & Bales, 1880-1890. Nephew of Stephen Gilbert. (Swinney)

GILBERT, RICHARD Rochester, New York, 1844d. Stockmaker. (Eich)

GILBERT, SAMUEL Mansfield, Massachusetts. Model 1798 contract muskets. (Gluckman)

GILBERT, STEPHEN (?-1885), Penn Yann, New York, 1848-1885. As Gilbert & Bales, 1848-1880.

GILBERT, W. Rochester, New York, 1837. Mule-ear locks marked "W. GILBERT PATENT, ROCHESTER.".

GILBERT, WILLIAM A. Jacksonville, Florida, 1883d-1895d.

GILBREATH, ROBERT (1823-?), Jamestown, North Carolina, 1850c. (Bivins)

GILCHRIST, RICHARD Troy, New York, 1840-1843. (Kauffman 2)

GILDNER see Reed & Gildner.

GILDNER, D.F. Williamsport, Pennsylvania, 1890d.

GILDNER, FREDERICK Philadelphia, Pennsylvania, 1816. Stockmaker.

GILES, RICHARDS & CO. Boston, Massachusetts, 1788-1797. Employed Amos and William Whittemore as gunsmiths. (Gluckman & Satterlee)

GILHAUS, G.E. Kansas City, Kansas, 1898d.

GILL & BLACKBURN Portland, Missouri, 1854d.

GILL, BENJAMIN D. (1790-1860), Lancaster, Pennsylvania, 1820-1860. Percussion fullstock. (Kauffman 2)

GILL, C. Grass Valley, California, 1878. (Shelton)

GILL, D.B. Lancaster, Pennsylvania, 1848d. Percussion fullstock.

GILL, HENRY Lancaster, Pennsylvania, 1843d.

GILL, JACOB Lancaster, Pennsylvania, 1819-1840. Percussion fullstock rifle. (Kauffman 2)

GILL, JOHN New Bern, North Carolina, 1830. (Bivins)

GILL, P. unlocated. Percussion 1/2 stock.

GILL, T.D. unlocated. Percussion fullstock.

GILL, WARREN Whitneyville, Connecticut, 1846. Underhammer pistol (some signed "W.G." only). (Logan)

GILLEAN, ROBERT (1825-?), Greene Co., Indiana, 1850c. (Lindert)

GILLEN, WILLIAM (1798-?), Lawrence Co., Ohio, 1820c, Jackson, Ohio, 1842-1852. Flintlock and percussion rifles. (Hutslar)

GILLESPIE, BRUCE Madison, Indiana, circa 1860. Percussion fullstock. (Lindert)

GILLESPIE, GEORGE H.D. New York, New York, 1848d-1870d. Derringers and locks. As Wolff & Gillespie, 1848-1852, importer and hardware dealer.

GILLESPIE, HARVEY (1821-?), Henderson Co., North Carolina, 1850c. Son of Matthew Gillespie. (Bivins)

GILLESPIE, J.P. New Albany, Indiana. Patent #33,481 October 15, 1861, cartridge. Made tip-up rifle to use these cartridges. (GR 10-72)

GILLESPIE, JAMES Choestoe, Georgia, 1879d-1883d.

GILLESPIE, JOHN Mills River, North Carolina, 1870c. (Bivins)

GILLESPIE, MATTHEW (1790-?), Henderson Co., North Carolina, 1815-1850. Flintlock Kentucky rifles. (Bivins)

GILLESPIE, PHILIP (1817-?), Henderson, North Carolina, 1850c. Worked with Phillip Sutton. (Bivins)

GILLESPIE, R.B. Aberdeen, Indiana, 1860d.

GILLESPIE, ROBERT Rehoboth, Ohio, 1875-1883. (Hutslar)

GILLESTON, SAMUEL Grayville, Illinois, 1860d.

GILLETT, FRANK N. Hampton, Virginia, 1890d-1893d.

GILLETTE, HIRAM B. Roseburg, Oregon. Patent #631,399 August 22, 1899, auxiliary barrel.

GILLFILLAN, ARCHIBALD Geddes, New York, 1870c.

GILLIAM & MILLER Jamestown, North Carolina, 1862. Confederate Mississippi rifle. (Hill-Anthony)

GILLINGHAM, GOLDING & CO. Trenton, New Jersey, 1862-1863. Converted flintlock muskets.

GILLIS & HARNEY Lexington, Kentucky, 1857-1860.

GILLMAN, DANIEL Maytown, Pennsylvania, 1779t-1812t. Flintlock Kentucky. (Dyke)

GILLMAN, NICHOLAS Maytown, Pennsylvania, 1801-1808. (Dyke)

GILLMOND, WILLIAM Tampico, Tennessee, 1860d.

GILLOGLY Savannah, Illinois. (Johnson)

GILMER, MARTIN (1827-1905), New Holland, Ohio, 1850-1899. (Hutslar)

GILMER, WILLIAM Cass Co., Illinois, 1850c. (Johnson)

GILMORE, C. unlocated. Percussion 1/2 stock.

GILMORE, HARVEY Edgertown, Ohio, 1859-1860c. (Hutslar)

GILMORE, HENRY & HARVEY Connellsville, Pennsylvania. Late percussion rifles. (MB 8-64)

GILMORE, J.B. (1827-1900), Shreveport, Louisiana, 1849-1860. For David Pabst, 1849-1853. Made percussion rifles and derringers. (MB 7-70)

GILMORE, JAMES J. Louisville, Kentucky, 1848-1870. As Dickson & Gilmore, 1848-1860. Derringers. (MB 12-49)

GILMORE, JOHN J. Columbus, Texas, 1873-1892d. As W.D. & J.J. Gilmore, 1884-1892.

GILMORE, W.D. & J.J. Columbus, Texas, 1884d-1892d.

GILMORE, W.T. unlocated. Altered Model 1841 rifles for the state of Mississippi in 1860. (Moller)

GILMORE, WILLIAM Edgertown, Ohio, 1860-1865. Percussion target rifle. (Hutslar)

GILMOUR, JAMES Tamaqua, Pennsylvania, 1872-1875. (Gardner)

GILPATRICK, J.C. Seattle, Washington, 1889d.

GILREATH, SAMUEL Covington, Kentucky, 1829-1834.

GILSON, L.G. Rockford, Illinois, 1869d, Fort Scott, Kansas, 1879d-1888d.

GILSON, SAMUEL (1796-?), Grayville, Illinois, 1860c. (Johnson)

GILSTON, J. & L. Lexington, Kentucky, 1821. Pair percussion duellers.

GINERICH, DANIEL Lancaster Co., Pennsylvania, 1785t-1801t. (Dyke)

GINGER, DAN Gettysburg, Ohio, 1870. (Hutslar)

GINGER, GEORGE W. (1837-?), Crawfordsville, Indiana, 1860c. Percussion 1/2 stock. Son of Joseph Ginger. (Lindert)

GINGER, GEORGE W. Bonneville, Missouri, 1879d. Same as George W. Ginger, Crawfordsville, Indiana?

GINGER, JAMES (1824-?), Newton, Indiana, 1860c, Gettysburg, Ohio, 1870. Percussion 1/2 stock and percussion fullstock. (Lindert, Hutslar)

GINGER, JOHN W. Winchester, Indiana, 1869-1890. (Gardner)

GINGER, JOSEPH (1812-?), Crawfordsville, Indiana, 1860. (Lindert)

GINGER, LEWIS (1790-1870), New Paris, Ohio, 1825-1853, Camden, Indiana, 1850-1870. Flintlock Kentucky pistol. (Hutslar, Lindert)

GINGER, OSCAR Ridgeville, Indiana. Son of Samuel Ginger. (Lindert)

GINGER, SAMUEL (1832-1900), Preble Co., Ohio, 1850c, Ridgeville, Indiana, 1855-1890, Gettysburg, Ohio, circa 1870. Son of Lewis Ginger. Conflict in dates may have resulted from dual residence. (Lindert, Hutslar)

GINGER, WESLEY Winchester, Indiana. Son of Samuel Ginger. (Lindert)

GINGERICH, GEORGE Pleasant Gap, Pennsylvania, 1861d.

GINGERICH, HENRY Lancaster, Pennsylvania, 1775-1778. For William Henry. (Hobbies 4-38)

GINNINGS See Peers & Ginnings.

GINNINGS, WILLIAM (1797-?), Pike Co., Ohio, 1850c. (Hutslar)

GINTER, C. Smith's Mills, Pennsylvania, 1861d.

GIPPERICH, ADOLPHUS Richmond, Virginia. Patent #210,115 November 19, 1878, sight.

GIPSON, S.M. Ash Grove, Illinois, 1860d.

GIROD, EMILE Newark, New Jersey, 1878d.

GIRSCH, JOSEPH Philadelphia, Pennsylvania, 1829d-1823d.

GIVIN, A. McCoysville, Pennsylvania, 1830-1845. Flintlock Kentucky.

GLAB, VALENTINE Shelbyville, Indiana, 1856-1892. (Lindert)

GLADDING, WILLIAM H. Savannah, Georgia. Patent #24,730 July 12, 1859, breechloading firearm with M.J. Gallager.

GLADHILL, W.J. Erie, Illinois, 1886d.

GLADIATOR trade name of Meriden on shotgun for Sears Roebuck & Co. (AR 2-74)

GLAKELER, G. Jacksboro, Texas, 1878d.

GLAKELER, T.J. Lopez Island, Washington, 1891d.

GLANZ, CHARLES A. Buffalo, New York, 1885d. Son of F. Glanz.

GLANZ, F. Buffalo, New York, 1854. For J.O. Robson. (Dean)

GLANZ, P.C. Buffalo, New York, 1880d-1882d.

GLARPS, GEORGE (1775-?), Washington, D.C., 1850c. For John Weaver. (Hartzler)

GLASMAN, CHARLES Indiana, Pennsylvania, 1861d.

GLASMAN, JOHN H. Denver, Colorado, 1884d. (Sellers-3)

GLASS, DANIEL Berks Co., Pennsylvania, 1848-1859. (Hobbies 5-37)

GLASS, JOHN Goughlersville, Pennsylvania, 1887d. Barrel maker.

GLASS, JOHN Pittsburgh, Pennsylvania, 1797. (Kauffman)

GLASS, JOHN Springfield, Ohio, 1812-1814 and 1818-1820, Putnam, Ohio, 1814-1817. Flintlock Kentucky rifles. (Hutslar)

GLASS, MICHAEL Allentown, Pennsylvania, 1772.

GLASS, PETER Putnam, Ohio, 1814-?. (Hutslar)

GLASS, SAMUEL Washington Co., Pennsylvania, 1807-1808, Springfield, Ohio, 1810-1814, Putnam, Ohio, 1814-1815. (Kauffman, Hutslar)

GLASS, VALENTINE Adams Co., Pennsylvania, 1850c. (Kauffman)

GLASSBRENER, DAVID (1798-1872), Dauphin Co., Pennsylvania, 1825-1860. Flintlock fullstock. (MB 2-71)

GLASSBRENNER, G. unlocated. Flintlock Kentucky rifle.

GLASSBRENNER, H. unlocated. Flintlock Kentucky rifle.

GLASSER, JASPER Livingston, Iowa, 1865d.

GLASSICK & CO. Memphis, Tennessee, 1840-1860. Derringer. Frederick G. Glassick. Became Schneider & Glassick in 1860, William S. Schneider and Frederick G. Glassick.

GLASSICK, FREDERICK G. Memphis, Tennessee, 1840-1864. Derringer and revolvers. As Glassick & Co., 1840-1860, and Schneider & Glassick, 1861-1864.

GLATT, NICHOLAS Salisbury, Maryland, 1880c. Percussion 1/2 stock. (Hartzler)

GLAYSMAN, D. unlocated. Flintlock Kentucky rifle.

GLAZE & RADCLIFFE Columbia, South Carolina, 1861. William Glaze and Thomas W. Radcliffe. William Glaze also owned and operated the Palmetto Armory.

GLAZE, CONRAD (?-1831), Hampshire Co., Virginia, ?-1831. (Bowers)

GLAZE, EARHART Hampshire Co., West Virginia, 1780-1820. (Whisker IV)

GLAZE, GEORGE W. (1780-?), Shanandoah Valley, Virginia, 1828, Belleville, Indiana, 1830-1850c. Percussion fullstock. (Lindert)

GLAZE, GEORGE (?-1823), Hampshire Co., Virginia, 1782-1823. Flintlock Kentucky. (Bowers)

GLAZE, GEORGE Hendricks Co., Pennsylvania. Flintlock Kentucky rifles and pistols.

GLAZE, WILLIAM Columbia, South Carolina, 1838-1870d. Military pistols, muskets, and swords. Guns marked "Wm Glaze & Co." on barrel, or "W.G. & Co.", on barrel. Owned and operated Palmetto Armory. Also operated as Glaze & Radcliffe, 1861.

GLAZIER, JOHN Bellville, Indiana. Percussion fullstock dated 1852.

GLEIST, HANIEL Bethlehem, Pennsylvania, 1770-1783t. (Dyke)

GLEN, THOMAS Lancaster, Pennsylvania, 1788. (Dyke)

GLENN J.D., Pleasantville, Pennsylvania, 1882d-1890d.

GLENN, WILLIAM (1796-?), Richmond, Virginia, 1850c. (MB 10-63)

GLENWOOD trade name on Fyrberg shotgun. (GR 12-67)

GLICK, RHINEHART (1815-?), Hancock Co., Ohio, 1850c. (Hutslar)

GLOBE MILLS lock marking on pistols and muskets made by Robert McCormick.

GLOKLER, BERNARD Pittsburgh, Pennsylvania, 1864d.

GLORE, J.R. Troy, Missouri, 1860d.

GLOVER & CUSHMAN New York, New York, 1879d.

GLOVER & SON, W. Cairo, Illinois, 1870-1872.

GLOVER, BENJAMIN Brownsville, Pennsylvania, 1832. (Whisker II)

GLOVER, S. unlocated. Iron mounted fullstock percussion.

GLOVER, SAMUEL Virginia, 1777. Committee of Safety repairs. (Gill)

GLOWERS, JERAH Elizabethtown, New York, 1820c.

GLUMPKE, J.W. San Francisco, California, 1893d.

GLUYAS, THOMAS (1826-1912), Guilford, North Carolina, 1847-1857, Charlotte, North Carolina, 1857-1912. Percussion fullstock, some signed "T.G.", some "T. Gluyas". (Bivins)

GLYNN, EDWARD M. Clarendon, Vermont, 1871-1885. Percussion 1/2 stock. (Horn)

GMEHLIN & SCHMIDT Bloomington, Illinois, 1859-1860. (Johnson)

GMEHLIN see Brown & Gmehlin.

GMEHLIN, CHARLES H. (1834-1914), Bloomington, Illinois, 1856d-1899d. Percussion parlor rifle and Martini action schuetzen rifle.

GNIBB, LEWIS (1776-?), Wytheville, Virginia, 1850c. (MB 10-63)

GOBBELS, MATHIAS St. Louis, Missouri, 1848d-1859d. As Gobbes, 1848, and Goebels, 1859.

GOBBLE, JOHN Houston, Virginia, 1871d.

GOBRECHT, DANIEL (1816-?), Adams Co., Pennsylvania. Flintlock Kentucky. Son of Samuel Gobrecht. (Kauffman)

GOBRECHT, DANIEL York Co., Pennsylvania, 1800. Flintlock Kentucky. (Kindig)

GOBRECHT, DAVID Hanover, Pennsylvania. Percussion fullstock. (Dean)

GOBRECHT, SAMUEL (1750-1836), York Co., Pennsylvania, 1807, Adams Co., Pennsylvania, 1810-1836. Flintlock Kentucky. (Bowers)

GODDARD & GLEASON Boston, Massachusetts (?). Flintlock lock makers.

GODDARD, EMERSON Brooklyn, New York. "Double Header"/"Perpetual Revolver" derringer. Patent #102,429 April 26, 1870, breechloading firearm with Samuel Perry. As Perry & Goddard, with Samuel Perry.

GODDARD, HENRY Taunton, Massachusetts, 1853-1856.

GODDARD, RESIN (1816-?), Montgomery Co., Indiana, 1850c. (Lindert)

GODDARD, SAMUEL A. New York, New York, 1858d. Imported locks from his factory in England.

GODFREY & HATT Paw Paw, Michigan, 1867d.

GODFREY & WELSH Albany, New York. Percussion shotgun. (Gluckman & Satterlee)

GODFREY, CHARLES J. New York, New York, 1875d-1907d. Importers and dealers.

GODFREY, JAMES New York, New York, 1844d-1884d. As James Godfrey & Son, 1867, Godfrey Bros, 1873-1874, and James W. Godfrey (son?), 1875-1884.

GODMAN, JOHN (1817-?), Freeport, Illinois, 1860c. (Johnson)

GODSCHALL, NICHOLAS Reading, Pennsylvania, 1767-1768. Lockmaker. (Gardner)

GODWIN, THOMAS W. Norfolk, Virginia, 1861. Invented a revolver with bayonet attached. (Albaugh 3)

GOEDEKE, HENRY (1849-1928), Olney, Illinois, 1873-1928. (Johnson)

GOEKEN, EWALD St. Louis, Missouri, 1859-1864d.

GOENAWEIN, CONRAD Frankfort, Michigan, 1891d.

GOETZ & TRYON Philadelphia, Pennsylvania, 1811 only. Frederick W. Goetz and George W. Tryon.

GOETZ & WESTPHALL Philadelphia, Pennsylvania, 1808-1813. Model 1808 contract muskets. Frederick Goetz and Charles W. Westphall. (Gluckman & Satterlee)

GOETZ, FREDERICK W. Philadelphia, Pennsylvania, 1805-1820. As Goetz & Westphall, 1808-1812 and Goetz & Tryon in 1811. Model 1808 contract muskets and flintlock fowler. (Gluckman)

GOFF, WILLIAM Pittsburgh, Pennsylvania, 1826. (Kauffman)

GOHRMANN, HENRY (1815-?), Pittsburgh, Pennsylvania, 1850c-1854d.

GOLBER, H. unlocated. Percussion over/under rifle.

GOLCHER & BUTLER Philadelphia, Pennsylvania. Lockplate on Kit Carson's Hawken.

GOLCHER & CO. see William Golcher.

GOLCHER & KAYE Philadelphia, Pennsylvania. Percussion rifles and derringers.

GOLCHER & SIMPSON see William Golcher.

GOLCHER see Goulcher.

GOLCHER, GEORGE W. Philadelphia, Pennsylvania, 1876d- 1892d.

GOLCHER, JAMES (?-1805), Philadelphia, Pennsylvania, ?-1805. Flintlock Kentucky.

GOLCHER, JAMES (1837-?), Joliet, Illinois, 1860c. (Johnson)

GOLCHER, JAMES Birmingham, England, 1820-1840, Philadelphia, Pennsylvania, 1840-1870. Operated the Eagle Gun Factory and Eagle Rifle Works. Made complete line of guns, as well as parts, for other gunsmiths. There is a pistol marked, "James Golcher Improved Patent", but there are no known patents by him.

GOLCHER, JOHN Easton, Pennsylvania, 1775-1800. Committee of Safety barrels, flintlock Kentucky, and flintlock revolving rifle. See John Goulcher. (Dillin)

GOLCHER, JOSEPH Philadelphia, Pennsylvania. Lockmaker only.

GOLCHER, MANUEL Philadelphia, Pennsylvania, 1824d.

GOLCHER, THOMAS L. Philadelphia, Pennsylvania, 1867d-1889d.

GOLCHER, THOMAS (1842-?), Joliet, Illinois, 1860c. (Johnson)

GOLCHER, WILLIAM (1834-1886), Philadelphia, Pennsylvania, 1851-1855, St. Paul, Minnesota, 1855-1873, San Francisco, California, 1878-1886. Patents #88,470 March 30, 1869, breechloading firearms, and #95,998 October 19, 1869, breechloading firearm. Son of James (Birm & Phila). As Golcher & Simpson, 1854-1857, Golcher & Co., 1857-1858, and Clabrough & Goicher, 1883-1886. (GR 11-77)

GOLD HIBBARD trade name of Hibbard, Spencer, Bartlett & Co. on imported rifles and shotguns.

GOLD, CALVIN Shawneetown, Illinois, circa 1810. (Johnson)

GOLDEN, GEORGE W. (1846-?), Harrison Co., West Virginia, 1880d. (Whisker IV)

GOLDEN, GEORGE (1833-?), Jeffersonville, Indiana, 1850-1860. Brother of Samuel. (Lindert)

GOLDEN, JAMES (1800-?), Waynesburg, Pennsylvania, 1823-1855, Craigmoor, West Virginia, 1855-1857. (Whisker II and IV)

GOLDEN, O. N. Criagmoor, West Virginia, 1900d.

GOLDEN, R. unlocated. Underhammer pistol.

GOLDEN, SAMUEL (1826-?), Jeffersonville, Indiana, 1850-1860. Brother of George. Percussion 1/2 stock. (Lindert)

GOLDEN, VICTOR Q. Bloodworth, Georgia, 1881d.

GOLDMARK, SAMUEL New York, New York, 1852-1877.

Patent #10,262 November 22, 1853, percussion caps. Made percussion caps and cartridges.

GOLDSBARRY, ANDREW Peru, Indiana, 1850-1925. (MB 7-53)

GOLDSBOROUGH, I. & F. Dover, Indiana, 1862d.

GOLDSMITH, EDWIN M. Philadelphia, Pennsylvania. Patent #657,344, September 4, 1900, pneumatic gun.

GOLDSOLL, MEYER St. Louis, Missouri, 1860d, Russell, Kansas, 1872-1873. Dealer.

GOME, FRANCOIS unlocated. Percussion fullstock.

GOMEZ, E. New York, New York. Patents #21,253 August 24, 1858, cartridge with W. Mills, and #34,056 January 7, 1862, fuse.

GOMPF, ANDREW J. see Andrew Gumpf.

GOMPF, C. Lancaster, Pennsylvania, Flintlock Kentucky.

GOMPF, JAMES Lancaster, Pennsylvania, 1826-1832. (Gluckman & Satterlee)

GONEL & SCHOTT Jackson, California, 1870. H. Gonel and L. Schott. (Shelton)

GONTER, JOHN (1762-?),Hagerstown, Maryland, 1790c-1801, Lancaster, Pennsylvania, 1810-1823, Reading, Pennsylvania, 1823-?. Son of John Peter Gonter, signed Kentucky rifles with "I.G." or "J. Gonter". (Kindig)

GONTER, PETER (1711-1768), Lancaster Co., Pennsylvania, 1750-1768. (Kindig)

GONTER, PETER (1751-1818), Lancaster, Pennsylvania, 1768-1818. Committee of Safety rifles, and contract rifles with Jacob Dickert, John Groff, and Henry DeHuff. Son of John Peter Gonter. (Kauffman)

GONYEA, JOHN Albany, New York, 1815. (Kauffman 2)

GONZALES, JOHN H. New York, New York, 1849d-1853d. As Miller & Gonzales, 1849.

GOOCH, A.F. Shelburn, Oregon, 1891d.

GOOCH, A.S. Malvern, Arkansas, 1878d.

GOOCH, M. (1820-?), Red Bluff, California, 1860c. (Shelton)

GOOCH, T.D. (1804-?), Red Bluff, California, 1860c. (Shelton)

GOOD, H. Feliciana, Kentucky, 1857-1860.

GOOD, J.J. Bloomery, Virginia, 1840. Percussion 1/2 stock (Bowers)

GOOD, J.J. Warrensburg, Missouri, 1860d, Cynthiana, Kentucky, 1879d-1896d.

GOOD, PETER Berks Co., Pennsylvania, 1850c. Flintlock Kentucky rifle. (Dillin)

GOODALE, JOHN W. Amherst, Massachusetts. Patent #90,741 June 1, 1869, breechloading firearm.

GOODALL, JOHN W. Hays, Kansas. Patent #258,051 May 16, 1882, breechloading firearm.

GOODELL, ABSALOM Otto, New York, 1846-1851. Percussion 1/2 stock.

GOODELL, BORDEN J. Otto, New York, 1870d-1882d.

GOODELL, FREDERICK New Rochelle, New York, 1844-1852. Patent #8,956 May 18, 1852, cartridge with William W. Marston.

GOODELL, GEORGE D. Middleton, Connecticut. Patent #197,773 December 4, 1877, breechloading firearm.

GOODELL, JAMES Olean, New York, 1866-1882d. Percussion 1/2 stock. (Swinney)

GOODELL, LAYTON B. Edinboro, Pennsylvania. Percussion fullstock.

GOODENVILL, ULRICK (1800-?), Stark Co., Ohio, 1850c. (Hutslar)

GOODHUE, J.W. Fort Fairfield, Maine, 1875-1879.

GOODLINE, J. St. Joseph, Missouri, 1869d-1873d.

GOODLING, GEORGE E. Lynn, Massachusetts, 1871-1879d. As Goodling & Taylor, 1876-1879. Percussion fullstock.

GOODLING, PETER Yorktown, Pennsylvania, 1792-1810. Flintlock Kentucky. (Kauffman 2)

GOODMAN & BALLOUGH Lynchburg, Virginia, 1871d-1875d. M.L. Goodman.

GOODMAN, HENRY St. Louis, Missouri, 1877-1899d. Patents #185,912, January 2, 1877, breechloading firearm, #212,459 February 18, 1879, breechloading firearm, #267,876 November 21, 1882, breechloading firearm, #274,093 March 13, 1883, revolver, #288,939 November 9, 1883, revolver, and #352,185, November 9, 1886, revolver.

GOODMAN, M. unlocated. Percussion fullstock.

GOODMAN, M.L. Lynchburg, Virginia, 1871d-1877d. As Goodman & Ballough, 1871-1875.

GOODMAN, NICHOLAS Westmoreland Co., Pennsylvania, 1826-1838. (Whisker II)

GOODREM, THOMAS Providence, Rhode Island. Patent #37,937 March 17, 1863, breechloading firearm with Charles Jackson.

GOODRICH, ASAPH Adair Co., Missouri, 1850c. (MB 11-66)

GOODRICH, HENRY Worcester, Massachusetts, 1865d.

GOODRICH, JOHN P. New York, New York, 1852d.

GOODRICH, R.S. Dayton, Oregon, 1891d.

GOODRICH, WILLIAM R. (1832-?), Kewanee, Illinois, 1864d-1888d.

GOODSELL, ALBERT B. Coudersport, Pennsylvania, 1844-1861d. (MB 7-46)

GOODSPEAD, THOMAS (1819-?), Ross Co., Ohio, 1850c. (Hutslar)

GOODSPEED, THOMAS Isadora, Missouri, 1889d-1898d.

GOODWIN, C.A. Terre Haute, Indiana, 1858d-1862d.

GOODWIN, CHARLES E. Saybrook, Ohio, 1885-1886, Geneva, Ohio, 1901. Patents #342,509 May 25, 1886, lock, and #665,634 January 8, 1901, single trigger. (Hutslar)

GOODWIN, G. unlocated. Flintlock double-barrel shotgun.

GOODWIN, JAMES P. Waterbury, Connecticut, 1860d-1889d. Percussion target rifles.

GOODWIN, JONATHAN Lebanon, Connecticut, 1775-1778. Committee of Safety muskets. (Gluckman & Satterlee)

GOODWIN, L.B. Surrey, Maine, 1871. (Demeritt)

GOODWIN, THOMAS W. (1817-?), Quincy, Illinois, 1860c-1864d, Springfield, Illinois, 1870. Goodwyn in 1864 directory. (Johnson)

GOODWIN, V.M. Newport, New Hampshire, 1869d-1875d.

GOODWYN, THOMAS W. Healdsburg, California, 1870-1885. (Shelton)

GOOL, ROBERT Abingdon, Illinois, 1860d.

GOOSLEY, EPHRAIM Yorktown, Virginia, 1748-1752. (Gill)

GOOT, B.F. Roland, Illinois, 1860d.

GOPPERT, GEORGE (1821-?), Baltimore, Maryland, 1850c-1852d. (Hartzler)

GORDON, ABNER (1826-?), Jamestown, North Carolina, 1850c. For Henry Ledbetter. (Bivins)

GORDON, ABNER North Salem, Indiana, 1860d, Jamestown, Indiana, 1862d. Same as Abner Gordon of Jamestown, North Carolina?

GORDON, CAPT. Bourbon, Indiana. (Lindert)

GORDON, EDWARD Hingham, Massachusetts. Patent #none, February 17, 1836, double-barrel cannon.

GORDON, ELI (1812-?), Jamestown, North Carolina, 1850c. Worked for Henry Ledbetter. (Bivins)

GORDON, FRANK D. (1858-?), Marysville, California, 1878-1900. (Shelton)

GORDON, G.A. Lansing, Michigan, 1879d, Bay City, Michigan, 1887d-1895d.

GORDON, GEORGE Annapolis, Maryland, 1776-1777. Committee of Safety muskets. (Hartzler)

GORDON, HARRY (1840-?), Galesburg, Illinois, 1860d.

GORDON, JAMES Jamestown, North Carolina. (Bivins)

GORDON, JOHN New London, Connecticut. Patent #72,844 December 31, 1867, spring operated revolver.

GORDON, JOHN San Francisco, California. Patent #129,334 July 17, 1872, revolver. (Sellers-1)

GORDON, L. Adams, Massachusetts, 1853d.

GORDON, STEVEN Clinton, Iowa. (MB 1-46)

GORDON, WILLIAM C. Maquoketa, Iowa, 1865d-1882d.

GORDON, WILLIAM (1820-?), Putnam Co., Ohio, 1850c. (Hutslar)

GORE see Sangre & Gore.

GORHAM, RICHARD, H. Shamokin, Pennsylvania, 1880d, Johnstown, Pennsylvania, 1889d.

GORMAN, DAVID (1785-?), Canton, Ohio, 1850c. (Hutslar)

GORMAN, FRANK (1805-?), Canton, Ohio, 1850c. (Hutslar)

GORMAN, JAMES New York, New York, 1847-1851.

GORMAN, RICHARD H. Shamokin, Pennsylvania, 1882d, Philipsburgh, Pennsylvania, 1887d, Johnstown, Pennsylvania, 1889d.

GORNER, PAUL see Paul Corner.

GORSCH, LOUIS New Orleans, Louisiana, 1871d-1872d.

GORSUCH, JOHN MANCHESTER (1821-1895), Mt. Pleasant, Ohio, 1850-1883. Percussion 1/2 stock. (Hutslar)

GORSUCH, THOMAS M. Mt. Pleasant, Ohio, 1858-1865. (Hutslar)

GORTON, B.H. Marion, Ohio, 1864d. (Hutslar)

GORTON, HENRY B. Friendship, New York. Patent #417,241 December 17, 1889, firearm.

GOSHAN, RUTH New York, New York. Patent #124,056 February 27, 1872, breechloading firearm.

GOSHMANN, HENRY (?-1854), Pittsburgh, Pennsylvania, 1854. (Whisker II)

GOSNELL, ANDREW J. Terre Haute, Indiana, 1858d-1860d.

GOSS, A. unlocated. Flintlock Kentucky.

GOSS, J. unlocated. Flintlock Kentucky.

GOSS, STEPHEN D. Devalls Bluff, Arkansas, 1878d.

GOTH, F. Ilion, New York. Percussion 1/2 stock.

GOTH, FRED (?-1922), Portland, Maine, 1882-1885. Son of F.R. Goth. (Demeritt).

GOTH, FREDERICK R. (?-1887), Biddeford, Maine, 1858-1866, Portland, Maine, 1866-1879. Patent #22,969 February 15, 1859, repeating gun. Percussion and cartridge rifles. (Demeritt)

GOTH, RICHARD Portland, Maine, 1882-1896. Son of F. R. Goth. (Demeritt)

GOTH, WILLIAM Portland, Maine, 1883-1895, Augusta, Maine, 1896. Son of F.R. Goth. (Demeritt)

GOTSCHEL, I. unlocated. Percussion 1/2 stock.

GOTT, H.C. Cincinnati, Ohio, 1880c. (Hutslar)

GOTT, ISAAC (1822-?), McLeansboro, Illinois, 1860. (Johnson)

GOTT, J.H. Cincinnati, Ohio, 1880c. (Hutslar)

GOTT, JOHN N. (1812-?), Gallatin Co., Illinois, 1850c. (Johnson)

GOTTSCHALCK, AUGUST Bozeman, Montana, 1886d-1892. Successor to Walter Cooper.

GOUBIL, BENJAMIN Mobile, Alabam, 1859d-1879d.

GOUCHER, THOMAS Philadelphia, Pennsylvania, 1774-1780. Committee of Safety musket barrels. (Gluckman & Satterlee)

GOUDIE, JAMES Atlas, Illinois, 1860d.

GOUGH, BENJAMIN C. Canton, Massachusetts. Patent #214,123 April 8, 1879, magazine gun.

GOUGHLER & HABERLING Berks Co., Pennsylvania, 1859-1862. Barrel maker. Bought Daniel Glass' shops. (MB 2-63)

GOUGHNOUR, DANIEL Pershing, Pennsylvania, 1861d.

GOULCHER see Golcher.

GOULCHER, EMANUEL Philadelphia, Pennsylvania, 1824d-1833. (Kauffman 2)

GOULCHER, GEORGE New York, New York. Percussion locks and one target rifle. (Swinney)

GOULCHER, JOHN Easton and Philadelphia, Pennsylvania, 1775-1781. Committee of Safety barrels. See John Golcher. (Gluckman & Satterlee)

GOULD, J. Salem and East Palestine, Ohio. Percussion fullstock. (MB 11-54)

GOULD, JOHN J. Newburyport, Massachusetts, 1886d-1889d.

GOULD, JOHN Clinton, Pennsylvania, 1882d-1890d. Percussion fullstock.

GOULD, NEHEMIAH Dixmont, Maine, 1875. (Demeritt)

GOULD, THEODORE P. Niagara Falls, New York, 1858-1861d. Patents #22,325 December 14, 1858, breechloading cannon with Edward S. Wright, and #26,734 January 3, 1860, breechloading firearm.

GOULDING, JOHN Worcester, Massachusetts. Patent #42,573 May 3, 1864, breechloading firearm.

GOULDING, WILLIAM Portland, Maine, 1830. (Demeritt)

GOVE, ALBERT F. Lincoln, Vermont, 1868-1882. Percussion 1/2 stock and target rifles. (Horn)

GOVE, CARLOS (1817-1900), St. Joseph, Missouri, 1852-1854, Council Bluffs, Iowa, 1840-1852 and 1854-1862, Denver, Colorado, 1862-1884. Percussion and cartridge guns. (Sellers-3)

GOVERNOR suicide special by Bacon.

GOVERNOR suicide special by Hopkins & Allen.

GOWDEY unlocated. All brass pistol.

GOWDEY, JAMES (?-1806), Charleston, South Carolina, 1801. (Kauffman)

GRABE, JOSEPH (1788-?), Philadelphia, Pennsylvania, 1808- ? For O. & E. Evans.

GRABOWSKY, MAX Detroit, Michigan, 1891d-1899d.

GRACE, HENRY S. San Francisco, California, 1881-1884. Percussion fullstock. (Shelton)

GRACE, J. unlocated. Flintlock Kentucky.

GRACE, ROBERT Philadelphia, Pennsylvania, 1867d-1886d. Percussion shotgun.

GRADDY, L.W. Batesville, Arkansas, 1892d.

GRADDY, WILLIAM Stafford Co., Virginia, 1762-1777. (Gill)

GRAEFELDER Reading, Pennsylvania. Percussion 1/2 stock.

GRAEFF, GEORGE Lancaster, Pennsylvania, 1785-1786. (Dyke)

GRAEFF, JOHN (?-1808), Lancaster, Pennsylvania, 1773-1808. Model 1798 contract muskets for Pennsylvania with Abraham Henry. (Kauffman)

GRAEFF, WILLIAM Lancaster, Pennsylvania, 1751, Reading, Pennsylvania, 1761-1802t. Flintlock Kentucky rifles. (Kauffman)

GRAEFF, WILLIAM Lancaster, Pennsylvania, 1807-1809. (Dyke)

GRAF & JORDAN Chicago, Illinois, 1889d. Break open shotguns. Louis Jordan.

GRAF, LOUIS Aurora, Indiana, 1879-1885, Cincinnati, Ohio, 1896-1900d. (Hutslar)

GRAFF, H.C. unlocated. Percussion fullstock.

GRAFF, THOMAS Fredericktown, Maryland. Model 1798 contract muskets with Nicholas White and Christopher Barnhizle. (Gluckman)

GRAFFELDER, PETER N. Reading, Pennsylvania, 1842. (Kauffman)

GRAH, WILLIAM & SON Toledo, Ohio, 1877-1883. (Knittle)

GRAHAM, A.M. unlocated. Flintlock Kentucky rifle.

GRAHAM, A.S. Hamilton, Ohio, 1863d. (Hutslar)

GRAHAM, EDMUND H. Biddeford, Maine. Patents #10,084 October 4, 1853, magazine gun, #10,944 May 16, 1854, magazine gun, #12,235 January 16, 1855, revolver, #15,734 September 16, 1856, pistol, and #40,687 November 24, 1863, revolver. (Demeritt)

GRAHAM, G.H. Defiance, Ohio. Percussion rifle. (Hutslar)

GRAHAM, GRAXTON Rochester, New York, 1855d. (Eich)

GRAHAM, HENRY H. Chicago, Illinois. Patent #386,535 July 24, 1888, magazine gun.

GRAHAM, JOHN (1810-?), Atwater, Ohio, 1850-1868. Percussion fullstock rifle. (Hutslar)

GRAHAM, JOSEPH (1818-?), Freedom, Pennsylvania, 1841-1854. Percussion fullstock. (Kauffman)

GRAHAM, M.H. Hodgensville, Kentucky, 1883d-1884d.

GRAHAM, RALPH Brooklyn, New York. Patents #41,960 March 15, 1864, explosive shell, and #43,881, August 16, 1864, grenade launcher.

GRAHAM, S. Allendale, Kentucky, 1879d-1884d.

GRAHAM, TAYLOR North Carolina, 1794. Flintlock Kentucky. Later moved to Elkhorn, Kentucky. Made "Daniel Boone's Kentucky". (AR 02-25) (Dean)

GRAHAM, W.B. Cedargrove, Tennessee, 1891d.

GRAMPS, JOHN H. Stone Arabia, New York. Patent #245,813 August 16, 1881, breechloading firearm.

GRANBERRY, WILLIAM Nansemond Co., Virginia, 1777. Committee of Safety repairs. (Gill)

GRANDSTAFF, GEORGE Edinburg, Virginia, 1812-1815. Flintlock rifles. (Dean)

GRANDSTAFF, JOHN (1789-1853), Edinburg, Virginia. Flintlock Kentucky. (Dillin, Bowers)

GRANGER, FRANK D. New York, New York. Patents #456,813 July 28, 1891, lock, and #572,480 December 1, 1896, single trigger.

GRANGER, HENRY R. (?-1882), New York, New York. Patent #266,133 October 17, 1882, breechloading firearm.

GRANGER, JAMES Robinson, Illinois, 1882d.

GRANGER, JOHN Guthrieville, Pennsylvania, 1860d-1861d.

GRANT & CO. Newark, New Jersey, 1869-1880. Henry L. Grant and Joseph Sherwood made parlor guns on Jacob Widmer's patent.

GRANT Louisville, Kentucky. Percussion 1/2 stock.

GRANT, CHARLES J. Willett, New York, 1879-1882d.

GRANT, D.C. Barnegat, New Jersey, 1878d.

GRANT, JOHN Baltimore, Maryland, 1801d. (Hartzler)

GRANT, SAMUEL Walpole, New Hampshire. 1798 contract muskets with Amasa Allen and Joseph Bernard. (Gluckman)

GRANT, W.L. see William P. Uhlinger & Co.

GRANT, WILLARD N. Greenfield, Massachusetts, 1854-1892d. Percussion 1/2 stock.

GRASS, DAVID Guilford Co., North Carolina, 1805. (Bivins)

GRATIOT MFG. CO. St. Louis, Missouri, 1860. Percussion revolvers of doubtful authenticity. (Sellers-1)

GRAUMAN, WILLIAM (1829-?), Marysville, Ohio, 1879-1883. Percussion 1/2 stock. (Hutslar)

GRAVE, JOHN Lancaster, Pennsylvania, 1769-1773. (Dean)

GRAVES & LONG Bangor, Maine, 1859-1861. Joseph Graves and Malcolm Long.

GRAVES, ASA W. West Killingly, Connecticut, 1849-1889d.

GRAVES, CALVIN L. Novi, Michigan, 1863d-1899d.

GRAVES, CONVERSE Fairfield, Illinois, 1882d-1884d.

GRAVES, J.C. Auburn, Alabama, 1861. Confederate gunsmith convention.

GRAVES, J.J. Spring Valley, Iowa, 1865d.

GRAVES, JOSEPH (1800-1876), Bangor, Maine, 1846-1876. Underhammer pistols, percussion 1/2 stock. As Graves & Long, 1869-1876. (Demeritt)

GRAVES, ROBERT S. Bangor, Maine, 1864-1868. (Demeritt)

GRAVES, THOMAS J. Pleasanton, Iowa, 1892d-1897d.

GRAVES, WILLIAM H. Syracuse, New York. Patent #208,810 October 8, 1878, spring gun.

GRAY & DUDLEY HARDWARE CO. Nashville, Tennessee. Dealers only.

GRAY & ROMANS Mt. Vernon, Ohio, 1870-1871. Carbine for U.S. trials. Gardner Gray and Joseph Romans.

GRAY, BENJAMIN Salem, Massachusetts, 1730. Son of Robert. (Dean*)

GRAY, BENNETT Sparta, Ohio, 1868d. (Hutslar)

GRAY, CHARLES J. Glouchester, Massachusetts, 1878d-1892d.

GRAY, DAVIS Greensboro, Indiana, 1860d-1885. Percussion 1/2 stock.

GRAY, DENSMORE & PHELPS Chicago, Illinois, 1853-1854. (Johnson)

GRAY, E. unlocated. Underhammer.

GRAY, GARDNER B. Mt. Vernon, Ohio, 1867-1872d, Cardington, Ohio, 1883d. Patents #106,983 August 2, 1870, breechloading firearm with Thomas D. Simpson and Joseph Romans, and #112,803 March 21, 1871, breechloading firearm with Joseph Romans. (Hutslar)

GRAY, GEORGE Frederick Co., Virginia, 1781. (Gill)

GRAY, J.B. Fredericksburg, Virginia, 1829-1836. Patent #none October 7, 1834, lock.

GRAY, J.H. Centralia, Illinois, 1886d-1893d.

GRAY, JOHN D. Columbus, Georgia, 1860-1865. Mississippi rifles and carbines for the Confederacy. Marked "J.P. Murray", who was the factory's master armorer. As Greenwood & Gray, 1862-1865. (Albaugh 1)

GRAY, JOSEPH (?-1690), Salem, Massachusetts, 1661. Son of Robert. (Dean*)

GRAY, JOSHUA Boston and Medford, Massachusetts. Patents #41,375 January 26, 1864, repeating firearm, #44,995 November 8, 1864, breechloading firearm, #45,560 December 20, 1864, magazine gun, #48,337 June 20, 1865, extractor, #48,622 July 4, 1865, magazine gun, and #54,068 April 17, 1866, magazine gun. Civil War and trial guns.

GRAY, LEE Russellville, Kentucky, 1879d.

GRAY, LORIN Lincoln, Ohio, 1853d, Bennington, Ohio, 1860-1864d. (Hutslar)

GRAY, ROBERT (?-1725), Salem, Massachusetts, 1679. Son of Robert. (Dean*)

GRAY, SAMUEL Salem, Massachusetts, 1730. Son of Robert. (Dean*)

GRAY, THOMAS Point of Fork, Virginia, 1786-1798. (Gill)

GRAY, W. unlocated. Percussion 1/2 stock.

GRAY, W.H. Philadelphia, Pennsylvania, 1862-1863. Converted flintlock muskets.

GRAY. ROBERT Salem, Massachusetts, 1650. (Dean*)

GRAYDON, JAMES W. Washington, D.C. Patent #399,882 March 19, 1889, pneumatic gun.

GRAYSON unlocated. Flintlock Kentucky.

GREAT WESTERN GUN WORKS Pittsburgh, Pennsylvania, 1865-1923. J.H. Johnston, retailer and manufacturer of all types of guns.

GREAT WESTERN suicide special by Great Western Gun Works. (Webster)

GREATHOUSE, ELIAS (1802-?), New Hope, Illinois, 1850c. (Johnson)

GREATHOUSE, PERRY (1829-?), New Hope, Illinois, 1850c-1860c. (Johnson)

GREATHOUSE, TIMOTHY (1831-?), Wabash Co., Illinois, 1850c. (Johnson)

GREATHOUSE, WILLIAM (1821-?), New Hope, Illinois, 1860c. (Johnson)

GREBLES, ALFRED Chicago, Illinois, 1866d-1869d, Muskegan, Michigan, 1873d. Air gun.

GREEN & ALLING Rochester, New York, 1873-1874. Charles Green, shotguns. (Eich)

GREEN & CO. Monument, Illinois, 1860d.

GREEN Red Clay, Georgia, 1800. (Dean)

GREEN, A.A. unlocated. Agent for Hilliard.

GREEN, ANDREW J. Hadley, Michigan, 1863d-1867d.

GREEN, B. Mattison, Michigan, 1887d.

GREEN, BENJAMIN Placerville, California, 1878-1881. (Shelton)

GREEN, CHAPIN Ross Co., Ohio, 1855d. (Hutslar)

GREEN, CHARLES Rochester, New York, 1860-1892. Patents #109,890 December 6, 1870, breechloading firearm, and #170,669 December 7, 1875, breechloading firearm. Percussion and cartridge guns. As Green & Alling, 1873-1874. (Eich).

GREEN, ELISHA Smoky Mountains, Tennessee. Percussion fullstock rifle.

GREEN, G.W. Readsboro, Vermont, 1870-1879. (Horn)

GREEN, HENRY Hendersonville, Illinois, 1850c. (Johnson)

GREEN, JAMES Connecticut, 1775-1777. Committee of Safety muskets. (Gluckman & Satterlee)

GREEN, JAMES Harpers Ferry, Virginia, Patent #none, October 3, 1817, boring gun barrels.

GREEN, JOHN H. (1815-?), Momence, Illinois, 1860c-1864d. (Johnson)

GREEN, KINSEY Yazoo City, Mississippi, 1885d.

GREEN, O. S. Havana, Illinois, 1860c. (Johnson)

GREEN, RILEY (1808-?), Crawford Co., Pennsylvania, 1850c.

GREEN, SAMUEL Greenwood, Wisconsin, 1879d.

GREEN, SAMUEL Troy, New York, 1841-1843d. (Kauffman 2)

GREEN, SAUL Vassar, Michigan. Falling block rifle. As Barnes & Green, 1890.

GREEN, W.D. Holton, Kansas, 1894d.

GREEN, WILLIAM E. Chicago, Illinois, 1893d.

GREEN, WILLIAM F. Port Huron, Michigan, 1863d-1867d, Speaker, Michigan, 1872d-1877d.

GREEN, WILLIAM S. Forrest Home, Illinois, 1893d.

GREEN, WILLIAM Crawford Co., Pennsylvania, 1850c.

GREENAMYER, E.D. Coldwater, Michigan, 1895d.

GREENE RIFLE WORKS Millbury, Massachusetts. J.D. Greene's rifles.

GREENE RIFLE WORKS Worcester, Massachusetts, 1865-1867, James Warner carbines.

GREENE, G.W. New York, New York. Made Keil V. Barnekov patent rifles for 1872 trials.

GREENE, JAMES DURRELL (1828-1902), Cambridge, Massachusetts. Patents #10,391 January 3, 1854, breechloading firearm, #11,157 June 27, 1854, breechloading firearm, #11,917 November 7, 1854, breechloading firearm, #18,143 September 8, 1857, cartridge, #18,634 November 17, 1857, breechloading firearm, #34,422 February 18, 1862, breechloading firearm, #88,161 March 23, 1869, breechloading firearm, and #312,201, February 10, 1885, breechloading firearm. Guns under patents #11,157 and #34,422 produced for both U.S. and British service by Massachusetts Arms Co. (GR 11-71)

GREENE, LOT Fayette Co., Pennsylvania, 1817-1844. (Kauffman)

GREENE, S.A., & SON Grants Pass, Oregon, 1881d-1889d.

GREENEWALD, JOSEPH Belleville, Illinois, 1867d-1868d.

GREENFIELD trade name of Hibbard, Spencer, Bartlett & Co. on shotguns. (Hinman)

GREENLAND, E.M. unlocated. Percussion fullstock.

GREENOUGH, JOHN J. Washington, D.C. Patent #645,292 March 13, 1900, automatic.

GREENSTRED, Z. Humbolt, Missouri, 1860d.

GREENTREE, ALEXANDER Philadelphia, Pennsylvania, 1776. For Lewis Prahl.

GREENUP, F.M. Mexico, Missouri, 1893d.

GREENWOOD & GRAY Columbus, Georgia, 1862-1865. Rifles for the Confederacy (marked "J.P. Murray", who was superintendent of the factory). Greenwood and Gray were not gunsmiths, only financiers. (Gluckman & Satterlee)

GREENWOOD IRON WORKS Cincinnati, Ohio, 1832-1886. Also known as Eagle Foundry and Eagle Iron Works. Rifled muskets, Gatling guns, and cannon. Miles Greenwood. (Hutslar)

GREENWOOD, CRAWFORD Tyrell, Ohio, 1883d. (Hutslar)

GREENWOOD, MILES (1807-1885), Cincinnati, Ohio, 1832-1885. As Eagle Iron Works and Greenwood Iron Works. (Hutslar)

GREENWOOD, NATHANIEL C. (1810-?), Vienna, Ohio, 1850c. (Hutslar)

GREER see Willey & Greer.

GREER, DAVID unlocated. Flintlock Kentucky pistol.

GREER, JAMES Philadelphia, Pennsylvania. Patent #none circa 1812, screw auger for boring pistol barrels. Flintlock pistols. A similar patent was subsequently obtained by Daniel Pettibone; resulting in a lawsuit between Greer and Pettibone which continued until the Civil War. (Boehret)

GREER, JOHN WILLIAM Austin, Texas. Patent #431,515 July 1, 1890, machine gun.

GREGG, D.S. Medicine Lodge, Kansas, 1888d.

GREGG, HAYDEN & CO. Charleston, South Carolina, 1835-1850. Importers.

GREGG, J. unlocated. Flintlock Kentucky pistol (possibly J. Gregory?).

GREGG, MYRON E. Washington, D.C. Patents #353,676 December 1, 1886, magazine gun, #374,597 December 13, 1887, magazine gun, #376,302 January 10, 1888, projectile, #386,245 July 17, 1888, magazine gun, and #430,799 June 24, 1890, magazine gun.

GREGOR, WILLIAM New York, New York, 1871d-1880d.

GREGORY, CHARLES P. Mount Vernon, Ohio, 1837-1876. Percussion rifles. (Hutslar)

GREGORY, CHARLTON M. Warren, Illinois. Patent #158,004 December 22, 1874, magazine gun with Peter Sheckler.

GREGORY, H. Bridgeman, Michigan, 1875d.

GREGORY, HENRY W. Amherst, Virginia, 1897d.

GREGORY, J. unlocated. Flintlock Kentucky pistol.

GREGORY, J.L. Peekskill, New York, 1849-1870d.

GREGORY, JAMES, JR. New York, New York, 1889-1890. Yacht cannon.

GREGORY, RICHARD Boston, Massachusetts, 1727.

GREINER, WILLIAM Hagerstown, Maryland, 1812, Franklin Co., Pennsylvania, 1814t-1846t. Apprenticed to George Kreps in 1802, took over the shop in 1812. (Bowers)

GRELL Logansport, Indiana. Percussion target rifle. (Lindert)

GRENINGER, THOMAS Booneville, Pennsylvania, 1890d.

GRESHEIM Lancaster, Pennsylvania, 1783. Flintlock Kentucky. (Dillin)

GRESS, GEORGE Easton, Pennsylvania, 1820t. (KRA II-3)

GRESS, JOHN Easton, Pennsylvania, 1820t. (KRA II-3)

GRETH, AUGUST San Francisco, California. Patent #378,091 February 21, 1888, revolving rifle.

GRETTON, GEORGE Virginia, 1774. (Gill)

GREYER, W. New York, New York. Air gun. (Wolff)

GRICE, J.P. Verona Mills, Michigan, 1887d.

GRICE, WILLIAM M. Lexington, Michigan, 1867d-1871, 1883d-1887d, Lapeer, Michigan, 1873d-1879d.

GRICE, WILLIAM, & CO. New York, New York, 1859-1860. Agents for Sharps revolvers. (Sellers-4)

GRIDNER, CHARLES St. Louis, Missouri, 1860d.

GRIEP, H.C. Freemont, Nebraska, 1893d.

GRIER, J.Y. Liberty Hill, Texas, 1884d.

GRIESLING, ALBERT Carroll, Iowa, 1895d-1897d.

GRIFFIN & ALBRIGHT Paris, Texas, 1885.

GRIFFIN, C.B. Dallas, Texas, 1878d.

GRIFFIN, CHARLES R. Bainbridge, Georgia, 1881d.

GRIFFIN, DANIEL Platteville, Wisconsin, 1884d-1889d.

GRIFFIN, LUKE Virginia, 1776. Committee of Safety repairs. (Gill)

GRIFFIN, PATRICK (1835-?), Connersville, Indiana, 1860c. (Lindert)

GRIFFIN, RICHARD Boston, Massachusetts, 1689. Flintlock rifle. (Dean)

GRIFFIN, T.B. Mitchell, South Dakota, 1884d-1886d.

GRIFFIN, T.B. Three Rivers, Michigan, 1899d.

GRIFFIN, W.C. Paris, Texas, 1884d-1885d, Ladonia, Texas, 1896d. As Griffin & Albright, 1885.

GRIFFITH & SEMPLE Louisville, Kentucky. Dealers after 1880.

GRIFFITH & TURNER Philadelphia, Pennsylvania, 1824d. John and Joseph Griffith. (Dean)

GRIFFITH, D.M. Washington, D.C., 1885d.

GRIFFITH, HENRY Maryland, 1776. Committee of Safety muskets. (Hartzler)

GRIFFITH, JOHN Philadelphia, Pennsylvania, 1824d. As Griffith & Turner. (Dean)

GRIFFITH, JOSEPH H. Louisville, Kentucky, 1843d-1878d. Locks and derringers. As Joseph Griffith & Son, 1874-1878.

GRIFFITH, JOSEPH Philadelphia, Pennsylvania, 1816d-1823d. Same address as John Griffith.

GRIFFITH, JOSEPH see Griffith & Turner.

GRIFFITH, KINZEY Alexandria, Virginia, 1831-1888d. Percussion rifles and pistols. (Hartzler)

GRIFFITH, R.C. Mineral Springs, Arkansas, 1885d.

GRIFFITH, SEMPLE & MILLS Louisville, Kentucky, 1890-1896d. Joseph H. Griffith(?), A.B. Semple(?), and Charles Mills.

GRIFFITHS & SIEBERT Cincinnati, Ohio, 1852-1854. John A. Griffiths and Henry L. Siebert. (Hutslar)

GRIFFITHS, CHARLES Little Rock, Arkansas, 1866. (Elias)

GRIFFITHS, HENRY Little Rock, Arkansas, 1838-1865. Percussion fullstock. (Elias)

GRIFFITHS, JOHN A. Cincinnati, Ohio, 1834-1866. Percussion 1/2 stock rifle and double-barrel shotgun. As Griffiths & Siebert, 1852-1854. (Hutslar)

GRIFFITHS, JOSEPH Tyler, Texas, 1864. At Tyler Arsenal. (Albaugh 2)

GRIFFITHS, SAMUEL (1808-?), Xenia, Illinois, 1847-1860. (Johnson)

GRIFFITHS, WILLIAM Philadelphia, Pennsylvania, 1860c. Percussion rifles and pistols.

GRIGGS, GEORGE E. Brooklyn, Connecticut, 1889d.

GRIGGS, J.L. Ft. Madison, Iowa, 1865d-1884d.

GRIGGS, PERRY Agency City, Iowa, 1865d.

GRIGGS, SETH E. Wapello Co., Iowa, 1850c. (MB 8-64)

GRILLET, ALEXANDER Philadelphia, Pennsylvania. Patent #45,152 November 22, 1864, breechloading firearm.

GRILLEY, WILLIAM Waterbury, Connecticut. See Jeremiah Peck.

GRIM, C.S. & L.S. Galion, Ohio, 1859d. (Hutslar)

GRIMES, A.E. Norwich, Connecticut. Percussion pistol.

GRIMES, ABEL (1829-?), Marion Co., Ohio, 1850c. (Hutslar)

GRIMES, ALVAH E. Norwich, Connecticut. Patent #619,565 February 14, 1899, ejector.

GRIMES, DANIEL Sheridan, Pennsylvania, 1850d-1887d, Newmanstown, Pennsylvania, 1887d-1890d. Rifle barrels. Sometimes listed as David Grimes.

GRIMES, JACOB (1819-?), Marion Co., Ohio, 1850c. (Hutslar)

GRIMES, JACOB Hutchinson, Kansas, 1894d.

GRIMES, JOHN Gainesville, Texas, 1885d-1890d.

GRIMM & STARKE Chicago, Illinois, 1872-1875d. Rudolph Grimm and William Starke.

GRIMM, FREDERICK Lancaster, Pennsylvania, 1857d.

GRIMM, JACOB Adamsburg, Pennsylvania, 1829. (Whisker III)

GRIMM, PHILIP Lake City, Iowa, 1884d.

GRIMM, RUDOLPH Chicago, Illinois, 1872d-1903d. Shotguns. As Grimm & Starke, 1872-1875.

GRIMMEL, JOHN Wheeling, West Virginia, 1867. (MB 9-60)

GRIMSLEY, A. Livingston and Overton, Tennessee, 1860d.

GRISEMAUER, C. St. Charles, Missouri, 1860d.

GRISHAM, JAMES M. Towash, Texas. Patent #152,990 July 14, 1874, lock.

GRISSOM, TIMOTHY M. (1827-?), Stokes Co., North Carolina. Apprenticed 1837. (Bivins)

GRISWOLD & GRIER alternate business name for Griswold & Gunnison. Samuel Griswold and E.T. Grier.

GRISWOLD & GUNNISON Griswoldville, Georgia, 1861-1864. Percussion revolvers for the Confederacy. Samuel Griswold and A.W. Gunnison. Also known as Griswold & Grier. (Albaugh 3)

GRISWOLD, ARTHUR B. New Orleans, Louisiana, 1845d-1870d. With Hyde & Goodrich, 1845-1860 and A.B. Griswold & Co., 1861-1870.

GRISWOLD, J. Hamburg, Iowa, 1865d.

GRISWOLD, JESSE Chambers Co., Alabama. Patent #1,938 February 1, 1842, barrels.

GRISWOLD, JOHN D. Avoca, New York, 1874d-1891d.

GRISWOLD, L.D. Avoca, New York, 1882d.

GRISWOLD, W.P. Maumee City, Ohio, 1859d. (Hutslar)

GROCE, H. unlocated. Percussion over/under rifle.

GROFF, B.C. Delaware City, Delaware, 1822d.

GROFF, H.D unlocated. Percussion fullstock.

GROFF, H.S. Fairmount, Pennsylvania. Flintlock and percussion rifles.

GROFF, H.W. unlocated. Flintlock Kentucky.

GROFF, HENRY C. (1818-?), Wayne Co., Ohio, 1850c. Percussion 1/2 stock. (Hutslar)

GROFF, HENRY Berks Co., Pennsylvania, 1767.

GROFF, HENRY Lancaster Co., Pennsylvania, 1847t. (Dyke)

GROFF, JOHN Lancaster, Pennsylvania, 1790-1793. Model 1792 contract rifles with Jacob Dickert and Peter Gonter, and flintlock Kentucky rifles.

GROFF, JOHN Lancaster, Pennsylvania, 1847t. (KRA IV-4)

GROGEN, SAMUEL Columbus, Kentucky, 1883d.

GROHNWALD, C.E. Richmond, Virginia, 1857-1859. (Albaugh 1)

GRONER, H.L. Jamestown, North Carolina. Percussion 1/2 stock. (Bivins)

GROOMES, BENJAMIN Carmichael's, Pennsylvania. Patent #14,017 January 1, 1856, repeating firearm.

GROOMS, LIGE Peebles, Ohio, 1890-1900. Percussion 1/2 stock. (Hutslar)

GROOMS, WILLIAM (1874-?), Pebbles, Ohio, 1890-?. (Hutslar)

GROOT, HENRY Pittsfield, Massachusetts, 1849d-1868d, Minneapolis, Minnesota, 1869-1872d. Shotguns.

GROPLEY, EDWARD (1829-?), Washington, D.C., 1850c. For John Weaver. (Hartzler)

GROSBERND, EDWARD Chicago, Illinois, 1894d.

GROSS ARMS CO. Tiffin, Ohio, 1849-1875. Rifles, pistols, revolvers, and muzzle loaders under Henry Gross' patents. Henry and Charles B. Gross. (AR 12-65)

GROSS, A.P.M. Sedalia, Missouri, 1898d.

GROSS, ALFRED FARRINGTON Sullivan Co., Tennessee. Flintlock Kentucky. (Hale)

GROSS, ARLEN (1835-?), Havana, Illinois, 1860c. (Johnson)

GROSS, CHARLES, B. (1810-?), Tiffin, Ohio, 1849-1870, Bowling Green, Ohio, 1872. With Gross Arms Co., 1849-1870. (Hutslar)

GROSS, GUSTAVE Chicago, Illinois, 1871-1888d.

GROSS, HENRY G. Union Co., Pennsylvania, 1820, Tiffin, Ohio, 1831-1842. Underhammer rifle. (Hutslar)

GROSS, HENRY, JR. (1813-1875), Tiffin, Ohio, 1841-1875. Patents #12,906 May 22, 1855, breechloading firearm, #15,072 June 10, 1856, breechloading firearm, #25,259 August 30, 1859, breechloading firearm, #33,836 December 3, 1861, revolver, #39,479 August 11, 1863, breechloading firearm, #39,645 August 25, 1863, revolver, #39,646, August 25, 1863, breechloading firearm, and #42,941 May 31, 1864, breechloading firearm. Operated as Gross Arms Co., 1849-1875. Gross carbines made by Gwyn & Campbell. (AR 12-65)

GROSS, J.R. Jonesborough, Arkansas, 1888d-1898d.

GROSS, JACOB (1797-?), Sullivan Co., Tennessee. Flintlock Tennessee. (ASAC 23)

GROSS, PHILLIPS H. (1817-?), Rutherford Co., North Carolina, 1850c. (Bivins)

GROSS, SAMUEL (1810-1886), Tiffin, Ohio, 1831-1838, Bloomville, Ohio, 1838-1886. Son of Henry Gross. (Hutslar)

GROSS, WILLIAM Burlington, Iowa, 1850c. (MB 8-64)

GROSZ, F.H. Albany, New York, 1861. Altered Model 1841 rifles for the state of New York.

GROTH, WILLIAM Appleton, Wisconsin, 1888d-1895d.

GROTJAN, J.A. Moberly, Missouri, 1898d.

GROTZ, SIGMUND Duquesne, Pennsylvania, 1860d-1864d, Rochester, Pennsylvania, 1887d. See Ziegmund Krotz, also listed as Edmund Krotz.

GROULEFF, ALBERT Grayling, Michigan. Patent #447,410 June 21, 1892, breechloading firearm with H.B. Williams.

GROUT, HENRY Pittsfield, Massachusetts, 1866-1868. (Lindsay)

GROUT, K.S. Ft. Collins, Colorado, 1883d. (Sellers-3)

GROVE, J. Hagerstown, Maryland. Flintlock Kentucky. (Hartzler)

GROVE, JOHN Greene Co., Pennsylvania, 1807-1808. Same as J. Grove, Hagerstown, Maryland?

GROVE, L. Lancaster, Pennsylvania, 1815-1835. Flintlock Kentucky rifles. (Gluckman & Satterlee)

GROVE, SAMUEL (?-1822), Lewisberry, Pennsylvania, 1767-1822. Flintlock Kentucky. (Kindig)

GROVE, SAMUEL, JR. (1782-1834), Lewisberry, Pennsylvania, ?-1834. Flintlock Kentucky. (Kindig)

GROVELL, J.C. Wheatland, Iowa, 1882d-1889d.

GROVER & LONG Augusta, Maine, 1871-1875. Malcolm W. Long. (Demeritt)

GROVER & LOVELL Boston, Massachusetts, 1841-1844. Flintlock musket. Leonard Grover and J.P. Lovell. (Demeritt).

GROVER, C.W. Bremen, Maine, 1877. (Demeritt)

GROVER, SIMON Showhegan, Maine, 1896-1898. (Demeritt)

GROVES, A.B. Mitchell, Tennessee, 1891d.

GROVES, ISAAC Chillicothe, Ohio, 1804-1817, Bidwell, Ohio, 1820. (Hutslar)

GROVES, O. Spencerville, Ohio, 1875d. (Hutslar)

GRUBB, DANIEL Meadville, Pennsylvania, 1824. (Whisker II)

GRUBB, GEORGE New York, New York. Percussion shotgun.

GRUBB, JOSEPH C. Philadelphia, Pennsylvania, 1839d-1886d. Retailer whose name was put on many guns.

GRUBB, O.A. Lenoir, North Carolina. Percussion 1/2 stock. (Bivins)

GRUBB, PETER Lancaster, Pennsylvania, 1775.

GRUBB, T. Philadelphia, Pennsylvania, 1822d. Flintlock pistols.

GRUBB, TOBIAS (1792-1872), Allentown, Pennsylvania, 1813-1872. Flintlock Kentucky. (Kauffman 2)

GRUDCHOS & EGGERS New Bedford, Massachusetts, 1854-1860. Whaling guns and percussion target guns. Patent #17,370 May 26, 1857, bomb lance. Julius Grudchos and Selmar Eggers.

GRUDCHOS, JULIUS New Bedford, Massachusetts, 1850-1860. Patent #17,370 May 26, 1857, bomb lance with Selmar Eggers. See Grudchos and Eggers.

GRUEBY, GEORGE H. Portland, Maine, 1844-1850. (Dcmeritt).

GRUENWALD, FRANK W. Belleville, Illinois, 1884. (Johnson)

GRUENWALD, JOSEPH Belleville, Illinois, 1864d-1880d.

GRULER, JOSEPH Norwich, Connecticut. Patent #26,641, December 27, 1859, revolver with Augustus Rebety. Gruler and Rebety were engineers in charge of the Manhattan Fire Arms Co. plant. (Nutter)

GRUNDER, FLORENTIN San Antonio, Texas, 1879d-1892d.

GRUNIGAL, FREDERICK Allegheny, Pennsylvania, 1858-1859. (Kauffman)

GRUP, PHILIP Northampton Co., Pennsylvania, 1792t. (Dyke)

GRYMES, WILLIAM Botetourt Co., Virginia, 1770. (Gill)

GUARDIAN suicide special by Bacon.

GUARINO, FRANK New Orleans, Louisiana, 1885d.

GUENTER, H. Racine, Wisconsin, 1870-1875.

GUENTHER, HERMAN San Diego, California, 1889-1893d. (Shelton)

GUENTZEL, AUGUST Golconda, Illinois, 1886d-1888d.

GUESE, ALBERT Wapakoneta, Ohio, 1896d. (Hutslar)

GUEST, J. unlocated. Percussion fullstock.

GUEST, JOHN Lancaster, Pennsylvania, 1802-1809. Model 1808 contract rifles and pistols, flintlock Kentucky. (Gluckman)

GUGER, JAMES R. Muncy, Pennsylvania, 1861d. See James Guyer.

GUGER, P. Murray, Pennsylvania. Flintlock Kentucky. (Di!lin)

GUIGNARD see Radcliffe & Guignard, and Thomas W. Radcliffe.

GUILBERT, SIVE New York, New York. Patent #44,303 September 20, 1864, sword revolver. (Sellers-1)

GUILD, G.S. Amenia, New York, 1874d.

GUILD, H.M. Springfield, Massachusetts, 1872d.

GUILLAM, BENJAMIN Massachusetts. Committee of Safety muskets. (Gluchman & Satterlee)

GUIN, JAMES Richland Co., Ohio, 1820c. (Knittle)

GUIN, JOHN Huron Co., Ohio, 1820c. (Knittle)

GUINTHER, HERMAN Wichita, Kansas, 1884d.

GUINZURG, FRANK DuBois, Pennsylvania, 1887d-1890d.

GUION, JAMES P. Lycoming Co., Pennsylvania, 1860c.

GUION, THOMAS F. New Orleans, Louisiana, 1838d-1861d. Retailer and importer. Percussion guns.

GULLETT, A. Northampton, Illinois, 1860d.

GULLICK, HENRY Jeffersonville, Iowa, 1865d.

GULLIVER FREDERICK Cleveland, Ohio, 1845-1847. (Kauffman 2)

GULLIVER, W. (1824-?), Chicago, Illinois, 1850c. (Johnson)

GUMP, A.A. Dayton, Ohio, 1874-1891. Dealers. (Hutslar)

GUMP, JONATHAN (1823-?), Plymouth, Ohio, 1843-1850c, Upper Sandusky, Ohio, 1850-1884. Percussion 1/2 stock. (Hutslar)

GUMPF, ANDREW J. Lancaster, Pennsylvania, 1869d-1894d. Son of Andrew Gumpf.

GUMPF, ANDREW Lancaster, Pennsylvania, 1843-1875d. Flintlock Kentucky. (Kauffman 2)

GUMPF, CHRISTIAN Lancaster, Pennsylvania, 1802-1843. Model 1809 contract rifles. (Kauffman)

GUMPF, CHRISTOPHER (1761-?), Lancaster, Pennsylvania, 1791-1820. 100 rifles for U.S. government in 1794, flintlock Kentucky. (Kauffman)

GUMPF, GEORGE Lancaster, Pennsylvania, 1825t-1849t. (Dyke)

GUMPF, HENRY Lancaster, Pennsylvania, 1820d-1843d. (Kauffman 2)

GUMPF, JACOB Lancaster, Pennsylvania, 1820-1843d. Flintlock Kentucky. (Kauffman 2)

GUMPF, JAMES (?-1887), Lancaster, Pennsylvania, 1814-1887. Flintlock Kentucky. (Di!lin)

GUMPF, JOHN Lancaster, Pennsylvania, 1819. (Kauffman 2)

GUMPF, MATHIAS Lancaster, Pennsylvania, 1789-1793. (Dyke)

GUMPF, MATHIAS Lancaster, Pennsylvania, 1843d-1857d. (Kauffman 2)

GUMPF, MICHAEL Lancaster, Pennsylvania, 1843d. (Kauffman 2)

GUMPH, STOPHEL Lancaster, Pennsylvania, 1793. (Kauffman)

GUMSTER, HIRAM Syracuse, New York, 1853-1855. (Kauffman 2)

GUNCKLE, JOHN D. Germantown, Ohio, 1860c. (Gardner)

GUNDERSON, G. Chicago, Illinois. Patent #145,998 December 30, 1873, breechloading firearm.

GUNDERSON, G.K. Sioux Falls, South Dakota, 1882d-1892d.

GUNKLE, H. unlocated. Percussion 1/2 stock.

GUNKLE, JOHN D. Germantown, Ohio, 1859d-1860c. (Hutslar)

GUNN, EDWIN F. Charlestown, South Carolina. Patents #68,736 September 10, 1867, breechloading firearm, and #85,442 December 29, 1868, breechloading firearm.

GUNN, GEORGE P. Herkimer, New York. Patents #337,395 March 9, 1886, air gun, #421,492 February 18, 1891, breechloading gun, and #541,085 June 18, 1895, air gun. With Haviland & Gunn, Quackenbush, and Atlas Gun Co.

GUNN, WILLIAM (?-1813), Charlestown, South Carolina, 1790-1811. (Kauffman 2)

GUNTEMAN, JOSEPH (1821-?), St. Louis, Missouri, 1850c. (Lewis)

GUNTEMAN, WILLIAM (1823-?), St. Louis, Missouri, 1850c. (Lewis)

GUNTER, A. New Orleans, Louisiana, 1867d.

GUNTER, PETER Franklin Co., Pennsylvania, 1813t-1837. Flintlock Kentucky rifle. (Bowers)

GUPTILL, R.P. Harrington, Maine, 1876-1879.

GURGAN, L.C. Terre Haute, Indiana, 1860d.

GURN, A. unlocated. Flintlock Kentucky rifle.

GUSTLE, METZ (1826-?), Marion, Ohio, 1850c. (Hutslar)

GUSTON unlocated. Percussion 1/2 stock.

GUT BUSTER suicide special.

GUTH, ADAM Brooklyn, New York, 1883d-1890d.

GUTHRIE, HUGH Leesville, Indiana, circa 1820. (Lindert)

GUTHRIE, SAMUEL Sackett's Harbor, New York. Patent #none August 21, 1834, pellet priming.

GUTTMAN, CHRISTIAN Havelock, Iowa, 1895d-1897d.

GUYER, CLINTON Muncy, Pennsylvania, 1875d-1890d. Patent #226,744 April 20, 1880, breechloading firearm. Son of J.P. Guyer.

GUYER, J.P. Muncy, Pennsylvania, 1867d-1882d. As J.P. Guyer & Son 1875-1882. Percussion rifles. See James Guger.

GWALTNEY, P.D. & CO. Norfolk, Virginia. Percussion 1/2 stock.

GWEETIES, CHARLES (1828-?), Washington, D.C., 1850c. For John Weaver. (Hartzler)

GWIMER, J.F. Ann Arbor, Michigan, 1865d.

GWIN & ELLSBERRY Cahaba, Alabama. Derringer. (Eberhart)

GWINN, ALEXANDER Juniata Co., Pennsylvania. Flintlock Kentucky rifle.

GWYN & CAMPBELL Hamilton, Ohio, 1861-1866. Patent #36,709 October 21, 1862, breechloading firearm. Made Gross patent and Gwyn & Campbell patent carbines, Edward Gwyn and Abner C. Campbell.

GYDE, HENRY (1813-?), Locust Point, Ohio, 1881-1886. (Hutslar)

GYPSY suicide special.

H SECTION

H & P see Hewes & Phillips.

H. & S. Co. see Hibbard & Spencer Co.

⊬. see J.B. Hixon.

H.B. see Henry Bruner.

H.C.M. unidentified. Percussion 1/2 stock.

H.D. unidentified. Percussion fullstock.

H.E. unidentified. Flintlock Kentucky.

H.G. see Henry Gilmore.

H.G. see Henry Griffiths.

H.H. unidentified. Flintlock Kentucky.

H.K. see Henry Kolb.

H.L. unidentified. Percussion fullstock.

H.L.B. unidentified. Percussion 1/2 stock.

H.M.C. & Co. unidentified. Flintlock Kentucky.

H.P.H. unidentified. Flintlock Kentucky rifle.

H.P.M. see Henry Mull.

H.S. see Henry Savory.

H.S. unidentified. Flintlock Kentucky rifle.

H.S.B. & Co. see Hibbard, Spencer, Bartlett, & Co.

H.S.F. unidentified. Percussion fullstock.

H.T. unidentified. Flintlock Kentucky rifle.

H.V.C. see Henry Clouse.

HAAG, CHRISTOPHER Pomeroy, Ohio, 1849-1868d. Percussion 1/2 stock. (Hutslar)

HAAG, GEORGE Evansville, Indiana, 1867d.

HAAS, C. Holden, Missouri, 1879d.

HAAS, GEORGE Berks Co., Pennsylvania, 1790. Flintlock rifles. (Dillin)

HAAS, JOHN A. Port Costa, California. Patent #363,955 May 31, 1887, shell crimper. (Shelton)

HAAS, NICHOLAS Philadelphia, Pennsylvania, 1837d-1847d.

HABERSTRO, JOSEPH Buffalo, New York, 1832-1844. (Swinney)

HABERSTROH, LAMBERT (1808-?), Fremont, Ohio, 1850-1869. (Hutslar)

HACKER, CHARLES F. Parsons, Kansas. Patent #493,084 March 7, 1893, breechloading firearm.

HACKETT, EDWIN New York, New York, 1877. Breechloading shotgun. (Hinman)

HACKETT, GOLDSBERRY Norfolk, Virginia, 1775-1776, Williamsburg, Virginia, 1776-1779. (Gill)

HACKETT, JOHN Virginia, 1776. Committee of Safety repairs. (Gill)

HACKMAN, H.H. (1847-1897), Vincennes, Indiana. Percussion 1/2 stock. Hardware dealer. (Lindert)

HACKNEY & SCHNEIDER Dayton, Ohio, 1858-1860 and 1879-1882. William Hackney and Charles E. Schneider. (Hutslar)

HACKNEY, WILLIAM W. Dayton, Ohio, 1856-1900. Percussion rifles. With Hackney & Schneider, 1858-1860 and 1879-1882. (Hutslar)

HACQUARD & SPRY Portsmouth, Ohio. Eugene Hacquard and Richard Spry. (Hutslar)

HACQUARD, CHARLES Portsmouth, Ohio, 1887d. (Hutslar)

HACQUARD, EUGENE Portsmouth, Ohio, 1858-1896. Percussion fullstock. (Hutslar)

HACQUARD, H.D. Portsmouth, Ohio, 1880. Percussion fullstock. (MB 3-65)

HADDEN, JAMES Philadelphia, Pennsylvania, 1769. (Kauffman)

HADE, WILLIAM (1817-?), Lithopolis, Ohio, 1850c. (Hutslar)

HADEN, THOMAS J. (1820-?), Harrodsburg, Kentucky, 1860c. For Benjamin Mills. Also R&S revolver marked "T.J. Haden Utica NY".

HADLEY & DAVIS Blue Earth, Minnesota, 1878-1881.

HADLEY, DANA G. Bethlehem, Pennsylvania. Patent #161,117 March 23, 1875, safety.

HADLEY, EZEKIEL H. Bradford, New Hampshire, 1887-1880.

HADLEY, GEORGE W. Chicopee Falls, Massachusetts. Patents #172,456 January 18, 1876, sight with William McFarland, #232,816 October 5, 1880, breechloading firearm, #275,377 April 10, 1883, breechloading firearm, and #362,956 May 17, 1887, breechloading firearm.

HADSTATE, HIRAM Birch Run, Michigan, 1863d.

HAEFELIN, JACOB West Point, Nebraska, 1886d.

HAEFFER, JACOB Lancaster, Pennsylvania, 1774-1821. Model 1798 contract muskets for Pennsylvania, Kentucky rifles. (Kindig)

HAEFFER, JACOB, JR. Lancaster, Pennsylvania, 1800. For Peter Brong. (Kauffman)

HAEFFER, JOHN Lancaster, Pennsylvania, 1803. With Jacob Haeffer. (Kindig)

HAEFFER, P. B. unlocated. Flintlock Kentucky rifle.

HAEGEN, E. Chicago, Illinois, 1881d.

HAENIG, BERNHARDT Marshall, Illinois, 1878d-1888d.

HAENY, SAMUEL Bushkill, Pennsylvania, 1823t. (Gabel)

HAFER, JOHN Pittsburgh, Pennsylvania, 1819. (Kauffman)

HAFFNER, JACOB (?-1827), Frederick, Maryland. Flintlock Kentucky. (Hartzler)

HAFORD, W. Amelia, Ohio, 1859d. (Hutslar)

HAFUSGER, W.M. unlocated. Percussion 1/2 stock.

HAGA, JESSE Clinton Co., Ohio, 1850-1854. (Hutslar)

HAGA, JOHN Lancaster Co., Pennsylvania, 1800-1809. Flintlock Kentucky. (Kindig)

HAGA, WOLFGANG (1716-1796), Reading, Pennsylvania, 1758-1796. (Kindig)

HAGADORN & COLE Detroit, Michigan, 1870d-1875d. Abraham Hagadorn and William Cole.

HAGADORN, ABRAHAM M. Ypsilanti, Michigan, 1865d-1869, Detroit, Michigan, 1870d-1887d. Percussion double rifle/shotgun. As Wicker & Hagadorn, 1865-1869, and Hagadorn & Cole, 1870-1875. Listed alone in 1869 Detroit directory.

HAGADORN, J.L. Detroit, Michigan, 1887d. Son of A.M. Hagadorn.

HAGAR, GEORGE I. Burlington, Vermont, 1870-1876.

HAGAR, J.S. St. Joseph, Michigan, 1863d.

HAGARD, THOMAS (1825-?), Pekin, Illinois, 1860c. (Johnson)

HAGE, WILLIAM Camden, New Jersey, 1878d.

HAGER, JONATHAN (1719-1795), Hagerstown, Maryland, 1740. Flintlock Kentucky. (Hartzler)

HAGERMAN, JAMES Philadelphia, Pennsylvania, 1824d.

HAGEY, J. unlocated. Flintlock Kentucky, probably John Hagy.

HAGGARD Oxford Mills, Iowa, 1889d. As Carlton & Haggard.

HAGGARD, THOMAS (1833-?). Canton, Illinois, 1854d-1893d.

HAGGARD, THOMAS Peoria, Illinois, 1856d-1857d. Same as Thomas Haggard, Canton?

HAGGENMILLER & SNYDER Philadelphia, Pennsylvania, 1862-1863. Converted flintlock muskets.

HAGUE, I.F. Salt Lake City, Utah, 1867-1876.

HAGUE, JAMES (1823-?), St. Louis, Missouri, 1850c-1852d. As Daft & Hague, 1852.

HAGUE, JAMES Salt Lake City, Utah, 1867d-1871d.

HAGY Lancaster, Pennsylvania, 1800-1806. Flintlock Kentucky. (Kauffman)

HAGY, JOHN Bay City. Michigan, 1859-1873d. Percussion 1/2 stock.

HAGY, S. unlocated. Flintlock Kentucky.

HAHN, F. Chicago, Illinois, 1859d.

HAHN, GEORGE A. Baltimore, Maryland, 1867-1880d. (Hartzler)

HAHN, GEORGE (1804-1864), Zanesville, Ohio, 1818-1864. (Knittle)

HAHN, HENRY Zanesville, Ohio, 1804. (Knittle)

HAHN, JOHN Warrensborough, Pennsylvania, 1860d-1882d. Percussion 1/2 stock.

HAHN, SAMUEL Winchester, Illinois, 1864d-1878d.

HAHN, WILLIAM New York, New York, 1858d-1889d. Percussion rifles and pistols.

HAIGHT, GEORGE Casscoe, Arkansas, 1888d-1892d. Percussion 1/2 stock.

HAIGHT, JABEZ Buffalo, New York, 1835d. For P. Smith. (Dean)

HAIGHT, JOHN Ionia, Michigan, 1895d-1899d.

HAILER, L. Washington, D.C. Patent #105,799 July 26, 1870, lock.

HAIMAN, LOUIS (1830-?), Columbus, Georgia, 1861-1865. As Columbus Fire Arms Mfg. Co. with his brother, Elias. (Albaugh 3)

HAIMANN, HERMAN (1818-?), Galena, Illinois, 1860c. (Johnson)

HAIMES, WILLIAM Harvey Towne, Maryland, 1688. (Hartzler)

HAIN, P.L. unlocated. Flintlock Kentucky.

HAINES, AMOS A. Belgrade, Montana. Patent #469,561 February 23, 1892, breechloading firearm.

HAINES, FRANCIS (?-1717), Marblehead, Massachusetts.

HAINES, GEORGE Avilla, Indiana, 1860d-1862d.

HAINES, GEORGE Snyder Co., Pennsylvania. Flintlock Kentucky rifles. (Gabel)

HAINES, ISAAC Lancaster, Pennsylvania, 1772-1792. Flintlock Kentucky rifle. (Kauffman)

HAINES, J. unlocated. Flintlock Kentucky.

HAINES, J., JR. Pekin, Illinois, 1880d.

HAINES, W.T. Chillicothe, Ohio, 1845-1860. Percussion rifles. (MB 12-51)

HAINRICH, DE GUFF (?-1799), Lancaster Co., Pennsylvania. (Whisker III)

HAKE, L. Frederick, Ohio, 1859d. Percussion fullstock rifle. (Hutslar)

HAKES, HENRY (1831-?), Bucyrus, Ohio, 1850c. Apprenticed to J.M. McClure. (Hutslar)

HALBACH & SONS Baltimore, Maryland, 1780-1790(?). Flintlock pistols. See Charles Halbach.

HALBACH, CHARLES (1810-?), Baltimore, Maryland, 1835d-1850c. Imported flintlock pistols. (Hartzler)

HALBURN, CASPAR Lancaster, Pennsylvania, 1775-1777. Committee of Safety repairs, worked for William Henry after 1777. (Hobbies 4-38)

HALDEMAN, DANIEL Union, Pennsylvania, 1840-1850, Morgantown, Virginia. Patent #12,351 February 6, 1855, alarm gun. Percussion fullstock. (Dean)

HALDEMAN, F. (?-1887), Heidelberg, Pennsylvania. Flintlock pistol. (Gluckman & Satterlee)

HALDEMAN, JOSEPH (1818-?), Fayette Co, Pennsylvania, 1839-1841, Reedsville, West Virginia, 1850-1860, Clinton, West Virginia, 1880c.

HALDEMAN, PETER S. (1832-1887), Fayette Co., Pennsylvania, 1872d-1887. Same as F. Haldeman? (Whisker II)

HALDEN, R. San Saba, Texas, 1878d-1892d. (Holden in 1878d)

HALE & HODSON New York, New York, 1860d-1861d.

HALE & TULLER Hartford, Connecticut. Underhammer pistol. (Logan)

HALE, H.J. Bristol, Connecticut, 1840-1852. Underhammer pistol. (Logan)

HALE, J.H. Worcester, Massachusetts. Underhammer pistol.

HALE, JOHN Occoquan, Virginia. Percussion revolving rifle.

HALE, LILUCIUS (1829-?), Wauconda, Illinois, 1850c. (Johnson)

HALE, MATHIAS Philadelphia, Pennsylvania, 1819d.

HALE, MICHAEL (1820-?), Chandlerville, Ohio, 1850-1898. (Hutslar)

HALE, S.A.J. Midland, Michigan, 1872d-1899d.

HALEY, A.W. unlocated. Percussion fullstock.

HALF BREED suicide special. (Webster)

HALIFAX MANUFACTORY Halifax, North Carolina, 1776-1778. Public gun factory operated by James Ransome. (Bivins)

HALL & COOK New Orleans, Louisiana, 1881d-1882d. Louis Hall and Louis Cook.

HALL & HODGSON New York, New York, 1858d. See Hale & Hodgson.

HALL & MOSES unlocated. Lock makers only. See also Moses & Hall, same persons?

HALL, A. Lyons, Ohio, 1882d. (Hutslar)

HALL, ALBERT Danville, Illinois. Patents #37,961 March 24, 1863, revolver, and #39,915 September 15, 1863, cartridge. (Sellers-1)

HALL, ALEXANDER New York, New York, 1854-1873. Patents #15,110 June 10, 1856, revolver, #37,961 March 24, 1863, pistol, and #138,751 May 13, 1873, powder flask. Made revolving rifles under his patent. (Sellers-1)

HALL, C.T. East Dayton, Michigan, 1863d.

HALL, CHARLES (?-1887), Lancaster, Pennsylvania, 1873-1880. (Dean)

HALL, CHARLES, JR. (1872-1927), Oquaga Lake, New York, 1893-1897, McClure, New York, 1897-1927. Percussion 1/2 stock. (Gardner)

HALL, DANIEL Richland Co., Ohio, 1800. (Knittle)

HALL, E. & W. New York, New York. Percussion pistol.

HALL, E. Middlebury, Vermont, 1843-1849.

HALL, EDWIN L. Springfield, Massachusetts, 1849d-1861.

HALL, ELIAS Montpelier, Vermont, 1840-1843, Middlebury, Vermont, 1849. Flintlock 1/2 stock. (Horn)

HALL, F.G. Manchester, New Hampshire, 1889d.

HALL, GEORGE A. Abbott Village, Maine, 1877d.

HALL, GEORGE W. Pittsylvania Courthouse, Virginia, 1861-1863. Confederate muskets. (Gardner)

HALL, GEORGE (1820-?), Mount Vernon, Indiana, 1858d-1860c. (Lindert)

HALL, H. Green Bay, Wisconsin, 1863-1875.

HALL, H.G. Newell, Iowa, 1897d.

HALL, HORACE Marquette, Michigan, 1863d.

HALL, HUGH Talbotton, Georgia, 1881d.

HALL, I. (1820-?), El Dorado Co., California, 1852c. (Shelton)

HALL, ISAAC New York, New York, 1852d-1853d.

HALL, J.T. New Bern, North Carolina, 1884-1890. With his brother Thomas as J.T. Hall & Bro.

HALL, J.T., & BRO. New Bern, North Carolina, 1884d-1890d. J.T. and Thomas Hall.

HALL, J.W. Leatherwood, Ohio, 1859d. (Hutslar)

HALL, JACOB J. (1817-?), Warren, Illinois, 1879-1890. (Johnson)

HALL, JOHN HARRIS (1778-1841), North Yarmouth, Maine. Patents #none March 21, 1811, breechloading firearm with William Thornton, and #none March 7, 1827, gun machinery. Model 1816 Experimental Hall rifle, the world's first officially adopted military breechloading rifle. Superintended the manufacture of guns under his patent at Harper's Ferry, 1816-1840. (Schmidt)

HALL, JOHN (1826-?), Morgan, Co., Ohio, 1850c. (Hutslar)

HALL, JOHN Greenleaf, Kentucky, 1883d-1884d.

HALL, JOHN New York, New York, 1849d-1851d.

HALL, JOHN Watertown, Massachusetts. Patent #71,162 November 19, 1867, magazine pistol.

HALL, JONATHAN Philadelphia, Pennsylvania, 1780-1785. Repaired U.S. arms. (Moller)

HALL, JOSEPH New York, New York, 1849d-1853d. Brother of John Hall.

HALL, JOSIAH Sterling, Colorado. Patent #497,874 May 23, 1893, shot spreader. (Sellers-3)

HALL, L.E., & CO. Oakland, California, 1892-1894. (Shelton)

HALL, LOUIS New Orleans, Louisiana, 1881d-1882d. As Hall & Cook.

HALL, M. Gobelville, Michigan, 1899d.

HALL, NELSON C. Blandford, Massachusetts, 1869d-1890d.

HALL, PERRY E. (1827-?), Ashtabula, Ohio, 1848-1854. Percussion 1/2 stock and four-barrel rifle. (Hutslar)

HALL, PHIDELLO W. Springfield, Texas. Confederate patent #8 August 10, 1861, revolving rifle. (Albaugh 3)

HALL, SAMUEL East Haddam, Connecticut, 1775-1778. Committee of Safety muskets. (Gluckman & Satterlee)

HALL, SAMUEL New York, New York, 1820-1851. Patent #1,461 December 31, 1839, breechloading firearm with Silas Day.

HALL, T. unlocated. New England flintlock Kentucky.

HALL, T.C. Gonzales, Texas, 1896d.

HALL, THOMAS New Bern, North Carolina, 1867d-1890d. As J.T. Hall & Bro., 1884-1890.

HALL, W.H. Boston, Massachusetts, 1854d-1857d.

HALL, WILLIAM B. Lancaster, Pennsylvania. Patents #264,827 September 19, 1882, breechloading firearm, #276,806 May 1, 1883, breechloading firearm, and #414,213 November 5, 1889, breechloading firearm. Breechloading over/under rifles/shotguns.

HALL, WILLIAM H. Portland, Maine, 1852. (Demeritt)

HALL, WILLIAM T. Fayetteville, Indiana. Patent #243,250 June 21, 1881, charge holder.

HALLADAY, FRANK E. Plover, Wisconsin, 1886-1895d. Patent #353,786 December 7, 1886, sight. As Halladay & Bean, 1895.

HALLARICH, JOHN La Crosse, Wisconsin, 1865d-1888d.

HALLIDAY, WILLIAM Hartford, Connecticut, 1847-1859. (Kauffman 2)

HALLOWELL & MEYERS Philadelphia, Pennsylvania, 1867d. Percussion over/under rifle. W.R. Hallowell and Paul Meyers.

HALLOWELL, HENRY (1846-?), Languille, Pennsylvania, 1880c-1915.

HALLOWELL, W.R. Philadelphia, Pennsylvania, 1866d-1867d. With Paul Meyers as Hallowell & Meyer, 1867.

HALLUM, B. Castalian Springs, Tennessee, 1881d.

HALLUM, GEORGE Bledsoe, Tennessee, 1891d.

HALLUM, HENRY Eastland, Texas, 1890d-1892d.

HALM, J. Warren, Pennsylvania, 1853-1875. Percussion fullstock rifle.

HALPEN, WILLIAM New Buffalo, Michigan, 1887d.

HALSEY, GEORGE Newport, Rhode Island, 1667. (Achtermier)

HALSEY, JAMES E. New York, New York. Patent #15,292 July 8, 1856, firearm.

HAM, DANIEL Iowa City, Iowa, 1856-1876. Percussion 1/2 stock.

HAMAKER, J. (or T.), unlocated. Flintlock Kentucky pistols.

HAMBETT & HEALD Milford, New Hampshire, 1875d.

HAMELIN, CHARLES W. (1817-?), Perry Co., Pennsylvania, 1850c. (Chandler 2)

HAMERLE, I. unlocated. Percussion fullstock.

HAMES, S. St. Charles, Missouri, 1867d.

HAMILTON RIFLE CO. Plymouth, Michigan, 1898-1945. Inexpensive .22 rifles. Clarence J. and son Coello Hamilton. (Perkins)

HAMILTON, ARNOLD Broad Brook, Connecticut. Patent #33,769 November 19, 1861, breechloading firearm.

HAMILTON, CLARENCE JAMES (?-1902), Plymouth, Michigan. Patents #390,297 October 2, 1888, air gun, #408,971 August 13, 1889, air gun, #427,313 May 6, 1890, air gun, #455,942 July 14, 1891, air gun, #631,010 August 15, 1889, air gun, #660,725 October 30, 1900, rifling with Coello Hamilton, #662,068 November 20, 1900, rifle with Coello Hamilton, #696,962 April 8, 1902, sight, #704,962 July 15, 1902, barrel, and #748,723 January 5, 1904, firearm. As Hamilton Rifle Co. after selling air rifle business to Daisy Mfg. Co. (Perkins)

HAMILTON, COELLO Plymouth, Michigan. Patents, with his father Clarence J. Hamilton, #660,725 October 30, 1900, rifling, and #662,068 November 20, 1900, rifle. Patents, individually, #739,412 September 22, 1903, rifle, and #863,171 August 13, 1907, rifle.

HAMILTON, E.R. Bloomington, Indiana, 1870c. Percussion 1/2 stock. (Lindert)

HAMILTON, E.R. Etna, Washington, 1886d-1891d.

HAMILTON, EDWARD G. (1839-?), San Francisco, California, 1870c. (Shelton)

HAMILTON, EDWARD Chicago, Illinois. Patent #32,768 July 19, 1861, breechloading firearm.

HAMILTON, F.M. Richmond, Pennsylvania, 1874d.

HAMILTON, H.B. Lebanon, New Hampshire, 1845. Underhammer rifle.

HAMILTON, J. St. Joseph, Missouri, 1860d.

HAMILTON, J.J. Tyler, Texas, 1878d-1896d.

HAMILTON, JAMES (1763-1842), York Co., Pennsylvania, 1797-1814, Cabarris Co., North Carolina, 1814-1842. (Hartzler)

HAMILTON, JAMES Little Rock, Arkansas, 1821.

HAMILTON, JOHN M. St. Louis, Missouri, 1850c-1859d, Denver, Colorado, 1860-1865. With Thomas Fea as Fea & Hamilton, 1854d. (Sellers-3)

HAMILTON, JOSEPH North Carolina, 1820c. (Bivins)

HAMILTON, W.D. Visalia, California, 1860. (Shelton)

HAMILTON, W.H. New York, New York. Imported double shotgun.

HAMLIN, J. Knob Lick, Missouri, 1889d.

HAMMELL, CHARLES New Orleans, Louisiana, 1842d.

HAMMELL, SAMUEL (1783-?), Hagerstown, Maryland. Apprenticed to John Gonter, 1800.

HAMMER, A. Trenton, New Jersey, 1878d.

HAMMER, HENRY CHARLES (1826-?), Mokelumme Hill, California, 1866-1873. (Shelton)

HAMMER, HENRY (1830-?), Edwardsville, Illinois, 1860d-1880d.

HAMMER, ISAAC Mossville, Illinois, 1860d.

HAMMER, JOHN H. Allegheny, Pennsylvania. Patents #584,222 June 8, 1897, cane gun, and #587,731 August 10, 1897, cannon muzzle.

HAMMER, JOHN John's Pass, Florida, 1883d-1884d.

HAMMERLE, FRANK (1838-?), Hamilton, Ohio, 1863-1896. Percussion 1/2 stock. (Hutslar)

HAMMERLEE, WILLIAM Cooperstown, Pennsylvania, 1861d.

HAMMERLY, FABIAN Philadelphia, Pennsylvania, 1780-1785. Repaired U.S. arms. (Moller)

HAMMOND & CRANE Blair, Nebraska, 1879d.

HAMMOND Cambridge City, Indiana. Marking on lockplate.

HAMMOND, A.F. Houston, Ohio. Patent #54,531 May 8, 1866, alarm gun. Guns made in Tiffin, Ohio.

HAMMOND, C. Cocoa, Florida, 1886d.

HAMMOND, EBENEZER K. West Derby, Vermont, 1846-1883d.

HAMMOND, GEORGE Clayton, New York, 1869d-1874d.

HAMMOND, GEORGE Hortonville, Wisconsin, 1857d.

HAMMOND, H.J. Kalamazoo, Michigan, 1891d.

HAMMOND, HENRY Providence, Rhode Island, Bridgeport, Connecticut, Hartford, Connecticut. Patents #44,798 October 25, 1864, breechloading firearm (Providence), #52,165 January 23, 1866, revolver extractor, #54,147 April 24, 1866, cartridge pouch, #61,007 January 8, 1867, sight, #62,415 February 26, 1867, cartridge pouch, #72,849 December 31, 1867, ejector, #112,589, March 14, 1871, breechloading firearm (Hartford), and #175,702 April 4, 1876, sight (Hartford). The Hammond "Bulldog" was made by Connecticut Arms & Mfg. Co. Patents #52,165, #54,147, #61,007, #62,415, and #72,849 at Bridgeport.

HAMMOND, J.A. Falls City, Nebraska, 1884d.

HAMMOND, JOSEPH (1813-1908), Geneseo, Illinois, 1860-1890d. (Johnson)

HAMMOND, LEVI (1811-?), Harrisville, West Virginia, 1870c-1872d.

HAMMOND, WILLIAM POTTER (1815-1886), San Francisco, California, 1859-1860, Napa, California, 1860-1886. (Shelton)

HAMMOND, WILLIAM York Co., Pennsylvania. Percussion fullstock. (Dean)

HAMPTON, FILSON J. (?-1910), Blair Mills, Pennsylvania, circa 1840-1906. Percussion fullstock rifle marked "F.J.H." on barrel. (MB 12-63)

HAMPTON, GEORGE Chicago, Illinois, 1860d.

HAMPTON, JOHN N. (1800-1900), Dauphin Co., Pennsylvania, 1837-1860. Flintlock Kentucky rifle. Marked "I.N.H." or "I.N.Hampton". (MB 4-63)

HAMPTON, ROBERT I. Athens, Georgia. Patent #375,626 December 27, 1887, breechloading firearm.

HANATTER, JACOB Allentown, Pennsylvania, 1842. (Kauffman)

HANAUER, CHARLES, & BRO. Cincinnati, Ohio, 1892d-1900d.

HANAUER, JOHN Appleton, Wisconsin, 1879d-1886d.

HANCOCK, GEORGE Providence, Rhode Island. Patent #42,471 April 25, 1864, breechloading firearm.

HANCOCK, JOHN New Market, Illinois, 1860d.

HANCOCK, M.S. Young's Creek, Indiana, 1878-1885. Percussion 1/2 stock. (Lindert)

HANCOCK, ROBERT Philadelphia, Pennsylvania, 1813.

HANCOCK, W. Valeene, Indiana, 1860d.

HANCOCK, WILLIAM M. (1825-?), Shelby Co., Ohio, 1850c. (Hutslar)

HAND, PATRICK Denver, Colorado, 1866-1870, Abilene, Kansas, 1870d-1880d. For M.L.Rood, 1866-1870. (Sellers-3)

HAND, PHILIP Frederick Co., Virginia. Apprenticed to George Brinker, 1776.

HANDCOCK, L. Ravenna, Michigan, 1860d.

HANDLYN, JOHN Pennsylvania, 1776. Committee of Safety repairs. (Hobbies 4-38)

HANDY, E.W. New Castle, Delaware, 1884d.

HANDY, J.S., & CO. Philadelphia, Pennsylvania, 1866d. Importer.

HANES, THOMAS Vineland, New Jersey, 1882d-1885d.

HANFORD see Bennett & Hanford.

HANFORD see Bennett & Hanford.

HANK, CHARLES Wapakoneta, Ohio, 1859d.

HANKINS, W.W. Bartow, Florida, 1886d-1895d.

HANKINS, WILLIAM C. Philadelphia, Pennsylvania, 1857-1865. Percussion and cartridge revolvers. Sold out to William Uhlinger in 1861 to go into partnership with Christian Sharps. (Sellers-4)

HANKS, URIAH Mansfield, Connecticut, 1776-1777. Committee of Safety locks. (Gluckman & Satterlee)

HANN, SAMUEL Winchester, Illinois, 1869. (Johnson)

HANNA, ISAAC Northumberland Co., Pennsylvania, 1782. (Whisker III)

HANNAH, JOHN (?-1781), Rockbridge Co., Virginia, 1754-1781. Apprenticed to J. Mitchell, 1754. (Gill)

HANNAH, JOHN Cumberland Co., Pennsylvania, 1769t-1770t. (Bowers)

HANNAH, T.A. unlocated. Percussion Tennessee fullstock.

HANNAH, WILLIAM W. Hudson, New York. Patent #127,873 June 11, 1872, spring gun.

HANNI, HIERRONIMUS Reading, Pennsylvania, 1824. (Kauffman)

HANNING, F. Lockhard, Texas, 1878d.

HANNIS, JOSEPH Philadelphia, Pennsylvania, 1829d.

HANOVER ARMS CO. trade name on shotgun, possibly Crescent. (Hinman)

HANSCOM, R.B. Lewiston, Maine, 1896. (Demeritt)

HANSCOMB trade name of Hanscomb Hardware Co., Haverhill, Maryland on shotguns. (Hinman)

HANSEN, H.C. Albert Lea, Minnesota, 1888d.

HANSEN, O. Cooperstown, Wisconsin, 1857d.

HANSFORD, CHARLES apprenticed to Peter Gibson, 1706.

HANSON, FREDERICK Baltimore, Maryland, 1834-1839, Paterson, New Jersey, 1839-1878d. Worked with John Pearson on Colt revolvers and made one of his own. (Sellers-1)

HANSON, GEORGE Maryland, 1776. Committee of Safety repairs. (Dean*)

HANSON, JOHN Hubbell, Nebraska, 1870-1882d. Patent #109,731 November 29, 1870, breechloading firearm.

HANSON, JOSEPH Crystal Falls, Michigan. Patent #590,834 September 28, 1897, magazine gun.

HANSON, OLE St. Joe, Indiana, circa 1900. (Lindert)

HANTZ, JACOB Berwick, Pennsylvania, 1800t-1810t. (Bowers)

HANY, CHRISTIAN (1805-?), Highland, Illinois, 1850c. (Johnson)

HAPGOOD, JOAB (1804-1890), Shrewsbury, Massachusetts, 1826-1864, Boston, Massachusetts, 1847-1864. Flintlock and percussion guns. (GR 7-76)

HAPPOLDT & MURRAY Charleston, South Carolina, 1850-1859, Columbus, Georgia, 1860-1863. Benjamin Happoldt and John P. Murray. (Kauffman 2)

HAPPOLDT, BENJAMIN G. Charlestown, South Carolina, 1850d-1859d. With Happold & Murray. (Kauffman 2)

HAPPOLDT, J.H. Charleston, South Carolina, 1852-1886d. Son of J.M. Happold.

HAPPOLDT, JOHN M. Charleston, South Carolina, 1826-1865, Columbus, Georgia, 1865-1868. Derringers and pistols. (Kauffman 2)

HAPWOOD, DAVID T. Baltimore, Maryland, 1840d. (Hartzler)

HARA, NICHOLAS Troy, New York, circa 1840. Percussion 1/2 stock.

HARANT & SWEJA Chicago, Illinois, 1896d-1897d, James Sweja

HARBAUGH, F.C. (1818-?), Van Wert, Ohio, 1846-1850c. (Hutslar)

HARCOURT, WILLIAM Covington, Kentucky, 1871d-1879d.

HARD PAN suicide special by Hood Fire Arms Co.

HARDAKER, JOSEPH Chicago, Illinois, 1893d. Shotguns.

HARDAWAY, ANDREW Dinwiddie Court House, Virginia, 1781. Son of John Hardaway. (Gill)

HARDAWAY, JOHN Dinwiddie Court House, Virginia, 1781. (Gill)

HARDAWAY, STITH Dinwiddie Court House, Virginia, 1781. Son of John Hardaway. (Gill)

HARDEN, ALFRED (1828-?), New Plymouth, Ohio, 1859d. Percussion 1/2 stock. (Hutslar)

HARDEN, G.W. Moulton, Iowa, 1853.

HARDEN, JASPER F. (1852-1879), New Plymouth, Ohio, 1872-1879. (Hutslar)

HARDEN, WALTER H. (1874-1958), Orland, Ohio, 1895-1935. Percussion 1/2 stock. (Hutslar)

HARDER, F. Green Bay, Wisconsin, 1857d.

HARDER, FRANK E. Lock Haven, Pennsylvania, 1870-1890d. Son of Jacob Harder, worked with him. (MB 12-44)

HARDER, GEORGE WASHINGTON (1852-1930), Tyrone, Pennsylvania, 1876-1885, Williamsport, Pennsylvania, 1855-1890d. Percussion and cartridge rifles. Son of Jacob Harder. (MB 12-44)

HARDER, HIRAM Watertown, Wisconsin, 1867d, Neenah, Wisconsin, 1879. Percussion 1/2 stock.

HARDER, JACOB (1820-1898), Athens, Pennsylvania, 1838-1860, Lock Haven, Pennsylvania, 1860-1888. Patent #319,482 June 9, 1885, breechloading firearm. Multi-barrel percussion rifles and patent breechloaders. (MB 12-44)

HARDER, JACOB Waverly, New York, 1856-1859. May be same as Jacob Harder from Lock Haven, Pennsylvania.

HARDER, JOHN E. Clearfield, Pennsylvania, 1860-1890. Son of Jacob Harder, made Jacob Harder patent rifles and percussion target rifles. (MB 12-44)

HARDESTY, CHARLES West Las Animas, Colorado, 1870-1871d. (Sellers-3)

HARDIN, E.H. Trewhitt, Tennessee, 1887d-1891d. As Hardin & Hixson, 1891.

HARDIN, ENOCH Soddy, Tennessee, 1860. Percussion fullstock. (ASAC 23)

HARDIN, W.E. Covington, Kentucky, 1869d.

HARDING, ALLEN, CRAIG & GEORGE Antrim, Ohio, circa 1900. (Hutslar)

HARDING, H. unlocated. Flintlock Kentucky.

HARDING, JOSEPH Lowell, Massachusetts, 1851-1856. Percussion rifles.

HARDING, JOSIAH Covington, Pennsylvania, 1882d-1890d. Underhammer Kentucky.

HARDING, THOMAS Detroit, Michigan. Patent #379,782 March 20, 1888, spring gun.

HARDINGER, PETER Berks Co., Pennsylvania, 1780. Flintlock Kentucky rifles. (Kauffman 2)

HARDKOFF, DANIEL (1816-?), Celina, Ohio, 1850c. (Hutslar)

HARDMAN, JOHN (1778-?), Lewis Co., West Virginia, 1816-1850. (Gardner)

HARDMAN, NATHAN H. (1847-?), Curtis, West Virginia, 1880c.

HARDSHELL, CHARLES Dry Creek, Missouri, 1889d.

HARDWAY, WILLIAM P. Charleston, West Virginia, 1900d. (Whisker IV)

HARDWICKE & SCHENKLE Boston, Massachusetts, 1857d-1866. John P. Schenkle.

HARDY, C.E., & CO. unlocated. Flintlock lockmakers only.

HARDY, GEORGE (?-1695), Isle of Wright Co., Virginia, 1695. (Gill)

HARDY, J. Lowell, Massachusetts. Percussion 1/2 stock.

HARDY, MOSES F. Seward, New York. Patent #36,148 August 12, 1862, revolving cannon.

HARDY, THOMAS A. Fernandina, Florida, 1883d-1884d.

HARE, JESSE (1793-?), Gates Co., North Carolina, 1850c. (Bivins)

HARE, RICHARD T. Springfield, Massachusetts. Patent #332,896 December 22, 1885, magazine gun.

HARGILL, J.D. Chicago, Illinois. Percussion target rifle. With J.H. Foster as J.H. Foster & Co., 1855-1879.

HARIG, FREDERICK Baltimore, Maryland, 1845d. (Hartzler)

HARKER, C.P. unlocated. Flintlock Kentucky.

HARLAN, JOSHUA (1833-?), Dog Creek, California, 1867-1880. (Shelton)

HARLE, JOSEPH Vancouver, Washington. Patent #601,097 March 22, 1898, magazine gun.

HARLEY BROS. Lima, Ohio, 1878-1883d. (Hutslar)

HARLEY, ANDREW J. Xenia, Ohio, 1870-1898. (Hutslar)

HARLOW, GILBERT V. Auburn, New York, 1879d.

HARLOW, JOHN R. Auburn, New York, 1874d-1887d. As Tomlinson & Harlow, 1874-1875.

HARLOW, N.L. Owensboro, Kentucky, 1867d.

HARLOW, T.W. Litchfield, Illinois, 1880d.

HARLOW, THOMAS Jersey Landing, Illinois, 1860d.

HARLOW, WILSON N. (1829-?), Staunton, Virginia, 1860c.

HARMON, ALPHEUS B. Havelock, Iowa. Patent #583,744 June 1, 1897, magazine gun.

HARMON, CHARLES (1810-?), Chesterfield, Illinois, 1860c. (Johnson)

HARMON, DAVID DeKalb, Missouri, 1891d-1898d.

HARMON, DAVID Lafayette, Indiana, 1814. (Lindert)

HARMON, JAMES Burlington, Indiana, 1860d.

HARMON, JOHN Sulphur Springs, Ohio, 1883-1888d. (Hutslar)

HARMON, JONAS Sulphur Springs, Ohio, 1853-1864. Percussion rifles. (Hutslar)

HARMON, L. unlocated. Flintlock southern rifle.

HARMON, MOSE Burlington, Indiana. (Lindert)

HARMON, SOLOMON Mockville, Kentucky, 1854-1860. Percussion fullstock rifle.

HARMON, STEPHEN Burlington, Indiana, 1860d.

HARNDEN, E. Brownstown, Michigan, 1863d.

HAROLD, CHARLES New York, New York. Patent #583,175 May 25, 1897, spring gun.

HAROLD, HENRY W. Alliance, Ohio, 1872, Akron, Ohio, 1880-1892. (Hutslar)

HARP, E.M. Waynesboro, Georgia, 1885d.

HARPER, ADOLPHUS D. Memphis, Tennessee, 1887d.

HARPER, EDWARD (1780-?), Chatham Co., North Carolina, 1850c. (Bivins)

HARPER, JAMES O. Park Co., Indiana, 1850c.

HARPER, JESSE H. Jackson, Tennessee, 1881d-1887d.

HARPER, JOHN (1815-?), Chatham Co., North Carolina, 1850c. (Bivins)

HARPER, S.H. unlocated. Percussion 1/2 stock and shotgun.

HARPER, W. New York, New York. Percussion target pistol.

HARPERS FERRY ARMORY Harpers Ferry, Virginia. U.S. martial guns. Also shown as Harper's Ferry in some sources. (Brown)

HARRING, CHRISTIAN Columbia Co., Pennsylvania, 1821t.

HARRINGTON & RICHARDSON ARMS CO. Worcester, Massachusetts, 1888-1986. Gilbert H. Harrington and William A. Richardson, successors to Wesson & Harrington. Cheap revolvers, rifles and shotguns.

HARRINGTON Skenesboro, New York, 1836. Percussion fullstock.

HARRINGTON, A.C. Armada, Michigan, 1863d-1865d, Vassar, Michigan, 1867d-1872, Lapeer, Michigan, 1872d-1877d, St. Louis, Michigan, 1879d-1895d. Percussion 1/2 stock.

HARRINGTON, BERNARD Worcester, Massachusetts, 1867d-1875d. (Grant)

HARRINGTON, ELI Shrewsbury, Massachusetts, 1850-1856d.

HARRINGTON, FRANCIS H. Springfield, Massachusetts. Patent #20,607 June 15, 1856, revolver.

HARRINGTON, GILBERT HENDERSON Worcester, Massachusetts. Patents #111,534 February 7, 1871, revolver ejector, and #360,686 April 5, 1887, revolver with W.A. Richardson. The first patent was used on Wesson & Harrington revolvers and the second on Harrington & Richardson revolvers.

HARRINGTON, H.B. Lebanon, New Hampshire. Percussion target rifle.

HARRINGTON, HENRY Southbridge, Massachusetts. Patent #297 July 29, 1837, breechloading firearm. Multi-barrel pistols and rifles.

HARRINGTON, J.C. Frumet, Missouri, 1893d.

HARRINGTON, JACKSON New London, Connecticut, 1877d-1886d. Percussion fowler.

HARRINGTON, LUKE (1789-1855), Sutton and Milbury, Massachusetts, 1829-1855. (GR 6-61)

HARRINGTON, MUNSON W. Homestead, Iowa, 1873, York Center, Iowa, 1882d-1884d. Patent #136,159 February 25, 1873, sight.

HARRINGTON, NATHAN S. Worcester, Massachusetts. Patent #25,926 October 25, 1859, breechloading firearm with Frank Wesson.

HARRINGTON, SETH New London, Connecticut, 1876-1880.

HARRINGTON, THOMAS Philadelphia, Pennsylvania, 1853-1860. Lockmaker.

HARRIS & BAPTIS San Francisco, California, 1872. William Harris. Also see Harris Bros.

HARRIS & DARLING Otsego, Michigan, 1867d-1868d. Percussion over/under rifles. C.H. Harris and W.K. Darling.

HARRIS & HOPKINS Hartford, Connecticut, 1854-1856d (1856-1857?). William R. Hopkins and William R. Harris.

HARRIS BROS. San Francisco, California, 1856-1871. Negro gunsmiths Benjamin and William Harris. (Shelton)

HARRIS, A.M. Floyd, Virginia, 1897d.

HARRIS, ANDREW Providence, Rhode Island, 1883d. Dealer.

HARRIS, B.V. Matanzas, Kansas, 1878d-1882d.

HARRIS, BENJAMIN (1820-?), San Francisco, California, 1856-1871. As Harris Bros. (Shelton)

HARRIS, C.A. Beebe Station, Arkansas, 1884d.

HARRIS, C.C. Georgetown, Colorado, 1875-1882d. (Sellers-3)

HARRIS, CALEB Scituate, Rhode Island, 1776. (Achtermier)

HARRIS, CHARLES H. Hartford, Connecticut, 1854-1855d, Otsego, Michigan, 1867d-1883d. As Harris & Darling, 1867d-1868d.

HARRIS, CHARLES W. Hartford, Connecticut, 1852-1855d, Pittsburgh, Pennsylvania. Patent #39,771 September 1, 1863, revolver. Used on Cooper revolvers. (Sellers-1)

HARRIS, CHARLES (1798-?), Hancock Co., Indiana, 1850c. (Lindert)

HARRIS, CYRUS Cadott, Wisconsin, 1884d-1886d.

HARRIS, D.R. Brownsville, Maine, 1877-1878. (Demeritt)

HARRIS, EDWIN S. New York, New York, 1868d-1883d. As Cooper, Harris & Hodgkins, 1868-1874.

HARRIS, EDWIN Springfield, Ohio, 1852. (Hutslar)

HARRIS, ELMORE A. Norwich, New York. Patent #394,691 December 18, 1888, breechloading firearm.

HARRIS, GEORGE J. Providence, Rhode Island, 1856d-1860d.

HARRIS, HENRY W. Detroit, Michigan, 1899d.

HARRIS, HENRY Middletown, Pennsylvania, 1779-1783. (Kauffman)

HARRIS, ISAAC Savagetown, Maryland, 1772-1777. Committee of Safety muskets, flintlock pistol. (Hartzler)

HARRIS, J.B. Marianna, Arkansas, 1898d.

HARRIS, JAMES Providence, Rhode Island, 1875d.

HARRIS, JASON L. unlocated. Flintlock Kentucky rifle.

HARRIS, JOHN New York, New York, 1848-1852.

HARRIS, JOHN York, Pennsylvania, 1799. (Kauffman)

HARRIS, R.H. Kirksville, Missouri, 1860d-1898d.

HARRIS, RALPH E. Macomb, Illinois, 1878d-1890.

HARRIS, ROBERT Palestine, Texas, 1890d-1896d.

HARRIS, RUSSELL Bourne, Massachusetts, 1892d.

HARRIS, S.H. Chetek, Wisconsin, 1888d-1895d.

HARRIS, SAMUEL Northumberland Co., Pennsylvania, 1782. (Kauffman)

HARRIS, T.J. Palestine, Texas, 1885d.

HARRIS, THOMAS Virginia, 1775, Point of Fork, Virginia, 1790. Committee of Safety repairs. (Gill)

HARRIS, W.M. Midway, Texas, 1896d.

HARRIS, WILLIAM R. Hartford, Connecticut, 1852d-1863d. Percussion pistols and rifles. As Harris & Hopkins, 1856-1857. (GR 1-77)

HARRIS, WILLIAM W. Sioux City, Iowa. Patent #468,803 February 16, 1892, sight.

HARRIS, WILLIAM (1760-1834), Seneca Co., Ohio, 1820-1834. (Hutslar)

HARRIS, WILLIAM (1820-?), Baltimore, Maryland, 1850c-1876d. Percussion shotgun. (Hartzler)

HARRIS, WILLIAM (1832-?), San Francisco, California, 1856-1874. As Harris Bros., 1856-1871, and Harris & Baptis, 1872. (Shelton)

HARRISON, A.Z. unlocated. L.H. Gibbs patent sporting rifle.

HARRISON, FRANK, ARMS CO. trade name of H & D Folsom on shotguns imported for Sickles & Preston, Davenport, Iowa. (AR 2-69)

HARRISON, G. Sand Gap, Kentucky, circa 1840. Son of John B. Harrison, signed guns "GH" on stock. (MB 2-68)

HARRISON, H.P. unlocated. Percussion fullstock and swivel breech.

HARRISON, J.W. Grass Creek, Indiana. (Lindert)

HARRISON, JOHN B. (1817-1888), Sand Gap, Kentucky, 1840-1888. Signed guns "JBH" on stock. (MB 2-68)

HARRISON, LEONARD S. Nashville, Ohio. Patents #278,546 May 29, 1883, auxiliary barrel, and #460,533 September 29, 1891, repeating firearm.

HARRISON, N.D. Marvin, New York, 1874d-1886d.

HARRISON, R.W. Le Mars, Iowa, 1887d.

HARRISON, SAMUEL T. San Jose, California. Patent #216,848 June 24, 1879, magazine gun.

HARRISON, T.J. Milan, Tennessee, 1885d.

HARRISON, THOMAS Des Arc, Arkansas, 1850. Percussion pistol. (Elias)

HARRISON, WILLIAM B. Berlin Heights, Ohio, 1883d. (Hutslar)

HARRISON, WILLIAM Baltimore, Maryland, 1888d. Importer and dealer.

HARRISON, WILLIAM Linneus, Missouri, 1850c-1860d.

HARRISON, WILLIAM Warren Co., Missouri, 1850c. (MB 11-66)

HARROLD, F.W. unlocated. Percussion fullstock.

HARSHAMM, GEORGE Fayette Co., Pennsylvania, 1835-1837. (Kauffman)

HARSIN, GERRIT (?-1754), New York, New York. Flintlock fowler. Note: a "Garrit" Harsin was in New York during the Revolution.

HARSON, SAMUEL Westmoreland Co., Pennsylvania, 1811-1824. (Kauffman)

HART & CO. Eaton, Ohio, 1859d. John Hart. (Hutslar)

HART & SLOAN Newark, New Jersey, 1878d.

HART Frewsberg, New York. Percussion 1/2 stock. (Clow)

HART, A.H. Ohio, 1834-1847, Neenah, Wisconsin, 1850c. (Hutslar)

HART, A.H., JR. Appleton, Wisconsin, 1865d-1867d. As Rose & Hart, 1867 and Dickerson & Hart, 1865.

HART, AARON Pittsburgh, Pennsylvania, 1810-1819. (Kauffman)

HART, ABEL Tiverton, Rhode Island, 1869d.

HART, ALFRED San Marcos, Texas, 1884d.

HART, ANDREW D. North Garden, Virginia. Patent #273,070 February 27, 1883, safety hammer.

HART, B.F. New York, New York, 1855-1865. Percussion target rifles. (Gluckman & Satterlee)

HART, BENJAMIN J. New York, New York, 1848-1865. As B.J. Hart & Bro., 1853-1860. Percussion pistols, revolvers, and rifles, mostly made by others. (Sellers-1)

HART, HENRY C. Detroit, Michigan. Patent #437,491 September 30, 1890, spring gun.

HART, JOHN (1832-?), Hay Fork, California, 1892-1894. (Shelton)

HART, JOHN Euphemia, Ohio, 1860-1864d. (Hutslar)

HART, JOHN Storm Lake, Iowa, 1889d-1892d.

HART, LEVI Lancaster, Pennsylvania, 1857d-1871d.

HART, LEWIS Providence, Rhode Island, 1867d-1873d.

HART, R.C. San Francisco, California, 1878-1879d. (Shelton)

HART, S. Fredonia, New York. On barrel of 1/2 stock rifle with J.H. Starr.

HART, S.L. Menasha, Wisconsin, 1857d-1879d, Tombstone, Arizona, 1881d-1895d. Converted trapdoor rifles.

HART, W.A. Cascade Hamlet, North Carolina. Flintlock Kentucky, eagle patchbox.

HART, WILLIAM AARON Fredonia, New York, 1823-1831. Patent #none February 20, 1827, pill lock. Percussion pistols. (Winant)

HARTELL, JOHN (?-1881), Chicago, Illinois, 1879d-1881d.

HARTENSTEIN, LEONARD (1825-?), Dallas City, Illinois, 1860c-1890d.

HARTER, S.K. Troy, Ohio, 1867-1883. (Hutslar)

HARTER, V. Chicago, Illinois, 1899.

HARTFKREFT, DANIEL New London, Missouri, 1867d.

HARTFORD ARMS CO. Norwich, Connecticut. Suicide specials.

HARTFORD ARMS CO. trade name of Crescent on shotguns for Simmons Hardware Co. and Shapleigh Hardware Co. (Hinman)

HARTIG, JOHN H. Dubuque, Iowa, 1880d-1889d. Son of Julius Hartig.

HARTIG, JULIUS E. Dubuque, Iowa, 1862-1878d.

HARTINGTON, ORRIN Coshocton, Ohio, 1885d. (Hutslar)

HARTLEY & GRAHAM New York, New York, 1880-1912. Successors to Schuyler, Hartley & Graham. Retailers only. Marcellus Hartley later acquired Remington and merged it with UMC.

HARTLEY, ABE Salineville, Ohio, 1860-1895. Percussion fullstock and 1/2 stock. (MB 11-54)

HARTLEY, GEORGE (1810-?), Jackson Co., Ohio, 1835-1850c. (Hutslar)

HARTLEY, HOWARD Pittsburgh, Pennsylvania. Patent #190,033 April 24, 1877, adjustable stock.

HARTLEY, MARCELLUS New York, New York. Patent #395,897 January 8, 1889, shot cartridge with A.J. Hobbs. President of Schuyler, Hartley & Graham, Remington Arms Co., U.M.C.Co. etc. (Hatch)

HARTLOVE, WALTER H. Wilmington, Delaware 1884d-1894d.

HARTMAN & KAHN Erie, Pennsylvania. Percussion shotguns. Peter Hartman and J. Kahn.

HARTMAN, C. Richmond, Virginia, 1871d.

HARTMAN, J. Pere Marquette, Michigan, 1860d.

HARTMAN, J.P. West Pikeland, Pennsylvania, 1890d.

HARTMAN, JOHN Weisenberg, Pennsylvania, 1800t. (KRA II-3)

HARTMAN, PETER Erie, Pennsylvania, 1856-1887d. Percussion 1/2 stock.

HARTOGENIS, HENRY S. Baltimore, Maryland, 1868-1884. (Hartzler)

HARTS, FRANKLIN Zanesville, Ohio, 1873d. (Hutslar)

HARTSEL, DAVID Cincinnati, Ohio, 1832-1836.

HARTSHORN, ISAAC Providence, Rhode Island. Patent #38,042 March 31, 1863, breechloading firearm. Used on Burnside carbines.

HARTSOCK, GEORGE Springhill, Pennsylvania, 1802-1824. Probably Hartzog. (Kauffman)

HARTSON, LAFAYETTE Wyoming, Iowa, 1865d.

HARTUNG, CHARLES New York, New York. Patent #6,871 November 13, 1849, breechloading firearm. Rifles made as "Klein's Patent".

HARTUNG, GOTFRIED Cape Girardeau, Missouri, 1889d-1898d.

HARTZOG, DAVID Springhill, Pennsylvania, 1823-1824.

HARTZOG, FREDERICK Georgetown, Pennsylvania, 1806-1810. (Kauffman)

HARTZOG, JACOB Georgetown, Pennsylvania, 1806-1810. (Kauffman)

HARVARD trade name of Crescent on shotguns.

HARVEL, G.W., & BRO. unlocated. Percussion 1/2 stock.

HARVEY & WEALE Louisville, Kentucky, 1857-1860.

HARVEY, ALBERT Nicholville, New York, 1877-1882.

HARVEY, H.T. unlocated. Percussion fullstock.

HARVEY, H.W. Green Bay, Wisconsin, 1867d.

HARVEY, H.W. Rockton, Illinois, 1884d.

HARVEY, HAYWOOD A. Orange, New Jersey. Patent #460,261 September 29, 1891, firearm.

HARVEY, J.M. Mound City, Missouri, 1889d.

HARVEY, JAMES (1819-?), Beaver Co., Pennsylvania, 1840-1880. (Whisker)

HARVEY, M. Racine, Wisconsin, 1857d.

HARVEY, SAMUEL Bushkill, Pennsylvania, 1850c. See Samuel Haeny (Gable)

HARVEY, THOMAS F. (1795-1854), New York, New York. Patent #6,537 June 19, 1849, lock.

HARWELL, J.F. Centersville, Georgia, 1879d-1885d.

HARWICK, W.G. Albion, Illinois, 1864d.

HARWOOD, HERBERT Littleton, Massachusetts. Patent #375,936 January 3, 1888, projectile.

HARWOOD, NATHANIEL H. Brookfield, Massachusetts, 1825-1840. (Roberts)

HARWOOD, REUBEN Somerville, Massachusetts. Percussion 1/2 stock.

HASDELL, THOMAS R. Chicago, Illinois, 1877d-1886d. Shotguns.

HASEMAN, WILLIAM Philadelphia, Pennsylvania, 1841d-1846d.

HASENJAGER, FREDERICK Holstein, Missouri, 1879d-1898d.

HASKELL, ASA G. North Andover, Massachusetts. Patent #175,702 April 4, 1876, sight.

HASKELL, C.A. Menomonee, Wisconsin, 1888d.

HASKELL, CHARLES Marshall, Minnesota, 1877-1882d.

HASKELL, GEORGE RICHARDS (1825-1897), Geneva, New York, 1850-1897. (Dean)

HASKELL, JAMES R. New York, New York, 1881d-1884d, Passaic, New Jersey, 1885d-1895d. Patents #241,978 May 24, 1881, machine gun, #484,007 October 11, 1892, mutli-charge gun, #484,009 October 11, 1892, machine gun, #484,010 October 11, 1892, machine gun, and #484,011 October 11, 1892, machine gun.

HASKELL, RILEY (?-1882), Painesville, Ohio, 1860-1871, Mentor, Ohio, 1872-1882. Percussion 1/2 stock. (Hutslar)

HASKELL, T.R. Painesville, Ohio. (Knittle)

HASKINS, D.W. Worcester, Massachusetts, 1867d.

HASKINS, GEORGE Osakis, Minnesota, 1888d.

HASKINS, JOHN Roxbury, Massachusetts. Patent #35,418 May 27, 1862, nipple protector.

HASKINS, WILLIAM G. Worcester, Massachusetts, 1867d. Pistols.

HASLETT, JAMES (1773-1833), Philadelphia, Pennsylvania, 1798-1803, Baltimore, Maryland, 1803-1827. Military and civilian flintlock guns.

HASSAM BROS. Boston, Massachusetts, 1838d-1860d. Percussion guns. Importers and dealers.

HASSELL, D.D. Plenitude, Texas, 1862-1864. Texas rifles. With John Billups.

HASSELMEYER, CHARLES New York, New York, 1849d-1851d.

HASSHAGEN, THEODORE Abilene, Kansas, 1894d.

HASSINGER, WILLIAM Ottawa, Ohio, 1860-1864d. (Hutslar)

HASSLOCK, A.R. Georgetown, Kentucky, 1896d.

HASSON, SAMUEL (?-1833), Westmoreland Co., Pennsylvania, 1811-1833. (Whisker II)

HASSON, WILLIAM (1802-?), Westmoreland Co., Pennsylvania, 1824-1860. (Whisker II)

HASTECKER, CHARLES D. Marengo, Iowa, 1865d.

HASTINGS, GARDNER P. Springfield, Missouri. Patent #576,964 February 9, 1897, magazine gun.

HASTINGS, J.L. Red Wing, Minnesota, 1882d-1898d.

HASTY, JOSEPH Bangor, Kentucky, 1883d.

HATCH, C.P. unlocated. Flintlock Kentucky.

HATCH, E.J. Litchfield, Minnesota, 1877-1881.

HATCH, J. Burlington, Vermont, 1844-1855. (Horn)

HATCH, JOHN Cazenovia, New York, 1848-1882d.

HATCH, WARREN Burlington, Vermont, 1848d-1860d, Plattsburg, New York, 1850. Percussion pistols and rifles. (Roberts)

HATCHER, J.F. Fremont, Nebraska, 1893d.

HATCHER, J.F. Hopkinton, Iowa, 1880d-1882d.

HATCHER, P.P. (1817-?), Morristown, Ohio, 1850c. Percussion rifles. (Hutslar)

HATFIELD, JOHN Martinsville, Indiana, 1860d-1862d.

HATFIELD, NOAH (1813-1884), Owensburg, Indiana, 1845-1884. (Lindert)

HATFIELD, R.P. Horse Creek, Missouri, 1860d.

HATFIELD, WASHINGTON (1815-?), Owensburg, Indiana. Percussion fullstock signed "W.H.". (Lindert)

HATHAWAY & BELLIS Berlin, Wisconsin, 1879d.

HATHAWAY, JOHN M. New York, New York. Patents #11,427 August 1,1854, shot pouch, #15,651 September 2, 1856, shot pouch, and #34,685 March 18, 1862, explosive shell.

HATHAWAY, S.B. Omaha, Nebraska, 1879d.

HATRICK, ROBERT Oswego, New York, 1859d.

HATT, S.S. Paw Paw, Michigan, 1867d-1873d, Argentine, Michigan, 1875d, Fenton, Michigan, 1879d. As Godfrey & Hart, 1867.

HATTEN, J.S. Atchison, Kansas, 1865d. As Hill & Hatten.

HATTERSLEY, HENRY Cleveland, Ohio, 1846-1878d. Percussion rifles. As H. Hattersley & Co., 1878. (Hutslar)

HATTERSLEY, RICHARD Cleveland, Ohio, 1861d. With Henry Hattersley. (Hutslar)

HATTICH, A. Houghton, Michigan, 1872d-1878d.

HAUCK, BERNARD York Co., Pennsylvania, 1800. Flintlock Kentucky. (KRA 76)

HAUG, GEORGE Evansville, Indiana, 1866d-1873d.

HAUGHIAN, PATRICK New York, New York. Patent #46,562 February 28, 1865, revolver.

HAUK, JOHN Newton, Illinois, 1882d-1893d.

HAUNUM & AVERY Northampton, Massachusetts, 1869d.

HAUPT, LOUIS Williamsville, New York, 1877-1882. Percussion 1/2 stock.

HAUPTMAN, GUSTAVE (1828-?), Chicago, Illinois, 1859d-1871d.

HAUPTMAN, JOSEPH St. Louis, Missouri, 1860d-1867d.

HAUSER, J. Canyonville, Oregon, 1873d.

HAUSER, JOHN Riverhead, New York, 1859d-1882d.

HAUSMAN, M.A. Huntington, Indiana, 1870c.

HAUSMANN, J. New Orleans, Louisiana. Derringer.

HAVEN, N. Put's Corner, New York, 1800. (Gardner)

HAVENS, GEORGE W. Ypsilanti, Michigan, 1876-1887d, Cheboygan, Michigan, 1891d, Grand Rapids, Michigan, 1895d. Patent #173,625 February 15, 1876, gun cover.

HAVENS, JOSEPH Reading, Pennsylvania, 1777. Flintlock Kentucky. (KRA 76)

HAVENS, WILLIAM Providence, Rhode Island, 1650. (Achtermier)

HAVEY, D.D. Worcester, Massachusetts, 1867d.

HAVILAND & GUNN Ilion, New York, 1871-1884. Patents #113,766 April 18, 1871, air gun, and #126,954 May 21, 1872, air gun. Benjamin Haviland and George C. Gunn made air guns and .22 rifles. (Wolff)

HAVILAND, FREDERICK Waterville, Maine. Patent #603 February 15, 1838, repeating rifle. (Demeritt)

HAWES & WAGGONER Charleston, South Carolina. Derringer. (Eberhart)

HAWES, A.C. Stamford, Connecticut. Patent #331,792 December 8, 1885, line throwing gun with Simon Ingersoll.

HAWES, C.A. Poland, Maine, 1877. (Demeritt)

HAWES, MILO C. Madison, Wisconsin, 1858-1859. (Kauffman)

HAWK, CHARLES Bushkill, Pennsylvania, 1835t. (Dyke)

HAWK, NICHOLAS (1782-1844), Chestnut Hill, Pennsylvania, 1809-1835t, Gilbert, Pennsylvania, ?-1844. Flintlock and percussion Kentucky rifles. (KRA 79)

HAWK, PETER S. Pleasant Valley, Pennsylvania, 1835t, Long Valley, Pennsylvania, 1861d. (Kauffman)

HAWKEN & CAMPBELL St. Louis, Missouri, 1854d-1856. William S. Hawken and Tristram Campbell. (Hanson 2)

HAWKEN, CHRISTIAN (1756-1821). Hagerstown, Maryland, 1784-1821. Flintlock Kentucky. (Hartzler)

HAWKEN, CHRISTOPHER MILLER (1825-1905), St. Louis, Missouri. Son of Jacob Hawken, although listed as a gunsmith in some works, he probably was not. His listings in directories are as a livery stable operator. (Hanson 2)

HAWKEN, DANIEL TURNEY (1814-1853), Piqua, Ohio, 1838-1850, Springfield, Ohio, 1850c-1853. Percussion fullstock. Son of Henry Hawken. (Hutslar)

HAWKEN, GEORGE (1811-1865), Vicksburg, Mississippi, 1840-1865. Son of John George Hawken. (Hartzler)

HAWKEN, HENRY CLAY (1829-1905), Springfield, Ohio, 1850-1852d. Son of John Hawken, machinist and musician after 1852. (Hutslar)

HAWKEN, HENRY (?-1835), Greensburg, Pennsylvania, 1796-1815, Columbus, Franklin Co., Ohio, 1815-1828, Springfield, Ohio, 1835. Son of Nicholas. Estate settled 1835, gunsmith tools bought by Daniel and John Hawken. (Hutslar, Hartzler)

HAWKEN, JACOB (1786-1849), Harper's Ferry, Virginia, 1808-1818, St. Louis, Missouri, 1818-1849. Percussion guns. With James Lakeman as Lakeman & Hawken, 1818-1825, and with his brother Samuel T. as J. & S. Hawken, 1825-1849. Son of Christian Hawken. (Hanson 1 & 2)

HAWKEN, JAMES M. (1836-?), St. Louis, Missouri, 1865d.

HAWKEN, JOHN C. Hagerstown, Maryland, 1840-1841. Son of John George Hawken, took over William Hawken's shop in 1840 and sold out the next year. (Hartzler)

HAWKEN, JOHN GEORGE (1781-1830), Hagerstown, Maryland, 1809-? Flintlock Kentucky rifles. Son of Christian Hawken, did not use his first name. (Hartzler)

HAWKEN, JOHN (1784-1820), Hagerstown, Maryland, Harper's Ferry, West Virginia. Son of Christian Hawken. (Hartzler)

HAWKEN, JOHN (1805-1847), Columbus, Ohio, 1823-1830, Piqua, Ohio, 1838-1842, Springfield, Ohio, 1842-1847. With brother Daniel in Piqua and Springfield. (Hutslar, Hartzler)

HAWKEN, NICHOLAS Hagerstown, Maryland, 1790c-1800c. Brother of Christian Hawken. (Hartzler)

HAWKEN, SAMUEL T. (1792-1884), Xenia, Ohio, 1816-1822, St. Louis, Missouri, 1822-1859, Denver, Colorado, 1859-1862. Flintlock and percussion guns. With brother Jacob in St. Louis as J. & S. Hawken, 1825-1849. Son of Christian Hawken. (Hanson 2)

HAWKEN, WILLIAM STEWART (1825-1900), St. Louis, Missouri, 1850c-1860, Denver, Colorado, 1860-1864. Son of Samuel T. Hawken. (Hanson 2)

HAWKEN, WILLIAM (1798-1885), Hagerstown, Maryland, 1821-1840 and 1846-1850. Flintlock Kentucky. Son of and successor to Christian Hawken. (Hartzler)

HAWKER, H. Saginaw City, Michigan, 1873d.

HAWKER, WILLIAM M. Saginaw City, Michigan, 1859-1887d.

HAWKEY, HENRY Hempfield, Pennsylvania, 1805-1815. Might be Hawken. (Kauffman)

HAWKEYE suicide special by Lee Arms Co.

HAWKINS, BENJAMIN L. (1875-1955), Cincinnati, Ohio, 1896-1940. (Hutslar)

HAWKINS, DAVID N. Lincoln Co., Georgia, 1820c.

HAWKINS, GEORGE Bedford, Pennsylvania, 1870-1876. Percussion fullstock rifle.

HAWKINS, HENRY Schenectady, New York, 1769-1775. Flintlock Kentucky rifles.

HAWKINS, HIRAM Edinboro, Pennsylvania, 1865. Percussion 1/2 stock.

HAWKINS, J. unlocated. Flintlock Kentucky.

HAWKINS, J.D. Ashland, Kentucky, 1857-1860.

HAWKINS, JOHN Charleston, South Carolina, 1699. (Kauffman 2)

HAWKINS, JOSEPH (?-1771), Frederick Co., Virginia. (Gill)

HAWKINS, L. & T.J. Piqua, Ohio, 1838d. Confused with J. & D.T. Hawken? (Hutslar)

HAWKS, C. Schuyler's Lake, New York, 1847, Exeter, New York, 1850d.

HAWKS, JACOB Rochester, New York, 1827d. For Ephraim Gilbert. (Eich)

HAWKS, THOMAS Philadelphia, Pennsylvania, 1837d.

HAWKSLEY, WILLIAM St. Louis, Missouri, 1859d-1860d.

HAWLEY, E.H. New Haven, Connecticut. Patent #90,749 June 1, 1869, air gun. Made as "Kalamazoo" by Snow & Coe.

HAWORTH, EUCLIDUS (1814-?), Darke Co., Ohio, 1850c. (Hutslar)

HAWS, WILLIAM Driggs, Idaho. Patent #650,461 May 29, 1900, rifling.

HAWTHORNE trade name of Montgomery Ward & Co.

HAY, PETER Bushkill, Pennsylvania, 1820t. (KRA II-3)

HAY, RANDALL D. Crooked Creek, North Carolina. Patents #109,513 November 22, 1870, safety, and #109,514 November 22, 1870, safety. (Sellers-1)

HAYDEN & GAY Jacksonville, Illinois, 1893. (Johnson)

HAYDEN & WHILDEN Charleston, South Carolina, circa 1840. Importers.

HAYDEN, A.R. & C.W. Skowhegan, Maine, 1891-1897.

HAYDEN, ALFRED Jacksonville, Illinois, 1872-1896d. Son of George Hayden. As Hayden & Gay, 1893d-1896.

HAYDEN, BEMISH unlocated. Percussion fullstock, dated 1838.

HAYDEN, CREED H. Dunbar, Pennsylvania, 1882d.

HAYDEN, DAVID S. (1831-?), Monmouth, Illinois, 1860d-1893d. As D.S. Hayden & Son, 1884.

HAYDEN, E.C. Cheasaning, Michigan, 1873d-1875d.

HAYDEN, ENOCH (1810-?), Ohio, 1843, Burlington, Iowa, 1850c. (MB 8-64)

HAYDEN, F.T. Gainesville, Texas 1890d.

HAYDEN, G. & A. Jacksonville, Illinois, 1880-1888d. Importers of shotguns. (Hinman)

HAYDEN, GEORGE Jacksonville, Illinois, 1872-1885d. As G&A Hayden, 1880-1885.

HAYDEN, GEORGE New York, New York, 1848-1879d. Firm continued as George Hayden's Sons until 1910.

HAYDEN, GEORGE Stoner, Kentucky, 1856-1860.

HAYDEN, HIRAM W. Waterbury, Connecticut. Patents #45,495 December 20, 1864, breechloading firearm, and #56,939 August 7, 1866, magazine firearm. Pistol with magazine in grip.

HAYDEN, HOSEA Union Co., Indiana, 1875. Percussion rifle and shotgun.

HAYDEN, JOSEPH Coffeyville, Kansas, 1894d.

HAYDEN, JOSEPH Galesburg, Illinois, 1884d-1888d. Percussion 1/2 stock. Son of David Hayden.

HAYDEN, JOSEPH Oxford, Ohio, 1848-1886. Percussion 1/2 stock. (Hutslar)

HAYDEN, LOUIS Manhattan, Kansas, 1882d-1888d.

HAYDEN, WILLIAM (1727-1823), Morris Co., New Jersey, 1774, Fredericksburg Arsenal, 1777, Hampshire Co., Virginia, 1781. (Bowers)

HAYDON, BLEMUS Cleves, Ohio, 1859d. (Hutslar)

HAYDON, EDWARD Camden, New Jersey, 1882d.

HAYE, HARRY Philadelphia, Pennsylvania. Percussion fowler.

HAYES, AARON (?-1854), Monroe Co., Kentucky. Gunsmith in Revolutionary War. (Sellers)

HAYES, CHARLES (1810-1850), Callaway Co., Missouri.

HAYES, J.H. The Rock, Georgia, 1881d.

HAYES, JOSEPH (1824-?), San Francisco, California, 1852d. (Shelton)

HAYES, WILLIAM E. Fulton, Tennessee, 1876d.

HAYES, WILLIAM Warsaw, Missouri, 1850c-1893d.

HAYMAKER, ADAM Winchester, Virginia, 1753-1804. (Gill)

HAYMAKER, JOHN Winchester, Virginia, circa 1800. Flintlock Kentucky pistol. Son of Adam Haymaker. (Bowers)

HAYNES, CHARLES Gonzales, Texas. (GR 8-59)

HAYNES, DAVID Hanover Co., Virginia, 1781-1783. Committee of Safety repairs. (Gill)

HAYNES, GIDEON, JR. Boston, Massachusetts. Patent #262,039 August 1, 1882, breechloading gun.

HAYNES, JOSHUA Waltham, Massachusetts, 1849d-1856d. Percussion target rifle.

HAYNES, M.M. Keelerville, Michigan, 1879d.

HAYNES, WILLIAM B. Chillicothe, Ohio, 1867-1900. Percussion 1/2 stock. (Hutslar)

HAYNES, WILLIAM C. Melrose, Texas. Patent #23,087 March 1, 1859, revolver. (Sellers-1)

HAYS, ANDREW J. Harrisburg, Oregon, 1867d-1871d.

HAYS, JOHN W. Henry Co., Iowa, 1850c. (MB 8-64)

HAYS, JOHN Nansemond Co., Virginia, 1781, Point of Fork, Virginia, 1789-1790. (Gill)

HAYTON, R.C. Ypsilanti, Michigan, 1872d-1899d. As R.C. Hayton & Son, 1872-1877.

HAYWARD & CUSHMAN Montpelier, Vermont, 1842. R.B. Hayward. (Kauffman 2)

HAYWARD, R.B. Montpelier, Vermont, 1840-1843. (Horn)

HAYWARD, R.S. Concord, Massachusetts, 1878d.

HAYWOOD, JOHN (1828-?), Natchez, Mississippi, 1860c.

HAYWOOD, WILLIAM P. West Creek, New Jersey, 1878d.

HAYWOOD, WILLIAM Milwaukee, Wisconsin, 1844-1861. Importer as well as gunsmith. (WGCA 6)

HAZARD & BLAIR unlocated. Percussion pistol.

HAZARD, HENRY T. (1844-?), Los Angeles, California. Patents #279,242 June 12, 1883, magazine gun, #296,563 April 8, 1884, reloading machine, #297,796 April 29, 1884, reloading machine, #301,887 July 15, 1884, reloading machine, #332,712 December 22, 1885, shell crimper, and #358,035 February 22, 1887, powder measure. (Shelton)

HAZELL, EDMOND (?-1737), Richmond, Virginia. (Gill)

HAZELTON, HAMILTON Philadelphia, Pennsylvania, 1780-1785. Repaired U.S. arms. (Moller)

HAZEN, ROCKWELL Homer, Michigan, 1860.

HAZEN, SAMUEL (1777-?), Mt. Gilead, Ohio, 1850c. (Hutslar)

HAZEN, WILLIAM Crittenden Co., Arkansas, 1850-1860. (Elias)

HEACOCK, J. Williamstown, Ohio, 1883-1887. (Hutslar)

HEAD, ANTHONY Washington Co., Indiana, before 1830. (Lindert)

HEAD, GEORGE R. Leesburg, Virginia, 1871d.

HEAD, H.G. Ashland, Ohio, 1860-1864. (Hutslar)

HEAD, L.D. Louisville, Missouri, 1860d.

HEAD, LORENZO (1809-?), Mann Co., Illinois, 1850c. (Johnson)

HEADMAN, JOHN Philadelphia, Pennsylvania, 1830d. Stockmaker.

HEAL, BENJAMIN Ilesboro, Maine, 1860-1880. (Demeritt)

HEAL, JOHN G. (1869-1945), Detroit, Michigan, 1899-1905. As Heal Rifle Co. and Detroit Rifle Co. (Perkins)

HEALD see Hambett & Heald.

HEARD, F.H. unlocated. Converted 1/2 stock.

HEARTMAN Concord, New Hampshire. Heavy percussion target rifle.

HEASLETT, WILLIAM Neillsville, Wisconsin, 1875d-1895d.

HEASLEY, JOSEPH Hempfield, Pennsylvania, 1815-1817. (Kauffman)

HEATH, A.B. Tyrigham, Massachusetts, 1890d.

HEATH, A.J. Gallatin, Texas, 1855-1862. (Albaugh 1)

HEATH, JOHN M. Atchison, Kansas, 1891d-1899d.

HEATH, LEVI N. (1826-?), San Francisco, California, 1852c. (Shelton)

HEATH, W. Bath, Maine, 1876. (Demeritt)

HEATH, W.H. Willow, Wisconsin, 1857d.

HEATHCOCK, N.G. Milan, Tennessee, 1885d.

HEATLY, ISIAH H. Jersey City, New Jersey. Patent #489,191 January 3, 1893, breechloading gun.

HEATON & OLIVIER New Orleans, Louisiana, 1859d. Dealers.

HEATON, A. New York, New York. Flintlock and percussion guns. (Swinney)

HEATON, J. (1804-?), Keithsburg, Illinois. (Johnson)

HEATON, MORGAN Putnam, Ohio, 1814, Warren Co., Ohio, 1820c. (Hutslar)

HEATON, T. unlocated. Underhammer rifle.

HEATONS, S.E. unlocated. Percussion 1/2 stock.

HEBARD, LEWIS Santa Clara Co., California. Patent #52,996 March 6, 1866, bullet machine with W.J. Brown. (Shelton)

HEBB, E.T. St. Louis, Missouri. Percussion fullstock.

HEBBARD, ALBERT H. Cambridge, Massachusetts. Patent #247,056 September 13, 1881, breechloading firearms.

HEBENER, ANTON St. Louis, Missouri, 1897d-1908d. (Pourie)

HEBER & MOLLER San Francisco, California, 1877-1879. Percussion 1/2 stock. William Heber and Herman Louis Moller. (Shelton)

HEBER, WILLIAM (1836-?), San Francisco, California, 1861-1905. Percussion 1/2 stock. With August Browning as Browning & Heber, 1873-1876. With Herman Louis Moller as Heber & Moller, 1877-1879. (Shelton)

HEBERER, FRANCIS (1814-?), Peoria, Illinois, 181857d-1861d.

HEBERLEIN, A. St. Louis, Missouri. Air gun.

HEBERLEIN, CHARLES (1822-1870), West Bend, Wisconsin, ?-1870. (MB 5-50)

HEBERT, ALEXIS S. New Orleans, Louisiana, 1870d-1879d.

HEBIG, HENRY C. Philadelphia, Pennsylvania, 1893d-1894d.

HEBLER, WILHELM New York, New York. Patent #173,540 February 15, 1876, air gun.

HECK, J.H. (1813-?), Sumner, Illinois, 1860c, Delaware, Ohio, 1869-1891. (Johnson-Hutslar)

HECK, K. unlocated. Flintlock Kentucky.

HECKENBACH, JOHN A. Mayville, Wisconsin, Kenosha, Wisconsin, 1875d-1879d, Milwaukee, Wisconsin, 1877-1880. Patents #91,624 June 22, 1869, breechloading firearm, and #178,636 June 13, 1876, breechloading firearm. (WGCA)

HECKER, ANDREW Carlisle, Pennsylvania, 1868-1871d. Lockmaker only.

HECKERT, PHILIP (?-1779), York, Pennsylvania, 1769-1779. Flintlock Kentucky rifles. (Kindig)

HECKERT, PHILIP, JR. (?-1812), York, Pennsylvania, 1783-1812. (Kindig)

HECKLA spur trigger revolver by Lee Arms Co.

HECKLEY, BENJAMIN (?-1781), Frederick Co., Virginia. (Gill)

HECKMAN, GEORGE M. Philadelphia, Pennsylvania, 1831d. Stockmaker.

HECKMAN, JOHN Philadelphia, Pennsylvania, 1819-1833d. Stocks only. (Kauffman 2)

HECLA suicide special.

HEDLUND, JOHN St. Cloud, Minnesota, 1882d-1898d.

HEDRICH, CHARLES Hermann, Missouri, 1879d.

HEED, ABRAHAM Bucks Co., Pennsylvania, 1796-1805. (Kauffman)

HEED, JOSEPH Lumberville, Pennsylvania, 1860d-1861d.

HEEHNARTS, CHARLES (1812-?), St. Louis, Missouri, 1850c. (Lewis)

HEEKLE, JOHN Point of Fork, Virginia, 1789-1790. (Gill)

HEEP, JOHN Briarwood, Illinois, 1878d-1884d.

HEETH, H.W. San Francisco, California, 1891-1900. With Herman Louis Moller as Moller & Heeth, 1891-1894. (Shelton)

HEFF, EDWARD Mattoon, Illinois, 1860d.

HEFFLEY, WILLIAM Jasper, Arkansas. (Elias)

HEFLIN, CHARLES R. Omaha, Nebraska, 1884d-1893d.

HEFNER, J. Marion, Ohio. Percussion 1/2 stock.

HEGAMAN, SAMUEL Philadelphia, Pennsylvania, 1808d-1813d.

HEGINBOTTOM, S.H. Saginaw, Michigan, 1895d.

HEGLER, WIRT Emporia, Kansas, 1888d.

HEHN, PETER Berks Co., Pennsylvania, 1805. (Kauffman)

HEIBERGER, GEORGE Philadelphia, Pennsylvania, 1780-1785. Repaired U.S. arms. (Moller)

HEIDENRICH, ERNEST Mt. Clemens, Michigan, 1879d.

HEIDER, HENRY Baltimore, Maryland, 1851d. (Hartzler)

HEILEN, C.V. (?-1890), Carlisle, Pennsylvania. (Whisker III)

HEIMANN, BERNARD Galena, Illinois, 1864d-1875d.

HEIMBAUGH BROS. Momence, Illinois, 1888d.

HEINBECK, G.H. Burlington, Iowa, 1865d.

HEINHOLD, SIMEON Strasburg, Pennsylvania, 1779t. (Dyke).

HEINRICH, LOUIS (1832-1910), Kings Co., New York, 1860, San Diego, California, 1871-1910. (Shelton)

HEINRICHS, CARL Fremont, Nebraska, 1884d-1893d.

HEINSE, C.F. Allardt, Tennessee, 1891d.

HEINZ & BERKELE Atlanta, Georgia, 1870d-1890d.

HEINZ, CHARLES Atlanta, Georgia, 1860-1905d. Converted flintlocks for the Confederacy. As Heinz & Berkele, 1877-1890, and Heinz & Sons, 1890-1905.

HEINZ, CHARLES, JR. Atlanta, Georgia, 1877d-1905d. As Heinz & Berkele, 1877-1890, and Heinz & Sons, 1890-1905.

HEINZ, RICHARD Baltimore, Maryland, 1884-1886d. (Hartzler)

HEINZEN, CHARLES A. & EDWARD Cincinnati, Ohio, 1868-1876d.

HEISEL, L. Cole Co., Missouri, 1850c. (MB 11-66)

HEISER, LEWIS (1829-?), Tiffin, Ohio, 1850-1866. Percussion 1/2 stock. (Hutslar)

HEISS, PHILIP St. Louis, Missouri, 1844-1845d.

HEISS, WILLIAM unlocated. Flintlock Kentucky. (Listed as Weiss by Kindig)

HELFENSTEIN'S GUN BARREL FACTORY Dayton, Ohio, 1837d. Edward Helfenstein and William Stoneberger.

HELFIN, WILLIAM New Buffalo, Michigan, 1891d. See W. Halpen.

HELFRICHT, OTTO Saginaw, Michigan, 1883d-1899d.

HELLER, D. unlocated. Percussion pistol.

HELLER, J. Carlisle, Pennsylvania, probably John Keller.

HELLERICH, JOHN see John Hallerich.

HELLINGHAUS, FREDERICK (1811-?), Baltimore, Maryland, 1832-1835, St. Louis, Missouri, 1840-1847d, Sacramento, California, 1851d, San Francisco, California, 1856-1857. Percussion guns. With John Pearson in Baltimore and St. Louis. (Shelton) Note: see Henry Morgan, with Hellinghaus, 1842-1844 per (Shelton).

HELM, CHARLES H. (1828-1868), Carlinville, Illinois, 1860d-1868.

HELM, E. Carlinville, Illinois, 1867d-1871d. Son of and successor to Charles Helm.

HELTON, JOAB unlocated. Percussion 1/2 stock.

HELWIG, W.J. Allegheny, Pennsylvania, 1887d.

HEMBEL, FREDERICK Yonkers, New York, 1870d.

HEMENWAY, LEVI J. Shrewsbury, Massachusetts, 1853d-1892d. Percussion 1/2 stock. Also spelled Hemmingway.

HEMENWAY, O. unlocated. Percussion 1/2 stock.

HEMING, L.M. unlocated. Percussion fullstock.

HEMIWORTH, RICHARD Troy, New York, 1831-1835. (Dillin)

HEMMES, STEPHEN St. Charles, Missouri, 1854d-1860d.

HEMMING, BENJAMIN New Haven, Connecticut. Patents #377,854 February 14, 1888, firearm, and #618,033 January 17, 1899, firearm.

HEMMINGER, A. Sandusky, Ohio, 1859d. Percussion fullstock rifle. (Hutslar)

HEMMINGWAY, L. see Levi J. Hemenway.

HEMSTREET, V.A. Augusta, Georgia, 1888d-1899d.

HENCH Pottsville, Pennsylvania. (Dillin)

HENDEE, D. Summum, Illinois, 1860d.

HENDEE, EDWIN B. San Francisco, California. Patent #410,360 December 20, 1870, lock.

HENDERSON & ANDREWS Denver, Colorado, 1861d. (Sellers-3)

HENDERSON, A.A. Okoboji, Iowa, 1895d-1897d.

HENDERSON, ABRAHAM (1762-?), Mecklenburg Co., North Carolina. (Bivins)

HENDERSON, C.C. Cherry Grove, Minnesota, 1898d.

HENDERSON, CHARLES Taylorstown, Pennsylvania, 1829-1831. (Whisker II)

HENDERSON, D. Andover, New York, 1850d. Percussion 1/2 stock.

HENDERSON, DANIEL Charleston, South Carolina, 1798-1809. (Kauffman 2)

HENDERSON, DAVID Holland, New York, 1856-1860c.

HENDERSON, L. Andover, New York, 1874d-1882d. Percussion target rifle.

HENDERSON, L.R. Vergennes, Vermont, 1880. (Horn)

HENDERSON, NELSON Lincoln Co., North Carolina. Apprenticed 1838. (Bivins)

HENDERSON, W. Dayton, Ohio, 1842. (Hutslar)

HENDERSON, W.H. Atlanta, Georgia, 1861. Confederate gunsmith convention.

HENDERSON, WILLIAM Oakland, Illinois, 1886d.

HENDERSON, ZINA Okoboji, Iowa, 1865d and 1882d-1889d, Spirit Lake, Iowa, 1880-1881d. As Middleton & Henderson, 1881.

HENDRICKS, B.F. Eugene, Oregon, 1878d, Junction City, Oregon, 1886d, McMinnville, Oregon, 1891d.

HENDRICKS, FRANCIS (?-1771), New York, New York.

HENDRICKS, HUMPHREY Virginia, 1776. Committee of Safety repairs. (Gill)

HENDRICKS, M.S. Arkansas City, Arkansas, 1888d.

HENDRICKS, MERTON S. (?-1930), Aurora, Illinois, 1868-1930. Altered breechloading rifles. (Johnson)

HENDRICKS, S.P. Dansville, Michigan, 1867d-1883d. As Hendricks & Fletcher, 1867.

HENDRICKSON, L. Ravenna, Ohio, 1878d, Brainerd, Minnesota, 1882d.

HENDRIE, W.C. Syracuse, New York, 1810. (Dean*)

HENG, BARTHOLOMEW Hudson City, New Jersey, 1856-1869.

HENKEL, WILLIAM St. Louis, Missouri, 1879d-1890d.

HENKELS, DANIEL Philadelphia, Pennsylvania, 1808-1817. Model 1812 contract muskets. (Gluckman)

HENLEY, W.H. unlocated. Percussion revolver, Confederate?

HENLY, LOUIS Cresco, Iowa, 1892d.

HENNCH, PETER Lancaster, Pennsylvania, 1770-1774.

HENNIG, AUGUSTUS Brooklyn, New York, 1889d.

HENNINGER, DANIEL Northumberland Co., Pennsylvania, 1841. (Kauffman)

HENNINGER, DANIEL Wallingford, Illinois, 1860d.

HENNINGER, J.S. Jewell, Kansas, 1882d-1894d. Percussion swivel breech.

HENNINGER, JOHN Sugar Valley, Pennsylvania, 1841. (Kauffman)

HENON, THOMAS Charleston, South Carolina, 1807-1809. (Kauffman 2)

HENRICH, ALONZO Bozrah, Connecticut, 1870d-1871d.

HENRICKS & FLETCHER Dansville, Michigan, 1867d.

HENRY ARMS CO. trade name of H & D Folsom on imported shotguns. Also known as Henry Gun Co. (AR 2-69)

HENRY REPEATING RIFLE CO. New Haven, Connecticut, 1865-1866. Became Winchester Repeating Arms Co., May 30, 1866.

HENRY, ABRAHAM (1728-1811), Nazareth, Pennsylvania, 1781t, Lancaster, Pennsylvania, 1795t-1811. Model 1798 contract muskets for Pennsylvania with John Graeff. Model 1798 contract muskets with Peter Brong and Henry DeHuff for Virginia. Model 1807 contract rifles and pistols. Kentucky rifles. (Gluckman-Dyke)

HENRY, BENJAMIN TYLER (1821-1898), New Haven, Connecticut. Patent #30,446 October 16, 1860, magazine gun. Made by Winchester as the Henry rifle.

HENRY, GEORGE Columbus, Mississippi. Confederate patent #108 September 27, 1862, breechloading firearm. (Albaugh 3)

HENRY, GEORGE Philadelphia, Pennsylvania, 1777-1779. At State Gun Factory.

HENRY, GRANVILLE (1835-1912), Boulton, Pennsylvania, 1860-1894. Patents #60,188 December 4, 1866, lockplate fitting, and #461,679 October 20, 1891, breechloading gun. Son of and successor to James Henry. (Gabel)

HENRY, J., & SON Boulton, Pennsylvania, 1830-1836 and 1860-1894. Large quantities of lesser quality 1/2 stock rifles. J.J. Henry II and James Henry 1830-1836. James Henry and Granville Henry, 1860. (Gabel)

HENRY, JAMES (1809-1894), Boulton, Pennsylvania, 1835t-1894. Son of and successor to J.J. Henry II. (Gabel)

HENRY, JOHN JOSEPH, I (1758-1811), Lancaster, Pennsylvania, 1775-1811. Son of William Henry.

HENRY, JOHN JOSEPH, II (1786-1836), Philadelphia, Pennsylvania, 1808-1820d, Boulton, Pennsylvania, 1820-1836. Son of William Henry, Jr. (Gabel)

HENRY, JOHN (?-1747), Lancaster, Pennsylvania, 1747. (Kindig)

HENRY, JOHN (?-1777), Lancaster, Pennsylvania, 1773-1777. Brother of William Henry.

HENRY, JOHN Cadillac, Michigan, 1895d.

HENRY, JOHN Elkton, Kentucky, 1860d.

HENRY, JOHN, JR. Bedford Co., Pennsylvania, 1876-1880. (Whisker II)

HENRY, JOSEPH Philadelphia, Pennsylvania, 1811-1816. Worked with his brother John Joseph Henry. (Gabel)

HENRY, L. unlocated. Percussion 1/2 stock.

HENRY, MICHAEL Moore, Pennsylvania, 1828t. (KRA II-3)

HENRY, MOSES Pittsburgh, Pennsylvania, 1766-1767, Frankfort, Ohio, 1769-1780. Gunsmith to Delaware Indians. (Hutslar)

HENRY, NOAH (1818-?), Henderson Co., North Carolina, 1850c. (Bivins)

HENRY, PIERRE New Orleans, Louisiana, 1822d-1823d.

HENRY, STEPHEN Providence, Rhode Island, 1859-1868.

HENRY, WILLIAM (1729-1786), Lancaster, Pennsylvania, 1750-1786. Committee of Safety muskets. (Kindig)

HENRY, WILLIAM, III (1796-?), Boulton, Pennsylvania, 1816-1822. Son of William Henry, Jr. (Gabel)

HENRY, WILLIAM, JR. (1757-1821), Nazareth, Pennsylvania, 1780-1817. Models 1798 and 1808 contract muskets with John Joseph Henry, II. Model 1797 contract muskets for Pennsylvania. Flintlock pistol. (Gabel)

HENSHAW, JOSEPH New York, New York, 1830-1836, Newark, New Jersey, 1836-? Gunsmith and engraver. (Sutherland)

HENSHAW, JOSHUA Vergennes, Vermont. Model 1798 contract muskets under Jonathon Nichols' contract. (At Middlebury, Vermont according to Moller)

HENSLAG, HERMAN (1802-?), St. Louis, Missouri, 1850c. (Lewis)

HENSLER, JOHN New Orleans, Louisiana, 1858-1861d. As Bujac & Hensler.

HENSLEY, SAMUEL J. (1849-1919), Weaverville, California, 1874-1885. (Shelton)

HENTZ, NICHOLAS Allegheny, Pennsylvania, 1859-1860. (Kauffman)

HEPBURN, JAMES H. Detroit, Michigan, 1871-1875d.

HEPBURN, L.L. Colton, New York, 1858-1882, Ilion, New York, 1883-1889, New Haven, Connecticut, 1889-1908. Patents #220,285 October 7, 1879, breechloading firearm, #290,426 December 18, 1883, breechloading firearm, #298,377 May 13, 1884, magazine gun, #354,059 December 7, 1886, magazine gun, #371,455 October 11, 1887, magazine gun, #400,679 April 2, 1889, magazine gun, #434,062 August 12, 1890, magazine gun, #463,832 November 24, 1891, magazine gun, #502,489 August 1, 1893, breechloading firearm, #525,739 September 11, 1894, magazine gun, #534,691 February 26, 1895, detachable barrel, #549,722 November 12, 1895, magazine gun, #560,032 May 12, 1896, magazine gun, #561,226 June 2, 1896, magazine gun, #584,177 June 8, 1897, magazine gun, #591,220, October 5, 1897, safety, #732,075 June 30, 1903, sight, #776,243 November 29, 1904, magazine gun, #776,332 November 29, 1904, safety, #918,447 April 13, 1908, magazine gun, #927,464 July 6, 1908, firearm, and #943,828 December 21, 1908, magazine gun. Made muzzle loading rifles at Colton. Worked for Remington at Ilion, and Winchester at New Haven.

HEPNER, JACOB Georgetown, Colorado, 1882d. (Sellers-3)

HEPPERT, HENRY Hannibal, Missouri, 1889d.

HEPTINSTALL, M.C. Enfield, North Carolina, Patent #53,144 March 13, 1866, alarm gun.

HERALD, LOUIS Little Rock, Arkansas, 1871d.

HERBERT, O.H. Albany, New York. Percussion fullstock rifle. (Clow)

HERCULES trade name of Iver Johnson and Montgomery Ward on shotguns. (Hinman)

HERDER Cincinnati, Ohio. Percussion lock.

HERDER see Chapman & Herder.

HERDER, AUGUST Marine, Illinois, 1875d.

HERDTFELDER, JOHN New York, 1873d-1890d.

HERFURTH & ANSCHUTZ Madison, Wisconsin, 1856-1858. Percussion double shotgun. August Herfurth and E. Anschutz. (WGCA 6)

HERFURTH & HOWARD Madison, Wisconsin. Percussion 1/2 stock, percussion shotgun. August Herfurth and J.P. Howard.

HERFURTH, AUGUST Fremont, Nebraska, 1882d. Same as above?

HERFURTH, AUGUST Madison, Wisconsin, 1856-1879d. Percussion schuetzen rifles. (WGCA 6)

HERGET, EMIL W. Oakland, California, 1880-1893d. (Shelton)

HERGET, JOHN (1821-?), San Francisco, California, 1854-1873. (Shelton)

HERIGER, SOLOMON (1829-1892), Clarion Co., Pennsylvania.

HERKSTROETER, FREDERICK St. Louis, Missouri, 1848d-1875d. As Herkstroeter & Stahlberg, 1870d.

HERMAN, F.H. Fenton, Michigan, 1891d.

HERMAN, JOHN St. Louis, Missouri, 1895-1905. Tip-up rifles and pistols.

HERMAN, PETER Lancaster, Ohio, 1864-1871. (Gluckman & Satterlee)

HERMANN, B. Galena, Illinois, 1867d.

HERMANN, E. Belleville, Illinois, 1888d.

HERMANN, LOUIS I. Pasadena, California, 1888d-1893d. (Shelton)

HERMES, AUGUST Rockport, Indiana, 1881-1885. (Gardner)

HERMITAGE ARMS CO. trade name of Crescent on guns made for Gray & Dudley Hardware Co., Nashville, Tennessee. Also known as Hermitage Gun Co. (AR 2-69)

HERMLE, JOHN Euclid, Ohio. Patent #311,755 February 3, 1885, stock.

HERNANDEZ, F. Laredo, Texas, 1885d.

HERNANDEZ, J.E. Jacksonville, Florida, 1886d.

HERNDON, JOSEPH Wilkes Co., North Carolina, circa 1780. (Bivins)

HERO trade name for percussion pistol by American Standard Tool Co.

HERO trade name for percussion pistol by Manhattan Firearms Co.

HERR Canton, Ohio, 1820. (Dean)

HERRERA, A. Visalia, California, 1874d. (Shelton)

HERRICK, EUGENE I. Rangely, Maine. Patent #426,015 April 22, 1890, reversible barrel.

HERRICK, H. Toledo, Ohio. Patent #323,810 August 4, 1885, alarm gun with W.L. Babcock.

HERRING, GEORGE Inland, Ohio, 1859d. (Hutslar)

HERRING, RICHARD Wilmington, North Carolina, 1776-1788. Public gun factory with John Devane, made muskets and rifles. (Bivins)

HERRINGTON, ALBERT Worthville, New York, 1870d.

HERRINGTON, HIRAM Macon, Georgia, 1881d-1883d.

HERRINGTON, WILLIAM Jefferson Co., Missouri, 1850c. (MB 11-66)

HERRIOTT, RUTHERFORD Independence Co., Arkansas, 1841-1860. (Elias)

HERRMANN, BRUNO S. Chicago, Illinois. Patent #415,509 November 19, 1889, breechloading firearm.

HERRON Zanesville, Ohio. Percussion fullstock.

HERRON, DANIEL New Castle, Ohio, 1859d. (Hutslar)

HERRON, N. Danville, Ohio, percussion 1/2 stock. (Hutslar)

HERSEY, ADAM Mason, Ohio, 1863-1872. Percussion 1/2 stock. (Hutslar)

HERSH, JACOB Pennsburg, Pennsylvania, 1860d-1861d. Percussion fullstock.

HERSTROETER & STAHLBERG St. Louis, Missouri, 1870d.

HERTHE, AUGUST unlocated. Flintlock Kentucky.

HERTING, F., & BRO. Wilmington, Delaware, 1882d.

HERTON, S.J. Dover Hill, Indiana, 1860d.

HERTZFELDT, CARL, JR. Chicago, Illinois. Patent #208,016 September 17, 1878, spring air gun.

HERTZOG, ANDREW (?-1794), York, Pennsylvania, 1777-1780, Fayette Co., Pennsylvania, 1790-1793. Committee of Safety repairs. (Gluckman & Satterlee, Whisker II)

HERTZOG, ANDREW (1804-1839), Fayette Co., Pennsylvania, 1825-1839. Son of George Hertzog. (Whisker II)

HERTZOG, DAVID (1799-1835), Fayette Co., Pennsylvania, 1823-1835. Son of George Hertzog. (Whisker II)

HERTZOG, FREDERICK Fayette Co., Pennsylvania. Flintlock Kentucky pistol. (KRA 76)

HERTZOG, GEORGE (1776-1849), Fayette Co., Pennsylvania, 1797-1849. Son of Andrew Hertzog. (Whisker II)

HERTZOG, JACOB (?-1823), Fayette Co., Pennsylvania, 1803-1823. Son of Andrew Hertzog. (Whisker II)

HERZEL, T.G. Philadelphia, Pennsylvania, 1863. Converted flintlock muskets.

HESKIT, H.H. Columbus, Ohio, 1879d. (Hutslar)

HESS, ADAM Lehigh Co., Pennsylvania. Son of Jonas Hess. (KRA II-3)

HESS, CHRISTIAN (?-1794), Lancaster, Pennsylvania, ?-1794. (Dean)

HESS, DAVID (1824-1898), Lehigh Co., Pennsylvania, 1850c, New Tripoli, Pennsylvania, 1861d, Lynnport, Pennsylvania, 1882d-1898d. Son of Jonas Hess. (Gabel)

HESS, DAVID Northampton Co., Pennsylvania, 1780t-1783t. (Dyke)

HESS, FLORIAN New Ulm, Minnesota, 1877-1882d.

HESS, JACOB Frease's Store, Ohio, 1852-1864, Wilmot, Ohio, 1868d. (Hutslar)

HESS, JOHN FREDERICK (?-1769), Lehigh Co., Pennsylvania, 1769. (Gabel)

HESS, JONAS M. Germanville, Pennsylvania, 1840-1861d. Underhammer swivel pistol presented to President Harrison, 1840, and flintlock swivel Kentucky rifles. Son of Jonas Hess. (Gabel)

HESS, JONAS (1799-?), Lehigh Co., Pennsylvania, 1832-? Son of and successor to Philip Hess. (Gabel)

HESS, PHILIP (1766-?). Northampton Co., Pennsylvania, 1780-1801. Son of John Frederick Hess. (Gabel)

HESS, PHILIP, JR. Lehighton, Pennsylvania, 1832. Flintlock Kentucky. (Gabel)

HESS, SAMUEL Lancaster Co., Pennsylvania, 1771.

HESS, SOLOMAN (1806-?), Lehigh Co., Pennsylvania, 1850c, Overton, Pennsylvania, 1861d. Son of Philip Hess. (Gabel)

HESS, THOMAS (1821-?), Schuylkill Co., Pennsylvania. Flintlock Kentucky rifles. Son of Jonas Hess. (Gabel)

HESS, THOMAS Lehigh Co., Pennsylvania. Flintlock Kentucky rifle. Son of Philip Hess. (Gabel)

HESS, THOMAS West Penn, Pennsylvania, 1882d, Leibyville, Pennsylvania, 1887d-1890d.

HESSE, FRED W. (1846-?), Santa Rosa, California, 1877-circa 1900. (Shelton)

HESTON, SAMUEL J. Reading, Pennsylvania, 1865-1870, Worthington, Indiana, 1882-1885. Percussion 1/2 stock.

HETRICK, JOHN (1829-?), Newark, Ohio, 1850-1896. Percussion rifles. (Hutslar)

HETRICK, L. Warsaw, Indiana, 1874-1880. (Gardner)

HETRICK, LEVI Lima, Ohio, 1880-1911. Breechloading rifles and shotguns. (Hutslar)

HETRICK, ROBERT Oswego, New York, 1856-1860.

HETTMANNSPERGER, A. Camden, New Jersey, 1878d.

HETZNER, THOMAS (1826-?), Peru, Indiana, 1860c. (Lindert)

HEUSER, J.J. (1820-?), New Orleans, Louisiana, 1850c-1853d.

HEUSER, MAX New York, New York. Patent #191,341 May 29, 1877, trigger.

HEUSIER, JACOB S. Salt Lake City, Utah, 1878d-1880d. As Heusier & Bro., 1878.

HEWES & PHILLIPS Newark, New Jersey, 1862-1864. Converted muskets marked "H&P" on bolster. (ASAC)

HEWES, JOSIAH Philadelphia, Pennsylvania, 1776. Committee of Safety muskets.

HEWITT, CHARLES B. Burlington, New Jersey. Patent #243,894 July 5, 1881, lock with W.H. Kimball.

HEXAGON trade name of Sears, Roebuck & Co. on shotguns. (Hinman)

HEYBERGER, G.W. & J.M. Philadelphia, Pennsylvania, 1856d-1857d. At separate addresses, 1865d.

HEYDE, WILLIAM Sherman, Texas, 1878d-1884d, Houston, Texas, 1889d-1899d.

HEYER see Duryea & Heyer.

HEYSINGER, ISAAC W. Philadelphia, Pennsylvania. Patents #194,679 August 28, 1877, breechloading firearm and #194,680 August 28, 1877, lock.

HIATT, JOSEPH (1848-?), Hampshire Co., West Virginia, 1880d. (Whisker IV)

HIB-SPE-BAR trade name of Hibbard, Spencer, Bartlett & Co.

HIBBARD & SPENCER CO. Chicago, Illinois, 1880-1883. Dealers only, successors to W.E. Spencer & Co.

HIBBARD, ALFRED T. Lincoln, Nebraska. Patent #371,886 October 18, 1887, stock.

HIBBARD, SPENCER, BARTLETT & CO. Chicago, Illinois, 1883-1929. Dealers only.

HIBNER, JOHN (1790-?), Baltimore, Maryland, 1837d-1853d. (Hartzler)

HICH, LEWIS (1842-?), Chicago, Illinois, 1860c. (Johnson)

HICKEY & DAVIDSON Nashville, Tennessee, 1871d.

HICKMAN, HENRY Omaha, Nebraska, 1866d-1867d. As McAusland & Hickman.

HICKMAN, L.M. Stockton, California, 1861-1870. Derringer. (Shelton)

HICKOK, T.A. Green Bay, Wisconsin, 1895d.

HICKS, A. unlocated. Percussion 1/2 stock.

HICKS, C.V. Oscoda, Michigan, 1883d.

HICKS, CHARLES Haverstraw, New York. Patents #16,587 February 10, 1857, percussion caps, and #16,646 February 17, 1857, percussion caps.

HICKS, GABRIEL Providence, Rhode Island, 1650. (Achtermier)

HICKS, W.B. Pittsburgh, Pennsylvania, 1890d.

HICKS, WALTER E. Brooklyn, New York. Patent #393,107 November 20, 1888, centrifugal gun.

HICKS, WILLIAM CLEVELAND New Haven, Connecticut. Patents #16,797 March 19, 1857, firing pin and extractor, and #41,814, March 1, 1864, breechloading firearm. The extractor patent was used on the Volcanic guns and was the subject of several lawsuits.

HICKS, WILLIAM Shelby Co., Kentucky, 1810, Greencastle, Indiana, 1820.

HIDDEN, ENOCH New Orleans, Louisiana, 1822d, New York, New York, 1823-1851. Patents #none April 26, 1826, elevating mechanism, #none January 14, 1831, cannon lock, #none December 16, 1831, cannon lock, and #none August 28, 1834, cannon lock. Made guns until 1830, cannons and locks thereafter.

HIDE, ELIJAH Connecticut, 1777. Committee of Safety repairs.

HIEKISCH, PAUL Decatur, Illinois, 1878d-1884d.

HIESTER, L. Reading, Pennsylvania. Barrell maker. (Kindig)

HIGBY, HIRAM Vienna, New York, 1856-1859.

HIGGENS, THOMAS Philadelphia, Pennsylvania, 1780-1785. Repaired U.S. arms. (Moller)

HIGGINS & SON West Chesterfield, Massachusetts, 1888-1890. Shotguns.

HIGGINS, D. Indian Springs, Georgia, 1861. Confederate gunsmith convention.

HIGGINS, EDWARD L. Fairfax, Vermont, 1882d.

HIGGINS, GEORGE F. Denver, Colorado, 1884d.

HIGGINS, H.H. Indian Springs, Georgia, 1861. Confederate gunsmith convention.

HIGGINS, JAMES M. Atlanta, Georgia, 1861. Confederate gunsmith convention.

HIGGINS, JOHN Hampshire Co., Virginia, 1809. Contract rifles for Virginia. (Cromwell)

HIGGINS, R.J. Beaumont, Texas, 1890d.

HIGGINS, WILLIAM unlocated. Flintlock lock.

HIGHSMITH, M.V. unlocated. Percussion 1/2 stock

HIGHT, ALLISON (1798-1873), Clermont Co., Ohio, 1816-1873. (Hutslar)

HIGHTOWER & ADAMS Denver, Colorado, 1859. G.W. Hightower and W.A. Adams. (Sellers-3)

HILDEN, GEORGE Keokuk, Iowa, 1880-1887d. Percussion fullstock.

HILDENBEITEL, JOHN Lancaster Co., Pennsylvania, 1835t-1850t. (Dyke)

HILDER, GOTTFRIED J. St. Cloud, Minnesota. Patent #493,382 March 14, 1893, multi-charge gun.

HILDRETH, LESTER C. Lowell, Michigan, 1863d-1879d. Percussion 1/2 stock.

HILER, SELAH Harlem, New York. Patent #34,961, April 15, 1862, gun barrels.

HILGAR, PHILIP (1822-?), Wayne Co., Ohio, 1850c. (Hutslar)

HILL & HATTEN Atchison, Kansas, 1865d. E. Hill and J.S. Hatten.

HILL, ALBERT V. Limestone, New York, 1859-1874d. Patents #24,936 August 2, 1859, breechloading firearm, and #32,421 May 28, 1861, breechloading firearm. Also in Hinsdale, 1859d and Carrollton, 1861d.

HILL, BRYON R. Cranston, Rhode Island. Patent #99,893 February 15, 1870, revolver.

HILL, EDMUND Baltimore, Maryland, 1840c. (Hartzler)

HILL, GEORGE W. Norfolk, Virginia, 1870-1888d.

HILL, GEORGE Washington Co., Pennsylvania, 1799-1808. (Whisker II)

HILL, ISAAC Circleville, Illinois, 1860d.

HILL, J.C. Tyler, Texas, 1863-1865. Took over Short Briscoe & Co. in 1863. Rifles marked "Hill Rifle Tyler C.S.". (Albaugh)

HILL, J.F. Newark, New Jersey, 1882d.

HILL, J.J. Johnstown, New York. Flintlock rifle. (Swinney)

HILL, JASON C. Rutland, Vermont, 1875-1894. (Horn)

HILL, JONATHAN Falmouth, Maine, 1689. (Dermitt)

HILL, JOSEPH A. Muncie, Indiana, 1881-1887. (Lindert)

HILL, LEMUEL G. Johnston, New York, 1861-1870. Son of S.W. Hill. (Swinney)

HILL, LYMAN E. Putnam, Connecticut, 1876d-1889d.

HILL, LYSANDER Chicago, Illinois. Patent #249,240 November 8, 1881, side trigger revolver with T.S.E. Dixon.

HILL, S.W. Johnston, New York. Percussion rifles. Son of J.J. Hill. (Swinney)

HILL, THOMAS Charlotte, Vermont, 1791-1800. Air guns and flintlock rifles.

HILL, WILLIAM Albany, New York, 1774. (Gardner)

HILL, WILLIAM Buffalo, New York, 1836. For P. Smith. (Kauffman)

HILL, WILLIAM Limestone, New York, 1870d.

HILLE, CHARLES (1810-?), New Orleans, Louisiana, 1842d-1859d. As Allen & Hille.

HILLEGAS, HENRY Harrisburg, Pennsylvania, 1840-1883. Flintlock and percussion rifles. (Dillin)

HILLEGAS, JOSEPH Pottsville, Pennsylvania, 1810-1841. Flintlock pistols and rifles. (Dillin)

HILLELAND, W.A. unlocated. Percussion fullstock.

HILLER, H.J. Los Angeles, California, 1893d.

HILLER, J.P. Woodhull, Illinois, 1884d.

HILLER, PRINCE Mattapoiset, Massachusetts. Patent #32,188 April 30, 1861, lock.

HILLIARD, CHARLES N. & GEORGE E. Cornish, New Hampshire, 1876-1879. Sons of D.H. Hilliard. Tip-up .38-40 rifle.

HILLIARD, DAVID HALL (1805-1877), Cornish, New Hampshire, 1842-1877. Underhammer guns. (GR 8-78)

HILLIARD, GEORGE E. Cornish, New Hampshire, 1873-1900. Brother of David and successor to his business. Underhammer pistols and rifles, tip-up rifles, and shotguns.

HILLIS, WILLIAM D. Joliet, Illinois. Patent #44,312 September 20, 1864, breechloading firearm. Multi-barrel tip-up rifle.

HILLMAN, DANIEL Mottville, Michigan, 1883d-1887d.

HILLS, BENONI Durham, Connecticut, 1728-1741, Goshen, Connecticut, 1741-1753. Flintlock guns.

HILLS, JOHN (1732-1808), Goshen, Connecticut, 1754-1774, Winchester, Connecticut, 1774-1784, Charlotte, Vermont, 1784-1810. Flintlock pistols and muskets. Son of Benoni Hills. (Hobbies 8-69)

HILLS, MEDAD (1729-1808), Goshen, Connecticut, 1750-1808. Committee of Safety muskets, and flintlock fowlers, rifles, and pistols.

HILLS, W.J. Uniontown, West Virginia, 1900d. (Whisker IV)

HILLSBORO MFG. CO. Hillsboro, North Carolina, 1776-1778. Contract for musket parts. (Bivins)

HILLSTEAD, F.W. Palmyra, Missouri, 1860d.

HILTON, ALEXANDER J.H. Boston, Massachusetts. Patent #66,709 July 16, 1867, breechloading firearm.

HILTON, GEORGE (1816-?), Hancock Co., Illinois, 1850c. (Johnson)

HILTON, JACOB Rochester, Iowa, 1865d.

HIMBER, J. San Antonio, Texas, 1878d.

HIMES, D.H. Crawfordsville, Indiana, 1860. Percussion 1/2 stock. (Lindert)

HIMES, JAMES (1819-?), Preble Co., Ohio, 1850c. (Hutslar)

HINCKLEY, A.F. Rockford, Illinois, 1877-1888. (Johnson)

HINCKLEY, H.W. Atchison, Kansas, 1873d.

HINDEN, MATHIAS J. Detroit, Michigan. Patent #92,048 June 29, 1869, breechloading firearm.

HINDERMYER, PHILLIP Philadelphia, Pennsylvania, 1875d.

HINDLEY, SOLOMON K. Springfield, Massachusetts. Patents #345,058 July 6, 1886, breechloading firearm with Edwin S. Field, #383,641 May 29, 1888, magazine gun, #384,161 June 5, 1888, magazine gun, and #391,953 October 30, 1888, magazine gun with Edwin S. Field. All patents were used by Bullard Repeating Arms Co.

HINDS, JOHN Boston, Massachusetts, 1745. (Gluckman & Satterlee)

HINDS, T. Whitesville, Kentucky. Percussion 1/2 stock.

HINE, JACOB (1782-?), Westmoreland Co., Pennsylvania, 1825-1832. (Whisker II)

HINE, JOHN Philadelphia, Pennsylvania. Musket barrels.

HINE, RILEY Croton, New York, 1874d-1882d.

HINELINE, THOMAS Washington, D.C., 1862d. (Hartzler)

HINES, EDWARD K. Poestenkill, New York, 1866-1882.

HINES, J.M. Newburg, Tennessee, 1887d-1891d.

HINGLE, JOHN St. Louis, Missouri, 1840d.

HINKLE, GEORGE J. Lancaster, Pennsylvania, 1857d-1875d.

HINKLE, WILLIAM Lancaster, Pennsylvania, 1875d.

HINKLES, DANIEL see Daniel Henkels.

HINKLEY, G.C. Sulphur Springs, Texas, 1890d-1892d.

HINMAN, B. Galena, Illinois, 1867d.

HINNAN, J.B. Sulphur Springs, Texas 1890d-1892d.

HINSDALE suicide special and taxidermy gun by Hopkins & Allen.

HINSDALE, SAMUEL DEXTER (1816-1875), Princeton, Illinois, 1838-1864d. (Johnson)

HINTSCHE, WILLIAM Kansas City, Missouri, 1888d-1898d.

HIRSCHY, H. Wooster, Ohio, 1888d. (Hutslar)

HIRTH, AUGUST Pittsburgh, Pennsylvania, 1880-1894. Percussion fullstock. With Brown & Hirth in Enterprise Gun Works after 1887. (Kauffman)

HIRTH, BERNARD Minneapolis, Minnesota, 1892d.

HISER, L. see Lewis Heiser.

HISMITH, FRANK & CO. San Antonio, Texas, 1884d.

HISTED, THADEUS C. Canon City, Colorado, 1883d, Cherryvale, Kansas, 1884d-1888d, Weir, Kansas, 1894d, Pittsburg, Kansas, 1903. Patent #727,363 May 5, 1903, gun boring machine. (Sellers-3)

HISTEL, GEORGE (1835-?), Freeport, Illinois, 1860c. (Johnson)

HITCHCOCK, ALEXANDER New York, New York, 1852d-1867d. As Hitchcock & Co., 1852-1857. Importer.

HITCHCOCK, DEXTER Worcester, Massachusetts, 1874-1875.

HITCHCOCK, FRANK W. Worcester, Massachusetts, 1874-1875. With Dexter Hitchcock.

HITCHCOCK, GAD Yarmouth, Maine, 1871. (Dermitt)

HITCHCOCK, J.H. New York, New York, 1862-1863. Converted flintlock muskets.

HITCHCOCK, MUZZY & CO. Worcester, Massachusetts, 1846-1857. Percussion pistols and rifles, Morse carbines, barrels. Failed February 17, 1857. (Owens)

HITCHCOCK, OAKLY (1820-?), Rock Island, Illinois, 1850c. (Johnson)

HITCHINGS, JOHN Colfax, California, 1877d. (Shelton)

HITCHINS, H. Denver, Colorado, 1861d. (Sellers-3)

HITTON, E.J. Clarksville, Missouri, 1850c. (MB 11-66)

HITZELBERGER, STEPHEN V. Westminster, Maryland, 1882d. (Hartzler)

HIVELY, W.H. Salem, Ohio, 1890d. (Hutslar)

HIX, DAVID Point of Fork, Virginia, 1786. (Gill)

HIXON, DANIEL (1818-?), Washington, Pennsylvania, 1840-1861. (Whisker II)

HIXON, J.B. Antrim, Ohio, 1859d. "H" marking on two of his rifles. (Hutslar)

HIXON, JOSEPH Westmoreland Co., Pennsylvania, 1816-1822. (Whisker II)

HIXSON, J. Trewhitt, Tennessee, 1881-1891d. As Hardin & Hixson in 1891.

HIZER, L. see Lewis Heiser.

HLUCHAN, JOHN Schulenburg, Texas, 1884d-1896d.

HOADLEY, LEMUEL Connecticut, 1775-1776. Committee of Safety muskets.

HOADY, J. unlocated. Sign dated 1824.

HOAG, C. Pomeroy, Ohio, 1859d. (Hutslar)

HOAKE, JACOB (?-1831), Lancaster, Pennsylvania, 1775-1831. Committee of Safety locks and Kentucky rifles. (Kindig)

HOAKE, MATTHIAS Lancaster, Pennsylvania, 1800-1816t. Flintlock Kentucky rifles. (Kauffman)

HOARD, CHARLES BROOKS Watertown, New York, 1861-1864, Pamelia, New York, 1864-1865. Model 1861 contract muskets and Freeman percussion revolvers. (Fuller, Sellers-1)

HOARD, F.H. Marquette, Michigan, 1899d.

HOBBES, JAMES Philadelphia, Pennsylvania, 1824d.

HOBBS, A.J. Bridgeport, Connecticut. Patent #395,897 January 8, 1889, shot cartridge with M. Hartley. Was superintendent of U.M.C.

HOBBS, J. West Ossipee, New Hampshire, 1870-1874.

HOBBS, JOHN L. Springfield, Massachusetts. Patent #635,705, October 24, 1899, safety with Joseph H. Wesson.

HOBBS, JOHN (1797-?), Zanesville, Ohio, 1850c. (Hutslar)

HOBBS, P. Monterey, Massachusetts, 1849d.

HOBERT, MILTON (1843-?), Ottawa, Illinois, 1860c. (Johnson)

HOBLIT, LYMAN Sheldon, Missouri, 1889d.

HOBRECKER, JOHN G. Charleston, South Carolina, 1806-1816. As Hobrecker & Roh in 1807. (Kauffman 2)

HOBSON, PETER Greenfield, Illinois, 1875d.

HOBSON, WILLIAM (?-1812), Wilmington, Ohio, ?-1812. (Hutslar)

HOCKBRUNN, FREDERICK New York, New York. Patent #660,437 October 23, 1900, breechloading firearm.

HOCKENSMITH, K.D. Jackson Co., Missouri, 1850c. (MB 11-66)

HOCKENSMITH, WILLIAM W. Lawson, Missouri, 1850c-1898d, Crab Orchard, Missouri, 1881.

HOCKETT, AARON L. Jonesboro, Indiana. Patent #435,833 September 2, 1890, breechloading firearm.

HOCKLEY, JAMES Chester Co., Pennsylvania, 1769-1771. (Gluckman & Satterlee)

HOCKSCHERN, GOTFRIED (1820-?), Nauvoo, Illinois, 1857-1860. (Johnson)

HOCUM, HENRY Denver, Colorado, 1864. Worked for Morgan Rood. (Sellers-3)

HODES, GUSTAV Corvallis, Oregon, 1866d-1891d.

HODGE, G.W. Clarence, Missouri, 1889d.

HODGE, J.T. New York, New York. Model 1861 contract muskets. (Fuller)

HODGES, JAMES C. Morristown, Tennessee. Patent #217,218, July 8, 1879, revolver with A.A. Hall.

HODGKINS & HAIGH New York, New York, 1875d-1884d. Importers.

HODGKINS, D.C. Macon, Georgia, 1862. Established Macon Armory with his three sons. (Hill-Anthony)

HODGKINS, WALTER C. Macon, Georgia, 1858-1865, New York, New York, 1868d-1888d. With D.C. Hodgkins & Son, 1858-1865, Cooper, Harris & Hodgkins 1868d-1874d, and Hodgkins & Haigh, 1875-1884.

HODGSON & THOMPSON Baltimore, Maryland, 1800d-1804d. Imported flintlock pistol. (Hartzler)

HODGSON, JOHN W. Washington, D.C., 1853d. (Hartzler)

HODIAMONT see George De Hodiamont.

HOEFFLER, GEORGE Sioux City, Iowa, 1892d.

HOEPNER, BENJAMIN Baltimore, Maryland, 1856d. (Hartzler)

HOEPNER, CASPAR B. Baltimore, Maryland, 1856d-1859d. (Hartzler)

HOERLE BROS. Naugatuck, Connecticut, 1883d.

HOEY, JOHN New York, New York. Model 1861 contract muskets. (Fuller)

HOFEDITY, H. Pleasantville, Indiana, 1882-1885. (Lindert)

HOFER, JOHN G. Philadelphia, Pennsylvania, 1846d. See John Hoffer.

HOFF, DAVID T. Mechanicstown, Maryland, Emmitsburg, Maryland, 1886-1895d. (Hartzler)

HOFF, PETER Hanover, Pennsylvania, 1856-1861d. Percussion fullstock.

HOFFEE, D. New Garden, Ohio, 1865-1880. (Hutslar)

HOFFENBRIDEL, LEWIS Baltimore, Maryland, 1851-1852d. (Hutslar)

HOFFER, JOHN Philadelphia, Pennsylvania, 1862-1863. Converted flintlock muskets.

HOFFMAN & CAMPBELL St. Louis, Missouri, 1845d-1848d. Plains rifles. Christian Hoffman and Tristram Campbell. (Hanson 2)

HOFFMAN, A.D. Belleville, Michigan, 1860d.

HOFFMAN, C. Denison, Texas, 1878d.

HOFFMAN, CHRISTIAN (?-1814), Woodstock, Virginia, ?-1806, Lancaster, Pennsylvania, 1807t-1811t, Ross Co., Ohio, 1811-1814. (Hutslar)

HOFFMAN, CHRISTIAN Philadelphia, Pennsylvania, 1824d-1833d, St. Louis, Missouri, 1836-1855. With Huber & Hoffman, 1836-1837, and Hoffman & Campbell, 1845-1847. (Kauffman 2, Hanson)

HOFFMAN, FREDERICK WILHELM New York, New York. Patents #14,710 April 22, 1856, revolver with G.A. Blittkowski, and #15,516 August 12, 1856, breechloading firearm. (Sellers-1)

HOFFMAN, J. Lancaster, Pennsylvania, percussion over/under.

HOFFMAN, J.H. Saltillo, Pennsylvania. Percussion fullstock rifle.

HOFFMAN, J.V. Attica, Indiana, 1858-1868. Percussion target rifles.

HOFFMAN, JACOB (1827-?), Mt. Vernon, Ohio, 1850c. (Hutslar)

HOFFMAN, JOHN Dauphin Co., Pennsylvania, 1828. See Bowers. (Kauffman)

HOFFMAN, JOSEPH St. Louis, Missouri, 1864d.

HOFFMAN, KILLIAN (1827-?), Jenner's Cross Roads, Pennsylvania, 1861d.

HOFFMAN, LOUIS FERDINAND ALEXANDER (1823-1914), Vicksburg, Mississippi, 1857-1886. Derringers and percussion 1/2 stock. (GR 8- 65)

HOFFMAN, LOUIS Brooklyn, New York, 1883d-1896d.

HOFFMAN, PHILLIP Hartford City, Indiana, 1860d-1862d.

HOFFMAN, R.A. Attica, New York. Percussion 1/2 stock. (Swinney)

HOFFMAN, SAMUEL Charleston, Illinois. Patent #12,295 January 23, 1855, repeating arms.

HOFFMAN, WILLIAM Pittsburgh, Pennsylvania, 1895d.

HOFFMANN, GEORGE Newport, Kentucky, 1884d-1890d.

HOFFMANN, JULIUS Minneapolis, Minnesota, 1886d.

HOFFSTETHER, J. (1825-?), St. Louis, Missouri, 1850c. (Lewis)

HOFNER, JOHN Marion, Ohio, 1859d-1860c. (Hutslar)

HOGAN, JOHN B. North Adams, Massachusetts, 1853d-1892d. Percussion 1/2 stock.

HOGAN, JOHN (1815-?), Washington, D.C., 1848-1860c&d. His son, James (1839), worked with him. (Hartzler)

HOGAN, JOSEPH M. St. Louis, Missouri, 1868d. As Shone & Hogan.

HOGG, ROBERT Delaware Co., Iowa, 1850c. (MB 8-64)

HOGHEN, WOLFKONG Northumberland Co., Pennsylvania, 1775-1777. Committee of Safety repairs. See W. Haga.

HOGLE, G.W. Cedar Springs, Michigan, 1873d-1879d.

HOGLUND, F.M. Ludington, Michigan, 1895d-1899d.

HOHENSHELL, HENRY E. Streator, Illinois, 1872. (Johnson)

HOHMAN, GEORGE Fredericksburg, Virginia, 1897d.

HOHN, W.E. Salem, Ohio. 1890d. (Hutslar)

HOISINGTON, ORANGE Leroy, Ohio, 1852-1859d, Seville, Ohio, 1875d. Percussion 1/2 stock. (Hutslar)

HOIT, ARTHUR A. Newburyport, Massachusetts, 1869d-1876d.

HOKE, CONRAD Strasburg, Pennsylvania, 1807-1809. (Kauffman)

HOLABIRD, W.H. Valparaiso, Indiana, 1880-1881. (MB 4-54)

HOLBECK, FRANCIS Chicago, Illinois, 1859d-1862d.

HOLBRON, M. Ogdensburgh, Wisconsin, 1857d.

HOLBROOK, MILTON J. Rochester, New York, 1837-1838d. (Eich)

HOLBROOK, THOMAS Sherborn, Massachusetts, 1780-1820. Flintlock rifles and pistols.

HOLBURN, CASPAR L. Lancaster, Pennsylvania, 1770. Flintlock Kentucky. (Dean)

HOLBURN, ROBERT Alpena, Michigan, 1893d. With Robert Holburn as Yake & Holburn, 1893.

HOLCOMB & BAKER Greenfield, Massachusetts, 1874d.

HOLCOMB, ALBERT Litchfield, New York. Patent #none October 31, 1822, firearm.

HOLDEN, ALEXANDER Marseilles, Ohio, 1845-1880. Percussion 1/2 stock.

HOLDEN, CYRUS BALDWIN (1827-1906), Worcester, Massachusetts, 1857d-1900d. Patents #34,859 April 1, 1862, breechloading gun, and #42,139 March 29, 1864, breechloading gun. Single shot rifles and shotguns. (GR 4-74)

HOLDEN, GEORGE W. Tabor, Vermont, 1855. (Horn)

HOLDEN, HENRY (1808-?), Hope, Indiana, 1860. (Lindert)

HOLDEN, S.W. Hutsonville, Illinois, 1860d.

HOLDEN, STOUGHTON B. Woburn, Massachusetts. Patent #25,788 October 11, 1859, alarm gun.

HOLDER, H. Hope, Indiana, 1860d.

HOLDER, J. Dunkirk, Ohio, 1886-1890. (Hutslar)

HOLDER, J.F. Macon, Georgia. Agent for Widmer's parlor guns.

HOLDRY, HIRAM Mohn's Store, Pennsylvania, 1861d. Barrel maker.

HOLEMAN, JOHN Lancaster, Pennsylvania, 1814-1816. (Kauffman)

HOLEY MFG. CO. Lakeville, Connecticut. Marking found on first model Reid revolver.

HOLGATE, GEORGE Oshkosh, Wisconsin, 1872d.

HOLLADAY, JOHN M. Holladay, Virginia. Patent #365,383 June 28, 1887, lock.

HOLLAND, J. unlocated. Flintlock lock, probably imported.

HOLLAND, LAWSON Cold Spring, Illinois, 1860d.

HOLLAND, W.A. Boston, Massachusetts. Percussion guns.

HOLLAND, WILLIAM Leadville, Colorado, 1880-1892. (Sellers-3)

HOLLAND, WILLIAM Leadville, Colorado, 1883, 1886, 1889-1890. As J. W. Webster & Co., 1883, Dougan & Co., 1884-1885.

HOLLAND, WILLIAM Point of Forks, Virginia, 1789-1790. (Gill)

HOLLAND, WILLIAM Washington, Illinois, 1860d.

HOLLAPETER, JOHN Covington, Ohio, 1859d. (Hutslar)

HOLLENBACK, WILLIAM Washington, D.C., 1822d. (Kauffman 2)

HOLLENBACK, WILLIAM, JR. (1818-?), Romney, Virginia, 1850c. (Bowers)

HOLLENBECK GUN CO. Wheeling, West Virginia, 1901-1903, Moundsville, West Virginia, 1903-1905. Succeeded by Three Barrel Gun Co. (AR 6-64)

HOLLENBECK, FRANK A. Homer, New York, Syracuse, New York, Batavia, New York, Wheeling, West Virginia. Patents #258,923 June 6, 1882, breechloading firearm, #446,166 February 10, 1891, safety, #461,182 October 13, 1891, lock, #481,327 August 23, 1892, breechloading firearm, #505,794 September 26, 1893, breechloading firearm, #537,203 April 9, 1894, breechloading firearm, and #752,492 March 1, 1904, breechloading firearm. Formed Hollenbeck Gun Co., Three Barrel Gun Co., and Royal Gun Co. to make his guns.

HOLLENBRINK, WILBUR Jacksonville, Illinois, 1899. (Johnson)

HOLLEY, ALEXANDER (1811-?), Lincoln Co., North Carolina. Apprenticed, 1819. (Bivins)

HOLLIDAY, THOMAS Washington, D. C., 1830c. (Hartzler)

HOLLINGSHEAD, WILLIAM Philadelphia, Pennsylvania, 1780.

HOLLINGSWORTH, HENRY Elkton, Maryland, 1773-1790. Committee of Safety muskets and barrels. (Hartzler)

HOLLINGSWORTH, JOHN Zanesville, Ohio. Patents #12,470 August 1, 1854, revolver, #12,471 August 1, 1854, revolver, and #39,825 September 8, 1863, revolver, all with Ralph Mershon. (Sellers-1)

HOLLINSHEAD, SAMUEL Fremont, Ohio, 1819, Port Clinton, Ohio, 1820. (Hutslar)

HOLLMANN, E.H. Navasota, Texas, 1890d.

HOLLOMAN, WILLIAM Warrenton, North Carolina. Percussion 1/2 stock. (Bivins)

HOLMAN Lind, Wisconsin, 1857d.

HOLMAN, F.C. Pontiac, Illinois, 1880d-1884d, Wellington, Kansas, 1887, Richfield, Kansas, 1894d. Patent #358,747 March 1, 1887, sight with Francis Orr.

HOLMAN, GEORGE Waterville, New York. Patent #75,016 March 3, 1868, revolver.

HOLMES, A.W. Utica, New York, 1865. (Dean)

HOLMES, CHARLES W. Colton, New York, 1873-1885. Percussion rifles. (Roberts)

HOLMES, FRANCIS G.D. Phillipsburg, New Jersey. Patent #380,682 April 10, 1888, breechloading firearm.

HOLMES, GEORGE H. Defiance, Ohio, 1860-1890d. (Hutslar)

HOLMES, GEORGE L. Lockport, New York, 1860-1870d. Percussion 1/2 stock.

HOLMES, ISAAC Q. Clarksville, Arkansas. Patent #273,684 March 16, 1883, breechloading firearm.

HOLMES, JACOB (1814-?), Kenton, Ohio, 1850c. (Hutslar)

HOLMES, JOHN V. Charleston, South Carolina, 1837-1852. (Kauffman 2)

HOLMES, M. Utica, Michigan. Percussion 1/2 stock, superposed loads.

HOLMES, NELSON Grattan, Michigan, 1867d-1871d.

HOLMES, ORVILLE Hudson, Wisconsin, 1891d.

HOLMES, R. Oswego, New York. Miller patent revolving rifle. (Sellers-1)

HOLMES, R., & SON Hudson, Wisconsin, 1857d-1879d.

HOLMES, REUBEN Bridgewater, Pennsylvania, 1837. (Kauffman)

HOLMES, SILVESTER Monroe Co., Missouri, 1850c. (MB 11-66)

HOLMES, W.M. Audubon, Iowa, 1887d.

HOLMES, WILLIAM Winchester, New Hampshire. Patent #none April 4, 1820, boring barrels.

HOLROYD, JOHN Washington, D. C. Patent #25,967 November 1, 1859, projectile.

HOLSAPPEL, PHILIP Pottsville, Pennsylvania, 1860d-1861d.

HOLSONBAKE, WILLIAM W.H. Sandersville, Georgia, 1881d. As Minton & Holsonbake.

HOLT, GARDNER L. Springfield, Massachusetts. Patent #138,157 April 22, 1873, breechloading firearm with J.C. Marshall. Fourth of July pistols. (GR 7-65)

HOLT, GEORGE Dixfield, Maine, 1875-1879.

HOLT, H. North Lewisburg, Ohio, 1857-1865. (Hutslar)

HOLT, J. Howell, Michigan, 1857-1862. Percussion over/under rifle/shotgun.

HOLT, JAMES W. (1853-1913), Bangor, Maine, 1881-1913. As Holt & Morrill, 1887-1896, Holt & Clewley, 1900-1908, and Holt & Kendall, 1909-1913. (Demeritt)

HOLT, JOHN B. Genesee, New York, 1870d.

HOLT, JUDSON Marion, Michigan, 1863d, Howell, Michigan, 1863d-1899d.

HOLT, OLE Eau Claire, Wisconsin, 1895d.

HOLT, P.N. Galena, Kansas, 1884d-1888d.

HOLT, PETER M. Ashtabula, Ohio, 1855. Percussion 1/2 stock.

HOLT, RUDOLPH D. Pikeville, Tennessee, 1856-1861. Percussion 1/2 stock.

HOLT, S., ARMS CO. trade name of Sears, Roebuck & Co. on imported shotguns.

HOLT, WILLIAM B. Estill Springs, Tennessee, 1881d-1891d.

HOLT, WILLIAM Seaville, Kentucky, 1883d.

HOLTER, PETER A. Worcester, Massachusetts. Patent #223,645 January 20, 1880, revolver.

HOLTRY, JOSEPH Berks Co., Pennsylvania, 1847-1875. Barrels only. (Hobbies 5-37)

HOLTZSCHEIDER, J. Philadelphia, Pennsylvania, 1873-1875d.

HOLTZSCHEIDER, LEONARD Philadelphia, Pennsylvania, 1876d-1896d.

HOLTZSCHEITER, F.J. Washington, North Carolina, 1873d-1890d. Percussion target guns.

HOLTZSHILD, JULIAN Tarboro, North Carolina, 1860c. (Bivins)

HOLTZWORTH, WILLIAM A. Lancaster, Pennsylvania, 1816-1830. Flintlock Kentucky rifle. (Kauffman)

HOLYOAKE, LOWNES & CO. Memphis, Tennessee, 1852d-1854d. Agent on Slotter and imported derringers. Succeeded by Lownes, Orgill & Co., same location.

HOLZGRAFF, GEORGE Jacksonville, Illinois, 1880. (Johnson)

HOLZMAN, E. unlocated. Percussion target rifle.

HOLZMANN, GEORGE New York, New York, 1873d-1888d.

HOMAN, JOHN F. Effingham, Illinois. (Johnson)

HOME & WHEELER Stevensburg, Virginia, 1799-1802. Flintlock muskets. George Wheeler and Patrick Home. (Gill)

HOMER, B. unlocated. Flintlock duelling pistols (English?).

HOMER, S. unlocated. Flintlock muskets (English?). (Boehret)

HOMERICH, CHRISTIAN (1855-1905), San Francisco, California, 1872-1882, San Jose, California, 1883-1905. Breechloading shotguns. (Shelton)

HONAKER, ABRAHAM Raleigh Co., West Virginia, circa 1820. son of Hans Honaker. (Whisker IV)

HONAKER, ALBERT Raleigh Co., West Virginia, circa 1890. Son of James Honaker. (Whisker IV)

HONAKER, ANDREW JACKSON (1844-1937), Raleigh Co., West Virginia, 1870c-1890c. Son of Hans Honaker.

HONAKER, HANS JACOB (?-1795), Botetourt Co., Virginia, 1749-1795. (Whisker IV)

HONAKER, JAMES BENJAMIN (1824-1912), Glen Daniel, West Virginia. (Whisker IV)

HONAKER, JAMES (1817-1898), Marsh Fork, West Virginia, 1870c-1898. (Whisker IV)

HONAKER, JASON Fayette Co., West VIrginia, late 19th century. Son of Joseph C. Honaker. (Whisker IV)

HONAKER, JOHN B. Wytheville, Virginia. (Whisker IV)

HONAKER, JOSEPH A. Wythe Co., Virginia, 1820. Flintlock Kentucky. (MB 3-65)

HONAKER, JOSEPH C. Fayette Co., West Virginia, circa 1861-1875. (Whisker IV)

HONAKER, THOMAS JEFFERSON Raleigh Co., West Virginia. Son of James B. Honaker. (Whisker IV)

HONAKER, WILLIAM Raleigh Co., West Virginia.

HONAKRE, JACOB (1812-?). Marion Co., Ohio, 1850c. (Hutslar)

HONEY, JOHN W. Herculaneum, Missouri. Patent #none February 10, 1819, shot table.

HONICKER, JOHN (1820-?), Brown Co., Ohio, 1850c. (Hutslar)

HOOD & FONCANNON Columbus, Ohio, 1848-1849. H.G. Hood and M.B. Foncannon. (Hutslar)

HOOD FIRE ARMS CO. Norwich, Connecticut, 1874-1889d. Suicide specials and shotguns, Freeman W. Hood. (GR 12-62)

HOOD, ARTHUR FRANCIS Hopkinton, Massachusetts. Patents #304,731 September 9, 1884, revolver, #391,612, October 23, 1888, revolver, and #391,613 October 23, 1888, revolver. Used by American Arms Co.

HOOD, FREEMAN W. Worcester and Boston, Massachusetts, Norwich, Connecticut. Patents #44,953 November 8, 1864, revolver (at Boston), #116,593, July 4, 1871, revolver, (at Norwich), #160,192 February 23, 1875, revolver, #161,615 April 6, 1875, revolver, #174,731 March 14, 1876, revolver, #235,240 December 7, 1880, revolver, #241,804 May 24, 1881, revolver, #268,489 December 5, 1882, and #316,622 April 28, 1885, revolver. Hood's first patent was used by Pond on their separate chamber revolvers, the others by Hood Fire Arms Co.

HOOD, H.G. Columbus, Ohio, 1847-1853. Percussion full-stock. With Hood & Foncannon, 1848-1849.

HOOEY, H. Charlotte, Michigan, 1863d.

HOOFMAN, JACOB Lancaster, Pennsylvania, 1750. (Dyke)

HOOGKIRK, GERRET Albany, New York, 1831-1832. (Kauffman 2)

HOOK, ELIJAH Booneville, Missouri, 1849, Florence, Missouri, 1860d-1889d.

HOOK, JACOB Lancaster Co., Pennsylvania, 1788t. (Dyke)

HOOKE, I. unlocated. Flintlock Kentucky.

HOOKER, H.B. Rochester, New York. Patent #126,962 May 21, 1872, reloading tool.

HOOKER, THOMAS Rutland, Vermont. Model 1798 contract muskets with Darius Chipman, Royal Crafts, and John Smith. (Gluckman)

HOOPER, JOSEPH Chester Hill, Ohio, 1860-1864d. (Hutslar)

HOOPER, ROBERT L., JR. Philadelphia, Pennsylvania, 1763. (Kauffman)

HOOPES, ISAAC (1823-?), Morgan Co., Ohio, 1850c. Son of Joseph Hoopes. (Hutslar)

HOOPES, JOSEPH (1800-1885), Morgan Co., Ohio, 1833-1885. (Hutslar)

HOOPES, NATHAN (1826-?), Morgan Co., Ohio, 1850c. Son of Joseph Hoopes. (Hutslar)

HOOPS, CHARLES Vermillion, South Dakota 1898d.

HOOVER, JACOB Waynesburgh, Pennsylvania, 1882d-1890d.

HOOVER, PETER Edwardsport, Indiana, 1862d.

HOOVER, THOMAS Readyville, Tennessee, 1860d.

HOPE Worcester, Massachusetts, 1865d.

HOPKINS & ALLEN Norwich, Connecticut, 1868-1917. General line of guns, including Merwin & Hulbert revolvers, Mauser rifles, and Berthier machine guns. Charles H. Allen and Samuel S. Hopkins. Purchased the Bacon factory in 1867. (ASAC 20)

HOPKINS & COMMINGS Jersey City, New Jersey, 1878d.

HOPKINS, CHARLES W. Norwich, Connecticut, 1861-1894. Patents #35,419, May 27, 1862, revolver, #165,098 June 29, 1875, revolver, #350,367 October 5, 1886, revolver, #489,366 January 3, 1893, firearm with Horace A. Briggs, and #505,569 September 26, 1893, safety with James Boland.

HOPKINS, D. New London, Wisconsin, 1857d.

HOPKINS, D.A. Brooklyn, New York. Patent #36,464 September 16, 1862, cartridge.

HOPKINS, DAVID Eagle, Missouri, 1860d.

HOPKINS, FRANK G. St. Joseph, Missouri, 1869d-1879d. As Eckhardt & Hopkins, 1869-1870.

HOPKINS, GERALD Maryland, 1776. Committee of Safety locks. (Dean*)

HOPKINS, HENRY H. Norwich, Connecticut. Patents #143,012 September 23, 1873, breechloading firearm, and #162,475 April 27, 1825, revolver.

HOPKINS, HILAND E. Barton, Vermont, 1883d.

HOPKINS, JEREMIAH Coventry, Rhode Island, 1775. (Dean*)

HOPKINS, REUBEN New York, New York, 1846d-1858. Percussion 1/2 stock. As Rose & Hopkins, 1846.

HOPKINS, SAMUEL S. Norwich, Connecticut. Patents #41,117 January 5, 1864, revolver with H.A. Briggs, #57,622 August 28, 1868, revolver with Charles Converse, #113,053 March 28, 1871, revolver, #297,80, April 29, 1884, ejector, and #311,323 January 27, 1885, folding hammer.

HOPKINS, TIMOTHY Athens Co., Ohio, 1820c, Morgan Co., Ohio, 1833-1886. (Hutslar)

HOPKINS, WILLIAM R. Hartford, Connecticut, 1856d-1858d. As Harris & Hopkins, 1856-1857. (GR 1-77)

HOPKINS, WILLIAM W. Milford, Michigan, 1863d-1867d.

HOPPENAU, HENRY Kansas City, Missouri, 1873-1878d, Paola, Kansas, 1884d. Patent #136,998 March 18, 1873, breechloading firearm.

HOPPER, R. Caverna, Missouri, 1898d.

HORD, AMBROSE Stafford Co., Virginia, 1781. (Gill)

HORMELL, JOHN, JR. Frederickstown, Pennsylvania, 1788-1798. (Whisker II)

HORN, CHARLES M. Eugene, Oregon, 1878d-1886d.

HORN, CONRAD Hazelton, Pennsylvania, 1820-1880. Flintlock and percussion swivel breech rifles. With brothers William and Thomas at times. (GR 8-62)

HORN, F. New York, New York, 1871-1876. (Gardner)

HORN, JOHN Cumberland Co., Pennsylvania, 1826-1833. Flintlock Kentucky rifles. (Gardner)

HORN, STEPHEN Easton, Pennsylvania, 1770-1782. (Dillin)

HORN, T.L. San Augustine, Texas, 1878d.

HORN, THOMAS (?-1921), East Hazelton, Pennsylvania, 1879. Brother of Conrad. (GR 8-62)

HORN, WILLIAM S. Bureau Co., Illinois, 1843-1850. (Johnson)

HORN, WILLIAM Hazelton, Pennsylvania, 1837-1839. Brother and associate of Conrad. (GR 8-62)

HORNBACK, WILLIAM A. Quincy, Ohio, 1853d. Percussion revolving rifle. (Hutslar)

HORNBERGER, CYRUS (1832-?), Berks Co., Pennsylvania, 1855. Barrel maker.

HORNBY, CHARLES W. (1848-?), Preston Co., West Virginia, 1880c. (Whisker IV)

HORNE, GEORGE A. Syracuse, New York. Patents #568,760 October 6, 1896, ejector, #572,755 December 8, 1896, ejector, #690,955 January 14, 1902, automatic, #731,904 June 23, 1903, ejector, #754,564 March 15, 1904, safety, and #782,248 February 14, 1905, breechloading firearm.

HORNE, W.T. Chicago, Illinois, 1890d.

HORNE, WILLIAM L. Meriden, Connecticut. Patents #357,960 February 15, 1887, electric firearm, and #406,667 July 9, 1889, magazine gun with Joseph M. Reams.

HORNER, FREDERICK Somerset Co., Pennsylvania, 1805-1834. (Kauffman)

HORNER, HENRY Horner's, Virginia, 1890d-1897d.

HORNER, J. Horner's, Virginia, 1890d-1897d.

HORNER, JACOB Jenner's Cross Road, Pennsylvania, 1832-1861d.

HORNER, JOHN, JR. Somerset Co., Pennsylvania, 1802-1806. (Kauffman)

HORNER, LEWIS Jenner's Cross Roads, Pennsylvania, 1861d.

HORNER, OSCAR A. Eureka, California. Patent #434,785 August 19, 1890, sight.

HORNER, T.J. Richmond, Virginia, 1897d.

HORNET suicide special by Prescott.

HORNET trade name on Deacon percussion pistol. (Nunnemacher)

HORNING, DAVID Marlboro, Ohio, 1866d. (Hutslar)

HORNUNG, LEWIS Schuykill Haven, Pennsylvania, 1835t-1861d. Four-barrel percussion rifle. (Sellers-2)

HORNUNG, PHILIP Portland, Oregon, 1867d-1878d.

HORR, AUSTIN Cape Vincent, New York, 1860-1882d. Percussion 1/2 stock.

HORR, OTIS WYMAN Chicopee Falls, Massachusetts. Patent #323,936 August11, 1885, breechloading firearm.

HORSLEY, JOHN Metamora, Indiana, 1860d-1862d.

HORSMER & CAMERON Colusa, California, 1878d. (Shelton)

HORST, GEORGE (1792-?), Baltimore, Maryland, 1850c-1853d. (Hartzler)

HORST, L.D. unlocated. Percussion 1/2 stock.

HORTON, HENRY B. Ithaca, New York. Patent #41,343 January 19, 1864, breechloading firearm with Eugene M. Mix.

HORTON, MOSES Morgan Co., Ohio, 1818, Monroe Co., Ohio, 1820c. (Hutslar)

HORTON, N. Lowell, Maine, 1869-1874.

HORTON, W. White Haven, Connecticut, 1840. (Dean*)

HORTON, WILLIAM New York, New York, 1801-1804, Philadelphia, Pennsylvania, 1810d. (Kauffman 2)

HORVETER, HENRY Lancaster, Pennsylvania, 1863d. See Henry Howerter.

HOSACK, E.L. Kimbolton, Ohio, 1852-1864d. Percussion 1/2 stock. (Hutslar)

HOSKINS, T.J. Ashland City, Tennessee, 1876d.

HOSLER, JONATHAN (1780-?), Canton, Ohio, 1850c. (Hutslar)

HOSLER, JONATHAN, JR. (1813-?), Steubenville, Ohio, 1850c. (Hutslar)

HOSS, GEORGE (1838-?), Urbana, Ohio, 1868d. (Hutslar)

HOSSE, A.F. Nashville, Tennessee, 1868-1891d.

HOSSLEY, T.J. Vicksburg, Mississippi, 1866-1875. Percussion 1/2 stock.

HOTCHINGS, THOMAS T. San Francisco, California, 1856-1857. Worked for A.J. Taylor. (Shelton)

HOTCHKISS, BENJAMIN BERKELEY (1826-1885), Watertown, Connecticut. Held over 100 patents, both U.S. and foreign on all types of firearms from handguns to cannon. His rifles and cannon were adopted by the U.S. and over 20 foreign governments. As Hotchkiss & Co., New York, New York, Paris, France, and England, 1882-1966. (G&A 7-61)

HOTZ, HENRY Cuero, Texas, 1892d.

HOUCHIN, ELLIS Traveler's Repose, West Virginia, 1882d. (Whisker IV)

HOUCKINS, WILLIAM (1822-?), Scioto Co., Ohio, 1850c. (Hutslar)

HOUDLETTE, FREDERICH M. St. Louis, Missouri, 1899d. (Pourie)

HOUGH, M.J. Alexander, Ohio, 1858-1861, Granville, Ohio, 1861-1865. Percussion 1/2 stock. (Hutslar)

HOUGHTON, JOHN Philadelphia, Pennsylvania, Trenton, New Jersey, 1860d. Buggy rifle in Philadelphia.

HOUGHTON, LEWIS T. Worcester, Massachusetts. Patent #609,233 August 16, 1898, safety.

HOUGHTON, RICHARD W. (1804-1863), Norway, Maine, 1838, Mechanics Falls, Maine, ?-1863. Percussion 1/2 stock. (Demeritt)

HOUGHTON, W.W. Augusta, Georgia, 1879d-1881d.

HOULNE, EDWARD New Orleans, Louisiana, 1886d-1897d.

HOUSE, T.J. Middleport, Illinois, 1859. (Johnson)

HOUSE, WILLIAM C. Easton, Maryland, 1887d. (Hartzler)

HOUSER, J. Canyonville, California, 1874d. (Shelton)

HOUSLEY, FERDINAND Nashville, Tennessee, 1874d.

HOUSMAN, S. Huntington, Indiana, 1860d.

HOUSTON, ADAMANTIUS C. Pickway, West Virginia. Patent #427,278 August 4, 1891, revolver.

HOUSTON, DAVID H. Hunter, North Dakota. Patent #593,890 November 16, 1897, stock.

HOUSTON, GEORGE (1825-?), New Orleans, Louisiana, 1850c. (MB 9-65)

HOUSTON, JAMES Philadelphia, Pennsylvania, 1780t. (Kauffman)

HOUSTUN, H.H. Van Buren, Arkansas, 1888d.

HOUY, C.P. Ashley, Illinois, 1884d.

HOVERMALE, SAMUEL J. Berkeley Springs, West Virginia, 1882d. (Whisker IV)

HOVEY, H. Watertown, New York. Percussion 1/2 stock and pistol.

HOVIS, CHARLES W. Parker City, Pennsylvania. Patent #184,079 November 7, 1876, loading tool.

HOWALTER, CHARLES Pittsburgh, Pennsylvania, 1864d.

HOWARD ARMS CO. Chicago, Illinois. Dealers only, possibly a trade name.

HOWARD BROS. Whitneyville and New Haven, Connecticut, 1859-1869. Sales organization for Charles and Sebre Howard, guns made by Whitney.

HOWARD, C.W. Hammonton, New Jersey. Patent #39,232 July 14, 1863, breechloading firearm.

HOWARD, CALEB Philadelphia, Pennsylvania, 1816d.

HOWARD, CHARLES New York, New York. Patents #50,125 September 26, 1865, breechloading firearm, #50,358 October 10, 1865, breechloading firearm, and #54,728 May 15, 1866, bayonet. Howard rifles made by Whitney. (GR 7-73)

HOWARD, D. Charleston, Missouri, 1860d.

HOWARD, H.G. Broadhead, Kentucky, 1883d.

HOWARD, HENRY (1839-?), Charleston, Indiana, 1860c. Apprentice. (Lindert)

HOWARD, HENRY Chattanooga, Tennessee, 1860-1870.

HOWARD, J.P. Madison, Wisconsin. Percussion 1/2 stock.

HOWARD, JAMES New Madrid, Missouri, 1850c. (MB 11-66)

HOWARD, JOHN A. Watsonville, California, 1864-1893d. Converted Spencer rifle with D. Morey.

HOWARD, JOSEPH P. Platform, Ohio, 1883d, New Hope, Ohio. (Hutslar)

HOWARD, LAWSON Louisiana, Missouri, 1879d-1889d.

HOWARD, MICAJAH Jamestown, North Carolina, circa 1860. (Bivins)

HOWARD, S.A. Bangor, Michigan, 1883d-1887d.

HOWARD, SANGER & CO. New York, New York. Agent for Slocum revolver.

HOWARD, SEBRE Elyria, Ohio. Patent #36,779 October 28, 1862, breechloading firearm. Howard rifles made by Whitney. (GR 7-73)

HOWARD, V.P. unlocated. Percussion 1/2 stock.

HOWARD, WILLIAM O. New York, New York. Patent #75,019 March 3, 1868, shot cartridge.

HOWARTER, J. Lishurn, Pennsylvania, 1861d. Barrel maker.

HOWAT, GEORGE (1810-?), Newport, Kentucky, 1855-1885. (Dean*, AR 1-24)

HOWDEN, A. Fairmount, Illinois, 1860d.

HOWE & FOLEK New York. Converted Kentucky rifle.

HOWE, AUSTIN see Austin Horr.

HOWE, BERNARD Vincent, Ohio, 1853-1854, Cleveland, Ohio. Apprenticed to John Vincent. (Hutslar)

HOWE, C.A. Niles, Michigan, 1887d.

HOWE, CHARLES H. Brattleboro, Vermont, 1882-1885. (Horn)

HOWE, FREDERICK W. (1822-1891), Providence, Rhode Island. Patents #36,466 September 16, 1862, breechloading firearm, #46,000 January 24, 1865, sight, and #46,671 March 7, 1865, breechloading firearm. Worked for many gun makers, 1865 trial carbines made by Providence Tool Co., of which he was superintendent. (GR 7-67)

HOWE, GEORGE A. Niles, Michigan, 1860d.

HOWE, H.B. unlocated. Mule ear double rifle.

HOWE, HARRY Lansing, New York. Percussion three-barrel rifle/shotgun.

HOWE, J. Lyon, Wisconsin, 1884d-1886d.

HOWE, JOHN C. Milwaukee, Wisconsin, 1853-1854, Worcester, Massachusetts, 1855-1892. Patents #11,852 October 31, 1854, breechloading firearm, #37,693 February 17, 1863, revolver, #43,851 August 16, 1864, cartridge, #357,710 February 15, 1887, revolver, #357,710 February 15, 1887, revolver, #363,948 December 7, 1886, revolver, #373,893 November 29, 1887, revolver, and #483,651 October 4, 1892, air gun. Percussion over/under rifle/shotgun, patent rifles, and revolvers.

HOWE, JOHN W. Clarkston, Michigan, 1867d.

HOWE, JOHN St. Johnsvile, New York, 1858-1882d.

HOWE, JOSEPH Appleton, Wisconsin, 1888d.

HOWE, OLIVER R. Amazonia, Missouri, 1850c-1891d.

HOWE, P.H. unlocated. Percussion 1/2 stock.

HOWE, W.N. Caroline, New York. Percussion rifle with B. Losey.

HOWE, WILLIAM Ellington, New York, 1870d.

HOWELL see Elliott & Howell.

HOWELL, CHARLES W. (1825-?), Martins Ferry, Ohio, 1850-1878d. Percussion 1/2 stock. (Hutslar)

HOWELL, JOHN Parkville, Missouri, 1860d.

HOWELL, LE GRAND M. Eldora, Iowa, 1897d.

HOWELL, THOMAS Cadwallader, Ohio, 1859d, Hunter, Ohio, 1875d. (Hutslar)

HOWELL, THOMAS Philadelphia, Pennsylvania, 1824d. Importer of hardware and locks.

HOWELL, WILLIAM B. Parkville, Missouri, 1850c. (MB 11-66)

HOWELL, WILLIAM T. & CO. Philadelphia, Pennsylvania, 1834d-1847d. Successors to Thomas Howell. Importers of hardware and locks. (GR 4-58)

HOWERER, CHARLES Lancaster Co., Pennsylvania, 1850t. Barrel maker. (Dyke)

HOWERER, GEORGE Lancaster Co., Pennsylvania, 1820t-1827t. (Dyke)

HOWERER, HENRY Lancaster Co., Pennsylvania, 1850t-1871d. Barrel maker. (Dyke)

HOWINGS unlocated. Percussion 1/2 stock.

HOWLAND, ISAAC South Valley, New York, 1879-1882d.

HOWLAND, RUFUS J. Binghamton, New York, 1840-1874d, Coudersport, Pennsylvania, 1887d-1890d. Patent #41,510, February 9, 1864, adjustable hammer with William H. Elliott. Percussion target and multi-barrel rifles.

HOWLETT, J. Augusta, Illinois, 1860d.

HOWLETT, J.W. Greensboro, North Carolina, 1862-1884d. Confederate patent #91 May 10, 1862, breechloading firearm. As Phillips & Howlett, 1884.

HOWLETT, ROBERT W. Hannibal, Missouri, 1860d, Barry, Illinois, 1864d-1880d.

HOWLING, W.M. St. Anthony, Minnesota, 1867d.

HOWLING, WILLIAM Portage City, Wisconsin, 1857d.

HOY, W.T. Saugatuck, Michigan, 1863d.

HOYER, ANDREW (?-1754), New York, New York.

HOYT, EBEN Chelsea, Massachusetts. Patent #12,795 May 1, 1855, projectile.

HOYT, PHILO W. Danbury, Connecticut. Patent #869 March 10, 1838, lock.

HSUEDER, HENRY Lancaster Co., Pennsylvania, 1848t-1849t. (Dyke)

HUACHT, E.M. Egg Harbor City, New Jersey, 1866d.

HUBBARD, COLEMAN S. Windsor, Vermont, 1845-1860. (Dean)

HUBBARD, EDWARD Lucas, Iowa, 1884d.

HUBBARD, HARVEY C. Manitowoc, Wisconsin. Patent #471,176 March 22, 1892, air gun.

HUBBARD, JOSEPH Hartford, Connecticut, 1848-1850. (Kauffman 2)

HUBBARD, LEONIDAS Cass, Michigan, 1863d, South Wright, Michigan, 1867d.

HUBBARD, S.H. Ilion, New York. (MB 2-53)

HUBBARD, SETH, JR. Fair Plains, Michigan, 1863d-1865d.

HUBBARD, SOLOMON Blackford Co., Indiana, 1860c. (Lindert)

HUBBELL, WILLIAM WHEELER Philadelphia, Pennsylvania, 1842-1867. Patents #3,649 July 1, 1844, breechloading firearm, and #65,812 June 18, 1867, breechloading firearm. Also numerous patents on cannon. (Bugle 79)

HUBER & HOFFMAN St. Louis, Missouri, 1836-1837d. J. Huber and Christian Hoffman. (Hanson)

HUBER, ABRAM York Co., Pennsylvania, 1799. (Kauffman)

HUBER, CHARLES Worcester, Massachusetts, 1865d.

HUBER, CHRISTIAN FREDERICK (1829-1878), Stockton, California, 1861-1862 and 1871-1878, Aurora, Nevada, 1863-1871. (Shelton)

HUBER, FELIX St. Louis, Missouri, 1879d.

HUBER, HENRY San Francisco, California, 1847. (Shelton)

HUBER, J. St. Louis, Missouri, 1836-1839. With Huber & Hoffman, 1836-1837. (Hanson)

HUCKLER, JOHN (1832-?), Marinetown, Illinois, 1860c. (Johnson)

HUDDLE, J.E. Paris, Texas, 1878d-1896d.

HUDSON & SIEBERT Cincinnati, Ohio. Percussion 1/2 stock rifle. William L. Hudson and Christian Siebert. (Hutslar)

HUDSON trade name of Hibbard, Spencer, Bartlett, & Co. on shotguns. (Hinman)

HUDSON, ALLEN (1797-?), Sycamore, Ohio, 1850-1865. (Hutslar)

HUDSON, ANDREW J. Syracuse, New York. Patent #187,280 February 13, 1887, breechloading firearm.

HUDSON, CHARLES Grand Haven, Michigan, 1873d-1875d.

HUDSON, DAVID Napoleon, Ohio, 1875-1896. Percussion rifles. (Hutslar)

HUDSON, EZRA L. (1829-?), Logan, Ohio, 1850-1853d. With William Stalter. (Hutslar)

HUDSON, G.L. Conneaut, Ohio, 1859d. (Hutslar)

HUDSON, GILBERT L. Romeo, Michigan, 1872d-1899d.

HUDSON, HENRY T. Portland, Oregon, 1880d-1889d. Percussion 1/2 stock.

HUDSON, SAMUEL see Samuel Hutson.

HUDSON, WILLIAM L. (1812-1865), Cincinnati, Ohio, 1845-1865. Percussion target rifle and revolving rifle (like Warner). (Hutslar)

HUDSON, WILLIAM Freetown, Indiana, 1851-1887. (MB 4-55)

HUDSON, WILLIAM New York, New York, 1844-1845. Percussion 1/2 stock.

HUDSON, WILLIAM Philadelphia, Pennsylvania, 1780-1785. Repaired U.S. arms. (Moller)

HUELS, FRED (?-1909), Madison, Wisconsin, 1875-1909. Worked for August Herfurth, 1875-1880. (GC 1)

HUER, W.H. Mexia, Texas, 1884d.

HUEY, ABE Root Hollow, Pennsylvania. Percussion full-stock.

HUFF, PETER unlocated. Percussion lockmaker.

HUFFMAN, CHRISTIAN Woodstock, Virginia, 1783-1815. Flintlock Kentucky. (Gill)

HUFFMAN, GEORGE (1831-?), Yreka, California, 1860c. (Shelton)

HUFFMAN, HENRY HOVIS (1829-?), Catawba Co., North Carolina, 1850c. Son of Henry Hoffman. (Bivins)

HUFFMAN, HENRY (1807-?), Catawba Co., North Carolina, 1850c. (Bivins)

HUFFMAN, PHILLIP (1824-?), Hartford City, Indiana, 1850c-1860c. (Lindert)

HUFFMAN, SAMUEL Charlestown, Illinois. Patent #12,295 January 23, 1855, revolving gun. See S. Hoffman.

HUG, BARTHOLOMEW Hudson City, New Jersey, 1866d, Jersey City, New Jersey, 1878d.

HUG, DANIEL New York, New York, 1873, Ula, Colorado, 1880, Denver, Colorado, 1879-1910. Patents #142,396 September 2, 1873, breechloading firearm, #232,035 September 7, 1880, breechloading firearm, and #691,056 January 14, 1902, breechloading firearm. Single shot rifles. (Sellers-3)

HUGGINS, EDWARD L. Fairfax, Vermont, 1882-1883. (Horn)

HUGGINS, F. Brandon, Oregon, 1880d-1881d.

HUGH, JOSEPH (1824-?), San Francisco, California, 1852c. (Shelton)

HUGHES & PHILLIPS see Hewes & Phillips.

HUGHES, ABELL V. unlocated. Percussion 1/2 stock.

HUGHES, BENJAMIN Wakarusa, Indiana, 1882-1885.

HUGHES, D.W. Memphis, Tennessee. Confederate patent #149 February 13, 1863, breechloading cannon. (Albaugh 3)

HUGHES, E. Santa Clara, California, 1861, McCartysville, California. Patent #44,630 October 11, 1864, percussion lock.

HUGHES, G.A. Perryville, Kentucky, 1896d.

HUGHES, G.W. Bloomington, Illinois. Patents #45,043 November 15, 1864, magazine gun, and #49,409 August 15, 1865, magazine gun with J.G. Pusey.

HUGHES, JAMES M. Independence Co., Arkansas, 1842-1860. (Elias)

HUGHES, JOHN (1818-?), Greene Co., Pennsylvania, 1850c.

HUGHES, MICHAEL Old Slip, New York, 1801, New York, New York, 1803. (Kauffman)

HUGHES, R.J. Monroe, Georgia, 1861. Confederate gunsmith convention.

HUGHES, R.P. Manchester, New Hampshire. Percussion pistol.

HUGHES, ROBERT (1788-?), Haywood Co., North Carolina, 1820c, Buncombe Co., North Carolina, 1850c. (Bivins)

HUGHES, T. Wheeling, West Virginia 1849d. Percussion fullstock.

HUGHES, THOMAS (1789-1849), Waynesburg, Pennsylvania, 1808-1809, Uniontown, Pennsylvania, 1813-1814, Wheeling, West Virginia, 1817-1849d. Percussion fullstock. (Whisker II & IV)

HUGHES, W.J. Galveston, Texas, 1884d.

HUGHES, W.N. (1814-?), Rusk, Texas, 1862-1896d. As Whitescarver, Hughes & Co., 1866-1870. (Holloway)

HUGHES, W.O. Pinkstaff, Illinois. Patent #662,761 November 27, 1900, machine gun with Mark Bowman.

HUGHLETT, J.F. Crofton, Kentucky, 1896d.

HUGHS, JACOB (1796-?), Reading, Illinois, 1860c. (Johnson)

HUGHSTEAD, A. Ripley, Ohio, 1845-1854. (Gardner)

HUGILL, WILLIAM (1797-?). Harrison Co., Virginia, 1820c-1850.

HUHN, C. Macon, Georgia, 1881d.

HUHN, FREDERICK Chicago, Illinois, 1859-1871d.

HUIFERNER, CHRISTIAN (1780-?), Perry Co., Pennsylvania, 1842t-1850c. Percussion fullstock. (Dyke)

HULBERT BROS. & CO. New York, New York, 1855d-1877d. Importers, William A. and M. Hulbert.

HULBERT, ANSEL (1836-?), Salinas, California, 1870c. (Shelton)

HULBERT, WILLIAM A. Brooklyn, New York. Patent #187,975 March 6, 1877, revolver. Merwin & Hulbert revolvers.

HULET, PHINEAS Shaftsbury, Vermont, 1840-1865, Pawlet, Vermont, 1868-1881. (Horn)

HULL, A.A. Morristown, Tennessee. Patent #217,218 July 8, 1879, revolver with Samuel Harrison.

HULL, BENJAMIN Philadelphia, Pennsylvania, 1819d-1833d. (Kauffman)

HULL, THOMAS South Kensington, Rhode Island, 1812. (Achtermier)

HULLETT, FLYN So. Shaftsbury, Vermont, 1880d. Percussion 1/2 stock. See P. Hulet.

HULME, GEORGE Weaverville, California, 1858-1860. (Shelton)

HULSE, JAMES R. Columbus, Ohio. (Hutslar)

HULSE, WILLIAM Bennetts Mills, New Jersey, 1878d.

HULTS, JAMES Delaware Co., Ohio, 1848-1854. Patent #10,927 May 16, 1854, lock.

HUMASON, J.W. Austin, Minnesota, 1867d.

HUMASON, L.H. & CO. Rochester, Minnesota, 1867d-1870d. As L.H. Humason & Bro., 1867d.

HUMBERGER, ADAM (1806-1865), Somerset, Ohio, 1834-1865. Son of Peter Humberger, made revolvers with brother Henry. (Sellers-1)

HUMBERGER, ADAM (1834-?), Somerset, Ohio, 1850c. Son of Adam Humberger. (Hutslar)

HUMBERGER, HENRY (1811-1879), Somerset, Ohio, 1832-1840. Son of Peter Humberger I, made revolvers in 1834 with brother Adam. (Hutslar, Sellers-1)

HUMBERGER, PETER (1767-1838), Lancaster, Pennsylvania, 1774-1802, Perry Co., Ohio, 1802-1820. (Hutslar)

HUMBERGER, PETER, III (1826-1899), Somerset, Ohio, 1850c. (Hutslar)

HUMBERGER, PETER, JR. (1796-1852), Perry Co., Ohio, 1802-1852. (Hutslar)

HUMBERGER, SAMUEL (1815-?), Kirkersville, Ohio, 1850-1887. Percussion fullstock. (Hutslar)

HUMBLE, MICHAEL (?-1819), Louisville, Kentucky, 1779-1819. Flintlock Kentucky rifle. (Dillin)

HUME, HUBBARD (1822-?), Plattsville, Ohio, 1848-1855, Shelby, Co., Ohio, 1855-1883. (Hutslar)

HUME, JOHN (1820-?), Shelby Co., Ohio, 1850c. (Hutslar)

HUMES, JOHN Philadelphia, Pennsylvania, 1800. (Kauffman)

HUMMEL, ADAM J. Johnstown, Pennsylvania, 1876d-1889d.

HUMMEL, ADAM Lebanon, Pennsylvania, 1860d.

HUMMEL, F. Lebanon, Pennsylvania, 1860c. (Kauffman)

HUMMEL, FERDINAND Paducah, Kentucky. Patents #235,771 December 31, 1880, breechloading firearm, and #258,759 May 30, 1882, breechloading firearm.

HUMMEL, FREDERICK S. Pennsylvania, circa 1850, Paducah, Kentucky. (Hist. KY,V5, P729)

HUMMEL, FREDERICK Hummelstown, Pennsylvania, 1777. Committee of Safety muskets. (Dean)

HUMMEL, JOHN JACOB (1756-?), Snyder Co., Pennsylvania, 1797. (Whisker III)

HUMMELL, ADAM Philadelphia, Pennsylvania, 1871-1874. (Kauffman)

HUMMELL, CHARLES San Antonio, Texas, 1850-1897d. As C. Hummell & Son 1887-1897. Percussion 1/2 stock. (T53)

HUMMELL, FERDINAND Paducah, Kentucky, 1879d- 1896d.

HUMMER trade name of H & D Folsom on shotguns imported for Lee Hardware Co. (AR 2-59)

HUMPHREY, DANIEL (1839-1884), Palmyra, Ohio, 1852-1884. Percussion 1/2 stock. (Hutslar)

HUMPHREY, GEORGE (1830-?), Darke Co., Ohio, 1850c, Belmont Co., Ohio, 1860-1880. Brother of Daniel Humphrey. (Hutslar)

HUMPHREY, JOHN Providence, Rhode Island, 1775. (Achtermier)

HUMPHREY, L. Hickey, Iowa, 1865d, Iowaville, Iowa, 1865d.

HUMPHREY, WILLIAM (1826-?). Darke Co., Ohio, 18 SOc. (Hutslar)

HUMPHREYS, HOSEA Pawtucket, Rhode Island, 1800. Model 1798 contract muskets with Stephen Jenks. (Gluckman)

HUMPHREYS, ROBERT (?-1837), Rutherfordton, North Carolina, 1837. (Bivins)

HUMPHREYS, WILLIAM ALBERT (1824-?). Rutherfordton, North Carolina. Apprenticed to A. Bechtler, 1838. (Bivins)

HUMPHRIES, CHARLES Yonkers, New York, 1866d. As Neal & Humphries.

HUMPHRIES, J. Sanford, Florida, 1884d.

HUMPHRYS, JOSHUA Augusta Co., Virginia, 1777. Committee of Safety muskets with Perry, Simpson, and Gabbott. (Gill)

HUNDT, A. unlocated. Percussion 1/2 stock.

HUNSICKER, HENRY Lehigh Co., Pennsylvania, 1821t. Flintlock Kentucky. (KRA II-3)

HUNT & JAMES Richmond, Virginia, 1861-1862. (Albaugh 1)

HUNT, CHARLES B. Springville, Pennsylvania. Patent #185,539 December 19, 1876, magazine gun.

HUNT, DAVID S. Cincinnati, Ohio, 1858-1860. Percussion shotguns.

HUNT, EDWIN Chicago, Illinois, 1854d-1857d. Percussion 1/2 stock.

HUNT, JAMES F. Brandon, Vermont, 1881d.

HUNT, JOHN Boston, Massachusetts, 1813-1816. (Kauffil an 2)

HUNT, JOHN Gentryville, Missouri, 1850c. (MB 11-66)

HUNT, JOHN Sacramento, California, 1873d. (Shelton)

HUNT, JONATHAN (1780-1865), Richland Co., Ohio, 1806-1812. (Knittle)

HUNT, LYMAN Williamstown, Massachusetts, 1888d.

HUNT, RICHARD New Berlin, New York, 1874d.

HUNT, S.A. Williamstown, Massachusetts, 1869d.

HUNT, THOMAS Clermont Co., Ohio, 1830. (Hutslar)

HUNT, W.M. unlocated. Percussion 1/2 stock.

HUNT, WALTER (?-1859), New York, New York. Patents #5,699 and #5,701 August 10, 1848, rocket ball, and #6,663 August 21, 1849, magazine gun. Guns based on these patents were eventually developed and produced by Volcanic and Winchester.

HUNTER & COMSTOCK ARMS CO. Fulton, New York, 1889. Assignee of Harry Comstock's patents, became Hunter Arms Co. in 1890.

HUNTER ARMS CO. Fulton, New York, 1890-date. Purchased L.C. Smith in 1890 and continued to make guns under that name until purchased by Marlin in 1918. Marlin resumed manufacture of L.C. Smith guns in 1969.

HUNTER trade name of Crescent on shotguns for Belknap Hardware Co.

HUNTER trade name of Hunter Arms Co. on shotguns.

HUNTER trade name on .22 derringer.

HUNTER, DAVID Berkley Co., Virginia, 1776. Committee of Safety muskets with Peter Light. (Gill)

HUNTER, GEORGE W. (1833-?), Merced, California, 1875-1878. (Shelton)

HUNTER, JAMES (?-1785), Stafford Co., Virginia, 1775-1780. As Hunter's Iron Works, also known as Rappahannock Forge, made muskets, pistols and swords during the Revolutionary War. (Swayze)

HUNTER, JAMES Macomb, Illinois, 1860d.

HUNTER, JOHN Philadelphia, Pennsylvania, 1781-1785. Repaired U.S. arms. (Moller)

HUNTER, LARS Stark, Minnesota, 1886d.

HUNTER, MICHAEL Dubuque, Iowa, 1850c. (MB 8-64)

HUNTER, WILLIAM Nevada, Missouri, 1891d.

HUNTINGTON, D.M. Grand Rapids, Wisconsin, 1888d.

HUNTINGTON, FRANK ATWOOD San Francisco, California. Patent #135,937 February 18, 1873, magazine gun with Alfred Swingle.

HUNTINGTON, GURDON Walpole, New Hampshire. Model 1798 contract muskets with John Livingston, Josiah Bellows, and David Stone. (Gluckman)

HUNTINGTON, HEZEKIAH Windham, Connecticut, 1775-1784. Committee of Safety muskets with Amasa Palmer. (Gluckman & Satterlee)

HUNTINGTON, JAMES Portland, Maine, 1866. (Demeritt)

HUNTINGTON, REUBEN Henderson, Illinois, 1864d.

HUNTINGTON, SIMON Connecticut, 1775. Committee of Safety repairs. (Gluckman & Satterlee)

HUNTINGTON, V. Allentown, Pennsylvania. Flintlock Kentucky rifle.

HUNTLEY, ABIEL Houlton, Maine, 1776-1780. (Demeritt)

HUNTLEY, F. Morrison, Illinois, 1871d.

HUNTLEY, GIBBS Bay City, Michigan. Patent #345,902 July 20, 1886, breechloading firearm.

HUNTLEY, JOHN C. Philadelphia, Pennsylvania. Patent #28,677 June 12, 1860, alarm gun.

HUNTLEY, STEPHEN A. Elk Point, South Dakota. Patents #654,895 July 31, 1900, firearm, #695,882 March 18, 1902, magazine gun, and #747,073 December 15, 1903, automatic.

HUNTOON, HARLEE J. Ludlow, Vermont, 1880. Worked for N. Brockway and later made percussion slug guns. (Horn)

HURD, HARRISON Hurd, Pennsylvania, 1887d.

HURD, JACOB Boston, Massachusetts, 1816-1825. (Kauffman 2)

HURLBERT, D. Okolono, Mississippi, 1885d.

HURLBUT, F. Fond du Lac, Wisconsin, 1879d.

HURRICANE trade name for Quackenbush air gun.

HURST, B.W., & CO. Danville, Virginia, 1871-1873.

HURST, J. MORGAN (1830-?), Vigo Co., Indiana, 1850c, Paris, Illinois, 1852-1882d. As Davis & Hurst, 1875d.

HURST, J.M. Rich Hill, Missouri, 1891d-1898d.

HURST, JACOB Syracuse, New York. Patent #312,564 February 17, 1885, breechloading firearm.

HURST, L.D. unlocated. Percussion 1/2 stock.

HURST, MORGAN H. Paris, Illinois, 1864d. Percussion fullstock. (MB 3-56)

HURST, RICHARD E. Bloomington, Illinois, 1894d-1899d. As Bentley & Hurst.

HURT, WILLIAM S. Richmond, Virginia, 1861. With Smith, Rhodes & Co. (Albaugh 1)

HUSE, RICHARD P. Manchester, New Hampshire, 1847-1852. Percussion pistol.

HUSEMAN, F.W. Columbia, South Carolina, 1886d.

HUSKY, D.F. California, Missouri, 1879d-1893d.

HUSLAGE, HERMAN G. St. Louis, Missouri, 1838d-1859d. As Huslage & Herman in 1854d, use of his first name probably an error.

HUSON, WILLIAM New York, New York, 1846d-1873d.

HUSS, FLORENT P. New Orleans, Louisiana, 1853d.

HUSS, JOHN A. St. Louis, Missouri, 1860d.

HUSS, MORITZ (1842-?), San Francisco, California, 1871-1872. Worked for A. Browning. (Shelton)

HUSTON, C. Macon, Georgia, 1885d.

HUSTON, GUY New Orleans, Louisiana, 1853d, San Francisco, California, 1856-1858, Victoria, British Columbia, 1858- ? (Shelton)

HUSTON, H.G. Boston, Massachusetts, 1894d.

HUTCHINGS, E., & CO. Baltimore, Maryland, 1836d. Underhammers, percussion 1/2 stock. Agents for Gibbs, Tiffany & Co., and A. Ruggles. (Hartzler)

HUTCHINGS, IVORY York, Maine, 1870-1874. (Demeritt)

HUTCHINS, GEORGE H. Derby, Vermont, 1883d.

HUTCHINSON, ANTHONY J. Rochester, New York, 1844d. For John Miller. (Eich)

HUTCHINSON, J.L. Cooper, Georgia, 1879d.

HUTCHINSON, JOHN W. New York, New York, 1873d-1884d. Manufacturer and importer.

HUTCHINSON, R.J. Williamsport, Pennsylvania, 1878. (Dillin)

HUTCHISON, G.G. Fulton, Kentucky, 1885d.

HUTSON, G. New Orleans, Louisiana, 1853d.

HUTSON, SAMUEL (1815-?), Logansport, Indiana, 1848-1862d. Percussion fullstock. Listed as Samuel Hudson in 1860 census. (Lindert)

HUTTEN, PHILIP Baltimore, Maryland, 1872d. (Hartzler)

HUTTLE, H. La Grange, Texas, 1878d.

HUTTON, JAMES Beemont, Missouri, 1879d.

HUTZ, BENJAMIN Lancaster, Pennsylvania, 1803, Lehigh Co., Pennsylvania. (Dillin)

HUXOL, SIMON Hermann, Missouri, 1898d.

HUYCK, G. LEVERENT Chicago, Illinois. (Johnson)

HUYSLOP, R. see R. Hyslop.

HYAMS, F. Charleston, South Carolina, 1867d.

HYATT, A.P. Crystal Lake and Rural, Wisconsin, 1857d with J. Vosburgh at both locations. New London, Wisconsin, 1872d, Rural, Wisconsin, 1879d. Percussion target rifle.

HYATT, W.H. Faribault, Minnesota, 1867d, Winneconne, Wisconsin, 1875d-1879d. Percussion 1/2 stock.

HYATT, WILLIAM H. Wasau, Wisconsin, 1857d-1875d. Same as W.H. Hyatt, Faribault, Minnesota?

HYDE & GOODRICH New Orleans, Louisiana, 1815d-1861d. Agents for Deringer and importers. Became A.B. Griswold & Co., in 1861.

HYDE & SHATTUCK Springfield, Massachusetts, 1876d, Hatfield, Massachusetts, 1877d-1880. "Queen" derringers and "American" shotguns. Became C.S. Shattuck in 1880. (AG 6-78)

HYDE & SLOAN MFG. CO. Springfield, Massachusetts, 1874d. Pocket pistols.

HYDE, ALBERT G. New York, New York. Patent #227,789 May 18, 1880, air gun.

HYDE, ANDREW Hatfield, Massachusetts, 1876-1886. Patents #221,171 November 4, 1879, revolver, #273,282 March 6, 1883, revolver, #315,413 April 7, 1885, revolver, and #326,986 September 29, 1885, firearm. As Hyde & Shattuck, 1876-1880.

HYDE, ASA E. Westville, New York, 1870d.

HYDE, CHARLES Hubbardstown, New York(?), 1842. Crude percussion revolving rifle with sliding bayonet, marked with this name, town (but no state), and date. (Sellers)

HYDE, E.H. Lancaster, Wisconsin, 1895d.

HYDE, EDWARD A. Washington, D.C. Patent #422,347 February 25, 1890, firearm.

HYDE, F.S. Sulphur Springs, Texas, 1885d.

HYDE, FRANK New York, New York. Worked for Sharps Rifle Co., 1873-1880 and then opened a shop in New York. (Sellers-4)

HYDE, GREGG & DAY Charleston, South Carolina, 1855. (Albaugh 3)

HYDE, HICKOCK & CO. unlocated. Lockmakers.

HYDE, JOHN S. (1801-?), Stanton, Indiana, 1860c. (Lindert)

HYER, HENRY (1832-?), Staunton, Virginia, 1858d-1897d.

HYSER, SAMUEL Philadelphia, Pennsylvania, 1847d.

HYSLOP, R. New York, New York, 1825-1850. As Smith & Huyslop, 1825-1830. Percussion 1/2 stock.

I SECTION

I.A.A.M. unidentified. Flintlock Kentucky.

I.A.F. see Israel Friend.

I.A.M. unidentified. Percussion fullstock.

I.D. unidentified. Percussion 1/2 stock.

I.E. unidentified. Percussion fullstock Bedford rifle.

I.G. see John Gonter.

I.G. unidentified. Flintlock Kentucky rifle.

I.G. unidentified. Percussion fullstock Tennessee rifle.

I.G.H. unidentified. Flintlock Kentucky rifle.

I.J. see Isaac Jones.

I.L. unidentified. Percussion 1/2 stock.

I.N. see John Nitchman.

I.N.H. see John Hampton.

I.R. unidentified. Percussion fullstock.

ICKES, JACOB (?-1897), Bedford, Pennsylvania, 1860, Spring Meadow, Pennsylvania, 1882d-1890d. Percussion over/under rifle/shotgun. (Whisker)

IDDINGS, JOHN S. (1810-1879), Milton, Ohio, 1838-1840, Peru, Indiana, 1844-1863. Percussion 1/2 stock. (MB 4-63)

IDDINGS, JOSEPH North Salem, Indiana, 1860d.

IDDINGS, SAMUEL (1827-1897), Lafayette, Indiana, 1850-1893. As Bixler & Iddings, 1850-1880. (Lindert)

IDE BROS. Waterford, Vermont, 1860-1870. (Dean*)

IDE, A.L. Springfield, Illinois, 1864d.

IHLENFELDT, WILLIAM Springfield, Illinois, 1892d.

ILLINGSWORTH, THOMAS New York, New York, 1850d-1867d.

ILLINOIS ARMS CO. trade name of Sears, Roebuck & Co. on shotguns.

IMFELD, ANTHONY Savannah, Georgia, 1811. (Kennedy)

IMHOFF, BENEDICT Middletown, Pennsylvania, 1759t-1800. Flintlock Kentucky pistol. (Dillin)

IMHOFF, J. Wausau, Wisconsin, 1879d.

IMPERIAL ARMS CO. trade name of Hopkins & Allen on owlhead revolvers.

IMPERIAL suicide special by Lee Arms Co.

INCE, H.E. Cairo, Illinois, 1882d-1895d.

INGALLS, ALBERT P. Eureka, Kansas, 1878d-1898d, St. Louis, Missouri, 1898d-1909d.

INGALLS, BARNEY Morgantown, Virginia. Percussion fullstock.

INGALLS, BROWN Bangor, Maine, 1846-1856, Bluehill, Maine, 1856-1859, Bucksport, Maine, 1859-1860, Portland, Maine, 1880-1889, Stewardson, Illinois, 1890. (Demeritt)

INGALLS, PHILLIP B. (1833-?), Lorain Co., Ohio, 1850c. (Hutslar)

INGER, JOHN (1822-?), Freeport, Illinois, 1850c. (Johnson)

INGERMAN, A.C. Ft. Madison, Iowa, 1884d.

INGERSOLL, A.R. Chamberlain, South Dakota, 1892d.

INGERSOLL, CALVIN E. Houston, Texas, 1884d.

INGERSOLL, E.Q. Bay City, Michigan, 1883d.

INGERSOLL, SIMON Stamford, Connecticut. Patents #331,792 December 8, 1885, line throwing gun with A.C. Howes, and #348,849 September 7, 1886, line throwing gun.

INGHAM, ALANSON Mexico, New York, 1871d.

INGLE, ARTHUR (1844-?), Ritchie Co., West Virginia, 1870c. (Whisker IV)

INGLES, DAVID St. Louis, Missouri, 1848d.

INGLES, SAMUEL Charleston, South Carolina, 1822-1832, Georgetown, South Carolina, 1832. Superintendent for John Shirer in Charleston, opened his own shop on Shirer's death. (Kauffman 2)

INGRAM BROS. Wahpeton, Dakota Territory, 1886d.

INGRAM, ISAAC Craven's Mills, Tennessee, 1860d.

INGRAM, WILLIAM H. Batesville, Arkansas, 1870c.

INMAN, CORNELIUS (1830-?), Grant Co., West Virginia, 1870c. 1/2 stock. (Whisker IV)

INMAN, WILLOUGHBY Mershon's Crossroads, Kentucky, 1896d.

INSE, TOME Bryantville, Indiana. (Lindert)

INSHAW New York, New York. Percussion fowler.

INSHAW, R.B. Springfield, Massachusetts, 1854-1860d.

INTERNATIONAL suicide special.

INTERNATIONAL trade name of E.C. Meacham on shotguns. (Hinman)

INTERSTATE ARMS CO. trade name of Crescent on guns made for Townley Metal & Hardware Co. (AR 2-69)

INTROWITZ, F.C.G. Chippewa Falls, Wisconsin, 1891d-1895d.

INTROWITZ, FRANK Waseca, Minnesota, 1884d, St. Peter, Minnesota, 1886d.

INVINCIBLE suicide special and shotguns by Iver Johnson.

IRELAND, A.B. Greene, New York. Patent #458,834 September 1, 1891, spring air gun.

IRELAND, J.F. St. Joseph, Missouri, 1859d-1860d.

IRION, MICHAEL Utica, New York, 1874d.

IRON CITY GUN WORKS Pittsburgh, Pennsylvania, 1856-1877. William Craig and Daniel J. McDonald, 1856-1857, McDonald alone, 1858-1864, and H.H. Schutte, 1864-1877. (Kauffman)

IROQUOIS suicide special by Remington.

IRVIN, E.W. Clifford, Virginia, 1890d-1897d.

IRVIN, JAMES (1832-?), McDonough Co., Illinois, 1850c. (Johnson)

IRVIN, RICHARD (1807-?), Rockville, Indiana, 1860c. (Lindert)

IRVING, WILLIAM New York, New York, 1862-1866. Cartridge derringers, percussion and cartridge revolvers. (Sellers-1)

ISAAC, GEORGE Buffalo, New York, 1832. (Gluckman & Satterlee)

ISAAC, JOHN Philadelphia, Pennsylvania, 1780. (Bean)

ISACHSON, NORMAN Marion, Idaho, 1891d.

ISBELL, J.J. Kendallville, Indiana, 1881-1885. (Gardner)

ISCH, CHRISTIAN (1753-?), Lancaster, Pennsylvania, 1774-1782. Flintlock pistol. Committee of Safety muskets with Peter Reigart (also listed as Peter Rugert). (Dillin)

ISCH, PETER Lancaster, Pennsylvania 1759. (Dyke)

ISDEL, JAMES (?-1731), Princess Anne Co., Virginia, 1727-1731. Apprenticed to David James, 1727. (Gill)

ISHAM, R.H. Greenwich, Connecticut. Patent #15,425 July 29, 1856, patching shot.

ISOM, JAMES Blandinsville, Illinois, 1860d.

ISOURD, J.B. New Orleans, Louisiana, 1842d.

ISRAEL, SAMUEL Greene Co., Pennsylvania, 1809-1810. (Kauffman)

ITH, RANDOLPH Fulton, Missouri, 1860d-1889d.

ITHACA GUN CO. Ithaca, New York, 1873-2005. Shotguns.

IVERS, G. unlocated. Converted fullstock dated 1824.

IVERSON, HANS New York, New York, 1845-1855. Patent #7,218 May 30, 1850, revolver.

IVES see Gaskin & Ives.

IVES, JOSEPH F. New Haven, Connecticut, 1847d-1889d.

IXL trade name of B.J. Hart on percussion revolvers. (Sellers-1)

IXL trade name of Davenport on rifles made for Witte Hardware Co. (AR 11-53)

J SECTION

J. & C.B. see Charles Chauncey Barstow.
J.A. see John Amos.
J.A. see John Armstrong.
J.A.H. see Joseph Honaker.
J.A.R. & CO. suicide special by Harrington & Richardson.
J.A.R. unidentified. Percussion fullstock.
J.B. see J. Betz.
J.B. see Joe Barkman.
J.B. see John Bonawitz.
J.B. see John Border.
J.B. see John Buchanan, North Carolina.
J.B. unidentified. Flintlock Kentucky.
J.B. unidentified. Percussion derringer.
J.B.H. see J.B. Harrison.
J.C. see John Clements.
J.C. see Joseph Clippinger.
J.C.G. & CO. see J.C. Grubb.
J.C.M. same marking on locks. (Note: this listing verbatim from First Edition, unsure if author was referencing that Edition's "J.C.M., Dayton, Ohio, percussion 1/2 stock." listing. Ed.)
J.C.M. unidentified. Dayton, Ohio. Percussion 1/2 stock. See other "J.C.M." listing.
J.D. see J. Dreisbach.
J.D. see J. Dunmeyer.
J.D. unidentified. Flintlock Kentucky.
J.D. unidentified. Percussion 1/2 stock.
J.D. unidentified. Percussion fullstock.
J.D.B. unidentified. Percussion 1/2 stock.
J.E. see Jacob Early.
J.E.B. unidentified. Derringer.
J.E.E. see James Engle.
J.E.N. unidentified. Percussion 1/2 stock.
J.F. see Jacob Fisher.
J.F. see John Furney.
J.F. unidentified. Percussion pistol.
J.F.B. see Jacob Brant.
J.F.G. unidentified. Percussion fullstock.
J.F.S. unidentified. Percussion fullstock.
J.G. see John Gillespie.
J.G.B. see Jacob Briggle.
J.G.B. unidentified. Percussion fullstock.
J.G.H. unidentified. Percussion fullstock.
J.G.U. unidentified. Flintlock Kentucky.
J.H. unidentified. Percussion fullstock.
J.H.F. unidentified. Fancy percussion fullstock.
J.H.H. see J.H. Hoffman.
J.I.H. unidentified. Percussion 1/2 stock.
J.J. unidentified. Flintlock Kentucky.
J.J.C. see John J. Carr.
J.J.P. see John Plank.
J.J.S. see John Suter.
J.K. see Jacob Kuntz.
J.L. see Jacob Lindemood.
J.L. see James Locke.
J.L. see John Long.
J.L. see Joseph Long.
J.M. see Joseph Mills.
J.M.C. see J.M. Caswell.
J.M.O. unidentified. Springfield, Massachusetts. Model 1808 pattern musket. (Gluckman)
J.N. unidentified. Flintlock Kentucky.
J.N.H. unidentified. Flintlock Kentucky.
J.N.L. see John Loughman.
J.N.M. see J.N. Medasia.
J.N.M. unidentified. Late Bedford double rifle.
J.P. unidentified. Flintlock Kentucky.
J.P. unidentified. Underhammer pistol.
J.P., JR. unidentified. Percussion fullstock.
J.P.B. see J.P. Beck.
J.P.L. unidentified. Percussion 1/2 stock.
J.P.M. see J.P. McRee.
J.R. see Jacob Ribelin.
J.R. see Jacob Rusley.
J.R. see John Rupp.
J.R.B. unidentified. Percussion 1/2 stock.
J.R.S. see Jacob R. Shawk.
J.S. see Jacob Sell.
J.S. see Jacob Snyder.
J.S. see Jacob Stoudenouer.
J.S. see John Shell.
J.S.H. unidentified. Percussion swivel.
J.S.T. & Co. suicide special by Iver Johnson
J.S.T. unidentified. Percussion fullstock.
J.T. unidentified. Converted fullstock.
J.T. unidentified. Percussion 1/2 stock.
J.V. see John Vogler.
J.W. see Jacob Welshantz.
J.W. see John Watts.
J.W. unidentified. Flintlock Kentucky.
J.W. unidentified. Tennessee fullstock percussion.

J.W.C. see J.W. Clements.

J.W.G. unidentified. Percussion fullstock.

J.W.H.G. unidentified. Percussion fullstock.

J.W.R. unidentified. Percussion fullstock.

J.W.S. see Jacob W. Shawk.

J.W.Y. see John W. Yerian.

JACK TAR spur trigger revolver.

JACKEL, CHRISTIAN F. Buffalo, New York, 1852d.

JACKER, JOSEPH Marquette, Michigan, 1873d-1875d, Livermore, California, 1878d. (Shelton)

JACKLE, JACOB Charlotte, Michigan, 1869d-1899d.

JACKSON & LOSEY see A.N. Jackson.

JACKSON ARMS CO. trade name of Crescent on guns made for C.M. McClung & Co. (AR 2-69)

JACKSON New York, New York. Pinfire double rifle.

JACKSON, A.N. unlocated. Flintlock 1/2 stock Kentucky rifle also marked "JACKSON & LOSEY" on the bottom of its barrel. (Sellers)

JACKSON, CHARLES (1797-1876), Providence, Rhode Island, 1859-1863. Patent #37,937 March 17, 1863, breechloading firearm with Thomas Goodrem. Made Burnside carbines.

JACKSON, CRAFT Guilford Co., North Carolina, 1811. (Bivins)

JACKSON, CYRUS Jamestown, New York, 1831, Buffalo, New York, 1834-1840.

JACKSON, CYRUS Lancaster, Pennsylvania, 1801, Rochester, New York, 1818-1827d. Flintlock Kentucky. (Dillin, Eich)

JACKSON, CYRUS Mercer Co., Pennsylvania, 1850c, Lancaster, Ohio. Percussion 1/2 stock. (GR 11-60)

JACKSON, DANIEL Providence, Rhode Island, 1776. (Achtermier)

JACKSON, DAVID Cincinnati, Ohio, 1831-1833. No directory listings as gunsmith. (Knittle)

JACKSON, DAVID Lee Co., Virginia, 1865-1881, Texas, 1881-1883. His father John, and brother Jim, also gunsmiths. (MB 5-52)

JACKSON, E.T. New Orleans, Louisiana, 1842d.

JACKSON, E.T. St. Louis, Missouri, 1838-1839d.

JACKSON, EDWARD T. Bangor, Maine, 1834. (Demeritt)

JACKSON, GEORGE R. Clinton, Missouri, 1879d-1893d, Chilicothe, Missouri, 1898d.

JACKSON, H.W. unlocated. Percussion fullstock.

JACKSON, J.L. Ypsilanti, Michigan. Percussion double rifle.

JACKSON, JAY Pine Plains, New York, 1877d-1882d

JACKSON, JESSE Beverly, New Jersey, 1866d-1869. Percussion rifles.

JACKSON, JOHN Jamestown, Virginia, 1623-1629. (Gill)

JACKSON, M. Shelbyville, Illinois, 1880d.

JACKSON, S. Palmyra, New York. Percussion rifles.

JACKSON, SILAS T. Philadelphia, Pennsylvania. Patent #45,830 January 10, 1865, cartridge.

JACKSON, TIMOTHY (?-1858), Rochester, New York, 1841d-1858. Numerous patents, but none on guns. (Eich)

JACKSON, WILLIAM (1820-?), San Francisco, California, 1852d. (Shelton)

JACOB, DAVID C. Washington, D.C., 1862d-1872d.

JACOB, JOSEPH Philadelphia, Pennsylvania, 1861d-1899d. Breechloading rifles and shotguns.

JACOBI HARDWARE CO. Philadelphia, Pennsylvania, 1890d-1914d. Dealers only.

JACOBI, NATHANIEL L. Wilmington, North Carolina, 1865-1867. (Bivins)

JACOBS, B. Selma, Alabama, 1866-1885d.

JACOBS, CORNELIUS Columbus, Ohio, 1842-1854d, Alton, Ohio, 1866d. Percussion fullstock. (Hutslar)

JACOBS, J.M. Cusseta, Texas, 1890d.

JACOBS, JOHN H. Curwensville, Pennsylvania, 1856, Benner, Pennsylvania, 1861d. (Kauffman)

JACOBS, MICHAEL York Co., Pennsylvania, 1807-1814. (Kauffman)

JACOBY, FRED O'Fallon, Missouri, 1889d.

JACOBY, MICHAEL Philadelphia, Pennsylvania, 1846d. Stockmaker.

JACOBY, P.E. Uniontown, Pennsylvania, 1887d-1890d.

JACOT, W. unlocated. Converted Kentucky rifle dated 1835.

JAEDICKE, F.W. Lawrence, Kansas, 1867d-1884d. Percussion 1/2 stock. As Gaston & Jaedicke, 1867.

JAEHNE, FREDERICK W. New York, New York, 1871-1884d. Schuetzen rifles. (MB 2-60)

JAHN, HENRY (1817-?), San Francisco, California, 1864-1885. As Jahn & Scholl, 1875-1880. (Shelton)

JALCHEL, G.G. unlocated. Percussion 1/2 stock.

JAMES & FERRIS Utica, New York, 1857-1859. Morgan James and George H. Ferris.

JAMES, DAVID Princess Anne Co., Virginia. Apprenticed to James Isdel, 1727.

JAMES, G. unlocated. Flintlock Kentucky.

JAMES, G. unlocated. Percussion fullstock.

JAMES, H. Nazareth, Pennsylvania, 1887d.

JAMES, H. Scopus, Missouri, 1898d.

JAMES, H.A. Sedalia, Missouri, 1889d-1898d. As White & James, 1889.

JAMES, JACK W. Memphis, Tennessee. Patent #600,787 March 15, 1898, magazine gun.

JAMES, MORGAN (1815-1878), Utica, New York, 1848-1878. Percussion target rifles. As James & Ferris, 1857-1859.

JAMES, ROBERT Baltimore, Maryland, 1796. (Gluckman & Satterlee)

JAMES, WILLIAM Virginia, 1783-1788. Committee of Safety repairs.

JAMESON, BENJAMIN FRANKLIN Mount Sterling, Kentucky, 1883d, Camargo, Kentucky, 1896d.

JAMESON, WILLIAM Philadelphia, Pennsylvania, 1810d.

JAMISON, ALLEN Gower, Missouri, 1898d.

JANKOFSKY, ANTHONY Charleston, South Carolina, 1777-1783. (Dean)

JANNASCH, CHARLES F. Kalamazoo, Michigan, 1863d-1895d.

JANNASCH, F.O. Schoolcraft, Michigan, 1872d-1879d.

JANSEN, DIEDERICH W. Joplin, Missouri, 1879d-1898d. Patent #341,751 May 11, 1886, breechloading firearm.

JANSMA, HERMAN Fulton, Illinois. (Johnson)

JANY, N. Sewellsville, Ohio. Percussion fullstock. (Hutslar)

JAQUITH, ELIJAH Brattleboro, Vermont. Patent #832 July 12, 1838, revolver. (Sellers-1)

JARECKI, HENRY (1826-?), Erie, Pennsylvania, 1849-1879. (Kauffman)

JARRETT, JOHN Rowan Co., North Carolina, 1820c. (Bivins)

JARVIS, LEWIS (1817-?), Athens, Ohio, 1850c-1853d. (Hutslar)

JARVIS, NATHAN, T. (1816-?), Sewellsville, Ohio, 1850c, Freeport, Ohio. Percussion 1/2 stock and fullstock signed "N.T.J.". (Hutslar)

JASPER Boston, Masschusetts, 1775.

JAUB, JOSEPH New Orleans, Louisiana, 1877d.

JEANNET, F. unlocated. Percussion schuetzen rifle.

JEANNET, H.F. Ashland, Wisconsin, 1895d.

JEANNOTAT, JULES Paterson, New Jersey, 1860d.

JEFFERSON, HENRY (1781-?), Cabell, West Virginia, 1860c.

JEFFREY, JOHN Lawrenceville, Pennsylvania, 1839. (Kauffman)

JEFFREY, RICHARD (1826-?), Roscoe, Illinois, 1850c. (Johnson)

JEHLE, AUGUST Highland, Illinois, 1893d. Percussion 1/2 stock.

JELFT, STEPHEN St. Louis, Missouri, 1848d.

JELINSKI, GUSTAVE St. Helena, California, 1893d.

JENISON, C.E. unlocated. Percussion target rifle.

JENKES, JOHN Gloucester, Rhode Island, 1754-1776. (Achternier)

JENKINS SAFETY CATCH GUN CO. Rock Hill, South Carolina, 1892-1894. Shotguns under William Jenkin's patent.

JENKINS, W.W. (1773-1881), North Carolina, Webster Co., Kentucky. His father was also a gunsmith in Virginia. (Hist KY, V5, P613)

JENKINS, WILLIAM E. Charlestown, South Carolina, 1886d, Rock Hill, South Carolina, 1891. Patent #465,764 December 22, 1891, hammerless shotgun.

JENKINSON, JAMES Brooklyn, New York. Patents #35,760 July 1, 1862, bayonet, and #37,075 December 2, 1862, revolver.

JENKS, ALFRED (?-1854), Bridesburg, Pennsylvania. Model 1861 contract muskets. Alfred and Barton Jenks operated Bridesburg Machine works until Afred's death, when Barton took over. (GR 5-62)

JENKS, BARTON H. (?-1896), Bridesburg, Pennsylvania. Patent #74,760 February 25, 1868, breechloading firearm. Son of and successor to Alfred Jenks. (GR 5-62)

JENKS, BENJAMIN Ludlow, Massachusetts, 1818. (Dean *)

JENKS, STEPHEN Providence, Rhode Island, 1770- ?, Pawtucket, Rhode Island, ?-1818. Model 1798 contract muskets with Hosea Humphries, Model 1808 contract muskets with son, Arnold Jenks. (Gluckman)

JENKS, WILLIAM Columbia, South Carolina. Patent #747 May 25, 1838, breechloading firearm. Produced by Ames and Remington. (GR 7-64)

JENN, C. Columbia, Texas, 1896d.

JENNER, CHARLES H. Rochester, New York, 1853d. (Eich)

JENNER, ELIJAH KIRMAN (1811-?), Rochester, New York, 1838d-1841d, San Francisco, California, 1855-1857. Percussion double rifle and John(?)/James(?) Miller patent revolving rifle. (Shelton)

JENNEY & GRAHAM GUN CO. Chicago, Illinois, 1887-1889d. Sales only.

JENNEY, SEMPLE, HILL & CO. Minneapolis, Minnesota. Shotgun.

JENNINGS, A.F. Springfield, Massachusetts, 1878d.

JENNINGS, BENJAMIN (1809-?), Coschocton, Ohio, 1834-1850c. (Hutslar)

JENNINGS, C.M. Amherst Court House, Virginia, 1884d-1893d.

JENNINGS, ELIJAH (1834-?), Spottsylvania, Virginia, 1850c. (MB 10-63)

JENNINGS, ISAIAH New York, New York. Patent #none September 22, 1821, repeating rifle. Breechloading and repeating flintlock rifles. (GR 6-77)

JENNINGS, J. Elmira, New York. Percussion 1/2 stock.

JENNINGS, JAMES Fredericksburg, Virginia, 1866-1875.

JENNINGS, LEWIS Windsor, Vermont. Patent #6,973 December 25, 1849, magazine gun. Produced by Robbins & Lawrence.

JENNINGS, NATHAN (1811-?), Keene, Illinois, 1838-1850. (Johnson)

JENNINGS, POLLARD (1813-?), Boutetourt Co., Virginia, 1850c. (MB 10-63)

JENNINGS, R.L. Astoria, Illinois, 1884d-1892d. As Willcock & Jennings, 1884.

JENNINGS, RICHARD (1816-?), Cleveland, Ohio, 1848-1882. Percussion 1/2 stock. (Hutslar)

JENNINGS, SOLOMON Richmond, Maine, 1752-1754, Ft. Halifax, Maine, 1754-1756. (Demeritt)

JENNINGS, WILLIAM Elmira, New York. Late flintlock. (Swinney)

JENNISON, JAMES Southbridge, Massachusetts. 1820-1850. Flintlock New England rifle and underhammer pistol.

JENSEN, JAMES T. Park Place, Arkansas, 1890, Chicago, Illinois, 1907d. Patent #418,951 January 7, 1890, breechloading gun.

JENSON, I. unlocated. Flintlock New England rifle.

JENSON, N. Washington, D.C. Patent #22,024 November 9, 1858, alarm gun.

JESTER, J.M. Smyrna, Delaware, 1882d.

JETER, HORATIO (1806-?), Lawrence Co., Indiana, 1850c. (Lindert)

JETT, JOHN San Francisco, California. Patent #276,593 May 1, 1883, combination stock and case. (Shelton)

JETT, PETER Virginia, 1778. Public arms repairs. (Gill)

JETTER, JACOB Buffalo, New York, 1862.

JETTZ, WASHINGTON Portwilliam, Kentucky, 1820c. (Gardner)

JEWEL suicide special by Hood Fire Arms Co.

JEWETT, JENKS & SONS Pawtucket, Rhode Island, 1818. Probably Sweet, Jenks & Sons. (Gluckman & Satterlee)

JICHA, FRANK St. Mary's, Missouri, 1879d.

JICHA, JOHN San Francisco, California, 1880-1893d. (Shelton)

JINNEY, B. Coshocton Co., Ohio, 1853d. Percussion 1/2 stock. (Hutslar)

JOB, L. unlocated. Percussion fullstock.

JOBES, MELVIN Moundsville, West Virginia, 1876. Percussion 1/2 stock.

JOHN, ADOLPH Chicago, Illinois, 1898d.

JOHN, WILLIAM Gretna, Louisiana, 1881d-1883d.

JOHNS, C.B. Elko, Nevada, 1871d.

JOHNS, ISAAC Philadelphia, Pennsylvania, 1778-1781. With Thomas Elton as Elton & Johns, repaired U.S. arms. (Kauffman)

JOHNS, JOHN (1804-?), Salineville, Ohio, 1834-1870. Percussion 1/2 stock and fullstock. (Hutslar)

JOHNS, LEVI (1834-?), Salineville, Ohio, 1850c. Son of John Johns, made similar guns. (Hutslar)

JOHNS, WILLIAM B. U.S. Army. Patent #17,792 July 14, 1857, cartridge shot.

JOHNSEN, J.C. (1830-?), Shasta City, California, 1860c. (Shelton)

JOHNSON & BRO. St. Paul, Minnesota, 1856-1870. Gunder and Johannes Johnson.

JOHNSON & McMANUS Sioux City, Iowa, 1889d.

JOHNSON & SMITH Middletown, Connecticut, 1864-1868d. Pistols.

JOHNSON BROS. Cincinnati, Ohio. Percussion fullstock.

JOHNSON, A. unlocated. Flintlock Kentucky and pill lock fullstock Kentucky dated 1833.

JOHNSON, A., & CO. St. Louis, Missouri. Percussion pistol.

JOHNSON, A.A. Kasson, Minnesota, 1877-1884d.

JOHNSON, A.L. Raleigh, North Carolina. Patent #60,897 January 1, 1867, alarm gun with Syd Allen.

JOHNSON, A.O. Helena, Arkansas, 1861. (Elias)

JOHNSON, ABIRAM (1793-?), Harrison Co., Ohio, 1822-1850c. Percussion fullstock. (Hutslar)

JOHNSON, ADOLPH F. Chicago, Illinois, 1898. (Johnson)

JOHNSON, ALEXANDER R. Hartford, Connecticut, 1847-1850. (Kauffman 2)

JOHNSON, ALFRED New Geneva, Pennsylvania, 1870-1883. Patent #233,100 October 12, 1880, lock. Single shot drop block rifles.

JOHNSON, BYE & CO. Worcester, Massachusetts, 1871-1883. Predecessor to Iver Johnson & Co.

JOHNSON, C. Kansas City, Missouri, 1898d.

JOHNSON, CHRIST Wausau, Wisconsin. Patent #532,380 January 8, 1895, automatic.

JOHNSON, DANIEL T. Lancaster, New Hampshire, 1850-1861.

JOHNSON, DAVID Augusta, Arkansas, 1863-1880. (Elias)

JOHNSON, EDWARD W. Columbus, Mississippi. Patent #116,078 June 20, 1871, revolver with John L. Moss.

JOHNSON, EDWIN H. San Francisco, California, 1864-1866. As Blewitt & Johnson. (Shelton)

JOHNSON, ERIC Hamden, Connecticut, 1927-1937. Barrels.

JOHNSON, EVAN (1823-?), Jamestown, North Carolina, 1850c. Percussion 1/2 stock and fullstock. (Bivins)

JOHNSON, EVANS Carthage, Indiana. Percussion 1/2 stock. (Lindert)

JOHNSON, F.B. DeWitt, Iowa, 1880d-1897d.

JOHNSON, FELIX Florence, Alabama, 1861. Percussion revolver. (Albaugh 3)

JOHNSON, GUNDER Cape Girardeau, Missouri, 1848d, St. Paul, Minnesota, 1856-1878d. As Johnson & Bro. in St. Paul.

JOHNSON, H.G. unlocated. Breechloading over/under rifle.

JOHNSON, HANS G. Waukon, Iowa. Patent #650,396 May 29, 1900, breechloading firearm.

JOHNSON, HENRY Buffalo, New York, 1842.

JOHNSON, IRA N. Middletown, Connecticut, 1850-1868. Model 1842 contract pistols. As Smith & Johnson, 1864-1868. (Gluckman)

JOHNSON, ISAAC New Philadelphia, Ohio, 1888d. (Hutslar)

JOHNSON, IVER (?-1911), Worcester, Massachusetts, 1867-1891, Fitchburg, Massachusetts, 1891-1911. Formed Johnson, Bye & Co. in 1871, Iver Johnson & Co. in 1883, and Iver Johnson Arms & Cycle Works in 1884. Moved factory to Fitchburg in 1891. Held numerous patents, mostly with other people. With Martin Bye: #176,003 and #176,004 April 11, 1866, air gun, #204,438 June 4, 1878, revolver, #212,606 February 25, 1879, revolver, and #253,292 February 7, 1882, revolver. By himself: #339,299 April 6, 1886, ejector, #339,300 April 6, 1886, revolver, and #391,144 breechloading firearm. With Andrew Fyrberg and R.T. Torkalson: #339,301 April 6, 1886, revolver, and #345,974 July 20, 1886. With Andrew Fyrberg: #350,681 October 12, 1886, firearm, #357,085 October 16, 1888, revolver, #362,631 #362,632, May 10, 1887, revolvers, #379,226 March 13, 1888, revolver, #379,227 March 13, 1888, safety, #391,153 October 16, 1888, revolver, #391,154 October 16, 1888, safety, #391,156 October 16, 1888, revolver, #465,179 December 15, 1891, revolver, #505,918 October 3, 1893, revolver, and #566,399 August 25, 1896, revolver.

JOHNSON, J. Weeping Water, Nebraska, 1884d.

JOHNSON, J.L. Fort Madison, Iowa, 1892d-1897d.

JOHNSON, J.L. Young American, Illinois, 1870-1872, Keithsburg, Illinois, 1878d-1888d. Choke bore shotguns.

JOHNSON, J.S. Oquawka, Illinois, 1875d.

JOHNSON, JAMES P. Washington, Arkansas, 1850, Des Arc, Arkansas, 1859. (Elias)

JOHNSON, JAMES Y. Louisiana City, Missouri, 1850c. (MB 11-66)

JOHNSON, JAMES (1801-?). Wake Co., North Carolina, 1850c. (Bivins)

JOHNSON, JAMES Mt. Union, Pennsylvania. Percussion fullstock.

JOHNSON, JAMES Virginia, 1777-1778. Public arms repairs. (Gill)

JOHNSON, JOEL M. (1822-?), Harrison Co., Ohio, 1850c. Son of Abiram Johnson. (Hutslar)

JOHNSON, JOHANNES see Johnson & Bro.

JOHNSON, JOHN S. McConnellsville, Pennsylvania, 1850c. (Kauffman)

JOHNSON, JONATHAN H. Houston, Delaware, 1891d.

JOHNSON, JOSEE Washington, D.C. Patents #13,574 September 11, 1855, charger, and #26,269 November 29, 1859, toy gun.

JOHNSON, JOSEPH Philadelphia, Pennsylvania, 1814. (Kauffman)

JOHNSON, L.L., & SON unlocated. Percussion 1/2 stock.

JOHNSON, L.W. Lake City, Florida, 1886d.

JOHNSON, LEMUEL (1824-?), Deersville, Ohio, 1850c-1859d. Son of Abiram Johnson. (Hutslar)

JOHNSON, LEVI North Plains, Michigan, 1865d.

JOHNSON, MARSH East Dorsett, Vermont. Patent #86, July 1, 1836, lock. (Horn)

JOHNSON, MEREDITH Cincinnati, Ohio, 1836-1842. (Gardner)

JOHNSON, O.D. Lancaster, Pennsylvania, 1873d.

JOHNSON, OSCAR (1836-?), Baltimore, Maryland, 1850c. Apprenticed to A. McComas. (Hartzler)

JOHNSON, PERLEY F. Detroit, Michigan, 1888d-1899d.

JOHNSON, ROBERT H. (1830-?), Santa Cruz, California, 1865-1875. (Shelton)

JOHNSON, ROBERT Middletown, Connecticut, 1812-1855. Model 1812 contract muskets, Model 1817 contract rifles, Model 1822 contract muskets, Model 1836 contract pistols. (Gluckman)

JOHNSON, S.R. Groveton, Texas, 1896d.

JOHNSON, SAMUEL WATSON (1838-1903), Newton, Massachusetts, 1874-1893. "Pocket Creedmoor" single shot pistols with extension stocks. Patents #154,871 September 8, 1874, sight, and #202,946 April 30, 1878, extension stock. (GR 2-77)

JOHNSON, SAMUEL Mount Jefferson, Indiana, 1860d.

JOHNSON, SETH Old Rutland, Massachusetts, 1773-1777. Committee of Safety muskets. (Gluckman & Satterlee)

JOHNSON, SPENCER & CO. Chicago, Illinois, 1857d-1860d. Became Hibbard, Spencer, Bartlett & Co.

JOHNSON, THOMAS ROSSLY (1862-1934), New Haven, Connecticut, 1885-1934. Firearms designer, 134 of his patents were assigned to his employer, Winchester. (Williamson)

JOHNSON, THOMAS Center Village, Ohio, 1860-1864d. Percussion 1/2 stock. (Hutslar)

JOHNSON, W.C. DeWitt, Iowa, 1887d.

JOHNSON, W.R. Oak Ridge, Illinois, 1880d-1884d, Tice, Illinois, 1886d.

JOHNSON, WESTLEY Ellisville, Illinois, 1860d.

JOHNSON, WILLIAM F. Ashland, Nebraska, 1879d.

JOHNSON, WILLIAM Hanoverton, Ohio, 1845-1886. Percussion 1/2 stock. Apprentice to Andrew Pettit, took over his shop in 1854, when Pettit was killed. (MB 11-54)

JOHNSON, WILLIAM Haverhill, Massachusetts. Underhammer pistols. (Logan)

JOHNSON, WILLIAM Lancaster, Pennsylvania, 1838t. (Dyke)

JOHNSON, WILLIAM Logansport, Indiana. (Lindert)

JOHNSON, WILLIAM Philadelphia, Pennsylvania, 1835d-1847d.

JOHNSON, WILLIAM Worcester, Massachusetts, 1787. (Gluckman & Satterlee)

JOHNSTON BROS. Cincinnatti, Ohio, 1834-1857. Locks only. (Hutslar)

JOHNSTON, COLUMBUS Clarksville, Missouri, 1879d.

JOHNSTON, GEORGE B. (1840-?), Waynesboro, Pennsylvania, 1866. Son of John H. Johnston, worked for brother James at Great Western Gun Works.

JOHNSTON, J.C. McConnellstown, Pennsylvania, 1890d.

JOHNSTON, J.C. Shasta, California. Percussion over/under rifle.

JOHNSTON, J.S. McConnellstown, Pennsylvania, 1887d-1890d.

JOHNSTON, JAMES HAMPTON (1863-1915), Waynesboro, Pennsylvania, 1850-1865, Pittsburgh, Pennsylvania, 1860-1890d. Percussion fullstock rifle. Son of John H. Johnston. As Great Western Gun Works, retired 1890 and succeeded by his son, John A. Johnston. (Kauffman)

JOHNSTON, JOHN A. (?-1923), Pittsburgh, Pennsylvania, 1888-1923. Son of and successor to James Hampton Johnston, as head of Great Western Gun Works.

JOHNSTON, JOHN H. (1811-1889), Waynesboro, Pennsylvania, 1832t-1889. Percussion fullstock rifles. (Bowers)

JOHNSTON, RICHARD Philadelphia, Pennsylvania, 1801. Model 1798 contract muskets with Robert McCormick. (Gluckman & Satterlee)

JOHNSTON, SAMUEL Pittsburgh, Pennsylvania, 1850. (Kauffman)

JOHNSTON, WILLIAM H. Felicity, Ohio, 1875d. (Hutslar)

JOHNSTON, WILLIAM (1796-1872), Shelocta, Pennsylvania, 1810-1841, Reynoldsville, Pennsylvania, 1841-1872.

JOHNSTON, WILLIAM Cincinnati, Ohio. Patents #35,241 June 13, 1862, breechloading firearm, and #44,868 November 1, 1864, breechloading firearm.

JOISSARD, RENE Philadelphia, Pennsylvania, 1780-1782. Continental Armory. (Moller)

JOKER suicide special by Marlin.

JOLLY, BENJAMIN R. Raleigh, North Carolina. Patent #383,814 May 29, 1888, trigger.

JONAS, F. McConnell's Grove, Illinois, 1860d. See Frederick Jones.

JONES & KELSALL Norwich, Connecticut, 1877d.

JONES & LYTTEL Cleveland, Ohio, 1875d. (Hutslar)

JONES & McBEAN Colorado, Texas, 1890d.

JONES & STUMP Hamlin, West Virginia, 1882d. (Whisker IV)

JONES, A. SHERIDAN Olivet, South Dakota. Patent #270,808 January 16, 1883, magazine gun.

JONES, A. Littleton, West Virginia. (Gluckman & Satterlee)

JONES, A.A. Aleppo, Pennsylvania, 1882d-1887d.

JONES, A.J. Augusta, Kentucky, 1856-1860. Percussion fullstock rifle, underhammer pistol.

JONES, ALBERT Gilmore, Pennsylvania, 1876. (Kauffman)

JONES, ALEXANDER Mobile, Alabama. Patent #none April 22, 1833, method of igniting gunpowder.

JONES, ALPHONSO C. South Paris, Maine, 1879-1900. (Demeritt)

JONES, AMOS Colchester, Connecticut, 1772-1782. Committee of Safety muskets.

JONES, C. Columbus, Ohio, 1840-1847. (Gardner)

JONES, CHARLES Lancaster, Pennsylvania, 1780.

JONES, DANIEL Williamsburg, Virginia, 1714-1717. (Gill)

JONES, EDWARD Bute Co., North Carolina, 1776-1779. Committee of Safety muskets. (Bivins)

JONES, ERASTUS New York, New York. Patent #480,587 August 9, 1892, recoil pad with Ralph Townsend.

JONES, EZEKIAL see Mendenhall, Jones & Gardner.

JONES, FREDERICK McConnells Grove, Illinois, 1860d. Patent #30,228 October 2, 1860, breechloading firearm.

JONES, G.G. Ada, Ohio, 1872-1873d. (Hutslar)

JONES, GEORGE W. Burlington, Iowa, 1850c. (MB 8-64)

JONES, H.E. Castalia, Ohio, 1860-1864d. (Hutslar)

JONES, H.L. unlocated. Percussion fullstock.

JONES, H.S. unlocated. Percussion fullstock.

JONES, HENRY H. Jefferson Co., Missouri, 1850c. (MB 11-66)

JONES, HENRY (1810-?), Shasta, California, 1870c. (Shelton)

JONES, HORACE St. Johnsbury, Vermont. (Horn)

JONES, HORATIO ROSS Addison, New York. Patent #35,524 June 10, 1862, percussion capper.

JONES, HUGH Philadelphia, Pennsylvania, 1813d.

JONES, I.N. Pine Bank, Pennsylvania, 1890d.

JONES, ISAAC (1797-?), Jamestown, North Carolina, 1820. Flintlock Kentucky rifles. (Bivins)

JONES, J.M. unlocated. Percussion derringer.

JONES, J.S. Peekskill, New York, ?-1874d.

JONES, J.W. unlocated. Percussion fullstock dated 1852.

JONES, JAMES H. Mt. Sterling, Ohio, 1878-1883. (Hutslar)

JONES, JAMES Concord, New Hampshire, 1844-1860.

JONES, JAMES Galway, New York, 1862-1882. Percussion fullstock.

JONES, JESSE P. Charlottesville, Virginia, 1893d-1897d.

JONES, JESSE Jefferson Co., Missouri, 1850c. (MB 11-66)

JONES, JOHN B. (1867-?), Brookville, Pennsylvania, 1888-1919. Percussion fullstock and tip-up cartridge pistol.

JONES, JOHN T. (1824-?), Savannah, Georgia, 1846-1860. As Rogers & Jones, 1846-1847. Percussion 1/2 stock rifle marked "I. T. Jones, Savannah.". (Kennedy)

JONES, JOHN (?-1699), Charleston, South Carolina, 1694-1699. (Kauffman 2)

JONES, JOHN Ayr, Kansas, 1882d-1884d, Potwin, Kansas, 1888d.

JONES, JOHN Cleveland, Ohio, 1845-1848. (Kauffman 2)

JONES, JOHN Pulaski, New York, 1874d.

JONES, JOHN Salineville, Ohio, 1848-1854.

JONES, JOSEPH H. (1818-?), Columbus, Ohio, 1843d, London, Ohio, 1850c-1868d, Mt. Sterling, Ohio, 1875d. Derringer. (Hutslar)

JONES, McELWAINE & CO. Holly Springs, Mississippi, 1859-1862. Confederate rifles.

JONES, MONROE (1821-?), Lorain Co., Ohio, 1850c. (Hutslar)

JONES, N. unlocated. Underhammer pistol.

JONES, OWEN Philadelphia, Pennsylvania, 1873-1880. Patents #151,882 June 9, 1874, extractor for revolver, #179,026 June 20, 1876, extractor for revolver, #189,360 April 10, 1877, revolver, #198,745 January 1, 1878, extractor for revolver with Frank Marston, #199,717 January 29, 1878, cartridge with Frank Marston, and #200,794 February 26, 1878, revolver. Moved to England in 1880 and became a gun designer for Enfield Arsenal.

JONES, PHILLIP Clarion, Pennsylvania, 1887. (Whisker)

JONES, R.M. Medina, New York, 1878-1882.

JONES, R.N. Holland, Michigan, 1891d.

JONES, ROBERT Lancaster, Pennsylvania, 1775-?. Flintlock Kentucky.

JONES, SIMPSON (1805-?), Guilford Co., North Carolina. (Bivins)

JONES, THOMAS A. (1844-?), Granville, Ohio, 1872-1893. (Hutslar)

JONES, THOMAS (1787-?), Harrison Co., Indiana, 1850c. (Lindert)

JONES, THOMAS Ohio Co., Virginia, 1777. Committee of Safety repairs. (Whisker IV)

JONES, THOMAS Shabbona's Grove, Illinois, 1860d.

JONES, W.A. Brick Mill, Indiana, 1862d.

JONES, W.E. Catawba Co., North Carolina. Percussion fullstock. (Bivins)

JONES, WILLIAM TREBEY Augusta, Maine, 1882-1900. (Demeritt)

JONES, WILLIAM Bedford, Pennsylvania, 1777-1803. Repaired U.S. arms. (Gluckman & Satterlee)

JONES, WILLIAM Kent Co., Delaware, 1774-1775. Lockmaker. (Gluckman)

JONES, WILLIAM Lineville, Iowa, 1870. Percussion 1/2 stock.

JORDAN, J. Denver, Colorado, 1864-1868. For M. L. Rood. (Sellers-3)

JORDAN, JERMIN (1793-?), Chillicothe, Ohio, 1823-1858. Flintlock and percussion rifles. (Hutslar)

JORDAN, JOHN Missouri Valley, Iowa, 1882d-1887d.

JORDAN, JOHN Windsor, Virginia, 1877d.

JORDAN, LEVI S. South Adams, Massachusetts, 1849d-1865d. Percussion target rifle.

JORDAN, LOUIS Chicago, Illinois, 1889d-1898d, St. Louis, Missouri, 1902-1906. Shotguns exhibited in both Columbian Exhibition and St. Louis World's Fair. As Graf & Jordan, 1889.

JORDAN, ROBERT Otho, Kentucky, 1896d.

JORDAN, W. Dubuque, Iowa, 1880d. Percussion 1/2 stock.

JORG, JACOB Reading, Pennsylvania, 1801-1820. Flintlock Kentucky rifle. (Kauffman)

JORGENSON, FREDERICK Brookston, Pennsylvania, 1882d-1890d.

JOSEPH, WILLIAM Lehigh Co., Pennsylvania, 1846-1848t. (KRA II-3)

JOSHUA (1741-1806), unlocated. Mohican Indian. (Hutslar)

JOSLIN, CHARLES M. Northville, Michigan. Patent #439,246 October 28, 1890, spring air gun.

JOSLIN, H.L. Stillwater, Minnesota, 1884d, Mankato, Minnesota, 1886d.

JOSLIN, H.V. Saugatuck, Michigan, 1863d.

JOSLIN, JOHN Harrison, Arkansas, 1898d.

JOSLIN, WILLIAM Cleveland, Ohio. Patent #24,031 May 17, 1859, centrifugal gun.

JOSLYN, BENJAMIN F. Worcester, Massachusetts, 1855-1861, Stonington, Connecticut, 1861-1879. Patents #13,507 August 28, 1855, breechloading firearm, #15,240 July 1, 1856, breechloading firearm, #33,435 October 8, 1861, breechloading firearm, #35,688 June 24, 1862, breechloading firearm, #39,405 August 4, 1863, revolver, #39,406 August 4, 1863, revolver, #39,407 August 4, 1863, revolver, #42,000 March 22, 1864, breechloading firearm, #42,379 April 19, 1864, revolver, #46.243 February 7, 1865, revolver, #48,073 June 6, 1865, breechloading firearm, #48,287 June 20, 1865, revolver, #48,288 June 20, 1865, breechloading firearm, #51,836 January 2, 1866, breechloading firearm, #51,837 January 2, 1866, breechloading firearm, #109,218 November 25, 1870, revolver, #109,417 May 30, 1871, revolver, #115,483 November 22, 1870, revolver, #180,037 July 18, 1876, revolver, #183,944 October 31, 1876, revolver, #202,350 April 26, 1878, revolver, #202,351 April 16, 1878, revolver, #204,334 May 28, 1878, revolver, #204,335 May 28, 1878, revolver, #204,336 May 28, 1878, revolver, #204,337 May 28, 1878, revolver, #211,743 January 28, 1879, revolver, and #222,912 December 23, 1879, magazine gun. Joslyn Firearm Co. made revolvers and carbines under these patents. (AR 7-66)

JOSLYN, ISAAC M. Batavia, New York, 1849-1882.

JOSSELYN, HENRY S. Roxbury, Massachusetts. Patent 52,248 January 23, 1866, chain revolver.

JOST White Plains, Pennsylvania, 1775-1776. Committee of Safety muskets.

JOST, CASPER Dauphin Co., Pennsylvania, 1785. (Bowers)

JOTUL, CARL Washington, D.C., 1858d. (Hartzler)

JOURDON, T. Neenah, Wisconsin, 1857d.

JOUSTAN, HENRI New Orleans, Louisiana, 1853d.

JOY, ANDREW S. Pittsburgh, Pennsylvania, 1838-1858. Percussion fullstock rifle. (Kauffman)

JUD, MORELAND, JR. (1840-?), Indiana, 1867, San Jose, California, 1870-1873. (Shelton)

JUDD & TOBEY Waterbury, Connecticut, 1887d.

JUDD, C.W. Woodcock, Pennsylvania, 1874d. Percussion over/under rifle.

JUDD, EDWARD M. New Britain, Connecticut. Patent #34,504 February 25, 1862, repeating firearm.

JUDD, F.N. Westhampton, Massachusetts, 1885d-1892d.

JUDD, G. Meadville, Pennsylvania, 1873. Percussion target rifle.

JUDD, ORANGE New York, New York. Percussion 1/2 stock target rifles. Partner of Homer Fisher.

JUDD, WILLIAM H. Ypsilanti, Michigan, 1887d-1899d. As Mallion & Judd, 1887d.

JUDSON & CO. Rochester, New York, 1872-1875.

JUDSON, ABEL New Lebanon, New York. Patent #none June 13, 1831, underhammer lock. Percussion underhammer rifle.

JUDSON, HENRY Avery, Iowa, 1875d, Harlan, Iowa, 1887d.

JUDSON, W.H. Union City, Pennsylvania, 1873d-1874d. As Novelty Iron Works.

JUFORGUL, PIERRE, R. New Orleans, Louisiana, 1838d-1853d.

JUGARN, LOUIS New Orleans, Louisiana, 1838d.

JUGE, ADOLPH New Orleans, Louisiana, 1870d-1878d.

JUGHARDT, CHARLES St. Louis, Missouri, 1859d, Fostoria, Ohio, 1859-1869.

JUNIUS, HENRY (1883-?), Harrodsburg, Kentucky, 1860c. For Benjamin Mills.

JUNKER, EDWARD St. Louis, Missouri, 1889d-1898d.

JUNKIN BROS. Red Oak, Iowa, 1880d-1884d.

JUNKIN Southport, Indiana. (Lindert)

JUSSELIN New Orleans, Louisiana, 1834d.

JUSTICE & STEINMAN Philadelphia, Pennsylvania, 1860c. Philip S. Justice.

JUSTICE, GEORGE W. Big Rapids, Michigan, 1875d.

JUSTICE, JOHN (1807-?), Rutherford Co., North Carolina, 1850c. (Bivins)

JUSTICE, P.S., & CO. Philadelphia, Pennsylvania, dates unknown. Philip S. Justice.

JUSTICE, PHILIP S. Philadelphia, Pennsylvania, 1860-1865. Model 1861 contract muskets. As Justice & Steinman, 1860. As P.S. Justice & Co., dates unknown. (Fuller)

JUZAN, JOSEPH New Orleans, Louisiana, 1884d.

JUZAN, LOUIS New Orleans, Louisiana, 1853d-1884d. For P. Bouron, 1853-1865.

K SECTION

K.A.T. unidentified. Percussion 1/2 stock.

K.K. trade name of Hopkins & Allen on shotguns made for Shapleigh Hardware Co.

K.S. unidentified. Flintlock Kentucky.

KABLER, JOHN G. Perry Co., Missouri, 1850c. (MB 11-66)

KABLER, W. Santa Fe, Kentucky, 1857-1860.

KACER, MARTIN V. St. Louis, Missouri. Patents #273,288 March 6, 1883, breechloading firearm and #282,328 July 31, 1883, magazine gun, both with William Kizer.

KACHELOFEE, JOHN G. Starke, Florida, 1884d.

KAEDING, CHARLES V.B. (1840-?). San Francisco, California, 1859-1889, as Liddle & Kaeding. (Shelton)

KAESE, AUGUST Oakland, California, 1870-1880. With Christian Rode as Kaese, Rode & Co.

KAESE, RODE & CO. Oakland, California, 1870-1880. August Kaese and Christian Rode. (Shelton)

KAFFKS, VINCENT Kansas City, Kansas, 1888d.

KAHL, E.H. Shelbyville, Tennessee, 1887d-1891d.

KAHN, J. Erie, Pennsylvania, 1860. Percussion shotguns. With Peter Hartman as Hartman & Kahn.

KAHN, W.T. Philadelphia, Pennsylvania, 1840d.

KAIL, WILLIAM unlocated. Flintlock and percussion rifles.

KAISER & BOWERSOX Monroe, Michigan, 1895d.

KAISER, HENRY San Francisco, California, 1880-1882. (Shelton)

KAISER, JOHN Fremont, Ohio, 1890-1897d. With Isaac G. Bower as Bower & Kaiser, 1890. (Hutslar)

KAISER, K.F. Monroe, Michigan, 1895d-1899d. As Kaiser & Bowersox, 1895.

KALAMAZOO trade name of Snow & Coe on air pistol made under E.H. Hawley's patent #90,749 June 1, 1869.

KALBITZ, JUSTICE Jefferson Co., Missouri, 1850c. (MB 11-66)

KALBITZ, ROBERT St. Louis, Missouri, 1857d-1870d.

KALINA, JOSEPH Cleveland, Ohio, 1894-1900. Patent #660,378 October 23, 1900, safety. (Hutslar)

KAMERER, MEINRAD Norwalk, Connecticut, 1874d-1876d.

KAMPF, HENRY Collomsville, Pennsylvania. Percussion fullstock. (Gluckman & Satterlee)

KAMPMANN, HENRY Chicago, Illinois, 1856d-1859d. With John Wettstein as Wettstein & Kampmann.

KAMPT, SOLOMON Hempfield, Pennsylvania, 1810-1825. (Kauffman)

KANE, B. Middle Fork, Ohio, 1881-1887. (Hutslar)

KANE, P. South Perry, Ohio. Patent #33,842 December 3, 1861, alarm gun with W. Floyd.

KANE, PETER (1816-1898), Buena Vista, Ohio, 1875-1878, Middle Fork, Ohio, 1881d. Percussion 1/2 stock. (Hutslar)

KANEN, P.J. Camden, Arkansas, 1892d.

KANSTEINER, WILLIAM (1827-?), Hannibal, Missouri, 1847-1890.

KANTLEHNER, FREDERICK Chelsea, Michigan, 1873d-1891d.

KANTZ, E. unlocated. Flintlock Kentucky.

KANTZ, GABRIEL Lancaster, Pennsylvania, 1863d. See Gabriel Kautz.

KAPP, ALFRED Sisterdale, Texas. Percussion revolver. (T 20)

KAPPAL, JOSEPH Philadelphia, Pennsylvania, 1855d-1858d.

KAPPLER, J. Evansville, Indiana, 1866d.

KARAS, SIGISMUND Wausau, Wisconsin, 1891d-1895d.

KARNES, L. Havana, Illinois, 1860d.

KARNS, LOUIS Oswego, Kansas, 1882d.

KARNS, LOUIS Pekin, Illinois, 1860d.

KARNS, M. Bloomfield, Iowa, 1865d.

KARSNER, JOHN Florida, Ohio, 1866-1883d. (Hutslar)

KARUTZ, ALBERT Brooklyn, New York. Patent #152,998 July 14, 1874, breechloading firearm.

KASCHELINE, PETER Northhampton Co., Pennsylvania, 1775-1776. Committee of Safety muskets. (Gluckman & Satterlee)

KASEL, G. Washington, Missouri, 1898d.

KASPERS, J.M. Houghton, Michigan, 1899d.

KASSAN, WILLIAM M. Columbus, Ohio, 1832-1835. (Knittle)

KAUEN, P.J. Santa Fe, New Mexico, 1882d.

KAUFFMAN, ANDREW (?-1785), Lancaster, Pennsylvania, 1770-1785. (Dean)

KAUFFMAN, JOHN (1810-?), Baton Rouge, Louisiana, 1850c. (MB 9-65)

KAUL, C. & PIUS Lancaster, Pennsylvania. Patent #298,982, May 20, 1884, breechloading firearm.

KAUP, ELI unlocated. Percussion fullstock.

KAUP, LEROY Union Co., Pennsylvania, 1850c. Flintlock Kentucky rifle. First name possibly Levi? (Kauffman)

KAUP, LEVI see Leroy Kaup.

KAUPERT, JOHN F. Philadelphia, Pennsylvania, 1861d.

KAUTZ, FREDERICK Urbana, Ohio, 1857-1866d. (Hutslar)

KAUTZ, GABRIEL Lancaster, Pennsylvania, 1863. Also known as Gabriel Kantz. (Dyke)

KAUTZKY, JOSEPH Perry, Iowa, 1895d, Ft. Dodge, Iowa, 1897d-1939. Patent #827,241 July 31, 1906, single trigger.

KAY, ALLEN B. Newark, New Jersey, 1871d. Patent #109,419 November 22, 1870, breechloading firearm. Possibly B. Kay & Co.?

KAY, B., & CO. Newark, New Jersey, 1874-1876. Possibly Allen B. Kay & Co.?

KAY, JOHN Nauvoo, Illinois, Salt Lake City, Utah, 1854-1857. With David Sabin as Sabin & Kay. See David Sabin.

KAYE & DEHAVEN Philadelphia, Pennsylvania. Flintlock Kentucky rifle. See Golcher & Kaye. (MB 4-63)

KAYE, S.R. Philadelphia, Pennsylvania, 1865d-1867d. Son of and successor to William W. Kaye.

KAYE, WILLIAM W. (?-1864), Philadelphia, Pennsylvania, 1856d-1864d. Percussion guns.

KAYSER, JOHN C. Georgetown, D.C., 1855-1872d.

KEAFFER, PETER Lancaster, Pennsylvania, 1759. (Dyke)

KEAN, J.B.M. unlocated. Percussion fullstock rifle.

KEAR, MOSE Wyandot Co., Ohio, 1820. (Hutslar)

KEARLING, SAMUEL Berks Co., Pennsylvania, 1779. See Samuel Kerlin. (Gluckman & Satterlee)

KEARRENBERG, F. Middletown, New York, 1870d.

KEATING & CO. New York, New York, 1874d.

KEATING, HENRY (1858-?), Namaqua, Colorado, 1880c.

KEATS, THOMAS Sturgis, Michigan, 1887d-1899d.

KEATS, WILLIAM Philadelphia, Pennsylvania, 1780-1782. Continental Armory. (Moller)

KEEFER, ISAIAH C. (1829-1861), Sylvan, Pennsylvania, 1850-1861d. Percussion fullstock. (Bowers)

KEEFER, JACOB (1821-?), Shippensburg, Pennsylvania, 1850c. Percussion fullstock. (Bowers)

KEEFER, JACOB Lancaster, Pennsylvania, 1802-1820. See Joseph Keffer. (Gluckman & Satterlee)

KEEHNART, CHARLES (1812-?), St. Louis, Missouri, 1850c. (possibly Heehnart)

KEELER, LUCIUS St. Albans, Vermont, 1823-1843. Underhammer pistol. Also see Lucius Keller. (Horn)

KEELEY, JACOB (?-1777), East Vincent, Pennsylvania, 1758-1777.

KEELEY, MATTHIAS (?-1780), East Vincent, Pennsylvania, 1776-1780. Committee of Safety muskets. Son of Jacob Keeley. (Gluckman & Satterlee)

KEELEY, SEBASTIAN M. Philadelphia, Pennsylvania, 1775. Committee of Safety muskets. (Hobbies 4-38)

KEELING, WILLIAM (1859-?), Holmans, Alabama, 1880c.

KEELY, JOHN Philadelphia, Pennsylvania, 1810d. (Whisker III)

KEEN & BEUTTENMULLER Joliet, Illinois, circa 1850. James C. Keen and Frederick Beuttenmuller.

KEEN, GEORGE Snyder Co., Pennsylvania. Flintlock Kentucky rifles. (Gabel)

KEEN, JAMES C. (1824-?), Joliet, Illinois, 1840-1880, North Platte, Nebraska, 1886d-1893d. With Frederick Beuttenmuller as Keen & Beuttenmuller, circa 1850. (Hobbies 3-36)

KEEN, WALKER & CO. Danville, Virginia, 1862-1863. Confederate "Perry" carbine. (Albaugh)

KEENE, JOHN W. Newark, New Jersey. Patents #147,945 February 24, 1874, magazine gun, #147,946 February 24, 1874, magazine gun, #147,947 February 24, 1874, magazine gun, #147,948 February 24, 1874, magazine gun, #148,614 March 17, 1874, magazine gun, #172,447 January 18, 1876, magazine gun, #172,448 January 18, 1876, magazine gun, #182,583 September 26, 1876, magazine gun, and #188,468 March 20, 1877, magazine gun. Guns made by Remington.

KEENE, PRINCE Providence, Rhode Island, 1775. (Dean*)

KEENER & SON Baltimore, Maryland, 1795-1806. (Hartzler)

KEENER, GEORGE P. (1824-?), Baltimore, Maryland, 1852-1860d. Son of John Keener. (Hartzler)

KEENER, JACOB Baltimore, Maryland, 1802.

KEENER, JOHN (1771-?), Baltimore, Maryland, 1796d-1851d. Son of Peter Keener. (Hartzler)

KEENER, JOHN (1821-?), Baltimore, Maryland, 1850c. With his father, John Keener. (Hartzler)

KEENER, PETER Baltimore, Maryland, 1777-1806d. Committee of Safety muskets, flintlock rifles and pistols. With his son John, 1795-1806. (Hartzler)

KEENER, SAMUEL Baltimore, Maryland, 1776. Committee of Safety muskets. (Hartzler)

KEENERT, LEWIS Stroudsburgh, Pennsylvania, 1868d.

KEENEY, J.T. Belton, Missouri, 1891d-1898d.

KEENISH, LEWIS Jackson Corners, Pennsylvania, 1870c.

KEEPORTS, GEORGE PETER Baltimore, Maryland, 1776-1781. Committee of Safety repairs. (Gluckman & Satterlee)

KEERAN & MATTLEN Bloomington, Illinois, 1853-1854d. Levi Keeran and Samuel Mattlen.

KEERAN, C.H. Corsicana, Texas, 1884d.

KEERAN, J.C. Shawnee, Kansas, 1884d-1894d.

KEERAN, LEVI (1824-?), Bloomington, Illinois, 1847-1862. Percussion 1/2 stock. With Samuel Mattlen as Keeran & Mattlen, 1853-1854.

KEES, F.D. Beatrice, Nebraska, 1879d-1884d.

KEESEY & APPLEBAY Steubenville, Ohio, 1875d. George Keesey and Alex Applebay. (Hutslar)

KEFFER, JACOB Lancaster, Pennsylvania, 1802-1820. Flintlock Kentucky rifles.

KEFFER, PETER Jamestown, Virginia, 1608. (Gill)

KEHLER, JOHN Lancaster, Pennsylvania, 1802-1803. (Kauffman)

KEHN, GREGORY New Albany, Indiana, 1850c. (Lindert)

KEIFEL, JOHN Quincy, Illinois. Percussion schuetzen.

KEIFFLER unlocated. Percussion fullstock.

KEIM, CHARLES Newport, Kentucky, 1880d-1882d.

KEIM, JOHN Berks Co., Pennsylvania, 1811-1839. Flintlock Kentucky. (Gluckman & Satterlee)

KEIM, W. & J.H. unlocated. Heavy flintlock fullstock target rifle.

KEINDER, DAVID (1820-?), Duncan's Mills, Illinois, 1860c. (Johnson)

KEIPP, P.C. Selma, Alabama, 1885d.

KEISSIG & SCHMIDT Kansas City, Missouri, 1868d.

KEITH & BUTTERFIELD Philadelphia, Pennsylvania, 1830. Flintlock Kentucky. Hiram A. Keith and B. Butterfield. (Kindig)

KEITH, BENHAM & DEZENDORF Chicago, Illinois, 1883d-1908d. Importers and dealers.

KEITH, F.C. Noble Co., Ohio. (Hutslar)

KEITH, HIRAM A. Philadelphia, Pennsylvania. Breechloading (Hall pattern) flintlock 1/2 stock. With B. Butterfield as Keith & Butterfield. (Kindig)

KEITH, JOHN S. Canton, Massachusetts. Patent #12,411 February 20, 1855, bullet mould with John Brooks.

KELKER & BRO. Harrisburg, Pennsylvania, 1861-1874. Lockmakers only. (Gluckman & Satterlee)

KELLAR, WILLIAM Maryville, Tennessee. 1860d, Corn, Tennessee, 1887d-1890d. Percussion fullstock.

KELLE, WALTER Ripon, Wisconsin, 1876.

KELLER, ALEXANDER M.S. unlocated. Southern Kentucky rifle.

KELLER, BENJAMIN Granville, Ohio. Percussion 1/2 stock.

KELLER, CHARLES (1826-1900). Evansville, Indiana, 1848-1900. Percussion 1/2 stock. (MB 12-52)

KELLER, CHRISTIAN New York, New York, 1871-1876d. Percussion schuetzen. (Swinney)

KELLER, ELIAS Yardleyville, Pennsylvania, 1860d-1861d.

KELLER, I. see John W. Keller.

KELLER, ISAAC Randolph, Ohio, circa 1830. (Hutslar)

KELLER, J.W. St. Anthony, Minnesota, 1867d.

KELLER, JAMES M. Liberty, Missouri, 1850c. (MB 11-66)

KELLER, JOHN W. Carlisle, Pennsylvania, 1823-1873. Flintlock and percussion guns. Early signature, "I. Keller". (Kauffman)

KELLER, JOHN (1828-?), Muskingum Co., Ohio, 1850c. (Hutslar)

KELLER, JOSEPH W. (1821-?), Meadville, Pennsylvania, 1850c, Casey, Illinois, 1860c. Percussion fullstock. (Johnson)

KELLER, JOSEPH W. Hagerstown, Maryland, 1841. Successor with William Cookman to William Hawken. (Hartzler)

KELLER, JOSEPH W. Little Rock, Arkansas, 1871d.

KELLER, L. Carlisle, Pennsylvania. Percussion double rifle.

KELLER, LUCIUS St. Albans, Vermont. Underhammer pistol. See Lucius Keeler.

KELLER, MOSES A. Batavia, New York. Patent #488,316 December 20, 1892, ejector.

KELLER, SAMUEL Blount Co., Tennessee. Percussion fullstock, signature "S.K.".

KELLER, T. Carlisle, Pennsylvania. Percussion 1/2 stock.

KELLERMAN, CHARLES C. New Orleans, Louisiana, 1876d-1877d.

KELLERMAN, E. Montesano, Washington, 1889d.

KELLERMAN, HENRY Chicago, Illinois, 1871d.

KELLERMAN, JOHN Eudora, Kansas, 1866d-1867d.

KELLERMAN, W. Meridian, Mississippi, 1885d.

KELLERMAN, WILLIAM (?-1869), Chicago, Illinois, 1852-1869. Percussion schuetzen. (MB 10-57)

KELLEY, J.E. Drayton, Georgia, 1881d, Marshallville, Georgia, 1883d.

KELLEY, JAMES W.D. Chicago, Illinois, 1877d. Dealer and importer.

KELLEY, JOSEPH W. New York, New York, 1886d-1888d.

KELLEY, PETER Claire, Michigan, 1895d-1899d.

KELLOG Indianapolis, Indiana. Lockmakers only.

KELLOGG BROS. New Haven, Connecticut, 1865-1870. Alfred and Henry Kellogg.

KELLOGG, ALFRED ANDREW (1845-1918), New Haven, Connecticut, 1862-1905d. Percussion target rifles and Sharps target rifles. (GR 5-76)

KELLOGG, COTTON New Hartford, Connecticut. Patent #none August 31, 1810, rifle with Elisha Strong.

KELLOGG, EBENEZER C.C. Hartford, Connecticut, 1859-1875d, Macelona, Michigan, 1833d-1887d, Ludington, Michigan, 1899d. Percussion rifles and shotguns. As Kellogg & Co., 1871-1875.

KELLOGG, HENRY S. Cincinnati, Ohio, 1834d-1840d, Indianapolis, Indiana. Locks and barrels. As Kellogg, Wells & Co., 1836-1837. (Hutslar)

KELLOGG, HENRY New Haven, Connecticut, 1858-1874. Patents #35,356 May 20, 1862, breechloading firearm, and #35,878 July 15, 1862, cartridge. As Crosby & Kellogg, 1860-1863 and Kellogg Bros. 1865-1870. (GR 2-79)

KELLOGG, SILVESTER Rochester, New York. Patent #none June 16, 1826, lock with Joseph Medbury.

KELLOGG, WELLS & CO. Cincinnati, Ohio, 1837. Hardware store, locks only. Henry S. Kellogg.

KELLUM, EBENEZER Hempstead, New York, 1850d-1872d.

KELLY see Norman & Kelly.

KELLY, DANIEL Detroit, Michigan. Patents #37,171 December 16, 1862, cartridge tearer, and #37,196 December 16, 1862, gun stocks.

KELLY, FERDINAND Iron Mountain, Michigan, 1895d.

KELLY, J.J. Hot Springs, Arkansas, 1898d.

KELLY, NATHANIEL Greenbrier Co., Virginia, 1810. Contract rifles (Model ?) for Virginia with George Dixon. (Cromwell)

KELLY, O.P. Hall, Illinois, 1860d.

KELLY, SAMUEL unlocated. Flintlock Kentucky.

KELLY, THOMAS San Francisco, California. Patent #342,363 May 25, 1886, breechloading firearm.

KELSAY, C.H. (1822-1882), Holt, Missouri. Percussion 1/2 stock. (MB 9-63)

KELSAY, JOHN (1819-1899), Ray Co., Missouri, 1841-1873, Kelseyville, California, 1873-1899. Percussion and breechloading rifles. (Shelton)

KELSAY, NATHANIEL (1825-?), Ray Co., Missouri, 1850c, Kelseyville, California, 1867-1873. (Shelton)

KELSEY, WILLIAM (1792-?), Pioneer and Huntington, Ohio, 1850c-1868d, Kelseyville, California, 1867-1879. (Shelton)

KELSO, JAMES Monroe Co., Kentucky, 1820c.

KELTING, SAM Brooklyn, New York, 1870-1876.

KELTON, JOHN C. (1828-1893), U.S. Army. Patents #280,484 July 3, 1883, sight, #313,212 March 3, 1885, sight protector, #313,213 March 3, 1885, magazine gun, #331,244 November 24, 1885, magazine, #333,416 December 29,

1885, revolver safety, #359,680 March 12, 1887, sight, and #331,891 December 8, 1885, cartridge pack. Kelton advanced to the rank of Adjutant General. Smith & Wesson revolvers were made with his safety and one of his magazine rifles was submitted to the 1890 trials. (Shelton)

KEMBLE & BUTLER Bowling Green, Kentucky, 1883d.

KEMBLE & DAVIS Wilmington, Delaware, 1884d.

KEMBLE, E.M. Buena Vista, Colorado, 1882d-1889d. (Sellers-3)

KEMMERER, DAVID Carbon Co., Pennsylvania. Flintlock Kentucky rifles.

KEMMERER, DAVID, JR. Lehighton, Pennsylvania, 1850. Underhammer pistols.

KEMMIS, JOHN W. Hartford, Connecticut, 1852-1853d.

KEMNITZ, GUSTAVE Kankakee, Illinois, 1864d.

KEMNITZ, K.G. Kankakee, Illinois, 1890d. Son of Gustave Kemnitz.

KEMP, ALEXANDER Helena, Montana, 1871d.

KEMP, DAVID (1813-?), New Albany, Indiana, 1850c-1858d. Percussion 1/2 stock. (Lindert)

KEMP, JOSEPH Chicago, Illinois, 1851-1856d.

KEMPER, G.W. Goodlettsville, Tennessee, 1870d-1874d. Percussion rifles for Bransford Hardware Co., Nashville, Tennessee.

KEMPF, BENJAMIN (1795-1879), Mount Pleasant, Pennsylvania, 1819-1879. (Whisker II)

KEMPF, SOLOMON (1790-1862), Westmoreland Co., Pennsylvania, 1809-1862. (Whisker II)

KEMPTON, EPHRAIM Boston, Massachusetts, 1677, Salem, Massachusetts, 1680.

KENDALL & LAWRENCE Windsor, Vermont, 1842-1844. Nicanor Kendall and Richard S. Lawrence.

KENDALL, EDWARD D. Jersey City, New Jersey. Patent #217,116 July 1, 1879, signal gun.

KENDALL, HUBBARD & SMITH Windsor, Vermont, 1835-1842. Underhammer pistols. Also known as Kendall, Hubbard & Story. (Horn)

KENDALL, HUBBARD & STORY Windsor, Vermont. Same as Kendall, Hubbard and Smith. (Horn)

KENDALL, N., & CO. Windsor, Vermont, 1838-1842. (MB 10-64)

KENDALL, NICANOR (1807-1861), Windsor, Vermont, 1835-1849. Underhammer guns in state prison. As Kendall, Hubbard & Smith, 1835-1838, N. Kendall & Co., 1838-1842, and Robbins, Kendall & Lawrence, 1842-1844. (MB 10-64, Horn)

KENDALL, WILLIAM Newton, Wisconsin, 1857d.

KENDRICK, W. Neosho, Missouri, 1860d.

KENESS, T. Chicago, Illinois, 1850. (Johnson)

KENIDY, A.S. Mound City, Illinois, 1867d. See A. Kennedy and Alex Kennedy.

KENISON, C.W. Freedom, New Hampshire, 1877d.

KENNEDY BROS. Minneapolis and St. Paul, Minnesota, 1867-1898d. Dealers.

KENNEDY see Logan & Kennedy.

KENNEDY, A. Monroe Co., North Carolina. (Bivins)

KENNEDY, A. Valley Forge, Illinois, 1860d.

KENNEDY, ALEX New Maysville, Illinois, 1860d.

KENNEDY, D. Mantua Center, Ohio, 1856-1861. (Hutslar)

KENNEDY, DAVID (1834-?), Robbins, North Carolina, 1850c. Flintlock Kentucky. (Bivins)

KENNEDY, E.E., & CO. unlocated. Converted fullstock rifle dated 1826.

KENNEDY, E.M. Robbins, North Carolina. (MB 5-65)

KENNEDY, ENOCH L. (1837-?), Robbins, North Carolina, 1860c. Percussion fullstock. (Bivins)

KENNEDY, GEORGE S. Philadelphia, Pennsylvania, 1888d-1899d. As Kennedy & Curtis, 1888-1895.

KENNEDY, JOHN A. Choteau and Browning, Montana. Patents #535,379 March 12, 1895, sight, #592,740 October 12, 1897, sight, and #937,244, October 14, 1908, sight.

KENNEDY, JOHN (1791-?), Robbins, North Carolina, 1850c. (Bivins)

KENNEDY, JOHN Pittsburgh, Pennsylvania, 1868d.

KENNEDY, MARTIN F. St. Paul, Minnesota, 1864-1898d. As Kennedy Bros., 1867-1898.

KENNEDY, SAMUEL V. New Haven, Connecticut. Patents #215,227 May 13, 1879, magazine gun, #218,462 August 12, 1879, magazine gun with F.W. Tiesing and W. Kennedy, #225,664 March 16, 1880, magazine gun with F.W. Teising and W. Kennedy, #235,829 December 21, 1880, magazine gun wtih F.W. Tiesing, and #235,830, magazine gun with F.W. Tiesing. (Maxwell)

KENNEDY, T.F. Providence, Rhode Island, 1869-1873.

KENNEDY, THOMAS J. New Co., Missouri, 1850c. (MB 11-66)

KENNEDY, W.W. Robbins, North Carolina, 1770-1800. (Bivins)

KENNER, ALEXANDER (1800-?), Hancock, Maryland, 1834-1893. (Hutslar)

KENNEY, MARTIN R. Bernardston, Massachusetts, 1885d-1890d.

KENO trade name on single shot .22 cal. pistol.

KENSTER, JOHN (1742-?), Georgetown, Maryland, 1777-?. (Kauffman 2)

KENT see Matthew Elliott.

KENT, A. unlocated. Flintlock Kentucky rifle.

KENT, ELIJAH Big Rapids, Michigan, 1884d-1887d.

KENT, P. unlocated. Percussion fullstock.

KENT, RICHARD Waverly, Illinois, 1888d.

KENTON, G.S. unlocated. Percussion pistol.

KENTUCKY suicide special by Iver Johnson.

KEPPERLING, LEWIS Berwick, Pennsylvania, 1850c. (Kauffman)

KERLIN, JOHN Bucks Co., Pennsylvania, 1773-1777. Committee of Safety muskets. (Hobbies 4-38)

KERLIN, JOHN, JR. Bucks Co., Pennsylvania, 1798-1826. Model 1798 contract muskets for Pennsylvania with Samuel Kerlin, Model 1808 contract muskets under John Miles, Jr's. defaulted contract. (Gluckman & Satterlee)

KERLIN, SAMUEL Bucks Co., Pennsylvania. Model 1798 contract muskets for Pennsylvania with John Kerlin, Jr. (Gluckman & Satterlee)

KERN, D.W. Shimerville, Pennsylvania, 1882d.

KERN, DANIEL Northampton Co., Pennsylvania, 1776-1790. Kentucky rifles. (Dillin)

KERN, FREDERICK R. Lancaster, Pennsylvania, 1853-1857. (Gluckman & Satterlee)

KERN, PETER Northampton Co., Pennsylvania, 1772-1790.

KERN, REINHARD Lancaster, Pennsylvania, 1857d.

KERNAGHAN, D., & CO. New Orleans, Louisiana, 1855-1860. Importers.

KERR, JOHN L. Allegheny, Pennsylvania. Patent #157,008 November 17, 1874, barrels.

KERR, JOHN Carlisle, Pennsylvania, 1778-1780. (Gardner)

KERR, MICHAEL Philadelphia, Pennsylvania, 1788-1800. (Kauffman)

KERR, W. Iredale Co., North Carolina. (Bivins)

KERSEY, LEVI CHARLES (1827-?), Rochester, New York, 1855-1857, Elmira, New York, 1859, St. Louis, Missouri, 1869d-1870d, San Francisco, California, 1874-1877, Red Bluff, California, 1877-1885. Percussion guns, primarily multi-barrel. (Shelton, Eich)

KERSHAW, J.H. Abilene, Texas, 1896d.

KERSTEINS, HENRY (1816-?), St. Louis, Missouri, 1850c-1854d. (Lewis)

KESLING, GEORGE Lebanon, Ohio, Patent #15,041 June 3, 1856, firearms. Roman candle gun.

KESSLER A. Trenton, New Jersey, 1878d.

KESSLER, ISRAEL Martindale, Pennsylvania, 1882d.

KESSLER, JOHN Weston, Missouri, 1848-1858.

KESSLER, P.O. Darien, Georgia, 1883d-1884d, Savannah, Georgia, 1885d.

KESSLER, PETER unlocated. Flintlock Kentucky rifle.

KESTER C. Weston, West Virginia, 1884d-1885d.

KESTER, COONRAD (1803-?), Lewis Co., West Virginia, 1847-1880c.

KESTER, JEREMIAH B. (1835-?), Coal, West Virginia, 1880c, Clarksburg, West Virginia, 1885d.

KESTER, JEROME B. (1831-1920), Lewis Co., West Virginia, 1850c, Clarksburg, West Virginia, 1882d. Son of Coonrad Kester.

KESTER, JOHN Weston (Kansas City), Missouri, 1860d-1879d.

KESTY & ROSENSTOCK Bloomsburg, Pennsylvania, 1890d.

KETCHIR, L. Tatumville, Arkansas, 1892d.

KETLAND, JOHN & THOMAS Birmingham, England, 1767-1789, Philadelphia, Pennsylvania, 1789-1800. Flintlock locks and muskets. From 1767 to 1789 Thomas Ketland operated this business as successor to his father, William Ketland. When Thomas moved to Philadelphia, the business continued to operate in both locations, and locks were made in England for export to America.

KETTERING, GEORGE (1802-1866), Hempfield, Pennsylvania, 1824-1844 and 1860-1866, Algerine Camp, California, 1849-1852. Flintlock Kentucky.

KETTLE, S. Grenada, Mississippi, 1885d.

KETTLER, EDWARD Cincinnati, Ohio, 1862d-1879d.

KETTNER, FRANCIS G. Baltimore, Maryland, 1840c. (Hartzler)

KEY, MINTER P. Memphis, Tennessee. Patent #241,671 May 17, 1881, machine gun.

KEY, R. unlocated. Percussion fullstock.

KEYES, E.L. Fostoria, Ohio, 1881d. (Hutslar)

KEYS, JESSE D. Fentonville, Michigan, 1860d-1865d.

KEYSER, C.B. Mount Gilead, Ohio. Percussion 1/2 stock.

KEYSER, WILLIAM W. Philadelphia, Pennsylvania, 1841d-1867d.

KEYSTONE FIREARMS CO. trade name, with Philadelphia, Pennsylvania address, of Edward K. Tryon (or of his various other companies) on single barrel shotguns made by Davenport.

KIBBEY, ERSKINE St. Louis, Michigan, 1863d-1867d.

KIBBLE Bluffton, Ohio, 1850. See Klay & Kibble.

KIBLER, JACOB (1807-?), Iredale Co., North Carolina. Apprenticed 1814. (Bivins)

KIDDER, WILLIAM New York, New York, 1854-1860. Pistol cases under patent of Ari Davis, Washington, D.C., #10,788, April 18, 1854.

KIEFFNER, ALBERT Haysville, Indiana, 1865-1890. (Lindert)

KIESSIG, CHARLES Central City, Colorado, 1860c-1871d, Denver, Colorado, 1876d-1880d, Leadville, Colorado, 1880d-1886d, San Diego, California, 1893d. (Sellers-3)

KIHM, WINAND Findlay, Ohio, 1875d. (Hutslar)

KILBOURN, HIRAM Waterloo, Iowa, 1865d.

KILBY, ROBERT (1824-?), California, 1852c. (Shelton)

KILE, NATHAN (1797-?), Jackson Co., Ohio, 1817-1837, Taylor, Indiana, 1840c-1850c. Flintlock and percussion rifles. (Hutslar-Lindert)

KILEY, F.J. Huntsville, Missouri, 1860d.

KILIAN, JOHN New York, New York. Percussion schuetzen rifle.

KILL BUCK trade name of Enterprise Gun Works on rifles.

KILLDEER trade name of Western Arms Co. on .22 cal. rifle.

KILLETS, CHARLES Lancaster Co., Pennsylvania, 1849-1850. Stockmaker. (Dyke)

KILLIAN, A. Pinckney, Illinois, 1867d-1868d.

KILLIAN, ELIGAH (1824-?), Catawba Co., North Carolina, 1850c. (Bivins)

KILLIAN, GEORGE Lancaster, Pennsylvania, 1857d.

KILLINGER, HENRY Wilna, New York, 1890d.

KILLINGSWORTH Crystal Springs, Arkansas. (Elias)

KILLINGSWORTH, HENRY Lewisburg, Tennessee, 1860d.

KILLMAN, T. unlocated. Percussion 1/2 stock.

KILLMON, T.H. Glenwood, Iowa, 1882d-1897d.

KILPATRICK, DANIEL Philadelphia, Pennsylvania, 1857d. Percussion 1/2 stock.

KIMBALL & BURLEIGH Fitchburg, Massachusetts, 1860d-1862d. Dealers.

KIMBALL, CHARLES N. Denver, Colorado, 1896d-1901d. (Sellers-3)

KIMBALL, CHARLES Milford, Nebraska, 1884d, Leslie, Colorado, 1890d. (Sellers-3)

KIMBALL, NARES O. Denver, Colorado, 1902d. Son of Charles N. Kimball. (Sellers-3)

KIMBALL, W.H. Burlington, New Jersey, 1878d-1881. Patent #243,894 July 5, 1881, lock with C.B. Hewitt.

KIMBALL, WILLIAM W. Washington, D.C. Patent #554,068 February 4, 1896, automatic rifle.

KIMBLE, DAVID (1828-?), Montepelier, Ohio, 1850c-1853d. (Hutslar)

KIMBLE, GEORGE (1860-?), Milroy, West Virginia, 1880c.

KIMBLE, J. Sumterville, Florida, 1886d.

KIMES, GEORGE W. (1821-?), Jackson Co., West Virginia, 1840c-1850c, Wood Co., West Virginia, 1860c. (Whisker IV)

KIMES, JOHN C. (1843-?), Tyner, West Virginia, 1865.

KIMMEL, ADAM Canton, Ohio, 1816-1820, Huron Co., Ohio, 1820c. (Hutslar)

KIMMEL, D.B. Sacramento, California, 1854d-1856d. (Shelton)

KIMMEL, D.B. West Unity, Ohio, 1861. (Hutslar)

KIMMELL, GEORGE Richland Center, Wisconsin, 1857d.

KINCAID, JOHN A. (1822-?), Trumbull Co., Ohio, 1850c. (Hutslar)

KINCAID, JOHN (1796-?), Girard, Ohio, 1829, Boone Co., Indiana, 1850-60. Percussion fullstock. (Lindert-Hutslar)

KINCHLER, EZEKIAL St. Francois Co., Missouri, 1850c. (MB 11-66)

KIND, H. Lansing, Iowa, 1880d.

KIND, HENRY Chippewa Falls, Wisconsin, 1888d-1895d. Same as H. Kind, Lansing, Iowa?

KIND, R. Dubuque, Iowa, 1883d.

KINDER, HENRY Racine, Wisconsin, 1857d.

KINDER, SAMUEL Philadelphia, Pennsylvania, 1775-1777. Committee of Safety locks. (Hobbies 4-38)

KINDLER, VINCENT Monroe, Michigan, 1868-1877d, East Saginaw, Michigan, 1879d-1899d. Breechloading double shotgun. As Mosser & Kindler 1868-1871.

KING & HISS Baltimore, Maryland, 1847-1855d. Henry S. King and George Hiss. (Hartzler)

KING & HUPMAN Baltimore, Maryland, 1860-1871. Successors to King & Hiss. (Hartzler)

KING & SMITH Celina, Ohio. Philip P. King and Louis Smith. (Hutslar)

KING & SMITH Middletown, Connecticut, 1862d-1865d. Revolver parts for S&W. (AG 11-79)

KING NITRO trade name of Davenport Fire Arms Co. on shotguns made for Shapleigh Hardware Co. (AG-75)

KING PIN .22 cal. derringer.

KING PIN suicide special. (Webster)

KING suicide special.

KING, A.S. Commerce, Michigan. Patent #34,303 March 4, 1862, cartridge.

KING, ALBERT (?-1931), Celina, Ohio, 1857-1890. Son of Philip P. King. (Hutslar)

KING, ANDREW L. Baltimore, Maryland, 1847d. (Hartzler)

KING, BENEDICT Providence, Rhode Island. Patent #34,579 March 4, 1862, breechloading firearm.

KING, C.H. & J.B. Hawkinsville, Georgia, 1881d. Charles H. and Joseph B. King.

KING, CHAMBERS (1840-1920), Dayton, Pennsylvania, 1863-1872. Percussion fullstock rifles. Father of Elmer King. (MB 1-67)

KING, CHARLES ALONZO (1837-1914), Middlefield (Rock Falls), Connecticut, 1862-1867, Springfield, Massachusetts, 1867-1874, Meriden, Connecticut, 1874-1914. Patents #94,003 August 24, 1869, revolver, #128,991 July 16, 1872, revolver with D.B. Wesson, #160,915 March 16, 1875, breechloading firearm, #175,862 April 11, 1876, gun barrels, #184,716 November 28, 1876, breechloading firearm, #201,618 March 26, 1878, attaching stocks, #213,760 April 1, 1879, breechloading firearm, #287,548 October 30, 1883, turning barrels. #356,321 January 18, 1887, breechloading firearm, #368,401 August 16, 1887, breechloading firearm, #402,675 May 7, 1889, breechloading firearm, #412,340 October 8, 1889, breechloading firearm, #470,157 March 1, 1892, ejector, #545,898 September 10, 1895, stock, #673,641 May 7, 1901, ejector with J.P. Hayes, and #797,123 August 15, 1905, breechloading firearm. As King & Smith, 1862-1865. Superintendent of Smith & Wesson, 1867-1874, and Parker Bros., 1874-1914. (AG 11-79).

KING, CHARLES H. Hawkinsville, Georgia, 1879d-1885d. With Joseph B. King as C.H. & J.B. King, 1881d.

KING, CHARLES M. Ann Arbor, Michigan, 1875d-1887d.

KING, CHARLES New London, Ohio, 1859-1888. Percussion guns. (Hutslar)

KING, CONRAD A. (1815-?), Circleville, Ohio, 1850c-1847d. Percussion 1/2 stock. (Hutslar)

KING, DAVID Otterville, Wisconsin, 1857d.

KING, ELMER (1881-1959), Dayton, Pennsylvania. Son of Chambers King. (MB 1-67)

KING, FREDERICK Lancaster, Pennsylvania, 1857d. Stockmaker.

KING, GEORGE (1809-1850), Armstrong Co., Pennsylvania, 1850. (Kauffman, Whisker III)

KING, HECTOR Petersburg, Indiana, 1880-1890. Percussion 1/2 stock. (Lindert)

KING, HENRY, & SON Baltimore, Maryland, 1873-1886d. Successor to King & Hupman. (Hartzler)

KING, ISAAC Somerset, Pennsylvania, 1818. (Kauffman)

KING, J.W. Manhattan, Kansas, 1878d.

KING, JAMES (1835-?), Melrose, Illinois, 1860c. (Johnson)

KING, JOHN N. (1819-?), Rollersville, Ohio, 1852-1854.

KING, JOHN Providence, Rhode Island, 1775. (Achtermier)

KING, JOHN Talbot Co., Maryland, 1755. Flintlock muskets. (Hartzler)

KING, JOSEPH B. Hawkinsville, Georgia, 1881d. With Charles H. King as C.H. & J.B. King.

KING, NELSON New Haven and Bridgeport, Connecticut. Patents #55,012 May 22, 1866, magazine gun, #57,636 August 28, 1866, magazine gun, and #177,852 May 23, 1876, breechloading firearm. Superintendent for both Winchester and Sharps. (Sellers-4, Williamson)

KING, NICHOLAS (1781-?), Baltimore, Maryland, 1835d. Apprenticed to Nicholas White, 1797. (Hartzler)

KING, NORMAN (1809-?), Defiance, Ohio, 1850c-1853d, Hampden, Ohio, 1859d. (Hutslar)

KING, P. Kenton, Ohio. Percussion 1/2 stock. (Hutslar)

KING, P.H. Thornville, Ohio, 1875. Percussion 1/2 stock. (Hutslar)

KING, PETER (1815-?), Farmington, Illinois, 1860c. (Johnson)

KING, PETER New Salem, Ohio, 1859d. Percussion fullstock. (Hutslar)

KING, PHILIP P. Celina, Ohio, 1845-1884, Shanes Crossing, Ohio, 1855-1886. Percussion 1/2 stock. With Louis Smith as King & Smith. (Hutslar)

KING, PHILIP (1827-?), Canal Winchester, Ohio, 1850c. (Hutslar)

KING, R.C. Ft. Dodge, Iowa, 1897d.

KING, SYLVESTUS, & CO. Bartless, Ohio, 1853d. (Hutslar)

KING, T. unlocated. Percussion 1/2 stock dated December 13, 1840. (MB 8-49a)

KING, THOMAS (1833-?), Madison, Ohio, 1857-1871. (Hutslar)

KING, WILLIAM D. Hawkinsville, Georgia, 1881d. Also a jeweler.

KING, WILLIAM E. Chase, Michigan. Patent #604,764 May 31, 1898, magazine gun.

KING, WILLIAM (1821-?), Rockingham Co., North Carolina, 1850c. (Bivins)

KING, WILLIAM Armstrong Co., Pennsylvania, 1867-1872. (Kauffman)

KING, WILLIAM Rush, Kentucky, 1800c. (MB 12-51)

KING, WILLIS L. Apponaug, Rhode Island. Patent #515,526 February 27, 1894, automatic firearm.

KINGMAN, LEVI C. Northampton, Massachusetts, 1887d.

KINGMAN, S.G. Bridgeport, Connecticut. Tools and barrels.

KINGSLAND 10 STAR trade name of Geller, Ward & Hasner on shotguns by Crescent. See also Kingsland and Kingsland Special.

KINGSLAND SPECIAL trade name of Geller, Ward & Hasner on shotguns by Crescent. See also Kingsland and Kingsland 10 Star.

KINGSLAND trade name of Geller, Ward & Hasner on shotguns by Crescent. See also Kingsland 10 Star and Kingsland Special. (Hinman)

KINGSLAND, J.H. Wellington, Kansas, 1894d.

KINGSLAND, R., & CO. unlocated. Lockmaker, flintlocks.

KINGSLEY, GEORGE LUMAN (1827-1890), St. Lawrence Co., New York, 1849-1855, Red Bluff, California, 1867-1886. Percussion 1/2 stock, percussion over/under rifle. (Shelton-Eich)

KINGSLEY, HENRY B. Hartford, Connecticut, 1865. Breechloading pistols.

KINKINGER, DAVID Allentown, Pennsylvania, 1797-1798t. (Dyke)

KINNARD, ASHER M., & BRO. West Chester, Pennsylvania, 1880d-1882d.

KINNEAR, G.W. Kane, Pennsylvania, 1887d.

KINNEY, GEORGE School, Illinois, 1882d-1886d.

KINSER, G.W. Plattsmouth, Nebraska, 1872d-1886d.

KINSEY, GIDEON (1829-?), Morrow, Co., Ohio, 1850c, Allen Co., Indiana, 1860c, Churubusco, Indiana, 1881-1885. Percussion 1/2 stock. (Lindert-Hutslar 2)

KINSEY, MOSES Newark, New Jersey, 1857-1899d. Percussion revolvers and rifles, .22 single shot pistol. Patent #20,496 June 8, 1858, revolver. (Sellers-1)

KINSEY, SAMUEL Galion, Ohio, 1859d. (Hutslar)

KINSEY, STEPHEN Gilmore, Ohio, 1890d. (Hutslar)

KINSLEY, ADAM Bridgewater, Massachusetts, 1799-1814. Model 1798 contract muskets with James Perkins and Model 1808 contract muskets with French, Blake, and Kinsley. With Jonathan Leonard as Leonard & Kinsley, Canton, Massachusetts, 1789-1800. (Gluckman)

KINSMAN, FRANK E. Plainfield, New Jersey. Patent #317,545 May 12, 1885, electric firearm.

KINSOR, JOHN Springville, Virginia, 1871d.

KINTER, JOHN SIMON (1800-?), Harrison Co., Indiana, 1833-1851.

KINTZY, L. unlocated. Percussion fullstock.

KINZY, CHRISTIAN Higginsville, Missouri, 1889d.

KIRBY, JOHN B. (1805-?), Galena, Illinois, 1850c. (Johnson)

KIRBY, JOHN B. Woodburn, Kentucky, 1883d.

KIRBY, WILLIAM Terrell, Texas, 1890d-1892d.

KIRCHBAUM, DAVID Canton, Ohio, 1850-1866. Percussion fullstock. (Hutslar)

KIRCHBAUM, E. Danville, Pennsylvania, 1830.

KIRCHBERG, WILLIAM Philadelphia, Pennsylvania, 1845d. Needlefire double-barrel shotgun. (Sotheby 4-82)

KIRK GUN CO. trade name of Farwell, Ozmun & Kirk on shotguns. (Hinman)

KIRK, E. CLARENCE Baltimore, Maryland, 1863-1867. Patents #53,306 March 20, 1866, lock, and #66,596 July 9, 1867, magazine gun, with C.E. Sneider.

KIRK, GRANVILLE (1833-?), Omaha, Nebraska, 1860c.

KIRK, JOHN L. Matoon, Illinois. Patent #116,066 June 20, 1871, magazine gun.

KIRKMAN & ELLIS Nashville, Tennessee, 1820-1854d. Derringers and locks.

KIRKMAN BROS. Nashville, Tennessee, 1835-1857.

KIRKMAN, H. & J. Nashville, Tennessee. Locks.

KIRKMAN, JOHN Nashville, Tennessee. Flintlock and percussion locks.

KIRKMAN, MAXFIELD & CO. New Orleans, Louisiana, 1842d. Flintlock duelling pistol. Importers & dealers.

KIRKSEY, J.E. Brownwood, Texas, 1892d.

KIRKWOOD BROS. Boston, Masschusetts, 1888-1924. Sons of and successors to David Kirkwood. (Kelver)

KIRKWOOD, AL unlocated. Flintlock Kentucky dated 1826.

KIRKWOOD, DAVID (1840-1897), Boston, Massachusetts, 1874-1897. Cartridge rifles and shotguns. Patents #169,710 November 9, 1875, lock with Henry Mortimer, #191,862 June 12, 1877, breechloading firearm, #233,256 October 12, 1880, breechloading firearm, #233,773 October 26, 1880, breechloading firearm, #240,147 April 12, 1881, breechloading firearm, #289,273 November 27, 1883, breechloading firearm, and #318,001 May 19, 1885, breechloading firearm. As Mortimer & Kirkwood, 1875-1879, and succeeded by his sons as Kirkwood Bros., 1888. (Kelver)

KIRLIN see Kerlin also.

KIRLIN, JOHN Berks Co., Pennsylvania, 1776-1785. Committee of Safety muskets. (Kauffman 2)

KIRLIN, JOHN New Lexington, Ohio, 1846-1853. Percussion fullstock rifle. (Hutslar)

KIRLIN, SAMUEL Philadelphia, Pennsylvania, 1801. (Kauffman 2)

KIRLIN, THOMAS (1805-?), St. Louis, Missouri, 1850c. (Lewis)

KIRLIN, THOMAS Northumberland Co., Pennsylvania, 1786t-1805t.

KIRNER, M. Cleveland, Ohio, 1856-1806d. (Hutslar)

KIRSCHMAN, E. Danville, Pennsylvania, 1830-1835. Also listed as Kirschbaum. (Gluckman & Satterlee)

KISER, A. unlocated. Flintlock and percussion rifles.

KISER, PETER Jefferson Furnace, Pennsylvania, 1850c. For John Shery.

KISH, M. Linden, Missouri, 1860d.

KISSLING, FREDERICK Salina, Kansas, 1894d.

KISTLER, GEORGE Berks Co., Pennsylvania, 1799-1800t. (Kauffman)

KITCHEN, J.B. (?-1890), Lawrenceburg, Tennessee, 1860d.

KITCHEN, WHEELER Broadway, Pennsylvania. Flintlock rifles. (Dillin)

KITTEMAUG suicide special.

KITTINGER, J. Charleston, Virginia, 1855. Percussion fullstock.

KITTINGER, LEVI (1820-?), East Greenville, Ohio, 1850c-1860c. Percussion 1/2 stock. (Hutslar)

KITTREDGE & FOLSOM New Orleans, Louisiana, 1860d-1861d.

KITTREDGE, BENJAMIN Cincinnati, Ohio, 1845-1891. Patent #41,848 March 8, 1864, revolver. Retail and wholesale dealer. As Eaton & Kittredge, 1850-1852, and various others after 1852. (Hutslar)

KITTREDGE, CHARLES St. Louis, Missouri, 1859d-1860d. Agent for Tranter Revolver.

KITTREDGE, JOHN H. (1851-1928), Augusta, Maine, 1871-1901. (Demeritt)

KLAMBERG, FREDRICH Indianola, Texas. Percussion shotgun.

KLASE, ABNER Ringtown, Pennsylvania, 1840. Flintlock Kentucky. (Dillin)

KLATTENHOFF, JOHN Colorado Springs, Colorado, 1878d-1881d. (Sellers-3)

KLAY & KIBBLE Bluffton, Ohio. Percussion 1/2 stock. Gideon Klay.

KLAY, ANDREW Allen Co., Ohio, 1893. Brother of Gideon Klay. (Hutslar)

KLAY, GIDEON Allen Co., Ohio, 1893. Locks. As Klay & Kibble. Brother of Andrew Klay. (Hutslar)

KLEABER, ALONZO B. Wayne, Michigan. Patent #440,638 November 18, 1890, spring air gun.

KLEIBACKER, CHRISTIAN B. Baltimore, Maryland, 1877-1880. With David B. Trimble as Trimble & Kleibacker. (Hartzler)

KLEIMEKEN, H. Trinidad, Colorado, 1870-1877d, Silver Cliff, Colorado, 1882-1885d. Not Kleineken. (Sellers-3)

KLEIN & CARR San Francisco, California, 1885-1887d. Possibly Howard W. Carr?

KLEIN, CHARLES Lancaster, Pennsylvania, Harrisburg, Pennsylvania. (Dean)

KLEIN, CHRISTIAN Lancaster, Pennsylvania, 1792t-1793t. See Christian Kline. (Dyke)

KLEIN, FERDINAND Newark, New Jersey. Patent #12,681 April 10, 1885, breechloading firearm. All metal needle fire pistols.

KLEIN, GEORGE New York, New York, 1800. Flintlock Kentucky rifle.

KLEIN, JOHN B. New York, New York. 1852d. Rifles and pistols using Charles Hartung's patent (#6,871 November 13, 1849), manufactured by George Pratt Foster, but marked "KLEIN'S PATENT".

KLEIN, JOHN EDWARD (1852-?), San Francisco, California, 1881-1902. (Shelton)

KLEIN, MAXWELL Lansing, Michigan, 1891d-1985d, Mt. Pleasant, Michigan, 1895d. Double-barrel shotgun.

KLEIN, PHILIP H. New York, New York, 1862-1824d. Percussion 1/2 stock.

KLEINFELTER, GEORGE Bushkill, Pennsylvania, 1820t. (KRA II-3)

KLEINHENN, AUGUST Washington, D.C., 1866-1872d. As Kleinhenn & Dudley, 1866. (Hartzler)

KLEINHENN, EMANUEL (1806-?), St. Louis, Missouri, 1845-1870d, East St. Louis, Illinois, 1874d-1884d.

KLEIST, DANIEL (1716-1792), Bethlehem, Pennsylvania, circa 1750, Easton, Pennsylvania, 1780t-1786, Bethlehem, Pennsylvania, 1788-1792. Flintlock rifles.

KLEPZIG, JOHN CHRISTIAN EBERHART (1817-1878), San Francisco, California, 1852-1878. Percussion 1/2 stock, derringer. (Shelton)

KLETTE, F. Stevensburg, Virginia, circa 1760. Flintlock Kentucky rifle.

KLINE, A. Dover, Pennsylvania, 1817-1818. Flintlock Kentucky. (Kauffman)

KLINE, CHARLES unlocated. Percussion fullstock.

KLINE, CHRISTIAN Lancaster, Pennsylvania, 1794, Harrisburg, Pennsylvania, 1811-1817. Flintlock pistols. See Christian Klein. (Kauffman)

KLINE, CONRAD York Co., Pennsylvania, 1818-1842.

KLINE, DANIEL (1830-?), Aledo, Illinois, 1860c, Henry, Illinois, 1865d. (Johnson)

KLINE, EDWARD (1821-?), Henry, Illinois, 1855-1880, Streator, Illinois, 1880d-1886d. Percussion 1/2 stock. (MB 2-50)

KLINE, EDWARD (1826-?), Harrodsburg, Kentucky, 1860c. For Benjamin Mills.

KLINE, HENRY (1802-?), Wilmington, Ohio, 1850c-1866d. Percussion 1/2 stock. (Hutslar)

KLINE, I.N. Winchester, Virginia, 1880d-1884d.

KLINE, JACOB (1792-?), Hampshire Co., Virginia, 1820c, Bloserville, Pennsylvania, 1828-1863. Flintlock Kentucky rifles. (Bowers)

KLINE, JACOB (1830-?), Crawford Co., Ohio, 1850c, McComb, Ohio, 1859d-1868d, Findlay, Ohio, 1870c. Son of Jacob Kline (1792-?). (Hutslar)

KLINE, P. St. Louis, Missouri. Percussion 1/2 stock.

KLINE, PHILIP Halifax, Pennsylvania, 1814-1861d. (Kauffman)

KLINEDINST, ANDREW York, Pennsylvania, 1825-1850. Kentucky rifle - stock type unknown.

KLING, MAGNUS Reading, Pennsylvania, 1854-1858. Patent #18,016 August 18, 1857, percussion powder. Percussion fullstock rifle. (Dillin)

KLINGE, WILLIAM Cincinnati, Ohio, 1888dc. (Hutslar)

KLINGELE, G. Burlington, Wisconsin, 1865d-1867d.

KLINGELHOFER, GEORGE Brooklyn, New York, 1858d-1896d. Percussion schuetzen rifle.

KLINGENSCHMIDT, ALEXANDER New York, New York, 1848-1851.

KLINGER, FRED Ft. Lee, New Jersey, 1878d.

KLINGER, H. Carthage, New York, 1870d-1882d. Percussion double rifle.

KLINGER, K. Carthage, New York. Percussion 1/2 stock.

KLINGLESMITH, JOHN F. St. Louis, Missouri. Patent #398,265 February 19, 1889, spring gun.

KLOCKER, JOHN Dyersville, Iowa, 1882d-1897d.

KLOCKER, JOHN St. Louis, Missouri, 1860d-1867d.

KLOER, HUGO A. (Prussia, 1853 -?), Denver, Colorado, 1880c-1883. As Kloer & Steuck, 1881-1882. (Sellers-3)

KLOKE, ANTON (1808-?), Baltimore, Maryland, 1837-1850c. (Hartzler)

KLUGE, FREDERICK (1813-?), Vandalia, Illinois, 1860c. (Johnson)

KNAPP unidentified, unlocated. Flintlock Kentucky.

KNAPP, A., & CO. Brighton, Ohio, 1860d-1864d. (Hutslar)

KNAPP, EDWARD Y. Blue Lake, California. Patent #403,432 May 14, 1889, spring gun.

KNAPP, JAMES Nashville, Tennessee, 1877d.

KNAPP, JOHN Morristown, Vermont, 1869-1874. (Horn)

KNAPP, LEE Denver, Colorado, 1886-1911. For J. P. Lower, 1886-1896, and for A.W. Peterson, 1890. (Sellers-3)

KNAPPENBERGER, HENRY Lehigh Co., Pennsylvania, 1818-1821t. (Kauffman)

KNAPPENBERGER, PHILIP Westmoreland Co., Pennsylvania, 1807-1816. (Whisker II)

KNAPPENBERGER, SOLOMON (1798-?), Cornersburg, Ohio, 1850c-1880d. (Hutslar)

KNAUF, HENRY Nippenose, Pennsylvania, 1861d-1879d.

KNAUS, J.H. Franklin, Missouri, 1879d.

KNAUS, WILLIAM Otterville, Missouri, 1850c-1889d.

KNAVE, JACOB Franklin Co., Pennsylvania, 1807. (Kauffman)

KNECHT, JOHN G. (1820-?), Tuscarawas Co., Ohio, 1878d. (Hutslar)

KNEL, PHILIP Baltimore, Maryland, 1847d. (Hartzler)

KNEPPER, JOSEPH Summerhill, Pennsylvania, 1834-1840. (Kauffman)

KNETZEL, ANTHONY Jerseyville, Illinois, 1880d-1888d.

KNETZEL, ANTOINE St. Louis, Missouri, 1859d. Same as Anthony Knetzel?

KNICKERBOCKER CLUB GUN trade name of Charles Godfrey on imported shortguns. (Hinman)

KNICKERBOCKER trade name of Crescent Fire Arms Co. on shotguns.

KNIGHT, ANDREW (1776-1856), Salem, Indiana, 1800-1856.

KNIGHT, C.J. unlocated. Percussion fullstock.

KNIGHT, D.K. Lane Depot, Illinois, 1860d.

KNIGHT, DANIEL (1809-?), Salem, Indiana, 1840-1855, Hazelton, Indiana, 1860d. Patent #11,483 August 8, 1854, salon rifle. Percussion fullstock, using his patent. (Lindert)

KNIGHT, J.W. Westminster, Maryland, 1878-1882d. (Hartzler)

KNIGHT, JAMES Cabot, Vermont, 1871-1879. (Horn)

KNIGHT, JOHN S. (1796-?), Olney, Illinois, 1860c-1864d.

KNIGHT, JOSEPH Wethersfield, New York, 1870d.

KNIGHT, R. EUGENE Worcester, Massachusetts, 1876d. Drop block single shot rifle.

KNIGHT, RICHARD Rochester, Indiana, 1881-1885. (Gardner)

KNIGHT, S. unlocated. Flintlock Kentucky.

KNIGHT, T.H., & CO. Bath, New York, 1859d.

KNIGHT, W.C. Onawa, Iowa, 1882d-1884d.

KNISS, JOSEPH Chicago, Illinois, 1850. (Johnson)

KNISTER, J. Charlotte, North Carolina, 1868-1876. (Bivins)

KNOBLAUCH, XAVIER Spring Bay, Illinois, 1864d.

KNOCK, EDWARD Adeline, Illinois, 1854d-1856d.

KNOCK, EDWARD Boston, Massachusetts, 1850c-1857d.

KNOCK, JOHN (1812-?), Ohio, 1843-1844, Charleston, Illinois, 1848-1850c. (Johnson)

KNOCK, MICHAEL (1836-?), Charleston, Illinois, 1860. Son of John Knock. (Johnson).

KNOCKABOUT trade name of Montgomery Ward & Co. on shotguns.

KNODDER, THEOPHILUS (1840-?), San Francisco, California, 1862-1864 and 1876-1894, Oroville, California, 1864-1866, Grass Valley, California, 1866-1869 and 1874-1876, Stockton, California, 1869-1874. (Shelton)

KNODER, JOHN Auburn, Indiana, 1877-1880. (Gardner)

KNOLLIN, T.H. Oswego, New York, 1857-1860. Percussion 1/2 stock. (Swinney)

KNOUS, FRANKLIN F. Hartford, Connecticut. Patents #313,001 February 24, 1885, safety, #316,899 April 28, 1885, magazine gun, #324,330 August 11, 1885, magazine gun, #332,203 December 8, 1885, magazine gun, #358,279 February 22, 1887, magazine gun, #372,153 October 25, 1887, magazine gun, and #933,254 September 7, 1908, automatic gun. All patents used by Colt.

KNOUSE, WILLIAM Philadelphia, Pennsylvania, 1847d-1855d.

KNOWLES, GRAVES Falmouth, Maine, 1722. (Demeritt)

KNOWLTON, W. Lee, Ohio, 1853d. Percussion 1/2 stock. (Hutslar)

KNOWLTON, W.D. Dodgeville, Wisconsin, 1884d-1886d.

KNOX ALL trade name of Crescent Fire Arms Co. and Iver Johnson Arms & Cycle Works on shotguns. (AR 2-69)

KNOX, ROBERT Chambersburg, Pennsylvania, 1800c. Flintlock Kentucky rifle. (Bowers)

KNOXVILLE ARMORY Knoxville, Tennessee, 1861-1863. Repairs only.

KNUDSON, ANDREW Ferrysburg, Michigan, 1879d.

KNUEKOLS, ROBERT (1812-?), Fayette Co., Ohio, 1850c. (Hutslar)

KNUPP, CHARLES MONROE (1863-1939), Bakersville, Pennsylvania. Percussion fullstock rifles. (Kauffman)

KNUTSON, IVER T. Audubon, Minnesota, 1875d.

KOBER, MARTIN Brownstown, Indiana, 1800-1902. (MB 4-55)

KOCH, A. Henrysville, Pennsylvania, 1861d. Flintlock Kentucky.

KOCH, BEN Rock Island Co., Illinois. (Johnson)

KOCH, CHARLES Mannheim, Pennsylvania, 1850. Barrelmaker. (Dyke)

KOCH, EDWARD Bowling Green, Ohio, 1853d. (Hutslar)

KOCH, GEORGE Tyrone, Pennsylvania, 1820. (Whisker III)

KOCH, HENRY (1780-?), Tyrone, Pennsylvania, 1820t. Flintlock Kentucky. Apprenticed to John Demuth, 1796. (Bowers)

KOCH, JOHN F. Cleveland, Ohio, 1878d. (Hutslar)

KOCH, JOHN N. (1829-1919), Rock Island, Illinois, 1850-1899. Percussion schuetzen. (Johnson)

KOCH, L. Henrysville, Pennsylvania, 1861d.

KOCH, RUDOLPH Temple, Texas, 1896d.

KOCKLER, PHILIP Lewisburg, Pennsylvania, 1868d-1882d. Percussion over/under rifle/shotgun.

KOEHLER & KIEFER Ottawa and Cairo, Illinois, 1860c-1865d. Percussion 1/2 stock. John Koehler.

KOEHLER, AUGUST (1858-?), Cincinnati, Ohio, 1875d-1881d, Newport, Kentucky, 1882d-1896d. Son of, and successor to, Hans Koehler. (Hutslar)

KOEHLER, GUSTAVE Syracuse, New York, 1860-1888. Percussion fullstock. For W. Malcolm, 1880-1888.

KOEHLER, HANS FREDERICK (1833-1880), Cincinnati, Ohio, 1860-?, Newport, Kentucky, ?-1880. For Kittredge & Bandle. (Hutslar)

KOEHLER, JOHN (1835-?), Ottawa, Illinois, 1860c, Cairo, Illinois, 1864d-1893d. Percussion fullstock. As Koehler & Kiefer, 1860-1865.

KOENIG & WERNER Lancaster, Pennsylvania, 1863. Frederick Koenig and John J. Werner.

KOENIG, FREDERICK W. Eau Clair, Wisconsin, 1879d-1896d.

KOENIG, FREDERICK Lancaster, Pennsylvania, 1857d-1888d. As Koenig & Werner, 1863.

KOENIGMACHER & CO. Philadelphia, Pennsylvania, 1807-1814. Lockmakers.

KOENIGSBERGER BROS. Deadwood, South Dakota, 1877-1886.

KOEPPENS, EDWARD St. Louis, Missouri, 1870d-1901d.

KOERSCHGEN, GOTFRIED K. Nauvoo, Illinois, 1884d-1886d.

KOFFLER, ADAM (?-1791), Washovia, North Carolina, 1762-1791. Mainly a weaver. (Bivins)

KOHL, CONRAD Reading, Pennsylvania, 1851-1862. Percussion pistols and rifles. (Hobbies 5-37)

KOHN, ISAAC Gilberts Mills, Ohio, 1883d. Percussion 1/2 stock. (Hutslar)

KOHN, J.T. Craigsville, Pennsylvania, 1887d-1890d.

KOHOUT, VEIT Ashland, Wisconsin, 1884d.

KOHR, WILLIAM Lancaster Co., Pennsylvania, 1837-1838. Barrelmaker. (KRA IV-4)

KOLB, HENRY M. Philadelphia, Pennsylvania, 1890-1911. Patents with Charles Foehl: #702,735 June 17, 1902, revolver, #818,177 April 17, 1906, revolver, #826,788 July 24, 1906, revolver, and #847,011 March 12, 1907 revolver. Patents #954,190 April 5, 1910, revolver, #954,191 April 5, 1910, revolver, #959,229 May 24, 1910, revolver, and #995,156 June 13, 1911. Percussion derringers and "Baby Hammerless" revolvers.

KOLL, PETER C. Walnut, Iowa. Patent #621,102 March 14, 1899, single trigger.

KOLLBERG & HARTMAN New York, New York, 1890d.

KOLLE, D. Ripon, Wisconsin, 1873d-1879d, Ellendale, North Dakota, 1888d.

KONCE, D. (1813-?), Venango Co., Pennsylvania, 1850c.

KONIG, FREDERICK Lancaster, Pennsylvania, 1857d. See Frederick Koenig, and Koenig & Werner.

KONIGMACHER, A. (?-1821), Philadelphia, Pennsylvania, 1807-1814, Chambersburg, Pennsylvania, 1814-1821. Lockmaker only. With Samuel Fahnestock in Chambersburg. Possibly Koenigmacher, and as Koenigmacher & Co.? (Bowers)

KONVALINKA, JOSEPH W. Mason City, Iowa, 1880d-1897d. As W.J. Konvalinka & Bro., 1880-1882.

KONVALINKA, W.J., & BRO. Mason City, Iowa, 1880d-1882d.

KOONS, F. Macungie, Pennsylvania, 1792t-1820t. (KRA II-3)

KOONS, FRANK A. Berks Co., Pennsylvania. Flintlock Kentucky rifles.

KOONS, GEORGE A. Marion, Ohio, 1840. Percussion fullstock. (Hutslar)

KOONS, HENRY Frederick Co., Maryland. Flintlock Kentucky. (Hartzler)

KOONS, ISAIAH Beaver Springs, Pennsylvania. Percussion fullstock rifle. (Gabel)

KOONTZ, A. unlocated. Flintlock Kentucky.

KOONTZ, J. unlocated. Flintlock Kentucky.

KOONTZ, JOHN Gallica Co., Ohio. (MB 11-44)

KOPP, ANDREW (1781-1875), York Co., Pennsylvania, 1809t-1811t, Franktown, Pennsylvania, 1823t-1850c. Flintlock Kentucky. (KRA VII-2)

KOPP, G. Burlington, Vermont. Flintlock and percussion rifles. (Horn)

KOPP, GEORGE (1810-1890), Frankstown, Pennsylvania, 1832t-1869. Flintlock and percussion rifles. Son of Andrew Kopp. (KRA 7-2)

KOPP, J. unlocated. Percussion fullstock.

KOPPIKUS, ADOLPH (1809-1882), Lexington, Kentucky, 1841, Sacramento, California, 1849-1874, San Francisco, California, 1874-1882. (Shelton)

KORNER, ALLBRIGHT (1802-?), Ohio Co., West Virginia, 1850c. (MB 10-63)

KORNMAN, A.D. unlocated. Percussion rifles.

KOSKI, MAXON M. (Poland, 1833-?), Omaha, Nebraska, 1860c.

KOSSE, LOUIS Houston, Texas, 1870d-1872d. Bookkeeper for E. Schmidt & Co., and after Ernst Schmidt's death, helped Schmidt's widow Christine operate as Schmidt & Kosse, 1870d-1872d.

KOTCH, H. unlocated. Percussion fullstock.

KOTLAND unlocated. Marking (Kotland?) on lock of flintlock Kentucky pistol.

KOUGHE, J.B. unlocated. Flintlock Kentucky rifles.

KRAFT, JACOB Lancaster, Pennsylvania, 1770-1782, Hagerstown, Maryland, 1786-1810c. (Hartzler)

KRAFT, JACOB York Co., Pennsylvania, 1807-1813.

KRAFT, JOHN H. (1821-?), Iowa, 1848, Eldorado Co., California, 1852c. (Shelton)

KRAFT, PETER W. Columbia, South Carolina, 1846-1886d. Percussion and cartridge guns. As P.W. Kraft & Sons, 1884-1886.

KRAFT, PHILIP Brooklyn, New York, 1890d-1896d.

KRAMMER unlocated. Percussion fullstock.

KRATSCH, A. Mankato, Minnesota, 1867d.

KRATTLI Hermann, Missouri, 1860d.

KRAUSGRIL, JACOB (1845-?), San Francisco, California, 1880c. (Shelton)

KRAUSKOPF, E. Fredericksburg, Texas, 1859-1865.

KRAUSPE, JULIUS A. Wilmington, Delaware, 1872d-1894d.

KRAUSPE, JULIUS Baltimore, Maryland, 1847-1860d. (Hartzler)

KRAUSSLICH, HENRY Chicago, Illinois, 1874d-1903d.

KREAMER, ANDREW (1825-?), Wooster, Ohio, 1850c. (Hutslar)

KREBS, RUBEN Windsor, Illinois, 1860d, Mattoon, Illinois, 1864d-1869.

KRECKER, J.P. Columbus, Mississippi, 1885d.

KRECKER, JOHN S. Columbus, Mississippi, 1854d.

KRELL, JOHN Clayton, Maryland, 1880-1882d. (Hartzler)

KREMER, J. Mishawaka, Indiana, 1874-1875d. (MB 4-54)

KRENKEL, AUGUST Memphis, Tennessee, 1873d.

KRENSER, ANDREW (1824-?), San Francisco, California, 1870c. (Shelton)

KREPPER BROS. Oakland, California, 1876-1884. Nicholas and Phillip H. Krepper. (Shelton)

KREPPER, NICHOLAS (1844-?), Oakland, California, 1876-1892. As Krepper Bros., 1876-1884. (Shelton)

KREPPER, PHILLIP H. (1843-?), Oakland, California, 1876-1886 and 1892-1898, Valejo, California, 1886-1892. As Krepper Bros., 1876-1884. (Shelton)

KREPS, GEORGE (?-1826), Hagerstown, Maryland, 1790c-1818, Winchester, Virginia, 1819-1826. Flintlock Kentucky rifles and pistols. (Bowers)

KREPS, GEORGE, JR. (1789-?), Hagerstown, Maryland, 1811-?. Rifles for Indiana department. (Hartzler)

KRESS unlocated. Percussion fullstock.

KRETZEL, A. Jerseyville, Illinois, 1857-1860. Percussion shotguns.

KREUGER, HENRY Spokane, Washington, 1889d.

KREULING, MATHIAS Northampton Co., Pennsylvania, 1805t. (KRA II-3)

KREUTNER, CHRISTIAN (?-1884), Montgomery, Alabama, 1863-1884. Model 1841 Mississippi rifles for the Confederacy. Percussion pistols and 1/2 stock rifles.

KRICHBAUM & SON Youngstown, Ohio, 1883-1891. J.G. Krichbaum.

KRICHBAUM, E. Danville, Pennsylvania, 1830. Percussion 1/2 stock.

KRICHBAUM, HENRY Dover, Delaware, 1882d.

KRICHBAUM, JOHN G. Youngstown, Ohio, 1877d-1890d. Percussion 1/2 stock. (Hutslar)

KRICK, ISAAC Wyomissing Creek, Pennsylvania. Barrelmaker. (MB 2-63)

KRIDER, JOHN H. (?-1889), Philadelphia, Pennsylvania, 1826d-1889d. Percussion guns. As Robinson & Krider, 1826-1834.

KRIDER, JOHN Philadelphia, Pennsylvania, 1769. (Gluckman & Satterlee)

KRIEGAR, GEORGE F. Springfield, Illinois, 1887, Chicago, Illinois, 1887d-1897d. Patent #368,924 August 23, 1887, breechloading firearm. As George F. Krueger in 1887d.

KRIEGBAUM, GEORGE Northumberland Co., Pennsylvania, 1832-1841. (Kauffman)

KRIGER, AUGUSTUS H. Rochester, New York, 1857. For Billinghurst. (Eich)

KRIM, D. Pennsylvania. Flintlock pistols.

KRINMAN, D. unlocated. Percussion swivel breech rifle.

KRITCH, JACOB Port Townsend, Washington, 1891d.

KRIZ, WILLIAM J. St. Louis, Missouri. Patents #273,288 March 6, 1883, magazine gun with Martin Kacer, #282,328 July 31, 1883, magazine gun with Martin Kacer, and #318,268 May 19, 1885, magazine gun.

KROGMANN, H.G. Saginaw, Michigan, 1899d.

KROHNE & RAQUET Ft. Wayne, Indiana, 1883-1885.

KROLL, CHARLES Garden City, Kansas, 1888d.

KRONENBERGER, ANDREW (1819-?), Bucyrus, Ohio, 1850c-1886d. (Hutslar)

KRONENBERGER, F. Bucyrus, Ohio, 1860d-1864d. Percussion 1/2 stock. (Hutslar)

KRONSHAGE, THEODORE Boscobel, Wisconsin, 1879d.

KROTZ, ZIEGMUND Duquesne, Pennsylvania, 1860-1861. See Sigmund Grotz, also listed as Edmond Krotz. (Kauffman)

KROUS, LAWRENCE (1805-?), Salisbury, Illinois, 1850c. (Johnson)

KROUSE, DAVID Ottawa, Illinois, 1867-1914. With Daniel S. Ebersol, 1875-1880, as Ebersol & Krouse.

KROUSE, WILLIAM Philadelphia, Pennsylvania, 1847d.

KROZIER, L.W. Knoxville, Iowa, 1880d.

KRUEGER, HENRY Aurora, Indiana, 1877-1880.

KRUEGER, HENRY Minneapolis, Minnesota, 1877-1886d.

KRUG, GOODLIP (Gotlieb), (1817-?), Cincinnati, Ohio, 1853-1857d, Mount Carmel, Illinois, 1860c-1925. (MB 8-44)

KRUG, J. HENRY Ilion, New York. Patent #304,008 August 26, 1884, magazine, used by Remington on Lee rifles.

KRUG, PHILIP Evansville, Indiana, 1873d.

KRUGER & CARLINE Hancock, Michigan, 1879d-1883d. William Carline.

KRUGER, A.O. Houghton, Michigan, 1887d.

KRUGIS, GEORGE F., & CO. Chicago, Illinois, 1895. (Johnson)

KRUMM Mt. Union, Pennsylvania. Flintlock Kentucky. (Dillin)

KRUSCHE, R.C. Duluth, Minnesota, 1883d-1890d.

KRUSCHKE, R.C. Appleton, Wisconsin, 1884d, Ashland, Wisconsin, 1884d-1888d.

KRUSE HARDWARE CO. Cincinnati, Ohio. Dealers only.

KRYDER, WILLIAM Wheeling, West Virginia, 1867d.

KRYNER, WILLIAM see William Greiner.

KRYTER, CHARLES A. Wheeling, West Virginia, 1873d-1876d. Possibly Kryder, and related to William Kryder, same location?

KUBICHEK, VACLAV Iowa City, Iowa, 1897d.

KUBLER, G.C. Hot Springs, Arkansas, 1876d.

KUBLER, JOHN Hot Springs, Arkansas, 1878d-1885d.

KUCK, WILLIAM New Knoxville, Ohio, 1885-1900. Percussion 1/2 stock. (Hutslar)

KUCKET, JOHN (1810-?), Highland, Illinois, 1850c-1860c. (Johnson)

KUEBLER, JOHN E. Belleville, Illinois, 1860d-1864d.

KUECK, MARTIN Fort Dodge, Iowa, 1876d-1897d.

KUEHLING, JOHN HENRY Washington, D.C., 1862-1872d.

KUENY, GEORGE Carmi, Illinois, 1888d.

KUERSTEN, J. FREDERICK Chicago, Illinois, 1894d-1898d.

KUESTER, CHARLES Raleigh, North Carolina, 1859-1870. As Kuester & Bro., 1866. (Bivins)

KUGLER, ADOLPHE Kingston, New York, 1862-1864. Air guns. (Wolff)

KUGLER, ALBERT Kingston, New York, 1857-1864d. Air guns and percussion 1/2 stock.

KUHN, C. Macon, Georgia, 1881d.

KUHN, F.P. Metamora, Illinois, 1884d-1886d.

KUHN, FRANCIS Philadelphia, Pennsylvania, 1866d-1899d. Percussion double shotgun.

KUHN, ULRICH (1821-1901), Nauvoo, Illinois, 1850-1901. (Johnson)

KUHN, WILLIAM Lancaster, Pennsylvania, 1869d-1884d, Mt. Joy, Pennsylvania, 1887d-1890d.

KUHRT, JOHN Highland, Illinois, 1854d-1860d.

KULL, JACOB Monroe, Michigan, 1860d-1892d.

KUMMER, VINCENT Columbus, Ohio, 1852d-1855d, Columbus, Nebraska, 1866d-1867d. Percussion 1/2 stock.

KUNKEL, JOHN H. Williamstown, Kentucky, 1879d-1885d.

KUNKLE Philadelphia, Pennsylvania, 1810-1814. Model 1808 contract muskets. (Gluckman)

KUNKLE, GEORGE Harrisburg, Pennsylvania, 1800-1830. (Dean)

KUNKLE, J.H. Warrensburgh, Missouri, 1889d-1898d. As Kunkle & Elk, 1898.

KUNKLE, LEONARD G. Harrisburg, Pennsylvania, 1831-1872. Son of George Kunkle. (Kauffman)

KUNKLE, WILLIAM Harwinton, Connecticut, 1877-1879.

KUNSTLER, CHARLES Luling, Texas, 1884d, San Antonio, Texas, 1887d.

KUNTZ & ROBINSON Philadelphia, Pennsylvania. Jacob Kuntz and William Robinson.

KUNTZ see Koons, and Koontz.

KUNTZ, CHRISTOPHER Lancaster, Pennsylvania, 1778. Furnished twelve gun locks to the Continental Armory. (Moller)

KUNTZ, DANIEL Philadelphia, Pennsylvania. Flintlock rifles. (Dillin)

KUNTZ, JACOB (1780-1876), Whitehall, Pennsylvania, 1807-1810, Philadelphia, Pennsylvania, 1811-1875. Air guns, flintlock and percussion guns. Brother of Peter Kuntz. (Dyke)

KUNTZ, MICHAEL Lancaster, Pennsylvania, 1802-1803. (Kauffman)

KUNTZ, P. Farmington, Illinois, 1860d-1864d.

KUNTZ, PETER (1791-1862), North Whitehall, Pennsylvania, 1817-1861d. Flintlock Kentucky. Brother of Jacob Kuntz. (Dyke)

KUNTZ, PETER Lehigh Valley, Pennsylvania, 1861d.

KUNTZMAN, JULES New Orleans, Louisiana, 1879d.

KUNZ, PETER see Peter Kuntz.

KUPFER, JOHN Corinne, Utah, 1869d-1871d, Dillon, Montana, 1876d-1896d.

KUPFERLE, W. Ft. White, Florida, 1886d.

KUPFERSCHMIDT, RICHARD Memphis, Tennessee, 1881d-1891d.

KURST, M.H. unlocated. Percussion 1/2 stock.

KURTH, WILLIAM Casselton, North Dakota. Patent #600,834 March 15, 1898, breechloading firearm.

KURTON, JULIUS Pottsville, Pennsylvania, 1871-1890d.

KURTZ, GEORGE Lancaster, Pennsylvania, 1759. Lockmaker. (Dyke)

KURTZ, SAMUEL Lancaster, Pennsylvania, 1837-1843. (Dyke)

KUSSMAUL, WILLIAM J. Baltimore, Maryland, 1847d-1867. Patent #66,919 October 15, 1867, lock. (Hartzler)

L SECTION

L & F see Loud & Farrington.

L. & M. see Morrison & Long.

L.A.B. unidentified. Flintlock Kentucky.

L.B. & CO. unidentified. Ashford, Connecticut. Model 1808 contract musket.

L.B. unidentified. Percussion fullstock.

L.C. & L. see Latimer, Colburn & Co.

L.C.E. unidentified. Percussion swivel breech dated 1850.

L.D. see L. Defibaugh.

L.F.M. unidentified. Percussion 1/2 stock.

L.G. & Y. see Lamson Goodnow & Yale.

L.G. unidentified. Percussion 1/2 stock.

L.G.B. unidentified. Percussion fullstock.

L.G.C. & L. see Latimer, Colburn & Co.

L.H.D. unidentified. Flintlock Kentucky rifle.

L.H.H. unidentified. Percussion fullstock double rifle.

L.J.W. & Co. see L.J. Webster & Co.

L.K. unidentified. Percussion fullstock.

L.N. see L. Nash.

L.N.D. see Lewis Donham.

L.P. unidentified. Percussion fullstock.

L.R.J. unidentified. Percussion fullstock.

L.S. see Leonard Snider.

L.S.M. marking of the Louisiana State Militia on Enfield and Winchester rifles.

L.T. unidentified. Percussion fullstock.

L.W.R. unidentified. Percussion fullstock.

L.Y. unidentified. Percussion fullstock.

L'HOMMEDIEU BROS. Mobile, Alabama, 1844d. Dealers and importers. (Neville)

LA BONE, WILLIAM LeClair, Iowa, 1867d.

LA MOTT, JOHN Cole Co., Missouri, 1850c. (MB 11-66)

LA RUE, DAVID E. (1828-?), Shelby Co., Ohio, 1850c. (Hutslar)

LA RUE, J.W. Globe Creek, Tennessee, 1860d.

LAAS, R.J. Benton Harbor, Michigan, 1895d.

LABADIE, JACOB Galveston, Texas, 1868d-1878d. Derringer. (AR 7-36?)

LABADIE, JOSEPH Galveston, Texas, 1878d-1884d. Son of, and successor to, Jacob Labadie.

LABAT, M. New Orleans, Louisiana, 1842d. Later worked for J.T. Latil.

LABO, GUSTAVUS Mapleton, Ohio, 1853d. (Hutslar)

LABORN, J.T. Good Hope, Alabama, 1881d.

LABOUNTY, EDWARD New Hampton, Iowa, 1897d.

LACAVE, CONSTANT Canton, Ohio, 1880-1883. (Dean)

LACAVE, J.B.C. Canton, Ohio, 1872d-1898. (Hutslar)

LACEY, GEORGE Bath, Illinois. (Johnson)

LACHER, LOUIS Harvard, Illinois, 1864d-1867d, Aurora, Illinois, 1882d-1886d.

LACHORSKY, A.A. Morrilton, Arkansas, 1888d-1898d.

LACKMAN, J.L. Cohoes, New York, 1891d.

LACKY unlocated. See Nolan & Lacky.

LACY, THOMAS Philadelphia, Pennsylvania, 1780-1785. Repaired U.S. arms. (Moller)

LADD & JOHNSON Westfield, Massachusetts, 1874d.

LADD & SMITH San Francisco, California, 1876-1879. Charles Douglas Ladd and Thomas L. Smith. (Shelton)

LADD, CHARLES DOUGLAS (1849-?), Stockton, California, 1871, San Francisco, California, 1872-1895. Patent #173,476 February 15, 1876, breechloading firearm. With Thomas L. Smith as Ladd & Smith, 1876-1879. Branch stores in Portland and Seattle. (Shelton)

LADD, GEORGE W. Sturgis, Dakota Territory, 1888d.

LADD, SAMUEL Waltham, Massachusetts. Patent # none October 14, 1835, tin plating.

LADD, WILSON Dorset, Vermont, 1846-1850. Percussion fullstock. (Horn).

LADE, G.C. Manitowoc, Wisconsin 1879d.

LADE, MAX G. Fort Wayne, Indiana, 1882-1885.

LADENSCHLAGER, J. Muncie, Indiana. (Lindert)

LADY, JOSEPH (1820-?), Troy, Indiana, 1850c. (Lindert)

LAFFERTY, SMITH (1824-?), Bellville, Ohio, 1850c-1853d, Bethany, Missouri, 1860c, Winterset, Iowa, 1882d-1892d.

LAFITTE, MARTILE Nachitoches, Louisiana. Derringer. (Eberhart)

LAFLIN, H.D. (1829-?), Chicago, Illinois, 1860c. (Johnson)

LAFLIN, MATTHEW Chicago, Illinois, 1839. (Johnson)

LAFLINS, SMITH & BOIES Chicago, Illinois, 1853-1854. (Johnson)

LAGOARGE, BERNARD (1824-?), San Francisco, California, 1854-1871. (Shelton)

LAGRAIN, WILLIAM South Fork, Missouri, 1889d-1891d.

LAIB, CHARLES Beaver Co., Pennsylvania, 1849-1851, Madison, Wisconsin, 1857d, Oshkosh, Wisconsin, 1865d-1867d. Also known as Charles Lamb.

LAIDLEY, JAMES G. Morgantown, West Virginia, 1811. Model (year?) contract rifles for the state of Virginia. (Cromwell)

LAIDLEY, THEODORE T.S. (1822-1886), U.S. Army. Patents #22,957 February 15, 1857, tape primer, #51,324 December 5, 1865, cartridge, #54,743 May 15, 1866, breechloading firearms with C.A. Emery, #55,676 June 19, 1866, cartridge, #77,988 May 19, 1868, tampion, and #240,319 April 19, 1881, heavy rifle(d?) guns. (GR 12-76)

LAING, CHARLES W. Anamosa, Iowa, 1865d.

LAIRD, D.C. Montgomery City, Missouri, 1891d-1893d.

LAIRD, J.P. Bowerstown, Ohio, 1896d. (Hutslar)

LAIRD, SAMUEL E. Covington, Kentucky, 1880d.

LAIRD, WILLIAM Montgomery City, Missouri, 1889d.

LAKE, EVERETT L. Syracuse, New York. Patents #284,213 September 4, 1883, breechloading firearm, #289,423 December 4, 1883, breechloading firearm, and #310,689 January 13, 1885, breechloading firearm.

LAKE, IRA Shamokin, Pennsylvania, 1832-1838. (Kauffman)

LAKE, JESSE Covalt, Pennsylvania, 1887d-1890d.

LAKE, LEWIS Forksville, Pennsylvania, 1860d.

LAKEMAN, JAMES (?-1825), Richmond, Virginia, 1802-1818, St. Louis, Missouri, 1818-1825. With Jacob Hawken as Lakeman & Hawken, 1818-1825. (Hanson 2)

LAKESIDE trade name of Crescent Fire Arms Co. on shotguns made for Montgomery Ward & Co. (AR 2-69)

LAKIN, HARTWELL Bennington, New Hampshire, 1876-1879.

LALLY, JOHN Fayette Co., Pennsylvania, 1811. (Kauffman)

LAMA, MICHAEL Milheim, Pennsylvania, 1861d. See Michael Lamey.

LAMARCHE, E. & H. New York, New York, 1851d-1858d. Importer and dealer.

LAMASTINE, J. (1816-?), Columbia, California, 1852-1860. (Shelton)

LAMB & ARMFIELD Jamestown, North Carolina, 1860. Percussion fullstock. (Bivins)

LAMB & SON Jamestown, North Carolina, 1790-1820.

LAMB & STEPHENS Guilford, North Carolina, 1840. Flintlock 1/2 stock.

LAMB & WRIGHT Jamestown, North Carolina, 1850c. William Lamb and Nathan Wright. (Bivins)

LAMB, A. & SON Jamestown, North Carolina, 1884d.

LAMB, A.B. & CO. unlocated. Percussion 1/2 stock.

LAMB, ALONZO R. Cassopolis, Michigan, 1863d-1867d.

LAMB, AMOS H. Royalton, Vermont, 1883d.

LAMB, ANDERSON (1815-?), Jameston, North Carolina, 1848-1875. (Bivins)

LAMB, C. Madison, Wisconsin. See Charles Laib.

LAMB, CLARKSON (1829-1912). Jamestown, North Carolina, 1850-1880. (Bivins)

LAMB, H.C., & CO. Jamestown, North Carolina. Mississippi rifles for Confederacy. Clarkson Lamb, son of William Lamb, operated this company. (Hill- Anthony)

LAMB, J.M. Covington, Georgia, 1861. Confederate gunsmith convention.

LAMB, JAY (?-1900), Deep River, North Carolina, 1860, Florence, North Carolina, and Lambsburg, North Carolina, 1870-1900. (Bivins)

LAMB, JEHU C. (1811-?), Jamestown, North Carolina, 1850c. (Bivins)

LAMB, JESSE (1831-?), Jamestown, North Carolina, 1850-1890. Son of William Lamb. (Bivins)

LAMB, JOAB Clay Co., Missouri. 1850c. (MB 11-66)

LAMB, LUTHER R. Waterville, Maine, 1846. Model 1808 contract muskets. (Demeritt)

LAMB, PHILETUS F. Climax Prairie, Michigan, 1863d-1867d.

LAMB, ROBERT (1792-?), Gallatin Co., Illinois, 1850. (Johnson)

LAMB, THOMAS B. Hamilton, Michigan. Patent #40,487 November 3, 1863, percussion cap holder.

LAMB, WILLIAM (1806-?), Jamestown, North Carolina, 1845-1870. Percussion rifles, flintlock 1/2 stock. (Bivins)

LAMB, WILLIAM, & SONS Jamestown, North Carolina, 1870. (Bivins)

LAMBERSON, C.M. Wamego, Kansas, 1894d.

LAMBERSON, D.H. Chicago, Illinois, 1874-1884d.

LAMBERSON, FURMAN & CO. New York, New York 1884d-1888d. Importers.

LAMBERT BROS. Kearney, Nebraska, 1886d-1893d.

LAMBERT, AARON North Carolina Committee of Safety gunsmith.

LAMBERT, GEORGE Philadelphia, Pennsylvania, 1829d-1831d.

LAMBERT, JOHN H. (1816-1896), Geneseo, Illinois, 1867d-1890d.

LAMBERT, JOHN (1829-?), San Diego, California, 1870c. (Shelton)

LAMBERT, JOHN Scott Co., Iowa, 1850c. (MB 8-64)

LAMBERT, PIERRE New Orleans, Louisiana, 1822d-1834d.

LAMBERT, ROGER N. Upton, Massachusetts. Patent #6,945x February 27, 1832, cane gun, made by E. Allen. (Mouilleseaux)

LAMBRECHT, J.V. Statesville, North Carolina 1885d.

LAMEY, MICHAEL Millheim, Pennsylvania, 1861d-1871d. Percussion fullstock and swivel breech. Also known as Michael Lama, and Michael Lamy. (GR2-61)

LAMOTE, ETIENNE New Orleans, Louisiana, 1822d.

LAMPHERE, X. Pittsfield, Massachusetts, 1885d.

LAMPORT, ALBERT G. Rochester, New York, 1870-1881, Syracuse, New York, 1882-1890. Patent #371,665 October 18, 1887, breechloading firearm with George Lewis. For Charles Green in Rochester. (Eich)

LAMSON, C.A. Hinsdale, New Hampshire, 1877d-1878d.

LAMSON, EBENEZER G. (?-1892), Windsor, Vermont, 1850-1869. Ball and Palmer carbines. As Lamson, Goodnow & Yale, 1858-1864, E.G. Lamson & Co., 1864-1865, and Windsor Mfg. Co., 1865-1869. (GR 8-66)

LAMSON, GOODNOW & YALE Windsor, Vermont, 1868-1864, Shelburn Falls, Massachusetts. Model 1861 contract muskets. Ebenezer G. Lamson. (GR 8-64)

LAMSON, J. Bennington, Vermont, 1814-1860. (Horn)

LAMSON, TRUMAN Bennington, Vermont, 1841-1865d. Percussion target rifle. (Horn)

LAMSON, WILLIAM Boston, Massachusetts, 1775. (Dean*)

LAMY, M. see Michael Lamey.

LANABIT, J. Idaho City, Idaho, 1866d.

LANCASTER ARMS CO. Lancaster, Pennsylvania, 1880d.

LANCASTER, AARON Princeton, Iowa, 1865d.

LANCASTER, H.S. Ellsworth, Maine, 1873-1900. (Demeritt)

LANCASTER, J.W. Ellsworth, Maine, 1876-1894. (Demeritt)

LANCASTER, PALMER (1824-?) Morrow Co., Ohio, 1850c, Burr Oak, Michigan. Patent #14,667 April 15, 1856, breechloading firearms. (Hutslar)

LANDER, C. unlocated. Flintlock lock makers.

LANDERS, JOHN S. Springfield, Massachusetts. Patent #323,873 August 4, 1885, revolver with D.B. Wesson.

LANDFEAR, WILLIAM R. Hartford, Connecticut. Patent #44,099 September 6, 1864, breechloading firearm.

LANDIS, BENJAMIN F. (1800-?), Cincinnati, Ohio, 1833d. (Hutslar)

LANDIS, DANIEL Mackinaw, Illinois, 1860d.

LANDON, J.W. Rockport, Indiana, 1850-1880. (Lindert)

LANDON, T.W. Fairmont, Maryland, 1884d.

LANDRUM, J.P. Taylor's Bayou, Texas, 1884d.

LANDRY, PIERRE New Orleans, Louisiana, 1822d-1823d.

LANE & READ Boston, Massachusetts, 1826-1849. Militia muskets, other firearms. William Read and (First Name?) Lane.

LANE, ABIJAH Mount Hope, New York, 1849-1859. (Gardner)

LANE, EDWARD Dunnville, Wisconsin, 1857d.

LANE, JOHN Paw Paw, Kentucky, 1879d-1880d.

LANE, MOSES Monroe Co., Kentucky, 1820c. (Gardner)

LANE, THOMAS W. Boston, Massachusetts. Patent #60,910 January 1, 1867, magazine gun.

LANE, THOMAS Monroe Co., Kentucky, 1820c.

LANE, WILLIAM Lancaster, Pennsylvania, 1776-1783. Flintlock muskets.

LANGDON, J.M. Rockport, Indiana, 1860d.

LANGDON, JACKSON Dayton, Ohio, 1843-1856d. Lockmaker. With brother Joseph, 1850-1856. (Hutslar)

LANGDON, JOSEPH Dayton, Ohio, 1850-1856. Lockmaker. Brother of Jackson Langdon. (Hutslar)

LANGDON, LEANDER W. Florence, Massachusetts. Patent #155,318 September 22, 1874, magazine gun.

LANGDON, W.G. Boston, Massachusetts, 1857-1864. Percussion target rifles. (Gluckman & Satterlee)

LANGE, FRITZ Hoboken, New Jersey, 1878d.

LANGE, L.G. Cannon Falls, Minnesota, 1884d.

LANGE, WILLIAM Warren Co., Missouri, 1850c. (MB 11-66)

LANGEAY, JOHN Philadelphia, Pennsylvania, 1775. (Kauffman)

LANGLEY, WILLIAM (1828-?), Aurora, Indiana, 1860. Percussion 1/2 stock. (Lindert)

LANGSDORF, OTTO Brooklyn, New York, 1883d-1896d. Percussion schuetzen rifle.

LANGTON, PATRICK Providence, Rhode Island, 1852-1858. For Charles Little. (Achtermier)

LANHAM, J.H. DeSoto, Georgia, 1881d-1883d.

LANHAM, J.W. Greensburgh, Indiana, 1881-1885.

LANNART, GEORGE Findlay, Ohio. Possibly G.W. Lannerd?

LANNART, HENRY (1812-?), Findlay, Ohio, 1850c-1853d. (Hutslar)

LANNERD, G.W. Findlay, Ohio, 1860d-1864. Possibly George Lannart. (Hutslar)

LANNING, E. unlocated. Flintlock Kentucky rifle.

LANNING, W.W. Flag Pond, Tennessee, 1891d.

LANTZ, FRANKLIN W. Washington, D.C., Patent #477,128 June 14, 1892, magazine gun.

LAONARD, WILLIAM (1825-?), New Orleans, Louisiana, 1850c. (MB 9-65)

LAPKEEHLER, HENRY Mifflinburg, Pennsylvania, 1850c. (Kauffman)

LAPOLD, P. unlocated. Percussion fullstock.

LAPPINGTON, WILLIAM Lawrenceville, Pennsylvania, 1839.

LAPTHORNE, S.J. St. Joseph, Missouri, 1898d.

LAPWORTH, HENRY Saginaw City, Michigan, 1875d.

LAQUEQUIST, CARL Macon, Georgia, 1861-1862. Confederate patent #58 January 21, 1862, breechloading firearm. Confederate Gunsmith convention.

LARAWAY, WILLIAM P. Hartford, Connecticut. Patent #597,096 March 16, 1897, ejector. For Lee Arms Co.

LARD, ALLAN E. St. Joseph, Missouri. Patent #630,06 1, August 1, 1899, single trigger, #636,050, October 31, 1899, single trigger, #668,526, February 19, 1901, single trigger, #674,508, May 21, 1901, single trigger and #747, 191, December 15, 1903, single trigger.

LARENAUDIE, ADRIEN L. San Antonio, Texas, 1889d. Son of Hippolite Larenaudie.

LARENAUDIE, HIPPOLITE San Antonio, Texas 1884d-1890d.

LARGE, JOSHUA New York, New York, 1850d-1851d.

LAROCHELLE, J. unlocated. Converted Kentucky rifle.

LAROSH, JESSE Lehigh Co., Pennsylvania, 1821t. (Kauffman)

LARRABEE & NORTH Chicago, Illinois, 1863d-1885d. Dealers. C.R. Larrabee and Robert L. North.

LARSEN, H.A. Faribault, Minnesota, 1875d.

LARSEN, IVERT Chicago, Illinois. Patent #458,704 September 1, 1891, breechloading firearm. Submitted magazine rifle to 1892 trials.

LARSON, W.H. Harrisburg, Pennsylvania, 1830. Flintlock Kentucky rifles.

LARTER, THOMAS Cleveland, Ohio, 1883-1888d. (Hutslar)

LASH, J.B. Marysville, Ohio, 1815-1882. Flintlock Kentucky.

LASH, JOHN H. (1840-?), Marysville, Ohio, 1854-1859d. Percussion 1/2 stock. Son of J.B. Lash. (Hutslar)

LASH, JOHN Ft. Scott, Kansas, 1866d-1876d, Girard, Kansas, 1884d-1888d.

LASKA, M.A., & SON New Orleans, Louisiana, 1889d-1899d. Mathias A. Laska.

LASKA, MATHIAS A. New Orleans, Louisiana, 1874d-1899d. As M.A. Laska & Son, 1889-1899.

LASKY, JOHN Iowa. Percussion fullstock.

LASSERRE, J.P. New Orleans, Louisiana, 1841d-1844d.

LASSETER, F.H. Fond du Lac, Wisconsin, 1870-1875.

LATHAM, GEORGE Gray, Maine, 1860c. (Demerritt)

LATHAM, JAMES DeWitt, Iowa, 1865d.

LATHAM, JAMES New York, New York, 1849d-1853d.

LATHAM, RICHARD Charleston, South Carolina, 1769-1776. Committee of Safety repairs. (Bivins)

LATHE, A. New York, New York, 1850d-1851d.

LATHROP, CURTIS G. Hollister, California, 1880-1881d. (Shelton)

LATHROP, EBENEZER Chicago, Illinois, 1876d. Dealer

LATHROP, GEORGE A. East Saginaw, Michigan. Patent #26,438 December 20, 1859, breechloading firearm.

LATHROP, NELSON Mineral Point, Wisconsin, 1857d. With Lyman Sprague as Sprague & Lathrop, Stevens Point, Wisconsin.

LATHROP, R.P. Albany, New York, 1858d-1867d. As Steele & Lathrop, 1862-1867.

LATIL & FRERE New Orleans, Louisiana, 1834d.

LATIL, ALEXANDRE New Orleans, Louisiana, 1842d. For Joseph Timecour Latil.

LATIL, HECTOR (1827-?), Baton Rouge, Louisiana, 1850c. Son of Louis Latil. (MB 9-65)

LATIL, JOSEPH TIMECOUR New Orleans, Louisiana, 1838d-1848d.

LATIL, LAZARE New Orleans, Louisiana, 1842d. For Joseph Timecour Latil.

LATIL, LOUIS A. (1798-?), Baton Rouge, Louisiana, 1838-1850c. Percussion revolvers for U.S. Government trials and other guns. (Sellers-1)

LATIL, T. New Orleans, Louisiana, 1841d.

LATIL, W.H. Beaumont, Texas, 1900. Son of Hector Latil. (Dean*)

LATIMER, COLBURN & CO. Cincinnati, Ohio, 1856-1861d. Hardware dealers, lockmakers. Locks marked "L.G.C. & L." or "L.C. & L." or "R.G.L. & Co.". (Hutslar)

LATIMER, HARRY High Bridge, New Jersey, 1885d.

LATIMER, P.E. Norwalk, Ohio, 1859-1865d. (Hutslar)

LATROBE, FERINAND C. Baltimore, Maryland, 1855-1859. As Merrill, Latrobe & Thomas. Son of John Latrobe. (Hartzler)

LATROBE, JOHN H.B. Baltimore, Maryland. Patent #14,319 February 26, 1856, priming hammer. (Hartzler)

LATTA, EMMET G. Friendship, New York. Patents #181,530 August 29, 1876, sight, and #507,278 October 24, 1893, sight.

LATTILE, A. Halletsville, Texas, 1878d.

LAU, J.H. New York, New York, 1873d-1900d. Importers and dealers, double-barrel shotguns. As Lau & Garlicks, 1873-1876. With Louis Struller as Struller, Lau, & Co., 1880-1884. As J.H. Lau & Co. 1885-1900.

LAUCK, JACOB (1794-1875), Winchester, Virginia. Son of Simon Lauck. (Bowers)

LAUCK, JOHN (1790-1826), Winchester, Virginia, 1811-1826. Flintlock Kentucky rifles. Son of Simon Lauck. (Bowers)

LAUCK, PETER (1753-1839), Winchester, Virginia, 1774-1839. Contract rifles for Virginia, with brother Simon. (Bowers)

LAUCK, SIMON (1760-1815), Lebanon, Pennsylvania, 1785t, Winchester, Virginia, 1794-1815. Flintlock Kentucky rifles, and contract rifles for Virginia (with and without his brother Peter).

LAUCK, SIMON, JR. (1784-1864), Winchester, Virginia, 1805-1815. Became minister and moved to West Virginia. (Bowers)

LAUCK, WILLIAM P. (1818-?), Winchester, Virginia, 1850c-1897d. (Bowers)

LAUCK, WILLIAM (1796-1826), Winchester, Virginia, 1815-1826. Son of Simon Lauck.

LAUDENSLAGER, HENRY (1839-1912), Fair Oaks, Pennsylvania, 1860-1912. (Kauffman)

LAUDENSLAGER, WILLIAM Snyder Co., Pennsylvania. Percussion fullstock rifle. (Gabel)

LAUDERMAN, WILLIAM H. Baltimore, Maryland, 1864-1867d. (Hartzler)

LAUDERVILLE, ANDREW St. Louis, Missouri, 1795. With Francois Migneron.

LAUFMAN, P.H. Pittsburgh, Pennsylvania, 1850d-1876d. Lockmakers only.

LAUGHLIN, G.O. Missouri City, Missouri, 1860d.

LAUMAN, P.S. Xenia, Ohio. Percussion 1/2 stock.

LAURAINE, E.G. Beeville, Texas, 1892d-1896d.

LAURENT, MICHAEL (1788-?), New Orleans, Louisiana, 1850c. (MB 9-65)

LAURWING, DERMENICO Washington, D.C., 1867d. (Hartzler)

LAUTER, JOHN (1823-?), Ripley Co., Indiana, 1860c. (Lindert)

LAUTZ, BECKET & MINET Boston, Massachusetts, 1857-1868d. Possibly Frank Minet, Boston, 1850?

LAUTZENHEISER, J. Louisville, Ohio. Flintlock Kentucky. (Lindsay 2)

LAVERY, D. Philadelphia, Pennsylvania, 1780-1785. Repaired U.S. arms. See David Lowery. (Moller)

LAVI, T.S. Portageville, Missouri, 1879d.

LAVIGNE, J.P. New Haven, Connecticut. Patent #386,995 July 31, 1888, breechloading gun. Signal guns made by R.H. Brown & Co.

LAVIZNE, J.J. (1819-?), New Orleans, Louisiana, 1850c. (MB 9-65)

LAW, JOHN Seward, Nebraska, 1872d-1886d.

LAW, WILLIAM (1816-?), Clarksville, Pennsylvania, 1838-1860c. (Whisker 2)

LAWARRE, BENJAMIN Cincinnati, Ohio, 1886-1900d. (Hutslar)

LAWDEN, THOMAS (1824-?), Morris, Illinois, 1850c. (Johnson)

LAWING, AMBROSE Winchester, Tennessee, 1858-1883d. Percussion Tennessee rifle.

LAWING, JOHN A. Winchester, Tennessee, 1881d-1891d. Son of Ambrose Lawing.

LAWLESS, JAMES Auburn, New York, 1856-1859. Percussion 1/2 stock.

LAWRENCE & BRO. Cincinnati, Ohio, 1863-1865. Dealers only. August and Charles Lawrence. (Hutslar)

LAWRENCE, A.S. Santa Anna, Illinois, 1860d.

LAWRENCE, ALBERT Denmark, New York, 1870d.

LAWRENCE, HENRY Little Cincinnati, Indiana, 1860-1895. Percussion 1/2 stock. (Lindert)

LAWRENCE, J.H. Yorkville, Tennessee, 1876d.

LAWRENCE, JOHN Antrim, Pennsylvania, 1786. (Kauffman)

LAWRENCE, JOHN Philadelphia, Pennsylvania, 1810d.

LAWRENCE, JOSEPH Franklinville, New York, 1858-1874d.

LAWRENCE, JOSEPH New Berlin, New York. Patent # none May 24, 1828, lock.

LAWRENCE, M. Cadiz, New York, 1880d.

LAWRENCE, PETER Ouray, Colorado. Patent #644,432 February 27, 1900, sight.

LAWRENCE, RICHARD S. (1817-1892), Windsor, Vermont, 1838-1856, Hartford, Connecticut, 1856-1872. Patents #8,637 January 6, 1852, breechloading firearm, #22,858 February 15, 1859, sight, #23,590 April 12, 1859, lock, #26,504 December 20, 1859, breechloading firearm, and #88,645 April 6, 1869, breechloading firearm. As Kendall & Lawrence, 1838-1844, Robbins, Kendall & Lawrence, 1844-1849, and Robbins & Lawrence, 1849-1856. Superintendent of Sharps Rifle Co., 1856-1872. (Sellers-4)

LAWRENCE, RICHARD Cumberland, Pennsylvania, 1783t-1794t. (Bowers)

LAWRENCE, S.B. Vacaville, California, 1878-1881. (Shelton)

LAWRENCE, SAMUEL B. Rochester, New York, 1851d. For Billinghurst. (Eich)

LAWRENCE, T.R. Seneca Falls, New York, 1880d.

LAWRENCE, THOMAS D. Lancaster, Pennsylvania, 1857d.

LAWRENCE, THOMAS Frederick, Maryland, 1778. For Jacob Reaser.

LAWRENCE, THOMAS Philadelphia, Pennsylvania, 1780-1830. Repaired U.S. arms. (Moller)

LAWRENCE, WALTER Williamsport, Pennsylvania, 1820c. (Gardner)

LAWRENCE, WILLIAM Clinton, Massachusetts. Percussion 1/2 stock.

LAWRENCE, WILLIAM Laconia, New Hampshire, 1862-1879, Farmington, Maine, 1858-1861. Tip up rifles and shotguns in Laconia. As Wheller & Lawrence, 1858-1861. (Demeritt)

LAWRENCE, WILLIAM Worcester, and Milford, Massachusetts, 1850d-1869d. Cased percussion pistol.

LAWS, A.D. unlocated. Underhammer pistol.

LAWSER, JOHN G. Harrisburg, Pennsylvania, 1871d-1889d. With his brother William H. Lawser.

LAWSER, WILLIAM H. Harrisburg, Pennsylvania, 1866-1889d. With his brother John G. Lawser, 1871-1889.

LAWSON, D.J. May Hill, Ohio, 1890d. (Hutslar)

LAWSON, JOHN Rushsylvania, Ohio, 1890d. (Hutslar)

LAWTON, ROBERT B. Newport, Rhode Island, 1833-1838. Patent #481 November 23, 1837, pepperbox sword. (Frost)

LAWTON, THOMAS Baltimore, Maryland, 1831-1835, Paterson, New Jersey, 1836-1837. Percussion double shotgun. Foreman at Colt's plant in Paterson, New Jersey.

LAYENDECKER, GEORGE Allentown, Pennsylvania, 1774-1783. State gun factory. See George Lydendecker.

LAYLAND, WILLIAM New York, New York, 1844-1846. (Kauffman 2)

LAYMAN, GODFREY (1831-?), Mt. Vernon, Ohio, 1850c. (Hutslar)

LAYPOLE, JOHN H. (1810-?), Weverton, Maryland, 1850c-1892. Percussion fullstock. (Hartzler)

LAZELL, J.M. Manchester, Michigan 1887d.

LE CONTE St. Louis, Missouri, 1804. (Hanson)

LE FAIRE, JOSEPH (1802-?), Muncie, Indiana, 1860c. (Lindert)

LE MAT, JEAN ALEXANDER FRANCOIS New Orleans, Louisiana. Patents #15,925 October 21, 1856, revolver, #16,124 November 25, 1856, revolver, #24,312 June 7, 1859, revolver, #24,313 June 7, 1859, cannon lock, and #97,780 December 14, 1869, revolver. Guns made in France. (AAC)

LE MONTE, L.E. Lancaster, Ohio, 1890d. (Hutslar)

LE VALLEY, SALEM G. Buffalo, New York, 1885d-1895d.

LEABO, ANDREW Philadelphia, Pennsylvania, 1807.

LEACH, CHARLES T., JR. Stockton, California, 1884-1888. (Shelton)

LEACH, J.B. Onarga, Illinois, 1875d.

LEACH, JAMES Fayette Co., Indiana, 1820c. (Lindert)

LEACH, JOHN New York, New York, 1849-1852.

LEACROFT, EDWIN S. Hartford, Connecticut. Patents #112,471 March 7, 1871, revolver, and #112,472 March 7, 1871, revolver. For National Arms Co.

LEADER GUN CO. trade name of Crescent Fire Arms Co. on shotguns for Charles Williams Stores. (AR 2-69)

LEADER suicide special by Harrington & Richardson.

LEADER trade name of Shattuck Arms Co. on shotguns. (AG 4-75)

LEADER, RICHARD Boston, Massachusetts, 1646. (Gluckman & Satterlee)

LEAMEY, MICHAEL unlocated. Percussion swivelbreech rifle.

LEAMING, F., & CO. Philadelphia, Pennsylvania, 1829d-1848d. Importer and dealer.

LEARNED, WALLACE Constable, New York, 1865-1867d.

LEAROCK, JOHN B. Boston, Massachusetts. Patents #37,512 January 27, 1863, sight, and #42,091 March 29, 1864, sight.

LEATHAM, W. New Philadelphia, Texas, 1890d.

LEATHER & CO. York, Pennsylvania, 1798. Model 1798 contract muskets for Pennsylvania. Jacob Leather and Conrad Welshantz. Also known as Lether & Co.

LEATHER, JACOB York, Pennsylvania, 1756-1807. Model 1798 contract muskets for Pennsylvania with Conrad Welshantz. As Leather & Co. with Conrad Welshantz. (Kindig)

LEATHERMAN, FREDERICK (1825-?), Dayton, Ohio, 1850c-1900d. Percussion fullstock. (Hutslar)

LEATHERMAN, T. Dayton, Ohio. Percussion fullstock.

LEAVITT, DANIEL Cabotville, Massachusetts. Patents #182 April 29, 1837, revolver, and #24,394 June 14, 1859, breechloading firearm. Revolvers made by Massachusetts Arms Co. (Sellers-1)

LEBAN, VALENTINE Bedford, Pennsylvania, 1820. (Hetrick)

LEBEAU, BAPTISTE St. Louis, Missouri, 1835. Probably John Baptiste Lebeau.

LEBEAU, G.F. unlocated. Percussion fullstock.

LEBEAU, JOHN BAPTISTE St. Louis, Missouri, 1823-1870d.

LEBETT, J.H. unlocated. Percussion fullstock.

LEBUHN, R. LeClaire, Iowa. Percussion shotguns. (Hobbies 11-34)

LECHLER, HARRY Springfield, Massachusetts, 1813-1815. Superintendent of Springfield Armory.

LECHLER, HENRY Carlisle, Pennsylvania, 1797-1843, Lancaster, Pennsylvania, 1843-1857. Percussion fullstock and 1/2 stock. (Kauffman)

LECHLER, HENRY, JR. Philadelphia, Pennsylvania, 1829d-1861d. Percussion duelling pistols. As H. Lechler & Son, 1857-1861. Percussion duelling pistols.

LECHLER, JACOB Philadelphia, Pennsylvania, 1829d. Kentucky rifle.

LECHLER, WILLIAM D. Waynesboro, Pennsylvania, 1846t. Dentist and gunsmith. Son of Henry Lechler. (Bowers)

LECHNER, JOHN (?-1835), Uniontown, Pennsylvania, 1802t-1835t. (Bowers)

LECKNER, JOHN York, Pennsylvania, 1778-1799. Flintlock Kentucky rifle. (Kindig)

LEDBETTER, A.C. Jamestown, North Carolina, 1855. (Bivins)

LEDBETTER, ALPHEUS (1831-?), Jamestown, North Carolina, 1850c. Son of Henry Ledbetter. (Bivins)

LEDBETTER, ALVEUS P. Jamestown, North Carolina, 1831-1862. With Henry Ledbetter. (Bivins)

LEDBETTER, CHESLEY E. (1830-?), Jamestown, North Carolina, 1850c-1884d. (Bivins)

LEDBETTER, FRANCIS (1835-?), Jamestown, North Carolina, 1850c. (Bivins)

LEDBETTER, HENRY (1809-?), Jamestown, North Carolina, 1850c. (Bivins)

LEDBETTER, JUDD F. (1834-?), Jamestown, North Carolina, 1850c. (Bivins)

LEDBETTER, MIRANDA (1831-?), Jamestown, North Carolina, 1850c. Stocker for James Gordon. (Bivins)

LEDBETTER, RANDY Jamestown, North Carolina. (Bivins)

LEDBETTER, Z.J. Friendship, North Carolina, 1884d.

LEDFORD, HENRY (1796-1856), Davidson Co., North Carolina. Percussion 1/2 stock and fullstock. (Bivins)

LEDFORD, R. unlocated, percussion fullstock.

LEDGWICK, C.J. Dayton, Ohio, 1880c. (Hutslar)

LEDLEY, GOTTLIEB Greenock, Pennsylvania, 1887d-1890d.

LEDUC, A. New Orleans, Louisiana 1838d.

LEDUC, LOUIS T. New Orleans, Louisiana, 1841d.

LEDUC, THEODORE (1799-?), New Orleans, Louisiana, 1850c-1859d. Imported percussion shotgun.

LEE ARMS CO. Bridgeport, Connecticut, 1879-1910. Sales organization for James Paris Lee's bolt action rifles. (Sellers-4)

LEE ARMS CO. Wilkes-Barre, Pennsylvania, 1877-1880. Suicide specials under many names. J. Frank Lee.

LEE FIRE ARMS CO. Milwaukee, Wisconsin, 1864-1866. Single shot rifles. James Paris Lee. (GR 6-67)

LEE HARDWARE CO. Salina, Kansas, 1895-1912. Dealers only.

LEE SPECIAL trade name of Crescent Fire Arms Co. on guns for Lee Hardware Co. (several variations in marking). (AR 2-69)

LEE, ALFRED New Whatcom, Washington. Patent #522,605 July 10, 1894, magazine gun.

LEE, DAVID Harford Co., Maryland. Committee of Safety muskets. (Hartzler)

LEE, G. unlocated. Percussion four-barrel swivel rifle.

LEE, J.A. unlocated. Percussion 1/2 stock.

LEE, JAMES PARIS (1831-1904), Stevens Point, Wisconsin, 1862-1864, Milwaukee, Wisconsin, 1864-1869, Ilion, New York, 1869-1880, Bridgeport, Connecticut, 1880-1904. Patents #35,941 July 22, 1862, breechloading firearm, #54,744 May 15, 1866, breechloading firearm, #114,951 May 16, 1871, breechloading firearm, #116,968 June 20, 1871, breechloading firearm, #122,470 January 2, 1872, breechloading firearm, #122,772 January 6, 1872, breechloading firearm, #160,919 March 6, 1875, breechloading firearm, #162,481 April 27, 1875, cartridge box, #193,524 July 24, 1877, primer, #193,821 August 7, 1877, breechloading firearm, #221,328 November 4, 1879, magazine gun, #295,563 March 25, 1884, magazine gun with Louis P. Diss, #383,363 May 22, 1888, magazine gun, #506,319 October 10, 1893, magazine gun, #506,320 October 10, 1893, magazine gun, #506,321 October 10, 1893, magazine gun, #506,322 October 10, 1893, magazine gun, #506,323 October 10, 1893, magazine gun, and #547,583 October 8, 1895, magazine gun. As Lee Fire Arms Co. in Milwaukee and Lee Arms Co. in Bridgeport. (Sellers 4, GR 6-57)

LEE, JOHN J. New Orleans, Louisiana, 1875d.

LEE, LEROY E. New Orleans, Louisiana, 1879d-1885d.

LEE, OAKLEY T. Norwich, Connecticut, 1874-1880d.

LEE, ROBERT Cincinnati, Ohio, 1880c. (Hutslar)

LEE, THOMAS New York, New York. Patent #20,073 April 27, 1858, breechloading firearm.

LEE, THOMAS Newark, New Jersey. Patent #33,745 November 19, 1861, breechloading firearm.

LEE, THOMAS Westport, Connecticut, 1871d-1873d. Patent #122,182 December 26, 1872, revolver extractor.

LEE, WILLIAM New York, New York, 1843-1845. (Kauffman 2)

LEE, WILSON (1802-?), Daviess Co., Indiana, 1850c. (Lindert)

LEECH & CO. Greensboro, Georgia, 1864-1865. Confederate revolvers after dissolution of Leech & Rigdon. Thomas S. Leech. (Albaugh 3)

LEECH & RIGDON Memphis, Tennessee, 1861-1862, Columbus, Mississippi, 1862-1863, Greensboro, Georgia, 1863-1864. Revolvers for the Confederacy. Thomas S. Leech and Charles H. Rigdon. (Albaugh 3)

LEECH, THOMAS S. Memphis, Tennessee. Agent for Deringer. As Thomas Leech & Co., with Charles H. Rigdon as Leech & Rigdon, Leech & Co., and Memphis Novelty Works.

LEEMANN, JULIUS St. Louis, Missouri. Patent #295,564 March 25, 1884, magazine gun.

LEET, CHARLES S. Bridgeport, Connecticut. Patents #282,997 August 14, 1883, extractor, and #288,459 November 13, 1883, wiper.

LEETE, J.R. Rochester, Minnesota, 1882d-1898d.

LEETE, WILLIAM B. New York, New York, 1846d-1853d.

LEFAVOUR, J. Muncie, Indiana, 1860d.

LEFEBVRE, T.B. New Orleans, Louisiana, 1834d.

LEFEVER & ELLIS Canandaigua, New York, 1863-1867. Percussion target rifle.

LEFEVER ARMS CO. Syracuse, New York, 1884-1948. See Daniel M. Lefever for predecessor and associated companies.

LEFEVER, CHARLES F. Syracuse, New York. Patents with Daniel Lefever: #732,420 June 30, 1903, breechloading gun, #795,991 August 1, 1905, single trigger, and #810,871 January 23, 1906, single trigger. Patents used by Union Firearm Co., Toledo, Ohio: #865,310 January 3, 1907, breechloading gun, and #944,448 December 18, 1908, revolver.

LEFEVER, D.M., SONS & CO. Syracuse, New York, 1901-1902. See Daniel M. Lefever for predecessor and associated companies.

LEFEVER, DANIEL M. (?-1906), Auburn, New York, 1853-1857 and 1870-1874, Canandaigua, New York, 1857-1867d, Syracuse, New York, 1874-1905, Bowling Green, Ohio, 1905-1915. Patents with F.R. Smith: #205,193 June 25, 1878, breechloading firearm, #229,429 June 29, 1880, breechloading firearm, and #264,173 September 12, 1882, breechloading firearm. Patents with J.H. Brown: #329,397 October 27, 1885, breechloading firearm, #343,040 June 1, 1886, breechloading firearm, #372,684 November 8, 1887, breechloading firearm, #385,360 July 3, 1888, breechloading firearm and #423,521 March 18, 1890, breechloading firearm. Patents with Charles Lefever: #475,873 May 31, 1892, lock and ejector, #536,636 April 2, 1895, ejector, and #810,871 January 23, 1906, single trigger. As Lefever & Ellis, 1863-1867, Dangerfield & Lefever, 1872-1874, Nichols & Lefever, 1876-1877, Barber & Lefever, 1877-1878, Lefever Arms Co., 1884-1906 (operations continued through 1948, acquired by Ithaca Gun Co. in 1915), D.M. Lefever & Sons, 1901, D.M. Lefever, Sons & Co., 1901-1902, and D.M. Lefever Co., 1905-1906.

LEFEVER, ISAAC Lancaster, Pennsylvania, 1731-1736. (KRA IV-4)

LEFEVRE, PHILIP (1710-?), Lancaster, Pennsylvania, 1731-1756. Kentucky rifles. (Dillin)

LEFEVRE, SAMUEL Strasburg, Pennsylvania, 1770-1771. (Gluckman & Satterlee)

LEFFEL, DAVID Shanesville, Pennsylvania, 1861d.

LEFFLER Memphis, Tennessee. Derringer. (Albaugh 3)

LEFFLER, CHRISTIAN (1823-?), Cincinnati, Ohio, 1850c.

LEGARD, M. Leavenworth, Kansas, 1873d.

LEGDEN, A. Atlanta, Georgia. Confederate patent #151 March 10, 1863, revolver. (Albaugh 3)

LEGG, JOSEPH Piqua, Ohio, 1859-1878d. Percussion 1/2 stock. (Hutslar)

LEGG, SAMUEL P. Springfield, Massachusetts. Patent #51,327 December 5, 1865, forging dies.

LEGG, T.C. Columbia, South Carolina. Percussion duelling pistol.

LEGGETT, WILLIAM Hampshire Co., West Virginia, circa 1865. See William Liggett. (Whisker IV)

LEGLER, FRANK (1865-1949), Nashville, Tennessee, 1887d-circa 1930. As J. Legler & Son, 1887-1891. Son of Joseph P. Legler.

LEGLER, JOSEPH P. (1829-?), Lockport, Illinois, 1850c-1864d, Nashville, Tennessee, 1867-1891d. As Bitterlick & Legler, 1867-1879, with Franz J. Bitterlick. As J. Legler & Son, 1887-1891, with Frank Legler.

LEHMAN, GEORGE F. Jerome, Ohio, 1850-1853d. (Hutslar)

LEHMAN, SAMUEL Philadelphia, Pennsylvania, 1780-1785. Repaired U.S. arms. (Moller)

LEHMANN, CHARLES Alma, Wisconsin, 1857d.

LEHMANN, CHRISTIAN Alma, Wisconsin, 1884d-1895d. Son of Charles Lehmann.

LEHMANN, FRITZ Pontiac, Illinois, 1888d-1891d.

LEHMPUL, ERNEST Chicago, Illinois, 1876d.

LEHNERT, GUSTAVE A. Louisville, Kentucky, 1880d-1886d. Son of, and successor to Julius Lehnert.

LEHNERT, JULIUS Louisville, Kentucky, 1865d-1878d.

LEHR, FRED Cleveland, Ohio, 1878d-1896. (Hutslar)

LEHR, JOSEPH Allentown, Pennsylvania, 1848t. (KRA II-3)

LEIB, ALPHEUS Lancaster Co., Pennsylvania, 1849-1850. Barrelmaker. (Dyke)

LEIB, JOHN Jeffersonville, New York, 1870d-1874d.

LEIB, JOHN Lancaster Co., Pennsylvania, 1842-1850. Barrelmaker. (KRA IV-4)

LEICH, GEORGE J.H. St. Louis, Missouri, 1889d-1898d.

LEICHT, JACOB Liberty, Texas, 1884d-1885d, Victoria, Texas, 1896d.

LEIDKE & BERTSCHE Sandusky, Ohio, 1859d. (Hutslar)

LEIDLE, J. (1827-?), Sacramento, California, 1852c. (Shelton)

LEIGLEY, GEORGE W. Orleans, Iowa, 1865d.

LEIMER, GUS C. Little Rock, Arkansas, 1881-1955. (Elias)

LEINBACH, ELIAS Lancaster Co., Pennsylvania, 1843-1846. (Dyke)

LEINBACH, PETER (1791-?), Bethania, North Carolina, 1850c. (Bivins)

LEINBACH, SIMON (1822-?), Bethania, North Carolina, 1850c. Son of Peter Leinbach. (Bivins)

LEINEWEBER, HERMANN South Chicago, Illinois. Patents #379,794 March 20, 1888, magazine gun, and #428,813 May 27, 1890, magazine gun.

LEISCHER, C. DuPlainville, Wisconsin, 1857d.

LEISENING, H.G. Philadelphia, Pennsylvania, 1862-1863. Converted flintlock muskets.

LEISHKO, WILLIAM Glencoe, Minnesota, 1898d. See William Leistiko.

LEISON, ALLEN J. Philadelphia, Pennsylvania, 1862-1863. Converted flintlock muskets.

LEISTIKO, WILLIAM Glencoe, Minnesota. Patent #564,525 July 21, 1896, breechloading gun. See W. Leishko.

LEITNER, ADAM York Co., Pennsylvania, 1779-1808. Flintlock pistols. (Kauffman)

LEITNER, IGNATIUS Yorktown, Pennsylvania, 1783-1800. See Ignatius Lightner - same person? (Kauffman)

LEITNER, JACOB Yorktown, Pennsylvania, 1799. (Kauffman)

LEKNER, JOHN (1831-?), Joliet State Penitentiary, Illinois, 1860c. Inmate. (Johnson)

LELAND & BROOKS Augusta, Maine, 1854-1860. Larkin M. Leland and C.C. Brooks (see Larkin M. Leland, 1836-1860 timeframe listed for this business).

LELAND, EDWIN A. New York, New York. Patent #199,915 February 5, 1878, machine gun.

LELAND, HENRY (1823-1846), Augusta, Maine, 1840-1846. Son of Moses Leland, worked for his brother, Larkin M. Leland. (Demeritt)

LELAND, LARKIN M. (1811-1894), Augusta, Maine, 1836-1871. Son of Moses Leland. With C.C. Brooks as Leland & Brooks, 1836-1860. (Demeritt)

LELAND, LEMUEL (1786-1860), Sherborn, Massachusetts, 1848-1860. Flintlock Kentucky. (ASAC 44)

LELAND, MOSES Sherborn, Massachusetts, 1800-1830. (Demeritt)

LELAND, WILLIAM Sherborn, Massachusetts, 1874d-1885d. Son of Moses Leland. (Demeritt)

LELAND, WILLIAM, JR. Sherborn, Massachusetts, 1853d-1873.

LEMAN, FRANK B. Lancaster, Pennsylvania, 1871d-1888. (Kauffman)

LEMAN, HENRY EICHOLTZ (1812-1887), Philadelphia, Pennsylvania, 1831-1834. Contract rifles and muskets, using the trade name Conestoga Rifle Works. For Tryon, Lancaster, Pennsylvania, 1834-1887. (Kauffman)

LEMAN, PETER (?-1741), Lancaster Co., Pennsylvania, 1717-1741. Barrels. (Dillin)

LEMAN, PETER Lancaster Co., Pennsylvania, 1740-1782. Son of Peter Leman. (Gluckman & Satterlee)

LEMM, HIRAM Storm Lake, Iowa, 1897d.

LEMMER, FREDERICK Washington, D.C., 1867d. (Hartzler)

LEMON, F. Mt. Vernon, Ohio, 1858-1859d. With A.F. Ely as Ely & Lemon, 1859. (Hutslar)

LENDER, LOUIS Charles City, Iowa, 1880d-1895d.

LENGSORF, GEORGE (1819-?), Ashland Co., Ohio, 1850c. (Hutslar)

LENHART, A.I. New Brunswick, New Jersey, 1878d.

LENNORD, CHARLES (1826-?), Petersburg, Virginia, 1850c. See Charles Leonard. (MB 10-63)

LENNOX, ANDREW Fairview, Pennsylvania, 1826-1837. (Kauffman)

LENOUR, H.R. Troy, Ohio, 1853d. (Hutslar)

LENTZ, A. Columbus, Wisconsin, 1879d.

LENTZ, J. Chillicothe, Ohio, 1855d. (Hutslar)

LENZ, MICHAEL Baltimore, Maryland, 1802-1804. (Gluckman & Satterlee)

LENZHANER & OTTO St. Louis, Missouri, 1864d. Frederick Lenzhaner and Augustus G. Otto.

LENZHANER, FREDERICK St. Louis, Missouri, 1857d-1866d. Percussion 1/2 stock. With Augustus G. Otto as Lenzhaner & Otto, 1864. Percussion 1/2 stock.

LEON, FRANK Missoula, Montana, 1892d-1898d.

LEONARD & KINSLEY Canton, Massachusetts, 1789-1800. Jonathan Leonard and Adam Kinsley.

LEONARD, A., & SONS Saxtons River, Vermont, 1849-1860. Percussion rifles and shotguns. Artemus Leonard. (Horn)

LEONARD, ARTEMUS Saxtons River, Vermont, 1840-1860d. Percussion rifles and shotguns. As A. Leonard & Sons, 1849-1860. (Horn)

LEONARD, C.W. Dearborn, Michigan, 1899d.

LEONARD, CHARLES Canton, Massachusetts, 1809-1826. Model 1808 contract muskets with his brother Robert. As R. & C. Leonard with Robert. Son of Jonathan Leonard. (Gluckman & Satterlee)

LEONARD, CHARLES Petersburg, Virginia, 1867-1877d. See Charles Lennord.

LEONARD, DAVID (1825-1908), Ellsworth, Ohio, 1865-1908. Percussion and cartridge rifles. (MB 4-60)

LEONARD, ELIPHALET Easton, Massachusetts, 1776-1778. Committee of Safety muskets. (Gluckman)

LEONARD, GEORGE OLIVER (1829-1887), Saxtons River, Vermont, 1849-1859, Keene, New Hampshire, 1859-1869, Red Bluff, California, 1869-1887. Son of George Leonard, Jr. (Shelton)

LEONARD, GEORGE, JR. Charleston, Massachusetts, 1849-1850. Patents #6,723 September 18, 1849, pepperbox, #7,493 July 9, 1850, pepperbox, #9,922 August 9, 1853, pepperbox, and #14,820 May 6, 1856, pepperbox. Pepperbox guns made by Robbins & Lawrence, Windsor, Vermont, after 1850. (Dunlap)

LEONARD, GIDEON North Granville, New York, 1870d.

LEONARD, HARDEN Nashville, Tennessee, 1876d-1877d.

LEONARD, HARVEY REID San Francisco, California. Patent #207,747 September 3, 1878, machine gun.

LEONARD, HENRY Buffalo, New York, 1835d. For Patrick Smith. (Dean)

LEONARD, HIRAM LEWIS (1831-1907), Bangor, Maine, 1854-1880, Central Valley, New York, 1880-1907. Percussion multi-shot single barrel guns. (Demeritt)

LEONARD, J.D. Grafton, Vermont, 1876-1879. (Horn)

LEONARD, JONATHAN (1759-1845), Canton, Massachusetts, 1788-1800. With Adam Kinsley as Leonard & Kinsley, 1789-1800. (Gluckman & Satterlee)

LEONARD, R. & C. Canton, Massachusetts. Model 1808 contract muskets. Brothers Robert and Charles Leonard.(Gluckman & Satterlee)

LEONARD, ROBERT Canton, Massachusetts, 1808-1826. Model 1808 contract muskets with his brother Charles. (Gluckman)

LEONARD, SAMUEL I. Grafton, Vermont, 1876-1880. (Horn)

LEONARD, WILLIAM (?-1905), Ft. Wayne, Indiana. 1858d-1905. Percussion 1/2 stock. (Lindert)

LEONHAGEN, FREDERICK Wausau, Wisconsin, 1888d.

LEOPOLD, J.A. Millersburg, Ohio, 1883d-1887. (Hutslar)

LEPAPE, DESBOIS New Orleans, Louisiana, 1841d-1842d.

LEPLEY, A. Ottawa, Ohio, 1881-1885d. As T. & A. Lepley, 1881d. (Hutslar)

LEPLEY, ADAM Somerset Co., Pennsylvania, 1842-1850. (Whisker II)

LEPLEY, T. & A. Ottawa, Ohio, 1881d. (Hutslar)

LEPLEY, WILLIAM (1830-?). Monroe, Ohio, 1850c. (Hutslar)

LEPLY, VALENTINE (1825-?), Monroe, Ohio, 1850c. (Hutslar)

LEPPELMAN, L. Fremont, Ohio, 1859d. Percussion 1/2 stock. (Hutslar)

LEPPER, HENRY G. Baltimore, Maryland, 1847-1854d. (Hartzler)

LEPPER, LEWIS Lancaster, Pennsylvania, 1857d. With Charles Pfeiffer.

LEPPLEY, JOSEPH Somerset Co., Pennsylvania, 1863-1874. (Kauffman)

LEROY, AUGUST Springfield, Illinois, 1892d.

LESCHER Philadelphia, Pennsylvania, 1730. Flintlock Kentucky rifle. (Gluckman)

LESH, EMANUEL (1824-?), Forsythe Co., North Carolina, 1850c. (Bivins)

LESHER, WILLIAM L. Philadelphia, Pennsylvania, 1846d.

LESLIE, A.J. & F.A. Mobile, Alabama, 1859d. Dealers.

LESLIE, J.D. Union Springs, Alabama, 1885d.

LESSEY, HENRY F. (1805-1850), Green Bay, Wisconsin, 1840-1850. (MB 5-50)

LESSIER Selma, Alabama, 1861. Partner of C. Suter. See Tissier. (Albaugh 3)

LESSLEY, PETER Philadelphia, Pennsylvania, 1780-1782. Continental Armory. (Moller)

LESTER, JOHN H. Niantic, Connecticut. Patent #161,343 March 30, 1875, safety.

LESTER, L.M. & H.H. New York, New York, 1875-1886. Lester safety pistols. (Gluckman & Satterlee)

LETHER & CO. see Leather & Co.

LETORT, JAMES Wytheville, Virginia. Patent #27,723 April 3, 1860, breechloading firearms with H.S. Mathews.

LETTOW, CONRAD Neenah, Wisconsin, 1884d-1886d, Rockford, Illinois, 1893d.

LEU, VALERIAN (1836-?), Philadelphia, Pennsylvania, 1860, Vallejo, California, 1875-1889, Watsonville, California, 1889-1893d. With his son, Charles William Leu, after 1878. (Shelton)

LEVERETT, WALTER Tallahassee, Florida, 1866d-1883d.

LEVERICH, JOHN B. New York, New York. Patent #35,456 June 3, 1862, lock cover.

LEVERIDGE, GEORGE New York, New York, 1850c.

LEVERING, JOSEPH Nazareth, Pennsylvania, 1779t-?, Bethlehem, Pennsylvania, 1782t-1784t. (Dyke)

LEVINE, PETER Charlottesville, Virginia, 1880d.

LEVY, I.M. Dayton, Ohio, 1880c. (Hutslar)

LEVY, WILLIAM M. St. Louis, Missouri. Patents #645,107 March 13, 1900, single trigger, and #656,822 August 28, 1900, single trigger.

LEWIS & SWAN St. Louis, Missouri, 1867d. (Pourie)

LEWIS & TOMES New York, New York. Derringers and revolvers. Importers and dealers.

LEWIS, A. Baltimore, Maryland, 1831d. (Hartzler)

LEWIS, A.H. unlocated. Percussion double rifle dated 1861.

LEWIS, ALLIE Spartansburg, Indiana.

LEWIS, C.C. Montpelier, Vermont, 1880-1881. (Horn)

LEWIS, C.G. Zanesville, Ohio, 1851. (Hutslar)

LEWIS, C.L. Concord, Missouri, 1860d.

LEWIS, CHARLES Buffalo, New York, 1836-1842. (Gluckman & Satterlee)

LEWIS, CHAUNCEY S. Lexington, Kentucky, 1840. (MB 12-51)

LEWIS, D.R., & BRO. Manchester, Iowa 1889d.

LEWIS, D.W. Chicago, Illinois, 1880d, Albert Lea Minnesota, 1884d-1886d, North Platte, Nebraska, 1893d.

LEWIS, D.W. Janesville, Wisconsin. Percussion 1/2 stock. Possibly same as D.W. Lewis of Chicago, Illinois, 1880?

LEWIS, DANIEL W. Pontiac, Illinois, 1878d.

LEWIS, E.C. Red Oak, Iowa, 1895d.

LEWIS, EDWARD R. Springfield, Massachusetts. Patent #362,096 May 3, 1887, spring gun.

LEWIS, FIELDING Rappahannock Forge, Virginia, 1775-1777. One of the partners in the armory. (Swayze)

LEWIS, GEORGE S. (?-1946), Syracuse and Fulton, New York, Chicopee Falls, Massachusetts. Patents #371,665 October 18, 1887, breechloading firearm with A.G. Lamport, #675,334 May 28, 1901, ejector, #694,654 March 4, 1902, breechloading firearm, #935,314 September 28, 1908, repeating gun, #939,142 November 2, 1908, repeating gun, and #1,459,108 June 19, 1923, breechloading firearm. As Page-Lewis Arms Co., 1921-1923, for Winchester 1924-1941, for High Standard 1942-1946. (Perkins)

LEWIS, HENRY Burlington, Ohio, 1880-1910. Negro gunsmith. (Hutslar)

LEWIS, IRA Mississipi Co., Missouri, 1850c. (MB 11-66)

LEWIS, J.B. Lone Dell, Missouri, 1891d-1893d.

LEWIS, J.H. Lewisville, Oregon, 1891d.

LEWIS, J.M. Westfield, Massachusetts, 1881d-1892d.

LEWIS, J.W. Alledonia, Ohio, 1888d. (Hutslar)

LEWIS, JACOB unlocated. Flintlock Kentucky.

LEWIS, JAMES M. Johnson Co., Arkansas, 1845-1860. (Elias)

LEWIS, JAMES Carter Furnace, Tennessee, 1881d.

LEWIS, JAMES Pierre, South Dakota, 1898d.

LEWIS, JAMES Troy, New York, 1852-1859, Rochester, New York, 1871-1874d. (Eich)

LEWIS, JOHN H. Leesburg, Virginia, 1897d.

LEWIS, JOHN Upper Sandusky, Ohio, 1808-1820. Repairs for Wyandot indians. (Knittle)

LEWIS, JOSEPH Groton, Connecticut, 1780. Repaired state arms. (Gluckman & Satterlee)

LEWIS, JOSEPH New York, New York, 1842-1865d. Percussion pistol.

LEWIS, JOSEPH Pike Co., Pennsylvania. Late flintlock period. (Dillin)

LEWIS, L.A. Wells, Vermont, 1876-1879. (Horn)

LEWIS, M.E. Albert Lea, Minnesota, 1882d.

LEWIS, MORGAN E. Youngstown, Ohio, 1880-1883d. (Hutslar)

LEWIS, NATHANIEL Stout, Ohio, Boone Co., Iowa, Muncie, Indiana. (MB 7-44)

LEWIS, NELSON (1811-1888), Troy, New York, 1843-1888. Percussion guns. (MB 11-51)

LEWIS, PETER Lawrence Co., Missouri, 1850c.

LEWIS, PETER Lecompton, Kansas, 1866d.

LEWIS, S.C. Whitneyville, Connecticut. Patent #24,942 August 2, 1859, revolver with F.P. Pfleghar. (Sellers-1)

LEWIS, SAMUEL C. (1804-?), Defiance Co., Ohio, 1850c. (Hutslar)

LEWIS, SAMUEL Rochester, New York, 1838d-1849d. (Eich)

LEWIS, THEOPHELUS Philadelphia, Pennsylvania, 1796d.

LEWIS, W. Leatherwood, Ohio, 1868d. (Hutslar)

LEWIS, W.N. Greeley Kansas, 1866d.

LEWIS, WARNER (1870-?), Tulip, Ohio, 1890-1947. Percussion 1/2 stock. Grandson of Nathaniel Lewis. (MB 7-44)

LEWIS, WASHINGTON Washington, D.C., 1822d. (Hartzler)

LEWIS, WEBSTER Lewisberry, Pennsylvania, 1836-1846. Made first percussion guns in York Co. With Isaac Loyd, 1836. (Dean)

LEWIS, WILLIAM N. (1810-?), Bartholomew Co., Indiana, 1850. (Lindert)

LEWIS, WILLIAM New Berlin, New York, 1872d-1882d.

LEWIS, WILLIAM Richmond Center, Ohio, 1859-1864d. Percussion 1/2 stock. (Hutslar)

LEY, FREDERICK Philadelphia, Pennsylvania, 1829d-1831d.

LEYDEN, A. Atlanta, Georgia. Confederate patent #151 March 10, 1863, revolver. (Albaugh 3)

LEYERZAPF, CHARLES Boise, Idaho, 1880d-1886d.

LIBBEY, A.R. Lawrence, Massachusetts, 1878d.

LIBBY, H.L. Norway, Maine, 1884. (Demeritt)

LIBEAU, CHARLES Cincinnati, Ohio, 1829-1844d. Percussion pistol. (Hutslar)

LIBEAU, V.G.W. New Orleans, Louisiana, 1832d-1847d. Percussion revolvers and derringers. (Sellers-1)

LIBEAU, VALENTINE Cincinnati, Ohio, 1825-1829d. Possibly V.G.W. Libeau. (Hutslar)

LIBERTY suicide special by O.A. Smith.

LIBIG, WILLIAM Baltimore, Maryland, 1884-1885d. Same as Liebig (No first name) who made air guns in Baltimore, Maryland, per (Wolff)? (Hartzler)

LICHTENMEYER, F. Blue Island, Illinois, 1860d. See George Luchtenmeyer.

LIDDELL, WILLIAM St. Johnsbury, Vermont. Single shot dropping block rifle.

LIDDLE & KAEDING San Francisco, California, 1873-1889. Derringers and tip-up rifles. Robert Liddle and C.H.V. Kaeding.

LIDDLE, JAMES HENRY (1846-?), San Francisco, California, 1865-1873, Visalia, California, 1873-?. Son of Robert Liddle. (Shelton)

LIDDLE, ROBERT (1824-?), Baltimore, Maryland, 1842-1855d, San Francisco, California, 1853-1898. Percussion derringer and cartridge guns. As Liddle & Co., 1859-1866 and 1889-1898. With C.H.V. Kaeding as Liddle & Kaeding, 1866-1889. (Shelton-Hartzler)

LIEBEENCUTH, GEORGE (1840-?), Ottawa, Illinois, 1860c. (Johnson)

LIEBEENCUTH, JOHN C. (1839-?), Ottawa, Illinois, 1860-1869. (Johnson)

LIEBIG Baltimore, Maryland. Air gun. Same as William Libig, Baltimore, Maryland, 1884-1885d? (Wolff)

LIEGE GUN CO. trade name of Hibbard, Spencer, Bartlett & Co. on imported shotguns. (Hinman)

LIEP, NICHOLAS Union City, Tennessee, 1876d.

LIFRED, JOHN Union Co., Pennsylvania, 1850c. Barrelmaker. (Kauffman)

LIGGETT, HENRY CLAY (1854-?), Wardensville, West Virginia, 1880d.

LIGGETT, WILLIAM Edinburgh, Virginia, 1853. Late flintlock rifles. (Bowers)

LIGGINS, THOMAS Philadelphia, Pennsylvania, 1835d.

LIGHT, ELMORE Shelby, Ohio, 1860. (Hutslar)

LIGHT, J.G. Burlington Flats, New York, 1862-1867. Percussion 1/2 stock.

LIGHT, PETER Berkeley Co., Virginia, 1776-1778. Committee of Safety muskets with David Hunter. (Gill)

LIGHTNER, IGNATIUS York Co., Pennsylvania, 1784-1786. Repaired U.S. arms. See Ignatius Leitner - same person? (Gluckman & Satterlee)

LIGON, E.T. Demopolis, Alabama. Confederate patent #24 September 24, 1861, breechloading gun. (Albaugh)

LIHIE, GEORGE Calistoga, California, 1880-1881d. (Shelton)

LILLIENDAHL, C.A. New York, New York. Patent #22,959 February 15, 1859, alarm gun.

LILLY, B.T. Greene Co., Pennsylvania, 1850-1861. Percussion 1/2 stock.

LILLY, DAVID H. (1826-?), Greene Co., Pennsylvania, 1848-1849, Marion Co., West Virginia, 1850c. (Whisker II)

LILLY, JAMES P. Fayette Co., Pennsylvania, 1845-1848. (Kauffman)

LILLY, JOHN P. Fayette Co., Pennsylvania, 1840-1852. See John Lilly, same location, 1816t-1817t. (Whisker II)

LILLY, JOHN Fayette Co., Pennsylvania, 1816t-1817t. (Gabel)

LILLY, M.C. Elmwood, Illinois, 1877d, Decatur, Illinois, 1888d.

LILLY, MARENZO C. (1828-?), Uniontown, Pennsylvania, 1850c-1851t. (Whisker II)

LILLY, ROBERT A. (1831-?), Carmichaels, Pennsylvania, 1850c. (Whisker II)

LILLY, THOMAS P. (1818-?), Carmichaels, Pennsylvania, 1846-1852, Morgantown, West Virginia, 1859-1880c. (Whisker II)

LILLY, THOMAS T. Grafton, West Virginia, 1885d. Percussion 1/2 stock. Son of Thomas P. Lilly.

LILLY, WILLIAM S. Morgantown, West Virginia. Son of Thomas P. Lilly.

LIMERICK, JAMES Philadelphia, Pennsylvania, 1798. (Kauffman)

LIMMERVAN, JOHN Philadelphia, Pennsylvania, 1823d.

LIMPER, EDWARD Houston, Texas, 1899d.

LINBERG, CHARLES J. St. Louis, Missouri. Patent #109,914 December 6, 1870, revolver with William J. Phillips.

LINCOLN, EDWIN M. Norwich, Connecticut, 1881d-1894d.

LINCOLN, JOSEPH Philadelphia, Pennsylvania, 1780-1782. Continental Armory. (Moller)

LINCOLN, N.B. Corunna, Michigan, 1879d.

LINDBARG, SWEN JOHN (1826-1873), Princeton, Illinois, 1852-1873. (Johnson)

LINDBERG, CHARLES A. Grand Rapids, Michigan, 1872d-1899d. Percussion and cartridge guns. Patent #614,532 November 22, 1898, spring air gun, with William Calkins.

LINDBURG, C. unlocated. Percussion over/under rifle/shotgun.

LINDE, A. Memphis, Tennessee, 1858-1867. Derringers. (T 47)

LINDE, J. unlocated. Percussion pistol.

LINDEMER, LOUIS Jackson, Michigan, 1869d-1899d.

LINDEMOOD, JACOB (1788-1874). Shenandoah Co., Virginia, 1814, Belmont Co., Ohio, 1828-1837, Monroe Co., Ohio, 1837-1874. Percussion fullstock. (Hutslar)

LINDEN, H.V. New York, New York, 1883d.

LINDLEY, JOHN Washington Co., Pennsylvania, 1811-1835. (Whisker II)

LINDLEY, STEPHEN West Sebena, Michigan, 1872d-1878d.

LINDNER & MOLO New York, New York. Air pistol.

LINDNER, EDWARD New York, New York. Patents #11,197 June 27, 1854, repeating pistol, #14,819 November 11, 1856, breechloading firearm, #17,287 May 12, 1857, cartridge, #17,382 May 26, 1857, breechloading firearm, #23,378 March 29, 1859, breechloading firearm, and #37,173 December 16, 1862, air gun. Lindner carbines made by Amoskeag Mfg. Co. (GR 11-66)

LINDNER, J.P. Helena, Montana, 1898d.

LINDSAY Chicago, Illinois, 1870-1890. Percussion 1/2 stock. (T 56)

LINDSAY, HIRAM W. (1808-?), North Putah, California, 1868-1877. (Shelton)

LINDSAY, JOHN P. Windsor, Vermont, 1840. (Horn)

LINDSAY, JOHN PARKER New York, New York, 1859-1861, New Haven, Connecticut, 1861-1867. Patents #28,090 July 24, 1860, cartridge, and #30,330 October 9, 1860, double trigger. Superposed load rifles and pistols. As Lindsay Mfg. Co. of New Haven, but actual manufacture by New Haven Arms Co. (ASAC 1)

LINDSEY, A.M. Spartansburg, South Carolina, 1885d.

LINDSEY, E.W. Spartansburg, South Carolina, 1886d.

LINDSEY, JOHHN unlocated. Gunsmith for Pottawatamie tribe, 1829-1836.

LINDSLEY & MOFFET unlocated.

LINDSLEY, WILLIAM Portsmouth, Ohio, 1828. (Knittle)

LINDTHON & BOMAN Fargo, North Dakota, 1884d.

LINGARD, JOSEPH Philadelphia, Pennsylvania, 1841d.

LINGLE, GORDON K. Burlington, Wisconsin, 1878d-1879d.

LINGO, J.A. Tyler, Texas, 1890d.

LINN, JACOB (1825-1878), San Antonio, Texas, 1846-1860. Percussion 1/2 stock. (T 68)

LINNARD, WILLIAM Colonel, U.S. Army(?), Philadelphia, Pennsylvania. Patent #none Month?, Day?, 1818, breechloading gun.

LINS, ADAM FREDERICK Philadelphia, Pennsylvania, 1859-1891d. Derringers and Model 1842 contract muskets. (AG 3-75)

LINS, FRANZ A. Philadelphia, Pennsylvania, 1855d-1867d. As F. & F. Lins, 1855-1857.

LINS, FREDERICK A. Philadelphia, Pennsylvania, 1855d-1861d. Percussion 1/2 stock.

LINSE, SOLOMON L. Philadelphia, Pennsylvania, 1891d-1899d.

LINSEY, JOHN St. John, Illinois, 1860d.

LINTHICUM, WILLIAM H. Baltimore, Maryland, 1887d. (Hartzler)

LINTON, WILLIAM Portland, Maine, 1829. (Demeritt)

LINZEL, AUGUSTUS EDWARD (1831-1904), St. Louis, Missouri, 1847-1869d, Little Rock, Arkansas, 1869-1904. Percussion and air guns. (Elias-Wolff)

LION suicide special by Iver Johnson.

LIONS, GEORGE Logana, Kentucky, 1896d.

LIPE see Spellings & Lipe.

LIPE, THOMAS Morristown, Ohio, 1859d. (Hutslar)

LIPEL, C. unlocated. Flintlock Kentucky.

LIPP, ABRAHAM Lancaster, Pennsylvania, 1850. (KRA IV-4)

LIPPHARDT, CHARLES New Richmond, Ohio, 1853d. (Hutslar)

LIPS, JOSEPH San Antonio, Texas, 1896d.

LIPSCOMB Greenbush, Michigan, 1860d.

LIPSCOMB, CHRISTOPHER Jerseyville, Illinois, 1864d-1884d.

LIPSCOMB, G.W. Jerseyville, Illinois, 1867d.

LISLE, HENRY Hunter, Ohio, 1857d. (Hutslar)

LISLE, MYRON C. Grand Rapids, Michigan. Patents #529,037 November 13, 1894, magazine gun, #536,960 April 2, 1895, magazine gun, #609,445 August 23, 1898, magazine gun, and #695,819 March 19, 1902, breechloading firearm. Moved to Toronto, Canada in 1905 and had patents in several gun areas.

LISTON, PERRY (1798-1882), Otway, Ohio, 1822-1882. (MB 5-46)

LITCHFIELD, ALEXANDER H. South Bend, Indiana, 1867d.

LITCHFIELD, EDWARD (1823-?), Lorain Co., Ohio, 1850c. (Hutslar)

LITCHFIELD, JAMES Grand Marsh, Wisconsin, 1867d.

LITHGOW, WILLIAM Thomaston, Maine, 1739-1740, Brunswick, Maine, 1742, Ft. Halifax, Maine, 1754. (Demeritt)

LITTIG, PETER see Peter Lydick.

LITTLE & PINKHAM see Charles T. Little.

LITTLE GIANT suicide special by Bacon.

LITTLE INJUN .22 cal. suicide special by Iver Johnson.

LITTLE JOHN suicide special by Hood Fire Arms Co.

LITTLE JOKER suicide special. (Webster)

LITTLE PAL trade name of L.E. Polhemus on knife pistol.

LITTLE PET suicide special. (Webster)

LITTLE, CHARLES T. (1805-1888), Providence, Rhode Island, 1828-1885d. Flintlock musket. As Pope & Little, 1836-1841 and 1860-1866, Little & Pinkham, 1841-1847, and C.T. Little & Co., 1866-1872. With Charles F. Pope, 1836-1841 and 1866-1872. With William R. Pope, 1836-1841 and 1860-1866. (Achtermier)

LITTLE, DANIEL Bellefonte, Pennsylvania, 1848, Pittsburgh, Pennsylvania, 1852-1860. Barrel maker, percussion 1/2 stock and fullstock target. With James as J. & D. Little.

LITTLE, J. & D. Pittsburgh, Pennsylvania, 1852-1860. Percussion fullstock target, barrels. James and Daniel Little. (MB 12-49)

LITTLE, JAMES (1809-?), Bellefonte, Pennsylvania, 1830-1834. Underhammer guns. (Kauffman)).

LITTLE, JAMES Columbus, Ohio, 1843-1845. For C. Jacobs. (Hutslar)

LITTLE, JAMES Pittsburgh, Pennsylvania, 1850-1860. Barrelmaker, with J. & D. Little. (Kauffman)

LITTLE, JOHN R. Colebrook, New Hampshire, 1876-1879.

LITTLE, WILLIAM Snyder Co., Pennsylvania, 1850. (Whisker III)

LITTLEFIELD, JOHN B. Lewiston, Maine, 1873-1892. (Demeritt)

LITTLER, JACOB unlocated, 1792-1793. Model 1792 contract rifles. (Moller)

LIVCY, CHARLES ROBERT (1820-1882), Healdsburg, California, 1866-1882. (Shelton)

LIVEGOOD, JACOB Lock Haven, Pennsylvania, 1855-1856. (Kauffman)

LIVERMORE, E.K. Ithaca, New York. Percussion 1/2 stock.

LIVERMORE, W.R. U.S. Army. Patent #221,079 October 28, 1879, magazine gun.

LIVESAY, MOSES (1829-1895). Jackson, Ohio, 1850-1895. Percussion rifles. (MB 6- 41)

LIVEZEY, EZRA (1812-1901), Morgan Co., Ohio. Percussion 1/2 stocks, dated 1877. (Hutslar)

LIVINGSTON, A.U. Quincy, Ohio, 1860-1864, Sidney, Ohio, 1866d-1867d. (Hutslar)

LIVINGSTON, A.W. Stuart, Iowa, 1884d-1897d.

LIVINGSTON, ANDREW W. San Francisco, California. Patent #477,976 June 28, 1892, firearm.

LIVINGSTON, FRANK Marathon, New York, 1865-1882. Percussion target rifles.

LIVINGSTON, HENRY Chicago, Illinois, 1880d. Dealer.

LIVINGSTON, JOHN Walpole, New Hampshire, 1796-1803. Model 1798 contract muskets with Gurdon Huntington, Josiah Bellows, and David Stone. (Gluckman & Satterlee)

LIVINGSTON, JOSEPH W. Syracuse, New York, 1877-1882d. Patents #198,669 and #198,670 December 25, 1877, lock with John A. Nichols and #227,907 May 25, 1880, breechloading firearm.

LIVINGSTON, T.E. West Plains, Missouri, 1893d-1898d.

LJUNGLOF, FREDERICK Smith's Flat, California, 1893d.

LLEWELLYN, MATTHEW Lancaster, Pennsylvania, 1792-1802. Model 1801 contract muskets for Pennsylvania with Jacob Dickert. (Gluckman, Dyke)

LLOCOMB, H. Worcester, Massachusetts. Flintlock Kentucy. See Hardin Slocomb.

LLOYD, JAMES Minersville, Pennsylvania, 1850c.

LLOYD, JOHN Madison, Indiana, 1868-1880. Percussion 1/2 stock. (Lindert)

LLOYD, WILLIAM Middleburg, Pennsylvania. Percussion fullstock rifles.

LOADER, WILLIAM (?-1946), Newcomerstown, Ohio, 1890-1946. Percussion 1/2 stock. (Hutslar)

LOAR, BENJAMIN B. (1822-?), Granville, Ohio, 1850-1864d. Percussion 1/2 stock. (Hutslar)

LOCHMEYER & BRO. Memphis, Tennessee, 1867-1876d.

LOCK, JAMES (1790-1870), Wellsboro, Pennsylvania, 1822-1861d. Percussion 1/2 and fullstock rifles, marked "J.L.". Patent #none April 6, 1834, lock cover. Also known as James Locke.

LOCK, JOHN (1815-?), Williamsburg, Ohio, 1850c. (Hutslar)

LOCKE, DANIEL Geneva, Wisconsin, 1857d.

LOCKE, H. unlocated. Flintlock Kentucky.

LOCKE, J.D. New York, New York, 1860. Agent for North & Couch pistol.

LOCKE, JAMES see James Lock.

LOCKWOOD, JOHN Eaton, Ohio. Lock maker.

LOCKWOOD, THOMAS J. Muncie, Indiana. Patents #468,002 February 12, 1892, lock, #468,003 February 12, 1892, lock, and #468,004, February 12, 1892, lock.

LODER Lancaster, Pennsylvania, 1770. Kentucky rifle. (Dillin)

LODETTI, FRANK EMILIUS Rondout, New York. Patent #545,512 September 3, 1895, magazine gun.

LODGE BROS. Columbia, Co., Pennsylvania, 1810-1830. Flintlock Kentucky. (Dillin)

LODGE, B.F. Idaho City, Idaho, 1889d-1891d.

LODGE, J.J. Junction City, Kansas, 1878d-1894d.

LODGE, JONATHAN Columbia Co., Pennsylvania, 1810. (Dillin)

LODGE, JOSEPH Exchange, Pennsylvania, 1860c-1861d. Percussion fullstock double rifle.

LODY, J. unlocated. Percussion 1/2 stock.

LOECHNER, B. Gilroy, California, 1871-1873. (Shelton)

LOESCH, JACOB (1722-1821), Christian Springs, Pennsylvania, 1780, Salem, North Carolina, 1781-1821. (Bivins, Kauffman)

LOEWEN BROS. Columbus, Kansas, 1884d.

LOGAN & KENNEDY Pittsburgh, Pennsylvania, 1831d-1847d. Lockmakers only.

LOGAN, ALEXANDER Warren Co., Missouri, 1850c. (MB 11-66)

LOGAN, G.S. unlocated. Percussion fullstock.

LOGAN, NEILL (1821-?), Stark Co., Ohio, 1850c. (Hutslar)

LOHNER, C. Philadelphia, Pennsylvania, Derringer.

LOHNES, ABRAHAM S. Lawrence, Massachusetts, 1874d.

LOLLIGER, JOHN Washington, D.C., 1858d. (Hartzler)

LOMBARD, H.C., & CO. Springfield, Massachusetts, 1859-1861. Cartridges and cartridge pistol.

LOMBARDI, SALVATORE New Haven, Connecticut, 1905d.

LONDON PISTOL CO. trade name of Manhattan Fire Arms Co. on percussion revolvers

LONDON unlocated. Flintlock Kentucky.

LONDON, BYRON Butler, Missouri, 1889d-1891d.

LONDON, C.M. Gober, Texas, 1884d-1896d.

LONE STAR suicide special.

LONEY, FRANCIS B. (1823-?), Baltimore, Maryland, 1860d-1872d. As Schaeffer & Loney, 1860, and F.B. Loney & Co., 1868-1872. (Hartzler)

LONG RANGE WONDER trade name of Sears, Roebuck & Co. on shotguns. (Hinman)

LONG TOM trade name of Sears, Roebuck & Co. on single barrel shotguns. (Hinman)

LONG, A., & SONS Davidson Co., North Carolina. Flintlock Kentucky rifle. Andrew Long and sons Felix and Solomon.

LONG, ANDREW (1793-?), Davidson Co., North Carolina, Forsythe Co., North Carolina, 1850c. (Bivins)

LONG, ARCHIBALD A. (1847-?), Staunton, Virginia, 1870c.

LONG, BARNHART Wooster, Ohio, 1878d. (Hutslar)

LONG, BENJAMIN Boulder, Colorado. Patents #370,344 September 20, 1887, sight, #410,422 September 3, 1889, sight, and #448,057 March 10, 1891, cartridge. (Sellers-3)

LONG, DANIEL Brookville, Pennsylvania, 1887d. (Whisker II)

LONG, FELIX (1811-?), Davidson Co., North Carolina, 1850c. With his brother Solomon and father Andrew as A. Long & Sons. (Bivins)

LONG, GEORGE P. (1821-1915), New Berlin, Pennsylvania, 1887d-1890d. (Chandler 2)

LONG, GEORGE P. Beaver Springs, Pennsylvania, percussion rifles. (Gabel)

LONG, J. Newport, Kentucky, 1866d.

LONG, J.E., & CO. Detroit, Michigan, 1877-1879. John E. Long.

LONG, J.S. Murphysborough, Illinois, 1890d.

LONG, JACOB (1808-?), Snyder Co., Pennsylvania, 1825, Westmoreland Co., Pennsylvania, 1835-1867. (Whisker II)

LONG, JAMES (1825-1887), Beaver Springs, Pennsylvania. Kentucky rifle. Son of Joseph Long. (Dillin, Chandler 2)

LONG, JESSE Beavertown, Pennsylvania. Percussion Kentucky rifles. (Gabel)

LONG, JOHN E. Detroit, Michigan, 1867-1879d. With Elam J. Fisher as Fisher & Long, 1867-1872. As J.E. Long & Co., 1877-1879.

LONG, JOHN F. Providence Rhode Island. Patent #175,613 April 4, 1876, butt plate.

LONG, JOHN (1815-?), Deerfield, Ohio, 1850c-1853d. (Hutslar)

LONG, JOHN York Co., Pennsylvania. Flintlock Kentucky. (Kindig)

LONG, JOSEPH (1799-1872), Beaver Creek, Pennsylvania, 1820-1872. Prolific maker of percussion rifles, inlays. (Kauffman)

LONG, MALCOLM W. (1834-1912), Bangor, Maine, 1855-1871, Augusta, Maine, 1871-1879, Harrisburg, Pennsylvania, 1880-1912. Hug type breechloading rifle. As Grover & Long, 1871-1875. (Demeritt)

LONG, PETER Turners, New York. Patent #429,631 June 10, 1890, stock.

LONG, PETER Westmoreland Co., Pennsylvania. Kentucky rifle.

LONG, RALPH Union Co., Pennsylvania, 1850c. (Kauffman)

LONG, ROBERT Fredericksburg, Virginia, 1877d.

LONG, ROBERT Kansas City, Missouri, 1859d-1870d.

LONG, S.S. Newmanstown, Pennsylvania, 1882d.

LONG, SOLOMON (1814-?), Davidson Co., North Carolina, 1850c. With his brother Felix and father Andrew as A. Long & Sons. (Bivins)

LONG, STOFIL Lehigh Co., Pennsylvania, 1810-1819. Flintlock Kentucky.

LONG, T.J. Howard Co., Indiana, 1842- ?. (Lindert)

LONG, W.T. Willis, Texas, 1896d.

LONG, WILLIAM H. Beaver Springs, Pennsylvania. Percussion Kentucky rifles. Same as William H. Long, Lewistown Pennsylvania? (Gabel)

LONG, WILLIAM H. Lewistown, Pennsylvania, 1870c. Same as William H. Long, Beaver Springs, Pennsylvania?

LONG, WILLIAM J. (1858-1948), Thornville, Ohio. Percussion rifles.

LONG, WILLIAM Augusta, Maine. Underhammer pistol. (Logan)

LONG, WILLIAM Millroy, Pennsylvania. (Dillin)

LONGANECKER, H.C. Kahoka, Missouri, 1889d-1891d. Possibly John F. Longanecker in 1881?

LONGANECKER, JOHN F. unlocated. Eureka Gun Works, 1881. Possibly H.C. Longanecker?

LONGDEN, W.H. Bridgeport, Connecticut, 1885d-1899d. As Longden Bros., 1885-?.

LONGER, JOHN Milton, Pennsylvania, 1833-1838. (Kauffman)

LONGSDORF, G. unlocated. Percussion fullstock.

LONGSTREET & COOK Philadelphia, Pennsylvania. Flintlock lock makers. Probably Longstreth & Cook.

LOOES, LOUIS Jersey City, New Jersey, 1878d.

LOOMIS, A. Hubbardsville, New York. Percussion 1/2 stock.

LOOMIS, A.W. Lebanon, Connecticut. Underhammer pistol. (Logan)

LOOMIS, ALONZO H. East Hamilton, New York, 1870d.

LOOMIS, B.G. Carson City, Michigan, 1891d.

LOOMIS, BENJAMIN T. New York, New York. Patent #52,582 February 13, 1866, revolver.

LOOMIS, C.E. Pioneer, Ohio, 1872d-1878d, Sparta Centre, Michigan, 1879d-1883d.

LOOMIS, E. Mt. Morris, New York, 1870d.

LOOMIS, EARL (?-1870), South Hamilton, New York, Golchester, New York, 1823-1860, Hubbardsville, New York, 1860c. Flint and percussion fullstock rifles. (Swinney)

LOOMIS, F.A. unlocated. Top-break double shotgun.

LOOMIS, J.D., & CO. unlocated. Percussion fullstock. (Hutslar)

LOOMIS, W.L. McPherson, Kansas, 1882d.

LOOMIS, WEBNER E. Springfield, Illinois. Patent #477,666 June 28, 1892, magazine gun.

LOOMMIRS, E. (1824-?), Sacramento, California, 1852c. (Shelton)

LOOS, F. Albany, New York. Percussion 1/2 stock. (Swinney)

LOOS, FREDERICK Cedar Falls, Iowa, 1880d-1884d.

LOPEX, DINZ (1825-?), Monterey, California, 1850c. (Shelton)

LOPEZ, A.E. St. Augustine, Florida, 1883d-1886d.

LORD, EDMOND B. Provincetown, Massachusetts, 1856-1861.

LORD, HORACE Hartford, Connecticut. Patents #73,351 January 14, 1868, extractor, #74,387 February 11, 1868, breechloading firearm, and #303,172 August 5, 1884, revolver. Worked for Colt.

LORD, J. Orwigsburg, Pennsylvania, 1838-1855. Kentucky and fullstock percussion rifles. (Dillin)

LORD, JAMES Minersville, Pennsylvania, 1850-1866d. Patent #28,677 June 12, 1860, firearm. Percussion swivel breech rifle.

LORD, JAMES Tamaqua, Pennsylvania, 1887d-1890d.

LORD, JOSEPH NATHAN (1852-1890), Santa Barbara, California, 1875-1890. (Shelton)

LORD, SAMUEL (1810-?), Harrison Co., Indiana, 1850c. (Lindert)

LOREN, FRANCIS M. Texarkana, Arkansas, 1898d.

LORING, JAMES Gales Creek Oregon, 1891d.

LORNEY, M. Boalsburg, Pennsylvania. Flintlock Kentucky. (Dillin)

LOSEY & LULL Caroline, New York, 1850c, Brooktondale, New York. Percussion shotgun and 1/2 stock. B. Losey and J.B. Lull.

LOSEY see Jackson & Losey.

LOSEY, B. Caroline, New York. Percussion three-barrel rifle/shotgun. Also percussion slug gun marked "B. LOSEY & W. N. HOWE".

LOSEY, J. & B. Caroline, New York, 1850c-1864d. Barrelmakers, 1864. As Losey & Lull in 1850 census.

LOSTY, JOHN Hartford, Connecticut, 1880d.

LOTZ, PETER Lancaster, Pennsylvania, 1857d-1863d.

LOUD & FARRINGTON Sanford, Florida, 1884d. Percussion lock marked "L & F/Sanford".

LOUDENSLAGER, H. unlocated. Flintlock Kentucky rifle.

LOUDENSLAGER, JACOB (1829-?), Suffield, Ohio, 1850c. Son of John Loudenslager. (Hutslar)

LOUDENSLAGER, JOHN (1803-?), Suffield, Ohio, 1850c-1853d. (Hutslar)

LOUDENSLAGER, SAMUEL Mexico, Pennsylvania, 1861d.

LOUDENSLAGER, SIMON Mexico, Pennsylvania. Flintlock and percussion fullstock.

LOUGHMAN, JOHN N. Licking Co., Ohio, 1850-1920. Percussion 1/2 stock marked "J.N.L.".

LOUIS, C. Ogdensburg, New York, 1870d-1882d.

LOUIS, VICTOR Shreveport, Louisiana, 1885d.

LOURIE, JOHN (1825-?), Kewanee, Illinois, 1850c-1860c. (Johnson)

LOUTHER, A. Kewanee, Illinois, 1860d.

LOUTZENHEISER, JOHN JACOB (1771-1810), Lewisville, Ohio, 1806-1810. Flintlock Kentucky. (Hutslar)

LOVE & TAYLOR Augusta, Maine, 1874. Robert C. Love and John Taylor. (Demeritt)

LOVE, L.B. Middletown, Missouri, 1854d.

LOVE, ROBERT C. Augusta, Maine, 1873-1876. With John Taylor as Love & Taylor, 1874. (Demeritt)

LOVEGROVE, THOMAS J. New Egypt, New York. Patent #441,676 December 2, 1890, firearm.

LOVEJOY, G.W. Menominee, Michigan, 1887d.

LOVELACE, DANIEL Argyle, Wisconsin, 1879d-1886d.

LOVELACE, P.L. Centerville, Tennessee, 1860d.

LOVELL & GROVER 1841-1846. See Grover & Lovell.

LOVELL & LATIMORE Savannah, Georgia, 1860d.

LOVELL, EDWARD (1816-1888), Savannah, Georgia, 1835-1860d. Percussion double shotgun. As Lovell & Latimore, 1860. Brother of J.P. Lovell.

LOVELL, JAMES Philadelphia, Pennsylvania, 1819d.

LOVELL, JOHN P., CO. South Portland, Maine, 1894-1904. Single barrel shotguns. Branch operation of John P. Lovell Arms Co., Boston, Massachusetts. (Demeritt)

LOVELL, JOHN PRINCE (1820-1897). Boston, Massachusetts, 1840-1897. Revolvers, rifles, and shotguns. As Grover & Lovell, 1841-1846, with Loenard Grover; Fairbanks & Lovell, 1848-1850, with Aaron B. Fairbanks; J.P. Lovell & Sons, 1868-1890; and John P. Lovell Arms Co., 1890-1897.

LOVETT, ISAAC (1832-?), Jamestown, North Carolina. Apprenticed in 1848. (Bivins)

LOVEWELL, SEWELL K. Gardner, Massachusetts. Patent #16,846 March 17, 1857, firearms.

LOW, WILLIAM (1827-?), Lone Pine, California, 1871-1872.

LOWE, JAMES A. New York, New York. Patent #22,881 February 8, 1859, lock.

LOWE, WILLIAM V. Fitchburg, Winchester, and Woburn, Massachusetts, 1875-1897.

LOWE, WILLIAM Ovid, New York. Model 1814 contract rifles marked "S.N.Y." on lock.

LOWELL ARMS CO. Lowell, Massachusetts, 1864-1868. Rollin White revolvers under contract to Smith & Wesson. (Jinks)

LOWELL, N. Danville, New Hampshire, 1868-1873.

LOWENBERG, EMIL Helena, Montana, 1880d.

LOWENSTEIN & SON Whitehall, Illinois, 1884d.

LOWER, JOHN P. (1833-1915), Denver, Colorado, 1868-1915. Retailer only. Apprenticed to J.C. Grubb & Co., August 1850. Moved to Denver in 1868 and then brought his family there in 1872. (Sellers-3, Antique Firearms, August 1911 Issue, pg. 16)

LOWER, JOSEPH NORRIS Denver, Colorado. Patent #535,384 March 12, 1895, cartridge. Son of John P. Lower. (Sellers-3)

LOWERY, DAVID Wethersfield, Connecticut, 1774-1777. Committee of Safety muskets. Also known as D. Lavery. (Gluckman & Satterlee)

LOWERY, J.M. unlocated. Percussion swivel breech.

LOWERY, JAMES B. Mayville, New York. Patent #none September 10, 1827, percussion lock and magazine.

LOWERY, M.T. New Point, Missouri, 1879d.

LOWMASTER, JOHN York, Pennsylvania, 1805, Fairfield Co., Ohio, 1816-1830c. (Kindig-Hutslar)

LOWNDES, EDWARD Greeley, Colorado, 1872-1879d. (Sellers-3)

LOWNES, ORGILL & CO. Memphis, Tennessee, 1858-1865d. Successors to Holyoake, Lownes & Co., Dealers.

LOWRY, NIMROD C. Pine Bluff, Arkansas, 1850. (Elias)

LOWRY, THOMAS Edinburg, Ohio, 1860d-1864d. (Hutslar)

LOWRY, THOMAS Lancaster, Missouri, 1860d.

LOWTHER, ELIAS Wirt Co., West Virginia, 1825-?. Born in West Milford, Ritchie Co., West Virginia.

LOYD, ISAAC Lewisberry, Pennsylvania, 1836. With Webster Lewis.

LUCAN Bellefonte, Pennsylvania, 1840. (Dillin)

LUCAS, A.S. Barnes' Corner, New York, 1872d-1880d. Percussion fullstock rifle.

LUCAS, J.B. Portland, Maine, 1870-1872. (Demeritt)

LUCAS, JOHN (1793-?), Cleveland Co., North Carolina, 1850c. (Bivins)

LUCE, GEORGE D. New Orleans, Louisiana, Tallahassee, Florida. Patents #136,660 March 11, 1873, magazine gun, and #156,431 November 3, 1874, magazine gun.

LUCHSINGER, FREDERICK Louisville, Kentucky.

LUCHTENMEYER, GEORGE Blue Island, Illinois, 1864d. See F. Lichtenmeyer.

LUCHY, EDWARD (1821-?), New Orleans, Louisiana, 1850c. (MB 9-65)

LUCY, D.E. Houlton, Maine, 1868-1879. Underhammer guns. (Demeritt)

LUDEKE, FRANCIS JOSEPH (1830-?), Georgetown, D.C., 1860c-1875d. (Hartzler)

LUDINGTON Lancaster, Pennsylvania, 1775. Flintlock rifles.

LUDKIN, WILLIAM Hingham, Massachusetts, 1635. (Dean*)

LUDLUM, JAMES M. New York, New York. Patent #none August 3, 1813, shot manufacture.

LUDRODA unlocated. Flintlock Kentucky rifle.

LUDUC, THEODORE New Orleans, Louisiana, 1853d.

LUDWICK, JOHN Pennsylvania, 1776. Committee of Safety repairs.

LUDWIG, ADOLPH Wausau, Wisconsin, 1884d-1886d.

LUDWIG, PAUL (?-1846), Allentown, Pennsylvania. Kentucky rifle. (Dyke)

LUERSSEN, HENRY Shiner, Texas, 1896d.

LUHNER, JOHN unlocated. Flintlock Kentucky.

LUKE, J.R. McDonald, Georgia, 1881d-1883d.

LUKENS, ISAIAH (?-1846), Philadelphia, Pennsylvania, 1790-1846. Air gun. (ASAC 35)

LULL & THOMAS Ilion, New York, 1850-1865. Percussion 1/2 stock, Gibbs carbines and shotguns, double rifles/shotguns.

LULL, CHARLES Rochester, New York, 1834d. (Eich)

LULL, J.B. Caroline, New York, 1848-1874. As Losey & Lull in 1850 census.

LULL, M.D. & A.G. Woodstock, Vermont, 1846-1849. Underhammer rifle.

LULL, ORRIN D. Watkins, New York. Patents #38,903 June 16, 1863, breechloading firearm, and #40,761 December 1, 1863, bullets.

LULL, TURNER & CO. Woodstock, Vermont. Underhammer guns. (Horn)

LULLMAN & VIENNA Memphis, Tennessee, 1865-1876d. Agents for Deringer. A.J. Vienna, Memphis, Tennessee, 1873d-1891d.

LUMAS, L. Philadelphia, Pennsylvania, 1816d.

LUMBARD, JOSEPH Springfield, Massachusetts, 1808. Pistol barrels at Springfield Armory.

LUND, E.H. Chipewa(?) Falls, (state?), 1879d.

LUNDBURGH, OLOF Osceola Mills, Wisconsin, 1857d.

LUNDEE, PETER River Vale, Indiana, 1860d.

LUNDGREN, JOHN W. Duluth, Minnesota. Patent #548,075 October 15, 1895, breechloading firearm with M.Z. Viau.

LUNDT, C.J. Malcom, Iowa, 1892d-1897d.

LUNDY BROS. Gosport, Indiana, 1862d.

LUNDY, DANIEL (1798-?), Martin Co., Indiana, 1850c. (Lindert)

LUNDY, H.E.M. Humboldt, Kansas, 1882d-1894d.

LUNDY, ISAAC, SR. (1780-?), Owen Co., Indiana, 1850c. (Lindert)

LUNDY, JAMES Linton, Indiana, 1862d, Switz City, Indiana, 1882-1885.

LUNDY, L. unlocated. Percussion fullstock.

LUNDY, PORTER B. (1833-?), Owen Co., Indiana, 1850c, Gosport, Indiana. (Lindert)

LUNDY, STOCKTON (1809-?), Mt. Tabor, Indiana, 1850c. (Lindert)

LUNDY, WILLIAM Gosport, Indiana, 1850. (Lindert)

LUNSMANN, FRANCIS (1820-?), St. Louis, Missouri, 1847-1870d. Percussion fullstock. (Lewis)

LUPUS, A. Dover, New Hampshire, 1867d. Percussion revolver and 1/2 stock.

LURCH, DAVID New York, New York, 1863d-1890d. Brother of Joseph Lurch. Percussion and air guns. (GR 12-57)

LURCH, JOSEPH New York, New York, 1868-1890d. Percussion 1/2 stock rifles and air guns, brother of David. (GR 12-57)

LUSCH, ANTON Ferdinand, Indiana, 1882-1885. (Lindert)

LUSK, FRANK B. Chicago, Illinois, 1874d-1886d.

LUTES, WILLIAM Bullitt Co., Kentucky, 1825, Mercer Co., Missouri, 1850c. (MB 11-66)

LUTHER, JAMES Hurricane, Illinois, 1860d.

LUTHER, JOHN Worcester, Massachusetts(?). Rifle and musket barrels. With Fredrick Allen and Andrew J. Brown as Allen, Brown & Luther, Worcester, Massachusetts, 1848-1858.

LUTNES, OLAUS West Superior, Wisconsin, 1895d.

LUTZ, C. & S. Reamstown, Pennsylvania. Barrelmakers. (MB 4-63)

LUTZ, D. St. Louis, Missouri. Percussion 1/2 stock, air gun. (Pourie)

LUTZ, DANIEL Z. Reinholdsville, Pennsylvania, 1861d. Barrelmaker.

LUTZ, GEORGE (1836-?), Lancaster, Ohio, 1883-1898. (Hutslar)

LUTZ, GEORGE Lancaster, Pennsylvania, 1842t-1850c.

LUTZ, JESSE Reinholdsville, Pennsylvania, 1850c-1861d. Barrelmaker.

LUTZ, JOHN Waterloo, Illinois, 1893d.

LYBARGER, EDWIN B. Granger, Ohio, circa 1900. Percussion 1/2 stock. (Hutslar)

LYCETT, JOHN Mt. Holly, New Jersey, 1860d.

LYDENDECKER, GEORGE Northampton Co., Pennsylvania, 1770t. See George Laydendecker, same person? (Dyke)

LYDICK, PETER Baltimore, Maryland, 1776-1810. Committee of Safety muskets and flintlock Kentucky rifles. Also known as Peter Littig. (Hartzler)

LYKES, JOHN W. Green Co., North Carolina, 1850c. (Bivins)

LYLE, WILLIAM (?-1782), Rockbridge Co., Virginia. (Gill)

LYMAN GUN SIGHT CORP. Middlefield, Connecticut, 1878-date. William Lyman (?-1898).

LYMAN, AZEL S. New York, New York, 1856-1885. Patents #16,568 February 3, 1857, accelerating gun, #200,740 February 26, 1878, accelerating gun, #321,043 June 30, 1885, gunnery, #321,042 June 30, 1885, cartridge, and #321,374 June 30, 1885, cartridge. Percussion single shot rifle with multiple charges for a higher projectile velocity. (GR 10-69)

LYMAN, WILLIAM (?-1898), Middlefield, Connecticut. Patents #211,753 January 28, 1879, sight, #298,305 May 6, 1884, sight, #327,957 October 6, 1885, sight, #341,426 May 4, 1886, sight, #348,224 August 31, 1886, sight, #366,121 July 5, 1887, sight, #368,598 August 23, 1887, sight, #396,043 January 8, 1889, sight, #447,886 March 10, 1891, sight, #455,911 September 22, 1891, sight, #541,558 June 25, 1895, sight, #558,402 April 14, 1896, sight, #558,403 April 14, 1896, sight, #3629,670 July 25, 1899, sight, and #629,671, July 25, 1899, sight. As Lyman Gun Sight Corp., Middlefield, Connecticut, 1878-date.

LYNCH, WILLIAM Salt Lake City, Utah, 1878d.

LYNE, JOHN Lancaster Co., Pennsylvania, 1751-1806. (KRA IV-4)

LYNE, WILLIAM Belleville, Ohio, 1860d-1866. (Hutslar)

LYON & BOYD Chadron, Nebraska, 1886d-1893d.

LYON & TROCH Watertown, Dakota Territory, 1886d. J.H. Troch, Watertown, Dakota Territory, 1886d-1889d, and Watertown, South Dakota, 1889d-1898d.

LYON, H.A. Sioux City, Iowa, 1877d-1887d. Percussion 1/2 stock.

LYON, JAMES (1833-?), Richmond, Virginia, 1850c. (MB 10-63)

LYON, WARREN (1789-1824), Providence, Rhode Island, 1824. (Achtermier)

LYONS unidentified. Percussion 1/2 stock.

M SECTION

M & B see Merwin & Bray.

M (in shield) Enfield pattern muskets, manufacturer uncertain, attributed to Blunt, Moore, McElwaine & Co., or Murdock Morrison. (Hill-Anthony)

M * L see Morrison & Long.

M.A. unidentified. Flintlock Kentucky.

M.B. unidentified. Percussion over/under rifle/shotgun.

M.D. see Milton Defibaugh.

M.F.A. Co. see Marlin Firearms Co.

M.G. see Matthew Gillespie.

M.H. unidentified. Percussion fullstock.

M.J. & G. see Mendenhall, Jones & Gardner.

M.M. unidentified. Flintlock Kentucky

M.R. unidentified. Converted Kentucky.

M.S. unidentified. Flintlock Kentucky.

M'CLALLAN, H. see H. McClallen.

MABERRY, JOHN (1818-?), Wilkes Co., North Carolina. Apprenticed 1822. (Bivins)

MABEY, T. Halcott Center, New York, 1869-1882d.

MAC FARLANE SONS New York, New York, 1872d-1890d. Percussion and cartridge guns.

MAC FARLANE, ANDREW New York, New York, 1844-1870d.

MACAULEY, D.H. Kalispell, Montana, 1898d.

MACHERDANE, GEORGE Covington, Kentucky, 1899d.

MACHTER, JOHN Glasgow, Missouri, 1860d.

MACK & MUNGER Dubuque, Iowa, 1860d-1868d. Jacob Mack and Luman Munger.

MACK, A. Rockville, Ohio, 1860-1864. (Hutslar)

MACK, JACOB F. Dubuque, Iowa, 1850c-1868d. With Luman Mack as Mack & Munger 1860-1868.

MACKENZIE, DUNCAN Philadelphia, Pennsylvania, 1731. (Lindsay 3)

MACKERAL, M. Shirland, Illinois, 1860d.

MACKLEM, J.B. Reinersville, Ohio, 1878-1888d. (Hutslar)

MACKLIN, J.B. see Macklem.

MACON ARMORY Macon, Georgia, 1862. Confederate arms manufacturer. (Albaugh 1)

MACY, GEORGE W. (1820-?), Guilford Co., North Carolina, 1850c. (Bivins)

MADDOX, G.W. Greenville, Texas, 1892d.

MADISON, EDWARD H. Brooklyn, New York, 1870d-1877d.

MAEDEL, ADOLPH (1807-?), Washington, D.C., 1860-1863d. (Hartzel)

MAEDEL, CHARLES B. (1825-?), Washington, D.C., 1860c-1863d. (Hartzler)

MAENDER, HENRY O. Memphis, Tennessee, 1881d-1887d.

MAENDER, W.F. Cincinnati, Ohio, 1886d.

MAER, WILLIAM Wooster, Ohio. (MB 11-60)

MAFIES, ABNER (1820-?), Cincinnati, Ohio, 1850c. (Hutslar)

MAGAHAN, ABRAHAM (1816-1870), Marklesburg, Pennsylvania, 1850c-1870. Percussion fullstock. (Whisker II)

MAGERS, LEVI Baltimore, Maryland. Patent #1,905 November 13, 1840, shot.

MAGILL unlocated. Percussion fullstock.

MAGINNIS, JOHN New Orleans, Louisiana, 1866d. Importer.

MAGNIEN, GEORGE Springfield, Missouri, 1898d.

MAGNOT, EDMOND unlocated. Percussion 1/2 stock.

MAGRUM, DAVID Philadelphia, Pennsylvania, 1824d. Also known as David Margrum?

MAHER & GROSH Toledo, Ohio. Retailers of suicide special made by Hood.

MAHER, EDMUND New York, New York. Patents #33,813 November 26, 1861, repeating firearm with William McCord, and #35,167 May 6, 1862, repeating firearm.

MAHLA, PHILIP Pittsburgh, Pennsylvania, 1856-1857. (Kauffman)

MAHLER, CAROLINE Port Clinton, Ohio, 1896d. (Hutslar)

MAHLINGER, LOUIS Galesburg, Illinois, 1864d-1868d.

MAHUN, J.H. Sheboygan, Wisconsin, 1857d. See John W. Mumm.

MAIER, CHARLES M. New Orleans, Louisiana, 1884d-1899d.

MAINE, GEORGE Perry, Pennsylvania, 1850c. (Kauffman)

MAIZE, HENRY B. (1806-?). Uniontown, Ohio, 1828-1863, Mansfield, Ohio, 1850c. Uniontown became Ashland. (Hutslar)

MAIZE, HENRY B., JR. (1834-?), Mansfield, Ohio, 1850c. (Hutslar)

MAJORS, RUSSELL & CO. St. Joseph, Missouri. Percussion double shotgun. Outfitters, later became the Pony Express.

MAKENZIE, DUNCAN Philadelphia, Pennsylvania, 1731- (Kauffman)

MALAMF, EZRA (1831-?), Allen Co., Indiana, 1860c. (Lindert)

MALCOLM & CRAIG Syracuse, New York, 1862-1864d.

MALCOLM, JOHN Philadelphia, Pennsylvania, 1776. Committee of Safety muskets. (Gluckman & Satterlee)

MALCOLM, WILLIAM (?-1913), Auburn, New York, 1855-1860, Syracuse, New York, 1862-1885. Percussion rifles. As Malcolm Telescope Co., 1862-1941. (AR 1-71)

MALETZ, CHARLES (1822-?), New Orleans, Louisiana, 1850c-1853d. (MB 9-65)

MALITZ, C.F. Victoria, Texas, 1896d.

MALLION & JUDD Ypsilanti, Michigan, 1887d. William Mallion and W.H. Judd.

MALLION, WILLIAM Ypsilanti, Michigan, 1883d-1887d. With W.H. Judd as Mallion & Judd, 1887.

MALLISON, JACOB Allegheny Co. Pennsylvania, 1800c. (Kauffman)

MALLONEE, EZRA Ovid, Michigan 1875d-1883d.

MALLORY, SAMUEL S. Rochester, New York, 1827d. For Ephraim Gilbert. (Eich)

MALLORY, WILLIAM G. (1850-?), Ruby City, Colorado, 1880c.

MALMGREN, CHARLES O. Chicago, Illinois, 1875d.

MALONE, D. Ovid, Michigan. Percussion double rifle.

MALONE, EZRA Decatur, Indiana, 1881-1885. (Gardner)

MALONE, MICHAEL New Orleans, Louisiana, 1860d-1898d. As Malone & Son, 1894-1898.

MALONE, T.C. Palmyra, Illinois, 1860d.

MALONEY, JAMES A. Providence, Rhode Island, 1868-1870d. (GR 9-72)

MALONEY, JAMES A. Washington, D.C. Patent #271,645 February 6, 1883, extractor.

MALSON, THOMAS Boston, Massachusetts, 1630. (Dean*)

MALTBY, CURTIS New York, New York. Patents #202,627 April 23, 1878, revolvers, #283,854 August 28, 1883, revolvers, and #294,188 Februrary 26, 1884, revolvers.

MALTBY, CURTIS, & CO. New York, New York, 1873-1887. Sales organization for low cost revolvers made by others. (AR 5-75)

MALTBY, HENLEY & CO. New York, New York, 1888-1893. Low cost revolvers. Successor to Curtis Maltby & Co.

MALTBY, JOSEPH ADALMON (1826-1867), Galena, Illinois, 1850c-1867. Jasper A. Maltby in some sources. (Johnson)

MANAHAN, JOHN F. Lowell, Massachusetts. Patent #436,062 September 9, 1890, safety.

MANGE, H. unlocated. Flintlock Kentucky.

MANGER, MICHAEL Honesdale, Pennsylvania, 1861d.

MANGOLD, SAMUEL New York, New York. Patent #197,042 November 13, 1877, alarm gun.

MANGUS, LEVI North Liberty, Indiana, 1860. Percussion 1/2 stock. (Lindert)

MANHART, THEODORE Hillsborough, Wisconsin, 1884d-1895d.

MANHATTAN ARMS CO. trade name of Schoverling, Daly & Gales on shotguns and revolvers.

MANHATTAN FIRE ARMS MFG. CO. New York, New York, 1855-1863, Newark, New Jersey, 1863-1868. Percussion and cartridge revolvers, "Hero" pistols. (Nutter)

MANLEY, DAVID Baltimore, Maryland, 1822d. (Hartzler)

MANLY, A. unlocated. Pre-Revolutionary War flintlock rifle.

MANLY, W.S. Reidsville, North Carolina. (Bivins)

MANN (1824-?), Brown Co., Indiana, 1860c. (Lindert)

MANN, ANDREW Griswold, Illinois, 1875d.

MANN, GEORGE Pittsburgh, Pennsylvania, 1826. (Kauffman)

MANN, H.F. La Porte, Indiana, 1861. Patent #31,985 February 24, 1861, breechloading cannon. (Lindert)

MANN, JACOB Coatesville, Indiana, 1860d-1862d.

MANN, JAMES (1838-?), Rectorville, Illinois, 1860c. (Johnson)

MANN, JOHN H. Syracuse, New York, 1848-1874. Percussion double rifle/shotgun.

MANN, L.W. Brown Co., Indiana, 1860c. Same as L.W. Mann, Ohio? (Lindert)

MANN, L.W. Napoleon, Ohio, 1859d. Same as L.W. Mann, Indiana? (Hutslar)

MANN, MOSES D. Buffalo, New York, 1817d-1820c.

MANN, TITUS L. Ottawa, Michigan, 1867d.

MANN, WILLIAM, JR. Juniata Co., Pennsylvania, 1835. (Whisker III)

MANNING & ANDERSON Boston, Massachusetts, 1744. (Dean)

MANNING, DANIEL J. Springfield, Massachusetts. Patent #584,698 June 15, 1897, revolver with John L. Murphy.

MANNING, FRANK El Paso, Texas, 1881. (El Paso Lone Star) (Gara)

MANNING, JACOB (?-1756), Salem, Massachusetts.

MANNING, NICHOLAS Salem, Massachusetts, 1763. (Dean)

MANNING, RICHARD Ipswich, Massachusetts, 1750.

MANNING, THOMAS Salem, Massachusetts, ?-1685, Ispwich, Massachusetts, 1685-1695. (Dean)

MANNON, R.W. Esper, Missouri, 1893d.

MANNY, POSTMAN Blairsville, Georgia. Percussion fullstock.

MANSAN, M. (1823-?), Shasta Co., California, 1852c. (Shelton)

MANSFIELD & LAMB Slatersville, Rhode Island, 1861-1865. Parts contractors. (Achtermier)

MANSON, W.C. Vienna, Ohio, 1883. Cased percussion 1/2 stock.

MANSUR, E. unlocated. Percussion underhammer rifle.

MANTLE, JOHN New Lebanon, New York, 1856-1859. (Gardner)

MANTON trade name of Eli Whitney on Model 1861 rifle muskets. (Fuller)

MANTON, J., & CO. trade name of H & D Folsom on imported shotguns. (AR 2-69)

MANVILLE, C.S. Atlantic, Iowa, 1892d.

MANVILLE, CYRUS New Haven, Connecticut, 1864-1867. Financial backer of J.P. Lindsay. (ASAC-1)

MANZ, GEORGE F. Wheeling, West Virginia, 1867, Bellaire, Ohio, 1878d. (MB 9-60, Hutslar)

MAPOTHER, D.H. Louisville, Kentucky. Patent #135,233 January 28, 1873, gun locks.

MARBARY, J.F. Murfreesboro, Tennessee, 1871d.

MARBLE ARMS & MFG. CO. Gladstone, Michigan, 1898-date. Mostly cutlery, but famous for the "Game-Getter" over/under combination gun. Walter L. Marble.

MARBLE, GEORGE W. Gainesville, Florida, 1886d-1895d.

MARBLE, LANSING Gladstone, Michigan. Patent #463,840 November 24, 1891, patched bullet.

MARBLE, SIMEON Sunderland, Vermont, 1840-1850. (Horn)

MARBLE, WALTER L. Gladstone, Michigan. Patents #451,499 May 5, 1891, sight, #741,920 October 20, 1903, sight, #931,328 August 17, 1908, sight, and #982,152 January 17, 1911, firearm.

MARBORGER, JOHN X. unlocated. Kentucky fullstock.

MARCELLUS, N.H. Belleview, Ohio, 1860-1864d. (Hutslar)

MARCH, MORRIS DEC. Baltimore, Maryland, 1840-1845. (Hartzler)

MARCHLEY, S. unlocated. Converted flintlock.

MARCKLEY, SAMUEL (?-1830), Rochester, New York, 1815-1830. With Ephraim Gilbert, 1822. Grandson of William Antes. (Eich)

MARCUM, J.E. Covington, Kentucky 1855d. Same as J.E. Marcum, New York?

MARCUM, J.E. New York, New York. Percussion 1/2 stock. Same as J.E. Marcum, Kentucky? (Van Rennselaer)

MARCUM, S.M. (1819-?), Cassville, West Virginia, 1880c.

MARCUM, STEPHEN Lawrence Co., Kentucky, Wayne Co., West Virginia, Boyd Co., Kentucky. (Hist KY, V4 P225)

MARCUM, THOMAS Loomisville, Missouri, 1860d.

MARCY, F.P. Keokuk, Iowa, 1847d. Percussion duellers.

MARDEN, CHARLES H. Hartford, Connecticut, 1852-1853d.

MAREAUX, P. San Antonio, Texas, 1878d.

MARGRUM, DAVID Philadelphia, Pennsylvania, 1824d. See David Magrum.

MARIN, NATHANIEL Savannah, Georgia, 1879d-1883d.

MARK, ANDREW Detroit, Michigan. Patent #none April 6, 1832, winged shot with William Pier.

MARK, CHARLES Visalia, California, 1878. (Shelton)

MARK, D. unlocated. Percussion fullstock.

MARK, F.H. Bellows Falls, Vermont, 1873-1906. (Horn)

MARK, GABRIEL & GODFREY Portland, Maine, 1850-1860. (Demeritt)

MARK, MILES (1793-?), Henderson Co., Illinois, 1850c. (Johnson)

MARKEL, SAMUEL (1810-1888), Butler Co., Pennsylvania, 1840-1888. Flintlock Kentucky. (Whisker II)

MARKER, DANIEL (1774-?), Sharpsburg, Maryland, 1797-1820t and 1824-1832, Martinsburg, Virginia, 1822-1824 and 1833-1855. Flintlock and percussion rifles. (Hartzler, Bowers)

MARKER, DANIEL, JR. Sharpsburg, Maryland, 1831-1841, Versailles, Ohio, 1835. With brother Paul in Ohio. (Hutslar, Bowers)

MARKER, GEORGE, JR. (1789-1854), Frederick Co., Maryland, 1801-1823, Montgomery Co., Ohio, 1823-1854. Flintlock Kentucky. (Knittle, Hartzler)

MARKER, JACOB (1832-?), Sharpsburg, Maryland, 1855-1890. Percussion fullstock. Son of, and successor to, James Marker. (Hartzler)

MARKER, JAMES (1810-1883), Sharpsburg, Maryland, 1833-1855. Percussion Kentucky rifles. Son of Daniel Marker. (Hartzler)

MARKER, PAUL (1793-1864), Sharpsburg, Maryland, 1816-1835, Versailles, Ohio, 1835-1864. Flintlock Kentucky, percussion fullstock. Brother of Daniel and George. (Hartzler)

MARKER, PAUL (1811-?), Gratis, Ohio, 1850c-1859d, Versailles, Ohio, Union City, Indiana, 1875d. Son of Paul. (Lindert, Hutslar)

MARKER, PETER Hagerstown, Maryland, 1822, Bedford Co., Pennsylvania, 1828. Flintlock Kentucky. (Hartzler)

MARKER, SAMUEL Sherman, Texas, 1896d.

MARKHAM, CARTER McDonald Co., Missouri, 1850c. (MB 11-66)

MARKHAM, T. unlocated. Percussion 1/2 stock.

MARKHAM, WILLIAM F. Plymouth, Michigan, 1886-1908. Patents #372,161 October 25, 1887, air gun, #473,633 April 26, 1892, spring air gun, #483,159 September 27, 1892, spring air gun, #557,849 April 7, 1896, air gun, #651,634 June 12, 1900, spring air gun, #655,170 July 31, 1900, air gun, #689,501 December 24, 1901, gun barrel, #689,502 December 24, 1901, rifled barrels, #696,461 April 1, 1902, spring air gun, #718,646 January 20, 1903, spring air gun, #842,324 January 29, 1907, air gun, #860,754 July 23, 1907, air gun, and #911,056 February 2, 1908, air gun with E.S. Roe. As Markham Air Rifle Co., founded in 1905.

MARKINS, TOM (?-1915), Sharps Creek, Ohio. (Hutslar)

MARKLEY, B. unlocated. Flintlock Kentucky.

MARKLEY, JACOB Northumberland Co., Pennsylvania, 1756. (Dean)

MARKLEY, L. unlocated. Percussion fullstock.

MARKLEY, O. Penn, Pennsylvania, 1887d.

MARKLOW, DAN (1837-?), Clark Co., Indiana, 1860c. (Lindert)

MARKMAN, J.H. Ithaca, Michigan, 1887d-1899d.

MARKS, ANDREW Washington, D.C., 1822d-1855d. (Hartzler)

MARKS, JACOB Washington, D.C., 1860d. (Hartzler)

MARKS, MARION Edna, Kansas, 1888d.

MARLIN FIREARMS CO. New Haven, Connecticut, 1870-1969, North Haven, Connecticut, 1969-date. Operated as J.M. Marlin, 1870-1881, Marlin Firearm Co., 1881-1915, Marlin-Rockwell Corp., 1915-1926, and Marlin Firearms Co., 1926-date. Acquired by Remington Arms Company, Inc., December 28, 2007. (ST 3-63)

MARLIN, JOHN MAHLON (1836-1901), New Haven, Connecticut, 1863-1901. Patents #99,690 February 8, 1870, revolver, #101,637 April 8, 1870, breechloading firearm, #140,516 July 1, 1873, revolver, #159,592 February 9, 1875, firing pin #222,064 November 25, 1879, magazine gun, #222,065 November 29, 1879, revolver, #222,066 November 25, 1879, revolver, #222,414 December 8, 1879, magazine gun, #234,309 November 9, 1880, magazine gun, #250,825 December 13, 1881, magazine gun with Andrew Burgess, #271,091 January 23, 1883, ejector, #297,424 April 22, 1884, magazine firearms, #308,183 November 18, 1884, revolver, #315,645 April 14, 1885, magazine gun, #316,554 April 28, 1885, magazine gun, #334,535 January 19, 1886, revolver, #367,535 August 2, 1887, revolver, #367,820 August 9, 1887, revolver, #367,821 August 9, 1887, revolver, #368,599 August 23, 1887, revolver, #371,608 October 18, 1887, revolver, #413,196 October 22, 1889, magazine firearm, #413,197 October 22, 1889, revolver, and #469,819 March 1, 1892, magazine. Founder of Marlin Firearms Co.

MARLOW, JAMES E. Guilford Co., North Carolina, 1860c-1884d.

MARLOW, THOMAS Jamestown, North Carolina. (Bivins)

MARNETTE, H.J. Carroll, Iowa, 1880d-1892d.

MARQUIS OF LORNE suicide special by T.E. Ryan.

MARRIOTT & BARSTOW Baltimore, Maryland, 1883-1886d. J.H.W. Marriott and Frederick Barstow. (Hartzler)

MARRS, ANDREW B. Hermitage, Illinois, 1860d.

MARS, ANDREW W. Berrien Co., Michigan, 1850-1860. Percussion 1/2 stock. (MB 2-50)

MARS, WILLIAM Pittsburgh, Pennsylvania, 1817. (Whisker II)

MARSH BREECH & MUZZLE LOADING ARMS CO. Washington, D.C., 1859-1862. (GR 12-78)

MARSH, C.S. Summit, Mississippi, 1885d.

MARSH, F.E. Calais, Vermont, 1894. (Horn)

MARSH, G.V. Mesopotamia, Ohio, 1868d. (Hutslar)

MARSH, HARRY Santa Maria, California, 1893d.

MARSH, J. Binghamton, New York, 1852-1870. Percussion target rifles.

MARSH, JAMES Leatherwood, Ohio, 1868d. (Hutslar)

MARSH, JOHNSON East Dorset, Vermont. Patent #none July 1, 1836, locks.

MARSH, O.B. Binghamton, New York. Percussion target rifle. (Swinney)

MARSH, SAMUEL W. Washington, D.C. Patents #26,362 December 6, 1859, breechloading firearm, and #33,362 November 5, 1861, breechloading firearm. (GR 12-78)

MARSHALL, ALFRED (1827-?), Alamance Co., North Carolina, 1850c. Brother of Mebane Marshall. (Bivins)

MARSHALL, CHARLES C. Norwich, Connecticut. Patent #176,412 April 18, 1876, revolver with Joseph C. Marshall and Dexter Smith.

MARSHALL, GEORGE C. Gallipolis, Ohio. (Hutslar)

MARSHALL, H., & CO. Atlanta, Georgia, 1862. Confederate Morse carbines. Sword manufacturer. (Hill-Anthony)

MARSHALL, J. PLYMTON Millbury, Massachusetts, 1857-1862. Patents #25,661 October 4, 1859, breechloading firearm, and #35,107 April 29, 1862, breechloading firearm.

MARSHALL, J.H. Columbus, Georgia, 1862. Confederate States barrelmaker. (Albaugh 3)

MARSHALL, JOB Luzerne Co., Pennsylvania. Flintlock Kentucky. (Dillin)

MARSHALL, JOSEPH C. Springfield, Massachusetts. Patents #138,157 April 22, 1873, breechloading firearm with G.L. Holt, #141,603 August 25, 1873, breech loading firearm with Dexter Smith, #162,863 May 4, 1875, revolver with Dexter Smith, #176,412 April 18, 1876, revolver with Dexter Smith, and #176,488 April 18, 1876, revolver with Dexter Smith.

MARSHALL, MEBANE (1826-?), Alamance Co., North Carolina, 1850c. Brother of Alfred Marshall. (Bivins)

MARSHALL, S.R., & CO. unlocated. Imported double-barrel shotgun.

MARSHALL, SIMEON Philadelphia, Pennsylvania. Patents #14,850 May 13, 1856, cartridge opener, and #24,372 June 14, 1859, self priming gunlock, both with Jesse Butterfield.

MARSHALL, W.F. Wellington, Kansas, 1884d.

MARSHALL, WILLIAM Howard, Indiana, 1862d.

MARSHALL, WILLIAM Jessup, Iowa, 1865d.

MARSHWOOD trade name of Crescent Fire Arms Co. on shotguns for Charles Williams Stores. (Hinman)

MARSON, JOHN Cambridge, Indiana, 1858d-1885.

MARSTEN, E. Concord, New Hampshire, 1849d.

MARSTERS BROS. New York, New York, 1867d. James F. Marsters.

MARSTERS, JAMES F. Brooklyn, New York, 1867d-1875d. As Marsters Bros., 1867.

MARSTERS, WILLIAM New York, New York, 1844d-1845d.

MARSTON & COHN New York, New York, 1853d. Swivel breech percussion pistols. S.W. Marston and J. Cohn.

MARSTON & KNOX New York, New York, 1851. W.W. Marston and Robert Knox. (ASAC 39)

MARSTON, C.H. Detroit, Michigan, 1899d.

MARSTON, DAVID Philadelphia, Pennsylvania, 1808d-1833d.

MARSTON, FRANK W. Philadelphia, Pennsylvania. Patents #198,745 January 1, 1878, revolver, and #199,717 January 29, 1878, cartridge, both with Owen Jones.

MARSTON, GEORGE T. Newman, Georgia, 1861. Confederate gunsmith convention.

MARSTON, JOHN Philadelphia, Pennsylvania, 1829d-1831d.

MARSTON, ROBERT New York, New York, 1849-1858. (ASAC 39)

MARSTON, STANHOPE WALKER New York, New York, 1844-1866. Patents #7,887, January 7, 1851, lock and #45,712, January 4, 1865, pepperbox. Pistols made by Cohn & Marston. (ASAC 39)

MARSTON, WILLIAM WALKER (1822-1872), New York, New York, 1844d-1872. Patents #6,514, June 5, 1849, lock, #7,443 June 18, 1850, breechloading firearm, #8,956 May 18, 1852, cartridge with Frederick Goodell, #13,581 September 18, 1855, pepperbox, #17,386 May 26, 1857, pepperbox, and #40,490 November 3, 1863, metallic cartridge. Made many different guns, mostly under his own patents. As Marston & Knox, 1847, and Sprague & Marston, 1848-1853. Son of Stanhope Marston. (ASAC 30, ASAC 39)

MARTENS, HENRY C. Fredericksburg, Virginia, 1877d-1897d.

MARTIC FORGE Colemanville, Pennsylvania, 1755-1883. Musket barrels.

MARTIN & DUNHAM Willimantic, Connecticut, 1886d. A.W. Dunham.

MARTIN & SMITH Philadelphia, Pennsylvania, 1840-1857d. Lockmakers.

MARTIN & WESTCOTT Marshalltown, Iowa, 1867d.

MARTIN P.J. Greenville, Illinois, 1886d-1888d.

MARTIN S. Hudson, New York. Percussion over/under rifle.

MARTIN, C.C. (1830-?), Whitely, Indiana, 1860c. (Lindert)

MARTIN, C.F. Bellefontaine, Ohio, 1875-1882. (Hutslar)

MARTIN, CHARLES Hartford, Connecticut, 1848-1850.

MARTIN, CHRISTIAN (1830-?), Toledo, Ohio, 1860c-1878d. (Hutslar)

MARTIN, DAVID Lancaster Co., Pennsylvania, 1847t. (Dyke)

MARTIN, DR. JOSEPH Louisville, Kentucky. Patent #1,713 August 3, 1840, centrifugal gun.

MARTIN, E.J.G. Milwaukee, Wisconsin, 1857d-1858d.

MARTIN, EDWARD Providence, Rhode Island, 1775. (Achtermier)

MARTIN, EDWIN Springfield, Massachusetts. Patent #48,820 July 18, 1865, priming metallic cartridges.

MARTIN, ELBERT Leesville, Indiana. Son of William Martin. (Lindert)

MARTIN, F.R. Anamosa, Iowa, 1887d.

MARTIN, FRANK N. Covington, Kentucky. Patent #41,162 January 5, 1864, sight.

MARTIN, G. Tiffin, Ohio, 1860-1864d. (Hutslar)

MARTIN, GEORGE H. Worcester, Massachusetts, 1848-1850. (Kauffman-2)

MARTIN, GEORGE (1826-?), Griggsville, Illinois, 1860c. (Johnson)

MARTIN, GEORGE Martinsville, Indiana. (Lindert)

MARTIN, H.T. Whitewater, Wisconsin, 1891d.

MARTIN, HARRY T. Ft. Robinson, Nebraska. Patent #271,883 February 6, 1883, auxiliary rifle barrels.

MARTIN, HENRY Fayette Co., Pennsylvania, 1802-1806t. (Kauffman)

MARTIN, HENRY Randolph Co., Virginia, 1810-1811. Contract rifles for Virginia with Henry Wallers and Lewis Schroyer. (Cromwell)

MARTIN, J. Atlanta, Georgia. Percussion fullstock.

MARTIN, JAMES Albany, New York, 1870d.

MARTIN, JAMES Philadelphia, Pennsylvania, 1837d.

MARTIN, JAMES Thomaston, Maine, 1758-1759. (Demeritt)

MARTIN, JOHN J. Clark Co., Missouri, 1850c. (MB 11-66)

MARTIN, JOHN (1766-?), Parke Co., Indiana, 1819.

MARTIN, JOHN (1806-?), Abingdon, Illinois, 1850c-1860d, Victoria, Illinois, 1864d.

MARTIN, JOHN (1829-?), Sacramento, California, 1850c. (Shelton)

MARTIN, JOHN (1830-?), Harrison Co., Ohio, 1850c. (Hutslar)

MARTIN, JOHN Charles Co., Maryland, 1682. (Hartzler)

MARTIN, JOHN Little Rock, Arkansas, 1832-1835.

MARTIN, JOHN New York, New York, 1788.

MARTIN, JOHN Watsons, Virginia, 1776-1781. (Gill)

MARTIN, JOSEPH Philadelphia, Pennsylvania, 1841d.

MARTIN, MICHAEL Lancaster Co., Pennsylvania, 1820-1839. Flintlock Kentucky. (Kauffman)

MARTIN, R. Hudson, New York. Percussion fullstock rifle.

MARTIN, ROBERT Baltimore, Maryland, 1808. (Hartzler)

MARTIN, ROY Delaney, Arkansas. (Elias)

MARTIN, SAMUEL Lancaster Co., Pennsylvania, 1847t-1850c. (KRA IV-4)

MARTIN, THOMAS C. Virginia. Committee of Safety repairs.

MARTIN, THOMPSON Elizabeth, Pennsylvania, 1839-1861. (Kauffman)

MARTIN, W.H. Tilton, Georgia, 1883d.

MARTIN, W.L. New Haven, Connecticut, 1873-1879.

MARTIN, WILLIAM (1810-1901), Medora, Woodville, and Leesville, Indiana, 1840-1891. Percussion 1/2 stock. (Lindert)

MARTINEZ, DIONISIO Philadelphia, Pennsylvania. Patent #168,404 October 5, 1875, sight.

MARTINOFF, JULES Chetopa, Kansas, 1884d.

MARTYR, TOMKINS Williamsburg, Virginia, 1777-1778. (Gill)

MARVEL trade name of J. Stevens Arms Co.

MARVIN, M. Salem, Oregon, 1867d.

MARWICK, JAMES Lamar, Missouri, 1889d-1898d.

MARX, CHARLES Abbott, Iowa, 1884d, Visalia, California, 1893d.

MARYLAND STATE GUN LOCK FACTORY Frederick, Maryland, 1777-1778. (Hartzler)

MASLIN, MICHAEL M. Baltimore, Maryland, 1822-1833d, Philadelphia, Pennsylvania, 1847d. Lockmaker only. (Hartzler)

MASON MACHINE WORKS Taunton, Massachusetts. See William Mason.

MASON Ashtabula, Ohio, 1812. Flintlock Kentucky. (Dillin)

MASON, ALONZO Monroeton, Pennsylvania, 1861d.

MASON, B. Windsor, Virginia, 1877d.

MASON, CHARLES F. Lewiston, Maine, 1859-1879. (Lindsay 3)

MASON, F.M. Springfield, Missouri, 1889d.

MASON, HENRY Lancaster Co., Pennsylvania, 1759t. (Dyke)

MASON, I.N. Lovelaceville, Kentucky, 1883d.

MASON, J. Taunton, Massachusetts, 1825. Flintlock 1/2 stock, converted fullstock. (Dean*)

MASON, J.C. Keene, New Hampshire. Percussion 1/2 stock.

MASON, JAMES M. Washington, D.C. Patents #112,523 March 7, 1871, breechloading firearm, and #117,906 August 8, 1871, breechloading firearm.

MASON, JOHN M. Raleigh, North Carolina, 1828. Plater. (Bivins)

MASON, JOHN, JR. (1775-1843), Sherborn, Massachusetts, 1796, Shrewsbury, Massachusetts, 1797-1843. (ASAC 44)

MASON, JOSEPH New Haven, Connecticut. Patent #414,651 November 5, 1889, breechloading firearm.

MASON, ROBERT Virginia, 1775. (Gill)

MASON, W.J. Detroit, Michigan, 1882d-1883d.

MASON, W.J. Paducah, Kentucky, 1885d.

MASON, WILLIAM Taunton, Massachusetts, 1860-1907. Patents assigned to E. Remington & Sons: #50,117 November 21, 1865, revolver, and #53,539 March 27, 1866, revolver. Assigned to Colt: #128,644 July 2, 1872, revolver, #155,095 September 15, 1874, revolver, #158,957 January 19, 1874, revolver, #247,373 September 20, 1881, breechloading firearm, #247,374 September 20, 1881, revolver, #247,375 September 20, 1881, revolver, #247,376 September 20, 1881, breechloading firearm, #247,377 September 20, 1881, breechloading firearm, #247,378 September 20, 1881, breechloading firearm, #247,379 September 20, 1881, breechloading firearm, #247,938 October 4, 1881, lock, #248,190 October 4, 1881, lock, #249,649 November 15, 1881, revolver, #250,375 December 6, 1881, revolver, #253,736 February 14, 1882, breechloading firearm, #260,586 July 4, 1882 revolver, #263,191 August 22, 1882, breechloading firearm, #263,551 August 29, 1882, revolver, #264,727 September 19, 1882, breechloading firearm, #278,987 June 5, 1883, magazine gun, #285,284 September 18, 1883, magazine gun, and #289,676 December 4, 1883, magazine gun. Assigned to Winchester: #295,031 March 11, 1884, magazine gun, #302,148 July 15, 1884, magazine gun, #305,093 September 16, 1884, magazine gun, #306,630 October 14, 1884, magazine gun, #311,079 January 20, 1885, magazine gun, #312,139 February 10, 1885, magazine gun, #354,327 December 14, 1886, magazine gun, #354,328 December 14, 1886, magazine gun, #354,329 December 14, 1886, magazine gun, #354,427 December 14, 1886, magazine gun, #373,298 November 15, 1887, magazine gun, #454,582 June 23, 1891, magazine gun, #487,486 December 6, 1892, takedown mechanism, #487,487 December 6, 1892, magazine gun, #487,488 December 6, 1892, takedown mechanism, #487,489 December 6, 1892, takedown mechanism, #498,983 June 6, 1893, takedown mechanism, #499,464 June 13, 1893, takedown mechanism, #511,631 December 26, 1893, breechloading firearm, #511,632 December 26, 1893, breechloading firearm, #511,633 December 26, 1893, breechloading firearm, #539,528 May 21, 1895, magazine gun, #545,708 September 3, 1895, magazine gun, #548,003 October 15, 1895, magazine gun, #548,715 October 29, 1895, magazine gun, #549,734 November 12, 1895, magazine gun, #551,393 December 17, 1895, magazine gun, #551,592 December 17, 1895, magazine gun, #564,441 July 21, 1896, magazine gun, #565,766 August 11, 1896, takedown mechanism, #565,767 August 11, 1896, safety, #599,587 February 22, 1898, magazine gun with Thomas Bennett, #605,734 June 14, 1898, takedown mechanism, #614,482 November 22, 1898, magazine gun, #616,719 December 27, 1898, magazine gun, #625,581 May 23, 1899, sight guard, #685,216 October 22, 1901, magazine gun, #695,784 March 18, 1902, magazine gun with Thomas Bennett, #748,395 December 29, 1903, magazine gun with Frank Burton, #846,591 March 12, 1907, automatic gun, #854,707 May 21, 1907, automatic gun, and #874,856 December 24, 1907, automatic gun. As Mason Machine Works, Taunton, Massachusetts, 50,000 Model 1861 contract muskets during the Civil War. Developed guns for Remington, Colt, and Winchester while maintaining a shop for custom work on other guns. Both muzzle loading and cartridge guns of the post war period carry his name. (Fuller, Williamson)

MASSA, GEORGE Lancaster, Pennsylvania, 1857d.

MASSACHUSETTS ARMS CO. Chicopee Falls, Massachusetts, 1849-1896. Percussion revolvers and breechloading carbines under several patents. The original company was dissolved in 1866, but the name was continued by T.W. Carter, who made only Maynard rifles. (Sellers-1)

MASSACHUSETTS ARMS CO. trade name of Stevens and Crescent Fire Arms Co. on shotguns.

MASSEY, BENJAMIN (?-1736), Charleston, South Carolina, 1730-1736. (Kauffman-2)

MASSEY, JOSEPH (or JOHN) (?-1736), Charleston, South Carolina, 1736. Also an engraver and printer of colonial currency. (Kauffman-2)

MASSEY, PHILIP (?-1739), Charleston, South Carolina, 1736-1739. (Kauffman 2)

MASTERMAN, D.S. Weld, Maine, 1869-1877. (Demeritt)

MASTERMAN, PETER S. Philadelphia, Pennsylvania, 1867d.

MASTERS, JAMES F. New York, New York, 1875d. See James F. Marsters.

MASTON, J. unlocated. New England flintlock.

MASUCH, EDWARD Kansas City, Missouri, 1860d-1871d.

MATER, M. Chippewa, New York. Percussion fullstock rifle. (Swinney)

MATER, W.B. Lincoln, Nebraska, 1882d-1886d.

MATHASIE, CHRISTIAN Lancaster, Pennsylvania, 1838t-1849t. (KRA IV-4)

MATHASSIE, GODFREY Evansville, Indiana, 1867-1872. (Lindert)

MATHASSIE, JOHN B. Evansville, Indiana, 1877-1880. (Gardner)

MATHEIS, JOHN Ottawa, Illinois, 1867d-1875d.

MATHENY, C. unlocated. Percussion fullstock.

MATHER & CARL Detroit, Michigan, 1875d. George B. Mather.

MATHER, EDWIN G. Ottumwa, Iowa, 1880d-1897d.

MATHER, GEORGE B. Detroit, Michigan, 1872d-1877d. As Mather & Carl, 1875.

MATHER, M. Ashtabula, Ohio, 1825. Flintlock Kentucky. (Hutslar)

MATHER, SAMUEL Kellogg, Idaho, 1891d, Butte, Montana, 1898d.

MATHESSIE, CHRISTIAN (1792-?), Evansville, Indiana, 1850c-1860d. (Lindert)

MATHESSIE, JOHN G. Evansville, Indiana, 1858d-1873d. Son of Christian Mathessie.

MATHEWS, HAROLD S. Wytheville, Virginia. Patent #27,723 April 3, 1860, breechloading firearm with James Letort.

MATHEWSON, GEORGE Rhode Island, circa 1770. Flintlock fowler. (Dillin)

MATHEWSON, WELCOME (1778-1872), Burrelsville, Rhode Island, 1796-1830. Flintlock guns. (Achtermier)

MATHIS, B. unlocated. Flintlock fowling piece.

MATHIS, W. Miribile, Missouri, 1860d.

MATON, FRANCES New York, New York. Patent #11,938 November 14, 1854, breechloading firearm.

MATSON, JOHN Boston, Massachusetts, 1662-1678. (Kauffman 2)

MATSON, THOMAS Boston, Massachusetts, 1655-1682. (Kauffman 2)

MATTES, CARL Chippewa Falls, Wisconsin, 1895d.

MATTESON, ELISHA Brooklyn, New York. Patent #33,478 November 11, 1861, projectiles.

MATTHEWS, ALBERT H. Augusta, Maine, 1867. (Demeritt)

MATTHEWS, CHARLES F. (1820-?), Burlington, Iowa, 1850c, Petersburg, Illinois, 18??-18??, Oquawka, Illinois, 1860c. (Johnson, MB 8-64)

MATTHEWS, J.A. St. Louis, Missouri. Patent #29,437 July 31, 1860, turret gun.

MATTHEWS, JAMES Johnson Co., Missouri, 1850c. (MB 11-66)

MATTHEWS, LEMUEL C. Johnson Co., Missouri, 1850c. (MB 11-66)

MATTHEWS, WASHINGTON Camp Bidwell, California. Patent #211,763 January 28, 1879, sight.

MATTHEWS, WILLIAM San Leandro, California, 1893d.

MATTHEWS, WILLIAM Sedalia, Missouri, 1879d-1893d.

MATTHIESSEN, E.R. Pontiac, Michigan, 1891d.

MATTHIS, ANSIL Wilkes Co., North Carolina, 1822. (Bivins)

MATTLEN, SAMUEL (1828-?), Springfield, Illinois, 1850c, Bloomington, Illinois, 1853, Springfield, Illinois, 1860-1870. As Keeran & Mattlen in Bloomington. (Johnson)

MATTON, JOSEPH (1805-?), Greencastle, Indiana, 1850c. (Lindert)

MATTOON, CHARLES B. Marshall, Michigan, 1855-1859, Allegan, Michigan, 1859-1877. Percussion rifles. For M.L. Rood, 1855-1857.

MATURKA, JOSEPH North Vernon, Indiana, 1856-1890. (Lindert)

MAUERMANN, B. San Antonio, Texas, 1878d.

MAUGER, HENRY (?-1827), Berks Co., Pennsylvania, 1762-1827. Flintlock Kentucky rifle. (MB 1-68)

MAUPIN, AMOS Franklin Co., Missouri, 1816-1820. Son of Mosias Maupin. (MB 3-71)

MAUPIN, JOHN (?-1843), Franklin Co., Missouri, 1804-1843. Son of Mosias Maupin. (MB 3-71)

MAUPIN, MOSIAS (?-1816), Franklin Co., Missouri, 1804-1816. (MB 3-71)

MAUPIN, W.A. Louisiana, Missouri, 1893d.

MAUPIN, WILLIAM (?-1880), Franklin Co., Missouri, ?-1880. (MB 3-71)

MAUPIN, WILLIAM Franklin Co., Missouri, 1820-?. Son of Amos Maupin. (MB 3-71)

MAURER, A. East St. Louis, Illinois, 1867d.

MAURER, B. St. Genevieve, Missouri, 1854d.

MAURER, JACOB East Saint Louis, Illinois, 1871d.

MAURER, JOHN Lancaster, Pennsylvania, 1803. For Peter Brong. (Kauffman)

MAUS, JACOB Berks Co., Pennsylvania, 1790-1798. Flintlock rifles. Son of Phillip Maus. (Diilin)

MAUS, PHILIP Berks Co., Pennsylvania, 1776-1798. Flintlock Kentucky rifles. (Dillin)

MAUSE, F.E. Mausdale, Pennsylvania. Flintlock Kentucky rifle. (Dillin)

MAUSER, FRANCIS C. Ilion, New York. Patent #148,476 March 10, 1874, breechloading firearm.

MAXEY, JOHN M. Albany, Ohio, 1872d, Athens, Ohio, 1883-1890d. (Hutslar)

MAXIM, HIRAM STEVENS (1840-1916). Patents #317,161 May 5, 1885, machine gun, #319,596 June 9, 1885, machine gun, #321,513 July 7, 1885, machine gun, #321,514 July 7, 1885, machine gun, #367,825 August 9, 1887, machine gun, #395,791 January 8, 1889, machine gun, #430,210 June 17, 1890, automatic gun, #430,211 June 17, 1890, automatic machine gun, #439,248 October 28, 1890, machine gun, #436,899 September 23, 1890, automatic gun, #551,779 December 24, 1895, automatic machine gun, #577,485 February 23, 1897, recoil operated gun, #579,401 March 23, 1897, recoil operated gun, #586,362 July 13, 1897, gas operated gun, #593,228 November 9, 1897, automatic gun, and #577,485 February 23, 1897, automatic gas operated gun. Inventor of the famous Great War/WW I "Maxim gun". (Chinn)

MAXIM, HUDSON (1855-1927), Pittsfield, Massachusetts. Brother of Hiram Stevens Maxim and interested primarily in gunpowder.

MAXWELL, A.L., JR., & CO. Knoxville, Tennessee, ?-1863. Model 1841 and Mississippi rifles for Confederacy. (Gluckman & Satterlee)

MAXWELL, SAMUEL Mossville, Illinois, 1864d.

MAY, C.A. Astoria, Oregon, 1889d-1891d.

MAY, J.P. Atlanta, Texas, 1896d.

MAY, JAMES (city?), Maryland, 1776. Committee of Safety repairs. (Dean*)

MAY, W.W. Lewisburg, Ohio, 1890-1896d. (Hutslar)

MAY, WILLIAM Philadelphia, Pennsylvania, 1829d-1831d.

MAYALL, THOMAS J. Roxbury, Massachusetts. Patents #26,197 November 22, 1859, scythe rifle, #30,335 October 9, 1860, turret gun, #30,742 November 27, 1860, ordnance, #32,376 May 21, 1861, ordnance, and #37,004 November 25, 1862, revolver. (Sellers-1)

MAYBACK, GOTTLEIB Buffalo, New York, 1856-1859.

MAYBERRY, J.C. White Rock, Illinois. Patent #35,699 June 24, 1862, cartridges.

MAYDAT, VICTOR San Francisco, California, 1852-1856. (Shelton)

MAYER & EACHUS West Chester, Pennsylvania, 1884d-1899d. Ernest Mayer and F.A. Eachus.

MAYER, ERNEST West Chester, Pennsyvlania, 1884d-1899d. As Mayer & Eachus.

MAYER, G.A., & SONS Henderson, Kentucky, 1837-1860d.

MAYER, GEORGE Lancaster, Pennsylvania, 1819-1861. Flintlock Kentucky. Locks only after 1838. (Kauffman)

MAYER, GOTTLEIB Cincinnati, Ohio, 1890-1900d. (Hutslar)

MAYER, WILLIAM Folsom, California, 1880-1881d. (Shelton)

MAYER'S SONS, G.A. Henderson, Kentucky, 1883d.

MAYES, MATTHEW Dinwiddie Court House, Virginia, 1781. Committee of Safety repairs. (Gill)

MAYESCH Lancaster, Pennsylvania, 1760-1775. (Dillin)

MAYFIELD, JOHN (1805-?), Baltimore, Maryland, 1824-1837d, Georgetown, D.C., 1850c-1855d. (Hartzler)

MAYHEW, G.H. Red Bluff, California, 1877-1878d. (Shelton)

MAYLOR, THOMAS Oak Harbor, Washington, 1886d-1891d.

MAYNARD & SLOCOMB Worcester, Massachusetts, 1818-1820. Flintlock New England rifle. Josiah Maynard and Hardin Slocomb. (ASAC 44)

MAYNARD, C.B. Bainbridge, New York. Percussion over/under rifle.

MAYNARD, C.C. Anthony Place, Florida, 1886d.

MAYNARD, CADISH Oxford, New York, 1845-1865. (Dean*)

MAYNARD, EDWARD Washington, D.C. Patents #4,208 September 22, 1845, primer, #8,126 June 27, 1851, breechloading firearm, #15,141 June 17, 1856, cartridges, #22,565 January 11, 1859, back sight, #25,663 October 4, 1859, back sight, #25,664 October 4, 1859, nipples, #26,364 December 6, 1859, breechloading firearm, #30,537 October 30, 1860, breechloading firearms, #32,896 April 2, 1861, cartridge loaders, #39,823 September 8, 1863, metallic cartridges, #40,111 September 29, 1863, cartridges, #40,112 September 29, 1863, metallic cartridges, #42,338 April 19, 1864, wad for metallic cartridges, #45,420 December 13, 1864, priming, #48,423 June 27, 1865, breechloading firearms, #48,966 July 25, 1865, retractor, #49,130 August 1, 1865, breechloading firearm, #59,044 October 23, 1866, priming, #83,194 October 20, 1868, double-barrel firearm, #86,566 February 2, 1869, breechloading firearm, #135,928 February 18, 1873, breechloading firearm, and #343,471 June 18, 1886, cartridge index. (GR 9 to 12-65)

MAYNARD, J.N. Deposit, New York, 1869d.

MAYNARD, JOHN Albany, New York, 1823-1825. For Henry Turner.

MAYNARD, JOSIAH (1791-1825), Worcester, Massachusetts, 1815-1825. Flintlock guns. Apprenticed to Silas Allen, 1806. With Hardin Slocomb as Maynard & Slocomb, 1818-1820. (ASAC 44)

MAYNARD, R. Springport, Michigan, 1875d.

MAYNARD, ROBERT Novi, Michigan, 1895d-1899d.

MAYNARD, WILLIAM C. Boston, Massachusetts, 1885, Aurora, Illinois, 1887, Mt. Pleasant, Michigan, 1889. Patents #318,899 June 2, 1885, sight, #371,850 October 18, 1887, breechloading firearm, and #398,065 February 19, 1889, breechloading firearm. Guns made in Mt. Pleasant and Durand, Michigan. (Perkins)

MAYO, J.W. Dunbar, Tennessee, 1887d.

MAYOTT, LAFAYETTE H. Springfield, Massachusetts, 1876d-1891d. Patent #436,100 September 9, 1890, safety lock.

MAYS, JAMES Lancaster, Pennsylvania, 1759-1790. (Dyke)

MAYWEG & NIPPES Philadelphia, Pennsylvania, 1814. Contract swords for U.S. Navy. Daniel Nippes.

MAYWEG, JOHN Philadelphia, Pennsylvania, 1829d-1831d.

MAYWEG, WILLIAM Philadelphia, Pennsylvania, 1829d-1841d.

MAZANGE, O., & CO. Mobile, Alabama, 1859d. Importers and dealers.

MAZE, HENRY Ashland, Ohio, 1856-1860.

McABOY, ISAAC E. Huntington, West Virginia. Patent #566,214 August 18, 1896, magazine gun.

McALISTER, C. Milledgeville, Ohio, 1878d. (Hutslar)

McALISTER, H. Tipton, Indiana, 1860d.

McALLISTER, ALBERT H. Cotton Plant, Mississippi. Patents #201,810 March 26, 1878, machine gun, and #674,811 May 21, 1901, machine gun. Both patents assigned to McAllister Machine Gun Co. of Memphis, Tennessee.

McALLISTER, BENJAMIN Lawrence, Massachusetts, 1859-1869d.

McALLISTER, C. Charleston, South Carolina, 1853-1855d. (Kauffman 2)

McALLISTER, CALL. Pittsburgh, Pennsylvania, 1813-1818. Also known as Call McCallister

McALLISTER, JOSIAH R. (1818-?), Williamsport, Ohio, 1850c-1864d. Percussion 1/2 stock. (Hutslar)

McALPIN, HENRY Xenia, Ohio. Lockmaker. (Hutslar)

McALPINE, JAMES New Haven, Connecticut. Lever action target rifle. Patent #204,674 June 11, 1878, breechloading firearm.

McAMMIN, JAMES (1777-?), Perry Co., Ohio, 1850c. (Hutslar)

McAMMIN, SAMUEL (1820-?), Perry Co., Ohio, 1850c. (Hutslar)

McARDLE, J. Boston, Massachusetts, 1858-1860.

McAUSLAND BROS. Deadwood, Dakota Territory, 1876-1879. John and Alexander D. McAusland, Jr.

McAUSLAND, ALEXANDER D. (?-1867), Omaha, Nebraska, 1857-1867. As McAusland & Hickman, 1866-1867. Succeeded by his three sons, Alexander, Jr., John, and William. (GR 1-64)

McAUSLAND, ALEXANDER D., JR. (1835-1919), Omaha, Nebraska, 1857-1876, Deadwood, Dakota Territory, 1876-1879, Miles City, Montana, 1879-1919. For his father, ?-1867. With his brothers John and William as McAusland Bros. 1867-1876. With his brother John, 1876-1879. By himself in Miles City. (GR 1-64)

McAUSLAND, JOHN Omaha, Nebraska, 1867-1876, Deadwood, Dakota Territory, 1876-1879. As McAusland Bros., 1867-1875 and 1876-1879. As Brady & McAusland, hardware dealers, 1875-1876.

McAUSLAND, WILLIAM Omaha, Nebraska, 1867-1876. Youngest son of A.D. McAusland, went into grocery business after his brothers left Omaha.

McBETH, JAMES E. New Orleans, Louisiana, 1866-1869. Patents #58,443 October 2, 1866, safety gunlock, #73,357 January 1, 1868, breech loading firearm, and #80,985 August 11, 1868, breechloading firearm.

McBRIDE, HENRY (1797-?), Mecklenburg Co., North Carolina. (Bivins)

McBRIDE, JOHN Mifflin Co., Pennsylvania, 1809. (Whisker III)

McBRIDE, THOMAS (1822-?), Maron, Ohio, 1850c. (Hutslar)

McBROOM, WILLIAM Hollister, California, 1874-1876. For E.J. Poole, 1874. (Shelton)

McCABE, THOMAS Lawrence, Massachusetts, 1874d-1891d.

McCAIN, HUGH Versailles, Pennsylvania, 1800c. (Kauffman)

McCALL & VAN LEAR Nashville, Tennessee, 1855-1899.

McCALL, WILLIAM A., & CO. Cincinnati, Ohio, 1864-1888. Hardware dealers, locks. (Hutslar)

McCALLA, JOHN Philadelphia, Pennsylvania, 1835d.

McCALLISTER, CALL Pittsburgh, Pennsylvania, 1820. Also known as Call McAllister. (Kauffman)

McCALLISTER, JOHN Carlisle, Pennsylvania, 1764-1765. (Bowers)

McCALY, JAMES Westmoreland Co., Pennsylvania, 1825.

McCAMANT, J.E. Tampa, Florida, 1895d.

McCAMANT, JAMES Washington, Pennsylvania, 1797. (Kauffman)

McCAMENT, SAMUEL Ipava, Illinois, 1860d-1893d.

McCAMERON, T.C. Lindale, Texas, 1884d.

McCAMMANT, JACOB I. (1824-?), West Lafayette, Ohio, 1850c-1878d. Percussion fullstock. (Hutslar)

McCAMMANT, JAMES Brooke Co., Virginia, 1811-1813. Contract rifles for Virginia. (Cromwell)

McCAMMANT, JOHN (1807-?), Brooke Co., Virginia, 1832-1850c. Percussion 1/2 stock and swivel breech.

McCAN, JOHN (1776-?), Lancaster, Pennsylvania, 1795. Ran away from Christian Klein. (Kauffman)

McCAN, JOSEPH E. Terre Haute, Indiana, 1862d-1867d.

McCANDLESS, JAMES W. Florence, Colorado. Patent #439,543 October 28, 1890, auxiliary barrels.

McCANN, J.E. Neosho, Missouri, 1879d.

McCARTNEY, ROBERT Boston, Massachusetts, 1805-1816. (Kauffman 1)

McCARTNEY, WILLIAM G. (1820-1872), Uniontown, Pennsylvania, 1841-1843, Pittsburgh, Pennsylvania, 1846-1871. Percussion fullstock. (Kauffman)

McCARTY, JOHN W. (1824-?), Rush Co., Indiana, 1850c. (Lindert)

McCARTY, JONAS Dexter, Ohio. (Hutslar)

McCARTY, M. (1842-?), Silver Cliff, Colorado, 1881d-1882d, Salida, Colorado, 1884d, Montrose, Colorado, 1885d-1889d. (Sellers-3)

McCARTY, ROBERT New York, New York. Patent #1,049 December 31, 1838, centrifugal gun.

McCARTY, THOMAS Elmira, New York. Patent #147 March 11, 1837, breechloading firearm.

McCAUGHIE, THOMAS (?-1859), St. Louis, Missouri, 1857d-1859d.

McCAULEY, JAMES Monongahela, Pennsylvania, 1825-1842. (Whisker II)

McCAVERY New York, New York, 1776-1777. Committee of Safety repairs.

McCAWLEY, J.A. Canton, Kentucky, 1896d.

McCHESNEY, REUBEN Ilion, New York. Patents #58,444 October 2, 1866, breechloading firearm, and #65,103 May 28, 1867, breechloading firearm.

McCLAIN, G. W. Circleville, Ohio. Percussion 1/2 stock.

McCLALLEN, H. Auburn, New York. 1850d. Percussion guns.

McCLANIN, DAVID Wainsburg, Pennsylvania, 1809. (Kauffman)

McCLARY, DAN Ashland, Ohio, 1885d. (Hutslar)

McCLEAN, SAMUEL N. Washington, Iowa, 1895-1905, Cleveland, Ohio, 1905-1908. Patents #575,265 January 12, 1897, magazine firearm, #601,838 April 5, 1898, magazine firearm, #601,840 April 5, 1898, magazine firearm, #601,843 April 5, 1898, magazine firearm, #601,844 April 5, 1898, magazine firearm, #601,839 April 5, 1898, magazine gun, #601,841 April 5, 1898, magazine gun, #601,842 April 5, 1898, magazine gun, #678,969 July 23, 1901, gun carriage, #691,912 January 28, 1902, gun mount, #691,913 January 28, 1902, gun recoil check, #723,706 March 24, 1903, magazine gun bolt, #735,131 September 4, 1903, gas operated firearm, #749,214 January 12, 1904, breechloading firearm, #722,248 October 12, 1904, gun training device, #780,216 January 17, 1905, gun, #783,453 February 28, 1905, gas operated firearm, #785,971 March 28, 1905, gas operated firearm, #785,972 March 28, 1905, gas operated firearm, #785,973 March 28, 1905, gas operated firearm, #785,974 March 28, 1905, gas operated firearm, #785,975 March 28, 1905, recoil control, #786,230 March 28, 1905, recoil control, #813,106 February 20, 1906, gun carriage, #816,591 April 3, 1906, automatic gas operated firearm, #827,259 July 31, 1906, discharge actuated firearm, #856,653 June 11, 1907, breech loading mechanism, #858,745 July 2, 1907, machine gun, #862,502 August 6, 1907, gun carriage, #933,098 September 7, 1908, breechloading gun, #1,003,632 September 19, 1911, gas operated gun, #1,005,263 October 10, 1911, gas operated gun, #1,042,135 October 22, 1912, gas operated gun, and #1,042,363 October 22, 1912, gas operated gun.

McCLELLAN, HUGH Albany, New York, 1819. (Kauffman 2)

McCLELLAN, RICHARD W. (1825- ?), Steubenville, Ohio, 1850c. (Hutslar)

McCLELLAN, W. Haven Run, Pennsylvania, 1882d. Percussion 1/2 stock.

McCLELLAND, ANDREW (?-1825), Fayette Co., Pennsylvania, 1811-1813, Greene Co., Pennsylvania, 1817-1825. (Kauffman)

McCLELLAND, ASA Greene Co., Pennsylvania, 1809-1821. (Kauffman)

McCLELLAND, DAVID Waynesburg, Pennsylvania, 1799. (Whisker II)

McCLELLAND, ENOS Fayette Co., Pennsylvania, 1802-1812. (Kauffman)

McCLELLAND, EPHRAIM Fayette Co., Pennsylvania, 1828-1829. (Whisker II)

McCLELLAND, HUGH Philadelphia, Pennsylvania, 1829d.

McCLELLAND, JAMES Fayette Co., Pennsylvania, 1798-1815. (Kauffman)

McCLELLAND, JOHN (1808-?), Morrow Co., Ohio, 1850c. (Hutslar)

McCLELLAND, JOHN Fayette Co., Pennsylvania, 1798-1799. With James McClelland. (Kauffman)

McCLELLAND, WILLIAM (?-1815), Uniontown, Pennsylvania, 1785-1798, Fayette Co., Pennsylvania, 1815. (Whisker II)

McCLELLAND, WILLIAM Albion, Indiana, 1860d-1862d.

McCLENDON, W.H. Lakesburgh, Arkansas, 1888d-1892d.

McCLINTOCK, GEORGE W. Brookline, Massachusetts. Patents #430,396 June 17, 1890, firearm lock, and #430,397, June 17, 1890, firearm lock. (Gardner)

McCLUER, W.L. (1833-?), Fairfield, Illinois, 1860c. (Johnson)

McCLUNG, C.M., & CO. Knoxville, Tennessee, 1891d-1914d. Dealers only.

McCLURE, A. Pacific, Missouri, 1860d.

McCLURE, J. & H. Raleigh, North Carolina, 1827-?. (Bivins)

McCLURE, J.M. (1817-?), Bucyrus, Ohio, 1850c-1853d. (Hutslar)

McCLURE, JAMES P. Oakland, California, 1878-1880. (Shelton)

McCLURE, JAY Spring Lake, Michigan, 1875d.

McCLURE, REUBEN (1812-?), Macon Co., North Carolina. Percussion rifles. (Macon County History, 1987)

McCLURE, WILLIAM Columbia, Pennsylvania, 1812. Flintlock Kentucky rifle. (Dean)

McCLURE, WILLIAM Fairfield, Illinois, 1860d.

McCOLISTER, JOSIAH (1818-?), Pickaway Co., Ohio, 1850c. (Hutslar)

McCOMAS, ALEXANDER (1821-?), Baltimore, Maryland, 1843-1889d. Largest maker of percussion guns in Maryland. (Hartzler)

McCOMAS, NICHOLAS A. Baltimore, Maryland, 1847d-1860d. Percussion guns (Hartzler)

McCOMBS, J.M., & CO. Memphis, Tennessee. Percussion lock only.

McCONKLIN, G. & H. unlocated. Percussion 1/2 stock.

McCONNELL, D. Centropolis, Kansas, 1866d.

McCOOK M., Philadelphia, Pennsylvania, 1780-1785. Repaired U.S. arms. (Moller)

McCOOK, THOMAS A. (1796-?), Richmond, Virginia, 1850c. (MB 10-63)

McCORD, DORASTAS (1797-?), St. Louis, Missouri, 1850c. (Lewis)

McCORD, MARCUS Nashville, Illinois. Patent #195,518 September 25, 1877, sight.

McCORD, RALPH Springfield, Illinois, 1893d.

McCORD, WILLIAM Ossining, New York. Patents #31,933 April 2, 1861, firearm, #33,813 November 26, 1861, repeating firearm with E. Mafer, and #39,940, September 15, 1873, projectiles.

McCORMICK, HENRY Oswego, New York, 1817-1822.

McCORMICK, JOHN St. Albans, Illinois, 1860d.

McCORMICK, ROBERT Philadelphia, Pennsylvania, 1798-1801. Model 1798 contract muskets and pistols. Defaulted on U.S. muskets contract and was put in debtors prison in 1801. Model 1799 contract muskets for Virginia. (Hobbies 10-34)

McCORY Canton, Ohio. (Knittle)

McCOSH, SAMUEL Gastonville, Pennsylvania, 1876. Son of Samuel McCosh of Pittsburgh. (Kauffman)

McCOSH, SAMUEL Pittsburgh, Pennsylvania, 1826-1861d. Flintlock and percussion rifles. With Jacob F. Brant as McCosh & Brant, 1854. (Kauffman)

McCOY & BAKER Princeton, Kentucky, 1860. Percussion double rifle/shotgun.

McCOY, ALEXANDER Philadelphia, Pennsylvania, 1779. (Kauffman 2)

McCOY, AMBROSE (1825-?), New Orleans, Louisiana, 1850c. (MB 9-65)

McCOY, CHARLES Little York, Illinois. (Johnson)

McCOY, DANIEL Utica, New York, 1850. As Adams & McCoy.

McCOY, GEORGE R. Elkader, Iowa, 1865d-1881d.

McCOY, GEORGE (1750-1820), Urbana, Ohio, 1804-1820. (MB 6-58)

McCOY, JOHN Independence, Missouri, 1842d-1854d. With William McCoy as McCoys & Lee, 1842.

McCOY, KESTER Lancaster Co., Pennsylvania, 1770-1773.

McCOY, WILLIAM T. Boston, Indiana, 1860d.

McCOY, WILLIAM Independence, Missouri, 1842d-1854d. With John McCoy as McCoys & Lee, 1842.

McCOYS & LEE Independence, Missouri, 1842. John McCoy and William McCoy.

McCRACKEN, WILLIAM G. Pittsburgh, Pennsylvania, 1850c.

McCRANER, ELISHA A. (1823-?), Willowdell, Ohio, 1850c. Percussion fullstock. (Hutslar)

McCREEDY, J.L. Anoka, Minnesota, 1878d.

McCRUM, JAMES Locust Grove, Ohio, 1858-1883d. (Hutslar)

McCULLOCH, JAMES H. St. Louis, Missouri, 1869-1870d.

McCULLOCH, JAMES Rochester, New York, 1880d.

McCULLOUGH, DENNIS (1819-?), Tyler Co., West Virginia, 1860c. (Whisker IV)

McCULLOUGH, GEORGE Lancaster Co., Pennsylvania, 1771-1773. (Gluckman & Satterlee)

McCULLOUGH, JOHN L. Brooklyn, New York. Patents #509,091 November 21, 1893, magazine gun, #509,548 November, 28, 1893, magazine gun, #514,490 February 13, 1894, magazine gun, #539,230 May 14,1895, magazine gun, #557,863 April 17, 1896, magazine gun, and #626,501 June 6, 1899, magazine gun.

McCULLOUGH, N.G. Muncie, Indiana. Percussion rifles. (Gluckman & Satterlee)

McCULLOUGH, WILLIAM (1812-1884), Brookville, Pennsylvania, 1847-1884d. Percussion over/under rifle. (Whisker II)

McCUNE, WILLIAM Lancaster Co., Pennsylvania, 1826-1846. (Dyke)

McDADE, WILLIAM (1819-?), Quincy, Illinois, 1860c. (Johnson)

McDANIEL BROS. Carlisle, Kentucky, 1883d-1884d. A.F. McDaniel.

McDANIEL Muffin Co., Pennsylvania. Flintlock Kentucky. (Dillin)

McDANIEL, A.F. Carlisle, Kentucky, 1879d-1884d. As McDaniel Bros., 1883-1884.

McDANIEL, A.V. Texarkana, Texas, 1884d-1892d.

McDERMIT, A.P. unlocated. Percussion 1/2 stock.

McDERMITT, J.M. unlocated. Percussion 1/2 stock.

McDONALD West Liberty, Iowa, 1880d. As Strattan & McDonald.

McDONALD, C.D. Alpena, Michigan, 1887d.

McDONALD, CHRISTOPHER Vance, Colorado. Patents #647,861 April 7, 1900, revolver, and #652,625 June 6, 1900, revolver. (Sellers-3)

McDONALD, D.W. Allenton, Missouri, 1898d.

McDONALD, DANIEL J. (?-1864), Pittsburgh, Pennsylvania, 1856-1864. Percussion 1/2 stock. With William Craig as Iron City Gun Works, 1856-1857. (Kauffman)

McDONALD, GEORGE Little Rock, Arkansas, 1888d. Son of Milton McDonald.

McDONALD, L.J. Carleton, Nebraska, 1898d.

McDONALD, MARTIN (1831-?), San Francisco, California, 1860c. (Shelton)

McDONALD, MILTON C. Little Rock, Arkansas, 1882d-1888d.

McDONALD, WILLIAM Romeo, Michigan, 1863.

McDONOUGH, L.H. Leesburg, Virginia, 1890d-1893d, Zumbrota, Minnesota, 1898d.

McDOUGALL, D.E. Springfield, Massachusetts. Patent #11,131 June 20, 1854, alarm gun.

McDOWELL, B. (1822-?), Westmoreland Co., Pennsylvania, 1843-1860c. (Whisker II)

McDOWELL, JAMES (?-1849), Sutter's Fort, California, 1845-1849. (Shelton)

McDOWELL, JAMES (1789-?), Vermillion Co., Indiana, 1850c. Percussion fullstock. (Lindert)

McELRATH, ROBERT Charles Town, South Carolina, 1786.

McELROY, JOHN Locke, New York, 1859d. Percussion rifles.

McELROY, TIMOTHY (1832-?), San Francisco, California, 1861, Bodie, California, 1862-1888. (Shelton)

McELROY, WILLIAM H. Kingston, New York, 1874d.

McELROY, WILLIAM JOHN (1824-1888), Macon, Georgia, 1850c-1864. Derringer. Mostly made swords and knives. (GR 11-75)

McELWAIN, R. G. Huntingdon, Pennsylvania. Percussion over/under rifle/shotgun.

McELWAINE, WILLIAM S. Holly Springs, Mississippi, 1859-1882. See Jones, McE1- waine & Co.

McEVOY, C.A. Richmond, Virginia. Patents #30,539 October 30, 1860, sabre bayonet fastening breech, and #31,815 March 26, 1861, loading firearms.

McEWEN, JOHN (1794-?), Pittsburgh, Pennsylvania, 1813. Runaway apprentice of Samuel Galbraith.

McEWIN, J.H. Trimbelle, Wisconsin, 1857d.

McFADDEN New York, New York. Percussion double shotgun.

McFADDEN, CHARLES (1805-?), Connelsville, Pennsylvania, 1827-1840, Portage, Ohio, 1860c. (Hutslar)

McFADDEN, JAMES Portage, Ohio, 1859d. (Hutslar)

McFALL, HUGH East Liverpool, Ohio, 1878-1986d. (Hutslar)

McFARLAND, ALBERT C. Upper Lisle, New York. Patent #370,966 October 4, 1887, lock.

McFARLAND, ANDREW New York, New York, 1844d-18 SOd.

McFARLAND, CHARLES Gardiner, Maine, 1867d.

McFARLAND, G.B. Zionville, Indiana, 1882-1885. Percussion 1/2 stock rifles.

McFARLAND, GEORGE W. Austin, Missouri, 1850c-1860d.

McFARLAND, R. Chamois, Missouri, 1860d.

McFARLAND, WILLIAM P. Chicopee Falls, Massachusetts. Patent #172,465 January 18, 1876, sight with George W. Hadley.

McFARLIN, CHARLES Gardner, Maine, 1867-1880. (Demeritt)

McFARLIN, DAVID Philadelphia, Pennsylvania, 1831d.

McGACKIN, ABE Huntington Co., Pennsylvania. Percussion fullstock.

McGARVEY, J.W. Seneca Falls, New York, 1877d-1882d.

McGAWGHRAN, PATRICK Troy, Pennsylvania, 1861d.

McGEE, HENRY Norwich, Connecticut. Patent #239,821 April 5, 1881, revolver.

McGILL, GEORGE W. Knoxville, Illinois, 1878d.

McGILLVERY, DANIEL Symme's Corners, Ohio, 1854-1864d. Percussion 1/2 stock. (Hutslar)

McGILVARY, ALEXANDER Harrisonburg, Virginia, 1820-1825. Flintlock and percussion rifles.

McGIRR, ALEXANDER C. (1825-1895), Marietta, Ohio, 1850-1888d. Percussion 1/2 stock. (Hutslar)

McGLINCHEY, J.B. Schuyler, Nebraska, 1879d-1884d.

McGONIGAL, CHARLES Philo, Illinois, 1893d.

McGOVEREN, JOHN New York, New York, 1852d-1869. Patent #88,890 April 13, 1869, breechloading firearm.

McGOVERN, ANTHONY Madison, Wisconsin, 1858-1876. (Kauffman 2)

McGOVERN, D. Madison, Wisconsin, 1872-1879d.

McGOWAN, ANTHONY (1831-?), Miamisburg, Ohio, 1850c. (Hutslar)

McGOWAN, JOHN PATRICK (1769-1812), Vincennes, Indiana, 1790-1812. (Lindert)

McGRAW, WILLIAM Duanesburgh, New York, 1874d.

McGREGOR, B. Cincinnati, Ohio, 1880c. (Hutslar)

McGREGOR, ELI Lebanon, Ohio. Percussion fullstock.

McGRUDER, JOHN B. Leadville, Colorado, 1886. For Dougan & Co., 1886. For William Holland, 1887.

McHARG, HILDRETH & CO. Rome, New York, 1866-1868. John B. McHarg.

McHARG, JOHN B. Rome, New York, 1859-1870d. Percussion 1/2 stock. Also as McHarg, Hildreth & Co., 1866-1868 and Armstrong & McHarg, 1870. (Swinney)

McHENRY, JACOB New Washington, Indiana, 1860d.

McHENRY, PETER Macon, Georgia, 1879d-1883d.

McHUGH, CORNELIUS Leadville, Colorado, 1891-1900d. (Sellers 3)

McILROY, J.W. unlocated. Percussion fullstock.

McINNES, JAMES St. Louis, Missouri, 1859d.

McINTOCK, WILLIAM, JR. Hagerstown, Maryland. Apprenticed to John Gonter, 1799. (Hartzler)

McINTOSH, C.C. Eau Claire, Wisconsin, 1891d.

McINTURF & SON Greenville, Tennessee, 1871d.

McINTURFF, MILTON Seven Fountains, Virginia, 1897d.

McJUNKIN, WILLIAM Luling, Texas, 1896d.

McK see William D. McKim.

McKAHAN, JOHN D. (1864), Washington, Pennsylvania, 1840-1864. Percussion rifles. With John C. Noble as McKahan & Noble, 1860. (Kauffman)

McKANE, JOSEPH W. Franklin, Indiana, 1882-1886. (Gardner)

McKEAN, HUGH (1763-1850), Allegheny Co., Pennsylvania, 1788-1801, Mercer Co., Pennsylvania, 1802-1850. (Whisker II)

McKEAN, JAMES B. (1832-?), Mercer, Pennsylvania, 1861d.

McKEAN, JAMES (1799-1851), Westmoreland Co., Pennsylvania, 1820-1851.

McKEAN, S.L. Mexico, Missouri, 1879d-1889d.

McKEAN, WILLIAM Westmoreland Co., Pennsylvania, 1839-1842. (Whisker II)

McKEE, DAVID Chicago, Illinois, 1839.

McKEE, JAMES (1788-?), Mecklenburg Co., North Carolina. Apprenticed, 1805. (Bivins)

McKEE, WILLIAM Baltimore, Maryland, 1817. (Gluckman & Satterlee)

McKELLER, J.F. Rockland, Maine, 1873. (Demeritt)

McKENNEY & BEAN Biddeford, Maine, 1867-1871. Henry H. McKenney and Samuel Bean. (Demeritt)

McKENNEY, HENRY H. Biddeford, Maine, 1855-1871. Percussion 1/2 stock. Patent #22,969 February 15, 1859, superposed loads firearm with Frederick Goth. With Samuel Bean as McKenney & Bean, 1867-1871. (Demeritt)

McKENNEY, J.F. Biddeford, Maine, 1850. (Demeritt)

McKENNEY, N.P. Dixon, Illinois, 1893d.

McKENZIE, ANDREW W. Providence, Rhode Island, 1881d-1888d.

McKENZIE, H.F. Chesaning, Michigan, 1899d.

McKIBBEN, WILLIAM Buck Valley, Pennsylvania. Patent #39,941 September 15, 1863, sights.

McKIM, WILLIAM D. Baltimore, Maryland, 1819-1841. Importer and hardware dealer. As McKim & Maslin, 1824-1833 and McKim & Bro., 1834-1841. (Hartzler)

McKINLEY, HUGH New Rome, Ohio. (Hutslar)

McKINLEY, J.W. Rochester, New York, 1870d.

McKINNEY & ALLING Madison, Indiana, 1860d.

McKINNEY, GEORGE Dayton, Ohio, 1850d. (Hutslar)

McKINNEY, J.R. Modoc, Missouri, 1860d.

McKINSTER, FRANK Adrian, Michigan, 1887d-1895d.

McKITRICK, JOHN Berne, Ohio, 1850c-1853d. (Hutslar)

McKNIGHT, ROBERT Girard, Illinois, 1860d.

McLAIN & THORP Weaverville, California, 1856. (Shelton)

McLAIN, G.W. Tabor, Indiana, 1879-1885. (Lindert)

McLAIN, J.T. Midland City, Michigan, 1879d.

McLANE, H.E. Fall River, Massachusetts, 1885d.

McLAREN, SAXTON & WILLIAMS St. Louis, Missouri, 1868d-1870d. Imported shotguns. Succeeded by McLaren, Williams & Co., 1870. (Pourie)

McLARTY, WILLIAM New York, New York, 1841d-1851d.

McLAUGHLIN & YOUNG Topeka, Kansas, 1872d-1873d. J.A. McLaughlin.

McLAUGHLIN, J.A. Topeka, Kansas, 1872d-1888d. As McLaughlin & Young, 1872-1873. (Hutslar)

McLAUGHLIN, JOHN W. (1826-?), Beamsville, Ohio, 1859d.

McLAUGHLIN, JOHN W. Indianapolis, Indiana, 1858d-1860d.

McLAUGHLIN, MICHAEL Yonkers, New York, 1866d.

McLEAN, DR. E.N. Washington, Iowa. Straight pull rifle in New York trials of 1896. See F.J. Evans. (GR 3-68)

McLEAN, DR. JAMES HENRY (1829-?), St. Louis, Missouri, 1880. Patents #282,548 August 7, 1883, breechloading gun, #282,549 August 7, 1883, machine gun, both with Myron Coloney. Patents #282,551 August 7, 1883, machine gun, #282,553 August 7, 1883, machine gun, #282,552 August 7, 1883, magazine gun, #282,554 August 7, 1883, magazine gun, and #290,905 December 25, 1883, breechloading firearm. (McLean)

McLEAN, T. unlocated. Percussion fullstock.

McLEISH, CHARLES Williamsburg, Ohio. (Knittle)

McLEMON, ADKIN Burke Co., North Carolina, 1776-1779. Committee of Safety muskets. (Bivins)

McLEOD, T.N. Lynn, Massachusetts, 1876d.

McLINE, JAMES Cumberland Co., Pennsylvania, 1776. Furnished 20 rifles and 43 muskets to Committee of Safety.

McLUE, ANDREW St. Louis, Missouri, 1850c. (MB 11-66)

McMAHON, JOHN (1815-?), New Orleans, Louisiana, 1850c-1853d. (MB 9-65)

McMAHON, JOHN New York, New York, 1841d-1845d.

McMANN, JOHN Wellsville, Virginia, 1835-1840. (Albaugh 1)

McMANUS see Johnson & McManus.

McMILLAN, EDWARD Bern, Missouri, 1860d.

McMILLIAN, W.R. Canaan, Missouri, 1881, Salem, Missouri, 1893d-1898d.

McMORAN, R.G. Ft. Collins, Colorado, 1882d. (Sellers-3)

McMULLEN, T.S. (1823-?), Farmington, Missouri, 1848-1860d, Mariposa Co., California, 1852c. (Shelton)

McNABB, J.A. Lambert, Tennessee, 1891d.

McNARY, J.B. Rome, New York, 1870d.

McNARY, THOMAS Martinsville, Illinois, 1864d.

McNAUGHT, JAMES Richmond, Virginia, 1810-1821. (Albaugh 1)

McNEAL Camba, Ohio, 1859d. (Hutslar)

McNEAL, JAMES C. Bowling Green, Kentucky, 1857-1860.

McNEARNY, MICHAEL Charleston, South Carolina, 1855. (Gluckman & Satterlee)

McNEELEY, WILLIAM Fayette Co., Pennsylvania, 1815t. (Whisker II)

McNEILL, MALCOLM (1802-?), Centerville, Illinois, 1839-1870. (Johnson)

McNELLY, JOHN Augusta Co., Virginia, 1764. (Gill)

McNICHOLS, JOSEPH (1808-?), Belmont Co., Ohio, 1828-1854. (Hutslar)

McNINCH, F.A. unlocated. Percussion 1/2 stock.

McNUTT, ROLLIN Franklin, Wisconsin, 1857d.

McPHAILS ARMORY Columbia, South Carolina. See Columbia Armory.

McPHERSON, SAMUEL Hanoverton, Ohio, 1888d. (Hutslan)

McQUAID, JAMES R. (1818-?), Canton, Illinois, 1844-1856. (Johnson)

McQUILKIN, THOMAS (1827-?), Terre Haute, Indiana, 1860c. (Lindert)

McRAE, ALEXANDER Richmond, Virginia. Model 1812 contract muskets.

McREE, J.P. unlocated. Marking on derringer with belt hook; another identical derringer has only "J.P.M." marking.

MEACHAM & POND Albany, New York, 1818-1830. Flintlock pistols. (Gluckman)

MEACHAM, E.C., & CO. St. Louis, Missouri, 1871d-1900d. Double barrel shotguns, retailers.

MEACHAM, H., & CO. Albany, New York. Flintlock pistol.

MEACHAM, I. & H. Albany, New York, 1802d. Flintlock muskets. (Swinney)

MEAD & ADRAINCE St. Louis, Missouri, 1835d-1840d. Agent for Allen underhammer.

MEAD, A. Brownville, Nebraska, 1866-1867d.

MEAD, EDWARD St. Louis, Missouri, 1835d-1864d. As Mead & Adraince, 1835-1840.

MEAKIN, BENJAMIN (1835-1907), New Paltz, New York, 1860c-1907. Double barrel percussion shotguns.

MEAKIN, GEORGE New York, New York, 1841d-1845d, Fulmerville, Pennsylvania, 1861d.

MEALOR, R.I. West Point, Georgia, 1879d.

MEALS, JOHN (1789-1852), Adams Co., Pennsylvania, 1821t-1852. Flintlock Kentucky and swivel breech rifles. (Bowers)

MEANLY, RICHARD Mecklenburg Co., Virginia, 1781. (Gill)

MEANS, B.L. Flora, Arkansas, 1888d-1892d.

MEANS, SAMUEL (?-1833), Washington Co., Pennsylvania, 1810-1825, Bridgeport, Ohio, 1829-1833. (Whisker II)

MEARS, JOHN Charleston, South Carolina, 1793. (Kauffman 2)

MEBAM, JOHN A. Orange Co., North Carolina, 1870c. (Bivins)

MEBANE, ALEXANDER (1808-?), Orange Co., North Carolina, 1870c. (Bivins)

MEBERGALL, JULIUS Brooklyn, New York, 1883d.

MECHLIUS, EDWARD Halifax, Pennsylvania, 1815. (Kauffman)

MECKLENBURG MANUFACTORY OF ARMS Mecklenburg, Virginia, 1776-1778. Operated by Thomas Rutherford.

MEDASIA, JOHN NICHOLAS (1815-1880), Bedford, Pennsylvania, 1840-1880. Percussion fullstock rifles signed "J.N.M.".

MEDBERY, CASPER (1803-1831), Rochester, New York, 1827d-1831. For brother Joseph Medbery. (Eich)

MEDBERY, JOSEPH (?-1882), Rochester, New York, 1818-1841. Flintlock and percussion rifles and pistols. Patent #none June 16, 1826, lock with S. Kellogg. Sold business to William Billinghurst in 1841. (Eich)

MEDBURY, ISAAC Erieville, New York, 1818-1828. Flintlock guns. Son of Thomas Medbury.

MEDBURY, THOMAS (1770-?), New Berlin, New York, ?-1818, Erieville, New York, 1818-1828. Flintlock rifles and fowlers. (Swinney)

MEDEER, BRUCE Brownsville, Pennsylvania, 1870d.

MEDLEY, N.B. Alexandria, Virgina, 1872d-1880d.

MEEKIN, GEORGE Pike Co., Pennsylvania. (Dillin)

MEEVES, D. unlocated. Flintlock Kentucky rifle.

MEFFORD, DANIEL M. Cincinnati, Ohio. Patents #34,285 January 28, 1862, bullet, and #47,317 April 18, 1865, cartridges for small arms.

MEFFORD, T. Maysville, Kentucky, 1803. Flintlock Kentucky. (Dillin)

MEGGENHOFFEN, FRED Franklin, Indiana, 1882-1885. (Gardner)

MEGLONE, W.W. Lexington, Kentucky, 1861. Percussion 1/2 stock.

MEHLIG, PETER Franklin, Indiana, 1867d. Same as Peter Mehlig, New York, New York?

MEHLIG, PETER New York, New York, 1847-1851. Same as Peter Mehlig from Franklin, Indiana?

MEHU, JOHN Sheboygan, Wisconsin, 1857d. See John W. Mumm.

MEICHINGER, MARTIN Brownwood, Texas, 1892d.

MEIER, ADOLPHUS St. Louis, Missouri, 1838d-1868d. Percussion double rifle/shotgun.

MEIER, WILLIAM C. Wooster, Ohio, 1859d-1897. (Hutslar)

MEIGS, HENRY, JR. Bergen Point, New Jersey. Patent #73,739 January 28, 1868, metallic cartridges.

MEIGS, JOSIAH V. Washington, D.C., 1862-1869, Lowell, Massachusetts, 1873-1875. Patents #36,721 October 21, 1862, breechloading firearm, #54,934 May 22, 1866, breechloading firearm, #81,100 August 18, 1868, breechloading firearm, #87,352 March 2, 1869, cartridge, #90,951 June 8, 1869, cartridge, #151,496 June 2, 1874, breechloading firearm. #157,621 December 8, 1874, carrier and extractor, #157,622 December 8, 1874, feed bar for magazine firearm, #157,623 December 8, 1874, magazine, #158,960 January 19, 1875, cartridge, #160,935 March 16, 1875, stock, #163,024 May 11, 1875, cartridge machine, #167,005 August 24, 1875, cartridge machine, #172,333 January 18, 1876, cartridge machine, and #340,234 April 20, 1886, cartridge machine. All cartridge patents used by U.S. Cartridge Co., Lowell, Massachusetts. (ICCA 7-78, AR 6-55)

MEINHEIM, JOHN (1815-?), Lewis Co., West Virginia, 1860c. (Whisker IV)

MEISENHEIMER, C. Jonesboro, Illinois, 1860d.

MEISGER, HENRY Ashland, Pennsylvania. Double barrel Kentucky. (Dillin)

MEISLANG, JOSEPH St. Louis, Missouri, 1866d-1868d.

MEISNER, AUGUST New Orleans, Louisiana, 1876d-1877d.

MEISSNER, C. & SON Zanesville, Ohio, 1875-1902. Charles Meissner. (Hutslar)

MEISSNER, CHARLES (1814-?), Adamsville, Ohio, 1840-1858, Zanesville, Ohio, 1858-1902. Percussion 1/2 stock, sometimes marked "C.M.". As C. Meissner & Son, 1875-1902. (Hutslar)

MELCHER, EDWARD O. Baltimore, Maryland, 1868d-1874d. Probably Edward Melchior.

MELCHER, H. Kirkwood, South Dakota, 1898d.

MELCHER, HARMAN Baltimore, Maryland, 1865d. (Hartzler)

MELCHIOR, EDWARD Baltimore, Maryland, 1876-1884d, Wilmington, Delaware, 1884d-1894d. Probably also known as Edward O. Melcher.

MELCHIOR, M. unlocated. Flintlock Kentucky.

MELCHIOR, NATHANIEL (1808-1870), Baltimore, Maryland, 1830-1879, Wilmington, Delaware, 1872d-1874d. Percussion fullstock. (Hartzler)

MELLEN, DUSTIN F. Manchester, New Hampshire. Patent #44,545 October 4, 1864, breechloading firearm.

MELLEY, HUGH Philadelphia, Pennsylvania, 1814d.

MELLIG, PETER Franklin, Indiana, 1860d-1862d.

MELLISH, W.E. Mount Holly, Vermont, 1869-1873. (Horn)

MELLOY, HUGH Lancaster, Pennsylvania, 1809. (KRA IV-4)

MELVIN, WILLIAM T. Vinton, Iowa, 1880d-1884d, Plattsmouth, Nebraska, 1886d.

MEMPHIS NOVELTY WORKS Memphis, Tennessee. Thomas Leech made swords and revolvers under this name. (Albaugh 3)

MENDENHALL, A.R. (1836-?), Des Ark, Arkansas, 1860c-1870c. Derringer. (Elias)

MENDENHALL, JONES & GARDNER Whitsett, North Carolina, 1861-1862, Jamestown, North Carolina, 1862-1864. Mississippi rifles, marked "M.J. & G.". Cyrus P. Mendenhall, E.P. Jones, and Nathan Gardner. (Bivins, Hill-Anthony)

MENEFEE, A.L. Coltharps, Texas, 1890d.

MENGAR, JOHN Madison, Ohio, 1859d. (Hutslar)

MENGES, E.E. Kansas City, Kansas, 1884d-1889d. Dealer.

MENSER, SAMUEL (1820-?), Ashtabula Co., Ohio, 1846-1850c. (Hutslar)

MENTZEL, HENRY New Orleans, Louisiana, 1871d-1872d.

MENZ, ALBERT J. (1839-?), Boston, Massachusetts, 1865, Marysville, California, 1868-1904. (Shelton)

MENZEL, GREGORY Milwaukee, Wisconsin, 1851-1852.

MEQUILLET, J. Mt. Eton, Ohio, Percussion 1/2 stock.

MERCER, A.J. Burdenville, Kansas, 1884d.

MERCER, ALFONSO Norfolk, Virginia, 1885d-1897d. Patent #477,764 June 28, 1892, magazine gun.

MERCKLEY, JACOB Philadelphia, Pennsylvania, 1781-1790. (Kauffman 2)

MEREDITH, BENJAMIN Baltimore, Maryland, 1810-1818d. (Hartzler)

MEREDITH, H. Baltimore, Maryland. Derringer. (Eberhart)

MERIAM, JOSEPH (1677-1750), Concord, Massachusetts, circa 1700-1750. Flintlock musket. (GR 11-73)

MERIAM, JOSIAH (1726-1809), Concord, Massachusetts, 1747-1809. Flintlock muskets. (GR 11-73)

MERIDEN MFG. CO. Meriden, Connecticut, 1863-1868. Made Triplet & Scott carbines and Miller conversion muskets.

MERKER, JOHN Petaluma, California, 1878d. (Shelton)

MERKLE, S. unlocated. Percussion fullstock.

MERLETT, JOHN Bound Brook, New Jersey. Patent #81,283 August 18, 1868, breechloading firearms.

MERMAN, D. Spring Mills, Pennsylvania. Percussion fullstock.

MERRIAM, LINCOLN A. New York, New York. Patents #86,091 January 1, 1869, firearm, #87,058 February 16, 1869, breechloading firearm, #212,105 February 11, 1879, magazine firearm, and #217,134 July 1, 1879, breechloading firearm.

MERRICK, JOHN St. Louis, Missouri, 1870d.

MERRIFIELD, THOMAS (1834-?), San Francisco, California, 1870c. (Shelton)

MERRIL, BENJAMIN Lexington, North Carolina, 1740-1771. Executed by the British for treason. (Bivins)

MERRILL PATENT FIRE ARM MFG. CO. Baltimore, Maryland, 1860-1867. Merrill carbines and Starr derringers. (Hartzler)

MERRILL, GEORGE H. Littleton, New Hampshire, 1876-1879d.

MERRILL, GEORGE East Orange, New Jersey. Patents #119,939 October 17, 1871, breechloading firearm, and #119,940 October 17, 1871, breechloading firearm.

MERRILL, H.P. unlocated. Percussion 1/2 stock dated 1864.

MERRILL, IRA M. Springfield, Massachusetts. Patents #137,786 April 15, 1863, hook attachments, and #174,634, March 14, 1876, implements for firearms.

MERRILL, JAMES H. (1816-?), Baltimore, Maryland, 1840d-1867d. Patents #14,077 January 8, 1856, breechloading firearms, #18,401 October 13, 1857, projectiles for rifled cannon, #20,954 July 20, 1858, breechloading firearm, #32,032 April 9, 1861, breechloading firearm, #32,033 April 9, 1861, breechloading firearm, #32,450 May 28, 1861, breechloading firearm, #32,451 May 28, 1861, breechloading firearm, #33,536 October 22, 1861, breechloading firearm, and #40,884 December 8, 1863, breechloading firearm. Merrill carbines made by Merrill, Latrobe & Thomas, 1856-1859, and Merrill Patent Fire Arm Mfg. Co., 1860-1867. (GR 5-59)

MERRILL, JEREMIAH (1780-?), Baltimore, Maryland, 1850c-1867d. (Hartzler)

MERRILL, JOSIAH P. Freeport, Maine, 1872-1890. Percussion fowler. (Demeritt)

MERRILL, LATROBE & THOMAS Baltimore, Maryland, 1856-1859. Carbines. James Merrill, Ferinond Latrobe, Lewen and Philip Thomas. (Hartzler)

MERRILL, LEONARD F. Woodford's Corner, Maine, 1878-1889. (Demeritt)

MERRILL, WILLIAM E.T. Philadelphia, Pennsylvania, 1879d-1880d.

MERRILL, WILLIAM Y. Baltimore, Maryland, 1864d. (Hartzler)

MERRIMAC ARMS & MFG. CO. Newburyport, Massachusetts, 1866-1872. Ballard rifles, Southerner derringers, Beach sights, and G. Merrill carving machine. Incorporated May 16, 1867; owned by Merwin & Bray - Joseph Merwin and Edward Bray. (AR 8-27)

MERRIMAN, J.F., & CO. Memphis, Tennessee, 1851d-1852d. Derringer.

MERRIMAN, SILAS Connecticut, 1777. Repaired public arms. (Gluckman & Satterlee)

MERRITT, ALLEN E. Randolph, Massachusetts, 1849d-1855d.

MERRITT, BENJAMIN Newton, Massachusetts, 1883-1886. Patents #233,363 October 19, 1880, revolving shotgun, and #338,760 March 30, 1886, 10 gauge four-shot revolving shotgun.

MERRITT, G. Peekskill, New York, 1775. (Dean*)

MERRITT, H. Randolph, Massachusetts, 1857-1860d.

MERRITT, IRA Abington, Massachusetts, 1859-1868.

MERRITT, JOHN Boston, Massachusetts, 1789-1798. (Kauffman 2)

MERRITT, RICHARD De Witt, Michigan, 1875d.

MERRITT, RICHARD Point of Fork, Virginia, 1789-1794. (Gill)

MERRITT, RICHMOND Bainbridge, New York, 1856-1859d.

MERRITT, THOMAS FLETCHER (1817-?), Jamestown, North Carolina, 1850c. (Bivins)

MERSHON, RALPH S. Zanesville, Ohio, 1853-1887. Patents #12,470 February 27, 1855, revolver, #12,471 February 27, 1855, revolver, and #39,825 September 8, 1863, revolver. All patents with John Hollingsworth. (Sellers-1)

MERWIN & BRAY Worcester, Massachusetts, 1862-1868. Also Merwin & Simpkins, 1867-1868 and Merwin, Taylor & Simpkins, in 1868. They were primarily sales agents for other manufacturers, with sales offices in New York City.

MERWIN, HULBERT & CO. New York, New York, 1868-1891. Sold revolvers under Daniel Moore's patents and Evans rifles. Successors to Merwin, Taylor & Simpkins.

MERWIN, JOSEPH (1821-1879), Worcester, Massachusetts, 1862-1868. Patents #41,166 January 5, 1864, firearm with Edward Bray, #175,293 March 7, 1876, cartridge, and British patent #1878-277, January 22, 1877, revolver with brothers M. and Wm. A. Hulbert. (GR 4-66)

MERZ, LOUIS Lock Haven, Pennsylvania, 1882d-1887d. Percussion double rifle/shotgun.

MESKE, DANIEL Port Townsend, Washington, 1889d-1891d.

MESLE, FRANZ J. Brooklyn, New York. Patent #207,056 August 13, 1878, breechloading firearm.

MESMER, C. Manitowoc, Wisconsin, 1857d. Percussion schuetzen rifle. See Caspar Messmer, same person?

MESMIN, AUGUSTUS Charleston, South Carolina, 1696. (Kauffman 2)

MESSENGER, WILLIAM Chase, Michigan, 1883d.

MESSER, C. Waynesville, North Carolina, circa 1870. (Bivins)

MESSER, CASPAR (1827-?), Toledo, Ohio, 1850c. (Hutslar)

MESSER, D. Bedford Co., Pennsylvania, 1860. Percussion swivel breech rifles. (Hetrick)

MESSER, ISAAC Waynesville, North Carolina, circa 1870. (Bivins)

MESSER, MELVIN Waynesville, North Carolina, circa 1890. Son of Isaac Messer. (Bivins)

MESSER, MILES Waynesville, North Carolina, circa 1890. Son of Isaac Messer. (Bivins)

MESSER, W.W. Boston, Massachusetts, during percussion era. (Roberts)

MESSERSMITH, GEORGE Lancaster, Pennsylvania, 1802t-1814. (Kauffman KRA IV-4)

MESSERSMITH, HENRY Lancaster, Pennsylvania, 1747. (KRA IV-4)

MESSERSMITH, JACOB Lancaster, Pennsylvania, 1779-1810. Flintlock Kentucky.

MESSERSMITH, JOHN Lancaster, Pennsylvania, 1776-1779. Committee of Safety locks. (Gluckman & Satterlee)

MESSERSMITH, SAMUEL Baltimore, Maryland, 1775-1778. Committee of Safety locks and muskets. (Hartzler)

MESSEX, BENJAMIN Polk Run, Indiana, 1860d.

MESSIX, S. Fisherville, Kentucky, 1857-1860. Percussion 1/2 stock rifles.

MESSMER, CASPAR Manitowoc, Wisconsin, 1843-1858. See C. Mesmer, same person? (WGCA 4)

MESSNER, JOEL Lancaster Co., Pennsylvania, 1837-1843. Barrelmaker. (KRA IV-4)

MESTIER, J.R. Galveston, Texas, 1875d-1878d, Corpus Christi, Texas, 1884d.

MESTREZAT, WILLIAM (1809-?), Mapleton, Pennsylvania, 1830-1836. (Whisker II)

METCALF, E.J. Fergus Falls, Minnesota, 1882d.

METCALF, WILLIAM Niles, Michigan, 1891d.

METCALFE, HENRY Springfield, Massachusetts. Patents #149,141 March 31, 1874, hook attachment to bands, and #167,006 August 24, 1875, attachment of magazines to firearms. Employed at the Springfield Armory. Also see Felix Chillingworth.

METLER, JOHN E. (?-1879), Easton, Pennsylvania, 1850-1879.

METROPOLITAN ARMS CO. New York, New York, 1859-1882. Copies of Colt revolver.

METROPOLITAN POLICE suicide special.

METROPOLITAN POLICE trade name of Curtis Maltby & Co. on owlhead revolvers.

METROPOLITAN trade name of Crescent Fire Arms Co. on guns made for Siegel-Cooper Co. (AR 2-69)

METTELKA, JOSEPH Marshfield, Wisconsin, 1891d-1895d.

METTLER, ELIAS Easton, Pennsylvania, 1860d. (Whisker II)

METZ Napoleon, Ohio, 1870c. (Hutslar)

METZGER, JACOB T. Lancaster, Pennsylvania, 1857d, Hamilton, Ohio, 1863d, Crawfordsville, Indiana, 1879-1885. (Hutslar-Lindert)

METZGER, JACOB (1765-1837), Lancaster, Pennsylvania, 1758-1777, Fredericktown, Maryland, 1788-1825. Model 1795 contract muskets with Nicholas White, Thomas Crabb, and Christopher Barnhizle. Flintlock Kentucky. (Kindig-Hartzler)

METZGER, PHILLIP Lancaster, Pennsylvania, 1814-1820. (Kauffman 2)

METZKER, J. Exeter, Illinois, 1860d.

MEUNIER, HERMAN New London, Wisconsin, 1878d-1879d.

MEUNIER, JOHN (1840-1919), Milwaukee, Wisconsin, 1857-1919. Percussion guns, mostly schuetzen. After John died the business was managed by his brother Stephen, 1919-1930. (WGCA 4)

MEUNIER, M. Hartford, Wisconsin, 1879d.

MEUNIER, STEPHEN Milwaukee, Wisconsin, 1919-1930. See John Meunier.

MEWHIRTER, JOHN Chambersburg, Pennsylvania. Flintlock Kentucky. Son of John Mewhirter. First name possibly Robert. (Bowers)

MEWHIRTER, JOHN Shippensburg, Pennsylvania, 1815-1836, Chambersburg, Pennsylvania, 1836-1841. Flintlock Kentucky. Son of William Mewhirter. (Bowers)

MEWHIRTER, WILLIAM (?-1814), Cumberland Co., Pennsylvania, 1779t-1790c, Shippensburg, Pennsylvania, 1811-1814. Flintlock Kentucky. (Bowers)

MEY, JAMES Maryland, 1781.

MEYER, BENJAMIN F. Jacksonville, Oregon, 1873d.

MEYER, CHARLES H.J. (1835-?), San Francisco, California, 1866-1876. (Shelton)

MEYER, GEORGE Lancaster, Pennsylvania, 1814. (KRA IV-4)

MEYER, JACOB (1822-?), New Orleans, Louisiana, 1850c-1874d. Percussion 1/2 stock.

MEYER, JOHN C.J. Baltimore, Maryland, 1856-1861d. Percussion guns. (Hartzler)

MEYER, JOHN Cambridge, Ohio, 1859d-1888d. 1/2 stock percussion rifles. (Hutslar)

MEYER, JULIUS W. St. Louis, Missouri, 1870c.

MEYER, PHILIP Newark, New Jersey, 1878d.

MEYER, WILLIAM Wooster, Ohio, 1858-1897. (Hutslar)

MEYERS, CHARLES A. Philadelphia, Pennsylvania, 1885d-1899d. Successor to Paul Meyers.

MEYERS, D. unlocated. Flintlock Kentucky.

MEYERS, JAMES Analomink, Pennsylvania, 1887d-1890d.

MEYERS, JOHN Cambridge, Ohio, 1850-1890. (Hutslar)

MEYERS, PAUL Philadelphia, Pennsylvania, 1866d-1888d. With W.R. Hallowell as Hallowell & Meyers, 1866d-1867d.

MEYLIN, MARTIN (1670-1749), Germantown, Pennsylvania, 1705, Lancaster Co., Pennsylvania, 1719-1749. Flintlock rifle. (Beck)

MICHAEL, CYRIL Van Buren, Maine, 1869-1873. (Demeritt)

MICHAEL, HENRY (1820-?), Baltimore, Maryland, 1847-1860d. (Hartzler)

MICHAEL, HENRY (1828-?), Xenia, Ohio, 1850c, Dowagiac, Michigan, 1872d-1887d. (Hutslar)

MICHAEL, JOHN Lancaster Co., Pennsylvania, 1812. Barrelmaker. (KRA IV-4)

MICHAELSON, O.H. Charleston, West Virginia, 1882d. (Whisker IV)

MICHELENA, GUILIERMO New York, New York. Patent #148,571 March 17, 1874, breechloading firearm.

MICHLER, WILLIAM San Francisco, California, 1850d. (Shelton)

MICHLIN, EDWARD Halifax, Pennsylvania, 1817. (Kauffman)

MICKEY, DANIEL (1812-1881), Confluence, Pennsylvania, 1876-1881. (Whisker II)

MICKSELL, MARTIN Leacock Twp., Pennsylvania, 1776. For Christian Werger.

MIDDAUGH, JESSE Farmerstown, Ohio, circa 1865. Percussion 1/2 stock. (Hutslar)

MIDDLETON & HENDERSON Spirit Lake, Iowa, 1880d-1881d. Zina Henderson.

MIDDLETON, JOSEPH T. Harveysburg, Ohio, 1878d. Son of Thomas J. Middleton.

MIDDLETON, THOMAS J. Harveysburg, Ohio, 1857-1860d. Percussion sporting rifle.

MIDDLETOWN BROS. South Bend, Indiana, 1875-1876d. (MB 4-54)

MIDNIGHT, I.E. unlocated. Percussion pistol.

MIELCAREK, W.S. Grand Rapids, Michigan, 1887d.

MIER, JACOB (1793-1873), Somerset, Pennsylvania, 1822-1873. Percussion 1/2 stock. (Kauffman)

MIER, JACOB Frederick Co., Maryland, 1762-?. (Hartzler)

MIER, JOHN (1829-1909), Somerset, Pennsylvania. Percussion fullstock. (Kauffman)

MIER, SAMUEL Frederick Co., Maryland, Somerset, Pennsylvania, 1852-1872. Percussion fullstock. Son of Jacob Mier. (Kauffman-Hartzler)

MIER, WILLIAM B. (1829-1909), Somerset, Pennsylvania. (Kauffman)

MIFORD, T. (1803-1890), Maysville, Kentucky, 1843-1896. Percussion rifles. (Dillin)

MIGNERON, FRANCOIS St. Louis, Missouri, 1795. With Andrew Lauderville.

MIGNERON, LOUIS SOLOMON St. Louis, Missouri, 1819-1821d.

MIGNERON, S.S. Manchester, Missouri, 1860d. Son of Louis Migneron.

MIGUA, JACOB (1804-?), Wayne Co., Ohio, 1850c. (Hutslar)

MILBANK, ISSAC M. Greenfield Hill, Connecticut, 1862-1875. Patents #37,048 December 2, 1862, breechloading firearm, #46,125 January 31, 1865, breechloading firearm, #52,734 February 20, 1866, breechloading firearm, #55,520 June 12, 1866, breechloading firearm, #61,082 January 8, 1867, breechloading firearm, #61,751 February 5, 1867, breechloading firearm, #62,283 February 19, 1867, priming metallic cartridges, #65,585 June 11, 1867, breechloading firearm, #84,566 December 1, 1868, breechloading firearm, #122,399 January 2, 1872, metallic cartridges, #123,351 February 6, 1872, metallic cartridges, #123,352 February 6, 1872, metallic cartridges, #125,829 April 16, 1872, breechloading firearms, #125,830 April 16, 1872, metallic cartridges, #131,016 September 3, 1872, metallic cartridges, #131,017 September 3, 1872, metallic cartridges, #131,018 September 3, 1872, metallic cartridges, #136,168 February 2, 1873, metallic cartridges, #136,850 March 18, 1873, breechloading firearm, #147,567 February 17, 1874, breechloading firearm, #157,856 December 15, 1874, explosive compound, and #157,857 December 15, 1874, explosive compound.

MILBURN, NATHAN L. St. Louis, Missouri. Patent #57,751 September 4, 1866, revolving cannon.

MILES, CHARLES M. Vineland, New Jersey. Patent #45,333 December 6, 1864, sight.

MILES, DON D. Aurora, Illinois, 1890-1899. Patent #618,116 January 24, 1899, magazine gun. Submitted a rifle to the 1892 trials.

MILES, E.J. Newton, Iowa, 1887d-1889d. As Frisbee & Miles, 1889.

MILES, H.S. unlocated. Percussion 1/2 stock.

MILES, JOHN (1752-1808), Philadelphia, Pennsylvania, 1790-1808. Model 1798 contract muskets for Pennsylvania, pistols. (Gluckman)

MILES, JOHN, JR. (1777-1852), Philadelphia, Pennsylvania, 1804-1805, Bordertown, New Jersey, 1808-1811. Model 1798 contract muskets for Virginia with Robert McCormick, Model 1808 contract muskets, and flintlock Kentucky rifles. Son of John Miles. (Gluckman)

MILES, MARY Philadelphia, Pennsylvania, 1824d. Widow of John Miles, Sr., listed as gunsmith in Deselven Directory in 1824.

MILES, THOMAS Philadelphia, Pennsylvania, 1775-1776. Committee of Safety pistols. (Cromwell)

MILES, WILLIAM A. Salisbury, Connecticut. Patent #129,976, July 30, 1872, machine gun.

MILES, WILLIAM C. Russell, Kansas, 1878d.

MILLAR, JOHN Rochester, New York. Percussion 1/2 stock. Early form of J. Miller signature.

MILLARD BROS. Williams, New York, 1872-1874d.

MILLARD, HENRY (1802-?), Culpepper Co., Virginia, 1850c. (MB 10-63)

MILLARD, JOHN (1832-?), Culpepper Co., Virginia, 1850c. Son of Henry Millard. (MB 10-63)

MILLARD, SETH Lockport, New York, 1868-1874d. Percussion target rifle.

MILLBURY COMPANY Worcester, Massachusetts. (James Durrell?) Greene underhammer rifles.

MILLEMANN, FREDERICK San Francisco, California, 1856-1857. (Shelton)

MILLEN, GEORGE South Salem, Ohio, 1853d. Percussion rifles. (Hutslar)

MILLER & BELL Leadville, Colorado, 1881-1882d. William P. Miller and William C. Bell. (Sellers-3)

MILLER & GONZALES New York, New York, 1849d. John F. Miller and John H. Gonzales. Also known as Muller & Gonzales.

MILLER, A. (1812-?), Milledgeville, Illinois, 1860c. (Johnson)

MILLER, A., JR. (1811-?), Illinois, 1833-1839. (Johnson)

MILLER, ABNER Easton, Pennsylvania. Flintlock Kentucky.

MILLER, ALBERT Detroit, Michigan, 1872d-1877d.

MILLER, B.C. New Haven, Connecticut. Percussion 1/2 stock.

MILLER, B.T. Fayetteville, Arkansas, 1884d. Same as B.T. Tyler, Tipton, Indiana?

MILLER, B.T. Tipton, Indiana, 1855-1870c. Derringer. Same as B.T. Tyler, Fayetteville, Arkansas? (Lindert)

MILLER, BENJAMIN Berks Co., Pennsylvania, 1821-1852.

MILLER, BENJAMIN Lancaster, Pennsylvania, 1841t. Percussion fullstock. (Dillin) (Dyke)

MILLER, BRYANT (1814-?), Raleigh, North Carolina, 1850c. (Bivins)

MILLER, C.A. New Haven, Connecticut. Breechloading rifles. (Lindsay)

MILLER, C.O. Hannibal, Missouri, 1860d. Percussion 1/2 stock.

MILLER, CALVIN Canadia, New York, 1857- ?, Honeoye, New York, 1858-1859d, Ontario, New York. Miller patent revolving rifle.

MILLER, CHARLES H. Ft. Wayne, Indiana, 188 l-1885d.

MILLER, CHARLES East Newark, Ohio, 1818-?. (Hutslar)

MILLER, CHARLES Greenville, West Virginia, 1850-1860. (Whisker IV)

MILLER, CHARLES Kansas City, Missouri, 1867d-1871d.

MILLER, CHARLES St. Louis, Missouri, 1860d-1869d.

MILLER, CYRUS Honeoye, New York, 1847-1850d. Percussion mule-ear over/under rifles.

MILLER, D.G. Anoka, Minnesota, 1867d.

MILLER, DANIEL (1801-?), Reading, Pennsylvania, 1850c. Flintlock Kentucky. (Whisker III)

MILLER, DAVID (1781-?), Fayette Co., Pennsylvania, 1802-1810. Apprenticed to Christian Hawken, 1796. (Kauffman)

MILLER, DAVID (1832-?), Monroe Co., Indiana, 1850c, Stanford, Indiana, 1854, Bedford, Indiana, 1879-1884. Percussion 1/2 stock. (Lindert)

MILLER, DAVID Pulaski Co., Missouri, 1850c. (MB 11-66)

MILLER, DAVID Springfield, Ohio, 1870-1878, Metamora, Ohio, 1883d. (Knittle, Hutslar)

MILLER, DAVID Troy, Ohio, 1875d-1898d. Percussion 1/2 stock rifles. (Hutslar)

MILLER, ENOCH East Newark, Ohio, 1818-1889. Son of Charles Miller. (Hutslar)

MILLER, FRANKLIN Wyomissing Creek, Pennsylvania, 1821-1856. Barrels only. Sold out to Franklin K. Schnader in 1856. (Hobbies 5-37)

MILLER, FREDERICK Cannelton, Indiana, 1860d.

MILLER, G.C., & CO. Kansas City, Missouri, 1876d-1898d. Successors to Charles Miller.

MILLER, G.G. New Haven, Connecticut. Percussion target rifles. (Lindsay)

MILLER, GEORGE E. (1824-?), Allen Co., Ohio, 1850c. (Hutslar)

MILLER, GEORGE W. (1824-?), West Meriden, Connecticut, 1850c. Patents #47,902 May 23, 1865, breechloading firearm, #51,739 December 26, 1865, breechloading firearm, #64,786 May 14, 1867, breechloading firearm, and #68,099 August 27, 1867, breechloading firearm. All patents with William H. Miller.

MILLER, GEORGE Columbia Co., Pennsylvania, 1821. (Kauffman)

MILLER, GEORGE Lancaster, Pennsylvania, 1766-1811. Two Georges, father and son. Flintlock Kentucky. (Kauffman)

MILLER, GEORGE Philadelphia, Pennsylvania, 1837d-1847d.

MILLER, H.M. Gainesville, Texas, 1884d.

MILLER, HENRY Lancaster, Pennsylvania, 1840-1850. (Kauffman)

MILLER, HENRY Mobile, Alabama, 1839d. (Neville)

MILLER, I. unlocated. Percussion fullstock.

MILLER, J.B. Monroeville, Indiana. Percussion 1/2 stock. (Lindert)

MILLER, JACOB M. Berlin Heights, Ohio, 1883d. (Hutslar)

MILLER, JACOB P. El Paso, Texas, 1884d-1890d, Santa Cruz, California, 1893d.

MILLER, JACOB Lancaster Co., Pennsylvania, 1773. (KRA IV-4)

MILLER, JAMES (?-1843), Rochester, New York, 1829-1843. Patent #none June 11, 1829, revolver. Percussion revolving rifles with brother John, 1829-1837. (Sellers-1)

MILLER, JOHN A. Paducah, Kentucky. Patent #46,257 February 7, 1865, breechloading gun.

MILLER, JOHN B. (1851-1938), Columbus, Ohio. (Hutslar)

MILLER, JOHN C. New York, New York. Patent #99,693 February 8, 1870, revolving rifle.

MILLER, JOHN D. Philadelphia, Pennsylvania, 1841d-1861d.

MILLER, JOHN DAVID (?-1816), Charleston, South Carolina, 1806-1816. Primarily a goldsmith, but worked as a gunsmith in his later years. (Dean)

MILLER, JOHN F. New York, New York, 1849d-1867d, Brooklyn, New York, 1868d-1896d. With John H. Gonzales as Miller & Gonzales, 1849. Also known as John F. Muller.

MILLER, JOHN (1739-1810), Lancaster Co., Pennsylvania, 1771-1810. Flintlock Kentucky. Committee of Safety member. (Gluckman & Satterlee)

MILLER, JOHN (1825-?), Shasta, California, 1860c. (Shelton)

MILLER, JOHN (1830-1893), New Jersey, 1850-?, Burlington, Iowa, ?-1860, Jacksonville, Oregon, 1860-1893. Percussion 1/2 stock. (GR 11-58)

MILLER, JOHN Bridgeport, Illinois, 1860d.

MILLER, JOHN East Newark, Ohio, 1818. Son of Charles Miller. (Hutslar)

MILLER, JOHN Lancaster, Pennsylvania, 1863. (Dyke)

MILLER, JOHN Penfield, Michigan, 1836-1868, Monroe, Michigan, 1868-1875. Percussion 1/2 stock. (Roberts)

MILLER, JOHN Rochester, New York, 1829-1853d, Battle Creek, Michigan, 1854-1856. Patent #none June 11, 1829, revolving rifle. Patent hand revolved rifles were made by many gunsmiths, notably Billinghurst, who apprenticed under Miller. (Sellers-1, Eich)

MILLER, JOSEPH Hermann, Missouri, 1850c. (MB 11-66)

MILLER, JOSEPH Watertown, Wisconsin, 1872d.

MILLER, JOSIAH Uniontown, Pennsylvania, 1814. (Whisker II)

MILLER, LOUIS Fairfield, Texas, 1878d-1890d, Mexia, Texas, 1892d.

MILLER, M. Eaton, Ohio, 1860-1864d. (Hutslar)

MILLER, M. South Hamburg, Pennsylvania, 1850. Percussion fullstock. (Gluckman & Satterlee)

MILLER, M.L. Hempstead, Texas, 1896d.

MILLER, MATHIAS (1794-?), Naperville, Illinois, 1860c. (Johnson)

MILLER, MATHIAS Easton, Pennsylvania, 1775t-1811t. Committee of Safety locks. (Kauffman 2)

MILLER, MICHAEL Philadelphia, Pennsylvania, 1780-1785. Repaired U.S. arms. (Moller)

MILLER, P.J. Tiffin, Ohio, 1881d. (Hutslar)

MILLER, PETER Berks Co., Pennsylvania, 1787-1790.

MILLER, PETER New Albany, Ohio, 1878d. (Hutslar)

MILLER, PIERRE New Orleans, Louisiana, 1834d-1838d.

MILLER, ROBERT Pittsburgh, Pennsylvania, 1860d-1864d. Barrelmaker

MILLER, S. Damascus and Danville, Ohio, 1853d. (Hutslar)

MILLER, S. Lawrence, Kansas, 1878d.

MILLER, SAMUEL C. New Haven, Connecticut, 1849-1860. Percussion 1/2 stock.

MILLER, SAMUEL (1810-?), Lawrence Co., Ohio, 1850c. (Hutslar)

MILLER, SAMUEL (1818-?), Upper Sandusky, Ohio, 1850c. (Hutslar)

MILLER, SAMUEL Boston, Massachusetts, 1730-1742. Successor to John Pim. Advertised a flintlock repeater. (Gluckman & Satterlee)

MILLER, SAMUEL Hamburg, Pennsylvania, 1823-1849. Flintlock Kentucky. (Kauffman 2)

MILLER, SIMON Hamburg, Pennsylvania, 1775-1806. Flintlock Kentucky rifles and pistols, signed either "S. M." or "S. Miller". (Dillin)

MILLER, STEPHEN (1805-?), Murry, California, 1866-1875. (Shelton)

MILLER, T.J. North Manchester, Indiana, 1882-1885. Percussion 1/2 stock. (Lindert)

MILLER, T.J. Sanford, Florida, 1886d.

MILLER, THOMAS Salem Center, Indiana, 1860d.

MILLER, W.G. unlocated. Percussion mule-ear fullstock rifle.

MILLER, WILLIAM D. Pittsburgh, Pennsylvania. Patent #169,465 November 2, 1875, recoil check.

MILLER, WILLIAM DEEDS Pittsfield, Massachusetts, 1849d-1867, New York, New York, 1867-1876. Derringer.

MILLER, WILLIAM H. West Meriden, Connecticut. Patents #47,902 May 23, 1865, breechloading firearm, #51,739 December 26, 1865, breechloading firearm, #59,723 November 13, 1866, breechloading firearm, #64,786 May 14, 1867, breechloading firearm, and #68,099 August 27, 1867, cartridge ejector. All patents with George W. Miller.

MILLER, WILLIAM P. Leadville, Colorado, 1881d-1882d. With William C. Bell as Miller & Bell. (Sellers-3)

MILLER, WILLIAM P. Rolling Prairie, Indiana, 1860d-1864d.

MILLER, WILLIAM R. Baltimore, Maryland. Patents #385,942 July 10, 1888, magazine gun, #387,531 August 7, 1888, charge indicator, #394,872 December 18, 1888, load indicator, #393,653 November 27, 1888, charge indicator, #395,913 January 8, 1889, hammer, and #404,921 June 6, 1889, changing center of gravity.

MILLER, WILLIAM T. Danville, Pennsylvania, 1861d.

MILLER, WILLIAM Chetopa, Kansas, 1878d-1882d.

MILLERON, D. Smicksburg, Pennsylvania, 1861d. (Possibly David Milliron)

MILLEY, EDWARD Lancaster, Pennsylvania, 1863. (Dyke)

MILLHOUSE, DAVID Montrose, Iowa, 1884d-1889d.

MILLIKEN, M.C. Charlestown, New Hampshire, 1872d-1874d. Underhammer buggy rifle.

MILLIRON, ANTHONY Indiana Co., Pennsylvania, 1805-1806. (Kauffman)

MILLIRON, C. Dayton, Pennsylvania. Percussion fullstock. (Gluckman & Satterlee)

MILLIRON, DAVID West Mahoning, Pennsylvania, 1850-1851. (Kauffman)

MILLIRON, JOHN Hempfield, Pennsylvania, 1802-1809. (Kauffman)

MILLNER, ELIZA Brooklyn, New York, 1864-1867d.

MILLNER, JOHN KEEN New York, New York. Patent #37,723 February 17, 1863, breechloading firearm.

MILLS & THOMPSON Pleasant Valley, Illinois, 1850. Lafayette Mills and James Thompson. (Johnson)

MILLS, B., & SON Lexington, Kentucky, 1870d-1889d. Benjamin Mills, Jr. and son Charles.

MILLS, BENJAMIN Charlottesville, North Carolina, 1784-1790, Harrodsburg, Kentucky, 1790-1814. (Gluckman & Satterlee)

MILLS, BENJAMIN, JR. (1810-1888), Harrodsburg, Kentucky, 1850-1860, Lexington, Kentucky, 1865-1889. Percussion and breechloading guns. At Harper's Ferry and Ashville Armories during the Civil War. With his son Charles as B. Mills & Son, 1870-1889.

MILLS, CHARLES (1845-1896), Lexington, Kentucky, 1870d-1889d, Louisville, Kentucky, 1889-1896. With his father Benjamin Mills Jr. as B. Mills & Son, 1870-1889. As Griffith, Semple & Mills, 1889-1896.

MILLS, EDWARD JAMES SMITH Jamestown, New York, 1873d.

MILLS, F.M. Charlottesville, North Carolina. Father of Benjamin Mills.

MILLS, GEORGE Cole Co., Missouri, 1850c. (MB 11-66)

MILLS, H.S. Coldwater, Michigan. Percussion 1/2 stock target rifle.

MILLS, HARVEY Springfield, Massachusetts. Patent #none July 12, 1834, barrels.

MILLS, ISAAC (1801-1836), Brookville, Pennsylvania, 1831. Percussion fullstock. Brother of Joseph Mills.

MILLS, J.R., & CO. Chicago, Illinois, 1853-1854. (Johnson)

MILLS, JASON Pittsfield, Massachusetts. Model 1795 contract musket, New England Kentucky flintlock.

MILLS, JOHN B. Fayetteville, North Carolina, 1831. Silversmith who repaired guns. (Bivins)

MILLS, JOSEPH W. Bangor, Iowa, 1865d.

MILLS, JOSEPH (1790-1876), Bedford Co., Pennsylvania, 1808t-1823t, Coshocton Co., Ohio, 1823d, East Union, Ohio, 1859d. Flintlock and percussion Kentucky rifles sometimes signed "J. M.". (Hutslar, Hetrick, AOLRC V II)

MILLS, L.F. Nord, California, 1893d.

MILLS, LAFAYETTE (1827-?), Pleasant Valley, Illinois, 1850-1868. With James Thompson as Mills & Thompson, 1850. (Johnson)

MILLS, O. Troy, New York, 1839. (Dillin)

MILLS, SIMEON Camden, Indiana, 1862d.

MILLS, WARDEN (1806-?), Ohio, 1831-1838, Pike Co., Illinois, 1845-1880c. (Johnson)

MILLS, WILLIAM (?-1844), Wheeling, West Virginia, 1839d-1844t. Barrelmaker. (Whisker IV)

MILLSPAUGH, A. Washington and Shreveport, Louisiana. A druggist who acted as agent for Deringer.

MILNOR, ISAAC Philadelphia, Pennsylvania, 1799-1800. Flintlock Kentucky rifles. (Kauffman)

MILNOR, JOHN (?-1749), Charleston, South Carolina, 1734-1749. (Hobbies 7-42)

MILNOR, JOHN, II Charleston, South Carolina, 1749-1790d. Son of John Milnor. (Hobbies 7-42)

MILSTEAD, J. Palmyra, Missouri, 1850c-1854d. Percussion 1/2 stock. As Milstead & Son, 1854.

MILSTED, A.I. Macon City, Missouri, 1879d.

MILSTED, INMENT Rochester, New York, 1838d-1841d. (Eich)

MILTIMORE, ALONZO E. U.S. Army. Patents #145,224 December 2, 1873, battery gun, and #181,093 August 15, 1876, battery gun.

MILTON, N.B. Monroe, Louisiana, 1885d.

MILWARD, J. Brooklyn, New York, 1872d.

MINARD, JOHN M. Norwalk, Ohio, 1881d. Percussion double shotgun. (Hutslar)

MINCH, GEORGE Stamford, Connecticut, 1886d.

MINER, GEORGE W. Syracuse, New York, 1850-1855. Mule-ear 1/2 stock. (Clow)

MINER, HENRY Cincinnati, Ohio, 1836-1844, Harrison, Ohio, 1845-1848. (Hutslar)

MINER, HENRY Huntingdon Co., Pennsylvania, 1800. (Whisker II)

MINESINGER, DAVID Beaver, Pennsylvania. Patent #6,139 February 27, 1849, breechloading firearm. Guns made by John White, Pittsburgh. (GR 8-57)

MINET, FRANK Boston, Massachusetts, 1850. (Dean*)

MINET, JOHN Brooklyn, New York, 1869-1878.

MINFIRT, ABRAHAM Erie Co., Pennsylvania, 1850c. (GR 11-60)

MINGES, JOHN (?-1893), Stockton, California, 1850-1859. (Shelton)

MINNEAPOLIS FIRE ARMS CO. Minneapolis, Minnesota, 1890-1892d. "Protector" palm pistols made by James Duckworth. (GR 1-67)

MINNESOTA ARMS CO. trade name of Farwell, Ozmun & Kirk on shotguns made by Crescent Fire Arms Co. (Hinman)

MINNICK, GEORGE Philadelphia, Pennsylvania, 1847d.

MINOT, H.P. unlocated. Underhammer rifle.

MINTON, SILAS Suckasunny, New Jersey, 1860d.

MINTON, WARREN D.S. Sandersville, Georgia, 1879d-1883d.

MINTY, JAMES Paris, Tennessee, 1873d.

MINTZER, GEORGE Philadelphia, Pennsylvania, 1874d-1896d. Revolvers.

MISEL, GEORGE A. Cole Co., Missouri, 1850c. (MB 11-66)

MISKEY, J. Galion, Ohio, 1872-1875d. (Hutslar)

MISNER, BENJAMIN D. (1819-?) Deerfield, Ohio, 1862. Also D.B. Misner, Berlin Center, Ohio? (Hutslar)

MISNER, D.B. Berlin Center, Ohio, 1859d-1864d. Probably Benjamin D. Misner.

MISSISSIPPI STATE ARMORY Panola, Brandon, and Meridian, Mississippi. Repairs and conversions. (Albaugh 1)

MISSISSIPPI VALLEY ARMS CO. trade name of Shapleigh Hardware Co. on shotguns made by Crescent Fire Arms Co. (GR 7-74)

MITCHELL & SIMPSON North Carolina, 1857. Entered rifle in state fair. (Bivins)

MITCHELL, B.C. Ottawa, Illinois, 1856-1858. As Bunker & Mitchell. (Johnson)

MITCHELL, D.D. St. Louis, Missouri, 1859-1860d.

MITCHELL, E.A. Bryan, Texas, 1878d, Belton, Texas, 1885d. Brother of M. Mitchell.

MITCHELL, E.J. Griswold, Iowa, 1897d.

MITCHELL, ELI Saline Co., Arkansas, 1860c. Percussion pistols.

MITCHELL, GEORGE Marshall, Missouri, 1879d.

MITCHELL, I.G. unlocated. Percussion fullstock.

MITCHELL, J.B. Cincinnati, Ohio. Lockmaker only.

MITCHELL, JOHN Augusta Co., Virginia. Apprenticed to John Hannah, November 21, 1754.

MITCHELL, JOSEPH (1798-?), Philadelphia, Pennsylvania, 1830-1841, Montgomery, Pennsylvania, 1860d-1861d. (Gluckman & Satterlee)

MITCHELL, M. Bryan, Texas, 1878d.

MITCHELL, N. Princeville, Illinois, 1860d.

MITCHELL, P.R., & CO. Cincinnati, Ohio, 1875d-1887d. As Mitchell & Whitelaw, 1875-1883. (Hutslar)

MITCHELL, R.S. Middletown, Kentucky, 1879d-1884d.

MITCHELL, WILLIAM Surry Co., Virginia, 1779. Committee of Safety repairs. (Gill)

MITTNACHT, E. Egg Harbor City, New Jersey, 1878d-1885d.

MIX, EUGENE M. Ithaca, New York. Patents #18,292 September 29, 1857, burglar alarm pistol with J. E. Mix, and #41,343 January 19, 1864, breechloading firearm with Henry B. Horton.

MIX, HARRISON, & CO. Cooper's Hill, Missouri, 1879d.

MIX, J. E. Ithaca, New York. Patent #18,292 September 29, 1857, burglar alarm pistol with Eugene Mix.

MIX, JOHN New York, New York. Patent #none June 3, 1813, cartridge box.

MIXTER, SAMUEL J. Boston, Massachusetts. Patent #391,811 October 30, 1888, magazine firearms.

MOAK, J.A. Spirit Lake, Iowa, 1884d.

MOATES, SAMUEL Barclay, Illinois, 1860d.

MOBLEY, FRANK PRESTON (1839-?), Stockton, California, 1871-1876. (Shelton)

MOCK, AUGUST New York, New York, 1873d-1883d. Air rifle. (Wolff)

MOCK, G.S. Lebanon, Kentucky, 1883d. Percussion 1/2 stock.

MOCK, JAMES R. Elizabethtown, Kentucky, 1856-1860. Patent #24,228 May 31, 1859, lock for repeating firearm.

MOCK, R. unlocated. Flintlock Kentucky.

MOCK, R.M. Paducah, Kentucky, 1879d.

MOCK, W.R. Ocala, Florida, 1886d.

MODLIN, NATHAN North Cumberland, Indiana, 1863-1865.

MOELLER, A. Milledgeville, Illinois, 1864d.

MOELLER, J.W. Waterloo, Illinois, 1864d.

MOENNING, HENRY J. Delphos, Ohio, 1878-1893d. (Hutslar)

MOFFATT, ARTHUR Washington, D.C. Patent #53,168 March 13, 1866, priming cartridge.

MOFFET unlocated. See Lindsley & Moffet.

MOFFIT, F.L. Raymond's Ohio, 1860. Worked with John Orahood. (Hutslar)

MOGG, L.N. Marcellus, New York, 1880-1900. Telescopes.

MOHAWK suicide special by Rome Novelty & Revolver Works.

MOHAWK trade name of Bish, Mize, Stillman & Co. on shotguns made by Crescent Fire Arms Co.

MOHAWK trade name of Otis Smith on suicide special by Mohawk Mfg. Co.

MOHEGAN suicide special by Hood Fire Arms Co. (Webster)

MOHN, BENJAMIN Wyomissing Creek, Pennsylvania, 1835-1859. Percussion fullstock. (Hobbies 5-37)

MOHN, HENRY Lincoln, Illinois, 1884d.

MOHNEY, VALENTINE (1827-?), Jefferson Co., Pennsylvania, 1860c.

MOHR, CHARLES Philadelphia, Pennsylvania, 1890d.

MOISSON, JOHN Charleston, South Carolina, 1813-1829. (Kauffman 2)

MOISSON, L. Charleston, South Carolina, 1831d. (Kauffman 2)

MOLAN & FINN Philadelphia, Pennsylvania. Model 1807 contract pistols and rifles, but no known deliveries. (Gluckman)

MOLIS, H. & CO. Muscatine, Iowa, 1865-1897. Henry Molis.

MOLIS, HENRY Muscatine, Iowa, 1850c-1897d. As H. Molis & Co. 1865-1897.

MOLITOR, JOSEPH St. Anthony, Minnesota, 1867d, Sauk Center, Minnesota, 1886d.

MOLL, DAVID (1807-1853), Hellertown, Pennsylvania, 1835-1853. As P. & D. Moll, with cousin Peter. (ASAC 25)

MOLL, EDWARD Algona, Iowa, 1865d.

MOLL, EDWIN Hellertown, Pennsylvania, 1853-1861d. Son of Peter Moll. Wiith his brother William took over the P. & D. Moll shop after the death of David Moll. After the death of William he took another David Moll into the business and quit making guns. His son John was last of the Moll gunsmiths. (ASAC 25)

MOLL, F.L. Franklin Co., Pennsylvania. Flintlock Kentucky. (Dillin)

MOLL, J. & W.H. Allentown, Pennsylvania, 1860d-1883d. John Moll, III and William Henry Moll.

MOLL, JOHN J. (?-1900), Hellertown, Pennsylvania. Son of Edwin Moll. (ASAC 25)

MOLL, JOHN (1716-1795), Allentown, Pennsylvania, 1762-1795. (ASAC 25)

MOLL, JOHN Knoxville, Iowa, 1882d-1884d.

MOLL, JOHN, II (1773-1867), Allentown, Pennsylvania, 1810-1820. Son of, and successor to, John Moll, 1. (ASAC 25)

MOLL, JOHN, III (1796-1883), Allentown, Pennsylvania, 1820-1883. Son of, and successor to, John Moll II in 1820. (ASAC 25)

MOLL, M. Hellerstown, Pennsylvania, 1861d.

MOLL, NATHAN Hellertown, Pennsylvania, 1838- ?. Flintlock and percussion target rifles. (ASAC 25)

MOLL, P. & D. Hellertown, Pennsylvania. Peter and David Moll.

MOLL, PETER (1779-?), Lehigh Co., Pennsylvania, 1835t. Son of John Moll I. (ASAC 25)

MOLL, PETER (1799-1879), Hellertown, Pennsylvania, 1820-?. Kentucky pistols. With his cousin David Moll as P. & D. Moll, 1835-1853. Son of John Moll II. (ASAC 25)

MOLL, WILLIAM HENRY (1825-?), Allentown, Pennsylvania, 1860-1884. Son of John III. (ASAC 25)

MOLL, WILLIAM Hellertown, Pennsylvania, son of Peter Moll; with brother, Edwin, took over the P. & D. Moll shop after David's death. (ASAC 25)

MOLLER & HEETH San Francisco, California, 1891-1894. Herman Louis Moller and H.W. Heeth. (Shelton)

MOLLER, HERMAN LOUIS (1851-?), San Francisco, California, 1875-1924. With William Heber as Heber & Moller, 1877-1881. With H. W. Heeth as Moller & Heeth, 1891-1894. Did not use his first name when signing his guns, "L. Moller" only. (Shelton)

MONAGHAN, JAMES Batavia, New York. Patent #498,070 May 23, 1893, spring gun.

MONARCH suicide special by Hopkins & Allen.

MONARCH trade name of Osgood Gun Works on double-barrel revolvers.

MONCKTON, JOSIAH New York, New York, 1848-1851, Plainfield, New Jersey, 1860d.

MONFERRER Philadelphia, Pennsylvania, 1810d. See Peloux & Monferrer.

MONFORT, EDGAR A. New York, New York. Patents #365,842 July 5, 1887, electric cartridge, #365,843 July 5, 1887, electric cartridge, and #365,843 July 5, 1887, electric breechloading firearm.

MONITOR suicide special by Whitney.

MONITOR trade name of Paxton & Gallagher on shotguns by Crescent Fire Arms Co. (Hinman)

MONK, HENRY Washington, D.C., 1855d. (Hartzler)

MONK, T.A. Sennamakoning, Pennsylvania. Patent #603,549, May 3, 1898, air gun with Elmer Bailey.

MONNIER, LOUIS (1820-?), Santa Clara, California, 1852c. (Shelton)

MONROE, ABIJAH Charleston, Massachusetts, 1837. (Dean*)

MONROE, EDWIN P. Charleston, Massachusetts. Patent #14,513 March 25, 1856, lock.

MONROE, ROBERT Wabash, Illinois, 1860d.

MONSON, W.S. South Bend, Indiana, 1871-1872d. (Lindert)

MONT STORM name by which guns and cartridges patented and manufactured by William Montgomery Storm became popularly known, due to a peculiarity in his signature. (Sellers-1)

MONTAGNY, THOMAS Vermont, 1810-1820. Flintlock pistols. (Horn)

MONTAGUE, J. unlocated. Flintlock Kentucky rifle.

MONTAGUE, J.B. Franklin, Kentucky, 1879d.

MONTAGUE, JAMES T. New Castle, Kentucky, 1835-1850. Percussion fullstock.

MONTAGUE, L.F. New Castle, Kentucky, 1857-1860.

MONTANA ARMORY Bozeman, Montana, 1874-1890. Operated by Walter Cooper until 1880 and the Gottschalk Bros. thereafter.

MONTEITH see Scott & Monteith.

MONTFORT, ABRAM Westfield, New York, 1866-1874d.

MONTGOMERY ARMS CO. Montgomery, Alabama, 1892-1893d. Shotguns made by Crescent.

MONTGOMERY ARSENAL Montgomery, Alabama, 1862-1863. Converted flintlock muskets for Confederacy. (Hill-Anthony)

MONTGOMERY WARD & CO. Various locations, 1897-date. Sales only.

MONTGOMERY, ALEXANDER (1762-?), Augusta Co., Virginia, 1808.

MONTGOMERY, THOMAS Vermont, 1812. Flintlock musket. (Dean*)

MONTGOMERY, WILLIAM Carroll Co., Missouri, 1850c. (MB 11-66)

MOOD, SAMUEL Augusta, Maine, 1867. (Demeritt)

MOODY, ALVAN South Hadley, Massachusetts, 1834-1851. (Mass. Arms)

MOODY, EDWIN A. Fort Valley, Georgia, 1881d.

MOODY, MOSES Andover, New Hampshire, 1877d.

MOON, CHRISTOPHER C. (1831-?), Martinsville, Ohio, 1850c-1853d. (Hutslar)

MOON, H. Valeene, Indiana, 1860d.

MOON, JESSE Cazenovia, Wisconsin, 1857d.

MOON, JESSIE Martinsville, Ohio, 1809-1820c. With William Moon. (Hutslar)

MOON, JOSEPH H. (1806-?), Martinsville, Ohio, 1850c-1853d. (Hutslar)

MOON, M.A. Buffalo, New York, 1828.

MOON, W.H. Rochester, New York, 1850c.

MOON, WILLIAM Martinsville, Ohio, 1809-1820c. With Jessie Moon. (Hutslar)

MOONEY, AARON SYLVESTER Lemore, California, 1877-1888. (Shelton)

MOONEY, ROBERT Greenville, Michigan, 1863d.

MOONEY, WILLIAM Waverly, Iowa, 1865d.

MOORE & BAKER New York, New York, 1849d-1853d. J.P. Moore and John Baker, importers.

MOORE & BEDWORTH Quincy, Illinois, 1878d.

MOORE & MANNING Portsmouth, Virginia, 1885d.

MOORE & NICHOLS New York, New York, 1867d. Importers and dealers.

MOORE ARMS CO. see D. Moore & Co.

MOORE, A.W. Kosciusko, Mississippi, 1885d.

MOORE, ABRAHAM Chester Co., Pennsylvania, 1770-1776. Committee of Safety muskets. (Kauffman 2)

MOORE, ANDREW P. (1883-?), Clearfield, Pennsylvania, 1860c. Son of John Moore. (Harriger)

MOORE, D., & CO. Brooklyn, New York, 1860-1863. Moore patent revolvers and derringers. Reorganized as Moore's Patent National Firearms Co., 1863 and Moore(?) Arms Co., 1866. Daniel Moore.

MOORE, D.A. Newtown, Missouri, 1860d.

MOORE, DANIEL De Witt, Michigan, 1860d.

MOORE, DANIEL Williamsburg, New York, 1852-1854, New York, New York, 1859, Brooklyn, New York, 1860-1882. Patents #11,870 October 31, 1854, cartridge, #11,871 October 31, 1854, powder flask, #30,079 September 18, 1860, revolver, #31,473 February 19, 1861, firearm, #33,848 December 3, 1861, breechloading firearm, #34,067 January 7, 1862, revolver, #38,321 April 28, 1863, revolver, #145,118 December 2, 1873, lock, #157,860 December 15, 1874, revolver, #187,980 March 6, 1877, revolver, #190,240 May 1, 1877, revolver, #193,269 July 17, 1877, revolver, #253,221 February 7, 1882, pistol handle, and #264,325 September 12, 1882, revolver. As D. Moore & Co., Moore's Patent National Firearms Co., and Moore(?) Arms Co.

MOORE, E. Jeffersonville, Indiana, 1862d.

MOORE, E.L. Slacks Canyon, California, 1880-1881d. (Shelton)

MOORE, EDWARD F. (1814-?), Baltimore, Maryland, 1850c-1855d. (Hartzler)

MOORE, EDWARD, SR. French Lick, Indiana, 1813-1820. (Lindert)

MOORE, F. M. Prairie City, Iowa, 1892d-1897d.

MOORE, GEORGE A. Mt. Vernon, Ohio, 1890-1910d. (Hutslar)

MOORE, GEORGE H. Charleston, South Carolina, 1837-1838d. (Kauffman 2)

MOORE, GEORGE Madison Co., Illinois. (Johnson)

MOORE, HENSZLEY & CO. Philadelphia, Pennsylvania, 1847d-1861d. Lockmakers only.

MOORE, HERMAN Rochester, New York, 1834d. (Eich)

MOORE, HOLLIS Lovell, Massachusetts, 1877. (Demeritt)

MOORE, I. T. New York, New York, 1810-1815. Flintlock pistols. (Gardner)

MOORE, J. B. Lovelaceville, Kentucky, 1896d.

MOORE, J. C. Monson, Maine, 1876-1879d. (Demeritt)

MOORE, J. P. Union, New York, 1844-1846. (Gluckman & Satterlee)

MOORE, J. S. Clarksville, Tennessee, 1881d-1891d.

MOORE, J. T. New Freeport, Pennsylvania, 1876. (Kauffman)

MOORE, JAMES D. Zanesville, Ohio. Patent #27,374 March 6, 1860, percussion magazine gun.

MOORE, JAMES Chester, Pennsylvania, 1860d-1861d.

MOORE, JOHN P. New York, New York, 1823-1888d. Mostly retail sales after 1865. With son George Moore and grandsons John P. Richards and Henry M. Richards in 1885.

MOORE, JOHN (1806-1872), Clearfield, Pennsylvania, 1850-1872. (Harriger)

MOORE, JOHN Albany, New York, 1820-1835. Flintlock fowler. (Swinney)

MOORE, JOHN New York, New York, 1801-1820.

MOORE, JOHN Sullivan Co., New York, 1870-1880. (MB 6-58)

MOORE, P.T., & CO. Richmond, Virginia, 1860-1863. Importer and dealer, 1862-1863.

MOORE, RENSSELAER R. (?-1884), Cincinnatus, New York, 1850-1866, Cortlandville, New York, 1866-1884. Percussion and cartridge guns. Patent #122,187 December 16, 1872, barrel. Patent information stamping appears on many of his guns. (Swinney)

MOORE, ROBERT (1815-?), Iredell Co., North Carolina, 1850c. (Bivins)

MOORE, S.B., & CO. Salisbury Center, Connecticut, 1848-1864. Barrelmakers.

MOORE, S.E. Burlington, Vermont, 1876-1878. (Horn)

MOORE, SAMUEL S. (1838-?), Clearfield, P{ennsylvania, 1860c-1870c. Son of John Moore. (Harriger)

MOORE, THOMAS Ottawa, Illinois, 1859. (Johnson)

MOORE, THOMAS Urbana, Ohio. (MB 12-51)

MOORE, W.D. Kellogg, Oregon, 1889d-1891d.

MOORE, W.H. Ludlowville, New York, 1870-1874d.

MOORE, W.J. Burnet, Texas, 1884d.

MOORE, W.M. Emmetsburg, Iowa, 1897d.

MOORE, WILLIAM H. Rochester, New York, 1845-1853. Miller patent revolving rifle. (Eich)

MOORE, WILLIAM (1833-?), Bedford, Pennsylvania, 1855. Percussion double rifle. (Hetrick)

MOORE, WILLIAM Madison Co., Illinois. (Johnson)

MOORE, WILLIAM Sullivan Co., New York, 1850. Flintlock fullstock. (MB 6-58)

MOORE, WILLIAM Windsor, Connecticut, 1859-1863.

MOORE'S PATENT NATIONAL FIREARMS CO. (also known as Moore's Pat. National Firearms Co., and/or Moore's Patent Fire Arms Co.) Brooklyn, New York, 1863-1866. Moore patent revolvers and derringers. Successor to D. Moore & Co., succeeded by Moore(?) Arms Co., 1866.

MOOREMAN, S. Milton, Pennsylvania. Percussion fullstock rifle.

MOORMAN, J.E. Corpus Christi, Texas, 1890d-1896d.

MOOS, JOHN (1830-?), Lincoln, Illinois, 1860d-1888d.

MOOSE, T. unlocated. Percussion target pistol. Last name not Moore.

MOOTS, JAMES (1824-?), Ottawa Co., Ohio, 1850c. (Hutslar)

MORAND, JUD Cleveland, Ohio, 1870d-1891. (Hutslar)

MORATH, L. Newark, Ohio, 1853d. Percussion 1/2 stock rifles. (Hutslar)

MORDECAI, JOSEPH Charleston, South Carolina, 1809d-1819. (Kauffman)

MORE, THOMAS Medina Co., Ohio, 1832-1841, Steuben Co., Indiana, 1850c. (Hutslar)

MORE, W.H. New Orleans, Louisiana, 1898d-1904d.

MOREAU, E.V. New Orleans, Louisiana, 1841d-1842d.

MORELLI, F.T. Galena, Illinois, 1880d-1893d.

MOREY, DAVID (1824-?), Watsonville, California, 1871-1881. Converted Spencer rifle with J.A. Howard. (Shelton)

MOREY, NATHAN Philadelphia, Pennsylvania, 1837d.

MORGAN & CLAPP New Haven, Connecticut, 1864-1867d. Single shot pistols. Lucius Morgan.

MORGAN, ANDREW (1818-?), Petersburg, Virginia, 1850c-1897d. (MB 10- 63)

MORGAN, B. Jacksonville, Illinois, 1881. (Johnson)

MORGAN, B.W. Rushville, Indiana, 1860d, Terre Haute, Indiana, 1868-1885. (Lindert)

MORGAN, GEORGE (?-1895), Lansing, Michigan, 1867d-1892d. Mule-ear over/under rifle.

MORGAN, GEORGE Galena, Ohio, 1866d. (Hutslar)

MORGAN, GEORGE Philadelphia, Pennsylvania, 1776. (Kauffman)

MORGAN, GEORGE Utica, New York, 1838-1867. Percussion 1/2 stock and target rifles.

MORGAN, HENRY (1822-?), St. Louis, Missouri, 1842-1854, Mt. Sterling, Illinois, 1858-1870. Percussion 1/2 stock. With Frederick Hellinghaus, 1842-1844. (GR 7-57) Note: Hellinghaus in St. Louis, Missouri, 1840-1847d, but no reference to association with Morgan, per (Shelton).

MORGAN, J. Belmont, Arkansas, 1860. (Elias)

MORGAN, J.W. Winchester, Kentucky, 1896d.

MORGAN, JAMES M. (1826-?), Bentonville, Ohio, 1850c-1864d, Washington Court House (city of), Ohio, 1872d, West Union, Ohio, 1888d-1890d. Percussion 1/2 stock. As J.M. Morgan & Co., 1872d. (Hutslar)

MORGAN, JAMES R. New York, New York, 1858d.

MORGAN, JEROME B. (1825-?), Wabash, Indiana, 1850c. Brother of Miles Morgan. (Lindert)

MORGAN, JOSEPH Morristown, New Jersey, 1779. (Gluckman & Satterlee)

MORGAN, JOSEPH Philadelphia, Pennsylvania, 1797-1800. Contract pistols. (ASAC 3)

MORGAN, LUCIUS New Haven, Connecticut, 1858-1877. As Morgan & Clapp, 1864-1867. (Gluckman & Satterlee)

MORGAN, MILES H.C. (1816-?), Wabash, Indiana, 1860-1880. (Lindert)

MORGAN, PHILAMON Springhill, Pennsylvania, 1818-1822t. (Kauffman)

MORGAN, WILLIAM (1811-?), Petersburg, Virginia, 1850-1876. Percussion double shotgun. (MB 10-63)

MORGAN, WILLIAM New York, New York, 1849d-1851d.

MORGAN, WILLIAM Richmond, Virginia, 1861-1863. (Albaugh 1)

MORGAN, WILLIAM Rochester, New York, 1845d-1847d. (Eich)

MORGANSTERN, WILLIAM Philadelphia, Pennsylvania, 1863-1867, Hartford, Connecticut, 1867-1868, New York, New York, 1869. Patents #40,572 November 10, 1863, breechloading firearm with Edward Morwitz, #45,262 November 29, 1864, breechloading firearm, #48,133 June 6, 1865, breechloading firearm, #72,526 December 24, 1867, breechloading firearm, #74,712 February 18, 1868, breechloading firearm, #79,291 June 22, 1868, breechloading firearm, #86,434 February 2, 1869, breechloading firearm, #87,190 February 23, 1869, breechloading firearm, and #93,330 August 3, 1869, breechloading firearm. Small quantities of rifles and carbines made under these patents.

MORGEL, JOHN C. Brazil, Indiana, 1881-1885.

MORIARITY, G.W. Opelousas, Louisiana, 1885d.

MORINEAU, PHILIP A. Philadelphia, Pennsylvania. Patents #none October 10, 1832, breechloading firearm, and #32,460 May 28, 1861, sword revolver.

MORITZ & KEIDEL Baltimore, Maryland, 1868-1886d. (Hartzler)

MORLEY suicide special by Bliss.

MORLEY, H.F. Brattleboro, Vermont, 1873-1874. (Horn)

MORLEY, WILLIAM Huntsville, Ohio, 1859d. Percussion fullstock rifles. (Hutslar)

MORLOCK, CHARLES F. Hillsdale, Michigan, 1872d-1887d.

MORR, A. Lancaster, Pennsylvania, 1830. Flintlock Kentucky.

MORRELL, C.T. Helena, Montana, 1888d-1892d.

MORRETT, L. Columbus, Ohio, 1848d-1850c. (Hutslar)

MORRETT, L. Columbus, Ohio, 1850c.

MORRILL, HENRY A. Amherst, Massachusetts, 1836-1839. With Silas Mosman Jr. and Charles Blair as Morrill, Mosman & Blair.

MORRILL, MOSMAN & BLAIR Amherst, Massachusetts, 1836-1839. Elgin cutlass pistols. Henry A. Morrill, Silas Mosman, Jr. and Charles Blair. Morrill and Blair only after July 1838. (GC 30)

MORRIS & BROTHER Baltimore, Maryland. Imported double-barrel shotgun.

MORRIS & BROWN New York, New York. Patent #26,919 January 24, 1860, "Conical repeater" rifle. William Hopkins Morris and Charles Liston Brown. (Sellers-1)

MORRIS, A.J. Vernon, Texas, 1892d-1896d.

MORRIS, C. Elmira, New York, 1878d.

MORRIS, C.L. Harrisburg, Oregon, 1891d.

MORRIS, DAVIDSON Norfolk, Virginia, 1877d-1890d.

MORRIS, G.W. Akron, Ohio, 1881d. Same as G.W. Morris, Corry, Pennsylvania? (Hutslar)

MORRIS, G.W. Corry, Pennsylvania, 1873d. Same as G.W. Morris, Akron, Ohio?

MORRIS, H.M. unlocated. Southern Kentucky rifle.

MORRIS, JAMES L. (1792-?), Orange Co., Virginia, 1850c. (MB 10-63)

MORRIS, JOHN A. Georgetown, Colorado, 1883d-1900d. (Sellers-3)

MORRIS, JOHN J. (1834-?), Healdsburg, California, 1865-1870. (Shelton)

MORRIS, JOHN Philadelphia, Pennsylvania, 1768-1785. Repaired U.S. arms. (Moller)

MORRIS, LEWIS Hampton, Virginia, 1781. (Gill)

MORRIS, M.W. Bean Blossom, Indiana, 1862d.

MORRIS, RICHARD Portsmouth, Rhode Island, 1643-1650. (Achtermier)

MORRIS, W.J. New York, New York. Patent #137,381 April 1, 1873, gunlock.

MORRIS, WILLIAM A. (1828-1912), Indiantown, Virginia, 1850c. Percussion fullstock and underhammer pistol. Son of James L. Morris. (MB 10-63)

MORRIS, WILLIAM HOPKINS New York, New York. Patent #26,919 January 24, 1860, "Conical Repeater" rifle" with Charles Liston Brown. As Morris & Brown with Charles Liston Brown.

MORRIS, WILLIAM Dexter, Michigan, 1867d.

MORRIS, WILLIAM Ripley, Ohio, 1859d. Percussion 1/2 stock. (Hutslar)

MORRISON & LONG Northumberland Co., Pennsylvania, 1840. Percussion mule-ear fullstock.

MORRISON, A. (1810-?), Scioto Co., Ohio, 1850c. Mule-ear fullstock. (Hutslar)

MORRISON, CALEB Stevensburg, Virginia, 1808. Model 1808 contract rifles with George Wheeler. (Gluckman)

MORRISON, DUNCAN Portland, Maine. Patent #63,552, April 6, 1867, breechloading firearm.

MORRISON, EBENEZER Franklin, New Hampshire, 1872d.

MORRISON, H.B. Britt, Iowa, 1884d-1887d.

MORRISON, J.S. Reidsville, North Carolina, 1884d.

MORRISON, JAMES A. Wahoo, Nebraska, 1886d-1893d.

MORRISON, JOHN T. Ft. Concho, Texas. Patent #206,475 July 30, 1878, breechloading firearm.

MORRISON, MURDOCK (1827-?), Wentworth, North Carolina, 1850-1863, Laurel Hill, North Carolina, 1863-1865. Percussion 1/2 stock marked M.M. With his father-in-law, John Buchanan, made rifles for the Confederacy. (Bivins, Hill-Anthony)

MORRISON, R.R. San Francisco, California, 1867-1868. (Shelton)

MORRISON, SAMUEL (?-1850), Pekin, Illinois, circa 1840. (Johnson)

MORRISON, SAMUEL Milton, Pennsylvania, 1826-1843. Patent #none February 10, 1836, superposed load gun. Flintlock and percussion Kentucky rifles, some with superposed loads.

MORRISON, WASHINGTON Salineville, Ohio, 1870-1890. Percussion 1/2 stock. (MB 11-54)

MORRISON, WILLIAM HENRY Indianapolis, Indiana, 1852-1855. Patent #11,698 September 19, 1854, revolver. (Sellers-1)

MORRISON, WILLIAM (1810-?), Thornton, Indiana, 1860c. (Lindert)

MORROW, ABRAHAM Philadelphia, Pennsylvania, 1776-1798. Committee of Safety muskets and Model 1792 contract rifles. (Gluckman & Satterlee)

MORROW, HENRY (1826-?), St. Louis, Missouri, 1850c. For Franz Lunsman. (Lewis)

MORROW, WILLIAM Uniontown, Pennsylvania, 1842-1843. (Whisker II)

MORSE & HASKELL Painesville, Ohio, 1861-1865. Percussion target rifle. Christopher Morse and Riley Haskell.

MORSE ARMS CO. Greenville, South Carolina, 1863-1865. Produced George W. Morse carbines for Confederacy. (Hill-Anthony)

MORSE, CHRISTOPHER (1815-?), Painesville, Ohio, 1843-1865. Percussion 1/2 stock. With Riley Haskell as Morse & Haskell, 1861-1865. (Hutslar)

MORSE, ENOCH E. (1808-?), Avon, Illinois, 1850c, Waukegan, Illinois, 1860c-1867d. Percussion 1/2 stock. (Johnson)

MORSE, GEORGE WOODWARD (?-1888), East Baton Rouge, Louisiana. Patents #15,995 October 28, 1856, breechloading firearm, #15,996 October 28, 1856, cartridge, #20,214 May 11, 1858, cartridge case, #20,503 June 8, 1858, breechloading firearm, and #20,727 June 29, 1858, cartridge. Muskets and carbines made by the Confederacy, 1861-1865, sporting guns by Hitchcock & Muzzy, and a limited number of muskets by Springfield Armory. (AR 3-55, Hill-Anthony)

MORSE, H.M. Pueblo, Colorado, 1880-1887d. (Sellers-3)

MORSE, R. unlocated. Flintlock Kentucky.

MORSE, T. Macon, Georgia. Percussion bench gun.

MORSE, THOMAS Lancaster, New Hampshire, 1866-1882. Percussion target pistol. (Roberts)

MORSE, THOMAS Richmond, Virginia, 1862-1864. Confederate patent #199 September 10, 1863, breechloading firearm. (Albaugh 3)

MORT, JAMES W. Bristol, Tennessee, 1880d-1897d.

MORTENSEN, H.P. Ashland, Michigan, 1887d-1891d, Grant Station, Michigan, 1892d-1895d.

MORTENSEN, T. & P. Grant Station, Michigan, 1896d-1899d. Sons of H.P. Mortensen.

MORTENSON, J. Denver, Colorado, 1894d. (Sellers-3)

MORTER, EMANUEL B. Pyrmont, Ohio, 1860-1864d, Brookville, Ohio, 1881d. Percussion fullstock. (Hutslar)

MORTER, GEORGE Lancaster, Pennsylvania, 1771-1779. Also known as George Moster. (Gluckman & Satterlee)

MORTIMER & KIRKWOOD Boston, Massachusetts, 1875d-1881d. Breechloading rifles and shotguns. Henry Mortimer and David Kirkwood.

MORTIMER, CHARLES Boston, Massachusetts, 1880-1881. Double shotgun. (Hinman)

MORTIMER, HENRY Boston, Massachusetts. Patent #169,710 November 11, 1875, lock with David Kirkwood.

MORTON & DEUTZ San Antonio, Texas, 1867d-1874d. Henry Morton.

MORTON, ALFRED Troupsburgh, New York, 1859-1864d.

MORTON, DAVID Westmoreland Co., Pennsylvania, 1811-1823. (Kauffman)

MORTON, HENRY San Antonio, Texas, 1859d-1874d. As H. Morton & Bro., 1859, and as Morton & Deutz, 1867-1874.

MORTON, J.H. Lake Wier, Florida, 1883d-1884d.

MORTON, JAMES Virginia City, Montana, 1868d, Seattle, Washington, 1871d.

MORTON, JOHN St. Louis, Missouri, 1869d. Percussion 1/2 stock.

MORWITZ, EDWARD Philadelphia, Pennsylvania. Patent #40,572 November 10, 1863, breechloading firearm with William Morganstern.

MOSCH, HERMAN St. Louis, Missouri, 1868d-1875d.

MOSER, H. unlocated. Percussion fullstock.

MOSES & HALL Columbus, Georgia. Derringer. See also Hall & Moses, same persons? (Eberhart)

MOSES, EDWIN A.F. Boston, Massachusetts. Patent #307,407 October 28, 1884, magazine firearm.

MOSES, ELIJAH Fayette Co., Pennsylvania, 1802-1803. (Kauffman)

MOSES, MYRON A. Malone, New York, 1857-1870d. Patent #36,571 September 30, 1862, breechloading firearm. Percussion 1/2 stock and patent rifles.

MOSES, OREN Malone, New York, 1824-1828. Patent #none May 3, 1828, lock.

MOSHER, CYRUS Hamilton, New York. Patent #none May 5, 1828, double shot rifle with Noble White.

MOSHER, GEORGE Presque Isle, Maine, 1856-1883. (Demeritt)

MOSHER, S. & S. unlocated. Percussion fullstock.

MOSHOLDER, S.H. Viroqua, Wisconsin, 1857d.

MOSIAN, JOHN Charleston, South Carolina, 1852d. (Dean)

MOSMAN, SILAS, JR. Amherst, Massachusetts, 1836-1839. With Henry A. Morrill and Charles Blair as Morrill, Mosman & Blair.

MOSS, ARNAL McLeansboro, Illinois, 1860d.

MOSS, EBENEZER Maryland, 1753. (Gluckman & Satterlee)

MOSS, ELIJAH Fayette Co., Pennsylvania, 1801-1803. (Whisker II)

MOSS, JAMES Nevada, Missouri, 1860d.

MOSS, JOHN L. Columbus, Mississippi. Patent #116,078 June 20, 1871, revolver with Edward W. Johnson. (Nutter)

MOSS, JOSIAH (1798-?), Cumberland, Maryland. Apprenticed to George Rizer, 1813. (Hartzler)

MOSS, THOMAS Virginia, 1776-1783. Committee of Safety repairs. (Gill)

MOSSBERG, G.P. New London, Minnesota, 1878d-1886d.

MOSSBERG, OSCAR F. (?-1937), New Haven, Connecticut. Patents #511,620 December 26, 1893, revolver, #651,177 June 12, 1900, repeating firearm, #697,516 April 15, 1902, firearm lock, #697,517 April 15, 1902, revolver, #670,862 March 26, 1901, revolver, #745,885 December 1, 1903, breechloading firearm, #754,080 March 8, 1904, hinge pin for break open revolvers, #756,039 March 29, 1904, breechloading firearm, #778,500 December 27, 1904, revolver, #778,501 December 27, 1904, revolver, #796,307 August 1, 1905, breechloading firearm with Charles P. Fay, #818,461 April 24, 1906, breechloading firearm with Charles P. Fay, #837,867 December 4, 1906, "Novelty"/Shattuck "Unique" four-barrel palm pistol, #840,507 January 8, 1907, breechloading firearm with Charles P. Fay, and #1,348,035 August 28, 1919, "Brownie" four-barrel derringer. Worked for Iver Johnson, Marlin, Stevens, and Shattuck Arms before forming his own company, O. F. Mossberg & Sons, in 1919.

MOSSBERG, R.P. New London, Maine, 1877-1880.

MOSSER & KINDLER Monroe, Michigan, 1868-1871d. Breechloading double shotgun. Vincent Kindler.

MOSSER, D.E. Danville, Pennsylvania. Superposed percussion rifles.

MOSSER, JOHN P. Dalton, Ohio, 1860-1864d. (Hutslar)

MOSSHOLDER, J.C. Lebanon, Oregon, 1880d-1881d.

MOSSHOLDER, WILLIAM Peking, Ohio, circa 1880. (Hutslar)

MOST, HENRY Philadelphia, Pennsylvania, 1813d-1814d.

MOSTER, GEORGE Lancaster Co., Pennsylvania, 1771-1779. Also known as George Morter. (Gluckrnan & Satterlee)

MOTE, A. & D. unlocated. Lockmakers.

MOTE, ELI K. (1817-?), Beamsville, Ohio, 1850c-1859d. Percussion rifles. (Hutslar)

MOTT, A. unlocated. Flintlock Kentucky.

MOTT, J.N. Sanderson, Florida, 1886d.

MOTTAZ, JOHN A. Hardin, Illinois, 1881d-1893d.

MOULD, THOMAS Saginaw City, Michigan, 1860d.

MOULTON & PIKE Worcester, Massachusetts, 1873-1875.

MOULTON, BENJAMIN S. New York, New York, 1872d-1875d.

MOULTON, GEORGE W. Bridgeport, Connecticut, 1873d.

MOULTON, R.B. Mt. Ogre, Iowa, 1875. Converted Sharps rifle.

MOULTON, R.B. Proctorsville, Vermont, 1838. Percussion harmonica rifle. (Horn)

MOUNTAIN EAGLE suicide special by Hopkins & Allen. (Webster)

MOURER, JOHN Philadelphia, Pennsylvania, 1847d.

MOWER, P. Columbia Co., Pennsylvania. Late-era flintlock Kentucky. (Dillin)

MOWRY, JAMES D. Norwich, Connecticut, 1861-1865. Mode 1861 contract muskets. (Fuller)

MOWRY, SMITH Providence, Rhode Island, 1847-1854. (Achtermier)

MOXLEY, MESHAL (1809-?), Bellafontaine, Ohio, 1853d-1873. Negro gunsmith, percussion rifles. (Hutslar)

MOXLEY, WILLIAM P. (1830-?), Bellefontaine, Ohio, 1860c-1881d. Son of Meshal Moxley. (Hutslar)

MOYAER, JOHN Washington Court House, Ohio, 1870c.

MOYER, ABSALOM Pittsburgh, Pennsylvania, 1860d-1864d. Barrelmaker.

MOYER, ANDREW Hepler, Pennsylvania, 1890. (Whisker III)

MOYER, DANIEL Kimberton, Pennsylvania, 1861d.

MOYER, GEORGE Lancaster, Pennsylvania, 1814-1821. Flintlock lockmaker. (Kauffman 2)

MOYER, J.H. Temple, Texas, 1892d.

MOYER, JOHN Mohntown, Pennsylvania. Percussion fullstock.

MOYER, WILLIAM Knapp, Pennsylvania, 1890d.

MOYLER, N. Vogler, Ohio. Percussion fullstock.

MT. VERNON ARMS CO. trade name of H & D Folsom on imported shotguns. (AR 2-69)

MUDGE, CARSON New Orleans, Louisiana, 1868d-1878d.

MUEGGE, W.H. Wheeling, West Virginia, 1884d.

MUELLER, ADAM St. Charles, Missouri, 1889d-1893d.

MUELLER, GEORGE St. Louis, Missouri, 1860d-1875d.

MUELLER, HIERONYMUS Decatur, Illinois, 1860d-1898d.

MUHL, WILLIAM HENRY (1871-1940), Bloomington, Illinois, 1886-1940. (Johnson)

MUIR, JAMES Andes, New York, 1874d-1882d.

MUIR, WILLIAM, & CO. Windsor Locks, Connecticut. Model 1861 contract muskets. (Fuller)

MULFORD & SPRAGUE New York, New York, 1869d. Importer and dealer.

MULGREW, WILLIAM Lancaster, Pennsylvania, 1841-1847. (KRA IV-4)

MULHOLLAND, JAMES Reading, Pennsylvania. Model 1861 contract muskets. (Fuller)

MULIER, F.W. Peoria, Illinois. Percussion 1/2 stock.

MULING, THEODORE Louisville, Kentucky, 1857-1860.

MULL, HENRY P. Lancaster, Pennsylvania, 1740-1751, York Co., Pennsylvania, 1783-1799. Flintlock Kentucky. (Kindig)

MULL, JOHN Northampton Co., Pennsylvania, 1786-1790. (Kauffman)

MULL, LUDWIG York Co., Pennsylvania, 1797, Adams Co., Pennsylvania, 1799. (Kauffman)

MULL, NATHAN Sellers' Tavern, Pennsylvania, 1860d.

MULLAN, H.J. & CO. New Orleans, Louisiana. 1866d-1883d. Derringer.

MULLEN, CYRUS Williamsburg, Indiana. (Lindert)

MULLEN, JOHN New York, New York, 1841d-1842d. Percussion fowler.

MULLEN, JOSIAH (1816-?), Washington, Indiana, 1850c, Williamsburg, Indiana, 1860d. (Lindert)

MULLENHOUR, HENRY Delphos, Ohio, 1850. Percussion 1/2 stock. (Hutslar)

MULLER & GONZALES see Miller & Gonzales.

MULLER, F.W. Peoria, Illinois, 1871d-1875d.

MULLER, FLORENT Hartford, Connecticut. Patent #74,119 February 4, 1868, breechloading firearm.

MULLER, FREDERICK Jersey City, New Jersey, 1878d.

MULLER, FREDERICK Nacogdoches, Texas, 1884d-1890d.

MULLER, GEORGE F. St. Louis, Missouri, 1864-1870d. Percussion locks.

MULLER, HUGH Philadelphia, Pennsylvania, 1831d.

MULLER, J. Watertown, Wisconsin, 1857d.

MULLER, J.H. New Orleans, Louisiana, 1853d.

MULLER, J.W. Waterloo, Illinois, 1867d.

MULLER, JOHANN New York, New York. See John Miller.

MULLER, JOSEPH Salem, North Carolina, 1774. (Bivins)

MULLER, W.J. Missouri Valley, Iowa, 1897d.

MULLIGAN, JOHN Galveston, Texas, 1870d-1878d.

MULLIN, ISRAEL W. Hamilton, Ohio, 1873-1883d. (Hutslar)

MULLIN, JOHN CLAY (?-1905), Mullican's Cove, Pennsylvania. Percussion fullstock. (Whisker)

MULLIN, JOHN New York, New York, 1841d-1858d. Percussion guns.

MULLIN, PATRICK (1835-1919), New York, New York, 1858d-1897d. Percussion and cartridge guns. (Clow)

MULLINS, JOHN W. London, Kentucky, 1885-1887, Fanston, Kentucky, 1890d-1896. Patents #349,282 September 14, 1886, magazine firearms, #373,410 November 15, 1887, repeating gun, #487,423 December 6, 1892, firearm, and #571,840 November 24, 1896, magazine firearm.

MULLOY, N.P. Worcester, Massachusetts, 1869-1872. (Gluckman & Satterlee)

MULY, DANIEL (1793-?), Guilford Co., North Carolina. Apprenticed 1807. (Bivins)

MUMM, JOHN W. Sheboygan, Wisconsin, 1868d. See also Mahun, Mehu, and Munn.

MUMM, WILLIAM Sheboygan, Wisconsin, 1879d.

MUNCASTER, T. Newark, Ohio, 1878d. (Hutslar)

MUNCASTER, THOMAS New York, New York, 1890d.

MUNCH, GEORGE Warren Co., Missouri, 1850c. Percussion 1/2 stock. (MB 11-66)

MUNCK, C.H. Washington, D.C., 1855-1866d. Air gun. (Hartzler)

MUND, HERMAN Chicago, Illinois, 1863d-1873d.

MUNDI, JOSEPH Huntingburgh, Indiana, 1881-1885. (Gardner)

MUNDY, E. Marengo, Ohio, 1859d. Percussion rifles. (Hutslar)

MUNGER, ALFRED J. Chicopee Falls, Massachusetts. Patent #62,873 March 12, 1867, breechloading firearm.

MUNGER, L.F. Rochester, New York. Patent #23,040 February 22, 1859, lock (key). Miller patent revolving rifle. (Sellers-1)

MUNGER, LUMAN Dubuque, Iowa, 1860d-1882d. With Jacob F. Mack as Mack & Munger, 1860-1868.

MUNN, A. Sheboygan, Wisconsin, 1872d. See John Mumm.

MUNN, FRANK E. Canon City, Colorado, 1871-1875d. (Sellers-3)

MUNN, MILES Ottawa Lake, Michigan, 1863d.

MUNRO, NATHANIEL Philadelphia, Pennsylvania, 1775. Committee of Safety repairs. (Dean*)

MUNROE, L.B. Curriesville, North Carolina, 1870c. (Bivins)

MUNSON, ALBERT L. New Haven, Connecticut. Patent #59,629 November 13, 1866, revolver. As Munson, Morse & Co., 1856-1868.

MUNSON, ALBERT Burlington, Vermont, 1826-1900. As Munson & Bro., 1884-1900. (Horn)

MUNSON, GEORGE C. Williston, Vermont, 1882d-1883d. Brother of Russell Munson. (Horn)

MUNSON, GEORGE Burlington, Vermont, 1884-1900. Brother of Albert Munson. (Horn)

MUNSON, H. Pittsburgh, Pennsylvania, 1847. (Kauffman)

MUNSON, LEVI Saybrook, Ohio. Percussion 1/2 stock.

MUNSON, MORSE & CO. New Haven, Connecticut, 1856-1868. Revolvers (under owner's patent). Albert L. Munson.

MUNSON, RUSSELL D. Williston, Vermont, 1890d. Percussion underhammer. Brother of George C. Munson. (Horn)

MUNSON, THEOPHILUS (1675-1747), New Haven, Connecticut, 1697-1747.

MUNSON, WILLIAM C. Vienna, Ohio, 1860-1864d. (Hutslar)

MUNZ, JACOB Detroit, Michigan, 1858-1867. Percussion 1/2 stock.

MURDEN, HENNING DANIEL (1815-1903). Crawfordsville (also known as Robinson), Georgia. Percussion 1/2 stock.

MURPHY & O'CONNELL New York, New York, 1857d-1858d. Derringer. Daniel O'Connell.

MURPHY, J.G. St. Clair, Missouri, 1860d.

MURPHY, JOHN L. Springfield, Massachusetts. Patents #427,239 May 6, 1890, machine gun, and #584,698 June 15, 1897, revolver with D.J. Manning.

MURPHY, JOHN Lancaster Co., Pennsylvania, 1817. (Dyke)

MURPHY, JOSEPH Washington, Pennsylvania, 1847. (Kauffman)

MURPHY, W.P. Dubuque, Iowa, 1867d.

MURRAY, ARCHIE J. Unity, Oregon. Patent #543,138 July 23, 1895, folding stock firearm.

MURRAY, C.W. (1819-?), Colorado Springs, Colorado, 1880d.

MURRAY, CHARLES W. Addison, Michigan, 1860d.

MURRAY, JOHN P. (?-1910), Columbus, Georgia, 1856-1889d. Pistols and rifles. With John M. Happoldt as Happoldt & Murray, 1856-1860. Superintendent of Greenwood & Gray during the Civil War and their guns carry his name. (Hill-Anthony)

MURRAY, JOHN Philadelphia, Pennsylvania, 1780-1785. Repaired U.S. arms. (Moller)

MURRAY, M. J. Chicago, Illinois, 1878d.

MURRAY, W. A. unlocated. Agent for Bacon percussion revolvers.

MUSA, GLODE Philadelphia, Pennsylvania, 1780-1782. (Moller)

MUSE Bath Co., Kentucky. Flintlock rifle. (MB 12-51)

MUSENKERNUT, J. C. (1835-?), Jonesboro, Illinois, 1860c. (Johnson)

MUSGRAVE, BENJAMIN Ironton, Ohio, 1850-1860. Percussion fullstock. (MB 3-55)

MUSGRAVE, SAMUEL Ironton, Ohio. Percussion rifles. (Roberts)

MUSHBACKER Clark City, Michigan, 1863d.

MUSKETNUSS, PETER Lancaster, Pennsylvania 1863d-1871d. (KRA IV-4)

MUSSER, H. Mulheim, Pennsylvania. Flintlock rifles. (Dillin)

MUSSER, JOHN (1827-?), Wayne Co., Ohio, 1850c. See John Mosser. (Hutslar)

MUSSER, JOSEPH (1793-?), Quincy, Illinois, 1850-1860. (Johnson)

MUSSER, WILLIAM (1832-?), Stark Co., Ohio, 1850c. (Hutslar)

MUSSMAN, FRANK Pittsburgh, Pennsylvania, 1866-1868d.

MUTH, D. E. unlocated. Percussion over/under rifle/shotgun.

MUTZ, JAMES Clare, Michigan, 1879d.

MUZZY & CO. Worcester, Massachusetts, 1857-1861. Percussion 1/2 stock and barrels. Successors to Hitchcock, Muzzy & Co.

MUZZY, N. M. Chicago, Illinois, 1874-1894d. As Muzzy & Trumbull, 1882, and Muzzy & Stafford, 1883-1885.

MY COMPANION suicide special.

MY FRIEND trade name of James Reid on Knuckleduster revolver.

MYER, F. (1832-?), St. Louis, Missouri, 1850c. (Lewis)

MYER, HENRY Lancaster Co., Pennsylvania, 1775-1790. For William Henry. (Hobbies 4-38)

MYER, JAMES Creston, Iowa, 1895d-1897d.

MYER, JOHN see John Meyer.

MYER, PHILLIP Pittsburgh, Pennsylvania, 1850. (Kauffman)

MYERS, ABRAHAM Boonesborough, Maryland. Patent #none November 11, 1832, sawing gunstocks.

MYERS, CHARLES (1872-1942), Canal Fulton, Ohio. Percussion 1/2 stock. Barrels marked "Fulton" only. With brother, Clayton Myers. (Hutslar)

MYERS, CLAYTON (1864-1939), Canal Fulton, Ohio. Brother of Charles Myers. (Hutslar)

MYERS, DANIEL Washington, Pennsylvania, 1847. (Kauffman)

MYERS, ELLIS Louisville, Ohio, 1866-1868d. (Hutslar)

MYERS, GEORGE S. Apple Grove, Pennsylvania, 1860d-1861d.

MYERS, J. C. Blue Rapids, Kansas, 1894d.

MYERS, J.W. Litchfield, Illinois, 1868d-1875d.

MYERS, JACOB (1807-?), Wayne Co., Ohio, 1850c.

MYERS, JACOB Pittsburgh, Pennsylvania, 1818. (Whisker II)

MYERS, JOHN G. L. Osceola Mills, Pennsylvania. Patent #650,411 May 29, 1900, crossbow gun.

MYERS, JOHN Bowne, Michigan, 1863d.

MYERS, JOHN Richmond, Virginia, 1775, Portsmouth, Virginia, 1775, Canada, 1776. (Gill)

MYERS, MATTHEW Lancaster Co., Virginia, 1758-1783. Committee of Safety repairs. (Gill)

MYERS, R. unlocated. Derringer.

MYERS, WILLIAM W. Portland, Michigan, 1887d.

MYERS, WILLIAM Maple Rapids, Michigan, 1860d.

MYHAN, PATRICK Georgetown, South Carolina, 1825. For B.T. Cuttino. (Kauffman 2)

MYRON, C. St. Anne, Illinois, 1864d.

N SECTION

N.C. unidentified. Flintlock swivel.

N.H. unidentified. Percussion 1/2 stock.

N.S. unidentified. Flintlock Kentucky.

N.T.B. unidentified. Percussion 1/2 stock.

N.T.J. unidentified. Percussion fullstock.

N.T.R. see N.T. Reed.

NACE, JOHN Philadelphia, Pennsylvania, 1841d.

NADLER, JOSEPH (1825-?), Peru, Illinois, 1860c-1886d.

NADLER, JOSEPH Winona, Minnesota, 1878d.

NAEHER see Werner & Naeher.

NAFF, D. Plattsburg, New York, 1868-1874d.

NAGEBAUER, JEAN New Orleans, Louisiana, 1853d. See Jean Neugbauer, same location, 1850-1853.

NAGEL, FRANZ San Antonio, Texas, 1878d-1897d. With Matthias Forder as Forder & Nagel, 1891-1892.

NAGEL, JOHN Brunersburg, Ohio, 1853-1870d. Percussion 1/2 stock. (Hutslar)

NAGLE, CHARLES Philadelphia, Pennsylvania, 1837d.

NAILER, JAMES Westmoreland Co., Pennsylvania, 1811-1812. (Kauffman)

NALL (1863-1953), Robbins, North Carolina. (MB 6-65)

NANCE, C.A. Webb's Hill, Illinois, 1893d.

NAPIL, A.O. Wilber, Nebraska, 1879d.

NAPOLEON suicide special by Ryan.

NAPP, LUDWIG Hackensack, New Jersey, 1866d-1882d.

NASH Rochester, New York, 1872d. (Eich)

NASH, JOHN New Haven, Connecticut, 1645. (Gluckman & Satterlee)

NASH, L. Iredell Co., North Carolina. Flintlock rifles. (Bivins)

NASH, SYLVESTER Harpers Ferry, Virginia. Patent #none April 11, 1818, gun barrel turning. (GR 9-60)

NASH, THOMAS (1589-1658), New Haven, Connecticut, 1638-1658. Colonial militia and town armorer. (Carey, Sellers)

NASHVILLE GUN FACTORY Nashville, Tennessee, 1861-1862. Mississippi rifles. (Gluckman & Satterlee)

NASON & EASTMAN Lewiston, Maine, 1896-1898. Charles F. Nason and Ivan F. Eastman.

NASON, CHARLES F. (?-1909), Lewistown, Maine, 1859-1887 and 1896-1902. Percussion and cartridge guns. With Ivan F. Eastman as Nason & Eastman, 1896-1897. (Demeritt)

NASON, ELBRIDGE G., JR. Bath, Maine, 1844-?, Lewiston, Maine, 1898. With C.F. Nason in 1898. (Demeritt)

NASON, G.W. Bath, Maine, 1876-1877. (Demeritt)

NATCHER, GABRIEL Sidney, Ohio. Patent #45,623 December 27, 1864, multibarrel cannon.

NATCHEZ & NATCHEZ San Francisco, California. Popular name for A.J. Taylor's shop.

NATHAN, JOSEPH St. Louis, Missouri, 1850c. (MB 11-66)

NATIONAL ARMS CO. Brooklyn, New York, 1866-1869. Moore revolvers and derringers. Successor to Moore's Patent Fire Arms Co., 1866. Sold out to Colt in 1869.

NATIONAL ARMS CO. trade name on imported shotgun.

NATIONAL FIRE ARMS CO. trade name of Crescent on double shotguns.

NATIONAL FIRE ARMS CO. trade name of Marlin on .22 cal. rifles and pump shotguns.

NATIONAL FIRE ARMS CO. trade name on Martini type shotgun.

NATIONAL suicide special.

NAUMAN, JACOB Lancaster, Pennsylvania, 1800-1822. (Kauffman)

NAVE, JACOB Franklin Co., Pennsylvania, 1804-1814t. (Bowers)

NAYLOR, JACOB Hedgesville, West Virginia, 1882d. (Whisker IV)

NAYLOR, PETER New York, New York. Patents #34,006 December 24, 1861, casting balls, and #34,844 April 1, 1862, compressing balls.

NAYLOR, WILLIAM Salt Lake City, Utah, 1857-1860. Copies of Colt revolvers. With David Sabin.

NEAL & HUMPHRIES Yonkers, New York, 1866d. John Neal and Charles Humphries.

NEAL, ALBERT Lawrence, Kansas, 1888d.

NEAL, ANDREW T. Lincoln, Maine, 1865. (Demeritt)

NEAL, DANIEL B. (1819-?), Mount Gilead, Ohio, 1850c. Patent #12,440 February 27, 1855, superposed loads. (Winant)

NEAL, JOHN F. Shelbyville, Tennessee, 1860d.

NEAL, JOHN H. (1842-1917), Bangor, Maine, 1861-1878. With Charles V. Ramsdell as Ramsdell & Neal, 1870-1881. Son of William Neal. (Demeritt)

NEAL, JOHN Yonkers, New York, 1866d-1870d. With Charles Humphries as Neal & Humphries, 1866.

NEAL, R.L. Parkersburg, West Virginia, 1882d. (Whisker IV)

NEAL, WILLIAM (1809-1853), Bangor, Maine, 1843-1853. Percussion rifles and pistols. (Demeritt)

NEALE, GEORGE (1805-?), Uniontown, Ohio, 1850c-1859d. (Hutslar)

NEAVE, THOMPSON Cincinnati, Ohio, 1819-1900d. Locks only. As T. Neave & Bros., 1819d, T. & C. Neave, 1829-1840, Neave & Free, 1849, T. Neave & Sons, 1856-1861, and T. Neave & Co., 1864-1867. (Hutslar)

NEEB, HENRY (1820-?) Hancock Co., Illinois, 1850c. (Johnson)

NEEDHAM, J. & G.H. Providence, Rhode Island. Patent #64,999 May 21, 1867, breechloading firearm. Needham conversions of Civil War muskets.

NEEDHAM, T.H. Glens Falls, New York, 1878-1882.

NEEF, AUGUST Detroit, Michigan, 1883d.

NEELY, RICHARD Bradley Co., Arkansas, 1850. (Elias)

NEEPER, JOHN Cumberland Co., Pennsylvania, 1800c. (Kauffman)

NEESE, W.G. Darlington, Wisconsin, 1888d.

NEESE, W.G. Stockton, Kansas, 1888d.

NEFF & BIRD Baltimore, Maryland, 1824-1829d. Importers, guns and locks. (Hartzler)

NEFF & BROS. Cincinnati, Ohio, 1829-1868d. Lock importers. (Hutslar)

NEFF, JOHANNES (1773-1853), Kutztown, Pennsylvania, 1808. Flintlock Kentucky rifle. (MB 9-67)

NEFF, JOHN South Poultney, New York, 1870d.

NEFF, JOHN St. Louis, Missouri, 1859-1860d. As Shillinger & Neff.

NEFF, PETER Baltimore, Maryland, 1819-1830, Cincinnati, Ohio, 1836-1868. Lockmaker and importer, guns and locks. As Bird, Nightingale & Neff, Baltimore, 1819-1823. As Neff & Bird, Baltimore, 1824-1829d. (Hutslar, Hartzler)

NEGUS, S.B. Plainwell, Michigan, 1883d.

NEIDNER, ADOLPH O. (1863-1954), Milwaukee, Wisconsin, 1883-1890, Malden, Massachusetts, 1890-1921, Dowagiac, Michigan, 1921-1940. Barrelmaker. (Kelver)

NEIHARD, CONRAD Lehigh Co., Pennsylvania, 1820-1835t. (KRA II-3)

NEIHARDT, PETER (1743-1813), Northampton Co., Pennsylvania, 1764-1813. Flintlock Kentucky rifle. (Gabel)

NEIL, FRANKLIN (1828-?), Nicholas Co., West Virginia, 1860c.

NEIL, JAMES Philadelphia, Pennsylvania, 1862-1863. Converted flintlock muskets.

NEILS, FRANK Davenport, Iowa, 1877-1880. Patent #562,846 June 30, 1896, machine gun.

NEIMEYER, GEORGE W. Elizabeth, New Jersey 1897d. Son of H.L. Neimeyer

NEIMEYER, HENRY LOUIS Elizabeth, New Jersey, 1878d- 1885d.

NEIMEYER, JACOB Trenton, Ohio, 1872d, Atlantic, Iowa, 1877-1880. Patent #225,412 March 9, 1880, gun wand. Percussion swivel breech.

NEIMEYER, T. unlocated. Percussion 1/2 stock.

NEITH, N. Middleton, Connecticut, 1845. (Dean*)

NELSON, ALEXANDER Philadelphia, Pennsylvania, 1776. Flintlock muskets for Colony of Virginia. (Gluckman & Satterlee)

NELSON, FRANCIS Philadelphia, Pennsylvania, 1776. Stockmaker. (Gluckman & Satterlee)

NELSON, G.H. Knoxville, Tennessee, 1876d.

NELSON, H. Shipman, Illinois, 1878d-1882d.

NELSON, JAMES E. (1831-?), Hampshire Co., West Virginia, 1869-1880c. (Whisker IV)

NELSON, JOHN D. Ball Ground, Georgia, 1881-1883d.

NELSON, NEIL Clifton, Texas, 1890d-1896d.

NELSON, NILS Carver, Minnesota, 1878d.

NELSON, O.B. Nevada, Iowa, 1889d.

NELSON, P.W. Kansas City, Missouri, 1871d.

NELSON, ROGER Medina Co., Ohio, 1825. (Knittle)

NELSON, ROGER, JR. Medina, Ohio, 1859d. (Hutslar)

NELSON, SETH IREDELL (1809-1905), Round Island, Pennsylvania. (Chandler)

NELSON, SETH IREDELL (1838-1934), Round Island, Pennsylvania. (Chandler)

NELZER, F. St. Louis, Missouri, 1860d.

NENNINGER, ROBERT Newark, New Jersey. Patent #113,194 March 28, 1871, breechloading firearm.

NEPPERHAN FIREARMS CO. Yonkers, New York, 1860. Percussion revolvers. (GR 7-71)

NEPPS, ABRAHAM Philadelphia, Pennsylvania, 1824d. Probably Abraham Nippes.

NERO trade name (of ?) on percussion single shot.

NERO trade name of Rupertus on suicide specials.

NESBITT, ROBERT McLane, Pennsylvania. Percussion fullstock.

NESTER, D.S. Anvil, West Virginia, 1900d. (Whisker IV)

NESTLE, FREDERICK (?-1884), Baltimore, Maryland, 1853-1884d. Percussion schuetzen. (Hartzler)

NETH, JACOB, W. Newton, Pennsylvania, 1861d.

NETHERCUT, GEORGE Grayson, Kentucky, 1856-1860d.

NETTER, JOSEPH Philadelphia, Pennsylvania, 1847d.

NETTER, SOLOMON Huntington Co., Pennsylvania. Flintlock Kentucky. (Dillin)

NETZ, JOHN (1815-?), Allegeny Co., Maryland, 1850c. (Hartzler)

NEUBECKER, PHILIP Lancaster Co., Pennsylvania, 1826. (KRA IV-4)

NEUGBAUER, JEAN (1805-?), New Orleans, Louisiana, 1850c-1853d. Also known as Jean Nagebauer in 1853 directory.

NEUHARDT, PETER see Peter Neihardt.

NEUKIRK, D. unlocated. Percussion fullstock.

NEUMAN, JOHN Yoakum, Texas, 1892d.

NEUMANN, R. San Antonio, Texas. Percussion bench gun.

NEVERMISS trade name of Marlin on derringers.

NEVINS, JOHN G. Buckhorn, Pennsylvania, 1861d.

NEVITT, DAVID R. (1830-?), Zionville, Indiana, 1860-1870, Noblesville, Indiana, 1885. (Lindert)

NEW AUBREY trade name of Sears, Roebuck & Co. on revolvers and shotguns.

NEW BABY trade name of Foehl & Weeks on revolvers. (Kolb)

NEW ENGLAND ARMS CO. trade name of Charles Godfrey on imported shotguns. (Hinman)

NEW ERA GUN WORKS trade name of Baker Gun Co. on shotguns.

NEW HAVEN ARMS CO. New Haven, Connecticut, 1857-1866. Successors to Volcanic Arms Co. Owned by Oliver Fisher Winchester and reorganized as Winchester Repeating Arms Co. in 1866. (Williamson)

NEW HAVEN lock marking of Whitney on flintlock muskets.

NEW LIBERTY trade name of Sears Roebuck & Co. on shotguns.

NEW RIVAL trade name of Crescent on guns for Van Camp Hardware. (AR 2-69)

NEW WORCESTER trade name of Torkalson Mfg. Co. on hammerless shotguns. (Hinman)

NEW YORK ARMS CO. trade name of Crescent on shotguns for Garnet-Carter Co. and Charles Altinger, and on Columbian revolvers. Also known as New York Gun Co. (AR 2-69)

NEW YORK CLUB trade name of Crescent Arms Co. on rolling block rifles.

NEW YORK GUN CO. see New York Arms Co. (AR 2-69)

NEW YORK MACHINE MADE trade name of Crescent on shotguns. (Hinman)

NEW YORK PISTOL CO. trade name of Otis Smith on revolvers.

NEW YORK SPORTING GOODS CO. New York, New York. Dealers only.

NEW, C.B. Three Creeks, Arkansas, 1898d.

NEWBECKER, PHILIP Halifax, Pennsylvania, 1817. Flintlock Kentucky. (Dillin)

NEWBERRY, WILLIAM Clarksville, Missouri, 1860d.

NEWBURN, D. & L. see David Newburn.

NEWBURN, DAVID Mt. Vernon, Iowa, 1865d-1882d. Percussion 1/2 stock. As D. & L. Newburn.

NEWBURN, JAMES C. Mount Vernon, Iowa, 1876-1894.

NEWBURN, W.G. Jefferson, Iowa, 1880d.

NEWBURY ARMS CO. Albany, New York, 1852-1866. Percussion revolvers and cartridge derringers. (Gluckman & Satterlee)

NEWBURY, FREDERICK D. Albany, New York, 1852-1866. Patents #12,555 May 20, 1855, revolver, #13,039 June 12, 1855, revolvers, #13,582 September 18, 1855, revolvers, #14,406 March 11, 1856, firearm, #14,774 April 29, 1856, firearm, #15,521 August 12, 1856, breechloading firearm, #16,629 February 10, 1857, patching bullets, #19,327 February 9, 1858, firearm, #19,739 March 23, 1858, revolver, #20,765 June 30, 1858, revolver, #27,868 April 10, 1860, #30,494 October 23, 1860, revolver, #46,131 January 31, 1865, revolver rammers, and #51,959 January 9, 1866, breechloading firearms. Also held "additional improvements" on patents. (Sellers-1, GC 18)

NEWBURY, JAMES Windham, New York, 1879-1882d.

NEWBURY, JOEL Poughkeepsie, New York. Patent #none April 27, 1830, underhammer gun.

NEWBY, WILLIAM C. Seymour, Indiana, 1867d-1872d. (Lindert)

NEWCOMB, ANDREW I. Staunton, Virginia, 1850c. For James A. Gardiner.

NEWCOMB, H.G. (1816-?), Natchez, Mississippi, 1860d-1867d. Agent for H. Deringer.

NEWCOMB, H.W. Eastport, Maine, 1863-1868. (Demeritt)

NEWCOMB, WILLIAM Johnsville, New York. Patent #308,513 November 25, 1884, firearm.

NEWCOMER, ABRAHAM Lancaster, Pennsylvania, 1764. (MB 8-65) (1761, Dyke)

NEWCOMER, CHRISTIAN Lancaster Co., Pennsylvania, 1803. Flintlock Kentucky. (Kindig)

NEWCOMER, JOHN (?-1782), Lancaster, Pennsylvania, 1767-1782. Flintlock Kentucky. (Kauffman)

NEWCOMER, JOHN, JR. Lancaster, Pennsylvania, 1780-1790, York Co., Pennsylvania, 1793-1807. Flintlock Kentucky. (Kindig)

NEWCOMER, M. Piketon, Missouri, 1860d.

NEWCOMER, MARTIN (1801-?), Gallia Co., Ohio, 1850c. (Hutslar)

NEWCUM, WILLIAM Mount Vernon, Kentucky, 1857-1860d.

NEWELL, GEORGE, H. Woodsville, New Hampshire, 1887d-1889d.

NEWELL, J.D.S. Tensas Parish, Louisiana. Patents #88,730 April 6, 1869, breechloading firearm, and #90,381 May 25, 1869, breechloading firearm.

NEWELL, W.H. Knoxville, Illinois, 1880d.

NEWHARDT, JACOB Allentown, Pennsylvania, 1774-1800. Flintlock Kentucky. (Dillin)

NEWHARDT, PETER see Peter Neihart.

NEWHOFF, FRANCIS B. San Francisco, California, 1856-1885. (Shelton)

NEWHOUSE BROS. Valparaiso, Indiana, 1895-1896d. (MB 4-54)

NEWHOUSE, SEWELL Oneida, New York. Percussion fullstock rifles and traps. (Swinney)

NEWKIRK, JOHN Jackson Co., Indiana. (Lindert)

NEWLIN, D. West Liberty, Ohio, 1870d. Negro gunsmith. (Hutslar)

NEWMAN, JAMES Amenia, New York, 1880-1882d.

NEWMAN, L. Seattle, Washington, 1880d.

NEWMARKET unlocated. Flintlock Kentucky.

NEWPORT suicide special.

NEWPORT trade name of Crescent Fire Arms Co. on shotguns for Hibbard, Spencer, Bartlett, & Co. (Hinman)

NEWTON, A.D. De Pere, Wisconsin, 1857d.

NEWTON, ABNER A. Richmond, Indiana, 1853-1857. Patents #10,950 May 23, 1854, primer, #11,198 June 27, 1854, breechloading firearm, #11,700 September 19, 1854, breechloading firearm, #12,556 March 20, 1855, cartridges, and #15,522 August 12, 1856, breechloading firearm. Also held numerous "additional Improvements" on these patents.

NEWTON, DENNIS unlocated. Percussion fullstock.

NEWTON, E.M. Skowhegan, Maine, 1858-1869. Percussion 1/2 stock rifles. (Demeritt)

NEWTON, EDMOND Worcester, Massachusetts, 1865d.

NEWTON, JOHN H. Athens, Georgia, 1861. Confederate gunsmith convention.

NEWTON, MILTON Little Valley, New York, 1870d.

NEWTON, MOSES Connecticut, 1776. Committee of Safety muskets and locks. (Gluckman & Satterlee)

NEWTON, PHILO S. Shrewsbury, Massachusetts, 1828-1832, Hartford, Connecticut, 1842d-1888d. Percussion target rifles and pistols. Patent #3,115 June 1, 1843, false muzzle. For J. Hapgood, 1828-1832.

NEWTON, SAMUEL Middleburg, Ohio, 1853d-1868d. Percussion guns. (Hutslar)

NICELY, JACOB (1810-1890), Beaver Co., Pennsylvania, 1834-1880, Enon Valley, Pennsylvania, 1880-1890d. Patent #377,531 February 7, 1888, lock.

NICHMAN, JOHN York Co., Pennsylvania, 1829. (Kindig)

NICHOL, JACOB Hagerstown, Maryland, 1800-1805. Flintlock Kentucky and locks. With John George as George & Nichol, 1802-1804. (Hartzler)

NICHOLAS, CELESTIAN New Orleans, Louisiana, 1822d-1823d.

NICHOLAS, JOHN Philadelphia, Pennsylvania, 1775-1789. See John Nicholson. (Boehret)

NICHOLAS, NORMAN (1841-?), Rushville, Indiana, 1860c. (Lindert)

NICHOLS & CHILDS Conway, Maine. Patent #707 April 24, 1838, revolver. Rufus Nichols and Edward Childs. (Sellers-1)

NICHOLS & LEFEVER Syracuse, New York, 1876-1878. Percussion rifles. John A. Nichols.

NICHOLS, C.P. Oil City, Pennsylvania, 1890d.

NICHOLS, G.L. Fergus Falls, Minnesota, 1876-1886d.

NICHOLS, JAMES Lake, Ohio, 1860-1864d. (Hutslar)

NICHOLS, JAMES Limestone, New York. Patent #36,358 September 2, 1862, revolver. (Sellers-1)

NICHOLS, JOHN A. Syracuse, New York, 1870-1880, Geddes, New York, 1880d-1882d. Patents #198,669 December 25, 1877, lock with Joseph W. Livingston, #198,670 December 25, 1877, breechloading firearm. As Nichols & Lefever, 1876-1878.

NICHOLS, JOHN Philadelphia, Pennsylvania, 1776-1789. (Gluckman & Satterlee)

NICHOLS, JONATHAN, JR. Vergennes, Vermont. Model 1798 contract muskets delivered by Joshua Henshaw. (Gluckman)

NICHOLS, M.T. Carrollton, Illinois, 1886d-1888d, Greenfield, Illinois, 1890d-1893d.

NICHOLS, MARCUS Erie, Pennsylvania, 1890d.

NICHOLS, RUFUS Conway, Massachusetts. Patent #707 April 24, 1838, revolver with Edward Childs.

NICHOLSON, JAMES (?-1836), Charleston, South Carolina, 1809d. Although listed in the 1809 directory as a gunsmith, other records indicate he was a lawyer who had a financial interest in John Schirer's gun shop.

NICHOLSON, JOHN (?-1799), Philadelphia, Pennsylvania, 1774-1799. Committee of Safety muskets and contract pistols, 1797-1798. (Kauffman)

NICHOLSON, L. unlocated. Percussion 1/2 stock.

NICHOLSON, R.B. Philadelphia, Pennsylvania, 1799. Son of John Nicholson.

NICHOLSON, WAYLAND B. Holly, Michigan, 1900-1902. Small quantity of .22 cal. revolving rifles. Patent #663,923 December 18, 1900, revolving rifle. (Perkins)

NICK BROS. El Paso, Texas, 1892d-1910d.

NICKERSON, CHARLES V. Baltimore, Maryland. Patent #8,690 January 27, 1852, firearms.

NICKERSON, ENSIGN ADAMS (1825-?), San Bernardino, California, 1872-1879. (Shelton)

NICKLIN, JOHN H. New York, 1873d-1888d.

NIEBELS, JACOB Waseca, Minnesota, 1876-1882d, Fergus Falls, Minnesota, 1883d-1886d. As Niebels & Watson, 1883-1884.

NIEHAUS, D. Jersey City, New Jersey, 1878d.

NIELL, JOHN (1805-?), Putnam Co., Ohio, 1850c. (Hutslar)

NIELSEN see Reinike & Nielsen.

NIEPER, AUGUST Leadville, Colorado, 1880-1884d, Aspen, Colorado, 1885d-1900. (Sellers-3)

NIES, LOUIS Buchanan Co., Missouri, 1850c. (MB 11-66)

NIGHTINGALE & NEFF Baltimore, Maryland, (1819d-1823d). Imported locks.

NILES, GEORGE H. Brattleboro, Vermont, 1875-1879. Percussion 1/2 stock rifles.

NILES, REUBEN C. (1812-?), Hancock Co., Indiana, 1850c. (Lindert)

NIMECK, P.J. Tipton, Missouri, 1860d.

NINEMEYER, CHARLES (1807-?), Greenville, Pennsylvania, 1833-1850c. (Whisker II)

NIPES, ABRAHAM Berks Co., Pennsylvania, 1800t. Probably Abraham Nippes. (Kauffman)

NIPPES, ABRAHAM (?-1812), Liberty, Pennsylvania. Father of Abraham and Charles.

NIPPES, ABRAHAM Philadelphia, Pennsylvania, 1813-1855. (Kauffman) (Whisker III, two men with the same names)

NIPPES, ALBERT S. Mill Creek and Philadelphia, Pennsylvania, 1848-1860. Sharps rifles, 1849-1851. Son of Daniel Nippes.

NIPPES, CHARLES Philadelphia, Pennsylvania, 1823d. Clerk for Abraham Nippes.

NIPPES, DANIEL Mill Creek and Philadelphia, Pennsylvania, 1796-1850. Model 1808 and 1840 contract muskets. Converted flintlock muskets to Maynard primer system. Model 1808 contract muskets marked "W.N. & S.", with James Winner and John Steinman. Winner, Nippes, and Steinman worked (together?) at the Harper's Ferry Armory. (Gluckman)

NIPPES, WILLIAM Philadelphia, Pennsylvania, 1796-1829d. Brother of Daniel Nippes.

NITCHMAN, JOHN (?-1828), Beavertown, Pennsylvania, 1813t-1828. Flintlock Kentucky, sometimes used "I.N." signature. (Bowers)

NITRO BIRD trade name of Richards & Conover Hardware Co. (Hinman)

NITRO HUNTER trade name of Belknap Hardware Co. on shotguns by Crescent.

NITRO KING trade name of Sears, Roebuck & Co. on shotguns. (AG 4-75)

NITRO SPECIAL trade name of Stevens on shotguns. (AG 4-75)

NIX, J.A. Jefferson, Texas, 1878d.

NIXON, AUSTIN Buffalo, New York, 1832.

NOBLE & BRADY Washington, Pennsylvania, 1863-1864. John C. Noble and Freeman Brady, Jr.

NOBLE & LITTLE Pittsburgh, Pennsylvania, 1856-1857. Barrels only. (Kauffman)

NOBLE, ALEXANDER (1814-?), Wellsville, Ohio, 1850c-1864d. (Hutslar)

NOBLE, ANTHONY Martinsburg, Virginia, 1777-1780. Arms factory with Adam Stephen. (Gill)

NOBLE, FLOYD Boardman, North Carolina. Percussion 1/2 stock.

NOBLE, GEORGE W. Galt, California, 1884d. (Shelton)

NOBLE, JOHN C. Claysville, Pennsylvania, 1861d. Patent #34,126 January 28, 1862, magazine gun, with Freeman Brady, Jr. With John D. McKahan as McKahan & Noble, 1860.

NOBLE, JOHN M. Hartford, Connecticut. Patent #541,654 June 25, 1895, automatic gun feeding device.

NOBLE, STILLMAN Kentland, Indiana, 1881d.

NOCK, JOSEPH Washington, D.C., 1866d. (Hartzler)

NOE, BARTHOLOMEW L. (1823-?), New York, New York, 1842-1845, Marysville, California, 1853-1860. Percussion rifles and pistols. (Shelton)

NOEL, B.F. St. Cloud, Minnesota, 1867d.

NOEL, J.R. Farmville, Virginia, 1897d.

NOGGLE, WASHINGTON New Burlington, Ohio, 1849-1855, Harveysburg, Ohio, 1860c. Percussion 1/2 stock and fullstock. (Hutslar)

NOLAN & LACKY unlocated. Flintlock New England rifle.

NOLAN unlocated. Flintlock New England rifle.

NOLAN, DENNIS New York, New York, 1850c.

NOLAN, JOHN New York, New York, 1850c.

NOLAN, MAURICE Traverse City, Michigan, 1883d-1899d.

NOLL, BENJAMIN Berks Co., Pennsylvania, 1850c.

NOLL, HENRY (1791-1855), Franklin Co., Pennsylvania, 1812t-1846. Flintlock Kentucky. Son of John Noll. (Bowers)

NOLL, JOHN (1747-1824), Lancaster Co., Pennsylvania, Franklin Co., Pennsylvania, 1788t-1824. Flintlock Kentucky. (Bowers)

NOLL, JOHN (1786-?), Bearsville, Ohio, 1850c. (Hutslar)

NOLL, PETER Berks Co., Pennsylvania, 1850c.

NON-XL suicide special by Hopkins & Allen.

NONPARIEL suicide special.

NORCOTT, WILLIAM New York, New York, 1848-1851. Gun implements. (Gardner)

NORCROSS, ALLEN (1815-?), Evansville, Indiana, 1850c. Percussion fullstock. (Lindert)

NORCROSS, G.E. Fremont, Nebraska, 1872d.

NORD, JACOB Philadelphia, Pennsylvania, 1859-1860d. Lockmaker.

NORDHEIM, GEORGE ANDREW (1818-1894), St. Louis, Missouri, 1850-1852d, Burlington, Iowa, 1856d, Yreka, California, 1862-1893. Percussion 1/2 stock and converted Spencer. (Shelton)

NORFOLK see Welch, Brown & Co. and W.W. Welch.

NORMAN & KELLY Kokomo, Indiana, 1867d. Benjamin R. Norman.

NORMAN, BENJAMIN R. Kokomo, Indiana, 1858d-1867d, Marion, Indiana, 1870. As Norman & Kelly, 1867. (Lindert)

NORMAN, BENJAMIN Morrow, Ohio, 1851-1854. (Gardner)

NORMAN, JOHN (?-1950), Gallipolis, Ohio. Percussion fullstock. (Hutslar)

NORMAN, JOHN Charleston, South Carolina, 1763. (Gluckman & Satterlee)

NORMAN, JOHN Springfield, Pennsylvania, 1861d.

NORMAN, WILLIAM Brooklyn, New York, 1855-1875.

NORRIS & BEATTY Baltimore, Maryland, 1835d-1842d. Importers. (Hartzler)

NORRIS & BRO. Baltimore, Maryland, 1840d-1864d. Percussion duellers, importers. Sons of Richard Norris. (Hartzler)

NORRIS & CLEMENT see Samuel Norris, and William T. Clement.

NORRIS, A.W. Atchison, Kansas, 1891d.

NORRIS, J.S. Atchison, Kansas, 1894d. Son of A.W. Norris.

NORRIS, JOHN T. Springfield, Ohio, 1880-1901. Finger guard for Chicago Palm pistol.

NORRIS, R.W. Piqua, Ohio, 1853d. Percussion fullstock. (Hutslar)

NORRIS, RICHARD Baltimore, Maryland, 1810d-1839d. Importers. As Norris & Sons, 1831-1839. (Hartzler)

NORRIS, SAMUEL Springfield, Massachusetts, 1862-1869. Model 1863 contract muskets for Massachusetts Militia marked "S.N. & W.T.C. MASS." with William T. Clement as Norris & Clement, Springfield, Massachusetts, 1862-1865. Patent #78,603 June 2, 1868, breechloading firearm (the Mauser-Norris 67-69) with brothers Wilhelm and Peter Paul Mauser. (Smith)

NORRIS, WILLIAM Brown Co., Ohio, 1853d. Percussion sporting rifle. (Hutslar)

NORTH & CHENEY Berlin, Connecticut, 1797. First U.S. contract pistols. Simeon North and Elisha Cheney. (North)

NORTH & COUCH Middletown, Connecticut, 1859-1861. Trap guns under owners Henry North's and John Couch's patent #24,573 June 28, 1859.

NORTH & SAVAGE Middletown, Connecticut, 1849d-1859. Revolvers under Henry North's patent. James North and Edward Savage. (Sellers)

NORTH CAROLINA GUN WORKS Halifax, North Carolina, 1776-1778. Muskets. (Gluckman & Satterlee)

NORTH, ANTHONY Essex Co., Virginia, 1706. Apprenticed to Henry Byron, May 11, 1706.

NORTH, FRANKLIN S. Hornellsville, New York, 1856-1859d.

NORTH, HENRY S. Middletown, Connecticut, 1844-1860. Patents #3,686 July 30, 1844, breechloading firearm with Edward Savage, #5,141 June 5, 1847, breechloading firearms, #8,982 June 1, 1852, revolver with Chauncey Skinner, #15,144 June 17, 1856, revolver, #19,868 April 6, 1858, revolver rammer, #22,566 January 18, 1859, revolving firearm with Edward Savage, #24,573 June 28, 1859, trap gun with John Couch, and #28,331 May 15, 1860, revolving firearm with Edward Savage. Son of, and successor to, Simeon North. Made guns alone, with Edward Savage, and with John Couch. (Sellers-1)

NORTH, JAMES Middletown, Connecticut, 1849d-1859. With Edward Savage as North & Savage. Son of Simeon North. (Sellers-1)

NORTH, L.C. Jefferson, Iowa, 1897d.

NORTH, REUBEN Middletown, Connecticut, 1811d. Son of Simeon North.

NORTH, SELAH Stow's Corners, Ohio, 1835. Flintlock rifles. (Knittle)

NORTH, SIMEON (1765-1852), Berlin, Connecticut, 1790-1840. First U.S. Government flintlock pistol contracts, also made Hall carbines. With Elisha Cheney as North & Cheney, Berlin, Connecticut, 1797. (North)

NORTH, THOMAS J. Boston, Massachusetts. Percussion 1/2 stock.

NORTH, THOMAS J. Hillsborough, Ohio, 1870c-1883d. Percussion 1/2 stock. (Hutslar)

NORTHFIELD KNIFE CO. marking (and trade name?) of Northfield Knife Co., Northfield, Connecticut on suicide specials made by Rome Revolver and Novelty Works, Rome, New York, circa 1870.

NORTHFIELD Louisville, Kentucky. Percussion fullstock rifle.

NORTHROP, E.A.B. Norwalk, Connecticut, 1866d-1881d.

NORTHUP, WARREN Hebbardsville, Ohio, 1859d. (Hutslar)

NORTON, D. Greensburg, Pennsylvania. Flintlock Kentucky. (KRA I)

NORTON, EBENEZER Goshen, Connecticut, 1777-1780. Stocker for Committee of Safety.

NORTON, FRANCIS Caledonia Centre, Wisconsin, 1857d.

NORTON, H.C. Guilford, Connecticut, 1869-1873.

NORTON, JOHN Chicago, Illinois, 1844d. For Peacock & Thatcher.

NORTON, L. Parish, New York, 1874d-1880d. Rifles.

NORTON, LYMAN Susquehanna, Pennsylvania, 1867d. Percussion 1/2 stock.

NORTON, STEPHEN Parish, New York, 1870d-1882d. Percussion sporting rifles.

NORTON, WILLIAM Virginia, 1777. Committee of Safety repairs. (Gill)

NORWICH ARMS CO. Norwich, Connecticut, 1861d-1865d. Model 1861 contract muskets. (Fuller)

NORWICH ARMS CO. Norwich, Connecticut, 1873-1881d. Suicide specials attributed to Bliss were made by this company, F.W. Hood, owner. Also known as Norwich Pistol Co.

NORWICH ARMS CO. trade name of Crescent on shotguns made for Sears, Roebuck & Co. (AR 2-69)

NORWICH FALLS PISTOL CO. Norwich, Connecticut, 1882d-1887d. Suicide specials for Maltby, Curtis & Co. Owned by Otis Smith.

NORWICH LOCK MFG. CO. Norwich, Connecticut, 1873-1878. Suicide specials. Alternate name used by Norwich Arms Co.

NORWICH lock marking of Nathan and Henry Cobb on Model 1798 contract muskets.

NORWICH, W.S. St. Albans, Vermont, 1879-1880. (Horn)

NORWICKI, FRANK New York, New York, 1890d.

NORWOOD, GEORGE W. Bayou La Chute, Louisiana. Patent #236,834 January 18, 1881, magazine firearm.

NOSS, J.A. New Castle, Pennsylvania, 1882d.

NOTESTINE, G.W. Kirksville, Missouri, 1893d.

NOTEWARE, NELSON Sheffield, Massachusetts, 1885d-1890d.

NOTNAC MFG. CO. trade name of Crescent on shotguns for Belknap Hardware Co. and Canton Hardware Co. (Hinman)

NOTT, HENRY Winchester, Virginia, 1893d-1897d.

NOVELTY IRON WORKS Union City, Pennsylvania, 1873d-1874d. W. H. Judson.

NOVOTNY, FRANK St. Paul, Minnesota, 1878d-1916d. Patents #288,618 November 20, 1883, breechloading firearm with P. Novotny and John Burkhard, #754,598 March 15, 1904, shell ejector, and #754,599 March 15, 1904, gun.

NOVOTNY, JOHN Jordan, Minnesota, 1878d.

NOVOTNY, P. St. Paul, Minnesota, 1878-1900. Patent #288,618 November 20, 1883, breechloading gun with Frank Novotny and John Burkhard.

NOWLIN, ABRAM CEPHUS (1825-1913), Cocke Co., Missouri, 1846-1861, Hickory Co., Missouri, 1865-1913. (MB 1-49)

NOWLIN, TOM (1879-1949), Fredonia, Missouri, 1889-1930. Son of Abram Nowlin. (MB 1-49)

NOYES, LUCIUS T. Houston, Texas, 1878d-1884. Dealer.

NOYES, WILLIAM H. Brattleboro, Vermont, 1873-1874, Brandon, Vermont, 1875-1879. As Taylor & Noyes, 1873-1874. (Horn)

NUDD, AMOS Waupun, Wisconsin. Patent #150,349 April 28, 1874, lock.

NULL, NATHAN Sellers Tavern, Pennsylvania, 1861d. See N. Mull.

NUNNAMACKER, GEORGE (?-1845), York, Pennsylvania, 1797, Emmitsburg, Maryland, 1798. Flintlock Kentucky. (Hartzler)

NUNNEMACHER, ABRAM (?-1791), York Co., Pennsylvania, 1779-1791. (Kindig)

NUNNEMACHER, ANDREW York, Pennsylvania, 1779. (Kindig)

NUTT, ROLLIN (1820-?), Eagleville, Ohio, 1850c-1854. (Hutslar)

NUTTER, ALBERT Barnstead, New Hampshire, 1876-1879.

NUTTING, EBENEZER (1700-?), Falmouth, Maine, 1722-1745. Public armorer, 1723-1726. (Demeritt)

NUTTING, GEORGE Huntington, Vermont, 1877-1885. (Horn)

NUTTING, MIGHILL Portland, Maine. Patent #713 April 25, 1838, revolving rifle. (Demeritt)

NUTTING, STEPHEN New Haven, Vermont, 1876-1878d. Percussion 1/2 stock rifles.

NUTTMAN, VICTOR W. (1826-1898), Alameda Co., California, 1867-1898. (Shelton)

NUTZ, L.N. St. Louis, Missouri, 1840d-1860d.

NYE, ALONZO Seville, Ohio, 1875d. (Hutslar)

NYE, JOHN C. Cincinnati, Ohio. Patents #36,852 November 4, 1862, breechloading firearm, and #37,356 January 6, 1863, breechloading firearm.

O SECTION

O.H. unidentified. Percussion 1/2 stock.

O.M. unidentified. Percussion 1/2 stock.

O'BEIST, JAC (1811-?), Stark Co., Ohio, 1850c. (Hutslar)

O'BRIEN, CHARLES C.C. (?-1842), Baltimore, Maryland, 1883d-1842. (Hartzler)

O'BRIEN, JOSEPH Brooklyn, New York, 1870d-1875.

O'BRIEN, P. Chandlerville, Pennsylvania, 1867d.

O'CONNELL, DANIEL New York, New York, 1852d-1858d. Derringer. As Murphy & O'Connell, 1857-1858.

O'CONNELL, MICHAEL Brooklyn, New York, 1870d-1875d.

O'CONNOR, MICHAEL W. Sanford, Maine, 1881-1890. (Demeritt)

O'DAY, THOMAS (1845-?), San Francisco, California, 1870c. (Shelton)

O'DONNELL, PATRICK Salina, Kansas, 1882d-1884d.

O'MARA BROS. Detroit, Michigan, 1865d-1870d. John O'Mara.

O'MARA, JOHN Detroit, Michigan, 1863d-1870d. With Frederick Ege, 1863. As O'Mara Bros., 1865-1870.

O'MEARA, DANIEL Milwaukee, Wisconsin, 1851-1852. (WGCA 4)

O'MEARA, J.D. (1874-1933), Lead, South Dakota, 1896-1933. Repairs and custom work.

O'NEAL, DAVID San Francisco, California, 1858. (Shelton)

O'NEIL, CHARLES Chambersburg, Pennsylvania, 1803. (Bowers)

O'NEIL, J. PALMER Pittsburgh, Pennsylvania, 1882d-1885d. Breechloading double shotgun.

O'NEIL, JAMES Sacramento, California, 1858-1859d. (Shelton)

O'ROURKE & BROWN Orange, New Jersey, 1878d.

O'ROURKE, JOHN Milwaukee, Wisconsin, 1851-1855. Percussion 1/2 stock. (WGCA 4)

OAHLE, WILLIAM Utica, New York, 1832d. (Kauffman 2)

OAK, CALVIN, & SON (1806-1881), Jacksonville, Florida, 1851-1860. Underhammer knife pistol, percussion double rifle/shotgun. (AG 12-74)

OAKES, SAMUEL Northumberland Co., Pennsylvania, 1787-1790, Ft. Washington, Pennsylvania, 1793, Philadelphia, Pennsylvania, 1800. (Kauffman)

OATIS, N. Little Osage, Missouri, 1860d.

OATS, LEVI Leesburg, Indiana, 1860d.

OBERHEU, LOUIS C. (1830-?), Cincinnati, Ohio, 1866d-1900d. Imported double shotgun. (Hutslar)

OBERHOLSER, CHRISTIAN Lancaster, Pennsylvania, 1775-1777. For William Henry, 1777. (Hobbies 4-38)

OBERTEUFFER, CHARLES A. (1811-?), Baltimore, Maryland, 1836-1840, Philadelphia, Pennsylvania, 1842d-1850c. Derringer. (Hartzler)

OBLINGER, CHARLES M. Piqua, Ohio, 1878d. (Hutslar)

OBLINGER, D. & SON Piqua, Ohio, 1890-1916. David and Walter W. Oblinger. (Hutslar)

OBLINGER, DAVID Piqua, Ohio, 1859-1916. With Walter W. Oblinger as D. Oblinger & Son, 1890-1916. (Hutslar)

OBLINGER, JOHN W. Troy, Ohio, 1878d. Percussion 1/2 stock rifles. (Hutslar)

OBLINGER, SOLOMON Troy, Ohio, 1867-1883d. (Hutslar)

OBLINGER, WALTER W. Troy, Ohio, 1887-1916. Son of David Oblinger. (Hutslar)

OCHS, CHARLES Bushkill Center, Pennsylvania, 1860t. Lockmaker. (Kauffman)

ODD FELLOW suicide special.

ODELL, STEPHEN (1820-?), Natchez, Mississippi, 1840-1860c. Percussion 1/2 stock rifles, and derringers.

ODENBAUGH, DANIEL (1812-?), Wheeling, West Virginia, 1833-1867d. Percussion 1/2 stock. (MB 9-60)

ODLE, A.M. Helena, Arkansas, 1878d.

ODLIN, JOHN Boston, Massachusetts, 1671-1682.

ODUM, S. Pikeville, Tennessee, 1860d.

OERTER, JOHN CHRISTIAN (1747-1777), Nazareth, Pennsylvania, 1771-1777. Flintlock Kentucky rifle. Master armorer at Christian Springs. (KRA IV-3)

OETZEL, J.A. Chicago, Illinois, 1884d.

OFFELT, E.A. unlocated. Percussion 1/2 stock.

OFFIELD, E. Ashley, Illinois, 1864d.

OFFREY, P. (1812-?), New Orleans, Louisiana, 1850c-1853d. (MB 9-65)

OFFUTT, NATHANIEL (?-1855), Hampshire Co., West Virginia, 1830c-1855. (Whisker IV)

OGDEN, C. Owego, New York, 1856-1859. Percussion 1/2 stock.

OGDEN, J. Owego, New York, flintlock rifles. (Gluckman & Satterlee)

OGDEN, WALTER E. Owego, New York, 1849-1870d. Also W. Ogden & Co. and W. & C. Ogden. (Swinney)

OGDEN, WILLIAM Burlington, Michigan, 1860d.

OGLE, A.J. Helena, Ohio, 1888-1890d. (Hutslar)

OHIO LOCK WORKS Perry Co., Ohio. Lockmaker. (Hutslar)

OHIO STATE PENITENTIARY Columbus, Ohio. Made fifty rifles in 1824. (Hobbies 4-39)

OHRING, R. Galveston, Texas, 1868d-1878d.

OK trade name on Cowles .22 cal. derringers.

OK trade name on Marlin revolvers and derringers.

OLBRICH, MORITZ Baker, Oregon, 1891d.

OLD HICKORY suicide special.

OLD HICKORY trade name of Hibbard, Spencer, Bartlett, & Co. on shotguns.

OLD RELIABLE trade mark of Parker Bros., 1900-1933.

OLD RELIABLE trade mark of Sharps Rifle Co., 1874-1881.

OLDEN, LEIGH Carbondale, Pennsylvania, 1861d.

OLDHAM, CHARLES Helena, Montana, 1880d-1898d. With his father Gabriel H. Oldham as G.H. Oldham & Son, 1886.

OLDHAM, GABRIEL H. Howard Co., Missouri, 1850c, Helena, Montana, 1880d-1886d. With his son Charles as G.H. Oldham & Son, 1886.

OLDHAM, THOMAS C. (?-1854), Bedford, Pennsylvania, 1847t-1854. Known primarily for side-by-side rifles signed "T.O.". (Hetrick)

OLDHAM, THOMAS Colesburg, Iowa, 1865d.

OLEACHEA, OCTAVIANO (1841-?), San Bernardino, California, 1871-1879. (Shelton)

OLENHAUSEN, F. Wooster, Ohio. Percussion 1/2 stock. (Knittle)

OLENHEUSEN, JACOB Pittsburgh, Pennsylvania, 1847d. (Kauffman)

OLIPHANT, JOHN Uniontown, Pennsylvania. Patents #37,406 January 13, 1863, safety nipple guard, and #37,407 January 13, 1863, breechloading firearm.

OLIVER & GRAHAM Council Bluffs, Iowa, 1868d-1887d.

OLIVER suicide special.

OLIVER, J.W. Warsaw, Kentucky, 1857-1860.

OLIVER, JOHN Baltimore, Maryland, 1810d. (Hartzler)

OLIVER, ROBERT Pittstown, Pennsylvania, 1890d.

OLIVER, THE taxidermy gun.

OLIVER, W.G. Buffalo, New York. Patent #55,588 June 12, 1866, safety.

OLIVER, WILLIAM Hempstead, New York, 1857-1859. Gun implements.

OLIVIER, A. New Orleans, Louisiana, 1870d.

OLMSTEAD & BENNETT Auburn, New York, 1858-1859. Morgan L. Olmstead. (Roberts)

OLMSTEAD & CHOATE Auburn, New York, 1865d-1867d. Nathaniel W. Choate and Morgan L. Olmstead. (GR 10-58)

OLMSTEAD, J.M. Prairie City, Illinois, 1862. (Johnson)

OLMSTEAD, JAMES Stevensville, Michigan, 1872d-1879d.

OLMSTEAD, L.W. Crescent City, California, 1875-1876. (Shelton)

OLMSTEAD, MORGAN L. (?-1872), Rochester, New York, 1827-1834d, Auburn, New York, 1834-1843 and 1849-1873d, Pontiac, Michigan, 1843-1849. For Ephraim Gilbert in Rochester. As Olmstead & Bennett, 1858-1859. With Nathaniel W. Choate as Olmstead & Choate, 1866-1867. (Massachusetts Arms, Eich)

OLMSTEAD, R. Winsted, Connecticut, 1867-1879d. Percussion 1/2 stock rifle.

OLMSTEAD, WALLER Melrose, Pennsylvania, 1833. Purchased right to make revolvers under David G. Colburn's patent. (Sellers-1)

OLNEY, ANTHONY Canton, Massachusetts. Patent #none August 24, 1818, lathe for turning gun barrels with Daniel Dana.

OLNEY, BENJAMIN Wayland, New York, 1874d.

OLNEY, L.B. Wayland, New York, 1879-1882d.

OLSEN, CHRISTOPHER Chicago, Illinois, 1876d-1932. For Frederick J. Abbey & Co., 1878. As C. Olsen & Sons, 1928-1932.

OLSEN, GNEABRAND Crookston, Minnesota, 1884d, Warren, Minnesota, 1886d.

OLSEN, MAGNUS Hastings, Minnesota, 1886d-1898d.

OLSEN, SEVERT Stoughton, Wisconsin, 1884d-1891d.

OLSTAD, MARTIN Stillwater, Minnesota, 1898d.

OLYMPIC trade name of Morley & Murphy Hardware Co., Green Bay, Wisconsin. (Hinman)

ONDERDONK, JOHN P. Philadelphia, Pennsylvania, 1883-1886. Patents #294,402 March 3, 1884, recoil mechanism, and #319,613 June 9, 1885, stock.

ONE POCKET CREEDMOOR see Samuel Watson Johnson.

ONG, E. Philadelphia, Pennsylvania, 1773-1777. At State Gun Factory during the Revolutionary War. (Gluckman & Satterlee)

ONIADOSI, EDWIN P. Fountain Co., Indiana, 1850c. (Lindert)

ONION & CORNWALL New York, New York, 1875d-1876d. Importers and dealers. Successors to Onion, Haight & Cornwall.

ONION & WHEELOCK New York, 1849d-1864d. Agents for Allen & Thurber and other makers.

ONION, BLISS & CO. New York, New York, 1864d-1867d. Successors to Onion & Wheelock.

ONION, HAIGHT & CORNWALL New York, 1867d-1874d. Successors to Onion, Bliss & Co. Importers and dealers only. (Mouillesseaux)

ONION, T.F. New Orleans, Louisiana. Agent for Lewis & Tomes percussion shotguns.

OPENSHAW, JAMES A. Houston, Texas, 1897d-1899d.

OPPELT, EDWIN A. Clarion, Pennsylvania, 1842-1847. (Kauffman)

OPPENHEIMER, MOSES (1824-?), Carrollton, Illinois, 1850c. (Johnson)

OPPENHEIMER, SOLOMON (1826-?), Carrollton, Illinois, 1850c, Greenfield, Illinois, 1851, Peru, Indiana, 1860c. (Johnson, Lindert)

ORAHOOD, JOHN (1834-?), Bellefontaine, Ohio, 1858, Raymond, Ohio, 1859d-1864. Percussion 1/2 stock rifles. (Hutslar)

ORBEN, MAX Port Jervis, New York, 1866d-1870d.

ORBEN, MICHAEL New York, New York, 1858d, Port Jervis, New York, 1873-1874d.

ORCUTT, SAMUEL Boston, Massachusetts, 1810. (Kauffman 2)

ORCUTT, WILLIAM Candor, New York, 1873-1882d.

ORDNANCE IMPROVEMENT CO. Watervliet, New York, 1895-1914. Cannon under patents of Gregory Gerdon.

ORDUNA, MANUEL Tucson, Arizona, 1884d.

OREAR, JOHN W. Downieville, California, 1878-1880. (Shelton)

ORGILL BROS. & CO. Memphis, Tennessee, 1860d-1887d. Dealers.

ORGILL BROS. New York, New York, 1875d-1876d. Importers and dealers. Joseph Orgill.

ORGILL, JOSEPH New York, New York, 1873d-1876d. As Orgill Bros., 1875d-1876d.

ORMAN, JOHN MICHAEL Lancaster, Pennsylvania, 1759. Lockmaker. (Dyke)

ORMSBY, COLLIS Louisville, Kentucky, 1857-1860d.

ORMSBY, E.S. unlocated. Miller patent revolving rifles.

ORMSBY, W.L. New York, New York. Engraved Colt cylinders.

ORR, FRANCIS J. Wellington, Kansas. Patent #358,747 March 1, 1887, sight with F.C. Holman.

ORR, HUGH (1717-1798), Bridgewater, Massachusetts, 1737-1798. Flintlock muskets and cannon. (GC 27)

ORR, HUGH Williamsburg, Virginia, 1761-1763. Public armorer. (Gill)

ORR, JAMES (1796-1887), Barnesville, Ohio, 1830-1864d. Percussion rifles. (Hutslar)

ORR, ROBERT Bridgewater, Massachusetts, 1775-1795. Master Armorer at Springfield Armory, 1795-1804. Son of Hugh Orr. (Gluckman & Satterlee)

ORR, WILLIAM New York, New York. Patent #148,742 March 17, 1774, revolver.

ORRAHOOD, SAMUEL (1791-?), Logan Co., Ohio, 1850c. (Hutslar)

ORTON, JOHN (1725-1795), Philadelphia, Pennsylvania. (Kauffman)

ORVELL, J.C. Carbondale, Illinois, 1864d-1867d.

ORVILLE, FAY A. Chicago, Illinois, 1869. (Johnson)

ORWAN, F. & C. Perry Co., Pennsylvania. Percussion 1/2 stock.

ORWAN, FREDERICK (1776-?), New Bloomfield, Pennsylvania. Flintlock Kentucky. (Chandler 2)

ORWAN, JOHN Carlisle, Pennsylvania, 1793t-1800t. Flintlock Kentucky rifle. (Bowers)

OSBORN Hamilton, Ohio, 1863d. (Hutslar)

OSBORN, AMOS (1830-?), Rockford, Illinois, 1858d-1882d.

OSBORN, B.P. Paragould, Arkansas, 1888d-1898d.

OSBORN, E.V. Pecatonica, Illinois, 1860d. With Eli Osom?

OSBORN, JESSE (1820-?), Davidson Co., North Carolina, 1850c. (Bivins)

OSBORN, JOHN (1789-?), Pope Co., Illinois, 1850c. (Johnson)

OSBORN, LOT Waterbury, Connecticut, 1776-1779. Committee of Safety muskets. (Gluckman & Satterlee)

OSBORN, S. Canton, Connecticut. Underhammer pistol. (Logan)

OSBORN, W.C. St. Johns, Michigan, 1883d-1893d, Grand Ledge, Michigan, 1895d-1899d.

OSBORN, WILLIAM E. Milton, New York. Patent #11,678 September 12, 1854, breechloading gun.

OSBORN, WILLIAM THOMAS (1831-1896), Madisonville, Kentucky, 1879d-1896d. (Hist. KY, V5, P514)

OSBORNE, BETHEL St. Johns, Michigan, 1863d.

OSBORNE, H. Springfield, Massachusetts, 1812-1830. Model 1808 pattern muskets and flintlock sporting rifles. (Gluckman)

OSGOOD & TOWNSEND Painted Post, New York, 1857d. Harmonica rifle.

OSGOOD GUN WORKS Norwich, Connecticut, 1880-1883d. "Duplex" and "Monarch" double-barrel revolvers. F.L. Osgood.

OSGOOD, F.L. Norwich, Connecticut, 1880-1883d. "Duplex" and "Monarch" double-barrel revolvers. As Osgood Gun Works.

OSGOOD, J.K. Houlton, Maine, 1875. (Demeritt)

OSGOOD, S.H. Toledo, Ohio, 1894, Mansfield, Ohio, 1895-1896. (Hutslar)

OSHKOSH TRAP GUN CO. Oshkosh, Wisconsin, 1896. Single shot shotgun. (GCI)

OSOM, ELI (1829-?), Pecatonica, Illinois, 1860c. See E.V. Osborn.

OSPREY trade name of L. Eppinger Hardware Co., Detroit, on shotguns.

OSSMAN, CHRISTIAN Cleveland, Ohio, 1863-1864d. (Hutslar)

OSTERMAN, CHARLES Covington, Kentucky, 1879d-1899d.

OSTERMAN, CHARLES Kansas City, Missouri, 1891d.

OSTRANDER REPEATING SHOTGUN CO. San Francisco, California, 1891-1897, Boston, Massachusetts, 1898-1900. Willis H. Ostrander. (Shelton)

OSTRANDER, JONATHAN F. New York, New York. Patent #4,568 April 3, 1849, bullet machine.

OSTRANDER, WILLIS H. Merced, California, 1890, San Francisco, California, 1891-1897, Boston, Massachusetts, 1898-1900. Patents #450,773 April 21, 1891, repeating breechloading gun, #469,90 March 1, 1892, magazine shotgun, #531,132 December 18, 1894, magazine gun, and #603,066, April 26, 1898, magazine firearm. As Ostrander Repeating Shotgun Co., 1891-1900. (Shelton)

OSWAN, FRED Harpers Ferry, Virginia, 1810-1816. Patent #none February 25, 1815, rifles.

OTT & PFAFFLE Dallas, Texas, 1878d. Charles Ott and E.C. Pfaffle.

OTT & TREILER Dallas, Texas, 1892d. Charles Ott.

OTT, CHARLES Dallas, Texas, 1878d-1892d. With E.C. Pfaffle as Ott & Pfaffle, 1878. As Ott & Treiller, 1892.

OTTEN & COKELY Palmer, Texas, 1884d.

OTTER, WILLIAM EDWARD Hamilton, Ohio, 1863d.

OTTO, A. Philadelphia, Pennsylvania, 1862-1863. Converted flintlock muskets.

OTTO, AUGUSTUS G. St. Louis, Missouri, 1859d-1864d. With Frederick Lenzhaner as Lenzhaner & Otto, 1864.

OUR JAKE suicide special by Dickinson.

OVER, B.D. Burbank, Ohio, 1872d. (Hutslar)

OVERBAUGH & STANTON Poughkeepsie, New York, 1862-1864. Percussion 1/2 stock. Charles E. Overbaugh and O.V. Stanton.

OVERBAUGH, CHARLES E. Poughkeepsie, New York, 1862-1864, Philadelphia, Pennsylvania, 1873-1875, New York, New York, 1876-1890, Bayonne, New Jersey, 1890-1898. Percussion and cartridge guns. Patents #408,857 June 6, 1893, cartridge, and #610,660, September 13, 1898, cartridge. With O.V. Stanton as Overbaugh & Stanton, 1862-1864, and Overbaugh & Daly, 1884.

OVERBECK, B.J. unlocated - possibly Virginia. Flintlock Kentucky.

OVERDORF, JOHN Brush Valley, Pennsylvania, 1861d.

OVERLY, PETER unlocated. Flintlock Kentucky rifle.

OVERTON, EDWARD St. Louis, Missouri, 1859d.

OVERTON, JESSE Arkadelphia, Arkansas, 1870-1885d. Percussion double shotgun with L. Braun. (Elias)

OVERTON, VAN Winchester, Illinois, 1890d.

OVERTON, W.M. Winchester, Illinois, 1890d.

OVREY, JOHN St. Louis, Missouri, 1838d.

OWEN, A. Trescott, Maine, 1877. (Demeritt)

OWEN, A.H. Red Bluff, Califorinia, 1861. (Shelton)

OWEN, G.E. Caro, Michigan, 1899d.

OWEN, H.V. unlocated. Percussion fullstock rifle.

OWENS, AMBROSE Ramsey, Illinois, 1864d.

OWENS, EVAN G. Philadelphia, Pennsylvania, 1860, Denver, Colorado, 1876d-1890d. Derringer. (Sellers-3)

OWENS, FLAVOS Montezuma, Tennessee, 1887d.

OWENS, GEORGE A. (England, 1837-?), Springfield, Massachusetts. Patents #602,870 April 26, 1898, revolver, and #678,274 July 9, 1901, revolver.

OWENS, LEMUEL Zanesville, Ohio, 1810-1823. (Knittle)

OWENS, NAPOLEON B. (1814-?), Bridgeport, Ohio, 1860c. (Hutslar)

OWENS, ROBERT Binghamton, New York, 1890. (Dean*)

OWENS, WALTER G. New York, New York. Patent #333,024 December 22, 1885, sight.

OWINGS, W. Iuke, Iowa, 1865d.

OXFORD ARMS CO. trade name of Belknap Hardware Co. on shotguns made by Crescent. (Hinman)

OXFORD, SAMUEL (1791-?), Lee Co., Virginia, 1850c. (MB 10-63)

OYLER, COOK Louisiana, Missouri, 1879d.

OZMENT, ALFRED (1820-?), Jamestown, North Carolina, 1850c. (Bivins)

OZMENT, J. Greensboro, North Carolina, 1855. (Bivins)

P SECTION

P. & B. unidentified. Percussion fullstock.

P. & G. trade name of Paxton & Gallagher Co. on shotguns made by Crescent. (Hinman)

P.A. see Philip Anglin.

P.A. unidentified. Percussion fullstock.

P.A.S. unidentified. Percussion fullstock.

P.B. unidentified. Flintlock Kentucky.

P.D. see Peter Dunmeyer.

P.F. unidentified. Flintlock Kentucky.

P.G. see Peter Geiger. Percussion fullstock.

P.G. see Philip Gillespie. Tennessee rifle.

P.G. unidentified. Percussion 1/2 stock.

P.G.F. unidentified. Percussion fullstock.

P.H. unidentified. Flintlock Kentucky.

P.K. see Peter Kuntz.

P.L.H. unidentified. Percussion fullstock.

P.R. unidentified. Flintlock Kentucky.

P.S. unidentified. Flintlock swivel breech.

P.S. unidentified. Percussion fullstock.

P.S.J. & Co. see P.S. Justice & Co. and Philip S. Justice.

P.W. see Peter White.

P.Y. see Peter Young.

PAALI, P.N. Westport, Wisconsin, 1857d.

PABST, HERMAN Chicago, Illinois, 1877d. Dealer?

PACKARD Enfield, Massachusetts, 1820-1830. Anson Chase apprenticed under Packard. (Massachusetts Arms)

PACKARD, ALONZO (1832-?), Elyria, Ohio, 1850c. Son of William Packard. (Hutslar)

PACKARD, WILLIAM M. (1802-?), Elyria, Ohio, 1850c-1866d. Percussion 1/2 stock rifles. (Hutslar)

PACKSON Kent Island, Maryland Colony, 1629-?. As Bennett & Packson, 1629-1631. (Gluckman & Satterlee, Hartzler)

PACOST, E.L. unlocated. Percussion fullstock.

PADDOCK, EDWARD Albany, New York, 1880d-1891d. Son of, and successor to, W.G. Paddock.

PADDOCK, MIRAN (1821-?), Fort Laramie, Nebraska Territory, 1860c.

PADDOCK, W.G., & CO. Albany, New York, 1880d-1885d.

PAGE, ALLEN W. New York, New York, 1801.

PAGE, D.J. Loudon, New Hampshire, 1872d.

PAGE, E.L. Hansen, Michigan, 1872d-1878d.

PAGE, JOHN Preston, Connecticut, 1768-1777. Committee of Safety locks. (Gluckman & Satterlee)

PAGE, STEPHEN PHILLIP (1836-?), Antioch, California, 1869-1890. (Shelton)

PAGE, WILLIAM I. Boston, Massachusetts. Patents #104,636 June 21, 1870, revolver, and #109,931 December 6, 1870, revolver cartridges.

PAGENHARDT, C.A. Westernport, Maryland, 1878d. (Hartzler)

PAGOMA trade name of Paxton & Gallagher Co., Omaha, Nebraska, on shotguns by Crescent. (Hinman)

PAIN, THOMAS (1800-?), Whiteside, North Carolina, 1850c. (Bivins)

PAINE, A.R. New Haven, Connecticut, 1877d.

PAINE, EDGAR H. Burlington, Vermont, 1857-1860d.

PAINE, ELIHU Knox Co., Kentucky. Percussion fullstock.

PAINE, JACOB Brainerd, Minnesota, 1892d.

PAINE, S.T. unlocated. Percussion 1/2 stock.

PAINE, SETH WHITE Rochester, New York. Patents #111,377 January 31, 1871, shot cartridge, and #136,336 February 25, 1873, shot cartridge.

PAINE, STEPHEN L. Farmington, Ohio, 1850c-1853d. (Hutslar)

PAINTER, CARL Chattanooga, Tennessee, 1887d-1891d.

PAINTER, ELISHA Marionville, Missouri, 1889d-1891d.

PAINTER, JACOB Somerset Co., Pennsylvania, 1805-1806t. (Kauffman)

PAINTER, JACOB Springfield, Missouri, 1850c-1889d.

PAINTER, JAMES, W. Lafayette, Missouri, 1850c-1854d.

PAINTER, JOHN, JR. (1814-?), Botetourt Co., Virginia, 1850c. Flintlock Kentucky (possibly by J. Painter, Sr.). (MB 10-63)

PALATINI, CONSTANTINO New York, New York. Patent #191,998 June 12, 1877, spring gun.

PALLISSARD, P. Kankakee, Illinois, 1871d-1875d.

PALM, DANIEL Bowmansville, Pennsylvania, 1875d.

PALM, FREDERICK Ulster Co., New York, 1769-1776. Flintlock rifles. (Gluckman & Satterlee)

PALM, JACOB Lancaster, Pennsylvania, 1764-1768, Esopus, New York, 1768-1776. Flintlock match rifles. (Dillin)

PALM, JOHN H. Chicago, Illinois. Patent #543,652 July 30, 1895, shell ejector.

PALM, JOHN Lancaster, Pennsylvania. Flintlock Kentucky rifles. (Dillin)

PALM, JOHN Womelsdorf, Pennsylvania, 1850c-1861d. (Kauffman)

PALMATEER & WRIGHT Poughkeepsie, New York, 1835-1846. Peter Palmateer and Alexander Wright. Also see A. Wright & Co., same time frame and location. (Swinney)

PALMATEER, PETER Poughkeepsie, New York, 1835-1846. With Alexander Wright as Palmateer & Wright.

PALMATER, PETER Sandusky, Ohio, 1854-1856d. With Isaac H. Robinson as Robinson & Palmater, 1854-1855. (Hutslar)

PALMER & ST. JOHN Fairmont, Minnesota 1898d.

PALMER, A.E Kansas City, Kansas, 1894d.

PALMER, A.M. Salisbury, Missouri, 1898d.

PALMER, AMASA Connecticut. Committee of Safety muskets with Hezekiah Huntington. (Gluckman & Satterlee)

PALMER, C.J. Newport, New Hampshire, 1877d, Whitefield, New Hampshire, 1878-1880d.

PALMER, CHARLES H. Lakeville, Connecticut. Patent #37,052 December 2, 1862, repeating gun.

PALMER, CHARLES H. New York, New York. Patent #332,741 December 22, 1885, machine gun.

PALMER, D.W. Andover, Massachusetts, 1854-1857.

PALMER, E.B. Stewartville, Missouri, 1860d.

PALMER, F.G. Ashland, Nebraska, 1893d.

PALMER, FREDERICK Philadelphia, Pennsylvania, 1837d.

PALMER, GEORGE W. Philadelphia, Pennsylvania, 1847d.

PALMER, H.M. Brooklyn, Michigan, 1860d.

PALMER, H.W. McMinnville, Tennessee, 1871d-1891d.

PALMER, HENRY A. Villisca, Iowa, 1880d-1884d, Atlantic, Iowa, 1887d-1889d.

PALMER, HENRY C. Chicago, Illinois, 1854d, St. Louis, Missouri, 1860d-1868d. Derringer, percussion 1/2 stock.

PALMER, HENRY F. Adrian, Michigan, 1860d-1895d. Percussion 1/2 stock. As H.F. Palmer & Bro., 1860-1864.

PALMER, HENRY Sextonville, Wisconsin, 1857d-1879d.

PALMER, J.W. Columbia, Missouri, 1854d, California, Missouri, 1860d.

PALMER, JOHN Manchester, Indiana 1860d.

PALMER, RAYMOND L. Tacoma, Washington. Patent #476,064 May 31, 1892, safety lock.

PALMER, STEPHEN Philadelphia, Pennsylvania, 1855-1857d. (Kauffman)

PALMER, THEODORE Philadelphia, Pennsylvania, 1770-1782. Committee of Safety muskets (Hobbies 4-38)

PALMER, THOMAS (?-1811), Philadelphia, Pennsylvania, 1772-1776. Committee of Safety muskets. (Hobbies 4-38)

PALMER, WILLIAM R. New York, New York, 1848-1864. Patents #21,623 September 28, 1858, revolver, #32,887 July 23, 1861, breechloading firearm, #41,017 December 22, 1863, breechloading firearm, and #41,857 March 8, 1864, revolver. Carbines made by E.G. Lamson. (GR 8-66)

PALMERTON, C.W. Leavenworth, Kansas, 1894d.

PALMETTO ARMORY Columbia, South Carolina, 1852-1865. Model 1842 muskets and pistols, (Albaugh)

PALMETTO trade name of E.K. Tryon on revolvers and shotguns.

PALMITER, WILLIAM M. West Edmeston, New York, 1878-1882d.

PAMMLER, AUGUST Chicago, Illinois, 1859d-1866d.

PAMMLER, HERMAN Chicago, Illinois, 1859d-1868d.

PANABACKER, J. unlocated. Flintlock Kentucky rifle.

PANAK, ALBERT Winona, Minnesota, 1892d.

PANCOAST, A.R. Morgantown, West Virginia.

PANCOST, E.L. Elizabeth, Pennsylvania, 1861d. Percussion fullstock.

PANE, E. Barboursville, Kentucky, 1857-1873. Percussion fullstock rifles.

PANET, CARLOUX, & CO. Philadelphia, Pennsylvania, 1780-1785. Repaired U.S. arms. (Moller)

PANGBURN, N.J. Trumansburgh, New York, 1874d-1882d.

PANNABECKER FAMILY (also Pennypacker, Panebacker, etc.) an extended family of barrelmakers in Berks and Lancaster Counties, Pennsyhlvania. See (KRA 76) for a complete article on this family.

PANNABECKER, DANIEL (?-1808), Wyomissing Creek, Pennsylvania, 1773-1808. (Hobbies 5-37)

PANNABECKER, DANIEL, I (1761-1825), Berks Co., Pennsylvania, 1800c, Lancaster Co., Pennsylvania, 1808-1825. (Kauffman)

PANNABECKER, DANIEL, II (1791-1872), Reinholdsville, Pennsylvania, 1825-1861d. Barrelmaker, son of Daniel Pannabecker.

PANNABECKER, DANIEL, III (1819-1894), Reinholdsville, Pennsylvania. Son of Daniel Pannabecker II.

PANNABECKER, JAMES Lancaster, Pennsylvania, 1833-1850. Son of Daniel Pannabecker.

PANNABECKER, JEFFERSON Hopeland, Pennsylvania, 1790-1810. Brother of Daniel Pannabecker, I.

PANNABECKER, JESSE R. (1783-?), Durlach, Pennsylvania, 1813-1861d. Patent #7,547 August 6, 1850, making barrels. Son of Daniel Pannabecker.

PANNABECKER, JOHN (1850-1926), Adamstown, Pennsylvania, 1875t-1926. Percussion fullstock target. Son of William Pannabecker Jr.

PANNABECKER, JOHN Lancaster Co., Pennsylvania, 1825-1831. Son of Daniel Pannabecker.

PANNABECKER, SAMUEL (1794-1876), Lancaster Co., Pennsylvania, 1815-1839. Flintlock Kentucky. Son of Daniel Pannabecker. (Kindig)

PANNABECKER, WILLIAM (1784-1870), Mohntown, Pennsylvania, 1800-1868d. Son of, and successor to, Daniel Pannabecker.

PANNABECKER, WILLIAM Lancaster Co., Pennsylvania, 1850. Barrelmaker. Same as Pannabecker at Mohntown? (KRA IV-4)

PANNABECKER, WILLIAM, JR. (1818-1880), Mohntown, Pennsylvania, 1845-1861, Trenton, New Jersey, 1861-1865. Percussion pepperbox.

PANTHER suicide special.

PAPPENHEIMER, LEOPOLD Cincinnati, Ohio, 1853-1900. Importers, various names. (Hutslar)

PAQUET New Orleans, Louisiana. LeMat revolvers.

PARAGON suicide special by Prescott Pistol Co.

PARAGON trade name of Baker Gun Co. on shotguns.

PARCEL see Williams & Parcel.

PARCELL, JOHN A. Corning, New York, 1891d. See J.A. Parsells.

PARCELL, P. Moscow Mills, Ohio, 1860-1864d. (Hutslar)

PARCHER, JOHN Ada, Ohio, 1859d. Percussion 1/2 stock. (Hutslar)

PARISH & FARRER Galena, Illinois, 1860. William Farrer. (Johnson)

PARISH, HENRY (1828-?), Jamestown, North Carolina, 1850c. (Bivins)

PARK & GARBER Columbus, Ohio, 1886-1888. (Hutslar)

PARK & IRWIN Columbus, Ohio, 1889-1891. (Hutslar)

PARK & MCLEISH Columbus, Ohio, 1878-1880d. Horace Park and Charles McLeish, shotguns. (Hutslar)

PARK, A.R. Columbia, Texas, 1878d-1896d.

PARK, G.H. & G.M. Adrian, Michigan, 1867d.

PARK, G.M., & SON Adrian, Michigan, 1868d-1871d.

PARK, GEORGE M. Adrian, Michigan, 1865d-1871d. As G.M. Park & Son, 1868-1871.

PARK, H.J. Velasco, Texas, 1896d.

PARK, HORACE Columbus, Ohio, 1880-1895. Patent #532,090 January 1, 1895, cocking mechanism. As Park & McLeish, 1880, Park & Garber, 1886-1888, and Park & Irwin, 1889-1891. (Hutslar)

PARK, JOHN (1815-1895), Williamsburg, Ohio, 1837-1882d. Single shot cartridge rifles. (Hutslar)

PARK, JOHN Huntington Co., Pennsylvania, 1821. Flintlock Kentucky. (Kauffman)

PARK, ROBERT (1829-?), DuQuoin, Illinois, 1860c. (Johnson)

PARKER BROS. Grand Rapids, Michigan, 1875d.

PARKER BROS. Milledgeville, Georgia, 1885d.

PARKER BROTHERS Meriden, Connecticut, 1868-1934. Formed by Charles Parker in 1868. Purchased by Remington in 1934. (Johnson 2)

PARKER SAFETY HAMMERLESS trade name of Maltby, Henley & Co. on revolvers.

PARKER Urbana, Ohio, 1883d. (Hutslar)

PARKER, A. Battle Creek, Michigan, 1867d-1877d. Percussion 1/2 stock.

PARKER, A. Desoto, Iowa. Percussion 1/2 stock.

PARKER, A. Keithsburg, Illinois, 1871. (Johnson)

PARKER, A. Ludlow, Vermont, 1850. Percussion rifles and pistols. (Horn)

PARKER, A.B. Three Mile Bay, New York. Percussion rifles. (Swinney)

PARKER, ALBERT Springfield, Massachusetts. Percussion revolvers and bar pistols. (Sellers-1)

PARKER, ALONZO Elkhart, Indiana, 1880-1881d. (MB 4- 54)

PARKER, ANDREW Philadelphia, Pennsylvania, 1780. (Whisker III)

PARKER, C., & CO. trade name of H. & D. Folsom on imported shotguns. (Hinman)

PARKER, CHARLES B. Hampton, Virginia, 1897d.

PARKER, CHARLES (1809-1902), Meriden, Connecticut, 1832-1902. Formed Parker Co. in 1832 to make coffee mills. Subsequently formed Parker, Snow, Brooks & Co., Parker, Snow & Co., Meriden Mfg. Co., and finally Parker Bros. in 1868. (Johnson 2)

PARKER, CHARLES Kelloggsville, Ohio, 1860-1864d. (Hutslar)

PARKER, E. Grand Haven, Michigan, 1867d.

PARKER, E.R. Scranton, Pennsylvania, 1887d.

PARKER, EDGAR Indianapolis, Indiana, 1860d-1862d.

PARKER, HENRY Liverpool, Pennsylvania, 1775. Committee of Safety muskets.

PARKER, HENRY Trenton, New Jersey, 1860d. Percussion 1/2 stock, also locks.

PARKER, I. unlocated. Flintlock Kentucky.

PARKER, J.R. McKinney, Texas, 1890d-1896d.

PARKER, JACOB New Bedford, Massachusetts, 1852-1856.

PARKER, JOHN M. Brunswick, Maine, 1867-1880. (Demenitt)

PARKER, JOHN Maryland, 1776. Committee of Safety muskets. (Hartzler)

PARKER, S.E. LaGrange, Georgia, 1879d-1881d.

PARKER, SAMUEL Philadelphia, Pennsylvania, 1773-1790. Committee of Safety muskets. (Hobbies 4-38)

PARKER, SNOW, BROOKS & CO. Meriden, Connecticut, 1860-1865. Model 1861 contract muskets. Succeeded in turn by: Parker, Snow & Co., Meriden Mfg. Co., and Parker Bros. (Fuller)

PARKER, THOMAS Oberling, Ohio, 1853d. (Hutslar)

PARKER, W.S. Jasper, Indiana, 1860d-1862d.

PARKER, WILBUR F. Mendan, Connecticut. Patent #161,267 March 23, 1875, breechloading firearm.

PARKER, WILLIAM L. (1829-?), Crawford Co., Indiana, 1850c.

PARKER, WILLIAM (1796-?), Mason City, Illinois, 1850c-1860c. (Johnson)

PARKER, WILLIAM Amsterdam, New York, 1849-1867d. Percussion schuetzen rifle.

PARKES, CHARLES (?-1694), Northampton Co., Virginia, 1675-1694. (Gill)

PARKESON, B.L. Parkersburg, West Virginia, circa 1840. Flintlock Kentucky rifles. (Gluckman & Satterlee)

PARKESON, THOMAS Yohogania Co., Virginia, 1777. Committee of Safety repairs with his brother William. (Whisker IV)

PARKHILL, ANDREW Philadelphia, Pennsylvania, 1778-1785. (Gluckman & Satterlee)

PARKHILL, JOHN Philadelphia, Pennsylvania, 1780-1785. Repaired U.S. arms. (Moller)

PARKHURST, CURTIS Lawrenceville, Pennsylvania. Patent #409 September 25, 1837, harmonica gun. (GR 9-56)

PARKHURST, EDWARD G. (?-1902), Hartford, Connecticut, 1878-1902. Patents #227,648 May 18, 1880, tripod for machine gun, #228,777 June 15, 1880, machine gun, #229,007 June 22, 1880, cartridge feed machine gun, #231,607 August 24, 1880, machine gun, #235,627 December 21, 1880, cartridge feeder machine gun, #341,499 May 11, 1886, carriage machine gun, #579,097 March 16, 1897, magazine gun, #599,287 February 15, 1898, magazine bolt gun, #604,904 May 31, 1898, magazine bolt gun, #679,908 August 8, 1901, magazine firearm, and #719,254 January 27, 1903, magazine bolt gun. Designer for Pratt & Whitney and Springfield Armory.

PARKHURST, HENRY Amherst, New Hampshire. Percussion 1/2 stock.

PARKHURST, WILLIAM Amherst, New Hampshire. Percussion 1/2 stock.

PARKINS, J. unlocated. Percussion fullstock.

PARKINSON, BENJAMIN F. Washington, Pennsylvania. Patent #48,201 June 13, 1865, magazine firearm.

PARKS, AARON (1833-1911), Valparaiso, Indiana, 1854-1911. (Lindert)

PARKS, GEORGE Chicago, Illinois, 1851d.

PARKS, JOHN Selins Grove, Pennsylvania, 1861d. Percussion 1/2 stock.

PARKS, JOHN, SR. Snyder Co., Pennsylvania. Flintlock and percussion rifles. (Gabel)

PARKS, JOSEPH Providence, Rhode Island, 1828-1830. (Achtermier)

PARKS, SAMUEL (1864-?), Valparaiso, Indiana, 1885-1894. (Lindert)

PARLIN, MATT Tuckaleechee Cove, Tennessee, 1860. (Dean*)

PARLY, J. unlocated. Flintlock Kentucky.

PARMALEE, PHINEAS unlocated. Armorer for Continental Army, 1775. (Gluckman & Satterlee)

PAROLE suicide special by Bacon.

PARPE & BOESSEL Ogden, Utah, 1871d.

PARR, L. New Alexandria, Ohio, 1859d. (Hutslar)

PARRE, J.C. Lamar, Missouri, 1860d.

PARRISS, W.A. unlocated. Flintlock Kentucky.

PARRON, ROBERT F. Quincy, Ohio, 1850-1875. (Hutslar)

PARROTT, L. Red Bud, Illinois, 1860d.

PARROTT, MATHEW ARTHUR (1842-?), San Francisco, California, 1875-1876, Reno, Nevada, 1878d-1886d. (Shelton)

PARRY FIRE ARMS CO. Ithaca, New York, 1889-1893. Sold to Charles Roth in 1892 after a few shotguns were produced.

PARRY, EDWARD GEORGE Ithaca, New York. Patents #395,849 January 8, 1889, breechloading firearm, #442,453 December 9, 1890, breechloading breakdown, #490,065 January 17, 1893, breechloading firearm with Martin Bye, #495,298 April 11, 1893, safety device with Martin Bye, and #554,002 February 4, 1896, ejecting mechanism.

PARSEL, JESSE Vinton, Iowa, 1887d.

PARSELLS, J.A. Corning, New York, 1872-1874. See John A. Parcell.

PARSONS, C. Plattsburgh, New York, 1857-1860.

PARSONS, C.M. Sumac, Tennessee, 1891d.

PARSONS, HIRAM Baltimore, Maryland, 1819d-1831d. (Hartzler)

PARSONS, JAMES Virginia, 1776. Committee of Safety repairs. (Gill)

PARSONS, JOHN H. Augusta, Maine, 1874-1899. With George E. Gay as Gay & Parsons, 1880-1884. With Charles Henry Safford as Safford & Parsons, 1874-1875. (Demeritt)

PARSONS, JOSEPH T. Elizabeth, New Jersey, 1875d-1888d.

PARSONS, REECE Leslie, Michigan, 1891d.

PARSONS, S. San Antonio, Texas, 1865d.

PARTELLO, CHARLES Watertown, New York, 1879-1882d.

PARTET, SERAPHIA Butte, Montana, 1898d.

PARTLOW, HORACE H. Johnson, Vermont, 1883d.

PASCOE, JEFFERSON (1855-?), San Francisco, California, 1876. (Shelton)

PASE, JAKE Kyler, Pennsylvania, 1872-1880. Percussion swivel breech. (MB 9-57)

PASLER, AUGUST Centralia, Illinois, 1868d.

PASPERSHILL, F.J. Lapeer, Michigan, 1860d, Detroit, Michigan, 1867d. As Paspershill & Bradford, 1867.

PASSAGE, CHRISTOPHER Rochester, New York, 1844d-1861. (Eich)

PASSAGE, HIRAM H. Plymouth, Michigan, 1890-1902. Patents #446,711 February 17, 1891, spring air gun, #638,751 December 12, 1899, firearm, and #695,485 March 18, 1902, firearm. Guns made by Heal Rifle Co.

PATCHEN, IRA Covington, Pennsylvania, 1882d. Percussion over/under rifle/shotgun.

PATCHEN, YORK Westfield, New York. Patent #465,088 December 15, 1891, telescopic sight.

PATCHIN, H.M. Springfield, Illinois, 1860d-1864d. Agent on Coon Alarm gun.

PATE, EDWARD Ann Arbor, Michigan, 1887d.

PATENT ARMS MFG. CO. Paterson, New Jersey, 1836-1842. First makers of Colt's arms. (Phillips)

PATH FINDER suicide special by Hopkins & Allen.

PATRICK, J. New York, New York. Percussion pistols.

PATRICK, J.M. Albany, Missouri, 1860d.

PATRICK, RICHARD New York, New York. Percussion double shotgun.

PATRICK, W.A. Ludlow, Vermont, 1868-1873. Percussion 1/2 stock rifles. (Horn)

PATRIOT suicide special.

PATT, CHRISTIAN (1847-1928), Alma, Wisconsin. Percussion and cartridge schuetzen rifle. (GR 1-61)

PATTERSON, E. unlocated. Percussion 1/2 stock.

PATTERSON, H.C. Marshall, Missouri, 1891d-1898d.

PATTERSON, J.F. Le Mars, Iowa, 1880d-1884d.

PATTERSON, J.R. Madison, Kansas, 1884d.

PATTERSON, JACOB Harrisville, Pennsylvania, 1861d.

PATTERSON, JAMES S. McCoysville, Pennsylvania, 1876-1890d. Patent #346,941 August 10, 1886, firearm lock.

PATTERSON, JOHN A. Lindley, Missouri, 1879d.

PATTERSON, NEWTON A. Kingston, Tennessee. Patent #40,498 November 3, 1863, barrels.

PATTERSON, ROBERT Washington, Pennsylvania, 1827. Flintlock Kentucky.

PATTERSON, SAMUEL J. Allegheny, Pennsylvania, 1858-1859. (Kauffman)

PATTERSON, W.H. Neligh, Nebraska, 1882d, Fremont, Nebraska, 1886d.

PATTERSON, WILLIAM P. Baltimore, Maryland, 1876d-1889d. (Hartzler)

PATTERSON, WILLIAM P. Dutch Valley, Tennessee, 1887. (ASAC 23)

PATTON, JOSEPH (?-1895), Montgomery, Ohio, 1873-1895. (Hetrick)

PATTON, ROBERT F. Quincy, Ohio, 1858-1865, Sydney, Ohio, 1875d. Percussion and cartridge guns. (Hutslar)

PATTON, THOMAS Stevensburg, Virginia, 1801. (Bugle 51)

PATTON, WILLIAM Springfield, Massachusetts, 1868d-1874d. Importer and dealer.

PATTON, WILLIAM Springfield, Ohio, 1850-1868. Percussion 1/2 stock. (Knittle)

PAUL, ANDREW Pennsylvania, 1831. Flintlock Kentucky. (Dillin)

PAUL, ISAAC (1802-?), Centerville, Indiana, 1850c. Percussion fullstock. (Lindert)

PAUL, JACOB Minisla, Ohio, 1881d. (Hutslar)

PAUL, JAMES Montgomery Co., Pennsylvania, 1796-1800. Converted Kentucky. (Kauffman)

PAUL, JOSEPH Newport, Kentucky, 1857-1867d. Percussion fullstock.

PAUL, LUDWIG unlocated. Flintlock Kentucky.

PAUL, U.S. West Richfield, Ohio. Percussion fullstock.

PAUL, WILLIAM (1833-?), Centerville, Indiana, 1850c. Son of Isaac Paul. (Lindert)

PAUL, WILLIAM Bedford, Pennsylvania, 1845, Summerhills, Pennsylvania, 1852. (Kauffman)

PAULEY, JONATHAN Clarksville, Iowa, 1865d.

PAULI, CHARLES Syracuse, New York, 1856-1882d. Percussion 1/2 stock. (Swinney)

PAULINS, ISAAC, JR. (1830-?), Ashland Co., Ohio, 1850c.

PAULINS, ISAAC, SR. (1790-?), Ashland Co., Ohio, 1850c. (Hutslar)

PAULINS, PETER (1825-?), Ashland Co., Ohio, 1850c. Son of Isaac Paulins. (Hutslar)

PAULMER, JACOB S. unlocated. Percussion 1/2 stock.

PAULSLEY, CHRISTIAN Cumberland Co., Pennsylvania, 1782. (Kauffman 2)

PAUTCH, JAMES New Albany, Indiana, 1858d.

PAWLEY, JOSEPH Cleveland, Indiana, 1860d.

PAXSON, W. & J.R. Philadelphia, Pennsylvania, 1800. Importer.

PAXTON & GALLAGHER CO. Omaha, Nebraska, 1880-1900. Trade name "PAGOMA" on shotguns made by Crescent. Dealers only. (Hinman)

PAYN, EDGER H. Burlington, Vermont, 1875d-1883d. Percussion 1/2 stock. (Horn)

PAYNE & SONS Springfield, Illinois, 1884d-1896d. Francis E. Payne.

PAYNE, BRIGHAM South Coventry, Connecticut. Patent #42,685 May 10, 1865, breechloading firearm.

PAYNE, CHARLES E. Gardner, Massachusetts. Patent #42,685 May 10, 1864, breechloading firearm.

PAYNE, E. SCOTT, & BRO. Baltimore, Maryland, 1876-1889. Double shotgun. (Hartzler)

PAYNE, FRANCIS E. Springfield, Illinois, 1860d-1896d. As Payne & Sons, 1884-1896.

PAYNE, J.R. Gainesville, Texas, 1896d.

PAYNE, JOEL Lockport, Kentucky, 1896d.

PAYNE, S.L. Erie, Pennsylvania, 1846-1851.

PAYNE, WILLIAM Virginia, 1776. Committee of Safety rifles and repairs. (Gill)

PAYNTER, BARNEY Arkadelphia, Arkansas, 1855-1868. (Elias)

PAYSON & NURSE Boston, Massachusetts. Importers and dealers.

PEABODY Newport, Rhode Island, 1759. (Achtermier)

PEABODY, CORNELIUS Buford, Ohio, 1859d. (Hutslar)

PEABODY, HENRY O. Boston, Massachusetts. Patents #35,947 July 22, 1862, Peabody breechloader, #2,197 March 13, 1866, reissue, #72,076 December 10, 1867, breechloader, and #76,805 April 14, 1868, breechloader. Guns made by Providence Tool Co.

PEABODY, JOHN J. Washington, D.C., 1862d-1885d. (Hartzler)

PEABODY, LOREN (1832-?), Georgetown, Ohio, 1850c, DeKalb, Missouri, 1860d. Percussion 1/2 stock. (Hutslar)

PEACE MAKER suicide special. (Webster)

PEACE, FRANK P. Knoxville, Tennessee. Patent #146,611 January 20, 1874, magazine firearms with James W.D. Williams.

PEACOCK & THATCHER Chicago, Illinois, 1839-1884. Percussion and cartridge guns. Joseph Peacock and David C. Thatcher. Sold to Frederick Abbey, 1870, but re-purchased in 1880.

PEACOCK, JOSEPH (1812-?), Chicago, Illinois, 1839-1884. With David C. Thatcher as Peacock & Thatcher. (Johnson)

PEACOCK, JOSHUA Haddonfield, New Jersey, 1878d.

PEACOCK, THOMAS Charleston, South Carolina, 1750. (Kauffman 2)

PEAK, JAMES (1819-?), Millersburg, Ohio, 1850c. (Hutslar)

PEAKE, DANIEL Madisonville, Missouri, 1854d.

PEARCE, JAMES DILLARD Lonoke, Arkansas, 1870-1884d. (Elias)

PEARD, JAMES J. Hartford, Connecticut. Patents #650,931 June 5, 1900, revolver with Carl Ehbetts, #671,609 April 9, 1901, sight, #680,274 August 13, 1901, revolver, and #761,706 June 7, 1904, sight. Employed by Colt. Son of Thomas Peard.

PEARD, THOMAS L. Hartford, Connecticut, 1848-1860d. (Kauffman 2)

PEARDEN, L.J.E. unlocated. Percussion 1/2 stock.

PEARE, STEPHEN Perth Amboy, New Jersey, 1878d.

PEARSE, HENRY (1833-?), Bloomfield, California, 1860c. Percussion swivel breech and 1/2 stock. (Shelton)

PEARSE, HENRY Palmyra, Wisconsin, 1857d-1867d, Whitewater, Wisconsin, 1872d-1879d.

PEARSE, L. unlocated. Percussion swivel breech rifle.

PEARSON, HERMAN (1828-?), San Francisco, California, 1860c. (Shelton)

PEARSON, JAMES Pennsylvania. Committee of Safety muskets, 1775. (Hobbies 4-38)

PEARSON, JOHN Baltimore, Maryland, 1830-1835d, St. Louis, Missouri, 1840-1845, Ft. Smith, Arkansas, 1845-1878d. Made first revolvers for Samuel Colt and percussion guns on his own. With Frederick Hellinghaus, Baltimore and St. Louis. (Sutherland-Elias)

PEARSON, JOSEPH Chester Co., Pennsylvania, 1767-1769. Gunsmith and cutler. (Gardner)

PEARSON, OLE Chicago, Illinois. Patents #434,522 August 19, 1890, target, and #440,190 November 11, 1890, spring gun.

PEARSON, W.C. Fort Smith, Arkansas, 1878d-1880d. Son of John Pearson.

PEARSON, WARREN Troy, Ohio, 1883d. (Hutslar)

PEASE, ADDISON Montevideo, Minnesota. Patent #228,778 June 15, 1880, magazine firearms.

PEASE, BRICE E. Gilmanton, New Hampshire. Patent #622,258 April 4, 1899, gun firing mechanism.

PEASE, H.A. Mankato, Kansas, 1894d.

PEASE, J.S., & CO. St. Louis, Missouri, 1831-1847d. Percussion pistol. (Pourie)

PEAVEY, THOMAS H. (?-1907), South Montville, Maine, 1850-1865, Epworth, Iowa, 1882d-1907. Patent #11,174 June 27, 1854, charger for firearms. (Demeritt)

PEAVY, ANDREW JACKSON (1832-1897), South Montville, Maine, 1856-?, Lawrence, Massachusetts, 1876. Patents #49,784 September 5, 1865, percussion knife pistol, #53,473 March 27, 1866, cartridge knife pistol, and #172,243 January 18, 1876, revolver with E.P. Boardman. Peavy made the knife pistols. The revolver was made by the All Right Fire Arms Co. (Demeritt)

PEAVY, H.A. Vicksburg, Mississippi. Derringer.

PECARE & SMITH New York, New York, 1847-1853. Patent #6,925 December 4, 1849, pepperbox. Jacob Pecare and Josiah M. Smith.

PECK & BOWMAN Atlanta, Georgia, 1861. John C. Peck. Confederate gunsmith convention.

PECK & GRILLEY New Haven, Connecticut. Dealers of Jeremiah Peck's patent revolvers. (Sellers-1)

PECK, ABIJAH Hartford, Connecticut. Model 1798 contract muskets. (Gluckman)

PECK, AMBROSE Swansea, Massachusetts, 1776. Flintlock muskets. (ASAC 35)

PECK, DANIEL Raleigh, North Carolina, 1809-1815. (Bivins)

PECK, ELI Philadelphia, Pennsylvania, 1819d.

PECK, ELIHU Providence, Rhode Island, 1806. (Achtermier)

PECK, G. Rockport, Indiana, 1860d.

PECK, I.D. Bedford, Iowa, 1880d.

PECK, JEREMIAH New Haven, Connecticut. Patent #10,930 May 16, 1854, revolver. Revolvers made by Whitney. (Sellers-1)

PECK, JOHN C. Atlanta, Georgia, 1857-1864. Percussion rifles for the Confederacy. As Peck & Bowman, 1861. (Hill & Anthony)

PECK, L.A. Newton, Massachusetts, 1868-1873.

PECK, LEVI Philadelphia, Pennsylvania, 1829d-1833d.

PECK, MILO New Haven, Connecticut. Patent #43,601 July 19, 1864, patched balls for firearms.

PECK, R.H. Austin, Texas, 1849.

PECKHAM & BARKER Providence, Rhode Island, 1823-1826. Flintlock New England rifle.

PECKHAM, A.C. Lockhart, Texas, 1896d.

PEDEN, D.T. Greenville, South Carolina. Percussion rifles.

PEDERSON, SIVERT Menominee, Wisconsin. Patent #264,897 September 26, 1882, machine gun.

PEEBLE, ROBERT Cumberland Co., Pennsylvania, 1776. Committee of Safety muskets. (Kauffman 2)

PEELER, HENRY Essex, Connecticut, 1848-1880d. Patent #6,088 February 6, 1849, boring gun barrels.

PEERLESS suicide special by Hood.

PEERLESS trade name of Crescent Fire Arms Co. on shotguns. (Hinman)

PEERS & GINNINGS St. Charles, Missouri, 1821.

PEFLEY, J.W. Perry, Iowa, 1897d.

PEIGHTAL, JOHN Phillipsburg, Pennsylvania. Patent #220,655 October 14, 1879, breechloading firearm.

PELCK, RUDOLPH OSWALD (1727-1886), Freeport, Illinois, 1859-1886d. Percussion rifles. As Pelck & Dittman, 1863-1883. (MB 4-46)

PELICAN trade name of Ogilvie Hardware Co., Shreveport, Louisiana, on shotguns.

PELOUX & MONFERRER Philadelphia, Pennsylvania, 1810d.

PELOUX, PETER Philadelphia, Pennsylvania, 1812-1857d. Flintlock rifles and pistols. (Kauffman)

PELTON & DAVY Lyons City, Iowa, 1867d. Martin V.B. Pelton.

PELTON, MARTIN V.B. (1834-?), Lyons City, Iowa, 1865d-1867d, Stockton, California, 1867. As Pelton & Davy, 1867. (Shelton)

PELTON, THEODORE G. Jersey Landing, Illinois, 1860d, Lyons City, Iowa, 1867d.

PENCE, A. Hemlock Grove, Ohio, 1861-1865. See A. Pense.

PENCE, JACOB (1793-?), Columbus, Indiana, 1850c-1862d. (Lindert)

PENCE, JACOB Lancaster Co., Pennsylvania, 1771. (Gluckman & Satterlee)

PENDERGRASS, A. Cleveland, Tennessee, 1860d.

PENDLETON, CALVIN C. (1812-?), Pottawattamie Co., Iowa, 1846-1850, Salt Lake City, Utah, 1852, Parowan, Utah, 1860. (MB 8-64)

PENDLETON, EDWARD Stevensburg, Virginia, 1801. State inspector of arms. (Bugle 51)

PENDLETON, FREEMAN W. (1855-1938), Parowan, Utah.

PENETRATOR suicide special by Bliss. (Webster)

PENFRO, JACOB (1825-?), Noble Co., Indiana, 1860c. Last name possibly Renfro. (Lindert)

PENHALLOW, JOHN Boston, Massachusetts, 1726-1730. Also spelled Penshallow. (Dean*)

PENN, GABRIEL Monroe Co., Missouri, 1850c. (MB 11-66)

PENN, H. Liverpool, Ohio, 1859-1864d. (Hutslar)

PENN, SAMUEL Monroe Co., Missouri, 1850c. (MB 11-66)

PENNELL, JOSHUA (?-1879), Bedford, Co., Pennsylvania, 1844-1879. (Whisker)

PENNEPACKER, WILLIAM Gouglersville, Pennsylvania, 1861d.

PENNIGAR & WARD Parker Co., Indiana, 1850c.

PENNSYLVANIA RIFLE WORKS Philadephia, Pennsylvania. Maker and dealer of percussion guns. G. Dunlap.

PENNSYLVANIA STATE GUN FACTORY Philadelphia, Pennsylvania, 1776-1779. Gun locks. (Gluckman & Satterlee)

PENNYPACKER see Pannabecker.

PENROD, R.C. Buncombe, Illinois, 1886d.

PENROSE & HARDIN Omaha, Nebraska, 1868d. Dealers. Percussion double shotgun.

PENSE, A. Hemlock Grove, Ohio, 1860-1864d. (Hutslar)

PENTIG, HENRY (1811-?), Iroquois Co., Illinois, 1843-1850. (Johnson)

PEORIA CHIEF suicide special by Lee Arms Co.

PEPPER, OLIVER Pine Bluff, Arkansas, 1850. (Elias)

PERCEY, FRANK Oshkosh, Wisconsin, 1870-1888d.

PERCIVAL, ORVILLE B. East Haddam, Connecticut. Patent #none, October 14, 1835, drill, #7,496, July 9, 1850, magazine gun with Asa Smith. (GC 24)

PERCY, J.G. Providence, Rhode Island, 1865d.

PERCY, JOHN P. Albany, New York. Brass frame tip up rifle. Patent #39,494 August 11, 1863, breechloading firearm.

PERFECT trade name of Foehl & Weeks on revolvers.

PERFECT, CHRISTOPHER (?-1791), Loudoun Co., Virginia, 1776-1791. Committee of Safety muskets and "large rifles". (Gill)

PERFECTION trade name of Crescent on shotguns.

PERIN & GAFF MFG. CO. Cincinnati, Ohio, 1861-1884. Importers and dealers. (Hutslar)

PERINE, OLIVER Bradley, Michigan, 1860d.

PERKIN, I. New York, New York. Queen Anne flintlock pistol. Same as Joseph Perkin?

PERKIN, JOSEPH Rappahannock Forge, 1776, Philadelphia, Pennsylvania, 1780-1793 and 1799-1802. Flintlock pistols. First armorer at Harpers Ferry in 1793. Supervisor at U.S. Armory, New London, Virginia, 1797. Master Armorer at Harpers Ferry Armory, Virginia, 1803. Repaired U.S. arms with Samuel Coulty and John Nicholson.

PERKINS unlocated. Lockmaker.

PERKINS, F.G., & CO. Waterbury, Connecticut, 1873-1884d.

PERKINS, HARVEY S. Delta, Ohio, 1870c. Percussion 1/2 stock. (Hutslar)

PERKINS, I. unlocated. Flintlock Kentucky.

PERKINS, J.P. Exeter, Rhode Island, 1869d.

PERKINS, JAMES Bridgewater, Massachusetts, 1795-1807. Model 1798 contract muskets with Adam Kinsley. (Gluckman)

PERKINS, LUKE Bridgewater, Massachusetts, 1800. (Gluckman & Satterlee)

PERKINS, R.H. Delta, Ohio. Percussion fullstock.

PERKINS, REUBEN (1767-1816), Belmont Co., Ohio, 1798-1816. (Hutslar)

PERKINS, RUFUS Bridgewater, Massachusetts, 1801-1812. Model 1808 contract muskets. (Gluckman)

PERKINS, W.L. Middlefield, Ohio, 1881d. (Hutslar)

PERL, JOHN E. Osage Mission, Kansas. Patent #555,582 March 3, 1896, auxiliary barrel.

PERLEY BROS. Boxford, Massachusetts, 1883d-1884d.

PERLEY, CHARLES New York, New York. Patent #37,764 February 24, 1863, breechloading firearm.

PERLEY, FRANK Oshkosh, Wisconsin, 1872-1886.

PERMMAREL, AUGUST Chicago, Illinois, 1864d. See August Pammler.

PERPETUAL REVOLVER trade name of Perry & Goddard on derringer made by E.S. Renwick. Also known as the "Double Header".

PERREIN, DENNIS Philadelphia, Pennsylvania, 1800. (Kauffman)

PERRIN, CASIMIR New Orleans, Louisiana, 1841d-1842d.

PERRIN, ISAIAH Rochester, New York, 1866-1867d. (Eich)

PERRY & GODDARD New York, New York. "Double Header"/"Perpetual Revolver" derringers made by E.S. Renwick. Samuel M. Perry and Emerson Goddard. (ASAC 21)

PERRY & SON Salem, Massachusetts, 1866d-1874d. Horatio B. and August H. Perry.

PERRY PATENT FIRE ARMS CO. Newark, New Jersey, 1850-1860. Alonzo D. Perry's patent breechloaders.

PERRY Albany, New York. Percussion fowler. (Clow)

PERRY, ALBERT Dutch Flat, California, 1875-1881. (Shelton)

PERRY, ALONZO D. Newark, New Jersey. Patents #6,945 December 11, 1849, breechloading firearm, #7,147 March 5, 1850, cartridge, #12,001 November 28, 1854, breechloading firearm, and #12,244 January 16, 1855, breechloading firearm. 200 carbines purchased by U.S. Government in 1855. As Perry Patent Fire Arms Co., 1850-1860.

PERRY, AUGUST H. Salem, Massachusetts, 1855-1883d. Percussion 1/2 stock. With his father Horatio B. as Perry & Son, 1866-1874. Successor to Horatio B. Perry in 1874.

PERRY, CHRISTIAN Kenton, Ohio, 1875d. (Hutslar)

PERRY, EDWARD L. Paterson, New Jersey. Patent #210,626 December 10, 1878, breechloading firearm.

PERRY, H.B. (1819-?), Mineral Point, Colorado, 1880c.

PERRY, H.B. (1821-?), Del Norte, Colorado, 1880c.

PERRY, H.P. Washington, Iowa. Percussion 1/2 stock.

PERRY, H.V. (?-1897), Fredonia, New York, 1850-1855, Pomfret, New York, 1858-1862, Ellicott, New York, 1863-1865, Jamestown, New York, 1875d-1897. Percussion rifles of all varieties, mostly target and multi-shot. (GR 4-71)

PERRY, HORATIO B. Salem, Massachusetts, 1857-1874d. With August H. Perry as Perry & Son, 1866-1874.

PERRY, J.A. unlocated. Underhammer pistol.

PERRY, J.W. Jamestown, New York, 1872-1874d, Fredonia, New York, 1875d, Del Norte, Colorado, 1879d-1886d. Percussion 1/2 stock and fullstock. Son of H.V. Perry.

PERRY, JOSHUA Augusta Co., Virginia, 1777, Staunton, Virginia, 1782-1784. Committee of Safety muskets and repairs with Jacob Gabbott, Joshua Humphrys, and Alexander Simpson, Augusta Co., Virginia. (Gill)

PERRY, OH. Rockland, Maine, 1857-1861. (Demeritt)

PERRY, P.P. Greenville, Michigan, 1872d-1879d, Howard City, Michigan, 1883d-1889d.

PERRY, SAMUEL M. Brooklyn, New York. "Double Header"/"Perpetual Revolver" derringers made by E.S. Renwick. Patents #43,259 June 21, 1864, breechloading firearm, #43,260 June 21, 1864, breechloading firearm, and #102,459 April 26, 1870, breechloading firearm with Emerson Goddard. As Perry & Goddard with Emerson Goddard. (ASAC 21)

PERRY, WYATT (1813-1906, Green Co., Ohio, 1840-1850, Westfield, Indiana, 1850-1906. Percussion 1/2 stocks marked either "W.P." or "W. Perry". Apprenticed to, and worked for, his step father, Greenbury Shaw. (MB 1-51)

PERSIGNON, F. Richmond, Virginia, 1860c.

PERSONS, H. Plattsburgh, New York. Percussion over/under rifle/shotgun and underhammer pistol.

PERSONS, J.L. Rutland, Vermont, 1857-1860.

PESSOU, ALPHONSE New Orleans, Louisiana, 1822d-1868d.

PET suicide special.

PETER, HERMAN F. (?-1920), Lima, Ohio, 1866-1870c, Lancaster, Ohio, 1872-1882d. Percussion 1/2 stock. Patents #154,804 September 8, 1874, primer, and #156,497 November 3, 1874, ramrod. (Hutslar)

PETER, J. unlocated. Flintlock Kentucky.

PETERMAN, ABRAHAM Philadelphia, Pennsylvania, 1847d-1899d. As Peterman & Son, 1886-1899. Percussion and cartridge guns.

PETERMAN, GEORGE (1775-?), Botetourt, Co., Virginia, 1850c. (MB 10-63)

PETERMAN, LEWIS C. Philadelphia, Pennsylvania, 1847d.

PETERS M. Covert, Michigan, 1883d.

PETERS, B.J. Chanute, Kansas, 1882d-1894d.

PETERS, CASPER Buffalo, New York, 1885d. With Nicholas Gerrins as Gerrins & Peters.

PETERS, JACOB Philadelphia, Pennsylvania, 1780-1785. Repaired U.S. arms. (Moller)

PETERS, JOHN Chester, Illinois, 1859. (Johnson)

PETERS, JONAS Heidelberg, Pennsylvania, 1795t. (KRA II-3)

PETERS, SELDON (1800-1900), Gateway, Ohio, 1893d-1896d. Negro gunsmith. Flintlock and percussion guns. (MB 3-55)

PETERS, WILLIAM Kingston, Wisconsin, 1857d.

PETERSON, AUGUST St. Charles, Minnesota, 1888d.

PETERSON, AXEL W. (1859-1946), Denver, Colorado, 1879-1946. With George C. Schoyen as Schoyen & Peterson, 1903-1916. With Roy Peterson as A.W. Peterson & Son, 1925-1946. (Sellers-3, AR 12-27, AR 1-28)

PETERSON, CHARLES New Harmony, Indiana, circa 1850. (Lindert)

PETERSON, G.W. Marion, North Carolina. Confederate patent #96 May 31, 1862, firearms. (Albaugh 2)

PETERSON, J.E. Algona, Iowa, 1887d.

PETERSON, JOHN (1820-?), Catawba Co., North Carolina, 1850c. (Bivins)

PETERSON, JONAS Bismark, North Dakota, 1877-1886d, Mora, Minnesota, 1888d-1898d.

PETERSON, LEWIS H. Logan, Iowa, 1892d-1895d, Woodbine, Iowa, 1897d, Madrid, Iowa, 1899. Patent #618,901 February 7, 1899, barrel.

PETERSON, PETER New Milford, Connecticut, 1869-1889d. Percussion 1/2 stock.

PETERSON, ROY Denver, Colorado, 1925-1954. With his father Axel until 1946. (Sellers-3)

PETERSON, SAMUEL (1770-?), Catawba Co., North Carolina, 1819-1850c. (Bivins)

PETERSON, WILLIAM Stuttgart, Arkansas, 1898d.

PETHMASS, G. unlocated. Percussion fullstock.

PETMECKY, JOSEPH C. Austin, Texas, 1865-1893d. Patents #193,670 July 31, 1877, breechloading firearm, #197,892 December 4, 1877, breechloading firearm, #210,144 November 19, 1878, breechloading firearm, #267,714 November 21, 1882, gun rack, and #289,132 November 27, 1883, barrel cleaner. As Petmecky & Todd, 1868.

PETREL all brass suicide special.

PETRI, AUGUST (1828-1902), Beardstown, Illinois, 1854-1867d.

PETRIE, O.M. Petoskey, Michigan, 1895d.

PETRIE, W.W. New York, New York, 1850d. Importers.

PETTENGILL, CARLTON Newark, New Jersey, 1850c. For Alonzo Perry.

PETTENGILL, CHARLES S. New Haven, Connecticut, 1856-1859, Ilion, New York, 1866-1870c. Patents #15,388 July 22, 1856, revolver, and #22,511 January 4, 1859, revolver. 5,000 Pettengill revolvers purchased by U.S. during the Civil War. For Remington after the Civil War. (Sellers-1)

PETTIBONE, DANIEL Philadelphia, Pennsylvania, 1799-1814. Patents #none 1802, welding cast steel with borax, #none November 10, 1813, bullet machine, and #none February 12, 1814, barrel drill. This last patent was stolen from James Greer, who sued Pettibone and eventually recovered damages. (Boehret)

PETTINGILL, ASA Keene, New Hampshire. Patent #204,167 May 28, 1878, spring air gun.

PETTIS, W.R. Troy, Alabama, 1885d.

PETTIT, ANDREW (?-1854), Salem, Ohio, 1828-1838, Hanoverton, Ohio, 1841-1854. Percussion 1/2 stock. (MB 2-66)

PETTIT, BENJAMIN F. San Luis Obispo, California, Patent #534,516 February 19, 1895, magazine gun.

PETTIT, H. unlocated. Percussion fullstock.

PETTIT, SETH Chautauqua Co., New York, 1873d, Cassadaga, New York, 1880d.

PETTMAN, G. unlocated. Percussion fullstock.

PETTY, ALBERT (1795-?), Hancock Co., Illinois, 1840-1844. (Johnson)

PETTY, JOHN W. Omaha, Nebraska, 1876d-1890d. Patent #328,713 October 20, 1885, machine gun barrel. As Collins & Petty, 1878-1880.

PETTY, JOSEPH M. Lancaster, Kentucky, 1857-1884d.

PETTY, JOSEPH La Crosse, Wisconsin, 1857d. Percussion 1/2 stock.

PEYTON, D.O. Harrisonville, Ohio, 1859-1864d. (Hutslar)

PFAFFLE, E.C. Dallas, Texas, 1878d-1884d. With Charles Ott as Ott & Pfaffle, 1878.

PFEFFERLY, JOHN Taylorsville, Illinois, 1858-1859. (Johnson)

PFEIFER, GEORGE Buffalo City, Wisconsin, 1867d.

PFEIFFER, CHARLES Lancaster, Pennsylvania, 1857d. With Lewis Lepper.

PFEIFFER, E.J. Woodland, California, 1884d-1886d. (Shelton)

PFEIFFER, GEORGE (1826-1893), Cincinnati, Ohio, 1856-1863d. (Hutslar)

PFEIFFER, JOHN W. San Francisco, California, 1856-1858. (Shelton)

PFISTERER, ERNST (1839-?), Chicago, Illinois, 1865d, Denver, Colorado, 1866d-1871d. (Sellers-3)

PFISTERER, GEORGE Elgin, Illinois, 1860d.

PFISTERER, JULIUS Rosita, Colorado, 1882d, Gunnison, Colorado, 1884d-1889d. (Sellers-3)

PFISTERER, L. Lincoln, Nebraska, 1879-1880d. As Scobel & Pfisterer.

PFLEGHAR, F.P. Whitneyville, Connecticut. Patent #24,942 August 2, 1859, revolver with S.C. Lewis. (Sellers-1)

PFLIEGER, H. unlocated. Flintlock Kentucky.

PFUETZNER, MORITZ Harrison, Ohio, 1866. Breechloading gun.

PHARRES, WILLIAM Broadheadsville, Pennsylvania, 1861d.

PHARRIS, ABSALOM Rocky Mount, Tennessee, 1860d.

PHEATT, DUDLEY G. & FRANK A. Toledo, Ohio, 1894-1900. Successors to Gideon Pheatt. (Hutslar)

PHEATT, GIDEON K. (?-1894), Toledo, Ohio, 1868-1894. Pinfire double shotgun. Patent #439,551 October 28, 1890, cartridge indicator. (Hutslar)

PHELAN, JOHN Pittsburgh, Pennsylvania. Patent #249,204 November 8, 1881, machine gun.

PHELPS, E.S. Rochester, New York, 1871-1876. As E.S. Phelps & Co., 1874-1876.

PHELPS, E.S., & CO. Rochester, New York, 1874-1876. E.S. Phelps.

PHELPS, JEDEDIAH Lebanon, Connecticut, 1773-1778. Committee of Safety locks. (Gluckman & Satterlee)

PHELPS, SAMUEL B. Norwich, Vermont, 1877-1879, Hanover, New Hampshire, 1879-1886. (Horn)

PHELPS, SILAS Lebanon, Connecticut, 1770-1778. Committee of Safety locks. (Kauffman 2)

PHENIX trade name of James Reid on revolvers. Also used "Phoenix".

PHILBRICK, S.C. Lagrange, Indiana, 1882-1885. Percussion 1/2 stock. (MB 2-50)

PHILBROOK & PYNE Bangor, Maine, circa 1880. Francis J. Philbrook. (Demeritt)

PHILBROOK, FRANCIS J. Bangor, Maine, 1871-1890. With Charles G. Staples as Staples & Philbrook, 1874d, and Philbrook & Pyne, circa 1880. (Demeritt)

PHILIP, J.G. unlocated. Percussion 1/2 stock.

PHILIP, WILLIAM H. Brooklyn, New York, Patent #142,175 August 26, 1873, revolver with 3 cylinders. (Winant)

PHILIPEE, JACOB Lebanon Co., Pennsylvania, 1842. (Kauffman)

PHILIPI, MOSES Portage Co., Ohio, 1829c. (Hutslar)

PHILIPPSON & SCHAFER Hamilton, Nevada, 1871d.

PHILIPS, EDWARD Providence, Rhode Island, 1847-1854. (Achtermier)

PHILIPS, J.G. Schofield, Wisconsin, 1865. Percussion fullstock.

PHILIPS, LEVAN Pittsburgh, Pennsylvania, 1791-1792. (Whisker II)

PHILIPY, J. Licking Co., Ohio. Flintlock Kentucky. (Dillin)

PHILIPY, SAMUEL C. (1841-?), Easton, Pennsylvania, 1887d. Son of and successor to Samuel Philipy.

PHILIPY, SAMUEL (1801-1877), Easton, Pennsylvania, 1828t-1877d. Various spellings for last name.

PHILLIP, G. Brooklyn, Iowa, 1880d.

PHILLIPPI, DANIEL Sunbury, Pennsylvania, 1826. (Kauffman)

PHILLIPS & BELMORE Skowhegan, Maine, 1896. (Demeritt)

PHILLIPS & HOWLETT Greensboro, North Carolina, 1884d.

PHILLIPS & VONTAUBE New York, New York, 1884d.

PHILLIPS, A. Geneva, New York, 1845. Precussion fullstock.

PHILLIPS, C.T. Glover, Vermont, 1854-1887. (Horn)

PHILLIPS, EDWIN New York, New York, 1840-1884d. Percussion target rifles.

PHILLIPS, FRANCIS (1801-?), Baton Rouge, Louisiana, 1850c. (MB 9-65)

PHILLIPS, FREDERICK H. Chattanooga, Tennessee, 1884d.

PHILLIPS, HENRY Jerry City, Ohio, 1883d. (Hutslar)

PHILLIPS, J.H. Greenville, Pennsylvania, 1872d.

PHILLIPS, J.L. Lawrence, Michigan, 1872d-1877d.

PHILLIPS, JAMES P. Yonkers, New York, 1866d.

PHILLIPS, JAMES Providence, Rhode Island, 1832d-1844d. (Kauffman)

PHILLIPS, JOHN G. Boone Co., Missouri, 1850c. (MB 11-66)

PHILLIPS, JOSIAH unlocated. Percussion target pistol.

PHILLIPS, O.H. Nashua, New Hampshire, 1878d.

PHILLIPS, ORSON D. Lisle, New York, 1874-1882. Patent #163,404 May 18, 1875, loading implement.

PHILLIPS, PRESTON Boone Co., Missouri, 1850c. (MB 11-66)

PHILLIPS, SAMUEL Onarga, Illinois, 1864d. Percussion double shotgun.

PHILLIPS, T. Maumee City, Ohio, 1859-1864d. Percussion guns. (Hutslar)

PHILLIPS, W.J. Pierceville, Georgia, 1883d.

PHILLIPS, WILLIAM J. St. Louis, Missouri. Patent #109,914 December 6, 1870, revolver with Charles J. Linberg. (Winant)

PHILPOT, WILLIAM H. (1815-?), Summerfield, Ohio, 1850c. (Hutslar)

PHIN, JOHN Rochester, New York. Patent #13,825 November 20, 1855, lock. Phin was a patent attorney and probably acting on behalf of a client. (Eich)

PHIPPS, ISRAEL Magnetic Springs, Ohio. (Hutslar)

PHIPPS, JOHN Washington, D.C., 1853d-1862d. (Hartzler)

PHIPS, JAMES (1615-1654), Pemequid, Maine, 1638-1643, Kennebec River, Massachusetts, 1643-1654. Doglock fowling piece. (Demeritt)

PHOENIX ARMORY trade name of W.W. Marston on percussion revolvers, pepperboxes, and pistols. (Sellers-1)

PHOENIX CO. New York, New York, 1870-1874. Breechloading shotguns. (Hinman)

PHOENIX suicide special by Crescent.

PHOENIX trade name of James Reid on percussion and cartridge revolvers. (Sellers-1)

PHOENIX trade name of James Reid on revolvers. Also used "Phenix".

PHOENIX trade name of Whitney on single shot rifles and shotguns. (Fuller)

PIATT, JOHN Portsmouth, Ohio, 1870c. (MB 2-43)

PICKEL, HENRY York, Pennsylvania, 1788-1809, Lancaster, Pennsylvania, 1811t. Model 1801 contract muskets for Pennsylvania with Jacob Doll and Conrad Welshanz, and Model 1798 contract muskets. Flintlock Kentucky rifles and fowling pieces. (Gluckman, Dyke)

PICKERING, JEREMIAH M. Leon, Iowa, 1882d-1884d.

PICKERING, TILGHMAN Cincinnati, Ohio, 1900. (Hutslar)

PICKETT unlocated. Tennessee percussion and flintlock.

PICKETT, ROBERT M. Ionia, Michigan, 1865d-1891d. Percussion rifles.

PICKETT, RUFUS S. New Haven, Connecticut. Patent #47,127 April 4, 1865, cap holder.

PIECHETCEK, JOHN New Orleans, Louisiana, 1876d-1899d.

PIEDMONT trade mark of Crescent on shotguns made for Piedmont Hardware Co., Danville, Pennsylvania.

PIELOP, AUGUST Brenham, Texas, 1892d-1896d.

PIEPER, ABRAHAM Lancaster, Pennsylvania, 1798-1803. (Gluckman & Satterlee)

PIER, WILLIAM B. Detroit, Michigan. Patent #none April 6, 1832, winged shot with Andrew Mark.

PIERCE, BALATIAH (1779-?), Medina Co., Ohio, 1850c. (Hutslar)

PIERCE, CHARLES Ithaca, New York. Patent #369,812 September 13, 1887, lock with Leroy H. Smith.

PIERCE, DAVID Almont, Michigan, 1860d-1867d.

PIERCE, EBENEZER New Bedford, Massachusetts, 1856-1890. Patents #200,338 February 12, 1878, breechloading firearm with Selmar Eggers, #211,777 January 28, 1879, harpoon gun, #255,330 March 21, 1882, breechloading firearm, #256,041 April 4, 1882, breechloading firearm, and #306,098 October 7, 1884, breechloading firearm. All patents covered guns used for whaling.

PIERCE, GEORGE RICHMOND (1830-1910), Rochester, New York, 1849d-1852, Grand Rapids, Michigan, 1852-1875. Percussion and cartridge guns. Patents #119,474 October 3, 1871, breechloading firearm, and #120,323 October 24, 1871, cartridge. As S. & G.R. Pierce in Grand Rapids. (Eich)

PIERCE, HARDIN (1801-?), Park Co., Indiana, 1850c. (Lindert)

PIERCE, HENRY (1811-?), Liverpool, Ohio, 1850-1872d, Grafton, Ohio, 1883d. Percussion rifle. (Hutslar)

PIERCE, HENRY Palmyra, Wisconsin, 1867d.

PIERCE, J.D. Lonoke, Arkansas, 1885d.

PIERCE, J.H. Leland, Illinois, 1860d.

PIERCE, J.J. Medina, Ohio. Flintlock Kentucky. (Van Rensselaer)

PIERCE, LYSANDER Clarksville, Iowa, 1865d.

PIERCE, S. & G.R. Grand Rapids, Michigan. Percussion revolving rifles. George Richmond Pierce. (Sellers-1)

PIERCE, S. Loomisville, Michigan, 1863d.

PIERREPONT, H.M. Westfield, Massachusetts, 1876d.

PIERSON BROS. Janesville, Wisconsin, 1882d-1886d. F.F. Pierson.

PIERSON, F.F. Janesville, Wisconsin, 1879d-1895d. As Pierson Bros., 1882-1886.

PIERSON, JOHN L. Rutland, Vermont, circa 1860. Percussion underhammer rifle. (Horn)

PIERSON, SILAS New York, New York, 1820d. (Kauffman 2)

PIETSCH, JOHN A. Pittsburgh, Pennsylvania, 1895d-1899d.

PIFFARD, HENRY G. New York, New York. Patents #272,581 February 20, 1883, cartridge, and #281,725 July 24, 1883, recoil pad.

PIKE & BARRETT Brattleboro, Vermont, 1856. Samuel Pike and Lockhart Barrett. (Horn)

PIKE, EDWIN Boscobel, Wisconsin, 1888d.

PIKE, ELIJAH (1824-?), John Co., Indiana, 1850c. (Lindert)

PIKE, SAMUEL Brattleboro, Vermont, 1845-1861. Underhammer. With Lockhart Barrett as Pike & Barrett. (Horn)

PIKE, SAMUEL Troy, New York, 1834d.

PILLMAN, W. unlocated. Percussion fullstock.

PILLSBURY, JOHN D. Rochester, New Hampshire, 1855-1861, Chatham, New Hampshire, 1871d-1877d. Underhammer pistol.

PILLSBURY, W. Long Pine, Nebraska, 1886d.

PILOUT, C. Richmond, Virginia, 1871-1873. (Gardner)

PILSILE Cedar Rapids, Iowa, 1865d.

PILSON, S.A. Snowflake, Illinois, 1888d-1893d.

PIM, JOHN (?-1729), Boston, Massachusetts, 1715-1729. Flintlock revolver. (Kauffman 2)

PINAFORE suicide special by O.A. Smith.

PINCALL, EMANUEL Charleston, South Carolina, 1777. (Kauffman 2)

PINCKNEY, CYRUS A. Plymouth, Michigan. Patent #390,311 October 2, 1888, spring air gun with Clarence J. Hamilton.

PINNEY & STRATTON Fredonia, Kansas, 1884d.

PIONEER ARMS CO. trade name of Crescent on guns for Kruse Hardware Co. (AR 2- 69)

PIONEER suicide special by several makers.

PIONEER trade name of Gamble Stores on .22 cal. rifles and shotguns. (Perkins)

PIPER, C.Y. Natchez, Mississippi, 1849-1860. Brass 1/2 stock. For Newcomb, 1849-1850.

PIPER, D. unlocated. Converted Kentucky rifle.

PIPER, DENNIS B. Keene, New Hampshire, 1874d-1884d.

PIPER, E.J. Battle Creek, Michigan, 1899d.

PIPER, EDWIN S. Springfield, Massachusetts. Patent #51,391 December 5, 1865, extractor.

PIPER, EDWIN Philadelphia, Pennsylvania, 1873-1882d.

PIPER, GEORGE (1783-?), Emmitsburg, Maryland. Flintlock Kentucky. Apprenticed to John Armstrong, 1801. (Hartzler)

PIPER, H.J. Emporia, Kansas, 1882d-1884d.

PIPER, JOHN Central City, Iowa, 1865d.

PIPER, S. Oswego, New York, 1856-1858. (Gluckman & Satterlee)

PIPER, S.P. Holden, Missouri, 1898d.

PIPER, WALTER F. Seattle, Washington, 1889d-1896d.

PIPER, WATSON unlocated. Name on stock of early flintlock fowler.

PIPER, WILLIAM S. Keokuk, Iowa, 1865d.

PIPINO, JACOB C. Baltimore, Maryland, 1847d-1871d, Quincy, Illinois, 1872d-1888d. Percussion guns. (Hartzler)

PIPINO, JOHN L. Baltimore, Maryland, 1847d-1868d, Cobden, Illinois, 1880d, Jonesboro, Illinois, 1882d.

PIPINO, LEWIS Baltimore, Maryland, 1860d. With Jacob Pipino. (Hartzler)

PIRTLE, JOHN B. Whiteville, Tennessee, 1860d.

PITCHER AUTOMATIC REPEATING FIREARMS CO. see Henry A. Pitcher.

PITCHER, HENRY A. Neillsville, Wisconsin. Patents #397,143 February 5, 1889, magazine gun, #433,420 July 29, 1890, magazine gun, #452,192 May 12, 1891, magazine gun, and #501,192 July 11, 1893, magazine gun. Dr. Pitcher formed Pitcher Automatic Repeating Firearms Co. in 1889 to promote his gun, which was declared unsafe in the Trials of 1890. (Hobbies 1-55)

PITCHER, JONATHAN S. (1831-1893), Chicago, Illinois, 1846-1859, Colorado, 1860-1861, Council Bluffs, Iowa, 1864-1870, San Diego, California, 1870-1893. (Shelton)

PITMAN, HILL Duplin Co., North Carolina, 1857. (Bivins)

PITMAN, J.W. Mayfield, Kentucky, 1883d.

PITT, T. Southport, Illinois, 1860d.

PITT, WILLIAM JONES Middletown, Connecticut. Patent #34,093 January 7, 1862, revolver.

PITTENGER, JOSHUA S. Wellsville, New York, 1856-1859. Percussion 1/2 stock. (Gluckman & Satterlee)

PITTMAN, W.C. Jacksonville, Florida, 1883d-1886d.

PITTS, THOMAS Sharon, Tennessee, 1876d.

PITTSBURGH FIREARMS CO. Pittsburgh, Pennsylvania, 1860-1885. Shotguns. (Kauffman)

PITTSFIELD trade name of Hibbard, Spencer, Bartlett, & Co. on shotguns by Crescent. (Hinman)

PLACE, GEORGE Richmond, Virginia, 1869-1873. As Place and Van Horn, 1871-1873.

PLACE, N.E.V. Will's Point, Texas, 1890d.

PLACE, WILLIAM S. Charleston, Maine, 1862-1879. Percussion 1/2 stock. (Demeritt)

PLAISE, WILLIAM (?-1646), Salem, Massachusetts, 1632-1646. Also known as William Plasse. (GR 12- 60)

PLANK, JOHN J. Winfield, Kansas, 1882d-1888d. Same as John J. Plank, Wooster, Ohio?

PLANK, JOHN J. Wooster, Ohio, 1875d. Percussion 1/2 stock. Same as John J. Plank, Winfield, Kansas?

PLANK, WILLIAM Columbia Co., Pennsylvania, 1821. (Kauffman)

PLANT'S MFG. CO. Southington, Connecticut, 1860-1861 and 1867d-1868d, New Haven, Connecticut, 1861-1866. Front loading cartridge revolvers under Ellis & White patents. Amzi P. and Ebenezer H. Plant. (AAC 4-57)

PLANTS, CHRISTIAN East Finley, Pennsylvania, 1861d-1873d. Percussion 1/2 stock.

PLASS, REUBEN H. New York, New York. Patent #46,023 January 24, 1865, revolver.

PLASSE, WILLIAM see William Plaise.

PLATE, A.F. & H.A. San Francisco, California, 1878-1882. Sons of, and successors to, Adolphus Joseph Plate.

PLATE, ADOLPHUS JOSEPH (1818-1878), San Francisco, California, 1850-1878. Percussion and cartridge guns. (Shelton)

PLATH, CHARLES New York, New York, 1853d-1879d. Percussion 1/2 stock. As Plath & Gruener, 1853-1855.

PLATT, ISAAC Centerville, Michigan, 1863d-1867d.

PLAYER, RICHARD North Carolina, 1776. Committee of Safety repairs. (Bivins)

PLEASANT & CHARNLER Philadelphia, Pennsylvania, 1845-1850. Lockmakers only.

PLETTNER, WILLIAM Trinidad, Colorado. Patents #295,425 March 18, 1884, sight, and #306,099 October 7, 1884, sight. (Sellers-3)

PLIMPTON, A.H. Honoeye Falls, New York. Percussion and cartridge guns. (Clow)

PLOTZ, J.C. Stockton, California, 1856-1859. (Shelton)

PLUG UGLY suicide special.

PLUMER, HENRY (England, 1824-?), Omaha, Nebraska Territory, 1860c.

PLUMMER, A., JR. Mystic Bridge, Connecticut. Patent #34,449 February 18, 1862, breechloading firearm.

PLUMMER, JOSEPH Wayne, Ohio. Patents #none May 17, 1832, magazine gun, and #none May 17, 1832, button rifling. Both with John Clark.

PLUNKET, LARKIN Bethany, Kentucky, 1879d.

PLUSHEL, F. Cedar Rapids, Iowa, 1866-1869.

PLYMOUTH trade name on double shotgun.

POAGE, JOHN Augusta Co., Virginia, 1798-1799. (Gill)

POBST, DAVID (1821-?), Shreveport, Louisiana, 1850c-1883d. Percussion 1/2 stock.

POCAHONTAS suicide special.

POCKET CREEDMOOR trade name of Samuel Watson Johnson, Newton, Massachusetts, on single shot pistol with extension stock.

POE, W.C.H. Smithwick, Texas, 1896d.

POEPPELMEYER, WILLIAM Cedar Fork, Missouri, 1889d-1893d.

POINT OF FORK ARSENAL Point of Fork, Virginia. State arsenal during the Revolutionary War. (Gill)

POINTER trade name on .22 cal. derringer.

POISSON, J. (1812-?), Natchitoches, Louisiana, 1850c. (MB 9-65)

POLE & CUTTER unlocated. Percussion fullstock. Probably Pope & Cutter.

POLE, EDWARD Philadelphia, Pennsylvania, 1775. (Kauffman 2)

POLEY, T. see Thomas Pooley.

POLK, ROBERT (1790-?), Guilford Co., North Carolina, 1825, Greensboro, Indiana, 1850c. (Bivins, Lindert)

POLLARD, JAMES A. Jonesboro, Arkansas, 1860. (Elias)

POLLARD, JOHN Pennsylvania, 1775-1777. Committee of Safety muskets. (Hobbies 4-38)

POLLARD, PHILIP Macon City, Missouri, 1889d-1898d.

POLLARD, ROBERT New York, New York, 1799-1801. Contract muskets for Virginia, imported from Germany. (Hobbies 8-34)

POLLEY, C.H. Wilmington, North Carolina, 1877d, Monroe, North Carolina, 1884d-1890d.

POLLEY, H.N. Wilmington, North Carolina, 1866d. (Bivins)

POLLEY, JAMES Memphis, Tennessee, 1860d. Percussion 1/2 stock.

POLLEY, S.P. Wilmington, North Carolina, 1838. (Bivins)

POLLITT, JOHN H. (1820-1895), Pittsburgh, Pennsylvania, 1842-1895. (Whisker II)

POLLOCK, BENJAMIN SMITH Lawrence Co., Pennsylvania, 1840-1849. (Whisker II)

POLLOCK, DAVID (1795-1876), Allegheny Co., Pennsylvania, 1820c-1860c, Lawrence Co., Pennsylvania, 1870c-1876. Flintlock Kentucky rifles and pistols. (Whisker II)

POLLOCK, S. New Castle, Pennsylvania, 1841. Percussion fullstock rifle. (Kauffman)

POLLOCK, THOMAS Virginia, 1776. Committee of Safety repairs. (Gill)

POLSZ, FREDERICK Philadelphia, Pennsylvania, 1874d.

POMEROY Canton, Ohio, 1820c. (Knittle)

POMEROY, EBENEZER (1669-1754), Northhampton, Massachusetts, 1690-1754. Son of Medad Pomeroy. (Gluckman & Satterlee)

POMEROY, ELDAD (England 1629-1662), Boston, Hampshire, and Northampton, Massachusetts, 1630-1662. Son of Eltwood Pomeroy. (Gluckman & Satterlee)

POMEROY, ELTWOOD (England, 1585-1671), Boston, Massachusetts, 1630, Dorchester, Massachusetts, 1633-1637, Hartford, Connecticut, 1640, Windsor, Connecticut, 1650, Northampton, Massachusetts, 1660-1671. Also known as Eltweed Pomeroy. (Gluckman & Satterlee, Carey)

POMEROY, LEMUEL, JR. (1778-1849), Pittsfield, Massachusetts, 1809-1849. Model 1808, 1821, 1831, and 1840 contract muskets. Grandson of Seth Pomeroy. (Gluckman)

POMEROY, MEDAD (1638-1716), Northampton, Massachusetts, 1659-1716. Son of Eltwood/Eltweed Pomeroy. (Gluckman & Satterlee)

POMEROY, SETH (1706-1777), Northampton, Massachusetts. Flint fowling piece. Son of Ebenezer Pomeroy. A General in the Continental Army, killed in the Revolutionary War. (Gluckman & Satterlee)

POMERY, CHARLES M. Fargo, North Dakota, 1877-1882d.

POND & CO. Albany, New York. Flintlock pistols.

POND, J. unlocated. Percussion shotgun.

POND, LUCIUS WILLSON (1826-1889), Worcester, Massachusetts, 1847-1870. Revolvers under patents #35,623 June 17, 1862, revolver, and #38,934 June 16, 1863, revolver. Also made revolvers under patents of A.J. Gibson and F.W. Hood. (AR 1-61)

PONSTORD, J.R. Cross Roads, Illinois, 1860d.

PONTIAC ARMS CO. Chicago, Illinois, 1892d.

POOL, H.R. Waukesha, Wisconsin, 1891d.

POOL, JESSE (1805-?), Alexander Co., North Carolina, 1850c. Percussion 1/2 stock. (Bivins)

POOL, LEMON Springfield, Ohio, 1875d. (Hutslar)

POOL, S., & SON Hudsonville, Kentucky, 1860. Sanford and Thomas Pool.

POOL, SANFORD Hudsonville, Kentucky, 1857-1860d. With his son Thomas as S. Pool & Son, 1860.

POOL, THOMAS Hudsonville, Kentucky, 1860d, Hawesville, Kentucky, 1879d. With his father Sanford as S. Pool & Son, 1860.

POOLE, J.E. Hollister, California, 1874. For William McBroom. (Shelton)

POOLE, JOHN New York, New York, 1852d. Percussion pistol.

POOLEY, JAMES Memphis, Tennessee, 1858-1860.

POOLEY, THOMAS Blackberry Station, Illinois, 1860d-1886d.

POOR, A.B. Lawrence, Massachusetts, 1878d.

POORMAN, HENRY B. St. Louis, Missouri, 1850c-1857. Patent #16,327 January 6, 1857, bullet mould with Tristam Campbell.

POORMAN, MICHAEL Dauphin Co., Pennsylvania, 1772t-1790. (Kindig)

POPE & CUTTER Providence, Rhode Island, 1847-1855. William R. Pope and Erastus W. Cutter.

POPE & LITTLE Providence, Rhode Island, 1836-1841 and 1860-1866. William R. Pope (1836-1841 and 1860-1866), Charles F. Pope (1836-1841), and Charles T. Little. (Achtermier)

POPE, ALBERT A. Boston, Massachusetts, 1875-1890. Air guns. Patents #172,582 January 25, 1876, spring air gun, and #172,583 January 25, 1876, spring air gun. (Wolff)

POPE, CHARLES F. Providence, Rhode Island, 1860-1901. With Charles T. Little as Pope & Little, 1836-1841. With Charles T. Little as C. Little & Co., 1866-1872. (Achtermier)

POPE, HARRY M. (1861-1950), Hartford, Connecticut, 1887-1901, Chicopee Falls, Massachusetts, 1901-1905, Jersey City, New Jersey, 1908-1950. Patent #384,277 June 12, 1888, breechloading firearm. Barrelmaker. (Kelver)

POPE, HEZEKIAH SPEAK (1826-1876), Indiana, 1848, Havilah, California, 1866-1870, Ventura, California, 1870-1876. (Shelton)

POPE, ICHABOD Providence, Rhode Island, 1860-1880. Brother of W.R. Pope. (Achtermier)

POPE, JOHN W. Philadelphia, Pennsylvania. Patent #none July 17, 1809, shot machinery.

POPE, LAWRENCE K. Chicago, Illinois, 1879d-1913d.

POPE, N. unlocated. Percussion schuetzen.

POPE, WILLIAM R. Providence, Rhode Island, 1836-1883. With Charles T. Little and Charles F. Pope as Pope & Little, 1836-1841. With Erastus W. Cutter as Pope & Cutter, 1847-1855. With Charles T. Little as Pope & Little, 1860-1866. (Achtermier)

POPPEN, J.H. Morrisonville, Illinois, 1893d.

POPPLEN, G.N., JR. Baltimore, Maryland. Percussion double shotgun. (Hartzler)

PORCHER, JOSEPH Patroon, Texas. Patent #502,389 August 1, 1893, magazine gun with Burrel Whitten.

PORTER & PRITCHITT Philadelphia, Pennsylvania. Percussion pistol.

PORTER, A.A. Dunksburg, Missouri, 1860d.

PORTER, ARCHIBALD A. Griffen, Georgia, 1861-1883d. Confederate gunsmith convention.

PORTER, C.M. Youngstown, Ohio, 1888d. (Hutslar)

PORTER, J.H. Philadelphia, Pennsylvania, circa 1830. Air gun. (ASAC 35)

PORTER, JAMES B. Girrard, Pennsylvania. Patent #none August 4, 1832, superposed load rifle.

PORTER, PATRICK W. Memphis, Tennessee, New York, New York. Patent #8,210 July 18, 1851, turret rifle. Guns made by G.P. Foster. (Bugle 46)

PORTER, RUFUS Billerica, Massachusetts. Patent #none 1826, revolver. Patent sold to Sam Colt in 1836. (Sellers-1)

PORTERFIELD, J.C., & CO. Dayton, Ohio, 1892-1900. (Hutslar)

PORTS, ISRAEL ALLISON (1810-1906), Sunbury, Ohio, 1871-1888d. Percussion 1/2 stock. (Hutslar)

POSEGATE, ISAAC F. Weston, Missouri, 1850c, St. Joseph, Missouri, 1860d.

POSEGATE, JOHN H. Fort Des Moines, Iowa, 1850c. (MB 8-64)

POSEGATE, WILLIAM J. St. Joseph, Missouri, 1869d-1876d, Maryville, Missouri, 1889d.

POST, EZRA Trinidad, Colorado, 1879d-1890d. Patent #263,575 August 29, 1882, stock. (Sellers-3)

POST, JACOB Newark, New Jersey. Patent #6,453 May 15, 1849, pepperbox. Percussion pepperbox. (Dunlap)

POST, SAMUEL B. (?-1947), Pleasant Grove, Pennsylvania. Percussion fullstock and 1/2 stock. (Kauffman)

POST, SAMUEL Washington, Pennsylvania. Percussion fullstock. (Hetrick)

POSTILL, ROBERT New York, New York, 1857d-1858d.

POSTLEY, NELSON & CO. Pittsburgh, Pennsylvania, 1852-1875. Barrelmakers, lockmakers. (MB 12-61)

POTEET, J.W. Mt. Levi, Arkansas, 1898d.

POTTER, A.J. Scottville, Michigan, 1883d-1891d.

POTTER, A.S. Carolina, Rhode Island, 1881d.

POTTER, CHARLES F. Lawrence, Massachusetts, 1878d.

POTTER, DANIEL Hartford, Connecticut, 1866-1868. Percussion target rifle and telescopes. (Roberts)

POTTER, ELAM O. New York, New York. Patent #35,949 July 22, 1862, cartridge.

POTTER, GEORGE D. Deming, New Mexico patents: #338,188 March 16, 1886, breechloading firearm, and #338,189 March 16, 1886, safety. Wallace, Idaho patents: #539,540 May 21, 1895, breechloading firearm, and #542,494 July 9, 1895, ejector. Spokane, Washington patents: #625,601 May 23, 1899, ejector, and #741,273 October 13, 1903, ejector.

POTTER, GEORGE W. New London, Connecticut, 1877d-1882d.

POTTER, H., & CO. New York, New York. (Roberts)

POTTER, JOHN Edgerton, Wisconsin, 1857d.

POTTER, JOSEPH Boston, Massachusetts, 1884d-1886d.

POTTER, NOADYER Dowagiac, Michigan, 1863d-1895d. Percussion 1/2 stock.

POTTER, S.H., & CO. Terre Haute, Indiana. Lockmakers.

POTTER, WILLIAM Providence, Rhode Island, 1775. (Achtermier)

POTTS & CORBY White Lake, New York, 1872-1874d.

POTTS, ALBERT Philadelphia, Pennsylvania. Patent #17,339, May 12, 1857, centrifugal cannon.

POTTS, JOHN H. (1843-?), Galena, Illinois, 1860c. (Johnson)

POTTS, RICHARD B. Edmond, Oklahoma. Patent #573,353 December 15, 1896, machine gun.

POTTS, WILLIAM B. Columbus, Ohio, 1855-1893. Percussion guns including Brettell & Frisbie revolvers. (Hutslar)

POTWIN, C.W. Granville, Ohio, lock marking.

POUCH, JAMES (1802-?), New Albany, Indiana, 1850-1885. (Lindert)

POULTNEY, THOMAS Baltimore, Maryland, 1860-1886. Patent #64,70 1, May 14, 1867, breechloading firearm with Silas Crispin. With David B. Trimble as Poultney, Trimble & Co., 1860-1876. As Poultney & Kleibacker (Christian B.?), 1876-1880. (Hartzler)

POULTNEY, TRIMBLE & CO. Baltimore, Maryland, 1860d-1876d. Sales agents for Smith carbines and other guns. Thomas Poultney and David B. Trimble. (Hartzler)

POULTOR, WILLIAM Grand View, Illinois, 1860d.

POUNDS, ISAAC D. (1817-?), Columbus, Ohio, 1843d-1855d. (Hutslar)

POWELL & BROWN Cincinnati, Ohio, 1856d. Palemon Powell and Ira Brown. (Hutslar)

POWELL & CLEMENT Cincinnati, Ohio, 1887d-1900. Imported shotguns. Palemon Powell and John B. Clement. (Hutslar)

POWELL & SON Cincinnati, Ohio, 1878d-1887d. Palemon Powell. (Hutslar)

POWELL, C.S. Macon, Missouri, 1898d.

POWELL, CHARLES L. Atlanta, Georgia, 1877d. With Arthur G. Wright as Wright & Powell.

POWELL, G. Cincinnati, Ohio, 1853d. (Hutslar)

POWELL, JACOB Ashland Co., Ohio, 1805-1825. (Knittle)

POWELL, JOHN & THOMAS Cincinnati, Ohio, 1864d. Related to Palemon Powell? (Hutslar)

POWELL, PALEMON Cincinnati, Ohio, 1835-1908. Patent #85,180 December 22, 1868, cartridge charger. With Ira Brown as Powell & Brown, 1856d. As Powell & Son, 1878d-1887d. With John B. Clement as Powell & Clement, 1887-1900. (Hutslar)

POWELL, PETER & CO. St. Louis, Missouri, 1836-1850d. Importers of locks and hardware.

POWELL, SAMSON Six Mile, South Carolina, prior to the Civil War.

POWELL, STACY W. Pemberton, New Jersey, 1878d-1882d.

POWELL, THOMAS (1837-?), Webster, West Virginia, 1880c.

POWELL, THOMAS Baton Rouge, Louisiana, 1850c. (MB 9-65)

POWELL, V. unlocated. Percussion fullstock.

POWELSON, CHARLES G. Stamford, Connecticut, 1880d.

POWER, THOMAS J. (?-1888), Santa Rosa, California, 1874-1888. (Shelton)

POWERS & HUME Pittsfield, Massachusetts, 1876d-1879d. H.M. Powers.

POWERS, CHARLES San Francisco, California, 1852-1853. For Charles Bauer. (Shelton)

POWERS, DANIEL C. Cleveland, Ohio, 1883d-1885d. With his father Michael as M. Powers & Son, 1883-1885. (Hutslar)

POWERS, EDWARD York Co., Virginia. Apprenticed to Peter Gibson, March 8, 1706.

POWERS, H.M. (?-1887), Pittsfield, Massachusetts, 1876d-1887d. As Powers & Hume, 1876-1879.

POWERS, M., & SON Cleveland, Ohio, 1883-1885. Michael and Daniel C. Powers.

POWERS, MICHAEL Cleveland, Ohio, 1857d-1885d. With Thomas Powers as M. Powers & Bro., 1870. With Daniel C. Powers as M. Powers & Son, 1883-1885. (Hutslar)

POWERS, THOMAS Cleveland, Ohio, 1856-1896d. With his brother Michael as M. Powers & Bro., 1870. (Hutslar)

POWERS, TIMOTHY J. New York, New York. Patents #47,246 April 11, 1865, cartridge machine, #50,536 October 17, 1865, cartridge, #54,254 April 24, 1866, cartridge, #54,255 April 24, 1866, cartridge, and #57,258 August 14, 1866, cartridge machine.

POWLTER, WILLIAM (1822-?), Grandview, Illinois, 1845-1860. (Johnson)

POWNALL, E.G. unlocated. Percussion pepperbox.

POYAS, FRANCIS D. Charlestown, South Carolina, 1825-1834. Flintlock and percussion guns. (Kauffman 2)

POYAS, J.D. Carrollton, Alabama. 1885d.

POYAS, JAMES, JR. Charleston, South Carolina, 1822. (Kauffman 2)

PRAHL, LEWIS Philadelphia, Pennsylvania, 1772-1790. Committee of Safety muskets and swords. (Gluckman & Satterlee)

PRAIRIE KING suicide special by Bacon and Crescent.

PRALSH, CHARLES Lancaster, Pennsylvania, 1857d.

PRANTZ, AUGUST Perry Co., Indiana. Percussion 1/2 stock. (Lindert)

PRATER, ROBERT (1812-?), Hollister, California, 1871-1877. (Shelton)

PRATER, WILLIAM (1844-?), Hollister, California, 1871-1877. Son of Robert Prater. (Shelton)

PRATHER, H.V. Palestine, Texas, 1878d-1884d.

PRATSH, CHARLES A. (1833-?), Millersburg, Illinois, 1860c. Same as Charles A. Pratsh, Aberdeen, Washington? (Johnson)

PRATSH, CHARLES A. Aberdeen, Washington, 1886d. Same as Charles A. Pratsh, Millersburg, Illinois?

PRATT & SIMMS Princeton, Missouri, 1860d.

PRATT & WHITNEY Hartford, Connecticut, 1860-date. Machine guns and cannon. Also working models of inventions for many inventors.

PRATT New Harmony, Indiana, circa 1860. Percussion 1/2 stock. (Lindert)

PRATT, A. unlocated. Model 1798 pattern musket.

PRATT, ALVAN (1790-1877), Watertown, Massachusetts, 1812-1813, Sutton, Massachusetts, 1813-1821, Concord, Massachusetts, 1821-1877. Flintlock and percussion guns. Brother of Nathaniel Pratt. (GR 1-77)

PRATT, AZARIAH Marietta, Ohio, 1788-1820c. (Hutslar)

PRATT, ELISHA (1798-1857), Marietta, Ohio, 1850c-1853d. Percussion 1/2 stock. Son of Azariah Pratt. (Hutslar)

PRATT, G.D. Attica, New York. Percussion target rifles. (Swinney)

PRATT, GEORGE Middleton, Connecticut. Patent #290,605 December 18, 1883, trapgun. (Winant)

PRATT, HENRY (1790-1880), Roxbury, Massachusetts, 1832-1861, Boston, Massachusetts, 1861-1880d. Flintlock and percussion rifles. Brother of Alvan Pratt.

PRATT, NATHANIEL W. Brooklyn, New York. Patents #430,086 June 10, 1890, pneumatic gun with M.W. Sewall, and #430,087 June 10, 1890, pneumatic gun.

PRATT, NATHANIEL Watertown, Massachusetts, 1812. Brother of Alvan Pratt. (GR 1-77)

PRATT, WILLIAM Baltimore, Maryland, 1853. English patents, #1855-1677 and #1855-1678, breechloading musket conversions. (Hartzler)

PRAY, WILLIAM L. Fort Dodge, Iowa, 1880d-1895d.

PRECHTEL, JOHN A. Cleveland, Ohio, 1888-1890. (Hutslar)

PREEKIT, RICHARD Ft. Madison, Iowa, 1850c. (MB 8-64)

PREMIER suicide special by Thomas E. Ryan Co.

PREMIER trade name of Crescent on rifles and shotguns made for Montgomery Ward Co., and Hibbard, Spencer, Bartlett, & Co. (Hinman)

PREMIER trade name of Harrington & Richardson on revolvers.

PREMIUM suicide special by Iver Johnson.

PRENTICE, A.W. Norwich, Connecticut, 1877d.

PRENTISS, CHENEY Waitsfield, Vermont, 1871-1879. (Horn)

PRENTISS, H. Union Village, New York. Locks, hardware, and firearms. As Dunbar & Prentiss, and H. Prentiss & Co. at various times. (Union Village became West Greenwich in 1878.)

PRENTISS, M. White Creek, New York, 1848-1850d.

PRESCOTT PISTOL CO. Hatfield, Massachusetts, 1874d-1876. Large variety of revolvers. Previously named Prescott, Porter & Co., ?-1874d. Edwin A. Prescott. (GR 4-71)

PRESCOTT, D.L. New Orleans, Louisiana, 1860d. Importer.

PRESCOTT, EDWIN A. Worcester, Massachusetts, 1850-1874d, Hatfield, Massachusetts, 1874d-1876. Muzzle loading rifles and pistols, percussion and cartridge revolvers. Patents #30,245 October 2, 1860, revolver, and #159,609 February 9, 1875, magazine gun. For Ethan Allen and Edwin Wesson, later on his own. (GR 4-71)

PRESCOTT, G.F. Sleepy Eye, Minnesota, 1884d.

PRESCOTT, PORTER & CO. Hatfield, Massachusetts, ?-1874d. Renamed Prescott Pistol Co., 1874. Edwin A. Prescott.

PRESTON, JAMES W. Newton, Massachusetts. Patent #61,865 February 5, 1867, breechloading firearm.

PRETZSCH, CHARLES New Harmony, Indiana, 1858d-1880, New Haven, Indiana, 1880-1885. Percussion 1/2 stock. (Lindert)

PRIBYL & SON Racine, Wisconsin, 1867d. Heinrich Pribyl.

PRIBYL BROS. Chicago, Illinois, 1875d-1877d. Ignatius M. and Joseph A. Pribyl.

PRIBYL, FRANK G. Houston, Texas, 1894d-1899d.

PRIBYL, HEINRICH Racine, Wisconsin, 1867d-1868d. As Pribyl & Son, 1867.

PRIBYL, IGNATIUS M. Chicago, Illinois, 1872d-1877d. With his father as Ignatz Pribyl & Son, 1872-1875. Successor to his father, with Joseph A. Pribyl as Pribyl Bros., 1875-1877.

PRIBYL, IGNATZ Chicago, Illinois, 1872d-1875d. With his son Ignatius M. Pribyl as Ignatz Pribyl & Son.

PRIBYL, IGNATZ, & SON Chicago, Illinois, 1872d-1875d. Ignatz and Ignatius M. Pribyl.

PRIBYL, JOHN M. Chicago, Illinois, 1888d-1910d.

PRIBYL, JOSEPH A. Chicago, Illinois, 1875-1877d. Son of Ignatz Pribyl. Successor to his father with Ignatius M. Pribyl as Pribyl Bros., 1875-1877.

PRIBYL, MARTIN J. Chicago, Illinois, 1882d-1890d.

PRIBYL, MATTHEW Chicago, Illinois, 1875d-1880d.

PRIBYL, RUDOLPH Chicago, Illinois, 1891d.

PRIBYL, STEPHEN Chicago, Illinois, 1872d-1893d.

PRICE & MOORE New York, New York, 1800. Importer.

PRICE, A.A. unlocated. Percussion 1/2 stock.

PRICE, A.W. Looney's Creek, Tennessee, 1860d.

PRICE, ALEXANDER (1829-?), Somerset, Ohio, 1850c. (Hutslar)

PRICE, CALVIN A. (1873-1942), Parsons, Kansas, 1894-1900, Orange, Texas, 1900-1942. Percussion fullstock rifles. (Gluckman & Satterlee)

PRICE, GEORGE (1832-?), Rochester, New York, 1850c. Gunsmith living with Wiliam Billinghurst. (MB 9-45)

PRICE, ISAAC Mecklenburg Co., North Carolina, 1776-1790.

PRICE, J. New York, New York, 1770. (Gluckman & Satterlee)

PRICE, J.D. Girard, Kansas, 1878d, La Cygne, Kansas, 1884d-1894d.

PRICE, JAMES C. Globe Creek, Tennessee, 1860d.

PRICE, JESSE (1851-1951), Pricetown, West Virginia, 1870-1904. (Whisker IV)

PRICE, JOHN Somerset Co., Pennsylvania, 1805-1806. (Kauffman)

PRICE, JOSEPH Philadelphia, Pennsylvania, 1800. (Kauffman)

PRICE, NEWLIN & CO. unlocated. Percussion lockmaker.

PRICE, RICHARD Riverhead, New York, 1865-1868.

PRICE, SAMUEL Winchester, Virginia, 1767-1784. (Gill)

PRICE, THOMAS Mecklenburg Co., North Carolina. Apprenticed in 1787. (Bivins)

PRICE, WAYNE H. Windsor, Connecticut. Patent #38,604 May 19, 1863, self loading firearm.

PRICKET, FREDERICK Richfield, Ohio, 1853d. Percussion target rifle. (Hutslar)

PRICKET, JOSEPH Oakdale, Indiana, 1858d-1860d.

PRICKETT, ENOS SAMUEL (1828-?), Marysville, California, 1865-1890. With David Thom, Jr. as Thom & Prickett, 1876-1880. (Shelton)

PRIEST, JOSEPH (1812-?), Cleveland, Ohio, 1845, Detroit, Michigan, 1850c. (Hutslar)

PRIEST, JOSIAH Cleveland, Ohio, 1840-1857d. (Hutslar)

PRIHL, FRANK Racine, Wisconsin, 1857d. Possibly Pribyl.

PRILLIMAN, MARTIN Tipton, Indiana, 1850-1860d. (Lindert)

PRILLING, MARTIN Tipton, Indiana, 1850. (Lindert)

PRIME, JOHN (1807-?), Washington Co., North Carolina, 1837-1850c. (Bivins)

PRIME, WILLIAM New Bern, North Carolina, 1872-1875. (Gardner)

PRINCESS suicide special by Hood.

PRINDLE, A. unlocated. Percussion 1/2 stock.

PRINDLE, FRANKLIN B. New Haven, Connecticut. Patents #21,149 August 10, 1858, magazine gun, and #57,213 November 28, 1865, breechloading firearm.

PRINDLE, J. Richmond, Missouri, 1854d.

PRINDLE, URI Charlotte, Michigan, 1872d-1879d.

PRINGLE, EUGENE Gloversville, New York. Patents #439,895 November 4, 1890, breechloading gun, and #484,457 October 18, 1892, cartridge holder.

PRINGLE, JOHN Cambria Co., Pennsylvania, 1838t. Bedford percussion Kentucky. (MB 4-70)

PRINGLE, JOHN Pennsylvania, 1775-1776. Committee of Safety locks. (Gluckman & Satterlee)

PRIOR, GEORGE W. Boeger's Store, Missouri. Patent #264,899 September 26, 1882, sight.

PRISS, BENJAMIN (1815-?), St. Louis, Missouri, 1843-1850c. (Lewis)

PRISSEY, ELIAS (1835-?), Hooversville, Pennsylvania, 1855-1874. Percussion 1/2 stock. (Roberts)

PRITCHARD, B. Centralia, Illinois, 1878d.

PRITCHARD, J.M. St. Louis, Missouri, 1861d. Percussion rifles.

PRITCHARD, THOMAS Onarga, Illinois, 1864d.

PRITZ, A. York Co., Pennsylvania. Flintlock Kentucky rifle. (Dean)

PROBST, DAVID see David Pobst.

PROCTOR, L. Washington Court House, Ohio, 1859d. Percussion fullstock. (Hutslar)

PROCTOR, V. McArthur, Ohio, 1860d. (Hutslar)

PROCTOR, WILLIAM Fayette Co., Pennsylvania, 1815-1819. (Kauffman)

PROEBSTING, J. & C. Peoria, Illinois, 1864d.

PROESCHEL, JULIUS N. Milwaukee, Wisconsin. Patent #246,817 September 6, 1881, breechloading firearm.

PROGRESS trade name of Charles J. Godfrey on shotguns. (Hinman)

PROPHAPER, GEORGE (1801-?), Cincinnati, Ohio, 1850c. (Hutslar)

PROSPECT, W.S. Jacksonville, Illinois, 1881. (Johnson)

PROSSER & HARVEY East Liverpool, Ohio, 1885d. (Hutslar)

PROTECTION trade name of Whitney on percussion revolvers. (Sellers-1)

PROTECTOR ARMS CO. Philadelphia, Pennsylvania, circa 1870. "Protector" suicide specials. Jacob Rupertus. Also see Rupertus Pat'd. Pistol Mfg. Co. (Sellers-1)

PROTECTOR palm pistol by Chicago Fire Arms Co. (GR 10-66)

PROTECTOR suicide special, maker unknown.

PROTECTOR trade name of Jacob Rupertus, Protector Arms Co., and Rupertus Pat'd. Pistol Mfg. Co. on suicide specials. (Sellers-1)

PROUT, GEORGE W. Pittsfield, Massachusetts, 1888d.

PROUTY, CHARLES B., & CO. Chicago, Illinois, 1892d.

PROVIANCE, S. New Alexandria, Ohio, 1859d. (Hutslar)

PROVIDENCE GUN LOCK CO. Providence, Rhode Island, 1865d.

PROVIDENCE TOOL CO. Providence, Rhode Island, 1850-1917. Peabody, Roberts, and Model 1861 contract muskets, Peabody rifles and carbines. (Gluckman & Satterlee)

PROVOST (?-1788), New York, New York, 1763-1788. Father of David Provost. (Kauffman 2)

PROVOST, DAVID Long Island, New York. Administrator of father's estate, in 1788. (Kauffman)

PRUETZMANN, A.C. Canton, Ohio, 1882d. (Hutslar)

PRYOR, SILAS D. (1795-?), Pittsburgh, Pennsylvania, 1819-1850. (Whisker II)

PSOTTA, FREDERICK Philadelphia, Pennsylvania, San Francisco, California, 1854-1857. As Wurffleim & Psotta in Philadelphia. For A.J. Plate in San Francisco. (Shelton)

PUBISKA, ANDREW Waukon, Iowa, 1865d.

PUFFER, A.D. Boston, Massachusetts, 1842-1868.

PUG suicide special, maker unknown.

PUGH, JAMES (?-1771), Burlington, North Carolina, ?-1771. Hanged for treason by British troops. (Dean)

PULASKI GUN WORKS Pulaski, Tennessee, 1861. Mississippi rifles. (Hill-Anthony)

PULING, J. unlocated. Flintlock Kentucky.

PULLIAM, T. unlocated. Percussion fullstock.

PUMILA, JOHN New Orleans, Louisiana, 1872d.

PUPKE, EBERHARD L. New York, New York. Patent #409,704 August 27, 1889, lock.

PURDOM, CALVIN Philadelphia, Pennsylvania, 1816d.

PURDY, E.K. Schoolcraft, Michigan, 1860-1871d. Percussion rifles.

PURMANN, THEODORE Detroit, Michigan, 1860d-1889d.

PURMONT, T.B. Huelveton, New York. Percussion target rifle. (Swinney)

PURMOT, BLAKE De Peyster, New York, 1871-1874d.

PURRINGTON, JOHN Rootstown, Ohio, 1850c-1853d. (Hutslar)

PURUCKER, JOHN W. Baltimore, Maryland, 1884d-1887d. (Hartzler)

PUSEY, J.G. Providence, Rhode Island. Patent #49,409 August 1, 1865, magazine gun with G.W. Hughes.

PUTERBAUGH, J.W. Clarinda, Iowa, 1887d-1892d.

PUTNAM, ENOCH Granby, Massachusetts, 1775. Committee of Safety repairs. (Gluckman & Satterlee)

PUTNAM, GEORGE L. New York, New York. Patents #609,211 August 16, 1898, magazine gun with C.H. Farmer, and #623,960 April 25, 1899, magazine gun.

PUTNAM, R. East Le Roy, Michigan, 1863d.

PUTNAM, WILLIAM Brockport, New York, 1865d.

PUTNEY, BERNARD Penwater, Michigan, 1872d-1887d, Ludington, Michigan, 1891d-1899d. Percussion 1/2 stock.

PUTNEY, E. Southbridge, Massachusetts. Underhammer pistol.

PYEATT & RAMAGE Independence, Kansas, 1878d. J.P. Pyeatt.

PYEATT, J.P. Independence, Kansas, 1878d-1882d. As Pyeatt & Ramage, 1878.

PYERS, JOHN Loudonville, Ohio, 1860-1890. (MB 4-45)

PYLE, C. unlocated. Flintlock Kentucky dated 1811.

PYLE, H.J. Minneapolis, Minnesota, 1882d-1886d.

PYLE, NATHAN Washington Co., Pennsylvania, 1827-1836. (Whisker II)

PYLE, T.J. Nairn, Ohio, 1883d. (Hutslar)

Q SECTION

QUACKENBUSH, HENRY MARCUS (1847-1933), Herkimer, New York, 1871-1933. Air guns and .22 cal. rifles. Patents #115,638 June 6, 1871, air gun, #156,890 November 17, 1874, air gun, #165,425 February 2, 1875, air gun dart, #188,028 March 6, 1877, spring air gun, #244,484 July 19, 1881, air gun, #302,283 July 22, 1884, spring air gun, #336,586 February 23, 1886, breechloading gun, #436,997 September 23, 1890, skeleton gunstock, and #562,487 June 23, 1896, adjustable firearm stock. (GR 5-76)

QUAIL trade name of Crescent Fire Arms Co. on shotguns. (AR 2-69)

QUALLS, THOMAS Benton Co., Arkansas, 1835-1860. (Elias)

QUEEN CITY trade name of Elmira Arms Co. on shotguns by Crescent and others. (Hinman)

QUEEN suicide special by Hood.

QUEEN trade name of Hyde & Shattuck on derringers.

QUICK, J.M. Lackwaxen, Pennsylvania, 1861d.

QUIGLEY, E.F. Unionville, Missouri, 1889d.

QUIKONER, J. unlocated. Flintlock swivel breech.

QUILLAN, NATHAN Rockwood, Michigan, 1879d.

QUIMBY, DENNIS Northfield, Vermont, 1864-1871. Percussion 1/2 stock rifles. (Horn)

QUINBY, ENOCH R. Lynn, Massachusetts, 1875-1878. Patent #195,690 September 25, 1877, magazine firearms.

QUINN & CLARK Philadelphia, Pennsylvania, 1861d-1863d. Kennedy Quinn.

QUINN, KENNEDY Philadelphia, Pennsylvania, 1860d-1863d. As Quinn & Clark 1861-1863.

QUINNEBAUG RIFLE CO. Southbridge, Massachusetts, 1850. Underhammer pistols. Alternate (trade?) name for Nathaniel Rider & Co. Underhammer pistols.

QUINNIE, SALATHIEL Williamsburg, Virginia, 1713-1714. Public armorer. (Gill)

QUIRK, WILLIAM Chester, Pennsylvania, 1873-1876.

R SECTION

R + MC unidentified. Flintlock Kentucky.

R.B. see Robert Blanchard.

R.B. unidentified. Percussion 1/2 stock.

R.B. unidentified. Percussion lock only.

R.F. unidentified. Percussion fullstock.

R.F.S. see R.F. Stunkard.

R.G.L. & CO. see Latimer, Colburn & Co.

R.H. see Robert Hughes.

R.H.P. unidentified. Percussion fullstock.

R.M.T. unidentified. Percussion fullstock.

RAABE, J.A. St. Louis, Missouri, 1893d-1898d.

RAACH, THOMAS see Thomas Roach.

RAAF, JACOB Halifax, Pennsylvania, 1820. (Kauffman)

RABBETH, FRANCIS J. Boston, Massachusetts. Patents #301,628 July 8, 1884, sight, and #308,699 December 2, 1884, sight.

RACKLIFF, WILLIAM Hartford, Connecticut, 1867d-1882d.

RADCLIFF, BEN R. Bement, Illinois, 1864d.

RADCLIFFE & GUIGNARD Columbia, South Carolina, 1846-1858. Importers and dealers. Thomas W. Radcliffe.

RADCLIFFE, THOMAS W. Columbia, South Carolina, 1846-1865. As Radcliffe & Guignard, 1846-1858. With William Glaze as Glaze & Radcliffe, 1861.

RADER, BENJAMIN Schuylkill Co., Pennsylvania, 1850c.

RADER, JOHN Columbus, Ohio. (Hutslar)

RADER, WESLEY Londonderry, Ohio, 1857-?, McArthur, Ohio, 1859d, Gillespieville, Ohio, ?-1886. Percussion 1/2 stock. (Hutslar)

RADER, WILLIAM Yorktown, Indiana, 1867d.

RADFANG see Frederick, or George, or Jacob Rathfong.

RADFORD, S. Newburn, Tennessee, 1887d.

RAESOR, DAVID (?-1774), Lancaster, Pennsylvania, ?-1774. (Kindig)

RAFFENSTEIN, P. North Topeka, Kansas, 1882d.

RAGG, H. Coleda, Missouri, 1898d.

RAIBLE, JACOB (1827-1905), Warren, Ohio, 1858 and 1875d-1905. Changed name to Ripley in 1890. (Hutslar)

RAIKE, H. unlocated. Percussion fullstock.

RAIKE, LEVI Lincoln Co., Kentucky. Percussion 1/2 stock. Probably Levi Rakes.

RAINES, BENJAMIN F. (1817-?), Greenfield, Indiana, 1850c-1860d. (Lindert)

RAINEY, JAMES Huntingdon Co., Pennsylvania, 1799-1818.

RAISON, HENRY Jelloway, Ohio, 1862d. (Hutslar)

RAISON, HENRY J. Wapakoneta, Ohio, 1875-1890d. Percussion 1/2 stock. (Hutslar)

RAKER, CHARLES Bedford Co., Pennsylvania, 1849t. (Kauffman)

RAKER, CONRAD Raker, Pennsylvania, 1887d-1890d.

RAKER, D. (1830-?), Wooster, Ohio, 1850c. Percussion fullstock. (Hutslar)

RAKES, LEVI (1809-?), Tazewell Co., Virginia, 1850c, Ironton, Ohio, 1860. (MB 10-63, MB 3-55)

RALLS, W.K. Maysville, Kentucky, 1850-1860.

RALPH & SCHRADER New York, New York, 1872-1879d. Frank Ralph and Herman Schrader.

RALPH, FRANK New York, New York, 1872d-1877. Patent #198,154 December 11, 1877, breechloading firearm. With Herman Schrader as Ralph & Schrader.

RALPH, JOHN (1810-?), Gallipolis, Ohio, 1850c. (Hutslar)

RALPH, NEAL N. Addison, Ohio, 1859d-1868d, Gallipolis, Ohio, 1871d-1890d. Percussion fullstock. (Hutslar)

RAMAGE see Pyeatt & Ramage. J.P. Pyeatt.

RAMAGE & CARRIER Trinidad, Colorado, 1877-1881. Asbel J. Carrier. (Sellers-3)

RAMBO, ABRAHAM (1824-?), Abingdon, Illinois, 1850c. (Johnson)

RAMEY BROS. Bloomington, Illinois, 1875d.

RAMEY, HIRAM Mohawk, New York, ?-1867d. See Hiram Ranney.

RAMEY, JACOB Heyworth, Illinois, 1860d, Bloomington, Illinois, 1867d-1884d. Percussion rifle. With Preston W. Bentley as Bentley & Ramey, 1867-1870, and J. Ramey & Sons, 1884.

RAMI, JOHN Mobile, Alabama, 1844d. (Neville)

RAMSDELL & NEAL Bangor, Maine, 1870-1881. Charles V. Ramsdell and John Neal. (Demeritt)

RAMSDELL & ROTH Bangor, Maine, 1873-1874. John W. Ramsdell and Ernest Roth. (Demeritt)

RAMSDELL, CHARLES S. Bangor, Maine, 1887-1890. Son of Charles V. Ramsdell. (Demeritt)

RAMSDELL, CHARLES V. (1821-1886), Bangor, Maine, 1855-1886. Percussion rifles and pistols. With John H. Neal as Ramsdell & Neal, 1871-1886. With Charles V. Ramsdell as C.V. & J.W. Ramsdell, 1867-1870. (Demeritt)

RAMSDELL, JOHN W. Bangor, Maine, 1870-1880. Brother of Charles V. Ramsdell. With his brother Charles V. as C.V. & J.W. Ramsdell, 1864-1872. With Ernest Roth as Ramsdell & Roth, 1873-1874. (Demeritt)

RAMSEY, H. Comanche, Texas, 1892d.

RAMSEY, JOHN Union Co., Indiana. (Lindert)

RAMSLEY, ROBERT Lancaster Co., Pennsylvania, 1796-1798. Barrelmaker. (KRA IV-4)

RANBOLD, EDWARD Chicago, Illinois, 1860d.

RAND, D.C., & CO. Perrington, New York, 1862-1864.

RANDAL, I.J. Bridgeville, Michigan, 1872d-1877d.

RANDALL, ENOCH Farmer, Ohio, 1888d. (Hutslar)

RANDALL, FRANCIS Chowan Co., North Carolina, 1786. (Bivins)

RANDALL, G.W. Centerville, Iowa, 1817d-1889d.

RANDALL, ISRAEL (1814-?), Huron Co., Ohio, 1850c. (Hutslar)

RANDALL, JACOB Philadelphia, Pennsylvania, 1837d.

RANDALL, JAMES Norwich, Connecticut. Patent #289,856 December 11, 1883, revolver.

RANDALL, JASON L. New Haven, Connecticut. Patent #343,492 June 8, 1866, magazine gun.

RANDALL, JOSEPH C. Philadelphia, Pennsylvania, 1847-1861. Lockmaker only.

RANDALL, MYRON (1878-1944), Waupaca, Wisconsin, 1895-1944. Percussion 1/2 stock and air guns. (GC 1)

RANDALL, VAN BUREN Rochester, New York, 1865-1886d. For Charles Green. (Eich)

RANDEGGER, JOHN Belleville, Illinois, 1864d-1869d. With George C. Bunsen as Bunsen & Randegger, 1869.

RANDLE, J.M. Bay City, Illinois, 1880d-1886d.

RANDOLPH & FAIRBANKS Anoka, Minnesota, 1867d.

RANDOLPH, C.A. Huntsville, Texas 1890d.

RANDOLPH, S.S. Cuba, New York, 1861-1880d.

RANEY, STEPHEN Huntington Co., Pennsylvania, 1809-1815. (Kauffman)

RANGER suicide special by E.L. Dickinson.

RANGER suicide special by Hopkins & Allen.

RANGER trade name of Sears, Roebuck & Co. on many guns. (Hinman)

RANGLER, GEORGE Racine, Wisconsin, 1871-1877.

RANKIN unlocated. Barrelmaker. As Clark & Rankin, also unlocated.

RANKIN & WERTER unlocated. Percussion barrel makers.

RANKIN, J.D. Monticello, Arkansas, 1884d.

RANKIN, JAMES B. Marion, North Carolina. Confederate patent #21 October 18, 1861, breechloading firearm. (Albaugh 1)

RANKIN, JOHN York Co., Pennsylvania, 1767t-1834. (Kindig)

RANNEY, HIRAM Mohawk, New York, 1861-1867d. See Hiram Ramey.

RANSIOR, J.L. Charleston, South Carolina, 1790d. (Kauffman 2)

RANSOM, JAMES Halifax, North Carolina, 1776-1778. Superintendent and master armorer of the public gun factory, also known as Halifax Manufactory. (Bivins)

RAPP & LUHRING Los Angeles, California, 1878d. (Shelton)

RAPPAHANNOCK FORGE Falmouth, Virginia, 1781-?. Flintlock muskets and pistols. (Swayze)

RAQUET & BANDLE Cincinnati, Ohio, 1861d-1864d. Christian R. Raquet and Jacob C. Bandle. Also see Bandle Arms Co. (Hutslar)

RAQUET, CHRISTIAN R. Cincinnati, Ohio, 1857d-1866d. Air guns. With Jacob C. Bandle as Raquet & Bandle, 1861-1864. (Hutslar)

RAQUET, PETER Cincinnati, Ohio, 1864-1866d. For Christian Raquet. (Hutslar)

RARICK, J.T. Harbor Springs, Michigan, 1899d.

RASH, A. Houston, Texas, 1878d.

RASH, B. unlocated. Percussion fullstock.

RASSMUSSEN, P. Springtown, Utah, 1878d.

RATCLIFF, FRANCIS Athens, Kentucky, 1860d.

RATCLIFF, JAMES Rochester, New York, 1871-1875.

RATCLIFF, THOMAS Kingman, Indiana. (Lindert)

RATE, JACOB White Deer, Pennsylvania, 1861d.

RATHBURN, GEORGE W. Bristol, Vermont, 1869-1885. Underhammer pistol. (Horn)

RATHBURNE, J.W. O'Neill, Nebraska, 1884d-1886d. Listed as Rathbone in 1886 directory.

RATHERS CO. Keene, New Hampshire. Percussion pistol.

RATHFONG, FREDERICK Lancaster Co., Pennsylvania, 1770-1777. (Gluckman & Satterlee)

RATHFONG, GEORGE (1750-1819), Lancaster Co., Pennsylvania, 1774-1819. For William Henry, 1774-1779. (Hobbies 4-38)

RATHFONG, JACOB (?-1839), Marietta, Pennsylvania, 1810-1839. Flintlock Kentucky rifles.

RATHVON, JACOB York, Pennsylvania, 1808-1811, Marietta, Pennsylvania, 1811- . See Jacob Rathfong. (Kauffman)

RATRAUFF, H.J. Warrensburg, Missouri. Percussion 1/2 stock.

RATTLER suicide special.

RATZ, WILLIAM Austin, Texas, 1878d.

RAUB, JOSEPH L. Nevada, Ohio. Patents #146,473 January 13, 1874, breechloading firearm, and #149,525, April 7, 1874, cartridge capper.

RAUB, JOSEPH L. New London, Connecticut, 1876d-1889d.

RAUBER, FEDER Berks Co., Pennsylvania, 1730. (Gluckman & Satterlee)

RAUBS, CHARLES New York, New York, 1888d-1896d. Son of William Raubs.

RAUBS, WILLIAM New York, New York, 1862-1887d. Percussion, cartridge, and air guns.

RAUCH, BENJAMIN Germansville, Pennsylvania, 1860d-1861d.

RAUCH, WOHLRAD Owensboro, Kentucky, 1883d.

RAUERT see Rinklaub & Rauert.

RAULT, HENRY New Orleans, Louisiana, 1882-1886d.

RAULT, JOHN New Orleans, Louisiana, 1853d.

RAULT, JOSEPH New Orleans, Louisiana, 1871d-1881d.

RAULTON Lancaster, Pennsylvania, 1794. Delivered one (1) Model 1792 contract rifle. (Moller)

RAUSSEAU, C. Murphys, California, 1867d. (Shelton)

RAVE, CHRISTIAN HEINRICH (1820-1915), Sacramento, California, 1850-1895. (Shelton)

RAVLIN, L.M. Burlington, Vermont, 1890-1900. (Horn)

RAWSELL, CHARLES (1813-?), Fayette Co., Pennsylvania, 1850c. First name John according to (Whisker II).

RAWSELL, JOHN see Charles Rawsell.

RAWSON see Rawson & Whipple.

RAWSON & WHIPPLE Norwich, Connecticut, 1873d-1875d.

RAWSON, JUDSON L. Jamaica, Vermont, 1880d-1884d. (Horn)

RAWSON, RALPH L. Brooklyn, New York, 1867-1875d.

RAY, DANIEL (1781-?), Moore Co., North Carolina, 1850c. (Bivins)

RAY, HORACE (1821-?), Mokelumne Hill, California, 1867-1878. (Shelton)

RAY, J.N. Jefferson, Indiana, 1856. Submitted breechloading rifle to Ordnance Department.

RAY, JAMES L. (1823-?), San Andreas, California, 1859-1860. (Shelton)

RAY, L. Hind's Creek, Tennessee, 1891d.

RAYMOND, C.H. see N.H. & C.H. Raymond.

RAYMOND, CHARLES Cambridge City, Indiana. (Lindert)

RAYMOND, EDWARD A. Brooklyn, New York. Patent #21,054 July 27, 1858, revolver with Charles Robitaille. Pettengill revolvers made under this patent. (Sellers-1)

RAYMOND, F., & CO. Lewiston, Maine, 1882d. (Demeritt)

RAYMOND, JOHN C. New York, New York. Patent #558,841 April 12, 1896, air gun.

RAYMOND, N.H. see N.H. & C.H. Raymond.

RAYMOND, N.H. & C.H. Cambridge City, Indiana. Percussion 1/2 stock.

RAYMOND, P. Winona, Minnesota, 1867d.

RAYMOND, R. Albion, New York. Percussion 1/2 stock.

RAYMOND, V.M. Roscommon, Michigan, 1887d.

RAYMOND, W. Albion, New York. Percussion 1/2 stock. (Swinney)

RAYMOND, WILLIAM Milwaukee, Wisconsin, 1854-1855. (WGCA 6)

RAYMOND, WILLIAM Winona, Minnesota, 1858-1886d.

RAYNES, H. New York, New York, 1851d.

RAYNOLDS, D.H. Mobile, Alabama. As Dade & Raynolds in flintlock and early percussion era.

RAZER, JOHN Fayette Co., Pennsylvania, 1798-1804. (Kauffman)

RAZEY, CHARLES Fife Lake, Michigan, 1891d.

RAZOLINI, ONORIO Maryland, 1740-1741. Colonial armorer. (Gardner)

RAZOR see Reasor.

RAZY, R. Benville, Illinois, 1886d-1888d.

REACH, T. Williamsburg, Ohio, 1859d. (Hutslar)

READ, GEORGE T. Belfast, Maine, 1876-1900. (Demeritt)

READ, JOHN B. Tuscaloosa, Alabama. Patents #15,999 October 28, 1856, projectile, #17,233 May 5, 1857, breechloading firearm, and #18,707 November 24, 1857, projectile.

READ, N.T. Danville, Virginia. Confederate patent #154 March 20, 1863, breechloading firearm. Carbines made by Keen, Walker & Co. Converted Hall rifles carry Read's monogram. (Hill-Anthony)

READ, O.H.P. Taney Co., Missouri, 1850c. (MB 11-66)

READ, ROBERT Chestertown, Maryland, 1775-1778. Committee of Safety muskets. (Hartzler)

READ, WILLIAM Boston, Massachusetts, 1826-1880. Militia muskets and other firearms. As Lane & Read, 1826-1849, and William Read & Sons, 1850-1880.

READ, WILLIAM Chesterton, Maryland, 1775-1776, Baltimore, Maryland, 1799d-1801d, Committee of Safety muskets. (Hartzler)

READE, CHARLES Fayette Co., Pennsylvania, 1814-1815. (Kauffman)

READING unlocated. Early flintlock Kentucky rifle.

REAGEN, JACOB West August, Virginia, 1774-1775, Fredrickstown, Maryland, 1778. (Boehret, Gill)

REAM, CHARLES Ream's Crossing, Pennsylvania, 1846.

REAM, DANIEL New Berlin, Ohio, 1882d. (Hutslar)

REAMS, JOSEPH M. Meriden, Connecticut. Patent #406,667 July 9, 1889, magazine gun with William L. Horne.

REAR, WILLIAM Nashville, Tennessee, 1877d-1891d.

REASOR, DAVID Lancaster, Pennsylvania, 1749-1780. (Gluckman & Satterlee)

REASOR, JACOB Frederick, Maryland, 1775-1785, Mercersburg, Pennsylvania, 1808. Committee of Safety muskets and rifles, flintlock Kentucky. (Hartzler)

REASURE, JOHN Lancaster, Pennsylvania, 1779-1781. (KRA IV-4)

REAVIS, GEORGE (1818-1881), Yadkinville, North Carolina, 1840-1881. (Bivins)

REAVIS, SAMUEL (1800-?), Davie Co., North Carolina, 1850c. (Bivins)

REBASZ, JOHN Lockport, New York, 1882d.

REBETY, AUGUSTUS Norwich, Connecticut. Patent #26,641 December 27, 1859, revolver with Joseph Gruler. Superintendent of Manhattan Fire Arms Co. Held several patents on gun making machinery. (Nutter)

RECK, GARRETT (1812-?), Rockport, Indiana, 1850c. (Lindert)

RECK, THOMAS (1821-?), Rockport, Indiana, 1850c. (Lindert)

RECKLING, H. Columbia, South Carolina, 1848-1860. (Albaugh 1)

RECTOR & ROBINSON Buffalo, New York, 1850-1853. Percussion 1/2 stock. James H. Rector and L.W. Robinson.

RECTOR & ROBSON Buffalo, New York, 1850-1853. John H. Rector and James O. Robson. (Kauffman)

RECTOR, CHARLES A. Syracuse, New York, 1851-1867d. With John H. Rector as J.H. & C.A. Rector, 1866-1867. (Swinney)

RECTOR, J.H. & C.A. Syracuse, New York, 1866-1867. John H. Rector and Charles A. Rector.

RECTOR, J.H., & SON Syracuse, New York, 1867-1868. John H. Rector.

RECTOR, JOHN H. (?-1868), Syracuse, New York, 1840-1850, Buffalo, New York, 1850-1853, Syracuse, New York, 1854-1868. Patent #5,402 December 18, 1847, false muzzle. With James O. Robson as Rector & Robson, 1850-1853. With Charles A. Rector as J.H. & C.A. Rector, 1866-1867. As J.H. Rector & Son, 1867-1868. Also see J.H. Rocketer. (Swinney)

RED CHIEFTAIN trade name of Supplee, Biddle Hardware Co. on shotguns. (Hinman)

RED CLOUD suicide special by Ryan Pistol Mfg. Co.

RED HOT suicide special.

RED JACKET suicide special by Lee Arms Co. and Hopkins & Allen.

REDACKER, WILLIAM Berks Co., Pennsylvania, 1850c. (Kauffman)

REDDICK, DAVID Baltimore, Maryland, 1776, Annville, Pennsylvania, 1800, Maryland Committee of Safety muskets, flintlock Kentucky. Also listed as Riddick, and as Reduk. (Hartzler)

REDFIELD GUNSIGHT CO. Denver, Colorado, 1900-date. Modified Ballard rifles, King sights, powder measures, and Redfield sights. John Redfield. (GR 7-75)

REDFIELD, EDWARD E. Linkville, Oregon, 1886d-1907d. Patents #362,110 May 3, 1887, firearm with John H. Redfield, #378,556 February 28, 1888, magazine gun, #772,746 October 18, 1904, magazine gun, #806,496 December 5, 1905, firearm, and #852,241 April 30, 1907, magazine gun.

REDFIELD, J. Galesville, Oregon, 1867d-1871d.

REDFIELD, JOHN Denver, Colorado. See Redfield Gunsight Company.

REDFIELD, JOHN H. Linkville, Oregon. Patents #362,110 May 3, 1887, firearm with Edward Redfield, and #403,959 May 28, 1889, breechloading firearm with Samuel H. Redfield.

REDFIELD, JOHN WATROUS Glendale, Oregon. Patent #356,961 February 1, 1887, breechloading firearm, and #358,071 February 22, 1887, breechloading firearm.

REDFIELD, SAMUEL H. Linkville, Oregon. Patent #403,959 Mary 28, 1889, breechloading firearm with John H. Redfield.

REDFIELD, SIDNEY, JR. Washington Co., Indiana, 1850c.

REDFIELD, THOMAS (1831-?), Washington Co., Indiana, 1850c. (Lindert)

REDFORD, ARTER Jefferson City, Missouri. Flintlock fullstock. (Dillin)

REDLICK unlocated. Flintlock Kentucky.

REDMON, M.A. Humboldt, Kansas, 1882d.

REDSECKER, G.W. Elizabethtown, Pennsylvania, 1890d-1896d.

REDUK see David Reddick.

REDWINE, C.F. Lynnville, Illinois, 1870-1888. Percussion 1/2 stock. (Johnson)

REDWINE, JOHN Lynnville, Illinois, 1860d-1864d.

REDWINE, JOHN F. Utica, Missouri, 1879d, Chillicothe, Missouri, 1881d-1898d.

REDWINE, WILLIAM J. Concordia, Kansas, 1884d-1900d. Patent #490,614 January 24, 1893, shotgun rifle attachment.

REECE, JASPER N. Springfield, Illinois, 1879-1885. Financial backer of Reuben S. Chaffee.

REED Seville, Ohio, circa 1850. (Knittle)

REED Valparaiso, Indiana, 1860c. (Lindert)

REED & GILDNER Philadelphia, Pennsylvania, 1874d-1890d. William H. Reed.

REED, A.H. East Liverpool, Ohio, 1875d. (Hutslar)

REED, CHARLES Fayette Co., Pennsylvania, 1816-1819. (Kauffman)

REED, E.M. unlocated. Percussion 1/2 stock target pistol.

REED, GEORGE W. Marion, Indiana, 1882-1885. (Gardner)

REED, ISAAC Cravensville, Missouri, 1860d.

REED, J. New Hampshire, 1800c. Flintlock Kentucky rifle. (Gardner)

REED, J. New York, New York, 1841d.

REED, J.P. unlocated. Percussion 1/2 stock.

REED, JACOB (?-1780), Augusta Co., Virginia, ?-1754, Hampshire Co., Virginia, 1754-1780. (Whisker IV)

REED, JAMES Lancaster, Pennsylvania, 1778-1781. Flintlock Kentucky rifles. (Dean)

REED, JOHN Chagrin Falls, Ohio, 1863-1878d. (Hutslar)

REED, JOHN Troy, New York, 1836. (Dillin)

REED, JOSEPH Lancaster, Pennsylvania, 1800-1808. Flintlock Kentucky rifles. (Dillin)

REED, PHILIP Philadelphia, Pennsylvania, 1898d.

REED, R.A. New York, New York. Imported percussion fowler.

REED, SAMUEL Philadelphia, Pennsylvania, 1829d-1841d. (Kauffman)

REED, SOLOMON unlocated. Percussion fullstock.

REED, THOMAS G. Ruby, Michigan, 1863d.

REED, WILLIAM H. Philadelphia, Pennsylvania, 1867d-1890d. As William Reed & Bro., 1867-1870, and Reed & Gildner, 1874-1890.

REED, WILLIAM M. (1844-?), Frease's Store, Ohio, 1850c-1864d. (Hutslar)

REED, WILLIAM, & BRO. Philadelphia, Pennsylvania, 1867-1870. William H. Reed.

REEDER, JOSEPH S. Canton, Ohio. Patent #30,760 November 27, 1860, magazine gun.

REEDY, B.E. (1818-?), Donaldson, Pennsylvania, 1862. Son of Leonard Reedy. (Kauffman)

REEDY, E. Dauphin Co., Pennsylvania, 1862. Percussion target rifle. (Kauffman)

REEDY, LEONARD (1772-1835), Berks Co., Pennsylvania, 1794-1810, Gratz, (Dauphin Co.), Pennsylvania, 1825-1835. (Kauffman)

REES, FRANK New York, New York. Patents #337,992 March 16, 1886, repeating gun, #337,993 March 16, 1886, repeating gun, and #473,179 April 19, 1892, repeating gun.

REESE Mt. Pleasant, Ohio. (Hutslar)

REESE, DAVID Buffalo, New York, 1804-1823. (Bingham)

REEVES, BUFORD (1810-?), Charleston, Indiana, 1846-1862d. (Lindert)

REEVES, GUSTON (1800-?), Ohio, 1842, Lee Co., Iowa, 1850c. (MB 8-64)

REEVES, W.F. Atlanta, Georgia, 1883d.

REGAN, JESSE (1815-?), Davidson Co., North Carolina, 1850c. (Bivins)

REGER, A.D. Buckhannon, Virginia, circa 1800. Signature "ADR" on modified militia rifle. (Whisker IV)

REICHARD, EDWIN D. Reading, Pennsylvania. Patent #198,044 December 11, 1877, alarm gun.

REICHENBACH, GEORGE Lancaster, Pennsylvania, 1850. (KRA IV-4)

REICHENBACH, WILLIAM Lancaster, Pennsylvania, 1820-1851. See William Reintenbach - same person? (Bugle 114)

REICHLING, FRANK (1821-?), Missouri, 1848, El Dorado Co., California, 1852c. (Shelton)

REICHWEIN, CORNELIUS Berks Co., Pennsylvania, 1838. Also known as C. Richwine. (Dean)

REID & TRACY New York, New York, 1858d-1862d. Hardware dealers, derringers.

REID, A.W. unlocated. Percussion 1/2 stock.

REID, ANDREW Wayne Co., Indiana, circa 1820. Percussion 1/2 stock.

REID, JAMES (1827-1898), New York, New York, 1857-1865, Catskill, New York, 1865-1883. Patents #38,336 April 28, 1863, revolver, #51,752 December 26, 1865, revolver. "My Friend" knuckleduster made in Catskill, revolvers in New York city. (GC 42)

REID, TEMPLETON Milledgeville, Georgia, 1824. Flintlock rifles.

REID, WILLIAM Spartansburg, South Carolina. Early flintlock. (Hobbies 10-31)

REIDERER, W. Chicago, Illinois, 1890d.

REIFF & McDOWELL Philadelphia, Pennsylvania. Patent #457,683 June 13, 1893 alarm gun.

REIFFSNYDER, JOHN Reading, Pennsylvania, 1779-1793t. Flintlock Kentucky. (Kauffman)

REIGART & SHELLENBERGER Maquoketa, Iowa, 1865d.

REIGART, PETER Lancaster, Pennsylvania, 1775-1778. Committee of Safety muskets with Christian Isch. See Peter Rugert. (Hobbies 4-38)

REIHL, WILLIAM Cincinnati, Ohio, 1880c.

REILLER, WILLIAM A. Houston, Texas, 1892d-1899d. As Culmore & Reiller, 1897d.

REILLY, HUGH Brooklyn, New York. Patent #245,015 August 2, 1881, rifling.

REIM, THOMAS New Orleans, Louisiana, 1841d-1844d.

REIN & MILLER Hamilton, Ohio, 1856. Percussion 1/2 stock.

REIN, A. Hamilton, Ohio, 1858d-1868d. Listed as August Rein in 1861-1862 directory, and Adam Reine in 1858. Percussion fullstock. (MB 6-62)

REIN, AUGUST see A. Rein.

REIN, JOHN New York, New York, 1863-1875, Brooklyn, New York, 1883d-1890d. Percussion rifles and shotguns.

REINDODT, F. Mendota, Illinois, 1860d.

REINE, ADAM see A. Rein.

REINE, JOSEPH Marshall, Missouri, 1893d.

REINEKE, FREDERICK St. Louis, Missouri, 1847d.

REINER, MICHAEL Lancaster, Pennsylvania, 1779-1790. Flintlock Kentucky. (Dillin)

REINFRIED, LEO Philadelphia, Pennsylvania, 1856d-1882d, Camden, New Jersey, 1884d-1890d. Percussion 1/2 stock and derringer.

REINFRIED, P.C. Bridesburgh, Pennsylvania. Patent #23,224 March 15, 1859, breechloading firearm with Joseph Barber.

REINHARD, FRANK Loudonville, Ohio, 1880-1890, Dayton, Ohio, 1891-1894. Son of Peter Albert Reinhard. (Hutslar)

REINHARD, PETER ALBERT (1827-1899), Loudonville, Ohio, 1848-1890, Dayton, Ohio, 1890-1899. Percussion guns. (MB 4-45)

REINHARD, WILL Loudonville, Ohio, 1880-1885. (MB 4-45)

REINHARDT, GOTTLIEB Leadville, Colorado, 1882d-1890d. (Sellers-3)

REINHART, J. Maddensville, Pennsylvania. (Gluckman & Satterlee)

REINIKE & NIELSEN Middletown, California, 1893d.

REINKE & WINNEMER Belleville, Illinois, 1860d. William Reinke and Hermann Winnemer.

REINKE, WILLIAM Belleville, Illinois, 1860d. With Hermann Winnemer as Reinke & Winnemer.

REINTENBACH, WILLIAM Lancaster, Pennsylvania, 1838-1847. See William Reichenbach - same person? (KRA IV-4)

REIS, JOHN T. Mount Vernon, Indiana, 1881-1885. (Gardner)

REISMULLER, BERNHARD Milwaukee, Wisconsin, 1858. (GC1)

REISS, A. Utica, New York. Percussion target rifle.

REITER, LEONARD Berks Co., Pennsylvania, 1800. (Kauffman)

REITZEL, PETER N. Canton, Ohio, 1846-1860. Percussion 1/2 stock. (Hutslar)

RELIABLE suicide special.

RELIANCE trade name of John Meunier on shotguns and revolvers. (Hinman)

REMBERT, S.S. Memphis, Tennessee. Patents #60,264 October 29, 1867, breechloading firearm, and #74,594 February 18, 1868, breechloading firearm.

REMINGTON ARMS & AMMUNITION COMPANY, INC. Ilion, New York, 1911-1916. Successor to Remington Arms Company.

REMINGTON ARMS - UNION METALLIC CARTRIDGE CO., INC. Ilion, New York, 1916-1920. Successor to Remington Arms & Ammunition Company, Inc.

REMINGTON ARMS COMPANY Ilion, New York, 1888-1911. Pistols, rifles, and shotguns. Corporate successor to E. Remington & Sons.

REMINGTON ARMS COMPANY, INC. Ilion, New York, 1920-date. Handguns, rifles, and shotguns. Corporate offices at Madison, Nortn Carolina, 1996-date.

REMINGTON, E., & SON Ilion, New York, 1847-1856. Eliphalet Remington, II, and Philo Remington. Succeeded by E. Remington & Sons.

REMINGTON, E., & SONS Ilion, New York, 1856-1888. Remington family members Eliphalet II, Eliphalet III, Philo, and Samuel operated under this name until the company's bankruptcy in 1886. Court appointed receivers controlled the business for two more years, when the assets were purchased by Marcellus Hartley and Thomas Gray Bennett. Succeeded by Remington Arms Company, 1888-1911.

REMINGTON, ELIPHALET, II (1793-1861), Litchfield, New York, 1816-circa 1828, Ilion, New York, 1816-1861. Founder of the Remington armaments empire. By himself, 1816-1847, as E. Remington & Son, 1847-1856, and as E. Remington & Sons, 1856-1861. Succeeded by E. Remington & Sons, 1856-1888, Remington Arms Co., 1888-1911, Remington Arms & Ammunition Co., Inc., 1911-1916, Remington Arms - Union Metallic Cartridge Co., Inc., 1916-1920, and Remington Arms Company, Inc., 1920-date. (Hatch)

REMINGTON, ELIPHALET, III (1828-1924), Ilion, New York, 1845-1889. Son of Eliphalet Remington, II. (Hatch)

REMINGTON, G.R. Buffalo, New York, 1866-1872. Assignee of W.G. Oliver's patent in 1866, submitted a rifle in the 1872 trials.

REMINGTON, GEORGE H. Rome, New York, 1862-1867, Dubuque, Iowa, 1867d-1870d, San Francisco, California, 1877-1879. With William H. Soper as Soper & Remington, 1877-1879. (Shelton)

REMINGTON, PHILO (1816-1889), Ilion, New York, 1839-1886. Son of Eliphalet Remington, II, and president of E. Remington & Sons, 1861-1866 and 1882-1886. (Hatch)

REMINGTON, SAMUEL (1819-1882), Ilion, New York, 1845-1882. Patents #37,921 March 17, 1863, revolver, and #86,690 Feburary 9, 1869, breechloading firearm. Son of E. Remington, II, and president of E. Remington & Sons, 1866-1882. (Hatch)

REMLEY, GEORGE J. Lancaster, Pennsylvania, 1871d-1875d.

REMLEY, JOHN H. Lancaster, Pennsylvania, 1857d-1875d.

REMLEY, JOHN Y. Lancaster, Pennsylvania, 1836-1850. (KRA IV-4)

REMMERER, DAVID unlocated. Flintlock Kentucky.

REMPT, CHARLES Paterson, New Jersey, 1878d-1885d. With his father Frederick as F. Rempt & Son, 1885.

REMPT, F., & SON Paterson, New Jersey, 1885d. Frederick and son Charles Rempt.

REMPT, FREDERICK Paterson, New Jersey, 1885d. With his son Charles as F. Rempt & Son.

RENDYLES, BERNARD Steubenville, Ohio, 1853d. Barrelmaker. (Hutslar)

RENICK, A. & G. Independence, Missouri, 1843-1861. Percussion 1/2 stock. Abram Renick and George Renick. (GR 4-62)

RENICK, ABRAM (1814-1861), Independence, Missouri, 1843-1861. Percussion 1/2 stock. With George Renick as A. & G. Renick. (GR 4-62)

RENICK, GEORGE (1816-1880), Independence, Missouri, 1843-1861. Percussion 1/2 stock. With Abram Renick as A. & G. Renick. (GR 4-62)

RENKER, RUDOLPH Lancaster, Pennsylvania, 1857d.

RENNICK, ROBERT (1823-?), Salem, Indiana, 1850c. (Lindert)

RENWICK, EDWARD S. New York, New York, 1864-1870, Milburn, New York, 1889-1905. Perry & Goddard's "Double Header" derringers. Patents #42,793 March 17, 1864, lock (key), #102,434 April 26, 1870, breechloading firearm, #628,356 July 4, 1889, revolver, and #792,077 June 13, 1905, revolver. Patent attorney involved in many other patents. (ASAC 28)

REPASSY, JOHN Lockport, New York, 1872-1882d.

REPERT, S. unlocated. Flintlock Kentucky.

REPHART, JACOB Newbern, Iowa, 1865d.

REQUA, JOSEPHUS Rochester, New York. Patent #36,448 September 16, 1862, machine gun with William Billinghurst. A dentist, not a gunsmith. (Eich)

REQUARTH, F.A. Dayton, Ohio, 1880-1910d. Toy guns. (Hutslar)

RESOR see Roesser.

RESOR, JACOB (1784-?), Cincinnati, Ohio, 1816d-1836d. Flintlock Kentucky rifles. Son of Peter Roesser. (Hutslar)

RESOR, JACOB Frederick, Maryland, Mercersburg, Pennsylvania, 1807-1809. Son of Mathias Roesser. (Hartzler)

RESOR, JOHN Fayette Co., Pennsylvania, 1798-1803. (Whisker II)

RESTILL, T. New York, New York. Patents #63,303 March 26, 1867, cane gun, and #139,190 May 20, 1873, breechloading firearm.

RETLINE, ADAM Cedar Falls, Iowa, 1897d.

RETNER & THOMAS Baltimore, Maryland. Percussion fullstock. (Hartzler)

RETRIEVER suicide special by T.E. Ryan.

RETTBERG, JACOB (1816-?), Hagerstown, Maryland, 1878d-1880c. (Hartzler)

RETTBERG, LEWIS H. Hagerstown, Maryland, 1882d-1884d. Son of Jacob Rettberg. (Hartzler)

REUTER, ANDREW (1809-?), Baltimore, Maryland, 1845d-1850c. (Hartzler)

REUTER, PETER Louisville, Kentucky, 1860d.

REUTHE, F. New Haven, Connecticut, 1854-1860. Large variety of trap guns. Patent #17,297 May 12, 1857, trap gun.

REUTTER, G.W. Iron Mountain, Michigan, 1887d.

REUTTERMANN, H. THEODORE Denver, Colorado, 1882d. (Sellers-3)

REV-O-NOC trade name of Hibbard, Spencer, Bartlett, & Co. on .22 cal. rifles and shotguns.

REVOL, JEAN BAPTISTE New Orleans, Louisiana, 1850d-1886d. Percussion guns, cartridge revolver.

REVOL, JOSEPH L. New Orleans, Louisiana, 1867d-1887d. Son of J.B. Revol.

REVOL, LEONARD (1832-?), New Orleans, Louisiana, 1850c. Son of J.B. Revol. (GR 9-650)

REW, W.O. Marianna, Florida, 1886d.

REX suicide special.

REXER Canton, Ohio, circa 1810. (Knittle)

REXER, JULIUS A. Galveston, Texas, 1874d-1885d.

REY, ALBERT Sherman, Texas, 1878d-1885d.

REYLAND, JOHN ADAMS (1862-1895), Sonora, California, 1880-1895. For H.H. Rowell. (Shelton)

REYNAL, RICHARD Philadelphia, Pennsylvania, 1797, Baltimore, Maryland, 1801d-1821d. (Hartzler)

REYNOLDS, DUDLEY Royal Oak, Michigan, 1863d-1867d.

REYNOLDS, F.W., JR. unlocated. Percussion fullstock.

REYNOLDS, FRANCIS (1833-?), Steubenville, Ohio, 1850c. (Hutslar)

REYNOLDS, FRANCIS New York, New York, 1841d-1867d. Percussion guns.

REYNOLDS, FRANCIS Troy, New York, 1837. (Dillin)

REYNOLDS, H.L., & CO. Mobile, Alabama, 1859d. (Neville)

REYNOLDS, HENRY New Haven, Connecticut. Plant's front loading cartridge revolvers (Ellis and White patents). Patents #42,688 May 10, 1864, revolver, #45,176 November 22, 1864, extractor, and #54,600 May 8, 1866, breechloading firearm. With Amzi Plant, Ebenezer Plant, and Alfred Hotchkiss as Reynolds, Plant & Hotchkiss. (AAC 4-57)

REYNOLDS, J.W. Hawkinsville, Georgia, 1883d.

REYNOLDS, JACOB B. (1816-?), Steubenville, Ohio, 1850c-1865. Barrelmaker, and percussion fullstock rifles.

REYNOLDS, JOHN A. Elmira, New York. Patents #13,292 July 17, 1855, machine gun, #13,293 July 17, 1855, machine gun, and #13,294 July 17, 1855, cooling device. Barrelmaker.

REYNOLDS, JOSEPH S. St. Georges, Delaware, 1859d.

REYNOLDS, PLANT & HOTCHKISS New Haven, Connecticut, 1859. Plant's front loading cartridge revolvers (Ellis and White patents). Henry Reynolds, Amzi and Ebenezer Plant, and Alfred Hotchkiss. Succeeded by Plant's Mfg. Co. (AAC 4-57)

REYNOLDS, RAUT Saranac Lake, New York, 1874d-1882d. Percussion fullstock.

REYNOLDS, STEPHEN unlocated. Percussion 1/2 stock dated 1855.

REYNOLDS, T. Rich Hill, Ohio, 1868d. (Hutslar)

REYNOLDS, THOMAS (1827-?), LaPorte Co., Indiana, 1850c. (Lindert)

REYNOLDS, THOMAS Troy, New York, 1835. (Dillin)

REYNOLDS, WILLIAM (1830-?), Pocahontas Co., West Virginia, 1880c. Percussion guns. As Wm. Reynolds & Son, and Wm. Reynolds & Co. (Whisker IV)

REYNOLDS, WILLIAM Lawrence, Kansas, 1867d-1888d. Percussion fullstock.

REYNOLDS, WILLIAM H. (1866-?), Point Pleasant, West Virginia. With his father William as Wm. Reynolds & Son.

REYNOLDS, WM, & CO. Pocahontas Co., West Virginia, 1880c-?. Percussion guns. William Reynolds.

REYNOLDS, WM., & SON Point Pleasant, West Virginia, 1880c-?. Percussion guns. William and William H. Reynolds.

REZNER see Williams & Rezner.

RHEINER, THEODORE Detroit, Michigan, 1896d-1910d. Son of William Rheiner.

RHEINER, WILLIAM A. Detroit, Michigan, 1858-1895d.

RHINEHART, RUDOLPH Bearwallow, Virginia, 1780. Flintlock Kentucky rifle.

RHODES, DANIEL Washington, D.C. Patent #368,307 August 16, 1887, spring gun.

RHODES, E.B. Anderson, Texas, 1892d.

RHODES, EDWARD H. Richmond, Virginia, 1861d. With Thomas M. Smith as Smith, Rhodes & Co. (Albaugh 1)

RHODES, F.B. New York, New York. Importer of locks and guns. (Swinney)

RHODES, FRED Allegheny, Pennsylvania, 1823. (Kauffman)

RHODES, J.E. Kaskaskia, Michigan, 1891d.

RHODES, J.G. Mount Pleasant, Michigan, 1887d.

RHODES, RICHARD Hartford, Connecticut. Patents #299,264 May 27, 1884, magazine gun, #299,282 May 27, 1884, magazine gun, and #308,702 December 2, 1884, magazine gun, with Christopher Miner Spencer.

RHODES, RICHARD New Orleans, Louisiana, 1871d-1897d.

RHODES, STEPHEN Pelham, Massachusetts, 1888d.

RHODES, WILLIAM Providence, Rhode Island, 1798-1801. Model 1798 contract muskets with William Tyler. Muskets marked "SCITUATE" only, for the township in which Tyler and Rhodes were located. (Gluckman)

RHODES, WILLIAM H. Janesville, Wisconsin, 1857d.

RHODES, WILLIAM HENRY (1822-?), Santa Cruz, California, 1865-1881. (Shelton)

RHONEY, MICHAEL (1824-?), Hagerstown, Indiana, 1850c. (Lindert)

RHYNE, ISAAC Schall's, Missouri, 1893d.

RIBELIN, ISAAC (1801-?), Salisbury, North Carolina, 1850c. (Bivins)

RIBELIN, JACOB (1780-1847), Salisbury, North Carolina. Percussion fullstock, signed "J.R.". (Bivins)

RIBELIN, JESSE (1821-?), Salisbury, North Carolina, 1850c. Son of Isaac Ribelin. (Bivins)

RIBELIN, MARTIN Salisbury, North Carolina, 1762. (Bivins)

RICE, C.A. Silver Creek, New York. Percussion rifle.

RICE, C.A. Weyauwega, Wisconsin, 1879d-1895d.

RICE, DAVID HALL Brookline, Massachusetts. Patents #316,485 April 28, 1885, magazine gun, #366,794 July 19, 1887, revolver, and #385,009 June 26, 1888, revolver.

RICE, GEORGE Caldwell, Ohio. (Hutslar)

RICE, JOSEPH Philadelphia, Pennsylvania, 1824d.

RICE, NATHAN E. Washington, D.C. Patent #237,444 February 8, 1881, rocket gun.

RICE, RALSA C. (1838-1911), Warren, Ohio, 1864-1911. Percussion slug gun. Patent #374,202 December 6, 1887, sight. (Hutslar)

RICE, SAMUEL Arcadia, Ohio, 1860-1864d. (Hutslar)

RICE, SAMUEL F. Talladega, Alabama, 1862. Mississippi rifles for the Confederacy. As Wallace & Rice. (Albaugh 1)

RICE, W.H. Duncan, Michigan, 1863d.

RICE, WAYNE H. Windsor, Connecticut. Patent #38,604 May 19, 1863, breechloading firearm.

RICE, WILLIAM Prince Edward, Virginia, 1774-1777. (Gill)

RICH, ABRAHAM L. Water Cure, Pennsylvania. Patent #253,628 February 14, 1882, magazine spring gun.

RICH, HENRY Canton, New York. Percussion pistol. (Swinney)

RICH, JULE Kaufman, Texas, 1890d.

RICH, WILLIAM Saco, Maine, 1741-1743. (Demeritt)

RICHARD, A. Washington, Missouri, 1860d.

RICHARD, P.H. Jamestown, California, 1856d. (Shelton)

RICHARDS & CONOVER HARDWARE CO. Kansas City, Missouri. Dealers only. (Hinman)

RICHARDS, CHARLES B. Hartford, Connecticut. Patents #81,290 August 18, 1868, breechloading firearm, #117,461 July 25, 1871, revolver, and #119,048, September 19, 1871, revolver. Patents used by Colt for Richards Conversion revolvers, and for Richards-Mason Conversion revolvers, circa 1870. See William Mason. (Sutherland)

RICHARDS, FRANCIS H. Hartford, Connecticut. Patents #506,339 October 10, 1893, magazine gun, and #515,130 February 20, 1894, magazine gun.

RICHARDS, G. Anaconda, Montana, 1886d.

RICHARDS, HARMON Somerset, Pennsylvania, 1852t. (Kauffman)

RICHARDS, HENRY Cincinnati, Ohio, 1880c.

RICHARDS, JOHN Savannah, Georgia, 1766-1799. With Jacob Russell as Russell & Richards, 1796. (Kennedy)

RICHARDS, JOHN C. Pittsburgh, Pennsylvania. Patent #179,609 July 4, 1876, breechloading firearm.

RICHARDS, JOSEPH Deer Lodge, Montana Territory, 1880d-1884, Deadwood, Dakota Territory, 1884d. Cartridge rifles.

RICHARDS, L.B. Lynchburg, Virginia, 1825-1835. Flintlock muskets.

RICHARDS, R. New Orleans, Louisiana. Flintlock and percussion locks and guns.

RICHARDSON & CONOVER HARDWARE CO. Chicago, Illinois, 1888d-1893d.

RICHARDSON & CUTTER Lowell, Massachusetts, 1857-1878d. Percussion target rifle. O.A. Richardson and Abijah Cutter.

RICHARDSON & DEXTER Lowell, Massachusetts, 1856d. O.A. Richardson.

RICHARDSON & OVERMAN Philadelphia, Pennsylvania, 1860-1865. Gallagher carbines. George J. Richardson.

RICHARDSON, C.H. Philadelphia, Pennsylvania. Patent #191,178 May 22, 1877, revolver.

RICHARDSON, C.Y., & BRO. Charleston, South Carolina, 1867d.

RICHARDSON, D. Moore's Prairie, Illinois, 1864d.

RICHARDSON, E.G. Memphis, Missouri, 1854d.

RICHARDSON, GEORGE J. Philadelphia, Pennsylvania, 1860-1865. Gallagher carbines. Patent #43,929 August 23, 1864, breechloading firearm. As Richardson & Overman, 1860-1865.

RICHARDSON, IRA Lamond, Minnesota, 1861. Percussion rifles.

RICHARDSON, ISRAEL P. Palmyra, New York, 1828-1832, Rutland, Vermont, 1842-1855. Percussion fullstock rifles. Patent #none February 17, 1832, lock. (Horn)

RICHARDSON, JAMES FLETCHER (1829-1902), Waverly, Illinois, 1870-1902. (Johnson)

RICHARDSON, JASON E. (?-1889), Skowhegan, Maine, 1876-1879. (Demeritt)

RICHARDSON, JOEL Boston, Massachusetts, 1816-1825d. (Kauffman 2)

RICHARDSON, JOHN J. Rutland, Vermont, 1839-1843. Percussion 1/2 stock. (Horn)

RICHARDSON, JONATHAN B. Mountain View, California. Patent #307,870 April 6, 1884, reloader. (Shelton)

RICHARDSON, MARK F. Rutland, Vermont, 1886-1893. Pistols with multiple magazines surrounding the barrel. Patents #410,609 September 10, 1889, magazine gun, #440,328, November 11, 1890, magazine gun, and #496,231 April 25, 1893, magazine gun. All patents with C.A. Woodbury. (GR 11-69)

RICHARDSON, O.A. Lowell, Massachusetts, 1849d-1879d. Percussion target rifle. As Richardson & Dexter, 1856. With Abijah Cutter as Richardson & Cutter, 1857-1878.

RICHARDSON, T.F. Knoxville, Tennessee, 1860d.

RICHARDSON, W.B. Wausau, Wisconsin, 1895d.

RICHARDSON, WILLIAM Lancaster, Pennsylvania, 1839-1850. (Dyke)

RICHARDSON, WILLIAM A. (1833-1898), Worcester, Massachusetts. Patents #177,887 May 23, 1876, revolver, #360,686 April 5, 1887, revolver with Gilbert H. Harrington, #552,699 January 7, 1896, revolver, #565,692 August 11, 1896, revolver, and #600,337 March 8, 1898, safety. With Gilbert Henderson Harrington as Harrington & Richardson Arms Co., founded 1871.

RICHART, EDWIN (1833-?), St. Louis, Missouri, 1850c. (Lewis)

RICHCON trade name of Richardson & Conover Hardware Co.

RICHE, HENRY Philadelphia, Pennsylvania, 1814d.

RICHERT, L. Tacoma, Washington, 1889d.

RICHMOND ARMORY Richmond, Virginia, 1797-1865. Flintlock and percussion military guns. See Virginia Armory, and Virginia Manufactory.

RICHMOND ARMS CO. trade name of Richmond Hardware Co. on shotguns imported by H. & D. Folsom. "Wilkinson Arms Co." was also used as a trade name by Richmond Hardware Co. on these shotguns. (AR 2-69)

RICHMOND HARDWARE CO. Richmond, Virginia. Dealers only. Used "Richmond Arms Co." and "Wilkinson Arms Co." as trade names on shotguns imported for them by H. & D. Folsom. (AR 2-69)

RICHMOND, J.R. Lewisburgh, Kentucky, 1883d.

RICHMOND, ROBERT Hamden, Connecticut, 1871d-1874d.

RICHMOND, ROMULUS R. Chariton, Iowa. Patent #572,771 December 8, 1896, machine gun.

RICHMOND, SHERMAN Alexander, New York, 1858-1882d. Percussion 1/2 stock, over/under rifle/shotgun.

RICHMOND, THERON Pine Valley, New York, 1871d.

RICHNER, FREDERICK Cape Girardeau, Missouri, 1850c. Probably A.F. Rickmers?

RICHTER, CHARLES New York, New York. Shotgun by Crescent Fire Arms Co. for New York Sporting Goods Co. (AR 2-69)

RICHTER, CHRISTIAN Lowville, New York, 1870d-1874d.

RICHTER, ROBERT Weimar, Texas, 1884d.

RICHWINE, C. Reading, Pennsylvania. Flintlock Kentucky rifles and barrels. See Cornelius Reichwein.

RICKARD ARMS CO. Schenectady, New York, 1890-1910. Shotguns and rifles (made by Crescent). J.A. Rickard. (AR 2-69)

RICKARD, J.A. Schenectady, New York, 1890-1910. Shotguns and rifles (made by Crescent). As Rickard Arms Co. (AR 2-69)

RICKETS, GEORGE W. Mansfield, Ohio, 1867d-1883d. With John Rickets in 1867. (Hutslar)

RICKETS, JOHN (1815-?), Mansfield, Ohio, 1850c-circa 1890. Percussion 1/2 stock. (Hutslar)

RICKETS, W.H. Village Creek, Alabama. Percussion fullstock.

RICKMERS, A.F. Cape Girardeau, Missouri, 1850-1860d, Kansas City, Missouri, 1888d-1894d. Also known as Frederick Richner?

RICKMERS, EDWARD H. New Melle, Missouri, 1879d-1898d.

RICKS, THOMAS Boston, Massachusetts, 1677-1681. (Kauffman 2)

RIDDELL Lancaster, Pennsylvania, 1770. Flintlock Kentucky rifles. (Dillin)

RIDDICK see David Reddick.

RIDDLEBERGER, MADISON Edinburg, Virginia. (Dean)

RIDENHOUER, RICHARD (1827-?), Springfield, Ohio, 1850c. (Hutslar)

RIDENOUR, DAVID LaCrosse, Wisconsin, 1891d-1895d.

RIDENOUR, JOHN Greenfield Mills, Indiana, 1882-1885. (Gardner)

RIDENOUR, PHILEMON (1826-?), Johnstown, Ohio, 1850c, Neward (Newark?), Ohio, 1853-1887d. Percussion fullstock. (Hutslar)

RIDEOUT, J. unlocated. Flintlock musket.

RIDEOUT, JAMES BUCHANAN (1857-1949), Long Lick, Ohio, 1881-1949. Flintlock and percussion guns. (Hutslar)

RIDER, CHARLES Newark, Ohio. Patent #400,712 April 2, 1889, breechloading firearm.

RIDER, E.C. Ridersville, West Virginia, 1884d.

RIDER, JOSEPH (1817-1901), Newark, Ohio. Patents #21,215 August 17, 1858, revolver, #23,861 May 3, 1859, revolver, #25,470 September 13, 1859, breechloading firearm, #40,887 December 8, 1863, breechloading firearm, #45,123 November 15, 1864, breechloading firearm, #45,797 January 3, 1865, breechloading firearm, #46,532 February 21, 1865, breechloading firearm, #51,269 November 28, 1865, revolver, #53,543 March 27, 1866, breechloading firearm, #74,427 February 11, 1868, barrel band, #74,428 February 11, 1868, breechloading gun, #118,152 August 15, 1871, magazine gun, #141,383 July 29, 1873, breechloading firearm, #141,384 July 29, 1893, breechloading firearm, #141,590 August 5, 1873, magazine gun, #215,507 May 20, 1879, revolver with Roswell Cook, #500,949 July 4, 1893, breechloading firearm, #571,362 December 26, 1893, breechloading firearm, and #532,096 January 8, 1895, ejector. All guns made by E. Remington & Sons.

RIDER, NATHANIEL Southbridge, Massachusetts, 1840-1858. Underhammer percussion rifles and pistols. As Nathaniel Rider & Co. Guns made by Quinnebaug Rifle Co., Southbridge, Massachusetts, circa 1850? (Carey)

RIDER, NATHANIEL, & CO. Southbridge, Massachusetts, 1840-1858. Underhammer percussion rifles and pistols. Guns made by Quinnebaug Rifle Co., Southbridge, Massachusetts, circa 1850? (Carey)

RIDGE, T.J. Mont Eagle, Tennessee, 1887d-1891d.

RIDGELY, HENRY Maryland. Committee of Safety muskets. (Hartzler)

RIDGEWAY, ZACK Calloway Co., Missouri, 1850c. (MB 11-66)

RIDGWAY, H.C. Trenton, Missouri, 1879d.

RIDINGER, J.W. New Richmond, Wisconsin, 1895d.

RIDLEY, C.E. Mapleton, Iowa, 1892d, Early, Iowa, 1895d.

RIEDEL, JULIUS Pleasant Hill, Kentucky. Patent #15,707 September 9, 1856, cartridge.

RIEGER, THEODORE Chicago, Illinois, 1888d.

RIEHL, JOSEPH (1844-?), Marysville, California, 1860-1861. Apprentice to P. George. (Shelton)

RIEHM, CHARLES Sacramento, California, 1870-1871. (Shelton)

RIESS, C.V. Shepherd, Michigan, 1899d.

RIFE, CHARLES Cadiz, Ohio, 1800-1812. (Knittle)

RIFE, CHARLES Cincinnati, Ohio, 1856d. Percussion 1/2 stock. (Hutslar)

RIFE, WILLIAM (1830-?), Circleville, Ohio, 1850c. Percussion 1/2 stock. (Hutslar)

RIFLEN, W.G. Reedfield, Wisconsin, 1857d.

RIGDEN, HENRY J. (1795-?), Georgetown, D.C., 1817, Brownsville, Pennsylvania, 1818-1850. (Whisker II)

RIGDON, ANSLEY & CO. Augusta, Georgia, 1864-1865. Copies of Colt 1851 percussion revolvers. Successor to Leech & Rigdon. Charles H. Rigdon and Jesse A. Ansley. (Albaugh 3)

RIGDON, CHARLES H. St. Louis, Missouri, 1848-1859, Memphis, Tennessee, 1861-1862, Greensboro, Georgia, 1863-1865. With Thomas S. Leech as Leech & Rigdon, 1861-1865. With Jesse A. Ansley as Rigdon, Ansley & Co., 1864-1865. (Albaugh 3)

RIGG, WILLIAM Kanawha Falls, West Virginia, 1816-?. Flintlock Kentucky. (MB 5-68)

RIGGAL, JOSEPH Newport, Kentucky, 1882d-1890d.

RIGGIN, JOHN St. Louis, Missouri, 1835.

RIGGINS, A.J. Cassville, Missouri, 1860d.

RIGGINS, THOMAS (1821-?), Knoxville, Tennessee, 1844-1863, McMinn Co., Texas, 1865-?. (Albaugh 1)

RIGGLEMAN, J. New Hamburg, Pennsylvania, 1870d.

RIGGS, B. Bellows Falls, Vermont, 1850.

RIGGS, BREESE Crowley, Oregon. Patent #497,607 May 16, 1893, animal gun.

RIGGS, JOSEPH, JR. Derby, Connecticut, 1776-1778. Committee of Safety repairs. (Gluckman & Satterlee)

RIGGS, R.A. Hiawatha, Kansas, 1894d.

RIGHTER, J. Cadiz, Ohio, 1800-1812. (Knittle)

RIGHTER, J.R. unlocated. Percussion 1/2 stock.

RIGHTER, JOHN G. (1816-?), Cadiz, Ohio, 1850c-1896d. Percussion 1/2 stock. Son of J. Righter. (Hutslar)

RIGHTS, N.N. unlocated. Percussion 1/2 stock.

RIKER, C.L. New York, New York, 1873-1880. Dealer only.

RILEY, EDWARD E. Philadelphia, Pennsylvania, 1814-1816d, Cincinnati, Ohio, 1819-1824. (Hutslar)

RILEY, FIELDING J. Macon, Missouri, 1850c-1891d.

RILEY, GEORGE unlocated. Percussion fullstock rifle.

RILEY, HUGH Rochester, New York, 1844d.

RILEY, JOHN New York, Iowa, 1865d.

RILEY, JOHN F. Randolph Co., Missouri, 1850c. (MB 11-66)

RILEY, JOHN W. Baltimore, Maryland, 1873-1878d.

RILEY, P. Menoham, New Jersey, 1866d.

RILEY, W.J. Portland, Oregon, 1886d-1889d.

RILEY, WILLIAM Colusa, California, 1850-1880. (Shelton)

RILEY, WILLIAM K. Ellsworth, Indiana, 1881-1885. (Gardner)

RILEY, WILLIAM L. (1819-?), Watertown, Ohio, 1850c-1853d. (Hutslar)

RILING, JOHN Altoona, Pennsylvania. Percussion fullstock target.

RILING, JOHN, JR. Eldorado, Pennsylvania, 1882d-1890d.

RINEER, MICHAEL Lancaster, Pennsylvania. Flintlock Kentucky rifle. See Michael Reiner.

RINEHART, J.W. Lexington, Missouri, 1889d.

RINEHART, JAMES Hampshire Co., Virginia, 1835-1840. (Bowers)

RINEHART, JAMES C. (1811-?), Ross Co., Ohio, 1850c. (Hutslar)

RINEHART, JESSE Bates Co., Missouri, 1850c. Percussion fullstock. (MB 11-66)

RINEHART, JOHN W. Hampshire Co., West Virginia, 1848-1853. Son of James Rinehart. (Whisker IV)

RINER, J. Lancaster, Pennsylvania. Percussion 1/2 stock.

RINER, MICHAEL see Michael Reineer.

RING, JAMES M. Morristown, New Jersey, 1866d.

RING, SETH C. (?-1806), Salem, Massachusetts.

RINGE, F. Philadelphia, Pennsylvania. Derringer.

RINGE, FREDERICK St. Charles, Missouri, 1860d-1879d. Same as F. Ringe, Philadelphia, Pennsylvania?

RINGE, HENRY St. Charles, Missouri, 1889d-1898d. Son of Frederick Ringe.

RINGE, J.H. Vandalia, Illinois, 1867d-1893d.

RINGE, J.H. Whalen, Minnesota, 1898d.

RINGE, LOUIS St. Charles, Missouri, 1879d-1893d. Son of Frederick Ringe.

RINGLE, A. unlocated. Flintlock Kentucky.

RINGLE, M. Bellefonte, Pennsylvania. Percussion fullstock.

RINGLE, MATHIAS Blairsville, Pennsylvania, 1835-1872. (Kauffman)

RINGLE, MATHIAS Farmington, Illinois, 1868d.

RINGLER, GEORGE Racine, Wisconsin, 1872d, Milwaukee, Wisconsin, 1875d.

RINK, EPHRAIM (1817-?), Catawba Co., North Carolina, 1850c. (Bivins)

RINKER Allentown, Pennsylvania, 1750c. Flintlock fowling piece.

RINKLAUB see Rinklaub & Rauert.

RINKLAUB & RAUERT Portland, Oregon, 1889d-1891d.

RINNA, HENRY Edwardsville, Illinois, 1860d.

RIOS, MICHAEL A. Brownsville, Texas, 1881d-1891d.

RIP RAP suicide special by Bacon.

RIPLEY BROS. Windsor, Vermont, 1835-1840. (Horn)

RIPLEY, CHARLES H. Nashville, Tennessee, 1887d.

RIPLEY, E.K. (1846-1918), Seattle, Washington, 1880-1918.

RIPLEY, EZRA Troy, New York. Patent #33,544 October 22, 1861, machine gun.

RIPLEY, J.F. Shinnston, West Virginia, 1900d. (Whisker IV)

RIPLEY, JACOB see Jacob Raible.

RIPLEY, JOHN B. Claremont, New Hampshire. Percussion rifles. Patent #1,084 February 20, 1839, magazine gun with Lebbeus Bailey and William Smith. (Demeritt)

RIPPY, HUGH Pittsburgh, Pennsylvania, 1789. (Kauffman)

RISE, WILLIAM H. Duncan, Michigan, 1865d.

RISHER, DANIEL (1810-?), Canton, Ohio, 1850c-1875d. Percussion bench gun. (Hutslar)

RISLEY, HIRAM (1804-1862), Sauquoit, New York, 1830-1840, Oriskany Falls, New York, 1840-1862. Flintlock fullstock rifle. (Swinney)

RISLEY, WILLIAM H. Berlin, Connecticut. Patent #53,490 March 27, 1866, cartridge.

RISON, MARCELLUS H. Paris, Tennessee, 1871d-1876d.

RITCHIE, HENRY Philadelphia, Pennsylvania, 1810d.

RITCHIE, J.S. Council Bluffs, Iowa, 1867d.

RITT, JULIUS St. Peter, Minnesota, 1898d.

RITTENHOUSE, BENJAMIN Philadelphia, Pennsylvania, 1776-1779. Committee of Safety muskets at State Gun Factory. Rittenhouse was not a gunsmith, but was famous for other manufacturing (clocks, chemistry, etc.). Brother of David Rittenhouse, the astronomer. (Hobbies 4-38)

RITTER, CONRAD Findley, Ohio, 1894d. (Hutslar)

RITTER, FERDINAND Virginia City, Nevada, 1878d-1880d.

RITTER, FERDINAND, JR. Virginia City, Nevada, 1884d.

RITTER, JACOB Philadelphia, Pennsylvania, 1775-1783. (Gluckman & Satterlee)

RITTER, PETER (1794-1876), St. Mary's, Pennsylvania, 1850c-1876.

RITZEL, P.M. see P.M. Reitzel.

RITZMANN, CHARLES L. New York, New York, 1879d-1884d. Importer, double-barrel shotguns.

RIVAL trade name of Van Camp Hardware Co. on shotguns made by N.R. Davis. (Hinman)

RIVERSIDE ARMS CO. trade name of Stevens on rifles and shotguns. (Hinman)

RIXON San Francisco, California. Percussion 1/2 stock.

RIZER, GEORGE Cumberland, Maryland, 1793-1813. Son of Martin Rizer I. (Hartzler)

RIZER, JACOB (1795-1859), Cumberland, Maryland and Bardstown, Kentucky, 1805-1859. Father of Mathias Rizer. (Hartzler)

RIZER, MARTIN L. (1788-?), Cumberland, Maryland. Flintlock Kentucky. Son of Martin Rizer II. (Hartzler)

RIZER, MARTIN, I (?-1796), Martinsburg, Virginia, 1782-1793, Cumberland, Maryland, 1793-1796. Probably not a gunsmith. (Hartzler)

RIZER, MARTIN, II (?-1815), Cumberland, Maryland, 1793-1815. Flintlock Kentucky. Son of Martin Rizer I. (Hartzler)

RIZER, MATHIAS Cumberland, Maryland, 1800-?. Apprenticed to George Rizer, 1800. Son of Jacob Rizer.

RIZER, WILLIAM L. (1818-?), Allegany Co., Maryland, 1850c.

ROACH, PETER Dalles, Oregon, 1873d-1878d, Spokane, Washington, 1886d-1891d.

ROACH, REUBEN (1816-?), Wyoming Co., West Virginia, 1860c. (Whisker IV)

ROACH, SOL Windber, Pennsylvania. (Van Rensselaer)

ROACH, THOMAS Williamsburg, Ohio, 1856-1860, Batesville, Ohio, 1860d-1864d. (Hutslar)

ROB ROY suicide special.

ROBBINS Scott Co., Tennessee. Tennessee flintlock (Dillin)

ROBBINS & LAWRENCE Windsor, Vermont, 1846-1857. Jennings rifles, Sharps rifles, Leonard pepperboxes, and Model 1841 contract rifles. Samuel E. Robbins and Richard S. Lawrence. Successor to Robbins, Kendall & Lawrence. (Sellers-4, Carey)

ROBBINS, C. New York, New York. Cartridge shotgun. (Swinney)

ROBBINS, C. Tioga, New York. Percussion fullstock rifle, 1826, martial pistol.

ROBBINS, CHARLES F. Brooklyn, New York. Percussion fullstock. Patents #190,782 May 15, 1877, sight, and #190,782 May 15, 1877, sight.

ROBBINS, IRA Hughsville, Pennsylvania. Patent #189,387 April 10, 1877, lock.

ROBBINS, KENDALL & LAWRENCE Windsor, Vermont, 1844-1846. Percussion pepperboxes. Samuel E. Robbins, Nicanor Kendall, and Richard S. Lawrence. Succeeded by Robbins & Lawrence, 1847. (Carey)

ROBBINS, SAMUEL E. Windsor, Vermont, 1844-1856. Not a gunsmith, but was the financial backer of Robbins, Kendall & Lawrence, and Robbins & Lawrence. (Sellers-4)

ROBBINS, WILLIAM E. Cherry Flats, Pennsylvania, 1847-1861, Elk Run, Pennsylvania, 1861d, Manesburg, Pennsylvania. Percussion rifles.

ROBELLAZ, JOHN L. New Albany, Indiana, 1881-1885. (Gardner)

ROBELLOY, LOUIS New Albany, Indiana, 1863-1867d.

ROBERS, J.W. Bramlette, Kentucky, 1879d.

ROBERSON & CO. Ames, Iowa, 1887d-1897d. George Roberson.

ROBERSON, GEORGE Ames, Iowa, 1887d-1897d. As Roberson & Co., 1889.

ROBERT, J.W. Prescott, Arizona, 1884d.

ROBERTI, AUGUST Topeka, Kansas, 1884d.

ROBERTS BREECH-LOADING ARMS CO. New York, New York, 1866-1870. Sales organization for Benjamin Stone Roberts converted muzzle loaders.

ROBERTS, A.T. Winfield, Kansas, 1884d.

ROBERTS, ALVIN Biddick, Iowa, 1895d-1897d.

ROBERTS, ARTHUR (1848-?), Denver, Colorado, 1870c. (Sellers-3)

ROBERTS, BENJAMIN STONE (1810-1875), U.S. Army. Patents #36,531 September 23, 1862, breechloading firearm, #37,979 March 24, 1863, cannon projectile, #52,887 February 27, 1866, breechloading firearm, #65,607 June 11, 1867, breechloading firearm, #87,297 February 23, 1869, cartridge, and #90,024 May 11, 1869, breechloading firearm. Conversions of Civil War rifle muskets under the 1866 patent were made by Providence Tool Co.

ROBERTS, C. unlocated. Mule ear 1/2 stock.

ROBERTS, GEORGE Fowlersville, New York, 1850d-1870d.

ROBERTS, HART Oramel, New York, 1870d.

ROBERTS, HENRY Cincinnatus, New York, 1870d.

ROBERTS, HENRY C. Rochester, New York, 1859-1860, Marysville, California, 1860-1864, Virginia City, Nevada, 1864-1865. With Christian Frederick Scholl as Scholl & Roberts, Virginia City, 1862-1864d. (Shelton, Eich)

ROBERTS, HILERY (1798-1874), Scott Co., Kentucky. (Hist. KY, V3, P688)

ROBERTS, L.D. McLean, Illinois, 1860d.

ROBERTS, MADISON Martinsburg, Indiana, 1860d-1862d.

ROBERTS, PETER Lancaster, Pennsylvania, 1871-1876.

ROBERTS, ROBERT Utica, New York. Patent #45,638 December 27, 1864, magazine gun. Percussion over/under rifle/shotgun with A. Clark.

ROBERTS, THOMAS Portsmouth, Virginia, 1871-1873d.

ROBERTS, WILLIAM A. Rochester, New York, 1849d, North Danville, New York, 1849-1859. Percussion four-barrel swivel breech. (Roberts, Eich)

ROBERTS, WILLIAM S. New York, New York, 1861. Model 1861 contract muskets. With John B. Sarson as Sarson & Roberts.

ROBERTSON, GUSTAVE ADOLPH (1835-?), San Francisco, California, 1872-1904. (Shelton)

ROBERTSON, J.W. Newton, Georgia, 1881d.

ROBERTSON, JAMES K. Morrison, Illinois, 1875d-1884d.

ROBERTSON, JOHN Lancaster, Pennsylvania, 1850. (KRA IV-4)

ROBERTSON, N.S. Mt. Clemens, Michigan, 1860d.

ROBERTSON, ROBERT York Co., Virginia, 1763. (Gill)

ROBERTSON, THOMAS Orderville, Utah, 1884d.

ROBERTSON, WILLIAM Philadelphia, Pennsylvania, 1814d-1860d. Percussion duellers, percussion 1/2 stock. Son of William O. Robertson. (Bugle 35)

ROBERTSON, WILLIAM A. (1805-?), Aurora, Illinois, 1860c-1864d.

ROBERTSON, WILLIAM F. Mt. Clemens, Michigan, 1865d-1870d.

ROBERTSON, WILLIAM H. Hartford, Connecticut, 1848d-1856d, New London, Connecticut, 1856d-1875. Patents #14,253 February 12, 1856, breechloading firearm, and #53,187 March 13, 1866, breechloading firearm, both with his nephew George W. Simpson. Submitted rifle on the latter patent to the 1872 trials. (Sellers-4)

ROBERTSON, WILLIAM O. (1846-?), Little Rock, Arkansas, 1870. Percussion 1/2 stock. (Elias)

ROBERTSON, WILLIAM O. Philadelphia, Pennsylvania, 1790-1829. Flintlock Kentucky rifles and duelling pistols, percussion rifles and pistols.

ROBESON, L.H. Jamestown, North Carolina. Percussion fullstock. (Bivins)

ROBIE, HENRY Winooskie, Wisconsin, 1857d.

ROBIE, I.S. Bristol, New Hampshire, 1872d.

ROBIN HOOD suicide special by Hood Fire Arms Co.

ROBINSON & KRIDER Philadelphia, Pennsylvania, 1840d. Percussion duelling pistols and derringers. William Robinson and John H. Krider.

ROBINSON & PALMATER Sandusky, Ohio, 1854-1856. Isaac H. Robinson and Peter Palmater. (Hutslar)

ROBINSON ARMS MANUFACTORY Richmond, Virginia, 1860-1863, Tallassee, Alabama, 1864. See Samuel C. Robinson.

ROBINSON, BERT Flint, Michigan, 1895d-1899d.

ROBINSON, CHARLES Cambridgeport, Massachusetts. Patent #182,330 September 19, 1876, arrow gun.

ROBINSON, E. Skowhegan, Maine, 1898. (Demeritt)

ROBINSON, E.A. Schell City, Missouri, 1893d-1898d.

ROBINSON, EDWARD New York, New York. Model 1861 contract muskets. (Fuller)

ROBINSON, F. Trinidad, Colorado, 1895d. (Sellers-3)

ROBINSON, G.H. Deadwood, Dakota Territory, 1884d.

ROBINSON, GREENLIEF Bridgton, Maine, 1885. (Demeritt)

ROBINSON, H. unlocated. Percussion 1/2 stock.

ROBINSON, ISAAC H. Sandusky, Ohio, 1850c-1868d. Percussion 1/2 stock. With Peter Palmater as Robinson & Palmater, 1854-1856. (Hutslar)

ROBINSON, JOHN (1808-1852), Lancaster, Pennsylvania. See John Robertson. (Whisker IV)

ROBINSON, JOHN Spring City, Utah, 1871d.

ROBINSON, JOHN St. Louis, Missouri, 1845d. Percussion shotgun.

ROBINSON, JOSEPH Frederick Co., Virginia, 1765. (Gill)

ROBINSON, JOSEPH Shreve, Ohio, 1863-1865. (Gardner)

ROBINSON, L. Watertown, New York, 1850d. Percussion rifles.

ROBINSON, L.M. Knobsville, Pennsylvania, 1887d-1891d.

ROBINSON, L.W. Syracuse, New York, 1850-1853. Percussion 1/2 stock. With James H. Rector as Rector & Robinson.

ROBINSON, LUTHER Chittenango, New York, 1848-1858d. Percussion 1/2 stock.

ROBINSON, MARCUS W. New York, New York, 1860d-1888d. Sales agent for Smith & Wesson. (Jinks)

ROBINSON, ORVILLE M. Upper Jay and Plattsburg, New York. Patents #103,504 May 24, 1870, magazine gun, #125,988 April 23, 1872, magazine gun, and #163,810 May 25, 1875, magazine gun. Guns made by Adirondack Arms Co.

ROBINSON, S. Cato, Wisconsin, 1878d.

ROBINSON, S. Saint Johnsville, New York, 1882d.

ROBINSON, S.D. Franklin, Wisconsin, 1857d.

ROBINSON, SAMUEL C. Richmond, Virginia, 1860-1863, Tallassee, Alabama, 1864. Copies of the Sharps carbine for the Confederacy, and muzzleloader carbines (after 1863 government control). As Robinson Arms Manufactory, 1860-1864. The Confederate government took control of the factory in 1863, and moved it to Tallassee, Alabama, 1864. (Albaugh 1, Carey)

ROBINSON, W., & SON Philadelphia, Pennsylvania, 1845d. William Robinson.

ROBINSON, W.C. Mount Clemens, Michigan, 1851-1871. (Gardner)

ROBINSON, WILLIAM Jay, New York, 1879-1882.

ROBINSON, WILLIAM Philadelphia, Pennsylvania, 1837d-1846d. Derringers and percussion target rifles. With John H. Krider as Robinson & Krider, 1826-1834. As W. Robinson & Son, 1845d. (Bugle 35)

ROBINSON, WILLIAM A. Aurora, Illinois, 1860d.

ROBISON, JOSEPH Shreve, Ohio, 1864d. (Hutslar)

ROBISON, W. Charleston, West Virginia, 1900d. (Whisker IV)

ROBITAILLE, CHARLES Brooklyn, New York. Patents #21,054 July 27, 1858, revolver (manufactured as the Pettengill) with E.A. Raymond, and #43,709 August 2, 1864, revolver with Florian Davis. (Sellers-1)

ROBSON, JAMES O. Buffalo, New York, 1850-1880d. With John H. Rector as Rector & Robson, 1850-1853.

ROCHAT, EMILE A. Hollister, California. Patent #274,279 March 20, 1883, trap gun with E.A. Crespin.

ROCHE, THEODORE Deadwood, South Dakota, 1882d-1884d, Sturgis, South Dakota, 1886d.

ROCHET, FRANCIS (1837-?), San Jose, California, 1874, Hollister, California, 1877-1881. (Shelton)

ROCK ISLAND ARSENAL Rock Island, Illinois, 1843-?. Model 1903 rifles. (Crossman)

ROCKETER, J.H. Syracuse, New York, 1845d-1856d. Probably J.H. Rector.

ROCKWOOD, AARON LELAND (1831-?), Hollister, California, 1876-1877. (Shelton)

RODA, ADOLPH Rochester, New York. Patent #200,667 February 26, 1878, sight.

RODDEN, J.L. Bowen, Arkansas, 1892d.

RODE, CHRISTIAN GOTTLEIB (1837-?), Oakland, California, 1868-1882. With August Kaese as Kaese & Rode, 1870-1880. (Shelton)

RODE, OTTO FREDERICK Oakland, California, 1892. (Shelton)

RODES, JOHN Schaefferstown, Pennsylvania, 1861d.

RODGERS ARMS CO. Norwich, Connecticut. Trade name used by Crescent Fire Arms Co. (GR 7-74)

RODGERS, HENRY Lamont, Michigan, 1899d.

RODGERS, J.A. Waverly, Illinois, 1880d-1893d.

RODGERS, J.W. Lyons, Michigan, 1860d. Same as William Rudgers, Lyons, Michigan, 1879d?

RODIER, LOUIS C. Springfield, Massachusetts. Patents #34,776 March 25, 1862, magazine gun, #41,864 March 8, 1864, lock (key), #48,775 July 11, 1865, revolver, #138,439 April 29, 1873, magazine gun with F.G. Bates, and #154,960 September 15, 1874, breech-loading firearm. The last patent was produced as a "4th of July" pistol.

ROEBER, HENRY St. Louis, Missouri, 1880-1890d. (Pourie)

ROEDLER, MAXIMILIAN Harrisburg, Pennsylvania, 1868-1870d.

ROEMER, J.F. Manitowoc, Wisconsin, 1895d.

ROEMER, O. E. unlocated. Percussion 1/2 stock.

ROESCHEN, C.A. unlocated. Percussion 1/2 stock.

ROESEN, JOHN Jefferson City, Missouri, 1879d.

ROESEN, WILLIAM Jefferson City, Missouri, 1879d-1891d.

ROESSER, MATHIAS (1708-1771), Lancaster, Pennsylvania, 1740-1771. (Kauffman)

ROESSER, PETER (?-1823), Lancaster, Pennsylvania, 1741-1785, Hagerstown, Maryland, 1785-1794, Mercersburg, Pennsylvania, 1796-1812t. Flintlock Kentucky. Son of Mathias. (Kauffman)

ROESSLER, C. Charleston, South Carolina, 1867-1886d. As C. Roessler & Son, 1886.

ROESSLER, C., & SON Charleston, South Carolina, 1886. C. Roessler.

ROESSLER, FREDERICK Charleston, South Carolina, 1855. (Dean)

ROESSLER, JOHN Beaufort, South Carolina, 1885d-1886d.

ROGERS & ABBEY Augusta, Georgia, 1842-1847. Elisha H. Rogers and Robert Abbey. (Kennedy)

ROGERS & BOWEN Augusta, Georgia, 1848-1861. Elisha H. Rogers and William Bowen. (Kennedy)

ROGERS & CONE Savannah, Georgia, 1839-1842. Elisha H. Rogers. (Kennedy)

ROGERS & FOWLER Dayton, Ohio, 1856d. Locks. (Hutslar)

ROGERS & HART Utica, New York, circa 1830. Pill lock pistols under Hart's patent. Riley Rogers and William Aaron Hart. (Winant)

ROGERS & HEARST Utica, New York, 1850-1860. This is probably the firm of Rogers & Hart, but they were much earlier. (Gardner)

ROGERS & JONES Savannah, Georgia, 1846-1847. C.W. Rogers and John T. Jones.

ROGERS & SPENCER Utica, New York, 1861-1865, Willow Vale, New York, 1863-1864. Improved Freeman percussion revolvers and Pettengill revolvers. (Sellers-1)

ROGERS BROS. Philadelphia, Pennsylvania, 1809-1846, Valley Forge, Pennsylvania, 1814-1830. Flintlock Kentucky rifles, flintlock pistols, Model 1816 contract muskets. John and Charles Rogers. (Gluckman, Carey)

ROGERS, AMOS Utica, New York. Son of Riley Rogers and partner of Julius Spencer. (Sellers-1)

ROGERS, C.W. Savannah, Georgia, 1846-1847. With John T. Jones as Rogers & Jones. (Kennedy)

ROGERS, CHARLES Philadelphia, Pennsylvania, 1809-1846. With his brother John as Rogers Bros. (Gluckman, Carey)

ROGERS, CHARLES H. Augusta, Georgia, 1879d. Son of Elisha H. Rogers.

ROGERS, ELISHA Utica, New York, 1832d. Son of Riley Rogers. (Kauffman 2)

ROGERS, ELISHA H. (1813-1891), Savannah, Georgia, 1839-1842, Augusta, Georgia, 1842-1891. As Rogers & Cone, 1839-1842. With Robert Abbey as Rogers & Abbey, 1842-1847. With William D. Bowen as Rogers & Bowen, 1848-1861. High quality percussion rifles and pistols. (Kennedy)

ROGERS, FRANK Lamont, Michigan, 1887d. Son of Henry D. Rogers.

ROGERS, GEORGE W. Competition, Missouri, 1879d.

ROGERS, HENRY (1831-?), Mishwaka, Indiana, 1850c. (Lindert)

ROGERS, HENRY Middletown, Ohio. Patent #none May 7, 1829, revolver. (Sellers-1)

ROGERS, HENRY D. Lamont, Michigan, 1863d-1867d. Percussion over/under rifle/shotgun.

ROGERS, HENRY S. Willow Lake, New York. Patent #36,861 November 4, 1862, revolver. Guns made by Rogers & Spencer. (Sellers-1)

ROGERS, J. Columbiana Co., Ohio, circa 1870. Percussion 1/2 stock. (Hutslar)

ROGERS, J. Highland, Illinois, 1875. (Johnson)

ROGERS, J. Utica, New York, 1830-1835. Percussion 1/2 stock. (Swinney)

ROGERS, JOHN Elkhart, Indiana, 1870d-1892d. Percussion 1/2 stock. (MB 4-54)

ROGERS, JOHN Philadelphia, Pennsylvania, 1805-1846, Valley Forge, Pennsylvania, 1814-1830. Model 1816 contract muskets with Brooke Evans. Model 1821 contract muskets alone. With his brother Charles, acquired Valley Forge Iron Works for firearms production, 1814. With Charles as Rogers Bros., 1809-1846. (Gluckman, Carey)

ROGERS, JONATHAN (1781-?), Greenfield, Ohio, 1850c. (Hutslar)

ROGERS, L. Xenia, Ohio, 1852-1879. Lockmaker and gunmaker.

ROGERS, L.H. Hudson, Michigan, 1879d.

ROGERS, LEWIS Raleigh, North Carolina, 1835-?. Percussion fullstock. (Bivins)

ROGERS, MARTIN Jacksonville, Wisconsin, 1857d-1870d.

ROGERS, RILEY Utica, New York, 1818-1860. Flintlock, pill lock, and percussion pistols and rifles. With William Aaron Hart as Rogers & Hart, circa 1830. Father of Elisha Rogers. (Winant)

ROGERS, RUSSELL Rensselaerville, New York, 1870d.

ROGERS, SAMUEL Coopersville, Michigan, 1863d.

ROGERS, SLOCUMB & CO. New Orleans, Louisiana, 1822-1885. Percussion fullstock, locks. Importer and dealer. Samuel B. Slocumb. Several other associated firms, see Samuel B. Slocumb.

ROGERS, W.D. New Lewisville, Arkansas, 1892d.

ROGERS, WILLIAM Philadelphia, Pennsylvania, 1829d.

ROGERS, WILLIAM G. Lawrence, Massachusetts, 1853d-1858d. Percussion 1/2 stock.

ROHNER, JOHN Miles City, Montana, 1881d.

ROHR, FERDINAN (1846-?), Staunton, Virginia. Apprenticed to Henry Hyer, 1860.

ROHR, JOHN FREDERICK Philadelphia, Pennsylvania, ?-1772. (Kauffman)

ROHRER, LEOPOLD (1851-1939), Chicago, Illinois, 1871-1873, Lancaster, Pennsylvania, 1873d, New Castle, Pennsylvania, 1873-1939. Percussion rifles. (MB 6-46)

ROLAND, HENRY Hazelton, Pennsylvania, 1882d-1890d.

ROLAND, THOMAS H. (1813-?), Brownsville, Pennsylvania, 1849-1854, Newcastle, Pennsylvania, 1854-1858, Pittsburgh, Pennsylvania, 1862-1867.

ROLFE, ANNANIES (1831-?), Seneca Co., Ohio, 1850c. (Hutslar)

ROLL, EDWARD Cincinnati, Ohio, 1880c. (Hutslar)

ROLL, F.M. Sault Ste. Marie, Michigan, 1891d-1895d.

ROLL, FRANCIS X. Liberty, Missouri, 1822-1865. (Hobbies 6-31)

ROLL, FRANCIS X. Liberty, Missouri, 1893d-1898d.

ROLLER & SPRECHER Lancaster, Pennsylvania, 1850. (KRA IV-4)

ROLLIN, DANIEL G. New York, New York. Patent #20,129 April 27, 1858, primer.

ROLLINS, JOHN B. San Francisco, California, 1876d. (Shelton)

ROLLINS, M.L. Providence, Rhode Island, 1868d.

ROLSTON, JAMES Kansas City, Missouri, 1889d.

ROMANS, JOSEPH H. Mount Vernon, Ohio. Patents #106,083 August 2, 1870, breechloading firearm with Thomas Simpson and G.B. Gray, and #112,803 March 21, 1871, breechloading firearm with G.B. Gray.

ROME REVOLVER & NOVELTY WORKS Rome, New York, circa 1870-187?. Suicide specials.

ROMINE, FRANCIS Clark Center, Illinois, 1860d.

ROMINES, WILLIAM F. (1831-?), Marshall, Illinois, 1853-1860. (Johnson)

RONE, JULIUS Milwaukee, Wisconsin, 1854-1855. (WGCA 6)

RONEY, M. (1824-?), Miamisburg, Ohio, 1850c. Percussion fullstock and 1/2 stock. (Hutslar)

ROOD, ALONZO H. New Haven, Connecticut, 1860.

ROOD, MORGAN L. (1816-1881), Marshall, Michigan, 1851-1859, Denver, Colorado, 1859-1881. Patent #10,259 November 22, 1853, revolver. Percussion guns of all varieties. (Sellers-3)

ROONEY, J.H. Chicago, Illinois, 1890d.

ROOP, I. unlocated. Flintlock Kentucky.

ROOP, J. Bellefonte, Pennsylvania, 1800-1840. Percussion fullstock. (Dillin)

ROOP, JACOB Dauphin Co., Pennsylvania, 1819. Percussion fullstock. (Hutslar)

ROOP, JOHN Allentown, Pennsylvania, 1766-1775. Flintlock Kentucky.

ROOSA, J. unlocated. Flintlock Kentucky rifle.

ROOT, EDWARD Waverly, Illinois, 1864d.

ROOT, ELISHA KING (1805-1865), Hartford, Connecticut. Patents #12,002 November 28, 1854, boring machine, #13,999 December 25, 1855, revolver, #22,675 January 18, 1859, cartridge pack, #44,660 October 11, 1864, cartridge, #65,509 June 4, 1867, breechloading firearm, and #65,510 June 4, 1867, revolver. Root was superintendent of Colt and its president after Colt's death in 1862. He also held many patents on machinery and cutlery. (Sutherland)

ROOT, SALMON New Haven, Connecticut, 1866d-1867d.

ROPER REPEATING RIFLE CO. Amherst, Massachusetts, 1866-1868, Hartford, Connecticut, 1868-1869. Roper revolving rifles and shotguns. Sylvester H. Roper and Charles Ethan Billings (company president). Succeeded by Billings & Spencer, 1869. (MB 12-52)

ROPER, JOHN St. Louis, Missouri, 1836-1860d.

ROPER, SYLVESTER H. Roxbury, Massachusetts. Patents #53,881 April 10, 1866, revolver, #79,861 July 14, 1868, detachable choke, #255,894 April 4, 1882, magazine gun with Christopher Miner Spencer, #316,401 April 21, 1885, magazine gun, #409,429 August 20, 1889, magazine gun and #413,734 October 29, 1889, magazine gun. Revolving rifles and shotguns made by Roper Repeating Rifle Co. and others by Spencer Arms Co.

ROPP, ADAM Lancaster, Pennsylvania, 1857d.

ROSAN, CHARLES (1834-?), San Francisco, California, 1870c. (Shelton)

ROSE & HART. Appleton, Wisconsin, 1867d. A.H. Hart, Jr.

ROSE & HOPKINS New York, New York, 1846d. Lodowick Rose and Reuben Hopkins.

ROSE, DAVID (1817-?), Liverpool, Ohio, 1853d, Rawsonville, Ohio, 1859d, Grafton Station, Ohio, 1860c-1875d. Percussion 1/2 stock. (Hutslar)

ROSE, E. New Plymouth, Ohio, 1853d. (Hutslar)

ROSE, EDWARD Ottawa, Illinois, 1866-1890d.

ROSE, JOSEPH New York, New York, 1849d-1858d. As Joseph Rose & Son, 1857-1858.

ROSE, JOSEPH, & SON New York, New York, 1857-1858.

ROSE, LODOWICK New York, New York, 1841d-1846d. With Reuben Hopkins as Rose & Hopkins, 1846.

ROSE, ORLANDO Crown Point, Indiana. Patent #611,977 October 4, 1898, safety.

ROSE, WILLIAM Cave in Rock, Illinois, 1860d.

ROSEBERRY, A. Guyandotte, West Virginia, 1885d.

ROSEBOROUGH, J. Elmore, Ohio, 1864-1872. Percussion 1/2 stock. (Hutslar)

ROSEE, WILLIAM New York, New York, 1857d-1884d. Patents #49,792 September 5, 1865, bullet, and #183,975 October 31, 1876, cheek rest.

ROSENBERG, A. Seymour, Indiana, 1867d.

ROSENBERG, L.J. (?-1859), Columbia, South Carolina.

ROSENBOROUGH, CHARLES Gibsonburg, Ohio, 1896d.

ROSENGRANT, G.H. Keene, Wisconsin, 1884d-1886d.

ROSER, ELI (1819-?), Harrison Co., Ohio, 1850c. Percussion fullstock. (Hutslar)

ROSIER, F. unlocated. Percussion fullstock.

ROSMER, J. Buffalo, New York. (Swinney)

ROSNER, ALBERT Dayton, Ohio, 1850c. Barrelmaker. (Hutslar)

ROSON, JOHN Jefferson City, Missouri, 1860d.

ROSS, ALEXANDER C. Zanesville, Ohio, 1810-1820. Flintlock rifles and pistols during the War of 1812. Son of Elijah Ross. (Knittle)

ROSS, B. Utica, New York. Percussion 1/2 stock.

ROSS, BENJAMIN D. Portland, Maine, 1823. (Demeritt)

ROSS, BOONE (1850-1930), Coxville, Indiana, 1870-1930. Percussion fullstock. (Lindert)

ROSS, ELIJAH (1785-1864), Zanesville, Ohio, 1804-1860d. Percussion fullstock marked "E.R.". (Hutslar)

ROSS, F. Hopkinsville, Kentucky, 1857-1860d.

ROSS, GEORGE (1841-?), Zanesville, Ohio, 1860c. Son of Elijah Ross. (Hutslar)

ROSS, GUSTAVUS Washington, Iowa, 1882d-1897d.

ROSS, J.R. Boston, Massachusetts, 1880-1900. Dealer.

ROSS, JAMES (?-1816), Steubenville, Ohio, 1803-1816. (Hutslar)

ROSS, JAMES (1801-?), Zanesville, Ohio, 1829, Clermont, Ohio, 1850c. (Hutslar)

ROSS, JAMES Eagle, New York, 1872-1874.

ROSS, JOHN (1829-?), Parke Co., Indiana, 1860c. (Lindert)

ROSS, JOHN B. Portland, Maine, 1817. (Demeritt)

ROSS, SAMUEL W. Pittsburgh, Pennsylvania, 1848-1850. (Kauffman)

ROSS, THOMAS Shenandoah, Iowa, 1884d-1897d.

ROSS, WILLIAM Fayette Co., Pennsylvania, 1796, New Richmond, Ohio, 1816-1828. (Kauffman, Hutslar)

ROSSEL, JOB Connellsville, Pennsylvania, 1849t. (Kauffman)

ROSSELL, H.M. unlocated. Percussion fullstock rifle.

ROSSELL, JOB, JR. (1813-?), Fayette Co., Pennsylvania, 1840t-1853t, Columbiana Co., Ohio, 1850c. (Hutslar)

ROSSIN, BRAD Bondville, Vermont, 1860. (Horn)

ROSSROCKER, FRANZ Shakopee, Minnesota, 1892d.

ROSTOCK, F.S., JR. Oregon, Missouri, 1889d.

ROSWELL, JOHN (1815-?), Washington Co., Ohio, 1850c. (Hutslar)

ROTH, CHARLES, JR. (1815-1903), Wilkes-Barre, Pennsylvania, 1840-1887d. Percussion 1/2 stock, percussion swivel breech. Son of Charles Roth Sr. (MB 9-60)

ROTH, CHARLES, SR. (?-1852), Wilkes-Barre, Pennsylvania. Father of Charles Roth, Jr. (Whisker III)

ROTH, ERNEST Bangor, Maine, 1874. With John W. Ramsdell (?) as Ramsdell & Roth. (Demeritt)

ROTH, ERNEST F. (1853-?), Wilkes-Barre, Pennsylvania, 1887-1917. Son of, the successor to, Charles Roth. (MB 9-60)

ROTH, GEORGE Northampton Co., Pennsylvania, 1820t, Lebanon Co., Pennsylvania, 1826t-1842. (KRA II-3)

ROTH, HENRY (1686-1774), Frederick Co., Maryland, 1749-1767, Ursina, Pennsylvania, 1771-1774. Flintlock Kentucky. (Hartzler)

ROTH, J. Bealsville, Ohio, 1890d-1910d. Percussion 1/2 stock. (Hutslar)

ROTH, SAMUEL Lancaster, Pennsylvania, 1830-1850. Barrelmaker. (Dyke)

ROTHANHEAFER, LAWRENCE J. Harmony, Maryland, 1878-1884d. (Hartzler)

ROTHENBERG, A.D. Bucks Co., Pennsylvania, 1737. (Van Rensselaer)

ROTHENBUHLER, JACOB (1837-?), Adolph, West Virginia, 1880c-1900d. (Whisker IV)

ROTHKAIG, STEPHEN Davenport, Iowa, 1867d.

ROTHROCK, EDWARD (1872-1934), Middle Creek, Pennsylvania, 1872-1934. Percussion over/under rifle.

ROTHROCK, EDWARD L. (?-1880), Middle Creek, Pennsylvania. (Whisker III)

ROTHROCK, JOHN DAVID (1816-?), Forsythe Co., North Carolina. Apprenticed, 1826.

ROTTON, WILLIAM (1826-1891), Nebraska City, Nebraska, 1857-1871. Percussion 1/2 stock. (MB 11-63)

ROUND, GEORGE St. Louis, Missouri, 1854d.

ROUND, JOHN (1816-?), St. Louis, Missouri, 1850c-1851d.

ROUNDS, MARK (?-1748), Searboro, Maine, 1681, Newcastle, Maine, 1684, Saco, Maine, 1699, Falmouth, Maine, 1715-1720. (Demeritt)

ROURKE, JOHN Norwich, Connecticut. Patent #519,875, May 15, 1894, revolver.

ROUSE, THOMAS Mohave City, Arizona, 1884d. Also listed as T. Bonse.

ROUSH, DAVID Freeburg, Pennsylvania. Flintlock Kentucky rifles. (Gabel)

ROVER suicide special.

ROW, EDWARD Penn Twp., Pennsylvania. Percussion fullstock. (Gabel)

ROW, ELIAS Penn Twp., Pennsylvania. Percussion fullstock. (Gabel)

ROW, JACOB Penn Twp., Pennsylvania. Percussion. (Gabel)

ROW, SAMUEL (1826-?), Morgan Co., Virginia, 1850c. (Whisker IV)

ROWARTH & LAKE Central City, Colorado, 1871d-1886d. William M. Rowarth. (Sellers-3)

ROWARTH, WILLIAM M. Central City, Colorado, 1871d-1886d. As Rowarth & Lake. (Sellers-3)

ROWE, A.H. Hartford, Connecticut, 1863-1865. Patent #42,227 April 5, 1864, breechloading rifle. Carbines made for trials. (ASAC 40)

ROWE, CONRAD (1826-?), Toledo, Ohio, 1850c. (Hutslar)

ROWE, E.P. unlocated. Flintlock Kentucky.

ROWE, J.W. Melrose, Illinois, 1878d-1888d.

ROWE, NATHANIEL (1821-1915, Emmitsburg, Maryland, 1842-1880. Flintlock and percussion Kentucky. Sometimes used "Row" as a signature. (Hartzler)

ROWE, REUBEN Dover, New Jersey, 1878d-1882d.

ROWE, WEBSTER (1844-1918), Skowhegan, Maine, 1859-1868 and 1891-1900, Hallowell, Maine, 1878-1880. (Demeritt)

ROWE, WILLIAM H. Hartford, Connecticut, 1832-1833. For Anson Chase, and for Colton & Snow. (Sellers-1)

ROWE, WILLIAM N. Washington, D.C. Patent #60,791 January 1, 1867, safety nipple.

ROWELL, HARVEY (?-1924), Columbus, Wisconsin, 1870-1883. Patents #187,319 February 13, 1877, breechloading firearm, and #266,206 October 17, 1882, sight.

ROWELL, HORACE HALL (1830-?), Columbia, California, 1856-1875, Sonora, California, 1875-1907. Percussion 1/2 stock. (Shelton)

ROWLAND, DENTLER Louisville, Illinois, 1886d-1890d.

ROWLAND, G.A. Waseca, Minnesota, 1898d.

ROWLAND, ROBERT (?-1800), Botetourt Co., Virginia, (Gill)

ROWLANDS, DENTON Ohio, 1834-1842, Neenah, Wisconsin, 1843-1850c. (Hutslar)

ROWLEY, JAMES Auburn, New York, 1885d-1886d.

ROWND Canton, Ohio, 1812-1864. (Knittle)

ROYAL suicide special by Lee and OAS(?).

ROYAL GUN CO. Wheeling, West Virginia, 1908-1910. Trade name of Three Barrel Gun Co. (AR 6-64)

ROYAL SERVICE trade name of Shapleigh Hardware Co. on shotguns by Crescent. (Hinman)

ROYAL, JARVIS Rochelle, Illinois. Patent #210,968 December 17, 1878, breechloading firearm.

ROYCE, A.J. (1834-?), Mt. Pleasant, Iowa, 1860c-1865d.

ROYDEN, JESSE Fentress Co., Tennessee, circa 1850. Percussion fullstock rifle. (Dillin)

ROYER, W.S. Pottstown, Pennsylvania, 1890d.

ROYET, LOUIS Reading, Pennsylvania, 1858-1890d. Percussion and cartridge rifles.

ROYON, EDWARD (1830-?), San Francisco, California, 1870-1872. (Shelton)

ROYS, THOMAS W. Southhampton, New York. Patent #31,790 January 22, 1861, harpoon gun.

ROYSDON, CHARLES W. Des Moines, Iowa, 1871d-1882d, Dayton, Washington, 1886d.

ROYSDON, WILLIAM Waterloo, Indiana, 1860d.

ROZZEL, THOMAS Grantville Hollow, Pennsylvania. Percussion fullstock.

RUBOTTOM, JOHN (1820-?), Greene Co., Indiana, 1860c. (Lindert)

RUBY, GEORGE Traverse City, Michigan, 1895d.

RUBY, JAMES (1815-?), Belmont Co., Ohio, 1850c, Galigher, Ohio, 1864d. (Hutslar)

RUCHEMEYER, L. Cincinnati, Ohio, 1880c. (Hutslar)

RUCKER, J.W. Bloomington, Illinois, 1872d. For P.W. Bentley.

RUDD & SPENCER Canon City, Colorado, 1877d-1885d. Anson Rudd. (Sellers-3)

RUDD, ANSON (1819-?), originally from Pennsylvania, Madison, Ohio, 1843, Canon City, Colorado, 1860-1885d. Percussion 1/2 stock. As Rudd & Spencer, 1877-1885. (Sellers-3)

RUDD, HENRY (1787-?), Highland, Illinois, 1850c. (Johnson)

RUDDELL, T. Henderson, Texas, 1878d.

RUDE, CHRISTIAN (1817-?), Salem, North Carolina. Apprenticed 1830. (Bivins)

RUDGERS, WILLIAM Lyons, Michigan, 1879d. Same as J.W. Rodgers, Lyons, Michigan, 1860d?

RUDISILL Lancaster, Pennsylvania, 1873d-1875d.

RUDOLPH & CO. St. Louis, Missouri, 1874-1879d. Successors to Horace E. Dimick. Victor Rudolph.

RUDOLPH, A.E. Canon City, Colorado, 1875d-1883d. (Sellers-3)

RUDOLPH, FORTUNAS (1856-?), San Francisco, California, 1870c. Apprentice at his father's shop. (Shelton)

RUDOLPH, G.M. Fayetteville, Arkansas, 1880. (Elias)

RUDOLPH, J.E. Roscoe, Missouri, 1893d.

RUDOLPH, VICTOR St. Joseph, Missouri, 1867d-1874d and 1879d-1893d, St. Louis, Missouri, 1874-1879. As Albright & Rudolph, 1872-1873. As Rudolph & Co., St. Louis. Rudolph and William Albright bought Horace E. Dimick's shop when Dimick died. (ASAC 7)

RUDOLPH, W.S. Canon City, Colorado, 1875. Percussion 1/2 stock. (Sellers-3)

RUDOLPH, WILLIAM (1832-?), Newark, New Jersey, 1856-1858, San Francisco, California, 1859-1873. Patents #54,021 April 17, 1866, lock, and #55,716 June 19, 1866, lock, both with Augustus Braun. (Shelton)

RUECKERT, FREDERICK W. Lake City, Minnesota, 1875d-1884d.

RUETSCHNER, A. Pueblo, Colorado, 1878d-1886d. (Sellers-3)

RUF, MICHAEL New York, New York, 1867d.

RUFFLEY, GEORGE E. Glenfield, Pennsylvania. Patent #381,821 April 24, 1888 magazine gun, and #399,464 March 12, 1889, magazine gun, both with R.M. Augenbaugh.

RUGENTHAL, S. Las Vegas, New Mexico, 1884d.

RUGERT, PETER Lancaster Co., Pennsylvania, 1775. Committee of Safety muskets with Christian Isch. Probably Peter Reigart.

RUGGLES, A. Stafford, Connecticut, 1830-1845. Percussion pistols.

RUGGLES, ALEXANDER (?-1888), Harrisburg, Pennsylvania, 1871d-1888d.

RUGGLES, FORDYCE Hardwick, Maine, 1823-1887. Percussion fullstock rifle. Patent #none November 24, 1826, firearm. (Demeritt)

RUGGLES, MARTIN Stony Creek, Michigan, 1879d.

RUGH & STOCK Peoria, Illinois, 1864d. Percussion 1/2 stock. William Rugh and Charles F. Stock.

RUGH, DANIEL (1812-?), Blairsville, Pennsylvania, 1836-1842, Galena, Illinois, 1850c-1854d. (Kauffman, Johnson)

RUGH, SAUL (1818-1894), Stephenson, Illinois, 1840-1841, Oroville, California, 1870c-1894. (Johnson)

RUGH, WILLIAM (1828-?), Indianapolis, Indiana, 1850c, Peoria, Illinois, 1864d. Percussion 1/2 stock. With Charles F. Stock as Rugh & Stock, 1864. (Lindert)

RUGHE, FRANCIS M. Frankfort, Indiana, 1882-1885. (Gardner)

RUHLAND, HENRY Philadelphia, Pennsylvania, 1893d-1895d.

RUHRER, LEOPOLD Chicago, Illinois, circa 1870. (Johnson)

RUMLEY, C. Onarga, Illinois, 1860d.

RUMMELL, A.J., ARMS CO. Toledo, Ohio, 1883-1896d. Shotguns made by Crescent. Dealer. (Hutslar)

RUMPLE, JOHN & PETER Milwaukee, Wisconsin, 1854-1855. (WGCA 6)

RUNFIELT, S.C. Lancaster, Pennsylvania, 1850. (Dyke)

RUNION, JOHN Brownlow, Tennessee, 1891d.

RUNKEL, M. San Francisco, California, 1854. For B. Lagoarde. (Shelton)

RUNYON, WILLIAM Springfield, Ohio, 1852d. Locks. (Hutslar)

RUP, CHARLES (1828-?), San Francisco, 1860c. (Shelton)

RUPERT, W. Rockport, Illinois, 1860d.

RUPERTUS, JACOB Philadelphia, Pennsylvania, 1858-1900. Cartridge derringers, percussion and cartridge revolvers, cartridge rifles. Patents #23,711 April 19, 1859, revolver, #23,852 May 10, 1859, priming device, #25,142 August 16, 1859, primer, #37,059 December 2, 1862, revolver, #43,606 July 19, 1864, revolver, #121,199 November 21, 1871, revolver, #165,369 July 6, 1875, revolver, #169,848 November 9, 1875, revolver, #209,925 November 12, 1878, breechloading firearm, and #633,734 September 26, 1899, revolver. Operated as Rupertus Pat'd. Pistol Mfg. Co. (Sellers-1)

RUPP, A. HERMAN (1756-1831), Lehigh Co., Pennsylvania, 1784-1809. Flintlock Kentucky rifle. (KRA IV-2)

RUPP, JACOB (1787-1858), Bellefonte, Pennsylvania, 1821-1829t. Nephew of Herman and John Rupp. (KRA IV-2)

RUPP, JOHN (1762-1836), Macungie, Pennsylvania, 1783-1800. Flintlock Kentucky rifle and pistol. Brother of Herman Rupp. (Kindig)

RUPP, JOHN (1786-1848), Lehigh Co., Pennsylvania, 1812-1848. Flintlock Kentucky. Nephew of Herman and John Rupp. (KRA IV-2)

RUPPERT, WILLIAM Lancaster, Pennsylvania, 1776. (Diilin)

RUPPRECHT, CARL Hustisford, Wisconsin, 1895d.

RUSH, J.Q.A. Elizabeth, Indiana, 1862d.

RUSH, JAMES (1679-1727), Byberry, Pennsylvania. (MB 12-68)

RUSH, JOHN (1712-1751), Philadelphia, Pennsylvania, 1740-1751. Son of James Rush. (MB 12-68)

RUSH, SOLOMON Reynoldsburg, Ohio. Patent #153,848 August 4, 1874, lock.

RUSH, WILLIAM Philadelphia, Pennsylvania, 1769-1771. (Dean)

RUSHMORE, HENRY C. Toledo, Ohio, 1888-1899d. As Venia & Rushmore, 1888. (Hutslar)

RUSHTON, FRANK Provo, Utah. Patent #323,368 July 28, 1885, extractor.

RUSLEY, JOHN JACOB Bedford, Pennsylvania, before 1844. Percussion double rifle. (Hetrick)

RUSLIN, JACOB Bedford, Pennsylvania, Flintlock Kentucky rifle. (KRA 76)

RUSO trade name of Hibbard, Spencer, Bartlett, & Co. on shotguns. (Hinman)

RUSS, M.B. Kansas City, Missouri, 1898d.

RUSSELL & CATLIN Bay City, Michigan, 1883d-1887d. Louis R. Russell and Willis Catlin.

RUSSELL & HAYDEN Jacksonville, Illinois, 1867. (Johnson)

RUSSELL & RICHARDS Savannah, Georgia, 1796. Jacob Russell and John Richards.

RUSSELL & TAYLOR Springfield, Massachusetts, 1853d.

RUSSELL ARMS CO. trade name of H & D Folsom on imported shotguns. (Hinman)

RUSSELL, A.T. unlocated. Percussion slug gun.

RUSSELL, ANDREW H. U.S. Army. Patents #221,079 October 28,1879, magazine gun with W.R. Livermore, #230,823 August 3, 1880, magazine gun, #295,285 March 18, 1884, magazine gun, #295,286 March 18, 1884, magazine gun, #396,835 January 29, 1889, magazine gun, #501,367 July 11, 1893, magazine gun, and #816,603 April 3, 1906, magazine gun.

RUSSELL, CHARLES F. New Haven, Connecticut. Patent #126,748 May 14, 1872, breechloading firearm.

RUSSELL, H.A.B. Augusta, Wisconsin, 1879d, Cadott, Wisconsin, 1884d-1888d.

RUSSELL, HORACE Meriden, Connecticut. Percussion target rifle.

RUSSELL, J. unlocated. Flintlock pistol.

RUSSELL, J.M. Minneapolis, Minnesota, 1886d.

RUSSELL, J.W. Bardstown, Kentucky, 1883d.

RUSSELL, JACOB Savannah, Georgia, 1796. With John Richards as Russell & Richards.

RUSSELL, JOHN Elizabeth, New Jersey, 1881d-1883d.

RUSSELL, JOHN M. (1793-?), Elizabeth, Indiana, 1850c-1858d. (Lindert)

RUSSELL, L.J. New Haven, Connecticut. Patent #316,880 April 28, 1885, magazine gun with Isaac Curtis.

RUSSELL, LEROY W. (1836-?), Taylor Co., West Virginia, 1860c-1870c. (Whisker IV)

RUSSELL, LOUIS R. Bay City, Michigan, 1883d-1891d. With Willis Catlin as Russell & Catlin, 1883-1887.

RUSSELL, N. Mayville, New York, 1850c.

RUSSELL, SAMUEL Brooklyn, New York. Patents #307,070 October 21, 1884, electric gun, #337,872 March 16, 1886, electric gun, and #337,873 March 16, 1886, electric gun. President of American Electric Arms & Ammunition Co.

RUSSELL, WILLIAM E. Buffalo, New York, 1832-1835. For A.V. Sill. (Dean)

RUSSIAN MODEL suicide special by Forehand & Wadsworth.

RUSSILY, JACOB Lancaster Co., Pennsylvania, 1820c. (Dillin)

RUST, HORACE (1818-?), Sonoma Co., California, 1860c. (Shelton)

RUTENFRANZ, A. St. Libory, Illinois, 1893d.

RUTES, JOHN H. Syracuse, New York, 1850c.

RUTH, JOHN Wyomissing Creek, Pennsylvania. Barrel-maker. (MB 2-63)

RUTHERFORD, ARCHIBALD Harrisonburg, Virginia, 1809-1815. Contract rifles for Virginia. (Cromwell)

RUTHERFORD, BENJAMIN Lexington, Kentucky, 1800-1810. (MB 12-51)

RUTHERFORD, DANIEL Rowan Co., North Carolina. Apprenticed 1819. (Bivins)

RUTHERFORD, THOMAS Mecklenburg, Virginia, 1776-1778. State gun factory. (Gill)

RUTROFF, JOSEPH W. (1838-?), Marsh Fork, West Virginia, 1870c. (Whisker IV)

RUTT, HENRY Lancaster Co., Pennsylvania 1820. (KRA IV-4)

RUYLE & BROWN Roodhouse, Illinois, 1877. (Johnson)

RYAN suicide special by Ryan Pistol Mfg. Co.

RYAN PISTOL MFG. CO. New York, New York, 1874-1876d, Norwich, Connecticut, 1876d-1890d. Suicide specials (30,000 mfg. in 1888). Thomas E. Ryan.

RYAN, J. San Antonio, Texas. 1878d-1880d.

RYAN, J.F. Maysville, Kentucky, 1883d-1896d.

RYAN, P. Pierce City, Missouri, 1898d.

RYAN, S. Jones Creek, Illinois, 1860d.

RYAN, T.O. Tarfork, Kentucky, 1896d.

RYAN, THOMAS E. New York, New York, 1874-1876d, Norwich, Connecticut, 1876d-1890d. Suicide specials (30,000 mfg. in 1888). As Ryan Pistol Mfg. Co.

RYAN, W.W., JR. Newark, Ohio. Percussion 1/2 stock. (Hutslar)

RYBACEK, FRANK Riverside, Iowa, 1884d-1897d.

RYBERG, ANDREW Jordan, Minnesota, 1877-1880d, Detroit Lakes, Minnesota, 1882d-1886d.

RYDBECK, SVEN Red Wing, Minnesota. Patent #104,775 June 28, 1870, breechloading firearm.

RYNE, REASON Lake City, Illinois, 1878d.

RYNES, MICHAEL Pequa Creek, Pennsylvania, 1778-1782. Flintlock Kentucky rifles. (Dillin)

RYON, P. Philadelphia, Pennsylvania. Flintlock pistol. (Dean)

S SECTION

S. & S. unidentified. Percussion fullstock.

S.B. see Samuel Baum.

S.B. see Samuel Border.

S.B. unidentified. Flintlock Kentucky.

S.B. & T. unidentified, but from Louisville, Kentucky. Percussion 1/2 stock.

S.B.J.D. unidentified. Flintlock Kentucky.

S.C. State of Connecticut marking on flintlock muskets, South Carolina marking on later guns.

S.D. unidentified. Flintlock Kentucky.

S.E.F. unidentified. Percussion fullstock.

S.G. see Stephen Gibson.

S.G. unidentified. Percussion fullstock.

S.G. & Co. see Scott, Gallagher & Co.

S.G.B. see Samuel Border.

S.G.F. marking of State Gun Factory, Fredericksburg, Virginia, 1775-1780.

S.H. & G. see Schuyler, Hartley & Graham.

S.J. see Sweet, Jenks & Co.

S.K. see Samuel Keller.

S.L. unidentified. Flintlock Kentucky.

S.L. unidentified. Percussion fullstock.

S.M. see Simon Miller.

S.M. unidentified. Flintlock Kentucky.

S.M. Co. see Springfield Mfg. Co.

S.M.B. unidentified, but from Old Salem, North Carolina. Flintlock Kentucky.

S.N. unidentified. Flintlock Kentucky.

S.N. & W.T.C. see Samuel Norris and William T. Clement. Marking on Model 1863 contract muskets.

S.N.Y. marking on contract arms made for the state of New York.

S.N.Y. see William Lowe.

S.R.F. unidentified, Waynesboro, Pennsylvania. Flintlock Kentucky.

S.S. unidentified. Flintlock Kentucky.

S.T.S. see Samuel T. Sherwood.

S.U. unidentified. Percussion 1/2 stock.

S.W.M. unidentified. Percussion 1/2 stock.

SABIN & KAY Nauvoo, Illinois, Salt Lake City, Utah, 1854-1857. David Sabin and John Kay. Primarily jewelers and die makers but made firearms. See David Sabin.

SABIN & NAYLOR Salt Lake City, Utah, 1857-1860. David Sabin and William Naylor. See David Sabin.

SABIN, DAVID Nauvoo, Illinois, Salt Lake City, Utah, 1854-1860. Copies of Colt revolvers, 1857-1860. Seven-shot percussion revolver for Brigham Young, Mormon leader. With John Kay as Sabin & Kay, both locations. With William Naylor as Sabin & Naylor(?), 1857-1860. (UTHQ)

SABIN, HENRY Newport, Rhode Island, 1733-1736. (Achtermier)

SABIN, HENRY Olympia, Washington, 1869d-1891d.

SACHS, GUSTAV A. Valley City, Dakota Territory/North Dakota, 1885-1890, Eugene, Oregon, 1890-1891. Patents #353,432 November 30, 1886, breechloading firearm, #410,678 September 10, 1889, ornamenting barrels, #495,639 April 18, 1893, breechloading gun, and #674,284, May 14, 1901, breechloading firearm.

SACK, CHRISTOPHER D. Savannah, Georgia, 1879d-1883d.

SACK, H. Savannah, Georgia, 1885d.

SACKET, D.S. Westfield, Massachusetts, 1850. Underhammer pistol. (Logan)

SACKETT, JACOB T. Woodcock, Pennsylvania, 1874d, Saegertown, Pennsylvania, 1880d-1887d. As Sackett & Robinson, 1880-1882. Percussion 1/2 stock.

SACKWITZ, LOUIS St. Louis, Missouri, 1896d. (Pourie)

SACRISTE, L.C. (1812-?), New Orleans, Louisiana, 1850c-1853d. (MB 9-65)

SADD, MATTHEW Hartford, Connecticut, 1750. (Lindsay)

SADDLER, W.O. Coffeyville, Kansas, 1884d.

SADLER, W. McKeen, Illinois, 1880d-1882d.

SAFE GUARD suicide special. (Webster)

SAFETY POLICE trade name of Hopkins & Allen on revolvers.

SAFFORD Burlington, Vermont. (Horn)

SAFFORD, CHARLES HENRY Augusta, Maine, 1871-1880. With John H. Parsons as Safford & Parsons, 1874-1875. As Safford & Co., 1876-1880. (Demeritt)

SAFFORD, HARRY Zanesville, Ohio, 1812. Swords. (Knittle)

SAFLEY, WILLIAM Goshen Township, Ohio, 1820c. (Hutslar)

SAFREED, JOSHUA (1814-1897), Hockingport, Ohio, 1850c-1897. (Hutslar)

SAGE, GEORGE W. Plymouth, Michigan. Patent #477,385 June 21, 1892, spring air gun.

SAGE, WILLIAM Redfield, New York, 1869-1874. Percussion rifles.

SAGE, WILLIAM H. Wahoo, Nebraska, 1882d-1884d.

SAGEL, NATHAN (1821-?), Harper's Ferry, West Virginia, 1880c.

SAGELSDORFF, G.R. Medford, Wisconsin, 1895d.

SAGER, C. Bethel, Oregon, 1880d.

SAGER, JOHN Lancaster Co., Pennsylvania, 1777. Converted Kentucky rifle. (Dyke)

SAGERS, BENJAMIN New York, New York, 1775. Runaway (from an apprenticeship?). (Kauffman)

SAGET, ARTHUR E. New Orleans, Louisiana, 1881d-1896d. Cartridge revolvers. Son of Julian Saget.

SAGET, JULIAN New Orleans, Louisiana, 1841d-1886d. Folding trigger revolvers. Patent #76,105 June 10, 1872, revolver.

SAHLMAN, AUGUST Marinette, Wisconsin, 1895d.

SAHLMAN, B.A. Marinette, Wisconsin, 1888d.

SAHN, C.F. unlocated. Percussion target rifle.

SAILOR, HENRY Harrisburg, Pennsylvania, 1792. (Kauffman)

SAILSGIVER, J.T. Onberg, Pennsylvania, 1887d.

SAINSBERRY, R. Cockeysville, Maryland, 1887d. (Hartzler)

SAKER, SAMUEL Ft. Scott, Kansas, 1897d.

SALEWSKI, L. Bloomington, Illinois. Patent #16,288 December 23, 1856, single shot breechloader with H. Schroeder and William Schmidt.

SALIERS, A.I. Grand Rapids, Michigan, 1895d.

SALISBURY Jamestown, New York. Percussion target rifle.

SALOLA Qualla Reservation, North Carolina, 1848. Indian gunsmith. (Bivins)

SALTER, JOHN H. (1845-1923), St. Mary's Pennsylvania. Patents #208,696 October 8, 1878, magazine firearm, and #232,766 September 28, 1880, magazine firearms with L.W. Gifford and C.C. Bigelow.

SALTER, WILLIAM J. Short Creek, Alabama. Flintlock. (Dillin)

SALTERSWAITE, BARCLAY New Lisbon, Ohio, circa 1830. Flintlock Kentucky. See Barclay Satterwaite. (MB 1-46)

SALTONSTALL, GURDON Connecticut, 1763-1776. State repairs. (Gluckman & Satterlee)

SALTONSTALL, NATHANIEL New London, Connecticut. Patent #none May 29, 1828, percussion gunlock.

SALTSMAN, D. Alexandria, Dakota Territory, 1884d.

SALVATORE, E.A. U.S. Navy. Patent #350,098 October 5, 1886, magazine gun.

SAMPLE, A.B. Fort Benton, Montana Territory, 1869.

SAMPLE, ROBERT M. South Bend, Indiana, 1867d. With J.W. Comper. (Lindert)

SAMPLES, A. Manchester, Illinois. (Johnson)

SAMPLES, BETHUEL (1780-?), Urbana, Ohio, 18i8-1853d. Flintlock and percussion Kentucky. (Hutslar)

SAMPLES, ROBERT (1814-?), Urbana, Ohio, 1850c. Son of Bethuel Samples. (Hutslar)

SAMPSON, C.M. Harrisonville, Kentucky, 1860d.

SAMPSON, D. Lancaster, Pennsylvania, 1820. (Dean)

SAMPSON, JAMES (1830-?), Jamestown, North Carolina. Apprenticed 1840. (Bivins)

SAMPSON, WILLIAM S. Lawrence, Massachusetts, 1870d-1873d.

SAMSON, E.V. or I.V., California, Ohio, 1878d, Flat Rock, Ohio, 1883d-1888d. (Hutslar)

SAMUELS, J.H. Hannibal, Missouri, 1889d.

SAN FRANCISCO ARMS CO. San Francisco, California. Used patents of Howard Carr and Robert Catlin.

SANBORN, CHARLES Concord, New Hampshire, 1850. (Kauffman 2)

SANDERS, LEWIS Bedford, Missouri, 1860d.

SANDERS, N.J. Carrollton, Illinois, 1884d.

SANDERS, WILLIAM Philadelphia, Pennsylvania, 1819d-1846d.

SANDERSON, AUGUSTUS Hamden, Connecticut, 1871d.

SANDERSON, B. unlocated. Underhammer rifle.

SANDERSON, E.A. Cheboygan, Michigan, 1884d.

SANDERSON, M.S. Proctorsville, Vermont. Underhammer rifles and pistols. With George V. Seaver, 1858. (Horn)

SANDOZ, JULES A. Grayson, Nebraska, 1893d. Sandoz was the subject of the book "Old Jules" by Marie Sandoz.

SANDS, JOHN Napa, California, 1870d. (Shelton)

SANDUSKY, JACOB Columbus, Ohio, circa 1830. (Hutslar)

SANDYRUST, J.J. Norwood, Minnesota, 1877-1884d.

SANFORD, PHILIP G. New York, New York, 1886d-1888d. Breechloading shotguns.

SANGER, FREDERICK Chicago, Illinois, 1895d.

SANGRE & GORE Auburn, California, 1893d.

SANKEY, WILLIAM Muffin Co., Pennsylvania, 1850c. (Kauffman)

SAPP, JOHN R. Quincy, Florida, 1883d-1885d.

SARGENT & SMITH Newburyport, Massachusetts, 1849d-1867d. Charles R. Sargent.

SARGENT, C.A. Lincoln, Maine, 1874-1900. (Demeritt)

SARGENT, CHARLES G. Graniteville, Massachusetts. Patent #36,891 November 11, 1862, breechloading firearm with Seymour Bostwick.

SARGENT, CHARLES R. Newburyport, Massachusetts, 1849d-1880d. As Sargent & Smith, 1849-1867.

SARGENT, EBENEZER (?-1797), Newburyport, Massachusetts. Also known as Ebenezer Sergeant.

SARGENT, EDWARD LEVI Watertown, New York. Patents #100,455 March 1, 1870, breechloading firearm, #104,502 June 21, 1870, breechloading firearm, and #109,255 November 15, 1870, breechloading firearm.

SARGOOD & GEPHART Elkhart, Indiana, 1887d. (MB 4-54)

SARONI, A.S. Boston, Massachusetts. Patent #9,943 August 16, 1853, breechloading gun with J.P. Schenkle.

SARSON & ROBERTS New York, New York, 1861. Model 1861 contract muskets. John B. Sarson and William S. Roberts. (Fuller)

SARSON, JOHN B. New York, New York, 1861. Model 1861 contract muskets. With William S. Roberts as Sarson & Roberts. (Fuller)

SARVEY, DANIEL (1829-?), Clarion, Pennsylvania, 1850c. For Nicholas Shennefelt. (Whisker II)

SASSE, G.F. Blue Earth City, Minnesota, 1884d-1886d, Devils Lake, North Dakota, 1892d.

SATER, J.F. Ft. Meade, Florida, 1884d.

SATTERWAITE, BARCLAY A. New Lisbon, Ohio, 1830-1860. Percussion fullstock rifle. With brother James Satterwaite. Also known as Barclay Salterswaite. (Hutslar)

SATTERWAITE, JAMES New Lisbon, Ohio, 1830-1860. Percussion fullstock rifles with brother Barclay.

SATTLER, ADAM Mt. Carmel, Illinois, 1834-1835. (Johnson)

SATTLER, AUGUST Chicago, Illinois, 1854d-1884d. As Uhrlaub, Sattler & Co., 1854.

SAUCERMAN, B. Sullivan, Indiana, circa 1860. Percussion guns. (Lindert)

SAUER, URIAS Lancaster, Pennsylvania, 1871d-1873d. Listed as Sowers in 1873 directory.

SAULET, ARMAND New Orleans, Louisiana, 1841d-1842d.

SAULNIER, EMIL P. Houston, Texas, 1899d.

SAUNDERS, CHAUNCY Marshall, Michigan, 1853-1857, Marengo, Michigan, 1858-1869. For M.L. Rood in Marshall. (Sellers-3)

SAUNDERS, F.W. Aberdeen, Mississippi, 1885d.

SAUNDERS, JAMES Salem, North Carolina, 1771. Tory gunsmith. (Bivins)

SAUNDERS, L.H. Galesburg, Illinois, 1884d.

SAUNDERS, L.H. Liberty, Nebraska, 1884d-1886d.

SAUNDERS, W.A. Boston, Massachusetts, 1856d.

SAUNDERS, WILLIAM (?-1742), Philadelphia, Pennsylvania.

SAUNDERS, WILLIAM Philadelphia, Pennsylvania, 1849d.

SAUPP, ANDREW (?-1855), Bedford, Pennsylvania, 1810-1855 (Whisker)

SAVAGE suicide special. (Webster)

SAVAGE & SMITH Middletown, Connecticut, 1868-1879. Revolvers under contract with Smith & Wesson. Successors to Smith & Johnson. Edward Savage and Otis A. Smith. (AR 5-75)

SAVAGE ARMS Westfield, Massachusetts, circa 1965-1981. Operated as Savage Arms Division of American Hardware Corporation (which became the Emhart Corporation). Succeeded by Savage Industries Inc., Westfield, Massachusetts, 1981-1989. (Murray, BBOGV)

SAVAGE ARMS CO. Utica, New York, 1899-1917. Succeeded by Savage Arms Corp., Utica, New York, 1917-1945, Chicopee Falls, Massachusetts, 1946-1959, Westfield, Massachusetts,1960- circa 1965. (Murray, BBOGV)

SAVAGE ARMS CORP. Utica, New York, 1917-1945, Chicopee Falls, Massachusetts, 1946-1959, Westfield, Massachusetts, 1960-circa 1965. Succeeded by Savage Arms Division of American Hardware Corp. (which became the Emhart Corporation), circa 1965-1981. (Muller, BBOGV)

SAVAGE ARMS, INC. Westfield, Massachusetts, 1989-date. (BBOGV)

SAVAGE INDUSTRIES, INC. Westfield, Massachusetts, 1981-1989. Succeeded by Savage Arms, Inc., Westfield, Massachusetts, 1989-date. (BBOGV)

SAVAGE REPEATING ARMS CO. Utica, New York, 1893-1899. Formed by Arthur W. Savage. Guns made by Marlin. Succeeded by: Savage Arms Co., Utica, New York, 1899-1917. (Murray, BBOGV)

SAVAGE REVOLVING FIREARMS CO. Middletown, Connecticut, 1860-1866. Percussion revolvers. (Sellers-1)

SAVAGE, ARTHUR WILLIAM (1857-1938), Utica, New York. Patents #366,512 July 12, 1887, magazine gun, #378,525 February 28, 1888, magazine firearm, #460,786 October 6, 1891, magazine firearm, #491,138 February 7, 1893, magazine firearm, #502,018 July 25, 1893, magazine gun, #611,284 September 27, 1898, firearm indicator, #634,034 October 9, 1899, firearms, #789,761 May 16, 1905, sight, #806,007 November 28, 1905, firearm, and #839,517 December 25, 1906, firearm. Savage was a British citizen living in New York when he patented his guns. Founder of Savage Repeating Arms Co., Utica, New York, 1893-1899. (Murray)

SAVAGE, C. Ford, Ohio, 1859d. (Hutslar)

SAVAGE, EDWARD Cromwell, Connecticut, 1843-1879. Patents #3,686 July 39, 1844, breechloading firearms with Simeon North, #22,666 January 18, 1859, revolver with Henry S. North, #28,331 May 15, 1869, revolver with Henry S. North, and #32,003 April 9, 1861, pistol stock. With Otis A. Smith as Savage & Smith, Middletown, Connecticut, 1868-1879. (Sellers-1)

SAVAGE, ISAAC Jefferson, Wisconsin, 1857d.

SAVAGE, JAMES Baltimore, Maryland, 1810d.

SAVAGE, M.R. Summit, Oregon, 1880d-1891d.

SAVAGE, SAMUEL Middletown, Connecticut, 1854-1856. Brother of Edward Savage.

SAVAGE, STILLMAN Temple, Maine, 1876-1879. (Demeritt)

SAVAGE, W.J. Columbus, Ohio, 1861-1868d. For William M. Savage. (Hutslar)

SAVAGE, WILLIAM M. Columbus, Ohio, 1861-1880d. (Hutslar)

SAVERY & CO. Philadelphia, Pennsylvania, 1855-1859d. Importers and makers of barrels.

SAVIDGE, WILLIAM (?-1777), Surry Co., Virginia, 1777. Committee of Safety repairs. (Gill)

SAVIN, HARVEY D. St. Albans, Vermont, 1869-1882d, Rutland, Vermont, 1894-1898. (Horn)

SAVORY, HENRY Bluebell, Ohio. Percussion 1/2 stock, "H.S." marking. (Hutslar)

SAWB, A. Guilford Co., North Carolina, 1860c. (Bivins)

SAWTELLE, LUCIUS (1846-?), Saxtons River, Vermont, 1860-1869, Red Bluff, California, 1869-1887. With George Leonard and George Kingsley. (Shelton)

SAWYER & DENNISON Haverhill, Massachusetts, 1865d-1871d. Breechloading rifles. Newell F. Sawyer and William C. Dennison.

SAWYER, JOSHUA W. Portland, Maine, 1844-1850. (Demeritt)

SAWYER, NEWELL F. Haverhill, Massachusetts, 1865d-1874d. With William C. Dennison as Sawyer & Dennison, 1865-1871.

SAWYER, PHINEAS (1746-1820), Harvard, Massachusetts, 1772-1800. Flintlock muskets. (GR 6-72)

SAWYER, SYLVANUS (1822-1895), Augusta, Maine, 1839-?. Circa 1853 granted patent for cannon projectiles, with his brother-in-law.

SAWYER, WILLIAM (1808-?), Brighton, Illinois, 1860c. (Johnson)

SAXON, A.G. (1875-?), Connersville, Indiana, 1891-1959. Percussion guns. (GR 12-57)

SAXONIA GUN WORKS Eugene, Oregon. Double-barrel shotgun.

SAXTON, G.S. St. Louis, Missouri, 1864d.

SAXTON, JAMES A. Canton, Ohio, 1845-1847. Hardware dealer, barrels and locks. (Hutslar)

SAXTON, JOSEPH (1799-1873), Philadelphia, Pennsylvania, 1824d. Percussion cane guns, which he had designed in Isaiah Lukens shop. (GR 7-68)

SAYER, ADOLF Naubuc, Connecticut. Patent #55,719 June 19, 1866, breechloading firearm.

SAYGER, C.W. Mexico, Indiana, 1860d.

SAYLES, STEPHEN D. (1828-1907), Washington Co., Indiana, 1850-1907. (Lindert)

SAYLOR, JACOB Bedford Co., Pennsylvania, 1771t-1790. Committee of Safety muskets. (Kauffman)

SAYMAN, J. or G., unlocated. Flintlock Kentucky.

SCAGGS, JAMES Caney Creek, Kentucky. Percussion fullstock.

SCAGGS, JAMES Waynesville, Illinois, 1864d.

SCALF, WILLIAM Gulnare, Kentucky, 1896d.

SCANLAND, J.W. Selma, Ohio, 1896d. (Hutslar)

SCANLIN, W.H. Holton, Kansas, 1894d.

SCARBROUGH, JAMES (1801-?), Caney Fork, Tennessee, 1824-1860. Flintlock rifles. (ASAC 23)

SCARBROUGH, WILLIAM Cumberland City, Tennessee, 1844. Brother of James Scarbrough.

SCHAAR, THEODORE Beardstown, Illinois, 1884d-1888d.

SCHACH, FRANK Sedalia, Missouri, 1898d.

SCHADE, JOHN (1822-1868), St. Louis, Missouri, 1850c, Sacramento, California, 1851-1868. (Shelton)

SCHAEFER & LONEY Baltimore, Maryland, 1847-1860d. Importers. Francis B. Loney. (Hartzler)

SCHAEFER & WERNER Boston, Massachusetts, 1867d. William R. Schaefer.

SCHAEFER, ANTON Moberly, Missouri, 1879d.

SCHAEFER, J.P. Canal Dover, Ohio, 1878-1888d. (Hutslar)

SCHAEFER, JOHN (1815-?), Waterloo, Illinois, 1850c. (Johnson)

SCHAEFER, JOSEPH unlocated. Flintlock Kentucky.

SCHAEFER, P. Kansas City, Missouri, 1869d.

SCHAEFER, WILLIAM R. Boston, Massachusetts, 1853d-1916. Percussion and cartridge guns. Patent #86,378 February 2, 1869, breechloading firearms with Julius Elston. As Schaefer & Werner, 1867. As Wm. R. Schaefer & Sons, 1879-1900. (MB 8-64)

SCHAERFF & BROS. St. Louis, Missouri, 1850-1854. Percussion 1/2 stock. Charles, Christopher, and John Schaerff.

SCHAERFF, CHARLES see Schaerff & Bros.

SCHAERFF, CHRISTOPHER (1820-?), St. Louis, Missouri, 1850c-1854d. Percussion 1/2 stock. With John and Charles Schaerff as Schaerff & Bros.

SCHAERFF, JOHN see Schaerff & Bros.

SCHAF, W.H. Paris, Texas, 1885d-1892d. As Frahner & Schaf, 1890.

SCHAFER, J.R. St. Louis, Missouri, 1866d.

SCHAFER, M. Beaver Dam, Wisconsin, 1879d-1884d.

SCHAFERMEYER, JOSEPH B. St. Louis, Missouri, 1896d. (Pourie)

SCHAFFER, HENRY C.G. (1811-1880), Sacramento, California, 1850-1855, Los Angeles, California, 1855-1872. (Shelton)

SCHAFFER, J.C. Fruitland, Missouri, 1893d.

SCHAFFER, JACOB (1820-?), Augusta Co., Virginia, 1860c.

SCHAFFER, JACOB A. Vicksburg, Mississippi, 1868-1877. Derringer, percussion 1/2 stock, agent for Deringer. As Warter & Schaffer, 1867. Also known as J.A. Shaffer, Vicksburg, Mississippi, 1830-1850.

SCHAFFER, KOTTER M. Highland, Illinois, 1860d.

SCHAFFNER, DANIEL Shoal Creek Station, Illinois, 1878d, Breese, Illinois, 1882d-1888d.

SCHAIRER, F.G. Greensburg, Pennsylvania. Percussion 1/2 stock.

SCHALCK, CHRISTOPHER Williamsport, Pennsylvania, 1825-1875. (Roberts)

SCHALCK, GEORGE (1821-1893), Pottsville, Pennsylvania, 1854-?. Percussion rifles. Patents #169,734 November 9, 1875, wad for rifles and guns, and #226,555 April 13, 1880, trigger. (MB 3-42)

SCHALK, ANDREW W. Pottsville, Pennsylvania, 1847-1858. Percussion arms. Son of George Schalk. (MB 5-60)

SCHALLER, F. Mattoon, Illinois, 1864. (Johnson)

SCHAMMEL, JOHN Palmyra, Missouri, 1850c-1860d, Blumfield, Michigan, 1863d.

SCHAND, FREDERICK and MOLTY St. Louis, Missouri, 1867d. (Pourie)

SCHANER, HENRY Berks Co., Pennsylvania, 1830-1845. Flintlock and percussion rifles. (Hobbies 5-37)

SCHANLIN, MARTIN (1804-?). Peoria, Illinois, 1850c-1856d. Listed as Martin Schaulin in 1850 and 1856 directories. (Johnson)

SCHANTZ, HENRY St. Louis, Missouri, 1857d-1869d.

SCHANTZ, PHILIP H. (1817-?), Stark Co., Ohio, 1850c-1865. Percussion 1/2 stock. (Hutslar)

SCHARF, WILLIAM C. New Haven, Connecticut. Patents #249,406 November 8, 1881, magazine firearm, and #354,757 December 21, 1886, magazine firearm with Eli Whitney.

SCHARFFE, AUGUSTUS Washington, D.C., 1867d. (Hartzler)

SCHARFFE, G. Washington, D.C., 1866d. (Hartzler)

SCHARFFE, GUSTAV New York, New York. Patent #16,070 November 11, 1856, breechloading firearms.

SCHARIO, JOHN Danville, Illinois, 1878d-1884d.

SCHARP, JACOB W. (1834-?), Sidney, Ohio, 1850c. Son of John Scharp. (Hutslar)

SCHARP, JOHN (1809-?), Sidney, Ohio, 1850c-1878d. Percussion 1/2 stock and fullstock.

SCHAUB, ADAM Lancaster, Pennsylvania, 1857d.

SCHAUB, ELIAS (1811-1881), Philadelphia, Pennsylvania, 1845d, Bethania, North Carolina, 1850c-1881. (Bivins)

SCHAULIN, MARTIN see Martin Schanlin.

SCHEANCK, S.J. Belmont, New York, 1865-1882d. Percussion over/under.

SCHEANCK, WILLIAM Angelica, New York, 1874d.

SCHEANER, WILLIAM Reading, Pennsylvania, 1779-1790. (Gardner)

SCHECKELS, J.W. Washington, D.C., 1866-1867d. (Hartzler)

SCHEER, A.F. Alpena, Michigan, 1883d.

SCHEETZ see Sheets, and also Sheetz. These surnames were used interchangeably in the 18th and 19th centuries.

SCHEFFIELD, E.A. Norvell, Michigan, 1883d-1891d.

SCHEITLIN, A. & E. New York, New York, 1852d-1858d. Importer and dealer.

SCHELL, VALENTINE La Crosse, Wisconsin, 1865d-1875d.

SCHELLOR, FREDERICK (1830-?), Kankakee, Illinois, 1860c. (Johnson)

SCHEMANN & WIRSING Cincinnati, Ohio, 1860-1868. Percussion and air guns. Theodore Schemann and August F. Wirsing. (Hutslar)

SCHEMANN, THEODORE Cincinnati, Ohio, 1855d-1896d. Percussion fullstock and air guns. With August F. Wirsing as Schemann & Wirsing, 1860-1868. With his son William as T. & W. Schemann, 1889-1892. (Hutslar)

SCHEMANN, WILLIAM Cincinnati, Ohio, 1889d-1892d. With his father Theodore as T. & W. Schemann, 1889-1892.

SCHENCK, AUGUST Taylor, Texas, 1890d-1896d.

SCHENCK, FREDERICK San Antonio, Texas. Patents #57,978 September 11, 1866, set trigger for revolver, and #94,036 August 24, 1869, set trigger for revolver. (Sellers-1)

SCHENCK, JACOB Chester, Illinois, 1882d-1893d.

SCHENCK, WILLIAM Angelica, New York, 1850c-1882. As Eldridge & Schenck, 1850.

SCHENDEL, WILLIAM Peru, Illinois, 1878d, Beardstown, Illinois, 1880d-1893d.

SCHENDEL, WILLIAM Wellington, Kansas, 1888d.

SCHENKL, JOHN P. (?-1863), Boston, Massachusetts, 1852-1863. Patents #9,943 August 16, 1853, breechloading gun with A.S. Saroni, #17,642 June 23, 1857, breechloading firearm, #21,802 October 12, 1858, breechloading firearm, #23,746 April 19, 1859, chamber, #35,061 October 16, 1861, fuze, and #45,951 January 17, 1864, breechloading firearm. As Hardwicke & Schenkl, 1857-1863. Also known as Schenkle. (GR 3-71)

SCHENKLE, JOHN P. see John P. Schenkl.

SCHENY, HENRY Xenia, Ohio, 1867-1870c.

SCHERICK, S.J. see S.J. Scheanck.

SCHESCH, HEINRICH A. Ilion, New York. Patent #125,620 April 9, 1872, breechloading firearm.

SCHIFFER BROS. & CO. Chicago, Illinois, 1858d. Dealers.

SCHIFFERDECKER, C.L. Mamaroneck, New York, 1869-1874d.

SCHILDT, L. unlocated. Percussion 1/2 stock.

SCHILEY, CHRISTIAN Celina, Ohio, 1859d. (Hutslar)

SCHILLER, J.H. unlocated. Flintlock Kentucky rifle.

SCHILLING St. Louis, Missouri, 1869-1874. Percussion target rifle.

SCHILLING, A. Washington, D.C., 1865d-1866d.

SCHILLING, CHARLES Chicago, Illinois, 1859d.

SCHILLING, CHARLES F. St. Louis, Missouri, 1875d-1879d, St. Paul, Minnesota, 1879-1892d. Air guns in St. Louis.

SCHILLING, DANIEL Gayoso, Missouri, 1860d-1879d. Percussion 1/2 stock.

SCHILLING, E. Sigourney, Iowa, 1880d, Mt. Carroll, Illinois, 1882d.

SCHILLING, ERNST Chippewa Falls, Wisconsin, 1884d-1886d.

SCHILLING, FRANK (1835-1916), San Francisco, California, 1858-1862, San Jose, California, 1862-1916. As F. Schilling & Son, 1898-?. (Shelton)

SCHILLING, FREDERICK Lancaster, Pennsylvania, 1857d.

SCHILLING, FREDERICK St. Charles, Missouri, 1850c, St. Louis, Missouri, 1869-1874. As Blickensdoerffer & Schilling in St. Louis.

SCHILLING, HERBERT EMILE (1861-?), San Jose, California, 1875-1913. Son of Frank Schilling.

SCHILLING, PETER Lancaster, Pennsylvania, 1857d.

SCHILLINGER, CHARLES St. Louis, Missouri, 1859-1864d. As Schillinger & Neff, 1859-1860.

SCHIMMING & EDDINGS Marlin, Texas, 1892d-1896d.

SCHIMPF, JOHN P. St. Louis, Missouri, 1865d-1893d.

SCHINNERER, FRED S. Columbus, Indiana, 1870c, Hope, Arkansas, 1884d-1917. (MB 10-50, Elias)

SCHIRER, JOHN (?-1828), Charleston, South Carolina, 1806-1828. Patent #none April 12, 1826, gunstock crooking by steaming. Also known as John Shires. (Kauffman 2)

SCHIRER, MARY CHARLOTTE Charleston, South Carolina, 1828-1829d. Widow and successor to John Schirer. (Hobbies 7-42)

SCHJAGEV, O.V.H. Wiota, Wisconsin, 1857d.

SCHLAGEL, N. Lakeview, Oregon, 1889d-1891d.

SCHLARBAUM, JOHN C. Ukiah, California, 1876-1880. (Shelton)

SCHLAT, ED Chicago, Illinois, circa 1860. (Johnson)

SCHLEGELMILCH, HERMAN (1830-1903), New York, New York, 1853, Bethlehem, Pennsylvania, Chicago, Illinois, Beaver Dam, Wisconsin, 1855-1860, Cedar Rapids, Iowa, 1860, Eau Claire, Wisconsin, 1860-1903. Percussion rifles and shotguns. (GR 10-58)

SCHLEICHER, JOHN Richmond, Virginia, 1868-1884d.

SCHLEY, JACOB (?-1811), Fredrickstown, Maryland, 1765-1811. Committee of Safety rifles and flintlock Kentucky. (Hartzler)

SCHLOERB, GEORGE CONRAD (1826-1895), Cleveland, Ohio, 1848-1850, Detroit, Michigan, 1850-1854, Oshkosh, Wisconsin, 1854-1895. Percussion rifles. (WGCA 4)

SCHLOTTERBACK, CHARLES (1814-?), Ottawa Co., Ohio, 1846-1850c. (Hutslar)

SCHMACHER, CHARLES see Charles Schumacher.

SCHMALTZERN New York, New York. Air gun. (Wolff)

SCHMEISER, GOTTLIPP Sacramento, California, 1855-1859. (Shelton)

SCHMELZER, J.F. Leavenworth, Kansas, 1855-1884d, Kansas City, Kansas, 1885d-1900. Percussion 1/2 stock. As Schmelzer Hardware Co. in Kansas City. Used Schmelzer Arms Co. as a trade name on shotguns.

SCHMEYKAL, WENZEL South Bend, Indiana, 1869d. (Lindert)

SCHMIDT & KOSSE Houston, Texas, 1870-1872d. Derringers and 1/2 stock rifles. Ernst Schmidt's widow Christine and bookkeeper Louis Kosse operated as successors to E. Schmidt & Co. under this name.

SCHMIDT & SON Memphis, Tennessee, 1891-1908. John G. Schmidt.

SCHMIDT, A. Hinckley, Ohio, 1894. Underhammer bench gun. (Hutslar)

SCHMIDT, ANDREW Ft. Smith, Arkansas, 1878d. Percussion fullstock. (Elias)

SCHMIDT, ANTON, E. Portland, Oregon, 1886d-1891d.

SCHMIDT, CHRISTINE Houston, Texas, 1870-1872d. Widow of Ernst Schmidt. See Schmidt & Kosse.

SCHMIDT, E., & CO. Houston, Texas, 1866-1870. Derringers and plains rifles. Ernst Schmidt. Succeeded by Schmidt & Kosse, 1870-1872d. See Christine Schmidt, Louis Kosse, and Schmidt & Kosse.

SCHMIDT, ERNST (?-1870), Houston, Texas, 1860-1870d. As E. Schmidt & Co., 1866-1870. Derringers and plains rifles. See Schmidt & Kosse.

SCHMIDT, G.B. Newark, New Jersey, 1878d.

SCHMIDT, G.R. Cedar Rapids, Iowa, 1884d-1887d.

SCHMIDT, GEORGE Salem, North Carolina, 1775. Barrelmaker. (Bivins)

SCHMIDT, HEINRICH Lancaster, Pennsylvania, 1857d.

SCHMIDT, JOHN Augusta, Missouri, 1860d.

SCHMIDT, JOHN G. Memphis, Tennessee, 1862-1908d. Repairs for the Confederacy. As Schmidt & Son, 1891-1908.

SCHMIDT, L. unlocated. Percussion 1/2 stock.

SCHMIDT, WILLIAM Jefferson City, Missouri, 1860d-1898d.

SCHMIDT, WILLIAM New York, New York. Patent #16,288 December 23, 1856, single shot breechloader with H. Schroeder & L. Salewski. (GR 10-63)

SCHMITZ, WILHELM Philadelphia, Pennsylvania. Patent #85,482 December 29, 1868, explosive cartridge.

SCHNADER, FRANKLIN K. (1831-1906), Mohn's Store, Pennsylvania, 1856d-1890d. Barrelmaker. (Hobbies 5-37)

SCHNADER, NATHANIEL (1869-?), Mohns Store, Pennsylvania, 1884-1890. Son of Franklin Schnader. With his father, 1884-1890. (Hobbies 5-37)

SCHNAUSS, GEORGE Coatsville, Illinois, 1860d.

SCHNAUT, T.G. (?-1838), Monmouth, New Jersey, 1822-1838. Rifles.

SCHNAUTZ, H.I. Garner, Iowa, 1887d.

SCHNECKENBERGER, JOHN New Orleans, Louisiana, 1874d-1879d.

SCHNEELOCH, OTTO Brooklyn, New York, 1868-1877d. Percussion guns. Patents #134,442 December 31, 1872, revolver, and #165,031 June 29, 1875, breechloading firearms. Revolver used triangular bullets! (Winans)

SCHNEGELER, G. unlocated. Flintlock Kentucky.

SCHNEGELSCHEIPEN, J.W. Warrensburgh, Missouri, 1889d-1893d.

SCHNEIDER & GLASSICK Memphis, Tennessee, 1860d-1862. Derringers and percussion revolvers. William S. Schneider and Frederick G. Glassick.

SCHNEIDER & SON(S) Dayton, Ohio, 1866-1876. Percussion 1/2 stock. Michael Schneider and sons Charles E. and/or Edward J. (Hutslar)

SCHNEIDER, ALOIS (1824-1886), San Francisco, California, 1859-1886. Percussion 1/2 stock and target guns. Patents #226,679 April 20, 1880, breechloading firearms, #228,560 June 8, 1880, magazine firearms with A. Rheude, #243,801 July 5, 1881, magazine firearms with C.F. Board, #252,145 January 10, 1882, magazine firearms, and #300,515 June 17, 1884, method of rifling guns. As Schneider & Browning, 1867-1871. (Shelton)

SCHNEIDER, C.G. Washington, D.C., 1864-1865d. (Hartzler)

SCHNEIDER, CHARLES (1820-?), Boonville, Indiana, 1855-1880, Mt. Vernon, Indiana, 1848-1854. Flintlock and percussion fullstock. (Lindert)

SCHNEIDER, CHARLES E. Dayton, Ohio, 1874-1883d. With William W. Hackney as Hackney & Schneider, 1858-1860. With his brother Edward J. and father Michael as Schneider & Son(s), 1866-1876. Successor to Michael Schneider. (Hutslar)

SCHNEIDER, EDWARD J. Dayton, Ohio, 1866-1882d. With his brother Charles E. and father Michael as Schneider & Son(s), 1866-1876. With William W. Hackney as Hackney & Schneider, 1879-1882. (Hutslar)

SCHNEIDER, F.A. Columbia, South Carolina, 1860. (Hutslar)

SCHNEIDER, FREDERICK ALEXANDER (1790-1864), Canton, Ohio, 1829-1857c. Barrels. (Hutslar)

SCHNEIDER, J. Hagerstown, Maryland, 1878-1880d. (Hartzler)

SCHNEIDER, JOHN Lancaster, Pennsylvania, 1793t. Flintlock Kentucky. (Dyke)

SCHNEIDER, JOHN Peoria, Illinois, 1878d-1893d.

SCHNEIDER, MICHAEL Columbus, Ohio, 1849-1850c, Dayton, Ohio, 1853d-1888d. Percussion 1/2 stock. As Schneider & Son(s), with Charles and/or Edward, 1866-1876. (Hutslar)

SCHNEIDER, PAUL F. Hartford, Connecticut, 1866-1889d. Patents #56,804 July 31, 1866, cartridge box, and #73,549 January 21, 1868, cartridge box.

SCHNEIDER, WILLIAM H. San Francisco, California, 1875-1892. Air guns. Son of Alois Schneider. (Shelton)

SCHNEIDER, WILLIAM S. Memphis, Tennessee. 1859d-1873d. Derringers. As Schneider & Co., 1859. With Frederick G. Glassick as Schneider & Glassick, 1860-1864.

SCHNEISITZER, CHARLES Mauch Chunk, Pennsylvania, 1873d.

SCHNELLHART, E. Jersey City, New Jersey, 1878d.

SCHNIDER, FREDERICK Philadelphia, Pennsylvania, 1797-1798. Contract pistols. (ASAC 3)

SCHNOUDS, L. Freehold, New Jersey, 1866d.

SCHOB, I. unlocated. Flintlock Kentucky rifle dated 1815.

SCHOBER, W. Jacksonville, Florida, 1886d.

SCHOBER, WILLIAM Columbus, Georgia, 1879d-1885d.

SCHODT, CHARLES Pottsville, Pennsylvania, 1880d.

SCHOENEMAN, FREDERICK (1833-?), San Francisco, California, 1859-1862, 1873-1898, Virginia City, Nevada, 1862-1873. Needlefire shotgun. (Shelton)

SCHOENEMAN, HERMAN Virginia City, Nevada, 1867d-1884d.

SCHOENER, HENRY Reading, Pennsylvania, 1850-1863. Percussion hunting rifle. (Kauffman)

SCHOENFELD, F. Denver, Colorado, 1873d. (Sellers-3)

SCHOENFELD, HENRY Baraboo, Wisconsin, 1879d-1895d.

SCHOENHEIT, JULE Falls City, Nebraska, 1886d.

SCHOENING, CHARLES J. Ravenswood, Illinois. Patent #350,565 October 12, 1886, magazine gun.

SCHOETTLER, CHRISTIAN (1822-?), Princeton, Illinois, 1871-1893d. (Johnson)

SCHOFIELD, B.D. Fowlerville, Michigan, 1872d-1883d.

SCHOFIELD, G.L. Lexington, Missouri, 1879d.

SCHOFIELD, GEORGE W. U.S. Army. Patents #104,211 June 14, 1870, breechloading firearm, #116,225 June 20, 1871, revolver, #138,047 April 22, 1873, revolver, #193,620 July 31, 1877, revolver, and #227,449 May 11, 1880, revolver. Model 3 Schofield revolvers made by Smith & Wesson.

SCHOFIELD, N.D. Fowlerville, Michigan, 1865-1883d. Percussion over/under rifle/shotgun.

SCHOFIELD, W.C. Caldwell, Ohio. (Hutslar)

SCHOLFIELD, NATHAN Norwich, Connecticut. Patents #16,819 March 10, 1857, bomb lance with W.W. Wright, #18,824 December 8, 1857, bomb lance, and #18,866 December 15, 1857, projectile.

SCHOLL & HOLMES Virginia City, Nevada, 1865d-1867d. Christian Frederick Scholl.

SCHOLL & ROBERTS Virginia City, Nevada, 1862-1864d. Christian Frederick Scholl and Henry C. Roberts.

SCHOLL, CHARLES (1833-?), Marysville, California, 1855-1862. (Shelton)

SCHOLL, CHRISTIAN FREDERICK (1821-?), Bellville, Illinois, ?-1849, Virginia City, Nevada, 1861-1869, Marysville, California, 1850-1861 and 1863-1864, Oakland, California, 1875-1885. Derringers. With Henry C. Roberts as Scholl & Roberts, 1864-1864d. As Scholl & Holmes, 1865-1867. With Henry Jahn as Jahn & Scholl, 1875-1880. (Shelton)

SCHOMBEL, HERMAN Chicago, Illinois, 1886d-1888d.

SCHONTZ, P.H. Canal Fulton, Ohio, 1849-1865. (Knittle)

SCHOOLER, THOMAS St. Stephens, South Carolina, 1809. (Kauffman 2)

SCHOOLEY, GEORGE W. Alliance, Ohio, 1876d-1898d. (Hutslar)

SCHOPP, FRANCIS Philadelphia, Pennsylvania, 1865, New York, New York, 1875d-1876d. Patent #51,225 November 28, 1865, harmonica gun.

SCHORER, ANDREW Lancaster Co., Pennsylvania, 1775-1780. (Gluckman & Satterlee)

SCHORER, FRANK Galveston, Texas, 1892d.

SCHORN, A.O.H.P. Murfreesboro, Tennessee. Patent #12,328 January 30, 1855, revolver cane. (Sellers-1)

SCHOTT, CARL Nashville, Tennessee, 1859-1867d.

SCHOTT, CHARLES Nashville, Tennessee, 1881d-1891d. Son of Carl Schott.

SCHOTT, L. Jackson, California, 1870. As Gonel & Schott. (Shelton)

SCHOVERLING & DALY New York, New York, 1865d-1939. Also operated as Schoverling, Daly & Gales after 1878.

SCHOVERLING, AUGUST New York, New York, 1887d-1899d. Warner type .22 rifle with "patent applied for" marking. Imported shotguns and pistols.

SCHOYEN, GEORGE C. (1845-1916), Denver, Colorado, 1872-1916. With Carlos Gove, 1872. With Daniel W. Butt as Schoyen & Butt, 1884-1887. With Fred A. Burgen as Schoyen & Burgen, 1887-1896. With Axel W. Peterson as Schoyen & Peterson, 1903-1916. Brother of Olaf Schoyen. (GD 28)

SCHOYEN, OLAF Denver, Colorado, 1881d-1893d. Brother of George Schoyen. (Sellers-3)

SCHRADE, C. Roanoke, Virginia, 1885d.

SCHRADER, HERMAN New York, New York, 1872d-1890d. With Frank Ralph as Ralph & Schrader 1875-1879.

SCHRAPEL, LOUIS (1845-?), Galesburg, Illinois, 1868d, Golden, Colorado, 1875d-1879d and 1881d, North Platte, Nebraska, 1878, Georgetown, Colorado, 1880c-1882d, Gunnison, Colorado, 1882-1885d, Aspen, Colorado, 1886d. Percussion 1/2 stock. Also listed as Louis Schrepel, and as L. Shrepel. (Sellers-3)

SCHRAUD, FRANZ San Antonio, Texas. Patent #295,437, March 18, 1884, breechloading firearm.

SCHRAYER, GEORGE see George Schroyer.

SCHRECKENGOST, DANIEL Connellsville, Pennsylvania, 1830-1835. (Harriger)

SCHRECKENGOST, LINCOLN (1865-1949), Putneyville, Pennsylvania. Son of William Schreckengost. (Kauffman)

SCHRECKENGOST, PETER Kittaning, Pennsylvania, 1870-1871. Son of William Schreckengost. (Kauffman)

SCHRECKENGOST, WILLIAM (1821-1897), Putneyville, Pennsylvania, 1857-1897d. Percussion 1/2 stock. (Whisker II)

SCHREIBEL, GEORGE LOUIS (1840-?), Sacramento, California, 1868-1873. (Shelton)

SCHREIBER, JOHN unlocated. Flintlock Kentucky.

SCHREIBER, LEONARD Cincinnati, Ohio, 1850-1875. (Hutslar)

SCHREIDT, JOHN Reading, Pennsylvania, 1758-1768. Same as John Schridt. Flintlock Kentucky. (Kauffman)

SCHREINER, FREDERICK New York, New York, 1886d-1889d.

SCHREPEL, LOUIS see Louis Schrapel.

SCHREYER, G. see George Schroyer.

SCHRIDT, JOHN Reading, Pennsylvania, 1758-1761. Flintlock Kentucky. (Dillin)

SCHRIEBNER, JOHN (1800-?), Lockport, Illinois, 1850c. (Johnson)

SCHRIENER, JOHN W. Mechanicsburg, Pennsylvania, 1866-1871.

SCHRIVER, DAVID Richmond, Virginia, 1859. For Samuel Sutherland. (Albaugh 1)

SCHRIVER, G.B. Camden, South Carolina, 1861. Breechloading gun, an improvement on the Maynard. (Albaugh 1)

SCHRIVER, J. see J. Shriver.

SCHRIVNER, JAMES A. Auburn, New York. Percussion target rifle. (Swinney)

SCHROCK, JACOB D. (1823-1918), Goshen, Indiana, 1852-1918. Percussion guns. (MB 3-47)

SCHROD, CHARLES Ellicott City, Maryland, 1884d-1885d.

SCHROEDER, CHARLES St. Louis, Missouri, 1889d.

SCHROEDER, G.H. LaGrange, Texas, 1890d.

SCHROEDER, HERMAN Bloomington, Illinois. Patents #16,288 December 23, 1856, single shot breechloading mechanism with L. Salewski and William Schmidt, and #32,653 June 25, 1861, breechloading firearm with Herman Schroder. (GR 10-63)

SCHROEDER, JOHN Tama City, Iowa, 1887d.

SCHROEDER, VALENTINE Buckstown, Pennsylvania, 1843t, Baltimore, Maryland, 1847d. (Hartzler)

SCHROYER, GEORGE Reading, Pennsylvania, 1758-1768, Hanover, Pennsylvania, 1775-1813. Flintlock Kentucky. (Kindig)

SCHROYER, GEORGE, JR. York Co., Pennsylvania, 1793, Franklin Co., Pennsylvania, 1804t-1805t, Baltimore, Maryland, 1810d-1815d. Flintlock Kentucky. (Hartzler)

SCHROYER, MATHIAS Taneytown, Maryland, 1796-1800. Model 1798 contract muskets. (Hartzler)

SCHUBARTH, CASPAR D. Providence, Rhode Island, 1855-1868. Patent #32,895 July 23, 1861, breechloading firearm. Model 1861 contract muskets and a few rifles on the Gallagher & Gladding patent. (Fuller)

SCHUBERT, ADOLPH Chicago, Illinois, circa 1860. (Johnson)

SCHUBERT, C.F. & W.B. Fredonia, Kansas, 1884d.

SCHUBERT, CARL F. Fredonia, Kansas, 1884d, Columbus, Nebraska, 1886d-1893d, Alma, Kansas, 1894d.

SCHUDELL, WILLIAM Sioux City, Iowa, 1882d-1884d.

SCHUDT, JOHN New York, New York. Patents #191,721 June 5, 1877, breechloading firearms, and #197,742 December 4, 1877, breechloading firearms with J.P. Schudt.

SCHUDT, MOREND Omaha, Nebraska, 1876d-1884d.

SCHULAR, DAN Round Head, Ohio, 1859d. (Hutslar)

SCHULER, JACOB Macungie, Pennsylvania, 1789t. (KRA II-3)

SCHULER, JOHN Quakertown, Pennsylvania, 1811. (Kauffman)

SCHULER, PETER Morris, Indiana, 1867-1885. Percussion 1/2 stock. Patents #85,616 January 5, 1869, breechloading firearms, and #108,836 November 1, 1870, breechloading firearms.

SCHULER, VALENTINE (1810-?), New Philadelphia, Ohio, 1850c-1853d. (Hutslar)

SCHULL, M. Lancaster Co., Pennsylvania, 1800-1838. Flintlock Kentucky.

SCHULT, M. Omaha, Nebraska, 1893d. See Morend Schudt.

SCHULT, MORGAN (1841-?), San Jose, California, 1870c. (Shelton)

SCHULTE, H.H. Pittsburgh, Pennsylvania, 1868d-1875. See H.H. Schutte.

SCHULTHEIS, JOHN Pekin, Illinois, 1850. (Johnson)

SCHULTZ, C. unlocated. Flintlock Kentucky.

SCHULTZ, C.A. Sauk City, Wisconsin. Percussion 1/2 stock.

SCHULTZ, CARL Alexandria, Dakota Territory (South Dakota), 1882d.

SCHULTZ, CHARLES Alexandria, Minnesota, 1878d-1886d.

SCHULTZ, FREDERICK Beardstown, Illinois, 1880d-1884d, Virginia, Illinois, 1884d-1893d.

SCHULTZ, GUSTAVUS Fort Madison, Iowa, 1876d. See Gustav Shulz.

SCHULTZ, HENRY Richland, Pennsylvania, 1860d. Percussion 1/2 stock.

SCHULTZ, HERMAN Syracuse, New York. Patent #312,564, February 17, 1885, breechloading firearm with Jacob Hurst.

SCHULTZ, J.S. Staunton, Illinois, 1860d.

SCHULTZ, JOHN (1824-?), Henry, Illinois, 1860c. (Johnson)

SCHULTZ, M. unlocated. Flintlock Kentucky.

SCHULTZ, R.A. Kansas City, Missouri, 1884d.

SCHULTZE, FREDERICK E. New York, New York. Patents #208,203 September 17, 1878, machine gun, and #208,204 September 17, 1878, machine gun.

SCHULZ, GUSTAV Ft. Madison, Iowa. Patent #89,947 May 11, 1869, breechloading firearm.

SCHUM, CHRISTIAN St. Louis, Missouri, 1857d.

SCHUMACHER, CHARLES Union, Humboldt Bay, California, 1856-1863, Walla Walla, Washington, 1863-1891d. Percussion 1/2 stock. (Shelton)

SCHUMACHER, CONRAD Baltimore, Maryland, 1858d-1887d. Also Schumachur. (Hartzler)

SCHUMACHER, PHILLIP Vincennes, Indiana, 1857-1874. (Lindert)

SCHUMANN, FRANK W. Memphis, Tennessee, 1876d-1891d. Derringer.

SCHUMANN, LOUIS Memphis, Tennessee, 1860d-1875. Percussion guns.

SCHURR, JOHN Henry, Illinois, 1878d-1893d.

SCHURY, HENRY GOTTLIEB (1823-1912), Xenia, Ohio, 1869-1912. (MB 10-58)

SCHUSLER, NICHOLAS Morgantown, Virginia, 1840-1860.

SCHUTT, ALOIS L. Cleveland, Ohio, 1871-1896. (Hutslar)

SCHUTT, MOREND see Morend Schudt.

SCHUTT, PETER Cleveland, Ohio, 1888-1890d. Son of A.L. Schutt. (Hutslar)

SCHUTTE, D.A. (?-1894), Chillicothe, Ohio, 1855d-1894d. Percussion fullstock. (Hutslar)

SCHUTTE, H.H. Pittsburgh, Pennsylvania, 1864-1877. As Iron City Gun Works after the death of D.J. McDonald, 1864-1877. Also listed as H.H. Schulte. (Kauffman)

SCHUYLER & DUANE New York, New York, 1881d. Importers and dealers.

SCHUYLER, HARTLEY & GRAHAM New York, New York, 1857d-1880d. Dealers, percussion and cartridge guns. Marking "S.H. & G." and others.

SCHWARTZ & MARIN Savannah, Georgia, 1868-1875. Percussion pistols and rifles.

SCHWARTZ, C. O'Quinn, Texas, 1884d-1892d.

SCHWARTZ, FREDERICK St. Louis, Missouri, 1854d-1898d.

SCHWARTZ, JOSEPH Bay City, Michigan, 1893d-1895d.

SCHWARTZKOPF, PAUL Philadelphia, Pennsylvania, 1862-1863. Converted flintlock muskets.

SCHWATKA, FREDERICK Vancouver Barracks, Washington Territory. Patent #305,537 September 23, 1884, folding gunstock.

SCHWEITZER, ABRAHAM (1769-1831), Lancaster, Pennsylvania, 1794-1795, Chambersburg, Pennsylvania, 1795-1831. Flintlock Kentucky. (Bowers)

SCHWEITZER, CONRAD (1824-1873), Canton, Ohio, 1848-1866d. With Louis P. Wikidal as Schweitzer & Wikidal, 1859, Schweitzer & Co., 1866. Percussion 1/2 stocks. (Hutslar)

SCHWEITZER, DANIEL Lancaster, Pennsylvania, 1790c. (Dean*)

SCHWEITZER, JACOB (1810-1864), Chambersburg, Pennsylvania, 1831-1840. Son of Abraham Schweitzer. (Kindig)

SCHWEITZER, JOHN (1805-?), Chambersburg, Pennsylvania, 1826t-1829t, Greenville, Ohio, 1850c. (Bowers)

SCHWENKE, HERMAN (1822-?), Chillicothe, Ohio, 1866-1868d, Circleville, Ohio, 1860c-1864d and 1894-1897d. Percussion 1/2 stock. (Hutslar)

SCHWERTZ, FREDERICK W. St. Louis, Missouri, 1879d-1899d. (Pourie)

SCITUATE lock marking on Model 1798 contract muskets by Rhodes & Tyler.

SCLATER, JOHN York Co., Virginia, 1776. (Gill)

SCOBEL & PFISTERER Lincoln, Nebraska, 1879d. L. Pfisterer.

SCOTT suicide special and taxidermy gun by Hopkins & Allen.

SCOTT Washington Co., Pennsylvania, 1800. Flintlock Kentucky. (Dean)

SCOTT & MONTEITH Albany, Oregon, 1880d.

SCOTT ARMS CO. suicide special.

SCOTT, ANDREW D. Merced, California, 1881d. (Shelton)

SCOTT, CHARLES B. Las Vegas, New Mexico Territory. Patent #299,686 June 3, 1884, machine gun.

SCOTT, CHARLES E. Albany, New York, 1883d-1891d. Son of R.H. Scott.

SCOTT, CORNELIEUS W. Constantia, Ohio. Patent #44,827 November 25, 1864, lock.

SCOTT, E. Albany, New York. Percussion target rifle. (Swinney)

SCOTT, E.E. Carson City, Nevada, 1871d.

SCOTT, GALLAGHER & CO. Louisville, Kentucky. Percussion fullstock rifle, and "S.G. & CO." marked locks.

SCOTT, GEORGE Dubuque, Iowa, 1850c. (MB 8-64)

SCOTT, GEORGE New Haven, Connecticut(?) or New Jersey(?), 1690.

SCOTT, GRANT Zanesville, Ohio, 1804-1820. (Knittle)

SCOTT, J.Q.A. Pittsburgh, Pennsylvania. Patent #36,174 August 12, 1862, magazine firearm.

SCOTT, JOHN (?-1759), Charleston, South Carolina, 1740-1759. Flintlock fowler. (Kauffman 2)

SCOTT, JOHN D. (1829-?), Mercer Co., Virginia, 1850c. (Whisker IV)

SCOTT, L.B. Waverly, New York, 1879-1882d.

SCOTT, MATTHEW Floyd Courthouse, Virginia, 1871d-1893d. Percussion fullstock. Repairs for the Confederacy. (Sellers)

SCOTT, MATTHEW Ohio, 1842, Dubuque, Iowa, 1850c. (MB 8-64)

SCOTT, PENNINGTON (1824-?), Millwood, Ohio, 1850c. (Hutslar)

SCOTT, R.H. Albany, New York, 1848-1891d.

SCOTT, RAY Wogansport, North Dakota, 1898d.

SCOTT, SYLVESTER Bristol, Vermont, 1846-1849d.

SCOTT, W.B. Albany, Oregon, 1880d-1886d. As Scott & Monteith, 1880d.

SCOTT, W.J. & R.H. Albany, New York, 1848-1874. Percussion guns.

SCOTT, WILLIAM M. Leadville, Missouri, 1860d.

SCOTTS, J.N. St. Louis, Missouri. Percussion guns. (MB 3-66)

SCOUT suicide special by Hood Fire Arms Co.

SCOUT, C.M. Baxter Springs, Kansas, 1878d-1882d.

SCOUT, JACOBUS (1736-1829), Bucks Co., Pennsylvania. Flintlock Kentucky with "J.S." marking.

SCRIBER, S.J. Syracuse, New York, 1866-1868. Same as Stephen J. Scriber, Elmira, New York?

SCRIBER, STEPHEN J. Elmira, New York, 1862d-1866d. With William P. Dewitt as Dewitt & Scriber. Same as S.J. Scriber, Syracuse, New York?

SCRIGGINS, GEORGE Dover, New Hampshire, 1869-1875d.

SCRIPTURE, OLIVER O. Prescott, Arizona. Patent #628,360 July 4, 1899, adjustable stock.

SCRIVENER, JAMES A. (1823-?), Pontiac, Michigan, 1843-1850, Auburn, New York, 1851. For Morgan Olmstead in Pontiac. (Massachusetts Arms)

SCRUGGS, HENRY (?-1793), Cumberland Co., Virginia, 1776. Committee of Safety repairs. (Gill)

SEABROOK, WILLIAM Lancaster Co., Pennsylvania, 1807t. (Dean)

SEABURY, J., & CO. Southbridge, Massachusetts, 1861. Underhammer. (Logan)

SEAGROVE, JOHN Neosho, Missouri, 1898d.

SEAMAN, CONRAD Lithopolis, Ohio, 1866-1888d. (Hutslar)

SEAMAN, E.J. Ashtabula, Ohio, 1888d. (Hutslar)

SEARCY, BARTLETT Knox Co., Missouri, 1850c. (MB 11-66)

SEARLES, DANIEL (1782-1860), Baton Rouge, Louisiana, 1836-1860. (AG 9-78)

SEARS, HENRY Rockford, Illinois.

SEARS, HENRY, & CO. Chicago, Illinois, 1872-1892d. Shotguns. (Johnson)

SEARS, ROEBUCK & CO. Many U.S. and Canadian locations. Sales only. Large quantities of inexpensive guns sold under the company or several trade names.

SEARS, WILLIAM P. (1820-?), Huntington, Indiana, 1850c. (Lindert)

SEAVER, E. Vergennes, Vermont, 1842-1843. Percussion fullstock and derringers. (Kauffman 2)

SEAVER, F.A. Lake Mills, Wisconsin, 1857d.

SEAVER, GEORGE V. Vergennes, Vermont, 1855-1860. Underhammer pistols. With M.S. Sanderson, 1858. (Horn)

SEAVER, W.A. New York, New York. Percussion 1/2 stock and derringer.

SEAVER, WILLIAM S. Brush's Mills, New York, 1862d. (Swinney)

SEAY Washington Co., Kentucky. Born in Ireland, pioneer gunsmith. (Hist KY, V4, P367)

SEBASTIAN, W.K. Clarendon, Arkansas, 1898d.

SEBBY, JAMES Washington, D.C., 1855d. (Hartzler)

SECHREST unlocated. Flintlock Kentucky.

SECONGOST, J.M. Booneville, Missouri, 1889d.

SECOR & CONNER Forest City, Iowa, 1892d.

SECOR, JEROME (1839-?), Peoria, Illinois, 1860c. Son of Oliver Secor. (Johnson)

SECOR, OLIVER P. Weston, Missouri, 1850c, Peoria, Illinois, 1860d-?, Chicago, Illinois, 1863d-1867d.

SECREST, J.R. (?-1888), Vinton, Iowa, 1876-1888.

SECRET SERVICE suicide special. (Webster)

SEDGEWICK & BRANDON Pittsfield, Massachusetts, 1869d.

SEDGLEY, R.F., INC. Philadelphia, Pennsylvania. See Reginald F. Sedgley.

SEDGLEY, REGINALD F. (?-1938), Philadelphia, Pennsylvania, 1897-1938. "Baby Hammerless" revolver. Patents #1,216,001 February 13, 1917, revolver #1,236,608 August 14, 1917, revolver, and #2,029,839 February 4, 1936, machine gun. Superintendent for, and successor to, Henry Kolb. As R.F. Sedgley, Inc.

SEDGWICK, C.J. Dayton, Ohio, 1880c. (Hutslar)

SEDWICK, G.S. Rimersburg, Pennsylvania, 1861d.

SEEBACH, EDWARD (1805-?), San Jose, California, 1870c. (Shelton)

SEEBACH, GEORGE W. New York, New York. Patent #441,512 November 25, 1890, spring gun.

SEEBROOKS, WILLIAM Lancaster Co., Pennsylvania 1803-1808. (KRA IV-4)

SEEL, CHARLES Charleston, South Carolina, 1885d-1886d.

SEELE, HENRY Rolla, Missouri, 1879d.

SEELEY, AUSTIN (1820-?), Walworth Co., Wisconsin, 1845-1849, Reedsburg, Wisconsin, 1849-1879d. Percussion rifles. (GC-1)

SEELEY, D.N. Dunkirk, New York, 1869-1882d. Over/under percussion rifles.

SEELEY, D.T. Bradford, Pennsylvania, 1882d-1890d.

SEELEY, EDGAR D. Brookline, Massachusetts. Patents #33,626 November 29, 1861, gun capping implement, and #35,783 July 7, 1862, cap priming attachment.

SEELEY, J.S. Delhi, New York 1870d.

SEELEY, SAMUEL J. New York, New York. Patents #5,845 October 10, 1848, shot plug, and #33,854 December 3, 1861, multi-barrel belt gun.

SEELEY, W. unlocated. Flintlock Kentucky.

SEES, JACOB (?-1812), Lancaster Co., Pennsylvania, 1800-1812. Flintlock Kentucky rifles and pistols. (Kindig)

SEES, WILLIAM P. Huntington, Indiana, 1858d-1862d. Percussion 1/2 stock.

SEESE & DUNCAN Petersburg, Illinois, 1864d.

SEEWALD, VALENTINE Tiffin, Ohio, 1830-1836. (Hutslar)

SEEWITHE, CHARLES Addison, New York, 1850c.

SEIBBLE see Christian Siple, also Jacob Sible.

SEIBER, EDWARD ROBERT Jacksonville, Illinois, 1865-1906. (Johnson)

SEIBERT, GEORGE Franklin Co., Pennsylvania, 1813-1824. Flintlock Kentucky rifle. (Bowers)

SEIDEL, CARL Cincinnati, Ohio, 1891d. (Hutslar)

SEIDNER, J. unlocated. Percussion fullstock.

SEIFERTH, FREDERICK E. St. Louis, Missouri, 1860-1890d.

SEIFRIT, I. unlocated. Percussion 1/2 stock.

SEIGLER, AMOS see Amos Sigler.

SEIGLER, CHARLES Nashville, Illinois, 1864d-1875d.

SEIGLING, W.C. Henderson, Kentucky, 1885d.

SEILER, CHARLES Springfield, Missouri, 1898d.

SEINIHER, C. St. Peter, Minnesota, 1867d.

SEINMAN, JOHN Philadelphia, Pennsylvania, 1824d. Middle name Frederick?

SEIPEL, JOHN Washington, D.C., 1864-1866d. Percussion 1/2 stock. Patent #50,502 November 17, 1865, ordnance rifling.

SEIPPLE see Christian Siple, also Jacob Sible.

SEITS, GEORGE Col. (U.S. Army?), Lancaster, Ohio, 1815-1826. For John Beaman. (John Seits in some sources) (Knittle)

SELBY, JAMES D. (1822-?), Washington, D.C., 1850c-1862d. (Hartzler)

SELDEN, A. Hampton, New York, 1860d.

SELDON, A. Dorset, Vermont, 1845-1847. (Horn)

SELDON, ALONZO Whitehall, New York, 1850-1874d. Percussion rifle and shotguns. (Clow)

SELF, BRADLEY Washington, D.C., 1855d.

SELKREY, JOHN H. Ithaca, New York, 1865. Breechloading carbine.

SELL, B. unlocated. Percussion 1/2 stock.

SELL, FREDERICK (1781-1869), Littlestown, Pennsylvania, 1807-1861d. Flintlock Kentucky. Son of Jacob Sell. (Kindig)

SELL, JACOB (1741-1825), Littlestown, Pennsylvania, 1793-1825. Flintlock Kentucky. (Kindig)

SELL, JACOB (1780-1855), Littlestown, Pennsylvania, 1800-1825. Flintlock Kentucky. Son of Jacob Sell. (Kindig)

SELL, JACOB Canton, Ohio, 1807-1825. (Hutslar)

SELLECK, W.W. Hastings, Nebraska, 1879d.

SELLEN, MICHAEL Brighton, Wisconsin. Patent #158,988 January 19, 1873, firearm.

SELLERS, J.J. Kingston, North Carolina, 1877d-1884d.

SELLS, BENJAMIN (1815-?), Augusta, Kentucky, 1830, Georgetown, Ohio, 1835-1883d. Percussion 1/2 stock. Brother of Michael Sells. (Hutslar)

SELLS, F.M. Laurel, Ohio, 1860-1902. Percussion 1/2 stock. (Hutslar)

SELLS, JAMES (1832-?), Coshocton, Ohio, 1865. (Knittle)

SELLS, JOHN (1807-?), Ohio, 1830-1849, Rush Co., Indiana, 1850c. (Lindert)

SELLS, M.B. Georgetown, Ohio, 1839. (Knittle)

SELLS, MICHAEL (1797-?), Augusta, Kentucky, 1827-1860. Percussion fullstock and 1/2 stock. Brother of Benjamin Sells. (MB 4-65)

SELLS, R. unlocated. Percussion fullstock.

SELMA ARSENAL Selma, Alabama, 1861-1865. Muskets, swords and possibly pistols. Confederate Arsenal. (Albaugh 1)

SELVRIDGE, JOHN (1808-1867), Cleveland, Tennessee, 1826-1848. Flintlock Tennessee rifles. (Cline)

SEMMENCE, ED Erie, Pennsylvania, 1890-1900. (Gluckman & Satterlee)

SEMMLER, E.R. Luling, Texas, 1885d.

SEMPLE, A.B. Louisville, Kentucky, 1842d-1880d. Flintlock and early percussion rifles. As A.B. Semple & Bro., 1850-1861 and A.B. Semple & Sons, 1862d-1880.

SEMPLE, A.B. & SONS Louisville, Kentucky, 1862d-1880d. Dealers.

SEMPLE, A.B., & BRO. Louisville, Kentucky, 1850-1861. Importers and dealers.

SEMPLE, ROBERT J. Steubenville, Ohio, 1868d-1897d. (Hutslar)

SENATOR suicide special.

SENN, JOHN F. Rochester, New York, 1897d.

SENSENY, JEREMIAH S. (1821-1873), Chambersburg, Pennsylvania, 1846t-1873. Percussion fullstock. (Bowers)

SENTINAL suicide special.

SEPOPEL, GEORGE (1812-?), New Orleans, Louisiana, 1850c. (MB 9-65)

SERESSOLE, EDWARD New Orleans, Louisiana, 1822d.

SERGEANT, C.A. Lincoln, Maine, 1876-1879. (Lindsay 3)

SERGEANT, EBENEZER see Ebenezer Sargent.

SERLES Wellston, Ohio, circa 1900. (MB 8-55)

SERLES, D. unlocated. Flintlock Kentucky rifle.

SERVOSS, HENRY S. Matteawan, New York, 1864d. Barrelmaker.

SESSLER, ADAM Jamestown, Ohio. (Hutslar)

SETTEL, JOHN (1803-1873), Cashtown, Pennsylvania, 1831t-1873. Flintlock Kentucky rifle. Also known as John Settle. (Bowers)

SETTER, J.V. unlocated. Tip-up single shot pistols similar to J. Stevens Arms Co. designs.

SETTLE, FELIX (1801-1871), Roseville and Glasgow, Kentucky. Percussion and flintlock rifles. Son of William Settle. (GR 12-61)

SETTLE, G.A. Russellville, Kentucky, 1883d-1896d.

SETTLE, JOHN New York, New York, 1850c.

SETTLE, SIMON (1823-1871), Greensburg, Kentucky, Bowling Green, Kentucky, 1857. Son of Felix Settle. (MB 1-64, Hist KY, V5, P456))

SETTLE, WILLIAM (1770-1808), Rocky Hill, Kentucky, 1798-1808. Flintlock Kentucky. (GR 12-61)

SETTLE, WILLIS F. Glasgow, Kentucky, Roseville, Kentucky, 1860-?. Percussion 1/2 stock. Son of Felix Settle. (GR 12-61)

SEUZHSINGER, FRED (1835-?), Indianapolis, Indiana, 1860c. (Lindert)

SEVENDOLLAR, G. Belle Meade, Kansas, 1884d.

SEVER, A.D.R. Galesburgh, Illinois, 1888d.

SEVER, JOSEPH & SHUBABEL Framingham, Massachusetts, 1775-1782. Committee of Safety repairs.

SEVERANCE, CHARLES Lake Ann, Michigan, 1899d.

SEVERIN, GEORGE FREDERICK THEODORE (1805-?), San Francisco, California, 1860-1868. Percussion 1/2 stock. (Shelton)

SEVIC, RUDOLPH Chicago, Illinois, 1886d-1932d.

SEWALL, M.W. Brooklyn, New York. Patent #430,086 June 10, 1890, pneumatic gun.

SEWARD, AUSTIN (1797-1872), Bloomington, Indiana, 1821-1872. Percussion 1/2 stock. (Lindert)

SEWARD, BENJAMIN Boston, Massachusetts, 1796-1803. (Kauffman 2)

SEWARD, BRYSON (1829-1875), Harrison Co., Indiana, ?-1875, Corydon, Indiana, 1850c. Son of Austin Seward. (Lindert)

SEWARD, R., E. Worcester, New York, 1870-1882. Percussion 1/2 stock.

SEWER, JACOB Philadelphia, Pennsylvania, 1780-1785. Repaired U.S. arms. (Moller)

SEYMOUR unlocated. Percussion swivelbreech.

SEYMOUR, DUDLEY S. Hartford, Connecticut. Double-barrel pump rifle. Patent #576,744 February 9, 1897, magazine firearms.

SEYMOUR, FREDERICK J. Cleveland, Ohio. Patent #376,168 January 10, 1888, making guns and ordnance.

SEYMOUR, JAMES M. Boston, Massachusetts. Patents #35,354 May 20, 1862, breechloading firearms. (GR 5-80)

SHACKLEFORD, ERASTUS (1815-?), Ohio, 1837, Rising Sun, Indiana, 1850c. (Lindert)

SHADLE, J. Ingraham Prairie, Illinois, 1860d.

SHAEFER, FREDERICK (1815-?), Stockton, California, 1850-1860.

SHAEFFER Washington, D.C., 1867. With G. Frederick Fisher as Fisher & Shaeffer. (Hartzler)

SHAEFFER, LEONARD Springfield, Ohio, 1852d-1859d. (Hutslar)

SHAFER, ELIAS Paulding, Ohio, 1853d. (Hutslar)

SHAFER, F.H. Waverly, Iowa, 1892d.

SHAFER, JOSEPH unlocated. Flintlock Kentucky.

SHAFF, CHRISTIAN (1830-?), St. Louis, Missouri, 1850c. (Lewis)

SHAFF, JOHN (1822-?), St. Louis, Missouri, 1850c. (Lewis)

SHAFFER, BALTZER Baltimore, Maryland, 1783-1787. (Hartzler)

SHAFFER, HENRY Lancaster, Pennsylvania, 1797-1798. (Kauffman)

SHAFFER, J.A. Vicksburg, Mississippi, 1830-1850. Agent for Deringer. Percussion 1/2 stock.

SHAFFER, JACOB (1784-?), Wythe Co., Virginia, 1825-1850c. Flintlock Kentucky. See Jacob Schaffer. (Lindsay)

SHAFFER, JACOB (1820-?), Burke's Mills, Augusta Co., Virginia, 1860c. See Jacob Shaver.

SHAFFER, SIMON B. Ekalaka, Montana. Patent #435,905 September 2, 1890, magazine gun.

SHAFFNER, JOHN Lancaster, Pennsylvania, 1788. (KRA IV-4)

SHAKANOOSA ARMS MFG. CO. see Dickson, Nelson & Co. Alternate/trade name.

SHALER, IRA W. Brooklyn, New York. Patent #36,197 November 18, 1862, bullet with Reuben Shaler.

SHALER, REUBEN Madison, Connecticut. Patents #32,844 July 16, 1861, bullet, #36,197 November 18, 1862, bullet with Ira Shaler, #36,968 November 18, 1862, centrifugal gun, and #41,943 March 15, 1864, toy gun.

SHALLENBERGER, DANIEL Fayette Co., Pennsylvania, 1822-1829, Connellsville, Pennsylvania, 1830-1838. (Kauffman, Whisker II)

SHAMELL, JOHN see John Schammell.

SHAMKER, SAMUEL S. unlocated. Flintlock Kentucky rifle.

SHAMP, E.T. Plattsmouth, Nebraska, 1866d.

SHANE, BENJAMIN FRANKLIN Hampshire Co., West Virginia, 1850-1860. Percussion fullstock. (Whisker IV)

SHANLEY, FRANK Pueblo, Colorado, 1891d. (Sellers-3)

SHANNON & SON Boone Co., Indiana, 1860c.

SHANNON, ALEXANDER New York, New York. Patent #34,615 March 4, 1862, cartridges for small arms.

SHANNON, HUGH Philadelphia, Pennsylvania, 1803-1820d. Model 1808 contract muskets. With his father William Shannon as W. & H. Shannon, 1808-1816. (Gluckman)

SHANNON, W. & H. Philadelphia, Pennsylvania, 1808-1816. Model 1808 contract muskets. William and Hugh Shannon, father and son.

SHANNON, WILLIAM (1745-1823), Philadelphia, Pennsylvania, 1800-1823. Model 1808 contract muskets. As W. & H. Shannon with son Hugh, 1808-1816. (Gluckman)

SHANNON, WILLIAM Thornton, Indiana, 1858d-1860d. As Shannon & Son, 1860.

SHANNON, WILLIAM Winterset, Iowa, 1880d.

SHAPELY, J. HAMILTON Exeter, New Hampshire. Patent #39,501 August 11, 1863, gun lock.

SHAPLEIGH HARDWARE CO. St. Louis, Missouri, 1868-?. Wholesalers only.

SHAPLEIGH, DAY & CO. St. Louis, Missouri, 1848d-1867d.

SHARLAVILLE, JOHN Little Rock, Arkansas, 1826-1831. As Shaw & Shereville, 1826. (Elias)

SHARP Crystal Springs, Arkansas. Possibly Scharps?(Elias)

SHARP, JOHN Shelby Co., Ohio, 1860.

SHARP, N. Ozaukee, Wisconsin, 1857d.

SHARP, NOAH A. unlocated. Percussion fullstock.

SHARP, ROBERT (1810-?), Wood Co., Virginia, 1850c. (Whisker IV)

SHARP, SAMUEL Upper Sandusky, Ohio, 1878d-1896d. (Hutslar)

SHARPIE, C. Old Washington, Ohio, circa 1840. Percussion fullstock. (Hutslar)

SHARPIE, P.F. St. Johns, Michigan, 1860d.

SHARPLESS, DANIEL Pennsylvania, 1775. Committee of Safety gunsmith. (Kauffman 2)

SHARPLEY, J. HAMILTON Exeter, New Hampshire. Patent #39,501 August 11, 1863, lock.

SHARPS & HANKINS Philadelphia, Pennsylvania, 1861-1867. Four-barrel pistols and single shot rifles and carbines. Christian Sharps and William Hankins.

SHARPS RIFLE CO. Hartford, Connecticut, 1874-1876, Bridgeport, Connecticut, 1876-1881. Sharps patent rifles. (Sellers-4)

SHARPS RIFLE MFG. CO. Hartford, Connecticut, 1851-1874. Sharps patent rifles and shotguns. (Sellers-4)

SHARPS, C. Portland, Oregon, 1846-1850.

SHARPS, C., & CO. Philadelphia, Pennsylvania, 1853-1861 and 1865-1874. Percussion and cartridge pistols under Sharps patents. (Sellers-4)

SHARPS, CHRISTIAN (1811-1874), Philadelphia, Pennsylvania, 1850-1851 and 1853-1874, Hartford, Connecticut, 1851-1853. Patent #5,763 September 12, 1848, breechloading firearm-basic Sharps patent, #6,960 December 18, 1849, four-barrel percussion pistol, #9,308 October 5, 1852, priming mechanism, #9,820 June 28, 1853, primers, #16,072 November 11, 1856, bolt action rifle, #22,752 January 25, 1859, tip-up rifle, #22,753 January 25, 1859, four-barrel pistol, #29,108 July 10, 1860, priming cartridges, #30,647 November 13, 1860, forming cartridges, #30,765 November 27, 1860, revolver, #32,790 July 9, 1861, Sharps & Hankins rifle, #33,546 October 22, 1861, Sharps & Hankins safety, #33,607 October 27, 1861, Sharps & Hankins sight, #34,987 April 15, 1862, cartridge, #37,057 December 2, 1862, rifling machine, #40,772 December 1, 1863, priming cartridges, #48,729 July 11, 1865, projectile, #62,077 February 12, 1867, breechloading firearm, #90,590 May 25, 1869, propeller, #95,150 September 21, 1869, propeller, #103,458 November 22, 1870, propeller, #118,752 September 5, 1871, revolver, and #137,625 April 8, 1873, breechloading firearm. Guns made under these patents by Sharps Rifle Mfg. Co., Sharps Rifle Co., C. Sharps & Co. and Sharps & Hankins. (Sellers-4)

SHARPULL, SAMUEL (1828-?), Sonora, California, 1870c. (Shelton)

SHATTOO, L. Deerfield, Ohio, 1853d. (Hutslar)

SHATTUCK ARMS CO. Hatfield, Massachusetts, 1880-1909. Shattuck patent revolvers, "Unique" four-barrel pistols (O.F. Mossberg patent), "Unique" four-barrel revolvers (Andrew Hyde patent), and side-break (side-opening?) shotguns. Charles S. Shattuck.

SHATTUCK, CHARLES S. (1840-1919), Springfield, Massachusetts, 1876d-1877, Hatfield, Massachusetts, 1877d-1915d."Queen" derringers, "American" shotguns, "Unique" revolvers under Andrew Hyde's patent, and "Unique," four barrel pistols under OF. Mossberg's patent. With Andrew Hyde as Hyde & Shattuck, 1876-1880. As Shattuck Arms Co., 1880-1909. (AR 2-73)

SHATTUCK, JOSEPH Mt. Pleasant, Ohio, 1821-1828. Patent #none November 10, 1827, percussion lock.

SHAUB, ADAM Lancaster, Pennsylvania, 1857d.

SHAVER, ISAAC (1829-?), Augusta Co., Virginia, 1850c. (MB 10-63)

SHAVER, JACOB (1823-?), Augusta Co., Virginia, 1850c. Same as Jacob Shaffer? (MB 10-63)

SHAVIER, I.R. St. Louis, Missouri, 1868d-1875d.

SHAW Massachusetts, 1775-1776. Committee of Safety muskets. (Dean*).

SHAW New York, New York. Percussion over/under rifle/shotgun.

SHAW & LEDOYT Stafford, Connecticut. Underhammer pistols.

SHAW, ALBERT S. Morrow Co., Ohio, 1840-1851. (Knittle)

SHAW, ALONZO E. (1823-?), Illinois, 1846, Keokuk, Iowa, 1850c. (MB 8-64)

SHAW, C.N. Alleyton, Michigan, 1872d-1879d.

SHAW, GREENBURY (1795-1840), Stokes Co., North Carolina, 1820-1830, Clinton Co., Ohio, 1830-1840. See Wyatt Perry. (MB 1-51)

SHAW, JACOB, JR. Hinckley, Ohio, 1853d-1857. Patent #17,698 June 30, 1857, underhammer revolver. (Sellers-1)

SHAW, JAMES (1831-?), Richland, Ohio, 1850c. (Hutslar)

SHAW, JOHN (1794-?), Ohio, 1831, Quincy, Illinois, 1850c. (Johnson)

SHAW, JOHN Annapolis, Maryland, 1776. Committee of Safety repairs and muskets. (Gluckman & Satterlee)

SHAW, JOHN W. (1823-?), Quincy, Illinois, 1850c. Son of John Shaw. (Johnson)

SHAW, JOSHUA (1777-1860), Philadelphia, Pennsylvania, 1817-1860. Patents #none June 19, 1822, percussion caps, #none June 24, 1822, percussion caps, #none October 24, 1828, cannon lock, #none May 7, 1829, percussion caps, #none December 3, 1832, cannon lock, #none December 3, 1832, cannon lock, #none December 3, 1832, percussion primer, #none March 17, 1833, percussion whip pistol, and #468 January 30, 1841, percussion lock. Shaw was the inventor of percussion caps, but never made guns. (Winant 2)

SHAW, LORING D. Melrose, Massachusetts. Patent #267,027 November 7, 1882, air gun.

SHAW, N. Briggsville, Wisconsin, 1872d.

SHAW, NATHAN Jamestown, New York, 1854.

SHAW, S. & J. unlocated. Percussion Tennessee fullstock.

SHAW, T.B. Dyersburg, Tennessee, 1871d.

SHAW, T.J. Little Rock, Arkansas, 1826. As Shaw & Shereville. (Elias)

SHAW, THOMAS Hartford, Connecticut. Patent #34,032 December 24, 1861, revolver.

SHAW, THOMAS M. Ypsilanti, Michigan, 1875d, Pontiac, Michigan, 1899d.

SHAWK & McLANAHAN St. Louis, Missouri, 1858d-1861. Although Abel Shawk and J.K. McLanahan were in St. Louis for many years, they were together only three years and made percussion revolvers.

SHAWK, JACOB RANDOLPH New Lisbon, Ohio, 1850-1880. Son of Jacob W. Shawk. Percussion 1/2 stock, "J.R.S." or "JR. Shawk" markings. (MB 3-53)

SHAWK, JACOB W. New Lisbon, Ohio, 1860. Percussion fullstocks, "J.W.S." marking.

SHAY, MICHAEL Lancaster, Pennsylvania, 1857d. Lockmaker only.

SHEAF, HENRY Lancaster, Pennsylvania, 1834-1857d. (Kauffman)).

SHEAFF, JEROME A. Fairbury, Illinois, 1878d-1893d.

SHEANER, WILLIAM see Shener.

SHEAR, WILLIAM H. Albany, New York. Patent #335,043 January 26, 1886, breechloading firearm.

SHEAR, WILLIAM H. Morrison, Illinois, 1886d-1890d.

SHEARD, WILLIAM F. Livingston, Montana, 1885-1895, Tacoma, Washington, 1895-1934. Patent #651,514 June 12, 1900, front sight.

SHEARS, J. Prophetstown, Illinois, 1860d.

SHECHT, E. unlocated. Percussion fullstock.

SHECKELIS, JOHN W. Washington, D.C., 1872d.

SHECKLER, JOHN Kirwin, Kansas, 1884d, Washington, Kansas, 1888d-1894d.

SHECKLER, PETER Oneca, Illinois, 1860d, Torrington, Connecticut, 1866, Orangeville, Illinois, 1867-1878d, Lincoln, Nebraska, 1879d, Stockton, Kansas, 1894d. Patents #63,564 April 2, 1867, magazine gun, #158,004 December 22, 1874, magazine gun with Chariton Gregory, and #521,624 June 19, 1894, magazine gun.

SHEEDER & BEEBE Denison, Texas, 1878. J.M. Sheeder and A.L. Beebe.

SHEEDER, J.M. Denison, Texas, 1878d. With A.L. Beebe as Sheeder & Beebe.

SHEESLEY, GEORGE Union City, Pennsylvania. Flintlock rifles. (Dillin)

SHEETS see Scheetz, and also Sheetz. These surnames were used interchangeably in the 18th and 19th centuries.

SHEETS BROS. Shepherdstown, Virginia, 1762-1776. Henry and Philip Sheets.

SHEETS, ASHER Union, Ohio, Dayton, Ohio. Percussion 1/2 stock. (Hutslar)

SHEETS, C. Decatur, Iowa, 1865d.

SHEETS, DANIEL (1811-?) Union, Ohio, 1850, Suisun, California, 1860-1875. (Shelton, Hutslar)

SHEETS, FREDERICK Hampshire Co., Virginia, 1809-1815. Contract rifles for Virginia. (Cromwell)

SHEETS, HENRY (1813-?), Union, Ohio, 1850c-1900. Percussion guns. As H. Sheets & Son, 1883-1890.

SHEETS, HENRY, & SON Union, Ohio, 1883d-1890d. (Hutslar)

SHEETS, I. unlocated. Percussion fullstock.

SHEETS, J. Stanton Co., Virginia, circa 1810. Flintlock Kentucky.

SHEETS, JOHN (1826-?), Union, Ohio, 1850c. Percussion fullstock. (Hutslar)

SHEETS, M. Shepherdstown, Virginia. Percussion revolvers similar to Cofer. (Albaugh 3)

SHEETS, MARTIN (1789-?), Union, Ohio, 1806-1850c. Flintlock fullstock. Brother of Henry Sheets. (MB 6-45)

SHEETS, S. unlocated. Percussion fullstock.

SHEETS, WILLIAM (1827-?), Union, Ohio, 1850c. Son of William Sheets. (Hutslar)

SHEETS, WILLIAM Union, Ohio, 1806-1830. (Hutslar)

SHEETY, J.P. Pilot Grove, Missouri, 1879d.

SHEETZ see Sheets, and also Scheetz. These surnames were used interchangeably in the 18th and 19th centuries.

SHEETZ & CLARK unlocated. Flintlock Kentucky.

SHEETZ, ADAM Shepherdstown, Virginia, 1766-1800. Flintlock Kentucky rifles. (Dean)

SHEETZ, D. unlocated. Southern Kentucky rifle.

SHEETZ, FREDERICK Hampshire Co., Virginia, circa 1800-1841. Flintlock Kentucky rifles. (Bowers)

SHEETZ, HENRY Lexington, Missouri, 1850c, Gallatin, Missouri, 1860d.

SHEETZ, HENRY Shepherdstown, Virginia, 1762-1777. Committee of Safety muskets. Brother of Philip Sheets. (Gill)

SHEETZ, HENRY & PHILIP Mecklenburg, Virginia, 1776. (Kauffman)

SHEETZ, I. Hartsville, Ohio. Flintlock(?) 1/2 stock. (Knittle)

SHEETZ, JACOB (1813-?), Charlestown, Virginia, 1838-1840. Son of Michael Sheetz. (Bowers)

SHEETZ, JOHN JACOB (1785-1860), Shepherdstown, Virginia, 1809-1860. Flintlock Kentucky. Son of Philip Sheetz. (Bowers)

SHEETZ, JOHN PHILIP (1774-?), Shepherdstown, Virginia. Son of Philip Sheetz. (Bowers)

SHEETZ, MARTIN (1776-1808), Shepherdstown, Virginia. Flintlock Kentucky. Son of Philip Sheetz. (Bowers)

SHEETZ, MICHAEL (1781-1836), Charlestown, West Virginia, 1810-1836. Flintlock and percussion Kentucky. (Bowers)

SHEETZ, O. & Z. Hampshire Co., Virginia. Flintlock Kentucky.

SHEETZ, OTHO (?-1833) Hampshire Co., Virginia, 1817-1820c, Belmont Co., Ohio, 1824-1833. Brother of Zebulon Sheetz. (Bowers)

SHEETZ, PHILIP (1738-1793), Shepherdstown, Virginia, 1754-1793. Committee of Safety muskets and repairs. Flintlock Kentucky. Brother of Henry. (Bowers)

SHEETZ, THOMAS Hampshire Co., Virginia, 1820c. (Bowers)

SHEETZ, WILLIAM MILLER (1810-1866), Shepherdstown, Virginia, 1832-1866. Flintlock Kentucky. Son of John Jacob Sheetz. (Bowers)

SHEETZ, WILLIAM MILLER, JR. Shepherdstown, Virginia, 1866-1882. (Bowers)

SHEETZ, ZEBULON Hampshire Co., Virginia, 1819-1835. Brother of Otho Sheetz. Flintlock and percussion Kentucky. (Bowers)

SHEFFIELD ARMS CO. Chicago, Illinois, 1878d-1879d. Imported shotguns.

SHEFFIELD, HIRAM (1811-?), Moore Co., North Carolina, 1850c. (Bivins)

SHEFFIELD, JEREMIAH South Kingston, Rhode Island, 1775-1776. Committee of Safety muskets.

SHEFFIELD, THE trade name of Baldwin & Co., New Orleans, Louisiana, on imported shotguns. (Hinman)

SHEFLER, GEORGE Westmoreland Co., Pennsylvania, 1817-1831. (Whisker II)

SHEIBNER, JOHN Mechanicsburg, Pennsylvania, 1860d-1861d.

SHELBERG, H. Naperville, Illinois, 1860d.

SHELDON Vermont, 1845. Percussion 1/2 stock. (Dean*)

SHELDON, PHELPS & CO. unlocated. Percussion lockmakers.

SHELL & EARLEY unlocated. Flintlock Kentucky.

SHELL, DANIEL Dauphin Co., Pennsylvania, 1825-1850. Percussion fullstock, Miller type revolving rifle. Son of Martin Shell, Jr. (Kauffman)

SHELL, J. Linglestown, Pennsylvania, 1860d-1861d.

SHELL, JACOB Dauphin Co., Pennsylvania. Son of Martin Shell. (Kindig)

SHELL, JOHN (1788-1922), Greasy Creek, Kentucky. Flintlock and percussion rifles. (Dillin)

SHELL, JOHN (1790-1875), West Hanover, Pennsylvania, 1817-1861d. Flintlock and percussion rifles. Son of Martin Shell, Jr. (Dean)

SHELL, MARTIN (1737-1796), Dauphin Co., Pennsylvania, 1770-1790c. Flintlock Kentucky, Committee of Safety muskets. Father of Daniel, Jacob, John, and Martin, Jr. (MB 9-70)

SHELL, MARTIN, III Dauphin Co., Pennsylvania. Flintlock Kentucky rifles. (Kindig)

SHELL, MARTIN, JR. (1763-1817), Dauphin Co., Pennsylvania, 1790c-1817. Flintlock Kentucky. (Kindig)

SHELL, SAMUEL Tennessee, 1782-1787. Father of John Shell. (Dillin)

SHELLENBERGER see Riegart & Shellenberger.

SHELLENGER, DANIEL Connellsville, Pennsylvania, 1830-1834. (Kauffman)

SHELTO WEE Shawnee Indians, Ohio, 1778. According to some sources Daniel Boone, while captured, acted as the tribe's gunsmith (probably apochryphal). (MB 9-63)

SHELTON, CLARK R. New Haven, Connecticut, 1880-1886. Double-barrel shotguns, "Shelton's Challenge Gun" marked on inserts. Patents #230,442 July 27, 1880, rifle barrel for shotgun, and #223,251 January 1, 1880, sight.

SHELTON, JOSEPH (1790-?), Lewis Co., Virginia, 1820-1850. (Gardner)

SHELTON, WILLIAM J. (1826-?), Lewis Co., Virginia, 1850c. Son of William Shelton. (Gardner)

SHENER, JOHN Reading, Berks Co., Pennsylvania, 1800c. (Kauffman)

SHENER, WILLIAM Reading, Pennsylvania, 1773t-1805t. Flintlock Kentucky pistol. (Kauffman)

SHENER, WILLIAM, JR. Reading, Pennsylvania, 1800c. (Kauffman)

SHENNEFELT, ANDREW (1832-1875), Clarion, Pennsylvania, 1850c-1875. Son of Nicholas Shennefelt. (Harriger)

SHENNEFELT, NICHOLAS (1799-1871), Huntington Co., Pennsylvania, 1823-1835, Redbank, Pennsylvania, 1835-1850, Clarion, Pennsylvania, 1850-1871. Flintlock and percussion rifles. (Kauffman)

SHENTENS, PATRICK (1825-?), Quincy, Illinois, 1850c. (Johnson)

SHEPARD, DAVID see Shepherd, David.

SHEPARD, R.R. Worcester, Massachusetts, 1872-1879. Cartridge guns.

SHEPHERD & IRVING New York, New York, 1857d. E.M. Shepherd of Sheffield, England and William Irving of New York. Manufacturers and Importers.

SHEPHERD, DAVID (1813-1903), Orleans, Indiana, 1830-1860, Martinsburg, Indiana, 1860d, Salem, Indiana, 1860-1872. Flintlock and percussion guns marked "D.S." or with full name. (Lindert)

SHEPHERD, JOHN J. Philadelphia, Pennsylvania, 1829d-1847d.

SHEPLER, HENRY South Bend, Indiana. Percussion 1/2 stock.

SHEPLER, JACOB (1806-?), Muskingum Co., Ohio, 1850c. (Hutslar)

SHEPLER, PETER, JR. Clarks, Ohio, 1842-1853d. Percussion 1/2 stock. (Hutslar)

SHEPPERD, WILLIAM Philadelphia, Pennsylvania, 1779. (Whisker III)

SHERICK, GEORGE C. Baltimore, Maryland, 1884-1887d. (Hartzler)

SHERMAN & SISSON New Bedford, Massachusetts, 1853d-1856d. Whaling guns. William R. Sherman and Daniel W. Sisson.

SHERMAN & VAIL Owatonna, Minnesota, 1867d.

SHERMAN, A.P. Portsmouth, Ohio, 1853-1857, Belpre, Ohio, 1860d-1905d. Percussion guns. (Hutslar)

SHERMAN, ABEL Crown Point, Indiana, 1868-1896. Percussion and cartridge rifles. Patent #181,289 August 22, 1876, adjustable gunstocks. (Lindert)

SHERMAN, B. & W.H. Woodstock, Illinois, 1861-1867d. Percussion rifles. Burnham Sherman.

SHERMAN, BURNHAM Woodstock, Illinois, 1861-1896d. As B. & W.H. Sherman, 1861-1867.

SHERMAN, GEORGE Minonk, Illinois, 1886d.

SHERMAN, H.N. Beloit, Wisconsin. Patent #144,872 November 25, 1873, breechloading firearm.

SHERMAN, J.W. Tekamah, Nebraska, 1884d-1893d. Son of W.H. Sherman.

SHERMAN, NATHANIEL Boston, Massachusetts, 1692. (Gluckman & Satterlee)

SHERMAN, W.H. Woodstock, Illinois, 1861-1867d, Tekamah, Nebraska, 1879d. With Burnham Sherman as B. & W.H. Sherman, 1879d.

SHERMAN, WILLIAM R. New Bedford, Massachusetts, 1853d-1876d. Whaling guns. With Daniel W. Sisson as Sherman & Sisson, 1853-1856.

SHERRIL, A. (1800-?), Iredell Co., North Carolina, 1850c. Three sons, Franklin, (1821), Jackson, (1833), and Jacob, (1835), were listed as laborers for him. (Bivins)

SHERRIT, JOSEPH Philadelphia, Pennsylvania, 1780t. (Dean)

SHERROD, J.H. Lancaster, Texas, 1862-1864. Percussion revolvers. With Labon E. Tucker as Tucker, Sherrod & Co.

SHERRY, HENRY (1850-1908), Clarion, Pennsylvania, 1870-1908. Son of Michael Sherry. (Whisker II)

SHERRY, JOHN (1773-1853), Lancaster, Pennsylvania, 1814-1830, Jefferson Furnace, Pennsylvania, 1830-1889(?). Flintlock and percussion Kentucky. For Leman, 1814-1830. (Dillin, Whisker III, date conflict between sources)

SHERRY, JOHN, JR. (1807-1893), Jefferson Furnace, Pennsylvania, 1848-1893. (Kauffman)

SHERRY, MICHAEL (1815-1884), Jefferson Furnace, Pennsylvania, 1844-1861d. Son of John Sherry.

SHERRY, PETER Westmoreland Co., Pennsylvania, 1810. (Kauffman)

SHERRY, X. Knox, Pennsylvania, 1877d. (Kauffman)

SHERTZ, CHRISTIAN Lancaster Co., Pennsylvania, 1779-1782. (KRA IV-4)

SHERWOOD, JOSEPH Newark, New Jersey. Percussion parlor rifles. See Grant & Co.

SHERWOOD, SAMUEL TODD (1828-1900), Smithburg, Virginia, Blandville, West Virginia. Percussion fullstock, "S.T.S." signature. (MB 3-49)

SHIEDT, JOHN Reading, Pennsylvania, 1786. (Dean)

SHIELDS, ABEL Stokes Co., North Carolina, 1837. (Bivins)

SHIELDS, D. unlocated. Percussion rifle.

SHIELDS, FRANCIS M. Coopwood, Mississippi. Patent #282,787 August 7, 1883, machine gun.

SHIELDS, FREDERICK Erie, Pennsylvania. Patent #654,850 July 31, 1900, revolver.

SHIELDS, JOHN Shenendoah Co., Virginia, 1790-1804. Member of the Lewis and Clark expedition. (Dean)

SHIELDS, W.H. Philadelphia, Pennsylvania, 1882d.

SHIELDS, ZACHARIAS W. Harrington, Washington. Patent #456,166 July 21, 1891, gunlock.

SHILLABER, JOHN F. Portsmouth, New Hampshire, 1858-1889d. Percussion fullstock rifles.

SHILLER, HENRY (1802-?), New Bremen, Ohio, 1850c. (Hutslar)

SHILLING, CHARLES (1828-?), Chicago, Illinois, 1859d-1860c. (Johnson)

SHILLINGER & MEFF St. Louis, Missouri, 1859d. Dealers only.

SHILLINGER, GEORGE Northampton Co., Ohio, 1828t, Roseland(?), Indiana, 1875. Percussion 1/2 stock. (Lindert, Dyke)

SHILLITO, SAMUEL (1793-1852), Fort Loudon, Pennsylvania, 1819t-1824t, McConnellsburg, Pennsylvania, 1825-1835t, Chambersburg, Pennsylvania, 1836-1852. Percussion fullstock. (Bowers)

SHILLITO, SAMUEL MILLER (1824-1904), Chambersburg, Pennsylvania, 1846t-1850 and 1863-1904, Mercersburg, Pennsylvania, 1850-1853. Percussion fullstock. Son of Samuel Shillito. (Bowers)

SHILLOCK, P.F. Minneapolis, Minnesota, 1878d.

SHILLS & CO. Boston, Massachusetts. Flintlock lockmaker.

SHINN, FREDERICK M. LeRoy, Kansas. Patent #162,582 April 27, 1875, magazine firearm.

SHINNER, ABRAHAM Camden, Arkansas, 1898d.

SHINNER, FRED Columbus, Indiana, 1870. (Lindert)

SHINNERER, FREDERICK Prescott, Arkansas, 1884d, Hope, Arkansas, 1898d.

SHIP, W. Henryville, Tennessee, 1860d.

SHIPPER, JESSE C. Hamilton, Ohio, 1863d-1866d.

SHIPPEY, ARNOLD K. Tinmouth, Vermont, 1881d.

SHIPPEY, I.B. Colchester, Illinois, 1880d.

SHIRES, JOHN Charleston, South Carolina. See John Schirer.

SHIRK, S. unlocated. Percussion 1/2 stock and fullstock.

SHIRLEY, E.W. Orleans, Indiana, 1860d-1862d. Percussion 1/2 and fullstock.

SHIRLEY, JEREMIAH Cloverdale, Ohio, 1870. Percussion rifles. (Knittle)

SHISLER, D. unlocated. Flintlock Kentucky.

SHISLER, NICHOLAS (1780-?). Monongahela Co., Virginia, 1850c. (MB 10- 63)

SHIVELY, CONRAD Ohio, 1832-1841, Keokuk, Iowa, 1850c. (MB 8-64)

SHNIDER, JACOB Northampton Co., Pennsylvania, 1805t. (KRA II-3)

SHOAFS, J., & CO. unlocated. Percussion fullstock.

SHOBEL, J.G. Washington, D.C., 1863d. (Hartzler)

SHOCK, EZRA Kokomo, Indiana, 1866-1890. (Lindert)

SHOCK, JOHN unlocated. Flintlock Kentucky. (Shumway)

SHOE FLY suicide special signed with an anagram.

SHOEMAKER, JACOB New Bethlehem, Pennsylvania, 1858-1868. (Kauffman)

SHOEMAKER, JONATHAN Canton, Ohio, 1893d. (Hutslar)

SHOEMAKER, M. Philadelphia, Pennsylvania, 1810d.

SHOFF, JACOB Berks Co., Pennsylvania, 1800c. Flintlock Kentucky rifle. (Kauffman)

SHOLETER, H.M. unlocated. Percussion fullstock.

SHOMO, DANIEL (1792-?), Barbour Co., Virginia, 1850c-1855. Son of John Shomo.

SHOMO, JAMES C. (1834-?), Barbour Co., Virginia, 1850c. Son of Daniel Shomo.

SHOMO, JOHN Berks Co., Pennsylvania, 1780-1782.

SHOMO, JOHN M. (1855-?), Barbour Co., West Virginia, 1880c. (Whisker III)

SHONE & HOGAN St. Louis, Missouri, 1868d. George Shone and Joseph M. Hogan.

SHONE, GEORGE St. Louis, Missouri, 1868d. With Joseph M. Hogan as Shone & Hogan.

SHONFELT, NICODEMUS Huntington Co., Pennsylvania, 1820. (Kauffman)

SHOOK, J.H. unlocated. Percussion 1/2 stock target.

SHORER, ANDREW Bethlehem, Pennsylvania, 1775-1776. (KRA IV-2)

SHORER, JOHN Liverpool, Pennsylvania, 1856-1860.

SHORES, JOHN Athensville, Illinois, 1864d.

SHORT, A. Arcola, Illinois, 1860d.

SHORT, BISCOE & CO. Tyler, Texas, 1862-1864. Rifles for the Confederacy. J.C. Short and William S.N. Biscoe. (Albaugh 2)

SHORT, FREDERICK Winchester, Virginia. Apprenticed to Adam Haymaker, March 2, 1763.

SHORT, J.C. Danville, Kentucky, Lexington, Kentucky, ?-1857, Tyler, Texas, 1858-1863, Dallas, Texas, 1866-1878d, Austin, Texas, 1878d. Percussion pistols and 1/2 stock. Apprenticed under Benjamin Mills and their guns look very much alike. With I. Wilson as Wilson & Short, Lexington, Kentucky,1855. With William S.N. Biscoe as Short, Biscoe & Co., 1862-1864. (Albaugh 2)

SHORT, J.C. Pleasant Hill, Missouri, 1870d.

SHORT, N.P. Independence, Kansas, 1882d.

SHOUGH, JACOB Philadelphia, Pennsylvania, 1814d.

SHOUGH, JOSEPH (1761-?), Fayette Co., Pennsylvania, 1809-1816. (Kauffman)

SHOUP, GEORGE (1798-?), Cambria Co., Pennsylvania, 1832, Indiana Co., Pennsylvania, 1842-1860c. (Kauffman, Whisker III)

SHOUP, J.H. Carmi, Illinois, 1884d.

SHOWALTER, ISAAC (1852-1905), Brookville, Pennsylvania, 1890d. Son of John Showalter.

SHOWALTER, JOHN (1814-1883), Lancaster, Pennsylvania, 1840, Brookville, Pennsylvania, 1861d-1883.

SHRACK, PINKNEY Orangeville, Illinois, 1860d.

SHREID, CASPER Lancaster Co., Pennsylvania, 1763. (KRA IV-4)

SHREIDER unlocated. Name appears on the barrel of a flintlock pistol with a Rappahannock Forge lock. (Swayze)

SHREPEL, L. North Platte, Nebraska, 1875d-1879d. See Louis Schrapel.

SHREVE & WOLF San Francisco, California, 1880-1886. George W. Shreve and Simon Wolf. (GR 9-72)

SHREVE, GEORGE WASHINGTON (1820-?), San Francisco, California, 1880-1908. With Simon Wolf as Shreve & Wolf, 1880-1886. With Charles A. and Howard. W. Carr, 1889d-1891. (Shelton)

SHREVES, D.Y. Shreves, West Virginia, 1882d-1900d. (Whisker IV)

SHRIVER, AARON Oscaloosa, Iowa, 1850c. (MB 8-64)

SHRIVER, DAVID Oscaloosa, Iowa, 1882d. Son of Aaron Shriver.

SHRIVER, J. Hanover, Pennsylvania, 1781-1793. Flintlock Kentucky. (Kindig)

SHRIVER, JOHN (?-1830), Mt. Pleasant, Pennsylvania, 1798-1830. Flintlock Kentucky. (Bowers)

SHRIVER, JOHN Lancaster, Pennsylvania, 1850-1860. (Gluckman & Satterlee)

SHROCK, JACOB D. Goshen, Indiana, 1846-1890. Percussion 1/2 stock. (Lindert)

SHROUT, HIDER (1843-?), Hardy Co., West Virginia, 1865-1880c. (Whisker IV)

SHROYER, ANTHONY (1815-1881), DeSoto, Indiana, 1836-1881. Brother of Melker Shroyer. (Lindert)

SHROYER, GEORGE Berks Co., Pennsylvania, 1768, Hanover (York Co.), Pennsylvania, 1775-1813. Two George Shroyers, father and son. (Kauffman)

SHROYER, JACKSON (1833-?), Taylor Co., West Virginia, 1850c. Son of John Shroyer.

SHROYER, JOHN (1811-?), Taylor Co., West Virginia, 1850c.

SHROYER, LOUIS Grafton, Virginia, 1800-1830. Contract rifles for Virginia with Henry Martin and Henry Walker. (Cromwell)

SHROYER, MELKER (1807-?), DeSoto, Indiana, 1836-?. Percussion fullstock. Son of Louis Shroyer. (Lindert)

SHUDHES, F. (1805-?), San Francisco, California, 1860c. (Shelton)

SHUE, IRA M. Hanover, Pennsylvania, 1880-1890. Shotguns made by Crescent. (Hinman)

SHULER, CALEB W. (1825-?), Liverpool, Pennsylvania, 1880d. Son of John Shuler.

SHULER, DANIEL Licking Co., Ohio, 1850, Hardin Co., Ohio, 1856, Chillicothe, Missouri, 1861. Percussion 1/2 stock. Son of John Shuler. (AOLRC IV-1)

SHULER, J.R. Keokuk, Iowa, 1880d-1887d

SHULER, JOHN (?-1828), Bucks Co., Pennsylvania, 1802, Lancaster, Pennsylvania, 1808-1809, Liverpool, Pennsylvania, 1817-1828. Flintlock contract pistols. (ASAC 3, Chandler 2)

SHULER, JOHN (1804-1879), Liverpool, Pennsylvania. Model 1808 contract pistols. Brother of Joseph and Samuel. (Kauffman)

SHULER, JOHN (1815-1870), Licking Co., Ohio, 1835-1870. Percussion rifles. Son of John Shuler. (Hutslar, AOLRC IV-1)

SHULER, JOHN Licking Co., Ohio, 1839. Flintlock Kentucky. (AOLRC IV-1)

SHULER, JOHN Milford, Pennsylvania, 1790-1810. Flintlock Kentucky. (KRA II-3)

SHULER, JOHN RAMSEY (1829-?), Liverpool, Pennsylvania, 1849-1870. Percussion rifles. Son of Samuel Shuler? (Chandler 2)

SHULER, JOSEPH (1811-1879), Liverpool, Pennsylvania, 1861d. Percussion fullstock. Brother of John and Samuel. (Kauffman)

SHULER, JOSEPH R. (1838-?), Liverpool, Pennsylvania. Son of Joseph Shuler. (Chandler 2)

SHULER, LEONARD (1804-?), Liverpool, Pennsylvania, 1825-1830, Lewistown, Pennsylvania, 1830-1832. (Chandler 2)

SHULER, LEONARD Philadelphia, Pennsylvania, 1829d-1830d.

SHULER, SAMUEL (1799-1875), Liverpool, Pennsylvania, 1825-1830. Flintlock and percussion guns. Brother of John and Joseph. (Kauffman)

SHULER, VALENTINE (1810-?), Licking Co., Ohio, 1830, New Philadelphia, Ohio, 1830-1850, Chillicothe, Missouri, 1860d. Percussion guns. Brother of John Shuler. Listed as Valentine Shuyler, New Philadelphia, 1850c-1853d. (AOLRC IV-1)

SHULL, THOMAS E. Millersburg, Pennsylvania. Patent #23,505 April 5, 1859, breechloading firearm.

SHULTHEISS, GOTTFRIED (1822-1872), Auburn, California, 1856-1872. (Shelton)

SHULTIE, HIRAM Wylie, Pennsylvania, 1860d.

SHULTZ, HENRY Missemer's Mills, Pennsylvania, 1861d.

SHULTZ, HENRY Richland, Pennsylvania, 1860d-1861d.

SHULTZ, JACOB (1817-?), Mahoning Co., Ohio, 1850c. (Hutslar)

SHULTZ, JOHN (1819-?), Mahoning Co., Ohio, 1850c. (Hutslar)

SHULTZ, WILLIAM Lansing, Iowa, 1865d.

SHULZ, DANIEL Washington, D.C., 1867d. (Hartzler)

SHULZ, R.G. Ft. Madison, Iowa, 1865d.

SHUMATE, KEMPER Shelbina, Missouri, 1889d-1898d.

SHUMEL, M. Palmyra, Missouri, 1854d.

SHUNK, ISAAC Taneytown, Maryland, 1801, Lancaster, Pennsylvania, 1810t-1811t. Apprenticed to Philip Creamer, 1801. (Hartzler)

SHUSLEY, GEORGE Union Co., Pennsylvania, 1880. (Whisker III)

SHUSTER, JOHN New Haven, Connecticut. Patent #211,674 January 28, 1879, magazine.

SHUYLER, VALENTINE (1810-?), New Philadelphia, Ohio, 1850c-1853d. See Valentine Shuler. (Hutslar)

SIBERT, G. unlocated. Flintlock Kentucky rifles.

SIBERT, LORENZO Mt. Solon, Virginia. Patent #32,316 May 14, 1861, magazine gun; with a forty-eight round capacity in multiple magazines mounted around the barrel. (Hill & Anthony)

SIBLE, JACOB Lancaster, Pennsylvania, 1770-1814t. Possibly also listed as Jacob Seibble or Seipple. (Dean)

SIBLEY, JOHN Sutton, Massachusetts, 1775. Flintlock fowler. (Lindsay)

SIBLEY, RUFUS Greenville, Connecticut. Patent #17,173 April 28, 1857, bomb lance.

SICHLER, STEPHEN Albany, New York, 1824d.

SICKELS, S. Buffalo, New York, 1836d. For Haberstro. (Dean)

SICKELS & PRESTON CO. Davenport, Iowa, 1865d-1881d. Dealers only.

SICKLES ARMS CO. trade name of H. & D. Folsom on shotguns imported for Sickles & Preston. (AR 2-69)

SIDEL, PHILIP Sharon Springs, New York, 1871-1874d. Percussion 1/2 stock.

SIDES, HENRY (?-1806), Bedford, Pennsylvania, 1788t-1806. (Whisker)

SIDOW, ADOLPH (1820-?), Lafayette, Indiana, 1850, North Platte, Nebraska, 1878. (Lindert)

SIEBENS, G., & SON Kansas City, Missouri, 1884d.

SIEBENS, GEORGE Storm Lake, Iowa, 1884d.

SIEBER, CHARLES R. St. Louis, Missouri, 1847d-1896d. For Hawken, 1847-1860. Same as Charles Sieber?

SIEBER, CLAUDE R. (1823-?), Denver, Colorado, 1870c-1872d. Derringer. (Sellers-3)

SIEBER, E.R. Nashville, Tennessee. Derringer.

SIEBER, EDWARD R. Jacksonville, Illinois, 1867d-1893d. Same as E.R. Sieber, Nashville, Tennessee?

SIEBER, FREDERICK R. Chicago, Illinois, 1898d-1903d.

SIEBER, ROBERT St. Louis, Missouri, 1857d-1867d. Worked for Hawken, 1857. Air gun marked Sieber & Heberlein. (Pourie)

SIEBERT, CHARLES M. (1839-1915), Columbus, Ohio, 1851-1870d, Circleville, Ohio, 1872d-1888d. For his brother Christian, in Columbus, 1851-1870. (Hutslar)

SIEBERT, CHRISTIAN (1822-1886), Cincinnati, Ohio, 1838-1841 and 1850c, Louisville, Kentucky, circa 1840, Columbus, Ohio, 1852d-1886. Percussion guns. (Hutslar)

SIEBERT, CHRISTIAN J. Columbus, Ohio, 1900d. Son of Charles M. Siebert. (Hutslar)

SIEBERT, FRANK L. Columbus, Ohio, 1887d-1889d. Son of Christian Siebert and succeeded him.

SIEBERT, HENRY L. (1827-?), Cincinnati, Ohio, 1849-1861d, Columbus, Ohio, 1866d-1867d. With John A. Griffiths as Griffiths & Siebert, 1852-1854. (Hutslar)

SIEBERT, JOSEPH Louisville, Kentucky, 1869d.

SIEFERTH, MORRIS Morristown, New Jersey, 1878d.

SIEGEL COOPER CO. New York, New York. Dealers only.

SIEGFRIED, ALEXANDER H. Snyder Co., Pennsylvania. Flintlock and percussion Kentucky. Same as Alexander H. Siegfried, South Bend, Indiana? (Gabel)

SIEGFRIED, ALEXANDER H. South Bend, Indiana, 1850c-1868d. Bought out by J.W. Camper. Percussion rifles and pistols.

SIEGFRIED, DANIEL Lancaster Co., Pennsylvania, 1846-1850, Mohn's Store, Pennsylvania, 1861d. Percussion 1/2 stock and barrels.

SIEGFRIED, DANIEL Lancaster, Pennsylvania, 1871d. Same as Daniel Siegfried, Lancaster Co.; or Daniel B. Siegfried, Berks Co.?

SIEGFRIED, DANIEL B. Wernersville, Berks Co., Pennsylvania, 1850c-1861d. Barrelmakers primarily. (Kauffman)

SIEGFRIED, HENRY Lancaster, Pennsylvania, 1871d.

SIEGFRIED, JOHN Berks Co., Pennsylvania, 1850c. (Kauffman)

SIEGFRIED, JOHN Snyder Co., Pennsylvania. Percussion Kentucky rifles. (Gabel)

SIEGFRIED, REUBEN Lancaster Co., Pennsylvania, 1850. Barrelmaker. (KRA IV-4)

SIEGFRIED, S. unlocated. Barrelmaker, percussion period.

SIEGLER, CHARLES Danville, Illinois, 1893d.

SIEGLING, CHARLES Sandusky, Ohio, 1867d-1868d. (Hutslar)

SIEGLING, WILLIAM C. Sandusky, Ohio, 1869d-1878d. Rifles and shotguns. (Hutslar)

SIEGMUND, LOUIS St. Louis, Missouri, 1864d-1870d.

SIEGRIST, CHARLES H. Memphis, Tennessee, 1881d.

SIESBUTTEL, DANIEL Oakland, California, 1875-1882. (Shelton)

SIEVERS Rome, Ohio, 1870-1882. (Hutslar)

SIFE, C.C. unlocated. Flintlock Kentucky.

SIFFLE, SILAS Altoona, Iowa, 1892d-1897d.

SIGLER, AMOS Philadelphia, Pennsylvania, 1819d-1847d.

SIGLER, CHARLES K. Nashville, Illinois, 1880d-1888d.

SIGLER, THOMAS (1829-?), Leipsic, Ohio, 1830c-1864d. (Hutslar)

SILGE, ALBERT Baltimore, Maryland, 1887d-1889d. (Hartzler)

SILKEY, JOHN Groveland, Kansas, 1878d.

SILKNITTER, SOLOMON Huntington Co., Pennsylvania, 1850c. (Kauffman)

SILL, ALEXANDER V. (1810-?), Buffalo, New York, 1828-1835, St. Charles, Illinois, 1844-1860. (Johnson)

SILL, ALFRED (?-1896), Philadelphia, Pennsylvania. Patent #596,244 November 13, 1896, breechloading firearms.

SILL, ENOCH Buffalo, New York, 1828-1835. With A.V. Sill. (Dean)

SILL, GEORGE (1828-?), St. Charles, Illinois, 1850c-1864d.

SILL, GEORGE N. St. Charles, Illinois, 1876d-1890d. Son of George Sill.

SILVERMAN, MORRIS Helena, Montana, 1886d.

SILVERS, M. West Branch, Wisconsin, 1857d.

SILVESTER BROS. Fargo, Dakota Territory, 1886d.

SILVIS, JACOB (1801-1891), Delmont, Pennsylvania, 1827-1891. Flintlock and percussion, "J.S." marking. (MB 3-62)

SIMCOCK, JOSEPH Philadelphia, Pennsylvania, 1780-1782. Continental Armory. (Moller)

SIMERS BROS. White Pine, West Virginia, 1900d. I.L. and W.L. Simers. (Whisker IV)

SIMERS, I.L. White Pine, West Virginia, 1900d. With W.L. Simers as Simers Bros. (Whisker IV)

SIMERS, P.L. unlocated. Percussion 1/2 stock.

SIMERS, W.L. White Pine, West Virginia, 1900d. With I.L. Simers as Simers Bros. (Whisker IV)

SIMMONS HARDWARE CO. St. Louis, Missouri, 1875-1930. Retailers only.

SIMMONS, DUDLEY Galena, Illinois, 1832. (Johnson)

SIMMONS, HENRY T. Denver, Colorado, 1892d-1920d. Single shot rifles. (Sellers-3)

SIMMONS, JAMES W.L. Cumberland, Maryland, 1878d-1884d, Baltimore, Maryland, 1885d-1889d. (Hartzler)

SIMMONS, JOHN P. San Francisco, California. Patent #275,085 April 3, 1883, magazine gun with Samuel Adams.

SIMMONS, JONAS (1805-?), Randolph Co., West Virginia, 1850c. (Whisker IV)

SIMMS, JAMES Mt. Nebo, West Virginia, circa 1860. (Whisker IV)

SIMMS, R.B. New York, New York, 1820.

SIMON, J.J. Santa Rosa, California, 1893d.

SIMON, JACOB Boonton, New Jersey, 1867-1869.

SIMON, JOSEPH Lancaster, Pennsylvania, 1794. Agent for other gunmakers who sold to the U.S. government.

SIMONDS, L. Big Rapids, Michigan, 1863d-1867d.

SIMONS, J.L. Madrid, New York, 1870d. Maynard type percussion guns.

SIMONS, WILLIAM O. (1825-1910), Seymour, Indiana, 1860-1891. Percussion 1/2 stock. (MB 4-55)

SIMONTON, FRANK H. Paterson, New Jersey. Patent #436,726 September 16, 1890, breechloading gun.

SIMPSON trade name of Iver Johnson on shotguns. (AG 4-75)

SIMPSON, ALEXANDER Augusta Co., Virginia, 1777. Committee of Safety muskets and repairs. With Joshua Perry, Joshua Humphreys, and Jacob Gabbott. (Gill)

SIMPSON, AUGUST Buffalo, New York, 1854. For J.O. Robson. (Dean)

SIMPSON, BARLEY (1834-?), Yreka, California, 1860c. (Shelton)

SIMPSON, G.W. Chicago, Illinois, 1867-1868d, Oakland, California, 1878d. For/with(?) Joseph Pratt & Co., 1868-1873. (Shelton)

SIMPSON, GEORGE E. Spokane, Washington, 1889d-1891d.

SIMPSON, GEORGE W. Hartford, Connecticut. For his uncle, William H. Robertson, 1850-1860. (Sellers-4)

SIMPSON, ISAIAH H. Brunswick, Maine. Patent #542,540 July 9, 1895, pneumatic firing device.

SIMPSON, J. New Britan, Connecticut. Percussion underhammer pistols.

SIMPSON, LaFOREST Waterville, Maine, 1861. (Demeritt)

SIMPSON, M.E. New York, New York, 1850c.

SIMPSON, MILES (1826-?), Keithsburg, Illinois, 1860c. (Johnson)

SIMPSON, OLIVER K. Pittsburgh, Pennsylvania, 1864d.

SIMPSON, PAUL J. New York, New York, 1838d-1851d. Derringer.

SIMPSON, THOMAS D. Mt. Vernon, Ohio. Patent #106,083 August 2, 1870, breechloading firearms with Gardner B. Gray and Joseph H. Romans.

SIMPSON, THOMAS J. Idaho City, Idaho, 1866d-1867d.

SIMPSON, W.J., & BRO. New York, New York, 1857d.

SIMS, WILLIAM (1780-?), Nicholas Co., West Virginia, 1850c. (Whisker IV)

SIMS, WINFIELD S. Newark, New Jersey. Patents #619,025 February 7, 1899, breechloading gun, and #619,026 February 7, 1899, gun breech mechanism.

SIMS-DUDLEY DEFENSE CO. New York, New York, 1898. Air guns under Mefford and Zalinski patents. Successors to Pneumatic Dynamite Gun Co. (G & A Annual 1971)

SINCLAIR, ALLEN G. Brooklyn, New York. Patent #178,806 June 13, 1876, recoil check.

SINCLAIR, C.H. Cadillac, Michigan, 1895d.

SINCLAIR, J. Wilmington, Illinois, 1860d.

SINCLAIR, JOHN Lancaster, Pennsylvania, 1794-1854. (Dyke)

SINER, JOHN T. Philadelphia, Pennsylvania, 1847d-1899d.

SINGER, E.C. Port Lavaca, Texas, 1861. Percussion repeating rifle. (Holloway)

SINGER, HIRAM J. LaSalle, Illinois, 1886d-1898d. Son of Peter Singer.

SINGER, JOSEPH (?-1924), Los Angeles, California, 1895-1924. Schuetzen rifle accessories. Patent #578,030 March 2, 1897, bores. As Southern California Arms Co., 1903. (Kelver)

SINGER, PETER P. (1819-?), Ottawa, Illinois, 1850c, LaSalle, Illinois, 1866-1884d. Percussion 1/2 stock.

SINGLAIR, JOHN Lancaster, Pennsylvania, 1814t. (Dean)

SINGLETON, BENJAMIN Portsmouth, Virginia. Patent #28,109 April 1, 1860, hammerguard.

SINGLETON, S.S. Middletown, Connecticut, 1881d-1882d.

SINGLEY, WASHINGTON Beetrace, Iowa, 1865d.

SINK, DAVID (1836-1910), Cameron, West Virginia, 1850c-1860c, Kittanning, Pennsylvania, 1882d, Punxsatawney, Pennsylvania, 1887d-1910. Son of William Sink. (Harriger)

SINK, JACOB (1842-1910), Cameron, West Virginia, 1860c, Indiana, Pennsylvania, 1882d-1887d. Son of William Sink. (Harriger)

SINK, JOHN (1826-?), Cameron, West Virginia, 1860c. Son of William Sink. (Harriger)

SINK, JOSEPH (1841-?), Cameron, West Virginia, 1860c. Son of William Sink. (Harriger)

SINK, WILLIAM Cambria Co., Pennsylvania, 1830, Cameron, West Virginia, 1850c-1860c. (Kauffman, Harriger)

SIPE, GEORGE (1828-?), Stark Co., Ohio, 1850c. With P. Schantz. (Hutslar)

SIPE, J.T. Woodsfield, Ohio, 1860. Percussion 1/2 stock. (Hutslar)

SIPES, CHARLES (1812-1876), Indiana, Pennsylvania, 1850c-1876. (Whisker II)

SIPES, CHARLES Allegheny Co., Pennsylvania, 1800. (Kauffman)

SIPLE, CHRIST unlocated. Percussion 1/2 stock, percussion fullstock. Same as Christian Siple, Jr./Christian Siple, ?

SIPLE, CHRISTIAN Lancaster, Pennsylvania, 1802, Middletown, Pennsylvania, 1797-1801. Flintlock Kentucky rifle. For Jacob Haeffer, 1797. "Christ Siple" signature. Possibly also listed as Christian Seibble or Seipple. (Kauffman, Gluckman & Satterlee)

SIRTERS, THEODORE Philadelphia, Pennsylvania, 1847d.

SISSON, ALBERT H. Lynn, Massachusetts, 1878d-1889d.

SISSON, DANIEL W. New Bedford, Massachusetts, 1853d-1878d. Whaling guns. With William R. Sherman as Sherman & Sisson, 1853-1856.

SISSON, FRANK North Stonington, Connecticut, 1869-1873.

SITES, ANDREW Jackson Co., Missouri, 1850c. (MB 11-66)

SITES, CHESTER P. Booneville, Missouri, 1850c, Osceolo, Missouri, Otterville, Missouri. Son of John P. Sites. (MB 7-69)

SITES, GEORGE Rockingham Co., Virginia, 1810-1812. Contract rifles for Virginia. (Cromwell)

SITES, JOHN P. (1784-1853), Fincastle, Virginia, 1804-?, Marion, Missouri, ?-1834, Booneville, Missouri, 1835-1853. Flintlock and percussion Kentucky. (MB 7-69)

SITES, JOHN P., JR. (1821-1904,) Clifton, Missouri, 1841-1844, Arrow Rock, Missouri, 1844-1900. (MB 7-69)

SITES, W. unlocated. Flintlock Kentucky.

SITTING BULL suicide special.

SITTON, PHILLIP Henderson Co., North Carolina, 1850. For Philip Gillespie. (Bivins)

SIX, FREDERICK Lebanon, Illinois, 1864d.

SIZE, ROSWELL Jackson Co., Iowa, 1850c. (MB 8-64)

SIZER, A.S. unlocated. Miller patent revolving rifle. (Sellers-1)

SKEED & SON Ft. Scott, Kansas, 1884d.

SKERL, ADOLPH Philadelphia, Pennsylvania. Patent #176,367 April 18, 1876, safety lock with T. Clark.

SKILLEN, CHARLES Allegheny Co., Pennsylvania, 1800. (Kauffman)

SKINKER, JOHN San Francisco, California, 1867-1885. (Shelton)

SKINNER, A.R. Watertown, New York, 1848-1850d.

SKINNER, B.F. Mystic Bridge, Connecticut. Patent #34,449 February 18, 1862, breechloading firearm with A. Plummer, Jr.

SKINNER, CALVIN B. Fairfield, Michigan, 1863d.

SKINNER, CHAUNCEY D. Haddam, Connecticut. Patents #8,982 June 1, 1852, revolver with Henry S. North, and #18,472 October 20, 1857, breechloading firearms with Dennis Tryon. (Sellers-1)

SKINNER, HOWARD (1803-?), Ashtabula Co., Ohio, 1850c. (Hutslar)

SKURLOCK, AL Wellston, Ohio, circa 1900. (MB 8-55)

SLACK & SON Springfield, Ohio, 1874-1892. Peter Slack.

SLACK, ALFRED J. (1852-?), Springfield, Ohio, 1874-1900. With his father Peter, 1874-1892. With his brother Charles, 1892-1898. (Hutslar)

SLACK, EDWIN K. Woodstock, Vermont, 1883d.

SLACK, PETER (1820-1892), Cincinnati, Ohio, 1851-1854, Springfield, Ohio, 1854-1892. As Slack & Son, 1874-1892. (Hutslar)

SLAGHER, JOHN New York, New York, 1850c.

SLANKES, SOLOMON Ronald Center, Michigan, 1863d-1867d.

SLATCHER, JOHN Dickinson, Dakota Territory, 1886d.

SLATE, JOHN D. Bernardston, Massachusetts. Patent #204,768 June11, 1878, breechloading firearm.

SLATELY, J. Dickinson, Dakota Territory, 1886d.

SLATER, JAMES New York, New York, 1788-1796.

SLATER, SAMUEL B. Tolland, Connecticut, 1868-1876d.

SLAUGHTER, CARPENTER & CO. Louisville, Kentucky, 1860d.

SLAYLER, HENRY B. North, Iowa, 1865d.

SLAYSMAN, CHARLES Indiana, Pennsylvania, 1850-1877. (Kauffman)

SLAYSMAN, GEORGE (1782-1862), Lewistown, Pennsylvania, 1821, Woodbury, Pennsylvania, 1825-1833, Punxatawney, Pennsylvania, 1861d. Percussion fullstock. (Kauffman)

SLEEPER, EDWIN Springfield, Massachusetts. Submitted a model to the 1872 rifle trials.

SLEGHEL, GOTTLIEB Washington, D.C., 1858d. (Hartzler)

SLERET, ENGLEHART Chillicothe, Ohio, 1853d-1864d. Percussion 1/2 stock and fullstock. (Hutslar)

SLINN, H.H. Chillicothe, Illinois, 1880d-1893d.

SLITERMAN, JEREMIAH Georgia, 1766-1768. Flintlock musket. (Dean)

SLOAN see Hart & Sloan.

SLOAN, M.J.C. Notchy, Tennessee, 1891d.

SLOAN, ROBERT Connecticut, 1775. Committee of Safety muskets. (Gluckman & Satterlee)

SLOAN, THOMAS J. Tuckahoe, New York. Patent #175,180 March 21, 1876, revolver.

SLOAT, DAVID A. Norvell, Michigan, 1860d.

SLOAT, G.P. Richmond, Virginia, 1861. As Sloat's Rifle Factory, which was also known as Union Manufacturing Co. (Albaugh 1)

SLOAT, JONATHAN D. Norwich, Connecticut. Patent #none October 19, 1818, magazine lock for muskets.

SLOAT, L.W. Mobile, Alabama, 1839d. Dealer and importer. (Neville)

SLOAT'S RIFLE FACTORY Richmond, Virginia, 1861. G.P. Sloat. Also known as Union Manufacturing Co. (Albaugh 1)

SLOCUM, FRANK P. Brooklyn, New York. Patents #37,551 January 27, 1863, revolver, and #38,204 April 14, 1863, revolver. Made by Brooklyn Arms Co. (GR 4-66)

SLOCUM, W.L. & B.F. Grand Rapids, Michigan, 1899d.

SLOCUMB New Orleans, Louisiana. Percussion guns.

SLOCUMB, C.H. New Orleans, Louisiana. As C.H. Slocumb & Co. Son of Samuel Slocumb.

SLOCUMB, C.H., & CO. New Orleans, Louisiana. Percussion pistol.

SLOCUMB, HARDIN Worcester, Massachusetts, 1818-1830, Homer, New York, 1831-1851. Flintlock and percussion guns. With Josiah Maynard as Maynard & Slocumb, 1818-1820. Also known as H. Llocomb. (ASAC 44)

SLOCUMB, HIRAM Worcester, Massachusetts. Percussion pistol. Probably a mis-reading of Hardin Slocumb.

SLOCUMB, MAYNARD unlocated. Percussion 1/2 stock. Probably Maynard & Slocumb.

SLOCUMB, SAMUEL B. New Orleans, Louisiana, 1822d-1885d. With his son C.H. Slocumb as Slocumb & Slocumb. As Brownson, Hopkins & Slocumb. As Rogers, Slocumb & Co., and as many other names. Importers and dealers.

SLOCUMB, Y.S. unlocated. Percussion 1/2 stock.

SLONAKER, CHRISTOPHER Hampshire Co., West Virginia, 1827-1856. (Whisker IV)

SLONAKER, GEORGE (1797-1870), Bedford, Pennsylvania, 1835-1870. (Hetrick, Whisker II)

SLOTTER & CO. Philadelphia, Pennsylvania, 1860-1870d. Slotterbek brothers, Samuel Burch, and William Carrigan. Derringers and percussion rifles. (Shelton)

SLOTTER, FREDERICK (?-1873), San Francisco, California, 1870-1873. Brother of Charles and Henry Slotterbek.

SLOTTER, HENRY (1867-1949), Lakeport, California, 1890-1949. Son of Frederick Slotter. (Shelton)

SLOTTERBEK, CHARLES S. (1831-?), San Francisco, California, 1858-1872 and 1882-1884, Lakeport, California, 1872-1882 and 1884-1886. Patents #84,224 November 17, 1868, drilling, #208,765 October 8, 1878, telescope attachment, #233,034 October 5, 1880, breechloading firearms, and #311,615 February 3, 1885, shooting glasses. With Leopold Joseph M. Villegia as Villegia & Slotterbek, 1868-1872. (Shelton)

SLOTTERBEK, HENRY (1836-1888), Philadelphia, Pennsylvania, 1860-1869, Los Angeles, California, 1869-1888. Percussion and cartridge guns. (Shelton)

SLOTTERBEK, JOSEPH San Francisco, California, 1861d. (Shelton)

SLOUGH, JACOB Philadelphia, Pennsylvania, 1810d.

SLUSSER, JOHN (1805-?), Canton, Ohio, 1824. Ran away from (apprenticeship with?) John Clark.

SLYTER, H.H. Mt. Etna, Indiana, 1840-1870c. (Lindert)

SMALL, DAVID New Lisbon, Ohio, 1806-1848. Son of John Small. (Hutslar)

SMALL, G., & SONS York, Pennsylvania, 1809-1820. Hardware dealers and importers, locks. Succeeded by P.A. & S. Small, 1820. (GR 8-77)

SMALL, JACOB Allegheny Co., Pennsylvania, 1800c. (Kauffman)

SMALL, JOHN (?-1823), Vincennes, Indiana, 1780-1823. Flintlock Kentucky. (Lindert)

SMALL, JOHN (1772-1825), New Lisbon, Ohio, 1804-1825. Flintlock Kentucky. (Hutslar)

SMALL, JOHN Fayette Co., Pennsylvania, 1820-1806. (Kauffman)

SMALL, JOHN Philadelphia, Pennsylvania, 1780-1882. Continental Armory. (Moller)

SMALL, JOHN West Augusta, Virginia, 1775. State repairs. (Gill)

SMALL, P.A. & S. York, Pennsylvania, 1820-date. Hardware dealers, lock makers. Sons of, and successors to, George Small.

SMALL, SAMUEL (1814-1900), New Lisbon, Ohio, 1835c-1875d. Flintlock and percussion rifles. Son of David Small. (Hutslar)

SMALL, SAMUEL New Lisbon, Ohio, 1804-1850. (MB 6-45)

SMALL, WILLIAM M. (1797-?), Lawrenceville, Illinois, 1847-1864d. (Johnson)

SMART & MITCHELL Dover, New Hampshire, 1896d-1898d. Eugene Smart.

SMART, ELISHA (1795-?), Mecklenburg Co., North Carolina. Apprenticed, 1810. (Bivins)

SMART, EUGENE Dover, New Hampshire, 1865-1898d. Percussion and cartridge rifles. As E. Smart & Co., 1871-1873. As Smart & Mitchell, 1896-1898.

SMART, ROBERT Minooka, Illinois, 1864d.

SMIGLEWICZ, PAUL Cincinnati, Ohio, 1890d. (Hutslar)

SMILES, JAMES Washington, D.C. Patent #110,505 December 27, 1870, breechloading firearm.

SMITH Frederick Co., Virginia, 1783. (Gill)

SMITH & BACHNER Minneapolis, Minnesota, 1867d.

SMITH & BAILEY Philadelphia, Pennsylvania, 1896d.

SMITH & DAVENPORT Worcester, Massachusetts, 1860. Barrelmakers. (MB 2-65)

SMITH & HYSLOP New York, New York, 1825d. Flintlock and percussion locks.

SMITH & JOHNSON Middlefield, Connecticut, 1864-1868. Pistols. Otis Smith and Ira N. Johnson. Succeeded by Savage & Smith. (AR 5-75)

SMITH & ROBERTS Richmond, Virginia, 1861. Importers and dealers.

SMITH & SQUIRES New York, New York, 1873-1874d. George Smith and Henry C. Squires.

SMITH & WESSON Norwich, Connecticut, 1855, Springfield, Massachusetts, 1857-date. Jennings rifles in Norwich, and revolvers, pistols, rifles, and shotguns. Handguns initially made under the Rollin White patent at Springfield. Horace Smith and Daniel B. Wesson, co-founders.

SMITH & WILKINSON Newburgh, New York. Percussion and cartridge rifles. (Swinney)

SMITH & WILLIAMS Rutland, Vermont, 1864-1868d. (Horn)

SMITH ARMS CO. New York, New York. Reported as the manufacturer of Silas Crispin's patent cartridge revolvers.

SMITH, A. Philadelphia, Pennsylvania. Agent for Bacon underhammer.

SMITH, A. Shelbyville, Kentucky, 1857-1860.

SMITH, ABIA BUTLER (1818-1900), Clinton, Pennsylvania, 1840-1900. Percussion fullstock. Patents #15,529 August 12, 1856, centrifugal cannon with William Weaver, and #39,359 July 28, 1863, breechloading cannon.

SMITH, ADAM Cincinnati, Ohio. Flintlock Kentucky.

SMITH, ALFRED A. (1808-?), Nelson, Ohio, 1850c-1853d, Garretsville, Ohio, 1859d. (Hutslar)

SMITH, ANDREW Smithland, Iowa, 1865d.

SMITH, ANTHONY Bethlehem, Pennsylvania, 1772-1790. (Dillin)

SMITH, ANTHONY Ft. Madison, Iowa, 1850c. (MB 8-64)

SMITH, ANTHONY Hartford, Connecticut. Patent #34,016 December 24, 1861, revolver.

SMITH, ANTHONY Henry Co., Virginia, 1782. Committee of Safety repairs. (Gill)

SMITH, ARGULUS Buffalo, New York. (Swinney)

SMITH, ARTEMAS unlocated. Percussion 1/2 stock.

SMITH, ASA New York, New York. Patent #7,496 July 9, 1850, magazine gun with O.B. Percival.

SMITH, B.F. Delina, Tennessee, 1881d.

SMITH, B.F. Niles, New York, 1878-1882d.

SMITH, B.J. Sandwich, New Hampshire, 1871-1873d.

SMITH, BENJAMIN Vienna, Kansas, 1866d, Wamego, Kansas, 1867d.

SMITH, BENJAMIN F. (?-1844), South Hadley, Massachusetts, 1830-1844. Patent #1,422 December 5, 1839, firearm. Also made a revolving rifle which was not patented. (Sellers-1)

SMITH, C. Scranton, Pennsylvania. Percussion 1/2 stock.

SMITH, C.F. Youngsville, Pennsylvania, 1882d-1890d.

SMITH, C.L. Des Moines, Iowa, 1892d.

SMITH, C.M. St. Cloud, Minnesota, 1898d.

SMITH, C.W. Waverly, Ohio, 1883d-1888d. (Hutslar)

SMITH, CATHERINE Union Co., Pennsylvania, 1776-1779. Widow of Peter Smith. Barrels only. (GR 5-62)

SMITH, CHARLES Boston, Massachusetts, 1857d.

SMITH, CHARLES Philadelphia, Pennsylvania, 1846d.

SMITH, CHARLES B. Staunton, Virginia, 1884d.

SMITH, CHARLES C. Dover, Maine, 1869-1878. (Demeritt)

SMITH, CHARLES W. Elyria, Ohio, 1883d-1895d. (Hutslar)

SMITH, CHARLES W. Silver Creek, New York, ?-1832, Cherry Creek, New York, 1832-?. Percussion rifles. (Swinney)

SMITH, CLARENCE H. Springfield, Illinois, 1891d-1893d.

SMITH, D. Griffin's Corners, New York, 1878-1882.

SMITH, D.S. Prescott, Wisconsin, 1857d.

SMITH, DANIEL (1777-?), Gibsonburg, Ohio, 1830-1853. (Hutslar)

SMITH, DANIEL Scipio, New York. Patent #6,124 February 20, 1849, false muzzle.

SMITH, DANIEL, JR. (1814-?), Rollersville, Ohio, 1848-1856. (Hutslar)

SMITH, DAVID (1780-?), Rollersville, Ohio, 1850c-1853d. (Hutslar)

SMITH, DAVID (1830-?), Licking Co., Ohio, 1850c. Apprenticed to Joshua Zartman. (Hutslar)

SMITH, DAVID Hartford, Connecticut, 1850c.

SMITH, DAVID New York, New York. Patent #6,400 May 22, 1849, drop shot.

SMITH, DAVID Richmond, Virginia, 1778. Committee of Safety repairs. (Gill)

SMITH, DAVID W. Boston, Massachusetts. Patent #19,213 January 26, 1858, nipple guard.

SMITH, DEXTER (1833-?), Norwich, Connecticut, 1850c, Springfield, Massachusetts, 1865-1874. Revolvers, shotguns, and rifles under his patents. Patents #60,074 November 27, 1866, cartridge machine, #111,814 February 14, 1871, breechloading firearms with Martin Chamberlain, #112,505 March 7, 1871, breechloading firearms with Martin Chamberlain, #129,433 July 16, 1872, breechloading firearms, #138,207 April 22, 1873, breechloading firearm, #141,603 August 5, 1873, breechloading firearm with Joseph C. Marshall, #160,551 March 9, 1875, revolver, #162,863 May 4, 1875, revolver with Joseph C. Marshall, #163,032 May 11, 1875, revolver, #171,059 December 14, 1875, revolver, #176,412 April 18, 1876, revolver with C.C. Marshall and Joseph C. Marshall, #176,448 April 25, 1876, revolver with Joseph C. Marshall, #193,836 August 7, 1877, revolver, #196,491 October 23, 1877, revolver, #221,000 October 28, 1879, revolver, #230,582 July 27, 1880, firearms, #247,217 September 20, 1881, revolver, #247,218 September 20, 1881, revolver, #238,223 October 11, 1881, revolver, #250,591 December 6, 1881, revolver, #279,197 June 12, 1883, revolver, #315,352 April 7, 1885, revolver, and #318,315 May 19, 1885, revolver. Son of Horace Smith, co-founder of Smith & Wesson.

SMITH, DONALD D. Springfield, Massachusetts. Patent #269,890 January 2, 1883, revolver.

SMITH, E. (?-1900), Cape, Alabama. (Dillin)

SMITH, E.E. Glenn Springs, South Carolina, 1886d.

SMITH, EDWARD G. South Bend, Indiana, 1862, Sonora, California, 1881d. (MB 10-50, Shelton)

SMITH, EDWIN Bridgeport, Connecticut, 1866-1891d.

SMITH, ELDRIDGE H. Raleigh Co., West Virginia, ?-1900, Missouri, 1901-?. (Whisker IV)

SMITH, ELISHA W. Des Moines, Iowa 1865d-1895d. As E.W. Smith & Co., 1882-1895.

SMITH, ENOCH Lexington, Kentucky, 1800-1810. (MB 12-51)

SMITH, F. unlocated. Flintlock, Kentucky.

SMITH, F. unlocated. Three-barrel percussion rifle.

SMITH, F.R. Syracuse, New York. Patent #264,173 September 12, 1882, breechloading firearm with D.M. Lefever.

SMITH, F.W. New Haven, Connecticut, 1905.

SMITH, FRANK M. Atchison, Kansas, 1880d, Independence, Missouri 1898d.

SMITH, FREDERICK Sulphur Springs, Ohio. Patent #158,221 December 29, 1874, breechloading firearm.

SMITH, FREDERICK Union Springs, New York, 1848-1874d, Fleming, New York, 1877d. Percussion rifles. (Clow)

SMITH, FREDERICK Worcester, Massachusetts. Patent #547,525 October 8, 1895, revolver.

SMITH, G.A. South Hadley, Massachusetts, 1839, Chicopee Falls, Massachusetts, 1857-1865. Submitted rifle to Ordnance Department in 1839.

SMITH, G.F. Heyworth, Illinois, 1867d.

SMITH, GAMALIEL Huntington Co., Pennsylvania, 1850. (Kauffman)

SMITH, GEORGE New York, New York, 1862-1888d. As Smith & Squires, 1873-1874. Percussion and air guns.

SMITH, GEORGE New York, New York. Patent #32,539 June 11, 1861, alarm gun.

SMITH, GEORGE South Bend, Indiana. Patent #179,075 June 20, 1876, stock.

SMITH, GEORGE Union Co., Pennsylvania. Flintlock Kentucky rifles. (Gabel)

SMITH, GEORGE A. Jackson, Michigan, 1872d-1887d, Pontiac, Michigan, 1895d.

SMITH, GEORGE M. Springfield, Massachusetts. Patent #136,871 March 18, 1873, revolver with John T. Smith and J.J. Sweeney.

SMITH, GEORGE R. (1786-?), Kingston, Ohio, 1850c. (Hutslar)

SMITH, GEORGE Y. Mt. Pleasant, Ohio. Percussion full-stock. (Hutslar)

SMITH, GILBERT Buttermilk Falls, New York. Patents #14,001 December 25, 1855, breechloading firearm, #15,496 August 5, 1856, breechloading firearm, #17,644 June 23, 1857, breechloading firearm, and #17,702 June 30, 1857, cartridges. Massachusetts Arms Co. made 30,362 Smith carbines which were purchased by U.S. government during the Civil War.

SMITH, GRANVILL unlocated. Percussion 1/2 stock.

SMITH, H.M. Algonac, Michigan, 1887d.

SMITH, HARVEY Lodi, California, 1881-1887. Percussion 1/2 stock target. (Shelton)

SMITH, HAZARD Victoria, Illinois, 1860d.

SMITH, HENRY Metropolis, Illinois, 1864d.

SMITH, HENRY Westmoreland Co., Pennsylvania, 1832t-1855t. (Kauffman)

SMITH, HORACE (1808-1893), Norwich, Connecticut, 1850 and 1852-1855, Springfield, Massachusetts, 1856-1873. Patents #8,317 August 26, 1851, magazine gun, #10,535 February 14, 1854, magazine gun with D.B. Wesson, #11,496 August 8, 1854, cartridge with D.B. Wesson, #14,147 January 22, 1856, primers for cartridges with D.B. Wesson, #24,666 July 5, 1859, revolver with D.B. Wesson, #27,933 April 17, 1860, mode of filling cartridges with D.B. Wesson, #30,990 December 18, 1860, revolver with D.B. Wesson, #38,921 June 16, 1863, revolver with D.B. Wesson, and #51,092 November 21, 1865, revolver with D.B. Wesson. Co-founder of Smith & Wesson. Although he was associated in various capacities with many gunmakers (Springfield Armory, Allen & Thurber, Robbins & Lawrence, etc.), Smith's fame rests on his partnership with Daniel Baird Wesson and his career at Smith & Wesson, 1856-1873. (Jinks)

SMITH, HORACE Utica, New York, 1832. (Gardner)

SMITH, I.W. Las Vegas, New Mexico, 1884d. Listed as J.W. Smith in 1887 directory.

SMITH, IRA W. (1825-1897), Onaquaga, New York. (Dean)

SMITH, ISAAC New York, New York. Patent #42,542 April 26, 1864, breechloading firearms.

SMITH, J. & P. Saltillo, Pennsylvania. Percussion full-stock. (Dean)

SMITH, J. HOMER Brewster Station, New York. Patent #33,371 September 14, 1861, lock.

SMITH, J.A. Mt. Carroll, Illinois, 1880d, Dixon, Illinois, 1888d-1890d.

SMITH, J.A. Reynolds, Georgia, 1879d-1883d.

SMITH, J.B. Alexandria, Louisiana. Percussion three-barrel gun. Possibly Josiah Smith, as there is great similarity in signatures.

SMITH, J.B. Elgin, Illinois, 1867d.

SMITH, J.D. Spencer, Iowa, 1887d.

SMITH, J.F. Huntington, Pennsylvania. Late flintlock period.

SMITH, J.H. Mt. Pleasant Village, Kentucky, 1857-1860.

SMITH, J.M. Nacoochee, Georgia, 1881d-1883d.

SMITH, J.R. El Paso, Texas, 1892d-1896d.

SMITH, J.T. unlocated. Percussion swivelbreech.

SMITH, J.W. Charlottesville, Virginia, 1897d.

SMITH, J.W. Las Vegas, New Mexico, 1882d.

SMITH, J.W. unlocated. Flintlock Kentucky.

SMITH, JACOB (1763-1847), Union Co., Pennsylvania. (Whisker III)

SMITH, JACOB (1819-?), Stockton, California, 1850c. (Shelton)

SMITH, JACOB Murrysville, Pennsylvania, 1861d.

SMITH, JACOB Newburgh, New York, 1860c.

SMITH, JACOB Snyder Co., Pennsylvania. Flintlock Kentucky rifles. (Gabel)

SMITH, JAMES Colfax, California, 1874-1878. (Shelton)

SMITH, JAMES Decorah, Iowa, 1865d.

SMITH, JAMES Philadelphia, Pennsylvania, 1780-1782. Continental Armory. (Moller)

SMITH, JAMES D. Bridgeport, Connecticut. Patents #52,933 February 27, 1866, magazine firearms, and #52,934 February 27, 1866, magazine firearms.

SMITH, JEREMIAH (1733-1818), Lime Rock, Rhode Island, 1770.

SMITH, JEREMIAH (1770-1854), Smithfield, Rhode Island, 1825-1837. Son of Jeremiah Smith of Lime Rock. (Dean*)

SMITH, JOHN (1802-?), Sandusky Co., Ohio, 1831-1850c, Hessville, Ohio, 1868-1869. (Hutslar)

SMITH, JOHN (1825-?), Erie Co., Ohio, 1850c. (Hutslar)

SMITH, JOHN (1827-?), Madison, Indiana, 1850c. (Lindert)

SMITH, JOHN Lancaster, Pennsylvania, 1850. (Dyke)

SMITH, JOHN Millroy and Reedsville, Pennsylvania. Flintlock Kentucky rifles. (Dillin)

SMITH, JOHN Rutland, Vermont, 1798-1804. 1798 contract muskets with Darius Chipman, Royal Crafts, and Thomas Hooker. (Gluckman)

SMITH, JOHN Sacramento, California. Percussion 1/2 stock. (Shelton)

SMITH, JOHN Spearville, Indiana, 1882-1885.

SMITH, JOHN Williamsburg, Virginia, 1777-1778. State arms repairs. (Gill)

SMITH, JOHN A. South Bend, Indiana, 1876d. (Lindert)

SMITH, JOHN B. Raleigh, North Carolina, 1827. (Bivins)

SMITH, JOHN C. Camden, New Jersey, 1848-1856. Percussion fullstock. Patent #14,034 January 1, 1856, magazine firearms.

SMITH, JOHN D. (1824-?), Trumbull Co., Ohio, 1850c. (Hutslar)

SMITH, JOHN G.S. Rome, Georgia, 1881d-1883d.

SMITH, JOHN H. Poor Fork, Harlan Co., Kentucky. (Hist KY, V4, P397)

SMITH, JOHN H. Wheelock, Vermont, 1869-1874. Percussion 1/2 stock. (Horn)

SMITH, JOHN JACOB (1857-?), Oakland, California, 1878-1892. (Shelton)

SMITH, JOHN M. Baltimore, Maryland, 1847d. Percussion over/under. (Hartzler)

SMITH, JOHN P. Exeter, New Hampshire. Breechloading rifles.

SMITH, JOHN T. Springfield, Massachusetts, 1873, Rockfall, Connecticut. Patents #136,871 March 18, 1873, revolver with George M. Smith and J.J. Sweeney, #251,306 December 20, 1881, revolver with Otis A. Smith, #295,064 March 11, 1884, revolver, #311,383 January 27, 1887, revolver, #314,067 March 17, 1885, revolver, #336,021 February 9, 1886, revolver, #346,327 July 27, 1886, revolver, #376,922 January 24, 1888, revolver, #394,027 December 4, 1888, revolver, #413,975 October 29, 1889, revolver, #530,730 December 11, 1894, revolver, and #556,653 March 17, 1896, revolver. Patents used by his brother Otis A. Smith for revolvers made for Maltby, Henley & Co.

SMITH, JOHN W. Cherry Springs, New York, 1873-1882d. Percussion 1/2 stock.

SMITH, JOHN W. Iowa Place, Kansas. Patent #53,370 January 30, 1866, cartridges.

SMITH, JOHN, JR. (1831-?), Sandusky Co., Ohio, 1850c. (Hutslar)

SMITH, JOHNSON Easton, Pennsylvania, 1776. Contracted for muskets for Virginia with John Young. (Cromwell)

SMITH, JOSEPH Hartford, Connecticut, 1850d.

SMITH, JOSEPH La Grande, Oregon, 1891d.

SMITH, JOSEPH N. Cincinnati, Ohio. Patent #39,591 September 18, 1863, magazine firearm.

SMITH, JOSEPH NOTTINGHAM Jersey City, New Jersey. Patent #35,548 June 10, 1862, magazine gun.

SMITH, JOSIAH B. Northfield, Vermont, 1855-1871. Percussion 1/2 stock target. (Horn)

SMITH, JOSIAH M. New York, New York, 1847-1853. Pepperbox revolver. With Jacob Pecare as Pecare & Smith.

SMITH, JULIUS Lyman, New Hampshire, 1868-1873d.

SMITH, L. Davidson Co., North Carolina. Flintlock fullstock. (Bivins)

SMITH, LAMBERT Wequoit, Wisconsin, 1857d.

SMITH, LEROY H. Ithaca, New York, 1887, Lisle, New York, 1888. Patents #369,812 September 13, 1887, breechloading firearms with Charles Pierce, #381,088 April 10, 1888, breechloading firearms, #381,324 May 22, 1888, breechloading firearms, #399,214 March 5, 1889, breechloading firearms, and #593,615, November 16, 1897, ejecting mechanism for breechloading firearms with H. and F.L. Cross. All patents were used by Ithaca Gun Co.

SMITH, LEVI Clyde, Ohio, 1864-1878d. (Hutslar)

SMITH, LORENS Scranton, Pennsylvania, 1861d.

SMITH, LOUIS (1816-?), Tiffin, Ohio, 1850c-1859d. (Hutslar)

SMITH, LYMAN CORNELIUS (1850-1910), Syracuse, New York, 1877-1890. Shotguns, initially the three-barrel and side-by-side "Baker Gun", circa 1880-1883. As L.C. Smith & Co., circa 1880-1888. L.C. Smith & Co. sold to Hunter Arms Co., 1890.

SMITH, M. Springfield, Massachusetts, 1869d.

SMITH, M.N. Denison, Iowa, 1897d.

SMITH, M.W. Fayette Co., Ohio, 1881d. (Hutslar)

SMITH, MAJOR, & SON New Haven, Connecticut, 1865-1868. (Gluckman & Satterlee)

SMITH, MARTIN (1797-?), Greenfield, Massachusetts, 1817-1836. Flintlock and percussion guns. Apprenticed to Silas Allen. (ASAC 44)

SMITH, MARTIN Falmouth, Kentucky, 1896d.

SMITH, MARTIN Lancaster, Pennsylvania, 1814t-1819t. (Dyke)

SMITH, MARVIN Perry, New York, 1874d-1882d.

SMITH, MORRIS F. Philadelphia, Pennsylvania. Patents #545,540 September 3, 1895, hydraulic recoil gun carriage, #548,096 October 15, 1895, machine gun, #784,966 March 14, 1905, gas operated machine gun, #814,242 March 6, 1906, automatic gas operated firearm, #817,134 April 3, 1906, gun, #817,197 April 10, 1906, gas operated machine gun, #817,198 April 10, 1906, gas operated firearm, and #1,291,690 January 14, 1919, gas operated gun. Patents used by Standard Arms Co.

SMITH, NEWBERRY A. Philadelphia, Pennsylvania. 1833d- 1870d. Hardware dealer. Derringer.

SMITH, O. Union Co., Pennsylvania. Flintlock Kentucky. (KRA 76)

SMITH, OBADIAH Brunswick Co., Virginia, 1810. (Gluckman & Satterlee)

SMITH, OLIVER E. Chicopee, Massachusetts. Patent #528,263 October 30, 1894, palm pistol.

SMITH, OLIVER H. Northampton, Massachusetts, 1857-1861.

SMITH, OTIS A. (1836-1923), Middlefield, Connecticut, 1862-1879, Rock Fall, Connecticut, 1879-1916. Inexpensive revolvers under his own and other names. Patents #135,377 January 28, 1873, revolver, #135,378 January 28, 1873, revolver, #137,968 April 15, 1873, revolver, and #251,306 December 20, 1881, revolver with John T. Smith. As Smith & King, 1862-1864. With Ira N. Johnson as Smith & Johnson, 1864-1868. With Edward Savage as Savage & Smith, 1868-1879. (AG 11-79)

SMITH, P.F. Saltillo, Pennsylvania. As J. & P. Smith.

SMITH, P.H. Hartford, Arkansas, 1888d.

SMITH, PATRICK (?-1881), Buffalo, New York, 1835-1881. Percussion and cartridge guns. (Swinney)

SMITH, PERLEY Lyman, New Hampshire, 1845-1849d. Percussion fullstock rifles.

SMITH, PETER (?-1773), New Berlin, Pennsylvania, 1772-1773. Flintlock Kentucky rifles. (Gabel)

SMITH, PETER (?-1837), Stone Valley, Pennsylvania, 1776-1800. Flintlock Kentucky rifle, Committee of Safety rifles. (Dean)

SMITH, PETER Ennisville, Pennsylvania, 1861d-1880.

SMITH, PETER, JR. New Berlin, Pennsylvania, 1795-1830. Flintlock Kentucky rifles. (Gabel)

SMITH, Q.D. Bath, Maine, 1852-1856d. (Demeritt)

SMITH, R.D.O. Washington, D.C. Patent #43,529 July 12, 1864, revolver.

SMITH, R.H. Bingham, Maine, 1869-1877. (Demeritt)

SMITH, R.M. Mineral Point, Wisconsin. Percussion 1/2 stock rifle. Also percussion revolvers as Elgar & Smith. (Sellers-1)

SMITH, REUBEN W. (?-1905), Bucksport, Maine, 1871-1905. As Wm. G. Smith & Son, 1871-1884. (Demeritt)

SMITH, RHODES & CO. Richmond, Virginia, 1861. Thomas M. Smith and Edward H. Rhodes. (Albaugh 1)

SMITH, S.F. Burlington, New Jersey, 1860d.

SMITH, S.N. Rockville, West Virginia, 1884d-1900d.

SMITH, SAMUEL (1802-?), Browning, Illinois, 1864d-1870c, Astoria, Illinois, 1879d.

SMITH, SAMUEL (1818-?), Ross Co., Ohio, 1850c. (Hutslar)

SMITH, SAMUEL Fayette Co., Pennsylvania, 1823-1831. Superposed load flintlock Kentucky. (Kauffman)

SMITH, SAMUEL New York, New York, 1846d.

SMITH, SAMUEL Philadelphia, Pennsylvania, 1780-1785. Repaired U.S. arms. (Moller)

SMITH, SETH (1803-?), Council Bluffs, Iowa, 1852-1865d, Castana and Exira, Iowa, 1865d.

SMITH, SILAS Lexington, Kentucky, 1833. Son of Enoch Smith. (MB 12-51)

SMITH, SIMEON Barnesville, Georgia, 1861. Confederate gunsmith convention.

SMITH, STEVEN R. New York, New York, 1881d.

SMITH, STOEFFEL Pennsylvania, 1790-1812. Flintlock Kentucky swivelbreech. (Kauffman)

SMITH, T. JOHN St. Louis. Missouri, 1836. (Pourie)

SMITH, THOMAS Harpers Ferry, Virginia, 1838-1848, Hartford, Connecticut, 1848-1849. For Harpers Ferry U.S. Armory. Partner of Edwin and D.B. Wesson in Hartford. (Jinks)

SMITH, THOMAS New York, New York, 1800-1801.

SMITH, THOMAS North Carolina, 1777. Committee of Safety repairs. (Bivins)

SMITH, THOMAS Pittsburgh, Pennsylvania. Patent #14,742 April 22, 1856, projectiles for firearms.

SMITH, THOMAS Washington Co., Pennsylvania, 1827-1828. (Whisker II)

SMITH, THOMAS J. Topeka, Kansas, 1884d.

SMITH, THOMAS L. San Francisco, California, 1876-1879. With Charles Douglas Ladd as Ladd & Smith. (Shelton)

SMITH, THOMAS M. Richmond Virginia, 1861. Percussion 1/2 stock. With Edward H. Rhodes as Smith, Rhodes & Co. (Albaugh 1)

SMITH, THOMAS S. (1823-?), Rockford, Illinois, 1854-1860. Percussion 1/2 stock. (Johnson)

SMITH, UPTON New Bern, North Carolina, 1818-1819. Flintlock Kentucky. (Bivins)

SMITH, VALENTINE Golconda, Illinois, 1860d-1864d.

SMITH, W.M. Van Buren, Arkansas, 1860. (Elias)

SMITH, W.N. Wichita, Kansas, 1872d.

SMITH, W.P., & CO. Richmond, Virginia, 1872-1875.

SMITH, W.W. Fitchburg, Massachusetts, 1875d-1899d.

SMITH, W.W. Saltillo, Pennsylvania, Lotta Grove, Pennsylvania, 1887d.

SMITH, WILEY B. Ray Co., Missouri, 1850c. (MB 11-66)

SMITH, WILLIAM (1802-?), Norwich, Connecticut, 1850c. Brother of Horace Smith.

SMITH, WILLIAM (1831-?), Cincinnati, Ohio, 1850c. With Palemon Powell. (Hutslar)

SMITH, WILLIAM Elizabethtown, Kentucky, 1860.

SMITH, WILLIAM Naillon, Tennessee, 1881d.

SMITH, WILLIAM Williamsville, Illinois, 1860d.

SMITH, WILLIAM York, Pennsylvania, 1853d. Locks only.

SMITH, WILLIAM B. Cornish, New Hampshire. Patent #1,084 February 20, 1839, percussion magazine rifle with Lebbeus Baily and John B. Ripley.

SMITH, WILLIAM D. Baltimore, Maryland, 1871d-1881d. (Hartzler)

SMITH, WILLIAM G. (1822-1884), Bucksport, Maine, 1858-1884. As William G. Smith & Son, 1879-1884. (Demeritt)

SMITH, WILLIAM G. Philadelphia, Pennsylvania, 1898d-1899d.

SMITH, WILLIAM H. Milwaukee, Wisconsin, 1847-1849. (WGCA 4)

SMITH, WILLIAM H. Rochester, New York, 1831d-1859d. Miller patent revolving rifles. For Billinghurst, 1831-1849. (Eich)

SMITH, WILLIAM H., & SONS Bath, Maine, 1867-1881. (Demeritt)

SMITH, WILLIAM H., & CO. Norwich, Connecticut, circa 1840, New York, New York, 1850-1860. Agents and importers.

SMITH, WILLIAM J. Charlottesville, Virginia, 1874-1888d.

SMITH, WILLIAM S. (1815-?), St. Marys, Ohio, 1850c-1853d, Ft. Wayne, Indiana, circa 1860. (Lindert, Hutslar)

SMITH, WILSON H. Birmingham, Connecticut. Patents #33,907 December 10, 1861, breechloading firearm, and #43,957 August 23, 1864, breechloading firearm. Rifles under first patent made by Sharps Rifle Manufacturing Co.

SMITH-WADSWORTH HARDWARE CO. Charlotte, North Carolina. Dealers only.

SMITHWICK, NOAH (1808-?), Texas, 1827-1861, Santa Ana, California, 1861-1893d. Was at many locations in Texas. (TGCA 61)

SMOCK, ISAAC Casstown, Ohio, 1860d. (Hutslar)

SMOCK, NEWTON Kansas City, Kansas, 1894d.

SMOKER suicide specials by Iver Johnson.

SMOKEY CITY suicide special by Harrington & Richardson.

SMOOT, WILLIAM SYDNEY Washington, D.C., 1868-1870, Ilion, New York, 1871-1880. Patents #68,250 August 27, 1867, breechloading firearm, #90,791 June 1, 1869, cartridge, #90,792 June 1, 1869, breechloading firearm, #97,821 December 14, 1869, repeating firearm, #116,105 June 20, 1871, metallic cartridges, #116,106 October 24, 1871, breech loading firearm, #120,338 November 7, 1872, breechloading firearm, #120,788 November 7, 1872, breechloading firearm, #133,063 November 12, 1872, revolver, #143,855 October 21, 1873, revolver, and #230,670 September 3, 1880, magazine gun. All patents used by Remington.

SMOOTS, JACOB Licking Co., Ohio, 1830c. (Hutslar)

SMOTHERS, G.W. Woodbine, Texas, 1890d-1896d.

SMUTS, JACOB Fayette Co., Pennsyvlania, 1823-1824, Piqua, Ohio, 1830c. (Hutslar)

SMUTZ, JACOB Dover, Ohio, 1830c. (Hutslar)

SMYTH, THOMAS Chester Town, Maryland, 1776. Committee of Safety muskets. (Gluckman & Satterlee)

SMYTHE, JOHN M., HARDWARE CO. Chicago, Illinois. Dealers only.

SNALLON, J. Shelbyville, Illinois, 1860d.

SNAPP, J.H. Coatesville, Indiana, 1870. Percussion 1/2 stock. (Lindert)

SNEAD, THOMAS Virginia, 1776. State arms repairs. (Gill)

SNEAD, W.W. Richmond, Virginia, 1869-1873d.

SNEDDEN, WILLIAM TAIT Johnstown, Pennsylvania. Patents #116,363 June 27, 1871, breechloading firearm, and #116,364 June 27, 1871, breechloading firearm.

SNEIDER ARMS CO. see Charles Edward Sneider.

SNEIDER, ANTHONY Lancaster, Pennsylvania. Flintlock era. (Dillin)

SNEIDER, CHARLES EDWARD Baltimore, Maryland, 1860-1889d. Patents #27,600 March 18, 1862, breechloading firearm, #34,703 March 18, 1862, revolver, #39,707 August 25, 1863, breechloading firearm, #44,692 October 11, 1864, priming cartridges, #45,210 November 22, 1864, priming cartridges, #46,054 January 25, 1865, breech loading firearm, #46,612 February 28, 1865, revolver, #47,755 May 16, 1865, breechloading firearm, #66,596 July 19, 1867, magazine firearm, #85,252 December 22, 1868, breechloading firearm, #97,717 December 7, 1869, sight for firearms, #149,352 April 7, 1874, breechloading firearm, #149,353 April 7, 1874, rebounding lock, #171,442 December 21, 1875, breechloading firearm, #202,126 April 9, 1878, breechloading firearm, #227,135 May 4, 1880, breechloading firearm, #257,097 April 25, 1882, breechloading firearm, #417,594 December 17, 1889, breechloading firearm, #417,594 December 17, 1889, magazine gun, #422,846 March 4, 1890, breechloading firearm, and #435,329 August 26, 1890, breechloading firearm. Most of the early patents were used by Poultney & Trimble. With Duncan C. Clark as Clark & Sneider, 1873-1884, shotguns. Sneider Arms Co. made small quantities of many of the Sneider patent guns. (Hartzler)

SNEIDER, CHARLES LOUIS Baltimore, Maryland, 1880d-1889d. Son of Charles E. Sneider. (Hutslar)

SNEIDER, CHARLES W. Baltimore, Maryland, 1875d-1889d. Patents #171,442 December 21, 1875, breechloading firearm with Charles Edward Sneider, #202,126 April 9, 1878, breech loading firearm, #227,135 May 4, 1880, breechloading firearm, and #257,097 April 25, 1882, breechloading firearm. Son of Charles E. Sneider.

SNEIDER, FRANK H. Philadelphia, Pennsylvania, 1870-1881. Breechloaders and needle guns.

SNEIDER, T. unlocated. Flintlock Kentucky.

SNELL, CHAUNCEY (1815-1870), Auburn, New York, 1832-1834, Corning, New York, ?-1870. Son of Elijah Snell. (Massachusetts Arms)

SNELL, ELIJAH (?-1834), Auburn, New York, 1820-1834. Percussion fullstock. Miller and Colburn revolving rifles. (Sellers-1)

SNELL, JAMES C. Binghamton, New York 1883d-1905d. Tip-up schuetzen rifle. As Eldridge & Snell, 1883-1894.

SNELL, JOSEPH Monroe Co., Missouri, 1850c. (MB 11-66)

SNELL, OSCAR Williamsburgh, Ohio. Patent #152,957 July 14, 1874, breechloading firearm. Submitted three different rifles to the 1872 trials.

SNELL, ROBERT La Plata, Missouri, 1860d.

SNEVELY, JACOB S. Harrisburg, Pennsylvania, 1817, Piqua, Ohio, 1824-1835. Flintlock Kentucky. (Kauffman, Hutslar)

SNIDAM, T. Leonidas, Michigan, 1863d.

SNIDER, JACOB, JR. (?-1867), Philadelphia, Pennsylvania. Patent #69,941 October 15, 1867, breechloading firearm.

SNIDER, JOHN unlocated. Flintlock Kentucky.

SNIDER, LEONARD (?-1823), Leitersburg, Maryland, 1794-1816, Franklin Co., Pennsylvnaia, 1816-1823. Barrelmaker, "L.S." marking. (Bowers)

SNIDER, LEWIS Lancaster, Pennsylvania, 1803. (KRA IV-4)

SNIDER, P. unlocated. Percussion fullstock.

SNIVELY, WILLIAM Flint's Mills, Ohio, 1854-1864d. As Jacob Snively in Knittle. (Hutslar)

SNODDERLY, GALEN B. Clarinda, Iowa, 1880d-1897d.

SNODDY, JAMES Lancaster Co., Pennsylvania, 1857. (KRA IV-4)

SNOW & COE New Haven, Connecticut, 1869-1880. Kalamazoo air guns. (Wolf)

SNOW & HEAP Osage Mission, Kansas, 1884d.

SNOW, E.A. Santa Barbara, California, 1893d.

SNOWDEN, DANIEL Dabney, Kentucky, 1857-1860d.

SNUFFIN, J.P. Glenwood, Iowa, 1859d.

SNYDER see Schneider, Sneider, Snider.

SNYDER, C.C. Canton, Ohio, 1883-1904d. (Hutslar)

SNYDER, D., & SON Charlotte, North Carolina, 1870c. (Bivins)

SNYDER, FREDERICK (1825-?), East Lewistown, Ohio, 1850c-1853d. (Hutslar)

SNYDER, G.R. Macomb, Illinois, 1893d.

SNYDER, GEORGE Lancaster Co., Pennsylvania. Flintlock Kentucky. (Dillin)

SNYDER, GRAND B. (1836-?), Bantam, Ohio, 1860d-1902d. (Hutslar)

SNYDER, HENRY Northampton Co., Pennsylvania, 1780t-1783t. Flintlock Kentucky. (KRA II-3)

SNYDER, IRA E. Woodward, Pennsylvania, 1850. Percussion over/under rifle.

SNYDER, JACOB (1821-?), Bedford Co., Pennsylvania, 1843-1860. Brother of Tobias Snyder. (Hetrick)

SNYDER, JOHN New York, New York. Patent #none January 26, 1832, buckshot.

SNYDER, JOHN Saxon, Pennsylvania, 1840-1850. Percussion fullstock. (Dean)

SNYDER, M.L. unlocated. Percussion target rifle.

SNYDER, P. unlocated. Percussion fullstock.

SNYDER, ROMAINE H. (?-1881), Rochester, New York, 1879d-1881. For Charles Green. (Eich)

SNYDER, SAMUEL Bushkill, Pennsylvania, 1820t. (KRA II-3)

SNYDER, TOBIAS Hollidaysburg, Pennsylvania, 1848-1849. (Hetrick)

SNYDER, W.H. (1800-?), Lexington, Illinois, 1860c. (Johnson)

SNYDER, WARD B. New York, New York, 1875d.

SNYDER, WILLIAM (1852-1905), Bedford Co., Pennsylvania. Percussion fullstock. (Whisker)

SNYDER, WILLIAM Flatwood, Pennsylvnnia, 1861d.

SNYDER, WILLIAM Philadelphia, Pennsylvania, 1824d.

SOBURY, H. unlocated. Percussion 1/2 stock.

SOEDING, GUSTAV Philadelphia, Pennsylvania, 1889d.

SOLDAN, W. Hempstead, Texas, 1878d. See W. Soltun.

SOLEIL, FRANCIS New Amsterdam, New York, 1656. (Gluckman & Satterlee)

SOLLACE, ROLAND D. New York, New York, 1850c. Percussion caps.

SOLLIDAY, BENJAMIN K. Jamestown, New York, 1883d.

SOLOMON, P.M. Cochran, Georgia, 1883d.

SOLOMON, R.A. Bull's Gap, Tennessee, 1887d.

SOLOMON, THEODORE Philadelphia, Pennsylvania, 1847d-1867d.

SOLTUN, W. Eagle Lake, Texas, 1884d. See W. Soldan.

SOMERS, H. Passumpsic, Vermont, Percussion underhammer rifle. May be either Harvey or Hugh.

SOMERS, HARVEY Barnet, Vermont, 1869-1875d. Percussion match rifles.

SOMERS, HUGH Barnet, Vermont, 1875d, Danville, Vermont, 1876d-1879. Underhammer target rifle. (Horn)

SOMES, DANIEL E. Washington, D.C. Patent #39,592 August 18, 1863, cannon. (Hartzler)

SONEY, JACOB Jersey City, New Jersey, 1878d.

SONNADECKER, EPHRAIM (1832-?), Mahoning Co., Ohio, 1850c. (Hutslar)

SONNEDECKER, C. Salem, Ohio, 1860-1870. Percussion 1/2 stock. (MB 11-54)

SONNENBERG, WILHELM Winona, Minnesota. 1887-1898d. Patent #371,390 October 11, 1887, breechloading firearm.

SONNENSCHEIN, HENRY St. Louis, Missouri, 1863d-1928d. (Pourie)

SONNER, J. unlocated. Percussion fullstock.

SONNETTI, F. Bremond, Texas, 1872d.

SONNSCHEIN, HERMAN Kansas City, Missouri, 1878d-1898d.

SOPAACH, SCHEPP Montra, Ohio, 1859d. (Hutslar)

SOPER & LYONS Sioux City, Iowa. Percussion 1/2 stock. (MB 9-46)

SOPER & REMINGTON San Francisco, California, 1877-1879. William H. Soper and George H. Remington. (Shelton)

SOPER, LOREN L. Theresa, New York, 1866-1874. (Roberts)

SOPER, R.W. Eureka, California, 1882-1886. Brother of William Soper. For California Arms Co. (Shelton)

SOPER, WILLIAM H. (1814-?), Traverse City, Michigan, 1875d, San Francisco, California, 1876 and 1877-1879, San Luis Obispo, California, 1876-1877, 1879-1882, and 1885-1888, Eureka, California, 1882-1885, Seattle, Washington, 1889d-1891d. With George H. Remington as Soper & Remington, 1877-1879. (Shelton)

SOREY & DEY Norfolk, Virginia, 1870-1875. P.A. Sorey and John Dey.

SOREY, E.N. Danville, Virginia, 1862-1870. Repairs for Confederacy. (Albaugh 1)

SOREY, P.A. Norfolk, Virginia, 1870-1880d. With John Dey as Sorey & Dey, 1870-1875. Son of E.N. Sorey.

SOREY, WILSON B. Norfolk, Virginia, 1885d-1897d. Son of, and successor to, P.A. Sorey.

SORRIES, A., & SON Maysville, Kentucky, 1896. Augustus Sorries.

SORRIES, AUGUSTUS Maysville, Kentucky, 1883d-1896d. As A. Sorries & Son, 1896.

SOSSAMAN, J.A. Long Creek, Arkansas, 1888d.

SOUBIEL, ARMAND New Orleans, Louisiana, 1883d-1862. Derringer. (T53)

SOUDERS, NATHAN Oak Hill, Missouri, 1889d.

SOUDIER, DANIEL Philadelphia, Pennsylvania, 1895d.

SOUL, H.M. Swan Creek, Illinois, 1860d.

SOULE, GEORGE Billings, Montana, 1892d.

SOULE, GEORGE H. Jersey City, New Jersey, 1843-1858. Patents #12,655 April 3, 1855, breechloading firearms, #15,347 July 15, 1856, breechloading firearms, and #20,825 July 6, 1858, breechloading firearms.

SOULE, JOHN W. Everett, Massachusetts. Patent #410,039 January 27, 1889, wind-gauge sights.

SOULE, W.H. Portland, Maine, 1896. (Demeritt)

SOURISSEAU, FELIX (1827-1909), Marysville, California, 1849 and 1855-1856, San Jose, California, 1849-1854 and 1856-1909. Son of Victor Sourisseau. (Shelton)

SOURISSEAU, LOUIS VICTOR (1869-1916), San Jose, California, 1884-1916. Son of Felix Sourisseau. (Shelton)

SOURISSEAU, VICTOR Marysville, California, 1849, San Jose, California, 1849-1859. (Shelton)

SOUSS, GEORGE (1808-?), Port Jefferson, Ohio, 1850c. (Hutslar)

SOUTHARD, A.M. Marshalltown, Iowa, 1882d.

SOUTHARD, WILLIAM (1801-?), Wilkes Co., North Carolina, 1850c. (Bivins)

SOUTHERLAND, C. Geneva, New York, 1850d.

SOUTHERN ARMS CO. trade name of Crescent on shotguns. (AR 2-69)

SOUTHERN CALIFORNIA ARMS CO. Los Angeles, California, 1903. Schuetzen rifle accessories. Joseph Singer. (Kelver)

SOUTHERN, HUGH Fifty-Six, Arkansas, 1900. (Elias)

SOUTHERNER suicide special.

SOUTHERNER trade name on derringer made by Brown Mfg. Co. or Merrimac Arms & Mfg. Co.

SOUTHGATE, PHILLIP W. Worcester, Massachusetts. Patent #660,227 October 23, 1900, extractor and ejectors.

SOUTHRON suicide special.

SOWDERS, DANIEL Putnam Co., Indiana, 1863-1870. (Gardner)

SOWERS & SMITH Philadelphia, Pennsylvania, 1855d. Importers.

SOWERS, GEORGE Pratt, Ohio, 1859d-1864d. As Sowers & Son, 1859-?. (Hutslar)

SOWERS, JOHN Philadelphia, Pennsylvania. Cased pair percussion pistols. (KRA 76)

SOYCE, WILLIAM Gray's Valley, Pennsylvania, 1868d.

SPAEDY, FRANK J. St. Louis, Missouri, 1900-1909. With/for(?) St. Louis Arms & Tool Co. (Pourie)

SPALDING, A.G., & BROS. Chicago, Illinois, 1874-1885d. Denver, Colorado, 1895-1918. (Sellers-3)

SPALDING, ABEL (1809-?), Buckfield, Maine, circa 1830-1848, Marietta, Ohio, 1850- circa 1870. Percussion 1/2 stock, underhammer pistols. Patent #148,150 March 3, 1874, lock. (Demeritt)

SPANG & WALLACE Philadelphia, Pennsylvania, 1830-1856d. Flintlock and percussion guns. Samuel T. Spang.

SPANG, SAMUEL T. Philadelphia, Pennsylvania, 1830d-1867d. As Spang & Wallace, 1830-1856.

SPANGENBERG, GEORGE F. Tombstone, Arizona, 1882-1900. (GR 2-76)

SPANGLE, J. unlocated. Percussion fullstock.

SPANGLE, P. unlocated. Percussion 1/2 stock.

SPANGLE, S. unlocated. Percussion fullstock rifle.

SPANGLER & WILLIAMS Monroe, Wisconsin. Percussion 1/2 stock and over/under rifle.

SPANGLER, D.W. Fort Smith, Arkansas, 1851.

SPANGLER, EMANUEL (1819-?), Harper's Ferry, West Virginia, 1880c.

SPANGLER, GEORGE (1826-1913), Monroe, Wisconsin, 1843-1900. Percussion guns. Son of Samuel Spangler. (WGCA 4)

SPANGLER, GEORGE Liverpool, Pennsylvania. Flintlock Kentucky. Sometimes signed "GS" instead of full signature.

SPANGLER, J.H. Toledo, Oregon, 1889d.

SPANGLER, SAMUEL Somerset, Pennsylvania, 1823-1834, Monroe, Wisconsin, 1844. Primarily a lockmaker in Pennsylvania although he did make some rifles. (Kauffman)

SPANGLER, T.C. Neonset, Illinois, 1877d, Annawan, Illinois, 1880d.

SPANGLER, WILLIAM Floyd Court House, Virginia, 1888d-1893d.

SPARKS & GALLAGHER Louisville, Kentucky. Derringer. (Eberhart)

SPARKS, THOMAS Philadelphia, Pennsylvania. Operated a shot tower founded by his father in 1808 and still standing (as of 1983).

SPARLING, LESLIE M. Fallsburg, New York, Montour Co., Pennsylvania, ?-1930. Son of Lewis Sparling. (Dillin)

SPARLING, LEWIS D. Fallsburg, New York, 1858. Flintlock rifles. (Dillin)

SPARRER, HENRY A. St. Louis, Missouri, 1900d-1933d. (Pourie)

SPAULDING & FISHER unlocated. Agents on Allen & Wheelock pistol.

SPAULDING, ABEL see Abel Spalding.

SPAULDING, ALEXANDER (1811-?), Swanton, Ohio, 1850c-1875d. (Hutslar)

SPAULDING, B.F. unlocated. Percussion underhammer pistol.

SPAULDING, ELISHA F. New Haven, Connecticut, 1860.

SPAULDING, F.M. Kalamazoo, Michigan, 1887d.

SPAULDING, HENRY C. New York, New York. Patent #46,034 January 24, 1865, metallic cartridge.

SPAULDING, J.R. Abilene, Texas, 1890d.

SPAULDING, JAMES Port Clinton, Ohio, 1872-1883d. (Hutslar)

SPAULDING, JOHN G. Lewes, New York, 1870d.

SPAULDING, JOHN G. Vergennes, Vermont, 1873-1885. Percussion over/under rifle. (Horn)

SPEAR, L. unlocated. Percussion fullstock.

SPECHT, ADAM (1788-1872), Beavertown, Pennsylvania, 1820-1860. Flintlock and percussion rifles. Also known as Adam Speight?

SPECHT, ARTHUR Beavertown, Pennsylvania, 1860-1880. Son of Moses Specht. (Whisker III)

SPECHT, ELIAS Beavertown, Pennsylvania, 1850-1890d. Percussion rifles and shotguns. Son of Adam Specht.

SPECHT, MOSES (1818-?), Beavertown, Pennsylvania, 1840-1880. Percussion fullstock. (Gabel)

SPECIAL SERVICE trade name of Shapleigh Hardware Co. on shotguns made by Crescent Fire Arms Co.

SPECK, DANIEL (1805-?), Statesville, North Carolina, 1850c. Flintlock Kentucky. (Bivins)

SPECK, JOB St. Louis, Missouri, 1870d.

SPECT, NOAH Belleville, Pennsylvania. (Dillin)

SPEED, ROBERT Boston, Massachusetts, 1820-1840.

SPEELMAN Peru, Indiana. (Lindert)

SPEER, W.H. Jersey City, New Jersey. Patent #136,162 September 2, 1873, breechloading firearms with Daniel Hug.

SPEIGHT, ADAM Union Co., Pennsylvania, 1850c. Probably Adam Specht. (Kauffman)

SPEIL, HENRY Susquehanna, Pennsylvania, 1882d-1890d.

SPELLERBERG, ANTON Philadelphia, Pennsylvania, 1861-1876, Beverly, New Jersey, 1882d-1885d. Underhammer breechloading rifle. Patent #32,929 July 30, 1861, breechloading firearm, and #180,803 August 8, 1876, breechloading firearm. (GR 12-59)

SPELLERBERG, WILLIAM Beverly, New Jersey, 1887d. Son of Anton Spellerberg.

SPELLIER, AUGUST Philadelphia, Pennsylvania. Percussion revolving rifle. Patent #30,260 October 2, 1860, revolver. (Sellers-1)

SPELLINGS & LIPE Milan, Tennessee, 1885d.

SPELLMAN, CHARLES Louisville, Tennessee, 1860d.

SPELLMAN, H.D. Kansas City, Kansas, 1889d.

SPELTER, JOHN (1853-?), Joliet, Illinois, 1885d-1915d. With Frederick Beutenmuller as Beuttenmuller & Spelter, 1886-1916.

SPENCE, PETER I. (1876-1968), Marietta, Ohio, 1898-1968. Percussion and cartridge guns. (MB 1-63)

SPENCER & ATKINS Cisco, Texas, 1890d.

SPENCER ARMS CO. trade name of Hibbard, Spencer, Bartlett & Co. on shotguns made by Crescent Fire Arms Co. (AR 2-69)

SPENCER ARMS CO. Windsor, Connecticut, 1883-1890. Pump shotguns. Acquired by Bannerman. (GR 2-78)

SPENCER GUN CO. trade name of Crescent on shotguns and revolvers.

SPENCER REPEATING RIFLE CO. Boston, Massachusetts, 1862-1869. Spencer carbines and rifles during the Civil War. Purchased by Oliver Fisher Winchester, 1869.

SPENCER, A.F. Winsted, Connecticut, 1852-1865. Percussion rifles and pistols.

SPENCER, CHRISTOPHER MINER (1841-1922), South Manchester and Hartford, Connecticut, Boston, Massachusetts. Patents #27,393 March 6, 1860, tubular magazine, #34,319 February 4, 1862, breechloading firearm, #36,062 July 7, 1862, cartridge retractor, #38,702 May 26, 1863, magazine firearm, #45,952 January 1, 1865, self loading firearm, #58,737 October 9, 1866, magazine firearm, #58,738 October 9, 1866, magazine firearm, #135,671 February 11, 1873, breechloading firearm, #255,894 April 4, 1882, magazine firearm with Sylvester H. Roper, #299,282 May 27, 1884, magazine gun with Richard Rhoades, and #386,614 July 24, 1888, safety lock. Guns made under these patents by Spencer Repeating Rifle Co., Roper Repeating Rifle Co., Billings & Spencer, Spencer Arms Co., and Bannerman.

SPENCER, DWIGHT W. West Hartford, Connecticut, 1855-1865. Percussion target rifles. (Roberts)

SPENCER, GEORGE NELSON New York, New York, 1882, Jackson, Michigan, 1885, Three Rivers, Michigan, 1887. Patents #258,491 May 23, 1882, magazine firearm, #310,328 January 6, 1885, magazine firearm, and #347,072 August 10, 1886, magazine firearm.

SPENCER, JOHN (1737-?), Kingstown, Rhode Island. Flintlock pistol.

SPENCER, JOHN Chicago, Illinois, 1864d. As Western Arms Co. Also known as "John Spencer, Arms Manufacturer".

SPENCER, JONAS Winchester, Indiana, 1860d. Percussion 1/2 stock.

SPENCER, LEWIS W. New York, New York. Patent #229,058 June 22, 1880, line throwing gun.

SPENCER, SAMUEL West Mills, Maine, 1880. (Demeritt)

SPENCER, WILLIAM Colfax, Indiana, 1862d.

SPENCER, WILLIAM E. Chicago, Illinois, 1859d-1916d. Importer and dealer. As Johnson, Spencer & Co., 1859 and various other names thereafter.

SPENCER, WILLIAM E., & CO. Chicago, Illinois, 1874d-1880d. Dealers. Predecessor to Hibbard, Spencer, Bartlett & Co.

SPERL, HENRY Susquehanna, New York, 1869d-1875d. Percussion over/under rifle/shotgun.

SPERLING, G. unlocated. Flintlock Kentucky.

SPERRY, A.C. Neodesha, Kansas, 1884d.

SPERRY, JOHN (1811-?), La Harpe, Illinois, 1834-1860d.

SPERRY, L.B. Spring, Pennsylvania, 1874d.

SPICKER, GOTTLIEB & FREDERICK Cincinnati, Ohio, 1857-1872. Importers of percussion shotguns and locks. Frederick carried on for several years after Gottlieb's death. (Hutslar)

SPIES, ADAM W. (1783-1863), New York, New York, 1823d-1863d. Dealer. As Spies, Kissam & Co., 1867d-1877 (business continued after Spies' death).

SPIES, KISSAM & CO. New York, New York, 1867d-1877. Dealers. Adam W. Spies.

SPIKER, BENJAMIN (1828-?), Allegeny Co., Maryland, 1850c. (Hartzler)

SPILLER & BURR Atlanta and Macon, Georgia, 1862-1865. Revolvers for Confederacy. Edward N. Spiller and David J. Burr. (Albaugh 3)

SPILLER, EDWARD N. Baltimore, Maryland, 1858-1860d, Atlanta and Macon, Georgia, 1862-1865. With David J. Burr as Spiller & Burr in Georgia.

SPINNING & STANSBERRY Findlay, Ohio, 1850. Percussion fullstock. (Hutslar)

SPITFIRE suicide special. (Webster)

SPITLER, HENRY Morrison, Illinois, 1860d.

SPITTLER, J.P. Salina, Kansas, 1894d.

SPITZ, R. Morrisania, New York, 1870d.

SPITZ, RICHARD New York, New York, 1875d-1886d.

SPITZER & SON New Market, Virginia, 1780-1821. Father and son worked for Committee of Safety and made guns after the Revolutionary War. (Dillin)

SPITZER, CHARLES (1807-1862), New Market, Virginia, 1828-1860. Son of Henry Spitzer. (Bowers)

SPITZER, HENRY (1767-1840), New Market, Virginia, 1795-1840. (Bowers)

SPITZER, WILLIAM A. (1815-1884), New Market, Virginia, 1838-1884. Flintlock fullstock target. (Bowers)

SPIVY, SAMUEL (1806-?), Rossville, Ohio, 1850c. (Hutslar)

SPLENDOR suicide special. (Webster)

SPOERL, C.R. Anaheim, California, 1893d.

SPOFFORD, JOSIAH Portland, Maine, 1846-1860, Boston, Massachusetts, 1867d. (Demeritt)

SPONSEL, CHARLES W. Hartford, Connecticut, Patent #487,432 December 6, 1892, magazine.

SPOON, JOEL Greenup, Illinois, 1860d.

SPORER, MATHIAS Hartford, Connecticut. Patents #320,186 June 16, 1885, magazine firearm, and #423,453 November 18, 1890, magazine firearm.

SPORLEDER, LOUIS B. Walsenburgh, Colorado, 1867d-1885d. (Sellers-3)

SPORT suicide special by T.E. Ryan.

SPORTSMAN suicide special.

SPORTSMAN trade name of W. Bingham Co. and other companies on shotguns made by Crescent. (Hinman)

SPRADLING, JOHN (1812-1887), Clinton, Illinois, 1843-1887. (Johnson)

SPRAGUE & LATHROP Stevens Point, Wisconsin. Percussion double shotgun. Nelson Lathrop and Lyman Sprague.

SPRAGUE & MARSTON New York, New York, 1848-1853. Pepperboxes and single shot guns. (ASAC 39)

SPRAGUE, CHARLES Loudonville, Ohio, 1846. (Knittle)

SPRAGUE, E.S. unlocated. Percussion target rifle.

SPRAGUE, H.J. Ashton, Illinois, 1886d.

SPRAGUE, H.J. Grand Rapids, Michigan, 1891d.

SPRAGUE, J.E. Athens, Michigan, 1873d.

SPRAGUE, J.L. Rochester, New York. Name found on Miller patent revolving rifle; may be original owner's name.

SPRAGUE, LYMAN Mineral Point, Wisconsin, 1878d. With Nelson Lathrop as Sprague & Lathrop.

SPRAGUE, NATHANIEL Nashua, New Hampshire, 1841. (Kauffman)

SPRAGUE, O.B. Prairie du Chien, Wisconsin, 1865d-1867d.

SPRAGUE, ORLANDO Chicago, Illinois, 1849d.

SPRAGUE, WILLIAM H. Jamestown, New York. Patent #380,361 April 3, 1888, revolver.

SPRAGUE, WOOSTER Montpelier, Vermont. Percussion underhammer pistol.

SPRAGUE, ZEBULON (1814-1888), San Francisco, California, 1859, Santa Cruz, California, 1860-1866, Stockton, California, 1866d-1888. (Shelton)

SPRANGLE, SAMUEL Oswego, Kansas, 1894d.

SPRATLEY, WILLIAM C. Norfolk, Virginia, 1855. Converted dueller. (Albaugh 1)

SPRATT, H.J. Galena, Illinois, 1888d, North Yakima, Washington, 1891d.

SPRAY, GUS Bobtown, Indiana, 1870-1895. (MB 4-55)

SPRECHER see Roller & Sprecher.

SPRENKEL, C.E. Harrisonburg, Virginia, 1897d.

SPRENKEL, GAMBLE Harrisonburg, Virginia, 1880d-1893d.

SPRENKEL, J.G. Harrisonburg, Virginia, 1871d.

SPRING Ashtabula, Ohio, 1838. Repeating rifle. (Kauffman 2)

SPRINGER, C. New Lexington, Ohio, 1859d. Percussion 1/2 stock. (Hutslar)

SPRINGER, CHARLES (1826-?), Rush Co., Indiana, 1850c. For his brother William. (Lindert)

SPRINGER, ISAAC W. (1808-?), Huntsburgh, Ohio, 1842-1856, Potter, Pennsylvania, 1860c-1861d. Percussion fullstock. (Hutslar)

SPRINGER, J.H. unlocated. Percussion 1/2 stock.

SPRINGER, J.W. Holt, Pennsylvania, 1882d-1890d. Percussion 1/2 stock.

SPRINGER, WILLIAM G. (1814-?), Rush Co., Indiana, 1850c. (Lindert)

SPRINGFIELD ARMORY Springfield, Massachusetts, 1782-1965. U.S. military weapons. (Fuller)

SPRINGFIELD ARMS CO. Springfield, Massachusetts, 1851-1869. Percussion revolvers under James Warner and E. Jaquith patents. (Sellers-1)

SPRINGFIELD ARMS CO. trade name of Crescent on shotguns and revolvers.

SPRINGFIELD ARMS CO. trade name of Stevens on rifles and shotguns.

SPRINGFIELD MFG. CO. Ludlow, Massachusetts, 1815-1830. Barrels marked "S.M. Co." produced for Springfield Armory. (Moller)

SPRINKLE, GEORGE Cole Co., Missouri, 1850c. (MB 11-56)

SPRINKLE, MICHAEL Shawnee Town, Illinois, 1803. (Johnson)

SPROULLE, R.H. St. Claire Co., Missouri, 1850c. (MB 11-60)

SPROWL, ALFRED R. Narragaus, Maine, 1859-1878. (Demeritt)

SPRUNG, A.E. Detroit, Michigan, 1895d.

SPRY, RICHARD S. (1809-1882), Norwich, New York, 1834, Honesdale, Pennsylvania, 1838, Portsmouth, Ohio, 1844-1858d. With Eugene Hacquard as Hacquard & Spry in Portsmouth. (Hutslar)

SPY suicide special.

SQUARE DEAL trade name of Crescent on shotguns for Stratton-Warren Hardware Co. (AR 2-69)

SQUIRE, JOHN N. Jackson, Michigan. Patent #268,374 November 28, 1882, gunstock.

SQUIRES, ALVIN R. Northampton, Massachusetts, 1858-1860.

SQUIRES, HENRY C. New York, New York, 1873d-1914d. As Smith & Squires 1873-1874. Importer and dealer.

SQUIRES, W.D. Midland, Michigan, 1883d.

SQUIRES, WILLIAM D. Sioux City, Iowa. Patent #157,034, November 17, 1874, gun barrels.

SREFEE, BOSEMORE (1817-?). Missouri, circa 1860, Gilroy, California, 1867-1879. (Shelton)

SROYER, LEWIS Fayette Co., Pennsylvania, 1806. (Kauffman)

ST. B., A. unlocated. Percussion 1/2 stock.

ST. B., S. unlocated. Percussion 1/2 stock.

ST. CLAIR, SAMUEL H. Snyder Co., Pennsylvania. Flintlock and percussion Kentucky. (Gable)

ST. JOHN, J.M. unlocated. Percussion fullstock.

ST. JOHNS, WILLIAM Lancaster, Pennsylvania, 1839-1854. (KRA IV-4)

ST. LOUIS ARMS & TOOL CO. St. Louis, Missouri, 1898d-1906d. Single shot rifle.

ST. LOUIS ARMS CO. trade name of H. & D. Folsom on shotguns imported for Shapleigh Hardware Co. and Sears, Roebuck & Co. (Hinman)

STABLER, EDWARD Sandy Springs, Maryland. Patent #45,356 December 6, 1864, extractor, and #46,828 March 14, 1865, magazine firearm. Patents used on the model 1865 Spencer. (Hartzler)

STACK, JOHN Annville, Pennsylvania, 1807. Barrelmaker. (Kauffman)

STACK, LEVIN T. (1827-1888), Jamestown, North Carolina, 1850-1888. (Bivins)

STACKHOUSE, JOSHUA W. (1830-?), Beallsville, Ohio, 1850c, Powhattan Point, Ohio, 1859d. (Hutslar)

STACY & ANGEL Knoxville, Tennessee, 1865-1871. Percussion fullstock.

STACY, M.H. Trace Creek, Missouri, 1889d.

STADDEN, RICHARD (1803-?), Dayton, Illinois, 1850c. (Johnson)

STAFFORD, J.F. Wichita, Kansas, 1882-1887. Double shotgun.

STAFFORD, S. & H. unlocated. Flintlock Kentucky.

STAFFORD, THOMAS J. New Haven, Connecticut, 1860d-1877d. Percussion pistols and break-open pistols under N.L. Babcock's patent.

STAHL, C.T. Lancaster, Pennsylvania, 1810-1817. Flintlock Kentucky.

STAHL, R. New York, New York, 1859-1860. Retailer of Walch twelve-shot revolvers.

STAHL, WILLIAM Philadelphia, Pennsylvania, 1855d-1861d.

STAKE, JOHN Hempfield, Pennsylvania, 1817-1830. Also known as John Steck? (Kauffman)

STALCUP, FRANK Densmore, Kansas, 1884d.

STALKER, ELI (1812-?), Highland Co., Ohio, 1850c. (Hutslar)

STALL, CHRISTIAN Harrisburg, Pennsylvania, 1817. (Kauffman)

STALLENT Edgewood, Illinois, 1864d.

STALTER, WILLIAM (1820-?), Logan, Ohio, 1850c-1875d. Percussion 1/2 stock. (Hutslar)

STAMM, BENJAMIN (1804-?), Stark Co., Ohio, 1850c. (Hutslar)

STAMM, CHARLES T. Milwaukee, Wisconsin, 1857-1858.

STAMM, JACOB Sardinia, Ohio, 1864d. Percussion sporting rifles. (Hutslar)

STAMM, JULIUS Aurora, Indiana, 1875-1880. (Lindert)

STAMM, PHILIP (1797-1862), Ripley, Ohio, 1842-1862. (Hutslar)

STAMM, PHILIP Ripley, Ohio, 1862, Georgetown, Ohio, 1883d-1896d. Son of Philip Stamm. (Hutslar)

STANBER, JACOB Houstontown, Pennsylvania, 1850c. (Dean)

STANBRA, CHARLES Creston, Iowa, 1889d-1892d.

STANDARD trade name of Marlin on revolvers.

STANDARD ARMS CO. trade name of Homer Fisher on imported shotguns. (Hinman)

STANFIELD, B.F. Hope, Arkansas, circa 1880.

STANFORD, G.B. Kalispell, Montana, 1892d.

STANLEY trade name of H. & D. Folsom Arms Co. on imported shotguns.

STANLEY, C.W. Springfield, Missouri, 1898d.

STANLEY, FRANK Dixfield, Maine, 1870-1873. (Demeritt)

STANLEY, FRANK C. Fulton, New York. Patent #510,999 December 19, 1893, ejector.

STANLEY, JOHN Laurel Fork, Virginia, 1871d.

STANLEY, LEWIS C. Millville, New Jersey, 1860d-1865d.

STANLEY, MERRITT F. Plymouth, Michigan, 1888-1890, Northville, Michigan, 1891-1905. Patents #420,316 January 28, 1890, spring air gun, #461,224 October 13, 1891, air gun, #454,081 June 16, 1891, spring air gun, #627,764 June 27, 1899, spring air gun, and #767,968 August 16, 1904, spring air gun.

STANLEY, N.C. Westford, Vermont, 1876-1879. (Horn)

STANNARD & MORAN Chicago, Illinois, 1910-?. Fremont P. Stannard. Preceeded by F.P. Stannard Gun Co.

STANNARD, F.P., GUN CO. Milwaukee, Wisconsin, 1893-?. Fremont P. Stannard. Succeeded by Stannard & Moran, 1910-?.

STANNARD, FREMONT P. Janesville, Wisconsin, 1874-1882, Milwaukee, Wisconsin, 1893, Chicago, Illinois, 1905-1918. Patent #805,588 November 28, 1905, firearm with W.D. Stannard. As F.P. Stannard Gun Co. in Milwaukee and Stannard & Moran after 1910.

STANNARD, W.D. Chicago, Illinois. Patent #805,588 November 28, 1905, firearm with F.P. Stannard.

STANSFIELD BROS. Texarkana, Texas, 1890-1893. J.W. Stansfield.

STANSFIELD, J.W. Texarkana, Texas 1890d-1896d. As Stansfield Bros., 1890-1893.

STANTON, HENRY Kings Co., New York. Patent #9,950 August 16, 1853, breechloading firearm.

STANTON, O.V. Wadhams, and Poughkeepsie, New York. Percussion target rifle, percussion and cartridge guns. With Charles E. Overbaugh as Overbaugh & Stanton, Poughkeepsie, New York, 1862-1864.

STANTON, SIMON F. Manchester, New Hampshire, 1852-1857. Patent #14,780 April 29, 1856, turret rifle.

STAPE, DANIEL Columbia, Pennsylvania, 1874-1884d.

STAPF, JULIAN Chicago, Illinois, 1896d-1899. Patent #626,310, June 6, 1899, firearm.

STAPH, G. (1790-?), St. Louis, Missouri, 1850c. (MB 11-66)

STAPLES & PHILBROOK Bangor, Maine, 1874d. Charles G. Staples and Francis J. Philbrook. (Demeritt)

STAPLES, CHARLES G. Bangor, Maine, 1874d-1875. With Francis J. Philbrook as Staples & Philbrook. (Demeritt)

STAPLETON, J. Adel, Georgia, 1883d.

STAPLETON, JAMES Todd, Pennsylvania, 1838-1890d. Flintlock and percussion guns.

STAPLETON, JOSEPH Orbisonia, Pennsylvania. Flintlock Kentucky. (Dillin)

STAPLETON, SOLOMON (1869-1950), Todd, Pennsylvania, 1890d. Son of James Stapleton. (Whisker II)

STAPLETON, WILLIAM B. (1864-?), Todd, Pennsylvania, 1887d-1916d. Son of James Stapleton.

STAR suicide special made by Prescott Pistol Co.

STAR trade name on .22 cal. derringer.

STAR LEADER suicide special. (Webster)

STAR LEADER trade name of Hibbard, Spencer, Bartlett & Co. on shotguns made by Crescent Fire Arms Co. (Hinman)

STARDTLEP, AUGUST (1828-?), St. Louis, Missouri, 1850c. (Lewis)

STARE, JOHN Harrisburg, Pennsylvania, 1792. (Kauffman)

STARK, D.C. Waddington, New York, 1859d-1882d.

STARKE, WILLIAM Chicago, Illinois, 1872d-1875d. Shotguns. With Rudolph Grimm as Grimm & Starke.

STARKEY, C.O. East Bonne Terre, Missouri, 1893d.

STARR Lancaster, Pennsylvania, 1750-1760. Flintlock Kentucky rifles. (Dillin)

STARR ARMS CO. Binghamton, and Yonkers, New York, 1860-1868. Starr patent revolvers and carbines. Army and Navy Model double-action revolvers purchased by the U.S. government during the Civil War. Ebenezer Townsend Starr. (Carey)

STARR, EBENEZER TOWNSEND Yonkers, New York. Starr double-action revolvers. Patents #14,118 January 15, 1856, revolver, #21,523 September 14, 1858, breechloading percussion firearm, #30,843 December 4, 1866, revolver, #42,697 May 10, 1864, firearm locks, #42,698 May 10, 1864, repeating firearm, #45,532 December 20, 1864, safety, #51,628 December 19, 1865, revolver, #51,629 December 19, 1865, gun locks, #150,201 April 28, 1874, breechloading firearm, #175,518 March 28, 1876, revolver, and #269,546 December 26, 1882, breechloading firearm. As Starr Arms Co., 1860-1868. (Carey)

STARR, J.H. Fredonia, New York. Marking on barrel of 1/2 stock rifle, "S. Hart" marking also.

STARR, NATHAN (1755-1821), Middletown, Connecticut, 1798-1821. Large quantities of swords and rifles under U.S. contracts. Firm name changed to N. Starr & Son in 1810. (Hicks)

STARR, NATHAN S., JR. (1784-1852). Middletown, Connecticut. Patent #1,141, May 3, 1839, breechloading firearms. Nathan, Jr. entered his father's shop in 1797 and took over after his father's death. Made U.S. rifles and Hall carbines. (Hicks)

STARR, SAMUEL R. New York, New York, 1884d-1886d.

STARR, W.O. & W.S. New York, New York, 1867d-1871d.

STARRETT, STEPHEN E. San Francisco, California. Patent #477,976 June 28, 1892, air gun with Andrew W. Livingston.

STARS marking on muzzle and rear sight, see Charles Bean.

STASSART, HENRY Leadville, Colorado, 1882d, Las Vegas, New Mexico, 1884d. (Sellers-3)

STASSART, J.G. Portland, Oregon, 1891d.

STATE ARMS CO. trade name of Crescent on shotguns for J.H. Lau & Co. (AR 2-69)

STATE GUN FACTORY Fredericksburg, Virginia, 1775-1780. Flintlock muskets. (Dean)

STATE RIFLE WORKS Greenville, South Carolina, 1863-1864. Morse and other rifles for the Confederacy.

STATE, J. New Haven, Connecticut, 1862. Percussion target rifle. (Dean*)

STATES, SAMUEL (1797-?), Bucks Co., Pennsylvania. Flintlock Kentucky. (Dillin)

STATES, T. Pennsylvania, 1818-1820. (Gardner)

STATLER, H. Atlas, Ohio, 1879-1882. (Hutslar)

STATLER, JOHN Moore, Pennsylvania, 1820t. (Dyke)

STATLER, WILLIAM Logan, Ohio, 1852-1871. (Knittle)

STAUDT, H. Murphysborough, Illinois, 1893d.

STAUF, C. St. Louis, Missouri. Patent #34,017 December 24, 1861, portable cannon with C.J. Steinbach.

STAUFFER, ESHLEMAN & CO. New Orleans, Louisiana, 1861d. Dealers only.

STAUS, A.J. Missoula, Montana, 1881-1886d, Spokane, Washington, 1886d.

STAVE, LEWIS A. Chicago, Illinois. Patents #232,214 September 14, 1880, breechloading firearm, and #364,446 June 7, 1887, firearm.

STEAD, GEORGE Cleveland, Ohio, 1872d. (Hutslar)

STEADINGS, JOSEPH (1813-?), Hancock Co., Illinois, 1844. (Johnson)

STEADMAN, F. unlocated. Percussion fullstock.

STEADMAN, J. unlocated. Percussion over/under rifle/shotgun.

STEAGER, JACOB South Bend, Indiana, 1881-1885. (Lindert)

STEARLING, CALVIN Moriah, New York, 1847-1850d.

STECK See John Stake.

STEDMAN, C. Medfield, Massachusetts, 1852-1856. Percussion over/under rifle/shotgun.

STEDMAN, C. Union, California, 1854-1856. (Shelton)

STEDMAN, F.J. South Bend, Indiana, 1886-1887. With his uncle James W. Camper as Camper & Stedman. (Lindert)

STEDMAN, J.F. Burlington, Kansas, 1882d, Arkansas City, Kansas, 1884d. As J.F. Stedman & Bro., 1884.

STEDMAN, JAMES (1818-?), Independence, Indiana, 1850c. (Lindert)

STEDMAN, JOHN (1810-?), Ohio, 1842, Independence, Indiana, 1850c. (Lindert)

STEED, EDWARD Steubenville, Ohio, 1859d. (Hutslar)

STEEL & LATHROP see Steele & Lathrop.

STEEL, JOHN Boston, Massachusetts, 1771-1787. Committee of Safety muskets with his two sons. (Gluckman & Satterlee)

STEEL, WILLIAM Philadelphia, Pennsylvania, 1858d.

STEELE & LATHROP Albany, New York, 1862-1867. Percussion locks, percussion saw-handle pistols. R.P.Lathrop. Also known as Steel & Lathrop. (Carey)

STEELE, L. East Concord, New York, 1880d.

STEELE, WARREN & CO. Albany, New York, 1840. Percussion guns.

STEENS, A.C. Hudson, New York, 1850-1852. Misprint for Stevens.

STEEPHENS, H.C. Paterson, New Jersey. Percussion three-barrel shotgun/rifle. See Henry C. Stevens.

STEEPHENS, H.C. Savannah, Georgia, 1879d-1885d. See Henry C. Stevens.

STEEVER, ADAM Huntington Co., Pennsylvania, 1824-1833. Flintlock fullstock. (Kauffman)

STEHLE, THOMAS Butler, Pennsylvania. 1882d-1887d. Percussion fullstock.

STEIGER, J.G. Cleveland, Ohio, 1863d-1864d. (Hutslar)

STEIGER, JOSEPH (1868-1924), Petaluma, California 1889-1924. Son of, and successor to, Peter Steiger. (Shelton)

STEIGER, PETER JOSEPH (1834-1907), New York, New York, 1858-1867, Petaluma, California, 1867-1907. Father of Joseph and William A. Steiger. (Shelton)

STEIGER, WILLIAM A. (1866-1912), Petaluma, California, 1886-1912, Son of and successor to Peter Steiger (Shelton)

STEIN, FREDERICK (1821-?), St. Louis, Missouri, 1850c. (Lewis)

STEIN, MATHIAS (1808-1896), Detroit, Michigan, 1834-1836, Milwaukee, Wisconsin, 1837-1896. (MB 5-49)

STEIN, THOMAS Edinburgh, Indiana, 1881-1885. (Lindert)

STEIN, WILLIAM (?-1892), Camden, New Jersey, 1860d-1890d. Air gun. (Wolff)

STEIN, WILLIAM, JR. Camden, New Jersey, 1891d-1923d. Successor to his father.

STEINBACH, C.J. St. Louis, Missouri. Patent #34,017 December 24, 1861, portable cannon with C. Stauf.

STEINER, A.B. Bushkill, Pennsylvania, 1860c. Lockmaker for Henry.

STEINER, J.H. Prescott, Arizona, 1884d.

STEINER, PETER Bushkill, Pennsylvania, 1820t-1828t. (KRA II-3)

STEINERT, ROBERT A. Washburn, Wisconsin. Patent #487,586 December 6, 1892, gun.

STEINHARDT, FRANK North Danville, New York, 1870d.

STEINMAN, FREDERICK Nazareth, Pennsylvania, 1779t, Philadelphia, Pennsylvania, 1825t-1836. Son of John Steinman. Possibly two men with same first and last name. (Sellers)

STEINMAN, JOHN Philadelphia, Pennsylvania, 1808-1845. Model 1808 contract muskets. With James Winner and David Nippes as Winner, Nippes & Steinman, 1808-1809. (Gluckman)

STEINMETZ, WILLIAM Philadelphia, Pennsylvania. Converted flintlock muskets.

STEKENIUS, JACOB (1810-?), Somerset and Bedford Co., Pennsylvania, 1859-1863. (Whisker II)

STELL, E.T. Manchester, Virginia, 1890d-1893d.

STELLE, A.H. Fort Worth, Texas, 1896d.

STEMPLE, LAWRENCE Carrollton, Missouri, 1893d-1898d. Son of Louis Stemple.

STEMPLE, LOUIS Carrollton, Missouri, 1866-1881d.

STENCE, I.M. unlocated. Percussion 1/2 stock.

STENGEL Lancaster, Pennsylvania, 1719. Reputed to have made the first "Kentucky" rifle.

STENGER, E.H. Cincinnati, Ohio, 1896d-1902d. With his brother F. Stenger, 1892d.

STENGER, F. Cincinnati, Ohio, 1892d. With his brother E.H. Stenger.

STENGER, T.S. Waterloo, Iowa, 1866-1868. (MB 1-46)

STENGER, THOMAS Lycoming Co., Pennsylvania, 1850. (Whisker III)

STENGER, THOMAS Oswego, Kansas, 1882d-1888d.

STENSLAND, CORNELIUS Negaunee, Michigan. Patent #143,729 October 14, 1873, machine gun.

STENZER Lancaster, Pennsylvania, 1776-1780. (Boehret)

STEPHEN, ADAM Martinsburg, Virginia, 1777-1782. With Anthony Noble. (Gill)

STEPHENS & PERKINS Watertown, New York, 1850c.

STEPHENS BROS. Milford, Michigan, 1887d-1899d.

STEPHENS, ANSON P. Brooklyn, New York. Patent #38,249 April 21, 1863, lock.

STEPHENS, CLARK Oak Grove, Florida, 1883d-1886d.

STEPHENS, DIONYSIUS V. Atlanta, Georgia, 1877d.

STEPHENS, EBENEZER Oshkosh, Wisconsin, 1868-1875. (GC 1)

STEPHENS, FIELDING (1836-?), Fayetteville, North Carolina. Son of Henry Stephens. (Bivins)

STEPHENS, HENRY (1820-?), Fayetteville, North Carolina, 1850c. (Bivins)

STEPHENS, JAMES Uniontown, Pennsylvania, 1810-1812. (Whisker II)

STEPHENS, JOHN Sidney, Ohio, 1878d-1896d. (Hutslar)

STEPHENS, JOHN, & CO. Philadelphia, Pennsylvania, 1777. Committee of Safety muskets. (Gluckman & Satterlee)

STEPHENS, W.H. unlocated. Persussion 1/2 stock.

STEPHENSON, A. Fort Worth, Texas, 1878d.

STEPHENSON, JAMES (1782-?), Petersburg, Illinois, 1831-1860. (Johnson)

STEPHENSON, R.A. Louisiana, Missouri, 1867d.

STEPHENSON, WILLIAM (1797-?), Aberdeen, Ohio, 1850c. Percussion 1/2 stock. (Hutslar)

STEPHENSON, WILLIAM (1826-?), Aberdeen, Ohio, 1850c-1900. Converted guns after the Civil War. With his father, 1850. (Hutslar)

STEREWITH Maryland, 1775-1776. Committee of Safety muskets. (Gluckman & Satterlee)

STERLING suicide special by Dickinson.

STERLING trade name on shotguns by many companies.

STERLING, H.J. trade name of Hibbard, Spencer, Bartlett & Co. on shotguns imported by H. & D. Folsom Arms Co. (also J.H. Sterling).

STERLING, R. Newburgh, New York. Percussion 1/2 stock. (Swinney)

STERNS & TAYLOR New Britain, Connecticut, 1885d.

STETSON, EDWARD New Bedford, Massachusetts, 1836. (Kauffman)

STETSON, GEORGE R. New Haven, Connecticut. Patent #116,642 July 4, 1871, breechloading firearm. Submitted a rifle to 1872 trials. Later patented cartridges and machinery while working for Winchester.

STEUCK, PAUL EDWARD Leadville, Colorado, 1878-1881d, Denver, Colorado, 1882-1937d. As Leadville Novelty Works, 1880-1881, Steuck & Kloer, 1882, Steuck & Bilz, 1889 (Sellers-3)

STEVENS, A.C. Washington, D.C., 1885d.

STEVENS, ABIJAH C. (?-1880), Hudson, New York, 1848-1874. Patent #89,699 May 4, 1869, breechloading firearm. Muzzle loading guns as well as single shot rifles under his patent. (Clow)

STEVENS, ALBERT A. (?-1882), Hudson, New York, 1870d-1882d. Son of A.C. Stevens.

STEVENS, CHARLES Providence, Rhode Island, 1777. (Achtermier)

STEVENS, CHARLES A. (1836-?), Arizona, New Mexico, 1870-1880. Born in Massachusetts.

STEVENS, EBENEZER Oshkosh, Wisconsin. (GCI)

STEVENS, EDGAR M. Medford, Massachusetts. Patents #31,560 October 22, 1861, breechloading firearm with Francis Vittum.

STEVENS, GEORGE A. see Wheeler & Stevens.

STEVENS, HENRY Watertown, New York, 1859d-1867d. Percussion guns.

STEVENS, HENRY C. Savannah, Georgia, 1879d-1885d. See both H.C. Steephens, Paterson, New Jersey; and Savannah, Georgia. Same person?

STEVENS, HENRY G. Hudson, New York, 1880d-1895d.

STEVENS, J., & CO. Chicopee Falls, Massachusetts, 1864-1886. Stevens patent breechloaders. Joshua Stevens, Wiliiam Fay, and Asher Bartlett. Succeeded by J. Stevens Arms & Tool Co., 1886-1920, and by J. Stevens Arms Co. (owned by Savage Arms Corp.), 1920-date.

STEVENS, J., ARMS & TOOL CO. Chicopee Falls, Massachusetts, 1886-1919. Joshua Stevens patent breechloaders, pistols, rifles shotguns. Preceeded by J. Stevens & Co., 1864-1886. Acquired by Savage Arms Corp., 1920, guns marked "J. Stevens Arms Co.", 1920-1990, and 1999-date.

STEVENS, J., ARMS CO. Chicopee Falls, Massachusetts, 1920-1990 and 1999-date. Successor to J.Stevens Arms & Tool Co. Owned by Savage Arms Corp.

STEVENS, JABEZ (1816-?), Jamestown, North Carolina, 1850c. (Bivins)

STEVENS, JOHN Philadelphia, Pennsylvania, 1777. Flintlock muskets for Pennsylvania.

STEVENS, JOSHUA (1814-1907), Chicopee Falls, Massachusetts. Patents #7,802 November 26, 1850, revolver, #8,412 October 7, 1851, revolver, #9,929 August 9, 1853, revolver, #12,189 January 2, 1855, revolver, #44,123 September 6, 1864, breechloading firearm, and #211,642 January 28, 1879, rifle barreled breechloading shotguns. For Allen, Whitney, and Massachusetts Arms Co. before 1864. With William Fay and Asher Bartlett as J. Stevens & Co., 1864-1886. As J. Stevens Arms & Tool Co., 1886-1920. (Sellers-1)

STEVENS, MARTIN Stoughton, Massachusetts, 1855d-1868.

STEVENS, ROBERT L. Albany, Oregon. Patent #264,361 September 12, 1882, gun barrel.

STEVENS, W.X. Worcester, Massachusetts. Patent #41,242 January 12, 1864, breechloading firearm.

STEVENS, WILLIAM S. DeSoto, Wisconsin, 1857d.

STEVENSON, ANDREW Ellensburg, Washington, 1886d-1889d. Same as Andrew Stevenson, New Mexico?

STEVENSON, ANDREW Silver City, New Mexico, 1884d. Same as Andrew Stevenson, Washington?

STEVENSON, GEORGE Cumberland Co., Pennsylvania, 1783-1785. Barrels. (Dean)

STEVES, EDWARD JR. San Antonio, Texas 1887d-1889d. As Steves Arms Co., 1888-1889.

STEVINS Ripley, Ohio, 1860. Percussion fullstock. (Hutslar)

STEWARD, T.M. Anson, Maine, 1875-1878d. (Demeritt)

STEWART, ADAM (1813-?), Blackford Co., Indiana, 1850c. (Lindert)

STEWART, G. York, Wisconsin, 1857d.

STEWART, GEORGE Lewistown, Pennsylvania, 1832-1850c. (Kauffman)

STEWART, GEORGE Norwich, Connecticut, 1857-1860d. Listed as gunsmith and cutler.

STEWART, GEORGE Providence, Rhode Island, 1878d-1886d.

STEWART, H. Clinton, Massachusetts, 1890d-1892d.

STEWART, HUGH Wichita, Kansas, 1884d.

STEWART, JAMES (1807-1883), Ireland, Indiana, 1830-1883. Flintlock and percussion rifles. Son of Robert Stewart. (Lindert)

STEWART, JAMES New York, New York, 1873d.

STEWART, JOHN (1778-1860), Richmond Co., North Carolina, 1800-1860. (Bivins)

STEWART, JOHN (1815-?), Piqua, Ohio, 1850c. Son of William Stewart. (Hutslar)

STEWART, JOHN (1850-?), Vallejo, California, 1871-1872, Pleasant Grove, California, 1875-1877. (Shelton)

STEWART, JOHN Baltimore, Maryland, 1810d-1819d. Flintlock Kentucky. (Hartzler)

STEWART, LAZRUS unlocated. Percussion fullstock with silver inlays and Nicholas Hawk styled patchbox.

STEWART, M.J. Aransas Pass, Texas, 1896d.

STEWART, ROBERT (?-1842), Ireland, Indiana, late 1700s. (Lindert)

STEWART, W.F. Star City, Indiana, 1878-1885. (Lindert)

STEWART, WILLIAM Piqua, Ohio, 1812-1816. (Hutslar)

STEWART, WILSON Bucyrus, Ohio, 1859d-1896d. With Wilson Stewart, Jr. as Wilson Stewart & Son, 1865-1873. (Hutslar)

STEWART, WILSON, JR. Chatfield, Ohio, 1859d-1864d, Bucyrus, Ohio, 1865-1873. With his father as Wilson Stewart & Son, 1865-1873. (Hutslar)

STICKEL, SAMUEL Hanover, Pennsylvania, 1793t. (Gluckman & Satterlee)

STICKENOUS, JACOB Mann's Choice, Pennsylvania, 1886d.

STICKNEY, CURTIS R. Ilion, New York, Patent #128,671, June 2, 1872, magazine gun.

STILES, JOHN (1788-?), Middletown, Pennsylvania, 1809. (Dean)

STILES, JOHN A. Savannah, Missouri, 1850c. (MB 11-66)

STILES, WILLIAM H. (1828-?), Zanesville, Ohio, 1850c. (Hutslar)

STILGENBAUER, ADAM C. (1828-1907), Winesburg, Ohio, 1854-1907. Percussion fullstock, "A.S." marking. (AOLRC 111-1)

STILLEY, PETER (1777-1819), Allegheny Co., Pennsylvania, 1800-1819. (Whisker II)

STILLINGS, I. Jefferson, New York, 1776. (Dean*)

STILLMAN, AMOS Farmington, Connecticut. Model 1798 contract muskets with his brother Ethan Stillman. (Gluckman & Satterlee)

STILLMAN, ETHAN (1768-?), Burlington, Vermont 1790-1797, Farmington, Connecticut, 1798-1803, Brookfield, New York, 1818-?. Model 1798 contract muskets with brother Amos. Model 1808 contract muskets. (Gluckman)

STILLMAN, J.H. Starkville, Mississippi, 1885d.

STILLMAN, JAMES Springfield, Massachusetts. Patent #50,507 October 17, 1865, breechloading firearm.

STILLMAN, WILLIAM J. Newburyport, Massachusetts. Patent #33,695 November 12, 1861, sights. Was U.S. consul in Rome, Italy when patent was issued.

STILLWELL, C. Oil City, Pennsylvania, 1853d-1875. Percussion 1/2 stocks.

STILWEL, HENRY (1824-?), Burke Co., North Carolina, 1850c. (Bivins)

STILWELL, WILLIAM (1817-?), Peoria, Illinois, 1860c. (Johnson)

STIMSON, JAPHET Wolf Creek, Michigan, 1863d.

STINER, A.B. unlocated. Percussion 1/2 stock.

STING, CHARLES H. Tiffin, Ohio, 1868-1890d. (Hutslar)

STINGER, THOMAS Emporia, Kansas 1869d. For B.J. Wright.

STINGER, THOMAS Jersey Shore, Pennsylvania, 1835-1850. (Dillin)

STIPES, ZACK Brunswick, Missouri, 1850c. (MB 11-66)

STITE, CASPER Lancaster Co., Pennsylvania, 1759. (Dyke)

STITES, JOHN Dennisville, New Jersey, 1866d.

STITH, OBEDIAH Quarlestown, Virginia, 1816-1819. Patent #none March 16, 1819, breechloading firearm.

STOAKES, JOHN T. Champlain, New York. Patent #92,393 July 6, 1869, breechloading firearm.

STOCK, CHARLES F. Peoria, Illinois, 1864d-1882d. With William Rugh as Rugh & Stock, 1864.

STOCK, THEODORE St. Louis, Missouri, 1857d-1860d.

STOCKER, KNEELAND Springfield, New Hampshire, 1875-1879.

STOCKETT, JOHN W. Washington, D.C. Patent #620,259 February 28, 1899, gun breech.

STOCKING & CO. Worcester, Massachusetts, 1849-1852. Percussion pepperboxes and pistols. Alexander Stocking.

STOCKING, ALEXANDER Worcester, Massachusetts, 1849-1852. Percussion pepperboxes and pistols. As Stocking & Co.

STOCKWELL, GEORGE Cumberland, Ohio. (Hutslar)

STOCKWELL, I.T. Chautauqua, New York, 1857-1861.

STOCKWELL, JOSEPH Sacramento, California, 1851. For P.B. Comins. (Shelton)

STOCKWELL, WILLIAM L. Ackerland, Kansas. Patent #637,043 November 14, 1899, breechloading firearm.

STODDART, A. Galena, Illinois, 1878. (Johnson)

STODDART, G. Galena, Illinois, 1854. (Johnson)

STOEHR, I. unlocated. Flintlock Kentucky rifles.

STOERMER, AUGUSTUS (1828-1882), Los Angeles, California, 1856-1882. (Shelton)

STOEY, GUSTAVUS Lancaster, Pennsylvania. 1806-1811. State inspector of arms. (Gluckman & Satterlee)

STOFEL, WILLIAM Cincinnati, Ohio, 1843d-1853d. Same as William Stofel, Illinois? (Hutslar)

STOFEL, WILLIAM Quincy, Illinois, 1867d-1868d. Same as William Stofel, Ohio?

STOFER, ELI T. Minster, Ohio, 1896d. (Hutslar)

STOKES & LEEMING Chicago, Illinois, 1893d. E.C. Stokes.

STOKES, CHARLES Pittsburgh, Pennsylvania, 1860d. Barrelmaker.

STOKES, E.C. Aberdeen, Dakota Territory, 1886d.

STOKES, E.C. Chicago, Illinois, 1889d-1893d. As Stokes & Leeming, 1893.

STOKES, ENOCH Lancaster, Pennsylvania, 1857d.

STOKES, F.U. Urbana, Ohio, 1875d. (Hutslar)

STOKES, ISAAC NEWTON PHELPS New York, New York. Patents #339,343 April 6, 1886, magazine gun, and #521,831 June 26, 1894, magazine gun.

STOKES, JOHN Baltimore, Maryland, 1847d-1886d. Percussion double shotgun. (Hartzler)

STOKES, JOHN Springfield, Massachusetts. Patent #84,314 November 24, 1868, lock.

STOKEY, C.J. Canton, Ohio, 1876d. (Hutslar)

STOLL, J.V. unlocated. Percussion double rifle/shotgun.

STONE, AMASA unlocated. Flintlock muskets, 1812-1815.

STONE, DAVID Walpole, New Hampshire, 1798-1801. Model 1798 contract muskets with Gurdon Huntington, John Livingston, and Josiah Bellows. (Gluckman & Satterlee)

STONE, J. Elizabethtown, New York, 1838-1850d. Flintlock and percussion arms.

STONE, JOHN Webster, Pennsylvania, 1874d, Polk, Pennsylvania, 1887d-1890d. Percussion 1/2 stock. (MB 8-43)

STONE, THOMAS Lexington, Missouri, 1850c. (MB 11-66)

STONEBERGER, WILLIAM Dayton, Ohio. Gun barrel factory with Edward Helfenstein.

STONER, JOHN Webster, Pennsylvania. (Whisker II)

STONER, S.D. unlocated. Percussion 1/2 stock.

STONESIFER, CHRISTIAN EMORY (1838-?), Boonsboro, Maryland, 1860c-?. Percussion fullstock. (Hartzler)

STONESIFER, JOHN (1813-?), Boonsboro, Maryland, 1838-1850d. Percussion fullstock. (Hartzler)

STONESIFER, JOHN Hagerstown, Maryland, 1782. (Bowers)

STONEWALL trade name of Marlin on derringers.

STONEWALL trade name on percussion derringers imported by T.F. Guion.

STOOTS, FREDERICK (1786-?), Monroe Co., Illinois, 1850c. (Johnson)

STORE, NATHAN Cleveland, Georgia, 1879d-1881d.

STORER, ALBERT Boston, Massachusetts. Patent #467,524 January 26, 1892, breechloading guns.

STORM, ANTHONY (1796-?), Martinsburg, Virginia, 1818-1826, Harper's Ferry, Virginia, 1826-1859. Father of George and Jerome Storm, who worked for Parker Bros. (Johnson)

STORM, WILLIAM MONTGOMERY New York, New York, 1853-1872. Patents #10,834 April 25, 1854, bullet molds, #10,846 May 2, 1854, chargers, #13,660 October 9, 1885, revolver, #14,420 March 11, 1856, revolving firearm, #15,307 July 8, 1856, breechloading firearms, #24,414 June 14, 1859, breechloading firearm, #32,607 October 29, 1861, skin cartridges, #132,740 November 5, 1872, breechloading firearm, and #210,976 December 17, 1878, magazine gun. These guns and cartridges are now known as "Mont Storm" products/models due to a peculiarity in Storm's signature. (Sellers-1)

STORRS, JOSEPH W. New York, New York, 1858d-1867d. Dealer.

STORY, ASA West Windsor, Vermont, 1830-1872. As Kendall, Hibbard & Story, 1835-1838. Percussion rifles and pistols. (Horn)

STORY, PASCHAL Windsor, Vermont, 1830-1845. Percussion 1/2 stock. Son of Asa Story.

STORY, WILLIAM Windsor, Vermont, 1850, Son of Asa Story. Percussion underhammer.

STOSSMEISTER, CHARLES Cincinnati, Ohio, 1848d-1867d. (Hutslar)

STOTZ, CHRISTIAN Williamsport, Pennsylvania, 1882d.

STOUDENOUR, JACOB (1795-1863), Rainsburg, Pennsylvania, 1821-1863. Flintlock and percussion Kentucky rifles, "J.S." usual signature. (Hetrick)

STOUDT, JOSEPH Bushkill, Pennsylvania, 1835t. (KRA II-3)

STOUP, ADAM (1792-?), Westmoreland co., Pennsylvania, 1835-1860c. (Whisker 2)

STOUT, JAMES Ramseur, North Carolina. (Bivins)

STOUT, PETER (1880-1963), Kadoka, South Dakota, 1897-1963. (MB 8-63)

STOUT, S. unlocated. Flintlock and percussion Kentucky rifles.

STOUTENBURGH, ISAAC (?-1770), New York, New York.

STOUTENBURGH, JACOBUS New York, New York, 1763. Executor of Barent Cool's (also spelled Koole) estate.

STOUTENBURGH, JOHANNES New York, New York. Resigned as executor of Barent Cool's (also spelled Koole) estate, 1791.

STOVER, FREDERICK York Co., Pennsylvania, 1781t-1824t, Adams Co., Pennsylvania, 1825t-1842t. Flintlock Kentucky. (Bowers)

STOVER, J.R. Eureka, Kansas, 1894d.

STOVER, WILLIAM Centralia, Illinois, 1860d.

STOWELL, ELSON J. Brooklyn, New York, 1870d-1878d. Single shot cartridge pistols.

STOWELL, JOHN Charlestown, Massachusetts, 1852-1855. Patent #12,836 May 5, 1855, lock.

STRAHORN, J.K. Hopewell, Missouri, 1860d.

STRAIT, RILEY Anamosa, Iowa, 1860, Fairview, Iowa, 1865d, Rockford, Iowa, 1880d-1882d and 1897d, Medford, Iowa, 1889d-1891d.

STRANG, WILLIAM G. Adeline, Illinois, 1864d.

STRASSER, JOHN Butte, Montana, 1898d.

STRATTAN & McDONALD West Liberty, Iowa, 1880d.

STRATTON, E. Philadelphia, Pennsylvania, 1841d.

STRATTON, GEORGE W. Macon, Georgia, 1879d-1883d.

STRATTON, J.W. Coal Grove, Kentucky, 1860d.

STRATTON-WARREN HARDWARE CO. Memphis, Tennessee. Dealers only.

STRAUB, JOHN see John Strave.

STRAUB, S.H. Kalamazoo, Michigan, 1899d.

STRAUBE, FRANK Schuyler, Nebraska, 1884d-1893d.

STRAUS, REUBEN Allentown, Pennsylvania, 1847t, Saegerstown, Pennsylvania, 1849-1860. (KRA II-3, Whisker II)

STRAUSS & SCHRAM Chicago, Illinois. Dealers only.

STRAVE, JOHN Monroe, Pennsylvania. Percussion Kentucky rifles. Also known as John Straub. (Gabel)

STRAW, EZEKIAL Manchester, New Hampshire. Magazine and single shot carbines. With William Wade as Straw-Wade. (GR 3-66)

STRAW-WADE Manchester, New Hampshire. Carbines made by Amoskeag Mfg. Co., both magazine and single shot. Ezekial Straw and William Wade. (GR 3-66)

STRAWBERRY, DAVID (1805-?), Anglaize Co., Ohio, 1850c. (Hutslar)

STRAWVICK, ANDREW (?-1832), Butler, Pennsylvania, 1810-1832. Percussion fullstock. (Whisker II)

STRAYER, JACOB South Bend, Indiana, 1879-1902. (MB 4-54)

STREET, CHARLES Portsmouth, Ohio, 1829. (Knittle)

STREET, CHARLES G. Brooklyn, New York. Patent #245,888 August 16, 1881, breechloading firearm with W.G. Eddy.

STREET, E.S. Kalamazoo, Michigan, 1850-1855. Multi-barrel rifles.

STREGLY, JOSEPH Philadelphia, Pennsylvania, 1841d.

STREUBER, G. San Francisco, California 1868d-1874d.

STRICKEL, SAMUEL York Co., Pennsylvania. (Kauffman)

STRICKLER, WILT & CO. Dayton, Ohio, 1837d. Barrelmakers. Jeremiah Wilt. (Hutslar)

STRIECER, E.J. unlocated. Flintlock Kentucky rifle.

STRIKER suicide special. (Webster)

STRIPLING see Farrell & Stripling.

STROBEL, JOHN G. Washington, D.C., 1864d-1867d. (Hartzler)

STROBLE & WILKEN Cincinnati, Ohio, 1883. C.A. Stroble.

STROBLE, C.A. Cincinnati, Ohio, 1883d, Hamilton, Ohio, 1888-1890d. As Stroble & Wilken, 1883. (Hutslar)

STROBLE, M.L. Hamilton, Ohio, 1896d. Son of C.A. Stroble. (Hutslar)

STRODE, JOHN Falmouth, Virginia, 1777, Culpepper, Virginia, 1796-1802. Manager of Rappahannock Forge and, later, inspector of arms. (Gill)

STROHECKER & EUBANK Charleston, South Carolina. Flintlock lock marking.

STROHECKER, H.F. Charleston, South Carolina, 1854d. Importer and dealer. Percussion duelling pistol.

STROHL, J. Fremont, Ohio, 1864-1875d. (Hutslar)

STROHL, JOHN Eprata, Pennsylvania, 1875d.

STROHWEG, ANDREW Butler, Pennsylvania, 1861d.

STRONACH, JOHN Frederica, Georgia, 1737-1749, Charleston, South Carolina, 1749. (Kauffman)

STRONG FIREARMS CO. New Haven, Connecticut, 1878-1890. Signal cannon, cartridges, breechloading rifles and shotguns.

STRONG, D. Ravenna, Ohio, 1860t-1870. (Hutslar)

STRONG, ELISHA Claridon, Ohio, 1830-1840. Patent #none August 2, 1831, percussion side lock. (Hutslar)

STRONG, ELISHA New Hartford, Connecticut. Patent #none August 31, 1810, rifles with Cotton Kellogg.

STRONG, H.A. unlocated. Percussion target rifle.

STRONG, JAMES Brady, Michigan, 1863d-1871d. Percussion 1/2 stock.

STRONG, JAMES Claridon, Ohio, 1853d-1859d. Son of Elisha Strong (Hutslar)

STRONG, JAMES A. Vicksburg, Michigan, 1867d, Scotts, Michigan, 1891d-1895d.

STRONG, R.H. Creston, Iowa, 1882d-1884d.

STRONG, SAMUEL Washington, D.C. Patents #37,208 December 16, 1862, breechloading firearm, #38,643 May 19, 1863, breechloading firearm, and #38,644 May 19, 1863, breechloading firearm.

STRONG, THEODORE F. Northampton, Massachusetts. Patent #698 April 21, 1838, revolver.

STRONG, W.S. unlocated. Percussion over/under rifle/shotgun.

STRONG, WILLIAM (1826-?), Ottawa, Illinois, 1850c. (Johnson)

STRONG, WILLIAM K. Big Rapids, Michigan, 1872d-1884d. Percussion guns, including over/under rifle/shotgun.

STROTHEL, WILLIAM Saltiville, Indiana, 1883-1885. (Gardner)

STROTHER, W.R. Owen Co., Indiana, 1867-1871. (Lindert)

STROUCH, CHARLES Pottsville, Pennsylvania, 1850c. (Gardner)

STROUP, D. unlocated. Flintlock Kentucky pistol. (KRA 76)

STROUP, O.M. Medina Co., Ohio, 1835, Wellington, Ohio, 1864d-1863d. (Hutslar)

STROUT, NATHANIEL Olympia, Washington, 1867d.

STRULLER, LAU & CO. New York, New York, 1880d-1884d. Louis Struller and J.H. Lau.

STRULLER, LOUIS New York, New York, 1849d-1884d. Importers. With J.H. Lau as Struller, Lau & Co., 1880-1884.

STRUVE, GEORGE Austin, Texas, 1878d-1896d.

STUARDT, JOSIAH unlocated. Flintlock Kentucky rifle dated 1808.

STUART & GAY Binghamton, New York, 1869d. Charles Stuart, Jr., and Eldridge Gay.

STUART, CHARLES Binghamton, New York, 1851-1883d. Percussion rifles. (Hobbies 11-38)

STUART, CHARLES Pinkbed, South Carolina, Iserd Co., Arkansas, ?-1861. (MB 12-50)

STUART, CHARLES, JR. Binghamton, New York, 1869d-1882d. With Eldridge Gay as Stuart & Gay, 1869-1870.

STUBBS, E.E. Jonesboro, Arkansas, 1898d. Captain Stubbs was a famous competition and exhibition shooter.

STUBBS, F. Sherman, Maine, 1877. (Demeritt)

STUCKHUSE, J.W. unlocated. Flintlock Kentucky.

STUDTE, F. (1805-?), Marysville, California, 1858-1859, San Francisco, California, 1860-1869, San Jose, California, 1870-1872. Operated his own shop in San Francisco only. (Shelton)

STUEBYEN, C. Saxonburg, Pennsylvania, 1861d.

STUFEGEN, G.A. unlocated. Percussion 1/2 stock.

STULL, B. Millwood, Ohio. Percussion 1/2 stock.

STULL, GEORGE (1821-?), Millwood, Ohio, 1841-1875d. Percussion fullstock. (Hutslar)

STULL, J.R. (1824-?), Trumbull Co., Ohio, 1850c. Percussion fullstock. (Hutslar)

STULL, PHILIP, Milwood, Ohio, 1865-1900. Son of Samuel Stull. (AOLRC V2)

STULL, SAMUEL (1808-1907), Millwood, Ohio, 1841-1865. Percussion 1/2 stock and flintlock fullstock. Brother of George Stull. (MB 12-55)

STUMPF, MICHAEL (?-1848), Indiana Co., Pennsylvania, 1826-1848. (Whisker II)

STUNE, GEORGE Austin, Texas, 1885d.

STUNKARD, ROBERT FERGUSON New Grenada, Pennsylvania, 1867. Percussion fullstock, "RFD" signature. (Kauffman)

STURDIVANT, LEWIS G. Talladega, Alabama, 1861-1863, Selma, Alabama, 1863. Mississippi rifles. (Hill-Anthony)

STURGEON, J.W. Colby, Kansas, 1894d.

STURGIS, JULIUS Lancaster, Pennsylvania, 1857d.

STURTEVANT, ALPHONSO T. Trinidad, Colorado, 1882-1885d. With Edwin A. Curtis as Curtis & Sturtevant. (Sellers-3)

STURTEVANT, EDWARD L. Boston, Massachusetts. Patent #66,751 July 16, 1867, breechloading firearm.

STURTEVANT, THOMAS L. Boston, Massachusetts. Patents #50,048 September 19, 1865, breechloading firearm, #50,854 November 7, 1865, cartridge retractor, #53,501 March 27, 1866, cartridge priming, #54,038 April 17, 1866, priming metallic cartridges, #55,552 June 12, 1866, cartridges, and #60,592 December 12, 1866, breechloading firearm.

STUTLER, ISAAC (1820-1896), Doddridge Co., Virginia, 1850c-1896. Percussion 1/2 stock.

STUTSMAN, J.G. (1819-?), Dayton, Ohio, 1850c-1854d. Percussion fullstock. (Hutslar)

STUTTS, C.C. Muffin, Tennessee, 1860d-1887d.

STUVER, T. Pyrmont, Ohio, 1878d. (Hutslar)

SUAN, JAMES B. see James Swan.

SUBERS, JAMES Philadelphia, Pennsylvania, 1855. (Kauffman)

SUBLETT, WILLIAM San Francisco, California. Patent #317,041 May 5, 1885, shot - cartridge. (Shelton)

SUCCESS suicide special. (Webster)

SUCHANEK, ANTON Silver Lake, Minnesota, 1898d.

SUCHE, MORITZ Crane's Mill, Texas, 1884d-1896d.

SUDBREINCK, WILLIAM, Duquesne, Pennsylvania, 1864d.

SUDDARTH, D.B. Marengo, Indiana, 1878-1885. (Lindert)

SUDDARTH, W.M. (1831-?), Marengo, Indiana, 1860c. (Lindert)

SUE, W. unlocated. Percussion fullstock.

SUESSMAN, AUGUST Buffalo, New York, 1854. (Dean)

SULLENBERGER, SAMUEL, A. Harrisburg, Pennsylvania. Patents #330,354 November 10, 1885, breechloading firearm, and #356,338 January 18, 1887, magazine gun.

SULLI VAN & PATTERSON Parsons, Kansas, 1884d.

SULLIVAN ARMS CO. trade name of Crescent Fire Arms Co. on shotguns. (AR 2-69)

SULLIVAN, J. Jeffersonville, Georgia, 1883d.

SULLIVAN, JAMES L. Xenia, Indiana. Flintlock fullstock rifle. (Lindert)

SULLIVAN, LEONARD Springfield, Massachusetts, 1872d.

SULLIVAN, T. Grafton, Wisconsin, 1857d-1870d.

SULLIVAN, W.H. Atlanta, Georgia, 1879d-1883d.

SUMERS, H. Barnet, Vermont. (Roberts)

SUMMERLIN, J.C. Visalia, California, 1866. (Shelton)

SUMMERS, JACOB, JR. Georgetown, Indiana, 1858d.

SUMMERSON, J.E. Charlottesville, Virginia, 1877d.

SUMNER ARMORY Gallatin, Tennessee, 1861-1862. Mississippi rifles and carbines for Confederacy. (Hill-Anthony)

SUMNER, MELVILLE Fall River, Massachusetts, 1874d.

SUMNER, THOMAS Augusta, Georgia, 1861. Confederate gunsmith convention.

SUNBY, HANS CHRISTIAN Chicago, Illinois, 1870. Originally from Norway. (GR 4-57)

SUNDERLAND & BLAIR Boulton, Pennsylvania. Flintlock Kentucky rifle. (Dillin)

SUNDERLAND, FERNANDO Y. Thorntown, Indiana. Patent #222,098 November 28, 1879, magazine gun.

SUPERIOR trade name of Paxton & Gallagher Co. on shotguns and revolvers.

SUPPE, J.L. Emporia, Kansas, 1894d.

SUPPLEE-BIDDLE HARDWARE CO. Philadelphia, Pennsylvania, 1880-1910. Dealers only.

SURE FIRE suicide special.

SURKAMER, FRED Chicago, Illinois, 1891d-1935.

SUSMAN & TOMBECK Cincinnati, Ohio, 1869. August Susman and Augustin Tombeck.

SUSMAN, AUGUST Cincinnati, Ohio, 1866d-1869d. With Augustin Tombeck as Susman & Tombeck, 1869. (Hutslar)

SUTER, C. Selma, Alabama, 1850-1866. Mississippi rifles for Confederacy, percussion guns before and after the Civil War. Partner of Lessier, 1861. As C. Suter & Co., 1863-1864.

SUTER, JOHN JAMES (1823-1902), Bucks Co., Pennsylvania, 1840-1902.

SUTER, THEODORE Philadelphia, Pennsylvania, 1847d.

SUTHARDS, WILLIAM (1804-?), Augusta Co., Virginia, 1850c.

SUTHERLAND, ANDREW J. Ann Arbor, Michigan, 1860d-1880. Percussion 1/2 stock.

SUTHERLAND, JOHN Flint, Michigan, 1860. Percussion 1/2 stock.

SUTHERLAND, SAMUEL Richmond, Virginia, circa 1830-1875. Importer and dealer. Succeeded by his sons, who maintained the business past the turn of the century.

SUTPHEN & BRO. Omaha, Nebraska, 1866-1875. D.C. and J.O. Sutphen.

SUTPHEN, D.C. Omaha, Nebraska, 1866d-1877d. With J.O. Sutphen as Sutphen & Bro., 1866-1875.

SUTPHEN, J.O. Omaha, Nebraska, 1866-1875. with D.C. Sutphen as Sutphen & Bro.

SUTTER, BENEDICT Highland, Illinois, 1893d.

SUTTER, HENRY Baker City, Oregon. Patent #196,399 October 23, 1877, breechloading firearms.

SUTTON see Waters and Whittemore.

SUTTON & DUNSETH Pittsburgh, Pennsylvania, 1799. (Kauffman)

SUTTON, GEORGE Pittsburgh, Pennsylvania, 1800. (Kauffman)

SUTTON, J.R. Kennedy, New York, 1880d. Percussion three-barrel swivelbreech.

SUTTON, JOHN Philadelphia, Pennsylvania, 1819d.

SUTTON, K. unlocated. Percussion slug gun.

SUTTON, R. Kennedy, New York, 1878-1882d.

SUTTON, W.C. Nashville, Arkansas, 1892d-1898d.

SUTVAN, ISAAC Bridesburg, Pennsylvania. Patent #46,866 March 14, 1865, breechloading firearm.

SVEJDA, JAMES Chicago, Illinois, 1896d-1910d. As Harent & Swejda, 1896-1897. Originally Voclav Swejda.

SWAIDNER, ANTHONY C. Salem, Ohio, 1830-1870. Percussion rifles.

SWAIN, J.M. Gladeville, Tennnessee, 1860d.

SWAIN, JOHN West Virginia. Flintlock Kentucky. (Dillin)

SWAIN, JOSEPH Concord, New Hampshire, circa 1775. For Samuel Barrett. (GR 4-75)

SWALLA, JOHN (1818-?), Fulton Co., Indiana, 1850c. (Lindert)

SWAMP ANGEL suicide special by Forehand & Wadsworth.

SWAN, JAMES B. Boston, Massachusetts, 1800. Imported Model 1798 contract muskets for the state of Virginia. (ASAC 35)

SWAN, JEFFERSON L. Loweville, New York. Patent #34,911 April 8, 1862, firearm.

SWARTCOOP New York, New York, 1786-1796. (Gluckman & Satterlee)

SWARTOUT, AARON Worcester, New York, 1882d.

SWARTZ, ABRAHAM Delaware, Ohio, 1859d, Tuscaroras Co., Ohio, 1870. (Hutslar)

SWARTZ, JOHN Arcola, Illinois, 1893d.

SWARTZ, PETER York Co., Pennsylvania, 1784-1786. Committee of Safety muskets. (Gluckman & Satterlee)

SWEENEY, JOSEPH J. Springfield, Massachusetts. Patent #136,871 March 18, 1873, revolver with George M. Smith and John T. Smith.

SWEENEY, JOSEPH L. New Haven, Connecticut. Patents #220,734 October 21, 1879, magazine firearm, and #223,409 January 6, 1880, magazine firearm, both with William Wetmore.

SWEET & ALLEN Kalamazoo, Michigan, 1867d.

SWEET, ALONZO LOUIS Norwalk, Connecticut, 1873-1874, Norwich, Connecticut, 1876-1881. Patents #210,725 December 10, 1878, revolver, and #243,993 July 5, 1881, firearms. Guns made by Bacon.

SWEET, D., & CO. unlocated. Percussion lock.

SWEET, E.S. Kalamazoo, Michigan. Percussion target rifle. (Roberts)

SWEET, JENKS & SON Rhode Island. Model 1808 contract muskets. (Gluckman & Satterlee)

SWEET, LEVI Wilson, New York, 1869-1874.

SWEET, WILLIAM A. Pompey, New York, 1847-1854, Syracuse, New York, 1855-1865. Patent #11,536 August 15, 1854, breechloading firearms. With William Malcolm in Syracuse. (GR 3-57)

SWEETSER, WILLIAM A. North Bridgewater, Massachusetts, 1874d.

SWEGER, H. Perry Co., Pennsylvania. Flintlock Kentucky.

SWEGER, WILLIAM ((1815-1892), Elliottsburgh, Pennsylvania, 1860-1890d. Percussion fullstock. (Chandler 2)

SWEIGART, ADAM Halifax, Pennsylvania, 1815-1817. (Kauffman)

SWEIGERT, WILLIAM Elliotsburg, Pennsylvania, 1850c-1861d. Percussion fullstock. (Kauffman)

SWEITSER, S. unlocated. Percussion fullstock.

SWEITZER, A. see Abraham Schweitzer.

SWEITZER, CHARLES Mauch Chunk, Pennsylvania, 1864-1875. Percussion fullstock.

SWEITZER, DANIEL & CO. Lancaster, Pennsylvania, 1808-1813. Locks only. (Dillin)

SWEITZER, JACOB unlocated. Flintlock Kentucky. (Dillin)

SWEITZER, JOHN (1805-?), Greenville, Ohio, 1850c-1860c. Percussion fullstock. (Hutslar)

SWEITZER, JOHN (1823-?), Attica, Indiana, 1858d-1880. (Lindert)

SWEITZER, S. Attica, Indiana, 1858d.

SWETT, DANIEL L. Vicksburg, Mississippi. Derringer. (Eberhart)

SWETT, L., & CO. Vicksburg, Mississippi. Agent on Deringer.

SWIFT trade name of Iver Johnson on double action revolvers.

SWIFT, DEXTER PETER, JR. (1838-1897), Starsboro, Vermont, 1871-1885. Percussion and cartridge guns. (MB 5-65)

SWINEHART, ANDREW (1829-?), Somerset, Ohio, 1850c-1853d. Percussion fullstock rifles. (Hutslar)

SWINEHART, WILLIAM Somerset, Ohio, circa 1890. (Hutslar)

SWINERTON, J. Dundee, Michigan, 1860d.

SWINFORD, J.B. Paxton, Indiana. Percussion fullstock.

SWINGLE, ALFRED (1810-?), San Francisco, California, 1870-1882. Lever action rifles. Patents #135,947 February 18, 1873, magazine firearms with Frank A. Huntington, #137,392 April 1, 1873, magazine firearm, #150,102 April 21, 1874, magazine firearm with Frank A. Huntington, and #224,742 February 17, 1880, revolving firearms. (GR 11-62)

SWISHER, ISAAC C. Marion, Kansas, 1882d-1888d, Coffeyville, Kansas, 1894d.

SWISHER, JOHN, Mifflin Co., Pennsylvania, 18134-1815. (Whisker III)

SWITZER, A. Bellefonte, Pennsylvania, 1861d.

SWOBE, ADAM Lancaster, Pennsylvania, 1785t-1802t. Delivered four Model 1792 contract rifles. (Moller)

SWOPE, ALFRED Taylorsville, Kentucky, 1879d. Percussion fullstock.

SWYNEY, JOHN Charlestown, Massachusetts. Patent #13,474 September 21, 1855, magazine breechloading firearm.

SYCO trade name of Wyeth Hardware Co. on shotguns. (Hinman)

SYDENHAM, A. Nebraska City, Nebraska, 1884d-1886d, Montrose, Colorado, 1891d. (Sellers-3)

SYFERT, JOHN Union Co., Pennsylvania, 1850c. Barrels. Same as John Syphers?

SYLVESTER, C.F. Fall River, Massachusetts, 1888d.

SYLVIS, ANTHONY Birmingham, Iowa, 1865d.

SYLVIS, JACOB Salem Cross Roads, Pennsylvania, 1861d.

SYMMES, JOHN CLEVES (1825-1895), Watertown, Massachusetts, 1853-1863. Patents #22,094 November 16, 1858, breechloaders, and #39,844 September 8, 1863, gas check. "Symmes" carbines purchased by U.S. government were actually patented by T.A. Washington. (AG 4-74)

SYMONS & SON Newark, Ohio, 1889d-1893d. William and Walter D. Symons. (Hutslar)

SYMONS, WALTER D. Newark, Ohio, 1889-1893. With William Symons as Symons & Sons.

SYMONS, WILLIAM Newark, Ohio, 1889-1893. With Walter D. Symons as Symons & Son.

SYMS, JOHN G. New York, New York. 1852d-1867d. Percussion guns.

SYMS, SAMUEL R. see Blunt & Syms.

SYMS, WILLIAM J. New York, New York, 1848-1867d. As W.J. Syms & Bro., 1858-1867.

SYNEK, CARL St. Paul, Minnesota, 1898d.

SYPHERS, JOHN Waynesburg, Pennsylvania, 1876d-1890d. Same as John Syfert?

SYRACUSE ARMS CO. Syracuse, New York, 1888-1908. Shotguns under Hollenbeck and Home patents. Trade names "Hollenbeck" and "Syracuse". Successor to Syracuse Forging & Gun Co. (Hinman)

SYRACUSE FORGING & GUN CO. Syracuse, New York, 1887-1888. Shotguns. Succeeded by Syracuse Arms Co.

T SECTION

T. & R. see Turner & Ross.

T.A.T. unidentified. Percussion fullstock.

T.B. unidentified. New Madrid, Missouri. Percussion 1/2 stock.

T.B. & CO. see E.K. Tryon.

T.B. & CO. unidentified. Philadelphia, Pennsylvania. Percussion derringer, percussion fullstock.

T.C.A. unidentified. Percussion fullstock.

T.F. see Thomas Fleming.

T.F.T. unidentified. Percussion 1/2 stock.

T.G. see Thomas Gluyas.

T.H. unidentified. Percussion fullstock.

T.H.B. unidentified. Percussion 1/2 stock.

T.H.B. & CIE unidentified. Derringer. Possibly T.B. & Co.?

T.J.C. unidentified. Percussion fullstock, Tennessee.

T.M. unidentified. Percussion fullstock.

T.M.Y. see Thomas Yerian.

T.O. see Thomas C. Oldham.

T.P. unidentified. Percussion fullstock.

T.R. unidentified. Percussion fullstock.

T.S. unidentified. Percussion fullstock.

T.W.A. unidentified. Percussion fullstock. (Bedford)

TABB, B.T. Norfolk, Virginia. Importers and dealers.

TABBUTT, A.J. Columbia, Maine, 1875. (Demeritt)

TABOR, WILLIAM J. (1834-?), Big Thompson, Colorado, 1880c.

TACHOLD, JACOB (1826-?), Leavenworth, Indiana, 1860c. (Lindert)

TAFFLINGER, ALLEN Marysville, Indiana, 1882-1885. (Lindert)

TAFT & FONDERSMITH Champaign, Illinois, 1878d-1882d.

TAFT, DANIEL F. New Bedford, Massachusetts, 1888d.

TAFTS, E. Westford, Massachusetts, 1869d.

TAGGART, WILLIAM Haverhill, Massachusetts. Patent #16,076 November 11, 1856, projectiles for firearms.

TAGLER, MARTIN Cincinnati, Ohio, 1880c. (Hutslar)

TAIT, ARTHUR F. Morrisania, New York. Patent #38,770 June 2, 1863, self-priming hammers. Tait was an artist, not a gunsmith.

TALIAFERRO, NICHOLAS Augusta, Kentucky. Patent #34,171 January 14, 1862, revolving cannon.

TALLASSEE ARMORY Tallassee, Alabama, 1863-1865. Percussion carbines for the Confederacy. (Hill-Anthony)

TALLEY Boston, Massachusetts, 1768-1776. Armorer to the colony, 1775-1776. (Gluckman & Satterlee)

TALLEY, ROBERT Rockdale, Texas, 1890d-1896d.

TALLY, MICAJAH Hanover Co., Virginia, 1781. Committee of Safety repairs. (Gill)

TAMABECKER, S. unlocated. Flintlock Kentucky rifles.

TAMPAUGH, SIMON Logansport, Indiana, 1867-1871. (Lindert)

TANNELLS, PETER Lawrence, Illinois, 1864d.

TANNER, AUGUST Brookfield, Missouri, 1889d-1898d.

TANNER, E.F. Edmore, Michigan, 1899d.

TANNER, N.B. Bastrop, Texas, 1862. Muskets and rifles for the Confederacy. As Tanner & Co.? (Hill-Anthony)

TAPKEN, HENRY Marquette, Michigan, 1883d-1887d.

TARPLEY, GARRET & CO. Greensboro, North Carolina, 1863-1864. Jere H. Tarpley's patent breechloading carbines. (Albaugh 1)

TARPLEY, JERE H. Greensboro, North Carolina. Confederate patent #148 February 14, 1863, breechloading firearm. (Albaugh 1)

TARR, MOSES B. Heath, Massachusetts, 1874d-1879d.

TARRATT, J. unlocated. Percussion 1/2 stock. See J. Tarratt & Sons.

TARRATT, J., & SONS unlocated. Marking on locks and barrels. See J. Tarratt.

TATE, JOHN Adair Co., Missouri, 1850c. (MB 11-66)

TAUBER, JOHN Cumberland, Maryland, 1878-1882d. (Hartzler)

TAUBER, JOHN McKeesport, Pennsylvania, 1887d.

TAUBER, JOHN New York, New York, 1851d.

TAUBERT Sandusky, Ohio, 1888d. As Rinkleff & Taubert.

TAYLOR & NOYES Brattleboro, Vermont, 1873-1874. (Horn)

TAYLOR & WOODBURY Corinne, Utah, 1871d.

TAYLOR MANUFACTURING CO. New Britain, Connecticut, 1876d. Pistols.

TAYLOR, A.J. Lebanon, Tennessee, 1876d.

TAYLOR, ALEXANDER McConnellsburg, Pennsylvania, 1808t-1832. Flintlock Kentucky. (Bowers)

TAYLOR, ANDREW J. (1813-1858), San Francisco, California, 1854-1858. Derringer. (Shelton)

TAYLOR, ARGULUS (1810-?), Auburn, New York, 1826-1835, Cato, New York, 1836-1880d. For his father-in-law Elijah Snell, Auburn. (Massachusetts Arms)

TAYLOR, BENJAMIN F. (1806-?), Ohio, 1831-1842, Illinois, 1846, Iowa, 1848-1850, Cottonwood, Utah, 1850, El Monte, California, 1852, San Bernardino, California, 1860, Springville, Utah, 1871d.

TAYLOR, C.C. Atlanta, Georgia, 1883d.

TAYLOR, C.G. Fort Worth, Texas, 1884d.

TAYLOR, CALVIN Triangle, New York, 1858-1874d. Percussion 1/2 stock.

TAYLOR, D.P. unlocated. Percussion 1/2 stock.

TAYLOR, DANIEL S.B. Eureka, California, 1877-1881. (Shelton)

TAYLOR, F.E. Ventura, California, 1893d.

TAYLOR, FERDINAND Danbury, Connecticut. Patent #166,947 August 24, 1875, lock.

TAYLOR, FREDERICK P. Chicago, Illinois, 1876d-1888d.

TAYLOR, GEORGE (?-1781), Easton Co., Pennsylvania, 1775-1781. Musket barrels. (Dillin)

TAYLOR, GEORGE A. Lynn, Massachusetts, 1878d-1884d.

TAYLOR, GROND Zanesville, Ohio, 1822. (Hutslar)

TAYLOR, H.H. Rochester, New York. Pill lock target pistol.

TAYLOR, HENRY Richland Co., Ohio, 1820c. (Hutslar)

TAYLOR, ISAAC Lesages, West Virginia, 1884d.

TAYLOR, J.A. Baxter Springs, Kansas, 1888d.

TAYLOR, J.A. Cairo, Illinois, 1890d.

TAYLOR, J.B. Boise, Idaho, 1891d.

TAYLOR, J.B. Franklin, Ohio, 1859d. (Hutslar)

TAYLOR, J.N. unlocated. Percussion barrelmaker.

TAYLOR, JAMES PATTON Elizabethton, Tennessee. Patents #116,775, July 4, 1871, repeating ordnance, #138,711 May 6, 1873, breechloading firearm, #174,872 March 14, 1876, machine gun, #174,873 March 14, 1876, machine gun, #177,030 May 2, 1876, machine gun, #189,811 April 17, 1877, machine feeder, #190,645 May 8, 1877, machine gun, and #206,365 July 23, 1878, machine gun.

TAYLOR, JOHN Augusta, Kentucky. Patent #37,025 November 25, 1862, breechloading firearm with James W. Armstrong.

TAYLOR, JOHN Pennsylvania, 1775-1776. Committee of Safety muskets. (Hobbies 5-37)

TAYLOR, JOHN A. Berlin, Michigan, 1863d-1867d.

TAYLOR, JOSEPH B. Greenbush, New York. Patent #561,360 June 2, 1896, sight.

TAYLOR, L.B., & CO. Chicopee, Massachusetts. Single shot cartridge derringers.

TAYLOR, N.B. Vienna, Ohio, 1840d. Probably N.B. Tyler. (Knittle)

TAYLOR, O.P. Elizabethtown, Indiana, 1862d.

TAYLOR, O.P. Rochester, Indiana, 1884-1886. (Lindert)

TAYLOR, OLIVER P. Peru, Indiana, 1882-1885. (Lindert)

TAYLOR, ROBERT W. Middlefield, New York, 1850c.

TAYLOR, S.W. Grenola, Kansas, 1884d.

TAYLOR, SYDNEY W. Newport, Rhode Island. Patent #316,416 April 21, 1885, sight.

TAYLOR, THEODORE E. Fremont, Nebraska, 1893d.

TAYLOR, TRAVIS Chester, Pennsylvania, 1887d-1889d.

TAYLOR, W.B. Charlotte, North Carolina, 1871-1884d. (Bivins)

TAYLOR, W.C. Union City, Ohio, 1866d. (Hutslar)

TAYLOR, W.W. Milan, Tennessee, 1885d.

TAYLOR, WILLIAM Bern, Missouri, 1860d.

TAYLOR, WILLIAM C. Sauk Center, Minnesota, 1878d.

TAYSMAND, G. Dauphin Co., Pennsylvania, 1790-1810. Flintlock Kentucky rifle. (Dean)

TEAFF, JAMES (1796-?), Steubenville, Ohio, 1816-1864d. Flintlock and percussion fullstock. (Hutslar)

TEAFF, JAMES, JR. (1827-?), Steubenville, Ohio, 1850c. (Hutslar)

TEAFF, MATTHEW Steubenville, Ohio, 1856d. Son of James Teaff. (Hutslar)

TEAFF, NIMROD Steubenville, Ohio, 1856d-1890d. With his father James Teaff, 1856-1864, alone thereafter. (Hutslar)

TEAFF, WILLIAM (1822-?), Steubenville, Ohio, 1850c. Son of James Teaff. (Hutslar)

TEALL, WILLIAM S. Little Falls, New York. Patents #308,216 November 18, 1884, breechloading firearm, and #322,568 July 21, 1885, breechloading firearm.

TEBODO, A. Holyoke, Massachusetts, 1876d-1889d.

TEDFORD, ALEXANDER (?-1781), Rockbridge Co., Virginia, ?-1781. (Gill)

TEED, CHARLES E. Pere Marquette, Michigan, 1863d.

TEEL, JOSEPH Kunkletown, Pennsylvania, 1882d-1890d.

TEETER, SAMUEL Elkhart, Indiana, 1850. Percussion 1/2 stock. (Lindert)

TEFF, GEORGE South Kingston, Rhode Island, 1775-1776. Committee of Safety muskets. (Gluckman & Satterlee)

TEGETHOFF, WILLIAM St. Louis, Missouri, 1857d. Name appears on Shawk & McLanahan revolvers although he was working for Hawken in 1857.

TEICHERT, ADOLPH Parsons, Kansas, 1888d.

TEINER unlocated. Lockmaker.

TEITUS, C.F. Mt. Eton, Ohio, 1860d-1864d. (Hutslar)

TELFORD, ANDREW Botetourt Co., Virginia, 1780. (Gill)

TELFORD, JAMES (?-1787), Amherst Co., Virginia, 1769-1787. (Gill)

TELL, FREDERICK Fredericktown, Maryland, 1790-?, Hagerstown, Maryland, ?- 1810. Flintlock Kentucky rifles. (Dean says this is mis-reading of Frederick Sell). (Dean)

TELSHAW, FRANK West Turin, New York, 1863-1864d.

TEN STAR trade name of H. & D. Folsom on imported shotguns for Geller, Ward & Hasner. (Hinman)

TENNEY, SYLVANUS Johnsonville, Illinois, 1878d-1882d, Elk Falls, Kansas, 1888d.

TENTA, MICHAEL Baltimore, Maryland, 1802-1804. (Dean*)

TERICK, I. Mohn's Store, Pennsylvania, 1882d-1887d. Gun barrels only.

TERK, MARTIN (1826-?), Peoria, Illinois, 1860c. (Johnson)

TERRELL, CHARLES C. Schullsburg, Wisconsin. Patents #14,215 February 5, 1856, revolving cannon, and #19,387 February 16, 1858, magazine gun.

TERRELL, EPHRAIM, JR. Hartstown, Pennsylvania, 1868d.

TERRIER suicide special by Rupertus.

TERRILL, E. Crossville, Tennessee, 1882-1886. Percussion fullstock.

TERRILL, LAFAYETTE Z. Chicopee, Massachusetts. Patent #89,705 May 4, 1869, magazine gun.

TERRILL, LAFAYETTE Z. Mt. Eden, Kentucky, 1883d.

TERROR suicide special by Forehand & Wadsworth.

TERRY, D.L. Philadelphia, Pennsylvania, 1862-1863. Converted flintlock muskets.

TERRY, ISAAC Riverhead, New York, 1850d-1859d.

TERRY, J.C. unlocated. "Patent Pending" .22 cal. single shot pistol.

TESTA, GIUSEPPE New York, New York. Patent #628,130 July 4, 1899, breechloading firearm.

TETLEY, JOHN Pittsburgh, Pennsylvania, 1848-1862. With James Bown as Bown & Tetley, 1848-1862. (Kauffman)

TETLEY, WILLIAM Leavenworth, Kansas, 1866d, Pana, Illinois, 1878d, 1884d, Virginia, Illinois, 1880d.

TETZEL, ALBERT (?-1948), Terre Haute, Indiana. Son of Edmund Tetzel. (Lindert)

TETZEL, EDMUND (?-1931), Terre Haute, Indiana, 1879-1931. (Lindert)

TETZEL, EDMUND, JR. (?-1958), Terre Haute, Indiana. (Lindert)

TEUTENBERG & DEISSNER San Francisco, California, 1877d. (Shelton)

TEUTSCH, AUGUST New Orleans, Louisiana, 1874d-1878d.

TEWKSBURY, JOSIAH Webb City, Missouri, 1898d.

TEXAN, A.M. St. Francisville, Missouri, 1860d.

TEXAS RANGER trade name of Montgomery Ward Co. on imported revolvers and shotguns.

THACHER, JOHN B. Albany, New York. Patent #504,820, September 12, 1893, air gun with E.C. Fasoldt.

THACKERS, F.L. Los Angeles, California, 1893d.

THACKSTON, BENJAMIN Virginia, 1776-1777. Army repairs. (Gill)

THAMES ARMS CO. Norwich, Connecticut, 1900c. Inexpensive revolvers.

THAMES ARMS CO. trade name of Harrington & Richardson on shotguns. (Hinman)

THANDON, JOHN unlocated. Flintlock Kentucky rifles.

THATCHER, DAVID C. (1816-?), Chicago, Illinois, 1839-1884. As Peacock & Thatcher. (Johnson)

THATCHER, J. Middletown Point, New Jersey, 1860d.

THATCHER, JOSEPH Brooklyn, New York, 1849-1886d.

THAYER, C.B. Boston, Massachusetts. Patent #21,109 August 3, 1858, centrifugal gun, and other patents for cannon.

THAYER, ORRIN G. (1838-1894), Chardon, Ohio, 1862-1878d. Percussion 1/2 stock. (Hutslar)

THAYER, ROBINSON & CARY Norwich, Connecticut, 1900. Inexpensive revolvers. Succeeded by Thames Arms Co.

THAYER, S. Hampden, Ohio, 1881d. (Hutslar)

THAYER, THADDEUS Pottsdam, New York, 1865-1867, Norwood, New York, 1868. (Swinney)

THEDE, CHRISTOPHER H. Ukiah, California, 1884. (Shelton)

THEILEN, HENRY A. Memphis, Tennessee, 1868-1876d. Percussion 1/2 stock.

THEIS, HENRY (1825-?), Greenup, Illinois, 1860c. (Johnson)

THIARD, CLAUDE Ahnapee, Wisconsin, 1884d-1886d.

THIBIDEAU, ALFRED Holyoke, Massachusetts, 1882d.

THIEDE, FREDERICK Centralia, Illinois, 1864d.

THIELEMANN, JULIUS Bastrop, Texas, 1890d-1892d.

THIELSEN, CHARLES Tacoma, Washington, 1891d.

THIEME, CHARLES H. North Vernon, Indiana. Patent #81,036 August 11, 1868, priming.

THISTLE, HEZEKIAH L. New Orleans, Louisiana, 1834-1838. Patent #865 August 1, 1838, breechloading firearm.

THOENEN, S.J., & SON Ithaca, Michigan, 1883d.

THOM & PRICKETT Marysville, California, 1876-1880. David Thom, Jr. and Enos Samuel Prickett.

THOM, DAVID, JR. (1847-?), Marysville, California, 1876-1881, San Francisco, California, 1882-1902. With Enos Samuel Prickett as Thom & Prickett, 1876-1880. (Shelton)

THOMAS & ANDERSON Louisville, Kentucky, 1858-1860.

THOMAS, BENJAMIN Hingham, Massachusetts, 1740-1750. (Roberts)

THOMAS, C.F.W. Lake, Pennsylvania, 1890d.

THOMAS, EDWIN, JR. Chicago, Illinois, 1867d-1916d. Breechloading shotgun.

THOMAS, ELISHA Luzerne, Michigan, 1891d.

THOMAS, FRANCIS Washington, Indiana, 1847-1856. (Lindert)

THOMAS, G.M. Williston, North Dakota, 1898d.

THOMAS, GRISWOLD & CO. New Orleans, Louisiana, 1861-1865. Henry Thomas, Jr., A.B. Griswold, and William Goodrich. Successors to Hyde & Goodrich.

THOMAS, H., & CO. Dayton, Ohio, 1859d. Barrelmakers. (Hutslar)

THOMAS, HORACE Kingman, Indiana, 1841-1872. Percussion pistol. (Lindert)

THOMAS, HORATIO (1804-?), Higginsport, Ohio, 1850c-1853d. Percussion 1/2 stock and target rifles. (Hutslar)

THOMAS, HORATIO Georgetown, Illinois, 1864d.

THOMAS, ISAAC Harford Co., Maryland, 1774-1776. Committee of Safety muskets with John Cunningham. (Gluckman & Satterlee)

THOMAS, ISAAC J. New York, New York, 1846d.

THOMAS, J. unlocated. Underhammer rifle converted to parlor gun.

THOMAS, J. Washington Co., Virginia. Percussion fullstock. (KRA 76)

THOMAS, J.H., & CO. Louisville, Kentucky. Percussion 1/2 stock.

THOMAS, J.M. Eldertown, Pennsylvania, 1882d-1887d.

THOMAS, JAMES (1796-?), Princeton, Indiana, 1850c-1858d. (Lindert)

THOMAS, JAMES R. Collingsworth, Georgia. Patent #1,611 May 19, 1840, detachable chamber rifle.

THOMAS, JEREMIAH Niles, Michigan, 1883d-1887d.

THOMAS, JOHN A. West Meriden, Connecticut, 1865-1886d.

THOMAS, JOHN F. Ilion, New York. Patents #22,911 February 8, 1859, alarm gun with J.P. Wilson, #19,328 February 9, 1858, cane gun, #125,229 April 2, 1872, breechloading firearm, and #127,386 May 28, 1872, breechloading firearm. Guns made by Remington.

THOMAS, JOHN, & SON Centre, Ohio, 1849-1854. Percussion fullstock rifle.

THOMAS, L. Freemont, Wisconsin, 1857d, Shiocton, Wisconsin, 1879d.

THOMAS, M.B. Bucksport, Maine, 1868-1873. (Demeritt)

THOMAS, MILTON Kingman, Indiana, 1867- ?. Son of Horace Thomas. (Lindert)

THOMAS, O. Woodbury, Vermont, 1884-1885. (Horn)

THOMAS, THEODORE Schultz Mills, Illinois, 1886d-1890d.

THOMAS, THOMAS New York, New York, 1875d.

THOMAS, W.H. Abingdon, Illinois, 1878d.

THOMAS, WILLIAM Bucks Co., Pennsylvania, 1800t-1801t, Philadelphia, Pennsylvania, 1814t. (Dyke)

THOMAS, WILLIAM M. Bridgeport, Connecticut. Patent #437,262 September 30, 1890, bullet.

THOMISON, SAMUEL F. (1810-?), Round Valley, California, 1860c. (Shelton)

THOMIZ, ANDREW (1811-?), Baltimore, Maryland, 1839-1960d. (Hartzler)

THOMPSON & BARLEY Hamilton, Montana, 1898d.

THOMPSON & JOHNSON Morris, Illinois, 1890d-1893d.

THOMPSON & McCRUM Locust Grove, Ohio, 1859d. Lewis Thompson and James McCrum. (Hutslar)

THOMPSON, ABIJAH Woburn, Massachusetts. Committee of Safety muskets. (ASAC 35)

THOMPSON, ALFRED (1813-?), Warren Co., North Carolina, 1850c. (Bivins)

THOMPSON, ANDREW J. Galesburg, Illinois, 1886d-1893d, Knoxville and Roseville, Illinois, 1893d.

THOMPSON, ARTEMUS (1814-?), Williamsburg, Indiana, 1850c. (Lindert)

THOMPSON, C.H. North Carolina, 1855. (Bivins)

THOMPSON, CHARLES I. Havana, Illinois, 1880d, Mason City, Illinois, 1881. Percussion 1/2 stock.

THOMPSON, DAVID Springfield, Pennsylvania, 1873d.

THOMPSON, E. Homer, New York, 1870d.

THOMPSON, F. St. Louis, Missouri, 1840d.

THOMPSON, GEORGE Fremont, Ohio, 1881d. Percussion 1/2 stock. (Hutslar)

THOMPSON, GEORGE W. Washington, Pennsylvania, 1870-1882d.

THOMPSON, H.R. Jackson, Michigan, 1863d-1899d.

THOMPSON, HARRY Erie, Pennsylvania, 1890d.

THOMPSON, HARRY Fremont, Ohio, 1875-1888d. (Hutslar)

THOMPSON, HENRY Rochester, New York, 1861d, Fredonia, New York, 1861-1864d. For Billinghurst, 1861. (Eich)

THOMPSON, ISAAC (1802-?), Mecklenburg Co., North Carolina, 1850c. (Bivins)

THOMPSON, J. Peebles, Ohio. Percussion 1/2 stock. (MB 1-60)

THOMPSON, J.M. Altoona, Pennsylvania. Percussion 1/2 stock.

THOMPSON, J.R. Jackson, Michigan. Percussion over/under rifle.

THOMPSON, JACOB Santa Ana, California, 1880-1881d. (Shelton)

THOMPSON, JAMES (1832-?), Derinda, Illinois, 1850c-1860d. With Lafayette Mills as Mills & Thompson.

THOMPSON, JAMES Marion, Indiana, 1858d.

THOMPSON, JAMES B. Watkins, New York, 1858-1874.

THOMPSON, JOHN Norwich, Connecticut, 1865-1867d.

THOMPSON, JOHN Philadelphia, Pennsylvania, 1780-1785. Repaired U.S. arms. (Moller)

THOMPSON, JOHN C. New Haven, Connecticut. Patent #213,307 March 18, 1879, stock.

THOMPSON, JOHN TALIAFERRO (1860-1940), Brigadier General, Ordnance Department, U.S. Army (Ret. 1918). Designer, with John Blish, of the Thompson submachine gun. Development by Auto-Ordnance Corp. Guns made by Colt, Savage, and Auto-Ordnance. For Remington Arms Company, as Chief Engineer, 1914-1917. (Hogg)

THOMPSON, LEWIS Peebles, Ohio, 1820, Locust Grove, Ohio, 1859d. As Thompson & Crum, 1859. (Hutslar)

THOMPSON, R.B. Karber's Ridge, Illinois, 1880d-1888d.

THOMPSON, RICHARD H.S. Lexington, Kentucky. Patent #309,262 December 16, 1884, electric gun.

THOMPSON, RUFUS (1827-?), Williamsburg, Indiana, 1850c. (Lindert)

THOMPSON, SAMUEL Westerly, Rhode Island, 1851-1856d. Percussion fullstock rifle.

THOMPSON, SAMUEL B. (1785-?), Lancaster, Pennsylvania, 1806-1820c, Columbus, Ohio, 1820-1850c. Flintlock rifles. (Hutslar)

THOMPSON, SANDY FORKS (1834-?), Chatham Co., North Carolina, 1850c. (Bivins)

THOMPSON, STEPHEN Haverhill, Massachusetts, 1853d-1856d.

THOMPSON, T.E. Passaic, New Jersey, 1878d.

THOMPSON, THOMAS Derby, Connecticut, 1881d-1889d.

THOMPSON, THOMAS Richmond, Ohio, 1853d. (Hutslar)

THOMPSON, THOMAS Seattle, Washington, 1878d.

THOMPSON, W. Jackson, Michigan 1867d, Fremont Center, Michigan, 1872d-1877d. As W. & H.R. Thompson, 1867.

THOMPSON, W. Snow Camp, North Carolina. Percussion fullstock. (Bivins)

THOMPSON, W.T. Jamestown, North Carolina. (Bivins)

THOMPSON, WILLIAM (1820-?), Catham Co., North Carolina, 1850c. (Bivins)

THOMPSON, WILLIAM (1840-1910), Fremont, Ohio, 1875d-? Percussion and cartridge guns. Patent #663,669 December 11, 1900, breechloading gun. (Hutslar)

THOMPSON, WILLIAM Xenia, Ohio, 1888d-1896d. Also known as William Thomson. (Hutslar)

THOPP, J. & J. Philadelphia, Pennsylvania, 1824d.

THORMANN, JOHANN St. Louis, Missouri, 1868d.

THORN, DAVID San Francisco, California, 1893d.

THORNBERRY, J. Georgetown, Kentucky, 1885d.

THORNE, CHARLES B. Glasgow, Illinois, 1864d.

THORNHILL, S.A. Waxahachie, Texas, 1890d-1892d.

THORNLEY, EDWARD H. Ilion, New York. Patents #568,285 September 22, 1896, single trigger, and #673,803 May 7, 1901, lock.

THORNSEN, HENRY Bakersfield, California, 1893d.

THORNSEN, OTTO Bakersfield, California, 1878-1881. (Shelton)

THORNTON, F.L. Aberdeen, Washington, 1891d.

THORNTON, WILLIAM Washington, D.C. Patent #none May 21, 1811, breechloading firearm with J.H. Hall. Original patent for Hall's rifles. Thornton was Patent Commissioner. (Huntington)

THORP, THOMAS J. Chicago, Illinois. Patent #473,370 April 19, 1892, magazine gun.

THORPE, ORLANDO B. (1812-?), Havana, Illinois, 1872-1888d.

THORSEN & CASSIDY Chicago, Illinois, 1892d. Dealers.

THORSEN, THEODORE M. Camden, New Jersey, 1894d-1899d, 1907, Philadelphia, Pennsylvania, 1900d-1906. Patents #696,118 March 25, 1902, automatic gun, #815,879 March 20, 1906, lock, and #867,685 October 8, 1907, automatic gun.

THORSTADT, ERIC La Crosse, Wisconsin, 1870-1875.

THORWALD, AUGUST St. Louis, Missouri, 1854d-1865d.

THOSS, EUGENE Mobile, Alabama, 1887d-1892d.

THRASHER, DAVID C. Freetown, Massachusetts. Patents #54,624 May 8, 1866, stock attachment, and #66,913 July 16, 1867, breechloading firearm with B.F. Aiken.

THRELKEL, M.F. Hadley, Kentucky, 1879d-1884d.

THRESHER, A. Stafford, Connecticut. Percussion underhammer pistol.

THROCKMORTON, JOHN A. (1832-?), Galion, Ohio, 1850c. Son of William A. Throckmorton. (Hutslar)

THROCKMORTON, WILLIAM A. (1810-?), Galion, Ohio, 1850c-1870c, Marion, Ohio, 1872d-1875d. Percussion 1/2 stock. (Hutslar)

THROE, H.P. Joseph, Oregon, 1889d.

THRUST, PETER M. (1814-?), Mineral Co., West Virginia, 1880c. Percussion fullstock. Last name possibly Thrush? (Whisker IV)

THUER, F. ALEXANDER Hartford, Connecticut. Revolvers and derringers. Patents #82,258 September 15, 1868, revolver, #98,529 January 4, 1870, revolver, and #105,388 July 12, 1870, breechloading firearm. For Samuel Colt.

THUMEN, CHARLES G. Oroville, California. Patents #573,725 December 22, 1896, sight, and #845,491 February 26, 1907, sight.

THURBER, BENJAMIN Providence, Rhode Island, 1775-1776. (Achtermier)

THURBER, CHARLES T. Grafton, Massachusetts, Norwich, Connecticut. Partner of Ethan Allen. (Mouilleseaux)

THURMAN, C. Lorimar, Iowa, 1879-1885. Percussion target rifles.

THURSTIN, A. Foley, Missouri, 1891d-1893d.

THURSTON, JAMES Virginia, 1761. Public arms repairs. (Gill)

THURSTON, RUSSELL R. Cuba, New York, 1863-1882. Percussion mule ear over/under rifle. (Swinney)

TIBBALS, WILLIAM South Coventry, Connecticut. Patents #51,243, November 28, 1865, breechloading firearm, #55,743 June 6, 1866, revolver, #56,466 June 17, 1866, revolver, and #78,337 May 26, 1868, cartridge. As Crittendon & Tibbals, cartridges.

TIBBET, S. Geneva, Ohio, 1888d. (Hutslar)

TIBBETS, GEORGE H. Augusta, Maine. Patent #123,595 February 13, 1872, breechloading firearm.

TICKLE, WILLIAM Paxton, Illinois, 1864d. See William R. Trickel.

TIDD, MARSHALL Woburn, Massachusetts, 1846-1867. Percussion guns. (Roberts)

TIEBEL, LOUIS B. Hudson City, New Jersey. Patent #89,955 May 11, 1869, breechloading firearm.

TIESING, FRANK W. New Haven, Connecticut. Patents #93,149 July 27, 1869, breechloading firearm with Eli Whitney and Charles Gerner, #113,470 April 4, 1871, breechloading firearm with Eli Whitney and Charles Gerner, #114,230 April 25, 1871, breechloading firearm with Charles Gerner, #129,637 July 16, 1872, breechloading firearm with Eli Whitney, #191,196 May 22, 1877, magazine gun, #191,197 May 22, 1877, breechloading gun, #193,574 July 24, 1877, magazine gun, #204,863 June 11, 1878, magazine gun, #206,367 July 23, 1878, magazine gun, #208,128 September 17, 1878, magazine gun, #218,462 August 12, 1879, magazine gun with W. and Samuel V. Kennedy, #222,749 December 16, 1879, magazine gun, #225,664 March 16, 1880, magazine gun with W. and Samuel V. Kennedy, #226,809 April 20, 1880, magazine gun, #235,829 December 21, 1880, magazine gun with W. and Samuel V. Kennedy, and #238,988 March 15, 1881, magazine gun. All guns made by Eli Whitney.

TIGER suicide special by Iver Johnson.

TIGER trade name of Crescent on shot guns for J.H. Fall & Co.

TIGNERES, G. Covington, Louisiana. Patent #26,538 December 21, 1859, magazine gun.

TIGNIERE, AUGUST New Orleans, Louisiana, 1867d-1872d, Wichita, Kansas, 1878d-1882d.

TIGNOR, JAMES C. Richmond, Virginia, 1893d-1897d.

TIGNOR, THOMAS W. Richmond, Virginia, 1858-1893d. Percussion double shotgun. Succeeded by his son in 1893.

TILESTON, THOMAS unlocated. Iron-mounted New England Kentucky rifle.

TILESTON, WILLIAM Georgetown, D.C. Patent #44,126 September 6, 1864, revolver safety. James Reid used this patent. (Sellers-1)

TILFORD, SAMUEL K. Lincoln Co., Missouri, 1850c. (MB 11-66)

TILGHMAN, MORRIS Ireland, Indiana, 1862d.

TILLMAN, J.H. Petersburgh, Indiana. Percussion 1/2 stock. (Lindert)

TILLMAN, M.A. Otway, Ohio, Jasper, Indiana. Percussion fullstock. (Lindert, Hutslar)

TILLMAN, WILLIAM Northumberland Co., Pennsylvania, 1860c.

TILLY, A. Grundy, Virginia, 1880d.

TILTON Georgia, 1861. Marking on (?) Mississippi rifle, maker unknown. (Albaugh 1)

TILTON, JOHN (1760-1849), Washington, Pennsylvania, 1790-1812, Stark Co., Ohio, 1812, Hocking Co., Ohio, 1831-1849. (Whisker II)

TILTON, JOHN Rock House, Ohio. Patent #16,761 March 3, 1857, cane gun with William Floyd.

TIMBLIN, C.O. Phoenix, Pennsylvania, 1882d.

TIMMER, JACOB Galveston, Texas, 1890d.

TIMMINS, EDWARD Ann Arundel Co., Maryland, 1776-1790c. Committee of Safety muskets. (Hartzler)

TINDLE, ROBERT Monticello, Kentucky, 1879d.

TINGLER, FRANK Dresden, Ohio, 1878d-1890d. (Hutslar)

TINGLER, MOSES (1818-?), Muskingum Co., Ohio, 1850. (Hutslar)

TINSLEY, G.W. Minneapolis, Minnesota, 1872d-1875d, Columbus, Indiana, 1882-1885. Percussion 1/2 stock. (Lindert)

TINSLEY, JOHN Goochland Co., Virginia, 1792-1804. Model 1798 contract muskets.

TINSLEY, JOSHUA Fredericksburg, Virginia, 1762. (Gill)

TIPPETT, GEORGE What Cheer, Iowa, 1887d-1897d.

TIREY, THOMAS A. (1862-1950), Mitchell, Indiana. (Lindert)

TIRRELL, J.P. North Bridgewater, Massachusetts, 1849. Percussion pepperbox. (Dunlap)

TIRY, WILLIAM E. Beaufort, Missouri, 1860d.

TISDALE, WILLIAM (1791-?). New Bern, North Carolina, 1850c. (Bivins)

TISDEL, LUTHER W. (?-1891), Scranton, Pennsylvania, 1848-1891. Percussion and cartridge rifles.

TISON, ALLEN Tarboro, North Carolina, 1835. For Henry Chamberlain. (Bivins)

TISON, W.H. Cuthbert, Georgia, 1881d-1885d.

TISSIER, CHARLES G. Selma, Alabama. 1871-1885. Patent #289,787 December 4, 1883, extractor with Peter Tissier. Percussion pistols by himself.

TISSIER, P. & CO. Selma, Alabama, 1871-1885d. Percussion double shotgun and single shot cartridge pistol. (GR 1-76)

TISSIER, PETER Selma, Alabama, 1871-1885. Patent #289,787 December 4, 1883, extractor with Charles Tissier.

TOBEY, LEMUEL Portland, Maine, 1823. With his son Lemuel, Jr. (Demeritt)

TOBIAS, FRANCIS Springfield, Illinois, 1864d-1888d.

TOBIAS, SAMUEL E. (1864-1927), Xenia, Ohio, 1882-1927. Percussion and cartridge guns. (AR 3-26)

TOBIAS, T. Quincy, Illinois, 1867d.

TOBIN, WILLIAM Detroit, Michigan, 1860d-1867d.

TOBLER, J.J. West Hoboken, New Jersey, 1885d.

TOBORG, GEORGE Chicago, Illinois, 1897d-1915d. Patent #784,193 March 7, 1905, breechloading firearm.

TODD, GEORGE H. (1837-1912), Austin, Texas, 1857-1861, Montgomery, Alabama, 1861-1912. Percussion revolvers in Austin, rifles and muskets for the Confederacy. Patents #87,990 March 16, 1869, cartridge, and #93,023 July 27, 1869, breechloading firearm. (Albaugh 3)

TODD, J.T. Neosho, Missouri, 1898d.

TODD, R.R. LaGrange, Texas, 1876d.

TOEPPERWEIN, EMIL ALBRECHT FERDINAND (?-1880), Boerne, Texas. Patents #167,712 September 14, 1875, magazine gun, #199,124 January 9, 1878, adjustable hammer, #215,695 May 20, 1879, set trigger. Single shot cartridge rifle. Father of A.D. Topperwein, famous exhibition shooter.

TOGGENBURGER, FREDERICK Chicago, Illinois, 1876d-1900d. Martini action scheutzen rifles. Patent #350,328 October 5, 1886, multi-barrel rifle.

TOLEDO FIRE ARMS CO. Toledo, Ohio, 1871-1905. Shotguns and automatic pistols (Hutslar)

TOLEDO FIREARMS CO. suicide special by Dickinson and Hopkins & Allen.

TOLIVER Manchester, Tennessee, 1860d.

TOLL, HERMAN H. Clarinda, Iowa. Patent #661,897 November 13, 1900, machine gun.

TOLLE, GEORGE, & CO. Chicago, Illinois, 1856d-1875d.

TOLLEY & SON Catskill, New York, 1870d-1874d. Percussion double rifle. John & George Tolley.

TOLLEY, GEORGE F. Catskill, New York, 1870d-1882.

TOLLEY, J. & W. New York, New York, 1875d-1876d.

TOLLEY, JOHN F. V. S. Catskill, New York, 1849-1874. Percussion 1/2 stock.

TOLMAN, EDGAR B. Chicago, Illinois. Patents #656,866 August 28, 1900, sight, and #656,867 August 28, 1900, sight.

TOMBECK, AUGUSTIN Cincinnati, Ohio, 1864d-1868d. With August Susman. (Hutslar)

TOMES, A.F. Leavenworth, Kansas, 1865-1866d. Importer and dealer.

TOMES, FRANCIS New York, New York, 1840d-1879d. As Francis Tomes & Sons, 1840-1858. As Tomes, Son, & Melvain, 1859-1866. As Tomes, Melvain & Co., 1867-1874. As Francis Tomes & Co., 1875-79. All firms were importers and dealers whose names appear on both American and foreign guns.

TOMES, HENRY New York, New York, 1847d-1857d. Importer and dealer. With James Eaton and Charles Folsom as Henry Tomes & Co., 1850-1856.

TOMES, HENRY, & CO. New York, New York, 1850-1856. Importers and dealers. James Eaton, Charles Folsom, and Henry Tomes.

TOMES, MELVAIN & CO. New York, New York, 1867d-1874d. Dealers. Name appears on Bacon revolvers and derringers.

TOMES, SON, & MELVAIN New York, New York, 1859d-1866d. Dealers.

TOMESKA, ANTON Chicago, Illinois, 1873d, Iowa City, 1880d-1882d, Kearney, Nebraska, 1882d-1886d.

TOMLINSON & HARLOW Auburn, New York, 1874d-1875d. Charles Tomlinson and John R. Harlow.

TOMLINSON & KELLOGG Auburn, New York, 1865d.

TOMLINSON, CARTER unlocated. Percussion lockmaker.

TOMLINSON, CHARLES Auburn, New York, 1865d-1880, Syracuse, New York, 1891. Patent #450,323 April 14, 1891, gun tool with C.E. Tomlinson. As Tomlinson & Harlow, 1874-1875. As Tomlinson & Kellogg, 1865.

TOMLINSON, JOSHUA (?-1777), Philadelphia, Pennsylvania, 1775-1777. Committee of Safety barrels. (Hobbies 4-38)

TOMPKINS & BATES Dallas, Texas, 1896d.

TOMPKINS & NORCROSS Tampa, Florida, 1883d-1886d.

TOMPKINS, A. Paris, Illinois. Percussion 1/2 stock.

TOMPKINS, M.J. Fremont, Nebraska, 1879d-1883d.

TOMS, JAMES Salt Lake City, Utah, 1871d-1878d.

TONE (1800-1879), Petaluma, California, 1858-1879. (Shelton)

TONKS, ALFRED Boston, Massachusetts, 1856-1888d. Percussion revolvers and double shotgun. Patent #16,411 January 13, 1857, revolver. (Sellers-1)

TONKS, JOSEPH Boston, Massachusetts, 1854-1880, Malden, Massachusetts, 1880-1890. Percussion guns (Boston), breechloading rifles, shotguns, and airguns (Malden). Patents #254,727 March 7, 1882, breechloading firearm, #254,728 March 7, 1882, breechloading firearm, #282,429 July 31, 1883, breechloading firearm with A.E. Whitmore, #333,795 January 5, 1886, breechloading firearm, and #435,334 August 26, 1890, breechloading firearm. Guns made by Whitmore Gun Co. (see Andrew E. Whitmore)

TONZE, JOHN Philadelphia, Pennsylvania, 1816d-1819d.

TOOKER, H.O. Rome, New York, 1874d-1882d.

TOOKER, JOSEPH S. Le Sueur, Minnesota, 1884d, Cleveland, Minnesota, 1884d-1886d.

TOOKER, JOSEPH S. Wilna, New York, 1860c, Carthage, New York, 1863d. Percussion double rifle. (Clow)

TOPE, H. Peru, Illinois, 1848-1849. (Johnson)

TOPPER, HENRY (?-1840), Adams Co., Pennsylvania, 1802t, Gettysburg, Pennsylvania, 1810-1813, Hampshire Co., Virginia, 1819-1820c, Bedford Co., Pennsylvania, 1832-1835, Youngstown, Pennsylvania, 1838-1840. Flintlock Kentucky rifle. (Bowers)

TOPPER, JOSIAH (1813-?), Youngstown, Pennsylvania, 1839-1851. Flintlock fowler. (Bowers)

TOPPIN, JOHNSON (1808-?), Carmichael, Pennsylvania, 1860c-1880c.

TOPPING & BRO. Alton, Illinois, 1853.

TOPPING, ALEXANDER Ravenna, Ohio, 1850c-1853d, Newburgh, Ohio, 1863d. (Hutslar)

TORGERSON, OLE Centralia, Illinois, 1878d-1880d.

TORKALSON MFG. CO. see Rheinhard T. Torkalson.

TORKALSON, RHEINHARD T. Worcester, Massachusetts, 1886-1888 and 1898, Hatfield, Massachusetts, 1891, Warren, Massachusetts, 1902-1908, Fitchburg, Massachusetts, 1908-1910. Patents #339,301 April 6, 1886, revolver with Iver Johnson and Andrew Fyrberg, #339,346 April 6, 1886, revolver, #339,347 April 6, 1886, revolver, #345,974 July 20, 1886, revolver with Iver Johnson and Andrew Fyrberg, #379,257 March 13, 1888, breechloading firearm with Iver Johnson, #391,213 October 16, 1888, revolver, #391,214 October 16, 1888, revolver, #452,126 May 12, 1891, revolver, #601,820 April 5, 1898, breechloading firearm, #715,903 December 16, 1902, ejector, and #903,919 November 17, 1908, revolver. Employed by Iver Johnson for several years before forming Torkalson Mfg. Co. to make shotguns.

TORONTO BELLE suicide special.

TORRANS, P.H. Atlanta, Texas, 1878d.

TORRE & BROS. Texas. Percussion 1/2 stock. (T 16)

TORRENCE, C.C. Marshall, Michigan, 1861. Breechloading shotgun.

TORREY, ALPHA H. (1820-?), Joliet, Illinois, 1850c, Middleport, Illinois, 1859-1860. As Torrey & House, 1859-1860d. (Johnson)

TORREY, MICHAEL Lawrence, Massachusetts, 1880d.

TOST, FREDERICK Ashford, Wisconsin, 1860d, Beaver Dam, Wisconsin, 1879d-1888d.

TOTTEN, CHARLES A.L. U.S. Army. Patent #187,432 February 13, 1877, sight.

TOTTEN, M.B. Colusa, California, 1878-1908. (Shelton)

TOTTEN, W.T. Sargent, Pennsylvania, 1887d-1890d.

TOULSON, ALEXANDER St. Mary's, Maryland Colony, 1663. (Hartzler)

TOUT, S.S. unlocated. Percussion fullstock.

TOUZE, JOHN Philadelphia, Pennsylvania, 1819d-1824d.

TOWER, DANIEL L. Brooklyn, New York. Patents #305,866 September 30, 1884, safety, #355,233 December 28, 1886, revolver, and #366,531 July 12, 1887, revolver.

TOWER, JOHN J. New York, New York, 1879d-1880d.

TOWERS POLICE SAFETY suicide special by Hopkins and Allen. (Webster)

TOWERS, ROBERT Philadelphia, Pennsylvania, 1775-1777. Continental armorer. (Gluckman & Satterlee)

TOWERY, J.H. unlocated. Percussion fullstock.

TOWN, ABNER Woodbury, Vermont, 1833-1836. Patent #none February 25, 1836, stock lathe. (Horn)

TOWN, ASPY unlocated. Flintlock Kentucky rifle.

TOWN, BENJAMIN Philadelphia, Pennsylvania, 1775. Committee of Safety muskets with John Willis. (Hobbies 4-38)

TOWNER, A.G. Ticonderoga, New York. Percussion pistol.

TOWNLEY METAL & HARDWARE CO. Kansas City, Missouri, 1880-?. Dealers only.

TOWNSEND, ALFRED H. Georgetown, Colorado. Patent #115,659 June 6, 1871, repeating ordnance.

TOWNSEND, FREDERICK Albany, New York. Patents #31,268 January 29, 1861, breechloading firearm, and #44,127 September 6, 1864, breechloading firearm with N.S. Clement.

TOWNSEND, G.S.C. Allamuchy, New Jersey, 1878d.

TOWNSEND, NICHOLAS (?-1694), Charleston, South Carolina, 1693-1694. (Dean)

TOWNSEND, RALPH New York, New York. Patents #488,855 December 27, 1892, recoil attachment, and #480,587 August 9, 1892, recoil pad with Erastus Jones.

TOWNSON, HENRY Rockingham Co., Virginia, 1783. (Gill)

TOWREY, J.H. Cleveland Co., North Carolina. (Bivins)

TOWSEY, CHARLES H. Portsmouth, Ohio, 1880c. (Hutslar)

TOWSEY, THOMAS Vergennes, Vermont, 1791-1801. Model 1798 contract muskets with Samuel Chipman. (Gluckman)

TOWSLEY, C.A. Battle Creek, Michigan, 1873d, Galesburgh, Michigan, 1875d.

TRABUE, WILLIAM Louisville, Kentucky. Patents #206,279 July 23, 1878, magazine gun, #207,782 September 9, 1878, magazine gun, #210,374 November 26, 1878, cartridge, #223,414 January 6, 1880, magazine gun, #223,660 January 20, 1880, magazine gun, #238,732 March 15, 1880, magazine gun, #253,641 February 14, 1882, magazine gun, #256,175 April 11, 1882, magazine gun, #276,308 April 24, 1883, magazine gun, #301,180 July 1, 1884, revolver, #301,181 July 1, 1884, revolver, #301,182 July 1, 1884, revolver, #314,494 March 24, 1885, revolver, #314,754 March 31, 1885, revolver, and #814,749 March 13, 1906, automatic firearm.

TRADOR, REGAL West Augusta, Virginia, 1774-1775. (Gill)

TRAFTON, CHARLES York, Maine, 1706. (Demeritt)

TRAHN, J.J. Cherokee, Iowa, 1882d-1897d.

TRAILL, THOMAS Marysville, California, 1855. For C.F. Scholl. (Shelton)

TRAMPS TERROR trade name of Western Gun Works, Chicago, Illinois on suicide special, 1877d.

TRANT, GEORGE B. Thornville, Ohio, 1877-1912. (Knittle)

TRASK, WILLIAM Round Top, Texas, 1884d.

TRAUDT, JOHN (1861-1945). Milwaukee, Wisconsin, 1881-1940. Target rifles. (MB 5-49)

TRAVAGLINI, ANTONIO Philadelphia, Pennsylvania. Patent #630,136 August 1, 1899, automatic firearm.

TRAVER, ALVA Ann Arbor, Michigan, 1868d-1871d. Percussion target rifle. With his brother Richard as R.C. Traver & Bro., 1868-1871.

TRAVER, R.C., & BRO. Ann Arbor, Michigan, 1868-1871.

TRAVER, RICHARD C. Ann Arbor, Michigan, 1860d-1871d. As Beutler & Traver, 1860-1867. As R.C. Traver & Bro., 1868-1871. (MB 9-66)

TRAYER, JOHN Fayette Co., Pennsylvania, 1802-1803. (Kauffman)

TREADWAY, WILLIAM M. Port Henry, New York. Patent #168,941 January 12, 1875, sight.

TREADWELL, NATHANIEL Ipswich, Massachusetts, 1635. (Dean*)

TREADWELL, REUBEN Muskegon, Michigan, 1875d.

TREAT, JOHN Thomaston, Maine, 1749-1759. (Demeritt)

TREAT, JOSEPH Boston, Massachusetts, 1730-1770. (Demeritt)

TREAT, JOSHUA Thomaston, Maine, 1759-1774. Son of Joseph Treat. Public gunsmith. (Demeritt)

TREBE, HENRY Olney, Illinois, 1862. (Johnson)

TREBER, JOHN (?-1830), Zanestrace, Ohio, 1798, West Union, Ohio, 1825-1830. (Hutslar)

TREBER, JOHN T. (1811-?), West Union, Ohio, 1872d-1875d. Son of Jacob Treber. (Hutslar)

TREBER, OLIVER C. (1811-?), Duncansville, Ohio, 1859d. Brother of John Treber. (Hutslar)

TREBLE, SHADRACK Halifax Co., Virginia, 1760. (Gill)

TREDWAY, JOHN W. Philadelphia, Pennsylvania. Patent #490,129 January 17, 1893, recoil operated gun with J. Wirth.

TREIBEL, HENRY Lancaster, Pennsylvania, 1857d.

TREISH, JOHN Lancaster Co., Pennsylvania, 1847-1850. Barrelmaker. (KRA IV-4)

TRENTON unlocated. Percussion lock marking.

TRENTON ARMS CO. Trenton, New Jersey, 1863-1865. Model 1861 contract muskets. A.M. Burt. (Fuller)

TRESSENE, CHARLES Joliet, Illinois, 1860d.

TREVOR, J.E. Hartford, Connecticut. Patent #541,654 June 25, 1895, automatic firearm (?) with Henry Cooley and John Noble.

TREXLER, JOHN Latona, Illinois, 1878d-1884d.

TRIAY, J.A. Savannah, Georgia, 1885t.

TRIBBEY, G.W. Marshfield, Illinois, 1889d.

TRICH, GEORGE Denver, Colorado, 1861d-1915. Dealer. (Sellers-3)

TRICKEL, WILLIAM R. Paxton, Illinois, 1878d-1890d. Same as William Tickle?

TRIEBEL, GEORGE JULIUS (1805-?), San Francisco, California, 1868-1873. (Shelton)

TRIELLER, JOHN Dallas, Texas, 1890d-1898d. As Ott & Trieller, 1892.

TRIELLER, P. Milwaukee, Wisconsin, 1879d.

TRIMBLE, DAVID B. Baltimore, Maryland, 1828-1880d. As Poultney & Trimble (paint), 1828-1848, Poultney & Trimble (guns), 1860-1876. With Christian B. Kleibacker as Trimble & Kleibacker (gunsmiths), 1877-1880. (Hartzler)

TRIMBLE, THOMAS (1810-?), Baltimore, Maryland, 1881d-?. Son of David Trimble, successor to Trimble & Kleibacker. (Hartzler)

TRIMBLE, THOMAS J. (1843-?), Baltimore, Maryland, 1885d. Son of, and successor to, Thomas Trimble.

TRINKHAM, W.D. Humboldt, Iowa, 1884d-1889d.

TRINKS, HENRY Ashville, North Carolina, 1884d.

TRIPLETT, LEWIS (1822-1902), Columbia, Kentucky. Patent #45,361 December 6, 1864, magazine gun. Triplet & Scott rifles and carbines made by Meriden Mfg. Co. (GR 6- 79)

TRIPLETT, WESLEY H. Redlands, California. Patent #606,493 June 28, 1898, turret gun.

TRIPP, SILAS GIFFORD (1809-?), Providence, Rhode Island, 1851, San Francisco, California, 1852-1856. (Shelton)

TRIPP, SYLVESTER Millerton, New York, 1870d-1882d.

TRISSLER, JOHN Lancaster, Pennsylvania, 1804t-1820. (Dean)

TRIUMPH trade name of Crescent on shotguns.

TROCH, J.H. Watertown, South Dakota, 1886d-1898d. As Lyon & Troch, 1886d.

TROJAN suicide special.

TROLL, HERMAN Fountain City, Wisconsin, 1884d-1886d.

TROMLEY, JOHN Mt. Vernon, Illinois, 1864d, Lawrenceville, Illinois, 1886d-1890d.

TROMLEY, MICHAEL Mt. Vernon, Illinois, 1847-1868. Patents #13,442 August 14, 1855, lock, #18,418 October 13, 1857, lock, #24,768 July 12, 1859, lock, and #85,233 November 17, 1868, lock.

TROSTEL, FREDERICK Lansing, Michigan, 1863d-1883d. Percussion over/under rifle/shotgun.

TROTH unlocated. Early flintlock Kentucky rifle.

TROTTER, H. Cameron, Texas. Derringer. (T 36)

TROUP, P.H. unlocated. Percussion double rifle.

TROUT, BALTZER (?-1782), Berks Co., Pennsylvania, ?-1782. (Whisker III)

TROUT, JOHN Williamsport, Pennsylvania, 1855-1875. Percussion over/under, rifle/shotgun. (Dillin)

TROUTMAN, BENJAMIN FRANKLIN (1781-1856), Frederick Maryland, 1808, Somerset Co., Pennsylvania, 1810t-1856. Apprenticed to George Rizer, 1805. (Kauffman, Hartzler)

TROUTMAN, DANIEL B. Bedford Co., Pennsylvania, 1856-1858, Wellersburg, Pennsylvania, 1864-1867. Son of Benjamin Troutman. (Bowers)

TROUTMAN, DANIEL. Ottawa, Kansas, 1882d-1888d.

TROUTMAN, HARRY Ottawa, Kansas, 1890d-1894d. Son of Daniel Troutman.

TROUTMAN, THOMAS Philadelphia, Pennsylvania, 1800. (Kauffman)

TROUTNER, WILLIAM D. Pittsfield, Illinois, 1884d-1890d.

TROWBRIDGE, CHARLES Kewanee, Illinois, 1877d-1888d.

TROWBRIDGE, H. Weathersville, Illinois, 1860d.

TROWBRIDGE, JOHN T. Hollis, New Hampshire, 1876-1879. Percussion shotgun.

TROWBRIDGE, JOSEPH M. U.S. Army. Patent #41,874 March 8, 1864, telescopic sight.

TROXLE, JOHN (1813-?), Reedsburg, Ohio, 1850c-1853d. (Troxal in census) (Hutslar)

TROXLE, PETER (1827-?), Reedsburg, Ohio, 1850c. (Hutslar)

TROYER, WILLIAM Lancaster, Pennsylvania, 1847-1875d.

TRUAX, R.W. Swanton, Vermont, 1876-1879. Percussion underhammer pistol. (Horn)

TRUAX, SAMUEL (1841-?), Fairfield, Illinois, 1860c. (Johnson)

TRUBY, JACOB German, Ohio, 1857-1864d. (Hutslar)

TRUBY, JACOB Kittanning, Pennsylvania, 1750-1756. (Gluckman & Satterlee)

TRUCAS, CHARLES New Orleans, Louisiana, 1878d.

TRUDELIND, WILLIAM Philadelphia, Pennsylvania, 1824d.

TRUE & DAVIS Albany, New York, 1832. Worked on Colt revolvers. (Sutherland)

TRUE BLUE suicide special.

TRUE, H.W. Hawkins, Wisconsin, 1895d.

TRUITT & CO. Philadelphia, Pennsylvania, 1862d-1863d. Lockmakers only.

TRUITT BROS. & CO. Philadelphia, Pennsylvania, 1847d-1861d. Lockmakers only.

TRULENDER, FREDERICK Salem, New Jersey. Patent #42,702 May 10, 1864, extractor.

TRUMAN, FRANK Iowa Falls, Iowa, 1897d.

TRUMBULL, DAVID Lebanon, Connecticut, 1775-1778. Committee of Safety repairs.

TRUMP, HENRY Fayette Co., Pennsylvania, 1807-1808.

TRUMP, J.V. Philadelphia, Pennsylvania. Percussion dueller.

TRUMPLER Madison, Georgia. Percussion 1/2 stock.

TRUMPLER & DABBS Little Rock, Arkansas, 1868-1874d. Jacob F. Trumpler and William Dabbs. (Elias)

TRUMPLER & DAY Little Rock, Arkansas, 1860. Derringer. Jacob F. Trumpler

TRUMPLER FIREARMS CO. Little Rock, Arkansas, 1887d. George M. Trumpler and Jacob Trumpler, Jr.

TRUMPLER, GEORGE M. (?-1894), Little Rock, Arkansas, 1872d-1894. With his father Jacob F. as Trumpler & Son, 1874-1882. With his brother Jacob, Jr. as Trumpler Firearms Co., 1887. (Elias)

TRUMPLER, JACOB F. Little Rock, Arkansas, 1855-1885d. Derringer. As Trumpler & Day, 1860. With William Dabbs as Trumpler & Dabbs, 1868-1874. With his son George M. as Trumpler & Son, 1874-1882. (Elias)

TRUMPLER, JACOB, JR. Little Rock, Arkansas, 1873d-1897d. With his brother George as Trumpler Firearms Co., 1887. Son of Jacob F. Trumpler.

TRUSTWORTHY suicide special.

TRY, JOHN Beaver Springs, Pennsylvania. Percussion fullstock rifles. (Gabel)

TRYON & GOETZ Philadelphia, Pennsylvania, 1811. George Tryon and Frederick Goetz.

TRYON, DENNIS Haddam, Connecticut. Patent #18,472 October 20, 1857, breechloading firearm with Chauncey Skinner.

TRYON, E.H. Perry, Iowa, 1887d-1889d.

TRYON, EDWARD K. (?-1904), Philadelphia, Pennsylvania, 1836-?. Muzzle loading guns and had other guns made for the business. As Tryon Bros. & Co. after Edward Tryon retired, 1864-1868 and various other names. Son of George Tryon. (GR 4- 67)

TRYON, F.J. Bolivar, Missouri, 1889d-1898d.

TRYON, GEORGE W. (1791-1878), Philadelphia, Pennsylvania, 1811-1841. Made Chambers repeating guns in 1814 and other military guns thereafter. With Samuel Merrick as Tryon, Merrick & Co., 1832-1837. (GR 4-67)

TRYON, MERRICK & CO. Philadelphia, Pennsylvania, 1832-1837. George Tryon and Samuel Merrick.

TRYONS, WILL Morrison, Illinois, 1880d-1890d.

TSCHERKI, JOHN Ft. Scott, Kansas, 1894d.

TSHOT, J.R. unlocated. Flintlock Kentucky lock.

TUASEUR, CHARLES Salina, Kansas, 1866d.

TUBBS, JOEL B. Waterloo, New York, 1857-1882d. Percussion over/under rifle/shotgun.

TUCKER unlocated. All metal percussion pistol.

TUCKER & TYLER unlocated. Flintlock Kentucky.

TUCKER, GEORGE B. Columbus, Mississippi, 1854d.

TUCKER, GEORGE D. Tecumseh, Nebraska, 1884d. Percussion 1/2 stock.

TUCKER, J.W. Carthage, Missouri, 1898d.

TUCKER, J.W. Tecumseh, Nebraska, 1882d.

TUCKER, JONATHAN Philadelphia, Pennsylvania, 1814d.

TUCKER, LABON E. Lancaster, Texas, 1861-1864, Weatherford, Texas, 1864. Percussion revolvers. With J.H. Sherrod as Tucker, Sherrod & Co., 1862-1864, and L.E. Tucker & Sons, 1864. (Albaugh 3)

TUCKER, R.D. (1815-?), Leavenworth, Indiana, 1860c. (Lindert)

TUCKER, SHERROD & CO. Lancaster, Texas, 1862-1864. Percussion revolvers. Labon E. Tucker and J.H. Sherrod.

TUCKER, T.B. Paris, Illinois, 1860d.

TUCKER, WILLIAM (1802-?), Forsythe Co., North Carolina, 1850c. (Bivins)

TUCKERMAN, ISAAC Providence, Rhode Island, 1776. Committee of Safety repairs. (Achtermier)

TUCKLE, WILLIAM Paxton, Illinois, 1860d. See William Tickle.

TUFTS & COLLEY New York, New York, 1858-1859. Derringers. Importers and dealers.

TUFTS, EBEN Westford, Massachusetts. Percussion 1/2 stock.

TUFTS, TIMOTHY Somerville, Massachusetts. Patent #46,762 March 7, 1865, repeating cannon.

TULLE, T. Philadelphia, Pennsylvania, 1824d.

TULLER, O.J. Mason City, Iowa, 1875d.

TULLY, WILLIAM A. Columbia City, Indiana, 1882-1885. Percussion 1/2 stock. (Lindert)

TUNNELL, SCARBURG Virginia, 1778. Committee of Safety repairs. (Gill)

TUNSTALL, MOSES Harrisburg, Wisconsin, 1857d.

TUNX, WILLIAM New York, New York, 1770-1775. Returned to England, 1775. (Gluckman & Satterlee)

TUPPER, A.N. Potsdam, New York, 1855-1868d. Percussion 1/2 stock. (Gluckman & Satterlee)

TUPPER, JAMES B. (1828-?), Canal Winchester, Ohio, 1850c, Columbus, Ohio, 1850c. Two men? (Hutslar)

TURK, JAMES (1811-?), Morrow, Ohio, 1850c-1853d. Percussion fullstock. (Hutslar)

TURK, JAMES Vernon, Michigan, 1887d-1891d.

TURK, JOHN C. (1832-?), Greencastle, Indiana, 1850c. Son of William Turk. (Hutslar)

TURK, WILLIAM (1809-?), Ohio, 1832-1847, Greencastle, Indiana, 1850c, Columbia, Missouri, 1860c. (Lindert)

TURLEY, THEODORE (1801-?), Nauvoo, Illinois, 1841. Fifteen-shot repeater mentioned in the April 30, 1845 edition of the "Nauvoo Messenger". (Johnson)

TURNBULL, WALTER J. New Orleans, Louisiana, 1885d-1900d. Patent #630,758 August 8, 1899, breechloading firearm.

TURNER & DORSEY Dresen, Ohio, 1883d. (Hutslar)

TURNER & ROSS Boston, Massachusetts, 1870-1888. Suicide specials and shotguns, both may carry the company name or the owners' initials. Dealers. George W. Turner and (first name?) Ross.

TURNER, B.F. Woodstock, Vermont, 1852. (Horn)

TURNER, CHESTER B. Grand Rapids, Michigan, 1860d-1876. Percussion guns.

TURNER, GEORGE Caroline Co., Virginia, 1779. Committee of Safety repairs. (Gill)

TURNER, HENRY Albany, New York, 1820-1823. Flintlock guns.

TURNER, JOHN Augusta, Virginia, 1777-1780. With Joshua Humphreys. (Gill)

TURNER, JOHN Boston, Massachusetts. Patents #287,740 October 30, 1883, breechloading firearm, and #321,923 July 7, 1885, breechloading firearm.

TURNER, JOSEPH Moorestown, New Jersey, 1860d-1866d.

TURNER, L.S. Adrian, Michigan, 1883d.

TURNER, NATHAN H. (1804-?), Lewistown, Illinois, 1832-1864d. (Johnson)

TURNER, R.C. Mendon, Michigan, 1863d-1879d.

TURNER, ROBERT Havana, Illinois, 1867. (Johnson)

TURNER, SAMUEL W. Cleveland, Ohio. Patent #37,159 December 16, 1862, centrifugal gun with G.C. Eaton. (Hutslar)

TURNER, WILLIAM New York, New York, 1850d.

TURNER, WILLIAM Rochester, Wisconsin, 1857d.

TURNER, WILLIAM H. Liberty, Missouri, 1850c-1898d.

TURNER, ZEPHENIAH (1813-?), Rowan Co., North Carolina, 1850c. (Bivins)

TURNPAUGH, MATT Burlington, Indiana. (Lindert)

TURNPAUGH, SIMON Anoka Junction, Indiana, 1870, Logansport, Indiana, 1867-1871. (Lindert)

TUSTIN, J. Pittsburgh, Pennsylvania, 1833. (Gluckman & Satterlee)

TUSTMAN, WILLIAM Philadelphia, Pennsylvania, 1799d. (Whisker III)

TUTTLE, C.W. New Haven, Connecticut, 1873d-1876d. As Fiske & Tuttle, 1873-1874.

TUTTLE, DANIEL L. (1823-?), Rockford, Illinois, 1850c. (Johnson)

TWICKELER, THEODORE Boston, Massachusetts. Patent #34,706 March 16, 1862, needle gun.

TWINING, DAVID Mount Sterling, Wisconsin, 1867d.

TWOMBLY, H.W. Dover, New Hampshire, 1874d-1875d.

TYCOON suicide special by Iver Johnson.

TYDICH, PETER Baltimore, Maryland, 1775. (Hobbies 1-33)

TYERYAR, FRANK Frederick, Maryland, 1888d. (Hartzler)

TYERYAR, FREDERICK F. Frederick, Maryland, 1895d. (Hartzler)

TYERYAR, WILLIAM Frederick, Maryland, 1878d-1886d. Percussion 1/2 stock. (Hartzler)

TYLER & MITCHELL Richmond, Virginia, 1860. Dealers.

TYLER ARSENAL Tyler, Texas, 1862-1865. Rifles and muskets. (Albaugh 2)

TYLER RIFLE WORKS Vienna, Ohio, 1858-?, Warren, Ohio, ?-1891. Guns and knives. Nathan B. Tyler. (Hutslar)

TYLER, C. Weybridge, Vermont, 1871-1880. (Horn)

TYLER, C.W., & CO. Warren, Ohio, 1875d. (Hutslar)

TYLER, CHARLES N. Worcester, Massachusetts. Patent #9,701 May 3, 1853, repeating firearm.

TYLER, D.A. Webster City, Iowa, 1880d-1884d, Bismarck, Dakota Territory, 1886d.

TYLER, GEORGE F. New Britain, Connecticut, 1886d-1894d.

TYLER, JOHN Philadelphia, Pennsylvania, 1770-1777, Allentown, Pennsylvania, 1777-1779. For state arms factory at Allentown, repaired public arms and operated his own shop. (Gluckman & Satterlee)

TYLER, JOHN E. Roxobel, North Carolina. Patent #325,878 September 8, 1885, revolver.

TYLER, NATHAN B. (1828-?), Vienna, Ohio, 1858-?, Warren, Ohio, ?-1896. Percussion 1/2 stocks. As Tyler Rifle Works, 1858-1891. (Hutslar)

TYLER, PHILO SHELTON Boston, Massachusetts. Patents #73,494 January 21, 1868, breechloading firearm, and #88,540 April 6, 1869, breechloading firearm; both with Francis Boyd.

TYLER, WILLIAM Providence, Rhode Island. Model 1798 contract muskets with William Rhodes, signed only "SCITUATE," the township in which they were located. (Gluckman)

TYNES, DANIEL Windsor, Virginia, 1877d.

TYNS, ROBERT Kerwin, Texas, 1884d.

TYRER, JAMES Petersburg, Pennsylvania. Patent #none June 3, 1825, firearm.

TYRER, THOMAS (1806-?), Richmond, Virginia, 1850c. Percussion guns. (MB 10-63)

TYRER, THOMAS, JR. (1832-?), Richmond, Virginia, 1850c-1884d. (MB 10-63)

TYSON & BRO. Philadelphia, Pennsylvania, 1863d-1866d. Listed at the same address as Tryon & Bro.

TYSON, J.H. York, Pennsylvania. (Gluckman & Satterlee)

U SECTION

U. A. Co. see Union Arms Co. located in New York.

U. M. C. ARMS CO. unlocated. Suicide special.

U.M.C. see Union Machine Co.

U.M.C. see Union Metallic Cartridge Co.

U.S. & Co. unidentified. Percussion 1/2 stock.

U.S. ARMS & CUTLERY CO. Rochester, New York, 1876-1880. Pencil and knife pistols, shotguns. (Hinman)

U.S. ARMS CO. trade name of H. & D. Folsom on shotguns for Supplee-Biddle Hardware Co.

U.S. ARMS CO. unidentified. Suicide special.

UFER, PETER Louisville, Kentucky, 1896d.

UHLINGER, WILLIAM P., & CO. Philadelphia, Pennsylvania, 1861-1865. Cartridge revolvers with many names - Cone, Grant, Lower, Uhlinger, Wheeler - as they were infringements of Rollin White's patent. Uhlinger was a sewing machine maker who purchased the gun factory of William Hankins. He also converted flintlock muskets to percussion on government contracts during the Civil War.

UHLMAN, AUGUST Cincinnati, Ohio, 1891d. (Hutslar)

UHRLAUB, SATTLER & CO. Chicago, Illinois 1854d-1858d. Percussion double shotgun. Importers and dealers. August Sattler.

ULLRICH, ANDREW Albany, New York, 1861d. Percussion fullstock and shotgun.

ULRICH, ANDREW Williamsport, Pennsylvania, 1866-1875. Percussion rifle makers. As Andrew Ulrich & Co., 1875.

ULRICH, D. unlocated. Flintlock Kentucky.

ULTANG, H.M. Callender, Iowa, 1897d.

UMBARGER, OBEDIAH unlocated. Flintlock Kentucky.

UMHOLTZ, JACOB Dauphin Co., Pennsylvania, 1825. (Kauffman)

UNANGST, ISAAC Snyder Co., Pennsylvania. Percussion Kentucky rifles. (Gabel)

UNANGST, ISAAC Union Co., Pennsylvania, 1850c. (Kauffman)

UNCLE SAM suicide special by Iver Johnson.

UNDERHILL, BENJAMIN F. New Albany, Indiana, 1882-1885. (Lindert)

UNDERWOOD, FRED Greensburg, Ohio, 1883d. (Hutslar)

UNDERWOOD, HENRY St. Louis, Missouri, 1860d.

UNDERWOOD, HENRY Tolland, Connecticut. Patents #38,772 June 2, 1863, breechloading firearm, and #44,476 September 27, 1864, lock.

UNDERWOOD, HUGH (1833-?), Washington Co., Ohio, 1850c. Apprentice to John Roswell. (Hutslar)

UNDERWOOD, SAMUEL (1834-?), Ritchie Co., West Virginia, 1860-1870c. Was at Harper's Ferry Armory until its destruction. (Whisker IV)

UNDERWOOD, THOMAS Lafayette, Indiana. (Gluckman & Satterlee)

UNDY, WALTER Youngstown, Ohio, 1875d. (Hutslar)

UNGER, CHARLES W. Salt Lake City, Utah, 1888-1892. Patent #475,640 May 24, 1892, gun rest.

UNGER, OS. & BENEDICT Utica, New York. Marking on lock.

UNGER, OSWALD Port Huron, Michigan, 1858-1899d. Percussion double rifle and 1/2 stock. (GR 1-74)

UNGLAUB, C. unlocated. Percussion 1/2 stock.

UNION .22 cal. single shot derringer.

UNION marking on percussion fullstock.

UNION suicide special by Hood (Fire Arms Co.?).

UNION 38 trade name of Prescott Pistol Co. on double action pistol.

UNION ARMS CO. Hartford, Connecticut, 1857-1861. Created to acquire the assets of Robbins & Lawrence, but made no guns. (Sellers-1)

UNION ARMS CO. New York, New York, 1861-1862. Model 1861 contract muskets. (Fuller)

UNION ARMS CO. Newark, New Jersey. Single shot cartridge pistols. (Gardner)

UNION ARMS CO. trade name used by W. W. Marston as Marston and Knox, and Bacon.

UNION ARMS CO., THE trade name used by W.W. Marston, as Marston & Knox, and Bacon.

UNION FIREARM CO. Toledo, Ohio, 1903-1913. Automatic shotguns and pistols. Purchased by Ithaca. (Hutslar)

UNION JACK suicide special by Norwich Lock Mfg. Co., or Hood Fire arms Co. (Gardner)

UNION KNIFE CO. Naugatuck, Connecticut, 1860-1865. Made Walch revolvers and sold Bliss & Goodyear revolvers. See John Walch and Walch Fire Arms Co. (Sellers-1)

UNION MACHINE CO. trade name on imported shotguns which were also marked "U.M.C.".

UNION MANUFACTURING CO. Richmond, Virginia, 1861. Factory operated by G.P. Sloat, known by this name and as Sloat's Rifle Factory. (Albaugh 1)

UNION METALLIC CARTRIDGE CO. Bridgeport, Connecticut, 1867-1912.

UNION RIFLE trade name of Cosmopolitan Arms Co. on rifles and carbines.

UNION RIFLE WORKS Philadelphia, Pennsylvania, 1858-1860. Locks and barrels.

UNION, N.Y. suicide special by Whitney.

UNIQUE trade name of C.S. Shattuck on revolvers and palm pistols.

UNITED STATES ARMS CO. Brooklyn, New York, 1874d-1878d. Sales outlet for Otis A. Smith.

UNIVERSAL trade name of Hopkins & Allen on owlhead revolvers.

UNIVERSAL ELECTRIC ARMS & AMMUNITION CO. New York, New York, 1887-1890. Firearms under Edgar Montfort's patents.

UNSELD, JOHN Hagerstown, Maryland, 1766, Frederick, Maryland, 1766-1777. Committee of Safety muskets. (Hartzler)

UNVERZAGT, WILLIAM Memphis, Tennessee, 1868-1876d. Percussion sporting rifles.

UPDEGRAFF, HORACE Ft. Laramie, Wyoming patents: #119,098 September 19, 1871, breechloading firearms, and #130,165 August 6, 1872, breechloading firearms. Smithfield, Ohio patents: #155,348 September 22, 1874, breechloading firearms, and #205,447 April 24, 1877, breechloading firearms. Hampton, Kansas patents: #291,111 January 1, 1884, breechloading firearms, and #325,369 September 1, 1885, magazine gun. Repeating rifles submitted to the Ordnance Dept. as early as 1867.

UPDEGRAFF, JACOB Schuylkill Co., Pennsylvania. Flintlock Kentucky rifles. (Dillin)

UPHAM, A. New Castle, Indiana, 1860d.

UPHAM, WILLIAM Cohoes, New York, 1869-1874d. Percussion 1/2 stock rifles.

UPPEN, NATHAN New Castle, Indiana, 1862d.

UPRIGHT, THOMAS Newport, New York, 1869d-1874d.

UPTON unlocated. Lock marking on Model 1808 contract musket.

URBAN, JOHN New Bern, North Carolina, 1826, Washington, North Carolina, 1829, Tarboro, North Carolina, 1832. (Bivins)

URIE, SOLOMAN Ashland Co., Ohio, 1814-1820. Flintlock rifles. (Knittle)

URIELL, D. unlocated. Flintlock Kentucky.

USHER, ROBERT Philadelphia, Pennsylvania, 1816d.

UTAH ARMORY trade name of Frank W. Freund.

UTICA FIREARMS CO. trade name of Simmons Hardware Co. on shotguns.

UTLEY & EASTMAN Concord, New Hamsphire, 1858-1860. Percussion bench rifles. John I. Eastman.

UTLEY, GREY Louisburg, North Carolina. Patent #20,229 May 11, 1858, repeating ordnance.

UTTER, GEORGE Newark, New Jersey. Percussion pistols.

UTTERBACK, MARTIN Claremont, Illinois, 1864d.

V SECTION

V.F.C. see Valentine Clouse.

V.L. see Valentine Leban.

V.L. & A. see Von Lengerke & Antoine.

V.L. & D. see Von Lengerke & Detmold.

VACHE, FRANCIS A. Philadelphia, Pennsylvania, 1824d.

VAIL, A.W. Browning, Illinois, 1860d.

VAIL, ABEL P. Hamilton, Illinois, 1878d-1888d.

VAIL, I. Oxford, Wisconsin, 1857d.

VAIL, ISAAC Bath, Illinois, 1864d-1867d.

VAIL, ISAIAH (1815-?), Oroville, California, 1870c. (Shelton)

VAIL, J.W. Erie Co., Pennsylvania, 1850c. (GR 11-60)

VAIL, STEPHEN (1831-?), Vermont, Illinois, 1860c. (Johnson)

VAIL, WARREN Vermont, Illinois, 1860d.

VAJEN, J.H., & CO. Indianapolis, Indiana, 1851-1900. Hardware store, locks. (Lindert)

VALE, T.A. unlocated. Flintlock Kentucky.

VALENTINE, F. (1784-?), Alton, Illinois, 1840-1845, Grafton, Illinois, 1860d, St. Louis, Missouri, 1860d-1864d. (Johnson)

VALENTINE, J.H. Danville, Virginia, 1884d. As J.H. Valentine & Bro.

VALENTINE, J.H., & BRO. Danville, Virginia, 1884d.

VALIANT trade name of Spear Co., Pittsburgh, Pennsylvania. (Fors)

VALKMAR, REINHOLD San Francisco, California, 1859. For A.J. Plate. (Shelton)

VALLEE, PROSPER Philadelphia, Pennsylvania, 1824d-1846d. Percussion guns.

VALLEREAUX, GUSTAVUS (1840-?), Ottawa, Illinois, 1860c. (Johnson)

VALLERY, NICHOLAS New Orleans, Louisiana, 1822d-1823d.

VALLEY FORGE IRON WORKS see John Rogers.

VALLUE, THOMAS Wexford, Michigan, 1879d-1891d.

VAN ANTWERP & NOBLE Alton, Illinois, 1836. John Van Antwerp.

VAN ANTWERP, HOWARD Mt. Sterling, Kentucky, 1883d.

VAN ANTWERP, JOHN Alton, Illinois, 1836-1837. As Van Antwerp & Noble, 1836.

VAN BIBBER, JOHN Greenbrier, Virginia, 1772. (Gill)

VAN BITTER Stow, Ohio, Percussion 1/2 stock. (Hutslar)

VAN BUREN New York, New York. Agent for Allen pepperbox revolver (also so marked on revolver?).

VAN CAMP HARDWARE & IRON CO. Indianapolis, Indiana. Dealers only.

VAN CHOATE, SILVANUS FREDERICK Boston, Massachusetts, 1867-1873. Patents #89,902 May 11, 1869, breechloading firearms, #94,047 August 24, 1869, breechloading firearms, #115,911 June 13, 1871, breechloading firearms, and #132,505 October 22, 1872, breechloading firearms.

VAN COONEY, WILLIAM Long Bottom, Ohio. Percussion fullstock. (Dean)

VAN DE WATER, HENRICK (?-1785), New York, New York, 1754-1785. (Kauffman 2)

VAN DER POEL Albany, New York, 1740. (Gluckman & Satterlee)

VAN DYKE Jamestown, New York, 1829.

VAN DYKE, D.W. Mason, Ohio, 1860d-1896d. (Hutslar)

VAN DYKE, OWEN Milwaukee, Wisconsin, 1847-1856. Miller patent revolving rifles and percussion 1/2 stock. (Sellers-1)

VAN ETTEN & STAPLES Erie, Pennsylvania, 1882d.

VAN GILDER, J.W. Vansburgh, Kansas, 1882d.

VAN GORKOM, HENRICK Pella, Iowa, 1884d-1897d.

VAN GRIESON, WILLIAM H. White Water, Wisconsin. Patent #226,893 April 27, 1880, breechloading firearm.

VAN HORN, JOHN Jackson Co., Missouri, 1850c. (MB 11-66)

VAN HORN, SYLVESTER A. Oneida, New York, 1856-1867. Percussion rifles and shotguns.

VAN HORN, WILLIAM Milledgeville, Georgia, 1881d.

VAN HOUGHTON, JAMES H. Savannah, Georgia. Confederate Patent #1 August 1, 1861, breechloading gun. (Albaugh 1)

VAN KEUREN, J. Allegan, Michigan, 1891d-1899d. As Bond & Van Keuren, 1899.

VAN LEAR, SAMUEL Nashville, Tennessee, 1859-1860. Importer and dealer. Successor to McCall & Van Lear.

VAN LEU, J.B. Gainsville, Michigan, 1863d.

VAN LOON, H.H. Mason City, Illinois, 1884d-1888d, Streator, Illinois, 1890d-1893d.

VAN METER, J.W. Richmondale, Ohio, 1855. Percussion 1/2 stock. (Hutslar)

VAN NEST, PETER Beallsville, Ohio, circa 1900. Percussion fullstock. (Hutslar)

VAN NORTRICK, I.H. Sturgis, Michigan, 1863d.

VAN RENESSELEAR, JACKSON ((?-1845), Rochester, New York, 1838d-1845. (Eich)

VAN RIPER, PHILIP Brooklyn, Iowa, 1865d.

VAN SCRIVER, J.B. Lancaster, Pennsylvania, 1850. (Dyke)

VAN SLYKE, P.C. Bloomfield, Indiana, 1862d.

VAN TASSEL, A.C. Bellaire, Michigan, 1887d.

VAN TREES, J.F. see J.F. Vandertrees.

VAN TROMP, JOHN Baltimore, Maryland, 1852d. Percussion 1/2 stock. (Hartzler)

VAN VALKENBURGH, J. Albany, New York, 1848-1850d.

VAN VLEAR, WILLIAM HUBBARD (1822-1904), Santa Clara, California, 1856-1860, Stockton, California, 1860-1898. Percussion 1/2 stock. (Shelton)

VAN VOORHIS, ABRAHAM Washington Co., Pennsylvania, 1791-1834. (Whisker II)

VAN WAGENEN, HUBERT G. Alton, Illinois, 1836-1837.

VAN WICKEL, JESSE New York, New York, 1848-1850d.

VAN ZANT, J. (1792-?), Jacksonville, Illinois, 1842-1850. (Johnson)

VANCE, LADD M. Indianapolis, Indiana, 1882-1885. (Lindert)

VANDANIKER, O. Omaha, Nebraska, 1887d.

VANDEGRIFT, ISAAC Elizabethtown, Illinois, 1867d.

VANDEMAN unlocated. Flintlock Kentucky.

VANDENBURG, J. Findlay, Ohio, 1881d. Percussion 1/2 stock. (Hutslar)

VANDERBURGER, F. unlocated. Percussion 1/2 stock.

VANDERBURGH, ELLIOT (1810-?), Wilmington, Ohio, 1850c-1866d. Percussion sporting rifles. (Hutslar)

VANDERBURGH, O.B. Findlay, Ohio, 1853d-1883d. Percussion 1/2 stock. As Vandenburgh Bros. in 1883. (Hutslar)

VANDERBURGH, WILLIAM Wilmington, Ohio, 1848-1853d. Percussion fullstock rifles. (Hutslar)

VANDERGRIFT, JEREMIAH Philadelphia, Pennsylvania, 1809-1815. Associated with Isaac Vandergrift. (Kauffman)

VANDERGRIFT, JOHN Bucks Co., Pennsylvania, 1773-1776. Committee of Safety muskets. (Gluckman & Satterlee)

VANDERHEYDEN, JOHN (1806-?), Auburn, New York, 1823-1850. For Elijah Snell, 1823-1830. (Massachusetts Arms)

VANDERSLICE, JACOB Philadelphia, Pennsylvania, 1847d-1855d.

VANDERTREES, J. Fort Recovery, Ohio, 1826-1855. Percussion fullstock. With son J.F., 1828-1843. Also known as J. Vantrees. (Hutslar)

VANDERTREES, J. & J.F. Fort Recovery, Ohio, 1828-1843. Percussion full stock. J. (father) and J. F. (son) Vandertrees. Also known as J. Vantrees, and J.F. Van Trees. (Hutslar)

VANDERTREES, J.F. Fort Recovery, Ohio, 1828-1843 and 1854-1864. Percussion fullstock. With his father, J., 1828-1843. Also known as J.F. Van Trees. (Hutslar)

VANHOY, ABRAHAM (1793-?), Forsythe Co., North Carolina, 1812-1850. (Bivins)

VANKEIRSBILCK, JOHN Patents #504,516 September 5, 1893, machine gun feed, and #504,517 September 5, 1893, machine gun, both with Clement Broderick.

VANSANT, J.A. Easton, Maryland, 1887d. (Hartzler)

VANSCRIVER, BENJAMIN Pittsburgh, Pennsylvania, 1859-1860. (Kauffman)

VANTREES, J. see J. Vandertrees.

VARE Alexandria, Virginia, 1800. (Dean*)

VARNER, JOHN Allegheny Co., Pennsylvania, 1800c. (Kauffman 2)

VARNEY, A.L. Watertown, Massachusetts. Patents #88,530 March 30, 1869, breechloading firearm, #88,531 March 30, 1869, breechloading firearm, and #95,395 September 28, 1869, breechloading firearm. Submitted altered muskets as early as 1867 (to Patent office?).

VARNEY, DAVID M. Burlington, Vermont, 1842-1875, Nevada City, California, 1861. Percussion 1/2 stock. For Z.P. Davis in Nevada City. (Horn, Shelton)

VARNEY, GEORGE Lincoln, Vermont, 1860. (Horn)

VAUGHN, AARON C. Bedford, Pennsylvania. Patent #35,404 May 27, 1862, double-barrel revolver. (GR 12-59)

VAUGHN, DANIEL Providence, Rhode Island, 1756. (Achtermier)

VAUGHN, DAVID F. Haddonfield, New Jersey. Patent #440,381 November 11, 1890, spring air gun.

VAUGHN, GEORGE W. (1834-?), Moultrie Co., Illinois, 1850c, Bryon, Ohio, 1888d. Percussion target fullstock. (Johnson, Hutslar)

VAUGHN, I.S. LeRoy, New York, 1861d.

VAUGHN, IRA S. Menasha, Wisconsin, 1872d.

VAUGHN, JAMES M. Rutland, Vermont, 1842-1843. (Kauffman 2)

VAUGHN, JAMES W. (1805-?), Marrow Bone, Illinois, Sullivan, Illinois, 1832-1860d.

VAUGHN, L.B. Quincy, Michigan, 1895d.

VAUGHN, O.L. Leslie, Michigan, 1875d.

VAUGHN, SIRAH Rutland, Vermont, 1840-1842. (Kauffman 2)

VAUX, W. Boston, Massachusetts, 1793d. Imported flintlock pistol.

VEACH, A.P. Ottawa, Illinois. (Johnson)

VEBER, W.F. Bowling Green, Ohio, 1896d. (Hutslar)

VEILED PROPHETS suicide special by T.E. Ryan.

VELTMAN & CO. Paris, Tennessee, 1891d.

VENIA & JOHNSTON Toledo, Ohio, 1883d. (Hutslar)

VENIA & RUSHMORE Toledo, Ohio, 1888d. Henry C. Rushmore. (Hutslar)

VENNER, O.H. Rockland, Maine, 1877. (Demeritt)

VENUS suicide special. (Webster)

VEON, ANDREW E. Brainerd, Minnesota. Patent #572,494 December 1, 1896, sight.

VER GENIUS, C.A. Galesburgh, Illinois, 1890d.

VERDIER, WASHINGTON Ralls Co., Missouri, 1850c. (MB 11-66)

VERGHO, RUHLING & CO. Chicago, Illinois, 1854d-1859d. Dealers. Charles Vergho and Adolph Ruhling.

VERMONT ARMS CO. trade name used by Robbins & Lawrence. (Horn)

VERNER, ANDREW Bucks Co., Pennsylvania, 1787t-1790c. Flintlock Kentucky. (Kindig)

VERNIER, LEWIS Louisville, Ohio, 1853d. Percussion 1/2 stock rifles. (Hutslar)

VERSILUS, S. Mancelona, Michigan, 1879d.

VERY, EDWARD W. (1847-1910), Washington, D.C., 1877. Signal cartridges. (Demeritt)

VESCELIUS, JOHN E. Vassar, Michigan 1870d-1879d.

VESI, WILLIAM Eaton, Ohio, 1860d-1866d. (Hutslar)

VETERAN suicide special.

VETO suicide special by H & R.

VETTER, FREIDRICH Brooklyn, New York. Patent #309,265 December 16, 1884, breechloading firearm with Hugo Vetter.

VIAU, M.Z. Duluth, Minnesota. Patent #548,075 October 15, 1895, breechloading firearm, with John W. Lundgren.

VICKERS, GEORGE R., JR. Baltimore, Maryland. Patent #287,741 October 30, 1883, gunstock.

VICKERS, JOHN H. Worcester, Massachusetts. Patents #35,657 June 17, 1862, revolver, #39,869 September 8, 1863, cartridge cases, #47,775 May 16, 1865, revolver, and #57,448 August 21, 1866, revolver. Cartridges and revolvers produced by L.W. Pond.

VICKERS, JOHN W. Charleston, West Virginia, 1880c-1882d. (Whisker IV)

VICKERS, JONATHAN (1801-?), Cleveland, Ohio, 1820, Perrysburg, Ohio, 1850c-1853d. (Hutslar)

VICKERS, JONATHAN Delphi, Indiana, 1860d-1862d.

VICKERY, WILLIAM H. Manchester, New Hampshire, 1876d-1879d.

VICTOR suicide specials by Harrington & Richardson.

VICTOR trade name of Crescent Fire Arms Co. on shotguns.

VICTOR trade name of Marlin on derringers.

VICTOR, JOSEPH Du Quoin, Illinois. Patent #300,743 June 17, 1884, lock.

VICTORIA suicide special by Hood Fire Arms Co.

VIEDENMAN, JOHN Buffalo, New York, 1842d.

VIENNA, A.J. Memphis, Tennessee, 1873d-1891d. As Lullman & Vienna, 1873-1876.

VIERECK, J.L. Columbus, Kansas, 1884d.

VIERGUTZ, OTTO HERMAN (Prussia, 1830 or 1832-1879), Leavenworth, Kansas, 1860d-1869d, Pueblo, Colorado, 1874-1879. (Sellers-3)

VIGNER, JOHN, JR. Kingston, New York, 1850d.

VILES, NATHAN (1820-?), Harrison Co., Indiana, 1850c. (Lindert)

VILLEGIA & SLOTTERBECK San Francisco, California, 1868-1872. Percussion guns. Leopold Joseph M. Villegia and Charles S. Slotterbeck. (Shelton)

VILLEGIA, LEOPOLD JOSEPH M. (1833-?), San Francisco, California, 1859-1881. Percussion guns. With Charles S. Slotterbeck as Villegia & Slotterbek, 1868-1872. (Shelton)

VILLWOCK, CHARLES Toledo, Ohio, 1871d-1878d. Percussion 1/2 stock. As Villwock & Orth, 1875d. (Hutslar)

VILLWOCK, ROBERT Blissfield, Michigan, 1872d-1877d.

VINCENT, ANDREW Defiance, Ohio, 1857-1888d. (Hutslar)

VINCENT, GEORGE (1833-?), San Francisco, California, 1880. (Shelton)

VINCENT, JOHN (1809-1882), Vincent, Ohio, 1844-1882. Percussion and cartridge guns. Father of John Caleb Vincent. (Hutslar)

VINCENT, JOHN CALEB (1841-1918), Vincent, Ohio, 1870-1918. With his father as John Vincent & Son, 1870-1882. Successor to John Vincent. (Hutslar)

VINCENT, JOHN, & SON Vincent, Ohio, 1870c-1882. Percussion 1/2 stock. John, and John Caleb Vincent. (Hutslar)

VINE, E.W. Albany, New York, 1891d.

VINERING, J.M. (1816-?), Shasta Co., California, 1852c. (Shelton)

VINSON, R.B. Fort Gaines, Georgia, 1881d.

VINTABLE, ABRAHAM Philadelphia, Pennsylvania, 1824d.

VIRDER, FRANCOIS (1845-?), San Jose, California, 1870c. For Felix Sourisseau. (Shelton)

VIRGINIA ARMORY see Richmond Armory, and Virginia Manufactory.

VIRGINIA ARMS CO. trade name of Crescent on shotguns for Smith-Wadsworth Hardware Co., Charlotte, North Carolina. Also see Carolina Arms Co. (AR 2- 59)

VIRGINIA MANUFACTORY Richmond, Virginia, 1797-1865. Flintlock and percussion military guns. Also known as the Richmond Armory, and as the Virginia Armory. (Cromwell)

VIRGINIA STATE GUN FACTORY Fredericksburg, Virginia, 1775-1783.

VITTUM, FRANCIS J. Boston, Massachusetts. Patent #33,560 October 22, 1861, breechloading firearms with Edgar M. Stevens.

VITTUR, D. Hartford, Connecticut, 1871d-1877d.

VIVROUX, C. San Antonio, Texas, 1878d.

VLIET, WILSON Clarkston, Michigan, 1879d.

VOCELLE, A. Charleston, South Carolina, 1850-1852. (Kauffman 2)

VOEBEL, CHARLES New Orleans, Louisiana, 1867d-1888d.

VOESTER, F.G. Denver, Colorado, 1868-1881d. (Sellers-3)

VOGEL St. Mienrads, and Princeton, Indiana. (Lindert)

VOGELREICH, CONRAD Moberly, Missouri, 1891d-1898d.

VOGELSANG, A.M. Fostoria, Ohio, 1864-1869. (Knittle)

VOGELSANG, HENRY (1810-?), St. Louis, Missouri, 1847d-1850c, Herman, Missouri, 1860d. (Lewis)

VOGLE, A. Storm Lake, Iowa, 1880d.

VOGLER & CO. Houston, Texas, 1878d. Edward Vogler.

VOGLER, CHRISTOPH (1765-1827), Salem, North Carolina, 1787-1826. Flintlock Kentucky. (Bivins)

VOGLER, EDWARD Houston, Texas, 1878d. As Vogler & Co.

VOGLER, GOTTLIEB Salem, North Carolina. Son of Christopher Vogler. (Bivins)

VOGLER, HENRY S. (1829-?), Salem, North Carolina, 1850c. Son of Nathaniel Vogler.

VOGLER, JOHN (1784-1881), Salem, North Carolina, 1803-?. Flintlock Kentucky. More active as a silversmith. (Bivins)

VOGLER, JULIUS ROLAND (1830-?), Bethania, North Carolina, 1850c. (Bivins)

VOGLER, MORTIMER (1834-?), Salem, North Carolina, 1850c. Son of Nathaniel Vogler. (Bivins)

VOGLER, NATHANIEL (1804-?), Salem, North Carolina, 1827-1850. Flintlock Kentucky. Son of, and successor to, Christopher Vogler. (Bivins)

VOGLER, PHILLIP (1725-?), Salisbury, North Carolina, 1777-1786. (Bivins)

VOGLER, T.M. Salem, North Carolina, 1885d.

VOGLER, TIMOTHY (1806-?), Salem, North Carolina, 1819-1842. Flintlock Kentucky. Brother of Nathaniel Vogler. (Bivins)

VOGLESANG, HENRY Pennsylvania, 1775-1776. Committee of Safety locks.

VOGT, CHARLES Bastrop, Texas, 1878d-1884d.

VOGT, CHRISTIAN, H. (1849-?), Piqua, Ohio, 1872-1897d. (Hutslar)

VOGUES, C.A. unlocated. Percussion pistol.

VOHS, WILLIAM Rochester, New York, 1869d-1887d. For Billinghurst, 1869-1874 and for Charles Green, 1882-1883. (Eich)

VOIGHT, HENRY Pennsylvania, 1775-1776. Committee of Safety locks.

VOIL, J.W. Forbestown, California, 1867. (Shelton)

VOLANSKI, HARRY Richmond, Virginia, 1884d-1893d.

VOLCANIC REPEATING ARMS CO. Norwich, Connecticut, 1855-1857. Purchased by Oliver Fisher Winchester and reorganized as New Haven Arms Co.

VOLENTINE, J. Washington, Missouri. Percussion fullstock.

VOLGER, GEORGE (1789-?), Salem, North Carolina, 1809-1824, Salisbury, North Carolina, 1824-1850c. Flintlock Kentucky. (Bivins)

VOLKEL, JOHN L. Sulphur Springs, Missouri. Patent #234,632 November 16, 1860, breechloading firearms.

VOLKIEM, H.J. Laporte, Indiana, 1861d.

VOLPIUS, H. Cincinnati, Ohio, Percussion revolving rifle. See Herman Vulpius. (Sellers-1)

VOLUNTEER suicide special.

VOLUNTEER trade name of Belknap Hardware Co. on shotguns by Crescent. (Hinman)

VOLVERT Lancaster, Pennsylvania. Revolutionary War period. (Billin)

VON ALLMAN, H. Fairfield, Illinois, 1878d.

VON BRECHT, AUGUST St. Charles, Missouri, 1854d.

VON JEINSEN, ERNST New York, New York. Patent #84,922 December 15, 1868, breechloading firearms.

VON KAPFF, J. HERMAN Baltimore, Maryland, 1887-1888d. Importer. As Walsh, Hoen & Von Kapff. (Hartzler)

VON LENGERKE & ANTOINE Chicago, Illinois, 1892d-1929d. Dealers.

VON LENGERKE & DETMOLD New York, New York, 1884d-1914d. Importers and Dealers.

VON SHIRER, BENJAMIN HENRY (1852-?), Lancaster, Pennsylvania, 1873. (Whisker III)

VON WESSELY, ZDEUKO RITTER New York, New York. Patent #92,673 July 13, 1869, breechloading firearm. Improvement on the Peabody Martini, made by Providence Tool Co.

VONDERLINDEN, HERMAN New York, New York, 1883d.

VONDERSMITH, J. Lancaster, Pennsylvania. Flintlock Kentucky. Probably John Fondersmith. (Dillin)

VOORHEES, JEREMIAH Avoca, New York, 1848-1852, Wellsville, New York, 1852-1874d. Percussion over/under rifle and target rifles.

VORE, BENJAMIN F. (1814-1889), Somerset Co., Pennsylvania, 1836-1840d, New Paris, Pennsylvania, 1882d-1889d. Percussion fullstock with "B.V." signature. Advertised as De Vore in Somerset Co. (Whisker)

VORSTER, CHARLES New Orleans, Louisiana, 1872d. Imported shotgun.

VOSBURG, IRWIN Port Allegheny, Pennsylvania, 1850c-1861d.

VOSBURG, J. Crystal Lake and Rural, Wisconsin, 1857d. With A.P. Hyatt at both locations.

VOSBURG, SELAH West Rush and Alabama, New York, 1845-1875. Percussion and cartridge guns.

VOSE, WILLIAM T. Newtonville, Massachusetts. Patent #306,563 October 14, 1884, pneumatic gun.

VOSS, CARL W. Pine Bluff, Arkansas, 1875-1888d.

VOSS, LOUIS Aurora, Illinois, 1886d-1888d.

VOTE, WILLIAM J. Trowbridge, Michigan, 1863d-1867d.

VOYIT, AUGUST San Francisco, California, 1870-1871d. (Shelton)

VOYLES, NATHAN Corydon, Illinois. See Nathan Viles.

VREDENBURGH, ALBERT C. Kingston, New York. Patent #203,799 May 14, 1878, breechloading firearm.

VREELAND, L.J. Ft. Scott, Kansas, 1897d.

VULCAN ARMS CO. trade name of Crescent on shotguns. (AR 2-69)

VULPIUS, HERMAN Pottsville, Pennsylvania, 1880d. Same as H. Volpius, Cincinnati, Ohio?

VULTZ, J.A. (1822-?), Chicago, Illinois, 1850c. (Johnson)

W SECTION

W. & H.S. see William & Hugh Shannon.

W.A. see William Ashton.

W.A.T. see William A. Tully.

W.B. see William Border.

W.B. see William Bourne (percussion revolver).

W.B. See William Briggs (underhammer rifles).

W.B. unidentified. Flintlock Kentucky.

W.B.K.J. unidentified. Percussion 1/2 stock.

W.D. see William Defibaugh.

W.D. see William Douglas.

W.F. unidentified. Flintlock Kentucky rifle.

W.F. unidentified. Percussion 1/2 stock.

W.G. see Warren Gill.

W.G. unidentified. Flintlock Kentucky.

W.G. & Co. see William Glaze.

W.G.M. unidentified. Flintlock Kentucky rifles.

W.H. see Washington Hatfield.

W.H. unidentified. Percussion 1/2 stock.

W.H. unidentified. Percussion fullstock.

W.H.M. unidentified. Percussion fullstock.

W.H.N. unidentified. Percussion 1/2 stock.

W.J. unidentified. Converted Kentucky rifle.

W.K. unidentified. Flintlock Kentucky.

W.L. unidentified. Percussion fullstock.

W.M. see William Meier.

W.M. see William Moore.

W.M. unidentified. Percussion fullstock.

W.M.H. unidentified. Percussion 1/2 stock.

W.N. & S. see Winner, Nippes & Steinman.

W.P. see Wyatt Perry.

W.P.J. unidentified. Flintlock Kentucky.

W.P.J. unidentified. Percussion fullstock.

W.S. unidentified. Percussion fullstock.

W.S. unidentified. Percussion swivelbreech.

W.S.B. see W.S. Blankenship.

W.W. unidentified. Flintlock Kentucky.

WACHTER, JOHN Glasgow, Missouri, 1870d-1893d. Percussion 1/2 stock. As J. Wachter & Bro., 1870.

WACKERMAN, FRANK Pittsburgh, Pennsylvania. Patent #516,417 March 13, 1894, recoil operated firearm.

WADDAM, CALEB (1838-?), Chico, California, 1872-1875, Alturas, California, 1885. With brother, William, in Chico. (Shelton)

WADDAM, WILLIAM H. (1841-1908), Chico, California, 1872-1907. With brother, Caleb, 1872-1875. (Shelton)

WADE, ABNER Salem, Ohio, 1811. (Knittle)

WADE, HAMILTON Point of Fork, Virginia, 1786. (Gill)

WADE, MATHEW Cincinnati, Ohio, 1857d-1858d.

WADE, TERRENCE P. Nashville, Tennessee, 1877d.

WADE, W.F. Norborne, Missouri, 1898d.

WADE, WILLIAM Manchester, New Hampshire. Magazine and single shot carbines. With Ezekial Straw as Straw-Wade. (GR 3-66)

WADSWORTH, HENRY C. (?-1892), Worcester, Massachusetts, 1871-1890. With Sullivan Forehand as Forehand & Wadsworth, 1871-1890. Henry Wadsworth and Sullivan Forehand were sons-in-law of Ethan Allen.

WADSWORTH, S.D. Plymouth, Massachusetts, 1885d.

WAECHTER, LOUIS (1808-?), St. Louis, Missouri, 1847d-1870d. (Pourie)

WAGENHORST, JOHANN (1787-1861), Kutztown, Pennsylvania, 1810-1861. Barrelmaker. (Whisker III)

WAGGONER, IMMANUEL (1816-?), Wayne Co., Ohio, 1850c. (Hutslar)

WAGGONER, ISAAC (1829-?), Wayne Co., Ohio, 1850c. (Hutslar)

WAGGONER, ISAAC Lovejoy, Missouri, 1891d.

WAGGONER, P. Schenectady, New York, 1836-1850d. Converted Kentucky. (Clow)

WAGNER & BIERMANN Ann Arbor, Michigan, 1895d. Frederick J. Biermann.

WAGNER & BRO. Yankton, South Dakota, 1874-1876. George Wagner.

WAGNER, AUGUST Chester, Illinois, 1860d-1867d.

WAGNER, DAVID Sandy Hill, Pennsylvania. Percussion rifles signed "DBW". (MB 12-63)

WAGNER, GEORGE Yankton, South Dakota, 1874-1898d. As Wagner & Bro. 1874-1876.

WAGNER, HENRY Prairie Du Chien, Wisconsin 1872d.

WAGNER, J. Upper Sandusky, Ohio, ?-1864d. (Hutslar)

WAGNER, JACOB Washington, D.C., 1860d-1863d. (Hartzler)

WAGNER, JOHN New York, New York, 1867d.

WAGNER, JOHN W. Mansfield, Ohio, 1885d. (Hutslar)

WAGNER, M. Bucyrus, Ohio, 1866-1875d. (Hutslar)

WAGNER, WILLIAM Warrenton, Virginia, 1871d.

WAGONHURST, JOHN unlocated. Percussion fullstock.

WAHLQUIST, CHARLES J. Ft. Assiniboin, Montana. Patent #450,900 April 21, 1891 magazine gun.

WAIBEL, B. Independence, Missouri, 1860d.

WAINWRIGHT, JOHN New Orleans, Louisiana, 1822d.

WAIT BROS. Austin, Minnesota, 1898d.

WAITE, HENRY M. Woodstock, Illinois, 1860d.

WAITE, PHINEAS Leicester, Massachusetts, 1767. (Dean*)

WAITES, TIMOTHY La Vega, Iowa, 1865d.

WAKEFIELD, C.H. unlocated. High quality 1/2 stock. Possibly Charles Wakefield?

WAKEFIELD, CHARLES (1831-?), Petersburg, Virginia, 1850c. (MB 10-63)

WAKEFIELD, G. Jacksonville, Illinois, 1880d.

WAKEMAN, HARVEY Buffalo, New York, 1827-1835d. For Patrick Smith in 1835.

WALCH FIRE ARMS CO. New York, New York, 1859-1862. Walch superposed-load revolvers. (Sellers-1)

WALCH, JAMES Richmond, Virginia. Derringer. See James Walsh (AG 5-78)

WALCH, JOHN New York, New York. Patent #22,905 February 8, 1859, revolver. (Sellers-1)

WALCK, JULIUS Valley City, Dakota Territory, 1886d.

WALD, E.O.S. Colchester, Illinois, 1886d-1890d.

WALDECKER, HENRY C. Austin, Minnesota, 1878-1898d. Patent #338,451 March 23, 1886, firearm safety.

WALDEN & MARSHALL Dayton, Ohio, 1859d. Hardware, locks. (Hutslar)

WALDEN, OTTO Wheeling, West Virginia, 1900d. (Whisker IV)

WALDER, NICHOLAS Peoria, Illinois, 1856d.

WALDREN, ALEXANDER Kittery, Maine, 1660-1676. Brother of William Waldren. Also listed at Pisquataqua River, Massachusetts, 1672. (Demeritt)

WALDREN, WILLIAM Scituate, Massachusetts, 1670, Boston, Massachusetts, 1671-1672. Brother of Alexander Waldren. (Gluckman & Satterlee)

WALDRON, A. Stafford Co., New Hampshire, 1869-1873.

WALDRON, MILTON H. Cassville, New York, 1874d. Percussion 1/2 stock. (Swinney)

WALFORD, THOMAS Charlestown, Massachusetts, 1623-1640. (Dean*)

WALHILL RIFLE WORKS New Paltz, New York, 1863-1864d.

WALKER & NUTTING Waterbury, Connecticut, 1884d-1886d.

WALKER, ASA Marshfield, Massachusetts, 1872-1885d. Percussion 1/2 stock.

WALKER, B.H. (1824-?), Galesburg, Illinois, 1860c. Percussion over/under rifle/shotgun. (Johnson)

WALKER, B.R. Lawrenceburg, Tennessee, 1860d.

WALKER, E.H. Monroe, Georgia, 1861. Confederate gunsmith convention.

WALKER, G. Philadelphia, Pennsylvania. Patent #20,776 July 6, 1858, breechloading firearm with E. Brooks.

WALKER, G.W.B. unlocated. Percussion 1/2 stock.

WALKER, GEORGE A. Boston, Massachusetts. Patent #179,984, July 18, 1876, air gun. (Wolff)

WALKER, H.L. New Madrid Co., Missouri, 1850c. (MB 11-66)

WALKER, ISAAC, HARDWARE CO. Peoria, Illinois. Dealers only.

WALKER, JABEZ Livonia, New York, 1872-1874d.

WALKER, JAMES Fayette Co., Pennsylvania, 1802-1803, Knox Co., Ohio, 1810-1830c. (Hutslar)

WALKER, JAMES, JR. Belfast, Maine, 1869-1873. (Demeritt)

WALKER, JOHN (?-1794), Rockbridge Co., Virginia. (Gill)

WALKER, JOHN Lancaster, Pennsylvania, 1780t-1807t. Flintlock Kentucky rifles. (Dyke)

WALKER, JOHN Rockbridge Co., Virginia, 1796t. Son of John Walker? (Gill)

WALKER, JOSEPH Fayette Co., Pennsylvania, 1799-1803, Mt. Vernon, Ohio, 1803-1816. (Hutslar)

WALKER, JOSEPH Shippensburg, Pennsylvania, 1842-1843. (Kauffman)

WALKER, LOUIS N. Ilion, New York. Patent #354,452 December 14, 1886, breechloading gun.

WALKER, P.H. Boston, Massachusetts, 1867d. Percussion double shotgun.

WALKER, SAMUEL Henderson, Illinois, 1860d.

WALKER, SAMUEL L. Cedarville, Ohio, 1857-1878. Percussion guns. (Hutslar)

WALKER, THOMAS Lancaster, Pennsylvania, 1799. (Dean)

WALKER, W.O. Eagle Point, Texas, 1884d.

WALKER, W.W. Belton, Texas, 1890d.

WALKER, WILLIAM (1838-1922), Tuckaleeche Cove, Tennessee, ?-1882. (Roberts)

WALKER, WILLIAM Livonia, New York, 1879-1882.

WALKER, WILLIAM H. Bourneville, Ohio, 1853d. Percussion 1/2 stock. (Hutslar)

WALKEY, SAMUEL Humblersburg, Pennsylvania, 1861d. Percussion fullstock rifle.

WALL New York, New York, percussion shotguns. (GR 1-63)

WALL, FREDERICK Spring City, Utah 1871d. Santaquin, Utah, 1884d.

WALL, GEORGE Mount Vernon, Indiana, 1860d.

WALLACE & OSBORN Canton, Connecticut, 1850. Underhammer pistol. S. Osborn? Predecessor to Andrus & Osborn (also at Canton, 1863-1867)?

WALLACE & RICE Talladega, Alabama, 1862. Mississippi rifles for Confederacy. Samuel F. Rice. (Albaugh 1)

WALLACE, D.P. East Liberty, Ohio, 1875d-1878d. (Hutslar)

WALLACE, DAVID Sardis, Pennsylvania, 1861d. Percussion fullstock.

WALLACE, J.A. Seneca, Missouri, 1879d.

WALLACE, JAMES Humboldt, Tennessee, 1887d.

WALLACE, JOHN Freeport, Pennsylvania, 1858-1890d. Percussion 1/2 stock.

WALLACE, ROBERT C. (1801-?), Perrysburg, Ohio, 1850c, Grand Rapids, Ohio, 1881d. (Hutslar)

WALLACE, SAMUEL R. Norwich, Connecticut, 1866d-1873d.

WALLACE, VICTOR M. West Topham, Vermont. Patent #none August 17, 1835, pocket pistol.

WALLACE, W.R. Leadville, Colorado, 1879d, Greeley, Colorado, 1879d. (Sellers-3)

WALLACE, WILLIAM Perrysburg, Ohio, 1859d-1864d, Toledo, Ohio, 1878d. (Hutslar)

WALLACH, MOSES A. Boston, Massachusetts, 1800-1825. (Gluckman & Satterlee)

WALLER, HENRY Randolph Co., Virginia, 1810-1811. Contract muskets with Henry Martin and Lewis Shroyer. (Cromwell)

WALLER, O.A. Salem, Oregon, 1881d-1886d.

WALLERICH, M. Independence, Missouri. Percussion 1/2 stock.

WALLERICH, MATHIAS Segourney, Iowa, 1880d-1887d, Des Moines, Iowa, 1895d-1899d. Same as M. Wallerich, Independence, Missouri?

WALLEY, HENRY Wyomissing Creek, Pennsylvania. Barrelmaker. (MB 2-63)

WALLEY, SAMUEL unlocated. Percussion fullstock.

WALLIS & BIRCH Philadelphia, Pennsylvania. Derringer.

WALLIS, THOMAS M. Philadelphia, Pennsylvania, 1856-1884. Patents #197,432 November 20, 1877, sub caliber chamber, #194,489 August 21, 1877, revolver, and #301,021 June 24, 1884, breechloading firearm. Percussion derringers and cartridge guns. For W. Wurfflein, 1877-1885.

WALLS, JOSEPH Ransom, Michigan, 1860d.

WALRAVEN, JOHN Baltimore, Maryland, 1800d-1810d. (Hartzler)

WALSER, EDWARD B. St. Louis, Missouri, 1893d-1916d.

WALSH, HOEN & VON KAPFF Baltimore, Maryland, 1887-1888d. Importers. J. Herman Von Kapff. (Hartzler)

WALSH, JAMES Philadelphia, Pennsylvania, 1775-1779. Committee of Safety locks. Flintlock pistol. (Hobbies 4-38)

WALSH, JAMES Richmond, Virginia. Imported percussion shotgun.

WALSH, JAMES T. Red Fork, Arkansas. Patent #433,260 July 29, 1890, breechloading gun.

WALSH, JOHN Philadelphia, Pennsylvania, 1776-1785. Committee of Safety stockmaker who repaired U.S. arms, 1780-1785. (Hobbies 4-38)

WALSH, P.J. Detroit, Michigan, 1865d.

WALSH, W.I. Baltimore, Maryland, 1885d.

WALSTAD, CHARLES Red Wing, Minnesota, 1898d.

WALSTON, JOHN Bell's Depot, Tennessee, 1887d-1891d.

WALTECK, JOHN Englewood, New Jersey, 1878d.

WALTER, HENRY (1821-?), Westmoreland Co., Pennsylvania, 1850c-1870c. (Whisker II)

WALTER, HENRY Columbiana Co., Ohio, 1800-1820c. Flintlock Kentucky. (Hutslar)

WALTER, HENRY Lancaster Co., Pennsylvania, 1820-1830. (Dyke)

WALTER, J.N. (1819-?), Evansport, Ohio, 1880-1890d, Marion, Ohio, 1850c. (Hutslar)

WALTER, JOHN (1808-?), Canton, Ohio, 1850c. Barrelmaker. (Hutslar)

WALTER, MATHIAS Columbiana Co., Ohio. (Hutslar)

WALTERHAVER, CHRIST Baltimore, Maryland, 1851-1854d. (Hartzler)

WALTERING, JOSEPH Wake Co., North Carolina, 1850c. Primarily a blacksmith. (Bivins)

WALTERS, A. New York, New York, 1822. (Gluckman & Satterlee)

WALTERS, JOHN ULRICH (?-1875), Sharpsville (?), Pennsylvania, 1840-1861d, Brighton, Missouri, 1867-1875. (MB 2-66)

WALTERS, R.W. Bonham, Texas, 1896d.

WALTERS, TRUMAN Jackson, Michigan, 1879d-1885d.

WALTHERS, C.F. Albuquerque, New Mexico, 1882d.

WALTON & NEAL New York, New York, 1889d.

WALTON, T. unlocated. Percussion fullstock.

WALTZ, DAVID Wadsworth, Ohio, 1850-1900. Percussion 1/2 stock. (Hutslar)

WALTZ, JOEL (1825-?), Wadsworth, Ohio, 1850-1900. Son of David Waltz. (Hutslar)

WALTZ, JOSEPH (1825-?), Wayne Co., Ohio, 1850c. (Hutslar)

WAMPLER, J. MORRIS Louden Co., Virginia. Patent #27,399 March 6, 1860, breechloading firearm.

WAMPOLE, A. Ord, Nebraska, 1893d.

WANDLE, JOHN Wells Co., Indiana. Percussion rifles. (Lindert)

WANE, WILLIAM P. Barry, Illinois, 1860d. Percussion 1/2 stock.

WANSTRUM, CHARLES Lewiston, Illinois, 1884d.

WANT, EDWARD New Bern, North Carolina, 1861. Contract for pistols but none delivered. (Bivins)

WAPPICH, MAXIMILLIAN Sacramento, California. Patent #37,882 March 10, 1863, gun carriage.

WARD BROS. Lincoln, Nebraska, 1880d-1893d.

WARD, BENJAMIN Wilson, North Carolina, 1870c-1877d. (Bivins)

WARD, D. unlocated. Flintlock Kentucky.

WARD, D.D. Oxford, Michigan, 1887d.

WARD, E.R. Prairie City, Iowa, 1884d, Ottumwa, Iowa, 1887d.

WARD, GEORGE N. Middletown, Connecticut, 1869-1874d. Lockmaker.

WARD, H.D. Pittsfield, Massachusetts, 1857-1864. Patent #38,850, September 8, 1863, double-barrel revolver.

WARD, HENRY (1800-?), St. Louis, Missouri, 1850c. (Lewis)

WARD, J.W. Atlanta, Georgia, 1883d.

WARD, JAMES Jamestown, North Carolina. Percussion fullstock. (Bivins)

WARD, JAMES N. New York, New York. Patents #15,262 July 1, 1856, magazine hammer, #16,503 January 27, 1857, conversion method, and #18,876 December 15, 1857, bayonet fastening.

WARD, JOHN Philadelphia, Pennsylvania, 1798-1813d. (Kauffman)

WARD, JOHN St. Louis, Missouri, 1850c. (MB 11-66)

WARD, MILLER & CO. York Co., Pennsylvania, 1838. Barrelmakers. (Kauffman)

WARD, OTIS East Arlington, Vermont, 1876-1880, Sunderland, Vermont, 1880-1881. (Horn)

WARD, SAMUEL Clarinda, Iowa, 1865d.

WARD, SOLOMON H. Jamestown, North Carolina, 1865-1884d. Percussion 1/2 stock. Son of James Ward. (Bivins)

WARD, THOMAS Rochester, New York, 1827d. (Eich)

WARD, WILLIAM G., U.S. Army. Patents #92,129 June 29, 1869, breechloading firearm, #94,458 August 31, 1869, breechloading firearm, #97,734 December 14, 1869, breechloading firearm, #99,504 February 1, 1870, breechloading firearm, and #111,994 February 21, 1871, breechloading firearm. Ward-Burton rifles made at Springfield Armory.

WARD, WILLIAM H. Auburn, New York. Patent #18,616 November 10, 1857, bullet machine.

WARDEN, LEWIS Paducah, Kentucky, 1857-1860d.

WARDEN, R.W. New Haven, Missouri, 1893d.

WARDWELL, FRANK A. Methuen, Massachusetts. Patent #349,864 September 28, 1886, cane gun.

WARE & MORSE Worcester, Massachusetts, 1833d. Joseph S. Ware and John R. Morse.

WARE & WHEELOCK Worcester, Massachusetts, 1825-1832. Joseph S. Ware. (Gluckman & Satterlee)

WARE, DAVIS Ely, Vermont, 1876-1879.

WARE, JOSEPH S. Worcester, Massachusetts, 1842d-1856d. Percussion guns. With Orlando as O. & J.S. Ware, 1842-1843. (Kauffman 2)

WARE, LYMAN DAVIS Fairlee, Vermont, 1876-1888. (Horn)

WARE, O. & J. S. Worcester, Massachusetts, 1842-1843. Orlando Ware, and Joseph S. Ware. (Kauffman)

WARE, ORLANDO Worcester, Massachusetts, 1842-1849d. With Joseph S. Ware as O. & J.S. Ware, 1842-1843.

WARE, WILLIAM W. Philadelphia, Pennsylvania, 1857d.

WAREHAM, D. & C.A. Belle Plaine, Kansas, 1884d.

WAREHAM, DAVID Stark Co., Ohio. (Knittle)

WAREHAM, GEORGE (1825-?), Stark Co., Ohio, 1850c, Uniontown, Indiana, 1870-1892. Percussion guns. (Lindert, Hutslar)

WAREHAM, PERCY Brooklyn, Michigan. Patent #612,071 October 11, 1898, revolver.

WARFEL, SAMUEL (1798-?), Uhrichville, Ohio, 1833-1850c. (Hutslar)

WARFIELD, A.M. Washington, D.C., 1875d. (Hartzler)

WARFIELD, AZEL Fredericktown, Maryland, 1777. Committee of Safety muskets. (Hartzler)

WARFIELD, C. Fruitland, Missouri, 1889d-1891d.

WARFIELD, L. & CO. unlocated. Barrelmakers, New England region.

WARFIELD, OLIVER D. Chicopee Falls, Massachusetts. Patents #214,331 April 15, 1879, firearm sight, and #217,717 July 22, 1879, firearm sight.

WARHAM unlocated. Percussion 1/2 stock.

WARIN, J.H. Syracuse, New York, 1870c.

WARNEKROS, ULRICH Petaluma, California, 1876-1885. (Shelton)

WARNER & LOWE Syracuse, New York, 1880-1888. Percussion sporting rifles, rebarreled single shot rifles. Horace Warner and William V. Lowe. (AR 12-39)

WARNER & WESSON Hartford, Connecticut, 1850. Percussion revolvers. Thomas Warner and D.B. Wesson. (Sellers-1)

WARNER, BENJAMIN FRANKLIN Seneca Co., Ohio, Ft. Gibson, Iowa, 1850c. For Seneca Indians. (Knittle)

WARNER, C.A. Hopkintown, New York, 1879-1882d.

WARNER, CHARLES Windsor Locks, Connecticut. Percussion revolvers. Brother of James Warner. (Sellers-1)

WARNER, DEWITT C., & BRO. Montrose, Pennsylvania, 1834. Purchased rights to make Colburn revolvers. (Sellers-1)

WARNER, FRANK P. Florence, Colorado. Patent #647,123 April 10, 1900, sight. (Sellers-3)

WARNER, GEORGE Lancaster, Pennsylvania, 1857d-1873d. Listed as George Werner in 1884 directory. See George Werner.

WARNER, GEORGE Philadelphia, Pennsylvania, 1819d.

WARNER, H. Grafton Station, Ohio. Percussion 1/2 stock With David Rose? (Hutslar)

WARNER, H. unlocated. Flintlock Kentucky.

WARNER, H.W. Liverpool, Ohio, 1850c-1864d. Percussion 1/2 stock. (Hutslar)

WARNER, HENRY Montgomery Co., Ohio, 1850c. (Hutslar)

WARNER, HIRAM (1833-1862), Wilcox, Pennsylvania, 1858d. Brother of Horace Warner. (Whisker II)

WARNER, HORACE (1832-1893), Ridgeway and Williamsport, Pennsylvania, 1850-1880, Syracuse, New York, 1880-1893. Patent #306,564 October 11, 1884, shot attachment for rifles. With William V. Lowe as Warner & Lowe, 1880-1888. (Roberts)

WARNER, ISAAC Philadelphia, Pennsylvania, 1780-1782. Continental Armory. (Moller)

WARNER, JAMES (1818-1870), Springfield, Massachusetts. Patents #7,894 January 7, 1851, revolver, #8,229 July 15, 1851, revolver, #15,202 June 24, 1856, revolver, #17,904 July 28, 1857, revolver, #37,782 February 24, 1863, sights, #41,732 February 23, 1864, breechloading firearm, and #45,660 December 27, 1864, breechloading firearms. Owner of Springfield Arms Co., which produced his revolvers. His carbines were made by Greene Rifle Works as well as himself. (Sellers 1, GR 5-60)

WARNER, JOSEPH Philadelphia, Pennsylvania, 1819d-1833d.

WARNER, RICHARD Maple Rapids, Michigan, 1895d-1899d.

WARNER, THOMAS (1793-1885), Springfield, Armory, 1810-1843, New Haven, Connecticut, 1843-1849, Hartford, Connecticut, 1849-1851, Springfield, Massachusetts, 1851-1857. Patent #9,999 September 6, 1853, twisted gun barrels. Superintendent of Springfield Armory, 1837-1843, Whitney Armory, 1843-1849, Edwin Wesson factory after Wesson's death, 1849-1851, Massachusetts Arms Co., 1851-1857 and Waters (?), 1857-1860. (Massachusetts Arms)

WARNER, WILLIAM C. (1826-?), Washington, Indiana, 1860d-1871. (Lindert)

WARREN & CO. Topeka, Kansas, 1873d. Breechloading shotguns. Abraham Warren.

WARREN & STEELE Albany, New York. Lockmakers only.

WARREN ARMS CORP. trade name of H. & D. Folsom on imported shotguns. (AR 2-69)

WARREN, A.L. Memphis, Tennessee, 1860c. (T 47)

WARREN, ABRAHAM Topeka, Kansas, 1873d-1894d. As Warren & Co., 1873.

WARREN, MILTON Abingdon, Virginia, 1860. (Dean*)

WARRING, W.W. Kansas, Ohio, 1883d. (Hutslar)

WARTER & SCHAFFER Vicksburg, Mississippi, 1867. Jacob A. Schaffer (also known as Jacob Shaffer).

WARUFF, HENRY Kalamazoo, Michigan, 1887d-1891d.

WARWICK, JAMES Philadelphia, Pennsylvania, 1837d.

WASHBURN IRON WORKS Worcester, Massachusetts. Gun barrels. Nathan Washburn. (Gluckman & Satterlee)

WASHBURN, F.C. Branch Store, California, 1867d. (Shelton)

WASHBURN, F.C. Wellsborough, Pennsylvania, 1882d-1887d.

WASHBURN, IRA South Gibson, Pennsylvania, 1861d.

WASHBURN, NATHAN Worcester, Massachusetts. Gun barrels. As Washburn Iron Works.

WASHBURN, R.C. Wellsborough, Pennsylvania. Tip-up rifle.

WASHBURN, R.H. Gatesville, Texas, 1884d-1890d.

WASHBURN, SOUTHWARD Turner, Maine, 1803. (Demeritt)

WASHBURN, THOMAS Richmond, Maine, 1740-1742. (Demeritt)

WASHBURN, V.R. unlocated. Percussion 1/2 stock.

WASHINGTON ARMS CO. trade name used by W. W. Marston on pepperboxes and percussion pistols.

WASHINGTON, LEWIS Washington, D.C., 1822d. (Kauffman 2)

WASHINGTON, READE M. Dallas, Texas. Patent #658,934 October 2, 1900, barrel.

WASHINGTON, THORNTON A. U.S. Army. Patent #15,990 October 28, 1856, breechloading firearms. John C. Symmes made "Symmes" carbines under this patent which were purchased by the U.S. Army. (AG 4-74)

WASNER, JOHN Salisbury, North Carolina. Apprenticed, 1816. (Bivins)

WASP suicide special.

WASSERMAN, BERNHARD Central City, Dakota Territory, 1877-1880.

WASSIN, BENJAMIN (1821-?), Shasta Co., California, 1852c. (Shelton)

WASSMAN, GEORGE F. Georgetown, D.C., 1860-1872d. Percussion 1/2 stock target rifle. (Hartzler)

WASSON, L. Fulton, Indiana, 1860d-1862d.

WASSON, THOMAS (1827-?), Shingle Springs, California, 1867-1880. (Shelton)

WATERBURY, C.A. unlocated. Bolt action magazine gun.

WATERMAN, A.P. Beloit, Wisconsin, 1857d-1865d.

WATERMAN, E. Rutland, Wisconsin, 1857d.

WATERMAN, JOHN O. (1820-?), Lacon, Illinois, 1850c-1860d. (Johnson)

WATERMAN, LYMAN (1821-?), Sycamore, Illinois, 1853-1860. (Johnson)

WATERS Dutchess Co., New York, 1775-1776. Committee of Safety repairs. (Gluckman & Satterlee)

WATERS & WHITMORE Sutton, Massachusetts, 1808-1812. Model 1808 contract muskets marked "Sutton". Elijah Waters, Asa Waters, Jr. and Nathaniel Whitmore. (Gluckman)

WATERS, A., & CO. Millbury, Massachusetts, 1812-1813. Asa Waters, I.

WATERS, A.H., & CO. Millbury, Massachusetts, 1843-1856. Asa H. Waters.

WATERS, ANDRUS (1752-1778), Sutton, Massachusetts, 1775-1776, Salisbury, Connecticut, 1776-1778. Committee of Safety gunsmith. Brother of Asa Waters, I. (GR 12-60)

WATERS, ASA HOLMAN (1808-1887), Millbury, Massachusetts, 1833-1850. As A.H. Waters & Co. Son of Asa Waters II. (GR 12-60)

WATERS, ASA, I (1742-1813), Sutton, Massachusetts, 1776-1812, Millbury, Massachusetts, 1812-1813. As A. Waters & Co., 1812-1813. (GR 12-60)

WATERS, ASA, II (1769-1841), Sutton, Massachusetts, 1790-1812, Millbury, Massachusetts, 1812-1841. Patent #none October 25, 1817, turning gun barrels. Son of Asa Waters, I. (GR 12-60)

WATERS, ELIJAH (1769-1814), Sutton, Massachusetts, 1785-1812, Millbury, Massachusetts, 1812-1814. Son of Asa Waters, I. (GR 12-60)

WATERS, G.H. suicide special.

WATERS, ISAAC L. Sutton, Massachusetts. Patents #349,244 September 14, 1886, breechloading firearm.

WATERS, JOHN Carlisle, Pennsylvania, 1779t-1791. (Bowers)

WATERS, RICHARD (?-1677), Salem, Massachusetts, 1632-1677. (GR 12-60)

WATERTOWN ARSENAL Watertown, Massachusetts, 1816-1995.

WATERVLIET ARSENAL Watervliet, New York, 1813-date.

WATKEYS, HENRY New Windsor, New York, 1772-1776. Flintlock muskets.

WATKEYS, HENRY Syracuse, New York. Patents #167,285 August 31, 1875, adjustable trigger, #245,888 August 23, 1881, breechloading firearm, and #246,052 August 23, 1881, break-open shotgun.

WATKINS, J.A. Windsor, Virginia, 1877d. Also listed in directory as Q.A. Watkins, 1880d-1884d.

WATKINS, J.F. Good Hope, Georgia, 1881d.

WATKINS, Q.A. Windsor, Virginia, 1880d-1884d. See J.A. Watkins.

WATKINS, S. Scotland, Florida, 1886d.

WATKINS, WILLIAM M. Monroe, Georgia, 1861. Confederate gunsmith convention.

WATKINSON, E.J. New Orleans, Louisiana, 1867d-1869d. As Dart & Watkinson, 1867d.

WATROUS, J.J. Cincinnati, Ohio, 1887d-1893d. Target rifles.

WATSLER, J.A. West Bay City, Michigan, 1899d.

WATSON, ALEXANDER T. Castleton, New York. Patent #12,567 March 20, 1855, breechloading firearm.

WATSON, BARON C. New York, New York. Patents #161,307 March 23, 1875, breechloading firearm, and #161,308 March 23, 1875, ordnance.

WATSON, GEORGE Bismark, North Dakota, 1898d.

WATSON, GEORGE Muncie, Indiana, 1867-1871. Percussion 1/2 stock. (Lindert)

WATSON, J.M. Altoona, Pennsylvania, 1882d-1887d. Percussion guns.

WATSON, JAMES Sulphur Springs, Tennessee, 1860d.

WATSON, JOHN Baltimore, Maryland, 1817-1818d. Barrels only. (Hartzler)

WATSON, JONATHAN Chester, New Hampshire, 1800.

WATSON, W.T. Green Ridge, Arkansas, 1884d.

WATSON, WALTER Fayetteville, North Carolina, 1864-1890d. Stock mark on imported (?) rifles. (Bivins)

WATT & BENNETT St. Louis, Missouri. Successors to W.S. Hawken. William L. Watt.

WATT, CHRISTOPHER Richmond, Virginia, 1804-1805, Philadelphia, Pennsylvania, 1814d. Percussion fullstock. For Virginia Manufactory. (Kauffman)

WATT, G. unlocated. Flintlock Kentucky.

WATT, GEORGE L. Philadelphia, Pennsylvania, 1847d-1849d.

WATT, J.W. Philadelphia, Pennsylvania, 1846d-1855d. Lockmaker.

WATT, JOHN Mifflintown, Pennsylvania, 1840-1850d. (Whisker II)

WATT, WILLIAM L. St. Louis, Missouri, 1860d-1870d. Successor to W.S. Hawken, as Watt & Bennett. (Hanson)

WATTERS, JOHN Carlisle, Pennsylvania, 1778-1785. Kentucky rifles.

WATTS, JAMES Sandy Hill, Pennsylvania, 1860-1887d. Son of John Watts. (MB 10-54)

WATTS, JOHN (1813-1885), Sandy Hill, Pennsylvania, 1850-1885. Percussion fullstock and swivelbreech, "J.W." usual marking. (MB 10-54)

WATTS, JOSEPH New Prospect, Ohio, 1850c-1853d. As Frank & Watts, 1853. Percussion fullstock. (Hutslar)

WATTS, JOSEPH Ransom, Michigan, 1863d-1865d.

WATTS, WILLIAM L. Baltimore, Maryland, 1835-1856d. (Hartzler)

WAUCH, G.W. Skookum Chuck, Washington, 1871d.

WAUGH, JOSEPH Levant, Maine, 1875. (Demeritt)

WAUGH, LEWIS Levant, Maine, 1875. (Demeritt)

WAUGH, THOMAS Starks, Maine, 1871. (Demeritt)

WAUTAUGA trade name of Wallace Hardware Co., Morristown, Tennessee, on shotguns. (Hinman)

WAY, ARAD Canfield, Ohio, 1803-1808 and 1820c, Middlebury, Ohio, 1812. Flintlock pistols. (Knittle)

WAY, DAVID S. Centre Point, Iowa, 1865d.

WAY, W. Natchez, Indiana, 1860d.

WAYMIRE, NORRIS O. Garfield, Kansas. Patent #299,302 May 27, 1884, extractor.

WAYMON, COLEMAN H. Princeton, Missouri. Patent #631,349 August 22, 1899, ejector.

WEANER, JOHN H. (1804-?), Washington, D.C., 1837-1850c. Employed three other gunsmiths. (Hartzler)

WEATHERBY, CHARLES PIERRE NEWTON New York, New York. Patents #409,889 April 27, 1889, magazine gun, and #410,621 September 10, 1889, magazine gun.

WEATHERBY, JOSEPH (1725-1809), Harvard, Massachusetts, 1750-1809. Committee of Safety muskets and flintlock rifles. (ASAC 44)

WEATHERBY, JOSEPH Philadelphia, Pennsylvania, 1819d.

WEATHERBY, O.B. Cedar Falls, Iowa, 1892d-1897d.

WEATHERHEAD, FRANK W. Hartford, Connecticut. Patent #358,237 February 22, 1887, magazine gun.

WEATHERLY, M. Ramsey, Illinois, 1875d.

WEATHERS, P.G. Denver, Colorado, 1890d. (Sellers-3)

WEAVER, ADAM Jonestown, Pennsylvania, 1771-1779. (KRA IV-4)

WEAVER, CHARLES Dayton, Ohio, 1850d. Barrels only. (Hutslar)

WEAVER, CYPRET unlocated. Kentucky rifles dated 1818 and 1834.

WEAVER, GEORGE A. Urbana, Ohio, 1860. (Hutslar)

WEAVER, GEORGE W. Ilion, New York. Patent #421,793 February 18, 1890, air gun.

WEAVER, H.B. South Windham, Connecticut, 1850-1856. Breechloading percussion shotguns. Patent #13,691 October 16, 1855, breechloading firearm.

WEAVER, HENRY Bedford Co., Pennsylvania, 1819-1837. (Whisker II)

WEAVER, HUGH Pleasant Ridge, Ohio, 1867-1870. (Hutslar)

WEAVER, JAMES Ashville, North Carolina, circa 1890.

WEAVER, JESSE D. Seymour, Indiana, 1867-1897. (MB 4-55)

WEAVER, JOHN AMOS (1830-?), New Frankfurt, Indiana, 1850c, Lexington, Indiana, 1862d. (Lindert)

WEAVER, LEMUEL (1808-1890), Urbana, Ohio, 1843-1878d. Hardware. With son George, 1875-1878. (Hutslar)

WEAVER, N.S. unlocated. Percussion pistol.

WEAVER, NICHOLAS S. (1831-?), Kenton, Ohio, 1850c-1896d. Percussion 1/2 stock. (Hutslar)

WEAVER, P.W. Paulding, Ohio, 1890d. (Hutslar)

WEAVER, SAMUEL unlocated. Flintlock Kentucky.

WEAVER, WILLIAM Clinton, Pennsylvania. Patent #15,529 August 12, 1856, centrifugal cannon with A.B. Smith.

WEAVER, ZACHARIAS Rochester, New York, 1841d-1883d, Syracuse, New York, 1884. For Billinghurst until Billinghurst's death in 1880, when he took over the shop. (Eich)

WEBB, AUSTIN (1841-?), Rock Island, Illinois, 1860c. (Johnson)

WEBB, CHARLES St. Louis, Missouri, 1855d-1859d. Percussion 1/2 stock. As Webb, Brison & CO., 1859.

WEBB, GEORGE Somerset, Kentucky, 1883d-1885d.

WEBB, GEORGE C. Greenford, Ohio, 1853d. (Hutslar)

WEBB, HARRY C. Tacoma, Washington. Patent #569,899 October 20, 1896, machine gun.

WEBB, JAMES Greenfield, Ohio, 1853d. Percussion full-stock. (Hutslar)

WEBB, JAMES R. (1828-?), Courtland, Illinois, 1860d-1864d.

WEBB, JOSEPH (1815-?), Rock Island, Illinois, 1855-1860. (Johnson)

WEBB, JOSEPH Harlan, Indiana, 1882-1885. (Lindert)

WEBB, SELBY S. (1862-1952), Salineville, Ohio. (Hutslar)

WEBBER, CARL Lapeer, Michigan, 1863d-1867d.

WEBBER, HENRY Hudson, New York, 1871-1874d.

WEBBER, J.H. Memphis, Tennessee, 1869-1875.

WEBEL, CHARLES New Orleans, Louisiana, 1853d.

WEBER, ADOLPH Victoria, Texas, 1885d.

WEBER, C. Goshen, Indiana, 1860-1861d, Elkhart, Indiana, 1862-1863d.

WEBER, C. Red Cloud, Nebraska, 1879d.

WEBER, CARL McMinnville, Oregon, 1886d.

WEBER, E.G. Parsons, Kansas, 1894d.

WEBER, MATTHIAS Chicago, Illinois, 1859d-1862. With Joseph Butler as Butler & Weber, 1859-1862.

WEBER, MATTHIAS Philadelphia, Pennsylvania, 1855-1870d.

WEBER, P. unlocated. Percussion 1/2 stock.

WEBER, WILLIAM Pekin, Illinois, circa 1885.

WEBERLEY, I.M. Somerville, New Jersey, 1866d.

WEBSTER, D.E. Galena, Illinois, 1886d-1888d.

WEBSTER, F. Chelsea, Massachusetts, 1867d.

WEBSTER, JOHN Colchester, Illinois, 1860d.

WEBSTER, L.J., & CO. New Orleans, Louisiana, 1849d-1850d. Importers and dealers. Percussion locks, "L.J.W. & CO." marking.

WEBSTER, THOMAS K. Lawrence, Massachusetts, 1857-1867d.

WECK, JOHN Baltimore, Maryland. Patent #146,445 January 13, 1874, breechloading firearm with Francis Fuss.

WEDDELL, PETER M. Zanesville, Ohio, 1823. Flintlock Kentucky. (Hutslar)

WEED, ALFRED Anderson, Indiana. Patent #642,858 February 6, 1900, sight.

WEED, HERSCHELL Niles, Michigan, 1863d-1871d. Percussion 1/2 stock.

WEED, JAMES New York, New York, 1851d.

WEED, T. unlocated. Percussion 1/2 stock.

WEEDMAN, JOHN Buffalo, New York, 1837d.

WEEDS, N.B. unlocated. Flintlock Kentucky.

WEEKS, CHARLES A. Philadelphia, Pennsylvania. Patents, all with Charles Foehl, #444,823 January 20, 1891, revolver, #447,219 February 24, 1891, revolver, #468,243 February 2, 1892, revolver, and #471,112 March 22, 1892, revolver. With Charles Foehl as Foehl & Weeks.

WEEKS, D. Dansville, New York, 1848-1850d.

WEEKS, DANIEL Erie, Pennsylvania, 1867-1890d. Percussion guns.

WEEKS, E.C. Erie, Pennsylvania, 1882d-1887d.

WEEKS, JOSEPH Marlin, Texas, 1892d.

WEEKS, THOMAS S. (1830-1910), Fond du Lac, Wisconsin, 1849-1890. Percussion rifles and shotguns. With Samuel Amory, 1849-1860. (WGCA 6)

WEGLE, J. Eminence, Indiana, 1858-1862. Percussion rifles. (Lindert)

WEGNER, AUGUST (1822-?), Chester, Illinois, 1860c-1864d.

WEHL, ABRAHAM Butte, Montana, 1888d.

WEHLI, JOHN Washington, Pennsylvania, 1847. (Kauffman)

WEHRLE, JOHN St. Louis, Missouri, 1865d-1879d.

WEHRLE, JOSEPH Denver, Colorado, 1884d-1888d. (Sellers 3)

WEHRMANN, HENRIETTA New Orleans, Louisiana, 1877d-1892d. See Henrietta Dittrich.

WEHRTE, S. Fountain, Wisconsin, 1857d.

WEIBEZAHN, CHARLES Pekin, Illinois, 1888d-1893d.

WEIBLE, J. Charleston, West Virginia. Percussion full-stock dated 1844.

WEIDERHOLD, CHARLES Bloom, Illinois, 1864d.

WEIDMAN, SOLOMON Lancaster, Pennsylvania, 1857d-1873d.

WEIDMANN, FELIX (?-1903), Mobile, Alabama, 1885d-1903.

WEIHOLD, HENRY (1830-1903), Greenville, Ohio, 1872-1896d. (Hutslar)

WEIKER, ADAM Bucks Co., Pennsylvania. Son of George Weiker.

WEIKER, GEORGE (1769-1853), Northhampton Co., Pennsylvania, 1800t-1806t, Bucks Co., Pennsylvania, 1806-1838, Wayne Co., Ohio, 1839-1853. Flintlock Kentucky. (Kindig, Whisker III)

WEIKUSAT, AUGUSTUS Kutztown, Pennsylvania, 1882d-1887d.

WEILERT, AUGUST Rochester, New York, 1866-1867d. (Eich)

WEIMAN, HENRY Lancaster Co., Pennsylvania, 1850. Barrelmaker. (KRA IV-4)

WEINBERGER, JOHN L. Johnstown, Pennsylvania, 1861d.

WEINBERGER, LEONARD Johnstown, Pennsylvania, 1876-1877. (Kauffman)

WEINBRECHT, WILHELM St. Louis, Missouri, 1864-1866d.

WEINER, A.G. St. Louis, Missouri, 1898d.

WEINRICK, WILLIAM (1800-?), Richland Co., Ohio, 1838-1850c, Perrysville, Ohio, 1860d-1864d. (Hutslar)

WEINSCHENK, LOUIS Chicago, Illinois, 1886d.

WEIR, FRED S. Monmouth, Illinois. (Johnson)

WEIRICK, WILLIAM Penns Creek, Pennsylvania. Flintlock Kentucky rifles. (Gabel)

WEIS, CHARLES (1831-1900), St. Mary's, Pennsylvania, 1882d-1890d. Cartridge guns. (Whisker II)

WEISBART, WILLIAM Houston, Texas, 1866d-1890d.

WEISER, B. unlocated. Flintlock Kentucky.

WEISER, G.W. Allentown, Pennsylvania, 1835-1839. Flintlock Kentucky.

WEISER, P. Delphi, Indiana, 1862d.

WEISER, PHILLIP Delaware, Ohio, 1853-1860. Percussion guns. Also spelled Wiser. (Hutslar)

WEISGERBER, A. Memphis, Tennessee, 1866-1870. Percussion 1/2 stock and derringer.

WEISHEIT, EDWARD A. New Haven, Connecticut. Patent #617,943 January 17, 1899, extractor.

WEISS, CHARLES Plainfield, Pennsylvania, 1828-1835t. (KRA II-3)

WEISS, ERNEST Carlinville, Illinois, 1867d-1886d.

WEISS, F. Port Jervis, New York. Percussion over/under. (Clow)

WEISS, GUSTAV Griggsville, Illinois, 1860d-1886d. (Name changed to Wise, 1880). Percussion fullstock.

WEISS, S. Port Jervis, New York. Percussion 1/2 stock. (MB 2-63)

WEISS, WILLIAM New Orleans, Louisiana, 1874d-1876d.

WEISS, WILLIAM Richmond, Virginia, 1804-1807, Lancaster, Pennsylvania, 1808-1821. At Virginia Manufactory, 1804-1807. (Kauffman, Cromwell)

WEISSERT, ANDREW (1809-?), Ohio, 1848, Sacramento, California, 1852c. (Shelton)

WEISTER, L. Bucks Co., Pennsylvania. Flintlock Kentucky. (MB 2-65)

WELBER, JESSE South Olive, Ohio, 1864d. Percussion 1/2 stock. (Hutslar)

WELCH & SON Santa Rosa, California, 1859. (Shelton)

WELCH, BROWN & CO. Norfolk, Connecticut, 1861-1865. Model 1861 contract rifles with "Norfolk" marking. William W. Welch and P. Brown. (Fuller, Carey)

WELCH, JAMES Philadelphia, Pennsylvania, 1779-1783. Flintlock pistols. (Gluckman & Satterlee)

WELCH, JOHN Cuero, Texas, 1878d-1892d.

WELCH, WILLIAM East Canaan, New Hampshire, 1873-1886. Percussion 1/2 stock.

WELCH, WILLIAM W. Norfolk, Connecticut, 1861-1865. Model 1861 contract muskets with "Norfolk" marking. With P. Brown as Welch, Brown & Co. (Fuller, Carey)

WELDAN, BENJAMIN Cass Co., Missouri, 1850c. (MB 11-66)

WELDON, ROBIN Mansfield, Ohio, 1812-1820c. (Knittle)

WELDY, D. (1809-1873), West Charleston, Ohio, 1829-1873. Percussion fullstock. (Hutslar)

WELLER, GEORGE W. Lewis Co., Missouri, 1850c. (MB 11-66)

WELLER, JESSE South Oliver, Ohio, 1860c.

WELLERDING, THEODORE Evansville, Indiana, 1882-1885. (Gardner)

WELLES, JOHN C. Milwaukee, Wisconsin, 1855-1910. Patent #177,905 May 23, 1876, breechloading firearm. As Wells & Hale, 1858-1870. (MB 5-49)

WELLINGTON, S.L. (1826-?), Portage Co., Ohio, 1850c. (Hutslar)

WELLS & HALE Milwaukee, Wisconsin, 1858-1870. Percussion double rifle. John C. Wells. (WGCA 4)

WELLS, C. Evansville, Indiana. Percussion fullstock. (Lindert)

WELLS, CHARLES S. New Haven, Connecticut. Patent #133,732 December 10, 1872, revolver.

WELLS, G.W. Oregon, Missouri, 1860d. Percussion fullstock.

WELLS, GEORGE L. Starksboro, Vermont, 1875-1885. (Horn)

WELLS, J.S. Virginia, 1776. Committee of Safety muskets and repairs. (Gill)

WELLS, JAMES H. (1826-?), Jennings Co., Indiana, 1850c. (Lindert)

WELLS, JOHN Providence, Rhode Island, 1777. (Achtermeir)

WELLS, JOHN C. Hartford, Connecticut, 1848-1850.

WELLS, JOHN C. Milwaukee, Wisconsin, 1858-1876. As Wells & Hale, 1858-1870.

WELLS, JOHN C. North Bridgeton, Maine, 1891. (Demeritt)

WELLS, JOHN H. Brooklyn, New York. Patent #33,867 December 24, 1861, automatic primer.

WELLS, JOHN H. Charlottesville, Virginia, 1869-1873d, Staunton, Virginia, 1840. (Dillin)

WELLS, LEMUEL Astoria, New York. Patent #18,217 September 15, 1857, bullet.

WELLS, LEWIS (1829-?), Dayton, Ohio, 1850c. (Hutslar)

WELLS, M.K. Cleveland, Ohio.

WELLS, RICHARD Philadelphia, Pennsylvania, 1780-1790. Committee of Safety muskets with Peter DeHaven. (Gardner)

WELLS, W., & BRO. Madison, Indiana. Percussion lock.

WELLS, WILLIAM R. Seneca, Kansas 1882d.

WELNER, HENRY Washington, D.C., 1855d. (Hartzler)

WELSAFER, JOSEPH (1810-?), Erie Co., Ohio, 1850c. (Hutslar)

WELSCHANTZ, ABRAHAM York, Pennsylvania, 1779-1782. (Kindig)

WELSH, O. (1826-?), Findlay, Ohio, 1850c. (Hutslar)

WELSHANTZ, CONRAD York, Pennsylvania, 1783t-1804. Model 1798 contract muskets for Pennsylvania with Jacob Leather. Model 1801 contract for Pennsylvania with Jacob Doll and Henry Pickel. With Jacob Leather as Leather & Co. (Gluckman)

WELSHANTZ, DAVID York Co., Pennsylvania, 1780-1783. (Kauffman)

WELSHANTZ, GEORGE Milton, Pennsylvania, 1826-1832. (Kauffman)

WELSHANTZ, JACOB York, Pennsylvania, 1777-1807. Arms for state of Pennsylvania, 1777-1780. (Kauffman)

WELSHANTZ, JACOB, JR. Harrisburg, Pennsylvania, 1807-1811, York, Pennsylvania, 1825-1831. Son of Jacob Welshantz. (Kindig)

WELSHANTZ, JOSEPH York, Pennsylvania, 1753-1800. There were two gunsmiths with this name, 1781-1783, father and son. (Kindig)

WELSHOFER, JOHN GEORGE Toledo, Ohio, 1868d. Percussion 1/2 stock. (Hutslar)

WELTON, ARD Waterbury, Connecticut, 1773-1801. Model 1798 contract muskets. (Gluckman)

WELTY, LOUIS Nickerson, Kansas, 1894d.

WELZHOFER, JOSEPH G. Buffalo, New York, 1842-1848. (Dean)

WENGER, FREDERICK Beatrice, Nebraska, 1872d.

WENTZEL, DANIEL Hereford, Pennsylvania, 1861d.

WENTZEL, W.H. Frederick, Maryland, 1850.

WENZEL, HERMAN Allegheny, Pennsylvania, 1872d-1882d.

WENZEL, HIRAM Allegheny, Pennsylvania, 1878-1879. (Kauffman)

WENZELL, J.H. Smithfield, Pennsylvania, 1870-1871. (Kauffman)

WERGER, CHRISTIAN Lancaster Co., Pennsylvania, 1776. Committee of Safety muskets.

WERKER, EBERT (1815-?), St. Louis, Missouri, 1850c. (Lewis)

WERNER see Schaefer & Werner.

WERNER & NAEHER Orange, New Jersey, 1866d. Charles F. Werner.

WERNER, C.L. Allegheny, Pennsylvania, 1874. (Kauffman)

WERNER, CHARLES F. Orange, New Jersey, 1866d-1870. As Werner & Naeher, 1866.

WERNER, CHARLES L. Rochester, New York, 1855d-1876d. Percussion target rifles and air gun. With his brother Otto, 1870-1871. (Eich)

WERNER, DANIEL St. Louis, Missouri. Patent #82,908 October 6, 1868, knife pistol. (Frost)

WERNER, GEORGE Lancaster, Pennsylvania, 1884d. Percussion pistol. Listed as George Warner, 1857d-1873d. See George Warner.

WERNER, GEORGE W. Lancaster, Pennsylvania. Patent #468,853 February 16, 1892, lock.

WERNER, J.G. Lancaster, Pennsylvania, 1880d-1882d.

WERNER, J.G. York, Pennsylvania, 1850. Percussion double rifle. (GR 6-58)

WERNER, J.H.T. Washington, D.C., 1846d. (Hartzler)

WERNER, JOHN J. Lancaster, Pennsylvania, 1863. With Frederick Koenig as Koenig & Werner.

WERNER, OTTO F. Kansas City, Missouri, 1889d.

WERNER, OTTO F. Rochester, New York, 1859d-1877d, Syracuse, New York, 1878-1880. Percussion guns, rim fire pistols, and revolving air guns. (Eich)

WERTHON, H. St. Louis, Missouri, 1853. Submitted muskets to Ordnance Department.

WERTSNER, C.S. Baltimore, Maryland, 1883-1888d. As Wertsner & Morris, 1885-1888. (Hartzler)

WERTZ, PETER Salem, Ohio, 1811. (Knittle)

WESCOTT, C.A. Marshalltown, Iowa, 1865d-1897d. See C.A. Westcott, and Martin & Westcott.

WESK, JOHN Baltimore, Maryland. Patent #146,445 January 13, 1874, breechloading firearm with Francis Fuss.

WESLE, NORBERT (1815-1898), Milwaukee, Wisconsin, 1854d-1881d. Percussion guns. Wesle's sons, Herman, (1874d) and August, (1879d), were both listed as gunsmiths working for him. (WGCA 6)

WESSELL, WILLIAM Concordia, Missouri, 1899d.

WESSELLS, IRVING Burlington, New Jersey, 1893d-1898d.

WESSELY see Von Wessely.

WESSON & HARRINGTON Worcester, Massachusetts, 1869-1874. Single shot pistols, 1869-1870. Frank Wesson and Nathan Harrington, 1869-1871. Gilbert Harrington inherited his uncle's part of the business in 1871. Succeeded by Harrington & Richardson in 1874.

WESSON & KING Grafton, Massachusetts. Percussion target rifles, Edwin Wesson.

WESSON & PRESCOTT Northboro, Massachusetts, 1840-1842. Edwin Wesson and Edwin Prescott. Percussion target gun.

WESSON & WARNER Hartford, Connecticut, 1850. Percussion rifles and revolvers in administration of the estate of Edwin Wesson. D.B. Wesson and Thomas Warner. (Sellers 1)

WESSON FIREARMS CO. Springfield, Massachusetts, 1867-1871. Breechloading shotguns under Daniel Wesson's patents. A subsidiary of Smith & Wesson. (Jinks)

WESSON, DANIEL BAIRD (1825-1906), Hartford, Connecticut,1848-1850, Norwich, Connecticut, 1854-1855, New Haven, Connecticut, 1855-1856, Springfield, Massachusetts, 1856-1906. Percussion rifles and revolvers as administrator of Edwin Wesson's estate; Volcanic pistols and rifles in Norwich and New Haven; revolvers and shotguns in Springfield. Patent #10,535 February 14, 1854, volcanic pistol with Horace Smith, #11,496 August 8, 1854, volcanic cartridge with Horace Smith, #14,147 January 22, 1856, cartridge with Horace Smith, #24,666 July 5, 1859, revolver with Horace Smith, #30,990 December 18, 1860, revolver with Horace Smith, #38,921 June 16, 1863, revolver with Horace Smith, #51,092 November 21, 1865, revolver with Horace Smith, #72,434 December 17, 1867, double barrel shotgun, #72,949 December 31, 1867, double barrel shotgun with John K. Blaze, #78,847 June 9, 1868, double barrel shotgun, #114,374 May 2, 1871, double barrel shotgun, #128,991 July 16, 1872, revolver with Charles King, #136,348 February 25, 1873, revolver, #158,874 January 19, 1875, revolver, #163,036 May 11, 1875, revolver, #186,509 January 23, 1877, revolver, #187,689 February 20, 1877, revolver with James Bullard, #198,228 December 18, 1877, revolver with James Bullard, #202,388 April 16, 1878, revolver with James Bullard, #217,562 July 15, 1879, magazine gun, #222,167 December 2, 1879, revolver, #222,168 December 2, 1879, revolver, #227,009 May 25, 1880, revolver, #284,786 September 11, 1883, revolver, #285,862 October 2, 1883, revolver, #289,875 December 11, 1883, grip safety, #323,837 August 4, 1885, revolver with Joseph Wesson, #323,838 August 4, 1885, grip safety, #323,839 August 4, 1885, grip safety, #323,873 August 4, 1885, grip safety with John S. Landers, #356,387 January 18, 1887, revolver, #360,263 March 29, 1887, revolver, #361,100 April 12, 1887, revolver, #361,101 April 12, 1887, revolver, #371,532 October 11, 1887, revolver, #377,877 February 14, 1888, revolver, #377,878 February 14, 1888, revolver, #401,087 April 9, 1889, revolver, #421,798 February 18, 1890, revolver, #429,397 June 3, 1890, revolver, #517,152 March 27, 1894, revolver, #520,468 May 29, 1894, revolver, #539,497 May 21, 1895, revolver with Joseph Wesson, #542,744 July 16, 1895, revolver, #542,745 July 16, 1895, revolver, #565,245 August 4, 1896, revolver with Joseph Wesson, #573,736 December 22, 1896, revolver with Joseph Wesson, #611,826 October 4, 1898, revolver with Joseph Wesson, #615,117 November 29, 1898, revolver, #682,397 September 10, 1901, revolver, #684,150 October 8, 1901, revolver, #684,331 October 8, 1901, revolver, #688,141 December 3, 1901, revolver, #689,260 December 17, 1901, revolver, #703,101 July 7, 1903, revolver, and #763,581 June 28, 1904, revolver. Brother of Edwin and Franklin Wesson. Co-founder of Smith & Wesson.

WESSON, EDWIN (?-1849), Grafton, Massachusetts, 1834-1840, Northboro, Massachusetts, 1840-1848, Hartford, Connecticut, 1848-1849. Patents #5,146 June 5, 1847, breechloading volley gun, and #6,669 August 28, 1849, revolver. Older brother of Daniel and Franklin Wesson. As Wesson & King in Grafton and Wesson & Prescott, 1840-1842. (Sellers-1, Jinks)

WESSON, FRANK (1826-?), Worcester, Massachusetts, 1854, 1869-1878d, Springfield, Massachusetts, 1855-1869. Civil War carbines, single shot cartridge pistols and rifles and revolvers. Patents #25,926 October 25, 1859, breechloading firearm with N.S. Harrington, #36,925 November 11, 1862, breechloading firearm, #84,976 December 15, 1868, revolver, #92,918 July 20, 1869, breechloading firearm, #103,694 May 31, 1870, breechloading firearm, #115,916 June 13, 1871, revolver, #125,640 April 9, 1872, breechloading firearm, and #193,060 July 10, 1877, breechloading firearm with C.N. Cutter. Brother of D.B. and Edwin Wesson. As Wesson & Harrington, 1869-1874.

WESSON, JOSEPH H. (?-1920), Springfield, Massachusetts. Patents #243,183 June 21, 1881, revolver, #251,750 January 3, 1882, revolver, #323,837 August 4, 1885, revolver with D.B. Wesson, #456,179 July 21, 1891, revolver, #539,497 May 21, 1895, revolver with D.B. Wesson, #565,245 August 4, 1896, revolver with D.B. Wesson, #573,736 December 22, 1896, revolver with D.B. Wesson, #611,826 October 4, 1898, revolver with D.B. Wesson, #635,705 October 24, 1899, revolver with J.L. Hobbs, #655,844 August 14, 1900, revolver, #702,607 June 17, 1902, revolver, #708,437 September 2, 1902, revolver, #743,784 November 10, 1903, revolver, #811,807 February 6, 1906, revolver, #818,721 April 24, 1906, revolver, #835,380 November 6, 1906, automatic with Harcourt Bull, #839,911 January 1, 1907, magazine gun, #897,806 September 1, 1908, revolver, #923,915 June 8, 1908, revolver, #961,188 June 14, 1910, revolver, #961,189 June 14, 1910, revolver, #978,092 December 6, 1910, automatic, #978,418 December 13, 1910, automatic, #1,181,417 May 2, 1916, automatic, and #1,290,855 January 7, 1919, automatic. Son of D.B. Wesson. (Jinks)

WESSON, STEVENS & MILLER Hartford, Connecticut, 1848. Percussion revolvers. (Sellers 1)

WEST BROS. Brooklyn, New York, 1874d-1875d.

WEST BROS. Napa, California, 1875d-1880d. James and William West (Shelton)

WEST, ALLEN W. Chillicothe, Ohio, 1858-1900d. (Hutslar)

WEST, B.B. Hartford, Connecticut, 1847d-1850.

WEST, B.F. Dardanelle, Arkansas, 1898d.

WEST, D.S. Auburn, Maine, 1894. (Demeritt)

WEST, DERRICK S. Great Falls, Montana. Patents #426,887 April 29, 1890, sight, #478,727 July 12, 1892, magazine gun, #478,728 July 29, 1892, magazine gun, and #478,729 July 12, 1892, magazine gun.

WEST, EDWARD King George Co., Virginia, 1761, Stafford Co., Virginia, 1770. (Gill)

WEST, EDWARD New Liberty, Kentucky, 1800-1820c. Patent #none July 6, 1802, lock.

WEST, FREDERICK H. Atlantic City, New Jersey, 1886d.

WEST, JAMES Napa, California, 1875d-1880d. With William West as West Bros. (Shelton)

WEST, JOHN Daviess Co., Missouri, 1850c. (MB 11-66)

WEST, JONATHAN Washington Co., Pennsylvania, 1809-1811. (Whisker II)

WEST, ROBERT Daviess Co., Missouri, 1850c. (MB 11-66)

WEST, SAMUEL Washington Co., Pennsylvania, 1807-1830. (Whisker II)

WEST, STEPHEN Woodward, Maryland, 1777-1783. Repaired public arms. (Hartzler)

WEST, W.B. (1790-1860), Lenoir Co., North Carolina. (Bivins)

WEST, W.F. Grass Valley, California, 1878-1888d. (Shelton)

WEST, WILLIAM (1850-1824), Napa, California, 1875-1924. With James West as West Bros., 1875-1880. (Shelton)

WEST, WILLIAM Millsboro, Pennsylvania, 1813-1818. (Whisker II)

WEST, WILLIAM I. Chillicothe, Ohio, 1888-1891d. (Hutslar)

WESTBERTH, WILLIAM Houston, Texas, 1878d.

WESTCOTT, C.A. Atlantic, Iowa, 1882d, Marshallton, Iowa, 1884d-1897d. As Martin & Westcott, 1867. See C.A. Wescott.

WESTERBROOK, W.H. Gainesville, Missouri, 1881d.

WESTERHOOD, BERNARD H. Philadelphia, Pennsylvania. Patent #15,397 July 22, 1856, trigger protection.

WESTERN ARMS & CARTRIDGE CO. Chicago, Illinois, 1888d. A.G. Spalding and C.E. Willard. Made cartridges, but only sold guns.

WESTERN ARMS CO. Chicago, Illinois, 1864d. "John Spencer, Arms Manufacturer" marking.

WESTERN ARMS CO. New York and Chicago. Bacon cartridge revolvers.

WESTERN ARMS CO. New York and Chicago. Trade name on .22 cal. single shot rifle.

WESTERN ARMS CO. New York and Chicago. Trade name on Baby Hammerless.

WESTERN ARMS CO. New York and Chicago. Trade name used on Marston percussion revolvers.

WESTERN FIELD trade name of Montgomery Ward & Co.

WESTERN GUN WORKS Chicago, Illinois, 1877d. Tramp's Terror suicide special. (Webster)

WESTERN LONG RANGE trade name of Montgomery Ward on shotguns. (Hinman)

WESTERVELT, PETER B. New York, New York, 1850c.

WESTHOFF, CHARLES (1839-?), San Francisco, California, 1870c. For Will & Finck. (Shelton)

WESTLAKE, PETER Iron Ridge, Wisconsin, 1857d.

WESTON & ULLERY Greenfield, Ohio, 1840-1852. Locks only. (Hutslar)

WESTON, A.G. Unadella, Michigan, 1883d.

WESTON, J.J. trade name on Crescent Fire Arms Co. shotgun.

WESTPHALL, CHARLES Philadelphia, Pennsylvania. Model 1808 contract muskets with Frederick Goetz. (Gluckman)

WETHERBEE, JOSEPH (1725-1809), Harvard, Massachusetts, 1755-1809. Committee of Safety muskets. (GR 10-71)

WETHERILL, SILAS Ft. Madison, Iowa, 1887d.

WETMORE, W.W. Lebanon, New Hampshire, 1870-?, Windsor, Vermont, ?-1895. Percussion target rifles. (Roberts)

WETMORE, WILLIAM W. New Haven, Connecticut. Patents #190,264 May 1, 1877, magazine gun with Thomas G. Bennett, #206,202 July 23, 1878, magazine gun, #213,538 March 25, 1879, magazine gun, #219,886 September 23, 1879, magazine gun, #220,734 October 21, 1879, magazine gun with Joseph L. Sweeney, #223,409 January 6, 1880, magazine gun with Joseph L. Sweeney, #229,662 January 20, 1880, magazine gun, #224,336 February 10, 1880, magazine gun with Thomas G. Bennett, #310,103 December 30, 1884, magazine gun, #338,898 March 30, 1886, sight, and #548,410 October 22, 1895, magazine gun. For Winchester as a designer.

WETS, CHARLES St. Mary's, Pennsylvania, 1882d-1890d.

WETTENSTEIN, I. Chicago, Illinois, 1866d. Percussion double rifle. Probably John Wettstein.

WETTSTEIN & KAMPMANN Chicago, Illinois, 1859d. John Wettstein and Henry Kampmann.

WETTSTEIN, JOHN Chicago, Illinois, 1859d. As Wettstein & Kampmann.

WETZEL, ANDREW Plainfield, Pennsylvania, 1800-1810t. (KRA II-3)

WETZEL, DANIEL Hereford, Pennsylvania, 1860d-1861d.

WETZEL, HENRY Union Co., Pennsylvania, 1850c. Barrelmaker. (Kauffman)

WETZEL, JOHN Macungie, Pennsylvania, 1781t-1788t. (KRA II-3)

WETZEL, JOHN Sheimersville, Pennsylvania, 1860d-1861d.

WETZEL, JOHN HENRY Snyder Co., Pennsylvania. Percussion Kentucky rifles. (Gabel)

WETZEL, JONATHAN Snyder Co., Pennsylvania. Flintlock and percussion Kentucky rifles. (Gabel)

WETZEL, LUDWIG Norfolk, Nebraska, 1886d-1893d. Percussion fullstock.

WEYERMAN, I. Ottawa, Minnesota, 1863-1867d.

WEYERMAN, ISAAC Mt. Eaton, Ohio, 1859d. (Hutslar)

WEYMOUTH, JOHN H. (1845-?), Randolph Co., West Virginia, 1870c. (Whisker IV)

WHAIL, WILLIAM Boston, Massachusetts, 1813-1819. (Lindsay)

WHALEN, JAMES A. Brooklyn, New York. Patent #35,052 April 22, 1862, revolver.

WHALL, WILLIAM Philadelphia, Pennsylvania, 1793.

WHARTON, JAMES C. Richmond, Virginia, 1871d.

WHARTON, JOSEPH Roseburg, Oregon, 1889d-1899d.

WHEAT, THOMPSON Palmetto, Georgia, 1885d.

WHEATLY, HENRY Washington Co., Pennsylvania, 1850.

WHEATLY, MICHAEL Virginia, 1776. Repairs. (Gill)

WHEELDON, JAMES Pomeroy, Ohio, ?-1940. Percussion 1/2 stock. (Hutslar)

WHEELER & BRANT Stevensburg, Virginia. Model 1798 contract muskets. George Wheeler and John Brant.

WHEELER & LAWRENCE Farmington, Maine. A.G. Wheeler and William Lawrence. (Demeritt)

WHEELER & MORRISON Stevensburg, Virginia, 1810-1814. Model 1808 contract muskets. George Wheeler and Caleb Morrison. (Gluckman)

WHEELER & STEVENS Farmington, Maine, 1872. Albert Gallitin Wheeler and George A. Stevens. (Demeritt)

WHEELER, A.J. Newville, California, 1893d.

WHEELER, A.W. New Orleans, Louisiana, 1877d.

WHEELER, ALBERT GALLITIN (1816-1883), Farmington, Maine, 1858-1883. As Wheeler & Stevens, 1872, A.G. Wheeler & Son, 1872-1873, Wheeler & Lawrence, 1858-1860, and A.G. Wheeler & Co., 1883. Percussion 1/2 stock and percussion fowler. (Demeritt)

WHEELER, ARTEMAS (1781-1845), Concord, Massachusetts, 1802-1821. Patents #none June 10, 1818, revolving rifle, and #none February 19, 1819, barrels. Flintlock revolving rifles which were developed as the Collier revolvers. (GR 4-78)

WHEELER, C. McPherson, Kansas, 1884d.

WHEELER, C. Mentor, Michigan, 1883d.

WHEELER, CHARLES Webb City, Missouri, 1893d.

WHEELER, CHARLES E. (1847-1916), Farmington, Maine, 1871-1916. Percussion and cartridge guns. Son of Albert Wheeler. (Demeritt)

WHEELER, E.G. Pleasant Hill, Missouri, 1891d.

WHEELER, F.G. New York, New York. Agent for Sharps pistols and Hankins revolvers. (Sellers-1)

WHEELER, G. Woolworth, Tennessee, 1887d-1891d.

WHEELER, GEORGE (?-1809), Stevensburg, Virginia, 1787-1809. Model 1798 contract muskets with Patrick Home in 1799, and John Brant in 1800. Model 1808 contract muskets with Caleb Morrison in 1808. (Gluckman)

WHEELER, H.G. Port Sanilac, Michigan, 1863d.

WHEELER, HENRY F. Boston, Massachusetts. Patents #46,286 February 7, 1865, magazine gun, #50,760 October 31, 1865, breechloading firearm, #55,752 June 19, 1866, breechloading firearm, #66,110 June 25, 1867, magazine gun, #196,749 November 6, 1877, breechloading firearm with George H. Fox, #422,930 March 11, 1890, revolver with George H. Fox, #430,243 June 17, 1890, revolver, #458,687 September 1, 1891, revolver (Peterborough, New Hampshire), and #546,369, September 17, 1895, magazine pistol. Guns made by American Arms Co. (AR 4-70)

WHEELER, HIRAM (1807-?), Richiand Co., Ohio, 1836-1850c. (Hutslar)

WHEELER, J.P. Kansas City, Missouri, 1859d.

WHEELER, JOEL B. Etna, Maine, 1877, Greenfield, Maine, 1878-1879. Percussion target rifle. (Demeritt)

WHEELER, JOHN H. Otego, New York, 1867-1882d.

WHEELER, M.W. Milan, Tennessee, 1885d.

WHEELER, MARSHAL Creston, Iowa. Patent #329,793 November 3, 1885, breechloading firearm.

WHEELER, S.A. Waterville, Maine, 1874-1883. As S.A. Wheeler & Son, 1877-1883. (Demeritt)

WHEELOCK & AMES Portland, Maine, 1832. (Demeritt)

WHEELOCK & DAWLEY Montpelier, Vermont, 1889d. Herbert Wheelock and Frank Dawley.

WHEELOCK & STEWART Montpelier, Vermont, 1880d. Underhammer pistol.

WHEELOCK, HERBERT R. Montpelier, Vermont, 1880d-1889d. As Wheelock & Stewart, 1880. As Wheelock & Dawley, 1889.

WHEELOCK, LUKE Hartford, Connecticut, 1855-1865, New Haven, Connecticut, 1866-1878. Patents #70,141 October 22, 1867, breechloading firearm, #84,598, December 1, 1868, magazine gun, and #111,500, January 31, 1871, magazine gun. Made the first Spencer carbines. For Winchester.

WHEELOCK, THOMAS PRENTISS Worcester, Massachusetts. Brother-in-law and partner of Ethan Allen. (Mouillesseaux)

WHETCROFT, WILLIAM (1735-1799), Annapolis, Maryland, 1775-1781. Committee of Safety muskets. (Hartzler)

WHETMORE, W.W. see W.W. Wetmore.

WHETSTONE, DAVID (1780-?), Washington Co., Maryland, 1796-1802, Bedford Co., Pennsylvania, 1802-1825. Flintlock Kentucky. Apprenticed to John Gonter, 1796. (Hartzler)

WHETSTONE, JOHN (1779-?), Cumberland Co., Pennsylvania, 1804t-1805, Martinsburg, Virginia, 1806-1824. Flintlock Kentucky. (Bowers)

WHIDDON, OLIVER Maryland, 1776-1777. Committee of Safety muskets. (Hartzler)

WHILDEN, CHARLES, E. Charlestown, South Carolina. Patent #580,538 April 13, 1897, breechloading firearm.

WHIPPET trade name of Hibbard, Spencer, Bartlett & Co. on shotguns by Crescent Fire Arms Co. (Hinman)

WHIPPLE see Rawson & Whipple.

WHIPPLE, J.B. Westford, Vermont, 1875d-1879.

WHIPPLE, THEODORE S. Cambridge, Vermont, 1864-1869. Percussion target rifles. (Horn)

WHIRLEY Lancaster Co., Pennsylvania, 1850. (KRA IV-4)

WHISNANT, J.O. Sunshine, North Carolina. Percussion guns. (Bivins)

WHISNANT, M.A. Sunshine, North Carolina, Percussion guns. (Bivins)

WHISNANT, W.O. Johnson, North Carolina, 1877d, Shelby, North Carolina, 1884d-1890d.

WHISTLER suicide special by Hood.

WHISTON, EPHREM New York, New York, 1820d. (Kauffman 2)

WHIT, J.R. Seneca Co., Ohio, 1812. (Knittle)

WHITCOMB & SOLOMON Alton, Illinois, 1842.

WHITCOMB, B. Stillwater, New York. Percussion target rifle.

WHITCOMB, HENRY Adams, New York. Patent #none November 24, 1826, lock.

WHITCOMB, JAMES O. New York, New York. Patent #38,350 April 28, 1863, magazine battery.

WHITCOMB, S.M. Albany, Illinois 1860d.

WHITE & JAMES Sedalia, Missouri, 1889d.

WHITE & MARIN Savannah, Georgia, 1885d.

WHITE ARMS CO. Lowell, Massachusetts. Copies of S & W revolver Models 1, 2, and 3.

WHITE JACKET suicide special. (Webster)

WHITE MAGAZINE RIFLE CO. Alexandria, Virginia, 1891-1892. Promotional agent for H.K. White's automatic rifle.

WHITE POWDER WONDER trade name of Sears Roebuck & Co. on shotguns made by Meriden. (AG 4-75)

WHITE STAR suicide special. (Webster)

WHITE, A.R. Leonidas, Michigan, 1867d.

WHITE, ABNER G. Brattleboro, Vermont, 1875-1887. Successor to L. Barrett. (Horn)

WHITE, ALBERT M. Port Chester, New York. Patent #47,350 April 18, 1865, breechloading firearm.

WHITE, BENJAMIN West Las Animas, Colorado, 1879d-1882d. (Sellers-3)

WHITE, D.J. Carbondale, Illinois, 1867d-1890d.

WHITE, DAVID Virginia, 1776. Committee of Safety repairs. (Gill)

WHITE, E.B. Independence, Kansas, 1878d-1894d. Underhammer pepperbox.

WHITE, E.D. unlocated. Percussion 1/2 stock.

WHITE, EPHRAIM R. (1843-1933), Waldoboro, Maine, 1860-1900. Percussion pistols and rifles. (Demeritt)

WHITE, F.W. unlocated. Percussion fullstock.

WHITE, FRANK W., JR. Norwich, Connecticut. Patent #532,931(date unknown), breechloading firearm.

WHITE, G.S. Greenwich, New York, 1861-1864.

WHITE, GEORGE W. New York, New York. Patents #34,325 February 4, 1862, breechloading firearm, and #37,369 January 6, 1863, breechloading firearm.

WHITE, HARRY K. Annapolis, Maryland. Patent #488,409 December 20, 1892, magazine gun.

WHITE, HIRAM W. (1818-?), Jackson, Ohio, 1850-1853d, Olney, Illinois, 1864d-1873, Yankton, Dakota Territory/South Dakota, 1877-1898d. Percussion 1/2 stock. Patent #247,451 September 20, 1881, stock.

WHITE, HORACE Springfield, Massachusetts, 1775-1776. Committee of Safety repairs. (Gluckman & Satterlee)

WHITE, J.A. Jackson, Ohio, 1854-1858. Percussion 1/2 stock. (Knittle)

WHITE, J.D. Williamstown, Vermont, circa 1850. Underhammer pistols, percussion 1/2 stock. (Horn)

WHITE, J.G. Midland, Texas, 1892d.

WHITE, J.H. Greenville, New York, 1870d.

WHITE, J.O.M. Dodge City, Kansas, 1888d, Salida, Colorado, 1890d.

WHITE, J.W. Hebron, Connecticut. Model 1812 flintlock musket.

WHITE, JAMES Harrison, Ohio, 1880-1890d. (Hutslar)

WHITE, JAMES Pittsburgh, Pennsylvania, 1816. (Bowers)

WHITE, JAMES D. (1814-?), Jamestown, North Carolina, 1850c. (Bivins)

WHITE, JESSE New Philadelphia, Ohio, 1878d. (John White in Knittle) (Hutslar)

WHITE, JOB Lancaster Co., Pennsylvania, 1848-1850. (KRA IV-4)

WHITE, JOEL Sutton, Massachusetts, 1810. Flintlock New England rifle.

WHITE, JOHN New Lisbon, Ohio, 1816-1829, Uniontown, Pennsylvania, 1829-1843, Pittsburgh, Pennsylvania, 1844-1859, Rochester, Pennsylvania, 1859-1861d, Pittsburgh, Pennsylvania, 1861-1867. David Minesinger's patent rifles. Flintlock Kentucky dated 1826. Partner of John Small in Ohio. Son of Peter White. (Kauffman, Hutslar, GR 8-57)

WHITE, JOHN Virginia, 1780. State arms repairs. (Gill)

WHITE, JOHN F. Gallatin, Tennessee, 1887d-1891d.

WHITE, JOHN N. New Haven, Connecticut. Patents #24,726 July 12, 1859, revolver, and #39,318 July 21, 1863, revolver. Both patents with Willard Ellis. Revolvers made by Plant's Mfg. Co. Southington, Connecticut.

WHITE, JOHN R. Reading, Pennsylvania, 1861d. Barrelmaker.

WHITE, JOHN, JR. Citronville, Alabama. All brass percussion pistol. Confederate patent #54 December 7, 1861, breechloading firearm. (Albaugh 3)

WHITE, JOSEPH J. Savannah, Georgia, 1879d-1881d. Joseph R. in 1881 directory.

WHITE, JOSEPH P. Richmond, Virginia, 1861, Savannah, Georgia, 1878-1881d. Patent #210,282 November 26, 1878, spade bayonet.

WHITE, L.B. Plymouth, Indiana, 1860d. Percussion 1/2 stock and underhammer.

WHITE, LEROY S. Waterbury, Connecticut. Patent #37,376 January 6, 1863, breechloading firearm.

WHITE, LEVI Allegheny, Pennsylvania, 1850. (Kauffman)

WHITE, MATTHEW B. Manchester, New Hampshire. Patent #193,061 July 10, 1877, sight.

WHITE, NICHOLAS Fredericktown, Maryland, 1775-1788 and 1797-1807, Berkeley Co., Virginia, 1788-?. Committee of Safety muskets. Model 1798 contract muskets with Thomas Crabb, Jacob Metzger and Christopher Barnhizle. (Hartzler)

WHITE, NOBLE Hamilton, New York. Patent # none May 5, 1828, double shot rifle with Cyrus Mosher.

WHITE, PETER (1777-1834), Bedford Co., Pennsylvania, 1806-1819, Uniontown, Pennsylvania, 1819-1834. Flintlock Kentucky. (Hartzler)

WHITE, PETER Annapolis, Maryland, 1778-1786. Flintlock rifles.

WHITE, R.A. Danville, Virginia, 1897d.

WHITE, ROBERT P. Ft. Wayne, Indiana, 1847. (Lindert)

WHITE, ROLLIN (1817-1892), Hartford, Connecticut, 1849-1857, Davenport, Iowa, 1857-1863, Lowell, Massachusetts, 1864-1892. Patents #12,528 March 13, 1855, breechloading firearm, #12,529 March 13, 1855, breechloading firearm, #12,638 April 3, 1855, breechloading firearm, #12,648 April 3, 1855, revolver, #12,649 April 3, 1855, revolver, #19,961 April 13, 1858, revolver, #33,805 November 26, 1861, cartridge, #45,290 November 29, 1864, revolver, #66,542 July 9, 1867, revolver, #93,572 August 10, 1869, revolver, #93,653 August 10, 1869, revolver, #99,505 February 1, 1870, revolver, #100,227 February 22, 1870, revolver, #119,633 July 4, 1876, revolver, #143,394 September 30, 1873, revolver, #162,208 April 20, 1875, revolver, #166,173 July 27, 1875, revolver, #179,084 June 20, 1876, revolver, and #179,633, July 4, 1876, revolver. Guns made by Smith & Wesson and Rollin White Arms Co.

WHITE, ROLLIN, ARMS CO. Lowell, Massachusetts, 1864-1869. Cartridge revolvers. (Jinks)

WHITE, S.M., JR. Sandusky, Ohio, 1882d. Dealer (Hutslar)

WHITE, SAMUEL Uniontown, Pennsylvania, 1828-1829t. (Bowers)

WHITE, SHATTUCK & CO. McDonough, New York, 1850c.

WHITE, W.C. Danville, Virginia, 1877d-1893d. As W.C. White & Bro., 1893.

WHITE, W.C. Williamsburgh, Kansas, 1884d.

WHITE, W.H. Brownville, Nebraska, 1884d-1886d.

WHITE, WILLIAM York, Wisconsin, 1857d.

WHITE, WILLIAM H Bem, Wisconsin, 1857d.

WHITE, WILLIAM HENRY Freeport, Ohio. Percussion fullstock. (AOLRC II-2)

WHITE, WILLIAM N. Portsmouth, Virginia, 1884d-1897d.

WHITE, Z.L., & SON Newberry, South Carolina, 1885d-1886d.

WHITEFORD, SAMUEL South Arm, Michigan, 1883d.

WHITEHEAD, MATHEW Pennsylvania, 1776. Repaired U.S. arms. (Gardner)

WHITEHEART, ALBERT (1817-?), Jamestown, North Carolina, 1850c. (Bivins)

WHITEHEART, C. (?-1829), Caswell Co., North Carolina, 1850c. (Bivins)

WHITELAW, HENRY W. San Francisco, California. Patent #449,988 April 7, 1891, breechloading firearm.

WHITESCARVER, CAMPBELL & CO. Rusk, Texas, 1861-1864. Mississippi rifles for the Confederacy. Succeeded by Whitescarver, Hughes & Co., 1866-1870. (Albaugh 1)

WHITESCARVER, HUGHES & CO. Rusk, Texas, 1866-1870. W.N. Hughes. (Holloway)

WHITESIDES, JOHN M. Abington, Virginia. Underhammer pistol. (Logan)

WHITING, A. New Orleans, Louisiana, 1825. Flintlock pistol. (Dean)

WHITING, E.D. Winona, Missouri, 1898d.

WHITING, JOHN Independence, Iowa, 1866-1868. (MB 1-46)

WHITMAN, BENJAMIN Stillwater, New York, 1859d-1874d.

WHITMAN, BYRON North Royalton, Wisconsin, 1857d.

WHITMAN, F.A. Macomb, Illinois, 1888d-1896d.

WHITMAN, HENRY Jamaica, Vermont, 1880-1881. (Horn)

WHITMAN, LORENZO F. Knoxville, Illinois, 1864d, Macomb, Illinois, 1867d-1884d.

WHITMORE & WOLFF Pittsburgh, Pennsylvania, 1837-1852. Lockmakers only. Christian Wolff. Succeeded by Whitmore, Wolff & Co.

WHITMORE, ANDREW E. Boston, Massachusetts, 1851d-1894d. Patents #117,843 August 8, 1871, breechloading firearm, #125,775 April 16, 1872, breechloading firearm, #153,509 July 28, 1874, breechloading firearm, #185,881 January 2, 1877, revolver, #238,821 March 15, 1881, breechloading firearm, #262,521 August 8, 1881, breechloading firearm, #266,245 October 17, 1882, lock, #282,941 August 7, 1883, breechloading firearm, #282,429 July 31, 1883, breechloading firearm with Joseph Tonks, #282,941 August 7, 1883, breechloading firearm, #386,174 July 17, 1888, breechloading firearm, and #433,262 July 29, 1890, breechloading firearm. Guns made by E. Remington & Sons, American Arms Co. (Boston), and Chicago Repeating Firearms Co.

WHITMORE, CHARLES New Boston, Illinois, 1890d-1893d.

WHITMORE, CHARLES Wapello, Iowa, 1887d.

WHITMORE, M.J. New York, New York. Percussion four-barrel swivelbreech.

WHITMORE, N. & N.G. Mansfield, Massachusetts, 1855-1881. Nathaniel and son, Nathaniel G. Whitmore.

WHITMORE, NATHAN (1805-1885), Potsdam, New York, ?-1885. Percussion target rifles. (Swinney)

WHITMORE, NATHANIEL (1770-?), Sutton, Massachusetts, 1808-1809, Mansfield, Massachusetts, 1828. Model 1808 contract muskets. With Elijah Waters and Asa Waters, Jr. as Waters & Whitmore. (MB 3-48)

WHITMORE, NATHANIEL (1804-1885), Boston, Massachusetts, 1850-1854, Mansfield, Massachusetts, 1855-1885. Son of Nathaniel (1770) Whitmore. For George Foster, 1824, and Alvan Clark, 1848, before opening his own shop. (MB 3-48)

WHITMORE, NATHANIEL GILBERT (1828-1917), Mansfield, Massachusetts, 1866-1882, Taunton, Massachusetts, 1882-1900, Eastondale, Massachusetts, 1900-1917. Patent #629,142 July 18, 1899, breechloading firearm. Son of Nathaniel (1804) Whitmore. Made President Grant's percussion 1/2 stock. (MB 3-48)

WHITMORE, WOLFF & CO. Pittsburgh, Pennsylvania, 1854-1858. Lockmakers only. Successors to Whitmore & Wolff.

WHITMORE, WOLFF, DUFF & CO. Pittsburgh, Pennsylvania, 1858-1872d. Lockmakers only. Christian Wolff and George J. Duff. Successors to Whitmore, Wolff & Co.

WHITNEY ARMORY, (WHITNEYVILLE ARMORY) New Haven, Connecticut, 1797-1888. Model 1798, 1812, 1822, 1861 contract muskets, Model 1841 and 1863 contract rifles, percussion revolvers, and many commercial arms. (Fuller)

WHITNEY ARMS CO. New Haven, Connecticut, 1863-1888. Same as Whitneyville Armory after incorporation on June 24, 1863. Purchased by Winchester, 1888. (Fuller)

WHITNEY BROS. Lewiston, Maine, 1887. F.R. and H.A. Whitney. (Demeritt)

WHITNEY SAFETY FIRE ARMS CO. Florence, Massachusetts, 1887-1894. Shotguns under William H. Whitney patents. (GR 4-67)

WHITNEY, A. Newburgh, New York, 1828. (Dean*)

WHITNEY, ARAD Fort Coyington, New York, 1870d.

WHITNEY, CHARLES Red Wing, Minnesota, 1870-1880d.

WHITNEY, CHARLES A. Fitchburg, Massachusetts, 1857-1861. Percussion fullstock.

WHITNEY, CORDIER & CO. Winchendon, Massachusetts, 1888d.

WHITNEY, ELI (1765-1825), New Haven, Connecticut, 1798-1825. Flintlock muskets under many U.S. and state contracts. Inventor of the cotton gin and one of the fathers of mass produced goods with component parts interchangeability. (Fuller)

WHITNEY, ELI, III (1847-?), New Haven, Connecticut, 1871-1888. With Whitney Arms Co. (Fuller)

WHITNEY, ELI, JR. (1820-?), New Haven, Connecticut, 1841-1888. Patents #11,447 August 1,1854, revolver, #44,991 November 8, 1864 breechloading firearm, #51,985 January 2, 1866, revolver, #59,110 October 23, 1866, percussion shotguns, #71,349 November 26, 1867, breechloading shotgun, #93,149 July 27, 1869, tip-up shotguns with Charles Gerner & F.W. Teising, #112,997 March 21, 1871, breechloading firearm, #115,258 May 23, 1871, revolver, #115,997 June 13, 1871, breechloading firearm, #124,994 March 26, 1872, breechloading firearm, #129,637 July 16, 1872, breechloading firearm with F.W. Teising, #137,989 April 15, 1873, sling swivel, #147,457 February 10, 1874, breechloading firearm, #151,458 May 26, 1874, breechloading firearm, #157,614 November 3, 1874, sling swivel, #191,734 March 9, 1875, breechloading firearm, #243,334 June 21, 1881, cartridge, #273,654 March 6, 1883, revolver, #354,757 December 21, 1886, magazine gun with W.C. Scharf, and #389,036 September 4, 1888, breechloading firearm. President of Whitney Armory, 1841-1888. (Fuller)

WHITNEY, F.R. Lewiston, Maine, 1885-1887. Reloading tools. As Whitney Bros., 1887. (Demeritt)

WHITNEY, G. Mexico, Ohio, 1859d. (Hutslar)

WHITNEY, HENRY (1822-?), Camden, Ohio, 1850c. (Hutslar)

WHITNEY, JAMES A. Maryland, New York. Patent #67,242 July 30, 1867, magazine gun.

WHITNEY, JAMES S. Lowell, Massachusetts. Patents #67,242 July 30, 1867, magazine gun, and #311,551 February 3, 1885, machine gun. Superintendent of Springfield Armory, 1854-1860.

WHITNEY, JOHN J. Independence, Iowa, 1867-1889d. Percussion 1/2 stock.

WHITNEY, JOHN M. (1810-?), Washington Co., Virginia, 1850c. (MB 10-63)

WHITNEY, WILLIAM E. Burlington, Vermont, 1875d-1894. (Horn)

WHITNEY, WILLIAM H. East Brookfield, Massachusetts. Patents #304,480 September 2, 1884, breechloading firearm, and #451,191, April 28, 1891, safety. Guns made by Whitney Safety Fire Arms Co.

WHITON BROS. & CO. suicide special by Iver Johnson.

WHITSON, GEORGE W. Ashville, North Carolina. Percussion 1/2 stock. (Bivins)

WHITTACKER, GEORGE Brooklyn, New York. Patent #187,244 February 13, 1877, revolver with William G. Ayres.

WHITTEMORE & ALT Salt Lake City, Utah, 1871d.

WHITTEMORE, AMOS Boston, Massachusetts, 1775-1797. Committee of Safety muskets and flintlock rifles. For Giles, Richards & Co., 1788-1797. (Gluckman & Satterlee)

WHITTEMORE, CALEB (1818-?), Peoria, Illinois, 1850c-1884d.

WHITTEMORE, D. Cambridge, Massachusetts, 1860. (Gluckman & Satterlee)

WHITTEMORE, JAMES M. Augusta, Maine. Patents #104,387 June 14, 1870, breechloading firearm, #131,487 September 17, 1872, breechloading firearm, #131,921 October 1, 1872, breechloading firearm. Bridesburg, Pennsylvania patent #201,970 April 2, 1878, breechloading firearm. Washington, D.C., patents, #572,919 December 8, 1896, magazine gun, #594,716 November 30, 1897, breechloading firearm, and #607,313 July 12, 1898, breechloading firearm. Submitted altered muskets in 1867 while he was at Watervliet Arsenal. (Demeritt)

WHITTEMORE, THOMAS J. Cambridge, Massachusetts, 1848d. Percussion 1/2 stock.

WHITTEMORE, THOMAS M. Eugene, Oregon, 1871d.

WHITTEMORE, WILLIAM Boston, Massachusetts, 1788-1797. Brother of Amos Whittemore. For Giles, Richards & Co., 1788-1797. (Gluckman & Satterlee)

WHITTEN, BURREL F. Patroon, Texas. Patent #502,389 August 1, 1893, magazine with Joseph Porcher.

WHITTENDON, WILLIAM (1808-?), Guilford Co., North Carolina. Apprenticed, 1820. (Bivins)

WHITTIER, OTIS W. Enfield, New Hampshire, 1829-1841. Patent #216 May 30, 1837, revolving rifle. Patent revolving rifles and percussion 1/2 stock. (Sellers-1)

WHORTON, CARTER (1829-?), Richmond, Virginia, 1850c. (MB 10-63)

WHYLEY, JOHN Portland, Maine, 1856d-1860d.

WHYLEY, LUTHER Portland, Maine, 1844-1846. (Demeritt)

WHYSONG, SAMUEL (?-1898), Pavia, Pennsylvania, 1875-1898. (Whisker)

WICHLEIN, JOHN Red Bud, Illinois, 1852-1855. (Johnson)

WICHMAN, JULIUS Decatur, Illinois, 1878d.

WICKELINE, G.L. see G.L. Wickline.

WICKER & HAGADORN Ypsilanti, Michigan, 1864-1867d. Percussion double rifle. Abraham M. Hagadorn and William W. Wicker.

WICKER, LUTHER Brownsville, Minnesota, 1867d.

WICKER, WILLIAM W. Ypsilanti, Michigan, 1863d-1867d. With Abraham M. Hagadorn as Wicker & Hagadorn, 1864-1867.

WICKERY, GEORGE Greene Co., Pennsylvania, 1813-1823, Washington Co., Pennsylvania, 1824-1827. (Whisker II)

WICKHAM & MATHEWS Emmitsburg, Maryland, 1802. Percussion fullstock. (Hartzler)

WICKHAM, J.D. South Riley, Michigan, 1863d.

WICKHAM, LEMUEL Fairmont, Minnesota 1882d-1886d.

WICKHAM, MARINE T. (1781-1833), Emmitsburg, Maryland, 1802-1804, Philadelphia, Pennsylvania, 1811-1832. Model 1822 contract muskets and barrel bands for Model 1812 pattern muskets and pistols. Flintlock Kentucky. (Hartzler)

WICKHAM, ROBERT Pawlet, Vermont, 1871-1881d.

WICKHAM, THOMAS Philadelphia, Pennsylvania, 1775-1776. Committee of Safety repairs. Father of Marine T. Wickham.

WICKIMIER, L. unlocated. Percussion fullstock dated 1847.

WICKLIM, JACOB Wilgus, Ohio, 1881d. (Hutslar)

WICKLIM, L. Red Bud, Illinois, 1860d.

WICKLINE, GEORGE LEWIS (1820-1903), Cadmus, Ohio, circa 1840, Sprikle Mills, Ohio, 1881d. Percussion rifles. (MB 11-44)

WICKS, I.S. Hamilton, Ohio, 1863d. (Hutslar)

WIDE AWAKE suicide special by Hood Fire Arms Co.

WIDEMAN, FRANCIS Jefferson Co., Missouri, 1850c. (MB 11-66)

WIDMER, JACOB Newark, New Jersey, 1866-1878d. Percussion schuetzen rifles and saloon gun. Patent #96,751 November 9, 1869, saloon gun. As Widmer & Co., 1867-1869. Guns sometimes marked "Grant & Co.".

WIER, BARNUBUS (1797-?), Davidson Co., North Carolina, 1850c. (Bivins)

WIER, CHRISTIAN (1821-?), Forsythe Co., North Carolina, 1850c, Taylorsville, Indiana, 1860c. (Lindert, Bivins)

WIER, HAMILTON (1823-?), Davidson Co., North Carolina, 1850c. (Bivins)

WIER, JACOB (1821-?), Davidson Co., North Carolina, 1850c. (Bivins)

WIER, JOHN (1835-?), Davidson Co., North Carolina, 1850c. (Bivins)

WIGAL, J.W. Alaska, Indiana, 1887-1890. (Lindert)

WIGEL, PETER York Co., Pennsylvania, 1777-1780. State gun factory.

WIGET, DOMINICK (1832-?), Alton, Illinois, 1853-1857, Highland, Illinois, 1857-1885, St. Louis, Missouri, 1885d-1893d. Percussion schuetzen rifles. Patent #466,209 December 29, 1891, powder flask.

WIGET, JOHN L. Mendota, Illinois, 1890d-1898d, St. Louis, Missouri, 1899d-1940. Son of Dominick Wiget.

WIGFALL, SAMUEL Philadelphia, Pennsylvania, 1770-1780. Committee of Safety locks. (Hobbies 4-38)

WIGHT, LYMAN Whitewater, Wisconsin, 1863-?. Single shot cartridge pistol. (GC 1)

WIGLE, JACOB Westmoreland Co., Pennsylvania, 1812-1816, Fayette Co., Pennsylvania, 1819-1822. Flintlock Kentucky. (Kauffman)

WIGLE, PETER York Co., Pennsylvania, 1777-1780. Committee of Safety repairs. (Dean)

WIKER, ADAM Union Co., Pennsylvania. Flintlock Kentucky rifles.

WIKIDAL, LOUIS P. Canton, Ohio, 1859d. With Conrad Schweitzer as Schweitzer & Wikidal. (Hutslar)

WIKLE, GEORGE Ottawa, Ohio, 1883d-1888d. (Hutslar)

WILBUR, R.J. Galesburg, Illinois, 1882d-1886d.

WILBUR, ROBERT Elk Co., Pennsylvania, 1870t-1872t. (Whisker II)

WILBUR, S. unlocated. Percussion target rifle.

WILCOCKS, JOHN Philadelphia, Pennsylvania, 1776. State gun lock factory.

WILCOX, JOHN (1860-?), Quaker City, Ohio, 1900d. (Hutslar)

WILCOX, JOHN Deep River, North Carolina, 1776-1779. Rifles, barrels, and cannon. (Gluckman & Satterlee)

WILCOX, LEONARD Chicago, Illinois, 1839. (Johnson)

WILCOX, M.M. Rochester, New York, 1834d. Percussion 1/2 stock. (Eich)

WILCOX, O. Fall Creek, Wisconsin, 1879d.

WILCOX, O.H. Lards, Idaho, 1891d.

WILCOX, SAMUEL Gridley, Illinois, 1860d.

WILD, LUTHER Brattleboro, Vermont, 1842-1843. (Kauffman 2)

WILDE, FERDINAND Portland, Oregon, 1853d-1866d, Oregon City, Oregon, 1867d-1886d.

WILDE, GEORGE Dayton, Ohio, 1872-1878d. (Hutslar)

WILDE, HERMAN Aurora, Illinois, 1868d-72d, Rochelle, Illinois, 1876d, Elgin, Illinois, 1878d.

WILDER, ELIHU (?-1896), Manchester, New Hampshire. Patents #182,729 September 26, 1876, machine gun, and #563,701 July 7, 1896, machine gun.

WILDER, F. unlocated. Percussion shotgun.

WILDER, R.M. Coldwater, Michigan. Three-barrel swivel-breech.

WILDES, F.L. Lake Washington, Minnesota, 1892d-1898d.

WILDRIDGE, JOHN Washington, Indiana, 1860d-1879.

WILDS, MERRILL F. West Topshan, Vermont, 1876-1879.

WILEY, JOHN, JR. Portland, Maine, 1831-1863. (Demeritt)

WILEY, THEODORE Philadelphia, Pennsylvania, 1775. Committee of Safety repairs. (Hobbies 5-37)

WILFONG, VINCENT W. Lancaster, Pennsylvania, 1871d-1875d.

WILHELM, DAVID Troy, Ohio, 1898d. (Hutslar)

WILHELM, JACOB B. Lancaster, Pennsylvania, 1857d.

WILKEN see Stroble & Wilken.

WILKENING, GUSTAV Houston, Texas, 1886d-1899d.

WILKERSON, JOHN Hatwood Co., North Carolina, 1820c. (Bivins)

WILKERSON, ROYAL B. Clyde, Iowa, 1865d.

WILKES, H. Camilla, Georgia, 1881d.

WILKES, JAMES Lancaster, Pennsylvania, 1871d.

WILKES-BARRE GUN CO. Wilkes-Barre, Pennsylvania, 1892-1895. Double-barrel and single barrel shotguns. Originally Parry Fire Arms Co., Ithaca, New York, which was moved to Wilkes-Barre. Business assets purchased by Ithaca Gun Co. at bankruptcy October 1, 1895. Charles and Ernest Roth.

WILKIN, JAMES C. Cedar Rapids, Iowa. Patent #654,336 July 24, 1900, firearm.

WILKINS, CHARLES W. Myrtle Point, Oregon, 1880d-1886d.

WILKINS, DIDRICK Shelbyville, Missouri, 1850c. (MB 11-60)

WILKINS, JOHN Burlington, Iowa, 1850c. (MB 8-64)

WILKINS, JOHN Shelbyville, Missouri, 1850c. (MB 11-66)

WILKINS, JOHN, JOSEPH & NORMAN Charleston, South Carolina, 1762. (Kauffman 2)

WILKINS, NEIL Zanesville, Ohio, 1804-1816. (Knittle)

WILKINSON ARMS CO. trade name of Richmond Hardware Co. on shotguns imported by H. & D. Folsom. "Richmond Arms Co." also used by Richmond Hardware Co. as a trade name on these shotguns. (AR 2-69)

WILKINSON BROS. Keeseville, New York, 1857-?, Plattsburg, New York, ?-1882. George C. and John D. Wilkinson. (Swinney)

WILKINSON, E. Newburgh, New York, 1882-1885. Brother of J.W. Wilkinson.

WILKINSON, G.C. St. Albans, Vermont, 1855. (Horn)

WILKINSON, GEORGE C. Keeseville, New York, 1857-1861. With his brother John D. as Wilkinson Bros.

WILKINSON, HENRY Newburgh, New York, 1861-1865.

WILKINSON, J.H. unlocated. Percussion fullstock.

WILKINSON, JOHN D. Keeseville, New York, 1857-1866, Plattsburg, New York, 1866-1882. Patent #118,569, August 29, 1871, breechloading firearm. Percussion and cartridge guns. With his brother George C. as Wilkinson Bros. (Swinney)

WILKINSON, JOHN W. (?-1881), Brooklyn and New York, New York, 1839-1859, Newburgh, New York, 1860d-1881. S.W. Woods carbines, 1861, percussion double rifle. (GR 2-61)

WILKINSON, WILLIAM M. Thomson, Georgia, 1881d.

WILKS, JOHN Albany, New York, 1815-1826. (Kauffman 2)

WILKS, JOSEPH M. New York, New York, 1883d.

WILKS, W. Quincy, Florida, 1883d-1884d.

WILL, WILHELM, JR. Zanesville, Ohio, 1800-1802. Locks. (Knittle)

WILL, WILLIAM C. (1808-?), Baltimore, Maryland, 1835d-1859d. (Hartzler)

WILLARD & CO. Boston, Massachusetts. Underhammer. (Logan)

WILLARD, A. Boston, Massachusetts, 1860. (Lindsay)

WILLARD, BARTHOLOMEW Burlington, Vermont, 1850. (Horn)

WILLARD, C.F. (1813-?), Muncie, Indiana, 1850c. Percussion 1/2 stock. (Lindert)

WILLARD, JULIUS Baltimore, Maryland. Patent #none July 10, 1830, bullet machine.

WILLCOCK & JENNINGS Astoria, Illinois, 1884d.

WILLERDING, S. Vincennes, Indiana, 1858d.

WILLERDING, THEODORE Evansville, Indiana, 1873d. Percussion rifles and pistols.

WILLERS, AUGUST Lawrenceburgh, Indiana, 1882-1885. (Lindert)

WILLET, D. unlocated. Percussion fullstock.

WILLET, JOHN Morenci, Michigan, 1863d.

WILLETS, A. & S. New York, New York, 1800. (Gluckman & Satterlee)

WILLETT, ALFRED Leadville, Colorado, 1882d. (Sellers-3)

WILLEY & GREER Watertown, South Dakota, 1892d.

WILLEY, ENOCH B. Cherryfield, Maine, 1852-1856. Percussion 1/2 stock. (Demeritt)

WILLEY, ENOCH S. Oakland, Washington, 1871d.

WILLEY, JULIUS Imlay City, Michigan, 1875d.

WILLIAM TELL suicide special by Lee.

WILLIAM, JOHANN (Germany 1732-1812), Berkshire Co., Pennsylvania, 1757.

WILLIAMS suicide special. (Webster)

WILLIAMS & PARCEL Corning, New York, 1870d. George Williams.

WILLIAMS & REZNER Mercer, Pennsylvania. Percussion 1/2 stock.

WILLIAMS STORES, CHARLES New York, New York. Dealers only. Note: this is a business entity listing, not an individual listing.

WILLIAMS, A. Washington City, Pennsylvania. Percussion fullstock.

WILLIAMS, A.R. Columbus, Ohio, 1866d-1867d. (Hutslar)

WILLIAMS, A.T. Beloit, Kansas, 1882d-1894d.

WILLIAMS, ABE Prosperity, Pennsylvania, 1830-1860, Oswego, New York, 1860-?. Percussion double rifle/shotgun. (Kauffman)

WILLIAMS, ABRAHAM Covington, Kentucky, 1845-1847.

WILLIAMS, ADIN W. (1804-?), Santa Ana, California, 1880-1882. (Shelton)

WILLIAMS, B.A. Bowling Green, Kentucky, 1885d.

WILLIAMS, BENJAMIN H. New York, New York, patent #150,120 April 21, 1874, revolver. Lawrenceville, Pennsylvania, patent #283,447 August 21, 1883, sight.

WILLIAMS, C., & BRO. Poplar Bluffs, Missouri, 1898d.

WILLIAMS, C.H. Ripley, Tennessee, 1887d-1891d.

WILLIAMS, CALEB B. (1812-?), Batavia, Ohio, 1850c. (Hutslar)

WILLIAMS, CHESTER (1813-?), Knox Co., Ohio, 1850c. (Hutslar)

WILLIAMS, CHESTER (1819-?), Lincoln, Illinois, 1860c. (Johnson)

WILLIAMS, DAVID Elizabeth, New Jersey, 1860d.

WILLIAMS, EDWARD Connecticut, 1774-1776. Committee of Safety locks. (Gluckman & Satterlee)

WILLIAMS, EDWIN Kenton Co., Kentucky. Patent #7,178 March 12, 1850, gain twist rifling machine with James Culbertson.

WILLIAMS, ELI (1750-1823), Williamsport, Maryland, 1791-1807. Model 1798 contract muskets, but none delivered. (Hartzler)

WILLIAMS, ELIJAH D. (?-1864), Philadelphia, Pennsylvania. Patents #35,273 May 13, 1862, bullet, #37,145 December 6, 1862, bullet, #43,615 July 19, 1864, bullet, and #44,492 September 27, 1864, bullet.

WILLIAMS, GEORGE Corning, New York, 1865-1870d. Percussion 1/2 stock. As Williams & Parcel, 1870.

WILLIAMS, GEORGE Oneca, Illinois, 1864d.

WILLIAMS, GEORGE EDWARD San Francisco, California. Patents #170,038 November 16, 1875, revolver, and #231,879 August 31, 1880, magazine gun. (Shelton)

WILLIAMS, H.B. Fremont Center, Michigan, 1883d, Grayling, Michigan, 1891d-1899d. Patent #477,410 June 21, 1892, breechloading firearm with Albert Gronleff.

WILLIAMS, H.N. Black Lick Station, Pennsylvania, 1887d-1890d.

WILLIAMS, HENRY (1810-?), Fulton Co., Ohio, 1850c. (Hutslar)

WILLIAMS, HIRAM Rockcastle, Kentucky, 1883d.

WILLIAMS, ISAAC (1818-?), Jamestown, North Carolina, 1850c. With Henry Parish. (Bivins)

WILLIAMS, J.A. Woodbine, Texas, 1884d.

WILLIAMS, J.H. Campbellsville, Kentucky, 1883d.

WILLIAMS, J.H. Wildwood, Florida, 1886d.

WILLIAMS, J.K. Akron, Ohio, 1888d. (Hutslar)

WILLIAMS, JAMES (1855-1942), Muncie, Indiana, 1880-1925. (Lindert)

WILLIAMS, JAMES Raleigh Co., West Virginia, circa 1870. (Whisker IV)

WILLIAMS, JAMES G. West Millgrove, Ohio, 1878d-1883d. (Hutslar)

WILLIAMS, JAMES W.D. Knoxville, Tennessee. Patent #146,611 January 20, 1874, magazine gun with Frank Peace.

WILLIAMS, JESSE Witherup's, Pennsylvania, 1887d, Scrubgrass, Pennsylvania, 1890d.

WILLIAMS, JOEL H. Skowhegan, Maine, 1860. Machine gun. (Demeritt)

WILLIAMS, JOHN Woodbury, Vermont, 1889d.

WILLIAMS, JOHN J. Jay, Indiana, 1860d-1862d.

WILLIAMS, JOHN R. (1832-1900), Columbus, Ohio, 1862-1866d. (Hutslar)

WILLIAMS, JOSEPH Lehigh Co., Pennsylvania, 1846t. See also William Josephs. (KRA II-3)

WILLIAMS, L. Clear Creek Landing, Illinois, 1860d.

WILLIAMS, LEVI Greene Co., Pennsylvania, 1820-1827. (Kauffman)

WILLIAMS, LEWIS Greene Co., Pennsylvania, 1820-1833. (Kauffman)

WILLIAMS, LORENZO Jamestown, Michigan, 1879d.

WILLIAMS, LYMAN Middlefield, Connecticut, 1881d. Percussion 1/2 stock.

WILLIAMS, M.D. Hornellsville, New York. Percussion rifle.

WILLIAMS, M.L. Maquoketa, Iowa, 1880d-1887d.

WILLIAMS, OLIVER P. Nashville, Tennessee, 1871d-1876d.

WILLIAMS, OSWALD Memphis, Tennessee, 1873d-1876d.

WILLIAMS, P.W. Lincoln, Illinois, 1860d.

WILLIAMS, RICHARD Frederick Co., Virginia. Apprenticed to Joseph Robinson, August 8, 1765.

WILLIAMS, RICHARD Washington Co., Pennsylvania, 1839-1841. (Whisker II)

WILLIAMS, RICHARD D. Baltimore, Maryland. Patent #197,708 November 27, 1877, revolver.

WILLIAMS, SAMUEL (1805-?), Carlisle, Ohio, 1850c. (Hutslar)

WILLIAMS, SOLOMON Plymouth, Ohio, 1859d. (Hutslar)

WILLIAMS, THOMAS (1810-?), Ohio, 1834-1836, Delaware, Indiana, 1838-1850c. (Lindert)

WILLIAMS, THOMAS (England 1848-?), Buena Vista, Colorado, 1880c.

WILLIAMS, THOMPSON Flat Creek, Tennessee, 1887d-1891d.

WILLIAMS, W.E. Maquoketa, Iowa, 1887d-1897d.

WILLIAMS, WILLIAM Connecticut, 1777. Committee of Safety repairs.

WILLIAMSON, ARGYLE (?-1807), Charleston, South Carolina, ?-1807. (Kauffman 2)

WILLIAMSON, BRILEY (1814-?), Randolph Co., North Carolina, 1850c. (Bivins)

WILLIAMSON, DAVID Brooklyn, New York. Patents #41,183 January 5, 1864, cartridge, #41,184 January 5, 1864, revolver, #42,823 May 17, 1864, revolver, #45,202 November 22, 1864, breechloading firearm with Alexander Bergen, #46,977 March 21, 1865, breechloading firearm, #58,525 October 2, 1866, breechloading firearm, #87,997 March 16, 1869, breechloading firearm, #137,043 March 18, 1873, revolver, #144,814 November 18, 1873, revolver, and #144,815 November 18, 1873, revolver. Revolvers, carbines, and derringers made by Moore and National.

WILLIAMSON, GEORGE Henrico, Virginia, 1769-1781, Richmond, Virginia, 1807. In Militia service, 1781. With Virginia Manufactory (Virginia Armory), 1807. (Gill)

WILLIAMSON, GRAY & CO. Chicago, Illinois, 1873d. Dealers.

WILLIAMSON, PEREGRINE Baltimore, Maryland. Patent #none May 12, 1813, manufacturing shot.

WILLIAMSON, WILLIAM (1835-?), Randolph Co., North Carolina, 1850c. Son of Briley Williamson. (Bivins)

WILLIAMSON, WILLIAM I. (1819-?), Moore Co., North Carolina, 1850c. (Bivins)

WILLINK, J.D. Savannah, Georgia, 1879d.

WILLIOME, JACOB St. Louis, Missouri, 1879d-1891d.

WILLIS, HENRY (?-1764), York Co., Pennsylvania, ?-1764. (Dean)

WILLIS, J.E. unlocated. Percussion 1/2 stock.

WILLIS, JOHN Philadelphia, Pennsylvania, 1775-1777. Committee of Safety muskets with Benjamin Town. (Kauffman 2)

WILLIS, RICHARD Lancaster, Pennsylvania, 1776-1778. Proclaimed Treasonous in 1778. (Kauffman 2)

WILLIS, WILLIAM Orange Co., New York, 1761.

WILLIS, WILLIAM Williamsburg, Virginia, 1768, Norfolk, Virginia, 1770-1772, Henrico Co., Virginia, 1791. (Gill)

WILLMAN, A.R. Charlotte, North Carolina, 1890d.

WILLS, DAVID Lebanon, Missouri, 1889d-1898d.

WILLS, J.B., CO. Keeseville, New York. Probably misreading of J.D. Wilkinson.

WILLS, J.T. Tacoma, Washington, 1886d-1891d.

WILLS, WILLIAM H. Boston, Massachusetts. Patent #45,292 November 29, 1864, cartridge.

WILLSTEIN & KAMPMAN Chicago, Illinois, 1857d. See Wettstein & Kampmann.

WILMONT ARMS CO. trade name of H. & D. Folsom Arms Co. on imported shotguns. (AR 2-69)

WILMOT GUN CO. unlocated. Breechloading rifle/shotgun.

WILMOT, NATHANIEL N. Boston, Massachusetts, 1847-1849, St. Louis, Missouri, 1850d-1859d, St. Paul, Minnesota, 1862-1864. Imported shotgun.

WILSHIRE ARMS CO. trade name of Crescent on shotguns made for Stauffer, Eshleman & Co. (Hinman)

WILSHIRE, W.H. Los Angeles, California, 1900. Breechloading shotguns.

WILSON & BRO. Lexington, Kentucky, 1879d-1896d.

WILSON & EVANS San Francisco, California, 1862-1865. Derringer. H.H. Wilson. (Shelton)

WILSON & SHORT Lexington, Kentucky. J.C. Short and I. Wilson. Percussion pistol.

WILSON, A. Shelby, North Carolina, 1877d-1890d.

WILSON, ALVA Wichita, Kansas. Patent #618,369 January 24, 1899, magazine gun.

WILSON, ANDREW New York, New York. Patent #none June 11, 1814, bayonet socket.

WILSON, BRO. & CO. Tipton, Indiana, 1860d. Dealer.

WILSON, CHARLES North Adams, Massachusetts, 1860d.

WILSON, CHARLES V. Augusta, Maine, 1876d.

WILSON, D.F. Parsons, Kansas, 1884d.

WILSON, E. Monmouth, Maine, 1871. (Demeritt)

WILSON, E.M. Savannah, Missouri, 1860d.

WILSON, F. Nicholsonville, Indiana, 1860d.

WILSON, FRANK R. Houlton, Maine, 1899. (Demeritt)

WILSON, GEORGE Easton, Connecticut, 1876-1879. Percussion 1/2 stock.

WILSON, GEORGE W. Martinsville, Illinois, 1860d.

WILSON, GEORGE W. Richmond, Virginia, 1857-1861. With Smith, Rhodes & Co. in 1861. (Albaugh 1)

WILSON, GEORGE W., & CO. St. Louis, Missouri, 1859d.

WILSON, HENRY San Francisco, California, 1878-1889. As H. Wilson & Son, 1878-84. (Shelton)

WILSON, HERMANN unlocated. Percussion fullstock.

WILSON, HUGH HARVEY (1828-?), Sacramento, California, 1854-1865, San Francisco, California, 1862-1889. As Wilson & Evans, (both locations), 1854-1874. As H.H. Wilson & Son, 1878-1884. (Shelton)

WILSON, I. Lexington, Kentucky. Percussion rifles like Benjamin Mills, under whom he apprenticed. With J.C. Short as Wilson & Short, 1855. (MB 12-51)

WILSON, J. Newcomerstown, Ohio, 1866-1868d. (Hutslar)

WILSON, J. FRED Worcester, Massachusetts. Patent #374,104 November 29, 1887, spring gun.

WILSON, J.L. Monkstown, Texas, 1896d.

WILSON, JAMES Callaway Co., Missouri, 1850c. (MB 11-66)

WILSON, JAMES St. John, Illinois, 1860d.

WILSON, JAMES EDWARD (1829-?), Visalia, California, 1867, Pajaro, California, 1868, Santa Barbara, California, 1871-1879. (Shelton)

WILSON, JAMES WENTZ San Francisco, California. Patent #241,446 May 10, 1881, breechloading firearm. (Shelton)

WILSON, JOHN Botetourt Co., Virginia. Converted flintlock fullstock.

WILSON, JOHN Mauch Chunk, Pennsylvania, 1828t. (Dyke)

WILSON, JOHN Philadelphia, Pennsylvania, 1780-1785. Repaired U.S. arms. (Moller)

WILSON, JOHN M. (1821-?), Ste. Marie, Illinois, 1853-1860. (Johnson)

WILSON, JOHN P. Ilion, New York, 1859-1864. Patent #22,911 February 8, 1859, alarm gun with John F. Thomas.

WILSON, JOHN R. Cincinnati, Ohio, 1880c. (Hutslar)

WILSON, JON unlocated. Tennessee fullstock.

WILSON, L.F. Pleasant Hill, Missouri, 1879d.

WILSON, L.P. Newcomerstown, Ohio, 1878d. (Hutslar)

WILSON, LEWIS E. Berlin, Wisconsin, 1884d-1895d. As Wilson Bros., 1895.

WILSON, M. Orangeville, Ohio, 1859d. Percussion 1/2 stock. (Hutslar)

WILSON, NATHANIEL Virginia, 1777. Committee of Safety repairs. (Gill)

WILSON, NATHANIEL N. Boston, Massachusetts, 1834d-1849d.

WILSON, P.L. Andrew Co., Missouri, 1850c. (MB 11-66)

WILSON, PHILIP Andrew Co., Missouri, 1850c. (MB 11-66)

WILSON, PHILIP, & CO. Philadelphia, Pennsylvania, 1859d-1867d. Percussion 1/2 stock.

WILSON, R.G. Richmond, Virginia, 1893d.

WILSON, ROBERT (1819-?), Caswell Co., North Carolina, 1850c. (Bivins)

WILSON, ROBERT Macomb, Illinois. Patent #45,105 November 15, 1864, magazine gun.

WILSON, SAMUEL Fairchild, Connecticut, 1835-1867.

WILSON, SAMUEL A. Columbus, Ohio, 1887d-1888d. (Hutslar)

WILSON, T. Antwerp, Ohio, 1860-1864d. (Hutslar)

WILSON, THOMAS Lexington, Kentucky, 1857-1860d. Percussion 1/2 stock.

WILSON, THOMAS B. Springfield, Massachusetts. Patents #571,608 November 17, 1896, breechloading firearm, #609,600 August 23, 1898, breechloading firearm, and #609,601 August 23, 1898, breechloading firearm.

WILSON, W.F. Bridesburg, Pennsylvania. Patent #49,463 August 15, 1865, breechloading firearm with Henry Flather.

WILT, J., & CO. Dayton, Ohio, 1832-1882. Gun barrels only. Jeremiah Wilt. (Hutslar)

WILT, JEREMIAH (1808-1882), Dayton, Ohio, 1832-1882. As Strickler, Wilt & Co., 1837. As J. Wilt & Son, circa 1860. Percussion fullstock. (Hutslar)

WILTFONG, ELIJAH (1815-?), Halfway House, California, 1873-1879. (Shelton)

WILTSHIRE ARMS CO. trade name of H. & D. Folsom on imported shotguns. (AR 2-69)

WILTZ, LOUIS E. New Orleans, Louisiana, 1876d-1877d.

WINANS, DANIEL M. Binghamton, New York. Patent #593,408 November 9, 1897, ejector.

WINANS, ROSS Baltimore, Maryland. Built Dickinson's steam operated cannon. (Hartzler)

WINANS, THOMAS J. Binghamton, New York. Patent #495,767 April 18, 1893, air gun.

WINBERG, JOHN H. St. Louis, Missouri, 1899d-1902d. (Pourie)

WINCHELL, JAMES D. Hillsdale, Michigan, 1863d-1865d. Percussion over/under rifle.

WINCHESTER REPEATING ARMS CO. New Haven, Connecticut, 1866-date. Rifles and shotguns. Founded by Oliver Fisher Winchester. Controlled by Western Cartridge Co., 1931-1992, by GIAT, France, 1992-1997, and by the Walloon region of Belgium, 1997-date. (Williamson, BBOGV)

WINCHESTER, OLIVER FISHER (1810-1880), New Haven, Connecticut, 1856-1880. Patents #57,808 September 4, 1866, magazine gun, and #60,814 January 1, 1867, cartridge. Founder of Winchester Repeating Arms Co.

WINDSOR CAR & RIFLE CO. Windsor, Vermont. (Horn)

WINDSOR MFG CO. Windsor, Vermont, 1864. Ball Carbines. Alternate name used by Ball & Lamson.

WINEBERGER, SAMUEL Richmond, Virginia, 1888d.

WINER, C.H. Frumet, Missouri, 1898d.

WINFIELD ARMS CO. suicide special.

WINFIELD ARMS CO. trade name of H. & D. Folsom on shotguns and revolvers made by Crescent.

WINFORD, S.A. Jefferson, Texas, 1890d.

WING, CHARLES Jackson, Indiana, 1850c. Percussion 1/2 stock. (Lindert)

WING, D.N. Waupun, Wisconsin, 1875d-1891d.

WING, ROBERT Charlestown, South Carolina, 1867-1874. (Albaugh 1)

WINGATE, GEORGE W. New York, New York. Patent #184,743 November 28, 1876, sight.

WINGATE, JESSE L. Mt. Pleasant, Iowa, 1884d-1887d.

WINGER, CHRISTIAN Lancaster Co., Pennsylvania, 1776. Member of Committee of Safety. Flintlock Kentucky.

WINGER, LAZ Lancaster, Pennsylvania, 1779. Furnished forty-nine locks to the Continental Armory. (Moller)

WINGER, RICHARD Lancaster, Pennsylvania, 1775-1777. Committee of Safety repairs. (Boehret)

WINGERHOLTER, MARTIN Pittsburgh, Pennsylvania, 1860-1861. (Kauffman)

WINGERT, JOHN A. Detroit, Michigan, 1845-1867. Brother of William Wingert. (MB 6-61)

WINGERT, WILLIAM Detroit, Michigan, 1837-1867. Percussion rifles and pistols with brother John A. Sold out to Fisher & Long in 1867. (MB 6-61)

WINGREN, R. Burlington, Kansas, 1884d.

WINK, CONRAD LaGrange, Texas, 1884d.

WINKLER, CHARLES Gutenburg, New Jersey, 1878d.

WINN, GEORGE W. (1828-?), Carrollton, Illinois, 1850-1871, White Hall, Illinois. Percussion 1/2 stock. (Johnson)

WINN, RICHARD B. (1843-?), Carrollton, Illinois, 1870c. (Johnson)

WINN, T. unlocated. Percussion 1/2 stock target rifle.

WINN, W.C. Somerville, Tennessee, 1873d.

WINN, W.H. Denison, Texas, 1878d.

WINN, WILLIAM (1804-?), Carrollton, Illinois, 1836-1864d.

WINNEMER, HERMANN Belleville, Illinois, 1860d. With William Reinke as Reinke & Winnemer.

WINNER suicide special. (Webster)

WINNER, JAMES Philadelphia, Pennsylvania, 1808-1814. As Winner, Nippes & Co., ?-1806 (unsure of date). With David Nippes and John Steinman as Winner, Nippes & Steinman to 1812 (1808-1809 according to Gluckman). Alone thereafter. (Kauffman)

WINNER, NIPPES & CO. Philadelphia, Pennsylvania, Model 1808 contract muskets. (Gluckman)

WINNER, NIPPES & STEINMAN Philadelphia, Pennsylvania, 1808-1809. Model 1808 contract muskets. James Winner, Daniel Nippes, John Steinman. (Gluckman)

WINNINGER, ADAM Rocky Fork, Ohio, 1813. (Knittle)

WINOCA ARMS CO. trade name of Crescent on shotguns for Jacobi Hardware Co. (AR 2-69)

WINSAUER, CASPAR (1829-?), Chicago, Illinois, 1860-1862d.

WINSHIP, GUSTAVUS L. Boston, Massachusetts. Patent #198,231 December 18, 1877, sight.

WINSHIP, WYNN Mansfield, Ohio, 1813. (Knittle)

WINSLOW see Bond & Winslow.

WINSTON & CO. Paducah, Kentucky, 1857-1860. Hardware, locks.

WINTABLE, ABRAHAM Philadelphia, Pennsylvania, 1814d-1837d.

WINTAFELD, ABEL Philadelphia, Pennsylvania, 1819-1833d.

WINTER, F.M. Chicago, Illinois, 1867d.

WINTER, GUSTAVE Denver, Colorado, 1876d-1900. As Winter & Fitting, 1883-1890. (Sellers 3)

WINTER, JOHN (1790-?), Cincinnati, Ohio, 1834d-1858d. Percussion fullstock. (Hutslar)

WINTER, JULIUS A. Chicago, Illinois, 1864d-1880d.

WINTER, PETER New Wells, Missouri, 1879d, Schall's, Missouri 1889d-1891d.

WINTER, THOMAS Green Bay, Wisconsin, 1879d-1886d.

WINTER, WILLIAM Baltimore, Maryland, 1885d. (Hartzler)

WINTERBERGER, FLORENCE (1820-?), Shawneetown, Illinois, 1860c. (Johnson)

WINTERBERGER, VALENTINE (1824-?), Shawneetown, Illinois, 1860c. (Johnson)

WINTERBOTTOM, JOHN Morris, Illinois, 1878d-1890d.

WINTERS, ELIJA Brady's Mill, Maryland, 1874-1881. (Hartzler)

WINTERS, ELISHA Chestertown, Maryland, 1775-1778. Committee of Safety muskets. (Hartzler)

WINTERS, G. Knoxville, Iowa, 1880d.

WINTERS, JOHN St. Clairsville, Ohio, 1820c. (Hutslar)

WINTERSTEIN, ERHARD (Germany 1835-?), Lincoln, Nebraska, 1872d, Trinidad, Colorado, 1874d-1889d. (Sellers-3)

WINTKLE, WASHINGTON (1809-?), Baltimore, Maryland, 1840d-1850c. (Hartzler)

WIRSING & SCHEMANN see Schemann & Wirsing.

WIRSING, AUGUST F. Cincinnati, Ohio, 1857d-1875d. With Theodore Schemann as Schemann & Wirsing, 1860-1868. Air guns and percussion 1/2 stock. (Hutslar)

WIRSING, CHARLES A. Waco, Texas, 1878d.

WIRSING, CHRISTIAN A. Cincinnati, Ohio, 1855d, St. Louis, Missouri, 1859d-1864d, Ft. Smith, Arkansas, 1875-1890. Air guns and percussion rifles. Son of August or Frederick. (Hutslar, Elias)

WIRSING, FREDERICK M. Cincinnati, Ohio, 1857d-1860d, Chicago, Illinois, 1864d-1869d.

WIRSING, WILLIAM A. (1860-1938), Ft. Smith, Arkansas, 1889-1938. Son of Christian A. Wirsing. (AR 9-37)

WIRTH, JOHN Philadelphia, Pennsylvania, 1874-1893. Patent #490,129 January 17, 1893, recoil pad. Tip-up single shot rifle.

WIRTH, MATHIAS Manitowoc, Wisconsin, 1865d-1875.

WIRTH, WILHELMINA Philadelphia, Pennsylvania, 1890d.

WIRTH, WILLIAM P. Lancaster, Pennsylvania, 1875d.

WIRTZ, ABRAM Maryville, Missouri, 1889d-1891d.

WIRWA, WILLIAM C. Somerville, Tennessee, 1876d.

WIRZ, GEORGE Brooklyn, New York, 1886d.

WISE, AUGUSTUS W. Griggsville, Illinois, 1860d-1886d. Changed name from Weiss.

WISE, HARRY San Francisco, California, 1893d, San Antonio, Texas, 1896d.

WISE, J.B. unlocated. Percussion over/under rifle.

WISE, JACOB Troy, Ohio, 1860d-1864d. Percussion fullstock. (Hutslar)

WISE, NATHANIEL Mifflin Co., Pennsylvania, 1850c. Flintlock swivelbreech. (Kauffman)

WISE, WILLIAM (1790-?), Staunton, Virginia, 1860c.

WISE, WILLIAM A. Griggsville, Illinois 1868d-1898d. Son of A.W. Wise.

WISEMAN, HONAKER Monroe Co., Virginia, 1811. Contract rifles for Virginia under contract of Andrew Beine. (Cromwell)

WISEMAN, JOHN Monroe Co., Virginia, 1809. Contract rifles for Virginia. (Cromwell)

WISER, PHILIP Delaware, Ohio, 1859d. Percussion fullstock. (Hutslar)

WISHON, JOHN (1801-?), Henderson Co., North Carolina, 1850c. (Bivins)

WISMAN, JOHN (1813-?), St. Louis, Missouri, 1850c. (Lewis)

WISPERT, JACOB Philadelphia, Pennsylvania, 1837d. (Whisker III)

WITERMAN, JOHN Buffalo, New York, 1836d. For Haberstro. (Kauffman)

WITHERS, JOHN Strasbourg, Pennsylvania, 1771-1790. (Kauffman 2)

WITHERS, MICHAEL (1733-1821), Lancaster, Pennsylvania, 1754-1805. Committee of Safety muskets, 1775-1780. (Dean)

WITHERS, MICHAEL unlocated. Nephew of Michael Withers, Lancaster, Pennsylvania.

WITHERS, WILLIAM Philadelphia, Pennsylvania, 1819d-1833. (Kauffman 2)

WITHINGTON, CHARLES B. Janesville, Wisconsin. Patents #467,217 January 19, 1892, breechloading firearm, and #485,313 November 1, 1892 ejector.

WITMAN, SOLOMON Lancaster, Pennsylvania, 1857d.

WITNEY, CHARLES Red Wing, Minnesota, 1872d-1878d. See Charles Whitney.

WITT, SILAS D. Brownsville, Texas, 1881d-1887d.

WITTE HARDWARE CO. St. Louis, Missouri. Dealers only.

WITTE, JOHN G. New York, New York, 1875d-1900d. Importer and dealer.

WITTMAN, JAMES M. Bridesburg, Pennsylvania. Patent #206,991 August 13, 1878, lock.

WM BOMEN see William Bowman. Marking on guns by William Bowman and Peter Albert Reinhard. (MB 9-44)

WOEHRLE, GEORGE New York, New York, 1851d.

WOERNER, C. Sutton, Nebraska, 1879d-1884d, McCook, Nebraska, 1886d-1893d.

WOERNER, CHRISTIAN, II Meadville, Pennsylvania, 1868d-1874d.

WOHLGEMUTH, FREDERICK New York, New York. Patents #90,214 May 18, 1869, breechloading firearm, and #96,373 November 2, 1869, cartridge. Submitted a rifle to the 1872 trials.

WOHRLE, JOSEPH Lincoln, Illinois, 1868d.

WOLCOTT, H.H. Yonkers, New York. Patents #48,227 June 13, 1865, breechloading firearm, and #60,106 November 27, 1866, breechloading firearm. Wolcott was president of Starr Arms Co., which made his patented carbines.

WOLF & DURRINGER Louisville, Kentucky, 1864d-1868d. Agent for Deringer. Charles Wolf.

WOLF, ADAM Boston, Massachusetts, 1805. (Kauffman)

WOLF, AMOS W. Terra Alta, West Virginia. Guns signed "AWW", dated 1847 and 1856. (Whisker IV)

WOLF, CHARLES Louisville, Kentucky, 1855d-1868d. As Wolf & Durringer, 1864-1868.

WOLF, DASH & FISHER New York, New York. Agent marking on derringers.

WOLF, ELMER (1868-?), Thurmont, Maryland. Percussion fullstock. Son of Herman Wolf. (Hartzler)

WOLF, EMILE Lancaster, Pennsylvania, 1850c. (Dyke)

WOLF, GEORGE New York, New York, 1879d.

WOLF, HENRY Pittsburgh, Pennsylvania, 1787-1808. (Kauffman)

WOLF, HERMAN Foxville, Maryland. Percussion fullstock.

WOLF, JOHN Troy, New York, 1859-1892d. For Nelson Lewis, 1859-1878.

WOLF, JOHN O. New York, New York, 1883d-1884d.

WOLF, LEONARD P. (1820-?), Ithaca, Ohio, 1850c-1860c. Percussion 1/2 stock. (Hutslar)

WOLF, MEREDITH Chattanooga, Tennessee, 1887d-1891d.

WOLF, OTTO Pittsburgh, Pennsylvania, 1852. (Kauffman)

WOLF, SAMUEL (1808-?), LaGrange Co., Indiana, 1850c. (Lindert)

WOLF, SIMON San Francisco, California, 1880d-1886d. With George W. Shreve as Shreve & Wolf. (Shelton)

WOLFANGER, WILLIAM New Orleans, Louisiana, 1874d-1875d.

WOLFARTH, ALANSON Salem, North Carolina, 1845. Bivins)

WOLFARTH, THOMAS Salem, North Carolina, 1819. (Bivins)

WOLFE & GILLESPIE see Wolff & Gillespie.

WOLFE, BISHOP & CO. New York, New York, 1830d-1857d. Importers and dealers. John Wolfe, Japtheth Bishop.

WOLFE, C. & D. New York. Over/under flintlock pistol.

WOLFE, JAMES Kinmundy, Illinois, 1860d.

WOLFE, MEREDITH (1833-1930), Cleveland, Tennessee, 1845-1856, Chattanooga, Tennessee, 1881-1930. Percussion fullstock. (Cline)

WOLFE, MEREDITH Dalton, Georgia, 1881d.

WOLFE, SAMUEL Middlebury, Indiana, 1862-1863d, Elkhart, Indiana, 1874-1876d. (MB 4-54)

WOLFERTZ, ROBERT Detroit, Michigan, 1883d-1885d.

WOLFF & GILLESPIE New York, New York, 1848-1852. Importers and hardware dealers. George H.D. Gillespie.

WOLFF & LANE Pittsburgh, Pennsylvania, 1850-1854. Lockmakers only. Christian Wolff.

WOLFF & MASCEK Memphis, Tennessee, 1860d. (T 47)

WOLFF, B., JR. unlocated. Percussion locks.

WOLFF, CHARLES Rock Island, Illinois, 1868d-1893d.

WOLFF, CHRISTIAN Pittsburgh, Pennsylvania. As Whitmore & Wolff, Whitmore, Wolff, Duff & Co., and Wolff & Lane, lockmaker only. C. Wolff (marking?) on percussion target rifle.

WOLFF, JOHN W. Winston, North Carolina. Patent #563,114 June 30, 1896, water gun.

WOLFF, LOUIS Rochester, New York, 1874d. (Eich)

WOLFF, ROBERT Memphis, Tennessee, 1855-1860d. As Wolff & Maschek, 1860.

WOLFFINGER, FRANK Mohnton, Pennsylvania, 1850. (MB 2-63)

WOLFGANG, MICHAEL Hegins, Pennsylvania, 1861d.

WOLFHEIMER, PHILIP Lancaster, Pennsylvania, 1774. Flintlock Kentucky. (Dillin)

WOLLAM, CLARENCE M. San Francisco, California, 1883-1885 and 1890-1900, Red Bluff, California, 1885-1890. Patent #498,043 May 23, 1893, breechloading firearm. (Shelton)

WOLLISTON, J.R. Williamsport, Ohio, 1881d. (Hutslar)

WOLTER & DILG Belleville, Illinois, 1865d. Percussion rifles. William E. Wolter.

WOLTER, WILLIAM E. Belleville, Illinois, 1865d-1890d. As Wolter & Dilg, 1865.

WOLTERING, JAMES Salisbury, North Carolina, 1849-?. (Bivins)

WOLVERINE ARMS CO. trade name of Crescent on shotguns for Fletcher Hardware Co. (AR 2-65)

WONACOTT, CHARLES San Francisco, California. Patent #347,455 August 17, 1886, loading machine. (Shelton)

WONDER suicide special. (Webster)

WOOD, A.C., & BRO. Oak Harbor, Ohio, 1875d. (Hutslar)

WOOD, ABRAHAM (1823-?), Belmont Co., Ohio, 1850c. (Hutslar)

WOOD, AMOS P. North Hamden, New York, 1850-1882d. Percussion 1/2 stock.

WOOD, BARRY C. Erwin, New York, 1848-1858, Painted Post, New York, 1858-1874. Percussion guns. As B.C. Wood & Sons, after 1870. (Swinney)

WOOD, CHARLES P. (1844-1918), Morgan Co., Ohio, 1865-1918. Percussion 1/2 stock. (Hutslar)

WOOD, CORBIN O. (1821-1904), Worcester, Massachusetts, 1852-1883. Patents #30,372 October 9, 1860, breechloading firearm, #31,050 January 1, 1861, breechloading firearm, and #219,336 September 2, 1879, chambering machine. For/with (?) Ethan Allen and Forehand & Wadsworth, 1852-1883. Made one single short drop block rifle. (Grant)

WOOD, DANIEL Rochester, New York, 1859-1864. Patent #42,983 May 31, 1864, telescopic sight.

WOOD, EDWARD L. Shreveport, Louisiana, 1882d.

WOOD, FELIX E. Columbia, Tennessee, 1881d-1887d.

WOOD, FRANCIS (1827-?), Rutherford Co., North Carolina, 1850c. (Bivins)

WOOD, GEORGE Vallejo, California, 1877-1893d. (Shelton)

WOOD, GEORGE W. Granville, New York. Patent #388,166 August 21, 1888, sight.

WOOD, H.C. Columbus, Ohio. Percussion 1/2 stock. (Hutslar)

WOOD, H.M. Brattleboro, Vermont, 1890-1898. (Horn)

WOOD, H.T. unlocated. Mule ear 1/2 stock.

WOOD, J.H., & SON Helena, Kentucky.

WOOD, J.M. unlocated. Percussion 1/2 stock.

WOOD, JAMES Crosswicks, New Jersey, 1878d.

WOOD, JAMES Lancaster, Pennsylvania, 1810.

WOOD, JAMES A. (1829-?), Jamestown, North Carolina, 1850c. For A. Lamb. (Bivins)

WOOD, JAMES D. Springfield, Massachusetts, 1874d-1876d. Pistols.

WOOD, JESSE (1805-?), Jamestown, North Carolina, 1850c. (Bivins)

WOOD, JOHAM (1798-?), Rutherford Co., North Carolina, 1850c. (Bivins)

WOOD, JOHN (1824-?), Paoli, Indiana, 1850c. Brother of Noah Wood. (Lindert)

WOOD, JOHN Boston, Massachusetts, 1724-1770. (Lindsay)

WOOD, JOHN Friendsville, Illinois, 1860d.

WOOD, JOHN H. Helena, Kentucky. 1879d-1884d. Percussion 1/2 stock. As J.H. Wood & Son.

WOOD, JOHN, JR. Roxbury, Massachusetts, 1775-1776, Boston, Massachusetts, 1800. Committee of Safety muskets. (Gluckman & Satterlee)

WOOD, JONATHAN B. Utica, New York, 1828d, Norwich, New York, 1867d. (GR7-57)

WOOD, JOSEPH (1830-?), Clark Co., Indiana, 1860c. (Lindert)

WOOD, JOSEPH Richmond, Maine, 1735-1741. (Demeritt)

WOOD, JOSHUA B. Norwich, New York, 1860-1867d. Percussion 1/2 stock and over/under rifle/shotgun. Patent #44,057 August 30, 1864, telescopic sight. (Clow)

WOOD, JOSIAH Norristown, Pennsylvania, 1775-1777. Committee of Safety muskets. (Gluckmand & Satterlee)

WOOD, LUKE Sutton, Massachusetts, 1815. Model 1808 pattern muskets. (Gluckman)

WOOD, M. Hennepin, Illinois. (Johnson)

WOOD, M.C. Bedford, Iowa, 1887d-1897d.

WOOD, MARSHALL Lewisburgh, West Virginia. Patent #130,098 July 30, 1872, machine gun.

WOOD, MASON Chatham Center, Ohio, 1853d. (Hutslar)

WOOD, MILTON (1831-?), Jamestown, North Carolina, 1850c. For Evan Johnson. (Bivins)

WOOD, MORRIS Hounsfield, New York, 1866-1867d.

WOOD, NICKOLAS Oak Harbor, Ohio, 1875-1881d. As A.C. Wood & Bro., 1875. (Hutslar)

WOOD, NOAH (1830-?), Paoli Co., Indiana, 1850c. (Lindert)

WOOD, ORSON Clinton, Illinois, 1878d.

WOOD, PINCKNEY P. Hot Springs, Arkansas 1884d-1920.

WOOD, R.A. Swainsboro, Georgia, 1885d.

WOOD, R.C. Winneconne, Wisconsin, 1857d.

WOOD, STEPHEN W. Cornwall, New York. Patents #34,854 April 1, 1862, breechloading firearm, #36,984 November 18, 1862, revolver, #39,619 August 18, 1863, revolver, #41,803 March 1, 1864, revolver, #44,363 September 20, 1864, revolver, #52,105 January 16, 1866, extractor, #126,607 May 7, 1872, cannon, #178,824 June 13, 1876, revolver, and #186,445 January 23, 1877, revolver. Revolvers made by Connecticut Arms Co.

WOOD, T.H. unlocated. Percussion 1/2 stock.

WOOD, W.N. New York, New York. Percussion 1/2 stock. (Swinney)

WOOD, WALTER W. Washington, D.C. Patent #620,524 February 28, 1899, magazine gun.

WOOD, WILLIAM M., JR. Washington, D.C. Patent #193,906 August 7, 1877, breechloading firearm.

WOODALL, JOHN Vallejo, California, 1871-1874d. (Shelton)

WOODBURY & TURNER Woodstock, Vermont, 1852. Nathan Woodbury and B.F. Turner. (Horn)

WOODBURY, CRAYTON A. Woodstock, Vermont, 1865d-1893, Sherborne, Vermont, 1875d. Percussion 1/2 stock and magazine pistols. Patents #410,609 September 10, 1889, magazine gun, #440,328 November 11, 1880, magazine gun, and #496,231 April 25, 1893, magazine gun. All patents with Mark F. Richardson.

WOODBURY, N. Amboy, Illinois, 1860d.

WOODBURY, NATHAN, & CO. Woodstock, Vermont, 1856-1879. Percussion 1/2 stock. (Horn)

WOODFIN, JOHN JAMES Virginia, 1777. State arms repairs. (Gill)

WOODHAM, ALFRED New York, New York, 1854d-1868d. Importer & dealer. Agent on derringer.

WOODLY, WILLIAM (1812-?), Jamestown, North Carolina, 1840. (Bivins)

WOODMAN, JOHN Arcadia, Ohio, 1859d-1860c. (Hutslar)

WOODMAN, W.E. Springfield, Massachusetts. .22 cal. single shot target pistols.

WOODMANCIE, JOSEPH (1831-?), Urbana, Illinois, 1860d. As Woodmancie & Allen.

WOODRING, ISAAC Waverly, Iowa, 1880d-1887d.

WOODROUGH & HANCHETT Chicago, Illinois, 1892. (Johnson)

WOODRUFF, A. Holly Springs, Pennsylvania, 1857. Percussion rifle/shotgun.

WOODRUFF, EZRA Cincinnati, Ohio, 1820. Gunsmiths supplies. (Hutslar)

WOODRUFF, W.W., & CO. Knoxville, Tennessee, 1865-?. Dealers only.

WOODS, A.D. Indianapolis, Indiana. Lockmaker. (Lindert)

WOODS, ABSOLOM Fayette Co., Pennsylvania, 1861-1818. (Kauffman)

WOODS, CHARLES Hamburgh, New Jersey, 1878d.

WOODS, ENOCH Chicago, Illinois, 1863-1864d. Dealer.

WOODS, JAMES Stockholm, New Jersey, 1878d.

WOODS, JAMES D. Springfield, Massachusetts, 1875d-1879d.

WOODS, JOHN New York, New York, ?-1775. Loyalist, left the colonies before the Revolutionary War.

WOODS, JOHN A. Provincetown, Massachusetts, 1869d.

WOODS, MOSES New Boston, New Hampshire, 1869-1875d.

WOODS, ROBERT Pocono, Pennsylvania, 1828t. Flintlock Kentucky rifles. (Dillin)

WOODS, T. Philadelphia, Pennsylvania, 1810. (Gluckman & Satterlee)

WOODS, WINFIELD SCOTT (1880-1961), Peeble, Ohio, 1898-1961. (MB 2-42)

WOODWARD, BENJAMIN F. (1828-1876), Clarksville, Missouri, 1850c, Napa, California, 1866-1876. (Shelton)

WOODWARD, C.F. Jasper, New York, 1869-1874. Percussion 1/2 stock.

WOODWARD, D.C. Randolph, Vermont, 1898. (Horn)

WOODWARD, DAVID F. Bath, New York, 1847-1853.

WOODWARD, E.W. Norway, Maine, 1884. (Demeritt)

WOODWARD, EDWARD Baltimore, Maryland, 1855d-1860d, Gettysburg, Pennsylvania, 1868d. (Hartzler)

WOODWARD, F.G. Worcester, Massachusetts. Percussion bolt action rifle and fowling piece. Patent #34,084 January 7, 1862, breechloading firearm.

WOODWARD, GILMAN Keene, New Hampshire, 1848-1860d.

WOODWARD, J.D. Phillips, Wisconsin, 1891d.

WOODWARD, SENECA E. Coloma, Indiana, 1877-1885. (Lindert)

WOODWARD, W.C. Abilene, Texas, 1884d.

WOODWARD, WILLIAM (1807-?), Johnson Co., Illinois, 1850c. (Johnson)

WOODWORTH, BYRON (1826-?), Watsonville, California, 1860-1875. Percussion 1/2 stock. (Shelton)

WOODWORTH, G. (1824-?), St. Louis, Missouri, 1850c. (Lewis)

WOOKEY, ALONZO Geneseo, Illinois, 1878d-1882d.

WOOKEY, S.G. Clarinda, Iowa, 1882d, Loup City, Nebraska, 1884d-1886d.

WOOLEY, A. Hilton, Indiana, 1862d.

WOOLEY, C.A. Flora, Indiana, 1877-1885. (Lindert)

WOOLSEY, JOHN S. Gilroy, California, 1874-1881. Patent #237,942 February 15, 1881, gopher gun. (Shelton)

WOOLWORTH, A. Salisbury, North Carolina, 1846. (Bivins)

WOOLWORTH, AZERIAH Waterbury, Connecticut. Patent #none June 13, 1820, gunstock lathe.

WORDEN, E.A. Dallas, Texas, 1884d-1896d.

WORDEN, WILLIAM H. Ypsilanti, Michigan, 1860d-1870d.

WORDEN, WILLIS Pleasant Vale, Illinois, 1860d.

WORDLEY, DAVID Chester Co., Pennsylvania, 1768-1771t. (Dean)

WORKMAN, F. (1827-?), St. Louis, Missouri, 1850c. (Lewis)

WORKMAN, JOHN Hamburg, Pennsylvania, 1838. Flintlock Kentucky rifles. (Kauffman)

WORL, H. unlocated. Flintlock Kentucky swivelbreech.

WORL, J. unlocated. Percussion 1/2 stock.

WORLDS FAIR trade name of Hopkins & Allen on shotguns.

WORLEY, CALEB Cumberland Co., Pennsylvania, 1800. (Kauffman)

WORLEY, DAVID (1797-?), Donegal, Pennsylvania, 1823-1841. (Kauffman)

WORLEY, HENRY (1833-1890), Mohn's Store, Pennsylvania, 1850-1890. Barrelmaker. Son of Jesse Worley. (KRA F76)

WORLEY, HENRY H. Mohn's Store, Pennsylvania, 1875. Son of Henry Worley.

WORLEY, I. signature of Jesse Worley.

WORLEY, JESSE (1788-1838), Wyomissing Creek, Pennsylvania, 1811-1838. Barrelmaker. Successor to Daniel Glass. (Hobbies 5-37)

WORLEY, JOHN Wyomissing Creek, Pennsylvania. Son of Jesse Worley. (KRA F-76)

WORLEY, JOHN G. Snyder Co., Pennsylvania. Flintlock and percussion Kentucky rifles. (Gabel)

WORLEY, L. unlocated. Percussion 1/2 stock.

WORLEY, THEOPHILUS Wyomissing Creek, Pennsylvania. Son of Jesse Worley. (KRA F-76)

WORLEY, THOMAS Berkeley Co., Virginia, 1776, Mecklenburg, Virginia, 1776, Washington Co., Maryland, 1779-1783. Flintlock military rifles and barrels. (Hartzler)

WORM, JAMES Whitewater, Wisconsin, 1857d.

WORM, T. unlocated. Percussion three-shot harmonica rifle.

WORMAN, JOHN Crescent City, Iowa, 1865d.

WORMER, MARK Sacramento, California, 1894-1899. For Charles Flohr. (Shelton)

WORTER & SCHAFFER Vicksburg, Mississippi, 1867d. Pius Worter and Jacob Schaffer.

WORTER, PIUS Vicksburg, Mississippi, 1867d-1875. With Jacob Schaffer as Worter & Schaffer, 1867.

WORTHEN, BARNEY San Francisco, California, 1860. (Dean*)

WORTHEN, WILLIAM Randolph, Vermont, 1886d.

WORTHING, F.G. Abrams, Wisconsin, 1884d-1891d.

WORTHINGTON ARMS CO. trade name of H. & D. Folsom on shotguns for George Worthington, Cleveland, Ohio. (AR 2-69)

WOTTRICK, RUDOLPH Caribou, Maine, 1886. (Demeritt)

WRATHWAN, GEORGE (1775-?) Morgan Co., Ohio, 1850c. (Hutslar)

WREGE & FLUES Bay City, Michigan, 1887d. Emil Flues.

WREN, I.G. unlocated. Flintlock 1/2 stock Kentucky.

WRIGHT & BRO. Philadelphia, Pennsylvania, Percussion single shot pistol.

WRIGHT & POWELL Atlanta, Georgia, 1877d. Arthur G. Wright and Charles Powell.

WRIGHT & RICE Florence, Alabama. Derringer. (AG 5-78)

WRIGHT ALBA C. Fitchburg, Massachusetts, 1847-1856. Underhammer pistol.

WRIGHT ARMS CO. Lawrence, Massachusetts. "Little All Right" revolvers, percussion and cartridge shotguns. (Hobbies 3-66)

WRIGHT, A., & CO. Poughkeepsie, New York, 1835-1846. Alexander Wright. Also with Peter Palmateer as Palmateer & Wright, same time frame and location.

WRIGHT, A.M. (1815-?), Cherry Fork, Ohio, 1850c-1900. Percussion fullstock. (Hutslar)

WRIGHT, AARON (1797-?), Greene Co., Pennsylvania, 1832-1851. (Whisker II)

WRIGHT, ALEXANDER Poughkeepsie, New York, 1835-1846, Newburgh, New York, 1857-1859d. Percussion guns. As A. Wright & Co. in Poughkeepsie. Also with Peter Palmateer as Palmateer & Wright, in Poughkeepsie.

WRIGHT, ARTHUR C. Fitchburg, Massachusetts, 1856d-1896d, Worcester, Massachusetts, 1898-1908. Percussion and cartridge rifles and pistols. Patents #615,467 December 6, 1898, revolver, #625,009 May 16, 1899, breechloading firearm, and #907,670 December 22, 1908, revolver.

WRIGHT, ARTHUR G. Atlanta, Georgia, 1877d. With Charles L. Powell as Wright & Powell.

WRIGHT, B.J. Emporia, Kansas, 1868d.

WRIGHT, BENJAMIN (1820-1874), Freeport, Ohio, 1850c. (Hutslar)

WRIGHT, BENJAMIN Peoli, Ohio, 1853d. Percussion fullstock with "B.W." marking. (Hutslar)

WRIGHT, BENJAMIN F. Cincinnati, Ohio, 1875d-1878d. With W.H. Wright. (Hutslar)

WRIGHT, CHARLES Paris, Michigan, 1872d-1877d.

WRIGHT, CHARLES J. Colorado Springs, Colorado, 1889d. (Sellers-3)

WRIGHT, CHRISTOPHER C. (1835-?), Harrison Co., West Virginia, 1850c. Son of Jerome Wright.

WRIGHT, DAVID unlocated. Revolutionary War claimant for gunsmith services. (Sellers)

WRIGHT, E. Staunton, Virginia, 1893d-1897d.

WRIGHT, EDWARD S. Buffalo, New York. Patents #22,325 December 14, 1858, breechloading cannon with Theodore Gould, and #45,126 November 15, 1864, breechloading firearm.

WRIGHT, FRANK Henderson, Kentucky, 1896d.

WRIGHT, G. unlocated. Percussion lockmaker.

WRIGHT, G.E. Newark, New Jersey, 1865. (Dean*)

WRIGHT, GEORGE Marion Co., Ohio, 1822. Repairs. (Hutslar)

WRIGHT, GEORGE Washington, D.C. Patent #7,675 September 24, 1850, percussion cap.

WRIGHT, GEORGE Winchester, Virginia, 1755-1760. (Gill)

WRIGHT, GEORGE W. Crofton, Kentucky, 1883d.

WRIGHT, HENRY (1807-?), Jamestown, North Carolina, 1850c-1860c. Percussion 1/2 stock. (Bivins)

WRIGHT, HENRY, A. Buffalo, New York, 1836d. With Patrick Smith. (Dean)

WRIGHT, J. Stevens Point, Wisconsin, 1879d.

WRIGHT, J.B. Anoka, Minnnesota, 1876-1882d. Percussion 1/2 stock.

WRIGHT, J.C. Lincoln, Missouri, 1898d.

WRIGHT, J.M. St. Joseph, Missouri, 1889d, Clinton, Missouri, 1893d, Kirksville, Missouri, 1898d.

WRIGHT, JAMES Arlington, Texas, 1884d.

WRIGHT, JEROME B. (1802-?), Harrison Co., West Virginia, 1850c.

WRIGHT, JOHN (1846-?), Randolph Co., West Virginia, 1870c. (Whisker IV)

WRIGHT, JOHN Lumberton, New Jersey, 1878d.

WRIGHT, JOHN Rutland, Ohio. (Hutslar)

WRIGHT, JOHN H. Vermillion, Illinois, 1864d.

WRIGHT, JOHN T. San Diego, California, 1886-1888. (Shelton)

WRIGHT, LOOMIS S. Waddington, New York, 1879-1883. (Roberts)

WRIGHT, M.H. McComb, Mississippi, 1885d.

WRIGHT, MITCHEL Cherry Fork, Ohio. Possibly A.M. Wright. (Hutslar)

WRIGHT, MOSES (1792-1854), Freeport, Ohio, 1816-1854. Converted Kentucky. (Hutslar)

WRIGHT, NATHAN (1817-1912), Jamestown, North Carolina, 1840-1870. With William Lamb as Lamb & Wright. (Bivins)

WRIGHT, THEODORE Bentley Creek, Pennsylvania. Patent #612,085 October 11, 1898, magazine gun.

WRIGHT, W.H. Cincinnati, Ohio, 1875d-1878d. With B.F. Wright.

WRIGHT, WASHINGTON Cherry Fork, Ohio. (Hutslar)

WRIGHT, WENDELL New York, New York. Patent #11,917 November 7, 1854, turret pistol. (Sellers-2)

WRIGHT, WILLIAM HENRY Copperdale, Ohio, 1840-1926. (Hutslar)

WRIGHT, WILLIAM R. (1822-?), Freeport, Ohio, 1878d-1890d. (Hutslar)

WRIGHT, WILLIAM W. Atlanta, Georgia, Patent #280,002 June 16, 1883, alarm gun.

WRIGHT, WILLIAM W. Norwich, Connecticut. Patent #16,819 March 10, 1857, bomb lance.

WRISLEY, LOREN H. (1813-1876), Norway, Maine, 1834-1876. Percussion 1/2 stock. (Demeritt)

WUENSCHE, A.O. Chicago, Illinois, 1884d-1886d.

WUERKER, C. & F. Alton Illinois, 1849-1875. Christian and Frederick Wuerker.

WUERKER, CHRISTIAN Alton, Illinois, 1849-1875. With Frederick Wuerker as C. & F. Wuerker.

WUERKER, FREDERICK (?-1908), Alton, Illinois, 1849-1908. With Christian Wuerker as C. & F. Wuerker, 1849-1875.

WUEST, CARL Newport, Kentucky, 1895d.

WUNDERLICH, CHARLES Washington, Missouri, 1889d-1893d.

WUNSH, ANDREW Wichita, Kansas, 1884d, Ashland, Kansas, 1894d.

WURFFLEIN & PSOTTA Philadelphia, Pennsylvania. Cased percussion buggy rifle.

WURFFLEIN, ANDREW Philadelphia, Pennsylvania, 1835d-1871d. Percussion guns. Patent #6,964 December 18,1849, lock. (Kauffman)

WURFFLEIN, JOHN Philadelphia, Pennsylvania, 1848d-1867d. Percussion guns. Patent #7,334 April 30, 1850, safety for Prussian needle gun. (Kauffman)

WURFFLEIN, WILLIAM Philadelphia, Pennsylvania, 1869-1915. Percussion and cartridge guns. Son of, and successor to, Andrew. (Bugle 61)

WURTS, J.B. unlocated. Percussion fullstock.

WURTZ, SAMUEL Lancaster, Pennsylvania, 1837. (Dyke)

WUTHE, WILLIAM Reno, Nevada, 1871d.

WYANT, A.H. Washington, Connecticut, 1869-1889d.

WYANT, I.S. Lebanon, Missouri, 1879d.

WYATT, E. unlocated. Flintlock Kentucky.

WYATT, THOMAS (1774-?), Shelby Co., Ohio, 1819t-1850c. (Hutslar)

WYCO trade name of Wyeth Hardware Co.

WYER, WILLIAM Wooster, Ohio, 1850d. (Hutslar)

WYETH HARDWARE CO. St. Joseph, Missouri, 1880-1900. Dealers only. (Hinman)

WYLER, J.L. unlocated. Percussion revolving rifle.

WYLIE, RICHARD Napa, California. Patent #220,325 October 7, 1879, spring gun.

WYLIE, THOMAS Carlisle, New Jersey, 1776-1780. Lockmaker. Lancaster, Pennsylvania according to Boehret. (Gardner)

WYLIE, WILLIAM Charleston, South Carolina, 1806. (Kauffman 2)

WYMAN, H.H. unlocated. Percussion slug gun.

WYMAN, ROSS (1716-1808), Shrewsbury, Massachusetts, 1755-1808. Flintlock muskets. (GR 6-74)

WYNKOOP, CORNELIUS unlocated. Early flintlock musket. (Dean)

WYOMING ARMORY trade name of Frank W. Freund.

WYSONG, SAMUEL see Samuel Whysong.

X SECTION

XCD suicide special by Hopkins & Allen.

XL trade name of Hopkins & Allen on pistols, revolvers, and shotguns.

XLCR suicide special.

XPERT trade name of Davenport on rifles for Witte Hardware Co. (Hinman)

XPERT trade name of Hopkins & Allen on single shot derringer.

Y SECTION

YAGER, CHARLES Lancaster, Pennsylvania, 1867-1870.

YAHNER, HENRY F. (1860-?), Cambria Co., Pennsylvania, 1880-1930. Percussion fullstock and swivel breech pistol. (Gluckman & Satterlee)

YAKE & HOLBURN Alpena, Michigan, 1893d. W.J. Yake and Robert Holburn.

YAKE, W.J. Alpena, Michigan, 1891d-1893d. With Robert Holburn as Yake & Holburn, 1893.

YALE, CHARLES O. New York, New York. Patent #424,043 March 25, 1890, loading and discharging guns.

YANKEY, GEORGE W. (1853-?), Pendleton Co., West Virginia, 1880c. (Whisker IV)

YANTIS, JOHN Washington, D.C., 1862d. (Hartzler)

YARBOROUGH, M. Briensburg, Kentucky, 1857-1860d.

YARBOROUGH, THOMAS J. Oakton, Kentucky, 1883d.

YARD, BENJAMIN Trenton, New Jersey, 1776-1777. Committee of Safety muskets. (Boehret)

YARKER, JOHN Wellsville, Ohio, 1888-1890d. (Hutslar)

YATES, J.A. Griffin, Georgia, 1879d.

YATES, J.B. Maple Rapids, Michigan, 1875d-1883d.

YATES, THEODORE Milwaukee, Wisconsin. Patents #46,417 February 14, 1865, breechloading ordnance, and #60,607 December 18, 1866, breechloading firearm.

YAW, M.B. Florida, Massachusetts, 1857-1860. (Gardner)

YAXLEY, R. Willoughby, Ohio, 1859d. Percussion guns. (Hutslar)

YEAGER, CHARLES F. Lancaster, Pennsylvania, 1875d.

YEAGER, JACOB Huntington Co., Pennsylvania, 1850c. Percussion 1/2 stock. (Kauffman)

YEAGER, STEPHEN Bedford, Kentucky, 1857-1860. Percussion fullstock.

YEAMAN, GEORGE Lenox, New York, 1866-1868.

YEAMANS, W.B. (1805-?), Athens, Illinois, 1859d-1860c. (Johnson)

YEAMANS, WILLIAM (1824-?), Springfield, Illinois, 1860c. (Johnson)

YEARIN, ADAM Chillicothe, Ohio, 1804. (Hutslar)

YEARWOOD, JOHN M. (1814-?), Mt. Vernon, Illinois, 1848-1860. (Johnson)

YEATES, ELIJAH S. Tuscarora, Nevada, 1880d.

YEISLEY, HENRY Lucas, Ohio, 1866d. Percussion rifles. (Hutslar)

YELLIG, JOSEPH D. Mariah Hall, Indiana, 1848-1927. (Lindert)

YEOMANS, DANIEL Lancaster, Pennsylvania, 1750. Flintlock Kentucky rifles. (Dean*).

YEOMANS, DAVID Charlotte, North Carolina. Flintlock Kentucky rifles. (Bivins)

YEORWOOD, JOHN Mt. Vernon, Illinois, 1864d.

YERIAN, FREDERICK (1837-1910), Noble Co., Ohio, 1872d, Sharon, Ohio. Son of, and successor to, John Yerian. (Hutslar)

YERIAN, JOHN W. (1816-1890), Morgan Co., Ohio, 1850, Washington Co., Ohio, 1878d-1883d, Sharon, Ohio, 1890. Percussion 1/2 stock. (Knittle)

YERIAN, L.M. Cumberland, Ohio, 1883-1902. Possibly M.L. Yerian. (Hutslar)

YERIAN, M. Columbia City, Indiana, 1862d.

YERIAN, M.L. see L.M. Yerian.

YERIAN, MOSES (1804-?), Allen Co., Indiana, 1850c, Columbia City, Indiana, 1861-1863, Greene Co., Indiana, 1888-1890. (Lindert)

YERIAN, THOMAS MADISON (1845-1928), Cumberland, Ohio, 1870-1928. (Hutslar)

YESLEY, H. Cincinnati, Ohio, 1840-1860.

YGLESIAS, JOSE New York, New York. Patent #114,742 May 5, 1871, breechloading firearm.

YITWELLER, ANTHONY Blair Co., Pennsylvania, 1850c. (Kauffman)

YOCHEM, MICHAEL Dubois Co., Indiana, 1870c. Percussion 1/2 stock. Also spelled Yoakum. (Lindert)

YOCUM, D. unlocated. Flintlock Kentucky rifles.

YOCUM, E.M. Reelsville, Indiana. Percussion 1/2 stock. (Lindert)

YOCUM, J.J. Orangeville, Pennsylvania, 1882d-1887d.

YOHN, PHILIP Montgomery Co., Pennsylvania, 1800c. (Kauffman)

YONLEY, ABSALOM Stark Co., Ohio, 1820c. (Hutslar)

YOPP, SAMUEL (?-1793), Lancaster Co., Virginia, 1756-1793. (Gill)

YORK, J.A. Mena, Arkansas, 1898d.

YORK, PARKER Caldwell, Kansas, 1868-1884d. For Draper Mercantile Co., 1884.

YORK, SANDERS Westerly, Rhode Island, 1854-1857.

YOST, CASPAR Lancaster Co., Pennsylvania, 1773-1778. Committee of Safety.

YOST, HENRY Frederick, Maryland, 1775-1776. Committee of Safety muskets with John Unsell. (Hartzler)

YOST, ISAAC Santa Ana, California, 1878-1881. (Shelton)

YOST, JOHN (1743-?), Georgetown, Maryland, 1775-1790c. Committee of Safety muskets and rifles. (Hartzler)

YOST, JOHN York, Pennsylvania, 1805. (Kauffman)

YOU BET suicide special.

YOULE, JAMES New York, New York, 1787-1792.

YOUMANS, I. unlocated. Flintlock Kentucky rifle.

YOUNG Boalsville, Pennsylvania, 1861d.

YOUNG & BERRY Liberty, Missouri, 1868d. A.J. Young.

YOUNG & LEAVITT New York, New York, 1850d-1855d. Dealers and Importers. Henry Young (1792-1874).

YOUNG AMERICA trade name of J.P. Lindsay on patent percussion pistols.

YOUNG AMERICAN trade name of (?) on double action revolver made by Harrington & Richardson.

YOUNG REPEATING ARMS CO. Columbus, Ohio, 1901-1903. Charles Addison Young's patent shotguns. Sears, Roebuck & Co. purchased factory in 1903. Charles Addison Young. (AR 9-66)

YOUNG, A. Marcellon, Wisconsin, 1857d.

YOUNG, A. Marion, Ohio, 1854d. (Hutslar)

YOUNG, A., & SONS Columbia, South Carolina. Imported percussion dueller.

YOUNG, A.J. Liberty, Missouri, 1867-1869d. As Young & Berry, 1868.

YOUNG, ALFRED Philadelphia, Pennsylvania. Patent #104,394, June 14, 1870, locks.

YOUNG, ARCANTHUS Barnstead, New Hampshire, 1865d-1873.

YOUNG, B.D. New Marion, Indiana, 1860d.

YOUNG, BRIGHAM Edgerton, Ohio, 1859d. (Hutslar)

YOUNG, C.E. Cumberland, Maryland, 1884d-1887d.

YOUNG, C.H. St. Charles, Iowa, 1865d.

YOUNG, CHARLES Lancaster, Pennsylvania, 1867d.

YOUNG, CHARLES Rochester, New York, 1871d. (Eich)

YOUNG, CHARLES A. (1834-?), Wheeling, West Virginia, 1850c, Weston, West Virginia, 1880c. (MB 10-63)

YOUNG, CHARLES ADDISON (1866-1951), Enon, Ohio, 1894-1906. Patents #543,366 July 23, 1895, ejecting gun, #676,809 June 18, 1901, magazine firearm, #709,385 September 16, 1902, magazine firearm, and #805,695 November 28, 1905, firearm. Shotguns made by Young Repeating Arms Co. (AR 9-66)

YOUNG, D. Birmingham, Kentucky, 1857-1860. Percussion 1/2 stock.

YOUNG, D. Boalsburg, Pennsylvania, 1861d.

YOUNG, D. Middleburg, Pennsylvania, 1816-1831. Percussion fullstock and swivel breech. (Dillin)

YOUNG, F.M. Camden, Maine, 1878. (Demeritt)

YOUNG, FRANKLIN K. Boston, Massachusetts, 1898-1905. Patents #624,145 May 2, 1899, automatic firearm, #624,146 May 2, 1899, cartridge, #691,040 January 14, 1902, firearm, #764,513 July 5, 1904, firearm, and #783,770 February 28, 1905, firearm with J.E. Sheriff.

YOUNG, GEORGE (1802-?), Perry Co., Illinois, 1840-1850. (Johnson)

YOUNG, GEORGE Eureka, Nevada, 1878d-1880d.

YOUNG, GEORGE Romney, Virginia, 1824-1833. Flintlock and percussion guns. (Bowers)

YOUNG, GUSTAVUS Hopkinsville, Kentucky, 1883d. Son of John Young.

YOUNG, H. Swanton, Ohio, 1860d-1864d. (Hutslar)

YOUNG, HENRY (1770-?), Michigan City, Indiana, 1850c. (Lindert)

YOUNG, HENRY (1792-1874), New York, New York, 1820-1858d. As H. Young & Co., 1830-1842, Young, Redfield & Leavitt, 1843-1849, Young & Leavitt, 1850-1855, and Young, Smith & Co., 1856-1858. Importers and dealers. (AG 3-75)

YOUNG, HENRY (1832-?), Lynn Grove, Indiana, 1860d. (Lindert)

YOUNG, HENRY Easton, Pennsylvania, 1774-1786t. (Dillin)

YOUNG, J.K. Easton, Pennsylvania, 1868d.

YOUNG, J.N. Independence, Iowa, 1882d-1889d.

YOUNG, JACOB Easton, Pennsylvania, 1835t. (KRA II-3)

YOUNG, JACOB Wilkes-Barre, Pennsylvania, 1805-1819. Flintlock Kentucky. (KRA 76)

YOUNG, JAMES Detroit, Michigan, 1860d-1863d.

YOUNG, JOE Proctor, West Virginia, 1884d. Percussion 1/2 stock.

YOUNG, JOHN (1825-?), Milton, Ohio, 1850c. Percussion fullstock. (Hutslar)

YOUNG, JOHN (1826-?), Michigan City, Indiana, 1850c-1871d, Kingsbury, Indiana, 1882-1885. Percussion 1/2 stock. (MB 4-54)

YOUNG, JOHN Annapolis, Maryland, 1728-1740. Armorer to the colony. (Gluckman & Satterlee)

YOUNG, JOHN Easton, Pennsylvania, 1770t-1805t. Committee of Safety rifles with Johnson Smith and Adam Foulke. Brother of Henry Young. (Kauffman)

YOUNG, JOHN Hopkinsville, Kentucky, 1879d.

YOUNG, JOHN New Hebron, Illinois, 1854d.

YOUNG, JOHN, JR. Easton, Pennsylvania, 1780t-1804t. (Dyke)

YOUNG, JOSEPH Harpers Run, West Virginia. Percussion fullstock. (Dillin)

YOUNG, L.G. Momence, Illinois, 1893d.

YOUNG, LEWIS V. St. Louis, Missouri. Patent #104,682 June 21, 1870, breechloading firearm.

YOUNG, M.R. Northfield, Minnesota, 1892d.

YOUNG, MARSHALL (1829-?), Nicholas Co., West Virginia, 1850c. (Whisker IV)

YOUNG, MICHAEL Bushkill, Pennsylvania, 1828t. (KRA II-3)

YOUNG, MILTON Watertown, New York, 1870d. Percussion 1/2 stock. (Clow)

YOUNG, N.G. Millbrook, Michigan, 1895d.

YOUNG, N.G. Northfield, Minnesota, 1882d.

YOUNG, NATHANIEL Fairfield Co., Ohio, 1803. (Knittle)

YOUNG, PETER Easton, Pennsylvania, 1807t-1835t. (KRA II-3)

YOUNG, PETER Philadelphia, Pennsylvania, 1800-1820. Flintlock Kentucky. (Kauffman)

YOUNG, SETH Hartford, Connecticut. Patent #none May 1, 1810, gun barrel turning.

YOUNG, SMITH & CO. New York, New York. Agents for Allen pepperbox. Henry Young (1792-1874).

YOUNG, THOMAS K. Easton, Pennsylvania, 1867-1876.

YOUNG, WILLIAM Hannibal, Missouri, 1893d.

YOUNG, WILLIAM E. Davenport, Iowa, 1865d-1882d.

YOUNG, WILLIAM, & BRO. Easton, Pennsylvania, 1861d.

YOUNG, WILLIAM, JR. Easton, Pennsylvania, 1804t-1835t. (KRA II-3)

YOUNGER, JOHN Terry, Tennessee, 1860d.

YOUNGMAN, JOHN A. Morris, New Jersey, 1867-1870.

YOUS, JOSHUA (1827-1905), Greencastle, Pennsylvania, 1854t-1861d. Percussion fullstock. (Bowers)

YOUTZE, GEORGE Wilmot, Ohio. (Knittle)

YOWELL, CHRISTOPHER (?-1762), Culpepper Co., Virginia. (Gill)

YUDER, REUBEN (1828-?), Catawba Co., North Carolina, 1850c. (Bivins)

YUNGLOFF, JACOB FREDERICK (1819-?), Placerville, California, 1858-1890. (Shelton)

YUTZY, RUBEN Winesburg, Ohio, 1839-1875. Percussion 1/2 stock. (Hutslar)

Z SECTION

Z.A. see Zachariah Albright.

ZAHM, GOTTFRIED Lancaster, Pennsylvania, 1810-1815. (Dean)

ZAHM, MATTHIAS Lancaster, Pennsylvania, 1814t-1816. (Kauffman)

ZAHN, CHARLES Elizabeth, New Jersey, 1875d.

ZAHRINGER, EUGENE Pittsburgh, Pennsylvania, 1860. (Kauffman)

ZALSMAN, J.F. Holland, Michigan, 1895d-1899d.

ZAMBA, JOSEPH (1830-?), Marysville, California, 1867-1875. (Shelton)

ZAMBONI, CARL Owatonna, Minnesota, 1877-1880.

ZAMBONI, JOHN St. Louis, Missouri, 1870d.

ZANNETTI, F.C. Bryan, Texas, 1890d.

ZARTMAN, JOSHUA (1816-1891), Newark, Ohio, 1850c-1889d. Percussion 1/2 and fullstock. (Hutslar)

ZARUBA, JOSEPH Terrell, Texas, 1878d and 1890d-1896d, Lampassas, Texas, 1884d.

ZEDICH, RODERICK St. Louis, Missouri, 1848d.

ZEECK, ANDREW New Madison, Ohio, 1853d-1883d. Rifles. (Hutslar)

ZEHR, CHRISTIAN Croghan, New York, 1870d.

ZEMAN, J.A. Davenport, Iowa, 1895d.

ZEPERNICK, CHARLES Mobile, Alabama, 1870d. Percussion pistol. As Danne & Zepernick.

ZETTLER BROS. New York, New York. Christian J. Zettler. See C.J. & B. Zettler.

ZETTLER, C.J. & B. New York, New York, 1868d-1893d. Percussion schuetzen rifle. Christian J. Zettler. Also as Zettler Brothers.

ZETTLER, CHRISTIAN J. New York, New York, 1858d-1893d. As C.J. & B. Zettler, 1868-1893. Also as Zettler Bros.

ZETTLER, IGNATZ Cincinnati, Ohio, 1870d-1892d.

ZETTLER, JOHN New York, New York, 1847-185?. Percussion and breechloading schuetzen rifles.

ZIEGLER, E.W. & J. Elgin, Illinois, 1888d.

ZIEGLER, H.D., & CO. Portsmouth, Ohio, 1858d-1878d. Henry D. Ziegler. (Hutslar)

ZIEGLER, HENRY D. Cincinnati, Ohio, Portsmouth, Ohio, 1853-1896. Percussion guns. As H.D. Ziegler & Co., 1858-1878. (Hutslar)

ZIEGLER, MICHAEL Aurora, Illinois, 1896d-1899d.

ZIEHM, AUGUST San Antonio, Texas, 1887d-1897d.

ZIETHEN, ALBERT Shakopee, Minnesota, 1898d.

ZIGG, JOSEPH (1836-?), St. Louis, Missouri, 1850c. Apprenticed to J. Hoffstether. (Lewis)

ZIMANSKI, NATHAN Chicago, Illinois, 1872d-1873d.

ZIMMER, EMIL Chicago, Illinois, 1872d-1873d.

ZIMMER, H.C. Pecos, Texas, 1890d.

ZIMMER, JACOB (1827-?), Tiffin, Ohio, 1850c. (Hutslar)

ZIMMERMAN Homerville, Ohio. (Hutslar)

ZIMMERMAN BROS. Hutchinson, Kansas, 1884d.

ZIMMERMAN, CHARLES Newport, Kentucky, 1895d.

ZIMMERMAN, E.G. (1810-?), Ross Co., Ohio, 1850c. (Hutslar)

ZIMMERMAN, E.T. unlocated. Percussion fullstock.

ZIMMERMAN, F.C. (1838-?), Dodge City, Kansas, 1872-1900.

ZIMMERMAN, J. Carlisle, Indiana, 1858d.

ZIMMERMAN, JOHN Sunbury, Pennsylvania, 1870c.

ZIMMERMAN, JOHN L. Chicago, Illinois, 1860d-1868d.

ZIMMERMAN, S. San Antonio, Texas, 1879d.

ZIMMERMAN, SAMUEL Westmoreland Co., Pennsylvania, 1827-1829. Flintlock Kentucky. (Whisker II)

ZINGG, CONRAD EUGENE (1849-1882), San Jose, California, 1873-1882. Operated shooting galleries in many locations. (Shelton)

ZINGG, JOHN JOSEPH (1857-?), San Jose, California, 1876-1900. (Shelton)

ZINGLER, WILLIAM (1820-?), Gilroy, California, 1869, San Jose, California, 1870-1872. Worked for other gunsmiths. (Shelton)

ZINGY, JOSEPH. Centralia, Illinois, 1867d.

ZINK, ALBERT (1837-?), Port Carbon, Pennsylvania, 1862. (Kauffman)

ZINK, J.M. Mixersville, Indiana, 1860. Percussion 1/2 stock. (Lindert)

ZINK, JOHN Panther Valley, Missouri, 1881d.

ZINK, JOSEPH Union, Missouri, 1850c-1860d.

ZINN, H.C. Leann, Missouri, 1898d.

ZISCHANG, AUGUST O. (1846-1925), Bridgeport, Connecticut, 1876-1879, Syracuse, New York, 1879-1925. Percussion rifles and cartridge alterations of highest quality. (Kelver)

ZISCHANG, WILLIAM O. (1878-1956). Syracuse, New York, 1892-1945. Son of August Zischang. (Kelver)

ZITTEL, FREDERICK Buffalo, New York, 1836. For Joseph Haberstro. (Kauffman 2)

ZITTEL, GEORGE Buffalo, New York, 1836. For Patrick Smith. (Kauffman 2)

ZOLLINGER, A. LaGrange Co., Indiana. (Lindert)

ZOLLINGER, GEORGE Harrisburg, Pennsylvania, 1811t, Carlisle, Pennsylvania, 1819-1842. Converted Kentucky. (Kauffman)

ZOLLMAN, S.B. Lexington, Virginia, 1890d-1897d.

ZORGER, C. York, Pennsylvania. Flintlock Kentucky. Son of Frederick Zorger. (Kindig)

ZORGER, FREDERICK (1734-1815), York, Pennsylvania, 1776-1807. Flintlock Kentucky rifles and pistols. (Kindig)

ZORGER, G. York, Pennsylvania, circa 1800. (Kindig)

ZUBERBEIR, AUGUST W. Logan, Minnesota. Patent #612,298 October 11, 1898, gun support.

ZUCCARELLE, N.B. Pulaski, Tennessee, 1884d. Percussion fullstock.

ZUENDORFF, JOHN New York, New York, 1851d-1886d. Patent #237,357 February 1, 1881, parlor gun. Air guns. (Wolff)

ZUIN & CLARK Philadelphia, Pennsylvania, 1860c. See Quinn & Clark.

ZULU trade name on imported, converted action, shotguns.

ZUZER, J.G. Arnheim, Pennsylvania, 1850-1858. (Gluckman & Satterlee)

ZWEIFEL & RIEDEL Council Bluffs, Iowa, 1869d.

ZWEIFUS, I. Cincinnati, Ohio, 1888d. (Hutslar)

ZWEIZ, BENJAMIN (1806-?), Columbia, Illinois, 1860c. (Johnson)

ZWIERZYNSKI, HERMAN St. Paul, Minnesota, 1878d.

BIBLIOGRAPHY

BOOKS

ACHTERMIER, WILLIAM O. *RHODE ISLAND ARMS MAKERS AND GUNSMITHS*, Man-at-Arms, Providence, Rhode Island, 1980.

ALBAUGH, WILLIAM A., III
1. *CONFEDERATE ARMS*, with Edward N. Simmons, The Stackpole Co., Harrisburg, Pennsylvania, 1957
2. *TYLER, TEXAS, C.S.A.*, The Stackpole Co., Harrisburg, Pennsylvania, 1958
3. *CONFEDERATE HANDGUNS*, with Hugh Benet, Jr. and Edward N. Simmons. Riling & Lentz, Philadelphia, Pennsylvania, 1963

BECK, HERBERT L.
1. "Martin Meylin" Vol. LIII No. 2 *PAPERS OF THE LANCASTER CO. HISTORICAL SOCIETY*, Lancaster, Pennsylvania
2. "William Henry" Vol. LIV No. 4, *PAPERS OF THE LANCASTER CO. HISTORICAL SOCIETY*, Lancaster, Pennsylvania
3. "Henry E. Leman, Riflemaker" Vol. LX, No.3, *PAPERS OF THE LANCASTER CO. HISTORICAL SOCIETY*, Lancaster, Pennsylvania

BIVINS, JOHN, JR.
LONGRIFLES OF NORTH CAROLINA, George Shumway, York, Pennsylvania, 1968

BOEHRET, PAUL C.
ARMING THE TROOPS, Hobson Printing Co., Easton, Pennsylvania, 1967

BOWERS, WILLIAM S.
GUNSMITHS OF PEN-MAR-VA, Irwinton Publishers, Mercersburg, Pennsylvania, 1979

CAREY, A. MERWYN
AMERICAN FIREARMS MAKERS, Thomas Y. Crowell Company, New York New York, 1953

CHANDLER, ROY F.
1. *KENTUCKY RIFLE PATCHBOXES*, David E. Little, Duncannon, Pennsylvania, 1972
2. *A History of Perry County Guns & Gunsmiths*, Author, Duncannon, Pennsylvania, 1969

CHANDLER, ROY F. & WHISKER, JAMES B.
PENNSYLVANIA GUNMAKERS, A COLLECTION, Old Bedford Press, Bedford, Pennsylvania, 1984

CLINE, WALTER M.
THE MUZZLE LOADING RIFLE, THEN & NOW, Standard Printing & Publishing Co., Huntington, West Virginia, 1942

CHINN, GEORGE M.
THE MACHINE GUN, Vol. I, U.S. Government Printing Office, Washington, D.C., 1951

CLOW, MILTON
CATALOG OF COLLECTION, Shephards Sales Service, Ithaca, New York, 1957

CROMWELL, GILES
THE VIRGINIA MANUFACTORY OF ARMS, University of Virginia Press, Charlottesville, Virginia, 1975

DEAN, HERMAN C.
Unpublished data gathered over fifty years of collecting, now in possession of William Myers. Those marked with an asterisk (*) were furnished to Dean by C.W. Sawyer

DEMERITT, DWIGHT B., JR.
MAINE MADE GUNS AND THEIR MAKERS, Maine State Museum, Hallowell, Maine, 1973

DEYRUP, FELICIA J.
ARMS MAKERS OF THE CONNECTICUT VALLEY, Smith College, Northhampton, Massachusetts, 1948

DILLIN, JOHN G.W.
THE KENTUCKY RIFLE, The National Rifle Association, Washington, D.C., 1924

DUNLAP, JACK
PEPPERBOX FIREARMS, H.J. Dunlap, Los Altos, California, 1964

DYKE, SAMUEL E.
THE PENNSYLVANIA RIFLE, Sutton House, Lititz, Pennsylvania, 1974. Mr. Dyke also has a vast amount of unpublished material on the early gunsmiths of Pennsylvania and New York. See also references in *AMERICAN ARMS COLLECTOR*, *ASAC BULLETIN*, and *KRA BULLETIN*

EICH, EDWARD L.
A CHECKLIST OF ROCHESTER, N.Y. GUNMAKERS AND GUNSMITHS, E.L. Eich, Auburn, New York, 1965

ELIAS, CHARLES H.
RIFLE MAKERS OF ARKANSAS, C.H. Elias, Little Rock, Arkansas, 1970

FJESTAD, S.P.
BLUE BOOK OF GUN VALUES, TWENTY-NINTH EDITION, Blue Book Publications, Inc., Minneapolis, Minnesota, 2008

FORS, W. BARLOW
COLLECTOR'S HANDBOOK-U.S. CARTRIDGE REVOLVERS, Barlow Book Co., Northbrook, Illinois, 1973

FROST, GORDON
BLADES AND BARRELS, Walloon Press, El Paso, Texas, 1972

FULLER, CLAUD E.
1. *THE WHITNEY FIREARMS*, Standard Publications, Huntington, West Virginia, 1946
2. *THE RIFLED MUSKET*, The Stackpole Company, Harrisburg, Pennsylvania, 1958

GABEL, RONALD G.
Unpublished data on the makers of East-Central Pennsylvania. See also articles in *ASAC BULLETIN* and *KRA BULLETIN*

GARDNER, ROBERT E.
SMALL ARMS MAKERS, Crown Publishers, Inc., New York City, New York, 1963

GILL, HAROLD B., JR.
THE GUNSMITH IN COLONIAL VIRGINIA, The Colonial Williamsburg Foundation, Williamsburg, Virginia, 1974

GLUCKMAN, ARCADI
UNITED STATES MUSKETS, RIFLES, AND CARBINES, Otto Ulbrich Co., Inc., Buffalo, New York, 1948

GLUCKMAN, ARCADI & SATTERLEE, L.D.
AMERICAN GUN MAKERS, The Ulbrich Co., Inc., Buffalo, New York, 1940

GRANT, JAMES J.
1. *SINGLE SHOT RIFLES*, The Gun Room Press, Highland Park, New Jersey, 1982
2. *MORE SINGLE SHOT RIFLES*, The Gun Room Press, Highland Park, New Jersey, 1976
3. *BOYS SINGLE SHOT RIFLES*, Wm. Morrow & Co., New York City, New York, 1967

HANSON, CHARLES E., JR.
1. *THE PLAINS RIFLE*, The Gun Room Press, Highland Park, New Jersey, 1976
2. *THE HAWKEN RIFLE*, The Fur Press, Chadron, Nebraska, 1979

HARTZLER, DANIEL D.
ARMS MAKERS OF MARYLAND, George Shumway, York, Pennsylvania, 1977

HETRICK, CALVIN
THE BEDFORD COUNTY RIFLE, George Shumway, York, Pennsylvania, 1973. NOTE: This originally appeared in the 4th Edition of Dillin's THE KENTUCKY RIFLE

HICKS, JAMES
NATHAN STARR, ARMSMAKER, James Hicks, Mt. Vernon, New York, 1940

HILL, R.T. and ANTHONY, W.E.
CONFEDERATE LONGARMS AND PISTOLS, R.T. Hill and W.E. Anthony, Charlotte, North Carolina, 1978

HINMAN, BOB
THE GOLDEN AGE OF SHOTGUNNING, Winchester Press, New York City, New York, 1971

HOGG, IAN V.
THE COMPLETE ILLUSTRATED ENCYCLOPEDIA OF THE WORLD'S FIREARMS, A&W Publishers, Inc., New York, New York, 1978

HORN, WARREN R.
GUNSMITHS AND GUNMAKERS OF VERMONT, The Horn Co., Burlington, Vermont, 1975

HUNTINGTON, R.I.
HALL'S BREECHLOADERS, George Shumway, York, Pennsylvania, 1972

HUTSLAR, DONALD A.
GUNSMITHS OF OHIO, George Shumway, York, Pennsylvania, 1973

JINKS, ROY
HISTORY OF SMITH & WESSON, Beinfeld Publishing, North Hollywood, California, 1978

JOHNSON, CURTIS L.
ILLINOIS GUNSMITHS, George Shumway, York, Pennsylvania, 1974

JOHNSON, PETER H.
PARKER, The Stackpole Co., Harrisburg, Pennsylvania, 1961

KAUFFMAN, HENRY J.
1. *THE PENNSYLVANIA- KENTUCKY RIFLE*, Bonanza, New York City, New York, 1960
2. *EARLY AMERICAN GUNSMITHS*, The Stackpole Co., Harrisburg, Pennsylvania, 1952

KELVER, GERALD O.
100 YEARS OF SHOOTERS AND GUNMAKERS OF SINGLE SHOT RIFLES, Gerald Kelver, Brighton, Colorado, 1975

KENTUCKY RIFLE ASSOCIATION
KENTUCKY RIFLES & PISTOLS 1750-1850, KRA, Columbus, Ohio, 1976

KINDIG, JOE
THOUGHTS ON THE KENTUCKY RIFLE, George N. Hyatt, Wilmington, Delaware, 1960

KNITTLE, RHEA M. & MARTIN, STUART M.
EARLY OHIO SILVERSMITHS AND PEWTERERS, The Calvert-Hatch Co. Cleveland, Ohio, 1943. NOTE: This information also appeared in an article in "The Magazine Antiques" May 1943 and "Muzzle Blasts" Feb-April, 1956

LEWIS, GORDON
Unpublished-census of Missouri

LINDERT, ALBERT W.
GUNMAKERS OF INDIANA, Albert Lindert, Homewood, Indiana, 1968

LINDSAY, MERRILL
1. *THE KENTUCKY RIFLE*, Arma Press, North Branford, Connecticut, 1972
2. *THE NEW ENGLAND GUN*, The New Haven Colony Historical Society, New Haven, Connecticut, 1975
3. *TWENTY GREAT AMERICAN GUNS*, Excerpt from "Armi Antichi," Rome, Italy, 1976

LOGAN, HERSCHEL C.
UNDERHAMMER GUNS, The Stackpole Co., Harrisburg, Pennsylvania, 1960

McLEAN, J.H.
DR. J.H. McLEAN'S PEACEMAKERS, Baker & Godwin, New York, New York, 1880

MASSACHUSETTS ARMS
SAMUEL COLT VS. MASS. ARMS CO., US. CIRCUIT COURT, BOSTON, MASS., JUNE 30, 1851, Daniel Steadman, Boston, Massachusetts, 1863

MAXWELL, SAMUEL
LEVER ACTION MAGAZINE RIFLES, S.E. Maxwell, Bellvue, Washington, 1976

MOLLER, GEORGE D.
Unpublished data on U.S. Military shoulder arms (see Arms Gazette for articles)

MOUILLESSEAUX, HAROLD R.
ETHAN ALLEN, GUNMAKER, Museum Restoration Service, Ottawa, Canada, 1973

MUELLER, CHESTER & OLSON, JOHN
SMALL ARMS LEXICON AND CONCISE ENCYCLOPEDIA, Shooter's Bible, Inc., South Hackensack, New Jersey, 1968

MURRAY, DOUGLAS P.
THE NINETY-NINE, Douglas P. Murray, Westbury, New York, 1976

NUTTER, WALDO
MANHATTAN FIREARMS, The Stackpole Co., Harrisburg, Pennsylvania, 1958

PARSONS, JOHN E.
HENRY DERRINGER'S POCKET PISTOL, William Morrow & Co., New York, New York 1952

PERKINS, JIM
AMERICAN BOYS RIFLES, ARA Corp., Koppel, Pennsylvania, 1976

PHILIPS, PHILIP R.
PATERSON ARMS, Jackson Arms, Dallas, Texas, 1979

POURIE, DeWITT
Unpublished studies of St. Louis Makers

ROBERTS, NED H.
THE MUZZLE-LOADING CAP LOCK RIFLE, The Clark Press, Manchester, New Hampshire, 1944

SELLERS, FRANK M.
1. *AMERICAN PERCUSSION REVOLVERS*, with Samuel E. Smith, Museum Restoration Service, Ottawa, Canada, 1971
2. *THE WILLIAM M. LOCKE COLLECTION*, The Antique Armory Inc., East Point, Georgia, 1973
3. *COLORADO GUNMAKERS*, American Society of Arms Collectors, Cincinnati, Ohio, 1981. Published previously in *COLORADO GUN COLLECTORS ASSOCIATION ANNUAL*
4. *SHARPS FIREARMS*, Beinfeld Publications, North Hollywood, California, 1978

SHELTON, LAWRENCE P.
CALIFORNIA GUNSMITHS, Far West Publishers, Fair Oaks, California, 1977

SMITH, FORREST
Unpublished studies of shotguns.

SMITH, W.H.B.
MAUSER RIFLES AND PISTOLS, Wolfe Publishing Company, Prescott, Arizona, 1990

STOCKBRIDGE, V.D.
DIGEST OF U.S. PATENTS, Government Printing Office, Washington, D.C., 1874

SUTHERLAND, ROBERT and WILSON, R.L.
THE BOOK OF COLT FIREARMS, R.Q. Sutherland, Kansas City, Missouri, 1971

SWAYZE, NATHAN L.
THE RAPPAHANNOCK FORGE, American Society of Arms Collectors, Cincinnati, Ohio, 1976

SWINNEY, HOLMAN J.
NEW YORK STATE GUNMAKERS, Fremans Journal Press, Cooperstown, New York, 1951

WEBSTER, DONALD B., JR.
SUICIDE SPECIALS, The Stackpole Co., Harrisburg, Pennsylvania, 1958

WHISKER, JAMES B. & VAUGHN E.
THE BEDFORD COUNTY PENNSYLVANIA RIFLE BOOK, Old Bedford Village Press, Bedford, Pennsylvania, 1982

WILLIAMSON, HAROLD F.
WINCHESTER, Combat Forces Press, Washington, D.C., 1952

WINANT, LEWIS
1. *FIREARMS CURIOSA*, Greenberg Publisher, New York, New York, 1955
2. *EARLY PERCUSSION FIREARMS*, Crown Publishers, Inc., New York, New York, 1959

WOLFF, ELDON G.
AIR GUNS, Milwaukee Public Museum, Milwaukee, Wisconsin, 1958

PERIODICALS

The codes used in the text are as follows:

AAC   *AMERICAN ARMS COLLECTOR*, The Collectors Press, Towson, Maryland, 1957-1958
4-57, Samuel E. Smith, "Plant Revolvers"
10-57, Samuel E. Dyke, "William Antes"
4-58, Samuel E. Dyke, "Cornelius Atherton"
10-58, James E. Fields, "Pioneer Guns of California"

AR   *AMERICAN RIFLEMAN*, National Rifle Assoc., Fairfax, Virginia, 1923-date. Monthly publications for members only
2-25, "Daniel Boone's Rifle"
8-27, L.D. Satterlee, "The Early Ballard"
3-26, L.D. Satterlee, "Tobias"
11-26, L.D. Satterlee, "Stevens Pistols"
12-32, L.D. Satterlee, "D.C.

Addicks"
9-37, L.D. Satterlee, "Will Wirsing"
12-39, W.V. Lowe, "Early Experiences," 2 parts.
12-40, Warner Ogden, "He's still making long Hog Rifles"
9-48, W.G.C. Kimball, "The Chicopee Falls Rifle"
9-55, John Dumont, "Harmon Fife"
2-56, M.D. Waite, "The White-Merrill Pistols"
3-55, B.R. Lewis, "Morse Arms and Ammunition"
12-57, Herschel C. Logan, "Bacon Arms"
4-58, H.L. Blackmore, "Chambers Repeating Flintlock"
1-61, Herschel C. Logan, "L.W. Pond Revolvers"
1-63, Thomas B. Rentschler, "Gwyn & Campbell Carbines"
3-64, Thomas B. Rentschler, "Cosmopolitan Arms Co. Rifle"
12-65, Thomas B. Rentschler, "Gross Revolvers"
9-66, Donald A. Hutslar, "Young Repeating Shotgun"
6-64, A.D. Lewis, "The Hollenbeck 3-Barrel Gun"
2-69, Harold E. McFarland, "Folsom Trade Branded Guns"
4-70, Elliott L. Minor, "American Arms Co."
2-73, Eugene L. Lyons, "C.S. Shattucks' Little Equalizer"
2-74, Eugene L. Lyons, "Where Sears Got Its Guns"
5-75, Kenneth L. Cope, "The Smith Who Wasn't with Wesson"

ASAC *AMERICAN SOCIETY OF ARMS COLLECTORS*, Cincinnati, Ohio, 1955-date. Bi-ennial publication for members only
1, Samuel E. Smith, "Lindsay Pistols"
3, R.C. Kuhn, "U.S. Martial Flintlock Pistols"
6, H.W. Williams, "Union Arms Co."
7, Clarence Fall, "St. Louis Guns"
17, J.C. McMurray, "U.S. Martial Flintlock Rifles"
21, L.D. Eberhart, "Perry & Goddard"
23, Robin Hale, "Tennessee Rifles"
25, S.E. Dyke, "The Moll Family of Gunsmiths"
30, L.D. Eberhart, "William W. Marston"
33, J. Altemus, "Hewes & Phillips"
35, R.C. Gabel, "Lehigh Kentuckies"
35, H.M. Stewart, "Philadelphia Air Guns"
35, Wm. Guthman, "Arms of the Revolutionary Period"
39, L.D. Eberhart, "W.W. Marston"
39, R.E. Neville, "James Conning"
40, Gerald Denning, "Rare Pairs"
44, F. Allen Thompson, "Gunmakers of Worcester County"

AG *ARMS GAZETTE*, Beinfeld Publishing Co., Inc., North Hollywood, California, 1973-1981
2-75, William Achtermeir, "Welcome Mathewson"
3-75, Herbert Rosenthal, "A. Frederick Lins Rifle Muskets"
3-75, Ernest D. Laube, "Henry Young, New York Pistols"
4-75, Eugene L. Lyons, "Collecting Single Barrel Shotguns"
6-77, William R. Williamson, "Daniel Searles of Baton Rouge"
5-78, Doug Eberhart and R.L. Wilson, "Deringers, Durringers, Diringers"
6-78, Herschell C. Logan, "E.A. Prescott"
6-78, Herschell C. Logan, "J.E. Evans of Philadelphia"
3-79, George D. Moller, "Proof and Inspection of U.S. Military Shoulder Arms" (3-parts)
11-79, Vern Ecklund, "King & Smith"
12-79, H.L. McDonell, "John Bassett's rifle"

AOLRC *ASSOCIATION OF OHIO LONGRIFLE COLLECTORS*
111-2, J. & B. Mast, "Holmes Co. Gunsmith"
V-2, Dewey Stull, "More Information On Sam Stull"

BUGLE *MONTHLY BUGLE*, Pennsylvania Antique Gun Collectors Assn., Pottstown, Pennsylvania, 1969-date. Monthly publications for members only
46, Henry M. Stewart Jr., "Mr. Porter of Memphis and His Rifle"
49, Henry M. Stewart Jr., "A Box of Goodies"
51, George E. Hunter, "The Wheeler Musket"
61, Author unknown, reference to William Wurfflein
72, Henry M. Stewart Jr., "Alarms of the 1800's"
79, Paul J. Leaser, "A Presentation Kentucky Breechloading Rifle"
114, Vincent Nolt, "William Reichenbach's Gun Making Tools"

GC *GUN COLLECTOR, THE*, G.C. Harrison, Madison, Wisconsin, 1946-1957
1, J.T. Teesdale, "Wisconsin Gun Makers"
18, Samuel E. Smith, "The Newbury Arms Company"
22, Paul Jahnke, "The Dance Brothers"
24, Samuel E. Smith, "The Percival & Smith Repeating Pistol"
24, "Philadelphia Gunsmiths in 1829"
27, Samuel E. Smith, "The Lancaster Texas Revolvers"
27, "The Gunsmiths of New Orleans, 1853"
30, C.M. Patterson, "George Elgins' Pistols"
42, Samuel E. Smith, "Reid's Knuckledusters"

BIBLIOGRAPHY, cont.

GD *GUN DIGEST*, Digest Publications Inc., Chicago, Illinois, 1944-date
7, James Grant, "Crazy Calibers"
16, Richard H. Chamberlain, "W. Milton Farrow"
20, Wallace Labisky, "Dan Lefever"
28, John Dutcher, "George C. Schoyen"

GR *GUN REPORT*, World Wide Gun Report Inc., 1955-date
12-57, G. Charter Harrison, "The Saloon Gun"
4-58, Robert McAfee, "The R. Ashmore Mystery"
10-58, Graham Burnside, "Herman Schlegelmilch"
11-58, J.H. Brooks, "Wurfflein Gallery Rifle"
12-59, C.M. Patterson, "Aaron Vaughan's Double-barreled Percussion Revolver"
12-59, Graham Burnside, "Anton Spellerberg, Philadelphia"
2-60, James Hicks, "Boynton Magazine Pistol"
8-60, Graham Burnside, "An Allen-Johnson Gun"
9-60, C.M. Patterson, "Gunstocking Genius" (2 parts)
12-60, C.M. Patterson, "Waters Gunmaking Family" (15 parts)
1-61, Richard H. Chamberlain, "Christian Patt, Wisconsin Gunmaker"
2-61, Andrew Lustyik, "The Wilkinson & Wood Carbine"
12-61, DeWitt Settle, "Settle Riflemakers of Kentucky"
4-62, R.H. Chamberlain, "Renick Bullet Mold"
8-62, R.T. Lyon, "Conrad Horn"
11-62, Tommy Bish, "The Swingle & Huntington Rifle"
10-63, Andrew Lustyik, "The Schroeder Carbine"
1-64, Art Chipman, "A Gunsmith of the Old West"
2-65, Charles Suydam, "Davenport's Fort Scott"
7-65, Andrew Lustyik, "4th of July Pistols"
8-65, R.L. Moore, "Louis Hoffman of Vicksburg"
9-65, Andrew Lustyik, "Dr. Maynard's Tape Primer" (4 parts)
3-66, Andrew Lustyik, "The Amoskeag Company's Fourteen Shooter"
4-66, A.W. Lawbaugh, "Merwin & Hulbert, Another Chapter"
7-66, Andrew Lustyik, "The Lamson Company Carbines" (2 parts)
10-66, Andrew Lustyik, "LeProtector"
11-66, C.M. Patterson & James Rasmussen, "Lindner's Magazine Repeater" (4 parts)
1-67, W.P. Smith, "Protector Revolver"
4-67, W.P. Smith, "The Whitney Safety Firearms Co."
4-67, Andrew Lustyik, "James W. Cruver"
6-67, H.L. Uphoff, "Lee's Fire Arms Co." (2 parts)
7-67, Andrew Lustyik, "The Howe Carbine"
8-67, W.E. Nutter, "Metropolitan Arms Co., New York" (2 parts)
4-68, Andrew Lustyik, "History of Military Pyrotechnics" (3 parts)
6-68, Warren Hay, "U.S. Amoskeag"
7-68, J.T. Teesdale, "Saxton's Cane Gun"
11-68, Art Chipman, "A Gunsmith of the Early West"
10-69, C.R. Suydam, "Accelerating Rifle"
5-70, Andrew Lustyik, "The Symmes Carbine"
5-70, J.P. Rehling, "Boyd & Tyler Shotgun"
9-70, A.F. Nehrbass, "Stephen Jenks & Sons"
9-70, J.A. Carderelli, "Briggs Underhammer Musket"
3-71, Andrew Lustyik, "John P. Schenkl"
4-71, Richard Wagner, "E.A. Prescott"
10-71, Willard C. Cousins, "Joseph Weherbee"
11-71, Andrew Lustyik, "The Breechloaders of James Durrell Greene" (3 parts)
1-72, C.E. Smith and Charles Suydam, "The DeGress 'Tiffany' Grips"
6-72, Willard C. Cousins, "Phinehas Sawyer"
9-72, Eugene L. Lyon, "Davenport Firearms Co."
11-72, Richard Wagner, "Frank Copeland, 1833-1927"
7-73, W.H. Johnson, "The Howard Thunderbolt"
11-73, Willard C. Cousins, "Josiah Meriam, Patriot Gunsmith"
6-74, Willard C. Cousins, "Captain Ross Wyman, Patriot Gunsmith"
7-74, Eugene L. Lyon, "The Last of the Norwich Gun Makers"
4-75, Willard C. Cousins, "Samuel Barret, Patriot Gunsmith"
7-75, A.M. Chernoff, "W.O. Robertson Cap Lock Rifle"
3-76, Willard C. Cousins, "Captain Silas Allen, Jr., Gunsmith, Shrewsbury, Mass."
5-76, Gerald Kelver, "Quackenbush"
7-76, Willard C. Cousins, "Captain Joab Hapgood, Gunmaker" (2 parts)
12-76, Edward A. Hull, "T.T.S. Laidley"
1-77, Willard C. Cousins, "Alvan Pratt" (2 parts)
2-77, F.K. Johnson, "Samuel Watson Johnson"
1-78, Edward A. Hull, "The Brand Patent Civil War Breechloaders"
4-78, Willard C. Cousins, "Captain Artemus Wheeler, Gunsmith" (4 parts)
8-78, Joe Race, "David Hall Hillard, Gunsmith"
12-78, Edward A. Hull, "The Marsh Breechloader"
2-79, Andrew F. Lustyik, "The Kellogg Carbine"
6-79, Andrew F. Lustyik, "Testing the Triplett & Scott Carbine" (2 parts)

G&A *GUNS & AMMO*, Peterson Publishing, Hollywood, California, 1955-date
7-61, R.H. Rankin, "The Hotchkiss Story"
1971 Annual, author unknown, reference to Sims-Dudley Defense Co.

HOBBIES *HOBBIES*, Hobbies Publishing Co., Chicago, Illinois, 1931-date
6-31, "Some Early Gunsmiths"
1-33, Carroll Dulaney, "Early Baltimore Gunsmiths"
8-33, "Who Can Answer"
9-34, L.D. Satterlee, "Elias Earle-Adam Carruth"
10-34, L.D. Satterlee, "Robert McCormick" (3 parts)
3-35, L.D. Satterlee, "A Convention of Gunsmiths"
5-37, Berks Co. Hist. Soc., "The Gun Makers Along Wyomissing Creek"
4-38, L.D. Satterlee, "The Committee of Safety Musket"
10-38, L.D. Satterlee, "Owen Evans and Valley Forge"
11-38, M.J. Cooper, "Gunmakers of Binghampton"
4-39, L.D. Satterlee, "Ohio Penitentiary Rifles"
7-42, Beatrice Ravenal, "Charleston Gunsmiths"
6-47, Harry Wandrus, "Chicago Gunmakers and Gunsmiths"
4-48, Arthur Ward, "The Conroy Breechloader"
8-69, Marius Peladeau, "John Hills, Gunsmith of Vermont"

KRA *KENTUCKY RIFLE ASSOCIATION*
VOL. I No. 1, S.E. Dyke, "John Armstrong"
VOL. I No. 2, C. Pippert, "Christian Hawken"
VOL. I No. 3, R.H. Mackintosh, "The Brunners of Salisbury, N.C."
VOL. I No.4, S.E. Dyke, "Henry Mauger"
VOL. II No. 1, R. Gabel, "Peter Neihardt"
VOL. II No.2, V.K. Goodwin, "The Hawkens Family"
VOL. II No. 3, S.E. Dyke, "Northampton and Lehigh County Gunsmiths"
VOL. II No.4, A.S. Berky, "Elias Brey"
VOL. III No. 1, S.E. Dyke, "Peter Smith"
VOL. III No. 2, S.E. Dyke, "Jacob Dubbs"
VOL. III No. 3, S.E. Dyke, "The Hess Family"
VOL. III No. 4, S.E. Dyke, "The Kuntz Brothers"
VOL. IV No. 1, S.E. Dyke, "The Moll Family"
VOL. IV No. 2, S.E. Dyke, "The Rupp Family"
VOL. IV No. 3, S.E. Dyke, "Christian Springs"
VOL. IV No. 4, S.E. Dyke, "Lancaster Gunsmiths"
VOL. V No. 1, R.G. Gabel, "The Hess Family"
VOL. V No.2, R.G. Gabel, "The Henry Family"
VOL. V No. 3, S.E. Dyke, "Why So Few Pre-Revolutionary Pa. Rifles Exist"
VOL. V No.4, Wm. Guthman, "New England Rifles"
VOL. VI No. 1, S.E. Dyke, "The Baker Family"
VOL. VI No. 2, S.E. Dyke, "Plans For A Revolutionary War Gun Factory"
VOL. VI No. 3, S.E. Dyke, "Controversial Indian Faces"
F-76 (Fall 1976?) Author unknown, reference to Jesse Worley

MB *MUZZLE BLASTS*, National Muzzle Loading Rifle Assn., Friendship, Indiana, 1939-date. Monthly publication for members only
6-41, W.C. Martin, "Early Gunsmiths of Jackson Co. Ohio"
3-42, Shooting & Fishing, "George Schalk, Gunsmith Plus"
7-44, Herman Dean, "Uncle George Brammer"
9-44, Duane Darling, "Bowman, Ohio Gunsmith"
11-44, Harry Kent, "George L. Wickline, Gunsmith"
4-45, F.A. Reinhard, "Peter Reinhard"
6-45, J.L. Secord, "Alfred Marion Cone"
9-45, James Serven, "William Billinghurst"
12-45, C. W. Everett, "William Bodenheimer, Gunmaker"
1-46, W.R. Felton, "Iowa Gunsmiths"
1-46, "Pittsburgh Gunsmiths"
4-46, Ralph Fischer, "Rudolph Pelck"
5-46, James Liston, "Perry Liston, Gunsmith"
10-46, Paul Fink, "The Beans of Tennessee"
10-46, W.R. Fulton, "William Bennett"
12-46, L.A. Remark, "James Day, Gunsmith"
3-47, Gerald Kelver, "Hoosier Gunsmith"
3-48, W.C. Overstreet, "A Presidents Rifle" (2 parts)
1-49, Thomas B. Hall, "Father & Son-Gunsmiths"
5-49, Harry Wandrus, "A Partial List of Milwaukee Gunmakers"
10-50, A.G. Saxon, "Indiana Gunsmiths"
1-51, C.W. Boswell, "Wyatt Perry, Gunmaker"
3-51, "James Fleenor, Gunsmith"
11-51, "Nelson Lewis, Gun Maker"
2-50, Clarence St. John, "Ten Nights in a Gun Room" (4 parts)
12-52, C.M. Patterson, "Roper Revolving Firearms"
1-53, S.L. Cullman, "Charles Cullman, Ohio Gunsmith"
4-54, "Indiana Gunsmiths"
10-54, Sam Woodside, "John Watts, Gunsmith of Pa."
12-54, T.W. Pike, "Columiana Gunsmiths"
4-55, Roy Beldon, "Early Gunsmiths of Jackson Co. Indiana"
12-55, Russ Waddell, "Stull Gunmaker"
10-57, "Chicago Gun

BIBLIOGRAPHY, cont.

Directory to 1880"
6-58, Elizabeth Hayward, "George McCoy"
8-58, "Pennsylvania Gunsmiths" (Boyds directory of 1861)
4-60, L.L. Cox, "David Leonard, Gunsmith 1825-1908"
9-60, James Pugh, "Charles Roth: Wilkes Barre Gunmaker"
1-63, H.K. Landis & G.D. Landis, "Lancaster Rifle" (4 parts)
9-63, Don Baird, "Ohio's Most Famous Gunsmith: Sheltowee."
10-63, Dennis Sebeck, "William Rotton, Nebraska Gun Maker"
11-63, Bob McAfee, "Iowa Gunsmiths in 1850"
8-64, Bob McAfee, "Iowa Gunsmiths in 1850"
2-65, Don Baird, "Research Column", ran until 5-68
9-65, Robert McAfee, "New Orleans Gunsmiths, 1850 Census"
11-66, Robert McAfee, "Missouri Gunmakers, 1850 Census"
1-67, W.C. Snyder, "Chambers King"
9-67, George Shumway, "A Long-rifle of Note"
2-68, R.W. Marcum, "Johnie B. Harrison"

NRA-GCN *NRA GUN COLLECTOR NEWSLETTER*, National Rifle Association of America, Fairfax, Virginia
8, Robert Sears, "Ballard's First Rifle"

T *TEXAS GUN COLLECTOR*, Texas Gun Collectors Assn., Dallas, Texas, 1950-date. Irregular publications for members only
20, R. Wipprecht, "Alfred Kapp-Sisterdale"
36, Harry Knode, "Texas Derringer Pistols"
53, C.C. Holloway, "San Antonio Letters of 1854-56"
58, C.C. Holloway, "American Gun Maker"
61, J.S. White, "Texas' First Gunmaker"
68, Herman Linn, "Jacob Linn, San Antonio"

WGC *A W.G.C.A. ANNUAL*, Wisconsin Gun Collectors Assn., Madison, Wisconsin, 1960-date. Annual publication for members only
4, John Nelson, "The Wisconsin Gun Maker"
5, Herb Uphoff, "James Lee's Percussion Breechloading Rifles"
6, John Nelson, "The Wisconsin Gun Maker" (Part 2)
7, John Nelson, "The Wisconsin Gun Maker" (Part 3)
9, H.M. Madaus, "Notes on the Thunderbolt"

AUTHOR'S PARTIAL/INCOMPLETE SOURCES

The following are shown as they appeared in the author's pre-publication master copy of the First Edition:

BAILEY & NIE, authors handwritten notation under BOOKS

Ballentine, reference to Frank W. Freund

El Paso Lone Star and Gara, reference to Frank Manning

Hist KY, V3, P259, reference to Chaney

Hist KY, V4, P367, reference to Seay

Hist KY, V4, P397, reference to John H. Smith

Hist KY, V5, P456, refrence to Simon Settle

Kolb, reference to NEW BABY (revolver)

Macon County History, 1987, reference to Reuben McClure

North, reference to Simeon North, and North & Chaney

North & North, author's handwritten notation under BOOKS

UTHQ, reference to David Sabin, Utah History Quarterly, V42, N1, P23

PERIODICALS

American Firearms Industry - 150 SE 12th Street, Suite #200, Ft. Lauderdale, FL 33316. Phone No.: 954-467-9994. Membership is $55 per year. Trade publications and related material.

American Gunsmith - P.O. Box 540638, Merrit Island, FL 32954. Phone No.: 321-459-1558. Published monthly. Subscription is $60 per year.

American Handgunner - Published by FMG. 12345 World Trade Center Drive, San Diego, CA 92128. Phone No.: 858-605-0253. Published bi-monthly. Subscription is $16.95 per year.

American Hunter - Published by the NRA. 11250 Waples Mill Rd., Fairfax, VA 22030. Phone No.: 800-672-3888. Subscription included in price of NRA Membership ($35). Published monthly.

American Rifleman - Published by the NRA. 11250 Waples Mill Rd., Fairfax, VA 22030. Phone No.: 800-672-3888. Subscription included in price of NRA Membership ($35). Published monthly.

Australian Shooter's Journal - Published by the Sporting Shooters Association of Australia, Inc., P.O. Box 2520, Unley, SA 5061, AUSTRALIA. Fax No.: 011-61-8-8272-2945. Web site: www.ssaa.org.au. Subscription is $50 per year in Australia, $60 per year elsewhere, published monthly.

Black's Wing & Clay - Published by the Ehlert Publishing Group. 6420 Sycamore Lane, Maple Grove, MN 55369. Phone No.: 800-848-6247. Published annually, $14.95.

The Clay Pigeon - P.O. Box 1022, Milford, PA 18337. Phone No.: 570-296-5768, Fax No.: 570-296-9298. Subscription is $18 per year (11 issues).

Combat Handguns - Published by Harris Publications. 1115 Broadway, 8th Floor, New York, NY 10010. Phone No.: 212-807-7100, Fax No.: 212-807-1479. Subscription rate: $35 for 1 year (8 issues).

Deutsches Waffen Journal - DWJ Verlags GmbH, Schmollerstrasse 31, Schwabisch Hall, D-74523, GERMANY, Phone No.: 011-49-791-956690, Fax No.: 011-49-791-95669-19, Web site: www.dwj.de, Email: info@dwj.de

The Double Gun Journal - P.O. Box 550, East Jordan, MI 49727-9636. Phone No.: 231-536-7439, Fax No.: 231-536-7450. Published quarterly.

Ducks Unlimited - One Waterfowl Way, Memphis, TN 38120. Phone No.: 901-758-3825, Fax No.: 901-758-3850. Membership rate: $25 per year, includes 6 issues.

Field & Stream Magazine - P.O. Box 55652, Boulder, CO 80322. Phone No.: 800-289-0639 or 212-779-5000. Subscription rate $25 annually. Published monthly (12 issues).

Gray's Sporting Journal - Published by North American Publications, Inc. 735 Broad Street, Augusta, GA 30901. Phone No.: 706-722-6060. Subscription is $36.95 for 7 issues.

Gun Report - P.O. Box 38, Aledo, IL 61231, Phone No.: 309-582-5311. $33.00 per year (USA), published monthly.

Guns and Ammo - Published by Primedia. 6420 Wilshire Blvd., Los Angeles, CA 90048. Phone No.: 323-782-2000. Subscription is $25 per year, published monthly.

Guns & Gear - Published by B.A.S.S., Inc. 5845 Carmichel Rd., Montgomery, AL 36117. Phone No.: 334-277-3940. Subscription is $35 per year, published monthly.

Gun List - Published by Krause Publications, 700 E. State St., Iola, WI 54990. Phone No.: 715-445-2214. $36.98 per year, published bi-weekly.

Gun Week - P.O. Box 488, Buffalo, NY 14209. Annual Subscription is $35. Published 3 times per month. Phone No.: 716-885-6408.

Guns Magazine - Published by FMG. 12345 World Trade Center Drive, San Diego, CA 92128. Phone No.:858-605-0252. Subscription is $19.95 per year (12 issues).

Handguns Magazine - Published by Primedia. 6420 Wilshire Blvd., Los Angeles, CA 90048. Phone No.: 323-782-2000. Subscription is $20 per year, published monthly.

Man at Arms - P.O. Box 460, Lincoln, RI 02865. Published bimonthly ($32 yearly). Phone No.: 401-726-8011.

Muzzle Blasts - Published by the National Muzzle Loading Rifle Association. P.O. Box 67, Friendship, IN 47021. Phone No.: 812-667-5131. Subscription is $35 per year, published monthly.

North American Hunter - 12301 Whitewater Dr., Minnetonka, MN 55343. Phone No.: 952-936-9333. Published 8 times per year (subscription included in membership).

Outdoor Guide Magazine - 505 S. Ewing, St. Louis, MO 63103, Phone No.: 314-535-9786. Subscription is $12 for 6 issues.

Outdoor Life Magazine - Two Park Ave., New York, NY 10016. Phone No.: 800-365-1580 or 212-779-5000. Subscription is $15.97 for 9 issues.

Petersen's Hunting - Published by Primedia. 6420 Wilshire Blvd., Los Angeles, CA 90048. Phone No.: 323-782-2000. Subscription is $25 per year, published monthly.

Pheasants Forever - 1783 Buerkle Circle, White Bear Lake, MN 55110. Phone No.: 651-773-2000, Fax No.: 651-773-5500. Membership is $25 per year, includes 5 issues.

Pointing Dog Journal/Retriever Journal - Published by the Village Press, 2779 Aero Park Dr., Traverse City, MI 49686. Phone No.: 231-946-3712, Fax No.: 231-946-3289. Subscription is $25.95 for 8 issues.

Quail Unlimited - P.O. Box 610 Edgefield, SC 29824. Phone No.: 803-637-5731, Fax No.: 803-637-0037. Membership is $25 per year, published bimonthly.

Rifle Shooter - Published by Primedia. 6420 Wilshire Blvd., Los Angeles, CA 90048. Phone No.: 323-782-2000. Subscription is $20 per year, published bimonthly.

Safari Club International - 4800 W. Gates Pass Rd., Tucson, AZ 85745. Web site: www.safariclub.org. Publications: *Safari Magazine*, *Safari Africa*, *Deer of the World*, *Sheep of the World*, *International Record Book of Trophy Animals*, *Record Book Field Edition*.

Shooting Industry - Published by FMG. 12345 World Trade Center Drive, San Diego, CA 92128. Phone No.: 858-605-0254, Subscription is $25 per year (USA). Published monthly.

Shooting Sportsman - Published by Down East Enterprise, Inc., P.O. Box 1357, Camden, ME, 04843. Phone No.: 207-594-9544, Fax No.: 207-594-5144. Subscription is $30 for 6 issues.

Shooting Sports Retailer - 130 W. 42nd St., New York, NY 10036. Phone No.: 212-840-0660. Free to retailers. Published 6 times per year.

Shooting Times - Published by Primedia, Inc. 2 News Plaza, Peoria, IL 61614. Phone No.: 800-727-4353. Subscription is $28.

Shotgun News - Published by Primedia, Inc. 2 News Plaza, Peoria, IL 61614. Phone No.: 800-345-6923. Subscription is $30 yearly (36 issues).

Shotgun Sports Magazine - P.O. Box 6810, Auburn, CA 95604. Web site: www.shotgunsportsmagazine.com. Phone No.: 800-876-8920, Fax No.: 530-889-9106. Subscription is $31 per year (11 issues).

Sporting Classics - P.O. Box 23707, Columbia, SC 29224. Phone No.: 803-736-2424.

Sporting Clays Magazine - 5211 S. Washington Ave., Titusville, FL 32780. Phone No.: 800-376-2237. Subscription is $29.95 per year (USA). Published monthly.

Sporting Goods Business - 1 Penn Plaza, New York, NY 10119. $65 per year.

Sports Afield Magazine - 15621 Chemical Lane, Huntington Beach, CA, 92649. Web site: www.sportsafield.com. Phone No.: 714-373-4910, Fax No.: 714-894-4949. Subscription is $32.95 per year (9 issues).

Turkey & Turkey Hunting - Published by Krause Publications, Inc. 700 E. State St., Iola, WI 54990. Phone No.: 715-445-2214. Published bimonthly for $14.95 (6 issues)

Varmint Hunter Magazine - Published by the Varmint Hunter's Association. 436 S. Pierre St., Pierre, SD, 57501. Phone No.: 605-224-6665, Fax No.: 605-224-6544. Subscription is $24 per year (4 issues).

Varmint Master Magazine - Published by the Vulcan Outdoor Group. 1 Chase Corp. Dr., Ste. 300, Birmingham, AL 35244.

Visier - International Waffen Magazine - Erich-Kastner-Strasse 2, D-56379, Singhofen, GERMANY. Phone No.: 011-49-2604-9780, Fax No.: 011-49-2604-978-703.

Waterfowl Magazine - Published by Ducks Unlimited. P.O. Box 50, Edgefield, SC 29824. Phone No.: 803-637-5767. 6 issues per year.

Western Outdoors - 3197-E East Airport Dr. Costa Mesa, CA 92626. Phone No: 714-546-4370. Published 9 times per year for $14.95

Wildfowl - Published by Primedia. 2 In-Fisherman Drive, Brainerd, MN 56425. Phone No.: 800-800-7724. Subscription is $25 for 6 issues. Published bimonthly.

Women & Guns - Published by Second Amendment Foundation. P.O. Box 488, Station C, Buffalo, NY 14209. $18 annual subscription. Published bimonthly.